The Search for Personal Freedom

The Search for Personal Freedom

Brief Edition
The Search

for Personal Freedom

Robert C. Lamm
Arizona State University

Neal M. Cross

Rudy H. Turk
Arizona State University

wcb Wm. C. Brown Publishers
Dubuque, Iowa

wcb

Wm. C. Brown Publishers, College Division

wcb group

Book Team

Wm. C. Brown
Chairman of the Board

Mark C. Falb
President and Chief Executive Officer

Lawrence E. Cremer
President

James L. Romig
Vice-President, Product Development

David A. Corona
Vice-President, Production and Design

E. F. Jogerst
Vice-President, Cost Analyst

Bob McLaughlin
National Sales Manager

Marcia H. Stout
Marketing Manager

Craig S. Marty
Director of Marketing Research

Marilyn A. Phelps
Manager of Design

Eugenia M. Collins
Production Editorial Manager

Karen Speerstra
Editor

Sharon R. Nesteby
Editorial Assistant

Catherine Dinsmore
Designer

Natalie Gould
Production Editor

Mary M. Heller
Photo Research Editor

Mavis M. Oeth
Permissions Editor

Cover image: *The Boating Party;* Mary Cassatt;
National Gallery of Art, Washington, D.C.,
Chester Dale Collection 1962

Printed in the United States of America
10 9 8 7 6 5 4 3 2 1

Contents

Colorplates xi
Preface xiii
Prologue: An Introduction to Integrated Humanities   3

Using This Book   4
A Common Basis for Understanding the Arts   7
An Introduction to Music Listening   16

Unit 1
Greece: The First Humanistic Culture   23

1 Early Greece: Preparation for the Good Life   25
2 Hellenic Athens: The Fulfillment of the Good Life   41
Literary Selection
    Perikles, *Memorial Oration*   51
Greece: From Hellenic to Hellenistic World   53
Literary Selection
    Plato, *Apology*   57
3 Greek Art: Gods, Temples, and the Greeks   69
4 Music in Greek Life and Thought   99
Poetry and Music   102
    from Sappho   102
Time Chart for Greek Civilization   107

Unit 2
Rome: The International Culture   **109**

5 A Thousand Years of Rome   111
Literary Selections
    Cicero, Scipio's Dream (Book VI, *On the Republic*)   127
    Lucretius, *On the Nature of Things*   130
    Catullus, Poems   132
    Martial, Epigrams   134
    Arrian, Discourses of Epictetus, Book 1, Chapter 1   135
    Marcus Aurelius, Meditations, Book II   136
6 Roman Art and Music: The Arts of Megalopolis   139

Unit 3
Judaism and Christianity: The Star and the Cross   **153**

7 Faith, Hope, and Love: The Judeo-Christian Tradition   155
Prophecy   156
    from Amos   157
    from Isaiah   157
    from Ezekiel   158
Literary Selections
    The Book of Job   160
    Psalms of David   161
    Ecclesiastes   162
    The Sermon on the Mount   162
    Paul's Letter to the Corinthians   164
    Five Parables   164
    Revelation   166
8 The Beginnings of Christian Art   169

Organum: "Alleluya (Nativitas)"[5]

Unit 4
The Age of Faith   **183**

9 Building Medieval Walls   185
The Assimilation of Cultures   190
    Boethius, from *The Consolation of Philosophy*   192
    from *The Song of Roland*   193
Literary Selections
    Beowulf's Fight with Grendel's Dam from *Beowulf*   195
    Everyman   197
10 The Late Middle Ages: Expansion and Synthesis   205
Literary Selections
    Songs and Poems of the Wandering Scholars   216
    Our Lady's Juggler   217
    Chaucer, The Prolog to *The Canterbury Tales*   219
    Chaucer, The Reeve's Tale from *The Canterbury Tales*   226
    Andreas Capellanus, from *The Art of Courtly Love*   229
11 The Medieval Synthesis in Art   231
12 Medieval Music: Sacred and Secular   251
Troubadours and Trouvères   256
    Duke William IX of Aquitaine, Troubadour Songs   256
    Bernart de Ventadorn, Troubadour Canso   257
    Beatriz, Countess of Dia, Troubadour Songs   258
Time Chart for the Middle Ages   264

Unit 5
The Renaissance, 1350–1600   267

13 New Ideas and Discoveries Result from a New Way of Looking at the World   269
   Literary Selection
       Pico della Mirandola, *Oration on the Dignity of Man*   270
   Time Chart for the Renaissance   283
14 Renaissance Art: A New Golden Age   285
15 Renaissance Music: Court and Church   315
16 Shadow and Substance: Literary Insights into the Renaissance   325
   Literary Selections
       Petrarch, Sonnets III, LXIX, XLVII, CCXCII, CCCXIII   326
       Niccolo Machiavelli, from *The Prince*   328
       Michelangelo Buonarotti, Sonnets XXX, XXXII, LXI   330
       Sir Thomas More, from *Utopia*   331

Unit 6
The Early Modern World, 1600–1789   339

17 Science, Reason, and Absolutism   341
   Literary Selections
       John Donne, Song, The Flea, The Good-Morrow, Holy Sonnet X   349
       Andrew Marvell, To His Coy Mistress   350
       John Milton, On the Late Massacre in Piedmont, On His Blindness   351
       Alexander Pope, from *Essay On Man*   352
       Jonathan Swift, *A Modest Proposal*   355
       Thomas Gray, Elegy Written in a Country Churchyard   358
       Thomas Jefferson, First Inaugural Address   360
   Time Chart for the Early Modern World, 1600–1789   362
18 Art: Baroque, Rococo, and Neoclassic   365
19 Music: Baroque, Rococo, and Classical   387

Unit 7
The Middle Modern World, 1789–1914   *403*

20 Revolution, Romanticism, Realism   405
    Literary Selections
        Lord Byron, Ode to Napoleon Bonaparte   406
        Alfred, Lord Tennyson, The Charge of the Light
            Brigade   408
        Abraham Lincoln, Second Inaugural Address   409
        Sir Walter Scott, Breathes There the Man   410
        Thomas Hardy, Cry of the Homeless   411
        Jean Jacques Rousseau, from *Émile*   412
        William Blake, Introduction, The Lamb, The Tiger   415
        William Wordsworth, Lines Composed a Few Miles above
            Tintern Abbey, The World Is Too Much With Us   416
        Samuel Taylor Coleridge, Kubla Khan   418
        Lord Byron, She Walks In Beauty, When a Man Hath No
            Freedom to Fight for at Home, Prometheus   419
        Percy Bysshe Shelley, To a Skylark, Ode to the West
            Wind   420
        John Keats, On the Elgin Marbles, Ode on a Grecian Urn,
            La Belle Dame Sans Merci   422
        Johann Wolfgang von Goethe, from Book of Timur   424
        Karl Marx and Friedrich Engels, from *Manifesto of the
            Communist Party*   426
        Charles Darwin, from *The Descent of Man*   428
        Alfred, Lord Tennyson, Mariana, Ulysses   430
        Matthew Arnold, Dover Beach   432
        Thomas Hardy, Neutral Tones, Drummer Hodge, The
            Darkling Thrush, Channel Firing   432
        Edgar Allan Poe, Annabel Lee   434
        Ralph Waldo Emerson, The Rhodora, Brahma, Concord
            Hymn   434
        Walt Whitman, I Hear America Singing, By the Bivouac's
            Fitful Flame   436
        Herman Melville, The Portent, Shiloh, On the Slain
            Collegians, A Utilitarian View of the Monitor's Fight,
            Pebbles   436
        Mark Twain, The Notorious Jumping Frog of Calaveras
            County   439
        Emily Dickinson, In a Library, I Had No Time to Hate, A
            Service of Song, Dying, I Never Saw a Moor, I Died for
            Beauty, Much Madness Is Divinest Sense, The
            Chariot   441
        Paul Laurence Dunbar, Sympathy   442
        Stephen Crane, War Is Kind, A Man Said to the
            Universe   443
    Time Chart for the Middle Modern World, 1789–1914   444
21 Romanticism in Music   447
22 Nineteenth-Century Art: Conflict and Diversity   463

Unit 8
The Twentieth Century   483

23 Things Fall Apart: The Center Cannot Hold   485
     Literary Selections
          Sigmund Freud, from *Civilization and Its Discontents*   490
          Thomas Stearns Eliot, The Love Song of J. Alfred
               Prufrock   492
          William Butler Yeats, The Second Coming   494
          Wilfred Owen, Dulce et Decorum Est   494
          Robinson Jeffers, Shine, Perishing Republic   495
          Countee Cullen, Yet Do I Marvel   495
          Richard Wright, The Ethics of Living Jim Crow, 1937   495
24 Ideas and Conflicts That Motivate the Twentieth Century   501
     Historical Overview, 1939–1980s   501
          Richard Eberhart, The Fury of Aerial Bombardment   501
          Langston Hughes, Harlem   502
     Literary Selections
          Jean Paul Sartre, The Wall   505
          Albert Camus, The Myth of Sisyphus   511
          Joan Didion, On the Road from *The White Album*   513
          Denise Levertov, Tenebrae   515
          Nadine Gordimer, A Soldier's Embrace   515
25 Art in the Twentieth Century: Shock Waves and Reactions   521
26 Modern Music   557
27 Twentieth-Century Literature   589
     Literary Selections
          e e cummings, anyone lived in a pretty how town   596
          Dylan Thomas, When All My Five and Country Senses
               See   596
          Ralph Ellison, Chapter 1 from *Invisible Man*   596
          John Berryman, Life, Friends, Is Boring. We Must Not Say
               So   602
          Kurt Vonnegut, Deer in the Works   602
          N. Scott Momaday, Flight on the Wind from *House Made of
               Dawn*   606
          Gail Godwin, A Sorrowful Woman   609
          Don L. Lee, Man Thinking about Woman, Mixed
               Sketches   611
          Nikki Giovanni, Nikki-Rosa   612
     Time Chart for the Twentieth Century   614
Glossary   G–1
Credits   C–1
Index   I–1

Colorplates

Colorplates follow page indicated.

1 Paul Gauguin, *Where Do We Come From? What Are We? Where Are We Going?* 10
2 Pieter Bruegel the Elder, *Winter (Return of the Hunters)* 10
3 Meindert Hobbema, *The Watermill with the Great Red Roof* 10
4 Vincent van Gogh, *The Starry Night* 10
5 Wassily Kandinsky, *Panel (3)* (also known as *Summer*) 10
6 Hyacinthe Rigaud, *Portrait of Louis XIV* 10
7 Pablo Picasso, *Girl Before a Mirror* 10
8 Giovanni Paolo Panini, *The Interior of the Pantheon* 146
9 *Head of Emperor Hadrian* 146
10 Interior, San Vitale, Ravenna 146
11 *Emperor Justinian and His Courtiers* 146
12 *Empress Theodora and Retinue* 146
13 "X–P (Chi-rho) Page," *Lindisfarne Gospels* 242
14 "Crucifixion Cover," *Lindau Gospels* 242
15 Reliquary in shape of head 242
16 "Capture of Christ and the Flagellation," *Psalter of St. Swithin* 242
17 High mass, nave of Notre Dame Cathedral of Coutances 242
18 Southern Rose and Lancets, Chartres Cathedral 242
19 Duccio, *The Calling of the Apostles Peter and Andrew* 242
20 Simone Martini, *Annunciation* 242
21 Giotto, *Lamentation* 242
22 Sandro Botticelli, *Birth of Venus* 306
23 Perugino, *Crucifixion with Saints* 306
24 Jan van Eyck, *Annunciation* 306
25 Leonardo da Vinci, *Ginevra de'Benci* 306
26 Michelangelo, *David* 306
27 Raphael, *The Alba Madonna* 306
28 Giorgione, *Adoration of the Shepherds* 306
29 Titian, *Venus with a Mirror* 306
30 Tintoretto, *Christ at the Sea of Galilee* 306
31 El Greco, *Laokoön* 306
32 Matthias Grünewald, *The Small Crucifixion* 306
33 Peter Paul Rubens, *The Assumption of the Virgin* 386
34 Peter Paul Rubens, *Rape of the Daughters of Leucippus* 386
35 Nicolas Poussin, *Holy Family on the Steps* 386
36 Jacob van Ruisdael, *Wheatfields* 386
37 Rembrandt van Rijn, *The Descent from the Cross* 386
38 Jan Vermeer, *The Girl with a Red Hat* 386
39 François Boucher, *Venus Consoling Love* 386

40 Eugene Delacroix, *Arabs Skirmishing in the Mountains* 466
41 John Constable, *Wivenhoe Park, Essex* 466
42 Winslow Homer, *Breezing Up* 466
43 Edouard Manet, *The Dead Toreador* 466
44 Edgar Degas, *Four Dancers* 466
45 Claude Monet, *Rouen Cathedral, West Façade Sunlight* 466
46 Auguste Renoir, *Girl with a Watering Can* 466
47 Paul Cézanne, *Le Château Noir* 466
48 Paul Gauguin, *Self-Portrait* 466
49 Georges Seurat, *Sunday Afternoon on the Island of La Grande Jatte* 466
50 Henri Matisse, *The Blue Window* 466
51 Pablo Picasso, *Still Life* 466
52 Piet Mondrian, *Composition in White, Black, and Red* 530
53 Marcel Duchamp, *The Bride Stripped Bare by Her Bachelors, Even* 530
54 Joan Miro, *Person Throwing a Stone at a Bird* 530
55 Jackson Pollack, *Number 1* 530
56 Willem de Kooning, *Woman I* 530
57 Mark Rothko, *Number 10* 530
58 Paul Klee, *Fish Magic* 530
59 Otto Duecker, *Russell, Terry, J. T., and a Levi Jacket* 530

Preface

The seventh edition of *The Search for Personal Freedom* is now available in two versions: a two-volume set and this briefer text in a single volume. This edition, like the original, is a text for the integrated humanities: the arts of literature, painting, music, sculpture, and architecture, and the discipline of philosophy. Though not an "art" in the strictest sense, philosophic ideas so consistently permeate each of the arts that theories of major philosophers are, of necessity, interwoven throughout the book. The components of the humanities—philosophy and the arts—are presented not as separate disciplines but as interrelated manifestations of human creativity. In such creativity men and women have found their freedom in the past, and are finding it now. Hence the theme of this book, a book about people and about "art's eternal victory over the human situation" (André Malraux).

In order to better understand why we are the way we are, we have centered our studies on our cultural heritage, from ancient Greece to the present day. The text is therefore organized chronologically; change, development, action, and reaction are, we feel, best understood within a chronological framework. The accomplishments of the past, however, are considered not as museum pieces but as living evidence of enduring responses to the perplexities of life. These achievements have become, in our day, a basic part of our attempts to make sense of the universe.

Because artists naturally respond to the issues of their own time, each unit of the text is prefaced by an overview of the social, scientific, religious, and philosophical climate of the period. Forming the core of the book are primary sources, the artworks themselves: poetry, short stories, sections of large works, hundreds of art illustrations—many in color—and numerous musical examples. Introduced with appropriate commentary, the selections are followed by practical exercises and questions. Additionally, there are maps, graphs, tables, and time charts plus a glossary of important terms in philosophy and the arts. There is more than enough material for a one-semester course based entirely on the book; for a two-semester course the book can be used as a central text enriched by additional primary materials.

In the final analysis this book is intended to develop an understanding of cultural diversity as well as cultural achievements. Meaningful exposure to a variety of arts and ideas is but the first step towards a lifelong appreciation of the joy, beauty, and artistic truth that are inherent in all of the arts.

This book could not have been written without the patience, forbearance, and expert editorial assistance of Katy Lamm.

We also wish to thank the following professors whose suggestions and careful reading of the manuscript proved invaluable for this brief edition.

Ruth E. Knier
San Francisco State University

Lois Muyskens
Richland College

Herbert J. Vandort
Pensacola Jr. College

Charles L. Hudson
Wilbur Wright College

Ralph A. Spaulding
Mount San Antonio College

Nirmala Varmha
Oklahoma City College

The Search for Personal Freedom

The Search for Personal Freedom

Prologue: An Introduction to Integrated Humanities

> Today, all the normal mischances of living have been multiplied, a million-fold, by the potentialities for destruction, for an unthinking act of collective suicide, which man's very triumphs in science and invention have brought about. In this situation the artist has a special task and duty: the task of reminding men of their humanity and the promise of their creativity.[1]
>
> Lewis Mumford

In Spain and in the modest mountains of southwestern France are numerous caves decorated with paintings that date from the late Old Stone (Paleolithic) Age (ca. 20,000–10,000 B.C.). In the caves of Lascaux there is, for example, a large chamber whose lofty ceiling is covered with paintings of antelope, horses, bulls, and other animals. Too deep and dark for human habitation, this may have been a sanctuary for religious rites or a setting for ritualistic magic to assure successful hunting, but no one knows for sure. No one knows the intentions of the people who created these images, but there is no question about what these people were. They were artists. Using intellect and imagination, late Paleolithic people had invented representation, a momentous step in the evolution of culture.

The invention of art symbolized major changes in the lives of people no longer at the mercy of the elements. Working together and planning ahead ("marking time") for seasonal changes, they hunted and gathered at optimum times and stored food for the long winters. It is now believed that they devoted as little as fifteen to twenty hours a week to the necessities of existence. There was time left over to make more efficient weapons and warmer clothing, to carve ivory and wood, to play, and to decorate cave sanctuaries. Late Paleolithic clans had created what every society must have if it is to advance its culture: free and unstructured time.

---

1. Lewis Mumford, *In the Name of Sanity* (New York: Harcourt, Brace, 1954), p. 141.

Figure P.1 Bull, ceiling painting, 18' long, caves of Lascaux near Montignac, France, ca. 12,000 B.C.

The creation of art also signified the emergence of individual artists. Lugging materials down through winding cave passages and erecting a scaffolding were undoubtedly communal efforts, but the artwork was done by an individual. That person, the artist, climbed atop the platform and painted a bull (fig. P.1) in sweeping, confident lines, elegantly capturing a sense of life and communicating the illusion of powerful motion. In today's high-tech, nuclear-threatened world, the art of Lascaux is a poignant reminder of our kinship with Stone Age artists who, along with a multitude of successors, inspire us to recall our humanity, our intellect and imagination, our creative potential for a better life.

It is because everyone is capable of living a more rewarding life that we study the humanities. From cave art to the present the arts and ideas of humans are beacons of hope, truth, and beauty for a world that needs to pay far more attention to the humanities, to the arts that teach us "nothing except the significance of life" (Henry Miller). In our integrated approach to the humanities, we study literature, painting, music, sculpture, philosophy, and architecture not as separate disciplines but as interrelated manifestations of human creativity. Nor do we study the arts and artists in isolation. Artists are individuals, coping with the stress and strain of everyday life and, perhaps more than other people, influenced by the ideas and values of their society. "Artists are," observed composer Ned Rorem, "like everyone else, only more so."

The humanities engage our intellect, our intuitions, and our emotions. Concerned with human values and the universal need of people to express themselves, they take us on a voyage of discovery. They not only widen our vision and provide insights into the human condition but they also fill us with wonder and delight. They take the materials of earthly existence and reach for the stars. History tells us, in varying degrees, what happened in past ages, but the humanities are individual creations that have outlasted the ages that produced them. Belonging as much to our world as to ancient Athens, Renaissance Florence, or Victorian London, the finest expressions of the human spirit continue to inform and to inspire.

This is a book about the present, the here and now. Only our imagination can take us backwards in time, back to the origins of our cultural heritage in ancient Greece and all the accomplishments since that Golden Age. We study past achievements not as museum pieces but as living evidence of enduring responses to the perplexities of life. In our own day this priceless legacy becomes a basic part of our attempts to make sense of the universe and of our own lives.

In the final analysis, our studies are intended to develop an understanding of cultural diversity as well as cultural achievements. Exposure to a variety of arts and ideas is but the first step towards a lifelong appreciation of the joy, beauty, and artistic truth that are inherent in all the arts. Only the beginning of an open-ended study of human creativity, the humanities are an indispensable part of a liberal, and liberating, education. Equipped with an understanding of some of the accomplishments of Western culture that shape the way we live today, students can begin to realize their full potential as human beings and to shape their own personal freedom.

Using This Book

This book has at least two purposes: (1) to help the student begin to find personal freedom and (2) to help construct a new society with an emphasis on human and life-giving values rather than materialistic and repressive ones. Fortunately, both can be approached through the arts and philosophy, for they are the means to discover human experience and yield new meanings for that experience and new significance for life itself.

First, what do we mean by personal freedom? A very simple analogy may help make this idea clear. One may consider the person first learning to swim and the expert swimmer. The learner does a tremendous amount of splashing and gets almost nowhere. The expert moves through the water with a minimum of disturbance, makes it look easy, and gets to the destination. So the person with a measure of freedom moves through life knowingly, arriving at predetermined goals with a minimum of disturbance.

The freedom we are talking about is not conditioned absolutely by political, social, and economic surroundings, although such factors may help or hinder a person. One can imagine a political prisoner in Siberia whose knowledge and personal values allow a free and independent spirit in the most squalid of surroundings. The prisoner's goals are not those of going somewhere, or of getting some material thing, but of being a particular person. The movement of the person toward Being measures an approach toward the personal freedom of which we are talking.

A person can come to self-knowledge, can establish an ever-expanding personal philosophy and value system, and can know much of life through the arts.

Of course, direct experience with all of life might be better, but waiting for enough immediate sensation would take forever.

Section 2 will discuss the personal humanistic value of literature, music, and the visual arts in more detail. The sincere artist confronts great problems of human experience, explores them, cuts away the irrelevancies that confuse us in direct experience, and leads us to new meanings. The greatest artists often present us with visible symbols of the highest human levels of Being or meaning as in Michelangelo's statue of *David,* the Parthenon, or Dante's *Divine Comedy.* Individuals, who make these meanings and these exaltations of the spirit a part of themselves, can make more discriminating value judgments and are on the way in the search for personal freedom.

In approaching the second goal of this book, building a culture based on human values, one needs to know how a culture is built. Philosophers of history have found many patterns that seem to account for the growth, flowering, and decay of civilizations. In this book we are using a modified and simplified form of the *culture-epoch theory* as a framework upon which to arrange our materials. This theory is neither more nor less "true" than any of a half-dozen other theories that attempt to account for changes throughout the recorded story of mankind.

According to the culture-epoch theory, a culture is founded upon whatever conception of reality is held by the great majority of people over a considerable period of time. This is true even though the majority may not be aware of any concept of reality or, more probably take it so much for granted that they are not aware it is simply a human idea, held on faith. Thus, for most people at the time this is written, a typewriter is real, a physical tree is real, and all things which can be seen, heard, smelled, felt, or tasted are real.

As a matter of fact, a number of scientists, philosophers, and religious thinkers have given us different concepts of reality, which have also been widely held. These thinkers have contemplated the millions of forms of life, many of them bearing resemblances to others, yet each one different; they have examined the forms of earth, air, fire, and water; they have wondered about the processes of change by which a tree today may, at some time in the future, disintegrate into earth and reappear in some totally alien form. They have watched such nontangible things as sunlight and air becoming leaf and branch. Pondering these things, they come inevitably to the ultimate question: "What is the nature of reality?"

To reach an answer, they usually focus on a few profound inquiries, some of which may be given here. For example, they might say, "We see change all around us. We see grass eaten and turn into cow. We see cow eaten and turn into human. We see humans disintegrate and turn into earth. If all these changes can take place, what are the universal elements of which all things are composed?" Or they might say, "We see an individual human, John Doe, as baby, as youth, as adult, as senile old man, as corpse. From one

moment to the next, he is never the same. Yet he is always the same, John Doe, a distinct being. Can it be that nothing is permanent, that reality is a process rather than a thing or group of things? If we have change, then, how does the process take place? And more important, we know that we live in a world of constant change, but what force directs the process?"

"Nonsense," retorts another group of thinkers. "That which is in a constant state of flow cannot be real. Only that which is permanent and unchanging can be real. What, then, in the universe is permanent, unchanging in itself, yet is able to transform itself, manifest itself, or produce from itself the countless forms we see around us?"

These are some of the basic questions the pure thinker contemplates. The answers are various concepts of reality.

Based upon the idea of reality accepted as "true," specialized thinkers build different thought-structures that underlie visible institutions. These include a philosophy of justice from which particular forms of law and government spring; a philosophy of education that dictates the nature of our schools and the material taught in them; a religious philosophy that becomes apparent in churches and creeds; and an economic philosophy that yields its particular ways of producing and distributing goods and services, including the token-systems used as money. Other philosophies and institutions could be named, but these are some that greatly affect our daily living.

When these are formed, we have a complete culture, but always by the time such a pattern is established, we have forces at work that tend to destroy it. The destroyers are new pure thinkers who note inconsistencies within the idea of reality itself, and who question postulates or find contradictions.

From these new thinkers (philosophers, scientists, theologians) comes a new idea of reality so convincing it cannot be brushed aside. It must be accepted. Suddenly the whole structure of the culture finds itself without foundation. The justice and the law appropriate in the old culture no longer fit on the new foundation; the old education is no longer appropriate; old religious beliefs no longer describe a person's position in relation to God; old ways of making things and distributing them no longer suffice.

At this time people are plunged into a *period of chaos,* the first step in the formation of a new epoch.

The symptoms of the period of chaos lie around us now in such profusion that they scarcely need description. In the latter part of the twentieth century this is where we live. New and shocking ideas, moralities, and beliefs are introduced and discarded; terrorists attack established governments; civil strife and wars of conquest rage; everyone damages the environment; and over everything looms the menace of nuclear obliteration. At the mercy of events beyond their control, some people try to turn back the clock to better, more peaceful days; others seek refuge and security in fundamentalist beliefs; still others retreat to paramilitary armed camps; many just mindlessly camp in front of their television sets, perhaps hoping that all of the problems will somehow vanish. In other words, we see in the late twentieth century a period of chaos that, nevertheless, gives some evidence of resolution.

Out of the turmoil and confusion of chaotic periods of past cultures emerges the *period of adjustment.* At this point, notable artists—whether painters, writers, sculptors, composers, or creators in some other medium—make their important contributions to society. Pheidias and Sokrates of ancient Athens; the master builders of the celebrated Gothic churches; Michelangelo, Beethoven, Goethe—these innovators begin to suggest the new line, shape, and pattern for a new culture.

Two ideas need to be stressed about the role of the artist in the development of a cultural pattern. First, the artist does not necessarily know all about new ideas of reality. For example, the artist in our time does not necessarily know all about Einstein's theory. The artist is simply a person of greater sensitivity than others, and with great skill in one medium. As a sensitive person, the artist probably feels more keenly than the rest of us the tensions of the time—the pulls of this belief and the pulls of another contradictory one. An artist will not rest until he or she has explored this confusing experience and discovered some meaning, some significance, therein. The great artist is always the composer (whether musician, writer, painter, choreographer, architect, or sculptor), the person who puts things together in new relationships and finds new meanings for experience.

A second idea about the artist's contribution to the formation of a cultural pattern is the important role of structure, rather than subject matter, conveying cultural meaning. For example, one may compare the structure of an Egyptian temple (see fig. 3.7) with that of the Parthenon in Athens (see fig. 3.44). The subject matter of both is roughly the same—they are temples built for the worship of a god. But what a difference! The Temple of Amon is enormous, both overpowering and intimidating, reflecting the total control of the populace by the pharaoh and a permanent priesthood. The temple of Athena, the Parthenon, is serene, rational, and exquisitely proportioned. Decorated with sculptured reliefs depicting gods *and* Greek citizens, it is a structure erected by the citizens of a democratic society in which there is no resident priesthood.

It comes down to this: styles in beauty change as the basic characteristics of people change. Or perhaps it works the other way; perhaps as new glimpses of beauty are caught by the artists, people themselves change to conform to the new beauty.

However it may happen, the artist, especially in the period of chaos and early in the period of adjustment within a culture-epoch, personally feels the stresses, tensions, and turmoil of the period. The artist explores conflicts within, which are the conflicts of the general population as well, and creates new structures, new designs, to synthesize the elements of conflict and to give new meaning to experience. Some works of art, probably depending upon the individual artist's breadth of vision and ability to compose insight into significance, are seized upon as symbols of new pattern and new truth in society. They express the new idea of beauty and truth.

At this point another element of the population—we may call them the *intellectuals*—enters the picture. They are people like ourselves, college students and faculty members, government officials, ministers, business executives, and many others who think seriously about things and who, like the artists, have been troubled by the conflict of their times. They still are working within the period of adjustment in an epoch. They become aware of new meanings and patterns produced by the artists, and they start reshaping these designs into new philosophies of justice, of economics, of religion, and the like, and begin to build concrete institutions out of the philosophies that they have created. Through their work, order slowly emerges out of chaos.

When their work is finished, we come to the third period within a culture-epoch, the *period of balance.* At this point, the idea of reality, the philosophies that underlie our basic institutions, and the institutions themselves are all in harmony. Early in a period of balance, life must be very satisfying; everyone must know the reason for getting up in the morning to face the day. But if balance lasts too long, life begins to get dull. The big jobs seem to be done, and decadence, boredom, and deterioration may set in. The long and painful decline of the Roman Empire was just such a period.

But change comes inevitably. At the beginning of the twentieth century, physicists were assuring young scientists that the great discoveries in physics had all been made and that only little tidying-up jobs remained. At the same time, Einstein was beginning his work, which was to supersede all our knowledge in physics. Just when people have been certain of everything in their periods of balance, new pure thinkers come along to upset the whole apple cart into a new epoch.

A word of caution should be appended here. This systematic description of an epoch makes it sound as if artists only function in a time of chaos or adjustment, or as if philosophers quit philosophizing until their proper time comes around. This, of course, is not true. While the epoch does divide itself into three rough periods, all of the functions occur with greater or lesser impact throughout the entire time period.

In this book, the various periods of history will be treated in the following way: The rise of Athenian democracy in the fifth century B.C. and its rapid decline will be treated as one culture-epoch. The Roman period from the time of the rule of Julius Caesar will be regarded as an attempt to maintain rationalistic Greek times, under law, and backed by strong military authority. It does not constitute an epoch of the type we have been describing. Because of their far-reaching importance, Judaism and Christianity will be treated separately, though inadequately because of limited space. Actually the teachings of Jesus represent the work of the pure thinker, and the Christian concept of God was a new concept of reality that served as the foundation for the Middle Ages. The Middle Ages, dating from about A.D. 450 to 1350 will be considered as a complete epoch. The time period from 1350 to the early twentieth century really constitutes another epoch, with the Renaissance as a large segment of the period of chaos within it. Because the Renaissance, using the approximate dates of 1350 to 1600, presents so much of interest for the student of humanities, however, it will be treated as a separate time period. Then, with the clash of rationalism and romanticism and the final emergence of the Faustian man, we will consider the period from about 1600 to the early twentieth century as a complete epoch. The last unit of this book will look as carefully as possible at the cultural changes with which we in the twentieth century are so deeply involved.

Summary

The humanities are the arts of literature, painting, music, sculpture, architecture, and dance, and the discipline of philosophy that permeates all of the arts and finally unites them all. As set forth in the next section, the arts, taken together, are a separate field of human knowledge with their own area of exploration and discovery, and with a method of their own. So these volumes will concentrate on the great artistic production of each of the time periods outlined above. Each unit is planned to give a chapter or two to the social, scientific, religious, and philosophic climate of the period in which the artists were working, for the artists usually accept the scientific and social world-picture of their time. Following these introductory discussions, direct attention is given to the arts themselves, with enough examples of each to reveal new answers to the great questions of mankind, new patterns, structures, and meaning the artists found for life in their time. By this treatment, the student will be able to trace the development and changes through history of the problems that plague us so sorely in our own time. Equipped with knowledge of the great answers found in the past that shape the way we live today, having come to know the exalted expressions of humanity revealed at their fullest, students can work to develop their own freedom and assist in the building of a new culture based on a combination of human values and the Greek ideals of *kalos k'agathos:* beauty and goodness.

A Common Basis for Understanding the Arts

In the humanities we take art seriously because, as Aristotle observed, "art is a higher type of knowledge than experience." Earlier in this century the arts were regarded as "the finer things of life" and were respected as a sort of polish the upper classes received as a part of their education. Art was show-off stuff, valuable precisely because it was of no practical good.

The upper middle-class child showed his status by wearing braces on his teeth and by taking piano lessons until he eventually learned to plunk out the *Moonlight Sonata* with little thought beyond the mechanical problem of getting the right fingers on the right notes. Another domestic status symbol was having a beautifully bound volume of the *Complete Works of Swinburne* (an "important" writer) resting casually on the coffee table, never opened let alone read, but advertising the good taste of the owner. As a matter of fact, this whole attitude towards art might well be called the coffee-table school of appreciation. The attitude still exists. But, as indicated earlier in our description of a culture-epoch, we now recognize that eminent artists actually help create patterns for a way of life; "The object of art is to give life a shape" (Jean Anouilh).

One might ask what area of the universe is the darkest, the most unknown. The universe itself? Einstein once said that the most incomprehensible fact about the universe is that it is so comprehensible. No, the most bewildering portion of the universe is yourself. As a member of the human race, you are (or should be) asking yourself such questions as "Who am I?" "What am I?" "Why am I here?" It is the artist who persists in reacting to these questions, who seeks answers from within, and who discovers answers that strike responsive chords in the rest of us. As Henry Miller said, "art teaches nothing, except the significance of life."

A Shakespearean scholar once made the statement that in his plays Shakespeare had made discoveries as important as those made by any scientist. At first, such an assertion seems to be an overreaction to the dominance of science in the modern world. Consider, however, Shakespeare's treatment of love and hate in *Romeo and Juliet,* good and evil in *King Lear,* and murder and revenge in *Macbeth,* for example. These aspects of the human condition, as they are dramatized on the stage, are artistic truths. This idea of discoveries by Shakespeare or any other artist can give us a basis for understanding the arts. In this respect, as Jean Cocteau observed, "art is science in the flesh."

Generally we can think of scientific knowledge and artistic truth in this way: The physical sciences explore the world outside humankind; the social sciences make discoveries about the behavior and activities of people in various groups; and the arts and humanities probe the area of inner meaning: humanity's fears, hopes, loves, delights as the individual and society act and react within their world. "All art is social," as James Adams noted, "because it is the result of a relationship between an artist and his time." Art is also exploration, and the discoveries artists make are expressed as *concepts* and *percepts.* Concepts are ideas that cannot be seen, like friendship, beauty, and justice. Percepts are what we perceive with our senses: line, taste, color, aroma, volume, pitch, and so forth. Artists express concepts by the unique manner in which they choose to arrange the percepts, that is, the sense-apparent objects and materials. Obviously this kind of vivid creativity can never be done by committee: "Art is the most intense mode of individualism that the world has known" (Oscar Wilde).

Because of differences in media and modes of expression, the arts differ from each other in many ways. Certainly a *time-art* such as music, which exists only as long as it is heard, differs from a *space-art* such as painting, which uses visual symbols as its means of expression. Both arts are separated from literature, a *word-art* that must be interpreted by the reader. The differences between Beethoven's Fifth Symphony, the *Mona Lisa*, and *Hamlet* are certainly obvious; what is not so obvious are their similarities. "Painting," wrote Emerson, "was called 'silent poetry,' and poetry 'speaking painting.' The laws of each art are convertible into the laws of any other." The common basis of all the arts is the exploration by means of sensory percepts into the emotion, the mind, the personality of humans; their common goal is to speak directly to our inner being. As Emerson also wrote: "Raphael paints wisdom; Handel sings it, Pheidias carves it, Shakespeare writes it." An examination of this common basis is the purpose of this section.

The artist deals subjectively with all materials as he or she draws upon a special store of personal experience. Moreover, artistic production depends as much upon the background and personality of the artist as it does upon the raw material of experience. It follows therefore that each artist is unique, an individual different from all other persons, and that the artist's production is equally unique. One might take, for example, the treatment two literary artists make of the same theme, the emptiness of the life of a woman who, in herself, is virtually a complete blank, but who moves from man to man, living only as a reflection of each man. Read Dorothy Parker's story, "Big Blonde," and Anton Chekhov's story, "The Darling" (filmed as *Darling*, starring Julie Christie). Although the experience is the "same" in both stories, the end result is quite different, and the experience of the reader is also very different, while reacting to the general idea in two different forms. The reader might protest, "But one of them must be right about this kind of person and one of them must be wrong." Actually both Parker and Chekhov are right, and any other artist who treated the same material with a different insight might also be right. The discovery of multiple truths is a personal matter and the corollary is that the realm of truth in personality, that prime area where the arts are focused, is inexhaustible. The person who understands any work of art grows with each facet of experience shared with the artist. In other words, our boundaries are expanded as we add the artist's experience to our own, thereby increasing the data in our own personal computer bank. Gabriel Marcel expressed a similar idea:

> Thanks to art, instead of seeing one world, our own, we see it multiplied and, as many original artists as there are, so many worlds are at our disposal.

Not always recognized is the fact that the artists in literature, painting, sculpture, music, and the other arts have a method of investigation in their field of knowledge that we may call the method of intuition or insight. In much the same way that scientists start out, artists become aware of a problem in the realm of human experience, or they sense some aspect of the human personality that is dark and unknown. Put more simply, they feel the need to create, and this compulsion is the first step in the artistic method. As a second step, they begin to gather materials, both conceptual (idea-stuff) and perceptual (physical-stuff: visual images, sequences of sound, etc.). The third step is the appropriate arrangement of materials, which comes as an insight or an intuitive perception of new and varied relationships among the materials with which they are working. Since artists are dealing with a problem of relationships, the truth they seek takes the shape of arranging materials in proper order with respect to each other. In other words, the form (arrangement and relationship) is a very necessary part of artistic truth; this form involves the arrangement of incident, character, or images in literature, of visual elements in painting or sculpture, of sounds or themes in musical composition so that they arrive at the point that artists have felt by insight. In other words, this is the step we call *composition,* a term that is common to all of the arts. From this step the art-object emerges—a song, a pot, a picture, a poem—which has both an aesthetic and a utilitarian function in the world (and frequently the best of the utilitarian productions have a very high degree of aesthetic value). But how can artists check results of their exploration? That is the job of the members of their audience. After the composition, artists turn their creations loose in the world. Many people examine these creations, both in terms of subject and explicit meaning, and in terms of the form in which they are presented. If an artwork is composed in such a way that the members of the audience *live through* the experience themselves and find that the artist has made a true statement of the experience in all of its relationships, then the discovery of the artist is accepted as a truth wrested from the dark ignorance of the human condition in the world. Two of the tests that might be applied are these: First, is it new? If the meaning (a combination of idea and formal structure) is old and trite, the artwork may be comfortable, but not of much artistic value. Second, is the emotional content proper for the subject? If the treatment is sentimentalized, then it is probable that the artist lacked either sincerity or a steady view of life.

One caution: The test of artistic truth cannot be made by the general public, although their criticism may be valuable. Scientists, for example, would not allow the validity of their conclusions to be tested by a plumber, a cab driver, and a meat cutter. They ask that these truths be tested by the experiments of scientists who are their equal in scientific knowledge. There is a little difference between scientists and artists, but the difference is not too marked. We could argue that since the butcher, the baker, and the candlestick maker are human personalities, they might be accepted as valid critics of the artist's discovery. To a certain extent this claim is true. On the other hand, certain people can read with more discernment than others. Some are excellent at understanding the language and symbolism of painting, sculpture, or music. Perhaps more important, some people are more sensitive than others to the problems of personality and experience. These people, those who can understand the medium of expression and who are sensitive to human problems, must constitute the group of judges for the validity of a work of art.

The next question for consideration is the nature of the raw materials for artistic investigation. These are sometimes hard to see. Most obvious are the many facets of such emotions as love, hatred, jealousy, contentment, sudden apprehension of the beauty in nature or people, and other emotional reactions. As a matter of fact, these materials from life are so common that it is probable that the great bulk of art is made from them, but there is much more material that has been explored in literature, art, and music. Artists present their explorations as experience that the members of the artistic audience may live through. Take, for example, the psychological experience confronting a young prince who has been humanely educated, who faces a problem of evil involving the murder of his father, the king, and the unfaithfulness, even incest, of his mother. (In other words, the problem Shakespeare explored in *Hamlet.*) The artist feels this problem within himself and composes its elements and its solution. Psychology and literature often run parallel to each other; the former gives facts, the latter gives truth-to-life. This truth is achieved because we become personally involved in the work of literature, live through the complexities of the problem with all their attendant, opposing emotions, and sense the logic, the rightness, and the freedom of the solution when it is reached.

Perhaps one more consideration is necessary before we turn to examples of the explorations and discoveries of the artists. This consideration is that of the place and importance of form. Let us put it this way: human experience is seldom simple or direct. Rather, its importance is usually clouded with events of no importance, many of which are totally irrelevant. Perhaps the best illustration of this may be found in the artist who is painting a landscape. The artist's purpose is not to make a direct copy from nature—a camera might provide a more exact representation than a human being. Rather, the painter is seeking to interpret an experience with beauty. The natural scene, however, is cluttered with objects detracting from the impression the artist seeks. Consequently, the artist leaves many out, rearranges them mentally, and paints on canvas the objects that individual sees, so that the picture, when complete, is not a copy of nature, but a picture of beauty, with the natural objects selected and arranged to make the meaning clear. But no critic, nor commentator, perhaps not even the artist, could give us a definite, final statement as to what that "meaning" is. Perhaps it is a sense of the

importance of peace, quiet, repose; perhaps it is the wonder of organization, order, design; perhaps it is the sheer joy of contrasting colors, the delight in appearances of objects, their texture and feel; perhaps the pleasure of a thing of beauty. If it could be expressed definitely in words, the picture would not be necessary, but since it cannot, it is the only means by which the artist can share a delight in the world. And the imperative need to share it, to get it "said," is the quality that makes artists; they not only do what they can, but what they must. Somehow, that creative urge, which everyone shares to some extent, is communicated to an audience; theorists of "aesthetic experience" do not agree on the "how," but something does happen. However little understood the process, the fact remains that people throughout the years have enjoyed (the word is too weak: they have *needed*) the making of pictures and the looking at them.

It is interesting that it is this element of form that all of the arts have in common, and it is this that gives them the "living-through" quality we have noted as distinctive of artistic truth. It is the process, not the end result, that is important. It is the form, not the final statement, that yields artistic truth, though this does not imply that the artist's final point is unimportant. The important thing is having gone through the experience with the artist and arriving at the discovery the artist wishes to communicate.

With this in mind, we are going to examine some examples of art in different mediums to see how the various artists have mined some truth from the darkness and chaos of the experiences of the human personality.

Every art form has much in common with other forms but each also has its own symbols, images, and materials, all used in ways that are unique for each medium. Written or spoken references to a painting, for example, are translations. If, as Gertrude Stein has written, "a rose is a rose is a rose," so also a painting is a painting is a painting. The mixture of paints on the canvas *is* the message; all else is translation in one way or another. "An artist cannot speak about his art," remarked Jean Cocteau, "any more than a plant can discuss horticulture." The literary arts resist translation just as obstinately as do the visual arts. Whether the poet, for example, uses familiar word sets ("Come live with me and be my love") or unconventional combinations ("love is more thicker than forget"), the exact arrangement of the precise words is what the poet has to say and nothing else, or the poet would have said that instead. In both arts a single work may have several levels of meaning, ranging deeper and deeper from the surface meaning, and lookers and readers can uncover greater depths of significance as they work through the symbols created by the artist. In both arts the interpretations are somewhat personal, depending upon the critical ability and background of the reader or the viewer. The response, however, *must be* within the limits set by the artist. In the arts, as in most other things, we can always arrive at some very mistaken interpretations.

Music amounts to pure form and is not amenable to any one "story" interpretation. Many untutored listeners have one of two responses to music. When they think they are listening perceptively they arrive at some sort of story, which usually sounds something like this: This person is in love, and then his girl leaves him, and right at the end she comes back and everything is just dandy. The other listening attitude is simply to be submerged in the sound, to, in other words, take a tonal bath. The latter listeners usually find their attention wandering off in a thousand directions before a musical selection of any length is finished. In other words, they find themselves thinking about everything but the music.

But music, except for program music, which has a story to tell in sound and sometimes employs sounds heard in everyday life (and the composer's "story" is not necessarily that of the listener), is, as said above, form in sound. It is a "time-art," which makes it particularly elusive, since by the time it is heard it is gone. For this reason we are devoting a special section to an introduction to music. Music makes greater demands on its audience, both in knowledge and attention, than do any of the other arts. The knowledgeable and attentive listener finds, however, that living through a musical selection yields as much meaning for life's experiences as do any of the other arts. In its structures one may find the grandeur of Bach, the elegance of Mozart, the serenity of Gregorian chant, or the sound of protest, which is sometimes characteristic of jazz. Whatever the significance of a piece of music, it is the composition that counts. As much as in any of the other arts, perhaps more, the composer must arrange materials so that the listener lives through an experience that lies deeper than words or the recognizable subject matter of painting. It is this process of composition that leads to "living through," our concern in this chapter, since it is the common basis for all the arts.

Examples from Literature

In order to see how this intricate interrelation of meaning and form is accomplished in literature, we can use some very simple illustrations for analysis. For example, a creative writing class once tried to make an "absolutely beautiful" line of poetry. This is what they came up with:

Rainy evening. Idle. Only music . . .

Most people would agree that this is a very pretty line. But what makes it so? You might ask yourself where the heavy accents fall. And then, what about the vowel sounds? Suddenly what appears at first to be only a nice lazy line begins to look like the work of a craftsman, for we discover that we are running down the long vowel sounds, exactly as they come in the alphabet *a, e, i, o, u,* and that these sounds occur exactly on the heavy accents. Now what about consonant sounds? The consonants are *r, n, v, ng, dl, l, m,*

hard *c* (a *k* sound). We could have had *p, b, k, g,* and all the rest. Are the ones that appear in the line purely accidental choices? Not on your life. Except for the last *c,* all the consonants are *liquid* consonants. The term is self-explanatory; they flow along without creating much stoppage. Only the last one (the *c* in *music*) is of a different sort, and it is put there exactly because it *does* stop the line. We have here a line that doesn't "say" much in terms of making a declaration or asking a question, but it certainly creates a mood. And the mood is created because of a lot of hard work in choosing sounds carefully and distributing them in terms of accentuation.

As another example, a student in the same class wrote a five-line poem about the Cain and Abel story. Here are the first two lines:

Oh Cain, you slay in vain. You may not stay.
East of Eden, East of Eden, flee for. . . .

Notice not only the vowel music, but the change in rhythm between the first and second line. Using the same pattern, you might try to write the last three lines.

The examples given above are really only one-finger exercises in the craft of writing poetry. Now we can choose a complete poem for the same kind of analysis to see the intricate relationships of form that create a sum of meaning greater than the arithmetical addition of the meanings of the words themselves. We might choose A.E. Housman's deceptively simple, eight-line poem, "With Rue My Heart is Laden."

With rue my heart is laden
    For golden friends I had,
For many a rose-lipt maiden
    And many a light-foot lad.
By brooks too broad for leaping
    The lightfoot boys are laid;
The rose-lipt girls are sleeping
    In fields where roses fade.

Of course Housman is saying that he grieves for the friends of his youth, now dead. Where does one attack the *form* of a poem like this? You might ask yourself why he chose the word *boys* in the second stanza when he used *lads* in the first. Then examine the first line of the second stanza:

By *b*rooks too *b*road for *l*eaping

Perhaps you begin to see that he chose *boys* in the second line to make an alliterative pattern with *brooks* and *broad.* What of the *l* in the first line of the second stanza? Suddenly one discovers that it forms a similar pattern with *lightfoot* and *laid* in the second line. In the first line of the second stanza we have two *b*s, one *l*; in the second line, two *l*s, one *b*. Is this purely accidental on the part of the composer? Try the last two lines of the first stanza, with its *m*s and *l*s. The same pattern reveals itself and, furthermore, the alliterative *l* of the first stanza carries over to repeat itself in the second stanza. In other words, the middle four lines of the poem form a unit by themselves, created by the alliterations.

Colorplate 1 Paul Gauguin, *Where Do We Come From? What Are We? Where Are We Going?* signed and dated 1897. Oil on canvas, 54¾ × 147½". Tompkins Collection. Arthur Gordon Tompkins Fund. Courtesy, Museum of Fine Arts, Boston.

Colorplate 2 Pieter Bruegel the Elder, *Winter (Return of the Hunters)*, 1565. Oil on panel, 46 × 63¾″. Kunsthistorisches Museum, Vienna.

Colorplate 3 Meindert Hobbema, *The Watermill with the Great Red Roof*, ca. 1670. Oil on canvas, 32 × 43⅛″. Collection of the Art Institute of Chicago.

Colorplate 4 Vincent van Gogh, *The Starry Night*, 1889. Oil on canvas, 29 × 36¼″. Collection, The Museum of Modern Art, New York. Acquired through the Lillie P. Bliss Bequest.

Colorplate 5 Wassily Kandinsky, *Panel (3)* (also known as *Summer*), 1914. Oil on canvas, 64 × 36¼". Collection, The Museum of Modern Art, New York. Mrs. Simon Guggenheim Fund.

Colorplate 6 Hyacinthe Rigaud, *Portrait of Louis XIV,* 1701. Oil on canvas, 9′ 1½″ × 6′ 2⅝″. The Louvre, Paris.

Colorplate 7 Pablo Picasso, *Girl Before a Mirror,* 1932. Oil on canvas, 64 × 51¼″. Collection, The Museum of Modern Art, New York. Gift of Mrs. Simon Guggenheim.

But that's not all. Examine the rhymes: *laden, maiden; leaping, sleeping; had, lad; laid, fade.* The first four of the rhymes listed here (lines 1, 3, 5, 7 in the poem) are weak endings; that is, they end in a dropping-off syllable that gets almost no accent at all. The second group of rhymes (lines 2, 4, 6, 8 of the poem) are strong endings; they end sharply on the accented syllable. This is strengthened even further by Housman's use of end punctuation after the lines with strong endings. Reason? Look at the subject matter of the lines with weak endings and that of the lines with strong endings.

One more example, this time in prose, for it is easy to jump to the conclusion that poets take this much care with their sounds, but that prose writers do not have to. In a story by Wilbur Daniel Steele,[2] we find the following sentence:

> Accept as he would with the top of his brain the fact of a spherical earth zooming through space, deep in his heart he knew that the world lay flat from modern Illinois to ancient Palestine, and that the sky above it, blue by day and by night festooned with guiding stars for wise men, was the nether side of a floor on which the resurrected trod.

An unskilled writer tried to communicate the "same" meaning with the following sentence:

> Although he accepted in his mind the fact that the earth was a sphere travelling through space, yet in his deepest emotions he knew that it was flat and that the sky was the under-side of the floor of heaven.

Why, for example, does Steele say that the world "lay flat from modern Illinois to ancient Palestine" instead of simply saying that it was flat, as the other writer did? Perhaps he wanted to suggest an expanse of time, from the modern world back to the time of Christ, as well as an expanse of space. Why did he describe the sky as he did rather than plainly using the word *sky,* as the unskilled writer did? There is the possibility that while he was stating a fact about a person's belief concerning the physical structure of the earth he also wanted to suggest a religious significance to the belief. So he mentioned the stars and the wise men to flood our memories with the story of the birth of Christ. The two sentences differ in at least one more phase of meaning. The unskilled writer's sentence has no rhythm, while Steele's sentence reads in long undulations of sound. This kind of rhythm puts us in a philosophic frame of mind, which creates the kind of atmosphere he wanted. It is for such reasons that the author chose exactly the words he did, and arranged them as he did. For its purpose in the story it is a much better sentence than that of the unskilled writer.

2. Wilbur Daniel Steele, "The Man Who Saw through Heaven," in *An Anthology of Famous American Stories,* ed. Angus Burrell and Bennett Cerf (New York: Modern Library, 1953).

An Example from Music

Music is sound moving in time, and therein lies its magical mystery. While listening to an unfamiliar piece of music, the listener does not know where the music is going until it gets there, that is, ceases to sound. From silence to sound to silence and what takes place in between is a mixture of sound and silence comprehended only in retrospect, after one musical section has followed upon another until silence reigns again. Readers can reread difficult passages in a book and art lovers can study a painting for hours, but music listeners have one ride on a merry-go-round. There is no way to stop the music or freeze a beautiful sound, even though some critics are fond of referring to architecture as "frozen music." Nothing is ever that simple.

Music is a structural art built out of a multiplicity of materials by the composer, who picks and chooses tones, colors, textures, rhythms, and patterns just as a writer selects words and phrases that best suit the purpose and the painter chooses lines and colors. Rarely are these infinite choices deliberately calculated or contrived, except in so-called "bad" art. The artist, each in his own way, is seeking expression, to communicate some feeling, truth, or emotion about experience as it is perceived.

Music is the envy of many artists because it is so abstract that it can never pretend to represent anything specific, or exactly portray one iota of the sensible world in which we live. Music is *free,* truly free, to soar to the heights or descend to the depths of intellectual-emotional experiences. This unfettered freedom is the constant delight of all good musicians and experienced nonmusicians (listeners). It is also the cause of utter despair of teachers and students who have yet to learn the basic skills and thus the joys of listening to music with some degree of understanding. Only after understanding can there be any real "appreciation," and this appreciation need not include approbation; many experienced listeners can understand and even appreciate music that they really do not enjoy. But then, how can people who are illiterate know whether or not they dislike a novel?

Literacy in music is no more a common heritage of all humans than is the ability to read and write. To become a reasonably knowledgeable listener is not very difficult because the listener has only to learn to "read"; the "writing" is left to professional musicians. And what is there to read in music: notes, scales, intervals, keys, chords? Not at all; these are merely the "grammar" of music and not its content. The listener begins with the larger units of music, with its structure. In the fullness of time a certain minimal knowledge of musical grammar will fall into place within the overall picture of musical design. For example, the following musical phrase has a beginning and an incomplete and unsatisfying ending:

Ein feste Burg

However, when the next phrase is added we have the completion of a musical idea, even though it is something less than a complete composition:

The two phrases add up to a musical period or a relatively complete musical idea called, for convenience, letter *A.* Then, for purposes of balance, the period (or paired phrases) is repeated before proceeding to the next section (section *B*). This section retains the strong, stern character of the first section, but introduces several new ideas for contrast (phrases indicated by dotted lines):

Formal Structure: *Ein feste Burg*

Bar Form (A–A–B)

Some Examples from Painting

A common plaint among laypeople is that they cannot understand "modern art" and that they prefer "realistic" works, that is, painting and sculpture that tell a story, look like something, and are easy to understand. The sad truth is that most people have never learned to understand much of anything about any kind of art, are very vague as to what "realism" might

be, do not know the story related in most figurative painting and sculpture (painting and sculpture presenting natural objects) and, if they do, are unaware that subject matter cannot make the art object beautiful, life-enhancing, or valuable by itself. Most painting, sculpture, and architecture *seem* to be easily understandable, but the qualities that make one work superior to another need to be learned, just as they must be learned in music and literature.

Some people refuse to take art seriously, being convinced that it is all a matter of taste. They fall back on that old bromide "There is no disputing taste." We answer, "Nuts." Taste is a learned, not innate, ability and all statements to the contrary are delusive and established in self-defense to soothe the ego. The vocabulary, subject matter, materials, and techniques of the visual arts cannot be reduced to the confines of this book, which serves a broader purpose. Nevertheless, imparting basic knowledge of the visual arts, stimulating aesthetic response, and encouraging further investigation into the arts are part of that purpose.

It is regrettable that in this century the words *beauty* and *beautiful* have taken on a narrow meaning for the general public, a meaning of prettiness and niceness, which makes the words *beauty* and *beautiful* incomprehensible to many people when they are applied to a highly abstract painting by Picasso; a nonobjective orgy of bright, explosive, and intermingling colors by Kandinsky; miles of earthwork constructions in the wilderness, or mounds of earthworks on the parquet floors of distinguished museums; and sculpture that moves, screeches, or destroys itself. For the moment, then, let us discard these words and investigate a fundamental term, *aesthetics.* A survey of dictionaries to discover the meaning of the word *aesthetics* generally will only add to the confusion, for the word usually is defined as a sense of beauty, love of beauty, or philosophy of beauty. It would seem that we are on a merry-go-round until we realize that the opposite of aesthetic is anaesthetic, which is the diminution and/or loss of communication and excitement of ideas and emotions, irrespective of what these ideas and emotions might be. The quality of art is determined by how well the ideas and emotions have been communicated.

People by nature are sentient, communicative beings—creators, artists. Everyone creates, but few produce anything unique, life-enhancing, or enduring. In this book we are concerned with the fine arts of literature, music, painting, sculpture, and architecture. But we must be aware that there are many other arts, including the art of cooking, the art of dancing, the art of gardening, and the art of living.

The French painter Paul Gauguin (go-GAN; 1848–1903) never saw a scene such as he portrayed in *Where Do We Come From? What Are We? Where Are We Going?* (colorplate 1), nor has or will anyone else. Certainly he drew the images of the gentle islanders, their birds and dogs, the beautiful landscape, from the world about him. But these perceptions could have been captured by a camera, which would have given us a clearer, more detailed, visually accurate representation. Gauguin, however, produced a painting in which his perceptions were simplified, distorted, abstracted, to present his vision of humanity asking the eternal questions. Carefully observe in colorplate 1 that the bodies vary in color from gold to brown to red; that the trees are undulating patterns of blues and purples; that there is a systematic interweaving of shapes and colors. Patterns, shapes, lines, and colors are arranged so as to establish a mood of enduring silence, gentleness, and reflection. Although the title aids us in understanding Gauguin's vision, it is not necessary for understanding the mood and the spirit of the painting. Obviously, this painting could not have been called *Joy and Celebration,* for it does not convey that mood. Likewise, *Natives on the Beach,* its elementary subject matter, fails to express the feeling this painting evokes. Of course philosophers, scientists, theologians, and historians have written books on the very questions Gauguin uses as his title and motif; this text will pursue these questions relentlessly. However, Gauguin painted instead of writing, because line, value, shape, form, color, and texture were his materials, which he used in repetition, opposition, dominance, and subordination, to produce a painting of unique rhythm and harmony.

How different, but equally challenging, is the *Return of the Hunters* (colorplate 2) by the Flemish painter Pieter Bruegel (BROO–gull; 1525–1569). Two moods are conveyed in this painting: the coldness and bleakness of nature, and the warmth and activity of humans. This painting is a wonderful study in linear and aerial perspective, for Bruegel was a master of illusion, convincingly conveying on a two-dimensional surface the illusion of the third dimension. Linear perspective is based on our visual memory, which tells us that two parallel lines eventually seem to meet in the distance; aerial perspective relies again on a visual memory, which tells us that objects seem to become obscure, faint, as we increase our distance from them. Our eyes tell us lies and Bruegel repeated the lies of visual memory. In this painting, which also is called *Winter,* our eyes are directed to the distant snow-covered mountains by strong diagonal lines, which lead away from the picture plane; likewise, people, buildings, even the mountains decrease in size and clarity as we move away from the returning hunters at the lower left-hand side of the painting. We have been brought up to understand perspective and proportion and thus appreciate Bruegel's mastery accordingly. An ancient Egyptian would not have understood this painting, since Egyptian art did not use these principles of perspective, and proportion was determined by the importance of the personages represented. Different cultures see and express themselves with different conventions.

Bruegel's work is considered a masterpiece not only because of his technical virtuosity, but also because the artist presented an image of his time, of life as he saw it. The day may be cold, the hunters and their dogs bent with fatigue after a long and arduous hunt, but within this little hamlet there is a variety of activity that shows the warmth and delights of human life. Bruegel presents a microcosm under the guise of a deceptively simple genre scene.

The Dutch painter Meindert Hobbema (MINE–dirt HOB–a–moh; 1639–1709) records a gentler nature in *The Watermill with the Great Red Roof* (colorplate 3). This scene of a countryside with soft, downy clouds in a baby-blue sky, gnarled trees with fuzzy foliage, sparkling water falling gently into the still pond, has a lyric quality that is enhanced by backlighting the scene. There is a gentle gradation from dark to light from foreground to background. Hobbema refined his work so that we can hardly see the brush strokes. The artist disappears in the image he creates. The artist is concerned with the beauty of domesticated nature as revealed by light. The scene is calm, quiet, and peaceful—a scene such as Wordsworth recounted in many poems.

The Dutch artist Vincent van Gogh (van–GO; 1853–1890) was no pastoral lyricist. He wanted to paint the world, people, and nature, with all the love, passion, and excitement that he failed to convey in personal relationships. In *Starry Night* (colorplate 4), nature is shown to be violent: the moon and stars of brilliant oranges and yellows are glowing, burning whirligigs that leave trails of golden streaks as they speed through the sky, which also moves in dashes, spots, and streaks of a variety of assertive blues. In the foreground the top branches of a cypress shoot into the sky like flames seeking to reach the highest heavens, devouring the very air in their pursuit. No camera could ever reproduce this scene; all knowledge of perspective and of natural color is disregarded; optical illusions and visual truths are forsaken. Van Gogh painted the scene not as he saw it, but as he felt it. And he painted it in heavy pigment (impasto) into which he gouged and scratched, so that in addition to the strength of color and violence of lines, the painting is rich in animated surface texture. Even cursory observation makes us keenly aware of the artist's physical activity in creating the work, and thus heightens our emotional response. Not for a moment, however, should we think of van Gogh as a madman, the popular conception of this great artist. Van Gogh was a driven man, indeed, but he planned his paintings in great detail, as his writings prove; and in this case he purposely established the small hamlet with its buildings composed of quiet squares and rectangles in the lower foreground to contrast with the turbulence of the heavens and the cypress. This painting relies very little on perception, very much on conception, in this case through very personalized abstractions.

The word *abstract* in relation to art is greatly misunderstood and commonly misused. All art is abstract—even the most naturalistic. Take a photo of a friend from your wallet and ask yourself how realistic it is. Quite obviously, your friend's body or head is not flat, not small enough to put in a wallet, and is not black, white, and gray. This photographic likeness is just that: a likeness or an abstraction of your friend. Painters or sculptors have always used abstractions in art; and society, as a group or as individuals, determines the degree to which it will accept these abstractions. Therefore, there are many degrees of abstractions, just as there are many languages, which are oral and written abstractions. Among some primitive tribes a high degree of abstraction from visual reality is so accepted that the primitives cannot recognize photographs of themselves or friends, but do "see" themselves and others in geometric signs and symbols. Some critics persist in claiming that the greatest art is that which is most illusionistic, that is, art that conveys the most convincing illusions of physical bulk and texture, visual recognition, and sense of three-dimensional space. Some of the greatest painters and sculptors in history have been superb illusionists, but illusionism by itself has little merit. There is no art form more illusionistic than the sculptured figures in a wax museum, but these figures lack vitality in that they resemble corpses rather than human beings.

When a painter chooses to forsake the perceptual world completely and paints on canvas with shapes, lines, and colors that draw upon no natural counterpart, the painting is called nonobjective. Wassily Kandinsky (va–SILL–ee can–DIN–ski; 1866–1944), a Russian painter, is often heralded as the first nonobjective artist. Without disclaiming his brilliance and importance to the development of modern art, it is important to note that the pottery painters of the geometric period of ancient Greece, the monks responsible for the medieval *Book of Kells,* the mosaicists who designed and executed the beautifully patterned floors of the public buildings of Byzantium, weavers from all periods of history, and your grandmothers who made patchwork crazy quilts were among the many thousands of artists who worked nonobjectively long before Kandinsky appeared upon the scene.

It was Kandinsky and the Dutch painter Piet Mondrian (Pete MOAN–dree–ahn; 1872–1944) who were the great pioneers of modern nonobjective art. Mondrian became the forerunner of the geometric nonobjective school and Kandinsky of expressionistic nonobjective art, both styles being carried to new and further directions by avant-garde artists today. Kandinsky's *Panel (3)* (colorplate 5) has all the turbulence of van Gogh's *Starry Night* without the subject matter drawn from nature. Colors and shapes move, impinge upon, and obliterate each other in this dynamic composition. For those who say, "I can't understand this kind of painting," here are a few questions: (1) Is this painting quiet or lively? (2) Is this painting somber or gay in mood? (3) Is this painting dull or bright? If your answers are (1) lively, (2) gay in mood, and (3) bright, you do understand the basic nature and elements of this painting. Keep asking questions of this type about any painting or work of art and you will learn a great deal. All that is needed is time and perseverance. One note of caution: whether or not you understand a work of art has little if any bearing on whether it is a good work.

We are brought to the problem, then, of how does one look at and judge a work of art? Just as with music and literature, there is no easy answer, but perhaps the following guidelines will be of some assistance.

First, look at the work and ask yourself what you *see.* Inventory the painting, not just for the figurative parts but also for all the shapes, colors, lines, textures, and spaces, and notice the manner in which these elements are put together, that is, the composition.

Second, almost at the same time you are asking yourself what you see, ask yourself what you *know.* There is an immense difference between seeing and knowing. For example, you might *see* a figure of a haloed man with a white beard carrying a key, but you might *know,* also, that the halo represents sainthood and that the key is the attribute (or symbol) through which we recognize St. Peter. You might see a tree form, but only special knowledge will define that particular tree as an oak, aspen, or willow.

Third, ask yourself what the artist was attempting to do. It is at this point that most amateurs falter, quite naturally. But the artist sets a mood for a painting, describes items in certain ways through color, shapes, lines, arrangements of many elements to create certain effects. For example, Bruegel bent the backs of his hunters to indicate their weariness, van Gogh painted stars in bright colors to make them seem like glowing orbs, and Kandinsky used white extensively to set off the bright reds, blues, and yellows of his painting. Each artwork, be it painting, sculpture, architecture, or craft item, has a composition that should function to make all parts work together in rhythm and harmony. The rules for judging any work are implicit in the work itself.

Fourth, judge how well the artist solves self-imposed problems. Remember that even the "Divine Michelangelo" goofed sometimes and that some tenth-rate artists turned out single works of inestimable merit. Do not hesitate to be critical. Do Bruegel's hunters give a convincing impression of weariness? Does the little and quiet hamlet afford a balancing contrast for the *Starry Night?* At this point you are evaluating or appreciating the painting, making a judgment on the basis of all that you *see* and *know,* and an analysis of how well the artist resolved the problems.

You have just received an elementary lesson in criticism. Try it often; you'll improve with practice.

Do not be discouraged or embarrassed if some of the world's greatest masterpieces leave you cold. If you can recognize the obvious merit of a work of art but find in it qualities distasteful to your temperament, you are developing discriminating personal taste. It is altogether possible to recognize the greatness of Raphael and van Gogh and at the same time dislike them because Raphael's figures are too saccharine for you and van Gogh's paintings are much too wild for you to live with comfortably. If you find, also, that you like paintings that have little artistic merit but are predominately orange (your favorite color) or whose subject matter is cats (and you love cats), recognize that there often are factors in a work of art that you value over the purely artistic values. In any case, you should begin to know how and why a work moves you. This is part of the process of learning how to judge a painting and yourself. Aesthetic understanding and appreciation is a give-and-take process involving you and the work of art. In undertaking the problem of criticism you should become a more knowledgeable, humanized individual.

Only a historian would know that the portrait (colorplate 6) by Hyacinthe Rigaud (REE–go; 1659–1743) of the imposing old man with the flowing wig, sumptuous robe, and red-heeled and red-ribboned shoes was the famous Louis XIV of France. Still, practically anyone would know that this gentleman was an overdressed, important personage posing in an elaborate setting. The French artist wanted to impress the viewer with the magnificence of the "Sun King," the elegance of his costume, and the majesty of his pose. Observe the artist's mastery in describing the fabrics, which are masterpieces of illusion. This is a beautiful painting of a homely old man, although the artist used every trick in the trade to de-emphasize the face. It is relatively easy to appreciate the quality of this painting, but it is difficult to like it because contemporary taste rejects the overblown extravagance of garb and ceremonial authoritarian poses. Remember that this painting was produced for a palace and now resides in a palace museum. It was not meant to hang over a television set and, despite its beauty as a painting, would have little relevance in most homes.

The Spanish artist Pablo Picasso (PAB–lo pea–KAH–so; 1881–1973) painted the *Girl Before a Mirror* (colorplate 7) in 1932. Like most of his works, it is a very controversial painting, which most people find difficult to understand; and even today it is seldom called beautiful. A cursory examination reveals only a series of circles and triangles in bright colors and patterns working on the picture plane. Perhaps you need to be told that the girl on the left is shown both in full-face and profile. Look carefully and you will see a profile view in pink and then its merging with a yellow side to describe a face frontally, a device now used by many comic strip artists. Picasso told us that he *knew* that each individual has profile views as well as a frontal view, that he painted not only what he actually saw but what he knew exists in a combination or "Picasso-view." That the colors of these sections do not coincide and are different again from the profile reflection in the mirror made no difference to Picasso because, in the last analysis, this painting is a highly abstracted study of a woman presented from many viewpoints and brightly colored and patterned to achieve a complex decorative composition. Pattern and color are the keys to this painting, but the psychological interpretations that may be made are numerous. This painting still seems new, unique, and

very intriguing; Picasso created new forms, a new way of seeing and presenting. Those of us who have been brought up with Picasso's works find them easy to understand, and we enjoy this painting for its decorative qualities, mystery of interpretation, and bold innovations. Art styles change as people's basic ideas and characteristics change. Picasso was one of the great artists of our century who not only reflected but produced these changes. All innovations seem heretical, sometimes even crazy, but often they become part of the mainstream of life, and inevitably are superseded by new and seemingly wilder innovations.

All the works illustrated and discussed were composed to communicate ideas and emotions; all differ from each other in style, degree of abstraction, and perceptual and conceptual understanding of people and nature. It is hoped, even anticipated, that you will appreciate or learn to appreciate each of these works, but it is unlikely you will like each of them. Remember, nevertheless, that each artist is sharing with you a vision of the world, a way of seeing, and in so doing communicates artistic truth.

Summary

In such fashions as those illustrated, artists, whatever their medium—music, painting, literature—have made form the vehicle of idea, have made the raw materials of art acquire significance by arrangement and handling. It is a different kind of meaning from that of scientists, which can be perceived and measured in an objective world, for this sort of meaning can be known only by the individual who can see the relationships the artists have formulated, and who can find them valid in terms of personal experience. It is not an easy process, sometimes; and just as the effectiveness of the scientist depends upon two things—the validity of the discovery, and the ability of the beholder to understand or comprehend it—so the effectiveness of the artist depends upon the validity of the discovery, and the sensitivity of the beholder to apprehend it. "I don't get it" is no refutation of either Einstein or Bach.

Not everyone will derive the same kind or degree of satisfaction from a particular art form, obviously; but the educated person is obligated to know that "there is something in it," even if that "something" does not deeply move that individual. And perhaps, with deeper acquaintance and wider knowledge, that "something" will become clearer and of greater value than before.

In this chapter we have made the assertion that the artist is an explorer and discoverer in the realm of the human personality. The artist uses the method of intuition and composition. The artist's raw material lies in the human personality and in human experience, with their vast and unknown reaches, their disrupting conflicts. The artist gives form to the component elements of personality and experience, and in so doing yields an artistic truth. No matter whether we speak of literature, painting, sculpture, music, or any of the other arts, this concept of creating form out of chaos is the single common basis and foundation for all aesthetics.

An Introduction to Music Listening

Prelude

Already the most universal of the arts, music can, through modern technology, span either national boundaries or centuries past with effortless ease. Whether rich or poor, all of us can enjoy, in our own homes, the Boston Symphony playing Beethoven or the musical life of medieval Paris or modern China. In fact, we live in a society saturated with music from supermarket to concert hall, however, quantity does not necessarily mean quality. Almost everyone has heard the everyday sounds of popular music and the murmer of Musak; but few know very much about Beethoven, or medieval, Chinese, or any other music that might be called classical.

Classical music is not drastically different from popular music. Both have unity and variety, and both use melody, harmony, rhythm, and tone color structured in recognizable musical forms. Quite simply, classical music just has more of everything: greater length, more unity, increased variety. It follows, then, that anyone who likes popular music—most of us—can learn to enjoy music a step beyond popular songs, music more intricate, complex, and considerably more interesting over a longer period of time. Popular hits are pleasurable and frequently delightful but they are also transitory. Classical music has an appeal that, with repeated listening, extends over months, years, or even a lifetime. And it all begins with nursery jingles, folk songs, hymns, marches, waltzes, and the popular songs of the day.

Music listeners tend to develop their musical tastes up a ladder of progressively more intricate and interesting music, a process usually more intuitive than deliberate. We become music lovers with the songs we sing and whistle as children. As teenagers we generally follow our peers and tune in to popular songs, rock, country-western, bluegrass, and the dance music of the time. At some point, however, nearly everyone develops a liking for more complex music—works like *Fiddler on the Roof, Hello Dolly, My Fair Lady,* and other marvelous American musicals—plus some jazz, which is also America's unique contribution to the world's music. At some other point we add Strauss waltzes, Sousa marches, *Finlandia,* the *Nutcracker Suite, Peter and the Wolf,* and, usually, some tuneful symphonies and concertos by Tchaikovsky and Rachmaninoff. At about this time some of the powerful music of Beethoven becomes attractive along with Chopin's romantic piano music. Further exploration leads to the elegance of Mozart and the lyricism of Schubert, and the music goes on and on.

The remarkable and wonderful fact about progressing up a ladder of musical taste is that *we can have it all:* everything we ever enjoyed as children and teenagers *plus* music of countless centuries and cultures. There are so many options when we appreciate a wide spectrum of music: music for romantic candlelight dinners, singing, dancing, jogging, studying, thinking, or dreaming. Modern technology has provided us with an incredible variety of recorded music—a whole world of listening experiences limited only by our musical tastes.

Throughout this book you will be introduced to music as it has developed in Western civilization, from medieval songs and dances to symphonic music by Beethoven, Tchaikovsky, and Stravinsky. As consumers of music—listeners rather than performers—you will have the opportunity to systematically develop your listening skills, to become sophisticated listeners. No one begins music listening from scratch. All our lives we are exposed to all kinds of music, some that we hear and some to which we listen. *Hearing,* sometimes described as taking a tonal bath, is a passive state, whereas *listening* is an active and alert activity. Throughout this text our focus will be on active listening, that is, conscious attention to musical content, melody, harmony, rhythm, tone color, and musical forms. As stated before and reiterated here, these elements are common to all music.

Characteristics of Musical Sounds

Musical tones are sounds of definite pitch and duration, as distinct from noises and other less definite sounds. Musical tones have the four characteristics of *pitch, intensity, tone color,* and *duration,* which may be described as follows:

Pitch   The location of musical sound from low to high or high to low.

Intensity   Relative degree of softness or loudness.

Tone Color   The quality of a sound that distinguishes it from other musical sounds of the same pitch and intensity; for example, the different tone quality of a flute as contrasted with a clarinet. Also called *timbre.*

Duration   The length of time a tone is audible.

The Four Elements of Music

Rhythm, melody, harmony, and *tone color* are the essential elements of music. Composers and performers are concerned with each, while for the listener, they are experienced as a web of sound that makes it difficult to single out any one element. Each can, however, be considered in isolation as a guide to understanding.

Rhythm

Though little is known about prehistoric music, the earliest music was probably the beating out of rhythms long before the existence of either melody or speech. There is rhythm in the universe: our heartbeat, alternating day and night, the progression of the seasons, waves crashing on a beach. Manufactured rhythm can be heard in train wheels clicking on rails, a Ping-Pong game, or the clacking castanets of a Spanish dancer.

Essentially, rhythm is the organization of musical time, that is, everything that takes place in terms of sound and silence, accent and nonaccent, tension and relaxation. Rhythm can also be defined as the "melody of a monotone"; music can be recognized just by hearing its rhythm. For example, tapping out the rhythmic patterns of "Dixie" can bring that familiar melody to mind.

Rhythm is the name of the whole and is not to be confused with *beat,* which results from a certain regularity of the rhythmic patterns. Beat, or pulse, can be compared with the heartbeat or the pulse rate. The beat will usually be steady but it may temporarily speed up or slow down. It may be *explicit* (the uniform thump of a bass drum in a marching band) or *implicit* (resulting from combinations of rhythmic patterns). As soon as one duration follows another, there will be rhythm but not necessarily beat. Certain types of music (such as Gregorian chant) do not produce the regular pulsation called beat.

When beats are produced by the music in a repeating pattern of accents, the result is *meter.* *Metered* music is *measured* music, with groupings of two, three, or four beats (or combinations of these) in each *measure,* or *bar.*

Time Signatures

When there is a regular pattern of accented and unaccented beats, it is customary to use a *time signature* in which the upper figure indicates the number of beats in a measure and the lower figure (though not in every case), the unit of beat; that is, the note value the composer has selected to symbolize one beat. For example:

2 = two beats per measure (duple meter)
4 = ♩ unit of beat (quarter note receives one beat)

3 = three beats per measure (triple meter)
8 = ♪ unit of beat (eighth note receives one beat)

Melody

A melody is a horizontal organization of pitches or, simply, a succession of musical tones. Melodies may move with:

Conjunct (Stepwise) Motion

Disjunct (Skipping) Motion

Disjunct and Conjunct Motion

Harmony

Harmony exists when two or more pitches are sounded together. Western music has used harmony since about the ninth century. However, harmony is still not commonly used in the music of the Near, Middle, or Far East or Africa.

Individual Harmonies

Melody with Harmony

Tone Color

Sometimes called timbre (TAM–ber), tone color is to music what color is to the painter. It is tone color that enables us to distinguish between a flute, a clarinet, and an oboe. A soprano voice is higher in pitch than a bass voice, but the tone color is also different. Through experience, everyone has learned to recognize the unique colors of many instruments. Further study leads to finer discriminations between similar instruments such as violin and viola, oboe and English horn, and so on. Composers select instruments for expressive purposes based largely on their coloration, whether singly or in combination. The full sound of a Beethoven symphony differs from a work by Richard Strauss, for example, because Strauss uses a wider range of instrumental colors.

Musical Literacy

The most abstract of the arts, music is sound moving in time. Factual information about music certainly helps the listener, but all the facts in the world can only assist the listening process; information about music can never replace the sound of music. One extremely useful method of instruction is to present major themes and ideas in musical notation, a practice common to virtually all books on music listening.

A practical approach to intelligent listening must include some instruction in musical literacy sufficient to read a single line of music. This is a simple process that can be quickly learned by young children and can be taught to an adult in a few minutes. The strangely prevalent folklore about musical notation being "too hard" or "too technical" has no foundation in fact, and probably refers to reading music as a performer, which is a very different matter that need not concern us here. As basic to music as the ABC's of written language but easier to understand, musical notation is an indispensable guide for music listeners. Learning to read music well enough to figure out a single line of music and to plunk it out on a piano is simply basic musical literacy.

Educated listeners quickly learn to enjoy picking out musical themes. This turns abstract sounds into tangible tunes, thus giving the listener an opportunity to preview the themes so that they can be anticipated in the music. Equally valuable is the repetition of themes after the listening experience. To summarize, picking out melodies is an aid to understanding, a helpful preview of music to be listened to, and a reminder of music already heard.

Approach the following material not with apprehension but with anticipation. Master the principles of musical notation with the positive attitude that this will materially assist not only in a better understanding of the music in this text but also lead, in time, to a lifetime of pleasurable listening.

Musical Notation

Pitch

The essential elements of our notational system were devised some ten centuries ago and subsequently altered and augmented to become a reasonably efficient means of communicating the composer's intentions to listener and performer. The system is based on the first seven letters of the alphabet and can best be illustrated by using a segment of the piano keyboard. The pitches range from low to high, from A through G in a repeating A–G pattern.

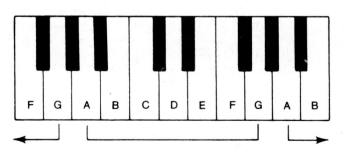

In order to know which of the eight A's available on the piano is the intended note, the following is necessary:

1. Use a musical *staff* of five lines and four spaces.

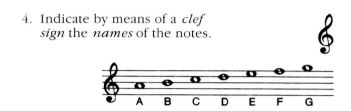

2. Use a symbol for a musical pitch, i.e., *note*.

3. Place the notes on the staff.

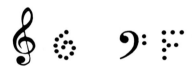

4. Indicate by means of a *clef sign* the *names* of the notes.

Clef (French, *key*) implies that the key to precise placement of the notes is the establishment of the letter name of *one* of the lines or spaces of the staff. There are two clefs in common use. Both are ornamental symbols derived from the letters G and F. The solid lines are the present clef signs and the dotted lines their original form:

The clefs are placed on the staff to indicate the location of the letters they represent. The lower portion of the G clef curls around the second line to fix the location of G; the two dots of the F clef are placed above and below the fourth line to show that this is the F line.

Once the five-line staff has received its pitch designations of G or F, the *staff* is subsequently identified as a *treble* or a *bass staff*.

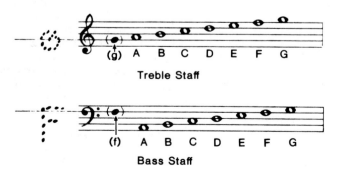

Treble Staff

Bass Staff

Both these staffs are segments of a complete system of lines and spaces called the *great staff*. The following illustration of the great staff includes notes arranged to form words, which is a quick way to learn to read music. Try putting your own words into notation.

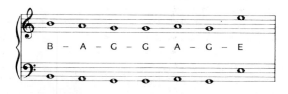

Not all melodies are composed so that they can be played on the white notes only of the piano. Sometimes another *key,* or different set of pitches, is used as demonstrated in the following examples:

Key of C

Key of D

In the second version the *key signature* indicates that all of the F's and C's have been raised a half step to the next closest note. A symbol called a sharp (♯) indicates raised notes. Key signatures can include up to seven sharps or flats.

The other common symbol that changes a note is the *flat* (♭), which lowers a note a half step to the next closest note. Following is the same melody written in the key of B♭. As indicated by the key signature, all the B's and E's have been lowered to B♭ and E♭.

Key of B♭

You will note that the staff given above has an added short line, a *ledger line,* used to accommodate the last two notes.

A piano keyboard has *white* keys and *black* keys, with the black keys grouped in alternating sets of two and three. The white note, or key, immediately to the left of the two black keys is always C. There are eight C's; the C closest to the center is *middle C.* It is from this C that you can locate the notes of the themes.

Middle C   Middle C

Below is a guide to the *chromatic scale,* which is all of the white and black keys in one octave.

Duration

The notation of the length of time of musical sounds (and silences) was developed in conjunction, more or less, with the notation of pitch. The modern *note-value* system consists of fractional parts of a whole unit, or *whole note* (𝅝), expressed in mathematical terms as 1/1. A *half note* (𝅗𝅥) is one-half the whole unit, or 1/2; a *quarter note* (𝅘𝅥) is one-quarter the unit, or 1/4; and so forth.

Chromatic Scale

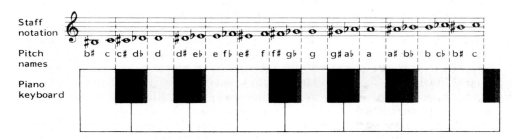

The *name* of the note value indicates the *number* of notes in the whole-note unit. There are four quarter notes (4 × 1/4 = 1/1), eight eighth notes (8 × 1/8 = 1/1), etc.

With note values smaller than the whole note, the relationships remain constant. There are two quarter notes in a half note (2 × 1/4 = 1/2), two eighth notes in a quarter note (2 × 1/8 = 1/4), etc.

Rhythmic notation is both relative and fixed. The duration of a whole note is dependent on the tempo (speed) and notation of music. It may have a duration of one second, eight seconds, or something in between. The interior relationships, however, never vary. A whole note has the same duration as two half notes, four quarter notes, and so forth. The mathematical relationship is fixed and precise. See table P.1 for an outline of the system.

Voices and Instruments

Choral ensembles are usually divided into four voice parts ranging from high to low: soprano and alto (women) and tenor and bass (men).

Instruments of the symphony orchestra and other ensembles are grouped by family, from highest pitch to lowest:

Strings	Woodwinds	Brass	Percussion
violin	piccolo	trumpet	snare drum
viola	flute	(and cornet)	timpani
cello	oboe	French horn	bass drum
bass	clarinet	trombone	cymbals
	bassoon	tuba	many others

Keyboard instruments include piano, harpsichord, and organ. The piano, originally called pianoforte, is based on the principle of hammers striking the strings; the harpsichord has a mechanism that plucks the strings. Built with two or more keyboards called manuals, organs either use forced air to activate the pipes or some version of an electronic reproduction of sound.

Musical Texture

The words for the three kinds of musical texture are derived from Greek and are virtually self-explanatory:

Monophonic (one sound)
Homophonic (same sound)
Polyphonic (many sounds)

Monophonic music has a single unaccompanied melody line. Much of the world's music is monophonic, including Chinese and Hindu music and, in Western civilizations, Gregorian chant and troubadour songs, as discussed in the chapter on medieval music. Homophonic music has a principal melodic line accompanied by harmony, sometimes referred to as chordal accompaniment. While it is relatively unknown outside Western culture, homophonic comprises the bulk of our music including nearly all popular music. Polyphonic music has two or more

Table P.1. Note and Rest Values

Note Value	Symbol
Whole note (basic unit)	𝅝
Half note	𝅗𝅥
Quarter note	𝅘𝅥
Eighth note	𝅘𝅥𝅮
Sixteenth note	𝅘𝅥𝅯
Rest Value	**Symbol**
Whole (note) rest	▬
Half rest	▬
Quarter rest	𝄽
Eighth rest	𝄾
Sixteenth rest	𝄿

melodies sounding simultaneously. Familiar rounds like "Three Blind Mice" and "Row, Row, Row Your Boat" are polyphonic, as is most Renaissance music. The music of baroque composers such as Bach, Handel, and many others is basically polyphonic.

Musical Form

Briefly stated, form in music is a balance of unity and variety. Too much unity becomes boring, while excessive variety leads to fragmentation and even chaos. Understanding form in music is a high priority for educated listeners. As Robert Schumann remarked, "Only when the form is quite clear to you will the spirit become clear to you."

The smallest unit of form is the *motive*, which to be intelligible must have at least two notes plus an identifiable rhythmic pattern. The principle motive in the first movement of Beethoven's Fifth Symphony has two different pitches in a four-note rhythmic pattern:

A musical phrase is a coherent group of notes roughly comparable to a literary phrase and having about the same function. Two related phrases form a *period,* in the manner of a literary sentence. In the period illustrated below, note that the first phrase has a transitional ending called a *half cadence,* while the second phrase ends solidly with a *full cadence.* Note also the extreme unity; the first three measures of both phrases are identical.

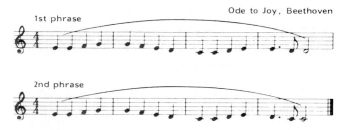

1st phrase

Ode to Joy, Beethoven

2nd phrase

In large works the musical periods are used in various combinations to expand the material into sections comparable to paragraphs, and these are then combined to make still larger units.

Musical structure can be comprehended only *after* the music has arrived at wherever the composer intends it to go. Look again at "Ode to Joy." You can "see" its form only because the music is notated, which is why learning some notation is so important. When the music is played, your ear follows the line to the half cadence, which is then heard as a statement that demands completion. As the second phrase begins, there is aural recognition of its relationship to the first phrase. When the second phrase concludes with a gratifying full cadence, there is a kind of flashback to the memory of the first phrase. In other words, the conclusion of the second phrase is satisfying because it completes the thought of the still-remembered first phrase. The music conforms to its own inner logic; that is, the second phrase is a logical consequence of the first.

As a general rule, most music is constructed around two different but logically related (inner logic) musical ideas. We can call one idea *A* and the other *B*. One common musical form is two-part (binary), or simply A–B. An even more common form is three-part (ternary), or A–B–A. In two-part form the composer makes a musical statement (A), which is followed by a new section (B), which is sufficiently different to provide variety but not so different as to destroy the balance. The following hymn tune is a complete composition in two-part form, with two phrases in each section. Section B has the same rhythm as Section A,

but the melody is a kind of inversion of the melody in A. The inner logic is maintained through the similarities.

St. Anne

The following complete hymn tune has a form related to two-part form: A–A¹–B, called A, A prime, B. Part A is followed by another A that is varied going into the cadence. Part B is properly different but related to A and A¹ by the similarity of measures 2, 6, and 10. In terms of measures, the structure of the piece can be diagrammed as:

A   A¹   B
2+2   2+2   2+2

Regent Square

Three-part form operates on the principle of closing with the melody that began the piece, a rounding off of the material: A–B–A. The following example can be analyzed as A–A¹–B–A¹ and diagrammed as:

A   A¹   B   A¹
4 + 4   4 + 4   4 + 4   4 + 4.

This is the thirty-two-measure form most commonly used for popular songs.

In the Gloaming

There are, of course, other variants of AB and ABA forms as well as several other structures. However, the examples given illustrate the principle of a balance between unity and variety, of which unity is paramount. Perhaps because it is rather amorphous, music, more than any other art, emphasizes repetition, restating the material again and again, but mixing with enough variety to maintain interest. The forms illustrated can also be heard in the larger context of longer compositions. For example, "In the Gloaming" has 32 measures in a basic ABA form; a large symphonic work could have, say, 200 measures and be diagrammed as follows:

$$\underset{\text{aba aba aba}}{\text{A B A}} \quad or \quad \underset{\text{aba}^1 \text{ aba aba}^1}{\text{A B A}^1} \quad or \quad \underset{\text{aa}^1\text{ba aba aa}^1\text{ba}^1}{\text{A B A}^1}$$

The Listening Experience

Listening to music begins with the question, What do you hear? This is an objective question that has nothing whatever to do with a story you may imagine the music is telling, random associations the music happens to trigger, or any meaning that may be attributed to the music. For the educated listener the procedure is to objectively identify the sounds you hear, to determine how the sounds are produced, and to try to determine how the sounds are organized.

Composers do not pour out notes as if emptying a glass of water on a tabletop. They arrange their sounds in a sort of container in a manner that molds the container to the material it holds. Learning to comprehend the musical structure leads inevitably to the ability to *anticipate* the next melody, cadence, section, or whatever. Being able to anticipate what is to happen next means that you are tuned in to the web of sound, listening along with the pace of the music. Almost everyone has already acquired the ability to follow the progress of popular music and to anticipate what comes next in favorite recordings. As stated before, the larger world of classical music is only a step beyond the listening expertise of most individuals.

Summary

It should be pointed out that it takes a long time to learn to speak; it takes about as long to learn to listen. However, listening comes as naturally as speaking, and the music listed in this chapter is just one of the many approaches to good music. You won't like everything at first and you may not start liking some things until a year or two later. You will, however, gradually build up listening skills without even being aware of it. When you hear something that you didn't hear before in the same record, you are indeed sharpening your ear. Moreover, there is no regression with this music; you don't fall out of love with it, so to speak. Instead, your understanding will increase and you will begin to view at least some of the music listed in this chapter as pleasant old friends and lifelong companions.

Unit 1

Greece
The First Humanistic Culture

1
Early Greece: Preparation for the Good Life

As nearly everyone knows, it was in Greece, particularly in Athens for a short time in the fifth century (ca. 500–400 B.C.), that human life developed a quality that has seldom if ever been equaled. Here for the first time—and most gloriously—personal freedom was achieved for a large percentage of the population, with a sense of justice embodied in laws and a political system that gave individuals the greatest possible freedom compatible with the coherence of the social group. Here, too, there was a sufficient amount of wealth and leisure to allow individuals to develop their capabilities to the fullest. A sufficient challenge in the differences between the various city-states and between the individuals within them kept many persons keenly alive in the development of their full selves.

It would be convenient for the reader, and certainly for the authors, if the development to the apex of culture had proceeded in some sort of regular progression from the beginning of our knowledge about the Greeks until its culmination during the reign of Perikles[1] (PAIR–i–kleez) in Athens or if all of the statesmen who brought change to the Greek social structure had been high-minded men with a clear vision of the ultimate goal of human values. Unfortunately this is not the case. Greek history— even Greek geography—represents the ultimate in confusion, and even the statesmen who made the greatest contributions in the development of the social structure were often self-seeking politicians, not above taking bribes or committing treason to accomplish their purposes. Out of all of this confusing history the evolution of a society devoted, even for a brief time, to human values becomes a tribute to the toughness of the human spirit.

---

1. Greek spelling is used throughout, removing what Robert Fitzgerald, translator of Homer, has called a "Roman screen." Some Latinized spellings have been retained (Helen, Priam, Troy, Crete); other inconsistencies are, we trust, equally deliberate. Rather than include Greek accent marks we have provided phonetic pronunciations, e.g., Hêphaistos = Hephaistos (Hay–FYCE–toss). As Fitzgerald suggests, "Pronounce it slowly and boldly, and savor every syllable."

This chapter will attempt to trace the development of Greek society from its earliest beginnings to the fifth century in what is necessarily an oversimplified version. Eventually the focus will be on the city of Athens, where the highest development took place and where ideas that were generated throughout Greece came into greater conflict than they did in their places of origin. This will necessarily be a long chapter, since the whole Greek period covers 2000 years and this chapter will cope with 1500 of them. This was a lively, even a brawling culture, whose history is hard to trace. Furthermore, during the two millenia of the epoch the seeds—and some of the finest flowers—of all Western art and philosophy reveal themselves.

In the first place, let it be made clear that there never was a nation called Greece. Instead, we find a group of people who called themselves Hellenes (HEL–e–neez), united by a common language, with several dialects; by a common though diversified religion; and a common heritage. Politically these people lived in independent city-states, each with its own form of government. Frequently there were alliances between these small states, and in the fifth century Athens put together a very loose Athenian Empire, opposing a strong coalition of city-states whose allegiance was to Sparta. Greece was not even confined to a single geographical location. The map shows that the mainland of Greece is the tip of the Balkan Peninsula, joined by a narrow isthmus to a fairly large land mass known as the Peloponnesus (pel–uh–puh–NEES–us). This is the heartland. But Greece was invaded from the north in the twelfth and eleventh centuries (1199–1000 B.C.), and many of the mainlanders fled to the Asiatic coast of the Aegean (i–JEE–an) Sea and the islands off the Asian coast to form a flourishing Greek cultural center with many important cities. Later, in the seventh and sixth centuries (699–500 B.C.), land poverty on the mainland encouraged many of the city-states to send out colonies to occupy new land. As a result, a great number of Greek cities were formed all the way from Byzantium (bi–ZANT–e–um), now Istanbul, along both shores of the Mediterranean Sea, in Sicily, and in Italy. For example, Syracuse in Sicily, and Sybaris and Paestum in Italy were important Greek cities. Although these cities were widely dispersed and frequently at war with each other, their common culture, heritage, religion, and language gave them a sense of kinship as Hellenes, while all other people were regarded as barbarians or strangers. The Hellenes felt that they were different from and better than the "barbarians" (which means non-Greek), a sense that created unity amid the vast diversity and a pride that led to the remarkable accomplishments of the people we know as the Greeks.

The Geography of Mainland Greece

Mainland Greece was a hard country in which to live. Ranges of mountains divided the area so that communication across the countryside was extremely difficult. Furthermore, the mountains were so eroded that little farmland was available. Only in the north were there any broad and fertile plains. For the remainder, sheep and goats grazed on the mountain slopes and bee-culture was common. The valleys between the mountains offered small plots of arable land on which olives and grapes were the chief crops. It was in these valleys that the first villages appeared that would later unite to become city-states.

Nor was the climate conducive to easy living. In the winter great storms blew down from the north bringing torrential rains and, on the mountain peaks, a good deal of snow. The summers were extremely hot and dry.

There was still another geographical influence on Greek life: the closeness of the sea. Nowhere is the sea more than a few miles distant, and communication by water was frequently much easier than overland travel.

All of these factors contributed to the Greek character. In a hard land, people must be ingenious and clever to survive. In a land where nature yields little, people must turn to manufacturing objects in order to make a living. As compared to other early civilizations, the Greek population contained many more artisans and artists than peasants. Finally, the proximity of the sea always offered the possibility of trade and commerce (and piracy) as a source of livelihood. Such commerce always broadens horizons; in addition to the bartering of goods, the traders barter ideas and bring them home. It is never possible to attribute the character of a people to geography and climate alone, yet the factors mentioned here must have done much to shape the personality of the Hellenes.

Some Steps in Greek History

The first people about whom we have much information and who lived in Greek lands were the Minoans (mi–NO–uns), so named after the fabled King Minos (MI–nus) who lived on the island of Crete. These were probably not "Greek" people, in that their language, as far as one can tell, does not seem to be related to the Indo-European family. (Of this language we have only clay tablets in the "Linear A" writing, which has not yet been deciphered.) This Minoan culture existed from about 2600 B.C. to about 1125 B.C., and reached its peak somewhere around the year 2000 with the building of the great palaces and the surrounding towns of Knossos (KNAWS–us), Phaistos (FEST–us), Mallia (MAL–ya), and others.

Despite the mystery of Linear A, we know a great deal about this culture because of the excavations by Sir Arthur Evans, Spyridon Marinatos, and others. From Evans's excavations and reconstructions at Knossos,

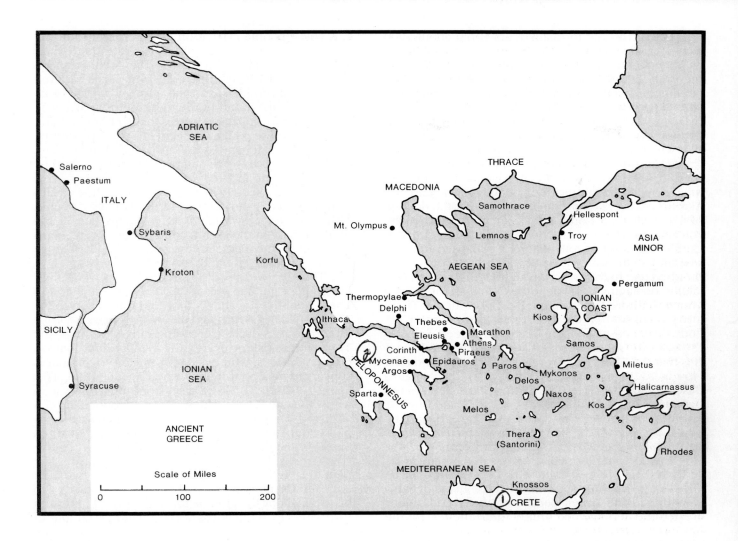

we see that this rich and sophisticated culture prospered because of trade and commerce. The excavations of Professor Marinatos at the buried Minoan city of Akrotiri on the island of Thira, beginning in 1967, furnish additional evidence of trade with Egypt and the Asian coast of the Aegean Sea.

Apparently life was peaceful on Crete itself, for the palaces were not fortified, and the Cretans seem to have trusted their maritime power to ward off enemies. This sense of peace is enforced by the art of the time, for the paintings depict athletic contests (the famous bull-dance), women gossiping, cup-bearers, and the like, rather than scenes of war. The designs on jars and vases were ornate and colorful, utilizing fish and animal designs, one of the most common of which is the octopus, as the flowing tentacles offered infinite possibilities for involved and convoluted spirals and circles.

The religion of these people seems to have been a fertility cult and a worship of the earth goddess. This, in turn, led to a matriarchal form of government, with the essential power lying with the queen as the earthly representative, indeed the incarnation, of the earth mother. A part of this worship involved the tradition of the year-king, a tradition that the king married the queen for a specified time—a year, four years, perhaps some other length of time—after which he was killed and the queen took another husband. This custom relates to the concept that the earth (the queen) must be refertilized to maintain continuing prosperity. It is important to mention this here because of the belief by many scholars, particularly Robert Graves, that much of Greek myth arises out of the clash between this earth worship and the matriarchy it produced and the worship of the sky gods, a religion that was brought into Greece by the people we will know as the Mycenaeans (mi–se–NE–uns), the first of the true Greeks, whose worship venerated the male and male symbols rather than the female.

So much has been discovered about the Minoan culture that it could be described at very great length, however, the student is directed to such fictional works as Mary Renault's books *The King Must Die* and *The Bull from the Sea* for a real grasp of the nature of this civilization.

The fact is that for many years (from about 1900 B.C. onwards) a group of tribes from northern Europe had been slowly invading and infiltrating Greece. By the year 1600 they occupied all of the Greek mainland including the Peloponnesus, where, at Mycenae (mi–SEEN–ee), their Great King established his palace and fortress. One of the Great Kings was Agamemnon (ag–a–MEM–non). These were warlike peoples who naturally came into contact and conflict with Cretan culture, and some time after about 1450 B.C. they conquered Crete. A persistent legend and mounting archaeological evidence, particularly at Akrotiri on Thera (Santorini), suggest that the decline of Crete resulted from a cataclysmic eruption of the volcano on Thera in about 1450 B.C. After the volcano's final mighty convulsion, it collapsed into the sea, and tidal waves possibly four hundred or five hundred feet high spread throughout the Aegean Sea, fatally damaging, among other things, the entire Minoan culture. The ongoing excavations on Thera also tend to support the theory that Thera was the legendary Atlantis; most of the island did indeed sink into the sea. Also, there are partially substantiated theories that the Thera catastrophe caused gases and dust clouds to reach Egypt, resulting in the plagues described in the Bible. The parting of the Red Sea has been explained by the tidal waves generated by the eruption. Whatever the cause may have been, the power of Crete was broken and the Mycenaean Greeks became the overlords of the Aegean world.

The deciphering of clay tablets in the "Linear B" script in 1953 showed that the Mycenaeans were true Greeks who not only spoke a Greek language but also worshipped the Greek pantheon of sky gods. They created the heritage that united the Hellenes, for the Mycenaeans fought the Trojan War that centuries later was to become the subject of the Homeric poems and the core of the Hellenic tradition. This Mycenaean culture lasted from the sixteenth century through the twelfth century (1599–1100 B.C.).

As far as the facts of this culture are concerned, we know a considerable amount. The people established themselves in small, warlike independent kingdoms whose kings lived in strongly fortified but rich palaces. Each king was independent, administering his rule through a group of officials who supervised the farmlands, collected taxes in produce, managed religious celebrations and sacrifices, and otherwise handled all the affairs of government. Although each king was independent, each owed a rough allegiance to the high king at Mycenae; although, as seen in Homer's *Iliad* (IL–ee–ad), a local ruler could disobey the high king—as Akhilleus (Ah–KILL–eoos) did with Agamemnon—and not be forced to follow the ruler. Each king had a group of well-armed troops, and the nobles rode chariots into battle, although most of the fighting was done on foot.

These people carried on extensive trade, mostly among the islands and Asia Minor, although their influence extended throughout the Mediterranean world. Gold, ivory, textiles, and spices were bartered for the local products, and the number of gold ornaments and cups found in the royal tombs at Mycenae and at other great palaces attests to the rather barbaric wealth of these kings. In general their prosperity seems to have depended upon trade, commerce, and barter, which is to be remembered as we see this civilization decline in later years.

This was a society in which the masculine virtues were honored, as evidenced in the Homeric poems. Although Homer wrote his epic poems late in the ninth or early in the eighth century, his poetry seems to reflect with considerable accuracy the knowledge we can piece together about the Mycenaeans.

The chief virtues of the early Greeks were physical courage and the preservation of individual honor. These qualities are shown time and time again in the *Iliad*, as when Diomedes (di–uh–MEED–eez) broke from the ranks of his troops and ranged through the Trojan forces risking everything in individual combat. Or by Akhilleus, who by twentieth-century standards appears to be a pouting boy when Agamemnon takes his girl, Briseis (bri–SEE–us), from him, but was in reality the Greek hero whose personal honor had been affronted. He refused to fight, not from cowardice or pique, but simply because Agamemnon had insulted his pride and belittled him in front of the entire Argive (the Greeks, led by the king from Argos) army. The hero must retaliate, and he did so by refusing to fight until he was moved, not by loyalty to his cause or to his king, but by the grief he felt at the loss of his friend Patroklos (Pa–TRO–kloss). The greatest example of all is the death of Hektor in Book XXII of the *Iliad*. Here was a man, the greatest and strongest of the Trojan warriors, who could easily have shirked this last individual battle. His aged father pled with him to stay within the city walls; earlier, in a touching scene with his wife and his little child he admitted he knew that he and his city were doomed. Yet, when the time came, he had to assert himself in a glorious action that would test all of his powers to the utmost, fulfill all of his capacities, and finally bring him immortality, not in heaven, but in the minds of men. For these Greeks, human worth and dignity lay in total self-fulfillment, usually on the battlefield where their exploits would bring death, perhaps, but certainly fame among their fellows and among people to come after them as their deeds were recounted in song and story.

Another aspect of the Greek character, much admired throughout the history of the people, was the use of a wily and tricky intelligence. For this quality, Odysseus (o–DIS–yews) stands as the supreme example. Thus, when Odysseus finally won his way home to his kingdom of Ithaka he was put ashore disguised as a beggar. Here Athena (uh–THEE–nuh) met him and heard his lying tale. Her response was typical of the Greek attitude:

> "What a cunning knave it would take," she said, "to beat you at your tricks! Even a god would be hard put to it."

> "And so my stubborn friend, Odysseus the arch-deceiver, with his craving for intrigue, does not propose even in his own country to drop his sharp practice and the lying tales that he loves from the bottom of his heart. But no more of this: we are both adepts at chicane. For in the world of men you have no rival as a statesman and orator, while I am pre-eminent among the gods for invention and resource."

And a few lines later:

> "How like you to be so wary!" said Athena. "And that is why I cannot desert you in your misfortunes: you are so civilized, so intelligent, so self-possessed."

Perhaps in our time we cannot so admire the man who was so smoothly deceitful to gain his own ends; even in classic Greece Sophokles (SOF-o-kleez) despised these qualities, as he pictured a rather despicable Odysseus in the drama *Philoktetes* (fil-OK-ti-teez). But for the Greek of the heroic age, this was simply another example of the idea of self-fulfillment. Odysseus had been given the quality and the capacity for sharp intelligence, and it was his purpose, a purpose of all people, to utilize all of his capacities to their utmost. He would be a fool, shirking his own fate, not to use this ability.

Greek Religion in the Heroic Age

The worship of the Olympian gods forms one of the most curious religions that we know of. This religion had no "revealer," divine or mortal; no Christ, no Mohammed, no Buddha. Neither did it have any sacred book such as the Bible, the Koran, or the Talmud. As far as we know, it simply grew as a collection of myths that were honored in various ways throughout the Greek world. Even the myths varied greatly, so that no single version of the history and the nature of the gods exists. Hesiod (HEE-see-ud) in his book *Theogony* (thee-OG-uh-nee), and other writers as well, attempted to systematize the story of the gods, but with only minor success. Vastly simplified, the genealogy of the gods can be presented in the following way: In the beginning was Chaos, composed of void, mass, and darkness. From Chaos emerged a male god, Ouranos (YOOR-uh-noss), who represented the heavens, and a female god, Gaea (JEE-ah), who represented earth. These gods had three types of offspring, one of which was the Titans, who represented earthquakes and other cataclysms of the earth. Kronos (KRO-nos), one of the Titans, led a revolt against his father and overthrew him. (It is interesting that from the drops of blood of Ouranos sprang the fearful hags known as the Furies, whose duty it was to pursue anyone who had shed the blood of his kindred; this type of superstition was important because it helped hold the clans together.) Kronos took his sister Rhea (REE-uh), another representation of the earth goddess, as his wife, and from this union, although not without some difficulty, came the Olympian gods. The difficulty alluded to was the fact that Kronos had a prophecy that one of his children would overthrow him; to prevent this, he swallowed all his children at birth (Kronos, of course, may be thought of as Time, which swallows all things). By a trick, Rhea saved Zeus from being swallowed and spirited him away to Crete where he grew to manhood. Then Zeus led the prophesied revolt and, aided by some of the Titans, managed to imprison his father in the dark cave of Tartarus, but not before Kronos had regurgitated the other children, Demeter (di-MEET-er), Hera (HAY-ra), Hades (also called Pluto), Poseidon (Po-SIDE-on), and Hestia. Zeus then took Hera as his wife and from this union came such gods and goddesses as Apollo, Aphrodite, Artemis, and others. (See box 1.1.)

In addition to these, many local gods and nymphs presided over particular streams and groves, and were worshipped locally. The whole Greek pantheon represents a most confusing array.

Just as confusing are the stories of the actions of the gods; we see Zeus almost constantly pursuing (and seducing) some mortal girl; all of the gods quarreled jealously among themselves; they all had favorites among the mortals, as we saw Athena protecting Odysseus; and they used all sorts of trickery to foil each other's designs for the success of their favorite mortals. How could such a group possibly be revered and worshipped?

If we can understand this worship, even faintly, then we may come to know something of the Greek character, and particularly some of its love for the very process of living. The gods were regarded as a race infinitely superior to human beings in that they were completely powerful, immortal, and always young and beautiful; they had the same characteristics as humans, but in a higher category. If people sometimes showed wisdom and nobility, so did Athena or Apollo (uh-POL-o), but to a vastly superior degree. If mortals were sometimes lustful, Zeus was much more so, and in his power, much more successful. If people were skilled artisans, so was Hephaistos (hay-FYCE-toss); if humans were crafty and skillful, so was Prometheus (pro-MEE-thee-us)—but the skill, wisdom, lust, or whatever quality one may choose of the gods was infinitely beyond that of mortals. For Greeks, death was a sort of dark oblivion, but the gods had life forever, and life in full beauty, full youth, and complete power.

Box 1.1 The Greek Pantheon

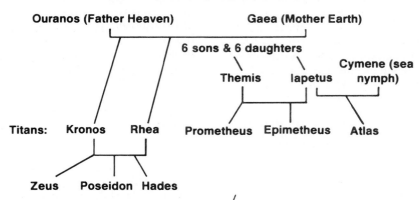

Zeus and his two brothers seized power from Kronos (Saturn) to originate "The Twelve," the Olympians who figure most prominently in Greek life. (The names in parentheses are Roman but these represent only approximations since Greeks and Romans had entirely different attitudes towards their respective gods, and towards most everything else for that matter.)

Zeus (Jupiter, Jove). Leader, god of the thunderbolt, representative of the power principle and chaser of women.

Hera (Juno). Long-suffering wife of Zeus, goddess of marriage and domestic stability.

Poseidon (Neptune). God of the sea and earthshaker (earthquakes).

Demeter (Ceres). Sister of Zeus and goddess of agriculture. Mother of *Persephone* and symbol of fertility.

Hades (Pluto, Dis). God of the underworld. Connected with nature myth by his marriage to Persephone who spends half her time on earth (the growing season) and half in the underworld (fall and winter). *Thanatos* represents death itself.

Pallas Athena (Minerva). Goddess of wisdom, warfare, arts and crafts. Sprang full-armed from the brow of Zeus. Patron goddess of Athens, representing the art of civilized living.

Phoibos Apollo (Sol). Son of Zeus and *Leto,* daughter of the Titans Krios and Phoebe. Sun god, archer, musician, god of truth, light, and healing. Represents principle of intellectual beauty.

Artemis (Diana, Cynthia). Sister of Apollo; virgin goddess of the moon and the hunt.

Aphrodite (Venus). Goddess of love and physical beauty. According to one version she was the daughter of Zeus and Dione; an alternate mythic version has her rising from the waves a la Botticelli.

Hephaistos (Vulcan). Lame blacksmith god who made armor for heroes, forged the thunderbolts of Zeus. Much-deceived husband of Aphrodite.

Hermes (Mercury). Son of Zeus and Maia, daughter of Atlas. Messenger and general handyman of Zeus. God of commerce, traders, travelers, and thieves.

Ares (Mars). Son of Zeus and Hera. God of war.

Hestia (Vesta). Virgin sister of Zeus and goddess of hearth and home. Later replaced among the Twelve by Dionysos.

Dionysos (Bacchus). Son of Zeus and mortal woman Semele. Like Demeter, connected with the principle of fertility and, like Persephone, represented the nature myth by dying in the autumn and being reborn in the spring. The Eleusinian Mysteries were dedicated to all three fertility deities and the festivals of Dionysos were periods of wild, Bacchic rejoicing, scheduled orgies so to speak. Since plays were usually performed at these festivals Dionysos also became god of the theatre. He represents the ecstatic principle as contrasted with the intellectual principle represented by Apollo.

LESSER OLYMPIANS

Eros (Cupid). Eternal child of Aphrodite and Hephaistos. Spirit of love with darts.

Pan (Pan). Son of Hermes, woodland god with goatlike horns and hoofs. Player of the pipes (panpipes).

Nemesis. Avenging goddess, the principle of retribution.

Hebe. Goddess of youth and cupbearer to the gods.

Iris. Goddess of the rainbow and sometimes messenger of the gods.

Hymen. Son of Aphrodite and Dionysos; god of the marriage festival.

The Three Graces: Aglaia (Splendor), *Euphrosyne* (Mirth), and *Thalia* (Good Cheer). Represented the principle of the happy life and always represented as a unit, which is a clear indication of the Greek version of the happy life.

The Nine Muses. Spirits of learning and of the arts. *Clio* (History), *Ourania* (Astronomy), *Melpomene* (Tragedy), *Thalia* (Comedy), *Terpsichore* (Dance), *Calliope* (Epic Poetry), *Erato* (Love Poetry), *Polyhymnia* (Sacred Poetry), and *Euterpe* (Lyric Poetry).

The Erinyes (Furies). *Tisiphone, Megaera,* and *Alecto.* Represented pangs of conscience; relentlessly hounded wrongdoers.

The Three Fates allotted to each man his destiny. *Clotho* spun the thread of life. *Lachesis* wove it into a pattern that determined the kind of life that would be led. *Atropos* cut the thread, terminating existence.

The worship of these gods during Mycenaean times and later may illustrate the point, for the formal ceremonies were always feasts. Animals were sacrificed, and a portion of the meat was burnt upon the fire. The rest was roasted and eaten by those performing the sacrifice. Wine was drunk, with a certain amount poured out first as a libation to the gods. Then the feast proceeded, with the assumption that the god was present as a guest at the meal, and that he enjoyed such things as well as the mortals did.

In what must seem to be a very diverse religious practice, one aspect of the life with the gods is of great importance. The Hellenes were never a priest-ridden group of people, as were the Egyptians. To us their religious practices seem relatively unstructured, almost casual; there was certainly plenty of room for freedom of thought. We will see later that in political organization the Greeks were not oppressed by despots, or at least not for very long. The Persians were, and culturally they produced only the monuments of an authoritarian state. In both religion and politics, the Greeks maintained the widest possible latitude for thought, questioning, and experimentation, which though turbulent and unstable, produced a great humanistic value system.

Such, greatly simplified, was the Olympian religion that existed from the fifteenth century throughout all of Greek history. During classical times and later, doubt may have existed about the nature and the presence of the gods but most people, excluding some of the intellectuals, believed in the gods, and for almost every important state decision one of the oracles was consulted, usually the oracle at Delphi. That the answers given by the oracles were frequently riddles that could be interpreted in any of several ways did not shake the faith of the people in the oracles themselves.

In this bewildering complexity of gods and people, what determined the events and the fate, or doom, of any individual? Here as before, we must rely on Homer, who wrote centuries after the heroic age and was none too certain himself of the answer to the question we have posed. In the first place, they had a vague belief that each of the people, or each of the heroes, had their own *moira* (MOY–ruh), or pattern of life, which they would fulfill. This may be illustrated as a sort of jigsaw puzzle that the hero's life would fill in—with the added complexity that the individual never knew what the picture would be when it was finished nor when it was completed. Within the individual's life we have the three forces of free will as determined by character, accident, and the intervention of the gods. These worked together, and sometimes in opposition, to determine the course of a person's life, and nothing could be counted on as certain until death finished the picture. This problem is considered in greater depth in *Oedipus the King* by Sophokles. Frequently the gods intervened and brought tragedy to a person who overstepped the limits of human action and, out of pride, attempted to act in the realm of the gods. Such action almost certainly brought about a doom. But for the most part it seems that in the heroic age a person's character *was* fate. The people did the things they did, receiving their attendant consequences, because of the kind of person they were. Thus Akhilleus, in spite of all sorts of ruses to outwit his predicted fate, had his short and glorious life just because he was the kind of person to whom personal honor was all important, because he took great risks in the hope of winning great fame. Odysseus, on the other hand, lived a long life not only because of his heroic strength, but also because of his ability to talk, to deceive, and to plan ahead for survival.

Such, then, is at least a suggestion of the nature of the Mycenaean civilization, the culture in which the Trojan War occurred, in which Agamemnon, Menelaos (men–uh–LAY–us), Helen, and the other fabled Greeks actually lived.

This Mycenaean culture began its decline in the twelfth century (the 1100s) as a result of many factors: a forced closing of trade with the Middle East; a series of wars between the kingdoms within the Mycenaean groups; and, most importantly, an invasion from the north by a group called the Dorians. These last were a people of the same racial stock as the Mycenaeans, but who were just now forced to migrate south because of the complicated folk movements of the time. They slowly occupied the mainland of Greece during the twelfth to the tenth centuries, overcoming the already spent civilization they found there. Two important consequences followed. First, a long "dark ages" descended upon Greece in which there was little cultural or artistic creation. Second, while retreating from the Dorians, the inhabitants of the Greek mainland emigrated to the Asiatic coast of the Aegean Sea where in the course of time, they developed a number of Greek cities in an advanced state of civilization. Because these last people spoke the Ionian dialect of Greek, this region became known as the Ionian coast and was later to become the center of the earliest Greek philosopher-scientists, as well as a land that was a sort of military football between the kingdoms of Lydia and Persia (the great Asiatic powers) and the city-states of Greece.

The Archaic Period (ca. 750–500 B.C.)

These dark ages move almost imperceptibly into the Archaic (ar–KAY–ic) times of historic Greece. We know quite a bit about the life of the period through the poems of Hesiod (HEE–see–ud), *Works and Days.* Hesiod was a farmer in Boeotia who, except for once winning a poetry contest, seems to have known nothing but bad luck. He gives us a picture of a landed aristocracy whose chief occupation was to squeeze the small farmer. Life was a continual round of jobs to be done with little or no reward or future in the work. Justice lay in the hands of the aristocrats who rendered their decisions almost entirely in terms of who could offer the largest bribe. Hesiod was always reverent towards the gods, but he neither expected nor got any reward in this life except for continuous toil, and Hesiod's plight was the common lot of most of the Greeks of his time.

Of course the latter part of the ninth century or the early part of the eighth was also the time when Homer wrote. While Hesiod was describing the life of his own time, Homer's work describes the departed glories of the heroic or Mycenaean period, which has already been discussed. We know little about Homer; computer analysis has shown that a single person, whom we call Homer, composed the tragedy of the *Iliad*. Analysis of the adventure tale that is the *Odyssey* is less conclusive, though Homer is the probable poet. However, precise knowledge about authorship is not as important as the fact that the *Iliad* and the *Odyssey* are at the very heart of the Greek heritage. Greek ideals, the idea of Greek superiority over the barbarians, and the overwhelming desire for personal honor were embodied in these works, and they became as close to a central religious book as the Greeks ever possessed. The works of Homer were memorized by every Greek student; they were recited at all of the great Greek festivals and games throughout the Hellenic world. Homer, of course, did not make up the stories he wrote. The poems were a collection of the legends that had their origins from time out of mind sung or recited by bards in the palaces. But they were brought together by the sure hand of a literary genius and transformed into the works that inspired the Greek mind from the time of their composition (fig. 1.1).

Figure 1.1 Portrait bust of Homer, marble, Roman copy of ca. 150 B.C. Certainly not a likeness, this is an idealized version of how a divinely inspired blind poet should look. National Museum, Naples.

But to return to the times of Hesiod. We witness first the rise of a landed aristocracy who, by force and guile, seized most of the land from the poor farmers. Not the least of the ways of acquiring land by the aristocrat was to lend money to the farmer, who used his own person as security for the loan. When he was unable to pay his debt, his land became the property of the aristocrat and the farmer became a slave. Numerous forms of governments arose at this time. Frequently the most powerful landowner became king; at other times the city-state was ruled by a committee of landowners, constituting an oligarchy. It was during this time that land poverty, simply the fact that there was not enough land to support the population, became painfully evident.

As a result of this land poverty the colonizing process that was mentioned earlier began to take place. Many city-states simply exported fairly large bands of adventurers to found colonies throughout the Aegean and Mediterranean world. Many colonies were established in northern Greece, including Byzantium, and a number of cities on the shores of the Black Sea. The present city of Marseilles in France was originally a Greek colony, as were a number of the cities of Sicily and Italy. The Greek world expanded greatly, and with the expansion came the development of trade and commerce among all of the Hellenic cities and an increasing flow of wealth into the original Greek cities. A large, important, and wealthy commercial class of people also began to form a part of the population of the cities, different from the landed aristocracy and opposed to them and different from the small-farmer group. This new group was to become a political faction to reckon with in the development of new governmental forms.

The first of the political changes came with the rise of *tyrants*. For us in the twentieth century, the term suggests a harsh military dictator, but at first, among the Hellenic cities, it was simply another word meaning "king." The tyrant was simply a man, sometimes chosen by the people, more usually a man who seized power and established himself as absolute ruler as long as he could hold office. Sometimes he came from the members of the old landowning families, a man who discerned the "wave of the future" and grabbed power either by allying himself with the merchant class or the farming class and promising political reforms, which would bring help to his political allies. Sometimes he rose from the merchant group; sometimes he was an outsider who came in to take over the rule of a city-state. No matter what his origin, he had to win over a good part of the population in order to try to hold his position, and he did this by effecting political, judicial, or economic reforms that would make him popular with a fairly large segment of the population. From this movement toward tyranny came the earliest reforms that were to lead, in Athens and some other cities, toward eventual democracy. None of this development was uniform through the cities of the Hellenic world; in none of them was progress a steady evolutionary process. From this point on in our discussion, we shall focus our attention on governmental changes in the city of Athens, which in most ways was to become the most glorious of the Greek cities. For our purposes in this chapter, we shall consider only the changes made under the rule of four leaders: Draco (DRAY–ko), Solon (SO–lon), Pisistratus (pi–SIS–truh–tus), and Kleisthenes (KLICE–the–neez). They will seem to have appeared in orderly succession but this did not happen. For example, two of Pisistratus's sons attempted to follow their father in the corridors of power but one was assassinated in 514 and the other was exiled in 510. The course of leadership never seems to run smoothly.

The Rise of Athens

In considering the political and economic development of Athens from the sixth century on, it is well to bear in mind a rather curious power structure. Three political factions, largely determined by economic status, struggled for power. They were the old landed aristocracy, the poor farmers who eked out a living on marginal land, and the growing commercial class. In addition to these economic groups, Athenian life was dominated by four family-clans, originally of the aristocracy, who controlled the individual lives of their members, and in a fairly large measure controlled as well the political developments within the city. As long as these four tribes remained powerful, political and economic advances would always be dominated by the traditions of the tribes.

The first of the reformers in the seventh century was an almost legendary figure, Draco (fl. 621 B.C.), one of the early tyrants. His great contribution was to publish a code of laws. This simple act was a great step toward freedom. Hesiod, for example, had complained that the aristocrats who were the judges of his time were the only ones who knew the laws, and it appears that they made up the rules as they went along. An ordinary citizen involved in a legal suit about land or homicide really cast himself on the mercy of the judges who rendered decisions as they saw fit; decisions that depended upon the economic status of the litigants, their family connections, and the size of the bribe that could be offered. Obviously justice cannot prevail in such a system. Draco's Code, although it is reputed to have been very severe, did offer a single standard of justice for *all* people, and since the law was published, individuals within the state could know their legal rights. No matter how harsh the laws may have been, the publication of the laws became a step forward in developing a *rational* system of justice rather than one based upon tradition, privilege, and wealth.

The second of the great reformers was Solon (ca. 639–559 B.C.), a man whose name has come down to us as the synonym for a wise lawgiver. Like Draco, he was a member of the nobility, but evidently in his youth he had travelled extensively and had developed interests in the possibilities of trade and commerce, and he also became aware of the injustice of land distribution in his native state of Attica. Perhaps his most important reform was to free all slaves who had reached that condition because of debt, and to abolish the custom that made debt-slavery possible. A man who sought moderation in all things, he was evidently pressured to break up the great estates and to distribute the land to the farmers, but he did not have sufficient faith in the poor and uneducated masses to take this step. He did, however, allow all people to become involved to some extent with the government. He limited the magistracies and important governmental offices to the upper classes, but he allowed members of the lowest class, even, to serve as jurors, and thus he began a process of educating all people in the processes of social action and social change. In running the day-to-day affairs of Athens he established an administrative council of four hundred members, and thus greatly broadened the civic responsibilities of the citizens. Shrewdly anticipating conservative resistance to change and liberal proclivities for tinkering with reforms, Solon stipulated that all reforms had to remain in force and unchanged for ten years.

In order to encourage trade and commerce, Solon adopted a much lighter coinage than Athens had used in the past, and also he imported many artisans, particularly potters, since pottery manufacture was one of the chief industries of Athens and one of its main exports. These last reforms began a series of developments that were to break Athens away from an economic dependence upon agriculture and land and to establish it as a city whose wealth depended upon manufactured objects that were more or less independent of the uncontrollable forces of nature.

The third great reformer was Pisistratus (ca. 605–527 B.C.), who governed Athens from 546 till his death. In his economic reforms he was to follow the precedent that had already been set by Solon in that he broke up the large estates and distributed the land to the almost landless peasants. Since voting privileges and participation in the government were determined largely by economic status, this single reform did much to broaden the base for government, and it allowed the people who had already been somewhat educated in social action by Solon's changes to take a more important role than before in the actual government of the state. He and his sons further increased employment by starting a number of great public works within the city. Perhaps the most important of Pisistratus's contributions to the city lay in the development of its art. Two of the greatest Hellenic poets of the time, Simonides and Anakreon, were brought to Athens, and Pisistratus and his sons also commissioned the preparation of the first careful edition of Homer's poems, which were later sung and recited at all of the important festivals and sacrifices within the city. This last step may not seem to be of great importance, but its significance is apparent when one realizes that the learning of these poems by most of the citizens and their recitation at public functions gave the people a sense of common heritage and a feeling of unity *as citizens of Athens* not as members of a particular family clan. These tyrants of Athens, consciously or unconsciously, were leading their city toward democracy, and, by educating them through increased responsibility made them ready for active participation in a truly democratic government.

This government came into being with the reforms of Kleisthenes (fl. 582 B.C.) who attempted to abolish the influence of the four old aristocratic tribes whose power had, for years, been the dominant political influence in Athens. To accomplish this he instituted ten new "tribes" whose membership was based simply on place of residence rather than upon heredity. In order to do this he first divided the city into "demes" or neighborhoods. These purely artificial units furnished the basis for the political structure. Then a number of demes were combined to form a tribe, of which there were ten within the city-state. Furthermore, the demes for any single tribe were selected at random, so that within any tribe one found neighborhoods composed of the shore (people connected with shipping and seafaring trades), the city itself, and the rural areas. Thus no tribe was dominated by any single economic group. To make a not-too-exact analogy, we might think of the city of Detroit as divided into ten political groups but within each group one would find neighborhoods from the inner city, neighborhoods from the regularly employed working class, and neighborhoods from suburbs like Grosse Pointe.

Kleisthenes abolished the old Council of Four Hundred, which had come into being with the reforms of Solon, and substituted a Council of Five Hundred, with fifty members representing each of the new political tribes. He did this since the old council had come to be simply the voice of the four traditional tribes, and Kleisthenes wished to break their hold upon political and judicial matters. In the new government, each artificial political tribe nominated a large slate of candidates for the Council, from which fifty were selected by lot, on the theory that any citizen who was nominated (the nomination process eliminated the obviously unfit) was just as capable as any other citizen to administer the affairs of the state, so that actual membership could be left to chance.

The executive branch of the government was placed in the hands of a committee of ten generals who were elected yearly by the Council, and in turn this committee-of-ten was headed by a commander-in-chief whose term was also for a single year.

While Athens was developing its political institutions the mighty Persian Empire was becoming increasingly irritated with the rebellious Greek cities in Asia Minor. Athens supported the Ionian Greeks in their refusal to pay tribute to Darius (da–RYE–us), the Persian King, which gave him all the excuse a despot needs to give rebels a lesson in power, and the free city-state of Athens some instruction in humility. The Persians invaded mainland Greece in 490 B.C., a date that became pivotal for the future of Western culture.

North of Athens, on the plain of Marathon, the mighty army of a totalitarian state was confronted by a badly outnumbered Athenian force. Led by General Miltiades (mil–TIE–uh–deez), the Greeks, like the wily Odysseus, plotted to outwit the Persians and in a swift and stunning dawn attack drove the Persians back into their ships. According to the historian, Herodotos, the Persians lost more than six thousand men, while Greek casualties were minimal. Free people had turned back the Asian hordes and changed the course of history. The messenger who ran the twenty-six plus miles from Marathon to Athens symbolized more than news of an incredible victory. Greek pride in Hellenism, in the superiority of their culture over that of the barbarians, was fully vindicated.

The Persians were not to give up easily, and a second invasion was planned, but held up for ten years while the Persians put down a revolt in Egypt. In 480, however, they effected their second invasion. In the meantime the Athenians had discovered rich silver deposits at Mount Laurium in Attica, and had achieved a fairly high degree of wealth. Themistokles (the–MIS–tuh–kleez), the commander-in-chief in Athens, sent a delegation to Delphi to ask how best to meet the Persians in their second invasion, and was told that they should protect themselves with "wooden walls." Themistokles, with the usual Greek intellectual twist, believed that the Athenians could best protect themselves with a strong navy, and convinced his fellow citizens that the "wooden walls" were ships. Consequently, the money from the silver mines was used to build a strong Athenian navy, which proved to be not only a military force but also the determining factor in establishing Athens as a great commercial center. The Persian invasion of 480 was conducted on an even larger scale than the earlier war, for Herodotos estimates the Persian forces at five million men—an obvious exaggeration—but indicative of the size of the invading army. This army crossed the Aegean Sea far in the north and marched down the Greek peninsula, closely attended by the great Persian navy. The first of the great battles was a Persian victory, but a glorious episode in the history of Greece. This was the battle at the pass of Thermopylai (Ther–MOP–a–lye).

Here, at a narrow pass between the mountains and the sea, three hundred Spartans (now actually allied with Athens as a part of the fighting force) under their king, Leonidas (lee–ON–uh–dus), faced the entire Persian army and fought magnificently. When the Spartans were told to surrender or the sky would be darkened with arrows, Leonidas calmly replied that the Spartans would therefore fight in the shade. As usual in Greek wars, they were betrayed by a traitor who showed the Persians an alternative route through the mountains so that the Spartans were surrounded, but even in the face of such odds, they kept on fighting until they were all killed. The inscription later carved on the tomb of the heroic Spartans, in tremendous understatement and compression of meaning, gives testimony to the spirit of the encounter:

Go tell the Spartans, thou that passest by,
That here, obedient to their laws, we lie.

In the meantime the Persian fleet sailing down the coast in support of the army had suffered defeats from the Greeks and from the storms, but it still overwhelmingly outnumbered the ships of Athens and its allies. Eventually this fleet reached the sea just off Athens near the bay of Salamis (SAL–a–mus), while the land army moved inexorably toward its goal. Themistokles abandoned the city and all of Attica, moved the population to the island of Salamis, and prepared to gamble everything on a single naval battle. By trickery he enticed the Persian fleet into the Bay of Salamis, where the fleet's very size was a disadvantage, since in the narrow waters it was impossible to maneuver so many ships, and the Greek fleet attacked around the edges of the Persian ships and destroyed the Persians. The war continued for a year more on land, but the Persian army was finally defeated by the Spartans at the Battle of Plataea (pla–TEE–uh), and the Persian threat was broken.

It is almost impossible to overestimate the feeling of pride the Greeks felt as a result of these victories. Persia controlled Egypt, the entire eastern end of the Mediterranean Sea, and all of the land as far east as India. The wealth of the Persian kings and their satraps is impossible to estimate. Yet a relatively few Greek men, poverty-stricken in comparison to the Persians, had beaten off the totalitarian enemy. The Greeks rightly felt that their tradition of personal freedom, their pride in personal honor, and the love they felt for their cities had been the decisive factor. As indeed it was. Although the old aristocratic, oligarchical party continued in Athens, the years following the Persian wars marked the complete triumph of democracy in Athens. Suddenly the idea of freedom had worked.

For us in the Western world in the twentieth century, these far-off wars are of equal importance, for the Greek tradition—principally the concept of the worth of the individual person—survived and has given form to the ideas we now hold as of greatest worth. If the Greeks had failed, that tradition might have been snuffed out.

Another Quest for Freedom: The Philosophers

Developments in Greece during these preclassical times were not only political, economic, and military. One important phase of individual freedom is always the liberation of the human mind, allowing the individual to ask all the important questions of the gods and the universe and to formulate new and original answers. This, too, had been going on during the time of more tangible and material progress of which we

have been taking note. Curiously, the abstract speculation about the nature of the universe was a Greek phenomenon, one not found in other parts of the Western world. The Egyptians had made astronomical observations, but always for such practical purposes as the prediction of the flooding of the Nile upon which their agriculture depended. So, too, in Babylon a number of astrologers had observed the stars, largely for use in making practical predictions about the affairs of the earth. But pure thought about the nature of things was uniquely Greek; Edith Hamilton attributes it to the loose, nonauthoritarian nature of Greek religion, which was never dominated by a priestly class. The miracle that was ancient Greece will never be satisfactorily explained anyway; the point is that the Greek philosopher-scientists, for whatever reason, were the first true philosophers (pure thinkers) in Western civilization.

The Ionian Philosophers

The first philosopher-scientists lived in the Ionian city of Miletus (my–LEET–us) with Thales (THAY–leez; ca. 636–546 B.C.) as their leading thinker. The *questions* they asked are always more important than the answers they found, for the questions are those that constantly return to challenge people's minds. The answers change as our knowledge of the universe becomes more varied.

One problem consistently bothered the philosophers of the Ionian (or Milesian) School. They were intrigued by the constant change of all the things they could see around them. Earth changed to plant life; plant life changed to animal; wherever one turned, one observed movement from one form of existence to another. They postulated that there must be one single basic substance of which all the forms of being are made, so that the process of change is simply the transformation of the basic element. The first question Thales asked, then, is *What is the single element, the basic stuff, of which the universe is composed?*

His answer was that this basic element is water, for all things need water for their existence, and water itself changes when heated or cooled to a gaseous nature—steam—or to a solid state—ice. These things being true and observable by our relatively coarse sensory equipment, all sorts of other changes and transformations that are not sense-apparent, could take place in water. Other philosophers, following the line of thought first explored by Thales, argued for earth or air as the basic world-stuff. But, as we have said before, the questions are important, not necessarily the answers.

A second of the Ionians, Anaximandros (a–NAKS–uh–man–dros; ca. 611–547 B.C.), a student of Thales, came up with the second question of importance, *How do specific things emerge from the basic element?* His answer, while it may seem unsatisfactory and vague, is probably more scientifically accurate than those of many of his contemporaries or successors. In the first place, he rejected the idea of a physical element such as water, earth, or air, and simply called his basic stuff "the Boundless." This, he suggested, was a form of being we cannot perceive with our senses; that is, it permeates everything and surrounds everything. In specific answer to the question he raised, he simply said that all forms that we can see—trees, living animal bodies, all specific things—are formed by "separating out" of this boundless element. Thus all forms that our senses can know, all physical things, simply coagulate out of the non-sense-apparent boundless and eventually lose their form and disappear back into it.

A later philosopher-scientist, not strictly a Milesian, since his native city was Ephesos on the Ionian coast and since he was doing most of his work right at the end of the sixth century (500 B.C.), was the philosopher Herakleitos (Hair–uh–KLY–toss; ca. 535–475 B.C.). Following the same line of thought as Thales and Anaximandros, he raised a third important question, *What guides the process of change?* He would grant a basic element from which all particular forms emerged, but he felt there must be some sort of controlling force to keep the process of universal change in order so that, let us say, an elm tree always produces elm trees rather than hippopotamuses.

Herakleitos denied the possibility of existence, for he felt that the universe was in a process of flow, not fixed. His basic belief is that nothing *is;* everything is *becoming.* Thus his famous statement that one can never step into the same river twice. The appearance of the river may be the "same," whatever that may mean, but by the time one has taken a foot out of the river and put it back, the water has changed, the bank has changed, nothing is exactly the same. The universe is in the same condition. Between *now* and *now* it has flowed, changed, varied; it is no longer the same even though its appearance may seem to remain.

Perhaps to illustrate this contention, he chose fire as his basic element. Thus one may watch a flame in a fireplace for half an hour and say to one's companion, "I have been watching that same flame for thirty minutes." Actually, though the shape of the flame may remain fairly constant, the burning gas that is the flame is never the same, even for the smallest fraction of a second. Thus is the universe envisioned by Heracleitus.

But such a universe needs a guiding force, for the human mind finds it hard to live with a picture of a changing world without some order and direction. So Herakleitos proposed a great *Logos* as the direct answer to his question of the guiding force. Now *logos* in Greek means *word.* Thus, the Gospel according to John, originally written in Greek, starts with the sentence, "In the beginning was the Word"—*logos* in Greek. But with John, as with Herakleitos, it obviously has a much more important significance than our

word, *word.* For Herakleitos it meant a great *Intelligence,* which permeated the world and somehow guided the constant change of its flamelike element of which all things were composed. This sense of all things "knowing" what shapes they should take, what forms they should assume, is one of the great mysteries of the universe. (How does each maple leaf differ from every other maple leaf in the world, yet take a characteristic shape so that we can identify it at a glance? How does it "know" the form it must fulfill?) Herakleitos's assumption of a great Logos or Intelligence is not far from the assumption of a single God as an intellectual Principle in the universe.

The line of thought of these Ionian philosophers seems reasonable enough in their attempt to explain the element that is One and yet so many, which seems to be always the same and yet so varied. However, the basic assumption here is one of constant change, and furthermore, all of the conclusions these thinkers reached are based on the testimony of the human senses. We see, hear, taste, feel, or smell the phenomena of the world and the changing nature of all things. The search for a basic element from which it is all made is essentially a quest for "That Which is Real."

But the human mind can take an entirely different tack in this same quest. For example, our mind can simply say that whatever is *real* cannot always be changing. The mind can equate *permanence* with reality and say that only the things, or thing, that are absolutely permanent and unchanging are real. Furthermore, it can easily be proven that our senses cannot be trusted. We know they give us varying reports about the "same" thing. For example, water at the same temperature as measured by a thermometer will be either "hot" or "cold," depending on the temperature of our hands as we feel the water. Perhaps only the "thought process," independent of the senses, can be trusted as a guide to truth. Here we have the difference between scientists—people who trust their senses as they can be refined through such instruments as they can make—and pure philosophers, those who trust their minds alone to lead them to truth. This distinction appeared early in Greek thought.

Pythagoras

Pythagoras (ca. 582–507 B.C.) was one of the most original, interesting, and least-understood Greek philosophers. He was an Ionian Greek from the Aegean Island of Samos but he was most influential in southern Italy (Magna Graecia), where he established a religious brotherhood in Krotona (fig. 1.2).

Pythagoras taught that number was the essence of all things, in the same sense that his predecessors saw ultimate reality as water or the boundless or fire.

Figure 1.2 Marble bust identified as a portrait of Pythagoras and placed in the Roman Forum in 343 B.C. The identification is probably correct, for what we see here is a religious mystic. Museum, Ostia.

He believed that number was more than a symbolic construction, that all matter was essentially numerical, and that all relationships in the universe could be expressed through number. Pythagoras was the first Greek philosopher to reject the geocentric theory that the sun revolved around the earth. He reduced the earth to the status of a planet that revolved around the fixed point of a central fire; he also saw the sun revolving around what he called the hearth of the universe.

In his search for *that-which-is-most-real,* Pythagoras kept returning to the universality of mathematical relationships. For example, most of us know the formula in plane geometry called the Pythagorean theorem: In right-angle triangles the square of the hypotenuse is equal to the sum of the square of the other two sides. Here are three such triangles:

Although the triangles are dissimilar in appearance, one fact about them is true: $AB^2 + AC^2 = BC^2$. In Euclidean geometry this relationship was true before it was ever discovered, and it will remain true when there is no one on earth to be aware of it. Furthermore, it is true no matter what sensory conditions surround it. In the hottest furnace or the coldest refrigerator it is true. Here is an "idea" that has no substance, that exists entirely apart from people's minds; yet any shape that fulfills the equation is inevitably a right triangle. In this numerical relationship we have the pattern for a physical thing. Pythagoras is therefore credited with the discovery of pure mathematics, with the development of mathematical proofs, and with the awareness that form and structure give objects individual identities. These monumental achievements provide the framework for the Eleatic philosophers and particularly Plato (see chap. 2), upon whom Pythagoras was the single most important influence.

Pythagoras was the first to prove a relationship between mathematics and the harmonies of music. He discovered, through experimentation, that vibrating strings had certain relationships that were dependent on the relative lengths of the strings. These relationships were as consistent and as true as the Pythagorean theorem. For example, a string that is, say, 30 cm long vibrates twice as fast as a string that is 60 cm in length. Further, the 30-cm string produces a tone or musical pitch that is eight notes higher (called *octave*); the name of the note is the same, but the pitch is an octave higher:

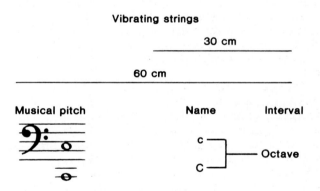

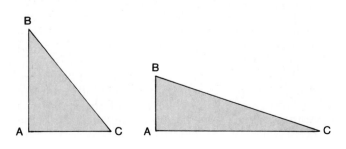

A string 20 cm long vibrates three times as fast as the 60-cm string and produces a pitch a 12th (octave plus five notes) above the lower string. Finally, a string 15 cm long vibrates four times as fast and produces a pitch two octaves higher. Though more and shorter strings can be used, Pythagoras chose to utilize the relationships as illustrated below:

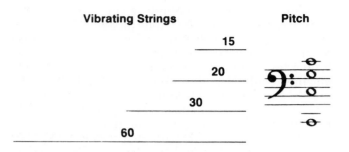

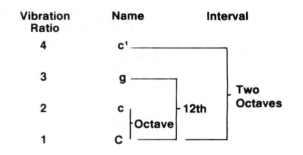

The longest string represents unity to which the other strings are related in vibration ratios of 2:1 (twice as fast), 3:1 (three times as fast), and 4:1 (four times as fast). This is a fact of nature that is always true, and its discovery acted upon Pythagoras like a mystic force. He based his philosophy of numbers upon a permanent reality symbolized by the unchanging relationships of the musical intervals. To Pythagoras these eternal truths proved that there was unity in the universe, that everything had its proper place, and that the universe and all within it could be understood in terms of numerical relationships.

You will notice that three of the four pitches have the same letter name; only the pitch level is different. The bottom *C* represents unity; the two higher *c*'s are derived from unity and related to unity by the even numbers of 2 (2:1) and 4 (4:1). The different note, the *g* represents diversity, for it is the next odd number (3) after unity (1). According to Pythagoras odd numbers are primary, strong, and masculine; even numbers are secondary, weak, and feminine, for they cannot exist independently.

Pythagoras, like most Greeks, considered 3 as the most logical number because it had a "beginning, middle, and end." Pythagoras's perfect number, however, was 10. He used a base 10 mathematical system (just as we do); ten has both a one for unity and a zero, which could be interpreted as representing eternity; ten terminates the one through ten sequence and all beyond this is reiteration of 1–2–3–4–5–6–7–8–9–10.

As previously demonstrated, the ratio of vibrations for the four strings is 1:2, 1:3, 1:4 (or 2:1, 3:1, and 4:1 since ratios can always be reversed). When arranged as superparticular ratios (each whole number differing by one) the three primary musical intervals are included: 1:2 (Perfect Octave), 2:3 (Perfect Fifth), and 3:4 (Perfect Fourth). Moreover, when 1:2:3:4 are added together the sum is ten, thus further confirming the perfection of ten.

Ten is the perfect number for a universe that has, according to Pythagoras, ten planets: sun, moon, Mercury, Venus, Mars, Jupiter, Saturn, the "dome of stars," earth, and counter earth. Of course he postulates a counter earth so that his so-called planets will add up to ten. He is also displaying a typically Greek determination to view the world as it should be rather than as it is. This Greek idealism will be discussed later, particularly in conjunction with Greek art.

Next, Pythagoras considers the 1:2:3:4 from the viewpoint of the "tetractys (tuh–TRACK–tus) of the decad (DEE–cad)," which translates as the "four quality of the ten." This is shown as an equilateral triangle of ten units in a 1:2:3:4 construction from each of the three points:

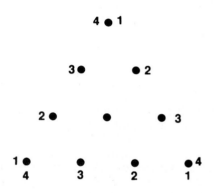

Each of the three sides has four units with a total of ten units in the triangle, and thus the tetractys of the decad. The equilateral triangle is the perfect figure, of course.

Pythagoras further emphasizes the fourness of this figure by pointing out that the figure represents the four mathematical qualities of point, line, plane, and solid. The *point* is one unit, the *line* is an outside lateral of four units, the *plane* (as in plane geometry) is the equilateral triangle (the perfect two-dimensional figure). Finally, the *solid* is the decad envisioned as three dimensional, i.e., as a pyramid, the perfect solid.

The heavenly bodies are pictured as revolving from west to east in an orderly circular orbit around the central fire. Agreement between nature and number has been proven (1:2:3:4) and so orbits are determined by relating them to musical intervals. The predictability of nature, like that of intervals on a vibrating string, was therefore musical and the wheeling arcs of the celestial globes was the *harmonia* of the *kosmos*, the music of the spheres.

From the theory of 10 as the perfect number Pythagoras applied numerical concepts to the world about him, using the concept that odd numbers were strong and masculine and even numbers were weak and feminine. Following are several of the less complicated concepts:

1 = unity
2 = female
3 = male
4 = justice (idea of retribution or 2 × 2)
5 = marriage (2 + 3)
7 = the goddess Athena because it is not generated by the numbers it contains (2 + 5 or 3 + 4). In other words, Athena was a virgin.

A basic thread in Greek thought is the idea that harmony is like a mean between two extremes. One of the first to promote the concepts of balance and control was Pythagoras, who set up the general parameters in his theory of the ten fundamental antitheses:

Odd Numbers (Perfect)	Even Numbers (Imperfect)
Limited	Unlimited
Odd	Even
Right	Left
One	Many
Male	Female
Rest	Motion
Straight	Crooked
Light	Darkness
Good	Evil
Square	Rectangular

A harmony between any of the two extremes listed above is never found precisely halfway in between. Situations change; what was reasonable one day might have to shift towards the other extreme the next day. Furthermore, since the odd numbers are perfect, the tilt will certainly favor the perfect numbers, particularly good over evil and light over darkness. In order to see how the ideas of Pythagoras were applied in everyday life it is now time to turn to the Pythagorean Order.

In the Pythagorean Order philosophy was a central part of a religious way of life, a life-style that was intellectual, political, religious, ethical. Small communities functioned within the larger community, each a social and religious unit as well as a scientific study group. Property was held in common, there was no discrimination based on sex, and music and mathematics were a regular part of social life.

The Pythagoreans are known especially for their doctrine of the transmigration of souls. They believed that souls were reincarnated in a series of lives as they tried to ascend to an ideal existence in a life of divine bliss. The ideal could be approached only through purification, emphasis upon intellectual activity, and renunciation of worldly sensuality. Salvation could be attained only after a final escape from the cycle of intermediate births.

The Pythagoreans were vegetarians who believed in the brotherhood of all living things. They believed in spiritual purification through music and science and physical purification through medicine and gymnastics. They advocated a humane society in which people would live always in harmony and friendship. Eventually they were either killed or forced to flee their communes by neighboring tribes who considered the Pythagoreans a threat to established religious practices.

Summary

In all these developments we see a culture emerging from chaos to a period of adjustment. A new political form, democracy, has appeared but still has to be tested by the stubborn aristocracy. There is great pride in Hellenism, in the great heritage celebrated in the Homeric poems and tremendously enhanced by the victories over the Persians. There is a loose religious structure and much philosophical speculation. Here is all the raw material for a great culture in which we will see the development of the arts and of philosophy as never before, or since.

2

Hellenic Athens: The Fulfillment of the Good Life

The city of Athens in 461 B.C. must have been an exciting place in which to live. It was prosperous and strong and, though no one knew it at the time, about to enter its Golden Age, that incredible era (ca. 460–430 B.C.) during which the resident artists, writers, statesmen, and philosophers would establish a society based on human values and on a commitment to truth, beauty, and justice. It was not a perfect society—far from it—but it did aspire to perfection. For a fleeting moment life was enveloped in the lusty embrace of a society that dared to compete with the gods.

Athenian Greeks may have been the most verbal people in the ancient world. Blessed with a sophisticated language rich in vocabulary and capable of infinite subtleties, they talked, discussed, argued, and debated everything under the sun: politics, society, love, and especially philosophy, because the intellectuals of the city were fascinated by the world of ideas. Herakleitean belief in constant change had its supporters, while others contended that reality could be expressed through numerical relationships, as Pythagoras had said. Entering into the debate came new ideas from Elea, the prosperous Greek colony in southern Italy. Led by Parmenides (par–MEN–uh–deez; born ca. 514 B.C.), the Eleatic School refused to accept the Herakleitean idea that nothing *is,* that the universe was in a constant state of *becoming.*

As the very basis of their thought they stated that whatever is *real* must be permanent and unchanging. If one turns the statement around, it may seem more logical: anything that constantly changes its state of Being cannot be real. Furthermore, they attacked the method of the Ionian philosophers by pointing out that the Ionians depended entirely upon their senses for the discovery of truth, trusting their sight, their sense of feeling, their hearing, the senses of smell and taste to lead them to valid conclusions. The Eleatics were quick to point out that the senses cannot be trusted. Of course this contention is easy to support; the sense impression that one receives depends quite as much on the state of the receiving sense organ as upon the thing itself. (The color-blind person sees a green traffic light as a sort of neutral gray; the person with "normal" sight sees it as green. Which is it really? For that matter, when one person sees "green" and another person agrees, are they really seeing the same color?) If the senses cannot be trusted as a guide to truth, what can? The Eleatic philosophers asserted that only the mind is a sure guide, and they could point to such truths as those found by the geometers like Pythagoras to support their theory that the mind, without the aid of the senses, can arrive at truth. As a matter of fact, these thinkers were much like the Pythagoreans, and form a sort of bridge between him and Plato, who will be discussed later. In the middle of the fifth century, Parmenides visited Athens at a time when Sokrates would have been about twenty years old. The two men could have met at that time.

The development of material philosophy reached its high point with the Athenian Leucippus, and his student, Demokritos (Di–MOK–ruh–toss; ca. 460–370 B.C.). Demokritos synthesized the attempts of the Milesians to understand the physical world and developed a theory of the material world that could not be verified until the twentieth century. He postulated Greek atomic theory, apparently using no more and no less than the power of his mind. According to Demokritos all matter consists of minute particles called *atoma* (unable to be cut). These atoms exist in space, combine and separate because of "necessity," and represent a strict conservation of matter and energy, i.e., the same number of atoms always exists; only the combinations differ. Contemporary nuclear physics confirms a strict conservation of matter and energy when taken together but identifies probability rather than necessity in terms of causality. As everyone knows, atoms do exist and some of them can be divided.

Following the Persian wars, Athens was optimistic and hopeful, filled with democratic pride and a confusion of ideas. Furthermore, the entire city had been burned by the Persians and needed to be rebuilt. The possibilities for growth and progress lay everywhere, but direction for human growth was needed. In terms of the development of the spirit, Aeschylus (ESK–i–lus), the playwright-artist in a time of chaos and early adjustment, was to point the way.

The Drama and Aeschylus

Before speaking specifically of the plays of Aeschylus, it might be well to mention something about the history of the drama. It began in Greece, as it was to do later in the Middle Ages in Europe, as a part of the worship service. Originally the priest spoke individual parts, while a chorus chanted responses. An original and almost mythical dramatist, Thespis (THES–pis), began to transform this rite into secular drama during the Archaic period.

The theatres were always in the open air, with the seats for spectators ascending the side of a hill. At the bottom of the hill a round flat area (the orchestra) provided a space in which the chorus danced and sang and chanted, and which had as its center the statue

Figure 2.1 Stone carving of theatrical mask at Ephesos, Turkey, where the Graeco-Roman theatre seated 25,000 spectators.

or altar of the god. Back of this and facing the audience was a long low building (the skene) with a room at either end and a platform between the two rooms. The rooms were for dressing and storage and the chief actors performed on the platform above and behind the chorus. (See fig. 4.7.)

Since they functioned as places of education and entertainment for most of the populace of a city-state, theatres were very large; seating was for 13,000 at Epidauros and 18,000 in Athens. These semicircular stadiums featured acoustics so fine that the actors could be understood fifty rows above the stage; however, because facial expressions could not be seen from this distance, performers wore large masks of easily recognizable character types (fig. 2.1). To compensate for distortions when viewed from high above, actors wore clog shoes that were about eight inches high, a convention that also contributed to the larger-than-life image of the subjects. Violence always took place offstage and was reported either by a messenger or another character. One stage set served throughout the play, and the only stage machinery was the *mechane,* a crane that transported the actors who played gods. This was the celebrated *deus ex machina,* or "god from a machine." Permanent stage sets, masks, clogs, offstage violence, dance, and music all challenged spectators to use their imaginations. (See also "The Art of Dance" and "Greek Theatre" in chap. 4.)

Drama festivals were held throughout Greece, but the one at Athens in honor of the god Dionysos (Di–uh–NYE–sos, and several other pronunciations) was the most important. Before the festival a number of playwrights would submit their plays to a board of judges, and the plays of four dramatists would be chosen for presentation, each one on a different day. In Aeschylus's time, each dramatist submitted a trilogy (a series of three plays on one theme) and a satyr play, which was a bawdy comedy presented at the end of the trilogy. A wealthy citizen paid the production costs for a playwright in the hope that his dramatist would win the first prize. A slight charge was made for seats at the drama, but in the fifth century the city paid for the admission of any citizens who could not afford it. Thus, if a writer had a message he wished to give to the entire population of his city, the drama was an almost perfect vehicle.

Aeschylus lived from 525 to 456 and was, therefore, a part of the great development of Greece as a whole, and Athens in particular. He was a soldier at the Battle of Marathon, a fact he had recorded on his tomb rather than that he was a dramatist. An aristocrat by birth, his drama presents a synthesis between the old ideas and those of the most enthusiastic democrats. Aeschylus has sometimes been accused of being much more of a preacher than a dramatist, for all of his plays carry a clearly stated message; yet Edith Hamilton points out that he was so much a dramatist that when the dramatic form did not exist, he invented it. Certainly before his time the cast contained only one speaking actor and the chorus. Aeschylus introduced a second speaking actor so that we could have the possibility of dialogue, real conflict, and resolution between two people and two ideas.

Aeschylus wrote about ninety plays, of which seven survive. Of these, only the trilogy called the *Oresteia* (O–res–TYE–ya), the story of Orestes, son of Agamemnon, will be discussed here. The trilogy consists of *Agamemnon,* the *Libation Bearers,* and the *Eumenides* (you–MEN–i–deez). They relate the story of the evolution of a system of justice dominated by

tradition, fear, and personal revenge into a new justice administered by the law courts of a free society.

Agamemnon begins in what Aeschylus must have regarded as the rural district of Argos, in front of the palace of Agamemnon, on what should be the most joyous day in ten years, for word has just been received that Troy has fallen, the ten-year Trojan War is over, the Greeks have been victorious, and Agamemnon, the great king, is returning. It should be a day of rejoicing, but the watchman on the palace who first sees the signal fires announcing the victory mutters darkly about the evil deeds that have been going on within the palace; the chorus refuses to believe in the message of the signal fires and spends much of the first part of the play recounting the sacrifice that was a part of the beginning of the war.

Their particular concern is with the death of Iphigeneia (If–i–je–NY–ya), the daughter of Agamemnon and Klytaimestra (Kly–tay–MES–tra) at Aulis (AW–lis) ten years before. The myth tells us that at the beginning of the war the brother kings, Agamemnon and Menelaos (Men–uh–LAY–os), had assembled the Greek army at the port of Aulis for embarkation to Troy, but after the troops were gathered Agamemnon had offended the goddess Artemis (ART–uh–mis) by violating her injunction against hunting. In retaliation she refused to grant favorable winds to the fleet unless Agamemnon offered his daughter as a sacrifice. Faced with a choice of standing firm against restless troops anxious for battle or sacrificing his daughter, Agamemnon, truly the son of his father, made the worst choice. He compounded the evil by sending for Iphigeneia on the pretext that she was to be married. (See box 2.1.)

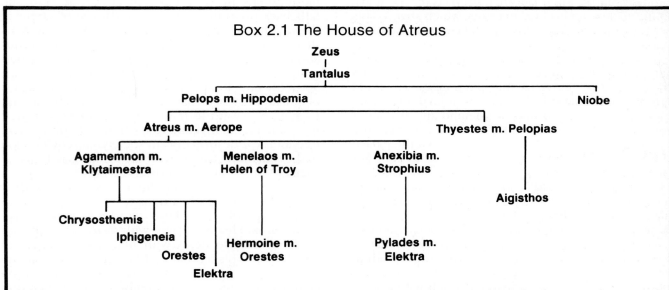

Box 2.1 The House of Atreus

Zeus
Tantalus
Pelops m. Hippodemia — Niobe
Atreus m. Aerope — Thyestes m. Pelopias
Agamemnon m. Klytaimestra — Menelaos m. Helen of Troy — Anexibia m. Strophius
Aigisthos
Chrysosthemis
Iphigeneia
Orestes
Elektra
Hermoine m. Orestes
Pylades m. Elektra

Like most old Greek families the roots go back to Zeus, in this case through Tantalus, a mortal who was permitted nectar and ambrosia at the table of the gods. In order to trick the gods and show them as fallible Tantalus hosted a banquet and served them a stew made of his son Pelops. The furious immortals dispatched Tantalus to Hades to suffer eternal hunger and thirst for he was guilty of *hubris*

(overbearing pride), the worst of all sins. The family curse continued with the sons of Pelops. Thyestes (thigh–ES–teez) seduced Aerope, his brother's wife; Atreus, in revenge, killed three of Thyestes' four sons (Aigisthos survived) and served them to their father as a meat course. In his *Oresteia* trilogy Aeschylus dramatizes the working out of the curse.

The chorus also calls our attention to Agamemnon's cousin, Aigisthos (i–JIS–thos), who now occupies the bed of the warring king. Moreover, Klytaimestra has not only taken a lover, she has dared to act as a man, to govern with a firm hand as a man would govern. What should be a day of rejoicing at the return of the victorious king starts as a day when all the dark collective guilt of the past is forced on the awareness of the chorus and the audience.

Finally Agamemnon himself returns, accompanied by Kassandra (Ka–SAN–druh), a princess from Troy who has received the unfortunate gift from Apollo that she can prophesy the future, but that no one will believe her prophesies. The last is not of immediate concern, though it will become important later in the play. What is of importance is that she has come on the same ship with the king, and now appears with him in his chariot. Of course Greek heroes were expected to take captive maidens as their mistresses, but the custom was that they would be brought home in a ship with the rest of the captured booty, and would serve as slaves in the household of their new master. Kassandra's appearance in Agamemnon's chariot is another act that will anger Klytaimestra.

Upon his arrival at the palace, Klytaimestra greets her husband so effusively that one recognizes this as a set speech, the sort of thing that is said when a returning hero is presented the keys to the city on the courthouse steps. Symbolically there follows one of the most important events of the drama, for the wife asks Agamemnon to enter the palace on a carpet dyed with a crimson (or purple) dye, which is so costly that it is reserved for the gods. Agamemnon refuses at first, but is persuaded by his wife. The act shows a pride too great for men; this mortal is stepping out of his proper zone and into the area reserved for the gods. Quite aside from his human errors, which angered his wife, this prideful act alone is sufficient to mark him for death.

After he has gone into the palace, we have one of the most interesting scenes of the play, for Kassandra tries to tell the chorus that Agamemnon is to be killed. Raging back and forth in an almost animal fury, probably in opposition to the strophe and antistrophe of the chorus, she tries to tell them of the murder being committed and urges them to break down the palace doors and prevent the deed. Casting aside all of her prophetic regalia, she finally shouts, "I say you shall see Agamemnon dead!" The chorus remains dumb and stupid, refusing to act. Then Kassandra, knowing she is to be murdered, meekly goes into the palace, hoping only that her death blow will be sure and swift.

Only when they hear Agamemnon cry out that he has been struck does the chorus nearly rouse itself to action. For the first time in Greek drama the members of the chorus speak as individuals, each with a short solo speech. The mood reaches a crescendo in the middle of this brief section when they are almost ready to break in and catch the murderers red-handed. Then apathy takes over, and at the end of the sequence they agree to wait until they really know what has happened. They do not have long to wait.

The palace doors are flung open, revealing the bodies of Agamemnon and Kassandra, with Klytaimestra proudly announcing that she has done this deed. The chorus mutters its protest, and Klytaimestra tries to calm them by suggesting that she is only the instrument of fate and the ancient curse on the house. Finally Aigisthos appears, rattles his sword a bit, and tells them to go home. The play closes as the chorus rather childishly tells the murderers just to wait until Orestes comes home to take his vengeance.

What does all this mean? It is interesting that the image most often presented in the play is that of a net or web. The purple carpet is referred to as a web, and Agamemnon has a net thrown over him in his bath so that he cannot resist while the murderous blows are being struck. Perhaps Aeschylus felt that this net was the old traditionalism, the belief in fate, and the idea of justice as revenge. Certainly the chorus is bound up in this web, since many of their speeches warn against pride, against wealth that breeds pride, and against any sort of innovation. Their wisdom follows the ancestral traditions hindering action. If they had acted by breaking down the door of the palace, they might have done more than merely break through a door; they might have broken the barrier between themselves and freedom. Curiously, Kassandra tries to inspire them to act, but she cannot do it. She, too, is caught in the net. The key to this lies in her entrance into the palace to meet her known fate. Even the chorus admonishes her that to delay her death even by a short time is to gain a small victory, but she answers that the time of her doom has arrived. She, too, is enmeshed by a belief in a fate that rules her life. Of all the characters in the play, only Klytaimestra seems free to act as a human being. True, she falls back upon the curse on the House of Atreus at the end, but this is only to placate the chorus in terms that they can understand. But her action is murderous and destructive, a type of freedom that cannot be permitted to survive in a community of human beings. So, at the end of the first play we have two conditions of human existence: that of the chorus, which is always looking backward to tradition for guidance in their lives, and that of Klytaimestra, whose wild destructive freedom will destroy human society. Aeschylus's job in the remaining two plays of the trilogy is to free one segment of society and restrict the other.

The second play in the trilogy, the *Libation Bearers,* is principally a transition play designed to bring the problem to a head. Orestes as a young man returns from Phocis (rhymes with *focus*) where he has been reared. He bears with him the command of Apollo to kill his mother and Aigisthos to avenge the murder of his father. It is interesting that this is the command of Apollo, a member of the new generation of progressive gods. On the other hand, we have the old tradition coming from clan and tribal governments that anyone who spills kindred blood will be hounded to his death by the Furies. Orestes is caught between two seemingly equally forceful commands; in his killing of his mother, he is damned if he does, and damned if he doesn't. But he does return, and in what must be the most awkwardly handled recognition scene in the history of drama, he is reunited with his sister Elektra (i–LEK–tra) and finally commits the murder. As the play ends he is set upon by the Furies and driven from the stage.

The word *Eumenides* may be translated as the *Gracious Ones,* and the change of the Furies (the Erinyes [i–RIN–e–eez]) to the Eumenides is the point of the third play in the series. The scene opens in Delphi at the shrine of Apollo, with the Furies temporarily sleeping, and with Orestes as a suppliant to the god having performed all the rites for the cleansing of guilt. He is told to go to the Temple of Athena on the Akropolis in Athens where he will receive justice. The movement in the trilogy is interesting to note at this point. *Agamemnon* started in the darkness with the gloomy mutterings of the watchman and the chorus in rural Argos. Now, in *Eumenides* we come to full light in the city of Athens. Because of the clash of ideas, the city is the place where new thought is generated, and Athens is chosen not only because it was the leading city of Greece, but also because it was Aeschylus's own city. The patriotic gesture is the appropriate one.

In Athens the chorus of Furies lament that they, the older gods, are being shamed and dishonored, and predict that if Orestes is allowed to go free, children will murder their parents at will, and that they, the Furies, will bring a blight upon the land. It is at this point that Athena arrives, and after hearing the preliminaries of the case asserts that the cause is too grave for a god to decide, and too grave, also, for a mortal man. She then sends out for a jury of twelve citizens of Athens to hear the case and render a verdict. What appears to be a contradiction may be resolved in this way. A trial by a jury transcends the judgment of a mortal man since, in the course of time, a jury will build up a body of law that will provide a rational basis for judgment, and thus go beyond the limits of on-the-spot mortal judgment.

With the jury selected and sworn in, the evidence in the case is presented, with Apollo acting as attorney for the defense. A modern reader must admit that his case—that the mother is not related to the child, but is only a sort of animated baby carriage—sounds pretty flimsy, but fortunately that is almost beside the point. After the presentation of evidence, Athena establishes the court (which is located at the foot of the Akropolis), the Areopagus (air–ee–OP–uh–gus), and charges it with its duties as the highest court of justice for all time. Her speech cannot be quoted often enough:

> Here reverence
> For law and inbred fear among my people
> Shall hold their hands from evil night and day,
> Only let them not tamper with the laws,
> But keep the fountain pure and sweet to drink.
> I warn you not to banish from your lives
> All terror but to seek the mean between
> Autocracy and anarchy; and in this way
> You shall possess in ages yet unborn
> An impregnable fortress of liberty
> Such as no people has throughout the world.

The tied vote of the jury follows, with Athena casting her vote for the acquittal of Orestes. There is, however, another interpretation of the voting process that is more closely attuned to the situation, more subtle, more Greek. This second version posits a jury of eleven persons and a vote of six to five for conviction. When Athena casts her vote for acquittal the result is a six–six division, which is, of course, a hung jury. Orestes is acquitted in either case but a hung jury, in a case of matricide, is as close as Orestes can come and still walk out of the court vowing a perpetual alliance between Argos and Athens. We must also consider the curious dramatic structure here when the hero of the drama can walk out with only two-thirds of the play finished. The reader must realize that Orestes is not the hero; *the real hero is an idea of justice*—of people getting along with people in such a way as to promote freedom and happiness for all.

The last third of the play deals with the conversion of the Erinyes to the Eumenides. These ancient and immortal hag-goddesses have real power, which cannot simply be taken from them by force; and they start the dialogue with their usual threats of civil violence and sterility in the city of Athens. But Athena is the goddess of wisdom and also of persuasion, and she slowly reveals to the Furies the role they can play and the worship they will receive as defenders of the city. Finally the Eumenides agree to accept their new role, and the drama closes with a procession, probably including the citizens of Athens, to the altar of the Eumenides on the site of the Areopagus.

As far as the significance of the play is concerned, Aeschylus probably had several specific messages for the Athens of his time. The court Athena founds is the old Areopagus, which represented the conservative element of the city as opposed to the more democratic Council. Four years before the production of the play, the Areopagus had been stripped of much of its authority, and perhaps Aeschylus is protesting this action. On the other hand, he may be considering the development of the Areopagus as the real birth of the polis (PO–lis), the city-state that through law was to give people freedom under a democratic government. For us, this latter is the significant interpretation.

In terms of the problem we noticed at the end of the discussion of *Agamemnon,* we have a much broader and more relevant meaning than the local Athenian one. The problem was that of bringing all the people out of the net of bondage to tradition and fate and, at the same time, limiting the freedom of such a person as Klytaimestra. The universal significance, which is our chief concern, may be described in the following way:

The people, as represented by the old chorus in *Agamemnon,* are set free simply because their eyes are turned forward rather than backward. No longer do they act under the shadow of old tradition and old superstition, since each case is tried in terms of its own evidence, and decided in terms of a law that has been made by human beings. In *Eumenides,* Aeschylus is setting forth the idea that people are to establish the limits for their own zone of action, limits determined by the amount of freedom each person can have while still maintaining the freedom of others. The same thing applies to the Klytaimestras of this new world. Their acts will also be brought to this tribunal to be checked by the same standard. Humanity—at least humanity in Athens—is now free for individual action for the best interests of the person and the state.

One more point is of interest here. The Furies insisted on rule by fear, and one is tempted to discard the element of fear in this new order toward which Aeschylus is pointing. But Athena insists that a certain amount of fear is still necessary. While Aeschylus was optimistic about human nature and human behavior in an atmosphere of freedom, he was not willing to go completely overboard with his hope. He knew that in spite of laws and courts there is in human nature a tendency to act completely selfishly, without any consideration for others. To curb this tendency an inbred fear must remain, more deeply felt than the purely intellectual respect for law. A number of critics have seen in the conversion of the Furies to the Gracious Ones a sort of birth of conscience. If this is true, the conversion must be to a very sophisticated conscience rather than the old primordial cultural fear. This must be an ethical conscience that while incorporating some element of fear, is chiefly concerned with the safety, even the total welfare, of the group. Conscience, of course, is the internal regulating force within each individual by which the morality of the culture is maintained. This may be the type of "fear" Athena maintains; perhaps we do not stretch the meaning of the play to think of the conversion of the old superstitious fears into household gods as the beginning of ethical conscience. At least it is a point to think about.

The Athens of Perikles

After the terms of office of a number of leaders such as Cimon and Ephialtes who made the laws of Kleisthenes ever more democratic, we come to the long and glorious rule of Perikles (PAIR–i–kleez). Perikles was first elected as general-in-chief in 461 and, with the exception of two years when he was voted out of office, directed Athenian affairs until his death in 429 (fig. 2.2).

One historian has estimated the population of Attica (the city of Athens and the surrounding territory it governed) at about two-hundred-thirty thousand people. Of these, forty thousand were free male citizens, the actual voting population that participated in the democracy; forty thousand were women who, at best, were second-class citizens; fifty thousand were foreign-born; and one hundred thousand were slaves. One must remember that in all of our discussion of the glories of Athenian democracy, we are

Figure 2.2 Marble bust from Tivoli inscribed with the name of Perikles. Roman copy after a bronze original of 450–425 B.C. The bronze original was possibly by Kresilas and placed on the Akropolis after the death of Perikles. Though the original work was probably a full figure this copy conforms to the Roman tradition of portrait busts, thus accounting for the feeling that this is an incomplete composition. British Museum, London.

talking about only the forty thousand free men. The rest of the free people participated only on the periphery, and the slaves had no voice at all. Nevertheless it is a miracle of history that a small group of less than a quarter of a million people, in about a single century starting with the second defeat of the Persians, could have produced three of the great writers of tragic drama and one of the great comedy writers in the history of literature, two or more of the philosophers whose ideas still give shape to our lives, great architecture, and magnificent sculpture. The music and the painting of the time are lost, but in the contemporary writings music is regarded as the highest and the best developed of the arts, and sculpture was thought of as a secondary art in comparison with painting.

Finally, and most significant of all, the people, at least in the first generation of this century, produced a life-style that in its freedom for the individual, coupled with a concern for the welfare of the state as a whole, has been envied and emulated by the Western world ever since. This was the life-style toward which the plays of Aeschylus pointed. The ideal of this life-style is nowhere better stated than by C. M. Bowra *(The Greek Experience),* who writes, "A man served his state best by being himself in the full range of his nobility, and not by sacrificing it to some abstract notion of political power or expediency."

Life at this time was largely out-of-doors. The courts and the council met on the Pynx Hill opposite the Akropolis and heard matters of state argued. The town assembly met also on the Pynx, which could seat up to eighteen thousand people. Life was vigorous in the Agora (AG–uh–ruh), a level area at the foot of the Akropolis, the marketplace for the city and also the place where the men went to meet each other and to argue politics and philosophy. Here visiting teachers would lecture to any audience they could attract, and one assumes that they did a thriving business. The Greeks were a dynamic and talkative people, and the issues of the day were thrashed out in the Agora with most of the free men listening and joining in the debate.

When not in the Agora, many men spent their time in the gymnasia. These were parks set aside for physical exercise not far from the city limits of Athens. These provided a running-track, a wrestling-ground, and other facilities for exercise, and provided, as well, for shady walks and places for discussion, since the ideal was the development of the whole man, with full development of both mind and body. Later, Plato's Academy and Aristotle's Lyceum were to be founded in surroundings like those of the gymnasia.

Home was the place where the Greek man went when there was no place else to go, and it is interesting that in all of the archeological remains, we have little indication of the nature of the private houses. Public buildings and palaces were built to last, while individual homes were not. We do know that Greek homes were built in the standard Mediterranean pattern of windowless walls adjoining the street with inner courts for coolness and privacy. The homes to which Greek men retired were, in effect, not their houses but those of their wives. Wives were not citizens and could not vote but they did run the household: raising children, supervising servants, going to market, and keeping household accounts.

Perikles did not make many great changes in the government of the city. His role, instead, was to maintain the democratic values and the human values that had already come into being. In order to do this, he rebuilt the city as a proper home for these ideals. Probably the Agora was first rebuilt, since it formed a marketplace for ideas as well as things, and later he commissioned the building of the Parthenon (447–438) and other temples on the Akropolis. The care with which the architect shaped the building to conform to human standards rather than rigid mathematical and physical rules suggests the complete devotion of the Athenians to the standard of human values.

The balance the Athenians maintained between individualism and the welfare of the state was a most delicate one. During the Age of Perikles there was a shift towards individuality and away from the general, especially in the welfare of other city-states. This was first noticeable in the international relations of the city, for it converted the Delian League into what was really an Athenian empire, and moved the treasury from the island of Delos to Athens. As a matter of fact, the Parthenon and other buildings were constructed

Figure 2.3 Athenian silver drachma, ca. 450 B.C. Obverse (heads): Archaic head of Athena wearing a crested helmet with three upright olive leaves. Reverse: Owl with olive spray at the left and A θ E at the right, standing for Athens. Known as the "owls of Athens," these coins dominated the Eastern Mediterranean for six hundred years. Museum of Fine Arts, Boston.

with money that belonged to this treasury. When member cities objected, they were simply told that if Athens were to assume the burden of protection for the league as a whole, Athens alone should be able to decide what to do with the money that was paid into the treasury (fig. 2.3).

As an international power, Athens became autocratic, and within the city the older values of reverence to the gods and to the state, ideas that had been triumphant at Marathon and that Aeschylus had preached in his plays, moved toward self-centered individuality. This metamorphosis probably had its start with the teachings of the atomists like Demokritos, who argued for complete materialism, even with the gods, and ascribed all change to accident. In such a world, the only human goal can be material pleasure, since with accident as the ruling force, nothing about the future can be predicted, and the gods who are material and subject to chance offer no guidance or inspiration.

Probably taking their cue from the atomists, the leading teachers of Athens became the sophists (sof [o as in *hot*]–ists). This group had a leader in Protagoras (pro–TAG–uh–rus), a high-minded thinker and teacher whose chief pronouncement was that *man is the measure of all things*. Taken by itself, this is simply a sloganlike reassertion of the idea of human values we have already praised so highly in this Greek state. But dangers also appear. If men, mankind, is the measure, then all may be well; if man the individual is the measure of all, then whatever the individual person may choose to do or believe is proper. The later sophists moved toward this last position, teaching, for example, that the laws were merely a set of people's opinions, so that if any people hold a different opinion, their conviction is as valid for them as are the laws. Much can be said in favor of the sophists' teachings, for they introduced a healthy questioning of the old traditions and the old veneration of the gods. On the other hand, their complete relativism, if taken seriously, undermined any coherence within the group and all thought or action became merely a matter of expediency.

Into this new and changing atmosphere came two of the great tragic writers to direct Athenian thought and feeling: Sophokles (SOF [as in hot]–uh–kleez; 496–406 B.C.) and his younger contemporary, Euripides (you–RIP–uh–deez; 484–406 B.C.).

Sophokles

Sophokles was a general, a priest, and the most popular dramatist in Athenian history (fig. 2.4). He is reputed to have written 123 plays and to have won first prize more than twenty times; he never placed lower than second. Of the seven complete plays that have survived, only *Oedipus the King* (ED–uh–pus, or EED–uh–pus) will be discussed here.

The plot of *Oedipus the King* concerns a plague in the city of Thebes, which the Delphic oracle says will be lifted only when the murderer of Laius (LYE–us), the former king, is discovered and punished. Oedipus, the new king, who has according to custom married the widowed queen, Jocasta (joe–KAS–ta), swears to find this murderer in order to save the city. This is done in the face of two prophecies. One was known to Jocasta and Laius, that their son would kill his father and marry his mother (box 2.2). Accordingly, when a son was born to them, Laius (without Jocasta's consent) had the baby exposed to die on the slopes of Mount Kithaeron (kee–the–RON). The second prophecy, known to Oedipus when he grew up in Corinth as the son of the king and queen there, was that he would kill his father and marry his mother. To avert this, he had fled the city of Corinth. On his flight he had an altercation with an old man and his bodyguard at the place where three roads come together, and in a fit of rage Oedipus had killed the whole group. He had then proceeded to Thebes

Figure 2.4 Portrait bust of Sophokles. Marble, ca. 340 B.C. British Museum, London.

where he solved the riddle of the Sphinx, was chosen king by the populace, and married Jocasta. The play is riddled with irony, for the audience and the readers know that in the search for the murderer, Oedipus is searching for himself, and that the curse he has pronounced on the killer of King Laius will fulfill itself on him. This expected event comes to pass; Jocasta commits suicide, and Oedipus blinds himself and exiles himself from the city. With these events the play of Oedipus ends.

The play is, of course, subject to a number of interpretations. It can be viewed as an exploration of man's fate; whether Oedipus because of a "fatal flaw" brought disaster upon himself, whether he was just a pawn of the gods, or whether the answer lies somewhere in between.

Professor Bernard Knox sees the play as an example of the power of the gods presented to the Athenians to stop them in their progress toward skepticism and atheism, and certainly this does constitute one level of meaning. Oedipus first quarrels with the ancient prophet, Tiresias (tie–REE–see–us), and ends up shouting angrily that all prophets are cheats. Several times Jocasta entreats Oedipus to put no faith in oracles, each time trying to show him how the oracles have lied. The final statement of her belief is given in the lines:

Why should we be afraid? Chance rules our lives,
And no one can foresee the future, no one.
We live best when we live without a purpose
From one day to the next.

The thought here is almost exactly the day-to-day philosophy of the atomic materialists, but each time Jocasta attempts to prove that the oracles are useless, Oedipus receives a new jolt that points to the fact that he is the murderer whom he is seeking.

This scoffing at the prophecies from the gods has an interesting effect on the populace as represented by the chorus of Thebans. One of their odes is a plea for reverence to the gods, ending with these lines:

If evil triumphs in such ways as these,
    Why should we seek, in choric dance and song,
To give the gods the praise that is their due?
    I cannot go in full faith as of old,
To sacred Delphi or Olympian vale,
    Unless men see that what has been foretold
Has come to pass, that omens never fail.
    All-ruling Zeus, if thou art King indeed,
Put forth thy majesty, make good thy word,
    Faith in these failing oracles restore!
To priest and prophet men pay little heed;
    Hymns to Apollo are no longer heard;
And all religion soon will be no more.

But the oracles are upheld; faith is restored. From the moment of Oedipus's highest hope when the messenger brings news that the king of Corinth has died and that the citizens there have chosen *him* king, he is dashed to the bottom of despair as he finally learns that he was the baby who was exposed to die, and that the old man he killed was his true father. Strained beyond endurance by her burden of knowledge, Jocasta commits suicide, and Oedipus, who has seen external things throughout his life, blinds himself as he comes to see himself and, with clear vision, sees truths that lie beyond the externals. He and the blind Tiresias, also one of the clear-sighted ones, reach equality at the end of the play. On this level of meaning this drama is a clear admonition that the gods are powerful and should receive worship and honor.

Until recently the view that Oedipus did not know he was seeking himself as the murderer was generally accepted. However, a conflicting interpretation, based on the text, is also possible. This alternate view contends that Oedipus had some knowledge (a lot?, a little?) of the truth *before* the fateful day with which the play begins.

Euripides

The third great tragedian of Athens, Euripides (484–406 B.C.), directed his tragic vision towards psychological drama with plots revolving around the plight of the underdog: the inferior status of women, the exploitation of peasants, the rejected wife, the exploited wife, those who lose wars. Aristotle said that Aeschylus composed properly without knowing it, that Euripides painted men as they were, and that Sophokles painted men as they should be. Euripides exposed the reality of suffering and suffered the usual fate of the artist who deals with unpopular truths. Euripides wrote ninety-two plays but won only four first prizes; the fourth one was awarded after Sophokles made an issue of the case. However, nineteen plays have survived, more than the combined extant dramas of Aeschylus and Sophokles, an ironic twist Euripides would have appreciated (fig. 2.5).

Elektra provides a good example of the different styles of the three dramatists. Aeschylus portrays Orestes and Elektra as vehicles for developing an idea of justice; Sophokles writes a classic study of a woman possessed and driven almost mad by the indignities that have been heaped upon her; Euripides presents Elektra and Orestes as cold-blooded butchers bent

Figure 2.5 Portrait bust of Euripides. Marble, Roman copy, ca. 320 B.C. Portraits of Euripides survived about as well as his plays; this is one of twenty-five replicas. National Museum, Naples.

solely on revenge. Orestes craftily insists upon staying close to the borders of Argos so he can escape should anything go wrong. Elektra is a proud, disdainful aristocrat who looks down upon Pylades, her peasant husband. The nobility of the poor is another of Euripides' themes; the peasant is as good a man as one can find, stoically suffering his wife's scorn.

In *Medea* two more of Euripides' great themes appear: the strength and greatness of a woman, and the hypocrisy and shabby ethics found so often in highly developed cultures. Medea is a raging woman, consumed by love turned to hate because of the sniveling opportunism of her civilized Greek husband. As she arranges for the murder of Kreusa, Jason's intended bride, and then murders her own sons in order to wipe out Jason's line, she is the magnificent Medea, destroyer of a decadent, materialistic civilization.

In *The Trojan Women,* Euripides shows us war as it really is. He does not treat the Trojan War as a glorious victory for the good Greeks; instead, he selects the time immediately after the victory and shows the misery of the women of Troy as they are parceled out to the conquerors and their heartbreak as they see their children murdered by the "heroic" victors.

During the last two years of his life, Euripides exiled himself from civilized Athens and went to live in primitive Macedonia, where he died. There he wrote *The Bacchae* (BOCK–ee), in which he repudiates all of the rationalistic civilization he had known—a civilization that had rejected him and that he had in turn rejected.

The antagonists in the play are the highly civilized, typically Greek, Pentheus (PEN–thee–us), King of Thebes, and the god Dionysos, who was born in Thebes (see box 2.2). As the play opens, Dionysos has assumed a homosexual role (he was also bisexual or asexual, as he wished) and come to Thebes to demand recognition and worship. The women are quickly enticed into the hills but Pentheus puts the god in prison and assumes that everything will become normal again. Even as Pentheus stands uncomprehendingly in the smoldering ruins of his palace he tries to keep the situation rational. Dionysos responds by tricking Pentheus into wearing women's clothing and then tricks Agaue, Pentheus's mother, into tearing off the head of her own son. At the end the kingdom is a total ruin and Dionysos is cooly dispensing justice. The point is that Dionysos is much more than just the god of wine; he also represents the nonrational aspect of human nature, that raging torrent within that man must recognize and to which he must give proper recognition. Euripides seems to be saying that men and women must maintain a delicate balance between emotion and intellect, and there must be both. Pentheus tried to suppress his emotions and was made a complete fool of before he was killed by his mother. On the other hand, emotion run riot is chaos. Though Dionysos is the god of the nonrational he certainly destroyed Thebes in a cool and calm

manner. Euripides did not live to see the play produced. The final irony is that Sophokles used his immense prestige to see that the play received the production it merited, in the city that deserved it.

Athenian Background after Perikles

Throughout the times of these dramatists, the cities of Athens and Sparta had each been growing in power until a confrontation between the two for dominance throughout the Hellenic world was inevitable. In 445 the two city-states signed a pact for a thirty-year truce, which was observed, more or less, for fourteen years. In 431 the Peloponnesian War broke out; it ended in 404 with Sparta's total conquest of Athens. Perikles believed that this would be a long war of attrition, and decided to abandon the land to Sparta, bringing all the people of Attica inside the walls of Athens, and trusting the Athenian navy to attack Sparta and her allies wherever a hit-and-run attack would do the most damage. Athens was almost immediately crippled when, in 430, plague broke out in the city and a third of the population died. Perikles himself died of the disease in 429. The conflict that followed furnishes almost a classic example of the stupidity of war. On two or three occasions Athens obtained the upper hand and could have made peace with Sparta without serious loss of honor, but the hawks within the government demanded total victory.

A number of Athenian acts during the war demonstrate the temper of the times. For example, in 416 the Athenians attacked the neutral island of Melos on the general principle that if you aren't for us, you are against us. The battle lasted a single day, with Athens winning, killing all the men on the island, and selling the women and children into slavery.

In the following year Athens mounted a great attack on the city of Syracuse in Sicily, an attack that was foolhardy and doomed to failure. Of the three generals in command, one of them, Alkibiades (Al–ki–BY–uh–deez), represents an extreme example of the new egocentric individualism that was becoming so prevalent in Athens. His self-indulgent actions and ethical relativism could be construed by the sophists of the city as proper (successful) behavior. In the first place, Alkibiades left Athens under a cloud, for after a series of farewell parties a number of the sacred shrines in the city were defaced, and it was generally supposed that Alkibiades and his followers committed this sacrilege. Before reaching Sicily, he defected to Sparta, and in Sparta became a leading citizen and military adviser. When he felt that his good fortune in Sparta was running out, he deserted to Persia, and even later he returned to Athens where he was greeted as a national hero and reelected to a generalship. This, as we have said, is an extreme case, but when such conduct could be tolerated, the moral fiber of the city must have been extremely weak. After the Sicilian disaster in which the navy and most of the army were lost, the war dragged on to what had become an inevitable victory for Sparta. Then, during the fourth century, the government vacillated between the strong antidemocratic element in the population, the democrats, and a moderate element, which sought to limit the voting power to a few thousand of the upper classes but still maintain some sort of democratic voice.

The Critics of Athens: Sokrates and Aristophanes

Probably the greatest questioner of the new value system in Athens was the philosopher, Sokrates, of whom we know little, since he never wrote and the only reports we have about him are from his pupils, principally Plato and Xenophon (ZEN–oh–fun). It is apparent, however, that he spent most of his life raising embarrassing questions and demanding that the Athenians examine their motives for their way of life. He was an extremely popular teacher for a group of the intellectual young men who shared his views about the decay of the old value systems, but he was certainly not popular with those whose motives were totally selfish. This last group finally had him arrested on the charge of corrupting the youth of Athens; in 399 a jury of his peers found him guilty of impiety and corrupting the youth and sentenced him to death. At his trial he described himself as the gadfly of Athens, and the description is probably very exact. He insisted that the only good life was the well-examined life, and he sought to help others by causing them to examine themselves by asking them what they meant by the words they used—what do you mean, "justice"?—and then by a series of other questions finally revealing to the individuals that they simply didn't know what they were talking about. His method was always the same: to ask a question and arrive at an answer that seemed to be true. Then, by further questions he would test each part of the original answer, paring away those parts that proved themselves to be false, until the original answer was refined to truth by the clear process of thought.

For Sokrates, the end of the good life is happiness, which is not only the avoidance of ignorance and its fruits, but the virtue that comes from knowledge. To know rightly, to make right choices, is virtue, for it alone can satisfy reason. Knowledge and virtue are inseparable. And happiness is the result of worthiness that comes when enlightenment and knowledge result, as necessarily they must in this highest good, which we call virtue.

The other great critic of late fifth-century Athens was Aristophanes (air–i–STOF–uh–neez; ca. 448–388 B.C.), the great writer of Greek Old Comedy. An aristocrat and a conservative, he sought to make Athens aware of its faults through the biting wit of his satires. In *The Clouds* he depicted Sokrates as a sophist who, for a fee, taught either right logic or wrong logic, which did not help matters at the trial of Sokrates. *The Wasps* poked fun at the Athenian passion for litigation and *The Frogs* was a literary satire involving Aeschylus and Euripides; he was sharply critical of Euripides. Perhaps his greatest play was *Lysistrata* (LIS–i–stra–ta or li–SIS–tra–ta) in which the war

between Athens and Sparta, or any war for that matter, was satirized. The Athenian woman Lysistrata enlists the cooperation of all the Greek women in a simple and wonderfully effective plan to stop warfare: no sex until all fighting stops. Given a choice between making love and making war the men, after considerable controversy and much pleading, opt for the former.

Thus was the great fifth century in Athens. It had started with the pride of victory over the Persians, with the triumph of democracy, and with the promise of the great life in the plays of Aeschylus. Within the early years of the leadership of Perikles that good life had been realized about as much as it ever can be. It ended in a time of military defeat; a time when selfish individualism was the dominant mood; a time when Athens could no longer listen to the voice of its best critic, and when even criticism-through-comedy turned from biting satire to simple comedy-for-amusement, which we see in the later plays of Aristophanes.

The highest assertion of the human spirit in these exhausted times came at the very end with the trial of Sokrates and a glimpse of the philosopher as hero. In his *Apology* (see complete text below) he spoke to his jury as a highly urbane and civilized man, disdaining high-flown rhetoric on the one hand, and sentiment on the other. Instead, he speaks almost in a conversational tone about his own life and his devotion to his own highest ideals for human conduct. Perhaps the highest statement comes after the vote has been taken that condemned him to death:

> . . . And there are many other ways of avoiding death in every danger if a man is willing to say and to do anything. But, my friends, I think that it is a much harder thing to escape from wickedness than from death, for wickedness is swifter than death. And now I, who am old and slow, have been overtaken by the slower pursuer: and my accusers, who are clever and swift, have been overtaken by the swifter pursuer—wickedness. And now I shall go away, sentenced by you to death; and they will go away, sentenced by truth to wickedness and injustice. I abide by my penalty, they by theirs.

Literary Selection

MEMORIAL ORATION
Perikles (?–429 B.C.)

This portion of Perikles' famous oration is taken from the history of the Peloponnesian War as written by Thucydides (thoo–SID–i–deez). Perikles made this address at the public funeral of a group of Athenian young men who had been killed in the war.

Some scholars contend that Aspasia exerted considerable influence not only on this notable speech but also on the political strategies of Perikles in general. An intelligent and highly educated foreigner from Ionia, Aspasia was a former hetaera (Gk., *hetaira*, female companion), Perikles' concubine (in effect, common-law wife), and the mother of his son Perikles, who was legitimized by vote of the people. The hetaerae of ancient Greece were companions—physically, intellectually, and emotionally—to influential men in Athenian society. Well-educated and adept in music, dancing, conversation, and other social graces, they fulfilled a role generally denied to Greek wives who, though undisputed mistresses of their households, were not permitted to partake fully in life outside the home.

Though criticized by some because of her former profession and her political influence, Aspasia established in the home of Perikles what might be called the first salon. Here she entertained notable artists, philosophers, and political leaders, including the more liberated women of Athens. Breaking with tradition, some men brought their wives to Aspasia's dinner parties to participate in discussions about the need for wives to be better educated and thus better able to be fit companions for their husbands. Since she was credited by Sokrates with teaching Perikles the art of rhetoric, it is likely that the brilliant Aspasia assisted Perikles in the composition of some of his speeches, most especially the Memorial Oration.

As you read this eloquent address, you should remind yourself of the questions about human aspirations that had been raised in the plays of Aeschylus. In the *Agamemnon* the chorus railed against great wealth, insisting that the most humble life was the best. In *Eumenides* we observed the question of whether justice should be by reason or by stern revenge within the family. The question of the conflict between maturing man and an absolute god who ruled through fear had been raised. Other questions we have not yet seen in the literature, but which were present in the Greek mind (and in our own) are whether the state needs to protect itself by universal military training or not, and whether a life of cultural pursuits does not enfeeble people in a nation. Perhaps the greatest question for our time and theirs is whether a democracy can really function. The argument on the one side is that an absolute government gets things done quickly and efficiently, while in a democracy, people talk so much that they have no time for action.

You will find some of the answers in which the Athenians believed in the following selection.

. . . Before I praise the dead, I should like to point out by what principles of action we rose to power, and under what institutions and through what manner of life our empire became great. For I conceive that such thoughts are not unsuited to the occasion, and that this numerous assembly of citizens and strangers may profitably listen to them.

Our form of government does not enter into rivalry with the institutions of others. We do not copy our neighbors, but are an example to them. It is true that we are called a democracy; for the administration is in the hands of the many and not of the few. But while the law secures equal justice to all alike in their private disputes, the claim of excellence is also recognized; and when a citizen is in any way distinguished, he is preferred to the public service, not as a matter of privilege, but as the reward of merit. Neither is poverty a bar, but a man may benefit his country whatever be the obscurity of his condition. There is no exclusiveness in our public life, and in our private intercourse we are not suspicious of one another, nor angry with our neighbor if he does what he likes; we do not put on sour looks at him, which though harmless are not pleasant. While we are thus unconstrained in our private intercourse, a spirit of reverence pervades our public acts; we are prevented from doing wrong by respect for authority and for the laws; having an especial regard to those which are ordained for the protection of the injured, as well as to these unwritten laws which bring upon the transgressor of them the reprobation of the general sentiment.

And we have not forgotten to provide for our weary spirits many relaxations from toil; we have regular games and sacrifices throughout the year; at home the style of our life is refined; and the delight which we daily feel in all these things helps to banish melancholy. Because of the greatness of our city the fruits of the whole earth flow in upon us; so that we enjoy the goods of other countries as freely as of our own.

Then again, our military training is in many respects superior to that of our adversaries. Our city is thrown open to the world; and we never expel a foreigner, or prevent him from seeing or learning anything of which the secret, if revealed to an enemy, might profit him. We rely not upon management of trickery, but upon our own hearts and hands. And in the matter of education whereas they from early youth are always undergoing laborious exercises which are to make them brave, we live at ease, and yet are equally ready to face the perils which they face. . . .

If, then, we prefer to meet danger with a light heart but without laborious training, and with a courage which is gained by habit and not enforced by law, are we not greatly the gainers? Since we do not anticipate the pain, although, when the hour comes, we can be as brave as those who never allow themselves to rest; and thus too our city is equally admirable in peace and in war. For we are lovers of the beautiful, yet simple in our tastes, and we cultivate the mind without loss of manliness. Wealth we employ, not for talk and ostentation, but when there is a real use for it. To avow poverty with us is no disgrace; the true disgrace is in doing nothing to avoid it. An Athenian citizen does not neglect the State because he takes care of his own household; and even those of us who are engaged in business have a very fair idea of politics. We alone regard a man who takes no interest in public affairs, not as a harmless but as a useless character; and if few of us are originators, we are all sound judges, of a policy. The great impediment to action is, in our opinion, not discussion, but the want of that knowledge which is gained by discussion preparatory to action. For we have a peculiar power of thinking before we act, and of acting too; whereas other men are courageous from ignorance but hesitate upon reflection. And they are surely to be esteemed the bravest spirits, who, having the clearest sense both of the pains and the pleasures of life, do not on that account shrink from danger. In doing good, again we are unlike others; we make our friends by conferring, not by receiving favors. Now he who confers a favor is the firmer friend, because he would fain by kindness keep alive the memory of an obligation; but the recipient is colder in his feelings, because he knows that in requiting another's generosity he will not be winning gratitude, but only paying a debt. We alone do good to our neighbors not upon a calculation of interest, but in the confidence of freedom and in a frank and fearless spirit.

To sum up: I say that Athens is the school of Hellas, and that the individual Athenian in his own person seems to have the power of adapting himself to the most varied forms of action with the utmost versatility and grace. This is no passing and idle word, but truth and fact; and the assertion is verified by the position to which these qualities have raised the State. For in the hour of trial, Athens alone among her contemporaries is superior to the report of her. No enemy who comes against her is indignant at the reverses which he sustains at the hands of such a city; no subject complains that his masters are unworthy of him. And we shall assuredly not be without witnesses: there are mightly monuments of our power, which will make us the wonder of this and of succeeding ages; we shall not need the praises of Homer or of any other panegyrist, whose poetry may please for the moment although his representation of the facts will not bear the light of day. For we have compelled every land and every sea to open a path for our valor, and have everywhere planted eternal memorials of our friendship and of our enmity. Such is the city for whose sake these men nobly fought and died: they could not bear the thought that she might be taken from them; and every one of us who survive should gladly toil on her behalf.

Exercises

1. What stand would Perikles take on the question of universal military training?
2. Here is raised an old question about men of words and men of action. It is frequently said that the democratic ways are terribly slow because people spend their time talking and never act. Is a compromise between words and action possible?
3. Why does Perikles speak of the individual Athenian when he is making a summary of the government?

Greece: From Hellenic to Hellenistic World

"The name Greek is no longer a mark of race, but of outlook, and is accorded to those who share our culture rather than our blood," said the Athenian orator Isokrates in 380 B.C. By then the Greek city-states no longer exercised political and military dominance in the Hellenic world of the eastern Mediterranean, but their culture spread not only throughout the Mediterranean but into Egypt and the vast Persian empire as well. What caused the decline of the Greek city-states? Their contentious fervor and pride had enabled them to soundly defeat the much larger forces of the Persian empire. However, this was because they were, for the first and last time, united against a common foe. Afterwards their pride and aggressive independence caused endless squabbles with each other, culminating in the disastrous war between Athens and Sparta and assorted allies on both sides. The Persian Wars (490–479 B.C.) inspired confidence but the internecine Peloponnesian War (431–404 B.C.) left despair and decay in its wake. Not one city-state was strong enough to take control, so a federation was

Figure 2.6 Portrait bust of Demosthenes. Roman marble copy, probably after a original bronze of 280/279 B.C. Ashmolean Museum, Oxford. This last great champion of Athenian liberty lived to see Athens free itself from Macedonia after Alexander's death in 323 B.C.

impossible. Sparta dominated for a time, followed by Thebes, Athens,[2] and Corinth, but always with the tireless Persians in the background manipulating events through bribery and coercion.

By the middle of the fourth century in a backwater of Greek civilization, King Philip of Macedonia began to move toward an empire that united all of Greece. Some purposes were gained by military strategy; however, most were through a series of wily political and diplomatic moves, accomplished despite repeated warnings by the Athenian orator Demosthenes (fig. 2.6). Upon Philip's assassination in 336 his brilliant young son, Alexander (fig. 2.7), who was a student of Aristotle's, became king. In one remarkable campaign Alexander brought all of Persia (including the territory of modern Turkey) as far east as India, Egypt, and all of Greece into one vast empire. In doing so he carried Greek culture as it had been influenced by many foreign sources throughout that vast territory. Significantly he established at least a half-dozen new cities named Alexandria throughout the empire, and in these he built libraries and other centers of culture. The Alexandria he built in Egypt

---

2. After ineffectual Spartan rule, Athens underwent a reign of terror under Kritias and the Thirty Tyrants, followed by a brief civil war. Democracy was restored in 401 B.C. It was the insecure government of a reestablished Athens that tried and condemned Sokrates in 399 B.C. (See the *Apology* on p. 57 for Plato's account of the trial.)

Figure 2.7 Portrait bust of Alexander the Great (356–323 B.C.) by Leochares (?). Original marble of 450–425 B.C., Akropolis Museum, Athens. The greatest military genius in history, Alexander conquered and Hellenized the then-known world in just twelve years.

Figure 2.8 Portrait bust of Plato. Boeringer Collection, Geneva. Roman copy (one of eighteen) of a bronze probably created by Silanion. Apparently the original was dedicated in the Academy after Plato's death in 347 B.C. Though his real name was Aristokles, Plato has always been known by his nickname, which means "the Broad."

was to supplant Athens as the cultural center of the world for centuries. Remnants of Alexander's empire survived until 146 B.C., when Rome finally conquered the last Achaean League, but the influence of Hellenistic art and thought was to flourish throughout most of the Roman period.

Our concern during this time must limit itself to the developments in art, which are discussed in chapter 3, and to the contributions of two philosophers, Plato and Aristotle.

Plato

Born in 427 B.C., two years after the death of Perikles, Plato (fig. 2.8) was a young man at the time of the Athenian defeat in the Peloponnesian War and an ardent student of Sokrates. It is impossible to distinguish between the thought of Plato and Sokrates in the early writings of Plato, for most of these are dialogues in which Sokrates is the principal speaker. It is probable that Plato included much of his own thought in these dialogues, or certainly that he reported the ideas of Sokrates with which he was in agreement. Only in the latter part of his life did he speak entirely for himself, as in the *Laws*.

Plato's thought about that-which-is-real is perhaps his most significant contribution to modern thought. In developing this he started with the work of Pythagoras and the Eleatic philosophers in that he

accepted permanence and unchangeability as the basic criteria for reality, and he accepted the mind as the only way to approach a knowledge of the real. In so doing, he denied the reality of all the sense-apparent objects around us, whether they be trees, animals, humans, or even such abstract concepts as the various manifestations of love or justice. All sense-apparent things he regarded as shadows of the Real, made imperfect by an alliance with material stuff.

For Plato, reality consisted of ideas or essences of all basic things that had their existence beyond the grasp of the human senses or even of the human mind. These ideas had no physical attributes, no material substance, but were the "pure form" for all things we see and know in our earthly existence. One must bear in mind that these forms are not ideas-in-the-minds-of-people. Thus when one imagines the perfect tree or the perfect human being, we are not dealing with Plato's essences. The ideas had existence, they were unchanging, and they were the source, in that they gave form, of all material things. But the material thing, because it is allied with matter or flesh, is always a distorted or impure shadow of its essence.

Probably this is clear enough, but a homely illustration might not be out of order. We can imagine that an architect is commissioned to design a building. Probably it does not happen this way, but assume that one morning, after wrestling with the problems for some time, he suddenly sees the building in his mind perfectly, exactly as it should be. "Eureka," he cries.

"This is *it*." So he dashes off to the drawing board. In drawing the plans, he has to make some changes in his original idea. For example, he has to stack the plumbing on the various levels directly above what is below. By the time the blueprints are finished, the building is no longer the same as it was when it was idea. Then comes the construction. Perhaps the builder faces a steel strike, and another material must be substituted for some of the steel members. The costs for the planned building may go beyond the money available, so sections must be cut out, and cheaper materials substituted for those in the original plan. But finally the building is complete and stands in its material form for people to see and use. When was the structure most real? A good argument can be made that it was most real when it was pure idea, and that it has become less real each time it became involved with substance or material. One suspects that the architect, at least, looking at the final product, will see it as only a shadow of what he had once seen in his mind. To avoid argument, let us accept these last statements as true. The physical building is but a clumsy manifestation of the "real" idea. Can we take another step now? Assume that the architect is God, and that the building is the universe. The ideas for all things existed in God's mind, and these forms, essences, or immaterial patterns exist forever, but as they are mixed with material substance—wood, mineral, flesh—they become distorted and changed. Now, perhaps, we have Plato's belief about reality with but one more step needed. From our last picture subtract the picture of God, for although Plato frequently spoke of the gods, and often of God, he did not believe that these ideas were created; they simply existed eternally.

For a further illustration of this concept of reality, the student is referred to Plato's dialogue, *The Symposium,* where the nature of love is discussed. The discussion turns on the thought that in the realm of ideas, there is one that is beauty—not a beautiful sunset, or a beautiful person, just pure beauty. Many physical things can reflect this idea, among them a person. So that when someone says, "I am in love with Isabella (or Henry)" what they really mean is, "I am attracted by beauty, and Henry (or Isabella) reflects that idea to me."

There are a great many important philosophic repercussions from this Platonic belief about reality. One of the most important is the separation of the soul from the body, and the belief that soul was related to the realm of the essences, and that body was evil because it imprisoned and distracted the soul. This has been a major bone of contention in all Christian religion, for St. Augustine, in formulating the first unified Christian theology, borrowed a great deal from Platonism. Specifically, Plato believed that in the realm of ideas a hierarchy existed, starting at the bottom with the essences of plants and animals, and ending at the top with the idea of the good (the light or fire one encounters in "The Allegory of the Cave"). This good, translated into early Christian theology, became the concept of God as the highest and best pattern for all things, and the goal toward which all

Christians should strive. The method of reaching it can easily become the method of despising the flesh as a hindrance to the soul in its aspiration.

The dialogue called the *Republic* gives us our best view of the Sokratic-Platonic idea of the nature of man on earth, and the nature of his government. A much later treatise, the *Laws,* gives the purely Platonic view of the same matter, differing somewhat from the beliefs stated in the *Republic.* In the first place, it should be made clear that the *Republic* is not Plato's formation of an ideal state as such. Instead, it is a discussion between Sokrates and his students concerning the nature of justice. Justice is not necessary when one has only an isolated individual, but it becomes more and more necessary within an ever-larger group. So in the *Republic,* the discussants formulate a picture of the luxurious state (one that goes beyond the provision of the barest physical needs of humans) in order to seek out the illusive quality, justice, that exists to a greater or lesser degree in the interrelationship of people.

In regard to humans themselves, Plato felt that people were dominated by one of three qualities: appetite, spirit, or intellect. For this reason he divided people into three classes, those of iron (or brass), those of silver, and those of gold. Those who were essentially people of appetite, iron, were to be the workers, including all who followed commercial pursuits. The silver, people of spirit, were to form the auxiliaries or soldier class, who had no property or money to distract them from their duty—the maintenance of order at home and protection from foreign enemies. The men or women of intellect, or the people of gold, were to be carefully educated to become the guardians of the state, the rulers, the philosopher-kings.

Education was to be the force that gave form to this state. The lowest class was to receive little or no education. The soldier or auxiliary group was to be taught gymnastics (to give them strong bodies, fit for their duties at all times), and music to make their personalities gentle toward their fellow citizens. In the discussion of this point, Sokrates uses the example of the good watchdog as an illustration of his point, for such a dog is gentle toward his master and friends, but fierce toward enemies. The soldier class should have such a nature, with their quality of spirit tempered by the study of music. The guardian class should have all of the education of the soldiers, then study methods of reasoning, and finally philosophy. After their years of study they were to be subjected to all sorts of trials and temptations to test their strength of character and their ability to make decisions on an unselfish basis, in terms of the general good. At about the age of fifty, after passing through this period of testing, the guardians would be called upon to rule the city. They would become the famous "philosopher-kings," and they would rule the state absolutely.

One notices immediately that this is a totalitarian state, with the exception that no lunatic would ever be able to rule. But the society is divided into strict classes; and Sokrates advocates a strict censorship of all stories and music the students are to hear, so that only the best and finest will enter into their souls. The classes of citizens are not controlled by birth or wealth, however, for Sokrates proposes the "great lie," which will be perpetrated on the citizens: all children will be told that the state is their mother, and they will be reared as wards of the city until they are about seven years of age. During these formative years they will be carefully observed in all their activities and their chief characteristics noted. At the end of this time they will be divided into the three classes according to their natural ability.

Insofar as the ultimate question of the nature of justice is concerned, Plato and Sokrates take the middle ground, the Golden Mean, which was ever a Greek ideal. In the qualities of men and women, wisdom should control the other qualities, so that appetite would be curbed to the point of temperance, spirit should be limited to the point of courage, and intellect should become wisdom. When these conditions are met, justice emerges. These—temperance, courage, wisdom, and justice were the great Platonic virtues. Later on, the Christians were to add faith, hope, and love to these to establish the seven cardinal virtues. The difference between the Platonic intellectual virtues and the Christian emotional and spiritual virtues illustrates a fundamental difference between the hopes and aspirations of the two cultures.

Aristotle

Aristotle came from a very different background than that of Plato, and although he studied with Plato at the academy, his answers to the important questions are quite different, perhaps because of the difference in youthful experience. Aristotle's father was a physician in northern Greece and early in Aristotle's life was called to the city of Pella to serve as a physician in the court of King Philip. Perhaps Aristotle's inquiring mind about sense-apparent things, his interest in experimentation, his concern in change rather than permanence, and his inability to accept the mind alone as a guide to truth came from his father's interest in similar things. As a matter of fact, exactly as Plato's thought had its source in the Eleatics and Pythagoras, Aristotle's mature conclusions have their roots in the Ionians.

Aristotle is one of the most extraordinary minds of all time; the keenness of his intellect, the range of his interests and studies, and the staggering amount of information and speculation in his enormous collection of writings, rouse the admiration and awe of any who read his work. Not the least of his distinctions was the fact that he served as tutor to the youthful Prince Alexander, and must have had a great influ-
· ence on the brilliant career of that monarch. After this period of tutoring, Aristotle went to Athens and founded his own school, the Lyceum. With Plato, he was to shape the course of Western thought: these two men are probably the most powerful influences from our Greek heritage.

As we have seen, Plato's quest for the permanent, the idea or form, rather than the actuality of experience, led him into a dualism that separates form from substance, soul from body. Aristotle, profoundly interested in the changing life about him, tried to reconcile the two. Perhaps the difference could be expressed in this way: when Plato wished to discuss his ideas of the state, he wrote the *Republic,* and later the *Laws,* theoretical speculations that construct the wholly imaginary idea of a state. When Aristotle wished to discuss his ideas of the state, he and his students collected and studied the constitutions of 158 Greek city-states as a prelude to the work known as *Politics.*

It is an impossible task, and not to the present purpose, to even mention the multitude of Aristotle's writings. His speculations ranged all the way from his logic, the proper process of thought, through biology, physics, metaphysics, ethics, law and politics, and literary criticism. Only two of his ideas concern us here: one is his view of the nature of reality; the other is his idea of the conduct of life in the light of that view. These last are drawn from the *Nicomachean Ethics* and the *Eudemian Ethics,* summaries of his thought about the proper conduct of life as written by his son and one of his students.

For Aristotle, the abstract idea or form of Plato's teaching could not be separated from the matter or substance by which it was known; the two must somehow come together as different aspects of the same thing. Thus Plato's "ideal" chair did not exist for Aristotle apart from the actual wood and metal that composed it. A brick is a brick only when the "idea" brick and the clay composing it come together; then the brick is "real." The brick then may become the matter or substance of another "idea," and become house; and the house, in turn, may be substance to the idea of town or city. At every stage, the union of substance and form, of matter and idea, is necessary to constitute "reality"; but there is a progression, upwards or downwards. The substance that Plato is not concerned with becomes for Aristotle the basis for higher, more complex realities when it is informed by idea or form. Such, at least, is the direction of the difference between the two men; Plato's static view becomes more dynamic in Aristotle's teaching.

The process of change (which Plato never satisfactorily explains) is accounted for, by Aristotle, in his theory of enteleche (en–TEL–uh–kee; the Greek word is made of the particles en, "within"; telos, "purpose or end"; and echaia, "having, possessing"). That is to say, it is in the nature of things that they have within them a goal, a destiny, to fulfill: the seed becomes the plant, for that is its "enteleche"; the clay becomes the brick, for that is its "enteleche." The movement upward through increasing complexity is the "enteleche" of the universe; and the cause of the process, drawing all things toward their own perfection, is God, the First Cause, who moved all things without being moved: the "Unmoved Mover," in Aristotle's phrase.

The motive power of Aristotle's God is apparently not love, as Christianity might contend, nor will, as Judaism might argue; it is rather that there seems to be a cosmic yearning toward perfection, and that perfection is, by definition, God. Aristotle's customary view of the necessity for the union of both form and matter to constitute reality here breaks down (or more kindly, "transcends itself"?) for such a God must be pure form, with none of the inherent weakness or imperfection of the material.[3] God is the only instance where pure form is separated from matter.

How does one lead the good life? It is interesting to note that Aristotle makes no apology for thinking that it must begin with sufficient means; he holds no ascetic views on the matter, and quite matter-of-factly begins with an assumption of enough material possession to allow one the choice of doing as he would. Granted, however, the adequate wealth, what does one do? The enteleche of which he speaks implies that there is a goal, or end, reached when the person or thing is functioning properly—that is, in accord with its own inner purposes; when conditions permit such functioning, there is a highest good, a summum bonum, attained. The enteleche of humans, then, would lead them to their own summum bonum, their own best functioning, the worthy and proper fulfillment of their humanity. And since humans are for Aristotle the "rational animal," that fulfillment would be the life of reason. When they are living harmoniously, using their minds, functioning in family and state (for Aristotle also calls humans a "political," i.e., social animal), they have achieved their greatest good. Such a life has two implications, among many others, that concern us here.

One is that such a life will be a life of virtue, or excellence. But virtues may fail by being deficient, or by being carried to excess; the middle ground between is what is to be desired. Courage, for instance, is a virtue; but it may be perverted through deficiency into cowardice, or no less perverted by being carried to the excess of foolhardiness, mere rashness. Generosity is a virtue, but it can be carried to the excess of prodigality and wastefulness, or perverted through deficiency to stinginess. To mediate between extremes, to discover the "Golden Mean"—which it is to be noted is a relative and not an absolute matter—that is to achieve virtue.

The other implication, then, is that people's best use of reason is in the life of contemplation. They must have time to read, to talk, to think about the whole idea of excellence, that they may achieve the high-mindedness that is their summum bonum; the word that Aristotle uses is "magnanimity." Such a quality is not to be won in the heat and dust of the marketplace; though good persons will perform their duties as a member of society, still the life of action is not as good as the life of contemplation.

With this brief discussion of a few of the ideas of Aristotle, we come to the end of our background of Greek civilization in Greece itself. The Hellenistic culture was to flourish for many years in such centers as Egyptian Alexandria and Pergamum in Asia Minor. Indeed, much of Roman culture formed itself around Hellenistic principles.

Greek civilization had started within the shadow of superstition and tradition in archaic times. Slowly those bondages had been cut away until a very delicate balance was achieved between the freedom of each individual person and the welfare of the group in Athens early in the reign of Perikles. The philosophers, the authors, and the artists of the time took an active part in politics, and conducted their affairs in the Agora, the marketplace.

But change is inevitable. In Athens it would seem that the knife-edge between individuality and the welfare of the group was too thin, the balance on it too precarious, for a group of people to maintain an equilibrium for a long period of time. The skeptical sophists taught that complete individuality was the goal—violating Aeschylus's doctrine of the mean between autocracy and anarchy. The original strength of the city was sapped, but to give rise to a new and different kind of strength in the broadened horizons of Hellenistic culture. It is interesting that both Plato and Aristotle (except for their brief efforts to educate a king: Plato as tutor for the Syracusan Dionysius, Aristotle as Alexander's tutor) stood apart from politics and the vigorous life of the time; they deserted the active marketplace. They were contemplatives, aware that something had gone wrong, that the dream had somehow failed, and each in his own way, introspected into himself and his culture to discover what had failed. Probably nothing had really gone "wrong." Change had simply taken place in the cultural milieu, leading to new forms of life, new types of exploration into human existence, new forms of freedom.

The Romans brought about a different type of balance in civilization, and this will be discussed later in our work.

---

3. "Such then is the principle upon which depend the heavens and the world of nature. And its life (i.e., the principle, or God) is like the best that we enjoy, and enjoy but for a short time; for it is ever in this state, which we cannot be. And if then God is always in that good state in which we sometimes are, this compels our wonder; and if in a better state, then this compels it yet more. And God is in a better state. We say therefore, that God is a living being, eternal, most good; so that life and a continual eternal existence belong to God; for this is God." (Aristotle, *Metaphysics,* XII, 7.)

Literary Selection

APOLOGY
Plato (427–347 B.C.)

Sokrates was tried in 399 B.C. before a generally hostile jury of 501 citizens on vague charges of impropriety towards the gods and corruption of the young. Long regarded as a suspicious character because of his relentless questioning of fellow Athenians, Sokrates, because of a general amnesty, could not be charged for any offenses prior to the defeat of Athens

Figure 2.9 Portrait bust of Sokrates. Roman marble copy of an original bronze supposedly created by Lysippos in ca. 350 B.C. Museo della Terme, Rome.

in 404 B.C. The unspoken charges were: (1) being the teacher of Alkbiades the traitor (interpreted as a corruptor of the young), (2) association with the Thirty Tyrants (viewed as possible collaboration), (3) accepting money for teaching argumentation (mistakenly taking him for a Sophist), and (4) causing general intellectual unrest. Sokrates (fig. 2.9) cheerfully admits to causing unrest, contending that the gods had commanded him to search into himself and other men to find the truth. This trial is his apology for his philosophical life. The translation is by F. J. Church and R. D. Cumming, whose spelling of proper names has been retained.

CHARACTERS

Socrates
Meletus

SCENE—The Court of Justice

Socrates. I cannot tell what impression my accusers have made upon you, Athenians. For my own part, I know that they nearly made me forget who I was, so persuasive were they; and yet they have scarcely uttered one single word of truth. But of all their many falsehoods, the one which astonished me most was when they said that I was a clever speaker, and that you must be careful not to let me deceive you. I thought that it was most shameless of them not to be ashamed to talk in that way; for as soon as I open my mouth they will be refuted, and I shall prove that I am not a clever speaker in any way at all—unless, indeed, by a clever speaker they mean a man who speaks the truth. If that is their meaning, I agree with them that I am an orator not to be compared with them. My accusers, then I repeat, have said little or nothing that is true; but

from me you shall hear the whole truth. Certainly you will not hear an elaborate speech, Athenians, dressed up, like theirs, with words and phrases. I will say to you what I have to say, without preparation, and in the words which come first, for I believe that my cause is just; so let none of you expect anything else. Indeed, my friends, it would hardly be seemly for me, at my age, to come before you like a young man with his specious phrases. But there is one thing, Athenians, which I do most earnestly beg and entreat of you. Do not be surprised and do not interrupt with shouts if in my defense I speak in the same way that I am accustomed to speak in the market-place, at the tables of the money-changers, where many of you have heard me, and elsewhere. The truth is this. I am more than seventy years old, and this is the first time that I have ever come before a law-court; so your manner of speech here is quite strange to me. If I had been really a stranger, you would have forgiven me for speaking in the language and the manner of my native country; and so now I ask you to grant me what I think I have a right to claim. Never mind the manner of my speech—it may be better or it may be worse—give your whole attention to the question, Is what I say just, or is it not? That is what makes a good judge, as speaking the truth makes a good orator.

I have to defend myself, Athenians, first against the old false accusations of my old accusers, and then against the later ones of my present accusers. For many men have been accusing me to you, and for very many years, who have not uttered a word of truth; and I fear them more than I fear Anytus and his associates, formidable as they are. But, my friends, those others are still more formidable; for they got hold of most of you when you were children, and they have been more persistent in accusing me untruthfully and have persuaded you that there is a certain Socrates, a wise man, who speculates about the heavens, and who investigates things that are beneath the earth, and who can make the worse argument appear the stronger. These men, Athenians, who spread abroad this report are the accusers whom I fear; for their hearers think that persons who pursue such inquiries never believe in the gods. Then they are many, and their attacks have been going on for a long time, and they spoke to you when you were at the age most readily to believe them, for you were all young, and many of you were children, and there was no one to answer them when they attacked me. And the most unreasonable thing of all is that I do not even know their names: I cannot tell you who they are except when one happens to be a comic poet. But all the rest who have persuaded you, from motives of resentment and prejudice, and sometimes, it may be, from conviction, are hardest to cope with. For I cannot call any one of them forward in court to cross-examine him. I have, as it were, simply to spar with shadows in my defense, and to put questions which there is no one to answer. I ask you, therefore, to believe that, as I say, I have been attacked by two kinds of accusers—first, by Meletus and his associates, and, then, by those older ones of whom I have spoken. And, with your leave, I will defend myself first against my old accusers; for you heard their accusations first, and they were much more forceful than my present accusers are.

Well, I must make my defense, Athenians, and try in the short time allowed me to remove the prejudice which you have been so long a time acquiring. I hope that I may manage to do this, if it be good for you and for me, and that my defense may be successful; but I am quite aware of the nature of my task, and I know that it is a difficult one. Be the outcome, however, as is pleasing to God, I must obey the law and make my defense.

Let us begin from the beginning, then, and ask what is the accusation which has given rise to the prejudice against me, which was what Meletus relied on when he brought his indictment. What is the prejudice which my enemies have been spreading about me? I must assume that they are formally accusing me, and read their indictment. It would run somewhat in this fashion: "Socrates is a wrongdoer, who meddles with inquiries into things beneath the earth and in the heavens, and who makes the worse argument appear the stronger, and who teaches others these same things." That is what they say; and in the comedy of Aristophanes[4] you yourselves saw a man called Socrates swinging round in a basket and saying that he walked the air, and sputtering a great deal of nonsense about matters of which I understand nothing, either more or less. I do not mean to disparage that kind of knowledge if there is any one who is wise about these matters. I trust Meletus may never be able to prosecute me for that. But the truth is, Athenians, I have nothing to do with these matters, and almost all of you are yourselves my witnesses of this. I beg all of you who have ever heard me discussing, and they are many, to inform your neighbors and tell them if any of you have ever heard me discussing such matters, either more or less. That will show you that the other common statements about me are as false as this one.

But the fact is that not one of these is true. And if you have heard that I undertake to educate men, and make money by so doing, that is not true either, though I think that it would be a fine thing to be able to educate men, as Gorgias of Leontini, and Prodicus of Ceos, and Hippias of Elis do. For each of them, my friends, can go into any city, and persuade the young men to leave the society of their fellow citizens, with any of whom they might associate for nothing, and to be only too glad to be allowed to pay money for the privilege of associating with themselves. And I believe that there is another wise man from Paros residing in Athens at this moment. I happened to meet Callias, the son of Hipponicus, a man who has spent more money on sophists than every one else put together. So I said to him (he has two sons), Callias, if your two sons had been foals or calves, we could have hired a trainer for them who would have made them perfect in the virtue which belongs to their nature. He would have been either a groom or a farmer. But whom do you intend to take to train them, seeing that they are men? Who understands the virtue which belongs to men and to citizens? I suppose that you must have thought of this, because of your sons. Is there such a person, said I, or not? Certainly there is, he replied. Who is he, said I, and where does he come from, and what is his fee? Evenus, Socrates, he replied, from Paros, five minae. Then I thought that Evenus was a fortunate person if he really understood this art and could teach so cleverly. If I had possessed knowledge of that kind, I should have been conceited and disdainful. But, Athenians, the truth is that I do not possess it.

Perhaps some of you may reply: But, Socrates, what is the trouble with you? What has given rise to these prejudices against you? You must have been doing something out of the ordinary. All these rumors and reports of you would never have arisen if you had not been doing something different from other men. So tell us what it is, that we may not give our verdict in the dark.

I think that that is a fair question, and I will try to explain to you what it is that has raised these prejudices against me and given me this reputation. Listen, then. Some of you, perhaps, will think that I am joking, but I assure you that I will tell you the whole truth. I have gained this reputation, Athenians, simply by reason of a certain wisdom. But by what kind of wisdom? It is by just that wisdom which is perhaps human wisdom. In that, it may be, I am really wise. But the men of whom I was speaking just now must be wise in a wisdom which is greater than human wisdom, or else I cannot describe it, for certainly I know nothing of it myself, and if any man says that I do, he lies and speaks to arouse prejudice against me. Do not interrupt me with shouts, Athenians, even if you think that I am boasting. What I am going to say is not my own. I will tell you who says it, and he is worthy of your respect. I will bring the god of Delphi to be the witness of my wisdom, if it is wisdom at all, and of its nature. You remember Chaerephon. From youth upwards he was my comrade; and also a partisan of your democracy, sharing your recent exile[5] and returning with you. You remember, too, Chaerephon's character—how impulsive he was in carrying through whatever he took in hand. Once he went to Delphi and ventured to put this question to the oracle—I entreat you again, my friends, not to interrupt me with your shouts—he asked if there was any one who was wiser than I. The priestess answered that there was no one. Chaerephon himself is dead, but his brother here will witness to what I say.

Now see why I tell you this. I am going to explain to you how the prejudice against me has arisen. When I heard of the oracle I began to reflect: What can the god mean by this riddle? I know very well that I am not wise, even in the smallest degree. Then what can he mean by saying that I am the wisest of men? It cannot be that he is speaking falsely, for he is a god and cannot lie. For a long time I was at a loss to understand his meaning. Then, very reluctantly, I turned to investigate it in this manner: I went to a man who was reputed to be wise, thinking that there, if anywhere, I should prove the answer wrong, and meaning to point out to the oracle its mistake, and to say, "You said that I was the wisest of men, but this man is wiser than I am." So I examined the man—I need not tell you his name, he was a politician—but this was the result, Athenians. When I conversed with him I came to see that, though a great many persons, and most of all he himself, thought that he was wise, yet he was not wise. Then I tried to prove to him that he was not wise, though he fancied that he was; and by so doing I made him indignant, and many of the bystanders. So when I went away, I thought to myself, "I am wiser than this man: neither of us knows anything that is really worthwhile, but he thinks that he has knowledge when he has not, while I, having no knowledge, do not think that I have. I seem, at any rate, to be a little wiser than he is on this point: I do not think that I know what I do not know." Next I went to another man who was reputed to be still wiser than the last, with exactly the same result. And there again I made him, and many other men, indignant.

Then I went on to one man after another, seeing that I was arousing indignation every day, which caused me much grief and anxiety. Still I thought that I must set the god's command above everything. So I had to go to every

---

4. *The Clouds.* The basket was satirically assumed to facilitate Socrates' inquiries into things in the heavens.

5. During the totalitarian regime of *The Thirty* which remained in power for eight months (404 B.C.), five years before the trial.

man who seemed to possess any knowledge, and investigate the meaning of the oracle. Athenians, I must tell you the truth; by the dog, this was the result of the investigation which I made at the god's bidding: I found that the men whose reputation for wisdom stood highest were nearly the most lacking in it, while others who were looked down on as common people were much more intelligent. Now I must describe to you the wanderings which I undertook, like Heraclean labors, to prove the oracle irrefutable. After the politicians, I went to the poets, tragic, dithyrambic, and others, thinking that there I should find myself manifestly more ignorant than they. So I took up the poems on which I thought that they had spent most pains, and asked them what they meant, hoping at the same time to learn something from them. I am ashamed to tell you the truth, my friends, but I must say it. Almost any one of the bystanders could have talked about the works of these poets better than the poets themselves. So I soon found that it is not by wisdom that the poets create their works, but by a certain natural power and by inspiration, like soothsayers and prophets, who say many fine things, but who understand nothing of what they say. The poets seemed to me to be in a similar situation. And at the same time I perceived that, because of their poetry, they thought that they were the wisest of men in other matters, too, which they were not. So I went away again, thinking that I had the same advantage over the poets that I had over the politicians.

Finally, I went to the artisans, for I knew very well that I possessed no knowledge at all worth speaking of, and I was sure that I should find that they knew many fine things. And in that I was not mistaken. They knew what I did not know, and so far they were wiser than I. But, Athenians, it seemed to me that the skilled artisans had the same failing as the poets. Each of them believed himself to be extremely wise in matters of the greatest importance because he was skilful in his own art: and this presumption of theirs obscured their real wisdom. So I asked myself, on behalf of the oracle, whether I would choose to remain as I was, without either their wisdom or their ignorance, or to possess both, as they did. And I answered to myself and to the oracle that it was better for me to remain as I was.

From this examination, Athenians, has arisen much fierce and bitter indignation, and from this a great many prejudices about me, and people say that I am "a wise man." For the bystanders always think that I am wise myself in any matter wherein I refute another. But, gentlemen, I believe that the god is really wise, and that by this oracle he meant that human wisdom is worth little or nothing. I do not think that he meant that Socrates was wise. He only made use of my name, and took me as an example, as though he would say to men, "He among you is the wisest who, like Socrates, knows that in truth his wisdom is worth nothing at all." Therefore I still go about testing and examining every man whom I think wise, whether he be a citizen or a stranger, as the god has commanded me; and whenever I find that he is not wise, I point out to him, on the god's behalf, that he is not wise. I am so busy in this pursuit that I have never had leisure to take any part worth mentioning in public matters or to look after my private affairs. I am in great poverty as the result of my service to the god.

Besides this, the young men who follow me about, who are the sons of wealthy persons and have the most leisure, take pleasure in hearing men cross-examined.

They often imitate me among themselves; then they try their hands at cross-examining other people. And, I imagine, they find plenty of men who think that they know a great deal when in fact they know little or nothing. Then the persons who are cross-examined get angry with me instead of with themselves, and say that Socrates is an abomination and corrupts the young. When they are asked, "Why, what does he do? what does he teach?" they do not know what to say; but, not to seem at a loss, they repeat the stock charges against all philosophers, and allege that he investigates things in the air and under the earth, and that he teaches people to disbelieve in the gods, and to make the worse argument appear the stronger. For, I suppose, they would not like to confess the truth, which is that they are shown up as ignorant pretenders to knowledge that they do not possess. So they have been filling your ears with their bitter prejudices for a long time, for they are ambitious, energetic, and numerous; and they speak vigorously and persuasively against me. Relying on this, Meletus, Anytus, and Lycon have attacked me. Meletus is indignant with me on the part of the poets, Anytus on the part of the artisans and politicians, and Lycon on the part of the orators. And so, as I said at the beginning, I shall be surprised if I am able, in the short time allowed me for my defense, to remove from your minds this prejudice which has grown so strong. What I have told you, Athenians, is the truth: I neither conceal nor do I suppress anything, small or great. Yet I know that it is just this plainness of speech which rouses indignation. But that is only a proof that my words are true, and that the prejudice against me, and the causes of it, are what I have said. And whether you investigate them now or hereafter, you will find that they are so.

What I have said must suffice as my defense against the charges of my first accusers. I will try next to defend myself against Meletus, that "good patriot," as he calls himself, and my later accusers. Let us assume that they are a new set of accusers, and read their indictment, as we did in the case of the others. It runs thus. He says that Socrates is a wrongdoer who corrupts the youth, and who does not believe in the gods whom the state believes in, but in other new divinities. Such is the accusation. Let us examine each point in it separately. Meletus says that I do wrong by corrupting the youth. But I say, Athenians, that he is doing wrong, for he is playing a solemn joke by casually bringing men to trial, and pretending to have a solemn interest in matters to which he has never given a moment's thought. Now I will try to prove to you that it is so.

Come here, Meletus. Is it not a fact that you think it very important that the young should be as good as possible?

Meletus. It is.

Socrates. Come then, tell the judges who is it who improves them? You care so much,[6] you must know. You are accusing me, and bringing me to trial, because, as you say, you have discovered that I am the corrupter of the youth. Come now, reveal to the gentlemen who improves them. You see, Meletus, you have nothing to say; you are silent. But don't you think that this is shameful? Is not your silence a conclusive proof of what I say—that you have never cared. Come, tell us, my good man, who makes the young better?

---

6. Throughout the following passage Socrates plays on the etymology of the name "Meletus" as meaning "the man who cares."

Mel. The laws.

Socr. That, my friend, is not my question. What man improves the young, who starts with the knowledge of the laws?

Mel. The judges here, Socrates.

Socr. What do you mean, Meletus? Can they educate the young and improve them?

Mel. Certainly.

Socr. All of them? or only some of them?

Mel. All of them.

Socr. By Hera, that is good news! Such a large supply of benefactors! And do the listeners here improve them, or not?

Mel. They do.

Socr. And do the senators?

Mel. Yes.

Socr. Well then, Meletus, do the members of the assembly corrupt the young or do they again all improve them?

Mel. They, too, improve them.

Socr. Then all the Athenians, apparently, make the young into good men except me, and I alone corrupt them. Is that your meaning?

Mel. Most certainly; that is my meaning.

Socr. You have discovered me to be most unfortunate. Now tell me: do you think that the same holds good in the case of horses? Does one man do them harm and every one else improve them? On the contrary, is it not one man only, or a very few—namely, those who are skilled with horses—who can improve them, while the majority of men harm them if they use them and have anything to do with them? Is it not so, Meletus, both with horses and with every other animal? Of course it is, whether you and Anytus say yes or no. The young would certainly be very fortunate if only one man corrupted them, and every one else did them good. The truth is, Meletus, you prove conclusively that you have never thought about the youth in your life. You exhibit your carelessness in not caring for the very matters about which you are prosecuting me.

Now be so good as to tell us, Meletus, is it better to live among good citizens or bad ones? Answer, my friend. I am not asking you a difficult question. Do not the bad harm their associates and the good, good?

Mel. Yes.

Socr. Is there any one who would rather be injured than benefited by his companions? Answer, my good sir; you are obliged by the law to answer. Does any one like to be injured?

Mel. Certainly not.

Socr. Well then, are you prosecuting me for corrupting the young and making them worse, voluntarily or involuntarily?

Mel. For doing it voluntarily.

Socr. What, Meletus? Do you mean to say that you, who are so much younger than I, are yet so much wiser than I that you know that bad citizens always do evil, and that good citizens do good, to those with whom they come in contact, while I am so extraordinarily ignorant as not to know that, if I make any of my companions evil, he will probably injure me in some way, and as to commit this great evil, as you allege, voluntarily? You will not make me believe that, nor anyone else either, I should think. Either I do not corrupt the young at all or if I do I do so involuntarily: so that you are lying in either case. And if I corrupt them involuntarily, the law does not call upon you to prosecute me for an error which is involuntary, but to take me aside privately and reprove and educate me. For, of course, I shall cease from doing wrong involuntarily, as soon as I know that I have been doing wrong. But you avoided associating with me and educating me; instead you bring me up before the court, where the law sends persons, not for education, but for punishment.

The truth is, Athenians, as I said, it is quite clear that Meletus has never cared at all about these matters. However, now tell us, Meletus, how do you say that I corrupt the young? Clearly, according to your indictment, by teaching them not to believe in the gods the state believes in, but other new divinities instead. You mean that I corrupt the young by that teaching, do you not?

Mel. Yes, most certainly I mean that.

Socr. Then in the name of these gods of whom we are speaking, explain yourself a little more clearly to me and to these gentlemen here. I cannot understand what you mean. Do you mean that I teach the young to believe in some gods, but not in the gods of the state? Do you accuse me of teaching them to believe in strange gods? If that is your meaning, I myself believe in some gods, and my crime is not that of complete atheism. Or do you mean that I do not believe in the gods at all myself, and that I teach other people not to believe in them either?

Mel. I mean that you do not believe in the gods in any way whatever.

Socr. You amaze me, Meletus! Why do you say that? Do you mean that I believe neither the sun nor the moon to be gods, like other men?

Mel. I swear he does not, judges; he says that the sun is a stone, and the moon earth.

Socr. My dear Meletus, do you think that you are prosecuting Anaxagoras? You must have a very poor opinion of these men, and think them illiterate, if you imagine that they do not know that the works of Anaxagoras of Clazomenae are full of these doctrines. And so young men learn these things from me, when they can often buy them in the theatre for a drachma at most, and laugh at Socrates were he to pretend that these doctrines, which are very peculiar doctrines, too, were his own. But please tell me, do you really think that I do not believe in the gods at all?

Mel. Most certainly I do. You are a complete atheist.

Socr. No one believes that, Meletus, not even you yourself. It seems to me, Athenians, that Meletus is very insolent and reckless, and that he is prosecuting me simply out of insolence, recklessness and youthful bravado. For he seems to be testing me, by asking me a riddle that has no answer. "Will this wise Socrates," he says to himself, "see that I am joking and contradicting myself? or shall I deceive him and every one else who hears me?" Meletus seems to me to contradict himself in his indictment: it is as if he were to say, "Socrates is a wrongdoer who does not believe in the gods, but who believes in the gods." But this is joking.

Now, my friends, let us see why I think that this is his meaning. Do you answer me, Meletus; and do you, Athenians, remember the request which I made to you at the start, and do not interrupt me with shouts if I talk in my customary manner.

Is there any man, Meletus, who believes in the existence of things pertaining to men and not in the existence of men? Make him answer the question, gentlemen, without these interruptions. Is there any man who believes in the existence of horsemanship and not in the existence of horses? or in flute-playing and not in flute-players? There is not, my friend. If you will not answer, I will tell both you and the judges. But you must answer my next question. Is there any man who believes in the existence of divine things and not in the existence of divinities?

Mel. There is not.

Socr. I am very glad that these gentlemen have managed to extract an answer from you. Well then, you say that I believe in divine things, whether they be old or new ones, and that I teach others to believe in them; at any rate, according to your statement, I believe in divine things. That you have sworn in your indictment. But if I believe in divine things, I suppose it follows necessarily that I believe in divinities. Is it not so? It is. I assume that you grant that, as you do not answer. But do we not believe that divinities are either gods themselves or the children of the gods? Do you admit that?

Mel. I do.

Socr. Then you admit that I believe in divinities. Now, if these divinities are gods, then, as I say, you are joking and asking a riddle, and asserting that I do not believe in the gods, and at the same time that I do, since I believe in divinities. But if these divinities are the illegitimate children of the gods, either by the nymphs or by other mothers, as they are said to be, then, I ask, what man could believe in the existence of the children of the gods, and not in the existence of the gods? That would be as absurd as believing in the existence of the offspring of horses and asses, and not in the existence of horses and asses. You must have indicted me in this manner, Meletus, either to test me or because you could not find any crime that you could accuse me of with truth. But you will never contrive to persuade any man with any sense at all that a belief in divine things and things of the gods does not necessarily involve a belief in divinities, and in the gods, and in heroes.

But in truth, Athenians, I do not think that I need say very much to prove that I have not committed the crime for which Meletus is prosecuting me. What I have said is enough to prove that. But I repeat it is certainly true, as I have already told you, that I have aroused much indignation. That is what will cause my condemnation if I am condemned; not Meletus nor Anytus either, but that prejudice and resentment of the multitude which have been the destruction of many good men before me, and I think will be so again. There is no fear that I shall be the last victim.

Perhaps some one will say: "Are you not ashamed, Socrates, of leading a life which is very likely now to cause your death?" I should answer him with justice, and say: "My friend, if you think that a man of any worth at all ought to reckon the chances of life and death when he acts, or that he ought to think of anything but whether he is acting rightly or wrongly, and as a good or a bad man would act, you are mistaken. According to you, the demigods who died at Troy would be foolish, and among them the son of Thetis, who thought nothing of danger when the alternative was disgrace. For when his mother—and she was a goddess—addressed him, when he was resolved to slay Hector, in this fashion, "My son, if you avenge the death of your comrade Patroclus and slay Hector, you will die yourself, for 'fate awaits you straightway after Hector's death' "; when he heard this, he scorned danger and death; he feared much more to live a coward and not to avenge his friend. "Let me punish the evildoer and straightway die," he said, "that I may not remain here by the beaked ships jeered at, encumbering

the earth."[7] Do you suppose that he thought of danger or of death? For this, Athenians, I believe to be the truth. Wherever a man's station is, whether he has chosen it of his own will, or whether he has been placed at it by his commander, there it is his duty to remain and face the danger without thinking of death or of any other thing except disgrace.

When the generals whom you chose to command me, Athenians, assigned me my station at Potidaea and at Amphipolis and at Delium, I remained where they stationed me and ran the risk of death, like other men. It would be very strange conduct on my part if I were to desert my station now from fear of death or of any other thing when God has commanded me—as I am persuaded that he has done—to spend my life in searching for wisdom, and in examining myself and others. That would indeed be a very strange thing. Then certainly I might with justice be brought to trial for not believing in the gods, for I should be disobeying the oracle, and fearing death and thinking myself wise when I was not wise. For to fear death, my friends, is only to think ourselves wise without really being wise, for it is to think that we know what we do not know. For no one knows whether death may not be the greatest good that can happen to man. But men fear it as if they knew quite well that it was the greatest of evils. And what is this but that shameful ignorance of thinking that we know what we do not know? In this matter, too, my friends, perhaps I am different from the multitude; and if I were to claim to be at all wiser than others, it would be because, not knowing very much about the other world, I do not think I know. But I do know very well that it is evil and disgraceful to do wrong, and not to be persuaded by my superior, whether man or god. I will never do what I know to be evil, and shrink in fear from what I do not know to be good or evil. Even if you acquit me now, and do not listen to Anytus' argument that, if I am to be acquitted, I ought never to have been brought to trial at all, and that, as it is, you are bound to put me to death because, as he said, if I escape, all your sons will be utterly corrupted by practising what Socrates teaches. If you were therefore to say to me, "Socrates, this time we will not listen to Anytus; we will let you go, but on this condition that you give up this investigation of yours, and philosophy; if you are found following those pursuits again, you shall die." I say, if you offered to let me go on these terms, I should reply: "Athenians, I hold you in the highest regard and affection, but I will be persuaded by the god rather than you; and as long as I have breath and strength I will not give up philosophy and exhorting you and declaring the truth to every one of you whom I meet, saying, as I am accustomed, "My good friend, you are a citizen of Athens, a city which is very great and very famous for its wisdom and power—are you not ashamed of caring so much for the making of money and for fame and prestige, when you neither think nor care about wisdom and truth and the improvement of your soul?" And if he disputes my words and says that he does care about these things, I shall not at once release him and go away: I shall question him and cross-examine him and test him. If I think that he does not possess virtue, though he says that he does, I shall reproach him for under-valuing the most valuable things, and over-valuing those that are less valuable. This I shall do to every one whom I meet,

---

7. Homer, Iliad, xviii, 96, 98.

young or old, citizen or stranger, but especially to citizens, for they are more closely related to me. For know that the god has commanded me to do so. And I think that no greater good has ever befallen you in the state than my service to the god. For I spend my whole life in going about and persuading you all to give your first and greatest care to the improvement of your souls, and not till you have done that to think of your bodies or your wealth; and telling you that virtue does not come from wealth, but that wealth, and every other good thing which men have, whether in public or in private, comes from virtue. If then I corrupt the youth by this teaching, these things must be harmful; but if any man says that I teach anything else, there is nothing in what he says. And therefore, Athenians, I say, whether you are persuaded by Anytus or not, whether you acquit me or not, I shall not change my way of life; no, not if I have to die for it many times.

Do not interrupt me, Athenians, with your shouts. Remember the request which I made to you, and do not interrupt my words. I think that it will profit you to hear them. I am going to say something more to you, at which you may be inclined to protest, but do not do that. Be sure that if you put me to death, who am what I have told you that I am, you will do yourselves more harm than me. Meletus and Anytus can do me no harm: that is impossible, for I am sure it is not allowed that a good man be injured by a worse. He may indeed kill me, or drive me into exile, or deprive me of my civil rights; and perhaps Meletus and others think those things great evils. But I do not think so: I think it is a much greater evil to do what he is doing now, and to try to put a man to death unjustly. And now, Athenians, I am not arguing in my own defense at all, as you might expect me to do, but rather in yours in order you may not make a mistake about the gift of the god to you by condemning me. For if you put me to death, you will not easily find another who, if I may use a ludicrous comparison, clings to the state as a sort of gadfly to a horse that is large and well-bred but rather sluggish from its size, and needing to be aroused. It seems to me that the god has attached me like that to the state, for I am constantly alighting upon you at every point to rouse, persuade, and reproach each of you all day long. You will not easily find anyone else, my friends, to fill my place; and if you are persuaded by me, you will spare my life. You are indignant, as drowsy persons are, when they are awakened, and, of course, if you are persuaded by Anytus, you could easily kill me with a single blow, and then sleep on undisturbed for the rest of your lives unless the god in his care for you sends another to arouse you. And you may easily see that it is the god who has given me to your city; for it is not human the way in which I have neglected all my own interests and endured seeing my private affairs neglected now for so many years, while occupying myself unceasingly in your interests, going to each of you privately, like a father or an elder brother, trying to persuade him to care for virtue. There would have been a reason for it, if I had gained any advantage by this, or if I had been paid for my exhortations; but you see yourselves that my accusers, though they accuse me of everything else without shame, have not had the shamelessness to say that I ever either exacted or demanded payment. To that they have no witness. And I think that I have sufficient witness to the truth of what I say—my poverty.

Perhaps it may seem strange to you that, though I go about giving this advice privately and meddling in others' affairs, yet I do not venture to come forward in the assembly and advise the state. You have often heard me speak of my reason for this, and in many places: it is that I have a certain divine sign, which is what Meletus has caricatured in his indictment. I have had it from childhood. It is a kind of voice which, whenever I hear it, always turns me back from something which I was going to do, but never urges me to act. It is this which forbids me to take part in politics. And I think it does well to forbid me. For, Athenians, it is quite certain that, if I had attempted to take part in politics, I should have perished at once and long ago without doing any good either to you or to myself. And do not be indignant with me for telling you the truth. There is no man who will preserve his life for long, either in Athens or elsewhere, if he firmly opposes the multitude, and tries to prevent the commission of much injustice and illegality in the state. He who would really fight for justice must do so as a private citizen, not as an office-holder, if he is to preserve his life, even for a short time.

I will prove to you that this is so by very strong evidence, not by mere words, but by what you value more—actions. Listen then to what has happened to me, that you may know that there is no man who could make me consent to do wrong from the fear of death, but that I would perish at once rather than give way. What I am going to tell you may be a commonplace in the lawcourt; nevertheless it is true. The only office that I ever held in the state, Athenians, was that of Senator. When you wished to try the ten generals who did not rescue their men after the battle of Arginusae, as a group, which was illegal, as you all came to think afterwards, the tribe Antiochis, to which I belong, held the presidency. On that occasion I alone of all the presidents opposed your illegal action and gave my vote against you. The orators were ready to impeach me and arrest me; and you were clamoring against me, and crying out to me to submit. But I thought that I ought to face the danger, with law and justice on my side, rather than join with you in your unjust proposal, from fear of imprisonment or death. That was when the state was democratic. When the oligarchy came in, the Thirty sent for me, with four others, to the council-chamber, and ordered us to bring Leon the Salaminian from Salamis, that they might put him to death. They were in the habit of frequently giving similar orders to many others, wishing to implicate as many as possible in their crimes. But, then, I again proved, not by mere words, but by my actions, that, if I may speak bluntly, I do not care a straw for death; but that I do care very much indeed about not doing anything unjust or impious. That government with all its power did not terrify me into doing anything unjust; but when we left the council-chamber, the other four went over to Salamis and brought Leon across to Athens; and I went home. And if the rule of the Thirty had not been overthrown soon afterwards, I should very likely have been put to death for what I did then. Many of you will be my witnesses in this matter.

Now do you think that I could have remained alive all these years if I had taken part in public affairs, and had always maintained the cause of justice like a good man, and had held it a paramount duty, as it is, to do so? Certainly not, Athenians, nor could any other man. But throughout my whole life, both in private and in public, whenever I have had to take part in public affairs, you will find I have always been the same and have never yielded unjustly to anyone; no, not to those whom my enemies falsely assert to have been my pupils.[8] But I was never anyone's teacher. I have never withheld myself from anyone, young or old, who was anxious to hear me discuss while I was making my investigation; neither do I discuss for payment, and refuse to discuss without payment. I am ready to ask questions of rich and poor alike, and if any man wishes to answer me, and then listen to what I have to say, he may. And I cannot justly be charged with causing these men to turn out good or bad, for I never either taught or professed to teach any of them any knowledge whatever. And if any man asserts that he ever learned or heard anything from me in private which everyone else did not hear as well as he, be sure that he does not speak the truth.

Why is it, then, that people delight in spending so much time in my company? You have heard why, Athenians. I told you the whole truth when I said that they delight in hearing me examine persons who think that they are wise when they are not wise. It is certainly very amusing to listen to that. And, I say, the god has commanded me to examine men, in oracles and in dreams and in every way in which the divine will was ever declared to man. This is the truth, Athenians, and if it were not the truth, it would be easily refuted. For if it were really the case that I have already corrupted some of the young men, and am now corrupting others, surely some of them, finding as they grew older that I had given them bad advice in their youth, would have come forward today to accuse me and take their revenge. Or if they were unwilling to do so themselves, surely their relatives, their fathers or brothers, or others, would, if I had done them any harm, have remembered it and taken their revenge. Certainly I see many of them in Court. Here is Crito, of my own deme and of my own age, the father of Critobulus; here is Lysanias of Sphettus, the father of Aeschines; here is also Antiphon of Cephisus, the father of Epigenes. Then here are others whose brothers have spent their time in my company—Nicostratus, the son of Theozotides and brother of Theodotus—and Theodotus is dead, so he at least cannot entreat his brother to be silent; here is Paralus, the son of Demodocus and the brother of Theages; here is Adeimantus, the son of Ariston, whose brother is Plato here; and Aeantodorus, whose brother is Aristodorus. And I can name many others to you, some of whom Meletus ought to have called as witnesses in the course of his own speech; but if he forgot to call them then, let him call them now—I will yield the floor to him—and tell us if he has any such evidence. No, on the contrary, my friends, you will find all these men ready to support me, the corrupter, the injurer, of their relatives, as Meletus and Anytus call me. Those of them who have been already corrupted might perhaps have some reason for supporting me, but what reason can their relatives have who are grown up, and who are uncorrupted, except the reason of truth and justice—that they know very well that Meletus is lying, and that I am speaking the truth?

Well, my friends, this, and perhaps more like this, is pretty much all I have to offer in my defense. There may be some one among you who will be indignant when he remembers how, even in a less important trial than this, he begged and entreated the judges, with many tears, to acquit him, and brought forward his children and many of his friends and relatives in Court in order to appeal to your feelings; and then finds that I shall do none of these things, though I am in what he would think the supreme danger. Perhaps he will harden himself against me when he notices this: it may make him angry, and he may cast his vote in anger. If it is so with any of you—I do not suppose that it is, but in case it should be so—I think that I should answer him reasonably if I said: "My friend, I have relatives, too, for, in the words of Homer,[9] "I am not born of an oak or a rock but of flesh and blood"; and so, Athenians, I have relatives, and I have three sons, one of them a lad, and the other two still children. Yet I will not bring any of them forward before you and implore you to acquit me. And why will I do none of these things? It is not from arrogance, Athenians, nor because I lack respect for you—whether or not I can face death bravely is another question—but for my own good name, and for your good name, and for the good name of the whole state. I do not think it right, at my age and with my reputation, to do anything of that kind. Rightly or wrongly, men have made up their minds that in some way Socrates is different from the multitude of men. And it will be shameful if those of you who are thought to excel in wisdom, or in bravery, or in any other virtue, are going to act in this fashion. I have often seen men of reputation behaving in an extraordinary way at their trial, as if they thought it a terrible fate to be killed, and as though they expected to live for ever if you did not put them to death. Such men seem to me to bring shame upon the state, for any stranger would suppose that the best and most eminent Athenians, who are selected by their fellow citizens to hold office, and for other honors, are no better than women. Those of you, Athenians, who have any reputation at all ought not to do these things, and you ought not to allow us to do them; you should show that you will be much more ready to condemn men who make the state ridiculous by these pitiful pieces of acting, than to men who remain quiet.

But apart from the question of reputation, my friends, I do not think that it is right to entreat the judge to acquit us, or to escape condemnation in that way. It is our duty to teach and persuade him. He does not sit to give away justice as a favor, but to pronounce judgment; and he has sworn, not to favor any man whom he would like to favor, but to judge according to law. And, therefore, we ought not to encourage you in the habits of breaking your oaths; and you ought not to allow yourselves to fall into this habit, for then neither you nor we would be acting piously. Therefore, Athenians, do not require me to do these things, for I believe them to be neither good nor just nor pious; and, more especially, do not ask me to do them today when Meletus is prosecuting me for impiety. For were I to be successful and persuade you by my entreaties to break your oaths, I should be clearly teaching you to believe that there are no gods, and I should be simply accusing myself by my defense of not believing in them. But, Athenians, that is very far from the truth. I do believe in the gods as no one of my accusers believes in them: and to you and to god I commit my cause to be decided as is best for you and for me.

(He is found guilty by 281 votes to 220.)
I am not indignant at the verdict which you have given, Athenians, for many reasons. I expected that you would find me guilty; and I am not so much surprised at that as at the numbers of the votes. I certainly never thought that the majority against me would have been so

---

8. E.g. Critias, a leader of The Thirty, and Alcibiades.

9. Homer, Odyssey, xix, 163.

narrow. But now it seems that if only thirty votes had changed sides, I should have escaped. So I think that I have escaped Meletus, as it is; and not only have I escaped him, for it is perfectly clear that if Anytus and Lycon had not come forward to accuse me, too, he would not have obtained the fifth part of the votes, and would have had to pay a fine of a thousand drachmae.

So he proposes death as the penalty. Be it so. And what alternative penalty shall I propose to you, Athenians?[10] What I deserve, of course, must I not? What then do I deserve to pay or to suffer for having determined not to spend my life in ease? I neglected the things which most men value, such as wealth, and family interests, and military commands, and popular oratory, and all the political appointments, and clubs, and factions, that there are in Athens; for I thought that I was really too honest a man to preserve my life if I engaged in these matters. So I did not go where I should have done no good either to you or to myself. I went, instead, to each one of you privately to do him, as I say, the greatest of benefits, and tried to persuade him not to think of his affairs until he had thought of himself and tried to make himself as good and wise as possible, nor to think of the affairs of Athens until he had thought of Athens herself; and to care for other things in the same manner. Then what do I deserve for such a life? Something good, Athenians, if I am really to propose what I deserve; and something good which it would be suitable to me to receive. Then what is a suitable reward to be given to a poor benefactor who requires leisure to exhort you? There is no reward, Athenians, so suitable for him as a public maintenance in the prytaneum. It is a much more suitable reward for him than for any of you who has won a victory at the Olympic games with his horse or his chariots. Such a man only makes you seem happy, but I make you really happy; and he is not in want, and I am. So if I am to propose the penalty which I really deserve, I propose this—a public maintenance in the prytaneum [town hall].

Perhaps you think me stubborn and arrogant in what I am saying now, as in what I said about the entreaties and tears. It is not so, Athenians; it is rather that I am convinced that I never wronged any man voluntarily, though I cannot persuade you of that, for we have discussed together only a little time. If there were a law at Athens, as there is elsewhere, not to finish a trial of life and death in a single day, I think that I could have persuaded you; but now it is not easy in so short a time to clear myself of great prejudices. But when I am persuaded that I have never wronged any man, I shall certainly not wrong myself, or admit that I deserve to suffer any evil, or propose any evil for myself as a penalty. Why should I? Lest I should suffer the penalty which Meletus proposes when I say that I do not know whether it is a good or an evil? Shall I choose instead of it something which I know to be an evil, and propose that as a penalty? Shall I propose imprisonment? And why should I pass the rest of my days in prison, the slave of successive officials? Or shall I propose a fine, with imprisonment until it is paid? I have told you why I will not do that. I should have to remain in prison, for I have no money to pay a fine with. Shall I then propose exile? Perhaps you would agree to

that. Life would indeed be very dear to me if I were unreasonable enough to expect that strangers would cheerfully tolerate my discussions and arguments when you who are my fellow citizens cannot endure them, and have found them so irksome and odious to you that you are seeking now to be relieved of them. No, indeed, Athenians, that is not likely. A fine life I should lead for an old man if I were to withdraw from Athens and pass the rest of my days in wandering from city to city, and continually being expelled. For I know very well that the young men will listen to me wherever I go, as they do here; and if I drive them away, they will persuade their elders to expel me; and if I do not drive them away, their fathers and kinsmen will expel me for their sakes.

Perhaps some one will say, "Why cannot you withdraw from Athens, Socrates, and hold your peace?" It is the most difficult thing in the world to make you understand why I cannot do that. If I say that I cannot hold my peace because that would be to disobey the god, you will think that I am not in earnest and will not believe me. And if I tell you that no greater good can happen to a man than to discuss virtue every day and the other matters about which you have heard me arguing and examining myself and others, and that an unexamined life is not worth living, then you will believe me still less. But that is so, my friends, though it is not easy to persuade you. And, what is more, I am not accustomed to think that I deserve anything evil. If I had been rich, I would have proposed as large a fine as I could pay: that would have done me no harm. But I am not rich enough to pay a fine unless you are willing to fix it at a sum within my means. Perhaps I could pay you a mina, so I propose that. Plato here, Athenians, and Crito, and Critobulus, and Apollodorus bid me propose thirty minae, and they will be sureties for me. So I propose thirty minae.[11] They will be sufficient sureties to you for the money.

(He is condemned to death.)

You have not gained very much time, Athenians, and, as the price of it, you will have an evil name for all who wish to revile the state, and they will say that you put Socrates, a wise man, to death. For they will certainly call me wise, whether I am wise or not, when they want to reproach you. If you would have waited for a little while, your wishes would have been fulfilled in the course of nature; for you see that I am an old man, far advanced in years, and near to death. I am saying this not to all of you, only to those who have voted for my death. And to them I have something else to say. Perhaps, my friends, you think that I have been convicted because I was wanting in the arguments by which I could have persuaded you to acquit me, if, that is, I had thought it right to do or to say anything to escape punishment. It is not so. I have been convicted because I was wanting, not in arguments, but in impudence and shamelessness—because I would not plead before you as you would have liked to hear me plead, or appeal to you with weeping and wailing, or say and do many other things which I maintain are unworthy of me, but which you have been accustomed to from other men. But when I was defending myself, I thought

---

10. For certain crimes no penalty was fixed by Athenian law, and, having reached a verdict of guilty, the court had still to decide between the alternative penalties proposed by the prosecution and the defense.

11. [One mina was a trifling sum, Sokrates's honest opinion of his just deserts but insulting to the court. A thirty minae fine was comparable to the dowry of a moderately rich man's daughter, as Plato later mentioned, but, by this time, totally unacceptable to the court.]

that I ought not to do anything unworthy of a free man because of the danger which I ran, and I have not changed my mind now. I would very much rather defend myself as I did, and die, than as you would have had me do, and live. Both in a lawsuit and in war, there are some things which neither I nor any other man may do in order to escape from death. In battle, a man often sees that he may at least escape from death by throwing down his arms and falling on his knees before the pursuer to beg for his life. And there are many other ways of avoiding death in every danger if a man is willing to say and to do anything. But, my friends, I think that it is a much harder thing to escape from wickedness than from death, for wickedness is swifter than death. And now I, who am old and slow, have been overtaken by the slower pursuer: and my accusers, who are clever and swift, have been overtaken by the swifter pursuer—wickedness. And now I shall go away, sentenced by you to death; and they will go away, sentenced by truth to wickedness and injustice. And I abide by this award as well as they. Perhaps it was right for these things to be so; and I think that they are fairly balanced.

And now I wish to prophesy to you, Athenians, who have condemned me. For I am going to die, and that is the time when men have most prophetic power. And I prophesy to you who have sentenced me to death that a far more severe punishment than you have inflicted on me will surely overtake you as soon as I am dead. You have done this thing, thinking that you will be relieved from having to give an account of your lives. But I say that the result will be very different. There will be more men who will call you to account, whom I have held back, though you did not recognize it. And they will be harsher toward you than I have been, for they will be younger, and you will be more indignant with them. For if you think that you will restrain men from reproaching you for not living as you should, by putting them to death, you are very much mistaken. That way of escape is neither possible nor honorable. It is much more honorable and much easier not to suppress others, but to make yourselves as good as you can. This is my parting prophecy to you who have condemned me.

With you who have acquitted me I should like to discuss this thing that has happened, while the authorities are busy, and before I go to the place where I have to die. So, remain with me until I go: there is no reason why we should not talk with each other while it is possible. I wish to explain to you, as my friends, the meaning of what has happened to me. An amazing thing has happened to me, judges—for you I am right in calling judges.[12] The prophetic sign has been constantly with me all through my life till now, opposing me in quite small matters if I were not going to act rightly. And now you yourselves see what has happened to me—a thing which might be thought, and which is sometimes actually reckoned, the supreme evil. But the divine sign did not oppose me when I was leaving my house in the morning, nor when I was coming up here to the court, nor at any point in my speech when I was going to say anything; though at other times it has often stopped me in the very act of speaking. But now, in this matter, it has never once opposed me, either in my words or my actions. I will tell you what I believe to be the reason. This thing that has come upon me must be a good; and those of us who

think that death is an evil must needs be mistaken. I have a clear proof that that is so; for my accustomed sign would certainly have opposed me if I had not been going to meet with something good.

And if we reflect in another way, we shall see that we may well hope that death is a good. For the state of death is one of two things: either the dead man wholly ceases to be and loses all consciousness or, as we are told, it is a change and a migration of the soul to another place. And if death is the absence of all consciousness, and like the sleep of one whose slumbers are unbroken by any dreams, it will be a wonderful gain. For if a man had to select that night in which he slept so soundly that he did not even dream, and had to compare with it all the other nights and days of his life, and then had to say how many days and nights in his life he had spent better and more pleasantly than this night, I think that a private person, nay, even the great King[13] himself, would find them easy to count, compared with the others. If that is the nature of death, I for one count it a gain. For then it appears that all time is nothing more than a single night. But if death is a journey to another place, and what we are told is true— that there are all who have died—what good could be greater than this, my judges? Would a journey not be worth taking, at the end of which, in the other world, we should be delivered from the pretended judges here and should find the true judges who are said to sit in judgment below, such as Minos and Rhadamanthus and Aeacus and Triptolemus, and the other demigods who were just in their own lives? Or what would you not give to discuss with Orpheus and Musaeus and Hesiod and Homer? I am willing to die many times if this be true. And for my own part I should find it wonderful to meet there Palamedes, and Ajax, the son of Telamon, and the other men of old who have died through an unjust judgment, and in comparing my experiences with theirs. That I think would be no small pleasure. And, above all, I could spend my time in examining those who are there, as I examine men here, and in finding out which of them is wise, and which of them thinks himself wise when he is not wise. What would we not give, my judges, to be able to examine the leader of the great expedition against Troy, or Odysseus, or Sisyphus, or countless other men and women whom we could name? It would be an infinite happiness to discuss with them and to live with them and to examine them. Assuredly there they do not put men to death for doing that. For besides the other ways in which they are happier than we are, they are immortal, at least if what we are told is true.

And you, too, judges, must face death hopefully, and believe this as a truth that no evil can happen to a good man, either in life or after death. His fortunes are not neglected by the gods; and what has happened to me today has not happened by chance. I am persuaded that it was better for me to die now, and to be released from trouble; and that was the reason why the sign never turned me back. And so I am not at all angry with my accusers or with those who have condemned me to die. Yet it was not with this in mind that they accused me and condemned me, but meaning to do me an injury. So far I may blame them.

---

13. Of Persia.

---

12. The form of address hitherto has always been "Athenians," or "my friends."

Yet I have one request to make of them. When my sons grow up, punish them, my friends, and harass them in the same way that I have harassed you, if they seem to you to care for riches or for any other thing more than virtue; and if they think that they are something when they are really nothing, reproach them, as I have reproached you, for not caring for what they should, and for thinking that they are something when really they are nothing. And if you will do this, I myself and my sons will have received justice from you.

But now the time has come, and we must go away—I to die, and you to live. Which is better is known to god alone.

Exercises

1. Sokrates could have saved his life by paying a moderate fine. Why didn't he do this? What is implied if he pays a fine?
2. Refusing to pay a reasonable rather than a token fine is one thing, but proposing lifetime maintenance at public expense is another matter. Why did Sokrates antagonize the court with this proposal? Was he serious?
3. Would Sokrates have taken this uncompromising position had he been, say, twenty years younger?

3
Greek Art: Gods, Temples, and the Greeks

According to Greek mythology, Daidalos (DED–uh–los) was the first and greatest of artists, a legendary Minoan artificer who created amazing figures in wood, bronze, and stone, and who even invented the mysterious Minoan maze that housed the fabled Minotaur. Although the story is fascinating, it is immaterial whether or not Daidalos actually existed, because the central idea the myth celebrates is the Greek commitment to creative activity: to invent, design, sculpt, and build. Daidalean Greeks studied nature and used their discoveries to create dynamic new images and structures radiating the illusion of vitality and life. This urge to create is the hallmark of Greek genius.

While the story of Daidalos has an unhappy ending, it does point to a primary artistic consideration of Greek artists. According to the legend, Daidalos had an undisciplined son named Ikarus, who prevailed upon his father to invent wings made of wax and feathers that enabled the lad to soar birdlike in the air. Disregarding the sober advice of his father not to fly too near the sun, the reckless aviator soared so high that his wings melted, plummeting him to his death in a sea that now bears his name. A charming fabrication that reveals a higher truth, this myth symbolizes Greek respect for the laws of nature. Thus, through the story of Daidalos and his hubristic son, Ikarus, we see reflected the Greek search for freedom in the arts through the study of nature, invention, and obedience to reason.

The Aegean Heritage

Chronological Overview

	Egyptian Civilization
2850–2200 B.C.	Old Kingdom[1]
2040–1786 B.C.	Middle Kingdom
1558–1075 B.C.	New Kingdom
3000–2000 B.C.	Cycladic Civilization
2000–1100 B.C.	Minoan Civilization
1550–1100 B.C.	Mycenaean Civilization
	(late Helladic)

Figure 3.1 Sphinx, ca. 2540–2514 B.C., original height 95′; top of the Great Pyramid of Khufu, ca. 2590–2568 B.C., original height 482′, Giza, Egypt.

Keenly aware of all the cultures of the eastern Mediterranean and the Middle East, the Greeks were influenced by all, especially by Egypt and the Aegean civilizations: Cycladic, Minoan, and the Greek-speaking Mycenaeans. Egyptian civilization, for the Greeks and the Romans, was unique in its longevity and continuity. When in the fifth century B.C. the Greek historian Herodotus gazed upon the two-thousand-year-old Sphinx and the pyramids (fig. 3.1), he was as awed by their antiquity as by their engineering and aesthetic effect. Though pyramid building was already part of Egypt's distant past, Egyptian artists did adhere to other long-established traditions, leading Plato to remark that Egyptian art had not changed in "ten thousand years" (*Laws* 656D–E).

The tenacity of Egyptian artistic conventions provided a large and compelling framework that influenced pre-Greek and Greek art down through the age of Alexander, albeit with uniquely Greek refinements. (An art "convention" is a consistent manner of seeing and depicting things that is generally understood and accepted: commonly held values that have taken form. The sum of all localized conventions is "culture.")

Egyptian artistic conventions can be seen in the statue of *Mycerinus* (MY–sir–reen–us) *and His Queen* (fig. 3.2), which shares qualities common to practically every Egyptian sculpture depicting life-sized standing or seated figures. Egyptian sculptors took a cubic view of the human form and prepared the statue by drawing its front and side views on the faces of a rectangular block, then working inward until the angular views met. The resultant image is one of startling clarity, but one that demands a 90° change of position every time the viewer desires another perspective. Egyptian statuary has a monumental frozen quality that can be observed from directly in front, directly in back, or squarely from the sides. Symbolizing the total control of an absolute ruler, this immobility is a visual counterpart of Egyptian belief in

Figure 3.2 *Mycerinus and His Queen,* ca. 2599–2571 B.C., Old Kingdom, Fourth Dynasty, from Giza. Slate schist, height 54½″. Shaw Collection. Museum of Fine Arts, Boston.

---

1. Of prime concern throughout all art chapters is the evolution of artistic styles; thus the various forms of the visual arts will be considered within the context of the historical development of Western civilization, as reflections of an overall cultural evolution. Careful attention should therefore be paid to all dates, particularly those given with the illustrations. Dates are historical guideposts, and they *are* important.

unalterable laws that govern man and nature. Also characteristic of Egyptian portraiture is the rectangularity of the figures, as if they were standing in a rectangular frame within a similar box, thus reinforcing the impression of calmly composed immobility. The illusion of massiveness is heightened by leaving as much stone intact as possible; as, for example, in the stone webbing that binds the rigid arms and clenched fists to the figure. By carving what amounted to very high reliefs, Egyptian sculptors consistently avoided openings in the stone. Finally, the conventions of portraiture required formal depictions of persons of high rank, as here in the figure of the pharaoh, while less-exalted personages are portrayed more realistically. The queen's clasping of her husband's waist and the touching hand on his left arm symbolizes, in a society in which property was inherited through the female line, the transfer of her power to the pharaoh.

In Egyptian painting, as illustrated by *Offering Bearers* (fig. 3.3), we see an even more pervasive convention. Egyptian painters and relief carvers almost invariably depicted the human body with the eyes and torso as viewed from the front, but with the face and legs in profile. This arrangement shows key body parts in their most telling and easily understood view, the way artists "know" rather than how they actually "see" the parts. Further, by avoiding specific settings and placing the boldly two-dimensional figures on a frontal plane, the artists emphasized the timelessness that characterizes Egyptian art.

Despite strong artistic influences, there were significant differences between Egypt and Greece, particularly in religion, government, topography, and climate (see "Geography of Greece," p. 26). In Egypt, with an absolute monarch and a powerful clergy, there was no power and no freedom for the common people. As the inventors of democracy, with neither an organized religion nor a lifetime clergy, the citizens of Greece, particularly the Athenians, enjoyed the only political freedom in the ancient world. Differences in topography and climate were also influential. Egypt was a vast, arid land with its agriculture, and thus its culture, confined to narrow fertile bands hugging the life-giving Nile. Greece was a semiarid land of pastures and olive groves, with rugged mountains guarding broad valleys that were closely linked to a seemingly endless seacoast.

Egyptian culture was immeasurably influenced by the geography and climate of the Nile Valley. Literally a "gift of the Nile," Egypt was generally only as stable as the smoothly flowing river that dictated the pattern of Egyptian life through predictable cycles of flood and retreat. Protected by mountains, the sea, and trackless deserts, inhabited Egypt averaged some 10 miles in width along 650 miles of the mighty river. Herodotus succinctly described Egypt as "all the country covered by innundations of the Nile" and Egyptians as "all men who drink Nile water" (*Histories*, II). Since their prosperous economy was based on the dependably bountiful river, it is no wonder that Egyptians viewed nature's laws and those of the gods as immutable and the afterlife as a continuation of the good life in the Nile Valley.

Once two warring kingdoms, Upper and Lower Egypt were united (in ca. 3100 B.C.) by a powerful ruler (King Menes?) who declared himself a god and claimed ownership of the river, land, and people as gifts of the gods. The exalted position of the pharaoh, which was never disputed by the people, is symbolized by the two statues of Amenhotep III (fig. 3.4) that originally flanked his funerary temple. Necessitated perhaps by the vastness of the desert landscape, the giant figures represented the significance of the pharaoh, while also serving to awe the subjects of the royal power.

Figure 3.3 *Offering Bearers* from Tomb of Sebekhotep, ca. 1500–1300 B.C., New Kingdom, Eighteenth Dynasty. Tempera on mud plaster, width ca. 30″, Thebes. Rogers Fund. Metropolitan Museum of Art, New York.

Figure 3.4 *Colossi of Memnon*, ca. 1400 B.C., New Kingdom, Eighteenth Dynasty. Quartzsite, originally 68′ high, Thebes.

Figure 3.5 Temple of Amon, dating from the twentieth century B.C. but constructed mainly from the sixteenth to twelfth centuries, New Kingdom, Karnak.

Figure 3.6 Mortuary Temple of Queen Hatshepsut, ca. 1480 B.C., New Kingdom, Eighteenth Dynasty, Deir el-Bahari.

Egyptian temples were not only designed on an enormous scale to make a distinctive statement in the vast landscape, but also as visual symbols of the power of the gods and the authority of the priests who served the pharaoh and the gods. Towering over the foreground figure, the Temple of Amon at Karnak (fig. 3.5) was the seat of the throne of Amon and the center of religious administration. It was the most extensive temple in Egypt and one of the largest sanctuaries in the ancient world, containing 134 columns in the Great Hall alone.

Constructed at the foot of sandstone cliffs on the western bank of the Nile at Thebes, the mortuary temple of Queen Hatshepsut (fig. 3.6) is a brilliantly

Figure 3.7 Temple of Amon-Mut-Khonsu, ca. 1390–1260 B.C., New Kingdom, Eighteenth Dynasty, Luxor.

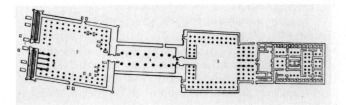

Figure 3.8 Floor plan of Temple of Amon-Mut-Khonsu: (1) entrance, (2) first court, (3) earlier sanctuaries, (4) great hall, (5) second court, and (6) sanctuaries of Amon, Mut, and Khonsu.

conceived complex designed as a memorial to the first woman to rule Egypt, the first illustrious female ruler of whom there is any record. In order to make the structure impressive, given the enormity of the setting, the architect Senmet has thrust the upper courtyard into the cliff face so that the towering mass can serve as a kind of natural pyramid.

Even in its ruined condition the Temple of Amon-Mut-Khonsu (fig. 3.7) clearly illustrates the nature of Egyptian religious architecture. Missing from the temple complex is the high wall that originally enclosed the entire aggregate of courts, halls, and temples. Egyptian temples were designed as a succession of spaces of increasing holiness, entered through a main portal flanked by ponderous slanting masses of stone called pylons (extreme left, fig. 3.7), which led to the first inner court (no. 1 in fig. 3.8). Passing through the 74' columns of the Great Hall (right center of fig. 3.7, no. 4 in fig. 3.8) ordinary worshippers assembled in the sequestered inner court (no. 5 in fig. 3.8), but were forbidden to go any farther. From here they could only marvel at the mysterious forest of columns that darkened the inner recesses, the exclusive preserve of the priesthood (far right of fig. 3.7, no. 6 of fig. 3.8). There the all-powerful clergy administered the temples of the local deity Amon, his wife Mut, and their son Khonsu. (In fig. 3.7 the structures to the right of the pylon are the dome and minaret of a medieval mosque.)

Figure 3.9 Cycladic Head, ca. 2500 B.C. Marble, height 11½". National Archeological Museum, Athens.

To summarize, the cubic view of Egyptian sculptors and the simultaneous profile/frontality of painting and relief carving strongly influenced Greek art. On the other hand, Egyptian geographical, political, and religious factors accounted for their monumental structures and sculptures, which were so vastly different from their Greek counterparts, as will be discussed later in this chapter.

Cycladic Civilization 3000–2000 B.C.

In the Aegean Sea north of Crete (see map on p. 27) lies a group of islands that are called the Cyclades because they "cycle" around the hub of the sacred island of Delos, birthplace of Apollo and his twin sister Artemis. A late Neolithic culture flourished here of which little remains beyond some remarkable marble idols. These strangely modern figures are characterized by rectangular angularity and an abstract, sophisticated simplicity. They include heads and, primarily, standing female figures, all carved of pure white Parian marble. The monumentally proportioned head in figure 3.9 can be favorably compared with the work of modern abstract sculptors. Here we have an artistic truth: all figurative art is essentially abstract, or a restatement of what the artist actually saw. Obviously this artist saw a nose as a dominant feature, and so we too are very aware of the nose. In addition, there are

Figure 3.10 Detail of the south front of the Palace at Knossos, ca. 1600–1400 B.C.

two tiny ears, an opened mouth, and two dimly perceived eyes. An abstracted version of the artist's perception, this is not the head of a specific person but rather an image of everyone, particularly all those with prominent noses.

Because the Cycladic figures as well as the entire Minoan and Mycenaean civilizations were all rediscovered during the past century or so, we have no way of knowing the full extent of their influence on Greek culture. We can only suggest that because of their proximity, the intensely curious Greeks knew more about Aegean civilizations than is indicated by current evidence.

Minoan Civilization, ca. 2000–1100 B.C.

Remarkably different from all other civilizations, the Minoans built no monumental showplace palaces for divine monarchs, no temples, and no fortifications of any kind. (See chap. 1 for an overview of Minoan history.) Minoan palaces were designed to be lived in comfortably and enjoyed. The palaces featured hundreds of small rooms, rambling corridors and staircases, walls gaily decorated with colorful murals, running water, bathtubs, a sewage system, terraces, open galleries, and numerous light wells to convey natural illumination to lower levels of the three- to five-story structures. They probably functioned also as administrative centers for the Minoan trade empire.

Probably the most important of the many palaces on Crete was that of the legendary King Minos at Knossos (fig. 3.10), the vastness of which can only be hinted at in the partial reconstruction by Sir Arthur Evans. The multiple levels, wandering corridors, and countless rooms (fig. 3.11) probably inspired the Greek legend of the labyrinth of Minos, which was guarded by the fearful Minotaur (half man, half bull). The monster was imprisoned there by Minos after his wife gave birth to it. The earthshaking roars attributed to the awesome beast can undoubtedly be linked to the earthquakes that periodically wracked Crete.

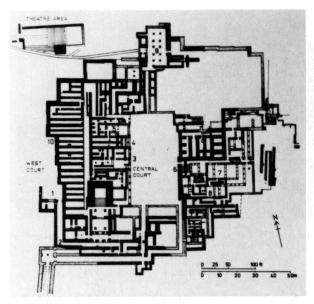

The Palace at Knossos

1. West Porch
2. Corridor of the Procession
3. Palace Shrine
4. Stepped Porch
5. Throne Room
6. Grand Staircase
7. Hall of the Double Axes
8. "Queen's Megaron"
9. Pillar Hall
10. Store-rooms
11. Royal Road, to Little Palace

Figure 3.11 Floor plan of the Palace at Knossos (after Reynold Higgins).

Figure 3.12 Throne Room, Palace of Minos, Knossos

Totally unlike that of an Egyptian king's, for instance, the Throne Room (fig. 3.12) is a small chamber at ground level containing a simple, high-backed alabaster throne with stone benches around three walls, including the wall with the throne. The fanciful griffin mural (white on red) is a modern reconstruction based on fragments found in the ruins. Opposite the throne is a colonnade separating the throne room from an open atrium, which adds air and light to an intimate and unpretentious setting.

Figure 3.13 Queen's Megaron, Palace of Minos, Knossos

Figure 3.14 *Snake Goddess,* ca. 1600 B.C., faience, height 17½". Archeological Museum, Heraklion, Crete.

Known as the legendary friend to all sailors, five dolphins frolic contentedly in a seascape mural in the Queen's Megaron (fig. 3.13). The queen's apartment, which is illuminated by a light well, also features ornamental floral designs on the door frames and an adjoining bathroom complete with bathtub. Even now there is an air of understated elegance, an ambience of good taste.

Whether she was a priestess, goddess, or queen, the so-called *Snake Goddess* (fig. 3.14) is typical of diminutive Minoan sculpture. A culture with neither divine monarch nor priesthood has no compelling need for monumental sculpture, and indeed none has been found. Though the rigid frontal pose of this small figure indicates an Egyptian influence, the raised arms plus the small animal on her head (panther?) lighten the mood to one akin to playfulness. Characteristic of feminine attire at the time, the colorful tiered skirt, tight bodice, and bared breasts are very stylish for a

Figure 3.15 Mask from Mycenae, ca. 1500 B.C. Funeral mask from the royal tombs. Beaten gold, ca. 12″ high. National Archeological Museum, Athens.

Figure 3.16 Lion Gate, citadel at Mycenae, ca. 1250 B.C. Limestone, height of relief 9′6″.

cult figure. Whatever her position or function was, she is a delightful work of art.

Mycenaean Civilization, ca. 1550–1100 B.C.

Occupying Crete after the sudden destruction of Minoan civilization in ca. 1450 B.C. (see chap. 1), the Mycenaean invaders adapted Minoan styles to their more robust tastes. The Mycenaeans were the Akhaians (uh–KAY–uns) of the fabled Trojan War depicted in Homer's *Iliad* and represented the final and highest stage of Helladic culture (after Hellas, the Greek mainland). Until the last century, historians had dismissed the *Iliad* as fanciful fiction, albeit a brilliant epic poem. They contended that Troy, Mycenae, and the epic heroes were products of Homer's fertile imagination. But in 1871, a wealthy German merchant named Heinrich Schliemann astounded everyone by announcing the discovery of Troy in northwest Turkey, just where his painstaking study of Homer indicated it would be.

Schliemann further astonished archeologists by discovering the Mycenaean civilization, including the great citadel at Mycenae with its grave circles full of precious jewelry and gold death masks, one of which Schliemann attributed to Agamemnon himself (fig. 3.15). It was soon determined, however, that this Mycenae predated the Homeric king, that the remains of "Agamemnon" were of someone from an earlier civilization. The undaunted German, realizing that argument was futile and acknowledging the lack of positive identification, jokingly renamed his Agamemnon "Schulze." Regardless of the appropriate name, the Mask from Mycenae is a superb example of the highly developed metal craftmanship called toreutics (to–RUE–tiks), the hammering of metals into representational form. The death mask (and weapons

and jewelry) represents a Mycenaean adaptation of the Egyptian funeral practice of burying their illustrious dead with items that were commensurate with their status in life.

The citadel of Mycenae, which is today in ruins, is a massive structure whose gigantic stones were placed, according to legend, by the Cyclopes (sigh–KLO–peas), a mythical race of one-eyed giants. A highly efficient fortress, its single entrance is protected by high walls on three sides. The lintel of this ponderous gate is topped by a stone relief of two lions, now headless, flanking a symbolic Minoan column (fig. 3.16). It is from this striking carving that the giant portal takes the name Lion Gate. Unlike the Minoans with their island isolation and protective seawall, closed palaces were a distinct necessity on the Greek mainland.

Greek Civilization, ca. 800–30 B.C.

The complexity and productivity of the Greek arts make it necessary to subdivide the balance of this chapter into the following artistic periods (all dates approximate):

Chronological Overview

800–660 B.C.	Geometric Period
660–480 B.C.	Archaic Period
480–323 B.C.	Classical Period
	Early 480–450
	High 450–400
	Late 400–323
323–30 B.C.	Hellenistic Period

Following a fairly strict chronology, the different media (sculpture, architecture, pottery) will be examined as manifestations of the evolving artistic styles of ancient Greece.

Geometric Period, ca. 800–660 B.C.

The invasions of Greek-speaking Dorians (ca. 1100–800 B.C.) not only abruptly terminated Mycenaean dominance and thoroughly disrupted the lives of all the Hellenes, but it also had a devastating effect on the arts of sculpture and architecture. Military invasions always disturb the arts, as political and economic turmoil is not conducive to the commissioning of such major works as temples and life-sized statues. While probably impoverishing many artists and interfering with the transmission of technology, the waves of Dorian invaders made relatively little impact upon the utilitarian arts of furniture, textiles, glassware, and, above all, pottery. Because most of the pottery produced during this chaotic period emphasized geometric decoration, this era is known as the Geometric period.

Even though it had been practiced since the Stone Age, the craft of making pots made a great leap forward with the invention (probably in Sumer—Iran—ca. 3250 B.C.) of the potter's wheel. The wheel was introduced into Crete around 2000 B.C. and enabled Minoan potters to lead the Aegean world in transforming the craft of making utilitarian vessels into an art form that reached its apex with the classic Greek vase.

As early as the ninth century, geometric conventions of pottery decoration had evolved into a vocabulary of meanders, concentric circles, horizontal bands, wheel patterns, shaded triangles, swastikas, and zigzags. Abstract animal and figure patterns were used in a two-dimensional form in either full front or profile views. Sophisticated, aesthetically appealing, and utilitarian, the *Amphora of the Dipylon* (fig. 3.17) is a masterwork of the potter's art. Because cremation had been abandoned, these monumental vases served as grave markers and also as receptacles for liquid offerings, which filtered down to the honored dead through openings in the base. The representational scene is a *prothesis* (PROTH–uh–sis), or lying-in-state of the deceased, flanked by triangulated geometric figures of mourners with their arms raised in grief. Alternating bands separate different versions of the meander[2] motif (also known as the Greek fret), with a band of grazing antelope highlighting the neck. Created about a quarter century after the inauguration of the Olympic Games in 776 B.C., this heroic vase can symbolically mark the beginning of the Homeric Age of ca. 750–700 B.C.

---

2. From the name of a winding river in Asia Minor. In Greek decoration it is a mazelike pattern of lines that wind in and out or cross one another.

Figure 3.17 *Amphora of the Dipylon,* ca. 750 B.C. Terra-cotta, height 61″ with base. National Archeological Museum, Athens.

Though it achieved its final form during the Archaic Period (ca. 600 B.C.), it is apparent that the Greek temple was known to Homer (*Iliad,* I, 39). Fragmentary terra-cotta models from the eighth century display three of the elements of the temple canon: rectangular floor plan, enclosed inner shrine, and porch supported by columns. The "canon" (Gk., *kanon,* rule) of Greek temples refers to fundamental procedures that help convert a concept into reality, in this case, buildings that look precisely like what they are: temples for the gods.

Among the most popular products of the Greek artisans were statuettes, which were produced throughout Greek history. Though they were not as impressive as life-sized statuary, the very smallness of miniature figures enables one to hold and turn them around in one's hands—a very personal relationship. The statuette shown in figure 3.18 is a votive offering bearing on its thighs the inscription, "Mantiklos dedicated me to the Far Darter of the silver bow, as part of his tithe. Do thou, Phoibos, grant him gracious recompence." As obvious as the geometric elements are, the unknown artist also demonstrates a concern for volume, modeling, and some anatomical details, design elements that place this work on the borderline between the Geometric and Archaic periods.

Archaic Period, 600–480 B.C.

Archaic is a term derived from a Greek word meaning *ancient* and is not to be confused with such contemporary definitions as antiquated, outdated, or old-fashioned. The sixth century saw Greek genius blossom with the production of brilliant works of art. This was one of the exalted periods in world art, a vigorous era that also produced the world's first democracy.

Throughout Greek art, beginning with the Archaic period, Greek sculptors evolved new representational modes that were different from all previous artistic conceptions. They were fascinated by the complex mechanics of the human body; this led to the creation of fully three-dimensional sculpture that more nearly represented the natural world. The ideal, as illustrated in the Pygmalion legend, was the creation of a marble figure that would step down from the platform and speak to its creator.

Two main subjects preoccupied sculptors throughout the sixth century: the standing nude male and the standing fully clothed female. Apparently serving as votive or commemorative statues, these figures were not personalized portraits but rather idealized representations placed somewhere between humankind and the gods. No one really knows why the men were always nude and the women fully clothed and, moreover, we can apply only vague and unsatisfactory names to these freestanding figures: *kouros* (KOO–rose; youth) and *kore* (KORE–ay; maiden). Probably adapted from Egypt and Mesopotamia, these two subjects were repeated again and again, never with the intention of exact repetition but rather with the competitive drive that leads to constant innovation. It is the degree of this ceaseless striving for something different, something better, that sets the Greeks apart from other cultures.

An early work, the *Kore of Auxerre* (fig. 3.19) stands as stiffly as an Egyptian statue, but compared with Egyptian conventions shows some significant differences (see fig. 3.2). Unlike his Egyptian predecessor, the sculptor has cut away some needless stone to outline the figure rather than encasing it. The hair is braided in the geometric manner, but a very human touch is conveyed by the way the waist is cinched by a wide belt. From the light shoulder covering to the swelling hips, there is a skillful contrast between curved and straight lines.

Compare the colossal statue of the *Kouros of Sounion* (fig. 3.20) with the pharaoh (fig. 3.2). We see that the Egyptian figure is "imprisoned" in stone in the manner of a very high relief, whereas the kouros statue has been liberated from unnecessary stone, with the exception of the hands. The pharaoh stands in repose with his weight on the back foot. The equal distribution of weight of the kouros figure gives the illusion that he is striding forward, an effect that is

Figure 3.18 Statuette of Youth, "Mantiklos dedicated me . . . ," ca. 700–680 B.C. Bronze, height 8". Francis Bartlett Donation. Courtesy, Museum of Fine Arts, Boston.

Based on the surviving pottery and statuettes, the Geometric can be viewed as an interlude rather than a major artistic period. The fact that Homer's *Iliad* and *Odyssey* were the greatest achievements of this era makes one wonder, however. Did the visual arts lag behind epic poetry, or have some important artworks been lost? In any event, the Geometric was a period in which the Greeks began to see and think and create as a Greek, not as an Egyptian or a Minoan or a Mycenaean. Borrowings from these civilizations are evident, but the unique forms introduced during the Geometric period clearly indicate an elementary process of producing art forms not bound to traditional conventions but subject to experimentation and invention, and above all, art that was dynamic rather than static.

Figure 3.19 *Kore of Auxerre,* ca. 630–600 B.C. Limestone with traces of paint, height 24″. The Louvre, Paris.

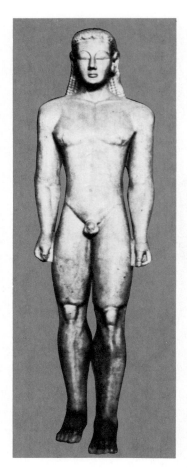

Figure 3.20 *Kouros of Sounion,* ca. 600 B.C. Marble, height 10′. National Archeological Museum, Athens.

heightened by the taut thigh muscles. Vestiges of geometric ornamentation remain in the rosette hair with meticulous braids and, especially, in the scrolls (volutes) that serve as ears. The most critical difference between the Egyptian and Greek sculptures lies in the eyes and facial expression. Displaying the typical relaxed serenity of Egyptian portraiture, the pharaoh gazes dreamily into an undefined distance. The *Kouros of Sounion* manifests the characteristic dynamism of Greek art, with tension present in every line of the face. Egyptian figures seem never to have known stress, whereas tension and striving are hallmarks of the restless Greeks.

Created shortly after the Greek triumphs over the Persians at Salamis and Plataea, the *Calf-Bearer* (fig. 3.21) was something new in Greek art, a composition of two figures so unified that neither figure is conceivable without the other. A bearded man with a cloak draped over his upper body is gently balancing a bull calf on his shoulders as he strides confidently forward. With the corners of his mouth lifted slightly in the so-called Archaic smile, he stares ahead with hollow eyes that once contained inlays, probably making them quite realistic. Characteristic of the

Archaic style, his braided hair and close-cropped beard are highly stylized, in contrast with the naturalistic depiction of the calf.

Larger than life size, the figure of *Hera of Samos* (fig. 3.22) is both subtle and strong. Basically cylindrical in shape, she was probably created by an Ionian sculptor who, among other things, was very interested in the interrelationship of the airy drapery of Ionian dress with the body underneath. Notice the contrast between the diagonal draping across the breasts and the delicate folds dropping lightly from the hips in a slightly concave mirroring of a Greek column.

Painting was, for the Greeks, one of the supreme art forms, and yet very little of it survives. We must focus instead on the superb achievements of Archaic vase painters, who raised that form of pictorial art to a level comparable to the best sculpture and architecture. That the Greeks themselves valued their vases is attested to by the number of painters (and potters) who signed their creations, which incidentally raised the value (and price) of the vase. They concentrated on lively interaction between individual gods, goddesses, and heroes; and using an incisive black-figure technique (silhouetted figures on a reddish background), vase painters like Exekias (e–ZEE–ki–as) set

Figure 3.21 *Calf-Bearer (Moschophoros),* ca. 575–550 B.C. Marble, height 66″. Akropolis Museum, Athens.

Figure 3.22 *Hera of Samos,* ca. 560 B.C. Marble, height 76″. The Louvre, Paris.

a standard that has not been surpassed (fig. 3.23). In this incident from the Trojan War, not related in the *Iliad,* Akhilleus is in the act of killing Penthesilea, Queen of the Amazons. At the very moment of his spear thrust, we can see that he has fallen in love with her. The hulking silhouette of the mighty hero looms over the vanquished but still proud queen, forming a tight and compact composition of striking power and intensity that contrasts with the delicate spirals. A tall, two-handled jar for wine or oil, the amphora itself was made by Exekias, who signed eleven vases but only two paintings, implying that he took more pride in making vases than in painting them. Exekias managed to misspell his own name on one of his two surviving paintings, possibly confirming the judgment of Plato and Aristotle that craftsmen were manifestly inferior to philosophers.

By the sixth century, Greek city-states had established colonies in North Africa and from Byzantium (Istanbul) westward to Italy, Sicily, France, and Spain. Magna Graecia (southern Italy) was particularly important, for it was here that Pythagoras founded his religious brotherhood (see chap. 1) and Parmenides and Empedokles established the Eleatic School of philosophy (see chap. 2). One of the better-preserved of the surviving Archaic temples is that of Hera

Figure 3.23 Exekias, amphora: "Akhilleus Slaying Penthesiles," ca. 540 B.C. Height 16¼″. British Museum, London. Reproduced by courtesy of the Trustees of the British Museum.

Figure 3.24 Temple of Hera I, ca. 550 B.C. Paestum, Italy.

Figure 3.25 *Kore in Dorian Peplos,* ca. 530 B.C. Marble with traces of paint, height 48″. Akropolis Museum, Athens.

at Paestum (fig. 3.24), the site of two religious centers of Magna Graecia. Though employing an unusual nine-column front, this structure has all the elements of the basic Greek temple: rectangular floor plan, columns on four sides, three steps rising from the foundation to the top level on which the columns rest, and an enclosed inner shrine. (As far as we know the odd number of columns was never tried again. Regularity was an important Greek concept, as exemplified in the six- or eight-column fronts of classical temples; see figs. 3.41 and 3.44.) Other archaic features are heavy, bulging columns that taper sharply as they near the oversize, pillowlike capitals. The whole effect is heavy because these features seem to create a sense of physical strain, unlike the Parthenon (see fig. 3.44), which appears to be light and free of stress.

By comparing the *Kore in Dorian Peplos* (fig. 3.25) with the *Kore of Auxerre* (fig. 3.19), one can observe a basic continuity while also noting significant changes. This is the last known archaic kore statue to wear the Dorian *peplos,* a heavy tunic reaching to the ground that was fastened at each shoulder and belted at the waist. It was commonly worn over a light, sleeved tunic called a *chiton.* Though there is still a rectangular frontality about this figure, there is no doubt about the presence of a young, nubile body beneath the woolen peplos. With its lovely natural smile and arched eyebrows, the softly rounded face exudes a serene kind of happiness. The remaining paint on the graceful braids indicates that the young woman was a redhead, a valued hue in ancient Athens.

The Ionian *himation* worn by the *Kore from Chios* (fig. 3.26) contrasts sharply with the severe Dorian peplos. This elegant mantle, which was worn over the chiton, was of much lighter material than the peplos and could be draped over the body in a variety of graceful arrangements. Based on the number of surviving works, it is obvious that artists were entranced

with the challenge of sculpting the sinuous lines of the garment. Moreover, the wholesale adoption by Athenian women of the stylish himation (see other styles in fig. 4.6) symbolizes the individualistic, pleasure-loving Ionian orientation of Athenian society, as compared with the sober peplos and stolid, group-oriented society of the Dorian city of Sparta. As we have already seen (p. 50), the clash of these disparate cultures was apparently inevitable.

The *Anavyssos Kouros* (fig. 3.27), which was placed over the grave of a warrior named Kroisos, signals a major advance towards *naturalism,* fidelity to the actual appearance of the natural world. The revolutionary changes were already apparent in the *Kouros of Sounion* (see fig. 3.20), but were realized in what is now more nearly a portrait of the finely tuned body of a youthful wrestler who had the misfortune to die on some unknown battlefield. Though the knees and calves are emphasized according to earlier conventions, the muscles of the powerful thighs and taut arms swell with lifelike vitality. Based on an increasing knowledge of skeletal structure and anatomical details, the sculptor has concentrated on portraying the body. Greek artists, from the very first efforts at monumental sculpture, were never interested in portrait busts, but instead were concerned with the depiction of the body. This does not imply

Figure 3.26 *Kore from Chios* (?), ca. 520 B.C. Marble with traces of paint, ca. 22″ high (lower part missing). Akropolis Museum, Athens.

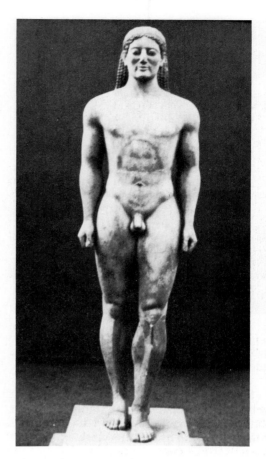

Figure 3.27 *Anavyssos Kouros,* ca. 525 B.C. Marble with traces of paint, height 76″. National Archeological Museum, Athens.

that the head was secondary—far from it. It simply means that Greek artists were intent on portraying the whole person, especially the vibrantly healthy body the Greeks so admired.

The ancient Greeks also seemed to possess a unique visual sensibility. Many factors may account for this, and a few will be mentioned. Meticulous observation was basic to Greek science, itself an area in which the Greeks had no rivals. In medical practice as exemplified by Hippokrates, there was an emphasis on the accumulation of sensory information. The Greek gods were conceived in the images of men and women and were thus immediately accessible for artistic representation. Perhaps most important, however, is the fact that the Greeks were not subjected to views of reality imposed from above by either a divine-right monarch or an organized religion.

During the discussion of the *Anavyssos Kouros* (fig. 3.27) it was pointed out that Greek sculptors portrayed the entire person, concentrating on the body, but without de-emphasizing the head. By deliberately selecting only the enchanting head of the kore figure that is sometimes called *La Delicata* (fig. 3.28), it is clearly apparent that the creator of this masterful

Figure 3.28 *Kore* (*La Delicata;* detail), ca. 500 B.C. Marble with traces of paint. Akropolis Museum, Athens.

Figure 3.29 Sosias painter, cup (detail): "Akhilleus Bandaging Patroklos's Wound," ca. 500 B.C. Attic red-figure cup, ca. 7″ high. Antikenmuseum Staatliche Museen Preussischer Kulturbesitz Berlin.

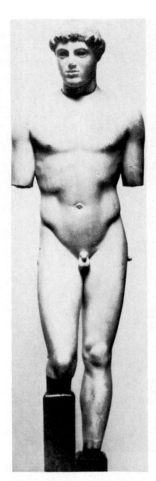

Figure 3.30 *Kritios Boy,* 481/480 B.C. Marble, height 34″. Akropolis Museum, Athens.

portrait of a beautiful woman wished to highlight her pensive, almost melancholy, mood. Also known as "the girl with the almond eyes," this work epitomizes the Archaic style at its best.

Around 530 B.C. vase painters began working with a color scheme of red figures against a black background, the reverse of black-figure technique. The luminous new *red-figure* technique permitted secondary markings like hair, muscles, details of dress, and even discreet shadings. The two styles coexisted for thirty or forty years, but the red-figure technique, with its greater opportunities for delicacy and subtlety, became the dominant style of the classical period. In the red-figure cup by the Sosias painter (fig. 3.29), we see the first example of eyes painted just the way they actually appear in profile. This significant advance marks a phase out of the Egyptian convention of always depicting the eyes as they are viewed frontally. In the painting Akhilleus is intent upon tending the wound, while in a very human reaction, Patroklos has turned his head away as if he were not even a party to this unhappy event—or wishes he weren't. Below the platform are three palmettes, a decorative motif invented by the Greeks based on a stylized rendering of a palm leaf. Some basic differences between red-figure and black-figure technique become apparent when this painting is compared with that of Exekias (fig. 3.23). It cannot be said that one of these works is better than another, only that different techniques lead to dissimilar styles. Black-figure painting is characteristic of the vigorous Archaic period, while red-figure vases typify the later Classical style.

Classical Period, 480–323 B.C.

The year 480 marked a critical turning point in the history of Athens. Invaded and humiliated by Xerxes' Persian forces, their city ravaged, and their culture in ruins, the Athenians and their allies struck back by destroying the Persian fleet at Salamis and defeating the army the following year. A resurgent Athens moved unerringly towards power, prosperity, and a legendary Golden Age epitomized by the confident Classical style.

The *Kritios Boy* (fig. 3.30), a prime example of the Severe style of early classicism, was created at about the same time as Aeschylus was gaining fame as a playwright. Somewhat like the innovations of Aeschylus, this statue represents a new principle in art. It is wearing an expression of composed, classical solemnity (compare this with the Archaic smile) and is truly a standing figure. Archaic sculptures were limited to a striding pose with an equal distribution of weight; here we have a formal composition with a fine balance of tense and relaxed muscles, the head turned slightly, one hip a bit elevated, and the weight on one leg with the other at rest. This is how any of us might stand in natural repose.

Figure 3.31 *Delphi Charioteer,* ca. 470 B.C. Bronze, height 71″. Archeological Museum, Delphi.

Figure 3.32 *Delphi Charioteer,* rear view, detail.

Figure 3.33 *Poseidon (Zeus?),* ca. 460 B.C. Bronze, height 82″. National Archeological Museum, Athens.

Also representing the Severe style is the *Delphi Charioteer* (fig. 3.31), which was once part of a large composition of a chariot and four horses. Chariot races were entered by the owners of racing teams and driven by highly skilled charioteers, much like thoroughbred horses today are ridden by professional jockeys. Overlooking the disheveled, dusty condition of a charioteer after a grueling race, the artist idealizes a proud champion, with his chiton falling in fluted folds like those of a Doric column (see fig. 3.39). Included, however, are such realistic details as a device to keep the chiton from billowing in the wind—a cord that passed over the shoulders, under the armpits, and crossed in back. The headband performed exactly the same function as a tennis player's sweatband (fig. 3.32).

One of the finest original Greek bronzes, *Poseidon* (*Zeus* according to some; fig. 3.33) stands majestically, prepared to hurl his trident (or thunderbolt). The figure is stridently asymmetrical: arms, legs, even the head, turn in different angles from the torso, which in turn shows the competing muscular strains and tensions. Unlike even the most naturalistic archaic statues, this body has rippling muscles

functioning beneath taut skin. The various concavities and convexities of the bronze surface reflect a shimmering light that further animates the figure. It matters little that if Poseidon's arms were lowered his hands would dangle at the knees; that the eyes are hollow sockets that were once filled with colored stones; or that the hair, beard, and eyebrows are highly stylized; the work exudes a kinetic energy never achieved in earlier sculptures.

Figure 3.34 Myron, *Discobolus (Discus Thrower),* reconstructed Roman marble copy of a bronze original of ca. 450 B.C. Height 60″. Museo della Terme, Rome.

The High Classical period (the Age of Perikles) was marked in part by the beginning of construction on the Akropolis, the early fame of Sophokles, and notable sculptures by Myron and Polykleitos. The *Discobolus (Discus Thrower;* fig. 3.34) is intended to be viewed when standing to the left of the figure in order to become totally involved with the moment leading to explosive action. Though a celebrated classical statue, the figure follows Egyptian conventions. It is designed on a frontal plane with head and legs in profile and the upper torso turned towards the front. It is balanced by the arced arms and the head and left leg, a formal composition that displays the harmonious proportions characteristic of the classical style. With simplified anatomical details and a stylized pose, all is in readiness for the athlete to wheel about and hurl the discus. Excellence of form, which counted as half of the scoring, was as important as marking the distance of the throw, a procedure comparable to the scoring in modern competitive diving. An athlete could win the olive wreath with a second-place throw, provided he displayed a form comparable to that of the *Discobolus.* (See also the discussion of the Olympic Games beginning on p. 122.)

One of the most highy acclaimed artists of the Golden Age was Polykleitos (polly–KLY–toss) of Argos, who is known today only through Roman copies of his work. This copy of his *Doryphoros* (dory–FOR–os; fig. 3.35) is of sufficiently high quality for us to see how it exemplified a "canon" (system of proportions), which became a model for several generations of artists. Displaying the powerful body of a finely conditioned athlete, the young man rests his full

Figure 3.35 Polykleitos, *Doryphoros (Spear Bearer),* Roman marble copy after a bronze original of ca. 450–440 B.C. Height 78″. National Museum, Naples.

weight on the right leg with the left bent at the knee and his toes lightly touching the ground. With the head barely turned to the right and the right shoulder dropped slightly, the whole body can be traced as a long **S** curve from the feet to the head. At rest as no sculpted figure had ever been before, the composition is still dynamic, a balance of tension and relaxation throughout the entire body. Harmoniously proportioned and with a classic balance of artistic and natural form, this is the confident style of the Golden Age.

Let us turn now to developments in architecture leading to the classical temples of the Age of Perikles. As discussed earlier, Greek temples had evolved into their canonical form during the early Archaic period (ca. 600). Fundamental to the temple canon is the architectural system of post and lintel (fig. 3.36). After planting a post at all four corners of the space to be enclosed, the builder then placed a beam (lintel) on top of and across the posts. Roof beams (joists) were placed at regular intervals to link the opposite lintels, and were then covered with a roof. Spaces between the posts were filled, as needed, with walls, windows, and doors. First employed in wood, then in brick, and eventually in stone construction, the post and lintel

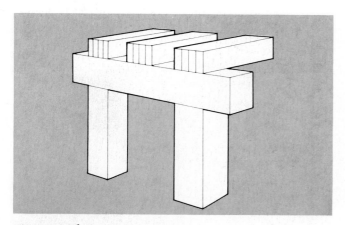

Figure 3.36 Post and lintel system

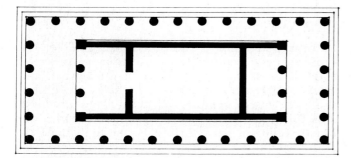

Figure 3.37 Typical Greek temple floor plan

Figure 3.38 Typical Greek temple facade

a.   b.   c.

Figure 3.39 Greek orders of columns: (a) Doric, (b) Ionic, and (c) Corinthian.

system was used for all major Greek buildings. The greater strength of arches and the arched vault (see Roman architecture, chap. 6) was known and used, but only for such minor works as the long arched corridor leading into the stadium at Nemea.

A typical temple floor plan (fig. 3.37) shows a *cella,* a central room where the statue of the diety was placed. This basic core was provided with a columned porch at the front and, usually, one at the back, with the latter sometimes enclosed to function as a treasury. Large, important temples had exterior columns on all four sides forming a colonnade or peristyle.

The plan appears to be simple, but a diagram of a facade (fig. 3.38) reveals a progression beyond the basic post and lintel. Because the Mediterranean area is subject to heavy winter rains, a sloping or saddle-back roof was developed to facilitate drainage. It was covered with terra-cotta or marble tiles, equipped with gutters and rain spouts, and adorned with decorative sculpture. The triangular space at each end, the *pediment,* was usually decorated with large-scale high reliefs or freestanding sculpture. Heavily ornamented pediments increased the weight of the superstructure and thus necessitated additional carefully spaced columns.

The Greeks constructed steps (usually three) on a stone foundation called a *stereobate* with the top level, the *stylobate,* forming the floor of the temple. (For the Greeks "three" was the perfect number because it represented a beginning, middle, and end.)

From the stylobate rose columns (shafts with capitals) that supported the lintel, also called an *architrave.* The ends of the roof joists are *triglyphs* (TRY–glifs), a term derived from the three vertical grooves that had become a decorative stone adaptation of the natural grain of wood joist ends. The spaces between the triglyphs were filled by plain, painted, or relief rectangles called *metopes* (MET–o–pays).

Determining the general mode of the basic temple plan was a problem that was brilliantly resolved with the inspired conception of three orders of columns, the classic Greek orders: Doric, Ionic, and Corinthian (fig. 3.39). The first to be invented, the

Figure 3.40 Marble drums, Eleusis

Figure 3.41 Temple of Hera II, ca. 460 B.C. Limestone. Paestum, Italy.

Doric order, is simple, solid, and serene. Placed directly upon the stylobate, the Doric column (shaft and capital) was about seven times as tall as its diameter, a ratio probably derived from the height of a man in relation to foot size. The column was fluted to provide visual depth and swelling in subtle convex curves (*entasis;* EN–ta–sis); it then rose to a capital (*echinus;* eh–KY–nus), or curved block under an *abacus* (AB–a–kus), which was a square block that joined the architrave. Surmounting the columns was a Doric frieze of alternating triglyphs and metopes. (For examples of Doric temples see figs. 3.41, 3.44, and 3.55.)

The contrasting Ionic order, the second temple style to be developed, is lighter than the Doric and more graceful, with a slender shaft about eleven times its diameter (approximately a woman's height in proportion to the size of her foot). Its components are a tiered base, softer flutes separated by narrow bands of stone, and a delicate shaft that terminates in a capital with paired scrolls (volutes) capped by a minute but highly decorated abacus. Usually subdivided into three projecting bands, the Ionic architrave normally consists of a continuous sculptural frieze. (For Ionic temples see figs. 3.52 and 3.54.)

A variant of the Ionic, the Corinthian order, adored by the Romans, is considerably more decorative, even opulent. Taller and more slender than the Ionic, its column culminates in an inverted bell shape encrusted with stylized acanthus leaves, an ingenious transition from a circular shaft to a rectangular architrave. (See fig. 3.66 for the only Corinthian temple in Greece.)

As illustrated by figure 3.40, the columns are made up of stone sections or drums, like multiple layers of a cake. Roughed out in the quarry, the drums were transported to the site, fitted with metal pegs that had been coated with lead to resist corrosion, and stacked into columns. The assembled columns were then finished under the supervision of the architect.

With only one form and three modes of expression, Greek architecture might appear to be a rather limited achievement, but the attainment of perfection

or near perfection is slow, tedious, and seldom achieved by *any* culture. For perfection of proportion and clarity of outline, subtlety of refinement, and visual appearance of solids and spaces in equilibrium, the Greek temple has never been excelled. Moreover, no two Dorian (or Ionian) temples are exactly alike; each is as distinctive and individualistic as the Greeks themselves.

Comparatively well preserved, possibly because it was out of the paths of marauding armies and barbarian incursions, the Temple of Hera II (fig. 3.41) is a Doric hexastyle (six-column front) structure of the Early Classical period. It stands next to the earlier Temple of Hera I (fig. 3.24), and although it is quite heavy and somewhat stolid, it nevertheless has the harmonious proportions so necessary to the classic unity of the Greek temple.

Most ancient Greek cities developed around an *akra* (high place), a fortified hilltop. As cities grew more prosperous and powerful, this people's high place *(akropolis)* became the center of religious and civic activity, suitably adorned with governmental buildings, libraries, and temples dedicated to the proprietary god or gods. According to legend the akropolis of Athens (fig. 3.42), the burial place of the fabled hero-king Erechtheus, was the site where Poseidon and Athena contended for authority over the city.

Under the leadership of Perikles, the Athenians completed a building and art program on the akropolis surpassing in splendor and artistic quality anything the world had ever seen. It signified the beginning of the Golden Age, in about 450 B.C., when Pheidias was appointed overseer of all works on the akropolis. By 405 the Parthenon, Erechtheion, Propylaia, and Temple of Athena Nike had been built, and the brief period of glory was at an end. These four buildings can be identified in the model (fig. 3.43): Temple of Athena Nike, tiny building on the right parapet above the stairs; Propylaia, at the top of the steps; Parthenon, largest building; and Erechtheion, two-part structure at the upper left near the wall. No other buildings have survived.

Figure 3.42 View from the west of the akropolis at Athens

Figure 3.43 Model of the classical akropolis at Athens. American School of Classical Studies at Athens: Agora Excavations.

Figure 3.44 Iktinus and Kallikrates, Parthenon (view from the northwest), ca. 447–432 B.C. Akropolis, Athens.

For a half century this small rocky plateau (ca. 1000′ long and 445′ wide) was a center of creative activity for the greatest painters, sculptors, and architects of the time, and one should not overlook the most skillful stonemasons in the Greek world. The ample funds of the Delian Treasury, which were entrusted to Athens for military preparedness, were lavished on an Athenian building project supposedly dedicated to the goddess Athena, but in reality devoted to proclaiming the power and glory of Athens.

Built under the direction of architects Iktinus (ik–TIE–nus) and Kallikrates (ka–LIK–kra–teas), the temple of Athena Parthenos (Parthenon; fig. 3.44) was created as the crowning glory of the akropolis, complete with sculptural reliefs and a massive gold and ivory statue of Athena created by Pheidias. Although it is the largest Doric temple ever built on the Greek mainland, with refinements so subtle that the building symbolized the Periklean ideal of "beauty in simplicity," its basic plan was still that of the sixth-century archaic temple. Even though they invented nothing new, its architects clearly saw just how refined the temple form could be. Despite the great size (228′ × 101′ with 34′ columns) this was still a rectangular box surrounded by columns and surmounted by a triangular prism. A temple in which the Doric order achieved perfection, the Parthenon is so unified and harmonious that its immense size is belied by its lightly poised serenity.

That the building has virtually no straight lines or true right angles is at first surprising. By using slight deviations from mathematical regularity, presumably to correct optical distortions, the architects succeeded in creating a building that gave the appearance of mathematical precision. This bothered Plato, who could not reconcile the discrepancy between perfection and the illusion of perfection that was projected by the masterful design.

Thus the cella walls lean slightly inwards; the stylobate rises 4¼″ at the center of the 228′ sides (fig. 3.45) and 2¾″ at the center of the other two sides. All columns lean inward about 2½″, except the corner columns, which lean diagonally, so much so that if they were extended, all four would meet at a point about a mile above the temple. Echoing the stylobate, the cornice, frieze, and architrave are all slightly higher in the center. The schematic drawing of some of the refinements (fig. 3.46) seems strange indeed, but through exaggeration it reflects these subtleties.

Further adjustments are found in the corner columns, each of which is of greater diameter and about two feet closer to its neighbors than the other columns. It is probable that these deviations were adopted so that the corner columns, which are seen most directly against the sky, would seem more supportive. Practically all Doric buildings show some signs of "correction," for the Doric column always had a slight outward curve called the entasis. In early Doric temples the entasis looks like a bulge about a third of the way up the column; but with the entire 34′ Parthenon column, the deviation from a straight line is only 11/16″. Established as a convention long before, fluted Doric columns were not only visually attractive

Figure 3.45 Stereobate and stylobate, north side of the Parthenon.

Figure 3.46 Schematic drawing of Parthenon refinements

Figure 3.47 Reconstruction of east pediment of Parthenon, central section. Akropolis Museum, Athens.

but they also made an optical correction; from a distance smooth-surfaced columns appear to be flat and without sufficient solidity and rigidity to perform support functions.

Adorned with some of the greatest marble carvings of antiquity, the Parthenon was virtually a visual encyclopedia of activities of the gods and of the Athenians themselves. A reconstruction of the east pediment (fig. 3.47) illustrates the story of the miraculous birth of Athena, who has just emerged from the brow of Zeus. All the gods at the center are astir, but Dionysos (fig. 3.48) is just awakening at the left corner as the sun god Apollo drives his chariot onto the scene. At the opposite end, three goddesses (fig. 3.49) are about to hear the good tidings, as Artemis, the moon goddess, begins her nightly travels. Dionysos and the goddesses are freestanding; larger than life size; and

carved in broad, clear planes and sharply delineated lines so that they could be seen from ground level. Whether they were carved by Pheidias or his assistants is of little concern. What is important is that these are masterpieces of monumentalized human form; graceful despite their amplitude; and animated, in the case of the goddesses, by garments that reveal as well as decorate the bodies.

A Parthenon metope depicting the *Combat between a Lapith and a Centaur* (fig. 3.50) is a skillfully executed high relief symbolizing the ascendancy of human ideals over the bestial side of human nature. Detailed studies of the ninety-two outer metopes reveal consistent improvement in quality from the early, rather crude carvings to the exceptional work of later pieces, like the metope of figure 3.50. The stonemasons obviously benefitted from some kind of on-the-job training under the direction of Pheidias.

Figure 3.48 *Dionysos,* from east pediment of Parthenon, ca. 438–432 B.C. British Museum, London. Reproduced by courtesy of the Trustees of the British Museum.

Figure 3.49 Three Goddesses: Hestia, Dione, Aphrodite, from east pediment of Parthenon, ca. 438–432 B.C. British Museum, London. Reproduced by courtesy of the Trustees of the British Museum.

Figure 3.50 *Combat between a Lapith and a Centaur,* metope from the Parthenon, ca. 447–443 B.C. Height 56″. British Museum, London. Reproduced by courtesy of the Trustees of the British Museum.

Figure 3.51 *Horsemen,* from the west frieze of the Parthenon, ca. 440 B.C. Marble, ca. 42″ high. British Museum, London. Reproduced by courtesy of the Trustees of the British Museum.

The inner frieze, about 3¾′ in height and over 500′ in length, ran along the outer walls of the cella. This marble bas-relief[3] depicted the gods and Athenians in the Greater Panathenaea celebration that took place every four years. This contemporary scene portrays a procession carrying a peplos, woven for the occasion, to the statue of Athena in the Parthenon. Apparently at the very moment that the procession is getting underway, the horsemen (fig. 3.51) ready their mounts to escort the singing maidens to the temple. With its six hundred persons and countless horses, this scene depicts but one moment of activity; this is "simultaneous narration," a sculptural version of the classic unities of Greek drama. Probably the most interesting aspect of this frieze is the fact that Athenians, hundreds of them, are depicted, in idealized versions, on a temple frieze, something unthinkable in other cultures of the ancient world. Of the few surviving portrayals of mortal activity on a temple wall, all of them Greek, this is the most significant example. One has only to think of the dark and forbidden recesses of the Temple of Amon-Mut-Khonsu at Luxor (see fig. 3.7) to understand some fundamental differences between the Egyptian and Greek civilizations.

---

3. The degree of projection of the sculpture from the surface is described as high, medium, or *bas* (the French word for low). High relief is almost detached from the surface and a bas-relief (BA–ri–leef) is only slightly raised. Seen from ground level as a bas-relief, the upper portion of the Parthenon frieze actually projected farther from the surface. This was, of course, one more optical refinement.

Figure 3.52 Mnesikles (ne–SEE–kleez), Erechtheion, ca. 421–405 B.C. View from the east. Akropolis, Athens.

Figure 3.53 Porch of the Maidens (view from the southwest), Erechtheion. Akropolis, Athens.

Figure 3.54 Kallikrates, Temple of Athena Nike, ca. 427–424 B.C. Akropolis, Athens.

The complex design of the Erechtheion (AIR–ek–thee–on; fig. 3.52) probably results from two factors: an uneven building site and the legendary contest between Athena and Poseidon. With both gods competing for the guardianship of the city, Poseidon struck a rock on the akropolis with his trident and sea water, symbol of Athenian sea power, gushed forth. Athena then struck the ground with her spear and a full-grown olive tree appeared. Judging olives more important because they were so useful, the other Olympians awarded the city to Athena. The cautious Athenians dedicated shrines to both within the same temple, however, and to cover all bets, named the building after the mythical King Erechtheus who had supposedly lived on the site.

The higher (eastern) level of this graceful Ionic temple was dedicated to Athena, while the lower level (right background) was the sanctuary of Poseidon. Three porticos, each of different dimensions and design, project from three sides. It is the south porch (fig. 3.53) with its six caryatids (karry–AT–ids; female figures used as columns) that is best known. Only 10′ × 15′, the porch, which is actually a veranda, has an architrave supported by young women whose drapery suggests the fluting of columns. They are grouped as if in a procession toward the Parthenon, with three figures on one side slightly bending their right legs and those on the other side bending their left legs to give the appearance of life and animation. All columns suggest physical strain; despite the individual beauty of these figures, substituting a human form for a supporting column tends to place an undue burden on our imagination. One might characterize these caryatids as an excellent solution for a less than satisfactory idea. The caryatid to the right of the figure on the left corner is a copy of the figure Lord Elgin carried off to England (along with considerable booty from the Parthenon and other buildings) as part of a questionable attempt to "save" Greek art.[4] Compounding the irony, all of the figures have now been moved to a protected environment and replaced with fiberglass copies, including a copy of the copy. Air pollution, rather than the Turks or an English lord, is the latest and most deadly threat to the Athenian akropolis.

A classic example of architectural unity, the exquisite Temple of Athena Nike (fig. 3.54) is a tiny building (17′9″ × 26′10″) of pentelic marble. Though architecture is usually defined as the art of enclosing space, Greek temples embody more than this. Each temple was designed as a series of receding planes

---

4. See Theodore Vrettos' *A Shadow of Magnitude; The Acquisition of the Elgin Marbles* (1974) about which Lawrence Durrell wrote, "So thoroughly researched and energetically executed, this is the first portrait in depth of that ignoble monomaniac Lord Elgin who lives in history as the man who despoiled the Parthenon." The Greek government has repeatedly pressed for the return of the Elgin Marbles.

Figure 3.55 Temple of Poseidon, ca. 440 B.C., Sounion.

from steps to columns to cella wall, with temple reliefs in comparable planes from surface to deepest recesses. Both a strongly defined form and a four-sided sculptural relief, the Greek temple is architectural but it is also a large sculptural composition. Rather than just enclosing space the temple also fills space, and none any better than the elegant temple of Nike, goddess of victory. Originally the temple housed a statue of the victory goddess with her wings clipped so that she could never leave Athens. Some twenty years after the completion of the building (in 404 B.C.) Athens fell to Sparta, never again to regain her political and military supremacy. Demolished by the Turks in the eighteenth century in order to build a fort, the Temple of Athena Nike was later reconstructed by retrieving the stone from the demolished fort. That the temple dedicated to the victory goddess could be reconstituted in something like its original form symbolizes the enduring quality of Athenian culture, which has survived invasions by Persians, Spartans, Romans, Venetians, Turks, Italians, and Germans.

The Classical style of the Golden Age, or Age of Perikles, was manifested not only in all the visual arts, and in literature, philosophy, music, drama, and dance but also in the finely balanced education and training of mind and body of Athenian citizens. Whenever the word *classical* is used, the basic reference point is Athens during the second half of the fifth century B.C., though the word may also be used to mean the best of its kind in any style. Whether considering original artworks, Roman copies, or even their ruined temples, we can feel some of the maturity, poise, and confidence of the Golden Age. Consider, for example, the Temple of Poseidon (fig. 3.55). Built to honor the god of the sea in grateful acknowledgement of the epochal victory at Salamis, the Doric temple is situated high on the promontory of Cape Sounion, where it replaced an earlier temple destroyed by the Persians. With 20′ columns that are considerably more slender than those of the Parthenon, the temple is poised lightly and elegantly, as if still awaiting the triumphant return of Theseus after the slaying of the dreaded Minotaur. Totally unlike ponderous Egyptian temples that attempt to fill desert landscapes, the Temple of Poseidon is more like a crown jewel placed, just so, on the tip of the hill.

Figure 3.56 Akhilleus Painter, white-ground lekythos (detail): "Muse on Mount Helicon," ca. 440–430 B.C. Height of vase 14½″. Staatliche Antikensammlungen und Glyptothek, Munich.

Vase painters of this period were just as skilled as the architects and sculptors, and their best work can, in fact, be favorably compared with paintings by Renaissance artists. Though red-figure paintings were preferred by most artists (see figs. 4.4, 4.5, and 4.6), some favored using a variety of colors on a white background in what is called the *white-ground* technique. Before being fired in the kiln, a white clay was added in the area to be decorated and the painting was done after firing. Though they were subject to fading because the color was not baked into the vase as in the red-figure technique, white-ground paintings are similar to easel paintings, but with the additional complication of working on curved surfaces. Some artists chose the permanency of red-figure painting, while others, like the Akhilleus Painter (fig. 3.56), favored the color range of white-ground decorations. Though he did not sign his work, the distinctive style of the Akhilleus Painter has been recognized in over two hundred vase paintings. Here, sitting quietly on the sacred mountain of the muses, Polyhymnia, the muse of solemn hymn and religious dance, is reverently plucking her seven-string kithara. Lightly decorated at top and bottom, the vase has

Figure 3.57 *Victory Untying Her Sandal,* from the parapet of the Temple of Athena Nike, ca. 410 B.C. Marble, height 42″. Akropolis Museum, Athens.

Figure 3.58 Paionios, *Nike,* ca. 421 B.C. Marble, height 76¾″ (85″ including base). Archeological Museum, Olympia.

nothing to draw our attention from the solitary figure with a lone bird at her feet. Through graceful line and harmonious composition we see a superb example of the Classical style.

In the relief of *Victory Untying Her Sandal* (fig. 3.57), we have a fine illustration of the celebrated wet drapery effect of Greek sculpture. Sculptors apparently dipped a filmy material in a starchlike substance, draped the female model, and arranged the folds for best artistic effect. Portrayed here is a rather awkward human action, but one accomplished so gracefully that the work is a marvel of softly flowing lines in a perfectly balanced design.

In a strikingly different portrait of Nike (fig. 3.58), we see the goddess descending so rapidly from the sky that the startled eagle has not yet made its escape. Wearing the diaphanous Ionic himation, Nike is moving so fast that the material covering her body is almost like a second skin. Originally balanced by a pair of large wings, the material billowing out behind is so skillfully carved that it appears to be undulating drapery rather than hard marble. Note also the exceptional skill that was used to create the illusion of an airborne figure not yet in contact with the ground. Discovered at Olympia in 1875, this is one of the all-too-scarce original marbles from the Periklean Age.

A sculptured gravestone known as the *Stele* (STEE–lee) *of Hegesco* (fig. 3.59) shows a serving

maid offering her seated mistress, the deceased who is commemorated, a casket of jewels. Common to Greek sculpture of the classical period is the serenity of facial expressions, whether the subjects are depicted as participating in a procession, a battle, or a meeting of the gods. Moreover, note that the heads of the standing servant and seated mistress are close to the same level; this same convention may also be noted in the Parthenon frieze (see fig. 3.51) whether the participants are standing, sitting, or riding horses. This isocephalic (I–so–se–FALL–ik) convention, that is, the tradition of keeping all heads on approximately the same level, brings to Greek relief art of the Classical period exceptional clarity; it is so subtly done that one's sense of rightness remains undisturbed.

With the defeat of Athens by Sparta in 404 B.C. the Golden Age came to an end. That both Sophokles and Euripides died at about the same time further marked the end of an era. Throughout the following century, until the death of Alexander in 323 B.C., the classical tradition was maintained, though in a somewhat more theatrical manner. Greek artists prided themselves on adhering to the high standards of the preceding century; although Athens no longer ruled the seas, it was still the center of the artistic world.

The more pleasing and personal qualities of Late Classical sculpture and the superbly executed naturalism are due, in large part, to Praxiteles (prax–SIT–uh–leas) of Athens, the most celebrated of all ancient Greek sculptors. In his *Hermes with the Infant Dionysos* (fig. 3.60) we see an example of the

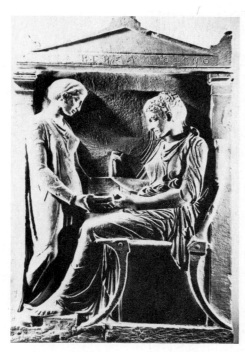

Figure 3.59 *Stele of Hegesco,* ca. 400–390 B.C. Marble grave-relief, height 58½". National Archeological Museum, Athens.

Figure 3.60 Praxiteles, *Hermes with the Infant Dionysos.* Marble copy of probable bronze original of ca. 340 B.C., height 73". Archeological Museum, Olympia.

Figure 3.61 Praxiteles, *Aphrodite of Knidos.* Roman marble copy of marble original of ca. 350 B.C., height 80". Vatican Museums, Rome.

artist's exceptional skill in working marble. Praxiteles was apparently among the first to exploit the shimmering, translucent quality of marble. There are no sharp angles; everything is smooth, rounded, polished. Compare, for example, the striking clarity of the *Doryphoros* (fig. 3.35) with the softly sensuous treatment of the *Hermes*. Slimmer and certainly more relaxed, the *Hermes* looks positively decadent compared with the earnest Spear Bearer. Among today's experts the argument continues as to the correct attribution of the *Hermes*. Long regarded as the sole surviving original by Praxiteles, the current consensus is that this lovely sculpture is most likely a Hellenistic copy of what was possibly a bronze original. The head of the infant is proportionately too small and the rumpled drapery is inconsistent with the Late Classical style. The most telling discrepancy, however, is the marble bar that braces the hip of Hermes. Greek sculptors usually designed their works to be self-supporting, but a marble copy of an inherently strong bronze original would need to be braced. The ongoing controversy over the 2500-year-old work points up the cogent definition of culture as what remains after the society that created it has vanished.

Definitely a copy, and quite a good one, the *Aphrodite of Knidos* by Praxiteles (fig. 3.61) is a revolutionary work. The single most popular statue in all antiquity, the *Aphrodite* was lavishly praised by the Roman historian Pliny (XXXVI, 20) as the finest statue in the world, so marvelous that it was placed in a shrine to be universally admired. (Pliny was equally enthusiastic about the Laokoön—fig. 3.69—and called *it* the finest sculpture in the world.) Abandoning the traditional concept of a figure occupying a rectangular space, Praxiteles designed a slender goddess with sinuous lines rising all the way from her feet to the quizzical tilt of her head. The slight outward lean of the right leg increases the sensuous curvature of the right hip. Echoing the swelling curve of the hip, the left leg is flexed so that the thighs are pressed gently together with the knees nearly touching. From the knees—the narrowest part of the composition—the figure ascends in an hourglass configuration to the slightly startled reaction of a woman surprised in the act of bathing. In line, pose, proportion, and structure Praxiteles has created an incomparable idealization of femininity, the essence of womanhood. It should be noted that although nude males were portrayed in a variety of activities, Greek artists invariably depicted women in normal situations that justified nudity: bathing, making love, functioning as flute girls, or as hetairai.

Lysippos, who was sculptor for the court of Alexander the Great, was probably the most revolutionary artist of the Late Classical period. His *Apoxyomenos* (apox–e–o–MAY–nos) in figure 3.62 was as important for the fourth century as the *Doryphoros* of Polykleitos (fig. 3.35) was for the fifth century; both works established new sculptural canons. Departing from the canon of Polykleitos, Lysippos introduced a new system of proportions in which the head was smaller, the body taller and more slender, and the limbs lithe and long. Using an **S**-shaped tool called a strigil, the athlete is scraping oil, dust, and sweat from his body, a standard procedure at the conclusion of athletic contests. Utilizing the space in front of the body, the extended arms break through the invisible barrier of the frontal plane, violating a convention dating back to the art of Egypt's Old Kingdom. There is a new sense of movement with trunk, head, and limbs turned in different directions; this is sculpture conceived, executed, and meant to be viewed in the round—all 360 degrees. As epitomized in the *Apoxyomenos,* these revolutionary ideas were not to be fully understood until the Italian Renaissance some seventeen centuries later.

Hellenistic Period, 323–30 B.C.

Symbolized by the death of Alexander, the long and enormously productive classical age had come to an end. Artists were no longer concerned with idealized portraits and classical harmony, but instead became increasingly interested in actual appearances and in the infinite varieties of human nature and experience.

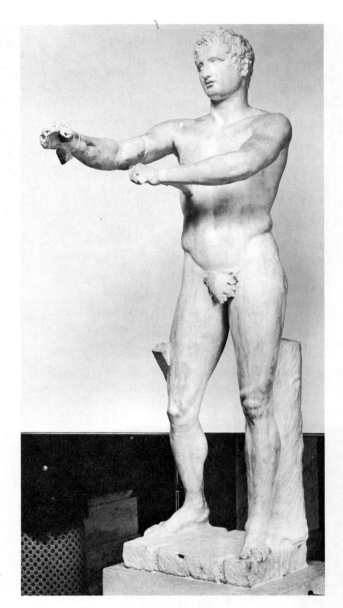

Figure 3.62 Lysippos, *Apoxyomenos (Scraper).* Roman marble copy of a bronze original of ca. 330 B.C., height 6'9''. Vatican Museums, Rome.

In the midst of the rapid disintegration of the Alexandrian empire, the emphasis was upon basic survival in a world beset by constant sectional strife. Sometimes described as decadent, Hellenistic art did indeed include banalities, trivialities, pathos, and empty virtuosity. Greek genius was not yet exhausted, however, for the age also saw the production of exceptional works of art that were no less admirable than those of the classical era but were certainly different.

A Celtic tribe that ravaged Asia Minor until subdued by Attalos I of Pergamon, the Gauls were immortalized in the remarkable figure of *The Dying Gaul* (fig. 3.63). Also known as the *Dying Trumpeter* because of the discarded battle trumpet in the right

Figure 3.63 *The Dying Gaul.* Roman marble copy of bronze original from Pergamon, ca. 230–220 B.C. Life-size. Capitoline Museum, Rome.

foreground, the hair, facial features, and ornamental collar about the neck realistically convey the idea of a Gallic tribesman. The figure, however, is in the heroic Greek tradition of the nude warrior; and the treatment of the vanquished barbarian is sympathetic, portraying a certain poignant nobility as the dying man braces his right arm against the ground in a futile effort to ward off an ignoble death.

Genre sculptures—works depicting everyday activities—were produced by the thousands for what today would be called a mass market. Sometimes charming, more often sentimental, favorite subjects were frisky cupids, children at play, cute children playing with adorable animals, and the like. Typical of these popular knickknacks is the *Child with a Goose*, quite charming in its own way but a far cry from the classical tradition.

At the other extreme is the *Nike of Samothrace* (fig. 3.64), not only one of the most dramatic and compelling works ever created but a prime example of the continuing power of classical themes. Attributed to Pythokritos (py–THOCK–ri–toss) and erected in a sanctuary on Rhodes in honor of a naval victory over King Antiochus III of Syria, Victory is portrayed at the moment of alighting on the symbolic prow of a ship. With her great wings still extended, she is moving into a wind that becomes a tangible presence as it shapes the flowing draperies into deep diagonal folds, carrying our eyes restlessly over the entire surface. Victory, who is aptly characterized as poetry in motion, communicates both the immediacy of the moment and a feeling for ongoing action in a pervasive atmosphere of wind and sea.

One of the wonders of the ancient world, the great Altar of Zeus (fig. 3.65), was built by the son and successor of Attalos I to commemorate his father's military victories. Even though it was designed as an Ionic structure for a site in Ionia, there is none of the delicacy of the classic Ionic style. With a base 100' square, this truly monumental altar is intended to impress

Figure 3.64 Pythokritos of Rhodes, *Nike of Samothrace,* ca. 190 B.C. Marble, height 8'. The Louvre, Paris.

rather than inspire. The immense frieze around the base is over 400' long and 7–8' high. Using the traditional Greek device of portraying actual historical events in mythological terms, this is a highly emotional and dramatic work. Here is a world of giants, an exaggeration of physical and emotional force that, in its own way, accomplishes its goals fully as well as the classic Parthenon frieze (see fig. 3.51). A comparison of the two friezes clearly defines the significant differences between the Classical and Hellenistic styles.

Figure 3.65 Altar of Zeus, west front, from Pergamon, ca. 180 B.C. (restored). Berlin State Museums.

Figure 3.66 Cossutius, Temple of the Olympian Zeus, ca. 174 B.C.–A.D. 131, Athens.

Figure 3.67 Signed by . . . andros of Antioch on the Maeander, *Aphrodite of Melos,* ca. 120 B.C. Marble, height 80″. The Louvre, Paris.

As dramatic as the Altar of Zeus and of equally monumental proportions, Hellenistic public buildings stressed sheer size over classic restraint and harmonious proportions. Even in the scanty remains of the Temple of the Olympian Zeus (fig. 3.66) one can detect some of the grandeur of a temple that originally had 104 columns over 56′ in height. Built in the Corinthian order and entirely of pentelic marble, the temple measured 130′ × 340′, as compared with the 101′ × 228′ dimensions of the Parthenon. In view of the Roman preference for the ornate Corinthian order, it is fitting that this architect was of Italic origin and that the grandiose project was completed by the Roman Emperor Hadrian.

The *Aphrodite of Melos* (fig. 3.67), formerly known by her Roman name of *Venus de Milo* and once highly praised, is a fleshy counterpart of the three goddesses from the Parthenon pediment (see fig. 3.49). She was once a fixture in pretentious Victorian parlors of the past century, usually cast in plaster and with a clock

Figure 3.68 *Portrait Head,* from Delos, ca. 80 B.C. Bronze, height 12¾″. National Archeological Museum, Athens.

Figure 3.69 Hagesandros, Polydoros, and Athenodoros of Rhodes, *Laokoön and His Sons,* 1st century A.D. Marble, height 8′. Vatican Museums, Rome.

in her tummy. Drawing more attention than her body, the abundant fabric and heavy folds of her gown demonstrate the awkwardness of a clothes-falling-off-a-figure motif.

The bronze head from Delos (fig. 3.68), originally part of a full-length statue, is a penetrating study of an apparently unhappy, fleshy-faced man who seems to be overwhelmed by doubt and anxiety. Though by no means limited to the Hellenistic age, this very private portrait seems to epitomize the predicament of helpless individuals in a chaotic and often violent world. A comparison of this face with that of the *Doryphoros* (see fig. 3.35) sums it up; the Golden Age has receded to the distant past.

The *Laokoön and His Sons* (lay–OK–o–on; fig. 3.69) is an extravagantly dramatic version of the fate of the Trojan priest. Supposedly punished by Poseidon's sea serpents because he warned his people of the Trojan horse strategy, the three Trojans writhe and struggle, their faces distorted with terror. Despite his powerful muscles the priest is helpless before the power of the gods. When this work was discovered during the High Renaissance (in 1506), its impressive virtuosity made an enormous impression on Michelangelo and other Renaissance artists. It is quite possible that the *Laokoön* was imported by the Romans because it represented an important episode in pre-Roman history. Supposedly forewarned of the fall of Troy by the punishment of the priest, Aeneas escaped from Troy to fulfill his destiny as the legendary founder of mighty Rome.

The Legacy of Greece

The Greeks of antiquity established the foundation for the development of Western art. During a cultural epoch of approximately a thousand years, they developed in many media a viable, complex art that changed constantly but generally in a rational and humanistic direction. Their achievements were by no means restricted to the sculpture, architecture, reliefs, and pottery and vase painting discussed in the limited space in this chapter. They also excelled in jewelry, coins, engraved gems, decorative metalwork, painting and mosaics, furniture, textiles, and glassware. When their contributions in philosophy, music, and the literary arts are added to this, we see a marvelously rounded culture. They established standards that serve as thesis or antithesis for contemporary judgments and achievements throughout our cultural life.

A skeptical, resilient, and frequently cantankerous people, the Greeks respected excellence and despised mediocrity. Constantly seeking an understanding of the world and everything in it, they not only asked "Why?" but they also asked "Why not?" And they expected sane, reasonable, and logical answers. There has never been anyone else quite like them.

4

Music in Greek Life and Thought

Music was a requisite for the good life in ancient Greece. The education of the young men of Athens was not complete without extensive instruction in the ethical qualities of music with approximately equal time devoted to the performance of music. Further, there must be instruction in gymnastics roughly equal to the time and effort expended on music. The question Glaucon posed for Sokrates was rhetorical: "After music our youth are to be educated by gymnastics?" For the record the Sokratic reply was a terse "Certainly."

The balanced regimen of music and gymnastics encouraged a harmonious adjustment of body and soul: a sound mind in a healthy body. According to Plato, overemphasizing gymnastics made men "more brutal than they should be." Conversely, overstressing music made men "softer than is good for them."

The Greek word for music encompassed at least five different meanings. Music was:

1. The art of singing and playing music, an art enjoyed by all free men. Public performance, however, was relegated to professionals, who were much less esteemed than educated amateurs.
2. "Of the muses," thus including all of the arts presided over by the nine muses. Misinterpretation of this particular reference has led to the false assumption that music was merely a minor art.
3. Music for the purpose of education; that is, performing and listening to music as a vital part of the ethical training necessary to inculcate virtue and "sobriety in the soul" (Plato). This is the *ethos* of music that occupied such a prominent place in Greek philosophy.
4. The study of the scientific basis of music with the attendant emphasis upon acoustics and mathematics.
5. Music and mathematics as a key to understanding the harmony of the universe: the Pythagorean "music of the spheres."

All free Athenian males were involved in music performance and music education. Scientists and speculative thinkers were concerned with the scientific, mathematical, and metaphysical implications of music.

Figure 4.1 Lyre Player "The Boston Throne" ca. 470–450 B.C. Three-sided marble relief, height 38″. H. L. Pierce Fund. Courtesy, Museum of Fine Arts, Boston. The lyre was always played from a sitting position (also see fig. 4.4).

Figure 4.2 Aulos Player of the Ludovisi Throne, ca. 460 B.C. Museo della Terme, Rome. One of the few female nudes from the Classical period, this lovely work is also notable for the relaxed and casual pose. Unlike the lyre, the aulos could be played standing or sitting.

Musical Instruments

The principal instruments were the *lyre,* a larger version of the lyre called the *kithara,* and the *aulos* (see table 4.1). According to mythology the infant Hermes, son of Zeus, killed a turtle and strung gut strings across the hollow shell. That the strings were made from intestines of oxen stolen from his brother Apollo complicated the situation. Hermes craftily avoided further trouble by permitting Apollo to play his lyre. Thus the beginning of the legendary lyre and with it the lyre-playing tradition of the cult of Apollo (fig. 4.1).

The seat of the Apollonian cult was the island of Delos and subsequently Delphi. The myths extol the virtues of the early musical life of the Greek mainland untouched by alien influences. Marvelous were the deeds of heroes and of divinely endowed musicians such as Orpheus, Amphion, Musaeus, and others, all with names connected with ancient tribes in the northern part of the mainland.

As the tribes migrated they carried their music with them. The Dorians moved as far south as Crete, the Aeolians settled in the eastern Aegean, and the Ionians moved from the west to the east central mainland and to Asia Minor.

The Ionians brought with them their music and their national instrument, the lyre. The influence of Oriental elements led to a synthesis of the two cultures which, in turn, led to the founding of Greek classical music, poetry, and dance. Mythology, characteristically, depicts the Ionian migration by relating how Orpheus accidentally dropped his lyre, which drifted eastward across the Aegean to the island of Lesbos.

The Near East produced the other national instrument, the reed pipe, or aulos (fig. 4.2). The inventors of this pungent-toned instrument came from Phrygia in Asia Minor. The aulos was associated with the Phrygian mode[1] or scale and with the cult of Dionysos. The lyre became associated with the Dorian mode or scale and with the Apollonian cult.

There was a notable conflict between the cult of the two instruments. The lyre was not fully accepted in the East, possibly because its tone quality was too delicate when compared with the nasal quality of the aulos. Legend recounts the musical competition between Olen the Lycian on the lyre and Olympos the Phrygian on the aulos. The results of that contest were inconclusive, indicating that the competing instruments attained a state of parity. The whole of Greek musical culture reflected this kind of balance of power between the Apollonian lyre and the Dionysian aulos, that is, the intellect versus the passions.

The earliest musicians were apparently the blind singers who performed the Homeric epics. Greek legends abound with accounts of singers who foolishly persisted in challenging the gods. Thamyris was blinded by the muses because of his boasting; the blind singer Tiresias (cf. Sophokles' *Oedipus*) had

---

1. An approximation of the Phrygian mode can be made by playing the white notes on the piano from *d* to the next *d* above or below. The Dorian mode is found from *e* to *e* on the white notes.

Table 4.1. Greek Musical Instruments

Instrument	Lyre	Kithara	Aulos
Basic form			
Tone production	string instrument	string instrument	wind instrument
Played	plucking	plucking	blowing through double reed into twin pipes
Size	small, hand-held	larger than lyre, hand-held	small, hand-held
Number of strings or air columns	usually seven strings	usually eleven strings	two pipes with up to eleven tone holes
Performance by	amateurs (usually aristocrats)	professional musicians	professionals and amateurs
Function	primarily to accompany solo songs	accompany solo and group singing	solo instrument and accompany group singing
Location	home, school	social and public gatherings	plays, orgiastic religious ceremonies, elegies
Tone quality	light, delicate, serene	louder than lyre but still delicate	loud, nasal, penetrating
Ethos (ethical quality)	intellectual, Dorian, Apollonian	intellectual, Dorian, Apollonian	emotional, Phrygian, Dionysian

suffered the same penalty by revealing things men should not know; Misenis lost a musical contest to the sea gods and was drowned in the Aegean. The satyr Marsyas was a spectacular loser. First, he picked up the aulos that Athena had discarded because she felt she looked undignified while playing it. She had Marsyas beaten for his impudence. Failing to take the celestial hint, he then challenged Apollo to a playing contest, for which presumption he was flayed alive (fig. 4.3).

The most famous singer-poet was Orpheus, reputedly the son of Apollo and Calliope. The powers attributed to Orpheus were staggering. In order to rescue Eurydice (you–RID–uh–sea), he enchanted the underworld with his lyre (fig. 4.4). He cast spells on all aspects of nature, and he was credited with inventing poetic meter and even the alphabet. The last attribute may refer to the fact that the Greeks used an elaborate musical notation based on their alphabet.

The earliest historical figure to emerge from the legendary past personified by the mythical Olympos is the kithara-player, Terpander of Lesbos (ca. 675

Figure 4.3 *Apollo and Marsyas,* marble relief from Manitinea, ca. 400–350 B.C. Width, ca. 4'. From the workshop of Praxiteles. National Archeological Museum, Athens. Marsyas is on the right, frantically playing, while a slave waits patiently with a knife. Holding a kithara, Apollo sits serenely at the left, waiting to execute the satyr for his hubris.

Figure 4.4 Orpheus Painter, red-figure krater (detail): "Orpheus Among the Thracians," ca. 440 B.C. Antikenmuseum Staatliche Museen Preussischer Kulturbesitz, Berlin. The power of Orpheus's music obviously failed to charm the vulgar Thracians. They murdered him, which tends to confirm the Greek thesis that their music was too sophisticated for barbarians to appreciate.

B.C.). His musical powers were so great that he was ordered to Sparta by the Delphic Oracle to help quell dissension within the state. As the first known musician, Terpander is regarded as the founder of Greek classical music.

Terpander's successors competed in the Olympic Games (776 B.C.–A.D. 393) in poetry and music. They sang variations on the *nomos* (nomos = law), or sung strains using fundamental melodic and rhythmic phrases. In his *Laws,* Plato described distinct classes of songs, such as kitharodic nomes, hymns, dirges, paeans, and dithyrambs, including the information that each type of song had its own special rules that even precluded the interchange of poetic texts. Terpander was credited with increasing the sections of the kitharodic nomes to the hallowed number of seven (cf. the seven-stringed lyre, the seven gates of Thebes and the—at that time—seven muses).

Archilochos (are–ki–LOW–kos) of Paros, another seventh-century musician, advanced the art of lyric music—music sung to the lyre—by introducing rhythmic variety. Much of his inspiration may have been drawn from folk song. Folk art was apparently widespread because literary sources mention a variety of work songs: songs for stamping barley, treading grapes, throwing pots, spinning wool; songs for watchmen, shepherds, drawers of water, and makers of rope.

The lyric works of the poet-musicians—Sappho, Alkaios, and Anakreon—were probably inspired by folk influences, as were many of the works performed at the great contests in Olympia and Delphi. Festival performances, however, were not limited to the lyre. At the Pythian Games at Delphi in 586 B.C., Sakadas of Argos won a celebrated victory with his *Nomos Pythikos* (*Pythian Nome*) for the aulos, depicting Apollo's triumph over the Python. While most nomes were written in praise of Apollo, the poet-musician

Pindar won a measure of fame for odes written in praise of victorious athletes.

From the Homeric age until the decline of Greek civilization, the lyre was the preferred instrument for the performance of epic and lyric poetry. The reedy and colorful aulos was used to accompany elegies and dramatic choruses.

Poetry and Music

When the arts of poetry and music were combined, which was the usual practice, the text dominated the music. The instruments were always designated as participants. Thus, *kitharodia* meant singing with the accompaniment of the kithara and *aulodia* meant singing with aulos accompaniment.

The principal musical-poetic type of composition was the *nomos,* which held a position analogous to the *epos* in literature. The nome was probably a melody originally, or perhaps a whole composition, but it later developed into a rather fixed style of words and music.

The nome is best understood by comparing it with architecture. A Doric temple, for example, is a kind of architectural nome. Architects were bound to a basic scheme and ornamentation called Doric but could assert their individuality by different organizations of the same elements.

The nome was usually associated with the name of one particular master but it was further developed, with certain restrictions, by other musicians without losing its basic melodic profile or rhythmic skeleton. The chief exponents of the nome from the mythic past were Olympos for the aulos nome and Terpander for the kithara nome.

Archilochos (fl. ca. 660 B.C.) must be added as the third major figure in Greek musical history. He instituted technical reforms that had far-reaching effects. Before his time, each note of the music was closely allied with the words. He added all sorts of embellishments that were improvised upon between songs. The musical accompaniment of the nomes followed the text, while instrumental solo playing now took place between the strophes or sections.

Archilochos even had the accompaniment play "dissenting" notes that were not in unison with the melody. These differing notes added considerable complexity to an already intricate musical style limited to three elements of music: melody, rhythm, and tone color. Harmony as we know it was never a part of Greek musical practice.

The profuse theoretical literature of classical antiquity did not deal with the laws of lyric poetry, that is, with rules about the metric structure of lyric verse. For the Greeks the union of lyric poetry and music was so complete that prosody and metrics did not belong to the domain of linguistics and poetry but rather formed part of the musical sciences practiced by the musician-poets.

The illustrious musician-poet (or poet-musician) Sappho was born on the Aegean island of Lesbos around 630 B.C. and lived most of her long life there. At a time when Solon was legislating in Athens and

Jeremiah was prophesying in Palestine, she was at the height of her fame and, moreover, fully aware of her reputation:

The Muses have made me happy
And worthy of the world's envy,
So that even beyond death
I shall be remembered.

Celebrated in both the Greek and Roman worlds, her poems were preserved until the third century A.D. by Alexandrian editors but were later almost totally destroyed along with other so-called pagan literature. The three surviving poems and numerous fragments remain to testify to the beauty of her lyric poetry, that is, poetry sung to the delicate sounds of the lyre.

Lead off, my lyre,
And we shall sing together.

Revolving mostly around Aphrodite, Sappho's themes focus on her passions and jealousies, but there are references to two brothers and to her daughter Kleïs. Though knowledge of her personal life is scanty, Sappho certainly enjoyed the social and domestic freedom of a society in which highly educated women mixed freely with men as their equals. Not confined to a haremlike existence like Ionian women or subject to a military discipline like the Dorians of Sparta, Aeolian women were devoted to the arts of beauty, especially poetry and music (fig. 4.5).

In the following complete poem, Sappho appeals to Aphrodite to help her win the affections of a reluctant girl. Aphrodite's response is good-natured but a bit impatient; Sappho has made this kind of request before and she will certainly make it again. Moreover, as Aphrodite points out, the girl refuses your gifts today but you will refuse hers tomorrow.

God's wildering daughter deathless Aphródita,
A whittled perplexity your bright abstruse chair,
With heartbreak, lady, and breathlessness
Tame not my heart.

But come down to me, as you came before,
For if ever I cried, and you heard and came,
Come now, of all times, leaving
Your father's golden house

In that chariot pulled by sparrows reined and bitted,
Swift in their flying, a quick blur aquiver,
Beautiful, high. They drew you across steep air
Down to the black earth;

Fast they came, and you behind them, O
Hilarious heart, your face all laughter,
Asking, What troubles you this time, why again
Do you call me down?

Asking, In your wild heart, who now
Must you have? Who is she that persuasion
Fetch her, enlist her, and put her into bounden love?
Sappho, who does you wrong?

If she balks, I promise, soon she'll chase,
If she's turned from gifts, now she'll give them.
And if she does not love you, she will love,
Helpless, she will love.

Come, then, loose me from cruelties.
Give my tethered heart its full desire.
Fulfill, and, come, lock your shield with mine
Throughout the siege.

Figure 4.5 "Alkaios and Sappho with Lyres," detail of red-figure vase, ca. 450 B.C. Glyptothek und Museum Antiker Kleinkunst, Munich. Standing as tall as her colleague, the poet Alkaios, Sappho is depicted as a poised and beautiful woman, fully the equal of a male poet-musician.

The next poem is also complete except for the last four words added by the translator. The theme is jealousy, a recital of physical torments brought about by the loved one's interest in conversing with a man. The emotions are strong but recollected in tranquility in carefully chosen words. Translated into Latin by Catullus, this work was praised by Plutarch as "a masterpiece among poems of passionate love."

He seems to be a god, that man
Facing you, who leans to be close,
Smiles, and, alert and glad, listens
To your mellow voice

And quickens in love at your laughter.
That stings my breasts, jolts my heart
If I dare the shock of a glance.
I cannot speak,

My tongue sticks to my dry mouth,
Thin fire spreads beneath my skin,
My eyes cannot see and my aching ears
Roar in their labyrinths.

Chill sweat slides down my body,
I shake, I turn greener than grass.
I am neither living nor dead and cry
From the narrow between.

But endure, even (this grief of love.)

Figure 4.6 "Young Girls Dancing Around the Altar," interior of red-figure bowl, ca. 450 B.C. The Hermitage, Leningrad. Note the elegantly curved chair (a Greek invention) on which the aulos player sits. The kithara player stands at the altar, while the girls circle about in a light and graceful dance. Note also the different hair styles and the variety of dress design and decoration.

The Art of Dance

The third art associated with music and poetry was that of dance. In fact, the three arts were so mutually interconnected that it is difficult to consider any one of them in isolation.

Human beings seem to have always enjoyed dance, and few people appreciated dance more than the ancient Greeks. Greek dance probably began as a form of worship, ritual, witchcraft, enchantment, and sex symbolism in association with fertility rites. Plato believed that dance was a natural expression of emotions and that it might have grown out of the use of gestures to imitate words and phrases.

All of our knowledge of steps and movements is based on the figures on vases, on architectural friezes, and, to some extent, on various writings referring to dance. The dancing figures in Greek art display a variety of design and gesture, but over many centuries certain positions occur consistently. Arm movements were built either upon a straight line of the arm from shoulder to fingertip or upon the angularity of bending the arm at the elbow to form a right angle. The designs could be somewhat curved by increasing the angle at the elbow, by adding a curve at the waist, or both at the same time. The basic design, however, was maintained. The straight lines and curves were normally associated with light and delicate dances (fig. 4.6). The angular designs were used in strongly dramatic dances.

Figure 4.7 Theatre at Epidauros, ca. 350 B.C. Designed by Polykleitos the Younger. This view from the top row shows the great size (13,000 capacity) typical of Greek theatres. Nevertheless, actors and chorus could be understood even from this height.

Dionysian dances were invariably dramatic and frequently frenzied. Dancers sometimes wore the animal skins of the Dionysian cult: bull, fawn, goat, fox, and panther. For the wild mountain dances the dancers carried snakes. The dancers were called Maenads, Thyiades, Bacchantes, and Satyrs.

The four Dionysian festivals held every year influenced everyday Greek life as well as the arts and literature. These festivals included much dancing, sacrificial processions, banquets, choruses conducted by the poets, and, most especially, performances of the tragedies and comedies.

Greek Theatre

Music played an important role in the theatre but the precise nature of that role is not clear. There is no question about the chorus; it performed vocal functions. On occasion, the individual actors sang their lines, and the aulos sounded at various times throughout the play. The aulos was the exclusive instrument for the theatre, never used except as a solo instrument and never replaced by the lyre.

Greek drama was, to a considerable degree, a musical experience and yet hardly comparable to an operatic production. In fact, nothing in our culture compares with the Greek amalgam of choric songs, spoken dialogues, solo songs, and aulos playing. Like other conventions of Greek tragedy—masks, stylized movement and speech, platform shoes—this unique form of theatre must be accepted on its own merits, which according to the Greeks themselves were quite sufficient.

Greek dramatic productions always utilized a circular or semicircular space in front of the stage on which the chorus danced. The theatre at Epidauros (fig. 4.7) exemplifies the classical Greek theatre where the chorus sang and danced in the circular *orkhestra* (from *orkheisthai,* to dance).

Greek plays are no longer performed in their original versions because all of the music has been lost. Over a long period of time, those who copied and recopied the manuscripts began omitting the musical notation because they were unable to read it. As a consequence, the words were transmitted to future generations but the music is gone forever.

Choric passages were an integral part of the plays of Aeschylus and were almost as important throughout the plays of Sophokles and Euripides. Towards the end of classical antiquity, however, tragedies were often performed without the choral parts. The reasons for this diminution of a major musical element are not clear but could be attributed to a decline in musical expertise in the chorus or lack of audience sophistication or both.

The high point of Greek drama, musically speaking, occurred with the plays of Aeschylus. Sophokles was a dramatist with a strong sense of plot and action, while Aeschylus was a musician, a choral lyricist, who composed his words and his music as inseparable parts of the whole. His *Agamemnon* was considered in his time to be a consummate example of tragedy because the two elements of choral song and narrative speech were combined into a powerful artistic unity.

The Doctrine of Ethos

Because music exerted a strong influence on the mood and spirits of the Greeks, the city-state assumed control of music education rather than leave such an important matter in the hands of performing artists. Sparta became the leader in this endeavor with Lycurgus ordering regular, supervised music education. No Spartan, regardless of age, sex, or rank, was to be excluded, and each was to do his or her part to further the moral, social, and political well-being of the state.

The songs to be sung must not offend the spirit of Sparta but rather praise the fatherland and lead to a sense of order, lawfulness, and dignity. The melodies should be in the Dorian mode because this evokes poise, temperance, and simplicity.

In Athens, the champion of music was Solon. All Athenian citizens received musical training until they were thirty, and all could be expected to sing on proper social, political, or religious occasions. Musical training was mandatory and universal but prohibited for slaves because it was considered a mark of nobility and of education reserved for free Athenians.

Plato was, next to Aristoxenus, the greatest writer on music in antiquity. The philosopher saw an analogy between movements of the soul and musical progressions and therefore felt the aim of music must be more than mere amusement; the goal must be harmonic education and perfection of the soul.

The primary role of music was a pedagogical one that implied the building of character and morals. The practice of music was therefore public rather than private, an affair of state rather than of the home. Every melody, rhythm, and instrument had its unique effect on the moral nature of man and therefore upon the morality of the state. Good music promoted the welfare of the state while bad music was harmful to the individual and to society.

The emphasis upon moral imperatives led to the Greek doctrine of ethos, a doctrine that brought order into the domain of music. This doctrine was derived from the effect that music had upon the will. According to the philosophers, music influenced the will in three ways: (1) it could prompt action; (2) it could strengthen character just as, conversely, it could undermine mental health; and (3) it could suspend normal willpower and thus make the person unaware of his actions.

Plato was the most eloquent and powerful exponent of the doctrine of ethos. In the *Republic,* he recognized the balance of music and gymnastics in the education of free men, but he felt that music should precede and dominate gymnastics. Music first enobles the soul, after which the soul should then build up the body.

Plato recommended the consistent practice of music by all generations. The entire male population was to be divided into choruses with a first chorus of boys, a second of men up to the age of thirty, and a third composed of men from thirty to sixty years of age.

The Dorian and Phrygian modes were considered by Plato and Aristotle to be morally superior to the other modes, but given a preference of both philosophers for rigor and austerity the Dorian might be considered superior because it was strong and dignified. Phrygian was ecstatic and religious and exerted a strong influence on the soul. Other modes were, respectively, piercing and suitable for lamentations or intimate and lascivious.

The two national instruments were naturally included in these ethical doctrines. The lyre was restrained and elegant and therefore proper for the performance of Dorian melodies. The aulos was strong and colorful and thus particularly suitable for the emotional intensity of Phrygian melodies.

In the final analysis, the doctrine of ethos, the lyre and the aulos, poetry, dance, drama, and music were all manifestations of the cults of Apollo and Dionysos. The Apollonian virtues of reason and rationality were balanced by the emotional drive of the Dionysian. As realists, the Greeks fully recognized the dualism, as they saw it, of the mind and body. As idealists, they preferred the dominance of the intellect over the passions.

Seikolos Song (A.D. 1st century)[2] Phrygian mode

Phrygian mode

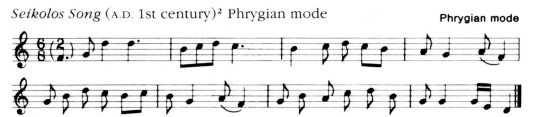

As long as you live, be cheerful; let nothing grieve you. For life is short, and time claims its tribute.

Musical Example

Unfortunately no music has come down to us from the Periklean age. In fact, only a few scattered works and some fragments have survived even from Hellenistic times. At the top of this page, in modern notation, is a brief composition that was found engraved on a tombstone in Asia Minor. Something akin to the sound of Greek music can be heard if the song is played on a guitar.

Summary

The Greeks yearned for reassurance that they lived in a rational and orderly universe in which there were certain eternal truths and, most important, an appropriate place for humanity. They based their rather unique realistic idealism quite heavily upon the multifarious approaches to music in terms of education, emotional communication, the ethical life, applied science, and metaphysics.

A proper balance of instruction in music and gymnastics provided the educational foundation for the citizens of ancient Greece. The study of music included the arts in general and music in particular, with special reference to its scientific basis (acoustics) and the comprehensive theory and tuning of music built on that basis. Music was also expected to further ethical instruction, which was designed to encourage rational behavior and intellectual control.

Through acoustics the Greeks determined the mathematical relationships of sounding bodies and built a theory resting on the conception of the unity and perfection of the vibrating string. This eventually led to the metaphysical concept of a universe that could be comprehended by the intellects of those philosophers who could go beyond the sensory data of the material world.

Music performance was allied with drama, dance, and especially poetry. Principal tone colors were the golden sounds of lyre or kithara (the instruments of Apollo) and the dark and pungent tone of the aulos (the instrument of Dionysos). Rhythm was almost entirely dependent on the rhythm and meter of poetry. Melody was developed to a fine art of subtle nuances. Harmony as such was unknown, but the melodic element has reigned supreme and unmatched by developments in Western music up to the present day.

The specialized art and craft of music notation achieved a notable degree of clarity and precision, almost all of which was lost during the centuries of copying and recopying Greek manuscripts. The precious little Greek music remaining can do no more than provide a tantalizing glimpse of the richness of Greek musical culture. Modern instruments distort beyond all recognition even this hint of past achievements. Only performances on lyre, kithara, and aulos in the original Greek tunings and in conjunction with poetry and drama can actually bring to life the glory that was Greece in the tonal art known as music.

2. T. Reinach, *La Musique Grecque,* 1926, p. 193.

Time Chart for Greek Civilization

Time	Government and Politics	Philosophers-Scientists	Literature and Art
2000 B.C.	Cretan-Minoan culture. About 2600 to 1125 B.C.	Worshippers of earth mother.	Highly sophisticated frescoes. Octopus designs on pots.
1500 B.C.	About 1600 B.C. onward, infiltration of Mycenaean Greeks. Between 1400 and 1125 these people conquered Crete. The heroic age of the Trojan War.	Worshippers of the sky gods— the traditional Greek gods. Spoke a true Greek language.	Gold death masks and other gold ornaments date from this period.
1184 B.C.	Traditional date for the fall of Troy.		
1000 B.C.	Dorian infiltration. Colonization of cities on Ionian coast. "Dark Ages" from about 1050 to 850, merging into Archaic period. Towns ruled by traditions of blood-related clans.		1000 to 700 B.C. Geometric period in Greek art.
900 B.C.	Lycurgus molds Spartan law; two kings; young men in constant military training.		
800 B.C.	Land poverty causes colonization throughout Mediterranean world.		*Iliad* and *Odyssey* of Homer. Hesiod writes *Works and Days* and *Theogony*.
700 B.C.	Revision of Spartan Constitution. Ephors rule.		
650–550 B.C.	Draco's Code: Written law, 621 B.C. Solon (638–558). Cancelled all debt; freed debt-slaves; established graduated income tax. Pisistratus (605–527 B.C.). Redistributed land. Homeric poems form Hellenic cultural tradition.	Ionian Philosophers. a. Thales (water as world-stuff). b. Anaximandros (the Boundless; separating out). c. Anaximenes. Pythagoras (580–500 B.C.). Form found in numerical relationships.	660 to 480 B.C. Archaic period in Greek art. Sappho: female lyric poet. Form of Greek temple fully established. Thespis: original dramatist.
550–500 B.C.	Kleisthenes (ca. 507). Abolished blood clans, substituting political demes. Assembly of all free Athenians. Senate of five hundred members; ten generals administer law.	Herakleitos (535–475 B.C.) "No thing abides." Fire as world-element. Logos or Reason rules change.	
500–450 B.C.	Persian Wars 490–480 B.C. Themistokles (514–449 B.C.) Income from silver mines used for fleet which defeated Persia and made Athens supreme sea power. Delian League founded, later to be transformed into Athenian empire.	The Eleatic Philosophers. a. Parmenides (510–?). b. Zeno (488–?). Nothing changes. Our senses lie to us. Only reason can be trusted. The Mediators: Many elements. Change occurs by combination.	Classical Age (480 B.C.–ca. 350). Charioteer of Delphi. Pindar (522–448). Odes to victors in Olympic Games. Aeschylus (525–456). First tragic dramatist. Celebrated greatness of men and Athens.

Time Chart for Greek Civilization (continued)			
Time	Government and Politics	Philosophers-Scientists	Literature and Art
450-400 B.C.	Perikles (490-429). Ruled in Athens 443-429. The height of Athenian glory. Rebuilt city after Persian Wars.	Demokritos (460?-362?). All things made of atoms which drift through space following no law but necessity. Completely materialistic. Sokrates (469-399). Teacher of Plato.	Sophokles (496-406). Second tragic dramatist. Euripides (484-406). Third tragic dramatist. Herodotos (484-425). Historian of Persian Wars. Parthenon built, 447-438 B.C. Ictinus and Kallikrates, architects. Phidias directed or executed sculpture. Thucydides (471-400). Historian of Peloponnesian Wars.
	Peloponnesian Wars (431-404).		Myron (480-407). Famed sculptor.
		The Sophists. Plato (427-347). Reality lies in the idea or essence of things. Virtues of temperance, courage, wisdom, from which comes highest good, justice.	Polykleitos (460-412). Famed sculptor. Aristophanes (448-380). Writer of comic drama satirizing life of Athens.
400-350 B.C.		Aristotle (384-322). Collected and wrote down all wisdom of his time. Principle of enteleche or purposivity. All things exist as they are, but move into higher forms. There must be a *summum bonum* or highest good.	Praxiteles (390-330). *Hermes.*
	Philip, King of Macedon, 359-336 B.C.	Epicureans—Pleasure the highest good.	Demosthenes (383-322). Orations to arouse Athenians against Philip. Hellenistic art.
350-146 B.C.	Alexander the Great, King of Macedon, 336-323 B.C. Rome conquers Greece 146 B.C.	Stoics—Virtue the highest good.	*Laokoön.* *Aphrodite of Melos.* *Victory of Samothrace.*

Unit **2**

Rome
The International Culture

5

A Thousand Years of Rome

The Roman Virtues

"So great a labor," wrote Virgil, "was it to found the Roman race." And it all began, according to legend, with Romulus and Remus, the twin sons of Mars, god of war, and of Rhea Silvia, daughter of King Numitor. It seems that Amulius, the wicked brother of Numitor, usurped the throne, forced his niece into service as a Vestal Virgin[1] and, to secure his rule against future claimants, ordered the infants placed in a flimsy basket and set adrift on the Tiber River. Rescued and suckled by a she-wolf, the ancient symbol of Rome, they were discovered by a shepherd couple and raised to vigorous manhood (fig. 5.1). Upon learning their true identity, they demonstrated their straightforward Roman nature by immediately killing Amulius and restoring Numitor to the throne. Choosing to ignore an omen of birds that pointed to Romulus as the sole founder of Rome, they resolutely set off to fulfill their destiny: to establish a mighty city on the seven hills by the Tiber. The inevitable quarrel between Romulus, the serious twin, and the light-hearted Remus led to the death of the latter; one version of the story has Remus making fun of a wall constructed by Romulus and falling victim to his brother's self-righteous anger. Subsequently, Romulus gathered an army about him, supplied them with Sabine wives (the Rape of the Sabines), and, to make a long story short, founded Rome right on schedule in 753 B.C. And, much as Moses received the tablets of law on the mountain, he accepted the first constitution from the gods and completed his imperative by becoming the first king of the Romans.

Establishing the Roman Republic was but the first step; the Roman Empire had its own legendary beginning as related by Virgil in his epic poem the *Aeneid*. "It is the nature," boasted Ovid, "of a Roman to do and suffer bravely," and Aeneas was the prototype of the stoic Roman hero.

---

1. Selected daughters of the best families served the goddess Vesta in chastity and obedience. Amulius undoubtedly forced Rhea Silvia into the arms of the goddess so that she would not bear a legitimate heir to the throne.

Figure 5.1 *The Capitoline She-Wolf* depicts Romulus, Remus, and an Etruscan wolf on Capitoline Hill in Rome. The figures were created during the Renaissance, but the wolf is a copy of an Etruscan original. Completing the symbolic representation of the Eternal City, the Colosseum looms in the background, accompanied by an early Christian bell tower and modern lighting fixtures.

After Troy fell to the Greeks under Agamemnon, Aeneas and a loyal band of Trojan warriors escaped the debacle and sailed to the west to confront their destiny. After a mighty storm at sea they found themselves on the coast of North Africa, from whence they made their way to the nearby city of Carthage where Dido (DIE–doe), the queen, received them with full honors while promptly falling in love with Aeneas. As much as stern duty would permit, Aeneas responded in kind while always knowing that, sooner or later, he would have to abandon her in order to fulfill his sacred mission of founding Rome. A despairing Dido chose suicide and, while she lay on her funeral pyre, still hopeful of a last-ditch rescue, Aeneas sailed resolutely to Sicily and finally to the banks of the Tiber. There he fought and defeated Turnus; married Lavinia, the beautiful daughter of King Latinus; and dutifully established "first among cities, the home of gods, golden Rome" (Ausonius).

Rome was fated to be a city of warriors, and of grandeur and glory; the legends of Romulus and Remus and of Aeneas were actually self-fulfilling prophecies. Romulus was descended from the god of war and Aeneas was the progenitor of the stalwart city that would restore Trojan honor by conquering the wily Greeks of the wooden horse. Rome was nourished by the forces of nature, symbolized by the she-wolf, and elevated to maturity by the good people of the soil, the peasant couple who had reared the twins. Rome pursued her imperative by seizing the Sabine lands and women, and established her legitimacy with a god-given constitution.

The Romans saw themselves as destined for world leadership; as Cicero said, "We were born to unite with our fellowmen, and to join in community with the human race." They would triumph because they were a no-nonsense, practical people with the exemplary virtues of thrift, honesty, loyalty, and dedication to hard work. Little interested in abstractions or theory, they had two questions: "Does it work?" and "How can we get the job done?" As Remus discovered, the task of building an illustrious city was no laughing matter, and obligations to the city took precedence over everything else, even passion, a lesson that was lost on the ill-fated Queen of Carthage. Duty to the state, in the final analysis, was the noblest virtue of all.

The legend of Aeneas was apparently based to a great extent on the Etruscans, the mysterious people who appeared in north central Italy during the ninth century B.C. Though the Etruscans used the Greek alphabet, their language was not an Indo-European dialect; according to the Greek historian Herodotos, they were an advanced culture from Asia Minor, a view modern historians have been unable to contradict. Leaving only partially deciphered inscriptions and no body of literature, their origins may never be known.

The Etruscans conquered most of central and northern Italy and ruled Rome itself during the sixth century B.C. From them Rome derived street plans for cities, the idea of the triumphal procession, divinations for foretelling the future, gladiatorial combat, and the masonry arch. But Rome did not accept all things Etruscan. Such Etruscan concerns as life after death, elaborate tombs, and, most especially, a luxurious style of living did not suit sober Roman sensibilities. Moreover, the Romans were so outraged about the nearly equal status of Etruscan women that they accused them of gross promiscuity including copulating in the streets, a judgment that says more about self-righteous Roman males than about Etruscan morality.

Rome came under Greek influence very early, in the eighth century B.C., when Greek colonies were established in southern Italy and Sicily in what the Romans called Magna Graecia. Syracuse, Naples, Paestum, Elea, the Pythagoreans of Krotona, the pleasure-loving Greeks of Sybaris—all were flourishing under the stern gaze of Rome. Throughout their long history the Romans were ambivalent about the Greeks. On one hand they were awed by a civilization so obviously superior, and yet there was hostility, for Greek culture amounted to a reversal of Roman values: literate, artistic, intellectual, sophisticated, delighting always in the pleasurable life, the good life. Roman enmity was not unexpected from an austere, rigid, and self-righteous society that stressed manly virtues, physical prowess, and duty to the state. From this point of view the Greeks were obviously effeminate and decadent.

Landmarks of Roman History

According to still another Roman tradition, the Republic began in 509 B.C. with the expulsion of the Etruscan king, Tarquin the Proud. In the absence of the deposed ruler the Romans were forced to devise a viable government. Never interested in abstractions or political theory, they pragmatically accepted the existing situation and made adjustments when they became necessary. It might be called the let's-try-it-this-way-and-see-if-it-stops-hurting theory of government. What existed after the hurried departure of Tarquin was an oligarchy (government by the few), and so this became the basis of the new state. The oligarchs, the land-owning aristocrats, established a republic with full citizenship reserved for the land-owning class, the patricians (Latin, *pater*, father). The other ninety percent or so of the population, the plebeians (pluh–BEE–uns; Latin *plebs*, the multitude), could neither hold office nor marry into the patrician class. They could make money, however, which meant that political adjustments were inevitable.

The patrician class supplied the executive heads of state, two consuls who governed with full power for one year (except that each had veto power over the other). The consuls appointed patricians to life terms in the three-hundred-member Senate and were, of course, senators themselves. The other legislative body, the Centuriate Assembly, had less power than the Senate but it did elect the consuls and passed on laws submitted to it by the consuls or Senate. From among the exconsuls the Assembly elected two censors who determined eligibility for military service and ruled on the moral qualifications of Senate nominees.

Consuls also served as commanders of the army, which meant that in time of war their mutual veto power could jeopardize the state. Of course the Romans invented another adjustment, a *dictator*, a supreme military commander who received his authority constitutionally and who relinquished it at the end of his six-month term. When Julius Caesar had himself voted dictator for life, his enemies had their worst fears confirmed.

The Roman oligarchy kept the plebeians in an intolerable situation; in effect they were minority stock-holders in a closed corporation. Growing financial power, however, forced the Senate to create the new office of tribune, protector of the people. Later in the century (fifth century B.C.) plebeian forces accused the judges of abusing their power; there were no written laws and thus a made-to-order situation for the party in power. The Roman response was most uncharacteristic; the Senate decreed that the best legal code in existence should be studied, and accordingly sent a commission to Athens to observe the rational legal system of Solon, the notable law-giver. The commission returned to compose the Twelve Tables of Law, at which point Roman conservatism reasserted itself; the adopted laws were fully as harsh as the fierce legal code of Draco of nearly two centuries earlier, the very system the Greeks had thankfully discarded in favor of the humane reforms of Solon.

Accomplished Roman pragmatists never solved the problem of ownership of the land, a failure that had much to do with the demise of the Empire. From the beginning of the Republic absentee landlords controlled a large part of the agricultural market, leaving the working farmer, with his small acreage, struggling to make ends meet. Competition from estate holders plus drought and pestilence forced him into debt and, finally, into a slavery decreed by the severe Twelve Tables. Large estates grew larger, operating with lower overhead because they used war booty slaves. The inexorable price for noncompetitive farmers was bankruptcy. (There were strikingly similar dilemmas in the American South prior to the Civil War.) Even after reforms barring debt-slavery and attempts to redistribute the land, many farmers ended up as urban poor: landless and unemployed. Unable to work on the land their ancestors had farmed for centuries and unfit for employment in a city that relied on slave labor, they became part of the permanent welfare program. It is estimated that by the first century B.C. about eighty percent of Rome's population was either slave laborers or subsisting on "bread and circuses." The welfare program was a failure because, as Plutarch observed, "The man who first ruined the Roman people was he who first gave them treats and gratuities."

Roman talent for organization was most spectacularly evidenced by their awesome military power. Reducing the ponderous 8,000-man phalanx to 3,600 men armed with javelin and short Roman sword, they created a mobile striking force that could march twenty-four miles in five hours, each man carrying a sixty-pound pack. Steely discipline honed a war machine that gave no quarter and asked none.

It has been said that Rome inadvertently became an empire, much as England did in the nineteenth century, but this is doubtful, because Roman conquest clearly became an end in itself during Republican days. The point at which Rome set out to deliberately conquer the world was probably 146 B.C., the final year of the Punic Wars with Carthage (264–146 B.C.). The First Punic War began when Carthage, the powerful Phoenician colony in North Africa, attempted to expand its trading empire in eastern Sicily. Responding to the appeals of their Greek allies, Roman armies found themselves opposing the Carthaginian navy. Hurriedly building their first fighting fleet, the Romans managed to defeat Carthage even though ineptness cost them more ships than did enemy action.

Spain, which had resisted Roman domination for two centuries, became the Carthaginian base for the Second Punic War (218–201 B.C.). Stating that "we will either find a way or make one," the remarkable general Hannibal negotiated the Alps with his elephants and attacked Rome from the rear. Unable to compete with his brilliant tactics, Rome, in desperation, attacked his vulnerable homeland and thus ended Carthage's dominance of the western Mediterranean. The Third Punic War, however, was a different kind of conflict.

Marcus Porcius Cato (Cato the Elder, the Censor; 234–149 B.C.) was a senator, consul, censor, and writer and, even more importantly, one of the prime instigators of the final attack on Carthage. Renowned for his devotion to Roman ideals of simplicity, honesty, courage, ability to endure hardship, rigorous sexual morality, and loyalty to Rome and the family, Cato opposed luxury, cultivation of the arts, and extravagance in any form; he hated the Greeks. He believed all children should be educated in the home and boasted of teaching his son reading, Roman law, and history, and training him in the arts of the javelin, riding, armoured combat, boxing, and swimming. Cato's maxim for slaves was that they should either be working or sleeping and they should be worked to death. Why not? Replacements were abundant and cheap.

Long since recovered from the Second Punic War but no longer a military threat to Rome, Carthage was another kind of target for Cato and other land-hungry Romans who lusted after her fertile soil and abundant harvests. After returning from a fact-finding mission to Carthage, Cato delivered an impassioned speech in the Senate about a resurgent foe that concluded, as did all subsequent speeches and writings, with a call to arms: "Delenda est Carthago!" (Carthage must be destroyed!). In 149 B.C. Rome launched an unprovoked attack upon an astonished and unprepared Carthage.

The conflict with Carthage was described by Rome as preventive warfare, but a more appropriate term would be armed robbery.[2] Carthage was not only captured but demolished and the area sown with salt. The men were killed and the women and children sold into slavery, actions that prompted Tacitus to write, "they make a desert and call it peace." This was in 146 B.C., the fateful year in which another rapacious Roman army administered the same treatment to Corinth, the richest city in Greece. "To the victors belong the spoils" is Ovid's comment, but Seneca wrote: "We are mad, not only individually, but nationally. We check manslaughter and isolated murders; but what of war and the much vaunted crime of slaughtering whole peoples?"

A new and very rich class of war-profiteering contractors, merchants, estate owners, province governors, and generals arose; they were known as *equites* (knights) because they could afford to buy equipment for the cavalry, the most expensive branch of the military. The city bulged with plunder, slaves, and increasing numbers of landless, jobless Romans. Reform was long overdue and, in the 130s and 120s, the patrician brothers Tiberius and Gaius Gracchus attempted to speak for the dispossessed. Although no one knew it then, it was the last opportunity the Senate would have to salvage the integrity of the state. The

Senatorial response was to murder Tiberius and force Gaius into suicide, thus unwittingly setting the stage for one-man rule.

The first of the generals to seize power, Marius, won victories against North African and Celtic tribes, but his reorganization of the army was the critical change. The requirement that Roman citizens had to pay for their own equipment was abolished. With the state furnishing battle gear, full-time professional soldiers began replacing the citizen-soldiers who returned to their peacetime occupations between campaigns. With the beginning of Rome's war against King Mithridates in 88 B.C., Marius emerged from retirement to claim command. When the Senate chose Sulla instead, a bloody civil war ensued, ending in 84 B.C. with Sulla's conquest of Mithridates in Asia Minor. The arrogant and ruthless Pompey, a veteran of Sulla's campaigns, next rose to power and eventually formed a ruling triumvirate with Crassus and Julius Caesar.

Gaius Julius Caesar (ca. 102–44 B.C.)[3] obviously viewed himself as the best-qualified man to rescue the foundering Republic. Not everyone agreed with him, then or now, because Caesar remains one of the most controversial figures in history. A man of enormous energy and even greater ambition, his mastery of power politics can be considered a textbook example on how to take over a state. He enjoyed spectacular success in war, politics, oratory, and statesmanship. Caesar's *Commentaries* on the Gallic campaigns were masterpieces of concise and lucid Latin and his social graces were remarkable. Cicero, who hated him, remarked that he would rather spend an evening conversing with Caesar than in any other way.

In tradition-minded Rome, family background was still important and Caesar had impressive credentials; the Julian *gens* (clan, family) was one of the oldest and most powerful in Rome. The patrician Caesar cast his lot, however, with the popular (democratic) party because he astutely saw the need to identify himself with those who opposed an entrenched and unpopular aristocracy. He passed rapidly through the usual offices, made dazzling orations, and, with a daring speech in defense of the legal rights of a treasonous conspirator, secured in one bold stroke the enmity of the Senate and the adulation of the people. He utilized a public office in Spain to add gloss to his growing reputation while also attempting to reduce some of his staggering debts which, it was said, resulted from his methodical program of paying huge bribes to the right people. He married his daughter to Pompey, the most successful general of the time, and completed an unbeatable combination by forming an alliance with Crassus, the richest man in Rome. The next step was by now inevitable: Caesar,

---

2. "From the Punic Wars on, [Rome's] internal history is that of a successful gang of cutthroats quarreling over the division of the swag." Basil Davenport, *The Portable Roman Reader* (Baltimore, Md.: Penguin Books, 1977), p. 7.

3. All Romans had three names: first name, family name, last name.

Pompey, and Crassus became a ruling coalition called the First Triumvirate, a short-lived association, however, because, as Lucan pointed out, "It is a law of nature that every great man inevitably resents a partner in greatness."

Caesar's self-improvement program was not yet complete because political power in Rome was necessarily based on military power. He had himself appointed governor of the portion of Gaul that the Romans had conquered, forged a seemingly invincible army to conquer the rest of Gaul, and established his reputation as one of history's remarkable troop commanders. What Tacitus referred to as "the terror of the Roman name" was confirmed by Caesar's statement that, "It is the right of war for conquerors to treat those whom they have conquered according to their pleasure." Though his military prowess was only too apparent to the Gauls, Caesar needed strong support back in Rome. His inspired solution was the carefully composed *Commentaries on the Gallic Wars* (what would Latin classes do without Caesar?), which received wide distribution in Rome, becoming a veritable best-seller.

By 49 B.C. Gaul was secured according to Caesar's pleasure, Crassus was dead in Parthia, Pompey had gone over to the Senate, and Caesar and his intensely loyal army were poised on the banks of the Rubicon in northern Italy. An apprehensive Senate reminded him of the standing order that all field commanders had to return to Rome without their troops whereupon Caesar, never known for indecisiveness, observed that "the die is cast," and invaded and conquered all of Italy in several weeks. Following his triumphant return to a wildly enthusiastic Rome (except the Senate and aristocracy, obviously), he won a war in Spain and then defeated his rival, Pompey, in Greece. He further solidified his power and filled his purse by campaigning in Egypt where he stabilized the reign of Cleopatra, Queen of Egypt (also fathering a child by her), and guaranteed almost the entire tax revenues of Egypt for himself. In four brief, brilliant years after crossing the Rubicon, Julius Caesar had triumphed in Italy, Spain, Greece, Syria, Egypt, and North Africa, strengthening and consolidating the Empire as he went. When he returned to Rome in 45 B.C. he was undisputed master of the Roman world and a legend in his, and our, time. Less than a year later, on the Ides of March, he died of multiple stab wounds on the Senate floor at the base of Pompey's statue. There were about sixty assassins.

The motives for murder ranged from genuinely patriotic concerns over constitutional violations to plain jealousy. Moreover, some of Caesar's reforms interfered with corrupt practices of the bloated aristocracy, providing additional incentive for murder. On the other hand the people, who supported Caesar throughout his meteoric career, regarded him as a martyr to the rapacity and greed of the aristocracy.

(According to Shakespeare, Caesar was "the noblest Roman of them all.") A curious and puzzling fact about the whole affair is that Caesar was almost certainly aware of the conspiracy and yet did nothing to protect himself.

Caesar's will left three-quarters of an enormous fortune to his adopted grandnephew, Octavian, but Octavian's true legacy was the opportunity to acquire Rome itself. Though only eighteen when Caesar died (and unaware of the will), Octavian reacted like a veteran politician. He formed a Second Triumvirate with Mark Antony and Lepidus, brutally suppressed all dissent and used terror and the threat of death to raise some fighting money. To his everlasting discredit he failed to stop Mark Antony from having Cicero murdered. In Macedonia he avenged Caesar by defeating and driving to suicide two of his assassins, Brutus and Cassius. (Shakespeare has Brutus say, "Not that I loved Caesar less, but that I loved Rome more.") After Lepidus was dropped from the triumvirate Antony and Cleopatra tried to use Caesar's son in their own bid for empire. After all the machinations and intrigue the final showdown was almost anticlimactic. In a naval battle off the northwest coast of Greece, near Actium, Octavian triumphed and the losers returned to Egypt to commit suicide.

Octavian became, in effect, the second emperor of the Roman Empire without most Romans even realizing that constitutional government had ended with Caesar. While prudently maintaining the appearance of restoring the Republic, Octavian orchestrated his power by redesigning the creaky governmental machinery to try to control the business of a vast empire. Careful to avoid the appellation of emperor, he did accept from the Senate the titles of Augustus (revered one) and *princeps* (first citizen). Although he ruled indirectly, he was just as much in control as any titled emperor.

Among many significant innovations, Augustus created a civil service based on merit, endowed a veterans pension fund from his own capital (secured by the taxes of Egypt), added a sales tax, rebuilt Rome ("I found Rome brick and left it marble"), created the first police and fire departments, overhauled the armed forces, and sponsored army construction of public works projects throughout the Empire. He adjusted the bureaucratic machinery of imperial Rome so it could continue to function under good, mediocre, or incompetent leadership. It survived even the tenures of murderous tyrants: Caligula, Nero, Commodus, and Caracalla (see box 5.1).

The *Pax Romana* (Roman peace) began with Caesar Augustus in 27 B.C. and ended with Marcus Aurelius in A.D. 180. (See the map of the Roman Empire in A.D. 180 on page 116.) For over two centuries the Roman world was relatively peaceful because there were no major wars. The Western world was stable and orderly for the first time in history, and people felt quite safe in their homes and even when traveling over

Box 5.1 Major Emperors of Rome

Julius Caesar (dictator)
(49–44 B.C.)

Caesar Augustus (princeps)
(27 B.C.–A.D. 14)

Julian Caesars
Tiberius (A.D. 14–37)
Caligula (37–41)
Claudius (41–54)
Nero (54–68)
Galba, Otho, Vitellius (69)

Flavian Caesars
Vespasian (69–79)
Titus (79–81)
Domitian (81–96)

Antoninus Caesars
Nerva (96–98)
Trajan (98–117)
Hadrian (117–138)
Antoninus Pius (138–161)
Marcus Aurelius (161–180)

Decline and Fall
Commodus (180–192)
Septimus Severus (193–211)
Caracalla (211–217)
Alexander Severus (222–235)
26 emperors (235–284)
Diocletian (284–305)
Constantine (312–337)
Constantius (353–361)
Julian (361–363)
Jovian (363–364)
Valens (364–378)
Theodosios (379–395)
Honorius (395–403)

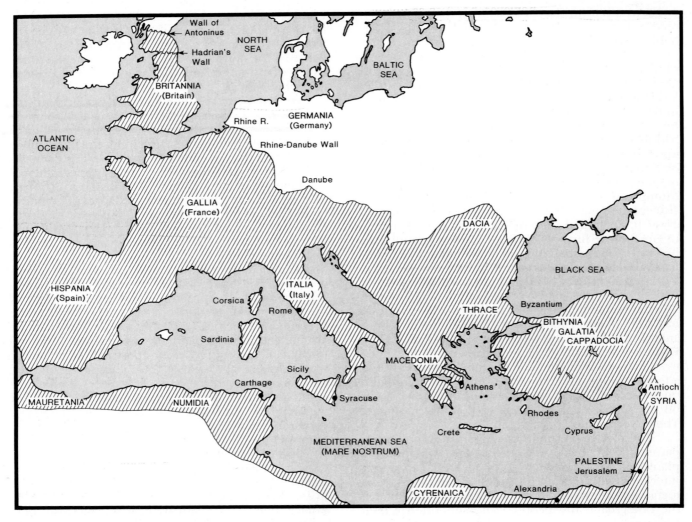

The Roman Empire in A.D. 180.

Figure 5.2 Roman coin, 17 B.C. Obverse: head of Augustus with the inscription "S.P.Q.R. IMP CAESARI." The reverse is characteristically Roman (more is better), featuring the emperor, Victory, and an elephant standing on a triumphal arch placed upon an aqueduct.

the roads and sea routes of the prosperous Empire. Roman coins (fig. 5.2) replaced the "owls of Athena" (see fig. 2.3) as the monetary standard of the ancient world. All was not rosy, however, because as Juvenal pointed out, "We are suffering the evils of a long peace. Luxury, more deadly than war, broods over the city, and avenges a conquered world."

After Marcus Aurelius, the position of emperor was usually decided by the army, with the legions supporting any general who would offer the largest benefits to the military. The problems all the emperors faced were very much the same: an increasing national debt because of military expense, a declining population in Italy, a growing disinclination to take public office in the cities outside Rome (the officers were held responsible for paying the cities' taxes to the central government, and with increasing rural poverty no one wanted to bankrupt himself by holding office), and growing rebellion on the borders of the Empire. A vast population movement from the north and east pushed Germanic, Gothic, and Vandal peoples west and south until they overran all of Italy and Spain.

The century of decline from Commodus to Diocletian (180–284) marked the beginning of the end even though the reforms of Diocletian temporarily halted the deterioration. The growth of Christianity posed an additional challenge to which Constantine responded with the Edict of Milan (313), granting freedom of worship throughout the Empire. Constantine also divided the Empire into west and east and located the capital of the Eastern Empire in the new city of Constantinople, built on the site of the old Greek colony of Byzantium. Theodosios made Christianity the official religion of the Empire, a decision that marked the beginning of vigorous Christian persecution of other religions. As the barbarian invasions intensified, the western emperor Honorius (395–403) moved to Ravenna, leaving the Pope to defend Rome as best he could. Rome was sacked in 410 and again in 455; in 476 the first non-Roman occupied the throne of Caesar and the Roman Empire passed into history. The painfully protracted decline led Emerson to comment, "The barbarians who broke up the Roman Empire did not arrive a day too soon."

Some Achievements of Rome

Rome's major and most enduring contribution to Western civilization was her legal system: the art and science of law. Administration of justice was an art, while science (jurisprudence) defined justice and injustice. There is no clearer evidence of Roman preference for facts as opposed to abstractions than in a body of law founded, as Cicero stated, "not on theory but on nature." Justice was a process rather than a concept, a way of dealing with practical problems in everyday life. "Law is nothing but a correct principle drawn from the inspiration of the gods, commanding what is honest and forbidding the contrary" (Cicero). Venality and rapacity were human characteristics the state had to control so that, "the stronger might not in all things have their way" (Ovid). Bertrand Russell once stated that an ideal society, for him, would be one in which everyone was honest and he was the only thief. Roman law stood guard against the thief in all of us. Moreover, Roman law used its experience of empire to build up a body of international law based on a rational appraisal of consistent human behavior in a variable environment.

Modern research has shown that, contrary to popular belief, the Romans were not masters of the arts of governance; that their legal system worked need not imply, by inference, a government of comparable efficiency. Until the time of Caesar Augustus government was a chaotic mess of inefficiency and corruption caused not by a Republic trying to administer an empire but by time-honored inequities and improbities. Augustus did institute some reforms, but he followed the Roman habit of shuffling parts around when what he needed was a new engine. Diocletian (284–305) did design an efficient new system, but by this time it was like installing a new motor in a disintegrating vehicle.

Province management was a permanent problem because there was little governing; the governors were responsible primarily for sending money to Rome. Charging whatever taxes the traffic would bear and rendering "unto Caesar that which is Caesar's," they pocketed the rest. Moreover, the vaunted Roman toleration of provincial cultures was more pragmatic than magnanimous: don't do anything that will jeopardize the tax-potential of conquered territories. Except for Greece,[4] Rome treated all foreign cultures with equal indifference.

Roman science dealt entirely with empirical data; theoretical science was something left to the Greeks. For example, Eratosthenes (air-uh-TOSS-thuh-neez), an Alexandrian Greek, used his reason rather than empirical data to theorize that the world was round. Pliny the Elder began with sensory evidence when he observed that the masts of ships approaching shore were visible before the hulls could

---

4. The love-hate relationship with Greece was largely involuntary. As Horace wrote, "Greece, taken captive, captured her savage conqueror, and carried her arts into clownish Latium."

Figure 5.3 Main thoroughfare, Ostia Antica. Leading from Rome to its port city, this three-lane highway is a typical Roman road. Even when driving in Europe today a Roman route can be recognized by the way it rolls on and on without a curve.

Figure 5.4 Great Bath, Roman bath complex, Bath, England, 54 A.D. Part of the finest group of Roman remains in England, this sumptuous pool is still fed by natural hot springs.

Figure 5.5 Snack bar, Ostia Antica. Located across the street from a large apartment house, this cozy bar featured a common room adjoined by a roomy patio. Fast foods were undoubtedly one of the specialties.

be seen; from this he deduced that the world had a curved surface. Roman medical science benefitted when their organizational talent was combined with their passion for war to produce the field hospital, a predecessor of the general hospital.

A fifty-thousand-mile network of paved roads linked Rome to all parts of the Empire. All roads did, in fact, lead to Rome. Originally designed as military roads, they carried the efficient postal service plus peripatetic Romans. Guidebooks, highway patrols, a stable every ten miles, and an inn every thirty miles made traveling easier and safer than at any other time prior to the late nineteenth century (fig. 5.3). Skillful engineering also produced the aqueducts that supplied the huge amounts of water needed for the luxurious public baths (fig. 5.4) and for the many affluent households that used water for cooking and sanitary facilities. Only a few aqueducts remain, such as the one still serving Segovia in Spain, and some of the plumbing—in the Pantheon, at Pompeii, and at Bath—still works. Almost everything else has vanished, like, for example, the vast irrigation system that watered productive farms in the northern Sahara.

As urbanization gradually supplanted Rome's early agrarian society, city building became a new specialty. Many residential units were five- and six-story apartment houses with such built-in services as nurseries, convenience markets, and neighborhood snack bars (fig. 5.5). Rome and other large cities always had extensive forums that served as civic centers (suitable backdrops for Roman pomp and ceremony) and open-air markets comparable to our shopping malls. Rome was not, however, a neat and orderly city. Except for several thoroughfares there were no names for the fifty-four miles of streets nor any house numbers. (Sample conversation: "See Marius in the leather shop behind the Pantheon; he knows where your friend, Sepulvius, lives.") There

was pollution ("cease to admire the smoke, wealth and noise of prosperous Rome."—Horace) and, as Sallust observed, corruption: "A city for sale and doomed to speedy destruction, if it finds a purchaser." City facilities always included public baths, but emperors who wished to improve their public image, which included most of those who stayed alive long enough, built elaborate facilities larger than several Grand Central Stations[5]; these hedonistic temples contained, in addition to the standard baths, indoor and outdoor swimming pools, gymnasiums, libraries, lounges, restaurants, bars, and numerous gardens. Sometimes included, apparently when in short supply in the community, were efficiently designed brothels. The center of each city featured a large amphitheatre, like the Colosseum, where the

5. The New York landmark was modeled after Rome's Baths of Caracalla.

entertainment was highlighted by gladiatorial combat; wild animal hunts; naval battles; and an occasional gladiator, in a bid for freedom, single-handedly killing an elephant.

Rome's bequest to the Western world was a curious compound of justice under law, military conquest, the Latin language, and Greek culture. Implicit in the laws that recognized the constitutional rights of citizens was the germinal idea that laws required the consent of the governed. Military conquest, on the other hand, was a devastating legacy of which the world has no need. In particular, Horace's pious statement, *dulce et decorum est pro patria mori* (it is sweet and glorious to die for one's country) has been used time and time again to justify enormous crimes against humanity.

In the final analysis, law and Greek culture were Rome's finest contributions to Western civilization. More imitative than inventive, Rome had the great good sense to copy Greek culture. The Greek temple style was adopted, though mainly the ornate Corinthian order; Greek sculpture was copied so often that most of what we know of Greek work exists only as Roman copies. The work of Greek artists, serving Roman tastes, appeared in the frescoes, murals, and mosaics of their houses and public buildings. Greek slaves tutored Roman children in the Greek language and the classics: Homer, Hesiod, and the plays of Aeschylus, Sophocles, and Menander. Roman tourists made the obligatory pilgrimage to Greece to view the centuries-old wonders of the Akropolis and to consult the oracle at Delphi. Rome contributed the language, organization, and law upon which the Church of Rome and the Middle Ages were built; at the same time, Rome preserved and transmitted the Greek humanism, which inspired the Renaissance and edified the Age of Reason.

Roman Religion and Philosophy

During the early days of the Republic, Roman religion encompassed household gods and earthly spirits appropriate to the simple life of a farmer. This traditional religion remained viable for those who clung to the land; the word *pagan* (literally, *country-man*) described those who adhered to the old religion of the city-state. Agrarian beliefs became inadequate, however, for urban life in an expanding empire, and the Romans again looked to Greece for suitable models. The Greek pantheon was adopted and given Roman names, albeit with somewhat different characteristics (see box 1.1 on page 30). For example, playfully amorous Aphrodite, who represented beauty and the pleasures of eroticism, became Venus, the mother of Aeneas, bringer of good fortune and victory and protector of female chastity; Athena, the Greek goddess of wisdom and patroness of the arts was transformed into Minerva, the goddess of learning and handicrafts; Poseidon, the powerful earthshaker and god of the sea became, for the Romans, Neptune, the god of water.

Jupiter, tho' called the best and the greatest, he was never, like Zeus, the supreme arbiter of the universe and the governor of the world. Zeus reigned from the heights of Mt. Olympus, Jupiter from a low and easily accessible hill. Zeus belonged to the shining space of the air, while Jupiter, as represented by the Romans, belonged to the earth as much as to the sky. Zeus was free. Jupiter was rigid. When we compare the two gods, we find we are comparing the imagination of the Greeks to the imagination of the Romans; they had almost nothing in common.[6]

The practical mind-set of the Romans also manifested itself in their religious practices. Dedicated pragmatist that he was, Ovid commented that "it is expedient that there should be gods, and as it is expedient, let us believe that they exist." In the interest of efficiency and the glory of the state, the Pantheon (from the Greek, meaning "of all gods") housed in one sumptuous structure the seven planetary gods (see fig. 6.21). Patriotism was promoted by elevating the emperors, usually during their lifetime, to godly status. After Caesar Augustus, most emperors were deified by Senate action and emperor worship became the official religion of the Empire.[7] When the Emperor Vespasian was at the point of death he wryly remarked, "Oh dear, I think I'm becoming a god."

Emperor worship and the adopted gods of the Greek city-states gradually evolved into Romanism, the worship of the state. Seneca noted that, "Religion is regarded by the common people as true, by the wise as false, and by the rulers as useful." The more personal spiritual needs of the common people, however, plus the diverse cultures within the Empire led to a variety of imported religious beliefs. Egypt contributed Isis, the wife of Osiris (fig. 5.6) and mother of Horus, the dynamic goddess who raised her husband from the dead. Much more than Diana or Minerva, she appealed to Roman women because she was a giver of health, beauty, wisdom, and love and, moreover, she needed priestesses as well as priests. Cybele, the Great Mother goddess of Phrygia (in Asia Minor), turned up in Rome during the war with Hannibal. According to the legend she loved the glorious youth Attis, who like Osiris was raised from the dead (the rebirth motif was standard for fertility cults). Her frantic grief over his death and abandoned delirium at his rebirth were followed by his unfaithfulness, at which point she castrated him. All of this dramatic spectacle was echoed in the ecstatic and bloody (including self-castration) rites of Cybele's followers. Even the Romans were sometimes aghast at the orgies and blood baths and attempted to regulate the mayhem.

aphrodite

---

6. Robert Payne et al., *Horizon Book of Ancient Rome* (New York: American Heritage Publishing Company, 1966), p. 68.

7. Little interested in the religions of other cultures, Rome was deeply concerned over the Christians who refused to place the emperor above their God; this threatened the state and was therefore heretical.

Figure 5.6 Priest of Serapis, ca. 170–180 A.D. J. Paul Getty Museum, Santa Monica, California. The sacred bull in Egyptian religion, Serapis was ruler of the underworld and supposedly the incarnation of Osiris. The priest is identified by the diadem and rosette.

The Eleusian mysteries and Dionysian rites, both Greek mystery religions, had their Roman adherents, but the vows of silence of both sects have been frustratingly effective. Dionysian ritual celebrated the nonrational but the particulars are obscure. The Eleusian mysteries are particularly intriguing because it appears that the worshippers were able to overcome their fear of death. Eventually the ceremonies at Eleusis (near Athens) were suppressed by Christianity; any religion that could conquer humanity's deepest fear could not be permitted to exist. Imported from Persia was the resolutely virtuous worship of Mithras, the unconquered intermediary between Ahura-Mazda, lord of life and light, and Ahriman, lord of death and darkness. Mithras was the protector of humanity whose believers had to be courageous and morally pure. Soldiers were strongly attracted to this male-oriented religion, which in the third century A.D. was Christianity's greatest rival.

Millions of believers looked to the stars as powerful deities on a par with Jupiter, Isis, and Cybele; astrology was the champion superstition of an age in which countless numbers preferred to believe the movements of heavenly bodies controlled their lives. Astrology, originating in Babylonia, had been known as early as Plato (he found it amusing) but it was not until Alexander's conquest of the Middle East that this persistent nonsense penetrated the Greek world and, ultimately, the entire Roman spectrum. The Eastern religions attracted different sectors of the populace but

Figure 5.7 Portrait bust of Epicurus. Roman marble copy, probably after a bronze original of ca. 275–250 B.C. Rogers Fund. Metropolitan Museum of Art. This is one of the finest of many copies. The long face marked by time and poor health is obviously an actual likeness, but in the wrinkled brow and deep-set eyes we also see "the philosopher."

astrology fascinated all classes, from slaves to emperors. Greek skeptics asked how it was that people fated to die at different times all went down in the same shipwreck, or how one-twelfth of humankind could share the basic characteristics of a Capricorn, but these rational queries simply bored true believers. Augustus and Tiberius, never ones to take chances, banned astrologers from Rome, not to put a stop to larceny, but out of fear of rivals whose horoscopes might predict an enticing throne in the offing. Practitioners of magic also did a thriving business. Spells, incantations, charms, curses, and hexes were for sale to an endless procession of fervently gullible Romans. Fraud flourished on its customary grand scale.

Epicureanism and Stoicism, two eminent Athenian schools of philosophy of the third century B.C., developed ethical systems that would assist individuals in feeling more secure in an unstable and hostile world. Materialistic and practical, both philosophies were suited to thoughtful, educated Romans who chose to face up to the problems of living an ethical life in a society plagued by dissension, vice, and corruption.

The philosophy of Epicurus (341–270 B.C.; fig. 5.7) was designed primarily to secure tranquility. He considered pleasure to be the ultimate good and adhered, with remarkable consistency, to the consequences of this view. "Pleasure," he said, "is the beginning and the end of the blessed life." And further, "I know not how I can conceive the good if I withdraw the pleasures of love and those of hearing and sight. The beginning and the root of all good is the pleasure of the stomach; even wisdom and culture must be referred to this." The pleasure of the mind is therefore the contemplation of the pleasures of the body. Sokrates and Plato would disagree of course, because of their insistence upon intellectual development as the chief good, but they did not have to contend with the unsettling problems of a violent age. For Epicurus one acquired virtue by "prudence in the pursuit of pleasure." Justice was not an abstract ideal as in Plato's *Republic* but a practical matter of acting so as not to cause fear and resentment in other people. Rather than a virtue in its own right, justice was essentially a defense mechanism against pain.

Epicureanism was on a considerably higher level than mere hedonism, the pursuit of physical pleasures. All materialistic philosophies contain elements of hedonism but Epicurus advocated intellectual pleasures as superior to purely sensual pleasures. He preferred quiet pleasures to violent joys. Eat moderately for fear of indigestion; drink moderately for fear of the morning after; avoid politics, love, and other turmoil; do not present hostages to fortune by marrying and having children; above all live so as to avoid fear. For Epicurus the safest social pleasure was friendship. Holding public office was dangerous because a man multiplied envious enemies as he achieved power. "The wise man will try to live unnoticed so that he will have no enemies."

Epicurus identified two of the greatest sources of fear as religion and the dread of death. He preferred to believe that the gods, if they existed, did not interfere in human affairs and that the soul perished with the body. Religion was not a consolation but a threat; supernatural interference with nature seemed to him to be a source of terror because immortality denied the hope of being released from pain. Death was both extinction and liberation.

In his long poem, *De Rerum Nature* (*On the Nature of Things*), the Latin poet and philosopher Lucretius (loo–KREE–shus; ca. 96–55 B.C.) explained the workings of the universe as seen by the Epicurean: a rational, materialistic interpretation of the ways in which all things came to be. The poet Horace (65–8 B.C.), known for his odes, exemplified Epicureanism in his life-style and recorded the ethical results of the philosophy in his poetry. He advocated moderation in all things though he did warn against the inconvenience of poverty; above all, he said, avoid high positions because lightning strikes the tallest trees and highest mountains. A lively sense of humor was Horace's chief Epicurean pleasure. As a sophisticated man he recognized the foibles of his time, laughed at most of them, and unashamedly participated in a goodly number. As the creed of a cultivated majority, Epicureanism survived about six hundred years, though with diminishing vigor.

Stoicism was taught by Zeno the Stoic (335?–263? B.C.), a Phoenician who lived and taught in Athens. He believed totally in *common sense* which, in Greece, meant *materialism*. He trusted his senses and had no patience with metaphysical subtleties. When the skeptic asked Zeno what he meant by the real world the reply was, "I mean solid and material, like this table." "And God," asked the skeptic, "and the soul?" "Perfectly solid," answered Zeno, "more solid than the table." In response to further questioning

Zeno added virtue and justice to his list of solid matter. Later Stoics like the Emperor Marcus Aurelius (A.D. 121–180) abandoned materialism but retained the ethical doctrines in virtually the same form. Stoicism was less Greek than any other doctrine because it was emotionally limited and somewhat fanatical. Moreover, its sober austerity contained religious elements the Greeks seemed unable to supply or endorse. In short, it had qualities that appealed to the Romans.

The main doctrines of Stoicism are concerned with cosmic determinism and human freedom. "There is no such thing as chance," said Zeno, "and the course of nature is determined by natural law." The natural world was originated by a Lawgiver, a supreme power called, variously, God or Zeus or Jupiter, who is the soul of the world. Each person has within a part of the Divine Fire. All things are part of a single system called Nature and the individual life is good when it is in harmony with nature. People are in harmony with nature, in one sense, because they cannot violate natural laws but in another, the stoic sense, a human life harmonizes with nature when the individual *will* is directed to ends that agree with nature. *Virtue*, therefore, is a *will* that is in agreement with nature. The wicked obey God's laws involuntarily, like a horse driven by a charioteer.

In an individual's life, virtue is the sole good; such things as health, happiness, possessions are of no account. Since virtue resides in the will, everything good or bad in a person's life depends entirely on that person. A person may be poor but virtuous; one can be sentenced to death, like Sokrates, who was looked upon as a patron saint by the Stoics. Other people may have power over externals; virtue, the only true good, is internal. Every person, therefore, has perfect freedom providing they free themselves from all mundane desires. The doctrine has a certain, non-Greek coldness; not only are bad passions condemned but all passions. The Stoic sage does not feel bereft when his wife and children die because his virtue is not disturbed. Friendship is all very well but don't let the misfortunes of your friend interfere with your detached calm. Participation in politics is permitted but helping other people does nothing for virtue.

Stoic doctrine does have some logical difficulties. If virtue is the only good then the Lawgiver must promote virtue; why, then, are there more sinners than saints? Also, how can injustice be wrong if, as Stoics liked to point out, it provided Stoics with more opportunities to endure and therefore more chances to be virtuous?

The Romans were acquainted with Stoicism mainly through the writings of Cicero, but the three most influential Roman Stoics were Seneca, Epictetus, and Marcus Aurelius: a minister, a slave, and an emperor, in that order. Seneca (ca. 3 B.C.–A.D. 65) was the teacher of Nero and also a multimillionaire, which casts some doubt on his reputation as a teacher and as a Stoic. Falsely accused of plotting Nero's assassination, he was ordered to commit suicide. His final words to his grieving family were, "Never mind, I leave you what is far more valuable than earthly riches, the example of a virtuous life."

Epictetus (ep–ik–TEE–tus; ca. A.D. 60–110) was a Greek and a slave though he did achieve his freedom. The Greek slave and Emperor Marcus Aurelius were in nearly complete agreement about the elements of Stoicism but their lives displayed some ironic contrasts. Marcus Aurelius was devoted to Stoic virtue, of which he had great need, since his reign was an endless procession of wars, insurrections, pestilence, and a few earthquakes. He was conscientious in his efforts but mainly unsuccessful and certainly frustrated. Out of political necessity he tried vainly to stamp out the Christian sect because their rejection of the state religion was an intolerable threat to the stability of the Empire. On the other hand, Epictetus lived a relatively short and uneventful life but his teachings had a profound effect on early Christianity. Consider, for example, the implications of the following:

On earth we are prisoners in an earthly body.
God is the Father of all men and we are all brothers.
Slaves are the equal of other men because all are alike in
    the eyes of God.
We must submit to God as a good citizen submits to the
    law.
The soldier swears to respect no man above Caesar but we
    are to respect ourselves first of all.
We must love our enemies.

Late Stoicism, in the philosophy of Epictetus and Marcus Aurelius, emphasized the idea of the brotherhood of all mankind; since the great intelligence (divine spark) is within each person, and each person is a necessary part of the rational scheme of things, then all men are brothers in the changing universe. Roman law interpreted this concept as all men being equal in the eyes of the law.

A third imported Greek philosophy was Neoplatonism, which became even more of a religion than did Stoicism. Its picture of an afterlife offered comfort to those Romans who enjoyed little satisfaction or self-fulfillment in their earthly existence. Neoplatonism was based on the doctrines of Plato and came to Rome from the Academy founded by Plato, the still-flourishing school in Athens (till A.D. 529). The Neoplatonists began with the Platonic concept of ideas as the true reality. Now, said the Neoplatonists, people can never know ideas in their pure form. For example, we always know and appreciate beauty in some of its manifestations in a beautiful person, or beautiful landscape or picture, but we can never imagine pure beauty apart from any of these things. To use another example, we can never imagine pure mind; we can only approach a knowledge of the mind as we see people acting according to the dictates of their mind. We see only the manifestations of the mind, never the reality. By the same token, the true reality of Good (God or Pure Idea) is something people can never conceive of on earth. A person's goal, therefore, is to approach as near as possible to an understanding of reality while on earth so that they may, upon death, be fit to enter the City of Good and finally contemplate the True Reality. With Neoplatonism there is the beginning of an idea of salvation and eternal life for those who lived their earthly lives in contemplation and with a desire for true wisdom. The influence of these ideas on Christianity can scarcely be overemphasized, for it was St. Augustine (354–430), a Neoplatonist in his youth, who laid the foundation for the doctrine of the early Christian church in his monumental volume, *The City of God*.

Games and Contests in Greece and Rome

This chapter has referred to the differences between Greek and Roman cultures. Consider now the athletic contests in the ancient world as a way of highlighting the differences. The Olympic Games and gladiatorial combat were both athletic contests, though we might refer to the Olympics as "games" and call battling gladiators something quite different, which already tells us something significant about the Greeks and the Romans. First we shall describe the games the Greeks played and then take a look at the Roman versions. By comparing the radically different approaches to athletics (sports), the reader can draw some conclusions about the two cultures in question.

The Greeks staged many festivals that featured contests in drama, music, poetry, and athletics, especially athletics. It seems that the cities of Sparta, Elis, and Pisa were always squabbling and, rather than settling their difficulties by the usual fractious methods, they decided upon a truce built around a foot-race to determine superiority. This worked so well that by 776 B.C. almost the entire Hellenic world was involved in footracing and other contests at the sacred site of Olympia. In fact, 776 was felt to be so significant that the Greeks began dating their entire history from that date. The contests were held every four years (the Olympiad) and so 776 was the first Olympiad, 772 the second Olympiad, and so on through the three hundred and twentieth Olympiad in A.D. 392: 1,168 years of Greek history.

From the beginning the truce was the critical factor and it was unique to the Olympic Games. The conditions were simple: no one was to bear arms in Elis (the province of the games); all athletes and spectators were guaranteed safe access to Elis from anywhere in the Greek world; all fighting would cease throughout that world. It is now thought that the truce lasted for ten months and probably included travel time to and from the games. True to style, the Greeks pledged on their honor to abide by these rules. The one time that Sparta violated the truce the entire Greek-speaking world was called upon to witness their shame; there were no further violations.

Athletic contests were staged throughout Greece and the greatest of these was at Olympia, not just because of the caliber of competition but because Olympia symbolized peace, the only extended periods of peace in the ancient world. Sportsmanship and brotherhood were also basic components of the

Figure 5.8 Stadium at Delphi. About the same length as the Olympic stadium, this is a fairly well-preserved site, whereas the Olympic facility was destroyed along with the statues and temples. This is a view from the semicircular end to the starting gates at the other end. The marble slabs with their etched starting line are still in place in the ground awaiting the next runners to "come up to scratch."

Figure 5.9 *Runner at the Starting Point, Two Wrestlers, Javelin Thrower.* Bas-relief, marble, ca. 500 B.C., 12¼″ × 26½″. National Museum, Athens. Originally decorating the base of a kouros, this illustrates the bound hair and heavily muscled bodies of the athletes.

games. Cheating was simply not permitted even though the Greeks were realistic enough to require from each athlete an oath of fair play. The kinship of all Greeks was recognized and competition was therefore open to all of Greek descent regardless of rank, class, or the city from which they came. Brotherhood was national rather than universal, however, because barbarians (from the Greek word for foreigner) could not compete. The dominating spirit of the games was precisely the same as it was for all Greek culture: *kalos k'agathos,* the beautiful and the good.

The best athletes in each city (selected by competition) started training exactly ten months before the festival; no one contestant had an unfair advantage. Because training was not permitted at the sacred site, final warm-ups were scheduled at Elis, after which everyone moved to Olympia for five days of competition dedicated to Zeus and Hera. Since the Olympiad was Greece's top event it had to be scheduled for both good weather and maximum attendance. Consequently, competition began on the third full moon of summer (in July or August), which placed the festivities after the grain and olive harvests and before the demands of fall planting. Adapting to the natural world was a consistent characteristic of Greek life.

The basic events of the games were footraces, primarily because all Greeks took great pride in their speed and stamina as runners.[8] The unit of distance was based on the length of the stadium at Olympia, which was about 200 yards (fig. 5.8). There were sprints of one-stade (200 yards), two-stade (400 yards), and so on up to distances of about three miles. There were no places (2d, 3d) in the Olympics; there was one winner and everyone else was an also-ran. The prize, a simple olive wreath,[9] was the most sought after in Greece; though the leaves soon withered and fell, the winner's name was recorded in the roll of the

Olympics and, ever after, his descendents would recall his name.

The winner of a footrace in the modern Olympics is, as everyone knows, the first to break the tape, unless disqualified because of a foul. The Greeks were more sophisticated; in the judging the position of finish counted only fifty percent. The other half was evaluated independently by judges who searched for that something special: grace, poise, rhythm, what we might call, in one word, style.[10] As usual, the Greeks had a word for it: *arete* (ARE–uh–tay), which can be translated as skill, or stylish grace or, more precisely, diligence in the pursuit of excellence.[11] Besides the quality of *arete,* the games differed from the modern version in one other significant respect. Though the Greeks honored tradition they were not bound by the past, preferring instead to live enthusiastically in the present. They kept meticulous records of each Olympiad but they never recorded winning distances or times; athletes competed with each other, not with the past.

Except for chariot racing the ancient Olympic events are still a basic part of the modern Olympics: footracing, broad jump, discus, javelin, and boxing and wrestling (fig. 5.9). The composite event, the pentathlon,[12] featured the kind of individual the Greeks

<hr />

8. Cross-country running was, surprisingly, not one of the Olympic events. The marathon, based on the Marathon-to-Athens run of Pheidippides to announce the wondrous victory over the Persians, was introduced at the modern Olympics which began at Athens in 1896.

9. The other games of the sacred circuit awarded the laurel at Delphi (Pythian), pine at Corinth (Isthmian), and wild celery at Nemea (Nemean). The olive branch of the Olympic Games remains as a nearly universal symbol of peace.

10. Athletes competed in the nude so that judges could better evaluate their performance. It should also be noted that women were forbidden to attend the games under penalty of death, a prohibition based on religious reasons rather than the fact of nudity, which was not a problem for the Greeks, who looked upon their readiness to strip in public as one of the traits that separated them from barbarians.

11. Style is a factor in judging modern Olympic events like diving, gymnastics, and ice skating.

12. Five events: sprint, broad jump, wrestling and boxing, discus, and javelin. The decathlon (ten events) of the modern Olympics dropped the wrestling and boxing and added shot put, pole vault, high jump, 110-meter hurdles, and 100-, 400-, and 1500-meter races.

Figure 5.10 Temple of Hera, ca. 600 B.C., Olympia. The column drums still lie where they were pushed over on orders of Theodosios or, as some would claim, toppled by an earthquake.

especially admired, a well-rounded person who could do many things well. The Romans admired specialists; Greeks, generalists.

During the 1,169 years of the Olympic Games the high point was reached, not unexpectedly, during the Golden Age of Perikles. There was a slight decline in quality and integrity after that time, which accelerated rapidly beginning in 146 B.C., the year in which Carthage and Corinth were razed, the year in which the Romans took over Olympia. Typical of the Roman way was the behavior of Nero, who had himself declared winner of any event he entered; there was no one who could deny him. The games came to an end in A.D. 393, after the three hundred and twentieth Olympiad, when the Emperor Theodosios, in the name of Christianity, issued an edict forbidding the games because they "promoted the worship of heathen and false gods." No mention was made of the ancient truce when the emperor completed his work by ordering the destruction of the statues and temples. *Arete, kalos k'agathos* (skill, beauty, and goodness) vanished from the sacred groves of the peaceful river valley at Olympia (fig. 5.10).

Roman games were originally conceived and produced to honor the gods but, by the time of the Empire, private individuals were sponsoring extravagant spectacles honoring themselves, with just passing references to the gods. While the Romans had frequent athletic contests the public was far more entranced by the giant spectacles staged in the Colosseum and Circus Maximus (see figures 6.13, 6.14, and 6.15). When the Romans discussed the *ludi* (games, from which we get the word *ludicrous*), they referred specifically to five types of extravaganzas produced for immense arenas: chariot races, gladiatorial combat, wild animal hunts, naval battles, and mythological pantomimes. These *ludi* were not competitive in the

Greek sense nor was there any concern for style or beauty. They were intended for the entertainment of vast crowds, and so we can credit the Romans with the invention of mass entertainment. As a part of the welfare program that also supplied food to the unemployed, the games were free. The familiar phrase "bread and circuses" aptly describes the Roman manner of controlling their constituency.

Most popular were the *ludi circenses* (games in a ring), the chariot races held at six racetracks in and about Rome. Racing was a frenzied and dangerous sport, if one can call driving four-horse chariots on a tight oval track that had only one rule—to the victor goes the spoils—a sport. The stakes were certainly high enough; the best drivers made a great deal of money and also enjoyed a status exceeding the combined charisma of a pro football star and a Grand Prix champion. There is no contemporary equivalent for a day at the races at the Circus Maximus in ancient Rome. Try to imagine an oval track 2,000 feet in circumference, four tense and tough racing teams (blues, greens, whites, reds) and 250,000 fanatical spectators who had millions riding on every race. Moreover, the races provided the ideal setting for the intrigues and assignations that were so much a part of Roman life.

Gladiatorial combat calls for a more extensive discussion, not only because it was unique to Roman civilization but also because it was so characteristic of Roman values. There has been a tendency, probably dating back to Napoleon, to ascribe the Roman virtues of nobility, courage, and honesty to the austere days of the Republic, and thus blame the Empire for much of the brutality and decadence for which Rome is justly infamous. It was the Republic, however, that brutally destroyed Carthage and Corinth in 146 B.C. and it was the Republic that bred gladiatorial combat, beginning in 264 B.C.

The ritual of mortal combat always began with the ceremonial march of the gladiators into the arena and the famous words to the royal box: *Ave, Caesar, morituri te salutant* (Hail, Caesar, we who are about to die salute you). Then there was the drawing of lots and the inspection of arms. A typical match-up, to start the show, would be a gladiator of the Thracian type versus one of the *hoplomachi* fighting style. The Thracian wore a heavy helmet, had leather and metal covering much of his body, and carried a small shield and curved sword. The *hoplomachi* wore a heavy helmet, was nearly naked, and carried a large, oblong shield and a Roman sword. Bodies were guarded by a variety of clothing and armament, all designed to protect the combatant from disabling minor wounds. What the crowd wanted was a skillful, courageous, and relatively even fight; given this kind of battle, public sentiment tended towards a thumbs-up verdict for the loser, who could then fight another day. The *editor,* the sponsor of the day's games, had the final say, however, and the verdict could just as well be thumbs-down. The loser was then expected to display his superb training and discipline (he was also trained in how to die) by presenting his naked throat to his conqueror's sword. Anguish and gore enough it would seem, but the Romans further embellished the bloody scene with an actor dressed as a god and brandishing a white-hot staff, which he pressed into the flesh of the fallen man to make certain he was dead. The tattered body was then hooked behind a horse and dragged away and the entire arena sprayed with perfume, after which the crowd settled contentedly back for the next contest.

The next pair, perhaps a *retiarius* and a *secutor,* were always great crowd pleasers. Possessing neither helmet nor shield, the *retiarius* had a dagger in his belt, while one hand gripped a net and the other a trident. His opponent, the *secutor,* wore a helmet and carried a long rectangular shield and a sword plus the standard dagger in his belt. The *retiarius* had to be very mobile because the contest amounted to a swift runner attacking a human tank; the advantage usually lay with the tank. Although the two pairs described above appeared at most spectacles, there was also fighting from chariots, dwarf gladiators, female combatants, and whatever else could be concocted to stimulate the interest of the common people in the upper tiers. Staging these extravaganzas was so expensive that the government had to assume the responsibility for special schools, which in Rome alone trained and housed some two thousand gladiators. Amphitheatre combat was probably scheduled only several times a year; this kept expenses down, helped maintain a full complement of gladiators (about six hundred pairs fought in each production) and, most importantly, heightened expectations for the next spectacular event.

Other spectacles involved elaborately staged hunts, which featured an African jungle, for example, in the Colosseum with hunters and assorted lions and tigers stalking each other, though it is doubtful the starved, frightened creatures wanted anything more than a place to hide from their tormentors. Many thousands of wild animals were slaughtered in this manner, so many in fact, that whole species were annihilated. Fought in pools built for the occasion, naval battles were reenactments of famous engagements, bloody reminders of the power of Roman arms at sea. Finally, there were dramatic pantomimes based on familiar mythological plots and starring condemned criminals in their first and last performance. Treated to mythology in action, audiences witnessed Herakles being consumed by flames, Dirce lashed to the horns of a maddened bull, Ikarus of the failing wings falling among wild beasts, and other edifying splendors. Roman efficiency was well-served; the mob was entertained and enlightened while, at the same time, justice was served.

The Roman games were so appallingly brutal that some apologists have tried to rationalize the whole bloody business into justifiable and necessary entertainment for restless and potentially dangerous mobs. Others have sought evidence that educated Romans disapproved of the institution; they have looked in vain, however, since Romans of every class and station attended and enjoyed the games. With the possible exception of Seneca and Pliny the Younger, we know of not a single Roman who ever voiced any concerns, humane or otherwise, about the events staged in the Colosseum. Death, in this ancient time, was not a significant consideration for those in power, particularly when the lower classes were doing the dying. Ironically, the one event that was vigorously denounced was the *sparsio,* the bonus episode that usually followed the final gladiatorial contest. While the upper class beat a hasty retreat, a machine with a rotating arm that hurled clay or wooden tablets in the general direction of the upper tiers was wheeled into the arena. Whatever was depicted on the tally was redeemable in kind: a water buffalo, ten pounds of ostrich feathers, an occasional elephant, two tickets in the lower tier for the next attraction, and so on. Horace spoke for the upper class when he wrote: "I hate the vulgar herd and hold it far."

It should be noted, in conclusion, that Roman spectacles were enthusiastically adopted throughout the Mediterranean world. Roman games, however, were never staged in Athens, Delphi, Delos, Epidauros, or, most especially, Olympia.

The Best of the Roman Ideal

Artistically and creatively, Rome reached its peak during the reign of Augustus. Virgil and Horace both lived during these years. The great orator, Cicero, had just died, and the passionate poet Catullus (kuh–TUL–us) had died only a few years before. Virgil, by the way, was almost adopted by Christianity, and during the Middle Ages was the only classic author who was read, largely because of his *Fourth Eclogue* in which he celebrated the birth of a child who, he predicted, would bring the world back to the Golden Age. His fame, however, rests on his celebrated epic poem the *Aeneid* (i–NEE–id).

To cut through the superficial judgments that may be made about the *Aeneid* is difficult. The first such judgment is that the poem provided "instant mythology" for the Roman empire, for it was apparent to Virgil that much of the greatness of Athenian life resulted from the tradition furnished by Homer's *Iliad* and *Odyssey.* Virgil knew these poems well and patterned his epic upon them to give Rome the same kind of golden past Greece had had, and to provide inspiration for the carrying on of great and noble works. Too clearly the reader gets the picture of Virgil thinking to himself, "Tomorrow we are going to start the old tradition of Roman greatness."

A second quick judgment is that the *Aeneid* presents a picture of the dutiful Stoic as epic hero, and somehow, the over-thoughtful, rather pompous figure of the middle-aged Aeneas (i–NEE–us) falls short of the glory-bound Akhilleus or Hektor, and especially the wily and resourceful Odysseus.

The good reader will accept these first judgments and then feel beyond them. The *Aeneid is* literature as propaganda for a great nation. But what's the matter with propaganda for a good cause? The hero is middle-aged and has gained the wisdom of maturity. Aeneas

Chronological Overview of Roman Literature

	PROSE	POETRY
Early Republic **ca. 300–80 B.C.**	Polybius (205–133 B.C.) Plautus (254?–184 B.C.) (Drama) Terence (190?–159 B.C.) (Drama)	Theocritus (310?–250 B.C.)
Age of Cicero **80–43 B.C.**	Cicero (106–43 B.C.) Caesar (102–44 B.C.) Sallust (86–34 B.C.)	Lucretius (ca. 96–55 B.C.) Catullus (84–54 B.C.)
Augustan Golden Age **42 B.C.–A.D. 17**	Livy (59 B.C.–A.D. 17)	Virgil (70–19 B.C.) Horace (65–8 B.C.) Ovid (43 B.C.–A.D. 17)
Silver Age **A.D. 17–130**	Seneca (4 B.C.–A.D. 65) Petronius (d. 66 A.D.) Pliny the Elder (23–79) Quintilian (35–ca. 100) Plutarch (46–120) Tacitus (55–120) Epictetus (ca. 60–110) Pliny the Younger (62–114) Suetonius (ca. 70–160) Lucian (ca. 117–180)	Lucan (39–65 A.D.) Martial (40–104 A.D.) Juvenal (ca. 60–140)
Decline and Fall **140–476**	Apuleius (fl. 155) Marcus Aurelius (121–180)	
Christian	Tertullian (160–230) St. Jerome (340–420) St. Ambrose (340–397) St. Augustine (353–430) Boethius (475–524)	

sees clearly that a kind of sadness underlies all heroic acts, and that many things people do result from choices that are forced upon them. Compared with Homer, Virgil loses much in dash; what he gains is a sad and chastened wisdom.

The poem recounts the legend of the founding of Rome by the Trojan hero Aeneas after the fall of Troy to Agamemnon and the Greeks. Aeneas, commanded by Jupiter and Aeneas's goddess mother, escaped from Troy with his aged father, his son Askanius (a–SKAY–nee–us; also called Ilus, and later Iulus to relate him to the Julian line of Caesars), and with the household gods that are to be the gods of the new city, Rome. The voyage is full of epic incident, storms at sea, battles, rather pleasant interludes, and the final war on Italian soil to conquer the kingdom of Latium and arrange for the marriage that will produce the Roman line.

Only two or three incidents need be mentioned to suggest the flavor of the epic. At the first of the book Aeneas, storm-tossed, landed on the shore near Carthage where he and his companions were made welcome by Dido, the queen of the city. As he recounted his adventures, Dido fell in love with him, and he with her. So satisfying was the affair that Aeneas lingered for a long time, while Dido tried to persuade him to settle there and make Carthage the city he was supposed to found. Aeneas, prodded by his stoic sense of duty, knew that he must push on, and so one morning before daybreak he and his companions set sail. Aeneas as a person hated his decision, but he was honor-bound to make it; Dido was so devastated that she had a great funeral pyre built and committed suicide in the flames. One of the ironies of the poem lies in the meeting of the lovers in the underworld in Book VI, when Aeneas tries to rekindle their love and she turns against him. Aeneas knew all there was to know about the founding of cities, but he understood little about the human heart.

Another of the little incidents occurs when the Trojans land on Sicily. The land is so beautiful that a number of Aeneas's group suggest that the city be founded there, but the hero knows that this is not the place, so he allows some of his party to stay while he again sails away to make war and cause death so that the city might be properly founded. Once again he realized the tragedy of his choice, but Duty, stern daughter of the voice of god, would not let him make the easy choice.

Many other events could be cited to illustrate the same point. Aeneas's chief adversary in Italy is a hero named Turnus, a thoroughly noble person; probably a better man than Aeneas. Turnus was patterned on the character of Hektor in the *Iliad*. Turnus must be destroyed, and Aeneas does it. Hektor, too, had to be killed. The difference is that Akhilleus, the youthful hero, fought his battle fiercely and killed his enemy in passion. Aeneas simply knew that the better man must be killed, and he did the job in full knowledge and for a greater good (the founding of the city of Rome) than would be accomplished by the saving of one good man.

Such is the tone of the whole poem except for some interludes, such as the funeral games for Ankhises when Virgil allows himself to relax and enjoy the deeds of physical strength and skill. The *Aeneid*, like the stoic philosophy, sees duty as the highest way of life, and the true Roman hero places duty above all other human values. Virgil wonderfully gave Rome its best and highest creed, when in the underworld, Ankhises told his son Aeneas:

Others, no doubt, will better mould the bronze
To the semblance of soft breathing, draw from marble,
The living countenance; and others plead
With greater eloquence, or learn to measure,
Better than we, the pathways of the heaven,
The risings of the stars: remember, Roman,
To rule the people under law, to establish
The way of peace, to battle down the haughty,
To spare the meek. Our fine arts, these, forever.

This was the highest of the Roman ideal. While it sacrificed much in the realm of human value, while it denigrated such qualities as imagination and joy, it furnished a noble code of conduct as long as the Romans adhered to it.

The pragmatic Romans cherished their flawed institutions and their proclivity for war, plunder, and profits, but they did have the saving grace of being able to laugh at themselves. Enthusiastically adapting satire to Roman tastes, they lambasted all that they held dear: politics, material possessions, manners, and morals. The Romans were, in the final analysis, rational and civilized people, and nowhere is there clearer evidence of this than in their literature. No more given to profundities than their society, Roman writers were, collectively, sophisticated, worldly-wise, and sometimes jaded. They sought to entertain and to inform rather than to enlighten, and they accomplished this with great style and a kind of lusty elegance. The literature is consistently entertaining, often irreverent, frequently lewd; it certainly makes lovely reading.

Literary Selections

ON THE REPUBLIC

from Book VI, *Scipio's Dream*
Marcus Tullius Cicero (106–43 B.C.)

In both his political career and his writing Cicero is the perfect embodiment of the noble Roman statesman and cultured man of letters. Metaphysics and aesthetics are Greek concerns and of no interest for a patriot committed to the austere business of being a Roman. Rather, practicality and devotion to the state are his central concerns; these support a Rome whose destiny is to establish order and to civilize the world.

In his *On the Republic* (54–51 B.C.), Cicero follows Stoic teaching on promoting the welfare of the state, but adopts some details from Plato's *Republic*. Although patterned after Plato's *Myth of Er* (*Republic*, Book X), Cicero's *Scipio's Dream* is unequivocally Roman. Plato's myth is a vision of aspiration towards the state as an absolute ideal; Cicero uses a dream device to illustrate duty, honor, and patriotism, for as Scipio is told, "the noblest of pursuits . . . are those undertaken for the safety of your country."

The narrator is Scipio Africanus the Younger, the adopted grandson of Scipio Africanus the Elder, the general who defeated Hannibal at Carthage (Second Punic War, 218–201 B.C.). Scipio the Younger totally destroyed Carthage at the end of the Third Punic War (149–146 B.C.). In this essay he is an officer under the consul Manius Manilius, who he later replaced. Widely read in the Middle Ages, this essay influenced both Chaucer and Dante; the geography and cosmology of the latter's *Hell* (see chap. 10) can be compared with Cicero's summary of the science of his day.

I served in Africa as military tribune of the Fourth Legion under Manius Manilius, as you know. When I arrived in that country my greatest desire was to meet King Masinissa, who had good reasons to be attached to my family. The old man embraced me tearfully when I called, and presently looked up to heaven and said, "I thank thee, sovereign sun, and ye lesser heavenly beings, that before I depart this life I behold in my realm and beneath my roof Publius Cornelius Scipio, whose very name refreshes my strength, so inseparable from my thought is the memory of that noble and invincible hero who first bore it." Then I questioned him about his kingdom, and he me about our commonwealth, and the day wore away with much conversation on both sides.

After I had been royally entertained we continued our conversation late into the night, the old man talking of nothing but Africanus and rehearsing his sayings as well as his deeds. When we parted to take our rest I fell into a deeper sleep than usual, for the hour was late and I was weary from travel. Because of our conversation, I suppose—our thoughts and utterances by day produce an effect in our sleep like that which Ennius speaks of with reference to Homer, of whom he used frequently to think and speak in his waking hours—Africanus appeared to me, in the shape that was familiar to me from his bust rather than from his own person. I shuddered when I recognized him, but he said: "Courage, Scipio, lay aside your dread and imprint my words on your memory. Do you see yonder city which I forced to submit to Rome but which is now stirring up the old hostilities and cannot remain at rest (from a lofty eminence bathed in brilliant starlight he pointed to Carthage), the city which you have come to attack, slightly more than a private? Within two years you shall be consul and overthrow it, and so win for yourself that which you now bear by inheritance. When you shall have destroyed Carthage, celebrated your triumph, been chosen censor, have traversed Egypt, Syria, Asia, and Greece as ambassador, you will be chosen consul a second time in your absence and will put an end to a great war by extirpating Numantia. But when you shall be borne into the capitol in your triumphal chariot, you shall find the government thrown into confusion by the machinations of my grandson; and here, Africanus, you must display to your country the lustre of your spirit, genius, and wisdom.

"But at this period I perceive that the path of your destiny is a doubtful one; for when your life has passed through seven times eight oblique journeys and returns of the sun; and when these two numbers (each of which is regarded as complete, one on one account and the other on another) shall, in their natural circuit, have brought you to the crisis of your fate, then will the whole state turn itself toward thee and thy glory; the senate, all virtuous men, our allies, and the Latins, shall look up to you. Upon your single person the preservation of your country will depend; and, in short, it is your part, as dictator, to settle the government, if you can but escape the impious hands of your kinsmen."—Here, when Laelius uttered an exclamation, and the rest groaned with great excitement, Scipio said, with a gentle smile, "I beg that you will not waken me out of my dream; listen a few moments and hear what followed.

"But that you may be more earnest in the defense of your country, know from me, that a certain place in heaven is assigned to all who have preserved, or assisted, or improved their country, where they are to enjoy an endless duration of happiness. For there is nothing which takes place on earth more acceptable to that Supreme Deity who governs all this world, than those councils and assemblies of men bound together by law, which are termed states; the governors and preservers of these go from hence, and hither do they return." Here, frightened as I was, not so much from the dread of death as of the treachery of my friends, I nevertheless asked him whether my father Paulus, and others, whom we thought to be dead, were yet alive? "To be sure they are alive (replied Africanus), for they have escaped from the fetters of the body as from a prison; that which is called life is really death. But behold your father Paulus approaching you."— No sooner did I see him than I poured forth a flood of tears; but he, embracing and kissing me, forbade me to weep. And when, having suppressed my tears, I regained the faculty of speech, I said: "Why, thou most sacred and excellent father, since this is life, as I hear Africanus affirm, why do I tarry on earth, and not hasten to come to you?"

"Not so, my son," he replied; "unless that God, whose temple is all this which you behold, shall free you from this imprisonment in the body, you can have no admission to this place; for men have been created under this condition, that they should keep that globe called earth which you see in the middle of this temple. And a soul has been supplied to them from those eternal fires which you call constellations and stars, and which, being globular and round, are animated with divine spirit, and complete their cycles and revolutions with amazing rapidity. Therefore you, my Publius, and all good men, must preserve your souls in the keeping of your bodies; nor are you, without the order of that Being who bestowed them upon you, to depart from mundane life, lest you seem to desert the duty assigned you by God. But, Scipio, like your grandfather here, like me who begot you, cherish justice and duty, a great obligation to parents and kin but greatest to your country. Such a life is the way to heaven and to this assembly of those who have already lived, and, released from the body, inhabit the place which you now see" (it was the circle of light which blazed most brightly among the other fires), "which you have learned from the Greeks to call the Milky Way." And as I looked on every side I saw other things transcendently glorious and wonderful. There were stars which we never see from the earth, and all were vast beyond what we have ever imagined. The least was that farthest from heaven and nearest the earth which shone with a borrowed light. The starry spheres were much larger than the earth; the earth itself looked so small as to make me ashamed of our empire, which was a mere point on its surface.

As I gazed more intently on earth, Africanus said: "How long will your mind be fixed on the ground? Do you not see what lofty regions you have entered? These are the nine circles, or rather spheres, by which all things are held together. One, the outermost, is the celestial; it contains all the rest and is itself the Supreme God, holding and embracing within itself the other spheres. In this are fixed those stars which ever roll in an unchanging course. Beneath it are seven other spheres which have a retrograde movement, opposite to that of the heavens. Of these, the globe which on earth you call Saturn, occupies one sphere. That shining body which you see next is called Jupiter, and is friendly and salutary to mankind. Next the lucid one, terrible to the earth, which you call Mars. The Sun holds the next place, almost under the middle region; he is the chief, the leader, and the director of the other luminaries; he is the soul and guide of the world, and of such immense bulk, that he illuminates and fills all other objects with his light. He is followed by the orbit of Venus, and that of Mercury, as attendants; and the Moon rolls in the lowest sphere, enlightened by the rays of the Sun. Below this there is nothing but what is mortal and transitory, excepting those souls which are given to the human race by the goodness of the gods. Whatever lies above the Moon is eternal. For the earth, which is the ninth sphere, and is placed in the center of the whole system, is immovable and below all the rest; and all bodies, by their natural gravitation, tend toward it."

When I had recovered from my amazement at these things I asked, "What is this sound so strong and sweet that fills my ears?" "This," he replied, "is the melody which, at intervals unequal, yet differing in exact proportions, is made by the impulse and motion of the spheres themselves, which, softening shriller by deeper tones, produce a diversity of regular harmonies. It is impossible that such prodigious movements should pass in silence; and nature teaches that the sounds which the spheres at one extremity utter must be sharp, and those on the other extremity must be grave; on which account that highest revolution of the star-studded heaven, whose motion is more rapid, is carried on with a sharp and quick sound; whereas this of the moon, which is situated the lowest and at the other extremity, moves with the gravest sound. For the earth, the ninth sphere, remaining motionless, abides invariably in the innermost position, occupying the central spot in the universe. But these eight revolutions, of which two, those of Mercury and Venus, are in unison, make seven distinct tones, with measured intervals between, and almost all things are arranged in sevens. Skilled men, copying this harmony with strings and voice, have opened for themselves a way back to this place, as have others who with excelling genius have cultivated divine sciences in human life. But the ears of men are deafened by being filled with this melody; you mortals have no duller sense than that of hearing. As where the Nile at the Falls of Catadupa pours down from lofty mountains, the people who live hard by lack the sense of hearing because of the cataract's roar, so this harmony of the whole universe in its intensely rapid movement is so loud that men's ears cannot take it in, even as you cannot look directly at the sun, your sense of sight being overwhelmed by its radiance." While I marveled at these things I was ever and anon turning my eyes back to earth, upon which Africanus resumed:

"I perceive that even now you are fixing your eyes on the habitation and abode of men, and if it seems to you diminutive, as it in fact is, keep your gaze fixed on these heavenly things and scorn the earthly. What fame can you obtain from the speech of men, what glory worth the seeking? You perceive that men dwell on but few and scanty portions of the earth, and that amid these spots, as it were, vast solitudes are interposed! As to those who inhabit the earth, not only are they so separated that no communication can circulate among them from the one to the other, but part lie upon one side, part upon another, and part are diametrically opposite to you, from whom you assuredly can expect no glory. You observe that the same earth is encircled and encompassed as it were by certain zones, of which the two that are most distant from one another and lie as it were toward the vortexes of the heavens in both directions, are rigid as you see with frost, while the middle and the largest zone is burned up with the heat of the sun. Two of these are habitable. The southern, whose inhabitants imprint their footsteps in an opposite direction to you, has no relation to your race. As to this other, lying toward the north, which you inhabit, observe what a small portion of it falls to your share; for all that part of the earth which is inhabited by you, which narrows toward the south and north but widens from east to west, is no other than a little island surrounded by that sea which on earth you call the Atlantic, sometimes the great sea, and sometimes the ocean; and yet with so grand a name, you see how diminutive it is! Now do you think it possible for your renown, or that of any one of us, to move from those cultivated and inhabited spots of ground, and pass beyond that Caucasus, or swim across yonder Ganges? What inhabitant of the other parts of the east, or of the extreme regions of the setting sun, of those tracts that run toward the south or toward the north, shall ever hear of your name? Now supposing them cut off, you see at once within what narrow limits your glory would fain expand itself. As to those who speak of you, how long will they speak?

"Let me even suppose that a future race of men shall be desirous of transmitting to their posterity your renown or mine, as they received it from their fathers; yet when we consider the convulsions and conflagrations that must necessarily happen at some definite period, we are unable to attain not only to an eternal, but even to a lasting fame. Now of what consequence is it to you to be talked of by those who are born after you, and not by those who were born before you, who certainly were as numerous and more virtuous; especially, as amongst the very men who are thus to celebrate our renown, not a single one can preserve the recollections of a single year? For mankind ordinarily measure their year by the revolution of the sun, that is of a single heavenly body. But when all the planets shall return to the same position which they once had, and bring back after a long rotation the same aspect of the entire heavens, then the year may be said to be truly completed; I do not venture to say how many ages of mankind will be contained within such a year. As of old the sun seemed to be eclipsed and blotted out when the soul of Romulus entered these regions, so when the sun shall be again eclipsed in the same part of his course and at the same period of the year and day, with all the constellations and stars recalled to the point from which they started on their revolutions, then count the year as brought to a close. But be assured that the twentieth part of such a year has not yet elapsed.

"Consequently, should you renounce hope of returning to this place where eminent and excellent men find their reward, of what worth is that human glory which can scarcely extend to a small part of a single year? If, then, you shall determine to look on high and contemplate this mansion and eternal abode, you will neither give yourself to the gossip of the vulgar nor place your hope of well-being on rewards that man can bestow. Virtue herself, by her own charms, should draw you to true honor. What others may say of you regard as their concern, not yours. They will doubtless talk about you, but what they say is limited to the narrow regions which you see; nor does talk of anyone last into eternity—it is buried with those who die, and lost in oblivion for those who come afterward."

When he had finished I said: "Truly, Africanus, if the path to heaven lies open to those who have deserved well of their country, though from my childhood I have ever trod in your and my father's footsteps without disgracing your glory, yet now, with so noble a prize set before me, I shall strive with much more diligence."

"Do so strive," replied he, "and do not consider yourself, but your body, to be mortal. For you are not the being which this corporeal figure evinces; but the soul of every man is the man, and not that form which may be delineated with a finger. Know also that you are a god, if a god is that which lives, perceives, remembers, foresees, and which rules, governs, and moves the body over which it is set, just as the Supreme God rules the universe. Just as the eternal God moves the universe, which is in part mortal, so does an everlasting soul move the corruptible body.

"That which is always in motion is eternal; but that which, while communicating motion to another, derives its own movement from some other source, must of necessity cease to live when this motion ends. Only what moves itself never ceases motion, for it is never deserted by itself; it is rather the source and first cause of motion in whatever else is moved. But the first cause has no beginning, for everything originates from the first cause; itself, from nothing. If it owed its origin to anything else, it would not be a first cause. If it has no beginning, it has no end. If a first cause is extinguished, it will neither be reborn from anything else, nor will it create anything else from itself, for everything must originate from a first cause. It follows that motion begins with that which is moved of itself, and that this can neither be born nor die—else the heavens must collapse and nature perish, possessing no force from which to receive the first impulse to motion.

"Since that which moves of itself is eternal, who can deny that the soul is endowed with this property? Whatever is moved by external impulse is soulless; whatever possesses soul is moved by an inner impulse of its own, for this is the peculiar nature and property of soul. And since soul is the only force that moves itself, it surely has no beginning and is immortal. Employ it, therefore, in the noblest of pursuits; the noblest are those undertaken for the safety of your country. If it is in these that your soul is diligently exercised, it will have a swifter flight to this, its proper home and permanent abode. Even swifter will be the flight if, while still imprisoned in the body, it shall peer forth, and, contemplating what lies beyond, detach itself as far as possible from the body. For the souls of those who have surrendered themselves to the pleasures of the body and have become their slaves, who are goaded to obedience by lust and violate the laws of gods and men—such souls, when they pass out of their bodies, hover close to earth, and do not return to this place till they have been tossed about for many ages."

He departed; I awoke from sleep.

ON THE NATURE OF THINGS
Titus Lucretius Carus (ca. 96–55 B.C.)

Nothing at all is known of Lucretius (Titus Lucretius Carus) beyond the fact that he is credited with a poem (excerpted below) extolling materialism and the philosophy of Epicurus, under whose disciples he probably studied. This is the most complete exposition of the materialistic basis of Epicureanism as well as being one of the world's outstanding poems.

In the following passage, Lucretius discusses the rise of ambition, of republican forms of government, of religions, the discovery of metals, of garments, of agriculture, of singing and dancing, and finally of the total development of luxurious civilization. Notice how carefully he suggests a materialistic origin for all of these things.

At several points during the selection he makes general statements about the nature of men and of human motives. Can you piece these together to discover Lucretius's basic thoughts about human nature and human motives, and about the nature of the best life? From these would you say that the author was essentially an optimist, a pessimist, or something in between? Compare the ideas with some of those expressed by Marcus Aurelius.

More and more every day men who excelled in intellect and were of vigorous understanding, would kindly show others how to exchange their former way of living for new methods. Kings began to build towns and lay out a citadel as a place of strength and of refuge for themselves, and divided cattle and lands and gave to each man in proportion to his personal beauty and strength and intellect; for beauty and vigorous strength were much esteemed. Afterwards wealth was discovered and gold found out, which soon robbed of their honors strong and beautiful alike, for men however valiant and beautiful of person generally follow in the train of the richer man. But were a man to order his life by the rules of true reason, a frugal subsistence joined to a contented mind is for him great riches; for never is there any lack of a little. But men desired to be famous and powerful, in order that their fortunes might rest on a firm foundation and they might be able by their wealth to lead a tranquil life; but in vain, since in their struggle to mount up to the highest dignities they rendered their path one full of danger; and even if they reach it, yet envy like a thunderbolt sometimes strikes and dashes men down from the highest point with ignominy into noisome Tartarus; since the highest summits and those elevated above the level of other things are mostly blasted by envy as by a thunderbolt, so that far better it is to obey in peace and quiet than to wish to rule with power supreme and be the master of kingdoms. Therefore let men wear themselves out to no purpose and sweat drops of blood, as they struggle on along the straight road of ambition, since they gather their knowledge from the mouths of others and follow after things from hearsay rather than the dictates of their own feelings; and this prevails not now nor will prevail by and by any more than it has prevailed before.

Kings therefore being slain, the old majesty of thrones and proud sceptres were overthrown and laid in the dust, and the glorious badge of the sovereign head bloodstained beneath the feet of the rabble mourned for its high prerogative; for that is greedily trampled on which before was too much dreaded. It would come then in the end to the lees of uttermost disorder, each man seeking for himself empire and sovereignty. Next a portion of them taught men to elect legal officers, and drew up codes, to induce men to obey the laws. For mankind, tired out with a life of brute force, lay exhausted from its feuds; and therefore the more readily it submitted of its own free will to laws and stringent codes. For as each one moved by anger took measures to avenge himself with more severity than is now permitted by equitable laws, for this reason men grew sick of a life of brute force. Thence fear of punishment mars the prizes of life; for violence and wrong enclose all who commit them in their meshes and do mostly recoil on him whom they began; and it is not easy for him who by his deeds transgresses the terms of the public peace to pass a tranquil and a peaceful existence. For though he eludes God and man, yet he cannot but feel a misgiving that his secret can be kept forever; seeing that many by speaking in their dreams or in the wanderings of disease have often we are told betrayed themselves and have disclosed their hidden deeds of evil and their sins.

And now what cause has spread over great nations the worship of the divinities of the gods and filled towns with altars and led to the performance of stated sacred rites, rites not in fashion on solemn occasions and in solemn places, from which even now is implanted in mortals a shuddering awe which raises new temples of the gods over the whole earth and prompts men to crowd them on festive days, all this is not so difficult to explain in words. Even then in sooth the races of mortal men would see in waking mind glorious forms, would see them in sleep of yet more marvellous size of body. To these then they would attribute sense, because they seemed to move their limbs and to utter lofty words suitable to their glorious aspects and surpassing powers. And they would give them life everlasting, because their face would appear before them and their form abide; yes, and yet without all this because they would not believe that beings possessed of such powers could lightly be overcome by any force. And they would believe them to be pre-eminent in bliss, because none of them was ever troubled with the fear of death, and because at the same time in sleep they would see them perform many miracles, yet feel on their part no fatigue from the effort. Again they would see the system of heaven and the different seasons of the years come round in regular succession, and could not find out by what cause this was done; therefore they would seek a refuge in handing over all things to the gods and supposing all things to be guided by their nod. And they placed in heaven the abodes and realms of the gods, because night and moon are seen to roll through heaven; moon, day and night, and night's austere constellations and night-wandering of the sky and flying bodies of flame, clouds, sun, rains, snow, winds, lightnings, hail, and rapid rumblings and loud threatful thunderclaps.

O hapless race of men, when that they charged the gods with such acts and coupled with them bitter wrath! What groanings did they then beget for themselves, what wounds for us, what tears for our children's children! No act is it of piety to be often seen with veiled head to turn to a stone and approach every altar and fall prostrate on the ground and spread out the palms before the statues of the gods and sprinkle the altars with much blood of beasts and link vow on vow, but rather to be able to look on all things with a mind at peace. For when we turn our gaze on the heavenly quarters of the great upper world and ether fast above the glittering stars, and direct our thoughts to the courses of the sun and moon, then into our breasts burdened with other ills that fear as well begins to exalt its reawakened head, the fear that we may haply find the power of the gods to be unlimited, able to wheel the bright stars in their varied motion; for lack of power to solve the question troubles the mind with doubts, whether there was ever a birth-time of the world, and whether likewise there is to be any end; how far the walls of the world can endure this strain of restless motion; or whether gifted by the grace of gods with an everlasting existence they may glide on through a never-ending tract of time and defy the strong powers of immeasurable ages. Again who is there whose mind does not shrink into itself with fear of the gods, whose limbs do not cower in terror, when the parched earth rocks with the appalling thunder-stroke and rattling runs through the great heaven? Do not people and nations quake, and proud monarchs shrink into themselves smitten with fear of the gods, lest for any foul transgression or overweening work the heavy time of reckoning has arrived at its fullness? When, too, the utmost fury of the headstrong wind passes over the sea and sweeps over its waters the commander of a fleet together with his mighty legions and elephants, does he not draw near with vows to seek the mercy of the gods and ask in prayer with fear and trembling a lull in the winds and propitious gales; but all in vain, since often caught up in the furious hurricane he is borne none the less to the shoals of death? So constantly does some hidden power trample on human grandeur and is seen to tread under its heel and make

sport for itself of the renowned rods and cruel axes.[13] Again when the whole earth rocks under their feet and towns tumble with the shock or doubtfully threaten to fall, what wonder that mortal men abase themselves and make over to the gods in things here on earth high prerogatives and marvelous powers, sufficient to govern all things?

To proceed, copper and gold and iron were discovered and at the same time weighty silver and the substance of lead, when fire with its heat had burnt up vast forests on the great hills, either by a discharge of heaven's lightning, or else because men waging with one another a forest-war had carried fire among the enemy in order to strike terror, or because drawn on by the goodness of the soil they would wish to clear rich fields, and bring the country into pasture, or else to destroy wild beasts and enrich themselves with the booty; for hunting with pitfall and with fire came into use before the practice of enclosing the lawn with nets and stirring it with dogs. Whatever the fact is, from whatever cause the heat of flame had swallowed up the forests with a frightful crackling from their very roots and had thoroughly baked the earth with fire, there would run from the boiling veins and collect into the hollows of the ground a stream of silver and gold, as well as of copper and lead. And when they saw these afterwards cool into lumps and glitter on the earth with a brilliant gleam, they would lift them up attracted by the bright and polished lustre, and they would see them to be moulded in a shape the same as the outline of the cavities in which each lay. Then it would strike them that these might be melted by heat and cast in any form or shape soever, and might by hammering out be brought to tapering points of any degree of sharpness and fineness, so as to furnish them with tools and enable them to cut the forests and hew timber and plane smooth the planks, and also to drill and pierce and bore, and they would set about these works just as much with silver and gold at first as with the overpowering strength of stout copper, but in vain, since their force would fail and give way and not be able like copper to stand the severe strain. At that time copper was in higher esteem and gold would be neglected on account of its uselessness, with its dull blunted edge; now copper lies neglected, gold has mounted up to the highest place of honor. Thus time as it goes round changes the seasons of things. That which was in esteem, falls at length into utter disrepute; and then another thing mounts up and issues out of its degraded state and every day is more and more coveted and blossoms forth high in honor when discovered and is in marvelous repute with men.

And now to find out by yourself in what way the nature of iron was discovered. Arms of old were hands, nails, and teeth, and stones and boughs broken off from the forest, and flame and fire, as soon as they had become known. Afterwards the force of iron and copper was discovered, and the use of copper was known before that of iron, as its nature is easier to work and it is found in greater quantity. With copper they would labor the soil of the earth, with copper stir up the billows of war and deal about the wide gaping wounds and seize cattle and lands; for everything defenseless and unarmed would readily yield to them with arms in hand. Then by slow steps the sword of iron gained ground and the make of the copper sickle became a by-word; and with iron they began to plough through the earth's soil, and the struggles of wavering war were rendered equal. . . .

---

13. A bundle of rods enclosing an axe was the emblem of magisterial authority at Rome.

A garment tied on the body was in use before a dress of woven stuff. Woven stuff comes after iron, because iron is needed for weaving a web; and in no other way can such finely polished things be made, as heddles and spindles, shuttles and ringing yarnbeams. And nature impelled men to work up the wool before womankind; for the male sex in general far excels the other in skill and is much more ingenious; until the rugged countrymen so upbraided them with it, that they were glad to give it over into the hands of the women and take their share in supporting hard toil, and in such hard work hardened body and hands.

But nature parent of things was herself the first model of sowing and first gave rise to grafting, since berries and acorns dripping from the trees would put forth in due season swarms of young shoots underneath; and hence also came the fashion of inserting grafts in their stocks and planting in the ground young saplings over the fields. Next they would try another and yet another kind of tillage for their loved piece of land and would see the earth better the wild fruits through genial fostering and kindly cultivation, and they would force the forests to recede every day higher and higher up the hillside and yield the ground below to tilth, in order to have on the uplands and plains, meadows, tanks, runnels, cornfields, and glad vineyards, and allow a gray-green strip of olives to run between and mark divisions, spreading itself over hillocks and valleys and plains; just as you now see richly dight with varied beauty all the ground which they lay out and plant with rows of sweet fruit-trees, and enclose all round with plantations of other goodly trees.

But imitating with the mouth the clear notes of birds was in use long before men were able to sing in tune smooth-running verses and give pleasure to the ear. And the whistlings of the zephyr through the hollows of reeds first taught peasants to blow into hollow stalks. Then step by step they learned sweet plaintive ditties, which the pipe pours forth pressed by the fingers of the players, heard through pathless woods and forests and lawns, through the unfrequented haunts of shepherds and abodes of unearthly calm. These things would soothe and gratify their minds when sated with food; for then all things of this kind are welcome. Often therefore stretched in groups on the soft grass beside a stream of water under the boughs of a high tree at no great cost they would pleasantly refresh their bodies, above all when the weather smiled and the seasons of the year painted the green grass with flowers. Then went round the jest, the tale, the peals of merry laughter; for the peasant muse was then in its glory; then frolick mirth would prompt to entwine head and shoulders with garlands plaited with flowers and leaves, and to advance in the dance out of step and move the limbs clumsily and with clumsy feet beat mother earth; which would occasion smiles and peals of merry laughter, because all these things then from their greater novelty and strangeness were in high repute, and the wakeful found a solace for want of sleep in this, in drawing out a variety of notes and going through tunes and running over the reeds with curving lip; whence even at the present day watchmen observe these traditions and have lately learned to keep the proper tune; and yet for all this receive not a jot more of enjoyment than erst the rugged race of sons of earth received. For that which we have in our hands, if we have known before nothing pleasanter, pleases above all and is

thought to be the best;[14] and as a rule the later discovery of something better spoils the taste for the former things and changes the feelings in regard to all that has gone before. Thus began distaste for the acorn, thus were abandoned those sleeping places strawn with grass and enriched with leaves. The dress too of wild beasts' skin fell into neglect; though I can fancy that in those days it was found to arouse such jealousy that he who first wore it met his death by an ambuscado, and after all it was torn in pieces among them and drenched in blood, was utterly destroyed and could not be turned to any use. In those times therefore skins, now gold and purple plague men's lives with cares and wear them out with war. And in this methinks the greater blame rests with us; but us it harms not in the least to do without a robe of purple, spangled with gold and large figures, if only we have a dress of the people to protect us. Mankind therefore ever toils vainly and to no purpose wastes life in groundless cares, because sure enough they have not learnt what is the true end of getting and up to what point genuine pleasure goes on increasing: this by slow degrees has carried life out into the deep sea and stirred up from their lowest depths the mighty billows of war.

But those watchful guardians sun and moon traversing with their light all around the great revolving sphere of heaven taught men that the seasons of the year came round and that the system was carried on after a fixed plan and fixed order.

Already they would pass their life fenced about with strong towers, and the land, portioned out and marked off by boundaries, be tilled; the sea would be filled with ships scudding under sail; towns have auxiliaries and allies as stipulated by treaty, when poets began to consign the deeds of men to verse; and letters had not been invented long before. For this reason our age cannot look back to what has gone before, save where reason points out any traces.

Ships and tillage, walls, laws, roads, dress, and all such like things, all the prizes, all the elegancies too of life without exception, poems, pictures, and chiselling of fine-wrought statues, all these things practiced together with the acquired knowledge of the untiring mind taught men by slow degrees as they advanced on the way step by step. Thus time by degrees brings each several thing forth before men's eyes and reason raises it up into the borders of light; for things must be brought to light one after the other and in due order in the different arts, until these have reached their highest point of development.

POEMS
Gaius Valerius Catullus (ca. 84–54 B.C.)

Gaius Valerius Catullus (ca. 84–54 B.C.), the leading Latin lyric poet, composed his love poetry for the enchanting Clodia (Lesbia in the poems), wife of Quintus Metellus. She became the most notoriously faithless beauty in Rome, while Catullus struggled with a virulent passion for her that slowly shriveled to despair before subsiding into bitter maledictions. Poems 5, 51, 58, 72, and 75 testify to the stages of his infatuation. The first three stanzas of poem 51 are a

---

14. Notice throughout this piece the philosophic generalization which Lucretius makes. Try reading them together without the intervening descriptions and see if you can get a fairly complete picture of his philosophy.

partial translation by Catullus of a poem by Sappho, the seventh-century Greek poet from the island of Lesbos. Poems 1, 22, 40, and 42 are concerned with poets and poetry; poem 42 refers to the stubborn muse of poetry who frustrates the best of poets by failing to provide the requisite inspiration.

1

Who do I give this neat little book to
all new and polished up and ready to go?
You, Cornelius, because you always thought
there was something to this stuff of mine,
and were the one man in Italy with guts enough
to lay out all history in a couple of pages,
a learned job, by god, and it took work.
So here's the book, for whatever it's worth
I want you to have it. And please, goddess,
see that it lasts for more than a lifetime.

5

Let's you and me live it up, my Lesbia,
and make some love, and let old cranks
go cheap talk their damn fool heads off.
Maybe suns can set and come back up again,
but once the brief light goes out on us
the night's one long sleep forever.
First give me a kiss, a thousand kisses,
then a hundred, and then a thousand more,
then another hundred, and another thousand,
and keep kissing and kissing me so many times
we get all mixed up and can't count anymore,
that way nobody can give us the evil eye
trying to figure how many kisses we've got.

22

Take Suffenus, now you know the guy, Varus,
handsome, good talker, knows his way around,
well he writes poetry also, in big shipments.
I think he's got thousands, maybe millions
copied out, I don't mean in rough draft either:
fancy imperial stock, new rolls, new pegs,
thongs of red leather, sheepskin slip covers,
lines ruled, edges trimmed, the whole works.
Then you read them. Suddenly your suave and
sophisticated Suffenus turns into a goat milker,
a shit shoveler from the mountains. It's grim!
What's going on anyway? Here he is, sharp,
looks like he could slice you down in a word,
but the minute he starts fooling with poetry,
watch out, he's clumsier than a hick is clumsy.
And he's never happier than when writing a poem,
or more pleased, he thinks he's just wonderful!
Okay, it's true, we all do it, there's nobody
who isn't a Suffenus in one thing or another.
Everybody has a pack of faults on his shoulders,
if heads were on backwards we'd all see our own.

40

Lost your mind Ravidus, you poor ass,
landing smack into one of my poems like this?
Is some god getting you into trouble
because you didn't say your prayers right?
Or are you just out to get talked about?
What do you want? To be famous, never mind how?
Okay you will, and being that it's my girl you're after,
you're going to suffer for a long, long time.

42

Calling all syllables! Calling all syllables!
Let's go! I need all the help I can get!
Some filthy whore's playing games with me
and won't give me back my manuscripts with
your pals inside! Are you going to let her?
Who is she, you ask? Well go take a look,
she's over there shaking her ass all around
and flashing smiles like a Pomeranian bitch.
Ready? Okay, line up and let her have it!
'O foul adulteress, O lascivious witch,
give me back my notebooks, you dirty bitch!'
What? Up yours, you say? You slut, tramp,
you've sunk so low you look up to see down!
Still, we can't let her get away like this,
if all else fails, at least let's see whether
we can force a blush from the hard-faced beast.
Try again, fellas, good and loud this time!
'O FOUL ADULTERESS, O LASCIVIOUS WITCH,
GIVE ME BACK MY NOTEBOOKS, YOU DIRTY BITCH!'
No use. It won't work. Nothing moves her.
We've got to switch to different tactics,
almost anything will work better than this.
'O maiden so modest, O virgin so pure . . .'

51

To me, that man seems to be one of the gods,
or to tell the truth, even more than a god,
sitting there face to face with you, forever
looking, listening
to you laughing sweetly, while poor me, I take
one look at you and I'm all torn up inside,
Lesbia, there's nothing left of me. I can't
make a sound, my tongue's
stuck solid, hot little fire flashes go
flickering through my body, my ears begin
ringing around in my head, my eyes black out,
shrouded in darkness . . .
This soft life is no good for you. Catullus,
you wallow in it, you don't know when to stop.
A soft life's already been the ruin of both
great kings and cities.

58

Caelius, our Lesbia, that Lesbia,
the Lesbia Catullus once loved
more than himself and all he owns,
now works streets and back alleys
groping big-hearted sons of Remus.

72

Time was you said only Catullus could touch you,
that God in heaven couldn't have you before me.
I loved you then, not just as a guy does a girl,
but the way a father loves his sons and grandsons.
Now I know you, Lesbia, and if my passion grows,
you're also much cheaper to me and insignificant.
How's that? Because, hurt a man in love and he
lusts for you more, but the less he really cares.

75

My mind's sunk so low, Lesbia, because of.you,
wrecked itself on your account so bad already,
I couldn't like you if you were the best of women,
or stop loving you, no matter what you do.

EPIGRAMS

Marcus Valerius Martialis (ca. A.D. 40–104)

MARTIAL (Marcus Valerius Martialis; ca. A.D. 40–104) wrote hundreds of epigrams, which are brief poems, often satiric, ending in a surprise twist or climax. His style can be described as terse, sardonic, sparse, ascerbic, sarcastic, witty, and, withal, strikingly and delightfully modern.

I, i

Here he is—the one you read,
the one you ask for—Martial,
recognized the world over
for his witty books of epigrams.
Learned reader, you've given him
(while he's still alive to enjoy it)
the glory poets rarely get
after they've turned to ashes.

I, xxxv

You take me to task for writing
poems that aren't as prissy
and prim as they might be, Cornelius.
Not the kind a schoolmaster
would read aloud in the classroom.
But my little books wouldn't satisfy
(anymore than husbands can
their wives) without a little sex.

Would you want me to write a wedding-song
without using the words that wedding-songs
always use? Would you cover up
Flora's nymphs with a lot of clothing
or let prostitutes hide their shamefulness
under ladies' robes? There's a rule
that merry songs can't be merry
unless they're a bit indecent.

So forget your prudishness, please,
and spare my jokes and my naughtiness,
and don't try to castrate my poems.
Nothing's worse than Priapus posing
as a eunuch of Cybele.

II, xxxvi

I don't say you should curl your hair,
but you could comb it.
I don't say your body should be oiled,
but you could take a bath.
You needn't have a eunuch's beard
or a jailbird's. I don't insist
upon too much manliness,
Pannychus, or too little.
As it is, your legs are hairy
and your chest is shaggy with bristles,
but your mind, Pannychus, is bald.

II, lxviii

Don't think me insolent, Olus,
for calling you by your name
nowadays instead of "Patron"
or "Master" as I used to do.
I've bought my freedman's cap
with everything I possessed.

A man needs patrons and masters
if he isn't master of himself
and covets the same things patrons
and masters covet. But once
he can get along without a slave,
he can get along without a master.

III, xxxviii

Tell me, what brings you to Rome
so self-confidently, Sextus?
What are you after, and what
do you expect to find there?
"First of all, I'll plead cases
more eloquently than Cicero
himself. There won't be anyone
in the three forums to touch me."
Atestinus and Civis
(you know them both) pled cases,
but neither one of them took in
enough to pay the rent.
"Well, if nothing comes of that,
I'll write poems. When you hear them,
you'll say they're Vergil's work."
You're crazy. Wherever you look
you'll see Ovids and Vergils—all of them
shivering in their thin cloaks.
"Then I'll cultivate rich men."
That sort of thing has supported
maybe three or four. The rest
of the crowd are pale with hunger.
"What *will* I do? Advise me.
I'm determined to live in Rome."
Well, Sextus, if you're honest,
you'll be lucky to stay alive.

IV, xlix

Believe me, Flaccus—anyone
who calls epigrams mere trifles
and frivolities doesn't understand
what they are. It's more frivolous,
really, when somebody writes
about Tereus' revolting dinner
or that undigestible meal
of yours, Thyestes, or Daedalus
fitting the meltable wings
to his son, or Polyphemus
grazing his Sicilian sheep.
That kind of windiness
won't be found in any of my poems.
My Muse doesn't puff herself up
with such tragic nonsense.

    "Still,
everybody praises that kind
of thing—admires it—worships it!"
Granted. They praise it, but
it's my kind of poem they read.

V, xiii

I'll admit I'm poor, Callistratus,
and always have been. And yet
two Emperors gave me a knighthood
and I'm not altogether unknown,
and my reputation isn't bad.

I've got a great many readers
everywhere in the world who will say
"That's Martial," and recognition
such as few receive after they're dead
has come to me while I'm alive.

On the other hand, your house-roof
is supported by a hundred columns,
and your money-boxes contain
a freedman's wealth, and wide fields
near Syene on the River Nile
call you master, and Parma in Gaul
shears its countless flocks for you.

That's what we are, you and I.
But you can never be what I am,
while anyone at all can be like you.

V, lvi

You've been wondering and worrying
and asking me every day
whom you ought to hand over your son to
for instruction, Lupus. I warn you:
stay away from all those grammarians
and professors of rhetoric.

Don't let him have anything to do
with Cicero's writings, or Vergil's,
and let Tutilius, the author
and advocate, earn his reputation
somewhere else. If the boy writes poems,
disown the young versifier!

Does he want to learn to make money?
Then have him take lessons in harping
or fluting. Or if the young fellow's
not too bright, you can turn him into
a salesman or an architect.

VI, xiv

You keep insisting, Labierus,
that you know how to write fine poems.
Then why is it you're unwilling
to try? Knowing how to write
fine poems and never doing it!
What will power, Labierus!

VI, xxxi

You know your wife's playing around
with your physician, Charidemus,
but you don't do anything about it.
My guess is you won't have to wait
for a fever to carry you off.

VIII, xii

Why don't I marry a rich wife?
Because I won't make my wife
my master. A wife should be
submissive to her husband, Priscus.
There's no other way to give men
an equal chance with their women.

XI, lxvi

You're a spy and a blackmailer,
a forger, a pimp, a pervert,
and a trainer of gladiators,
Vacerra. I can't understand
why you aren't rich.

On the Dedication of the Colosseum in Rome

Barbaric Egypt, boast no more
    The wonders of your pyramids!
Babylon, vaunt no longer now
    The gardens of Semiramis!
Let not the soft Ionians swell
    With pride for their great Artemis
Whose temple splendor long has been
    The claim and fame of Ephesus.
Let Delos hide its head in shame
    And say no more Apollo
Himself did rear the altar there
    (A claim both weak and hollow).
Let not the Carians wildly praise
    The wondrous, sculptured tomb
The Queen at Halicarnassus raised
    When Mausolus met his doom.
Let every wonder of the past
    Yield now to this great wonder.
Fame shall cling to this at last,
    Her applause as loud as thunder.

(Mills, 1969)

DISCOURSES OF EPICTETUS, BOOK I, CHAPTER 1
Arrian (b. A.D. 108)

This lecture of Epictetus (ca. A.D. 60–110), as recorded by his student Arrian, together with the meditations of Marcus Aurelius (121–180), which follows, present the Stoic point of view. This philosophy assumes that the great *Logos* (Intelligence) pervades the entire world and directs all that happens. Therefore, as will be seen in the selections, it is essentially a stern philosophy of acceptance, duty, and brotherhood of all men.

On Things in Our Power and Things Not in Our Power

Of our faculties in general you will find that none can take cognizance of itself; none therefore has the power to approve or disapprove its own action. Our grammatical faculty for instance: how far can that take cognizance? Only so far as to distinguish expression. Our musical faculty? Only so far as to distinguish tune. Does any one of these then take cognizance of itself? By no means. If you are writing to your friend, when you want to know what words to write grammar will tell you; but whether you should write to your friend or should not write grammar will not tell you. And in the same way music will tell you about tunes, but whether at this precise moment you should sing and play the lyre or should not sing nor play the lyre it will not tell you. What will tell you then? That faculty which takes cognizance of itself and of all things else. What is this? The reasoning faculty: for this alone of the faculties we have received is created to comprehend even its own nature; that is to say, what it is and what it can do, and with what precious qualities it has come to us, and to comprehend all other faculties as well. For what else is it that tells us that gold is a goodly thing?

For the gold does not tell us. Clearly it is the faculty which can deal with our impressions. What else is it which distinguishes the faculties of music, grammar, and the rest, testing their uses and pointing out the due seasons for their use? It is reason and nothing else.

The gods then, as was but right, put in our hands the one blessing that is best of all and master of all, that and nothing else, the power to deal rightly with our impressions, but everything else they did not put in our hands. Was it that they would not? For my part I think that if they could have entrusted us with those other powers as well they would have done so, but they were quite unable. Prisoners on the earth and in an earthly body and among earthly companions, how was it possible that we should not be hindered from the attainment of these powers by these external fetters?

But what says Zeus? 'Epictetus, if it were possible I would have made your body and your possessions (those trifles that you prize) free and untrammelled. But as things are—never forget this—this body is not yours, it is but a clever mixture of clay. But since I could not make it free, I gave you a portion in our divinity, this faculty of impulse to act and not to act, of will to get and will to avoid, in a word the faculty which can turn impressions to right use. If you pay heed to this, and put your affairs in its keeping, you will never suffer let nor hindrance, you will not groan, you will blame no man, you will flatter none. What then? Does all this seem but little to you?'

Heaven forbid!

'Are you content then?'

So surely as I hope for the gods' favour.

But, as things are, though we have it in our power to pay heed to one thing and to devote ourselves to one, yet instead of this we prefer to pay heed to many things and to be bound fast to many—our body, our property, brother and friend, child and slave. Inasmuch then as we are bound fast to many things, we are burdened by them and dragged down. That is why, if the weather is bad for sailing, we sit distracted and keep looking continually and ask, 'What wind is blowing?' 'The north wind.' What have we to do with that? 'When will the west wind blow?' When it so chooses, good sir, or when Aeolus chooses. For God made Aeolus the master of the winds, not you. What follows? We must make the best of those things that are in our power, and take the rest as nature gives it. What do you mean by 'nature'? I mean, God's will.

'What? Am I to be beheaded now, and I alone?'

Why? Would you have had all beheaded, to give you consolation? Will you not stretch out your neck as Lateranus did in Rome when Nero ordered his beheadal? For he stretched out his neck and took the blow, and when the blow dealt him was too weak he shrank up a little and then stretched it out again. Nay more, on a previous occasion, when Nero's freedman Epaphroditus came to him and asked him the cause of his offence, he answered, 'If I want to say anything, I will say it to your master.'

What then must a man have ready to help him in such emergencies? Surely this: he must ask himself, 'What is mine, and what is not mine? What may I do, what may I not do?'

I must die. But must I die groaning? I must be imprisoned. But must I whine as well? I must suffer exile. Can any one then hinder me from going with a smile, and a good courage, and at peace?

'Tell the secret!'

I refuse to tell, for this is in my power.

'But I will chain you.'

What say you, fellow? Chain me? My leg you will chain—yes, but my will—no, not even Zeus can conquer that.

'I will imprison you.'

My bit of a body, you mean.

'I will behead you.'

Why? When did I ever tell you that I was the only man in the world that could not be beheaded?

These are the thoughts that those who pursue philosophy should ponder, these are the lessons they should write down day by day, in these they should exercise themselves.

Thrasea used to say 'I had rather be killed to-day than exiled tomorrow'. What then did Rufus say to him? 'If you choose it as the harder, what is the meaning of your foolish choice? If as the easier, who has given you the easier? Will you not study to be content with what is given you?'

It was in this spirit that Agrippinus used to say—do you know what? 'I will not stand in my own way!' News was brought him, 'Your trial is on in the Senate!' 'Good luck to it, but the fifth hour is come'—this was the hour when he used to take his exercise and have a cold bath— 'let us go and take exercise.' When he had taken his exercise they came and told him, 'You are condemned.' 'Exile or death?' he asked. 'Exile.' 'And my property?' 'It is not confiscated.' 'Well then, let us go to Aricia and dine.'

Here you see the result of training as training should be, of the will to get and will to avoid, so disciplined that nothing can hinder or frustrate them. I must die, must I? If at once, then I am dying: if soon, I dine now, as it is time for dinner, and afterwards when the time comes I will die. And die how? As befits one who gives back what is not his own.

MEDITATIONS, BOOK II
Marcus Aurelius (121–180)

Begin the morning by saying to thyself, I shall meet with the busybody, the ungrateful, arrogant, deceitful, envious, unsocial. All these things happen to them by reason of their ignorance of what is good and evil. But I who have seen the nature of the good that it is beautiful, and of the bad that it is ugly, and the nature of him who does wrong, that it is akin to me, not only of the same blood or seed, but that it participates in the same intelligence and the same portion of the divinity, I can neither be injured by any of them, for no one can fix on me what is ugly, nor can I be angry with my kinsman, nor hate him. For we are made for cooperation, like feet, like hands, like eyelids, like the rows of the upper and lower teeth. To act against one another then is contrary to nature; and it is acting against one another to be vexed and to turn away.

2. Whatever this is that I am, it is a little flesh and breath, and the ruling part. Throw away thy books; no longer distract thyself: it is not allowed; but as if thou wast now dying, despise the flesh; it is blood and bones and a network, a contexture of nerves, veins, and arteries. See the breath also, what kind of a thing it is, air, and not always the same, but every moment sent out and again sucked in. The third then is the ruling part: consider thus: Thou art an old man; no longer let this be a slave, no longer be pulled by the strings like a puppet to unsocial movements, no longer be either dissatisfied with thy present lot, or shrink from the future.

5. Every moment think steadily as a Roman and a man to do what thou hast in hand with perfect and simple dignity, and feeling of affection, and freedom, and justice; and to give thyself relief from all other thoughts. And thou wilt give thyself relief, if thou doest every act of thy life as it were the last, laying aside all carelessness and passionate aversion from the commands of reason, and all hypocrisy, and self-love, and discontent with the portion which has been given to thee. Thou seest how few the things are, that which if a man lays hold of, he is able to live a life which flows in quiet, and is like the existence of the gods; for the gods on their part will require nothing more from him who observes these things.

9. This thou must always bear in mind, what is the nature of the whole, and what is my nature, and how this is related to that, and what kind of a part it is of what kind of a whole; and that there is no one who hinders thee from always doing and saying the things which are according to the nature of which thou art a part.

11. Since it is possible that thou mayest depart from life this very moment, regulate every act and thought accordingly. But to go away from among men, if there are gods, is not a thing to be afraid of, for the gods will not involve thee in evil; but if indeed they do not exist, or if they have no concern about human affairs, what is it to me to live in a universe devoid of gods or devoid of Providence? But in truth they do exist, and they do care for human things, and they have put all the means in man's power to enable him not to fall into real evils. And as to the rest, if there was anything evil, they would have provided for this also, that it should be altogether in a man's power not to fall into it. Now that which does not make a man worse, how can it make a man's life worse? But neither through ignorance, nor having the knowledge, but not the power to guard against or correct these things, is it possible that the nature of the universe has overlooked them; nor is it possible that it has made so great a mistake, either through want of power or want of skill, that good and evil should happen indiscriminately to the good and the bad. But death certainly, and life, honour and dishonour, pain and pleasure, all these things equally happen to good men and bad, being things which make us neither better nor worse. Therefore they are neither good nor evil.

16. The soul of man does violence to itself, first of all, when it becomes an abscess and, as it were, a tumour on the universe, so far as it can. For to be vexed at anything which happens is a separation of ourselves from nature, in some part of which the natures of all other things are contained. In the next place, the soul does violence to itself when it turns away from any man, or even moves towards him with the intention of injuring, such as are the souls of those who are angry. In the third place, the soul does violence to itself when it is overpowered by pleasure or by pain. Fourthly, when it plays a part, and does or says anything insincerely and untruly. Fifthly, when it allows any act of its own and any movement to be without an aim, and does anything thoughtlessly and without considering what it is, it being right that even the smallest things be done with reference to an end; and the end of rational animals is to follow the reason and the law of the most ancient city and polity.

17. Of human life the time is a point, and the substance is in a flux, and the perception dull, and the composition of the whole body subject to putrefaction, and the soul a whirl, and fortune hard to divine, and fame a thing devoid of judgement. And, to say all in a word, everything which belongs to the body is a stream, and what belongs to the soul is a dream and vapour, and life is a warfare and a stranger's sojourn, and after-fame is oblivion. What then is that which is able to conduct a man? One thing and only one, philosophy. But this consists in keeping the daemon within a man free from violence and unharmed, superior to pains and pleasures, doing nothing without a purpose, nor yet falsely and with hypocrisy, not feeling the need of another man's doing or not doing anything; and besides, accepting all that happens, and all that is allotted, as coming from thence, wherever it is, from whence he himself came; and, finally, waiting for death with a cheerful mind, as being nothing else than a dissolution of the elements of which every living being is compounded. But if there is no harm to the elements themselves in each continually changing into another, why should a man have any apprehension about the change and dissolution of all the elements? For it is according to nature, and nothing is evil which is according to nature.

6

Roman Art and Music: The Arts of Megalopolis

Etruscan Civilization

Chronological Overview

800s B.C.	Etruscans in Italy
ca. 800–700 B.C.	Conquest of central Italy
ca. 650–550 B.C.	Conquest of Rome
509 B.C.	Romans expel Tarquin the Proud and begin final destruction of the Etruscan city-states

Although strongly influenced by their constant contacts and conflicts with Greek city-states but generally lagging behind Greek innovations, the Etruscans developed a distinctive kind of art. Provincial, sometimes homespun, their work has an earthy vigor, which in turn influenced their Roman conquerors. With no literature and little more than some massive stone walls remaining of their fortified hilltop cities, our scanty knowledge of Etruscan culture is based almost entirely on the contents of the thousands of tombs found throughout central Italy. Etruscan skill in making terra-cotta objects is exemplified by the funerary sculpture (fig. 6.1) found in the *necropolis* (city of the dead) outside Cerveteri, northwest of Rome. A deceased couple is shown resting their left elbows on a couch as if they are attending a celestial banquet. The smooth bodies, braided hair, and archaic smiles in the Greek manner are typical of the Etruscan style, as is the display of mutual affection and the individualized features of the couple. The exact meaning of festive banquet scenes in tomb paintings and as depicted on numerous sarcophagi is unknown, but continuation of the good life after death may have been intended.

Constantly at war with the Phoenicians and the Greeks over trade routes in the western Mediterranean, the Etruscans nevertheless valued the arts of Greece, especially Greek vases; most Greek pottery recovered

Figure 6.1 Etruscan sarcophagus, from Cerveteri, Italy, ca. 510 B.C. Painted terra-cotta, length ca. 80″. Museo Nazionale della Villa Giulia, Rome.

to date has been found in Etruscan tombs. Unconcerned with art objects, the Romans apparently learned utilitarian skills from the Etruscans: how to plan cities and how to build fortifications, monumental gateways, bridges, and aqueducts.

Roman Civilization, ca. 753 B.C.–A.D. 476

Chronological Overview

753 B.C.	Traditional date of the founding of Rome
ca. 509 B.C.	Founding of the Republic
264–146 B.C.	Three Punic Wars with Carthage and (214–146 B.C.) four wars with Macedonia and Dyria
133–27 B.C.	Disintegration of the Republic
27 B.C.– A.D. **180**	*Pax Romana*
27 B.C.– A.D. **17**	Augustan (Gold) Age
A.D. **17–130**	Silver Age
180–284	Age of Revolutions
284–337	Reorganization and division into East and West Empires.
330	Constantine transfers the capital to New Rome (Constantinople)
337–476	Decline and Fall of Western Empire

For the stern Romans, art was a corrupting influence that could undermine the moral fiber of the people, especially the citizen-soldiers of the republic. As late as the third century B.C., Rome was, according to Plutarch, a drab and dreary city full of battle trophies, barbarous weapons, triumphal monuments, and bloodstained hostages—a metropolis devoid of refinement and beauty. The penetration of Greek culture, especially Greek art, was a slow process that gathered momentum with Roman triumphs over Greek territories. During the conquest of the luxurious cities of Magna Graecia (southern Italy) in 212 B.C., for example, one general returned bearing Greek statues and paintings with which to adorn the city, while another general displayed gold and jewels, which according to the old guard was the only proper kind of booty. With the conquest of the Greek mainland in 146 B.C., a huge volume of confiscated artworks flooded the city, overwhelming the hostility of the die-hard conservatives and establishing Rome as the prime custodian of the Hellenic artistic tradition. Geared more to copying than creating, doing rather than theorizing, the native arts in Rome were produced by an army of anonymous artisans, with most efforts directed at a burgeoning mass market.

Though much of what we call Roman art is derived from Greek models and often created by Greek artists, the Romans did make some significant and original contributions with their realistic portrait busts, landscape painting, and, especially, their architecture. Justly famous for the monumental architecture of the imperial period, the Romans must also be credited with developing the "art" of civilized living. During the early days of the Republic, more attention was paid to the efficient design of military camps than to the urban planning of Rome and other growing cities of the rapidly expanding Republic. With the shift from a simple rural to an affluent urbanized society, the Romans had to come to grips with the problems of city planning. Taking their cue from Etruscan hill towns, they learned how to design and build the basic requirements for urban life: fortifications; streets; bridges; aqueducts; sewers; town houses; apartment houses; and recreational, shopping, and civic centers.

Figure 6.2 West portico of the forum, Pompeii

Figure 6.3 Atrium, House of the Vetti, Pompeii

With no art and very little architecture remaining from the early centuries of the Republic, we will begin our study of the arts of Rome with Pompeii, which through an accident of history is the only surviving city of the Roman Republic. The eruption of Mount Vesuvius in A.D. 79 buried Pompeii under cinders and ashes that, in effect, preserved the city as a museum of Roman civilization. Probably founded in the sixth century B.C., Pompeii was inhabited by Italic Oscans and Samnites, plus some Greeks, until its conquest by Rome in about 80 B.C. Containing the earliest extant amphitheatre and public baths, Pompeii was built in a modified Greek grid plan around the most important early forum outside Rome (fig. 6.2). Reflecting Greek influence, the Doric colonnade with superimposed Ionic columns was a device that was later extended to four levels in the design of the Colosseum (see fig. 6.14). There are, in fact, so many different elements of Etruscan, Greek, and Italic contributions to Pompeiian decoration that it is impossible to precisely determine who did what. The civic center, or forum, is, however, typically Roman. Combining religious, commercial, and civic functions, forums are found in every Roman city, reflecting Roman concerns for centralized authority and control.

Because the city-center forum was always closed to vehicular traffic, the network of streets began at the perimeter and expanded outward to the suburbs. Much as old Italian towns are today, the streets nearer the forum were lined by shops, which were flanked by houses of shopkeepers and other citizens. The *domus,* single-family residence, was entered through a front doorway set in a windowless wall that guaranteed privacy and shut out city noise and dirt. An

entrance hall led to the *atrium* (fig. 6.3), a typical Italic-Roman design for larger houses and for the still more elaborate villas in the surrounding countryside. A rectangular, windowless court that kept out heat while admitting light and air, the atrium had an inwardly sloping roof that drained rainwater into the pool below, from which it was piped to a cistern. Surrounding the central atrium were the kitchen, parlors, and other rooms for everyday living. Beyond the atrium were the bedrooms, with porches fronting on an open courtyard surrounded by a peristyle of, in this case, Doric columns. As was customary with Roman houses, the numerous blank walls were either brightly painted or decorated with murals like those on the two square columns and exterior bedroom walls in figure 6.3. The combination of Roman atrium and Hellenistic Greek peristyle court, which was adopted in the second century B.C., makes the Roman house or villa an ideal design for hot Mediterranean summers.

Maintaining a strong sense of identity was a major concern for Roman families; they preserved collections of exact portrait masks in wax of their ancestors. Recognizable portrayals were therefore required, accounting for the long tradition of starkly realistic marble portrait busts as represented, for example, by the bust of Julius Caesar (fig. 6.4). As the man responsible for the final demise of the embattled Republic, Caesar is depicted as history has revealed him to be: imperious, ruthless, a charismatic leader of men. With their no-nonsense approach to reality, the Romans insisted upon an exactitude that included every wart, pimple, line, and blemish. This bust may have been done from life; if so, it is possible that Caesar relished the portrait, particularly the commanding tilt of the head.

Figure 6.4 Bust of Julius Caesar, first century B.C. Marble, height 38″. National Museum, Naples.

Figure 6.6 Three portrait busts of Caesar Augustus. British Museum, London. Reproduced by courtesy of the Trustees of the British Museum.

Figure 6.5 *Augustus of Primaporta,* ca. 20 B.C. Marble, height 81″. Vatican Museums, Rome.

There are no blemishes on the commanding statue of Caesar Augustus from the Imperial Villa at Primaporta (fig. 6.5). Idealized in the Greek manner, this is how Augustus intended to be seen and to be remembered—a noble ruler. Based on the *Doryphoros* (see fig. 3.35), with the commanding gesture probably derived from Near Eastern art, this is an official portrait. With his likeness on Roman coins and

with thousands of busts like those in figure 6.6 distributed throughout the Empire, Augustus created the imperial image of powerful Rome. Based on Virgil's tracing of his ancestry to Aeneas, founder of Rome, Augustus's divine origins are revealed here in the cupid and the dolphin, symbols of Venus, mother of Aeneas. Indicating the secular history, the statue's cloak has fallen low enough to reveal the relief sculpture on the armor detailing the emperor's road to power. The only realistic elements are the tactile illusions of leather, metal, and cloth that give the feeling of actuality prized by Romans but considered trite by Greeks. Becoming a stock device for depicting kings, emperors, and dictators, the commanding gesture will also be seen in the figure of Christ in the Royal Portal of Chartres Cathedral (see fig. 11.31) and in Michelangelo's Christ of the *Last Judgment* in the Sistine Chapel (see fig. 14.31). The *Augustus of Primaporta* is a superb example of a didactic art form probably forever after destined to serve church and state.

Though no intact Augustan temples remain in Rome, the remarkably well preserved temple nicknamed the Maison Carrée (marble house; fig. 6.7) embodies the qualities advocated by the emperor. Unlike their Greek counterparts, Roman temples stand on high podiums and are entered from the front by a single flight of steps. The open form of the Greek temple, with a walkway and three steps on all four sides, has been converted to the closed form of buildings designed to enclose space. This temple uses the rich Corinthian order (fig. 6.8) favored by most Roman architects and engaged columns attached to the cella walls in a decorative device from Republican days. A small building measuring 59′ × 117′ with 30′ columns, the Maison Carrée became a prototype of temples honoring notable emperors, much as the Jefferson Memorial in Washington memorializes an illustrious

Figure 6.7 Maison Carrée, ca. 19 B.C., Nîmes, France.

Figure 6.8 Corinthian capital

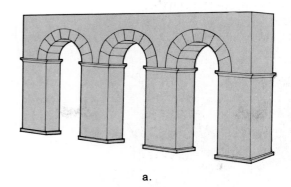

a.

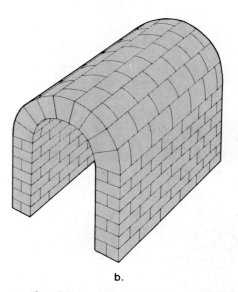

b.

Figure 6.9 (a) Semicircular arch arcade (b) Semicircular arch vault.

president. This building, in fact, inspired Thomas Jefferson to utilize the classic style of Rome in his neoclassic designs of the Virginia State Capitol, the University of Virginia, and his own home of Monticello.

Rome made a lasting contribution to the development of the rounded arch and vault as structural architectural principles. Used for centuries in Asia Minor and Greece for lesser works like gates, storage areas, corridors, and sewers, the arch was exploited by Roman engineers on a massive scale. They were concerned with spanning and enclosing space, and thus used arches to build bridges, aqueducts, baths, and basilicas, the secular structures necessary for the efficient operation of Roman cities. A semicircle of stone blocks, or bricks and mortar (fig. 6.9), spanning spaces between piers or walls, the arch was better suited to the utilitarian needs of Roman engineering than the post and lintel system. Not intended to bridge large spaces, the lintel is the weaker portion of the system because it can support a limited amount of weight. To bear greater loads it must be enlarged, the columns moved closer together, or both. In the arch, the wedge-shaped blocks called *voussoirs* (voo–SWAHR) curve up to the keystone at the apex

of the arch, giving strength and stability because of the mutually supporting pressures from pier to keystone. From the keystone the thrust is transmitted through the voussoirs down through the pier, or wall, to the ground. When the arches are side by side they form an arcade, as in the Pont du Gard (see fig. 6.10). When extended longitudinally along its axis, the arch is called a barrel or tunnel vault, as in the Arch of Titus (see fig. 6.18).

Representing Roman engineering and power, aqueducts were a highly visible portion of the network of waterways and roadways that interconnected the empire. Built by Agrippa, a lieutenant under Augustus, the Pont du Gard (fig. 6.10) is 180′ high and in its present condition about 900′ long. It carried water some twenty-five miles from the mountains, across the gorge of the Gard River, and into Nîmes. Spanning over 80′, each massive arch supports an arch of similar dimensions but with much less masonry, which in turn undergirds the watercourse itself. Supported by three small arches for each large one, the water flowed steadily down an approximate 1 percent grade, dropping about one foot every hundred feet.

Figure 6.10 Pont du Gard, ca. 20–10 B.C., near Nîmes, France.

Figure 6.11 Roman Mausoleum, ca. A.D. 40, St.-Rémy-du-Provence, France.

Figure 6.12 *Herakles Discovering the Infant Telephos in Arcadia,* wall painting from Herculaneum, ca. A.D. 70, approximately 86″ × 74″. Roman copy of a Hellenistic painting of second century B.C. National Museum, Naples.

Using stones weighing up to six tons each and assembled without mortar, the bridge of the lowest arcade has been in continuous use for two thousand years.

The best-preserved of all Roman funerary memorials, the so-called Mausoleum (fig. 6.11) is actually a cenotaph that honors the dead but does not contain the remains. Erected in honor of two grandsons of Augustus who died in childhood, the three-stage structure has reliefs on the solid base and engaged Corinthian columns flanking the second-level arches. Statues of the two children are within the circular third level. The combination of reliefs, projecting cornices, squared-off arches, and rounded forms is eclectic rather than classical and illustrates how far removed Roman opulence is from Greek restraint.

In *Herakles Discovering the Infant Telephos in Arcadia* (fig. 6.12) we see an example of the continuing interest in classical themes, which formed one of the bridges between Greek and Roman cultures. The powerful nude figure stands before a classically conceived woman representing the mythical Arcadia, where everyone lived at peace with one another and with nature. The lion is painted in a vaguely impressionistic manner, while the doe in the left foreground is light, lovely, and graceful. The disparate figures look like they have been placed in a preexisting space with

Figure 6.13 Reconstruction of fourth-century Rome (detail) by I. Gismondi. Museum of Roman Civilization, Rome.

Figure 6.14 Colosseum, A.D. 72–80, 513′ × 620′ × 161′ high, Rome.

little concern for how they relate to each other or to the overall unity of the painting. In common with much Roman painting, the work does display, however, great technical skill in the manipulation of light, lines, and shapes, and in the illusion of three-dimensional space.

A comparison of the assemblage of visual images of the *Herakles* with the figure of the *Doryphoros* (see fig. 3.35) illustrates some fundamental differences between Greek and Roman cultures. More concerned with practice than theory, the Romans itemized rather than conceptualized. The *Herakles* is a kind of visual catalog of a specific event: Herakles finding his son in Arcadia. The *Doryphoros* is not a specific person but a realization of the ideal athlete, the embodiment of a concept against which individual athletes measured themselves. The Romans portrayed people as they were and the Greeks depicted them as they should be. The Romans were practical, the Greeks theoretical. It is no wonder that the Romans viewed the Greeks with awe, contempt, envy, and suspicion. The Romans accepted the world, with its imperfections as it was; the Greeks wanted something better. The quarreling Greek city-states were forcibly united by Alexander; Rome conquered the world.

That Greek culture was generally superior to any other was acknowledged by the Romans, and Greek literature, art, and architecture became basic strands in the fabric of Roman civilization. The empire was, in fact, administered in both languages—the Latin of the ruling Romans and the Greek of the conquered Hellenes. (Try to imagine Napoleon administering the French Empire in French *and* German.) Where the two cultures differed significantly was in sheer size. Athens of the Golden Age had a population of about

100,000; Imperial Rome had a much larger population and greater wealth. It also had the endless problems that plague large cities in any culture. Shown in figure 6.13 is part of the central section of a city with over fifty miles of streets, almost none with names, and a population in the second century A.D. of about 1,200,000. Much of the area shown was constructed by the Flavian emperors (A.D. 69–96); the monumental civic structures were completed by Nerva, Trajan, and Hadrian (A.D. 96–138).

In the far upper left of the model can be seen the Baths of Trajan; with a central complex of thermal rooms surrounded by thermal rooms further enclosed by peripheral rooms, this became the model for all subsequent imperial baths. Near the bottom of the model is the Circus Maximus, the primary stadium for chariot racing and the common meeting ground for all levels of Roman society. Achieving its final form in about 329 B.C. the stadium enclosed a race course measuring 220 yards × 650 yards. Seating about 250,000 spectators and operating a full racing program on 240 days of the year, the Circus Maximus could, with full houses, total about seventy million admissions a year. Thinking big was the Roman way.

Directly above the Circus Maximus are the Imperial Forums and the Claudius Aqueduct leading to the Palatine, highest of the seven hills of Rome and urban abode of the aristocracy. Seen at the upper left is the Colosseum, the single most representative building of the Roman Empire, then and now. Designed for the staging of battles between various combinations of animals and gladiators, the Colosseum seated about 50,000 spectators around an arena measuring 156′ × 258′. With underground corridors for gladiators, animals, and technicians, and elaborate stage equipment for crowd-pleasing effects, the Colosseum was a complete entertainment center. Built on four levels, the exterior is unified by four superimposed orders of columns (fig. 6.14). Beginning with a simplification

Figure 6.15 Colosseum, Rome (aerial view)

Figure 6.16 Roman amphitheatre, ca. 46 B.C., 21,000 capacity. Arles, France.

of the Doric column called Tuscan, the columns mount upwards through the Ionic and Corinthian orders to flat Corinthian piers called *pilasters.* Topping the wall are sockets for pennants and for a removable canvas covering that helped keep off the sun and rain. A key design unit in the exterior wall is the characteristic combination of a Roman arch flanked by a Greek order. Called the Roman arch order, the basic elements are a Roman arch set in a Greek post and lintel frame. Used in triumphal arches and other structures, this device was revived in the Italian Renaissance and can be seen today in neoclassic building facades in Europe and America.

Invented by the Romans as a derivation of Greek theatre design, the Colosseum is an amphitheatre (Gk., *amphi,* both; *theatron,* theatre). As the name indicates, this building is actually two theatres facing each other to form an oval-shaped bowl (fig. 6.15). Brilliantly designed and executed, the Colosseum exemplifies the qualities the Roman architect Vitruvius (first century B.C.) considered basic for superior design: firmness, commodity, and delight. Structurally sound in its own day (firmness), the Colosseum functioned exceptionally well as a grand arena with eighty portals for easy ingress and egress, comfortable seating, and unobstructed sightlines (commodity). Though not a prime Roman concern, it does have a quality of "delight," an aesthetic appeal that makes a work of art exalted and memorable.

Erected by the Flavian emperors, the Colosseum, also known as the Flavian Amphitheatre, was largely built by prisoners of the Jewish Wars, which had ended in A.D. 70 with the conquest of Jerusalem and the destruction of the Temple of Solomon. Dedicated by Titus in A.D. 80, the Colosseum opened with inaugural ceremonies that lasted 100 days and that were, according to contemporary accounts, very successful, costing the lives of some 9,000 wild animals and 2,000 gladiators.

The Colosseum was the largest Roman amphitheatre, but its basic design was anything but innovative. Apparently the amphitheatre concept was first realized at Pompeii in about 80 B.C. and copied throughout the empire before finally appearing in Rome. The Roman procedure was to develop a workable design and then to increase the efficiency of later structures through improved engineering. Amphitheatres are still used today in Verona, Italy and in France at Nîmes and Arles (fig. 6.16), testifying to the remarkable stability of Roman structural engineering. The amphitheatre at Verona is used for operatic productions, but the one at Arles is mainly a bullring.

With stability restored after the murderous excesses of Caligula and Nero, the Flavian emperors (Vespasian, Titus, and Domitian, 69–96) presided over an ever larger and richer empire. Despite attempts, especially by Vespasian, to return to the austerity of sober Republican days, Flavian artists became highly proficient in the dynamic sculptural techniques of Praxiteles and the Hellenistic sculptors. Representative of the high fashion of the Flavian age, the portrait of a Flavian woman (fig. 6.17) is notable both for the towering coiffure and for its relentless Roman realism. Undoubtedly a Flavian aristocrat, the lady is as homely as she is stylish.

Julius Caesar contended that the only truly effective way of controlling conquered people was to execute every man, woman, and child. However, the practical Roman alternative to extermination was the conversion of prisoners of war into a tractable slave labor force. One of the most effective propaganda devices for impressing their bondage on the slaves was the triumphal arch, a symbolic representation of the yoke of oxen. In a ritualistic dramatization of Roman might, victorious generals marched their prisoners through hastily erected temporary arches to the accompaniment of Roman battle trumpets and drums. The overall effect was meant to be awesome and intimidating.

To commemorate his brother Titus's destruction of Jerusalem in A.D. 70, Domitian had a permanent version of the triumphal arch erected where the Via Sacra enters the Roman Forum (fig. 6.18). (By the end of the empire there would be over sixty triumphal arches in Rome and many more throughout the

Colorplate 8 Giovanni Paolo Panini, *The Interior of the Pantheon*. Samuel H. Kress Collection. National Gallery of Art, Washington, D.C.

Colorplate 9 *Head of Emperor Hadrian.* Bronze, height 16″. Roman provincial work of second century A.D. British Museum, London. Reproduced by permission of the Trustees of the British Museum.

Colorplate 10 Interior, San Vitale, Ravenna

Colorplate 11 *Emperor Justinian and His Courtiers*, ca. 547. Mosaic, San Vitale, Ravenna

Colorplate 12 *Empress Theodora and Retinue,* ca. 547. Mosaic, San Vitale, Ravenna

Figure 6.17 *Flavian Woman,* ca. A.D. 80. Marble, life-size. J. Paul Getty Museum, Santa Monica, California.

Figure 6.18 Arch of Titus, A.D. 81, Rome

empire.) Constructed of concrete with a marble facing, the Arch of Titus utilized a Roman arch order similar to that of the Colosseum. Massive piers with dual-engaged columns provided a post and lintel frame for a deep Roman arch vault (see fig. 6.9). With a superstructure called the *attic* bearing the commemorative inscription, the walls of the vault were decorated with high reliefs depicting Titus's successful campaign against the Jews. Symbolizing a major Roman victory, the arch was also a graphic reminder for all slaves, especially the Jews who labored on the Colosseum, of the futility of opposing the might of Rome.

The assassination of Domitian in A.D. 96 ended the Flavian dynasty and ushered in the era of the so-called good emperors: Nerva, Trajan, Hadrian, Antoninus Pius, and Marcus Aurelius (96–180). The first non-Italian to occupy the throne, the brilliant Spanish general, Trajan, led Rome to the maximum expansion of her empire. Among the monuments commemorating his phenomenal successes is the Column of Trajan (fig. 6.19), an unprecedented conception. Carved in low relief in 150 scenes, the 658′ frieze narrates the highlights of Trajan's two campaigns into Dacia (modern Romania and Hungary). To "read" the story it is necessary to walk around and around the column, but it soon becomes impossible to read it without binoculars. How and if this story was read in its entirety has never been satisfactorily explained. Perhaps there were special viewing balconies or perhaps slaves were stationed at the base of the monument delivering illuminating lectures and selling guidebooks.

Figure 6.19 Column of Trajan, ca. A.D. 106–113. Marble, height 125′ with base, Rome.

Figure 6.20 Column of Trajan, detail

Figure 6.21 The Pantheon, ca. A.D. 118–125, Rome.

Though the inspiration for this unusual monument is unknown, it is perhaps significant that it was placed between the Latin and Greek libraries of Trajan; the column is quite similar to library books of the time—*rotuli* (scrolls), which were wound on two spindles. The basic inspiration, however, is the "continuous narration" technique, which is so typically Roman, as opposed to Greek "simultaneous narration." The Greek unities of time, place, and action as observed in the Parthenon frieze (see fig. 3.51) were apparently not suitable for the day-to-day world of empire building. Reflected in the Column of Trajan is Roman interest in biography and history; the basic unity is the focus on the leadership of Trajan while history is served by the unfolding scenes of campaigns. A detail from the bottom of the column (fig. 6.20) depicts a river god, symbolizing the Danube, and landscapes as stylized stage sets. Artistic details are minimized, making the soldiers the prime figures of the Roman conquest. Executed under the direction of a single artist, the frieze is a masterpiece of didactic art in the tradition of the *Augustus of Primaporta* (see fig. 6.5). The column was originally topped by a statue of Trajan, which was destroyed during the Middle Ages; the figure now standing at the top is a sixteenth-century statue of St. Peter. The first pope of the Church of Rome is positioned over a visual record of two bloody Roman campaigns, symbolizing the Church's triumph over Rome.

Probably the best educated of all Roman emperors and certainly the most cosmopolitan, Hadrian (117–138) was more interested in improving the cultural life of the empire than in extending political frontiers. Indicating the extent of the Roman Empire at that time, Hadrian lived and worked in Britain, southern France, Spain, Morocco, Asia Minor, Greece, Tunisia, Greece (again), Syria, Palestine, and Egypt. He finally returned after ten years abroad to build Hadrian's Villa at Tivoli near Rome. A student of all

things Greek, Hadrian was more concerned with supporting the intellectual life of Greece than with whatever took place in the mercantile environment of Rome. He did, however, strongly support the most advanced concepts of Roman architects in their designs of interior space.

One of the most revolutionary and authoritative structures ever built, the Pantheon (fig. 6.21) has influenced the architecture of every age from ancient Rome to the present day. The inscription on the frieze, "M. AGRIPPA L.F. COS TERTIUM FECIT" (Marcus Agrippa, son of Lucius, consul for the third time, built this), does not refer to this building but to previous structures erected in 27–25 B.C. by Agrippa, son-in-law of Augustus. Because the original buildings included baths and a temple called Pantheon (Gk., to all the gods), Hadrian, displaying his fine sense of Roman history, had the original inscription repeated on the new temple. With a portico 59' high and measuring 143' in the interior (diameter and height), the Pantheon is topped by one of the largest domes ever built. (St. Peter's dome is 140' in diameter and that of Florence Cathedral averages 137½'.) Twenty feet thick at the outside edge, the poured concrete dome decreases to less than five feet at the center. Resting on eight enormous piers and providing interior lighting with a circular opening (*oculus*) that is nearly 30' in diameter, the dome is coffered (indented panels) to decrease the weight without sacrificing structural strength. The water from rainstorms can be drained away in a matter of minutes by a plumbing system that still works. The Pantheon is the best preserved of all Roman buildings because it was converted into a Christian church early in the history of the Church of Rome.

The eight-column front of Corinthian capitals topping polished granite columns is, in effect, a Greek portico opening into a massive drum derived from the circular Greek tholos. One of the most astounding spatial accomplishments in architecture, the impressiveness of the interior is communicated better by the

Figure 6.22 *Equestrian Statue of Marcus Aurelius,* ca. A.D. 161–180. Bronze, over life size. Piazza del Campidoglio, Rome.

Figure 6.23 *Head of a Bearded Man,* ca. A.D. 250. Marble, life size. J. Paul Getty Museum, Santa Monica, California.

Panini painting (colorplate 8) than by any contemporary photograph. Originally painted blue, the hemisphere of concrete was highlighted with rosettes of gilded bronze set into each coffer. Softly colored columns alternate with marble panels, pilasters, and niches, forming a harmonious blend within a single, self-sufficient, uninterrupted space. Dedicated to the worship of the seven planetary gods, the Pantheon is a stunning human version of the sky itself, the Dome of Heaven.

The bronze head of Hadrian (colorplate 9), which wears a trim beard in the Greek manner, was probably created during the enlightened reign of that remarkable monarch. A combination of the staid portrait style of Republican tradition and the glamorous, more sensuous Hellenistic imperial style, the bust was found in the Thames River under London Bridge. That a masterful portrait of this most urbane of Roman rulers should be found in the outermost reaches of empire symbolizes the international culture of Rome. Writing during the reign of Trajan, the Greek biographer Plutarch remarked, "I am a citizen, not of Athens or of Greece, but of the world."

The last of the illustrious Antonine emperors,[1] Marcus Aurelius (161–180) was an unusual combination of distinguished general and Stoic philosopher. Most un-Roman in his detestation of war, he confined his military activities to defending the borders against barbarian incursions, particularly in the Balkans. It was on that distant frontier that the philosopher-king died in the performance of his stoic duty towards the state. As depicted in the only equestrian statue surviving from the ancient world (fig. 6.22), the emperor wore a beard in the Greek style first adopted by Hadrian. With his right arm extended

in the characteristic gesture of a general about to address his troops, the emperor is both commanding and resigned to the necessity of fulfilling his responsibilities. Vigorous and impatient, the high-spirited war-horse displays the artist's exceptional knowledge of equine anatomy. Originally the head of a conquered warrior was under the raised right hoof of the charger as a symbol of Roman dominance. That the imperial bronze survived at all was due to a case of mistaken identity; Christians mistook it for a depiction of the Emperor Constantine.

After the death of Marcus Aurelius in 180, the empire was in an almost continual state of disruption. Between 235 and 284 there were no less than 26 "barracks emperors" sponsored by various army factions. The accession of Diocletian in 284 replaced anarchy with a rigid despotism under which the Roman Senate lost the last vestige of its by then ephemeral powers. A time of agony and despair, the chaotic third century saw the flourishing of many mystery cults as people sought spiritual salvation in the midst of nihilism. Representative of the malaise of the time, the *Head of a Bearded Man* (fig. 6.23) is a study in ambivalence: hopefulness coupled with despair, spiritual aspirations conflicting with the problem of sheer physical survival. It was the worst of times.

Seizing power from his corulers, Constantine (312–337) represented the last effective authority in an empire doomed to destruction from external assaults and from internal corruption and decadence. Built to celebrate his assumption of sole imperial power, the Arch of Constantine (fig. 6.24) was wholly dependent on its predecessors for its impressive appearance. In an attempt to recapture the glorious past, the three-arch design was copied from the Arch of Septimus Severus (ca. 203) in the Roman Forum,

---

1. The very last Antonine was Commodus (180–192), the son of Marcus Aurelius. Anything but illustrious, he was corrupt, demented, and, ultimately, the victim of a household conspiracy.

Figure 6.24 Arch of Constantine, A.D. 312–315, Rome.

Figure 6.25 *Constantine the Great,* ca. A.D. 330. Marble, height 8'. Palazzo dei Conservatori, Rome.

while the eight Corinthian columns are literally from the time of Domitian (81–96). The freestanding statues, with heads recarved to resemble Constantine, were lifted from monuments to Trajan, Hadrian, and Marcus Aurelius. Despite the borrowed design and transferred columns and statues, there is little trace of the Hellenic tradition. The inferior craftsmanship of the carved reliefs can be explained by a shortage of skilled artists; there had been no official relief sculpture in nearly a century. Despite the technical inadequacies, the shift from classical to a new Constantinian style appears, however, to have been deliberate. Compare, for example, the classical style of the Augustus of Primaporta (see fig. 6.5) with the head of Constantine the Great (fig. 6.25). In addition to the notable stylistic differences, it is clear that the latter is intended as a much more obvious symbol of imperial majesty *and* spiritual superiority. Part of a colossal statue enthroned in his basilica, the masterful modeling of the head demonstrates a total awareness of the Hellenistic tradition with the significant exception of the remarkably large eyes. Carved even with a marble fleck representing light reflecting from the cornea, these are not the eyes of a mere man; this is an exalted being, unique in authority and vision, with godlike eyes fixed upon infinity. Symbolizing sanctity and sometimes saintliness, oversized eyes become a convention in Early Christian and Byzantine art.

Though a miniature in fact and truly miniscule when compared with the head of Constantine, the *Diptych of Consul Boethius* (bow–E–thi–us; fig. 6.26) is similar to the bust in that the artist has denied the physical reality of Boethius and emphasized instead his authority and spirit. Costume, body, and space are reduced to patterned lines that are more emotional than representational. One of the last Roman consuls and the author of *Consolation of Philosophy* (A.D. 524), the other-worldliness of Boethius can be compared to the physical reality of the *Augustus of Primaporta* (see fig. 6.5). Both share the commanding arm gesture— a symbol of authority—but all else has changed. In the *Augustus* we see a man with supreme authority and in the *Boethius* there is depicted supreme authority that happens to be a man.

The Artistic Legacy of Rome

Roman achievements in architecture were notable and still act upon the modern world. The first to achieve mastery of enclosing space, Roman prototypes are visible today in grandiose train stations, monumental public buildings, and the ubiquitous football and soccer stadiums patterned after the Colosseum. In fact, one essential difference between the Astrodome and the Colosseum is that the latter had a removable canvas roof. With their superbly designed roads, bridges, and aqueducts, Roman engineers made essential contributions to civilizing and humanizing people that were fully as important as their monuments, buildings, and stadiums. Indeed, roads, bridges, and sewers may be as essential for the development of civilization as art, music, and literature.

Sculpture was as common in the Roman world as billboards are in the United States, but considerably more attractive. Streets, buildings, and homes were filled with portrait busts and freestanding statues or reliefs of the gods of all major and minor religions. Included were masterpieces confiscated from Greece and Egypt and mass-produced copies of Greek works of all periods. A compelling urge to create was characteristic of Greek artists, while the Romans were

Figure 6.26 *Diptych of Consul Boethius,* ca. A.D. 487. Ivory miniature. Brescia Museum, Italy.

often content to copy. It was in portraiture and historical narrative that Roman artists excelled, precisely because they were copyists of the world as they saw it.

The little that is left of Roman painting was found mainly in the ruins of Pompeii and Herculaneum (see fig. 6.12), which were buried by the eruption of Vesuvius in A.D. 79. Excavations beginning in the eighteenth century have revealed at least four major styles of painting. Whether this work was accomplished by Greek, Hellenistic, or Roman artists cannot be determined. Furthermore, later development of painting during the enlightened regimes of the Antonines may never be known. Deeply indebted to Greek developments in painting techniques, it is safe to assume that Roman painters produced works comparable to the Pantheon and the *Augustus of Primaporta.*

Roman Music

No Roman music survives nor are there any extant musical documents or theoretical treatises. With nothing original to contribute, the Romans were content to use the brass instruments of the Etruscans and to adopt the whole of Greek musical culture. Though

some musical instruments have survived, our knowledge of Roman music has been derived from sculptures, mosaics, wall paintings, and references to music by Cicero, Seneca, and Quintilian. According to the evidence, music was highly esteemed, particularly in association with poetry. Interested in the visual arts mainly as collectors, the patrician class left the messy business of painting and sculpting to artisans and slaves. Writing verse and singing to lute accompaniment was, however, a worthy pursuit for wealthy amateurs of both sexes. The arts of poetry and music added to the social graces of patricians and emperors alike. Hadrian wrote poetry in Latin and Greek and, like Antoninus Pius and the tyrant Caracalla, was an accomplished performer on the kithara and the hydraulis.[2] A kind of chamber instrument with clear and delicate tones, the effect of the hydraulis was described by Cicero as a "sensation as delectable to the ears as the most delicious fish to the palate."

Music of a public nature provided appropriate settings for acrobats, pantomime, popular theatre, dancing, chariot racing, gladiatorial combat, and the maneuvers of Roman troops. Commensurate with Roman ideas of grandeur, instruments were increased in number and size, particularly the trumpets and drums that relayed battle commands to the Roman legions. Quintilian, in fact, equated the brassy loudness of Roman trumpets with the supremacy of Roman arms. Audiences in amphitheatres were treated to musical spectacles featuring huge choral and instrumental groups that sometimes outnumbered the spectators. The limpid-toned hydraulis was converted to an advertising medium for the proclaiming of gladiatorial contests. Traveling on a large wagon and with vastly increased air pressure supplied by hordes of toiling slaves, the now strident tone had a reputed range of over three miles.[3]

Roman drama omitted the Greek choruses but used musical interludes throughout, all of which were composed by specialists rather than by the dramatists themselves, as had been the case with Greek drama. The aulos, called *tibia* in Latin, and the kithara were still employed much as they were in Greek plays and generally played by Greek musicians, who were usually more skilled than Roman musicians. Nero fancied himself an outstanding instrumentalist and had coins minted depicting him playing the kithara. He did not start the great fire that burned most of Rome

---

2. Hydraulis (Gk., *hydor,* water; *aulos,* pipe) invented ca. 300 B.C. Of Near Eastern origin and improved on by the Greeks, this was actually a pipe organ. Air was pumped into an inverted bowl with air pressure controlled by the volume of water holding the bowl in place. Adding water increased the pressure of the air supplied to the pipes and thus the volume of sound. Though no instruments have survived, a precise clay model found in the ruins of Carthage has provided enough information for modern reconstructions.

3. The association of the hydraulis with the so-called games in the arena, especially those with assorted lions and Christians, delayed for many centuries the introduction of the pipe organ into Christian services.

in 64 nor, contrary to legend, did he "fiddle while Rome burned." He was blamed for the fire, however, and launched the first persecution of the new Christian sect to divert attention from himself.

Using a variety of drums plus trumpetlike instruments such as the buccina, lituus, and tuba, official bands were important components of military establishments throughout the empire. With their ceremonial music they effectively proclaimed the magnificence of the state, much as military bands have done in just about every culture since ancient times.

Unit 3

Judaism and Christianity
The Star and the Cross

7

Faith, Hope, and Love: The Judeo-Christian Tradition

It was pointed out in the preceding unit on Rome that life in the later years of the Empire was a matter of increasing disillusionment and pessimism. Epicureanism is grounded on pessimism; Stoicism is at best a resignation to the evil of the world; popular cults provided little abiding satisfaction. The discontent and dissatisfaction were not found only among thinkers and philosophers, but were shared by the common people. A Roman epitaph found rather frequently reveals the spirit of cynicism and disillusion; it reads

I was not

I was

I am not

I do not care

One could scarcely go further in general world-weariness; yet the sentiment was not uncommon.

There were two conflicting tendencies during this period and earlier. One was the general disbelief in the old Olympian religion, and a cynical attitude toward emperor worship; the intellectual element in the population was skeptical about religion in general. The other was, contradictorily, the appeal of mystical cults and religions, usually of oriental origin: Mithraism, the worship of Isis, the cult of Cybele, and the like. However much scoffing or indifferent disregard there may have been at the upper level of society, the poor and uneducated were ready for the emotional appeal of any religiosity that softened their uncertainties and insecurities; there was a need for comfort and reassurance.

The genius of the Greeks was intellectual rather than moral or spiritual, and the Romans had little to add on the latter score to what they inherited from the Greeks. Both peoples had advocated the life lived according to reason. For a Plato, an Aristotle, a Cato, such a life could be worthy and satisfying, but not many men in any generation are of such caliber, and even those few are often felt to be wanting in human warmth. At best, the God whom Aristotle finds the sum of perfection is cold, distant, and aloof from human affairs: a noble concept, but again lacking warmth.

Reason, important as it is, has never been the only tool in man's possession. Call it emotion, belief, faith, there is something that is not in the same category. No one will seriously give six good reasons why he or she loves the beloved, for love is not "reasonable." That is not to say that it is necessarily contrary to reason; it simply moves in another category. That "something" beyond reason may be considered the compulsion of a moral ideal, or a yearning for spiritual satisfaction; it is more pronounced in some people than in others, but hardly ever totally absent in any individual. It is precisely such a range of human experience that the perhaps overly intellectualized philosophical traditions of Greece and Rome failed to satisfy.

While the Greek and Roman cultures were developing—cultures devoted to two forms of rationalism—a third and entirely different type of society had come into being in Palestine. A vast amount of pure intellectual power has gone into the development of Jewish doctrine, but the core of Judaism is faith, as faith is different from, though not opposed to, reason. The Hebrew religion itself, and as it has had wider influence through Christianity, wove another strand into the great amalgam we call Western civilization.[1]

The Chosen People

The Hebrews would have been just another set of Near Eastern tribes, small in number and lacking talent for art and invention, had it not been for their remarkable religion. Other civilizations have come and gone; they alone have maintained their culture essentially intact for four thousand years.

Following the leadership of Abraham, the Hebrews emigrated (ca. 1950 B.C.) from the Sumerian city of Ur in the Euphrates valley to the west, eventually arriving in the "Land of Canaan" (later called Palestine). Probably prompted by famine, many Hebrews followed Joseph to Egypt and into slavery, from which they were delivered by Moses. Leading the Children of Israel into Sinai (ca. 1300 B.C.), Moses gave them the concept of a single tribal God, Yahweh (or Jehovah), and a covenant with the deity based on their acceptance of his commandments.

The Promised Land of "milk and honey" was taken by conquest, with the key city of Jericho falling to Joshua in 1230 B.C. By 1020 they had formed a monarchy with Saul as king. The height of Hebrew political power was reached with the United Kingdom of Palestine under David (1000–960) and Solomon (960–922), followed by a division into Israel (933–722) and Judah (933–586). Conquered by the Assyrians in 722 B.C., they were later carried into exile by King Nebuchadnezzar (Babylonian Captivity, 586–538 B.C.). Allowed to return to Jerusalem by the Persian king Cyrus the Great, they rebuilt the Temple of Solomon but were politically subservient to three successive empires: Persian, Hellenistic, and Roman. During the first century A.D. the Jews rebelled against Rome. Jerusalem was totally destroyed and much of the population was killed or driven from the land, a Diaspora (Dye–AS–po–ra; "scattering") that was to last nearly two thousand years.

The will to resist and to survive was based on their religion, Judaism,[2] four aspects of which were different from all other Near Eastern religions.

1. Monotheism: There was only one God and he came to be viewed as universal.
2. Covenant: God chose Israel to be his people and they accepted him as their God.
3. Graven images: Images of God or of any living thing were prohibited.
4. The name of God (Yahweh, meaning "he causes to be" or "the creator") was not to be taken "in vain," i.e., was not to be spoken.

Let us examine each of these concepts. Beginning with the Mosaic period in the Sinai, Yahweh was the primary God among many: "You shall have no other gods before me" (Exodus 20:3). This concept gradually evolved into a monotheism in which there was one Hebrew God and, later, one universal God. The first people to insist upon monotheism, the Jews found this to be, throughout their history, their greatest source of strength.

The covenant was a religious bond that the Hebrews made of their own free will with Yahweh. Moses climbed the mountain and returned with knowledge of God's will—"commandments" inscribed on tablets of stone and subsequently amplified in the Torah. In a narrow sense the Torah consists of the first five books of the Bible, the so-called Pentateuch, or Books of Moses. Torah means Law but it also means "teaching" or "direction." In the broad modern sense, Torah refers to the total content of God's unending revelation to and through Israel.

The prohibition of graven images separated Judaism from all other religions, which represented their gods in a variety of ways. This stricture, designed to guard against idolatry, had the effect of nullifying any significant artistic development.

The injunction against using the Lord's name in vain emphasized a reverence unknown to other ancient religions.

In sum, Judaism was a People in covenant with God, a Book (the Hebrew Scriptures), a Way of Life, and a Hope grounded in Faith.

Prophecy

The Hebrew prophets of the eighth to fifth centuries B.C. emerged from a tradition of augurs and seers who, as they did in other religions, sought to ascertain the divine will and to forecast the future through dreams,

---

1. See chap. 11 for an overview of Islam and its culture.

2. A term coined by Greek-speaking Jews to distinguish their religious way of life from that of the Hellenes. Though the term is late, the religion to which it refers goes back to the beginnings of Jewish spiritual life.

divinations, and induced ecstasy. Eventually these professionals were denounced as "false prophets" and replaced by a succession of preachers, mystics, moralists, and poets who felt themselves to be speaking for Yahweh. Prophets like Amos and Isaiah spoke as instruments of Yahweh's creative purpose in the lives of his people. Ethical considerations were primary and the predictive element secondary, an extension of ethical and religious tendencies into a foreseeable future. Stressing righteousness and justice, the prophets spoke and, more importantly, wrote as restorers and conservators of Israel's inspiring spiritual heritage. Not always accepted by various classes of society, they preached an uncompromising and lofty doctrine of ethical monotheism.

The first and perhaps most important of the notable eighth-century prophets, Amos preached against luxury, corruption, and selfishness, pointing the way to altruism and a higher form of religion.

> [11]Therefore because you trample upon the poor
>   and take from him exactions of wheat,
> you have built houses of hewn stone,
>   but you shall not dwell in them;
> you have planted pleasant vineyards,
>   but you shall not drink their wine.
> [12]For I know how many are your transgressions,
>   and how great are your sins—
> you who afflict the righteous, who take a bribe,
>   and turn aside the needy in the gate.
> [13]Therefore he who is prudent will keep silent in such a
>   time;
>   for it is an evil time.
> [14]Seek good, and not evil,
>   that you may live;
> and so the LORD, the God of hosts, will be with you,
>   as you have said.
> [15]Hate evil, and love good,
>   and establish justice in the gate;
> it may be that the LORD, the God of hosts,
>   will be gracious to the remnant of Joseph.
>
> Amos 5:11–15

> [4]"Woe to those who lie upon beds of ivory,
>   and stretch themselves upon their couches,
> and eat lambs from the flock,
>   and calves from the midst of the stall;
> [5]who sing idle songs to the sound of the harp,
>   and like David invent for themselves instruments of
>   music;
> [6]who drink wine in bowls,
>   and anoint themselves with the finest oils,
>   but are not grieved over the ruin of Joseph!
> [7]Therefore they shall now be the first of those to go into
>   exile,
>   and the revelry of those who stretch themselves shall
>   pass away."
> [8]The Lord GOD has sworn by himself
> (says the LORD, the God of hosts):
> "I abhor the pride of Jacob,
>   and hate his strongholds;
> and I will deliver up the city and all that is in it."
>
> Amos 6:4–8

Active around 740–700 B.C., Isaiah[3] was the prophet of faith, preaching an abiding trust in the providence of God. Also a prophet of doom like the other preachers, Isaiah saw that a purging was necessary in the interest of spiritual betterment in a kindlier and more loving world. He was among the first to picture a warless world under the benign rule of a Prince of Peace, a Messiah ("anointed one") descended from the House of David.

> [1]There shall come forth a shoot from the stump of Jesse,
>   and a branch shall grow out of his roots.
> [2]And the Spirit of the LORD shall rest upon him,
>   the spirit of wisdom and understanding,
>   the spirit of counsel and might,
>   the spirit of knowledge and the fear of the LORD.
> [3]And his delight shall be in the fear of the LORD.
> He shall not judge by what his eyes see,
>   or decide by what his ears hear;
> [4]but with righteousness he shall judge the poor,
>   and decide with equity for the meek of the earth;
> and he shall smite the earth with the rod of his mouth,
>   and with the breath of his lips he shall slay the
>   wicked.
> [5]Righteousness shall be the girdle of his waist,
>   and faithfulness the girdle of his loins.
> [6]The wolf shall dwell with the lamb,
>   and the leopard shall lie down with the kid,
> and the calf and the lion and the fatling together,
>   and a little child shall lead them.
> [7]The cow and the bear shall feed;
>   their young shall lie down together;
>   and the lion shall eat straw like the ox.
> [8]The sucking child shall play over the hole of the asp,
>   and the weaned child shall put his hand on the
>   adder's den.
> [9]They shall not hurt or destroy
>   in all my holy mountain;
> for the earth shall be full of the knowledge of the LORD
>   as the waters cover the sea.
>
> Isaiah 11:1–9

> For unto us a child is born,
>   to us a son is given;
> and the government will be upon his shoulder,
>   and his name will be called
> "Wonderful Counselor, Mighty God,
> Everlasting Father, Prince of Peace."
>
> Isaiah 9:6

During the Babylonian Captivity when his people were far from home, their city and Temple destroyed, Ezekiel preached the universality of the faith and of the personal relationship between the individual Jew and his God. God existed wherever the people were; the city and the Temple were not indispensable. Each person had the option of selecting good over evil or even turning from evil ways to a righteous life.

---

3. The Book of Isaiah contains prophecies attributed to Isaiah (chaps. 1–39) and those by an unknown prophet of the fifth century, known today as Second Isaiah (chaps. 40–66).

²⁵"Yet you say, 'The way of the Lord is not just.' Hear now, O house of Israel: Is my way not just? Is it not your ways that are not just? ²⁶When a righteous man turns away from his righteousness and commits iniquity, he shall die for it; for the iniquity which he has committed he shall die. ²⁷Again, when a wicked man turns away from the wickedness he has committed and does what is lawful and right, he shall save his life. ²⁸Because he considered and turned away from all the transgressions which he had committed, he shall surely live, he shall not die. ²⁹Yet the house of Israel says, 'The way of the Lord is not just.' O house of Israel, are my ways not just? Is it not your ways that are not just?

³⁰"Therefore I will judge you, O house of Israel, every one according to his ways, says the Lord GOD. Repent and turn from all your transgressions, lest iniquity be your ruin. ³¹Cast away from you all the transgressions which you have committed against me, and get yourselves a new heart and a new spirit! Why will you die, O house of Israel? ³²For I have no pleasure in the death of any one, says the Lord GOD; so turn, and live."

Ezekiel 18:25–32

The celebrated unknown prophet of the exile, known as Second Isaiah, was the great architect of Jewish ethical monotheism. Climaxing the prophetic movement, his ethical and religious insight set the sufferings of the Jews against a background of God's eventual redemption of the entire world. He saw the Jews as a people chosen to exemplify in their characters and lives the spiritual presence of the Lord. "A light to the nations" (Isaiah 42:1), their suffering had not been in vain. The world would say of Israel:

³He was despised and rejected by men;
    a man of sorrows, and acquainted with grief,
and as one from whom men hide their faces
    he was despised, and we esteemed him not.
⁴Surely he has borne our griefs
    and carried our sorrows,
yet we esteemed him stricken,
    smitten by God, and afflicted.
⁵But he was wounded for our transgressions,
    he was bruised for our iniquities;
upon him was the chastisement that made us whole,
    and with his stripes we are healed.
⁶All we like sheep have gone astray;
    we have turned every one to his own way;
and the LORD has laid on him
    the iniquity of us all.

Isaiah 53:3–6

They were to return to the New Jerusalem where the work of redemption would be a model for all the world.

¹Comfort, comfort my people,
    says your God.
²Speak tenderly to Jerusalem,
    and cry to her
that her warfare is ended,
    that her iniquity is pardoned,
that she has received from the LORD's hand
    double for all her sins.
³A voice cries:
    "In the wilderness prepare the way of the LORD,
    make straight in the desert a highway for our God.

⁴Every valley shall be lifted up,
    and every mountain and hill be made low;
the uneven ground shall become level,
    and the rough places a plain.
⁵And the glory of the LORD shall be revealed,
    and all flesh shall see it together,
    for the mouth of the LORD has spoken."
⁶A voice says, "Cry!"
    And I said, "What shall I cry?"
All flesh is grass,
    and all its beauty is like the flower of the field.
⁷The grass withers, the flower fades,
    when the breath of the LORD blows upon it;
    surely the people is grass.
⁸The grass withers, the flower fades;
    but the word of our God will stand for ever.
⁹Get you up to a high mountain,
    O Zion, herald of good tidings,
lift up your voice with strength,
    O Jerusalem, herald of good tidings,
    lift it up, fear not;
say to the cities of Judah,
    "Behold your God!"

Isaiah 40:1–9

The profound insights of Second Isaiah strongly influenced later Judaism but were even more significant for early Christianity. His writings were studied and pondered by those who awaited the coming of the Messiah. In particular the story of the sufferings of Israel (see Isaiah 53:3–6 above) was so specific and individualized that later generations came to believe that he was speaking of a particular person, a Messiah who would redeem the world through his suffering. In Jesus of Nazareth the early Christians found that Messiah.

Some of the Teachings of Jesus

Jesus was born in the year we now call 4 B.C., or possibly 6 B.C.,⁴ a time that was ripe for his message of hope and love. He preached for possibly three years, but in the two thousand years since that time—whether people have believed his teachings or not, whether they have acted upon them or not—men and women throughout what was once called "Christendom" have been hearing the teachings of Jesus. What are the cardinal points of his teaching? These: that One God (a Personal Spirit, not an abstract idea nor a principle) is not only the Creator, but also the living Father of all humankind; that all people are consequently the children of God, and that as a result all men and women are brothers and sisters; that as children of God, human beings are capable of better lives than they lead; that their human inadequacies, imperfections, and shortcomings can be forgiven if they are repentant; that life is eternal, and death is not extinction; that "all the Law and the Prophets" hangs upon the joint commandment to "Love thy God, and thy neighbor as thyself"; and that the intention—the

---

4. The idea of denominating the years of the Christian era was introduced in A.D. 525 by Dionysius Exiguus; the B.C. sequence extending backwards from the birth of Christ was not added until the seventeenth century.

act of the personality—is of greater importance than the deed—the act of the person.

Not the least of the appeals of Christianity is the joy and hope that it carries with it because of its doctrine of Christ as Redeemer. Theologically, one of several explanations may be stated in this way: because of the sin of Adam, humankind as a whole carried with it the taint of original sin, a sort of moral disease. But God, loving all people, sought to redeem them. This was accomplished through the mystery of Incarnation in which God became man, taking to himself all of humankind's inherent guilt. Then, in Christ's death as a mortal, the guilt is atoned, and human beings are set free. The possibility of salvation and eternal life with God, from that moment on, lies before each person. In a world-weary and guilt-ridden time like that of the late Roman Empire, even as in our own time, such a possibility can bring hope and joy to the believer.

All of these teachings affect the world of here and now, for Christianity is a "social" religion; that is, its effects are seen in the daily acts of people in relation to other people. It is not essentially a religion in which the believers isolate themselves from others and seek individual salvation through private contemplation. It is a religion of involvement for most Christians. Love must prompt the worshipper to present acts of love, mercy, and compassion as evidence of an inward change. The act of the believer in Christ cannot wait upon another world. If three words could be used to sum up this teaching, those three, with their many implications, might be those Jesus addressed to Peter: "Feed my sheep."

Early Christianity

Jesus left no written record of his work nor are there any surviving accounts contemporary with his ministry. A collection of his sayings, written in Aramaic, disappeared before A.D. 60, and scholars are still debating some of the references to Jesus in the Dead Sea Scrolls. His life, character, and message inspired hope and joy but this, coupled with the absence of documentation, was not sufficient for a theology. By definition, Christian theology is a discipline concerned with God and God's relation to the world. It remained for the followers of Jesus to construct a systematic theology as a solid foundation for the propagation of the new faith.

Written accounts in Greek began to appear several decades after Christ's death: Saint Paul's epistles to the Corinthians (ca. A.D. 55); the Acts of the Apostles (ca. 60); the four Gospels telling the story of Jesus: Mark (ca. 70); Matthew and Luke (ca. 80–85); and John (ca. 100–120). By about A.D. 200 the texts were revised in Alexandria into a canonical Christian text.

An upper-class Jew of Orthodox parentage, Saint Paul (Saul of Tarsus) was first a persecutor of Christians and later one of the most ardent missionaries of the faith. A Hellenized Jew, Paul took the position that "there is neither Jew nor Greek" (Galatians 3:28). Contending at first with Paul, Saint Peter believed instead that the Christian message was intended only for Jews and converted Gentiles. Paul argued (and Peter later agreed) that the Law was no longer valid, even for Jews; it could only bring people to an understanding of their dependence on Christ in a new covenant with Christ the Saviour. Sweeping aside Jewish rituals and practices, Paul, the "apostle to the Gentiles," carried the message of salvation through faith in Christ throughout the eastern Mediterranean and into Rome itself.

An enthusiastic teacher, organizer, and administrator, Paul was neither a theologian nor a logician. He was convinced that Christian faith was not a matter of reasoning but rather an act of faith. Confirmed by his own conversion experience on the road to Damascus, Paul believed that faith was a gift of God. Christians had only to accept the discipline of the Church and to lead quiet, faithful, and firmly Christian lives.

A synthesis of Judaic, Greek, and Christian ideas, Christian theology developed separately from the work of the Apostle Paul. In his Prologue, which introduces the fourth Gospel, John states that:

In the beginning was the Word, and the Word was with God, and the Word was God. ²He was in the beginning with God; ³all things were made through him, and without him was not anything made that was made. ⁴In him was life, and the life was the light of men. ⁵The light shines in the darkness, and the darkness has not overcome it.

John 1:1–5

In the Greek of the New Testament, "word" is a translation of *logos,* a word as old as the Greek language. Introduced by Herakleitos in the fifth century B.C., logos was a principle of cosmic interpretation. Constantly changing, the cosmos was a total process becoming controlled by an agency called logos. To avoid chaos, change had to conform to fixed patterns; logos was thus an intelligent and eternal agent that imposed an orderly process upon change.

Though the concept of logos is vague and unspecified in Plato and Aristotle, the Stoics took it from them but used logos to designate a divine element present in all men. It remained for Philo Judaeus of Alexandria (ca. 30 B.C.–A.D. 50) to go beyond the Stoics and to consciously construct a synthesis of Hebraic and Hellenic philosophy. Philo saw logos as a mediator between God and man and as a translation of the Hebrew word for "wisdom." As a personal agent of God in the creation of the world, logos was not identical with God but distinctly separate from him.

The Prologue of John is thus a creation story; Jesus is a divine being whose existence antedates the world itself. God's relation to this imperfect world was through the intervention of the logos; in Christ "the Word became flesh and dwelt among us, full of grace and truth" (John 1:14). It can be said that Herakleitos and Second Isaiah meet in John, representing two contrasting civilizations, which are synthesized into a Christian philosophy of history.[5]

---

5. See chap. 9 for subsequent developments in Christian theology.

The Impact of Christianity

Objective study of the historical Jesus and the facts about his life and death yields no clear-cut answers to some basic questions. Was he the Messiah, "Son of God," "son of man," a religious reformer, prophet, humanitarian, inspired teacher? Or was he, as his Jewish critics claim, a blasphemer and an imposter? Based on currently available sources there has been no final answer acceptable to everyone. The multiplicity of Christian beliefs (Catholic, Orthodox, varieties of Protestantism) testifies to the different interpretations of the evidence.

Nevertheless, the Christian emphasis on the importance of the human personality carries a religious sanction weightier than the speculations of the philosophers. The worth and dignity of the individual soul, and its responsibility to itself, has been a shaping influence in Western thought.

It is small wonder that Christianity spread from an obscure, remote province of the Roman Empire to practically throughout the known world within the first century of its existence; its message of hope, joy, salvation, and a merciful and loving God in a world that knew only the sterner aspects of justice made its welcome assured. Encompassing the whole of life, and able to take to itself the good things of any civilization, Christianity could appropriate to itself the best of Greek thought, as well as the most notable product of Rome: its law and organization. With the passage of time, it produced such diverse offshoots as the elegance and beauty of Chartres Cathedral and the horror and brutality of the Inquisition; but its impact upon the Western world is fundamental.

Literary Selections

The Bible (Greek, Ta Biblia, The Books) has exercised a more profound and continuous influence upon Western civilization than has any other literary work. By its style alone it has burnished the tongues of poets and writers from Chaucer to Shakespeare to Lincoln, and its ethical tenets have become basic to the codes and customs of Western culture. Of its two main divisions, the Old Testament (thirty-nine books in the King James Version) was written almost entirely in Hebrew (with a little Aramaic) from the eleventh to the second century B.C. The New Testament (twenty-seven books in the King James Version) was written in Greek from about A.D. 40 to 150.

Divided into three parts, the Hebrew Scripture (Old Testament) consists of the Law (Pentateuch or Torah), the Prophets, and the Hagiographa (Writings). The Book of Job is from the Hagiographa.

THE BOOK OF JOB

Because the Book of Job is not included in this text, the reader is referred to any version of the Bible that may be available.[6] The following comments and "Some Topics for Discussion" may be used in conjunction with your Old Testament reading about the incredible trials of Job.

The problem of human suffering, particularly the suffering of the innocent, the just, and the good, has confused humankind since the beginning of time, particularly when people believe in a just and benevolent God. The Book of Job, written sometime after the seventh century B.C., tackles this problem as few books do. The author is unknown (indeed there is a strong possibility that the prose, prologue, and epilogue were originally a unit, and that the poetic drama is an interpolation), and the hero, Job, may or may not have been a historical character. It seems probable that the book is addressed to all of Israel after one of the frequent persecutions of the Jews. Perhaps the author is attempting to explain to his people the nature of their suffering. If one considers the final answer from a completely rational point of view—as the Greeks, the Romans, and twentieth-century Americans would—one is left unsatisfied, for the attempt to probe God's secrets with the unaided human mind has seldom brought satisfactory results. If the reader can somehow translate his or her questioning into the realm of faith and mystery, an intuitive understanding may be reached.

From verses 1–5 in chapter 1, we must accept the fact that Job is a completely good man, and totally loyal to God. Job's comforters hold to an old religious concept of a simple cause-and-effect relationship between God and man: if man is upright, God will reward him; if he is evil, God will punish him. The generation gap is quite apparent when the youth, Elihu, speaks in chapter 32 and begins to introduce a totally new idea of the nature of the God-man relationship, an idea that is developed as God speaks out of the whirlwind.

The reader should not expect a logical development of ideas up to chapter 32. Rather, Job's searing doubts are explored with ever-greater intensity, and the arguments for the old religious idea are reiterated by the three comforters. Although this is not a drama in the strict sense of the word, the reader should try to imagine the tone of voice of the speakers. Notice, for example, the timid way in which Eliphaz begins his argument in chapter 4 after sitting on the ground for seven days and seven nights, or how Bildad's argument in chapter 25 sputters to a quick conclusion. What is Elihu's tone after listening to the lengthy discussions of Job?

---

6. The translations included in this chapter are all from the American Revised Standard Version (RSV).

Some Topics for Discussion

1. The reader might question the role of Satan at the first of the book. As one of the children of God, what force does he represent? A force for evil, almost as powerful as God himself?

2. One of the central arguments of Job's comforters is that the wicked are always destroyed, while the good prosper. In chapter 21 Job answers this argument. What is the basis for the argument of the comforters? What is the basis for Job's final answer?

3. In all the discussion up to Elihu's outburst the four men are searching for something not understood in the governing of the world. Sometimes this takes the form of sinfulness, which Job does not recognize, sometimes a question about the ways of God in determining the course of the universe. Using this search for the "something not understood" as a key question, follow all of the speeches.

4. How does Elihu's rebuke to the three old men foreshadow the revelation given from God in the voice out of the whirlwind? Question very carefully God's answer to the problem that is faced in the book. What is He really saying?

5. Do you find the final rewarding of Job with the twofold return of everything that he has lost a satisfactory conclusion to the book?

6. This Hebrew book and the play *Oedipus the King* have much in common in that both represent the downfall of a good man through the intervention of God or gods. Do you see any difference in the spirit of the inquiry between the Hebrew and the Greek exploration of the problem?

PSALMS OF DAVID

The third part of the Hebrew Bible is a collection of late writings, including the Psalms, a hymnal (Psalter) reflecting the whole history of Hebrew worship. The Psalmists sing Israel's praise of God the creator, intone their sorrow for national guilt and tribulations, and carol the songs of salvation. Following are two Psalms of salvation and glory.

24 The earth is the LORD's and the fulness thereof,
the world and those who dwell therein;
²for he has founded it upon the seas,
and established it upon the rivers.
³Who shall ascend the hill of the LORD?
And who shall stand in his holy place?
⁴He who has clean hands and a pure heart,
who does not lift up his soul to what is false,
and does not swear deceitfully.
⁵He will receive blessing from the LORD,
and vindication from the God of his salvation.
⁶Such is the generation of those who seek him,
who seek the face of the God of Jacob. *Selah*

⁷Lift up your heads, O gates!
and be lifted up, O ancient doors!
that the King of glory may come in.

⁸Who is the King of glory?
The LORD, strong and mighty,
the LORD, mighty in battle!
⁹Lift up your heads, O gates!
and be lifted up, O ancient doors!
that the King of glory may come in!
¹⁰Who is this King of glory?
The LORD of hosts,
he is the King of glory! *Selah*

150 Praise the LORD!
Praise God in his sanctuary;
praise him in his mighty firmament!
²Praise him for his mighty deeds;
praise him according to his exceeding greatness!
³Praise him with trumpet sound;
praise him with lute and harp!
⁴Praise him with timbrel and dance;
praise him with strings and pipe!
⁵Praise him with sounding cymbals;
praise him with loud clashing cymbals!
⁶Let everything that breathes praise the LORD!
Praise the LORD!

Apparently composed during the Babylonian Captivity (586–538 B.C.), Psalm 137 is a Lamentation. Though the condition of the Jews in Babylon was relatively favorable, the mourning is caused by the destruction of Jerusalem and by their own separation from the homeland. This magnificent poem was especially prominent in the worship services of American slaves, who viewed slavery as Babylonian or Egyptian captivity, an enforced exile from the African homeland.

137 By the waters of Babylon,
there we sat down and wept,
when we remembered Zion.
²On the willows there
we hung up our lyres.
³For there our captors
required of us songs,
and our tormentors, mirth, saying,
"Sing us one of the songs of Zion!"
⁴How shall we sing the LORD's song
in a foreign land?
⁵If I forget you, O Jerusalem,
let my right hand wither!
⁶Let my tongue cleave to the roof of my
mouth,
if I do not remember you,
if I do not set Jerusalem
above my highest joy!
⁷Remember, O LORD, against the E'dom-
ites
the day of Jerusalem,
how they said, "Rase it, rase it!
Down to its foundations!"
⁸O daughter of Babylon, you devastator!
Happy shall he be who requites you
with what you have done to us!
⁹Happy shall he be who takes your little
ones
and dashes them against the rock!

ECCLESIASTES

From the Writings part of the Old Testament, Ecclesiastes (Greek, the preacher) is representative of pessimistic Oriental wisdom (teaching) literature. It dates from the third century B.C. and reflects some of the inroads of Greek civilization, but not enough to disturb the basic philosophy that all is vanity and that a young man should enjoy his youth.

3 For everything there is a season, and a time for every matter under heaven:
²a time to be born, and a time to die;
a time to plant, and a time to pluck up what is planted;
³a time to kill, and a time to heal;
a time to break down, and a time to build up;
⁴a time to weep, and a time to laugh;
a time to mourn, and a time to dance;
⁵a time to cast away stones, and a time to gather stones together;
a time to embrace, and a time to refrain from embracing;
⁶a time to seek, and a time to lose;
a time to keep, and a time to cast away;
⁷a time to rend, and a time to sew;
a time to keep silence, and a time to speak;
⁸a time to love, and a time to hate;
a time for war, and a time for peace.
⁹What gain has the worker from his toil?

¹⁰I have seen the business that God has given to the sons of men to be busy with. ¹¹He has made everything beautiful in its time; also he has put eternity into man's mind, yet so that he cannot find out what God has done from the beginning to the end. ¹²I know that there is nothing better for them than to be happy and enjoy themselves as long as they live; ¹³also that it is God's gift to man that every one should eat and drink and take pleasure in all his toil. ¹⁴I know that whatever God does endures for ever; nothing can be added to it, nor anything taken from it; God has made it so, in order that men should fear before him. ¹⁵That which is, already has been; that which is to be, already has been; and God seeks what has been driven away.

¹⁶Moreover I saw under the sun that in the place of justice, even there was wickedness, and in the place of righteousness, even there was wickedness. ¹⁷I said in my heart, God will judge the righteous and the wicked, for he has appointed a time for every matter, and for every work. ¹⁸I said in my heart with regard to the sons of men that God is testing them to show them that they are but beasts. ¹⁹For the fate of the sons of men and the fate of beasts is the same; as one dies, so dies the other. They all have the same breath, and man has no advantage over the beasts; for all is vanity. ²⁰All go to one place; all are from the dust, and all turn to dust again. ²¹Who knows whether the spirit of man goes upward and the spirit of the beast goes down to the earth? ²²So I saw that there is nothing better than that a man should enjoy his work, for that is his lot; who can bring him to see what will be after him?

THE SERMON ON THE MOUNT
Matthew 5–7

The New Testament contains four sections: (1) the Gospels and Acts of the Apostles, (2) the Epistles of Paul, (3) the pastoral and general Epistles, and (4) the Book of Revelations. Mark's Gospel emphasizes the human aspect of Jesus, while Matthew and Luke include substantial additions dealing mainly with the birth and teaching of Jesus, including the Sermon on the Mount and the parables. The basic ethical teachings of Christ are presented in the Sermon on the Mount, in which the Mosaic Ten Commandments are compared with a new ethic. Beginning with the statement "You have heard that it was said to the men of old," Jesus takes each commandment in turn and contrasts it with his own commandment. As presented by Matthew, Jesus is the new Moses expounding a new Torah, which commands a higher righteousness than that found even in the best of Judaism.

Seeing the crowds, he went up on the mountain, and when he sat down his disciples came to him. And he opened his mouth and taught them, saying:

"Blessed are the poor in spirit, for theirs is the kingdom of heaven.

"Blessed are those who mourn, for they shall be comforted.

"Blessed are the meek, for they shall inherit the earth.

"Blessed are those who hunger and thirst for righteousness, for they shall be satisfied.

"Blessed are the merciful, for they shall obtain mercy.

"Blessed are the pure in heart, for they shall see God.

"Blessed are the peacemakers, for they shall be called sons of God.

"Blessed are those who are persecuted for righteousness' sake, for theirs is the kingdom of heaven.

"Blessed are you when men revile you and persecute you and utter all kinds of evil against you falsely on my account. Rejoice and be glad, for your reward is great in heaven, for so men persecuted the prophets who were before you.

"You are the salt of the earth; but if salt has lost its taste, how can its saltness be restored? It is no longer good for anything except to be thrown out and trodden under foot by men.

"You are the light of the world. A city set on a hill cannot be hid. Nor do men light a lamp and put it under a bushel, but on a stand, and it gives light to all in the house. Let your light so shine before men, that they may see your good works and give glory to your Father who is in heaven.

"Think not that I have come to abolish the law and the prophets; I have come not to abolish them but to fulfill them. For truly, I say to you, till heaven and earth pass away, not an iota, not a dot, will pass from the law until all is accomplished. Whoever then relaxes one of the least of these commandments and teaches men so, shall be called least in the kingdom of heaven; but he who does them and teaches them shall be called great in the kingdom of heaven. For I tell you, unless your righteousness exceeds that of the scribes and Pharisees, you will never enter the kingdom of heaven.

"You have heard that it was said to the men of old, 'You shall not kill; and whoever kills shall be liable to judgment.' But I say to you that every one who is angry with his brother shall be liable to judgment; whoever insults his brother shall be liable to the council, and whoever says, 'You fool!' shall be liable to the hell of fire. So if you are offering your gift at the altar, and there remember that your brother has something against you, leave your gift there before the altar and go; first be reconciled to your brother, and then come and offer your gift. Make friends quickly with your accuser, while you are going with him to court, lest your accuser hand you over to the judge, and the judge to the guard, and you be put in prison; truly, I say to you, you will never get out till you have paid the last penny.

"You have heard that it was said, 'You shall not commit adultery.' But I say to you that every one who looks at a woman lustfully has already committed adultery with her in his heart. If your right eye causes you to sin, pluck it out and throw it away; it is better that you lose one of your members than that your whole body be thrown into hell. And if your right hand causes you to sin, cut it off and throw it away; it is better that you lose one of your members than that your whole body go into hell.

"It was also said, 'Whoever divorces his wife, let him give her a certificate of divorce.' But I say to you that every one who divorces his wife, except on the ground of unchastity, makes her an adulteress; and whoever marries a divorced woman commits adultery.

"Again you have heard that it was said to the men of old, 'You shall not swear falsely, but shall perform to the Lord what you have sworn.' But I say to you, do not swear at all, either by heaven, for it is the throne of God, or by the earth, for it is his footstool, or by Jerusalem, for it is the city of the great King. And do not swear by your head, for you cannot make one hair white or black. Let what you say be simply 'Yes' or 'No'; anything more than this comes from evil.

"You have heard that it was said, 'An eye for an eye and a tooth for a tooth.' But I say to you, Do not resist one who is evil. But if any one strikes you on the right cheek, turn to him the other also; and if any one would sue you and take your coat, let him have your cloak as well; and if any one forces you to go one mile, go with him two miles. Give to him who begs from you, and do not refuse him who would borrow from you.

"You have heard that it was said, 'You shall love your neighbor and hate your enemy.' But I say to you, Love your enemies and pray for those who persecute you, so that you may be sons of your Father who is in heaven; for he makes his sun rise on the evil and on the good, and sends rain on the just and on the unjust. For if you love those who love you, what reward have you? Do not even the tax collectors do the same? And if you salute only your brethren, what more are you doing than others? Do not even the Gentiles do the same? You, therefore, must be perfect, as your heavenly Father is perfect.

"Beware of practicing your piety before men in order to be seen by them; for then you will have no reward from your Father who is in heaven.

"Thus, when you give alms, sound no trumpet before you, as the hypocrites do in the synagogues and in the streets, that they may be praised by men. Truly, I say to you, they have their reward. But when you give alms, do not let your left hand know what your right hand is doing, so that your alms may be in secret; and your Father who sees in secret will reward you.

"And when you pray, you must not be like the hypocrites; for they love to stand and pray in the synagogues and at the street corners, that they may be seen by men. Truly, I say to you, they have their reward. But when you pray, go into your room and shut the door and pray to your Father who is in secret; and your Father who sees in secret will reward you.

"And in praying do not heap up empty phrases as the Gentiles do; for they think that they will be heard for their many words. Do not be like them, for your Father knows what you need before you ask him. Pray then like this:
'Our Father who art in heaven,
Hallowed be thy name.
Thy kingdom come,
Thy will be done,
    On earth as it is in heaven.
Give us this day our daily bread;
And forgive us our debts,
    As we also have forgiven our debtors;
And lead us not into temptation,
    But deliver us from evil.'

"For if you forgive men their trespasses, your heavenly Father also will forgive you; but if you do not forgive men their trespasses, neither will your Father forgive your trespasses.

"And when you fast, do not look dismal, like the hypocrites, for they disfigure their faces that their fasting may be seen by men. Truly, I say to you, they have their reward. But when you fast, anoint your head and wash your face, that your fasting may not be seen by men but by your Father who is in secret; and your Father who sees in secret will reward you.

"Do not lay up for yourselves treasures on earth, where moth and rust consume and where thieves break in and steal, but lay up for yourselves treasures in heaven, where neither moth nor rust consumes and where thieves do not break in and steal; for where your treasure is, there will your heart be also.

"The eye is the lamp of the body. So, if your eye is sound, your whole body will be full of light; but if your eye is not sound, your whole body will be full of darkness. If then the light in you is darkness, how great is the darkness!

"No one can serve two masters; for either he will hate the one and love the other, or he will be devoted to the one and despise the other. You cannot serve God and mammon.

"Therefore I tell you, do not be anxious about your life, what you shall eat or what you shall drink, nor about your body, what you shall put on. Is not life more than food, and the body more than the clothing? Look at the birds of the air: they neither sow nor reap nor gather into barns, and yet your heavenly Father feeds them. Are you not of more value than they? And which of you by being anxious can add one cubit to his span of life? And why be anxious about clothing? Consider the lilies of the field, how they grow; they neither toil nor spin; yet I tell you, even Solomon in all his glory was not arrayed like one of these. But if God so clothes the grass of the field, which today is alive and tomorrow is thrown into the oven, will he not much more clothe you, O men of little faith? Therefore do not be anxious, saying, 'What shall we eat?' or 'What shall we drink?' or 'What shall we wear?' For the Gentiles seek all these things; and your heavenly Father knows that you need them all. But seek first his kingdom and his righteousness, and all these things shall be yours as well.

"Therefore do not be anxious about tomorrow, for tomorrow will be anxious for itself. Let the day's own trouble be sufficient for the day.

"Judge not, that you be not judged. For with the judgment you pronounce you will be judged, and the measure you give will be the measure you get. Why do you see the speck that is in your brother's eye, but do not notice the log that is in your own eye? Or how can you say to your brother, 'Let me take the speck out of your eye,' when there is the log in your own eye? you hypocrite, first take the log out of your own eye, and then you will see clearly to take the speck out of your brother's eye.

"Do not give dogs what is holy; and do not throw your pearls before swine, lest they trample them underfoot and turn to attack you.

"Ask, and it will be given you; seek, and you will find; knock, and it will be opened to you. For every one who asks receives, and he who seeks finds, and to him who knocks it will be opened. Or what man of you, if his son asks him for a loaf, will give him a stone? Or if he asks for a fish, will give him a serpent? If you then, who are evil, know how to give good gifts to your children, how much more will your Father who is in heaven give good things to those who ask him? So whatever you wish that men would do to you, do so to them; for this is the law and the prophets.

"Enter by the narrow gate; for the gate is wide and the way is easy, that leads to destruction, and those who enter by it are many. For the gate is narrow and the way is hard, that leads to life, and those who find it are few.

"Beware of false prophets, who come to you in sheep's clothing but inwardly are ravenous wolves. You will know them by their fruits. Are grapes gathered from thorns, or figs from thistles? So, every sound tree bears good fruit, but the bad tree bears evil fruit. A sound tree cannot bear evil fruit, nor can a bad tree bear good fruit. Every tree that does not bear good fruit is cut down and thrown into the fire. Thus you will know them by their fruits.

"Not every one who says to me, 'Lord, Lord,' shall enter the kingdom of heaven, but he who does the will of my Father who is in heaven. On that day many will say to me, 'Lord, Lord, did we not prophesy in your name, and cast out demons in your name, and do many mighty works in your name?' And then will I declare to them, 'I never knew you; depart from me, you evil-doers.'

"Every one then who hears these words of mine and does them will be like a wise man who built his house upon the rock; and the rain fell, and the floods came, and the winds blew and beat upon that house, but it did not fall, because it had been founded on the rock. And everyone who hears these words of mine and does not do them will be like a foolish man who built his house upon the sand; and the rain fell, and the floods came, and the winds blew and beat against the house, and it fell; and great was the fall of it."

And when Jesus finished these sayings, the crowds were astonished at his teaching, for he taught them as one who had authority, and not as their scribes.

LETTER TO THE CORINTHIANS
(1 Corinthians 13:1–13)

The Apostle Paul wrote his letters to the Corinthians during the years A.D. 54 to 56. Perhaps the most familiar of all his Epistles is chapter 13 of 1 Corin-

thians in which Paul speaks eloquently of the place of love in Christian living.

13 If I speak in the tongues of men and of angels, but have not love, I am a noisy gong or a clanging cymbal. And if I have prophetic powers, and understand all mysteries and all knowledge, and if I have all faith, so as to remove mountains, but have not love, I am nothing. ³If I give away all I have, and if I deliver my body to be burned, but have not love, I gain nothing.

⁴Love is patient and kind; love is not jealous or boastful; ⁵it is not arrogant or rude. Love does not insist on its own way; it is not irritable or resentful; ⁶it does not rejoice at wrong, but rejoices in the right. ⁷Love bears all things, believes all things, hopes all things, endures all things.

⁸Love never ends; as for prophecy, it will pass away; as for tongues, they will cease; as for knowledge, it will pass away. ⁹For our knowledge is imperfect and our prophecy is imperfect; ¹⁰but when the perfect comes, the imperfect will pass away. ¹¹When I was a child, I spoke like a child, I thought like a child, I reasoned like a child; when I became a man, I gave up childish ways. ¹²For now we see in a mirror dimly, but then face to face. Now I know in part; then I shall understand fully, even as I have been fully understood. ¹³So faith, hope, love abide, these three; but the greatest of these is love.

FIVE PARABLES — *moral lesson*

I

(Matthew 18:23–35)

"Therefore the kingdom of heaven may be compared to a king who wished to settle accounts with his servants. When he began the reckoning, one was brought to him who owed him ten thousand talents; and as he could not pay, his lord ordered him to be sold, with his wife and children and all that he had, and payment to be made. So the servant fell on his knees, imploring him, 'Lord, have patience with me, and I will pay you everything.' And out of pity for him the lord of that servant released him and forgave him the debt. But that same servant, as he went out, came upon one of his fellow servants who owed him a hundred denarii; and seizing him by the throat he said, 'Pay what you owe.' So his fellow servant fell down and besought him, 'Have patience with me, and I will pay you.' He refused and went and put him in prison till he should pay the debt. When his fellow servants saw what had taken place, they were greatly distressed, and they went and reported to their lord all that had taken place. Then his lord summoned him and said to him, 'You wicked servant! I forgave you all that debt because you besought me; and should not you have had mercy on your fellow servant, as I had mercy on you?' And in anger his lord delivered him to the jailers, till he should pay all his debt. So also my heavenly Father will do to every one of you, if you do not forgive your brother from your heart."

II

(Matthew 20:1–16)

"For the kingdom of heaven is like a householder who went out early in the morning to hire laborers for his vineyard. After agreeing with the laborers for a denarius a day, he sent them into his vineyard. And going out about the third hour he saw others standing idle in the market place; and to them he said, 'You go into the vineyard too, and whatever is right I will give you.' So they went. Going out again about the sixth hour and the ninth hour, he did the same. And about the eleventh hour he went out and found others standing; and he said to them, 'Why do you stand here idle all day?' They said to him, 'Because no one has hired us.' He said to them, 'You go into the vineyard too.' And when evening came, the owner of the vineyard said to his steward, 'Call the laborers and pay them their wages, beginning with the last, up to the first.' And when those hired about the eleventh hour came, each of them received a denarius. Now when the first came, they thought they would receive more; but each of them also received a denarius. And on receiving it they grumbled at the householder, saying, 'These last worked only one hour, and you have made them equal to us who have borne the burden of the day and the scorching heat.' But he replied to one of them, 'Friend, I am doing you no wrong; did you not agree with me for a denarius? Take what belongs to you, and go; I choose to give to this last as I give to you. Am I not allowed to do what I choose with what belongs to me? Or do you begrudge my generosity?' So the last will be first, and the first last.''

III

(Luke 10:30–37)

"A man was going down from Jerusalem to Jericho and he fell among robbers, who stripped him and beat him, and departed, leaving him half-dead. Now by chance a priest was going down that road; and when he saw him he passed by on the other side. So likewise a Levite, when he came to the place and saw him, passed by on the other side. But a Samaritan, as he journeyed, came to where he was; and when he saw him, he had compassion, and went to him and bound up his wounds, pouring on oil and wine; then he set him on his own beast and brought him to an inn, and took care of him. And the next day he took out two denarii and gave them to the innkeeper, saying, 'Take care of him; and whatever more you spend, I will repay you when I come back.' Which of these three, do you think, proved neighbor to the man who fell among the robbers?" He said, "The one who showed mercy on him." And Jesus said to him, "Go and do likewise."

IV

(Luke 15:11–32)

"There was a man who had two sons; and the younger of them said to his father, 'Father, give me the share of property that falls to me.' And he divided his living between them. Not many days later, the younger son gathered all he had and took his journey into a far country, and there he squandered his property in loose living. And when he had spent everything, a great famine arose in that country, and he began to be in want. So he went and joined himself to one of the citizens of that country, who sent him into his fields to feed swine. And he would gladly have fed on the pods that the swine ate; and no one gave him anything. But when he came to himself he said, 'How many of my father's hired servants have bread enough and to spare, but I perish here with hunger! I will arise and go to my father, and I will say to him, "Father, I have sinned against heaven and before you; I am no longer worthy to be called your son; treat me as one of your hired servants."' And he arose and came to his father. But while he was yet at a distance, his father

saw him and had compassion, and ran and embraced him and kissed him. And the son said to him, 'Father, I have sinned against heaven and before you; I am no longer worthy to be called your son.' But the father said to his servants, 'Bring quickly the best robe, and put it on him; and put a ring on his hand, and shoes on his feet; and bring the fatted calf and kill it, and let us eat and make merry; for this my son was dead, and is alive again; he was lost, and is found.' And they began to make merry.

"Now his elder son was in the field; and as he came and drew near to the house, he heard music and dancing. And he called one of the servants and asked what this meant. And he said to him, 'Your brother has come, and your father has killed the fatted calf, because he has received him safe and sound.' But he was angry and refused to go in. His father came out and entreated him, but he answered his father, 'Lo, these many years I have served you, and I never disobeyed your command; yet you never gave me a kid, that I might make merry with my friends. But when this son of yours came, who has devoured your living with harlots, you killed for him the fatted calf!' And he said to him, 'Son, you are always with me, and all that is mine is yours. It was fitting to make merry and be glad, for this your brother was dead, and is alive; he was lost, and is found.' ''

V

(Matthew 25:14–30)

"For it [the Kingdom of Heaven] will be as when a man going on a journey called his servants and entrusted to them his property; to one he gave five talents, to another two, to another one, to each according to his ability. Then he went away. He who had received the five talents went at once and traded with them; and he made five talents more. So too, he who had the two talents made two talents more. But he who had received the one talent, went and dug in the ground and hid his master's money. Now after a long time the master of those servants came and settled accounts with them. And he who had received the five talents came forward, bringing five talents more, saying, 'Master, you delivered to me five talents; here I have made five talents more.' His master said to him, 'Well done, good and faithful servant; you have been faithful over a little, I will set you over much; enter into the joy of your master.' And he also who had the two talents came forward, saying, 'Master, you delivered to me two talents; here I have made two talents more.' His master said to him, 'Well done, good and faithful servant; you have been faithful over a little, I will set you over much; enter into the joy of your master.' He also who had received the one talent came forward, saying, 'Master, I knew you to be a hard man, reaping where you did not sow, and gathering where you did not winnow; so I was afraid, and I went and hid your talent in the ground. Here you have what is yours.' But his master answered him, 'You wicked and slothful servant! You knew that I reap where I have not sowed, and gather where I have not winnowed? Then you ought to have invested my money with the bankers, and at my coming I should have received what was my own with interest. So take the talent from him, and give it to him who has the ten talents. For to every one who has will more be given, and he will have abundance; but from him who has not, even what he has will be taken away. And cast the worthless servant into the outer darkness; there men will weep and gnash their teeth.' ''

Exercises

The East has always been fond of teaching by parable, the brief narrative that by comparison provides a way of getting at a truth. It is not quite like an algebraic problem, to be solved by substituting terms: "x = y," "a = b," and the like. It is rather a way of stimulating the imagination, of getting at the point by *insight.* Jesus was following an ancient, well-established tradition in teaching by parables. These stories must be understood on an exceedingly literal level; they mean what they say; but they do not stop there—the mind goes on to seize upon the inherent likenesses, the points to be compared. Here are some questions over the parables in the text.

1. "The Wicked Servant." What prompted the action of the servant's lord, at the beginning and at the end? What is the specific fault of the servant? What was the point that Jesus was trying to convey?

2. "The Vineyard." Imagine a disciple of Plato, who wrote the whole treatise of the *Republic* in order to consider the question "What is Justice?", commenting upon this story. In two or three sentences, what would his opinion be? Imagine a disciple of Jesus trying to answer, again in two or three sentences. Where is the point of departure between the two?

3. "The Good Samaritan." Why does Jesus make a *Samaritan* the subject of his tale? In trying to modernize it, what word would you pick instead? (On second thought—better *not* answer that question!) What fault or shortcoming among his contemporaries was Jesus pointing out?

4. "The Prodigal Son." It is always tempting to feel a great deal of sympathy for the elder brother in this story. When you do so (or when you side with the workers in the vineyard who had worked all day), what *basis* of judgment are you using? How does this measuring rod of what is just differ from that of Jesus?

5. "The Talents." Which of the other parables is this most like? As a story it is harsh and forbidding; how would you answer the argument that it does not portray a merciful and loving God?

♀REVELATION

For several centuries before and after Christ, there flourished a distinctive writing known as apocalypse or revelation. Apocalyptic thought was based on the Jewish eschatological[7] view of history. A portion of the Book of Daniel is an apocalypse, and Paul included

---

7. Eschatology (Gk., *eschatos,* furthest) is a branch of theology dealing with the last things, such as death, judgment, resurrection, and immortality.

Figure 7.1 *The Fourth Horseman of the Apocalypse,* Angers Tapestries, Angers Castle, France. Height ca. 8'. Woven by Nicolas Bataillel in 1375/80 in Paris, this is the oldest known French tapestry.

several apocalyptic verses in 2 Thessalonians. The last book of the Bible, called Revelation or Apocalypse of John, is the only full apocalypse in the New Testament. Writing to seven beseiged churches around A.D. 93 during Domitian's savage persecution of Christians, John of Patmos declares, in visionary terms, the ultimate triumph over the empire and his perception of a new heaven, a new earth, and a new Jerusalem after all souls have been raised from the dead for the Last Judgment. In the early Church there was a widespread belief that the Second Coming of Christ was imminent.

In the following selection, Christ opens four of the seven seals, releasing the Four Horsemen of the Apocalypse: Conquest, War, Famine, and Death (fig. 7.1).

6 Now I saw when the Lamb opened one of the seven seals, and I heard one of the four living creatures say, as with a voice of thunder, "Come!" [2]And I saw, and behold, a white horse, and its rider had a bow; and a crown was given to him, and he went out conquering and to conquer.

[3]When he opened the second seal, I heard the second living creature say, "Come!" [4] And out came another horse, bright red; its rider was permitted to take peace from the earth, so that men should slay one another; and he was given a great sword.

[5]When he opened the third seal, I heard the third living creature say, "Come!" And I saw, and behold, a black horse, and its rider had a balance in his hand; [6]and I heard what seemed to be a voice in the midst of the four living creatures saying, "A quart of wheat for a denarius, and three quarts of barley for a denarius, but do not harm oil and wine!"

⁷When he opened the fourth seal, I heard the voice of the fourth living creature say, "Come!" ⁸And I saw, and behold, a pale horse, and its rider's name was Death, and Hades followed him; and they were given power over a fourth of the earth, to kill with sword and with famine and with pestilence and by wild beasts of the earth.

Revelation 6:1–8

Following the Last Judgment, John presents a golden vision of the world to come.

21 Then I saw a new heaven and a new earth; for the first heaven and the first earth had passed away, and the sea was no more. ²And I saw the holy city, new Jerusalem, coming down out of heaven from God, prepared as a bride adorned for her husband; ³and I heard a great voice from the throne saying, "Behold, the dwelling of God is with men. He will dwell with them, and they shall be his people, and God himself will be with them; ⁴he will wipe away every tear from their eyes, and death shall be no more, neither shall there be mourning nor crying nor pain any more, for the former things have passed away."

Revelation 21:1–4

8

The Beginnings of Christian Art

Chronological Overview

306–337	Reign of Constantine
313	Edict of Milan guaranteed Christians freedom of worship
325	First Council of Nicea condemned Arian heresy
330	Constantine established a new capital at Constantinople
410; 455	Rome sacked by Visigoths and by Vandals
476	Last Roman emperor deposed
ca. 493–527	Theodoric and Ostrogothic Kingdom
527–565	Emperor Justinian; First Byzantine Golden Age
726–843	Iconoclastic Controversy
ca. 900–1100	Second Byzantine Golden Age
1204	Destruction of Constantinople by Fourth Crusade
1453	Constantinople falls to Ottoman Turks; end of Eastern Roman Empire

---

The first two centuries of Christianity had little need for art in any form. Meeting in small groups in private homes, early Christians conducted simple services centered around the Eucharist, the consecrated bread and wine commemorating Christ's sacrifice on the cross. Dating from about 250, the earliest known church building is a Greek peristyle house in Dura-Europos, Syria. Suitable for a congregation of no more than sixty, this was a private home converted to liturgical use though it possessed neither decorations nor architectural distinction. There is, in fact, no surviving Christian art from the first two centuries and very little from the third century, and that almost entirely from the catacombs of Rome.

Christianity in Rome

Initially and during most of the first two centuries, Christians were buried in regular Roman cemeteries. Rejecting cremation (the usual procedure for the lower classes) because of their belief in the Resurrection, Christians continued burying their dead in surface cemeteries except in the outskirts of Rome, Naples, and Syracuse, where porous stone (tufa) was easily excavated for subterranean tombs. During the late second century Christian communities became increasingly interested in separate burial areas where they could, in privacy, perform rites for the dead and also safeguard the tombs. Because Roman law permitted no burials within city limits, Christian families or groups bought land on hillsides alongside the major highways leading into Rome, sites that already contained the funerary monuments of wealthy Roman families. Utilizing surface buildings and subterranean passages, these cemeteries were ideally suited to Christian concerns for seclusion and security. At no time, however, were the catacombs exclusively Christian nor were they used as secret meeting places; Roman officials knew the location and extent of the burial grounds. There were, after all, some thirty-eight subterranean cemeteries outside Rome in which were interred about four million bodies.

The Roman catacombs had up to five subterranean levels with superimposed niches for sarcophagi eight to ten deep in each passage. Each cemetery included small chapels for burial and commemorative services. In the chapels and sometimes over the burial niches are found the earliest examples of Christian figurative art. Executed by artisans working by lamplight in a dark, dank, and undoubtedly malodorous environment, the representations were generally simple and often hastily executed. However, neither the client nor the artist was preoccupied with aesthetics; Christians were mainly interested in conveying a message or a prayer that would be understood by the Christian community and, above all, by God.

The most common representation in the catacombs was the *orant* (OR–an; from the Latin word for *praying*; fig. 8.1), a figure presented in full frontality, standing with arms raised in prayer or supplication. The orant can symbolize the soul of the deceased praying for salvation or it can reflect the Hellenistic view, a personification in human form of abstract ideas like resurrection or salvation.

The figure of Jesus as *The Good Shepherd* (fig. 8.2), a commonly used representation of Christ throughout the centuries, appears frequently in catacomb frescoes. As might be expected, the Good Shepherd motif can be found in most cultures in which sheepherding is an important occupation. There is, for example, the *Calf-Bearer* (see fig. 3.21) of Archaic Greek sculpture and, in the Hebraic tradition, David the shepherd boy, giant-killer, psalmist, and king. Christ as the Good Shepherd is a symbol of the guardian of the faithful of his church; further, Jesus was a descendent of the David who tended sheep in Palestine.

Figure 8.1 *Orant,* ca. A.D. 300. Catacombs of St. Priscilla, Rome.

Figure 8.2 *The Good Shepherd,* ca. A.D. 250. Ceiling painting, Catacombs of St. Callixtus, Rome.

Ιησους
Χριστος
Θεου
Ὑιος
Σωτηρ

Figure 8.3 Anagram as derived from the Greek for "Jesus Christ, the Son of God, Savior."

Artistic representation of the concepts inherent in the new religion caused difficulties never dreamed of by Egyptian, Greek, and Roman artists. The Greeks, for example, had created the gods in their own image, thus making the divinities instantly available for artistic representation: Zeus with a thunderbolt symbolizing the power principle; Poseidon with his trident; Aphrodite as the Goddess of Love, and so forth. How, then, was the Christian artist to depict such abstractions as the Trinity, the Holy Spirit, salvation, redemption, the Eucharist, immortality? In time, artists worked out a variety of solutions using biblical stories, parables, and symbols. The idea of immortality, for example, could be represented through biblical scenes of salvation: Moses leading his people out of Egypt; Jonah released from the whale; Daniel escaping from the lion's den; Lazarus rising from his tomb. The anchor came to represent hope, the dove was peace or the Holy Spirit, and the palm meant victory through martyrdom. Symbolizing Christ is the Khi–Rho (KYE–ro) monogram, which superimposes the first two letters of Christ's name (Khristos) in Greek: ☧ . The first and last letters of the Greek alphabet, Alpha (A) and Omega (Ω), symbolize infinity as in Christ's statement, "I am Alpha and Omega, the Beginning and the End." Multiple meanings are found in the symbol of the fish: (1) the Last Supper; (2) Christian evangelism as represented in Christ's exhortation to his fishermen disciples to be "fishers of men"; and (3) an anagram upon a Greek phrase, the initial letters of which form the Greek word *ikhthys,* or *fish* (fig. 8.3).

The one event that was not symbolized in catacombs paintings was the Crucifixion. The most ignoble and horrible method of Roman execution, crucifixion was reserved for criminals judged guilty of foul and heinous acts; Christ was crucified by the Romans as an "enemy of the state," treason being the worst of all crimes. For early Christians, the simple geometric form of the cross was all that was needed to symbolize Christ's sacrifice. Perhaps the earliest extant crucifixion scene produced for a public place

Figure 8.4 *Crucifixion,* from the west door of the Church of Santa Sabina, ca. A.D. 430, Rome. Wood, 11″ × 15¾″.

is a small, wooden, low-relief panel on one of the doors of the Church of Santa Sabina (fig. 8.4). Set amidst a door rich with elaborately carved panels this, the simplest panel, appears to be a deliberate attempt to tone down the horror of the crucifixion.

Early Christians also refrained from producing sculpture in the round, especially life-size figures. God's commandment to Moses that "Thou shall not make unto thee any graven images" remained basic to Christianity though religious conservatives chose to interpret this injunction literally. The recognition by the early church fathers of the didactic and educational value of art was summed up by Pope Gregory the Great (ruled 590–604): "Pictures are used in the church in order that those who are ignorant of letters may, merely by looking at the walls, read there what they were unable to read in books." Supplementing this realistic position was the theological argument that since Jesus was "made flesh and dwelt among us," he had a human likeness and nature that could be represented in art. Conservatives were nevertheless suspicious of freestanding statues because they associated these with the gods of other religions, which is the main reason why there was very little monumental sculpture between the fourth and tenth centuries.

Two very rare three-dimensional sculptures do survive from fourth-century Rome. Classical in pose and reminiscent of the catacomb painting in figure 8.2, the *Good Shepherd* (fig. 8.5) is as carefully detailed as the finest Hellenistic genre sculpture. Stylistically it still relates to the *Calf-Bearer* (see fig. 3.21) that was created about a thousand years earlier.

The statue of *Christ Enthroned* (fig. 8.6) depicts Christ as a young, clean-shaven philosopher or emperor. Features, clothing, and gestures are classical, as is the smooth, idealized face. Not accepted

Figure 8.5 *Good Shepherd,* ca. A.D. 350. Marble, height 39″. Vatican Museums, Rome.

Figure 8.6 *Christ Enthroned,* ca. A.D. 350–360. Marble, smaller than life size. National Museum, Rome.

until the Byzantine era, though certainly the universal image today, the concept of a bearded Christ was probably Syrian in origin. Because this was art of the spirit rather than the flesh, literal depiction was not the goal; this is Christ the symbol, the Son of God. Just as the image of Christ is venerated as if it were the person, so too can a cross or relic be venerated. Nevertheless, the existence of these two sculptures is unusual and might even be construed as images from another religion if very similar figures did not also appear on innumerable early Christian sarcophagi.

By the middle of the third century important church leaders were entombed in stone sarcophagi, but the practice was not widely accepted until Christianity was legalized in the fourth century. Drawing on both classical sources and catacomb paintings, the superb *Jonah Sarcophagus* (fig. 8.7) depicts the Jonah story in a continuous narration, a series of successive episodes in which Jonah appears three times and the strangely serpentine whale twice. Reading from left to right: Jonah is cast naked into a swirling sea by the sailors and heads directly into the mouth of the waiting whale; after the confused whale disgorges Jonah, the latter ends up sleeping nude under a protective arbor of gourds. Noah appears in a miniscule box floating on the sea to the right of the second whale, while in the upper left-hand corner Jesus addresses a tiny mummy standing in front of a tomb, thus paralleling the raising of Lazarus with the Noah

and Jonah stories. Though using biblical material to communicate the idea of salvation, the artist was clearly influenced by classical sculptors.

By the middle of the fourth century, sarcophagi began to emphasize New Testament scenes, as evidenced in the *Sarcophagus of Junius Bassus* (fig. 8.8). The front panel, illustrated here, is divided into ten reliefs on two levels. The top level includes: (1) the Sacrifice of Isaac, (2) the Arrest of St. Peter, (3) Christ Enthroned between St. Peter and St. Paul, and (4–5) Christ before Pilate. The bottom level shows: (1) the Misery of Job, (2) Adam and Eve after the Fall, (3) Christ's Entry into Jerusalem, (4) Daniel in the Lion's Den, and (5) St. Paul Led to His Martyrdom. Many interpretations are possible for a series this complex: The sacrifice of Isaac is in response to God's command, as is the testing of Job; Daniel, Abraham, and Job represent salvation; the fall of Adam and Eve represents the condition of humanity that is redeemed by Christ's sacrifice; the triumphal entry into Jerusalem signals the eternal triumph of the Resurrected Christ, depicted directly above. The implications are

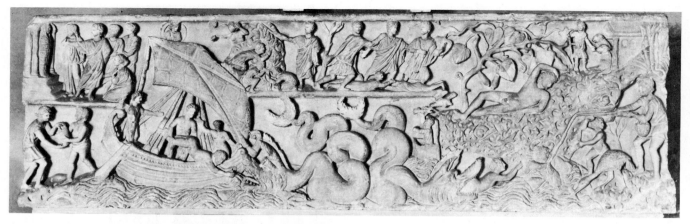

Figure 8.7 *The Jonah Sarcophagus,* late third century A.D. Lateran Museum, Rome.

Figure 8.8 *The Sarcophagus of Junius Bassus,* ca. A.D. 359. Marble, 46½″ × 96″, St. Peter's, Rome.

endless. All of the Old and New Testament figures look like Romans of the time and, indeed, the central top panel shows the Roman sky god Caelus holding up the firmament on which Christ is resting his feet.

The Age of Constantine

For a document of such critical importance, the Edict of Milan is a typical example of the urbane and low-keyed Roman approach to affairs of state:

> When we, Constantine Augustus and Licinius Augustus, met so happily at Milan, and considered together all that concerned the interest and security of the State, we decided . . . to grant to Christians and to everybody the free power to follow the religion of their choice, in order that all that is divine in the heavens may be favorable and propitious towards us and towards all who are placed under our authority.
> From a rescript issued at Nicomedia
> by Licinius, June 13, 313.[1]

Though it came soon after the two most severe and methodical persecutions of Christians, by Decius in 249–251 and by Diocletian in 303–305, this declaration of religious freedom found organized Christianity ready to build churches and otherwise assume a prominent role in the empire. For centuries the

---

1. Laotantius, *De mortibus persecutorum,* xlviii. Constantine did not assume sole leadership of the empire until 324, when he had Licinius, his coregent, executed.

Figure 8.9 Roman basilica, Volubilis, Morocco, third century A.D.

Figure 8.10 Basilica of St. Clement, interior of lower church, fourth century A.D., Rome.

Romans had constructed basilicas, large buildings that served as meeting halls, mercantile centers, halls of justice, and the like. The basilica was a prototype of the kind of large, dignified structure Christians needed for worship services. For example, the basilica at Volubilis (fig. 8.9) originally had five aisles and four rows of arcades like the one pictured here. Serving as a hall of justice for a large Roman colony, the building has the usual Roman arches with Corinthian pilasters punctuating the heavy columns. By removing the pillar and letting the column carry the thrust of the arch (fig. 8.10), Christian architects developed a lighter and more graceful setting for the Christian liturgy. St. Clement, one of the smaller early churches, has only one aisle on each side and a single triumphal arch framing the altar. It is called a basilica because it contains the relics of a saint; it is not, however, a true basilica as an architectural type.

None of the great basilica-type churches erected in Constantine's Rome have survived as such. Old St. Peter's was replaced by the present church, and hardly anything original remains of St. John Lateran after numerous restorations. St. Paul's Outside the Walls was destroyed by fire in 1823 and faithfully reconstructed by 1854, insofar as that was possible. However, the etching by Piranesi (fig. 8.11) is of the original church and clearly illustrates a basic design used for nearly all Western churches throughout the entire medieval period. The secular basilica was usually entered from its longitudinal sides, but Christians shifted the entrances to a shorter side, usually the western end, thus orienting the building along a longitudinal axis. The interior space was divided into a large area called the *nave*, because it seemed to symbolize a ship (*navis*, the ship of souls), flanked by two aisles on each side (see fig. 8.12). The nave joins a secondary space, the *transept*, which is placed at right angles to the nave proper and forms an interior Latin cross. Later churches would lengthen the transept so that even the exterior walls assumed a cruciform shape, the most characteristic church design in

Western Christendom. Behind the transept is a semicircular space called an *apse* (aps) in which the altar is placed on a raised platform. The nave was covered with an **A**-shaped truss roof; at a level well below the nave roof the aisles were covered by lean-to truss roofs so that the clerestory, or clearstory, windows could be set in the upper nave wall to illuminate the interior. Corinthian columns connected a nave arcade above which was the *triforium,* usually painted or covered with mosaics; above that was the clerestory area with alabaster windows. Aesthetically, the basilica interior is complex and stimulating, for there is no single point from which one can comprehend the space. The strong rhythm of the nave arcade seems to march inexorably towards the eastern end and the triumphal arch that frames the ultimate focus of the design: the high altar where the sacraments are celebrated.

An obvious choice for Christian use, the basilica had imperial associations that suited the triumph of Christianity and a spacious interior that could accommodate thousands of worshipers; Old St. Peter's was said to have a capacity of 40,000. In addition to the interior space, large churches like St. Paul's and Old St. Peter's were fronted by an open courtyard called an *atrium,* which was surrounded on three sides by a covered arcade called an *ambulatory,* or walkway. On the fourth side of the atrium was a porch, or *narthex,* that led to the front doors of the church. Adapted from Roman house plans (see fig. 6.3), the atrium was later moved to the south side of monastic churches to become the medieval cloister. Traversing the entire complex from the ambulatory into the arcaded courtyard (atrium), going through the narthex, entering the church proper, and walking

Figure 8.11 Interior, St. Paul's Outside the Walls, begun 386 A.D., Rome. Etching by Giambattista Piranesi, 1749.

down the nave to the altar is curiously suggestive of the layout of Egyptian temples (see figs. 3.7 and 3.8).

With a deliberately plain exterior of brick or rubble construction, Christian churches reserved glorious interiors—embellished structural materials, marble panels, paintings, and mosaics—for their congregations. Very little of early Christian mural painting has survived, and what remains is not as striking as the incredibly beautiful mosaics. As created by Hellenistic and Roman artists, mosaics were composed of small bits of marble called *tesserae* (TES–ser–ay). Almost always designed as floor mosaics, artists incorporated subtle gradations of color into designs, some of which were reproductions of existing paintings. Early Christian mosaics were, on the other hand, unprecedented. Designed entirely as wall or ceiling decorations, the tesserae were made of bits of glass cubes that had a wide range of color and intensity, including transparent pieces backed with glittering gold leaf. With shiny, irregular glass faces, the tesserae were set into plaster at slightly varying angles, turning a flat wall surface into a shimmering screen of color. Depicting Christ enthroned and raised above the Apostles, the much renovated mosaic of Santa Pudenziana (fig. 8.13), asserts Christ's authority and, by implication, the institutional authority of the church. In the background are buildings representing the Heavenly Jerusalem, while in the sky are

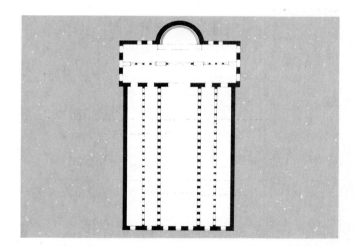

Figure 8.12 Schematic floor plan of St. Paul's, Rome

winged symbols of the four evangelists: the lion of St. Mark, the ox of St. Luke, the eagle of St. John, and the winged man of St. Matthew. Of unknown origin but widely employed by this time, these evangelical images continued throughout Christian iconography. Not meant to be read as a historical event, this scene is an essay on salvation as assured by Christ's death

Figure 8.13 *Christ Teaching the Apostles in the Heavenly Jerusalem,* mosaic in the apse of Santa Pudenziana, ca. A.D. 401–407, Rome.

Figure 8.14 *Abraham and the Celestial Visitors,* mosaic from the second quarter of the fifth century, Church of Santa Maria Maggiore, Rome.

on the cross, of which we have been informed by the evangelists, and which is available through the church, the representative of God on earth.

What is believed to be the oldest cycle of evangelical and biblical mosaics is found in the fifth-century church of Santa Maria Maggiore in Rome. One scene depicts, on two levels, the encounter of Abraham with the three celestial visitors at Mamre and his subsequent vision of the Trinity (fig. 8.14). On the lower level Sarah prepares food, which Abraham then sets before the three young men, whose celestial status is marked by halos. On the upper level Abraham bows before his visitors, who now appear in a vision; this time the central figure of Christ is completely surrounded by an oval field of light called an *aureole* (OR–e–ol). This manner of representing the Holy Trinity was common in the West into the Gothic period and even in today's Byzantine world.

Ravenna

Serving briefly as an imperial city for the Romans, Ostrogoths, and the Byzantine Empire, provincial Ravenna was, when compared with Rome, a most unlikely capital. Located south of Venice in the midst of extensive swamps, the port of Ravenna did provide the Western emperors with an easily defensible site and, perhaps more importantly, a low profile compared with the once mighty city of Rome, now the natural target of every barbarian invader. Becoming

Figure 8.15 *The Good Shepherd,* mosaic; Mausoleum of Galla Placidia, ca. 425–450, Ravenna, Italy.

Figure 8.16 Interior, Church of Sant' Apollinare Nuovo, ca. 493–526, Ravenna.

the capital of the West under Honorius in 404, Ravenna fell to Odoacer in 476 but emerged as the capital of Theodoric's Ostrogothic Kingdom (489–526), and concluded its royal career as the Western capital of Justinian's Byzantine Empire (527–565). Modern Ravenna contains notable artworks from all three imperial periods.

The mausoleum Empress Galla Placidia, half sister of Honorius, built for members of her family contains some of the best-preserved and splendid mosaics of the fifth century. Set in a *lunette* (lew–NET), a semicircular wall of a vaulted room, the mosaic of *The Good Shepherd* (fig. 8.15) depicts a majestic Christ watching over six attentive sheep, who balance him in pyramid formations of three on each side, thus symbolizing the Trinitarian doctrine. The regal pose spirals upwards from the right hand feeding a sheep to the left hand, which grasps a knob-ended cross signifying the earthly death of the King of Kings. In the Hellenic tradition of classical painting, the forms are positioned in a real space and give the illusion of having three-dimensional bulk. Particularly notable is the rocky landscape, which though increasingly stylized remained in the repertoire of landscape painting throughout the Byzantine tradition and into the late medieval style of such painters as Giotto. Often overlooked are the funnel-shaped tubes along the lower border that represent footlights illuminating a liturgical tableau.

Theodoric, King of the Ostrogoths, built some notable churches in Ravenna. Originally dedicated by Theodoric to "Our Lord Jesus Christ" to serve his Arian sect, the Church of Sant' Apollinare Nuovo (fig. 8.16) was later renamed by the Orthodox church after Apollinarus, a disciple of St. Peter and the patron saint of Ravenna. Though the teaching of Arius of Alexandria (ca. 256–336) was condemned by the 325 Council of Nicea over which Constantine presided, many Germanic tribes like the Ostrogoths persisted in the Arian heresy. Briefly, the Arians held to the rationalistic belief that since Christ was created by God the Father, he must be subordinate and not of the same divine substance as his creator. Jesus was therefore the highest of created beings but human rather than divine. The orthodox Byzantine view was that Christ, as the Word Incarnate, was of single substance with the Father and thus wholly divine. The popes of the Western church held to a middle ground: the Word was made flesh, and so Christ was both divine and human and a full member of the Holy Trinity. Reflecting the controversy between Arianism and Byzantine orthodoxy, the mosaics of Sant' Apollinare Nuovo are arranged in three levels. Created by Roman artists for Theodoric, the top band includes scenes from the life of Christ, while the figures between the clerestory windows represent Old Testament patriarchs and prophets. After the Byzantine conquest of Ravenna, Bishop Angellus ordered the lowest band removed, presumably because Arian beliefs were depicted. These were replaced with Byzantine-style saints in procession, women on the north wall (left in fig. 8.16) and men on the south. The nave itself has an arcade of columns with ornate capitals topped by blocks from which spring the semicircular arches. With only one side aisle and no transepts, the plan is that of a small and unpretentious basilica, which further highlights the splendid mosaics.

The Byzantine World

Marking the true beginning of the Byzantine style, the reign of Justinian (527–565) was notable for artistic production and for the Justinian Legal Code, plus the dubious distinction of closing, after a thousand years, Plato's Academy in Athens. Operating from his capitals of Constantinople in the East and Ravenna in the West, Justinian was both an emperor in the Roman tradition and an Oriental potentate in what was to later

Figure 8.17 San Vitale, ca. 526–547, Ravenna

become the Byzantine Empire. Except for some architecture in Constantinople, most Byzantine art created prior to 1402 can be found in Ravenna. The rape of Constantinople by the Fourth Crusade (1204) destroyed most of the art and much of the city, which was not retaken from the Latins until 1261.

The most "Byzantine" of the many religious buildings in Ravenna is the octagonal domed church of San Vitale (fig. 8.17), a prototype of the central-plan churches that were to dominate the world of Orthodox Christianity just as the basilica plan prevailed throughout Western Christendom. The brick exterior is a complex and subtle interplay of angular patterns around a central core, marred only by the addition of a Renaissance doorway. The interior is a veritable jewel-box (colorplate 10), with walls of polychromed marble, pierced marble screens, hundreds of decorative and pictorial mosaics, marble floor mosaics, and numerous carved alabaster columns. San Vitale is an octagonal structure surmounted by an octagonal drum on which the circular dome rests. The transition from the octagonal drum to the round dome was accomplished by using *squinches,* stone lintels placed diagonally across corners formed by the octagonal walls. Topping the aisle that surrounds the nave is a vaulted triforium gallery reserved for women, as was customary for Orthodox Christianity. Compact and intimate, San Vitale functioned for the imperial court somewhat like a diminutive, luxurious theatre.

Facing the altar from opposite sides are the two justly celebrated mosaics of Emperor Justinian (colorplate 11) and Empress Theodora (colorplate 12). Though extensively reconstructed, these ceremonial works are still the best extant examples of early Byzantine mosaics. Illustrating the new ideal of the Byzantine style, the figures are tall and slim with small feet, solemn faces, and large oval eyes. Frozen in time without a hint of movement, the grave figures are depicted in full frontality, highly stylized, but nevertheless revealing individual differences. Flanked by twelve companions suggesting the twelve Apostles, Justinian stands in the exact center holding the offering of bread for the mass. He is crowned with both the imperial diadem and a halo, representative of the unity of the spiritual force of the church and of the temporal power of the state. At Justinian's left is Bishop Maximianus, who was responsible for the completion of San Vitale and whose importance is signified by the label over his head. The composition of the work delineates the threefold structure of the empire: the six soldiers represent the army, the three staff members the state, and the three clergymen the church. One of the soldiers holds a shield with the Chrismon insignia that symbolizes not only the name of Christ but allegorically becomes a combination of the cross and shepherd's crook, indicating Christ's death and his pastoral mission.

Unlike the emperor, Theodora is depicted in a more specific setting, probably the narthex of San Vitale. About to pass through a doorway to which she is beckoned by an attendant, she is carrying the offering of wine in a gold chalice encrusted with precious stones. With her huge diadem, ropes of pearls, and luxurious ceremonial gown in royal purple, Theodora is portrayed as the strong-willed, intelligent, and beautiful empress history has revealed her to be, and considerably removed from her early career as circus performer and courtesan. Pictured on her gown are the Magi bringing their offerings to the infant Jesus, suggesting a parallel with her gift-bearing activity. Both mosaics achieve some of their clarity by conforming to the Greek isocephalic convention of placing all heads on about the same level.

The City of Constantine

Dedicated by Constantine in 330 as "New Rome," Constantinople, as the city quickly came to be known, was the sumptuous center of Byzantine civilization for over a thousand years. Typical of central-plan churches, St. Irene was only one of Justinian's many building projects for the imperial city. Contrasting with the extended longitudinal axis of the basilica plan, central-plan churches are built around a vertical axis which extends from the floor to the ceiling mosaic of the central dome. Figure 8.18 illustrates the psychological impact of the head of Christ as the ultimate focus of the vertical axis, and symbolizes the total dominance of the Orthodox faith under the aegis of the emperor who built the churches and appointed the patriarch of Constantinople.

Figure 8.18 *Christ Pantocrater,* dome mosaic, ca. 532, Church of St. Irene, Constantinople (Istanbul).

Figure 8.19 Anthemius of Tralles and Isodorus of Miletos, Hagia Sophia, 532–537, Constantinople (Istanbul).

Justinian's building program for Constantinople began in 532 as a matter of necessity. It was in that year that the Blues and Greens, rival chariot-racing factions, had combined in a powerful revolt against the autocratic rule of Justinian and Theodora. Before the imperial troops put down the revolution by slaughtering about 30,000 people, most of the public buildings had been destroyed, including the Constantinian Basilica of Hagia Sophia (HA–jeh SO–fee–ah; Church of Holy Wisdom).

Disdaining the usual procedure of selecting an architect for a building project, Justinian appointed the noted mathematician Anthemius of Tralles to design the new Hagia Sophia. Assisted by Isodorus of Miletos and possibly Justinian himself, Anthemius invented a revolutionary new design unlike anything in either the Roman or Byzantine world (fig. 8.19). Combining the longitudinal axis of the basilica plan with the domed structure of a central plan, abutted on east and west by half domes, the new Hagia Sophia was a beautiful and inspiring building, truly a majestic architectural achievement. No wonder Justinian is said to have exclaimed as he rode up to the church for its consecration, "O Solomon, I have excelled thee!"

The interior of Hagia Sophia is breathtaking (fig. 8.20). The dome seems to float on light, as it rests upon a tightly spaced ring of forty windows. The entire interior is, in fact, flooded with light from hundreds of windows in the thin, shell-like walls. Adding to the magical effect of all this light were thousands of tesserae that were set into the walls, but later covered with plaster and paint when the Turks converted the building into a mosque. With an interior measuring 240' x 270', crowned by a dome 112' in diameter and extending to 184' above the pavement, this is one of the largest space enclosures achieved prior to this century. At the corners of a 100' square area under the dome are 70' piers that support massive

Figure 8.20 Interior of Hagia Sophia, Constantinople (Istanbul).

Figure 8.21 Greek Orthodox church, from the fourth century A.D. Naxos, Greece.

Figure 8.22 Aerial view of St. Mark's Cathedral, begun 1063, Venice.

arches. They in turn are connected by *pendentives* (pen–DEN–tivs), which effect the transition from the basic square to the circular rim of the dome. Best described as concave spherical triangles, two of the four pendentives can be seen in figure 8.20. A more graceful transition from a square base to a round dome than squinches, pendentives also facilitate the covering of more floor space. Their origin remains unknown and their use on the monumental scale of Hagia Sophia is unprecedented. Henceforth used in most Byzantine architecture, pendentives became standard structural devices from the Renaissance to the present day.

As sometimes happens with highly original buildings, there were some technical problems, the most serious being the collapse of the dome twenty-one years after its completion. The present higher-arched dome solved that problem. Byzantium never produced another structure to equal Hagia Sophia. Though it inspired similar designs that can be seen all over Istanbul, it remains unique—the first and best of its kind. First a church and then a mosque, Hagia Sophia is now a museum.

Typical of the more modest churches throughout the empire is the small Orthodox church on the Greek island of Naxos (fig. 8.21). It was built of local field-stone and displays the Byzantine central-dome plan at the left, but this diminutive church also features domes over the other arms of the Greek cross plan, such as those used much later and on a far-greater scale in the Cathedral of St. Mark's in Venice (see fig. 8.22).

Brutally terminating the first Byzantine golden age, the Iconoclastic Controversy lasted off and on, mostly on, from 726 to 843. Issuing an imperial decree forbidding idolatry, Leo III ordered the destruction of all images of Christ, saints, prophets, and the like. Representations of all sorts, including mosaics in Hagia Sophia, were destroyed along with the entire legacy of pictorial art of Justinian's age, except in Byzantine Italy and on Mount Sinai. Iconoclasts

(image-destroyers) mutilated, blinded, tortured, and sometimes executed those who tried to protect sacred images. Ostensibly a religious issue based on the biblical commandment forbidding graven images, the controversy was essentially a conflict between Church and State. The monastic movement had achieved great wealth and power and won considerable respect from the faithful, much to the consternation of the emperors; furthermore, monasteries were diverting revenue from the state and paying little or no taxes. As principal repositories for sacred images, monasteries were attacked, sometimes confiscated, and their resident monks executed, without, however, stamping out the image-worshipping monks (iconodules) in the West. A later Empress Theodora allowed images again in 843, but the Western and Eastern branches of Christianity were already launched on a parting of the ways, which led, in 1054, to a schism that has yet to be healed. Though the extent of the loss of priceless artworks can never be known the disaster was not total. The controversy did help to spark a renewed interest in secular art and Late Classical motifs, setting the stage for the Second Byzantine Golden Age of ca. 900–1100.

The Second Golden Age

The largest and most profusely decorated church of the Second Golden Age, St. Mark's of Venice is also the most ambitious structure outside the empire. St. Mark's differs from Hagia Sophia in that the Greek cross form is clearly visible from within and that in addition to the central dome, each arm of the cross is capped by a full dome. From the exterior and especially from the air (fig. 8.22), St. Mark's, with each of its five domes encased in wood covered by gilt copper sheathing and topped by ornate lanterns, is the splendid showcase the Republic of Venice intended it to be. As required by law, every ship's captain had to return to Venice with something of value for construction or decoration of the cathedral. Because of

Figure 8.23 *Crucifixion,* mosaic. ca. 1100, Monastery Church, Daphné, Greece.

the law many treasures from the 1204 sack of Constantinople found their way to Venice. Despite Romanesque and Gothic elements, the Greek cross plan, multiple domes, strong interior lighting, and glittering mosaics make St. Mark's a Byzantine masterpiece.

After the victory of the iconophiles (image-lovers) in 843, Byzantine painting and mosaics began to blend the otherworldly beauty of Justinian's time with a renewed interest in classical Greek art. Perhaps the finest examples of art of the Second Golden Age are to be found in the monastery church at Daphne, Greece. In the *Crucifixion* mosaic (fig. 8.23) there are no Apostles, soldiers, or thieves, only the grief-stricken Mary looking up at Christ and John gazing on in sorrow. The suffering is intense but restrained, reflecting an adaptation of classical Greek sculptural elements to the linear Byzantine style. The skull at the base of the cross represents Golgotha, the "place of the skull." Symbolizing the sacraments of the Eucharist and Baptism, the blood spilling from Christ's side also nourishes the flowers, which represent a new life in Christ. Controlled and compassionate, this is not a historical representation but a humanized portrayal of the Passion of Jesus Christ, his ultimate sacrifice for all of humankind.

The Byzantine style spread throughout the Balkans, Russia, and as far west as Sicily. Strongly influencing some of the Western art of the Middle Ages, it flourished in Eastern Europe for centuries beyond the demise of the Byzantine empire in 1453.

Unit

4

The Age of Faith

9

Building Medieval Walls

The so-called Middle Ages extended for approximately a thousand years from about A.D. 410 to around 1400. Furthermore, they divide themselves sharply at about the year 1000, for reasons that will become apparent. This long period constitutes an amalgamation of various cultures—some features of the Arabic and Moslem, the Eastern civilization that had its source in Byzantium (Constantinople), and principally the crude northern way of life of Germany and the Scandinavian countries—into the old Graeco-Roman institutions. As such, the gestation of the Middle Ages constitutes an almost new start for Western culture, with only a memory of past glories, with written records that lay dormant for centuries, and with the Roman Church as foci of centralizing forces. The rather glorious medieval culture, which reached maturity during the twelfth and thirteenth centuries, represents a fusion of seemingly contradictory ways of life, and of opposition in ways of feeling and thought. Once again we can witness a testimony to the toughness of the human spirit, which lives, survives, changes itself, and finally triumphs over darkness and confusion, expressing itself in magnificent symbols of new growth.

We have already said that Rome "fell" sometime in the fifth century—the arbitrary dates of 410 or 476 do not make much difference. It should be remarked, however, that the average Roman citizen living at the time did not know that Rome had fallen. Life went on much as it had before; life got tougher and tougher, but the government and the Emperor, whether he be Italian or Ostrogoth, were still there. For example, the philosopher Boethius (Bo–EE–thi–us; ca. 475–524), who wrote the famous *Consolation of Philosophy* during the last year of his life, held the office of Roman consul about fifty years after the final "official" date for the fall of Rome.

As a matter of fact, the power of Rome dwindled until it was virtually nonexistent. For centuries the Roman legions had been replaced by barbarian mercenaries, and Rome, unable to defend its borders, either pulled back the soldiers who had been stationed on the extreme boundaries of the Empire or allowed them to become integrated with the local peoples. An ever-increasing number of tribesmen were settled in Italy when the original Italian peoples deserted the land. The capital of the Empire was moved, once to Milan and later to Ravenna, and under the Emperor Constantine the Empire was split into an eastern and a western section, with a growing sense of independence in each area. The "fall" was simply a slow disintegration of power, not a sudden cataclysm. But as civil power failed, the Church gained in strength until it became the great unifying power in Western civilization. The development of this power needs to be considered.

The Early Church: St. Augustine

Christianity had its source in the teachings of Christ, but it became an institutionalized church largely through the efforts of two men. The first of these was the apostle Paul, who traveled widely and kept up a very active correspondence with the communities of Christians throughout the Roman world. Largely through his efforts, the various congregations in the important cities were held together. After his work, a centralized doctrine and a widely accepted institution for the preservation and the propagation of the faith were still lacking. This last work was accomplished in large measure by St. Augustine (354–430).

Augustine was a North African who was very well educated in the arts of logic and dialectic in his native town of Thagaste and in Carthage. The chief Christianizing influence on the young man was his mother, Monica, who admonished him and prayed for him so much that she must have been a real millstone around the neck of the high-spirited young man. He was not baptized until he came under the influence of St. Ambrose and other Christians in Milan in 387. The following year he returned to North Africa, where he founded a monastic order, was made Bishop of Hippo in 396, and spent the rest of his life in that post, writing and preaching in defense of the faith against various heretical groups and against pagans, particularly those who attacked Christianity after the sack of Rome in the year 410. His greatest work, *The City of God,* was written in part as a refutation of the pagan claim that Rome's failure resulted from the Christian influence.

All of his life Augustine was a searcher for a firm belief. As a young man he became a Manichaean, a sect with a strong dualistic belief in a power of good and a power of evil conflicting in the world and in people. His logical mind could not, however, accept all the doctrine of this sect, and later, in Rome, he became a skeptic, a believer in nothing, not even his own existence. Finally he read some of the Neoplatonists and was strongly influenced by them, so much so that he regarded his Neoplatonic period as the most important stepping stone to his acceptance of Christianity, for his doctrine incorporated much of Neoplatonism (minus Greek rationalism). This was in Milan, where he was serving as a municipally appointed teacher (his students in Carthage had been too unruly for him to put up with; the students were better behaved in Milan but they seldom paid their tuition), where his Christian mother, Monica, had joined him, and where he heard the impressive preaching of Bishop Ambrose, a critical influence on his eventual conversion to Christianity. After experiencing his famous mystical experience in the garden (as recounted in his noted autobiography, *The Confessions*), he was baptized in 387 by St. Ambrose. Although he preferred to lead a contemplative life, his later duties as Bishop of Hippo forced him into vigorous activity as a powerful advocate of the Roman Church against the Manichaeans, the Arians and, especially, against the Donatist heresy, which he energetically persecuted.

The Arian and Donatist heresies represented practical and philosophical problems of the early Christian church, problems that were still of great concern to Augustine and his contemporaries. Roman persecution of Christians after A.D. 303 forced many priests to collaborate with authorities by handing over sacred texts. After Constantine's edicts of toleration in 311 and 313, these "handers-over" (*traditores*) resumed their roles as priests only to be challenged by Donatus, bishop of Carthage. Donatus advocated punishing weak, collaborationist priests by declaring their administration of the sacraments invalid, a politically dangerous position because it gave believers opportunities to judge which priests were dispensing valid sacraments. Because of the political nature of the controversy, Constantine utilized his imperial prerogative by ruling that once a priest has been properly ordained, his administration of the sacraments remains valid even though his actions may become reprehensible. The problems of dissent and violence over the Donatist heresy continued to plague North Africa even after Augustine's tenure as Bishop of Hippo.

Heresy also involved such philosophical principles as Arianism, named after Arius, an Alexandrian priest who maintained that God the Son could not be precisely of the *same* essence as God the Father because the begetter must be somehow superior to, as well as necessarily earlier in time than, the begotten. This view threatened to diminish the divinity of Christ and to break up the Holy Trinity, as emphasized by Arius's bitter opponent, Athanasius, bishop of Alexandria. Disdaining logic and espousing mystery, Athanasius and his followers exhorted Christians to simply accept on faith that the Trinity of Father, Son, and Holy Ghost was both equal and contemporary. Unable to settle the quarrel, in 325 Constantine called the first meeting to involve the whole church, an ecumenical council (Greek, *oikoumene,* the inhabited world). Meeting at Nicaea, across the straits from Constantinople, the assembled bishops backed Athanasius's view, resulting in the famous Nicene Creed ("We believe in one God"), which was issued by Constantine with all the force of an imperial decree.

Augustine was not only a theologian but also a very busy administrator as Bishop of Hippo and propagandist for the Roman Church. In this respect he was faced with the problem of the efficacy of the sacraments when performed by priests who belonged to heretical sects or who led impure lives. His judgment in the matter was that the efficacy of the sacraments (it must be remembered that only through the sacraments did one find salvation) lay in the office of the priesthood, not in the man who performed them. The basis for this decision rested in the argument that if the benefit of the sacraments lay in the quality of the man who performed them, then people themselves would be placed in judgment of God's grace. The promulgation of this doctrine did much to establish the concept of the infallibility of the Church, since its power was inherent within its offices. This power, it was argued, descended directly from the apostles, who were the original bishops of the Church. From them it passed to other bishops, and from the bishops to the priests through the "laying on of hands." Through this act, the power to administer the sacraments was given and could not be revoked.

When considering Augustine as a philosopher and theologian we are confronted with the vast number of books written about the whole body of his thought. Here we shall give a very summary treatment of his ideas about the nature of God, of the creation, of free will, his philosophy of history, and the infallibility of the Church, for these beliefs provide the backbone for European civilization up to the late Middle Ages.

Earlier in our study we made the point that a culture is based upon the idea of Reality that is held by that culture. According to Augustine, God was the only reality, who created the world out of nothingness. This God was a mystic being, not an intellectual principle as was the case with the Neoplatonists, so that knowledge of God and life in him was available to all human beings, whether they were philosophers or not. Although Augustine regarded his own early philosophic speculations as stepping stones to belief, he felt that his conversion came about through the grace of God, not through human efforts, and that this grace is available to all people. For Augustine and all believers throughout the Middle Ages, union with God is the only true goal and the only true happiness for people, all of which takes place in the hereafter.

The process of creation-from-nothingness took place because of two aspects of the mind of God, roughly corresponding to the Platonic essences, but with significant differences. One such aspect corresponds to the eternal truths, such as the truth that the sum of the angles of a triangle always equals 180°. Such truths, existing before creation and after the destruction of the world, constitute the basic patterns and harmonies of the universe. Another aspect of God's mind consists of the "seminal (or seed) reasons" for created things. These are the patterns that acquire physical substance and form the visible things of the world: the visible people, trees, earth, and the myriad things that are apparent to our senses. These sense-apparent things exist in time; they rise, disintegrate, and pass away, and because of their transitory nature are the least important of God's creations.

Implicit in the last statement is Augustine's dualistic concept of time. He believed in a direct flow of time in which humanity's activities (never repeating themselves in spiral or circular patterns) moved upward toward eventual perfection, toward the godlike.

The flow of time and all the changes that occur within it are characteristic of the temporal world. God, however, with all the attributes of his mind, dwells in eternity, which is really a timeless instant. In this realm past and future have no meaning; all is present.

In this way, Augustine reconciled the problem of God's foreknowledge of all events and humanity's free will. He asserted that people, with the exception of original sin that could be washed away with baptism, had free will; yet God knew every event that would take place. How does one avoid fatalism and the idea of predestination if all of a person's actions are known in advance? The answer is that God's seeing all things as present-time allows for foreknowledge in what *we* call time, yet the "seeing" of things does not influence them. All events are simultaneous for God, and thus he can know them without influencing them. A person's vision is shackled by past, present, and an inscrutable future, but in the temporal world there is complete free will.

In his attitude toward the body and the whole world of matter, Augustine was somewhat ambivalent. If this world is God's creation then it must be good. On the other hand, being overly concerned with the acquisition of worldly goods can turn a person away from God, and that is of course sinful. The matter of bodily pleasures was especially disturbing. Before his conversion Augustine had lived a lusty life of fleshly pleasures; his proclivities were dramatized in his famous prayer: "O Lord, make me chaste, but not yet." He shifted to the other extreme after his conversion and condemned sexual pleasure (music was included in this censure because, like the sex act, it kept the mind from contemplating God).

His view of the material world was strongly influenced by Platonic doctrine, but not entirely. He believed that the physical things of the world are all passing away and changing. For example, in *The City of God* he makes the point that in Rome in 410 many people lost all of their worldly possessions, yet Christians remained happy since their "possessions" were in their spirit and could not be taken away. The conclusion is that a concern with worldly things is a concern with nothing, since these things are ephemeral. The only vital concern is with the things of the spirit, which have their existence in the realm of eternity. This type of thought is not completely dualistic in that it does not despise the flesh and the things of the world, yet it tends in that direction. Many later Christian thinkers were to turn completely against the world and the flesh, asserting even more strongly than Plato and Augustine that these things were traps for the mind and the spirit of humanity. Much of the puritanical thought of our time comes from this basic reasoning.

Augustine, in the first complete formulation of a Christian philosophy of history, viewed the story of humanity as a conflict between two cities. (He used the word *city* as we might use the word *community* in such a phrase as the "business community.") One of these was the City of God, the other the City of Man.

In the beginning, when time was created, he stated, everything belonged to the good city, yet with the revolt of the angels and Satan's expulsion from heaven, the other city came into being. From that time until the birth of Christ, almost all of humanity belonged to the Earthly City. Only a few Hebrews who had faith in the coming of a Savior belonged to the City of God. With Christ's coming for the redemption of mortals, and with the formation of the Church, the membership in the two cities was more sharply divided, since all members of the City of God were also members of the Church. This, he was careful to assert, did not work conversely—all members of the Church were not necessarily members of God's City. The end of history will come with the Last Judgment and the final and complete separation of the two cities. The saved will be reclothed in their perfect bodies and take their place with God; the damned will undergo eternal torture with Satan. Since the members of the good city are already known to God, we find here the basis for the doctrine of the elect, a tenet that was to be completely enunciated by Calvin after the Reformation.

This philosophy of history has at least one other important consequence. If the original members of the City of God are to be found only among the Hebrews, they alone knew truth. Thus all pagan learning, that of the Greeks, for example, is falsehood and is not to be studied. The loss of the Graeco-Roman heritage had an incalculable effect on the course of Western civilization.

Sometime after the death of Augustine final authority of the Church in Rome was achieved, for the bishops of Rome had asserted their supremacy over the other bishops. The argument for this was that St. Peter had founded the Church in Rome, and that he was Christ's spiritual successor. Biblical authority was given for this claim from Christ's words concerning Peter, "Upon this rock (petras) will I build my church." Leo, Bishop of Rome from 440 to 461, first made this claim to ecclesiastical authority, and Pope Gregory the Great, slightly more than a century later, was such an able diplomat and churchman that the primacy of the Pope became universally accepted for the Western Church.

These were the moves that established a body of doctrine incorporating the infallibility of the Church, and a strong and revered institution that was able to maintain its authority throughout the troubled and confused years of the early Middle Ages as the only source of order throughout all of Europe. Very early on the Church was divided into two branches: the regular clergy (from the Latin regula or rule) composed of the monks and those who retreated from the active life, and the secular clergy, the Pope, the bishops, and parish priests who lived among the people and sought to lead them to a better life. During the time of the decline of the Roman authority, a very great number of men, particularly among the intellectual class, retreated from the world to live and work in the communal life of monasteries leading the contemplative existence. This is not an unusual phenomenon during any time of cultural upheaval, including our own.

Feudalism and Manorialism

Following the withdrawal of Roman military and governmental stability, the people of western Europe had to find ways by which they could govern themselves with some semblance of justice, and by which they could make a living. The governmental system, feudalism, did not develop fully until the tenth century, but it can be described here as the slowly evolving political system of the Middle Ages. Manorialism, the economic arrangement by which the people made a living, actually had its beginnings during late Roman times when the peasants were forced to stay on the land and became serfs. Furthermore, the two systems, at the lowest level—the demesne, or land-holding of a single knight—are so intertwined that they are scarcely distinguishable.

In its essence, feudalism is simply an arrangement by which the whole territory of the former empire was divided up into small enough units so that a single man could rule each one. It also created a fighting society, since the lords constantly raided adjoining territories, and all of them were subject to the forays of the northern tribes from Germany and Scandinavia.

In what had once been the civilized Roman Empire, we find a number of kings who lacked both the money and the power to hold their kingdoms together. These rulers proceeded to split up their kingdoms among the nobility, the highest ranking of which were the barons. The barons accepted the land from the king, and in return swore allegiance to him and agreed to furnish a certain number of fighting men when the kingdom was attacked. Thus a baron became a vassal of the king. But since the barons also lacked power to administer their lands, they took vassals under them, further subdividing the land. This successive division of land continued down to the knight, who owned one estate or demesne consisting of a village and the rather extensive farmlands surrounding it. Each member of the nobility was thus a despotic ruler over the land that he actually controlled, subject only to the oaths of loyalty he swore to the lord immediately over him. One knight could control his one small village and the farms that surrounded it and provide some form of rough justice for the inhabitants.

The manorial system was simply the totality of the life within one of these villages. Here, unless he was away at war, resided the lord in his manor house. A priest took care of the spiritual needs of the community, and the church and parish house usually occupied the center of the village. In addition to these buildings, one usually found a community bake-oven, a winepress, and a mill for grinding grain. The farming land (one can assume that an average demesne comprised about a thousand acres) was divided into three main sections, two of which were planted each year and the third allowed to lie fallow. The lord retained a certain area as his personal property (though it was farmed by the serfs), the priest was given a small allotment of land, a section was retained as common

Figure 9.1 Aigues-Mortes, France. Located on the Mediterranean coast, this perfectly preserved medieval town was founded as a staging area and supply base for the crusades. Medieval walls were a common denominator throughout Europe.

Figure 9.2 Inside the walls, Carcassonne, France. When inside the restored walls of this fortified town, the overwhelming masses of masonry give a comforting feeling of security and community.

woodland, and another section was used as a common meadow. Each farmer or serf was given certain strips of land in each of the three fields—each strip was usually an eighth of a mile in length and about seventeen feet wide.[1] The serf and his family were ''attached'' to the land, that is, they could not leave, but neither could they be turned away. The serf gave a certain portion of his produce to the lord and was also obligated to work a certain number of days on the lord's land. The lord, in his turn, was obliged to protect his villagers and to provide justice, though he was the only judge in the case of disputes, and his word was final.

The manorial system gives us a picture of a poverty-stricken and almost totally isolated life. All of the bare necessities were provided within the single manor, and the serf scarcely ever traveled beyond it. No news of the world came in except when the lord returned from a war, or when an occasional itinerant peddler came through. One can safely assume that none of the peasants could read, and that formal education was unknown. Life on the manor slowed to the regular round of work, religious holidays, births, marriages, and deaths. Life was maintained at a minimal level behind medieval walls, which shut out hostile forces but also, figuratively speaking, kept out ideas that might disturb the rigid order enforced by the church and the barons (figs. 9.1 and 9.2). It is little

wonder that the people came to regard this world as a vale of tears and that they lived in anticipation of a glorious afterlife in heaven.

Charlemagne

The most important political and humanistic period of the early Middle Ages was the reign of Charlemagne (Charles the Great, ruled 768–814). The first bright spark in the so-called Dark Ages, the Carolingian Renaissance proved that the light of civilization had not been entirely extinguished.

Charles was the second of the Carolingian Kings of the Franks, and his father had already gained the support of the Roman Church by defeating the Lombards in Italy and granting a very considerable area of land to the Papacy. When Charles came to the throne he set about to expand and solidify the kingdom of the Franks, fighting the Moslems in Spain, the Norsemen up to the border of Denmark, and against the Lombards in Italy. The battle of Roncevaux in 778 in which Charles's knight, Count Roland, was ambushed and killed furnished the kernel for the great cycle of songs and stories relating to the exploits of Charles. In return for this warring activity against the pagans, and as a shrewd political move, the Pope crowned Charles as ''Emperor of the Romans'' on Christmas day in the year 800.

Important as these political events are, they cannot be our main concern. The significant factor here is that Charles had a great respect for learning and brought scholars from all Europe to his court at

---

1. Replacing the scratch plow, a new kind of plow was invented (late seventh century) which was equipped with a vertical knife to cut the furrow, a horizontal plowshare to slice under the sod, and a moldboard to turn it over. Pulled by eight oxen (communally owned), it attacked the land with such violence that cross-plowing was unnecessary and fields tended to be shaped in long strips. Found nowhere else in the world (for centuries to come), this plow marked the beginning of a technological revolution that would change the European from nature's partner to an exploiter of natural resources, leading to today's ecological problems.

Figure 9.3 Aachen, Germany. Four periods of history are represented here. At the right is a modern building constructed after Aachen was almost totally demolished during World War II. The tower is twelfth century Romanesque, to the left of which is Charlemagne's eighth century domed chapel, with the fourteenth century Gothic choir at the far left.

Aachen (Aix-la-Chapelle). The architecture of this court itself is a landmark in Western culture, for Charles had been to Ravenna where he had seen the magnificent architecture and the gleaming mosaics, the ideas for which had come directly from Byzantium. The chapel at Aachen is modeled after the Church of San Vitale in Ravenna, and it was responsible for introducing Eastern ideas of beauty and Roman stone construction to the Western world (fig. 9.3; also see fig. 8.17, colorplate 10, and fig. 11.10).

Most important of all in this revival of learning was the establishment of the Palace (or Palatine) School. To direct it, Charles imported the English scholar Alcuin from the cathedral school at York, and in addition to teaching and directing the school itself, Alcuin collected a considerable number of manuscripts of ancient learning and revived the monastic practice of copying manuscripts, both for the palace library and for distribution to other seats of learning. The Palatine School did not generate much original thought, but it was the first center of scholarship since the collapse of classical civilization and thus very important in terms of later intellectual development.

Under Charles, all of Italy, northern Spain, all of modern France, and southern Germany were united under a single rule, though Charles did not attempt to impose a single code of law on the diverse people. He did, however, have all of his counties inspected regularly to see that the lands were well governed and that justice was administered. Further than that he strengthened the power of the Church, since he forcibly Christianized all of the pagans whom he conquered. One consequence of his being crowned as emperor by the Pope lay in the development of the idea that the Church was superior to all secular authority, an idea that was to give all sorts of trouble in later centuries.

After Charlemagne's death in 814, and the short rule of his ineffective son Louis the Pious, his empire was divided among his three grandsons, none of whom was able to continue the tradition that each had inherited. The empire rapidly fell apart, particularly under the invasions of the Norsemen, the Vikings, who ravaged all of Europe and even sailed to the continent that was later to be named America.

The Assimilation of Cultures

Earlier in this chapter it was pointed out that the most important development during the early Middle Ages was the digestion of several very different and opposed cultures. No one can deny that the old classic tradition of Greece and Rome had run its full course and that it was no longer fruitful. If life was to become meaningful, new ideas, new ways of life, new blood needed to be transfused into the cultural body. The dark period from the fifth to the tenth centuries, full of fear, doubt, confusion, and strife was the result of these clashing cultures. From the vantage point of not having to live in those times, this can now be seen as a period of transition leading to a new culture.

In the main, Byzantine and Moslem cultures remained as storehouses that would be drawn upon by European civilization in the later Middle Ages. Except for a brief conquest of Italy and North Africa under the Eastern emperor Justinian and the influence we have already noted during the rule of Charlemagne, Byzantium was chiefly important as a bastion against eastern infringement upon Europe by the Persians, and by the Slavic and Magyar peoples who settled in what is now Hungary, the Balkans, and southern Russia. These peoples were Christianized and civilized chiefly by missionaries from the Eastern Catholic Church. Another and rather unusual influence of the East came through the Christianizing of Ireland according to the Eastern ritual. For a time at least, Ireland enjoyed a higher and more enlightened culture than did the rest of Europe, and subtle influences of this civilization reached the mainland.

The strongest influence on Western culture was the rise of Islamic religion and culture, a powerful movement that threatened to engulf all of Europe. Originally the Arabs were an uncultured polytheistic people, and they, in themselves, did little to produce enlightenment, but under the general peace and stability of their rule, Hellenistic, Persian, and Syrian art and intellect were permitted to expand.

Mohammed was born in Mecca in about the year 570 and worked as a merchant there until his then unpopular religious beliefs forced him to flee the city in 622. This last date is accepted as the beginning of the Muslim faith. Very soon after this flight, he returned to Mecca in triumph and succeeded in converting many Arabs to his belief.

Mohammed regarded his religious insight as an extension and culmination of the Judeo-Christian tradition, and the faith shares much with those two religious beliefs. Islam stresses the oneness of God and the equality of all men before God. For this reason, it developed no priesthood and no central institutional authority other than the political rulers, the caliphs, under whose rule and warlike spirit the faith was propagated. Particularly important for the development of Western culture was the Muslim banning of statues and images, which was to send many refugee artists to Europe when the Muslims captured Constantinople in 1453.

The Arabs, united for the first time in their new religious belief, set out to conquer most of the world, and were remarkably successful. Very early they overran Persia and the lands to the east, including India. They also occupied Egypt and all of North Africa, and by 720 had conquered all of Spain. They crossed the Pyrenees and invaded France. Here they were met by Charles Martel, grandfather of Charlemagne, near the city of Poitiers in 732, and driven back to Spain. Much of Charlemagne's time was spent fighting in Spain in his attempt to drive the Moors out of Europe.

The contribution of Islam lay not in the wars, but in the peace and prosperity that followed them. Trade routes were opened clear to China so that material goods and immaterial ideas flowed freely through the Islamic world. They were great builders, synthesizing the Roman dome with features of Persian architecture to produce the pointed dome, which we usually associate with Islamic construction. Because images were banned for religious reasons, they developed decorative forms based on geometric designs, which we now call *arabesques*. Most important of all, learning flourished under the rule of these people, and such great universities as those at Cairo and Toledo came into being, both preserving older knowledge and developing new. The works of Plato and Aristotle were translated into Arabic and studied with great zeal; mathematics was developed, particularly with the use of the Arabic system of numbers rather than the clumsy Roman system; and the study of medicine was greatly advanced. While Italy and northern Europe were slogging along in the mud, a very high culture flourished in Asia, Africa, and Spain, the riches of which would not be known until after the Crusades began.

By far the greatest cultural fusion in the early Middle Ages was that of the Celto-Germanic peoples of the north with the Graeco-Romans of the south. We have already become well acquainted with the balanced and intellectual culture of the Greeks and Romans, whose horizontal-linear architecture and predictable designs in art and architecture give a clue, at least, to their reposeful, rational character. We have already seen, too, that many of the northern people had come into the Roman Empire either by invitation, infiltration, or military conquest. But these people were vastly different in basic character from the Romans. Their architectural line was energetic, vertical, and angular; their decorations were twisted and unpredictable. Just about the time of the removal of Roman authority, we witness a great folk-wandering of these peoples, with tribes from the east pressing upon the Germanic tribes, and they, in turn, moving outward both as colonizers and as warlike raiders through all of the continent of Europe. This restless movement of peoples was to continue for centuries, with an inevitable clash and subsequent fusion of the two cultures.

The basic social organization of these northern peoples was the *comitatus,* which was the banding together of a group of fighting men under the leadership of a warrior chieftain. The men pledged their loyalty and their strength to the chief, and he, in turn, promised to give them rewards from captured plunder. Thus in the early Germanic poem of *Beowulf,* both the hero and another leader, Hrothgar, are frequently called "ringgivers" from their roles as leaders distributing gold to their fighting men. Once the comitatus was formed, it had only one function: to fight, to capture, and to plunder. The dragonships of the Norsemen were frequent and fearful visitors in England and all Europe.

But there is another aspect to these people that is revealed in their religion. The contemporary philosopher Lewis Mumford has spoken of the Graeco-Romans as "pessimistic of the body and optimistic for the soul," and of the Celto-Germanic peoples as "optimistic of the body but pessimistic for the spirit." The distinction is a valid one. The classic and Christian southern peoples regarded life here on earth only as a short period of pain and sorrow to be followed, they hoped, by a joyous afterlife in heaven. The Celto-Germanics ate greatly, drank deeply, raped widely, but were ultimately pessimistic about the afterlife. Theirs was perhaps the only religion that pictures the ultimate defeat of the "good" gods by the forces of evil and darkness.

The Norsemen worshipped a group of anthropomorphic "good" gods who lived in a celestial residence called Valhalla. Wotan was the king of the gods; the most active, certainly, was Thor, the thunder god. Baldur represented the idea of beauty, springtime, and warmth; Loki was the trickster. Even in the heavenly abode the pessimistic nature of these gods appears, for, through a trick of Loki's, Baldur was slain. For the fighting men on earth, an afterlife among the gods was promised, but far different from any heaven conceived of by Christians, Muslims, or Jews. If a warrior was killed in battle, semidivine maidens (the Valkyrie) swooped over the battlefield to take him to Valhalla. Here the hero simply continued his earthly life of fighting, eating, and drinking.

For the gods and heroes, however, an awful fate was predicted, for Valhalla was surrounded by the land of the giant Jotuns, probably representing the cold and the darkness of the northern climate. The gods and the Jotuns were engaged in constant small warfare and trickery, but in the Norse religion, the future held a great battle between the two forces, with the Jotuns winning and bringing about the downfall of the gods. Thus the ultimate and total pessimism of the spirit of the Scandinavian-Germanic people.

The difference between the Graeco-Roman and the Celto-Germanic personalities has been suggested earlier with a comparison between the structural line and the type of ornamentation that each found beautiful and which, therefore, may give a clue to the differences in character. A comparison between the type of literature each culture produced may strengthen our awareness of the clash of cultures. No better example of the Graeco-Roman literature of the very early Middle Ages can be found than Boethius's *Consolation of Philosophy*. Boethius, one remembers, was a Roman consul, serving under the Roman emperor (actually an Ostrogoth) Theodoric. The *Consolation* was written in the year 524 while he was languishing in prison awaiting death after being accused by his emperor of treason.

Boethius gives his work the form of a highly rational dialogue between himself as a man who is deeply distressed by his fate in the world, and a vision of philosophy as a stately woman. The dialogue is interspersed with poetical passages that serve to sum up the previous discussion and form a bridge into their next topic. The subjects for discussion range from the nature of fortune and chance, of happiness, the existence of evil, of free will, and the paradox of humanity's free will and an all-knowing God. In reading the whole discussion, one is reminded of a Sokratic dialogue, and indeed Boethius draws heavily on Platonic thought. While the ideas themselves are not new, the reader is constantly aware of a classic coolness and dignified withdrawal from the passions of life. Perhaps a brief quotation may make this clear. The excerpt is drawn from book III, prose X. Philosophy speaks first:

> "But it has been conceded that the highest Good is happiness?"
>
> "Yes," I said.
>
> "Therefore," she said, "it must be confessed that God is Happiness itself."
>
> "I cannot gainsay what you premised before," said I, "and I perceive that this follows necessarily from those premises."
>
> "Look, then," she said, "whether the same proposition is not proved more strongly by the following argument: there cannot be two different highest Goods. For it is clear that where there are two different goods the one cannot be the other; wherefore neither one can be the perfect Good while each is wanting to the other. And that which is not perfect is manifestly not the highest; therefore, if two things are the highest Good, they can by no means be different. Further, we have concluded that both God and happiness are the highest Good; therefore the highest Deity must be identical with the highest happiness."
>
> "No conclusion," said I, "could be truer in fact or stronger in theory or worthier of God."
>
> "Over and above this," she said, "let me give you a corollary such as geometricians are wont to do when they wish to derive a deduction from the propositions they have demonstrated. Since men become happy by attaining happiness, and happiness is identical with divinity, it is plain that they become happy by attaining divinity. And as men become just by attaining justice and wise by attaining wisdom, so by the same reasoning they become godlike by attaining divinity. Every happy man, then, is God-like; but, while there is nothing to prevent as many men as possible for being God-like, only one is God by nature: men are God-like by participation."[2]

Nothing could be more urbane, civilized, classic, or rational than this discussion. To become aware of the difference in spirit between this and the Celto-Germanic personality, one may look briefly at two of the hero-epics from the northern people. *Beowulf* and the *Nibelungenlied* will serve as examples. The very sound of the harsh lines, much smoothed and rounded in modern English translation, reveals something of the lusty vigor of the people. Consider, for example, the alliteration of crashing consonants in the line, "Bit his bone-frame, drank blood from his veins." This is a far cry from the epics of Greece and Rome in its very tone.

The story of Beowulf is almost equally harsh. It tells of Beowulf, a warrior from the south of Sweden who went to the court of his uncle in Denmark. There he slew a monster, Grendel, who had been devastating the uncle's kingdom. As a trophy of the fight, Beowulf brought home the arm and shoulder of the monster as it had been wrenched from the giant's torso. Following the victory, a great banquet was held in the hero's honor. Having eaten and drunk until they could hold no more, Beowulf and his men lay down on the floor of the banquet hall, their war gear hanging by them, for the night's rest. But when all was quiet, Grendel's mother entered the hall, killed some of the men, and took the bloody arm and shoulder of her son back to the home she had beneath the waters of a dismal fen.

On the next morning Beowulf set out and tracked Grendel's mother to the shore of a swamp. Fearlessly he donned his armor and plunged into the water, down to the opening of the cave. Here he grappled with the hag-monster and finally killed her with a weapon forged by the giants of old. (See the Literary Selections.)

The last episode of the poem tells of Beowulf's last days when, as king or chief of his Swedish tribe, his own land was threatened by a dragon. As a warrior hero and leader, he went forth, killed the dragon, and was mortally wounded himself. The poem ends with his funeral pyre as a Viking chieftain, and the construction of his tomb as a monument that would serve as a landmark for Viking ships at sea.

Beowulf was never tender, never kind, never sympathetic. When his friends were slain in battle or in the great hall of Heorot, he never wept for them or extolled their virtues. Rather, he swore vengeance and went forth to do it. He was the mighty warrior, the great adventurer. Such was the Germanic hero.

Another example is at once older and younger; it is the German tale called the *Niebelungenlied,* or *Song of the Niblungs*. It was not written down in its present form until the 1200s, but its materials hark back to the days of Attila the Hun, in the fifth century.

2. Boethius, *The Consolation of Philosophy,* ed. James J. Buchanan (New York: Frederick Ungar Publishing Co., Inc., 1957), 31–32.

The Scandinavian version of the tale is known as the *Volsunga saga;* Wagner freely adapted the tale in his four music-dramas, *The Ring of the Nibelung.*

The epic is concerned with the hero Siegfried, who loved Kriemhild, sister of the Burgundian king, Gunther. In order to win her, Siegfried promised his help in Gunther's wooing of Brunhild, the warlike queen of a distant country. By magical means Siegfried assisted him in the feats of strength that won her. On their wedding night, Brunhild tied Gunther up in knots, and hung him behind the door; again it was Siegfried who came to the rescue, and on the second night, wrapped in his cloak of invisibility, wrestled with her and subdued her, without Brunhild's being aware that her adversary was Siegfried, not Gunther. How he took from her then a ring and a girdle, giving them to Kriemhild; how the two queens quarreled; how Kriemhild, in haughty anger, revealed the trick of Brunhild's conquest; and how Brunhild plotted revenge, is quickly recounted. The climax of the first part is the treacherous murder of Siegfried by Hagen, the loyal henchman of Gunther, and the villain of the piece. The last half of the story concerns Kriemhild's revenge against the Burgundians. Married, after many years, to Etzel (Attila), King of the Huns, she invited the Burgundians to visit her, and there follows a general massacre in which they are all slain, including Kriemhild.

One sees in these epics the warrior's world of the first half of the medieval period, its spirit of adventure, courage, bravery, harshness, and blood.

Perhaps these examples can help one to visualize the difference between the character of the two peoples who encountered each other during the early Middle Ages. So important was it that Dorothy Sayers in her introduction to the translation of the *Divine Comedy* attributes the origin of the two great political factions that tore Italy apart in late medieval times, the Guelfs and the Ghibellines, to this cultural difference. She contends that the Ghibellines represented the descendants of the northern stock with all of their vigorous energy, and that the Guelfs were essentially the native Italian land-owning, placid southern people.

Be that as it may, by the tenth century the two cultures achieved a physical amalgamation. Many of the northerners had moved to the south, had become Christianized, and had given up some of their savage ways. The Angles and Saxons settled in England, other Norsemen took over the great province of Normandy in France. Throughout all of Europe the Germanic people settled and took land, so that the northern chieftain moved into the already evolving feudal system, becoming a baron or a count, a duke or a knight, holding land from his suzerain and granting fiefs to those under him. It was still a warlike society, the difference being chiefly in its fairly settled nature. The leader gave up his wooden hall for a castle built of stone. The highest virtue became a mutual loyalty between the lord and his vassals. The *Song of Roland* furnishes a good example of this new civilization. This minor epic was written in French at about the time of the first crusade (the 1090s), but the written version

simply records a hero-story that had been sung and recited concerning the events that happened (legendarily) three centuries before in the days of Charlemagne. The persons of the story are Franks, the Germanic conquerors who gave their name to France; the central figure is Roland, the emperor's nephew. The great event of the poem is the ambush by Saracens of the rear guard of Charlemagne's army in the passes of the Pyrenees at Roncevaux. The ambush was arranged by Roland's treacherous kinsman Ganelon, inspired by envy and revenge. Roland and his companion, Oliver, together with the militant Archbishop Turpin, are the last survivors of the Frankish host; they too are killed, facing overwhelming odds. One of the best-known episodes is that of Roland's refusal to blow his ivory horn (oliphant), despite the urging of Oliver, to recall Charlemagne's host before the battle begins. When he realizes that he and his Franks are doomed, he does at last blow three mighty blasts that Charlemagne hears, thirty leagues away, and the Emperor returns to rout the Saracens and avenge the death of Roland and his companions. The epic concludes with the trial and punishment of Ganelon.

It is a truly feudal poem, full of the vigorous, active, restless spirit of the northern warrior. Roland is the man-at-arms, the warrior, unsoftened by the chivalry of later knighthood; he is a splendid barbarian, courageous in the face of overwhelming odds, loyal to his friends, utterly devoted to God, his spiritual overlord, and to Charlemagne, his temporal one. He is blood brother to his earlier northern kinsmen, Beowulf; both heroes represent the all-out, do-or-die, go-for-broke spirit of the heroic age.

There are many magnificent scenes: the pathetic one in which the wounded Oliver, dazed and blinded by blood, strikes his best friend Roland, and the two are immediately reconciled; the striking one in which Roland tries to shatter his sword, "Durendal," against a rock lest its hilt, which is a reliquary with sacred relics in it, fall into pagan hands. Let us read only one, the one hundred and seventy-sixth stanza, or "laisse," of the poem:

Count Roland lies under a pine tree,
Towards Spain has he turned his face.
Many things he recalls to remembrance:
How many lands, hero-like, he has won;
Sweet France; the men of his lineage;
Charlemagne his lord, who reared him.
At this he sighs and weeps, nor can he restrain himself.
But he does not wish to go into oblivion;
He confesses his fault, and prays God's mercy:
"True Father, Who never lies,
Who raised St. Lazarus from the dead,
Who preserved Daniel from the lions,
Keep my soul from all dangers,
Despite all the sins I have committed in my life!"
He raises towards God the glove from his right hand;
St. Gabriel from his hand receives it.
On his arms his head falls back;
His hands clasped, he goes to his end.
God sends his angel Cherubin
And St. Michael of the Peril;
Together with these comes St. Gabriel.
The count's soul they carry into Paradise.

The similarities and differences between this story and that of *Beowulf* are immediately apparent. Roland, with its heavy Christian overlay, is much more "civilized" than the early epic. But it is still a very masculine, savagely militaristic poem, extolling the glories of war, of bravery, and of loyalty. Not least interesting in the poem is the role of the Archbishop Turpin, who is a great Church leader, at least in title. Throughout the battle, however, he ranges through the ranks of fighting men, wielding his great mace (at this time it was illegal for a churchman to wield a sword) and breaking heads with the best of them. We see here a new role of the Church, with churchmen active in feudal society, holding great areas of land, and as much concerned with battle and secular affairs as with the religious life. The final act of Roland reveals much of the spirit of the time, for his offer of his glove to God is the very act of pledging loyalty to a feudal lord. Roland, always a vassal of Charlemagne, has now accepted a new suzerain in God, and the acceptance of the glove signifies God's acceptance of Roland as a vassal in the celestial feudal system.

Summary

It is almost symbolic that the people of the early Middle Ages built walls around their villages; wooden palisades in the early days, later, with feudalism, the walls were constructed of stone and the lord's house and the whole village became a fortified enclave. The total way of life at the time paralleled those confining fortifications, because early medieval people built battlements of equal strength around their minds.

The universe was based on the Church of Rome, which allowed no questioning of its tenets or of its actions. Further, the Church, through a contraction of the Augustinian doctrine, took a very dim view of all worldly pleasure and carefully restrained any questioning of the physical world. Science as we know it was lost completely, so that the natural world was a closed book, to be interpreted only as a vague shadow of the intention and mind of God. Life here and now was viewed as a brief and transitory journey through a dismal land, with true life and true happiness coming only after death. Furthermore, as is particularly apparent in the morality play of *Everyman* (see the Literary Selections), the only way to reach the blissful afterlife lay in the faithful acceptance of the doctrines and the sacraments of the Church.

The economic system of manorialism bound the greatest part of the population to the thousand acres or so of the manor itself. They could not escape; the few who traveled any distance at all had to have special permission. In fact, the average serf never strayed as much as one mile from the demesne. Food, clothing, and meager physical comforts were limited to what the manor could produce. Not even the mind could escape the narrow confines; reading was almost unknown because there was so little literacy (not even all of the clergy could read and write). Illiteracy and minimal travel meant also that news of the outside world almost never penetrated the closed miniworld of the manor.

The political system of feudalism was equally narrowing. Justice lay entirely in the hands of the feudal lord or, more often, his deputy. Except for the specific obligations of serf to lord and vassal to suzerain, which were generally known and accepted, the law was made up on the spot, and the individual never knew what to expect.

The narrow confines of Church, manorialism, and feudalism provided the walls that closed in upon the human spirit. Creativity and freedom of thought were almost unknown. But, with the withdrawal of Roman protection and with all the dangers from bands of marauders, these walls provided protection for the individual. If ordinary serfs could not live well, they could at least live safely.

Perhaps Elinor Wylie's twentieth-century poem "Sanctuary" expresses the same problem:

This is the bricklayer; hear the thud
Of his heavy load dumped down on stone,
His lustrous bricks are brighter than blood,
His smoking mortar whiter than bone.

Set each sharp-edged, fire-bitten brick
Straight by the plumb-line's shivering length;
Make my marvelous wall so thick
Dead nor living may shake its strength.

Full as a crystal cup with drink
Is my cell with dreams, and quiet, and cool . . .
Stop, old man! You must leave a chink;
How can I breathe? *You can't, you fool!*

But the human spirit is never content with mere security. Particularly with gaining of a little freedom as it did in the tenth century, it clamors more and more for expansion. (The twentieth-century movement towards equality of opportunity is a similar phenomenon.) The seeds that were to germinate and eventually break down medieval walls were already planted. Some of the directions for that growth may be indicated.

First, the human spirit has never long been content to *not* examine the world around it. The varied forms of the world, its beauties, and reason for being demand attention. Both art and science express this quest for an exploration of the world of the senses.

Second, the two personality types of Europe, the rational Graeco-Roman and the emotional and energetic Germanic lived side by side but not in unison by the year 1000. Some form of synthesis between these two personality types, almost exactly opposite each other, needed to be found.

Third, a problem limited largely to politics: the question of supremacy of church or state demanded settlement. At a time when the secular power was so weak as to be almost nonexistent, the Church could and did assert its authority over kings and lords. But with the growth of the powers of the world a struggle was inevitable, a bitter conflict of church and state that has been waged all over the Western world and which is still not fully resolved.

Fourth, and perhaps most important, people demand and need joy in the present life, but this was sternly denied by the Church. A desire for immediate physical and intellectual pleasure in life now would necessarily conflict with the doctrine that life here was nothing, the afterlife was everything. The pull of life as opposed to the Church-dictated pull of death was bound to tear the human personality apart until some synthesis could be effected.

These are the latent problems one sees at the end of the early Middle Ages. Their solutions will be dealt with in subsequent chapters.

Beowulf's Fight with Grendel's Dam
from BEOWULF

The oldest of English epics, *Beowulf* probably dates from early in the eighth century. Written by an unknown author of exceptional talent, the poem is a brilliant example of the masculine code, the embodiment of the heroic tradition.[3] In the brief excerpt given below (see p. 192 for a synopsis of the plot), Beowulf tracks Grendel's hag-mother to her cave in the depths of a swamp where he battles her to the death. The modern translation in alliterative verse is by Charles W. Kennedy; the line numbers are from Klaeber's Old English text.

> Beowulf spoke, the son of Ecgtheow:
> 'Sorrow not, brave one! Better for man
> To avenge a friend than much to mourn.
> All men must die; let him who may
> Win glory ere death. That guerdon is best
> For a noble man when his name survives him.
> Then let us rise up, O ward of the realm,
> And haste us forth to behold the track
> Of Grendel's dam. And I give you pledge
> She shall not in safety escape to cover,
> To earthy cavern, or forest fastness,
> Or gulf of ocean, go where she may.
> This day with patience endure the burden
> Of every woe, as I know you will.'
> Up sprang the ancient, gave thanks to God
> For the heartening words the hero had spoken.
>
> Quickly a horse was bridled for Hrothgar,
> A mettlesome charger with braided mane;
> In royal splendor the king rode forth
> Mid the trampling tread of a troop of shieldmen.
> The tracks lay clear where the fiend had fared
> Over plain and bottom and woodland path,
> Through murky moorland making her way
> With the lifeless body, the best of thanes
> Who of old with Hrothgar had guarded the hall.
> By a narrow path the king pressed on
>
> [1384–1408]
>
> Through rocky upland and rugged ravine,
> A lonely journey, past looming headlands,
> The lair of monster and lurking troll.
> Tried retainers, a trusty few,
> Advanced with Hrothgar to view the ground.
> Sudden they came on a dismal covert
> Of trees that hung over hoary stone,
> Over churning water and blood-stained wave.
> Then for the Danes was the woe the deeper,
> The sorrow sharper for Scylding earls,
> When they first caught sight, on the rocky sea-cliff,
> Of slaughtered Æschere's severed head.
> The water boiled in a bloody swirling
> With seething gore as the spearmen gazed.

3. The warrior code of *Beowulf* should be compared with the courtly code of the age of chivalry in chapter 10 (*The Art of Courtly Love*) and in chapter 12 (troubadour-trouvère tradition).

> The trumpet sounded a martial strain;
> The shield-troop halted. Their eyes beheld
> The swimming forms of strange sea-dragons,
> Dim serpent shapes in the watery depths,
> Sea-beasts sunning on headland slopes;
> Snakelike monsters that oft at sunrise
> On evil errands scour the sea.
> Startled by tumult and trumpet's blare,
> Enraged and savage, they swam away;
> But one the lord of the Geats brought low,
> Stripped of his sea-strength, despoiled of life,
> As the bitter bow-bolt pierced his heart.
> His watery-speed grew slower, and ceased,
> And he floated, caught in the clutch of death.
> Then they hauled him in with sharp-hooked boar-spears,
> By sheer strength grappled and dragged him ashore,
> A wondrous wave-beast; and all the array
>
> [1409–1440]
>
> Gathered to gaze at the grisly guest.
> Beowulf donned his armor for battle,
> Heeded not danger; the hand-braided byrny,
> Broad of shoulder and richly bedecked,
> Must stand the ordeal of the watery depths.
> Well could that corselet defend the frame
> Lest hostile thrust should pierce to the heart.
> Or blows of battle beat down the life.
> A gleaming helmet guarded his head
> As he planned his plunge to the depths of the pool
> Through the heaving waters—a helm adorned
> With lavish inlay and lordly chains,
> Ancient work of the weapon-smith
> Skillfully fashioned, beset with the boar,
> That no blade of battle might bite it through.
> Not the least or the worst of his war-equipment
> Was the sword the herald of Hrothgar loaned
> In his hour of need—Hrunting its name—
> An ancient heirloom, trusty and tried;
> Its blade was iron, with etched design,
> Tempered in blood of many a battle.
> Never in fight had it failed the hand
> That drew it daring the perils of war,
> The rush of the foe. Not the first time then
> That its edge must venture on valiant deeds.
> But Ecglaf's stalwart son was unmindful
> Of words he had spoken while heated with wine,
> When he loaned the blade to a better swordsman.
> He himself dared not hazard his life
> In deeds of note in the watery depths;
> And thereby he forfeited honor and fame.
>
> [1440–1471]
>
> Not so with that other undaunted spirit
> After he donned his armor for battle.
> Beowulf spoke, the son of Ecgtheow:
> 'O gracious ruler, gold-giver to men,
> As I now set forth to attempt this feat,
> Great son of Healfdene, hold well in mind
> The solemn pledge we plighted of old,
> That if doing your service I meet my death
> You will mark my fall with a father's love.
> Protect my kinsmen, my trusty comrades,
> If battle take me. And all the treasure
> You have heaped on me bestow upon Hygelac,
> Hrothgar beloved! The lord of the Geats,
> The son of Hrethel, shall see the proof,
> Shall know as he gazes on jewels and gold,
> That I found an unsparing dispenser of bounty,
> And joyed, while I lived, in his generous gifts.

Give back to Unferth the ancient blade,
The sword-edge splendid with curving scrolls,
For either with Hrunting I'll reap rich harvest
Of glorious deeds, or death shall take me.'
    After these words the prince of the Weders
Awaited no answer, but turned to the task,
Straightway plunged in the swirling pool.
Nigh unto a day he endured the depths
Ere he first had view of the vast sea-bottom.
Soon she found, who had haunted the flood,
A ravening hag, for a hundred half-years,
Greedy and grim, that a man was groping
In daring search through the sea-troll's home.
Swift she grappled and grasped the warrior

[1471–1501]

With horrid grip, but could work no harm,
No hurt to his body; the ring-locked byrny
Cloaked his life from her clutching claw;
Nor could she tear through the tempered mail
With her savage fingers. The she-wolf bore
The ring-prince down through the watery depths
To her den at the bottom; nor could Beowulf draw
His blade for battle, though brave his mood.
Many a sea-beast, strange sea-monsters,
Tasked him hard with their menacing tusks,
Broke his byrny and smote him sore.
    Then he found himself in a fearsome hall
Where water came not to work him hurt,
But the flood was stayed by the sheltering roof.
There in the glow of firelight gleaming
The hero had view of the huge sea-troll.
He swung his war-sword with all his strength,
Withheld not the blow, and the savage blade
Sang on her head its hymn of hate.
But the bold one found that the battle-flasher
Would bite no longer, nor harm her life.
The sword-edge failed at his sorest need.
Often of old with ease it had suffered
The clash of battle, cleaving the helm,
The fated warrior's woven mail.
That time was first for the treasured blade
That its glory failed in the press of the fray.
But fixed of purpose and firm of mood
Hygelac's earl was mindful of honor;
In wrath, undaunted, he dashed to earth
The jewelled sword with its scrolled design,

[1502–1532]

The blade of steel; staked all on strength,
On the might of his hand, as a man must do
Who thinks to win in the welter of battle
Enduring glory; he fears not death.
The Geat-prince joyed in the straining struggle,
Stalwart-hearted and stirred to wrath,
Gripped the shoulder of Grendel's dam
And headlong hurled the hag to the ground.
But she quickly clutched him and drew him close,
Countered the onset with savage claw.
The warrior staggered, for all his strength,
Dismayed and shaken and borne to earth.
She knelt upon him and drew her dagger,
With broad bright blade, to avenge her son,
Her only issue. But the corselet's steel
Shielded his breast and sheltered his life
Withstanding entrance of point and edge.
    Then the prince of the Geats would have gone his
        journey,
The son of Ecgtheow, under the ground;
But his sturdy breast-net, his battle-corselet,

Gave him succor, and holy God,
The Lord all-wise, awarded the mastery;
Heaven's Ruler gave right decree.
    Swift the hero sprang to his feet;
Saw mid the war-gear a stately sword,
An ancient war-brand of biting edge,
Choicest of weapons worthy and strong,
The work of giants, a warrior's joy,
So heavy no hand but his own could hold it,
Bear to battle or wield in war.

[1533–1562]

Then the Scylding warrior, savage and grim,
Seized the ring-hilt and swung the sword,
Struck with fury, despairing of life,
Thrust at the throat, broke through the bone-rings;
The stout blade stabbed through her fated flesh.
She sank in death; the sword was bloody;
The hero joyed in the work of his hand.
The gleaming radiance shimmered and shone
As the candle of heaven shines clear from the sky.
Wrathful and resolute Hygelac's thane
Surveyed the span of the spacious hall;
Grimly gripping the hilted sword
With upraised weapon he turned to the wall.
The blade had failed not the battle-prince;
A full requital he firmly planned
For all the injury Grendel had done
In numberless raids on the Danish race,
When he slew the hearth-companions of Hrothgar,
Devoured fifteen of the Danish folk
Clasped in slumber, and carried away
As many more spearmen, a hideous spoil.
All this the stout-heart had stern requited;
And there before him bereft of life
He saw the broken body of Grendel
Stilled in battle, and stretched in death,
As the struggle in Heorot smote him down.
The corpse sprang wide as he struck the blow,
The hard sword-stroke that severed the head.
    Then the tried retainers, who there with Hrothgar
Watched the face of the foaming pool,
Saw that the churning reaches were reddened,

[1563–1593]

The eddying surges stained with blood.
And the gray, old spearmen spoke of the hero,
Having no hope he would ever return
Crowned with triumph and cheered with spoil.
Many were sure that the savage sea-wolf
Had slain their leader. At last came noon.
The stalwart Scyldings forsook the headland;
Their proud gold-giver departed home.
But the Geats sat grieving and sick in spirit,
Stared at the water with longing eyes,
Having no hope they would ever behold
Their gracious leader and lord again.
    Then the great sword, eaten with blood of battle,
Began to soften and waste away
In iron icicles, wonder of wonders,
Melting away most like to ice
When the Father looses the fetters of frost,
Slackens the bondage that binds the wave,
Strong in power of times and seasons;
He is true God! Of the goodly treasures
From the sea-cave Beowulf took but two,
The monster's head and the precious hilt
Blazing with gems; but the blade had melted,
The sword dissolved, in the deadly heat,
The venomous blood of the fallen fiend.

EVERYMAN

Medieval drama began in the tenth century as liturgical drama (discussed in detail in chap. 12), out of which grew plays in the vernacular called mysteries or mystery plays (a corruption of the Latin *ministerium,* service). Performed by trade guilds, mystery plays were cycles depicting the history of humanity from damnation to redemption. The various guilds enacted episodes associated with their own craft; thus, the shipwright's guild was responsible for the building of the ark, the water drawers for Noah's flood, the goldsmiths for the story of the magi, and so on.

Performed outdoors from dawn to dusk on "pageants" (L. *paginae),* wagons consisting of roofed platforms on wheels, the plays used scanty scenery but often elaborate costumes. Cycles like, for example, *The Second Shepherd's Play* included a large repertoire of acting conventions, comic elaboration, and considerable opportunity for improvisation. During the sixteenth century the plays became more and more secular, with increasing elements of comedy and outright buffoonery until, during the reign of Elizabeth I, they were suppressed. By this time they had been superseded by the plays of Marlowe and Shakespeare.

On the continent miracle plays dealt with miracles worked by the saints; in England the word was interchangeable with mystery. A completely separate category, but developing along with mystery plays, the morality play was a single work rather than a cycle. Mystery plays dramatized biblical events to show their relevance to everyday life; morality plays were more directly didactic, enacting the conflict between good and evil, the constant struggle within each person between virtue and vice.

The contest was presented as an allegory with virtues and vices personified: Patience vs. Anger, Pride vs. Humility, and so forth. A key element was penance, the recognition and confession of sin to the priest followed by absolution, on condition of the performance of assigned penances. One of the primary themes of *Everyman* is the necessity of penitence for sin before death within the discipline of the church.

Everyman was written about 1485 and may be a translation of a Dutch play on the same theme or possibly the Dutch play was a translation from the English. The most famous of its type, *Everyman* is not a battle between opposites but rather a somber stripping of worldly goods from a man, concentrating on his increasing isolation as he descends into the grave. Only Good Deeds is left as a mediator between him and Judgment. *Everyman* is a moral allegory of preparation for death, a solemn statement of the human predicament, and, no less important, an exposition of church doctrine.

CHARACTERS:

Messenger
God (Adonai)
Death
Everyman
Fellowship
Kindred
Cousin
Goods
Good-Deeds
Knowledge
Confession
Beauty
Strength
Discretion
Five-Wits
Angel
Doctor

HERE BEGINNETH A TREATISE HOW THE HIGH FATHER OF HEAVEN SENDETH DEATH TO SUMMON EVERY CREATURE TO COME AND GIVE ACCOUNT OF THEIR LIVES IN THIS WORLD AND IS IN MANNER OF A MORAL PLAY.

Messenger: I pray you all give your audience,
And hear this matter with reverence,
By figure a moral play—
The *Summoning of Everyman* called it is,
That of our lives and ending shows
How transitory we be all day.
This matter is wondrous precious,
But the intent of it is more gracious,
And sweet to bear away.
The story saith,—Man, in the beginning,
Look well, and take good heed to the ending,
Be you never so gay!
Ye think sin in the beginning full sweet,
Which in the end causeth thy soul to weep,
When the body lieth in clay.
Here shall you see how *Fellowship* and *Jollity,*
Both *Strength, Pleasure,* and *Beauty,*
Will fade from thee as flower in May.
For ye shall hear, how our heaven king
Calleth *Everyman* to a general reckoning:
Give audience, and hear what he doth say.
God: I perceive here in my majesty,
How that all creatures be to me unkind,
Living without dread in worldly prosperity:
Of ghostly sight the people be so blind,
Drowned in sin, they know me not for their God:
In worldly riches is all their mind,
They fear not my right wiseness, the sharp rod:
My law that I shewed, when I for them died,
They forget clean, and shedding of my blood red:
I hanged between two, it cannot be denied:
To get them life I suffered to be dead:
I healed their feet, with thorns hurt was my head:
I could do no more than I did truly,
And now I see the people do clean forsake me,
They use the seven deadly sins damnable;
As pride, covetise, wrath, and lechery,
Now in the world be made commendable;
And thus they leave of angels the heavenly company;
Everyman liveth so after his own pleasure,
And yet of their life they be nothing sure:
I see the more that I them forbear
The worse they be from year to year;

All that liveth appaireth[4] fast,
Therefore I will in all the haste
Having a reckoning of Everyman's person
For and I leave the people thus alone
In their life and wicked tempests,
Verily they will become much worse than beasts;
For now one would by envy another up eat;
Charity they all do clean forget.
I hoped well that Everyman
In my glory should make his mansion,
And thereto I had them all elect;
But now I see, like traitors deject,
They thank me not for the pleasure that I to them meant
Nor yet for their being that I them have lent;
I proffered the people great multitude of mercy,
And few there be that asketh it heartily;
They be so combered with worldly riches,
That needs of them I must do justice,
On Everyman living without fear.
Where art thou, Death, thou mighty messenger?
Death: Almighty God, I am here at your will,
Your commandment to fulfil.
God: Go thou to Everyman,
And show him in my name
A pilgrimage he must on him take,
Which he in no wise may escape;
And that he bring with him a sure reckoning
Without delay or any tarrying.
Death: Lord, I will in the world go run over all,
And cruelly outsearch both great and small;
Every man will I beset that liveth beastly
Out of God's laws, and dreadeth not folly:
He that loveth riches I will strike with my dart,
His sight to blind, and from heaven to depart,
Except that alms be his good friend,
In hell for to dwell, world without end.
Lo, yonder I see Everyman walking;
Full little he thinketh on my coming;
His mind is on fleshly lusts and his treasure,
And great pain it shall cause him to endure
Before the Lord Heaven King.
Everyman, stand still; whither art thou going
Thus gaily? Hast my Maker forgot?
Everyman: Why askst thou?
Wouldest thou wete?[5]
Death: Yea, sir, I will show you;
In great haste I am sent to thee
From God out of his majesty.
Everyman: What, sent to me?
Death: Yea, certainly.
Though thou have forget him here,
He thinketh on thee in the heavenly sphere,
As, or we depart, thou shalt know.
Everyman: What desireth God of me?
Death: That shall I show thee;
A reckoning he will needs have
Without any longer respite.
Everyman: To give a reckoning longer leisure I crave;
This blind matter troubleth my wit.
Death: On thee thou must take a long journey:
Therefore thy book of count with thee thou bring;
For turn again thou can not by no way,
And look thou be sure of thy reckoning:
For before God thou shalt answer, and show
Thy many bad deeds and good but a few;

How thou hast spent thy life, and in what wise,
Before the chief lord of paradise.
Have ado that we were in that way,
For, wete thou well, thou shalt make none attournay.[6]
Everyman: Full unready I am such reckoning to give.
I know thee not: what messenger art thou?
Death: I am Death, that no man dreadeth.
For every man I rest and no man spareth;
For it is God's commandment
That all to me should be obedient.
Everyman: O Death, thou comest when I had thee
    least in mind,
In thy power it lieth me to save,
Yet of my good will I give thee, if ye will be kind,
Yea, a thousand pound shalt thou have,
And defer this matter till another day.
Death: Everyman, it may not be by no way;
I set not by gold, silver, nor riches,
Ne by pope, emperor, king, duke, ne princes.
For and I would receive gifts great,
All the world I might get;
But my custom is clean contrary.
I give thee no respite: come hence, and not tarry.
Everyman: Alas, shall I have no longer respite?
I may say Death giveth no warning:
To think on thee, it maketh my heart sick,
For all unready is my book of reckoning.
But twelve year and I might have abiding,
My counting book I would make so clear,
That my reckoning I should not need to fear.
Wherefore, Death, I pray thee, for God's mercy,
Spare me till I be provided of remedy.
Death: Thee availeth not to cry, weep, and pray:
But haste thee lightly that you were gone the journey.
And prove thy friends if thou can.
For, wete thou well, the tide abideth no man,
And in the world each living creature
For Adam's sin must die of nature.
Everyman: Death, if I should this pilgrimage take,
And my reckoning surely make,
Show me, for saint charity,
Should I not come again shortly?
Death: No, Everyman; and thou be once there,
Thou mayst never more come here,
Trust me verily.
Everyman: O gracious God, in the high seat celestial,
Have mercy on me in this most need;
Shall I have no company from this vale terrestrial
Of mine acquaintance that way me to lead?
Death: Yea, if any be so hardy,
That would go with thee and bear thee company.
Hie thee that you were gone to God's magnificence,
Thy reckoning to give before his presence,
What, weenest thou thy life is given thee,
And they worldly goods also?
Everyman: I had wend so, verily.
Death: Nay, nay; it was but lent thee;
For as soon as thou art go,
Another awhile shall have it, and then go therefro
Even as thou has done.
Everyman, thou art mad; thou hast thy wits five,
And here on earth will not amend thy life,
For suddenly I do come.

---

4. Is impaired.
5. Know.

---

6. Mediator.

Everyman: O wretched caitiff, whither shall I flee,
That I might scape this endless sorrow!
Now, gentle Death, spare me till to-morrow,
That I may amend me
With good advisement.
Death: Nay, thereto I will not consent,
Nor no man will I respite,
But to the heart suddenly I shall smite
Without any advisement.
And now out of thy sight I will me nie;
See thou make thee ready shortly,
For thou mayst say this is the day
That no man living may scape away.
Everyman: Alas, I may well weep with sighs deep;
Now have I no manner of company
To help me in my journey, and me to keep;
And also my writing is full unready.
How shall I do now for to excuse me?
I would to God I had never be gete![7]
To my soul a full great profit it had be;
For now I fear pains huge and great.
The time passeth; Lord, help that all wrought;
For though I mourn it availeth nought.
The day passeth, and is almost a-go;
I wot not well what for to do.
To whom were I best my complaint to make?
What, and I to Fellowship thereof spake,
And showed him of this sudden chance?
For in him is all mine affiance;
We have in the world so many a day
Be on good friends in sport and play.
I see him yonder, certainly;
I trust that he will bear me company;
Therefore to him will I speak to ease my sorrow.
Well met, good Fellowship, and good morrow!
Fellowship: Everyman, good morrow by this day.
Sir, why lookest thou so piteously?
If any thing be amiss, I pray thee, me say,
That I may help to remedy.
Everyman: Yea, good Fellowship, yea.
I am in great jeopardy.
Fellowship: My true friend, show to me your mind;
I will not forsake thee, unto my life's end,
In the way of good company.
Everyman: That was well spoken, and lovingly.
Fellowship: Sir, I must needs know your heaviness;
I have pity to see you in any distress;
If any have ye wronged he shall revenged be,
Though I on the ground be slain for thee—
Though that I know before that I should die.
Everyman: Verily, Fellowship, gramercy.
Fellowship: Tush! by thy thanks I set not a straw;
Show me your grief, and say no more.
Everyman: If I my heart should to you break,
And then you to turn your mind from me,
And would not me comfort, when you hear me speak,
Then should I ten times sorrier be.
Fellowship: Sir, I say as I will do in deed.
Everyman: Then be you a good friend at need:
I have found you true here before.
Fellowship: And so ye shall evermore;
For, in faith, and thou go to Hell,
I will not forsake thee by the way!
Everyman: Ye speak like a good friend; I believe you well;
I shall deserve it, and I may.

Fellowship: I speak of no deserving, by this day.
For he that will say and nothing do
Is not worthy with good company to go;
Therefore show me the grief of your mind,
As to your friend most loving and kind.
Everyman: I shall show you how it is;
Commanded I am to go a journey,
A long way, hard and dangerous,
And give a strait count without delay
Before the high judge Adonai.[8]
Wherefore I pray you, bear me company,
As ye have promised, in this journey.
Fellowship: That is matter indeed! Promise is duty,
But, and I should take such a voyage on me,
I know it well, it should be to my pain:
Also it make me afeard, certain.
But let us take counsel here as well as we can,
For your words would fear a strong man.
Everyman: Why, ye said, If I had need,
Ye would me never forsake, quick nor dead,
Though it were to hell truly.
Fellowship: So I said, certainly,
But such pleasures be set aside, thee sooth to say:
And also, if we took such a journey,
When should we come again?
Everyman: Nay, never again till the day of doom.
Fellowship: In faith, then will not I come there!
Who hath you these tidings brought?
Everyman: Indeed, Death was with me here.
Fellowship: Now, by God that all hath bought,
If Death were the messenger,
For no man that is living today
I will not go that loath journey—
Not for the father that begat me!
Everyman: Ye promised other wise, pardie.
Fellowship: I wot well I say so truly
And yet if thou wilt eat, and drink, and make good cheer,
Or haunt to women, the lusty company,
I would not forsake you, while the day is clear,
Trust me verily!
Everyman: Yea, thereto ye would be ready;
To go to mirth, solace, and play
Your mind will sooner apply
Than to bear me company in my long journey.
Fellowship: Now, in good faith, I will not that way.
But and thou wilt murder, or any man kill,
In that I will help thee with a good will!
Everyman: O that is a simple advice indeed!
Gentle fellow, help me in my necessity;
We have loved long, and now I need,
And now, gentle Fellowship, remember me.
Fellowship: Whether ye have loved me or no,
By Saint John, I will not with thee go.
Everyman: Yet I pray thee, take the labour, and do so
      much for me
To bring me forward, for saint charity,
And comfort me till I come without the town.
Fellowship: Nay, and thou would give me a new gown,
I will not a foot with thee go;
But and you had tarried I would not have left thee so.
And as now, God speed thee in thy journey,
For from thee I will depart as fast as I may.
Everyman: Whither away, Fellowship? Will you forsake
      me?
Fellowship: Yea, by my fay, to God I betake thee.

---

7. Been gotten, been born.

---

8. God.

Everyman: Farewell, good Fellowship; for this my
heart is sore;
Adieu for ever, I shall see thee no more.
Fellowship: In faith, Everyman, farewell not at the end;
For you I will remember that parting is mourning.
Everyman: Alack! shall we thus depart indeed?
Our Lady, help, without any more comfort,
Lo, Fellowship forsaketh me in my most need:
For help in this world whither shall I resort?
Fellowship herebefore with me would merry make;
And now little sorrow for me doth he take.
It is said, in prosperity men friends may find,
Which in adversity be full unkind.
Now whither for succour shall I flee,
Sith that Fellowship hath forsaken me?
To my kinsmen I will truly,
Praying them to help me in my necessity:
I believe that they will do so,
For kind will creep where it may not go,
Where be ye now, my friends and kinsmen?
Kindred: Here be we now at your commandment.
Cousin, I pray you show us your intent
In any wise, and not spare.
Cousin: Yea, Everyman, and to us declare
If ye be disposed to go any whither,
For wete you well, we will live and die together.
Kindred: In wealth and woe we will with you hold,
For over his kin a man may be bold.
Everyman: Gramercy, my friends and kinsmen kind.
Now shall I show you the grief of my mind:
I was commanded by a messenger,
That is an high king's chief officer;
He bade me go a pilgrimage to my pain,
And I know well I shall never come again;
Also I must give a reckoning straight,
For I have a great enemy, that hath me in wait,
Which intendeth me for to hinder.
Kindred: What account is that which ye must render?
That would I know.
Everyman: Of all my works I must show
How I have lived and my days spent;
Also of ill deeds, that I have used
In my time, sith life was me lent;
And of all virtues that I have refused.
Therefore I pray you go thither with me,
To help to make mine account, for saint charity.
Cousin: What, to go thither? Is that the matter?
Nay, Everyman, I had liefer fast bread and water
All this five year and more.
Everyman: Alas, that ever I was bore![9]
For now shall I never be merry
If that you forsake me.
Kindred: Ah, sir; what, ye be a merry man!
Take good heart to you, and make no moan.
But one thing I warn you, by Saint Anne,
As for me, ye shall go alone.
Everyman: My Cousin, will you not with me go?
Cousin: No, by our Lady; I have the cramp in my toe.
Trust not to me, for, so God me speed,
I will deceive you in your most need.
Kindred: It availeth not us to tice.
Ye shall have my maid with all my heart;
She loveth to go to feasts, there to be nice,
And to dance, and abroad to start:
I will give her leave to help you in that journey,
If that you and she may agree.

Everyman: Now show me the very effect of your mind.
Will you go with me, or abide behind?
Kindred: Abide behind? Yea, that I will and I may!
Therefore farewell until another day.
Everyman: How should I be merry or glad?
For fair promises to me make,
But when I have most need, they me forsake.
I am deceived; that maketh me sad.
Cousin: Cousin Everyman, farewell now,
For verily I will not go with you;
Also of mine own an unready reckoning
I have to account; therefore I make tarrying.
Now, God keep thee, for now I go.
Everyman: Ah, Jesus, is all come hereto?
Lo, fair words maketh fools feign;
They promise and nothing will do certain.
My kinsmen promised me faithfully
For to abide with me steadfastly,
And now fast away do they flee:
Even so Fellowship promised me.
What friend were best me of to provide?
I lose my time here longer to abide.
Yet in my mind a thing there is:—
All my life I have loved riches;
If that my goods now help me might,
He would make my heart full light.
I will speak to him in this distress.—
Where art thou, my Goods and riches?
Goods: Who calleth me? Everyman? What haste thou
hast!
I lie here in corners, trussed and piled so high,
And in chests I am locked so fast,
Also sacked in bags, thou mayst see with thine eye,
I cannot stir; in packs low I lie,
What would ye have, lightly me say.
Everyman: Come hither, Good, in all the haste thou
may,
For of counsel I must desire thee.
Goods: Sir, and ye in the world have trouble or
adversity,
That can I help you to remedy shortly.
Everyman: It is another disease that grieveth me;
In this world it is not, I tell thee so.
I am sent for another way to go,
To give a straight account general
Before the highest Jupiter of all;
And all my life I have had joy and pleasure in thee.
Therefore I pray thee go with me,
For, peradventure, thou mayst before God Almighty
My reckoning help to clean and purify;
For it is said ever among,
That money maketh all right that is wrong.
Goods: Nay, Everyman, I sing another song,
I follow no man in such voyages;
For and I went with thee
Thou shouldst fare much the worse for me;
For because on me thou did set thy mind,
Thy reckoning I have made blotted and blind
That thine account thou cannot make truly;
And that hast thou for the love of me.
Everyman: That would grieve me full sore,
When I should come to that fearful answer.
Up, let us go thither together.
Goods: Nay, not so, I am too brittle, I may not endure;
I will follow no man one foot, be ye sure.

---

9. Born.

Everyman: Alas, I have thee loved, and had great pleasure
All my life-days on good and treasure.
Goods: That is to thy damnation without lesing,
For my love is contrary to the love everlasting
But if thou had me loved moderately during,
As, to the poor give part of me,
Then shouldst thou not in this dolour be,
Nor in this great sorrow and care.
Everyman: Lo, now was I deceived or I was ware,
And all I may wyte[10] my spending of time.
Goods: What, weenest thou that I am thine?
Everyman: I had wend so.
Goods: Nay, Everyman, I say no;
As for a while I was lent thee,
A season thou hast had me in prosperity;
My condition is man's soul to kill;
If I save one, a thousand I do spill;
Weenest thou that I will follow thee?
Nay, from this world, not verily.
Everyman: I had wend otherwise.
Goods: Therefore to thy soul Good is a thief;
For when thou art dead, this is my guise
Another to deceive in the same wise
As I have done thee, and all to his soul's reprief.
Everyman: O false Good, cursed thou be!
Thou traitor to God, that has deceived me,
And caught me in thy snare.
Goods: Marry, thou brought thyself in care,
Whereof I am glad,
I must needs laugh, I cannot be sad.
Everyman: Ah, Good, thou hast had long my heartly love;
I gave thee that which should be the Lord's above.
But wilt thou not go with me in deed?
I pray thee truth to say.
Goods: No, so God me speed,
Therefore farewell, and have good day.
Everyman: O, to whom shall I make moan
For to go with me in that heavy journey?
First Fellowship said he would with me gone;
His words were very pleasant and gay,
But afterward he left me alone.
Then spake I to my kinsmen all in despair,
And also they gave me words fair,
They lacked no fair speaking,
But all forsake me in the ending.
Then went I to my Goods that I loved best,
In hope to have comfort, but there had I least:
For my Goods sharply did me tell
That he bringeth many into hell.
Then of myself I was ashamed,
And so I am worthy to be blamed;
Thus may I well myself hate,
Of whom shall I now counsel take?
I think that I shall never speed
Till that I go to my Good-Deed,
But alas, she is so weak,
That she can neither go nor speak,
Yet will I venture on her now.—
My Good-Deeds, where be you?
Good-Deeds: Here I lie cold on the ground;
Thy sins hath me sore bound,
That I cannot stir.

Everyman: O, Good-Deeds, I stand in fear;
I must you pray of counsel,
For help now should come right well.
Good-Deeds: Everyman, I have understanding
That ye be summoned account to make
Before Messias, of Jerusalem King;
And you by me[11] that journey what[12] you will I take.
Everyman: Therefore I come to you, my moan to make;
I pray you, that ye will go with me.
Good-Deeds: I would full fain, but I cannot stand verily.
Everyman: Why, is there anything on you fall?
Good-Deeds: Yea, sir, I may thank you of all;
If ye had perfectly cheered me,
Your book of account now full ready had be.
Look, the books of your works and deeds eke;
Oh, see how they lie under the feet,
To your soul's heaviness.
Everyman: Our Lord Jesus, help me!
For one letter here I can not see.
Good-Deeds: There is a blind reckoning in time of distress!
Everyman: Good-Deeds, I pray you, help me in this need,
Or else I am for ever damned indeed;
Therefore help me to make reckoning
Before the redeemer of all thing,
That king is, and was, and ever shall.
Good-Deeds: Everyman, I am sorry of your fall,
And fain would I help you, and I were able.
Everyman: Good-Deeds, your counsel I pray you give me.
Good-Deeds: That shall I do verily;
Though that on my feet I may not go,
I have a sister, that shall with you also,
Called Knowledge, which shall with you abide,
To help you to make that dreadful reckoning.
Knowledge: Everyman, I will go with thee, and be thy guide,
In thy most need to go by thy side.
Everyman: In good condition I am now in every thing,
And am wholly content with this good thing;
Thanked be God my Creator.
Good-Deeds: And when he hath brought thee there,
Where thou shalt heal thee of thy smart,
Then go you with your reckoning and your Good-Deeds together
For to make you joyful at heart
Before the blessed Trinity.
Everyman: My Good-Deeds, gramercy;
I am well content, certainly,
With your words sweet.
Knowledge: Now go we together lovingly,
To Confession, that cleansing river.
Everyman: For joy I weep; I would we were there;
But, I pray you, give me cognition
Where dwelleth that holy man, Confession.
Knowledge: In the house of salvation:
We shall find him in that place,
That shall us comfort by God's grace.
Lo, this is Confession: kneel down and ask mercy,
For he is in good conceit with God almighty.

---

10. Blame.

---

11. If you go by me.
12. With.

Everyman: O glorious fountain that all uncleanness
    doth clarify,
Wash from me the spots of vices unclean,
That on me no sin may be seen;
I come with Knowledge for my redemption,
Repent with hearty and full contrition;
For I am commanded a pilgrimage to take,
And great accounts before God to make.
Now, I pray you, Shrift, mother of salvation,
Help my good deeds for my piteous exclamation.
Confession: I know your sorrow well, Everyman;
Because with Knowledge ye come to me,
I will you comfort as well as I can,
And a precious jewel I will give thee,
Called penance, wise voider of adversity;
Therewith shall your body chastised be,
With abstinence and perseverance in God's service:
Here shall you receive that scourge of me,
Which is penance strong, that ye must endure,
To remember thy Savior was scourged for thee
With sharp scourges, and suffered it patiently;
So must thou, or thou scape that painful pilgrimage;
Knowledge, keep him in this voyage,
And by that time Good-Deeds will be with thee.
But in any wise, be sure of mercy,
For your time draweth fast, and ye will saved be;
Ask God mercy, and He will grant truly,
When with the scourge of penance man doth him bind,
The oil of forgiveness then shall he find.
Everyman: Thanked be God for his gracious work!
For now I will my penance begin;
This hath rejoiced and lighted my heart,
Though the knots be painful and hard within.
Knowledge: Everyman, look your penance that ye fulfil,
What pain that ever it to you be,
And Knowledge shall give you counsel at will,
How your accounts ye shall make clearly.
Everyman: O eternal God, O heavenly figure,
O way of rightwiseness, O goodly vision,
Which descended down in a virgin pure
Because he would Everyman redeem,
Which Adam forfeited by his disobedience:
O blessed Godhead, elect and high-divine,
Forgive my grievous offence;
Here I cry thee mercy in this presence.
O ghostly treasure, O ransomer and redeemer
Of all the world, hope and conductor,
Mirror of joy, and founder of mercy,
Which illumineth heaven and earth thereby,
Here my clamorous complaint, though it late be;
Receive my prayers; unworthy in this heavy life,
Though I be, a sinner most abominable,
Yet let my name be written in Moses' table;
O Mary, pray to the Maker of all thing,
Me for to help at my ending,
And save me from the power of my enemy,
For Death assaileth me strongly;
And, Lady, that I may be means of thy prayer
Of your Son's glory to be partaker,
By the means of his passion I it crave,
I beseech you, help my soul to save.—
Knowledge, give me the scourge of penance;
My flesh therewith shall give a quittance:
I will now begin, if God give me grace.
Knowledge: Everyman, God give you time and space:
Thus I bequeath you in the hands of our Saviour,
Thus may you make your reckoning sure.

Everyman: In the name of the Holy Trinity,
My body sore punished shall be:
Take this, body, for the sin of the flesh;
Also thou delightest to go gay and fresh,
And in the way of damnation thou did me bring;
Therefore suffer now strokes and punishing.
Now of penance I will wade the water clear,
To save me from purgatory, that sharp fire.
Good-Deeds: I thank God, now I can walk and go;
And am delivered of my sickness and woe.
Therefore with Everyman I will go, and not spare;
His good works I will help him to declare.
Knowledge: Now, Everyman, be merry and glad;
Your Good-Deeds cometh now; ye may not be sad;
Now is your Good-Deeds whole and sound,
Going upright upon the ground.
Everyman: My heart is light, and shall be evermore;
Now will I smite faster than I did before.
Good-Deeds: Everyman, pilgrim, my special friend,
Blessed be thou without end;
For thee is prepared the eternal glory.
Ye have me made whole and sound,
Therefore I will bide by thee in every stound.[13]
Everyman: Welcome, my Good-Deeds; now I hear thy
    voice,
I weep for very sweetness of love.
Knowledge: Be no more sad, but ever rejoice,
God seeth thy living in his throne above;
Put on this garment to thy behove,
Which is wet with your tears,
Or else before God you may it miss,
When you to your journey's end come shall.
Everyman: Gentle Knowledge, what do you it call?
Knowledge: It is a garment of sorrow:
From pain it will you borrow;
Contrition it is,
That getteth forgiveness;
It pleaseth God passing well.
Good-Deeds: Everyman, will you wear it for your heal?
Everyman: Now blessed be Jesu, Mary's Son!
For now have I on true contrition.
And let us go now without tarrying;
Good-Deeds, have we clear our reckoning?
Good-Deeds: Yea, indeed I have it here.
Everyman: Then I trust we need not fear;
Now, friends, let us not part in twain.
Knowledge: Nay, Everyman, that will we not, certain.
Good-Deeds: Yet must thou lead with thee
Three persons of great might.
Everyman: Who should they be?
Good-Deeds: Discretion and Strength they hight,
And thy Beauty may not abide behind.
Knowledge: Also ye must call to mind
Your Five-wits as for your counsellors.
Good-Deeds: You must have them ready at all hours.
Everyman: How shall I get hither?
Knowledge: You must call them all together,
And they will hear you incontinent.
Everyman: My friends, come hither and be present,
Discretion, Strength, my Five-wits, and Beauty.
Beauty: Here at your will we be all ready.
What will ye that we should do?
Good-Deeds: That ye would with Everyman go,
And help him in his pilgrimage,
Advise you, will ye with him or not in that voyage?

---

13. Season.

Strength: We will bring him all thither,
To his help and comfort, ye may believe me.
Discretion: So will we go with him all together.
Everyman: Almighty God, loved thou be,
I give thee laud that I have hither brought
Strength, Discretion, Beauty, and Five-wits; lack I nought;
And my Good-Deeds, with Knowledge clear,
All be in my company at my will here;
I desire no more to my business.
Strength: And I, Strength, will by you stand in distress,
Though thou would in battle fight on the ground.
Five-Wits: And though it were through the world
    round,
We will not depart for sweet nor sour.
Beauty: No more will I unto death's hour,
Whatsoever thereof befall.
Discretion: Everyman, advise you first of all;
Go with a good advisement and deliberation;
We all give you virtuous monition
That all shall be well.
Everyman: My friends, hearken what I will tell:
I pray God reward you in his heavenly sphere.
Now hearken, all that be here
For I will make my testament
Here before you all present.
In alms half my good I will give with my hands twain
In the way of charity, with good intent,
And the other half still shall remain
In quiet to be returned there it ought to be.
This I do in despite of the fiend of hell
To go quite out of his peril
Ever after and this day.
Knowledge: Everyman, hearken what I say;
Go to priesthood, I you advise,
And receive of him in any wise
The holy sacrament and ointment together;
Then shortly see ye turn again hither;
We will all abide you here.
Five-Wits: Yea, Everyman, hie you that ye ready were,
There is no emperor, king, duke, ne baron,
That of God hath commission,
As hath the least priest in the world being;
For of the blessed sacraments pure and benign,
He beareth the keys and thereof hath the cure
For man's redemption, it is ever sure;
Which God for our soul's medicine
Gave us out of his heart with great pine;
Here in this transitory life, for thee and me
The blessed sacraments seven there be.
Baptism, confirmation, with priesthood good,
And the sacrament of God's precious flesh and blood,
Marriage, the holy extreme unction, and penance;
These seven be good to have in remembrance,
Gracious sacraments of high divinity.
Everyman: Fain would I receive that holy body
And meekly to my ghostly father I will go.
Five-Wits: Everyman, that is the best that ye can do:
God will you to salvation bring,
For priesthood exceedeth all other thing;
To us Holy Scripture they do teach,
And converteth man from sin heaven to reach;
God hath to them more power given,
Than to any angel that is in heaven;
With five words he may consecrate
God's body in flesh and blood to make,
And handleth his maker between his hands;
The priest bindeth and unbindeth all bands,
Both in earth and in heaven;

Thou ministers all the sacraments seven;
Though we kissed thy feet thou were worthy;
Thou art surgeon that cureth sin deadly:
No remedy we find under God
But all only priesthood.
Everyman, God gave priests that dignity,
And setteth them in his stead among us to be;
Thus be they above angels in degree.
Knowledge: If priests be good it is so surely;
But when Jesus hanged on the cross with great smart
There he gave, out of his blessed heart,
The same sacrament in great torment:
He sold them not to us, that Lord Omnipotent.
Therefore Saint Peter the apostle doth say
That Jesu's curse hath all they
Which God their Saviour do buy or sell,
Or they for any money do take or tell.
Sinful priests giveth the sinners example bad;
Their children sitteth by other men's fires, I have heard;
And some haunteth women's company,
With unclean life, as lusts of lechery:
These be with sin made blind.
Five-Wits: I trust to God no such may we find;
Therefore let us priesthood honour,
And follow their doctrine for our souls' succour;
We be their sheep, and they shepherds be
By whom we all be kept in surety.
Peace, for yonder I see Everyman come,
Which hath made true satisfaction.
Good-Deeds: Methinketh it is he indeed.
Everyman: Now Jesu be our alder speed.[14]
I have received the sacrament for my redemption,
And then mine extreme unction:
Blessed be all they that counselled me to take it!
And now, friends, let us go without longer respite;
I thank God that ye have tarried so long.
Now set each of you on this rod your hand,
And shortly follow me:
I go before, there I would be; God be our guide.
Strength: Everyman, we will not from you go,
Till ye have gone this voyage long.
Discretion: I, Discretion, will bide by you also.
Knowledge: And though this pilgrimage be never so
    strong,
I will never part you fro:
Everyman, I will be as sure by thee
As ever I did by Judas Maccabee.
Everyman: Alas, I am so faint I may not stand,
My limbs under me do fold;
Friends, let us not turn again to this land,
Not for all the world's gold,
For into this cave must I creep
And turn to the earth and there to sleep.
Beauty: What, into this grave? Alas!
Everyman: Yea, there shall you consume more and
    less.
Beauty: And what, should I smother here?
Everyman: Yea, by my faith, and never more appear.
In this world live no more we shall,
But in heaven before the highest Lord of all.
Beauty: I cross out all this; adieu by Saint John;
I take my cap in my lap and am gone.
Everyman: What, Beauty, whither will ye?
Beauty: Peace, I am deaf; I look not behind me,
Not and thou would give me all the gold in thy chest.

---

14. Speed in help of all.

Everyman: Alas, whereto may I trust?
Beauty goeth fast away hie;
She promised with me to live and die.
Strength: Everyman, I will thee also forsake and deny;
Thy game liketh me not at all.
Everyman: Why, then ye will forsake me all.
Sweet Strength, tarry a little space.
Strength: Nay, sir, by the rood of grace
Though thou weep till thy heart brast.
Everyman: Ye would ever bide by me, ye said.
Strength: Yea, I have you far enough conveyed;
Ye be old enough, I understand,
Your pilgrimage to take on hand;
I repent me that I hither came.
Everyman: Strength, you to displease I am to blame;
Will you break promise that is debt?
Strength: In faith, I care not;
Thou art but a fool to complain,
You spend your speech and waste your brain;
Go thrust thee into the ground.
Everyman: I had wend surer I should you have found.
He that trusteth in his Strength
She him deceiveth at the length.
Both Strength and Beauty forsaketh me,
Yet they promised me fair and lovingly.
Discretion: Everyman, I will after Strength be gone,
As for me I will leave you alone.
Everyman: Why, Discretion, will ye forsake me?
Discretion: Yea, in faith, I will go from thee,
For when Strength goeth before
I follow after evermore.
Everyman: Yet I pray thee, for the love of the Trinity,
Look in my grave once piteously.
Discretion: Nay, so nigh will I not come.
Farewell, every one!
Everyman: O all thing faileth, save God alone;
Beauty, Strength, and Discretion;
For when Death bloweth his blast,
They all run from me full fast.
Five-Wits: Everyman, my leave now of thee I take;
I will follow the other, for here I thee forsake.
Everyman: Alas! then may I wail and weep,
For I took you for my best friend.
Five-Wits: I will no longer thee keep;
Now farewell, and there an end.
Everyman: O Jesu, help, all hath forsaken me!
Good-Deeds: Nay, Everyman, I will bide with thee,
I will not forsake thee indeed;
Thou shalt find me a good friend at need.
Everyman: Gramercy, Good-Deeds; now may I true
friends see;
They have forsaken me every one;
I loved them better than my Good-Deeds alone.
Knowledge, will ye forsake me also?
Knowledge: Yea, Everyman, when ye to death do go:
But not yet for no manner of danger.
Everyman: Gramercy, Knowledge, with all my heart.
Knowledge: Nay, yet I will not from hence depart,
Till I see where ye shall be come.
Everyman: Methinketh, alas, that I must be gone
To make my reckoning and my debts pay,
For I see my time is nigh spent away.
Take example, all ye that this do hear or see,
How they that I loved best do forsake me,
Except my Good-Deeds that bideth truly.

Good-Deeds: All earthly things is but vanity:
Beauty, Strength, and Discretion, do man forsake,
Foolish friends and kinsmen, that fair spake,
All fleeth save Good-Deeds, and that am I.
Everyman: Have mercy on me, God most mighty;
And stand by me, thou Mother and Maid, holy Mary.
Good-Deeds: Fear not, I will speak for thee.
Everyman: Here I cry God mercy.
Good-Deeds: Short our end, and minish our pain;
Let us go and never come again.
Everyman: Into thy hands, Lord, my soul I commend;
Receive it, Lord, that it be not lost;
As thou me boughtest, so me defend,
And save me from the fiend's boast,
That I may appear with that blessed host
That shall be saved at the day of doom.
In manus tuas—of might's most
For ever—*commendo spiritum meum.*[15]
Knowledge: Now hath he suffered that we all shall
endure;
The Good-Deeds shall make all sure.
Now hath he made ending;
Methinketh that I hear angels sing
And make great joy and melody,
Where Everyman's soul received shall be.
Angel: Come, excellent elect spouse to Jesu:
Hereabove thou shalt go
Because of thy singular virtue:
Now the soul is taken the body fro;
Thy reckoning is crystal-clear.
Now shalt thou into the heavenly sphere,
Unto the which all ye shall come
That liveth well before the day of doom.
Doctor: This moral men may have in mind;
Ye hearers, take it of worth, old and young,
And forsake pride, for he deceiveth you in the end,
And remember Beauty, Five-wits, Strength, and
Discretion,
They all at the last do Everyman forsake,
Save his Good-Deeds, there doth he take.
But beware, and they be small
Before God, he hath not help at all.
None excuse may be there for Everyman:
Alas, how shall he do then?
For after death amends may no man make,
For then mercy and pity do him forsake.
If his reckoning be not clear when he do come,
God will say—*ite maledicti in ignem aeternum.*[16]
And he that hath his account whole and sound,
High in heaven he shall be crowned;
Unto which place God brings us all thither
That we may live body and soul together.
Thereto help the Trinity,
Amen, say ye, for saint Charity.
THUS ENDETH THIS MORALL PLAY OF EVERYMAN.

---

15. Into your hands I commend my spirit.
16. Be damned to the eternal fire.

10

The Late Middle Ages: Expansion and Synthesis

It is impossible to pinpoint any particular reason for the liberation of a whole social structure, but as we look back over the centuries, we know that it happened in eleventh-century Europe. Perhaps not the least of the reasons was a release from a sense of doom; the end of the world had been predicted for the year 1000 and the prediction was widely believed by the peasantry. One must imagine the wonder of a whole culture when people woke up on New Year's morning of the year 1001, pinched themselves, and found that they were still alive in the flesh, and felt the pangs of hunger, not for spiritual food, but for a very physical breakfast. Such a reprieve may have been one of the causative factors in the general awakening of Europe. The people were still in the Middle Ages; God was still the accepted Reality, but what a difference was soon to be discovered in the lives and the thoughts of men and women!

The difference expresses itself in various ways. One can notice a change from the code of feudalism to the code of chivalry, closely associated with the rising Cult of the Virgin, which became the dominant popular religious force in late medieval times. Another factor to be considered is the rise of cities. The Crusades, still another leavening influence, brought about an increasing knowledge of the relatively luxurious life of Islamic culture. Within the new cities we also witness the revival of humanistic learning with the rise of the great universities. Last to be mentioned, though perhaps basic to the whole movement, was the philosophic ferment about the nature of reality itself, which culminated in the "Battle of Universals" in philosophic circles.

Historians attribute the rise of cities to a number of causes, all of which were probably significant. One reason lay in the increase of land available for agriculture because of the drainage of swamps, for it must be remembered that cities need agriculture to supply food. The needs of the great nobility for central fighting forces gave another impetus to the gathering of people, for as wars became bigger and landholdings wider, the barons needed men in a central place who could be mobilized immediately. Perhaps the most important force in the development of cities was the rise of trade and commerce (though one who asks for the causative force in this development cannot find a specific answer except that it happened). At any rate, the itinerant peddler, traveling from manor to manor, had been known throughout the early Middle Ages. Sometime about the eleventh century this trade became somewhat stabilized as the peddlers-become-merchants set up stalls under the protection of the great churches or abbeys, and the Church law that governed the place insured peaceful transactions. This brought about another change. If trade were to flourish, the old barter system was no longer adequate, and money was reintroduced to Europe. The nobility was quick to seize upon this change and to foster it. For centuries they had collected their feudal dues in produce and goods, but money offered them much greater freedom in carrying on their activities. They were willing, therefore, to grant charters to the cities, giving them varying degrees of freedom from feudal responsibilities in return for tax money. Thus did the towns grow, and whatever the immediate forces that made them flourish, their development was but a symptom of a general stirring of the human spirit.

Throughout Europe the word went around, "City air is free air," for in free cities the custom was established that a serf who could maintain his residence for a year and a day became a free man. The more adventurous and intelligent serfs flocked to the city. Here men of common interests—interests centered in their trades—formed themselves into guilds to regulate the quality and price of their goods and to provide insurance and a measure of social life for the members and their families.

As these guilds—first craft guilds, later merchant guilds—became wealthy, the grand guildhalls flanked the great church to form a quadrangle about the open marketplace; these became the distinguishing feature of the medieval city. After the towns were founded, came the great expansion of the merchants, plying their trade with the East and returning to Europe with the silks and spices they were able to buy there. In 1241, nearly three centuries after the first movement toward city growth, came the great Hanseatic League, the guild of merchants of the German coastal towns, uniting to carry on their trade. The cities, already founded, formed a safe outlet for their goods. Trade could be carried on. The increase in wealth, for the Church, for the producers of goods in the craft guilds, and for the merchants, was such that it found an outlet in drama, processions, and parades—one answer to the need for beauty in a world that had for centuries been sparse and bare.

The Crusades were another of the forces that enlightened the Middle Ages. The first Crusade took place at the end of the eleventh century, and was followed by many others even into the Renaissance. The last Crusade was led by Don John of Austria (1571). In carrying on these holy wars to free the Holy Land from the Muslims, various groups of crusading knights (the Knights of St. John, for example) set up permanent bases on such islands as Rhodes and Malta, and even on the eastern shores of the Mediterranean. As was noted in the consideration of the early Middle

Ages, a flourishing culture and a luxurious civilization had been alive in the Near East, parts of North Africa, and Spain during the first five hundred years of medieval times in Europe.

Well before the Crusades, Europe had been influenced by contacts with Islam in Sicily and Spain. Its agriculture and commerce, already expanding rapidly, were further stimulated by crusader encounters with the heart of Islamic culture. The luxurious booty carted home by the soldiers, as is the ancient custom of all soldiers, contributed to the rising expectations for a better life. First imported as luxuries, food (sugar, saffron, rice, citrus, melon) and manufactured goods (silk, damask, muslin, cotton) quickly became necessities. More important than food and textiles, however, was the rich reservoir of Islamic science, medicine, and mathematics and the carefully tended heritage of ancient Greece. The way was still long and tortuous but semibarbaric Europe began, finally, to develop the arts of civilized living.

One of the most interesting transformations was that from feudalism to chivalry, a movement from a masculine to a feminine code of behavior. Feudalism, according to the historian Henry Adams, was the code of men-at-arms. With the later Middle Ages, however, especially in France, women assumed a more prominent role in matters of taste and manners. Men were away from home for great stretches of time, trading, fighting, and crusading. In their absence their wives had opportunities to expand their limited roles by introducing poetry and music to the courts and elevating the standards of behavior, dress, and manners. If we must have one name to fix this movement in our memory, Adams gives us that of the remarkable Eleanor of Aquitaine (1122–1204), Queen of France and then of England. Insisting on accompanying her husband, King Louis VII of France, on the Second Crusade in 1147, Eleanor was especially impressed by the sophistication of Constantinople, and undoubtedly incorporated elements of Byzantine and Muslim culture into her already extensive education. Along with her daughter, Marie of Champagne, and granddaughter, Blanche of Castile, Eleanor established Courts of Love that were to write legal-sounding codes of etiquette. Epic tales of bloody battles and mighty heroes were replaced by lyrical love songs composed and performed by aristocratic troubadours and trouvères (fig. 10.1; see also chap. 12). This change may be seen in the contrast between Roland's lament over the fallen Franks at Roncevaux, representative of the ideals of feudalism, and the lament over the dead Lancelot, representative of the chivalrous knight. Roland, surveying the field of death where lie his comrades in arms, says:

> Lords and barons, now may God have mercy upon you, and grant Paradise to all your souls that you may rest among the blessed flowers. Man never saw better men of arms that ye were. Long and well, year in and year out, have you served me, and many wide lands have ye won for the glory of Charles. Was it to such an end that he nourished you? O France, fair land,

Figure 10.1 "Music and Her Attendants" from Boethius, *De Arithmetica*, Biblioteca Nazionale, Naples. Holding a portable pipe organ, the elegant lady who symbolizes the civilized art of courtly music is surrounded by an ensemble of female court musicians. In the circle at the top King David plays a psaltery, the instrument named after the Psalms (Psaltery) of David.

today art thou made desolate by rude slaughter. Ye Frankish barons, I see you die through me, yet I can do naught to save and defend you. May God, who knows no lie, aid you!

Yet when Lancelot, the almost perfect knight of chivalry, lies dead, we hear the following lament:

Thou wert the courtliest knight that ever bare shield, and thou were the truest friend to thy lover that ever bestrode horse, and thou wert the truest lover among sinful men that ever loved woman, and thou wert the kindest man that ever struck with sword, and thou wert the goodliest person that ever came among the crowd of knights, and thou wert the meekest man and the gentlest that ever are in hall among ladies, and thou wert the sternest knight to thy mortal foe that ever put spear in breast.

From this we see the transformation from a fighting code to a courtly and courteous one. Both are found in the lament over Lancelot, but the virtues of mildness, of love, and of humility always stand before the virtues of strength or the recognition of human weakness.

Given the vagaries of human nature, the elaborate codes of courtly love were undoubtedly violated about as often as they were observed, there being few Lancelots in this world. They assisted nevertheless in the long process of civilizing barbaric Europe.

Closely allied to the evolution of chivalry was the development of beauty and warmth within the Church. As has already been pointed out, the official doctrine of the Church was a vast intellectual monument. It centered in the Trinity—the Father, the Son, and the Holy Ghost—a Three who were always One, administering the rigid justice found in the development of doctrine from the time of Augustine. For sinful people, justice is the last thing to be desired, and medieval men and women, guilt-ridden by the absolutism of the time, were convinced that they were sinful. They sought not justice, but mercy, turning to the Virgin, the highest of the Saints, the Queen of Heaven. She was the essence of purity, an idealized version of love, warmth, and beauty. A manifestation of the polarized medieval view of women, the Cult of the Virgin venerated one woman, pure in body and soul, possessor of all the womanly virtues. Her diametric opposite was Eve the temptress, the "fallen" woman who had been beguiled by Satan, a concept that was to have disastrous consequences in later centuries, including our own.

The Virgin was nevertheless the loving Mother who could mercifully intercede for the faithful, and it was to her that the great cathedrals were dedicated. Indeed, in France one asks not how to get to the cathedral, but how to get to Notre Dame, the church of "Our Lady." The two are almost synonymous. As Adams points out:

The measure of this devotion [to the Virgin], which proves to any religious American mind, beyond possible cavil, its serious and practical reality, is the money it cost. According to statistics, in the single century between 1170 and 1270, the French built 80 cathedrals and nearly five hundred churches of the cathedral class, which would have cost, according to an estimate made in 1840, more than five thousand millions to replace. Five thousand million francs is a thousand million dollars,[1] and this covered only the great churches of a single century. . . . The share of this capital which was—if one may use a commercial figure—invested in the Virgin cannot be fixed . . . but in a spiritual and artistic sense, it was almost the whole. . . .

Expenditure like this rests invariably on an economic idea. . . . In the thirteenth [century] they trusted their money to the Queen of Heaven— because of their belief in her power to repay it with interest in the life to come.

Therein lay the power of the Virgin in bringing human understanding and human sympathy into the cold philosophic structure of Church doctrine. While the philosophers wrangled about the nature of the

---

1. This is the money values of 1840. If we multiplied the figure by fifty, it would still be low for the late twentieth century.

universal substance, the common people found comfort and a release of pent-up energies in the addition of a Person with human sympathy and warmth to the austere Trinity. Such faith reveals itself in the great body of stories of the mysteries of the Virgin, one of the most widely known and touching of which is "Our Lady's Juggler," given on page 217.

Most important of all in terms of a basic way of life were the continual attacks and modifications of the doctrine of the Church itself, for the Church insisted upon absolute authority. In spite of his early philosophic gropings, St. Augustine had finally said, "I believe in order that I may know." Thus *faith* in the Scripture and the writings of the early churchmen and total submission to these sources was the first necessity for Christian life. Knowledge came second, and if at any point the doctrine seemed contrary to reason or inexplicable by it, the doctrine was to be believed and intellect was to be denied.

Upon this basis was built the great structure of Christian Scholasticism, the way of thought of the late Middle Ages. Most simply, Scholasticism can be explained in this way: If a thinker had any question for which he wanted an answer, he went first to the Bible and the writings of the Church Fathers to discover all the passages that pertained to his subject. This was his only source for basic data; experimentation in the world of his senses was not permitted. Then, as a second step, he used Aristotelian logic to work on his source material. Such logic is built upon the three-part syllogism: a major premise, *all men are mortal;* a minor premise, *Sokrates is a man;* a conclusion, *therefore Sokrates is mortal.* Then this conclusion can be used as a major or minor premise in further syllogisms until the thinker reaches an answer to his problems.[2]

As early as the ninth century the conflict between faith and reason had been pointed up by John Scotus Erigena who insisted that both reason and the Scriptures had come from God, and that there could be no conflict between them. After his time, the Church's stand on faith alone had been reaffirmed, particularly by Anselm of Canterbury in the eleventh century.

This reaffirmation was not to stand unchallenged for long. In the late eleventh century a philosophic conflict broke out that was called the Battle of Universals. The "battle" involved a lengthy philosophic dispute, greatly simplified here, about the nature of reality. Twentieth-century students may view this as a dry wrangle between a number of ivory-towered philosophers, but it was not. In the first place it has been pointed out that the idea of reality that is held at any time determines the nature of civilization, and that a change in this idea will bring about a change in the way people think and live. We are dealing with thinkers as important to their time as Einstein and Freud have been to ours. Second, the philosophers were important Churchmen, and since the Church was the central institution of the time, any change in its position would and did have a very great effect on life itself. True, the peasant on the farm or the craftsman in his shop neither knew nor cared about the Battle of Universals, but the men concerned in it were the men who made and moved society as a whole.

To see the nature of this "battle" we may remember that one of the strongest foundations of Church doctrine was a Christian adaption of the Neoplatonist belief that reality was permanent, unchanging, without any body or material substance, existing in the mind of God. This position sprang from Plato's belief in essences (forms, ideas) as the ultimate reality. Thus body and substance, all physical things subject to change were only illusory shadows, imperfect copies, of the Idea. According to this accepted doctrine, the human body was to be disregarded and a study of the physical world wasted time that should be spent seeking eternal truths. This Neoplatonic, Augustinian doctrine was accepted, up to the eleventh century, by the "Establishment" and became known as the *Realist* position.

The philosopher Roscellinus first challenged this doctrine and established what was called the *Nominalist* position, very close to the belief of most people today. He said that physical things were the only reality. For example, each sense-apparent tree is real and as far as trees are concerned, no higher reality exists. The question then arises, "How can we know the 'idea' tree?" Certainly we know these insubstantial ideas, for we can speak of trees, or people, or elephants, or justice when no specific one is present to our senses. Roscellinus answered that these "ideas" were only names (hence the word *Nominalist*), and that we form the idea as a generalization only after experience with a great number of individual things. We experience, he said, specific examples of elms, pines, palms, and all kinds of trees. In our mind we then generalize and form the "idea" tree so that we can talk about the species—and understand each other—in the middle of the ocean, with no specific tree within a thousand miles.

The two positions in the battle were thus established, as opposite as any two opposites can be. William of Champeaux stoutly defended the Realist position, the standard doctrine of the Church. If he should fail, the Church itself would be in danger, and indeed it was.

A middle position was suggested by the brilliant thinker Peter Abelard, probably the most popular teacher in the early University of Paris. (Abelard is shown as a hero for the twentieth century as well as a brilliant thinker of the eleventh and twelfth centuries in the contemporary play, *Abelard and Heloise.*)

---

2. Modern students tend to scoff at this type of reasoning until they remember that *every* culture sets similar limits to its thought process. For example, in the early twentieth century, the searcher for truth drew the basic material for investigation from the world of the senses (one was not encouraged to go outside of this realm) and then used the scientific method to refine the raw data and find answers to the questions. The type of knowledge found through the use of this technique of research is totally different from that found in the Middle Ages, but the limitations are equally severe. A God-centered society results from one method, a completely materialistic society comes from the other.

Abelard had studied with both Roscellinus and William of Champeaux and knew their arguments thoroughly and, as a matter of interest, he defeated William in a public debate on the nature of the universals. (Henry Adams in *Mont-St. Michel and Chartres* gives an imaginary debate between the two, which is not too difficult to follow.) Abelard's compromise became known as the *Conceptualist* position, and anticipates an Aristotelian view of the problem even before the whole body of Aristotle's works was known to Europe. The Conceptualist view can be stated rather quickly, for it will become much better developed with the work of St. Thomas a century or so later. Briefly, Abelard held that the *idea* is *real,* but that it does not exist either before a particular physical thing or after it. That is, reality as idea exists only in the physical, sense-apparent object.

Abelard's intellectual daring was condemned by the Church, but the Battle of Universals was debated without conclusion for a century. The Realist, the Nominalist, and the Conceptualist positions remained at loggerheads and were a sore point in Church doctrine until the great synthesis, which was to be made by St. Thomas, who established what was to become the official dogma of the Church.

Abelard not only developed one of the sides in the Battle of Universals, but he threw another bombshell into the religious thought of the time when he published his book *Sic et non* (Yes and No). One remembers that the source of all knowledge at the time lay in the Scriptures and the writings of the early commentators on the Bible, the Church Fathers. In *Sic et non* Abelard proposed a number of important religious questions, then in opposite columns set down what the Fathers had written on the subject. In doing so, he demonstrated that one could find contradictory answers in this body of writings. If this body was the source of knowledge, and if contradictions existed within it, as Abelard clearly showed, how wrong must conclusions be that were based on this writing. The whole way of thought of Scholasticism was threatened if its original source of knowledge was self-contradictory, and all answers to questions that had been derived by the method must be suspect.

Still another fire broke out in the structure of the Church with the rediscovery of all of Aristotle's works in the last part of the twelfth century. Because his logic had been universally used as the method of thinking, Aristotle, though a pagan, was perhaps the most venerated name among all of the world's philosophers throughout the early Middle Ages, but only his work on logic was known to the philosophers of the time. About the year 1200 almost the entire corpus of his works was brought into Europe through a curious process. Aristotle had written in Greek, Syrian scholars had translated him into Syriac, then Arabic writers had converted those translations into Arabic. Finally, through the Muslims in Spain, the body of thought was discovered, turned into medieval Latin, and made available to all of Europe. The discovery of this trove of scientific knowledge posed several touchy questions, but the most important was that it revealed that Aristotle had developed considerable knowledge of the world by investigating and classifying *physical* things. The Church had stood against any studies of the physical world, yet here was a man more revered by scholars than were most of the saints, who had developed his knowledge by such investigation. The impact was about as great as if we discovered that one of our most revered scientists received his knowledge and made his discoveries by consulting a witch doctor. What was the Church to do?

The first reaction was to ban the newly discovered works entirely, and in 1210 and for the next few years we have records of the books being banned at the University of Paris. The discovery of the books was sufficiently well known, however, that they could not so conveniently be done away with. The next step was the publication of "authorized" versions from which all of Aristotle's ideas that were directly contradictory to Church doctrine had been expurgated. Since the minds of the scholars were hungry for new material, this step did not work either, and finally the entire body of knowledge was made available to the scholars of the late Middle Ages.

The Church had preached complete otherworldliness and disdained earthly knowledge except as it seemed to be a symbol or testimony of scriptural knowledge and heavenly life. Yet these books revealed that the most revered mind of the Middle Ages had dissected animals to discover similarities and differences between species; had classified plants according to their structure. Thus another problem was presented, demanding synthesis if the Church were to maintain its authority.

The rise of the universities is the last of the symptoms of new life we will consider here. Actually their origin is very obscure, for we have little knowledge of them until their formal charters were issued. In Christian Europe (as different from Spain) the University of Salerno, which specialized in medicine, was probably the earliest, for we have records of its existence in the middle of the eleventh century, yet situated in southern Italy, it had little influence on the general dawn of culture. The University of Bologna with its great law school was given a formal grant of rights in 1158; the University of Paris was granted a royal charter in 1200 and a Papal license in 1231. Oxford was formed in the twelfth century when a group of teachers and students seceded from Paris, and Cambridge came into being somewhat later when a dissident group left Oxford. The growth was so rapid that by the end of the Middle Ages we find eighty universities scattered throughout Europe. The actual founding dates for the universities are of relatively little importance, since it is probable that schools had existed in connection with cathedrals and abbeys where the universities were founded at least a century before formal charters were granted; this, at least, was the case with the University of Paris, which had a long history as the Cathedral School of Notre Dame before it was licensed as a university. Nor did the schools have a smooth course throughout; the occasion for the Papal license of the University of Paris in 1231 was the reopening of the University that had been closed for two years following a riot between students and the city authorities. Few things are new under the sun!

The word *universitas* is Latin for a corporation such as a trade guild. When teachers (or students) joined together as a legal body, a university came into existence. Operating under the protection of a charter granted usually by the pope or a king, universities were generally freed from local jurisdiction, though they could not avoid "town and gown" conflicts that seem to be endemic to university communities. Their operation paralleled that of craft guilds, with guild masters (professors) awarding qualifying certificates (degrees) to apprentices (students), who were working to become masters in the teaching corporation (university). Graduation of the apprentices marked their "commencement" as certified teachers.

Offering instruction in all recognized fields of knowledge, the University of Paris was the leading institution of the time, with faculties of medicine, law, theology, and liberal arts. As a prerequisite for professional courses, the liberal arts curriculum followed the seven liberal arts pattern of monastic schools: trivium (grammar, rhetoric, logic) and quadrivium (arithmetic, geometry, astronomy, and music, plus the works of Aristotle). In today's terms the subjects of the trivium were humanistic and those of the quadrivium mathematical.

Initial studies were devoted to the trivium (including analyses of works of philosophy, literature, and history) but with no prescribed hours or units of credit. Achievement was measured solely by comprehensive oral examinations, after which the bachelor of arts (B.A.) degree was awarded as the necessary prerequisite for studying the quadrivium. Passing the second set of examinations certified the student as a master of arts (M.A.), and thus qualified to teach the liberal arts curriculum. The higher degrees of doctor (in law, medicine, and theology) were also teaching degrees, with the doctor of philosophy (Ph.D.) added later for advanced study in the liberal arts. Usually based upon four years of study beyond the M.A., doctorates were awarded after passing another set of rigorous examinations and successfully defending a "thesis," or proposition, before a faculty board. The comparative few who survived this ordeal were granted not only a doctorate but also the opportunity to put on a banquet for the examiners.

Though some women had been admitted to Plato's Academy and some Hellenistic scholars were women, medieval universities were operated solely by and for the masculine sex. The medieval assumption that women had no need for formal education resulted, of course, in an incalculable loss of the brain power of half the human race, a cultural deprivation still not entirely rectified.

As guilds of teachers and scholars, universities at first had no campus and no buildings. With classes meeting wherever rooms could be found, usually in churches, early regulations specified charges for room and board, the price of books (usually rented because manuscripts were expensive), the minimum number of classes students had to attend to be "official" (usually two a week), and the number of lectures and their length that a professor had to give to collect his fees. Students could fine professors for absences or for lecturing too long and, by not attending his classes, cost him a portion of his fees.

The *collegium* (L., community, society) was a residence hall that private benefactors began providing for students who were too poor to pay room and board. Robert de Sorbon, royal chaplain to Louis IX, endowed a hall in 1257 called the College de Sorbonne, now the college of arts and sciences of the University of Paris.

This was a new group of people who had been unknown in the early Middle Ages. They were eager for all sorts of knowledge and questing for experience. Their motto may well have been Abelard's famous teaching, "for by doubting we come to inquiry, by inquiry we discover the truth." These people would not tolerate a culture that walled itself in by authority and allowed no questioning of that authority. Here, as in most areas of life in the late Middle Ages, we see life bursting out at the seams.

At the end of the preceding chapter we saw that medieval men and women had sheltered themselves within the narrow walls of the authoritarian church and of feudalism and manorialism. These provided a measure of physical and psychological safety but little room in which to grow. With the rise of cities and the increasing intellectual ferment in the universities, we see the breeching of medieval walls in the search for knowledge of the physical world. Contacts with Muslim and Byzantine cultures and the civilizing effects of chivalry and the courts of love indicated that life here on this earth could be made immeasurably better. In the ferment of city life and in the idea-ferment of the universities all established modes of existence were called into question, a questioning that is revealed in the literature of the time.

Life's Questions as Seen in Literature

In the preceding chapter the morality play *Everyman* was presented. *Everyman,* to review briefly, faced either eternal damnation or eternal bliss; there is no middle ground and the fear of death hangs like a pall over all of life.

Chaucer, in his "Prolog" to *The Canterbury Tales,* illustrates this problem, though his tone and outlook are essentially realistic. While he is not seeking to illustrate anything, while he is trying only to describe an assortment of people with their too human weakness, he poses the problem nevertheless. The basic nature of the gathering of the pilgrims is a case in point. The pilgrimage to the Shrine of St. Thomas is, or should be, a religious exercise. Yet these people, or some of them at any rate, seem to be there for an extended picnic and nothing else. In the characters, again, we see the division of personality. On the one hand we have the poor and virtuous Parson; on the other we see the Friar, the Summoner, and the Pardoner, who are devoted entirely to the gratification of the flesh, and all of whom exploit their religious affiliation to make these gratifications possible.

In some instances we see the city men, the new class of merchants, lawyers, doctors, and guildsmen. Their aim is profit and they will achieve their purpose regardless of any nice concerns about religion. They partake of the upsurging spirit that denies the balance of the old Graeco-Roman tradition. Chaucer draws no moral from this collection of people, nor does he attempt to state a problem with the exactness of a mathematician or a social worker. What does the reader make of this collection of medieval men and women?

Nowhere is the spiritual conflict of the time better illustrated than in the student songs, for the universities themselves were products of the new and stirring life. The pulls upon the personality are particularly evident in one of the student creeds in which the dying goliard burlesques the creed of the Church. With almost savage vigor he takes each word of the Church's creed and turns it to a flaunting of his vices. Then the student faces the last moment and is gripped by a fear of the unknown to which he is committing himself: a fear that is supported by five hundred years of religious tradition. With an anguish that strikes home to the reader, he commits his soul to God and begs for the last sacrament of the Church.

The Medieval Synthesis

To summarize the conflicts in the late Middle Ages that have been suggested, the clash of the times came about in new secular ways of thinking and living that challenged the older religious and mystic ways. Where was the art that could bring these together in a new synthesis? Where were the people who could define new relationships between human beings and the universe, human beings and God, the individual person and society as a whole? Where could be found artists to suggest new purposes for life since the old were so sorely challenged?

It would seem that this new synthesis came about in three places. In philosophy, it was St. Thomas Aquinas who built a new philosophic structure that could accommodate the divergent points of view. In art, the medieval Gothic cathedral furnished a synthesis at the point when the artist's skill and the function came together. Chartres Cathedral is the prime example of such a structure. In literature, the new balance was suggested by Dante Alighieri in *The Divine Comedy*. Let us look briefly at the ways in which the synthesis was achieved in these three forms.

It cannot be our purpose here to go into detail in a discussion of the doctrines of St. Thomas. Rather, we shall show how he reconciled some of the contradictions of the time. In discussing Thomas's thought, one can scarcely avoid using the symbol of the equilateral triangle as a representation of the individual person, of the nation, and of the universe, for all of his ideas seem to shape themselves around that symbol. It was no accident that this is also the symbol of the Trinity of God; it may have been accident that

it is also a shape that suggests both stability and upward motion. In its visual form it unifies the energy of the Celto-Germanic spirit with the desire for stability of the Graeco-Roman world where it first appeared as the perfect two-dimensional figure of Pythagoras (see pp. 212 and 38).

In Thomas's unification of Aristotelian thought with that of the Church, he accepted the central Aristotelian doctrine, similar to that of the Conceptualists. This doctrine was that matter and form (or idea) cannot exist separately. Matter, he said, had only potentiality, that is the possibility of being itself, until it was entered into by the idea of the thing. Then it became that thing. For example, "clay" is not "brick," nor is there "brick" without "clay"; but when "clay," which has only potentiality by itself, is joined with the form or idea of "brick," then the "brick" exists. Next, he said, lower forms of existence are only matter in the formation of higher forms. And everything, he said, was moving, changing, growing, turning into something else. This movement is the movement toward perfection, which is God. Thus the First Mover, God, does not move things from behind, but is the purpose toward which all things are moving. Since things must desire the thing toward which they move, then the motive force is the love of God.

This argument involves the most important of Thomas's proofs of the existence of God. (He proposed five such proofs, bearing out his belief that all things accepted by faith could be proved by reason.) His most famous proof is that of motion. Very briefly stated, this proof proceeds in this way: We see motion. If there is motion, there must be a mover. If we think backward, for example, I roll a stone; something causes me to move to roll it; but something causes the mover which moves me, etc.; we have an endless and infinite series of movers. On the other hand, consider the first mover as a force that attracts rather than pushes from behind. Then we can come to a first "attracting force" (like a magnet), which sets all other things in motion. This First Mover, or if you will, the Unmoved Mover, is God, pulling all things toward himself.

Furthermore, in the idea that both *form* and *matter* are necessary for reality, Thomas brought together the conflicting arguments in the Battle of Universals. Here we may consider the question of whether form (or Idea) has existence *before*, or only *in* a specific thing, and whether it exists *after* the specific has vanished. All three, said Thomas. The Idea exists (as potentiality) before the thing; it exists in the thing, and in its continuing progress upward, it exists after the particular thing. Thus, borrowing heavily from the Conceptualist view, he brought the three positions into harmony.

It was with the doctrine of lower and higher forms, all in motion toward perfection, that Thomas brought together the conflict between the growing desire of people for natural knowledge and the doctrine of the Church that such knowledge was a study of nothingness, for, said Thomas, the highest human studies are philosophy and law. He considered philosophy as a study of the humanly knowable laws for the discipline of the spirit, and law, of course, as the study of the rules for the governing of our physical nature. Both, according to the Aristotelian concept of reality, are necessary and equal. To reach a knowledge of these subjects, a study of all forms and all matter is necessary. It is in this way that people attain their highest perfection—through knowledge.

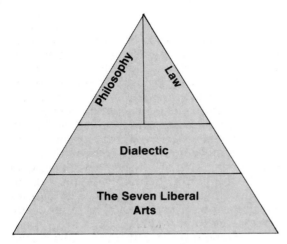

Thomas's Plan of Education

Then, he continued, there is another realm of knowledge, complementary to philosophy. This is theology, which has its source in God. It cannot be understood through natural learning, but only by revelation. The two, however, are not opposed to each other. Rather, a knowledge of philosophy leads to the possibility of receiving revelation and revelation presupposes a knowledge of philosophy. Finally, he said that true knowledge, the union with the divine science, came only after death. It was the duty of people, therefore, during their lifetimes to acquire as much natural knowledge as possible that they might be fit to receive the final revelation of God after their death.

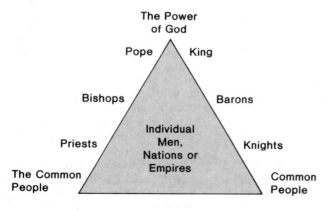

The Separate, Equal Roles of Church and State

The settlement of the opposition of Church and State came with a justification of feudalism on the basis of the lower forms constantly seeking the higher. However, in the governing of people he believed Church and State equal, with both the king and the pope receiving their power directly from God. It was the duty of the king to administer God's laws for the physical nature of human beings; of the pope and the Church to administer the law for the spirit of humankind. This solution, which justified the status quo, ran contrary to the secular spirit of the time and the growing nationalism. Thomas's argument would not stand for long against the moving social and political forces.

The pull of life and death, perhaps the greatest question of all, was solved by St. Thomas, first with the Aristotelian doctrine of matter and form existing only when they were together and in each other. With this, and with Thomas's insistence that natural knowledge, gained through the use of human senses, was necessary for the perfection of the human being, he banished the dualism that had existed since the time of Augustine and the idea of the City of God. Hereafter, both body and soul were necessary for earthly perfection, the one as important as the other.

Thus it was that the Middle Ages, in this final great synthesis, found freedom and opened the way for people to develop themselves, like the medieval city, outside of its early walls, yet still in keeping with the fundamental pattern. The way for science was now open, hate for the body was banished, the State was recognized as one of the forms of order leading to the highest order, that of the kingdom of God.

Without becoming too technical, this may suggest the kind of synthesis that was made in philosophy. For the common people, however, the involved thinking of philosophers has little meaning. In the Middle Ages, it was the common person, as well as the serious thinker, who needed a solution to the problems that were splitting the personality.

For these common people it is probable that the Gothic cathedral effected this synthesis. The thrust of the cathedral was upward. Standing before it, the beholder's eye moved up its great towers, impelled by the pointed arches, until the eye reached the spire, which directed it even farther upward—toward heaven. In this way was the need for the otherworldly satisfied. So, too, did the figures in the stained-glass windows tell the stories of the Bible and the lives of saints and satisfy the religious needs of the time. It is foolish to argue that people could "read" the stories told in the windows. Even with binoculars we cannot clearly read the upper pictures. However, the profuse beauty of colored light, like the echo of the unintelligible Latin ecclesiastical chants echoing through the arches, filled the onlooker with a sense of beauty and awe (see colorplate 18).

So there was more to the cathedral than lessons, for here was beauty. Not only did the windows preach the gospel, but their colors also brought joy to the beholder. The pageantry of the Church was a thing of splendor made colorful by the rich garments of the bishop and those who assisted him at the mass, by the heaviness of the incense, and by the chant of the choir. All these brought richness to the life of the medieval person who sought such satisfaction in day-to-day living. Even the task of building these cathedrals, a great communal effort shared alike by nobility, wealthy burghers, and common people, furnished a creative outlet for the energies of these people of the Middle Ages.

Architecturally, the Gothic cathedral furnished a symbol of balance between classic and energetic. It achieved balanced tension and unity, yet it had the thrust, the upward push, which we have remarked as characteristic of the northern personality. The elongated statuary of the portals, the pointed arches, the flying buttresses, beautiful in themselves and symbolic of the desire to go upward beyond the limits wall and column could support, all these are marks of the Gothic style.

Among the thousands of symbols connected with the Gothic cathedral, one significance of the tower deserves mention. The lower, heavy square tower represented earthly life. The spire signified human aspiration toward the divine. And finally, the elevation of the eye from the last point of physical stone toward the sky suggested union with God. The architect of the south tower at Chartres (see fig. 11.30) had the right idea when he created a transition between the square tower and the octagonal spire that is almost imperceptible. In a truly Thomistic sense, the things of this world blend perfectly with those of the next; the physical and the spiritual are united. The transition triumphs both as architecture and as symbol of the best thought of the time.

In one other aspect the cathedral was the symbol of the synthesis of the Middle Ages, for it was here that the Cult of the Virgin reached its height. The sudden flowering of this cult may be ascribed to the sense of sin that obsessed the people, convinced as they were of their moral deformity from Adam, and of their weakness to withstand the pulls of the world around them. For them, the justice of the Trinity was a thing to flee from, and they fell back upon the mercy of the Mother. Miracles were needed to insure their salvation, and a whole body of literature has grown up to tell of the miracles wrought by the Gracious Lady. Mary provided comfort, solace, and understanding for nobility and common people alike. Thus people could believe that a juggler doing his act for her amusement was as important as the learned friar writing scholarly books according to the formulas of Scholasticism.

A three-dimensional medieval synthesis, the Gothic cathedral was church, school, meeting place, concert hall, a place of beauty in the present life, and an inspiration to heaven. It represented the golden moment in the development of an art form when artists were masters of achieving what they had envisioned. In addition to the cathedral, there were other great syntheses of medieval life. We have already spoken of the notable work of St. Thomas, which brought the doctrines of the church together into a coherent whole. Still another synthesis, in the realm of literature, was the *Commedia* of Dante.

For the present study, the important aspect of the *Commedia* was the removal of restrictions that earlier centuries had imposed upon people. The goal and final purpose of human beings was still the attainment of heaven and the bliss of that afterlife, but people were left free to achieve this goal through their own power and through the discipline of their own will. Dante's God was no accountant; rather, he was perfect wisdom, which in Dante's mind was almost synonymous with love. The purpose and goal of humankind, like the enteleche of Aristotle, was perfect union with this God. For Dante, this heavenly state is the true home of humankind, which must ever be earned anew because of Adam's fall from grace. Furthermore, people, while they are alive, cannot know the wisdom or order or love of God; for salvation, the final union was still a matter of God's grace rather than a result of human effort. It was as if God's wisdom were a different category of wisdom from that of human beings, one to which people may aspire, but to which they can be admitted only by the will of God.

While people may not achieve union with God through their own efforts, they may prepare themselves for it by gaining the maturity that accompanies earthly wisdom. This mature nature is called innocence by Dante, by which he meant the happy state of Adam and Eve before the fall. It is for this reason that Dante places the Garden of Eden, the Earthly Paradise, at the top of the mountain of Purgatory. It is here that men and women, after having attained their full maturity, the totality of human wisdom, may await the act of God that will transport them into the category beyond.

Mystery plays represented an emotional approach to God, while morality plays like *Everyman* were didactic. Dante's vision, on the other hand, was intellectual. For him human beings were part of God's rational order, which was love; so it was through the pull of the love of God that individual human beings, exercising their own free will, ascended the ladder of love. The choice was made on earth and that choice, expressed in faith and good works, determined the destiny of each person in the afterlife.

What were the choices? Since the way of God is discipline and orderliness, the way of Satan is disorder and lack of proportion. God himself is perfect freedom, and the way toward him is the constant increase of one's personal freedom. Essential sin is the loss of freedom. This idea can be illustrated with the simple and not *too* sinful example of smoking—or any other addiction.

At first—in relation to cigarettes—the individual is ignorant, knowing neither the pleasures or the harms of smoking. So, for one reason or another, the person tries one. *The act in itself is not sinful,* nor are subsequent experiences with smoking. The person always says, "I can quit any time." And, for a time, that is true. A time comes, however, when given a choice of smoking or not smoking, true addicts will always choose to smoke; they have lost the power to say no, and if cigarettes are denied, they will end up climbing the wall. Thus they have sacrificed one aspect of their freedom of choice, and this, for Dante, is sin. Godlike freedom is the ability to say yes, no, or any of the choices between. Sin is loss of that ability, and in Dante's Hell we see that the degree of sin is measured by the extent to which the person consciously twists a body or an intellect away from free choice. The person who loses hope of making free choices is destined for Hell, and the inscription Dante envisions over the mouth of Hell, "Abandon hope, all ye that enter here," is an expression of the state the condemned ones have reached. In their choice, they have abandoned all hope and all desire to be anything or anywhere else. The punishments Dante saw for the souls in Hell are symbolic of the nature they have made for themselves. With the body removed, in other words, we see them exactly as they have made themselves to be. Step by descending step we traverse the cone of Hell, in each lower depth viewing the souls who are deeper and deeper in sin. Step by descending step we see these souls deprived of more and more freedom, until at the very bottom of the pit we find Satan, the greatest sinner of all, deprived of movement, frozen, as he is, in ice. So is he bound by his sins.

Emerging with Dante at the base of the mountain of Purgatory, we find another picture. Here are the souls who have erred, who have somehow strayed in their earthly lives from the path of wisdom. The difference is that these people still have hope; they aspire toward their own true selves and toward God. Their labors are difficult as they expiate their sin, but through all the labor they are joyous, for they know that the end will be full wisdom and maturity, the Garden of Eden, and the state of Earthly Paradise. It is of utmost importance to realize that each soul decides for itself when it is completely purged of any sin and is ready to move upward to another cornice of the mountain. The decision is never made by an angel or any other outside force. So free of envy are all the souls on the mountain that they chant *Gloria in excelsis* in unison when an individual moves upward.

This is explicitly stated when Dante and Virgil, toiling up the mountain, encounter the spirit of the Latin poet Statius, who has just moved from a lower cornice to a higher one. The occasion is so momentous that the whole mountain has shaken, and all the souls have shouted the *Gloria*. (The word *inn* in the fifth line quoted simply means "resting place.") It is of great importance to note that while the soul moves upward through its own free choice, it disciplines itself so that the movement is never made until it feels that the stain of former sin is completely removed (see the seventh through the thirteenth quoted lines).

But when some spirit, feeling purged and sound,
    Leaps up or moves to seek a loftier station,
    The whole mount quakes and the great shouts resound.
The will itself attests its own purgation;
    Amazed, the soul that's free to change its inn
    Finds its mere will suffice for liberation;

True, it wills always, but can nothing win
    So long as heavenly justice keeps desire
    Set toward the pain as once 'twas toward the sin;
Thus I, who've languished in this torment dire
    Five hundred years and more, felt only now
    The enfranchised will urge me to thresholds higher;
Then didst thou feel the shock, then heardest how—
    God send them happy—the kind souls to speed me
    Gave praise from mountain-foot to mountain-brow.

Finally in Heaven, and guided by Beatrice, Dante receives instruction in theology, the science of God. It is here that he sees the perfect order of the whole universe, both of humans and of angels. He sees the Church and its officers as the guardians of the human spirit and he sees the kings' importance to God, for they maintain temporal order on earth. Here, too, he finds freedom, as opposed to the ever-increasing bondage he witnessed in Hell, for in Heaven, though the souls are symbolically assigned to different spheres as a result of their different capacities for joy and love, yet they are actually free to pass through all the spheres and to approach the throne of God itself. There is no bondage here. In the final Cantos of the *Paradiso*, Dante comes as close as any human being can to communicating the mystic union of the soul with God as actual living experience.

Is this only a poem of death, or does Dante have something to say for living people? We believe that he has much to say to us. He says that people must make their choice, for which they have their own wills. If they choose wisely, they will choose a life of order and discipline. Throughout their life, they will gain knowledge, for that and its resultant wisdom will make them free. Finally, he tells us, our studies should turn to philosophy and law, the fields of knowledge that represent the best possible concepts of order on earth; the former disciplines and instructs the spirit, the latter has the same function in our temporal dealings with each other. This life will be one that is joyously led, and leads to the final realization of the true self when, by the will of God, the soul is united with the perfect wisdom.

These ideas, too, are stated clearly in Canto 27 of the *Purgatory* with Virgil's farewell to Dante. The mountain has been climbed and we have reached the point of perfect *human* wisdom. Since Virgil was a pagan, he can go no farther, and the "fair eyes" of Beatrice will guide Dante farther on his way. Incidentally, the "temporal fire" referred to is that of Purgatory; the "eterne" is that of Hell. Further, the mitre is the hat worn by a bishop; the crown is a king's hat. Thus from this point onward, Dante, through his free choices, has complete control over both his spiritual and physical natures, in accordance with his own and St. Thomas's philosophy.

So when the stair had dropped, long flight on flight,
    Away beneath us, then did Virgil turn
    On the top step and fix me with his eyes,
Saying: "The temporal fire and the eterne
    Thou hast beheld, my son, and reached a place
    Where, of myself, no further I discern.

I've brought thee here by wit and by address;
   Make pleasure now they guide—thou art well sped
   Forth of the steep, forth of the narrow ways.
See how the sun shines here upon thy head;
   See the green sward, the flowers, the boskages
   That from the soil's own virtue here are bred.
While those fair eyes are coming, bright with bliss,
   Whose tears sent me to thee, thou may'st prospect
   At large, or sit at ease to view all this.
No word from me, no further sign expect;
   Free, upright, whole, thy will henceforth lays down
   Guidance that it were error to neglect,
Whence o'er thyself I mitre thee and crown."

What has Dante brought together here? In the first place, he envisions a life at once balanced and aspiring. These are the Gothic and classic elements of the Middle Ages. He brings together the desire for broad worldly knowledge and religion, for his poem itself is scientific according to the science of his time, and he counsels the widest possible earthly knowledge as a necessary condition for heavenly bliss. He brings together the pulls of life and death, for his concept of the full life is one that is joyous and in which people use their full powers, yet use them as they aspire to the greatest possible happiness and freedom both now and in the hereafter. Finally, he unites the rival claims of pope and king as he sees each working God's will and God's order on earth, each in his own way and in his own place.

This is the final answer of the Middle Ages to the great question of the search for freedom. It started with the building of walls, for people needed their protection. It has progressed through the stage where they found their walls no longer necessary for protection and found them cramping in the human desire for the good life. It emerges in a great synthesis in which human nature is free, by nature divine, but in which human beings have freedom of choice. The *Commedia* unites body and soul in the process of discipline—one individuals must choose for themselves, a discipline that must occur in the present life. This discipline, in its order, produces freedom here and prepares the spirit for freedom in the afterlife. Particularly in the cathedrals and in the *Commedia* we see the artist at work, proposing new answers to the great questions of humankind. It is upon these answers that the institutions are to be reshaped, and upon them that a new pattern for existence is to be built.

What was the nature of human freedom within this new design? The period of synthesis during the late Middle Ages was brief. Dante lived from 1265 to 1321. St. Thomas lived from 1225 to 1274. Chartres dates from the thirteenth century. Yet by the beginning of the fifteenth century, the Renaissance had burst upon Europe. The forces that had challenged the old walls of life that had been built during the Dark Ages (the years 500 to 1000) were too strong to be held in check, and the secular spirit was to go ahead to new triumphs. But in those 200 years, we can witness a new freedom toward which many world-weary people of the twentieth century look back with longing. It is worthy of at least a brief examination.

The single and fundamental characteristic of medieval freedom lies in the sense of unity that provided strict rules for all types of human behavior, and yet furnished complete individual freedom to create within those rules. This seems to be a paradox, a contradiction. At least it can be seen as a most delicate balance between individual aspiration and endeavor and community solidarity, which offers stability.

Perhaps better than anywhere else, this balance can be seen in the art of the late Middle Ages. Consider, for example, the cathedral. Its pattern was extremely strict. It had to be oriented with the altar toward the east. It had to be cruciform. Each part of the structure carried some symbolic meaning, so that the symbols had to be exactly treated. All this was a part of the strict rule that governed art and life in the period of balance.

Yet consider the freedom of the individual within this rule. The stonecarver was free to do as he wanted. If he wanted to carve little fat angels or animals he had seen or imagined, that was his decision. One sees much of this type of work on the miserere seats in the choir stall. Here a woodcarver thought that it would be fun to carve a pig playing a fiddle. No sooner thought of than started! Or somewhere else, the carver wished to caricature a fat burgher of the town. He could do it because he was a free man, working within the limits of the grand design. These were no machine-made units to be put up as they came from the factory. They were the work of free and independent craftsmen.

This same freedom, within strict limits, is found in all spheres of activity during the late Middle Ages. For example, the craftsman necessarily belonged to his guild. It was the association that regulated the quality of his work, the price that could be charged, and many other things. Beyond that, the guild served as an insurance and burial society for its members, a social group, and a dramatic society, since the mystery and miracle plays that amused and inspired the city-dwellers were functions of the guilds. The guild-hall was not only a place of business, but was also a social center where banquets, weddings, and balls were held. The guild also very strictly regulated the membership within itself and established stringent rules for the training of the craftsmen. All these point to the strict communal regulation of the individual.

But within those limits, the member of a guild, the shoemaker, let us say, was absolutely free. He had his own shop, which was part of his home. He did his work only on order, so that when there was no business, he could lock up and take the members of his family, together with the apprentices and journeymen in his shop, and go for an outing in the country. Furthermore, and one suspects that this is the important aspect of the whole system, each pair of shoes was an individual creation. The pride of craft and of creation entered into all of the work done, and the master craftsman developed a sense of pride in each item of his work. The very fact that he did the whole job, from heel to toe, from sole to the very top of the uppers, gave him a sense of responsibility and of pride.

The story of "Our Lady's Juggler" reveals the same type of freedom within religion. The Catholic creed was strict, and its rules were absolute. But within them people were free. There was sufficient opportunity for individual practice of the religious observances to satisfy each person. Dante's idea of freedom as participation in the wisdom, the order, and the love of God are of great importance here. The person who was not free was the one who, by his or her own choices, had become inhuman in outward form and in nature. The order of God, however, was of sufficient latitude that people could make a comfortable life within it. In addition to this, there was the one provision of the Christian scheme of things that has always been a source of strength for that faith. This was the idea that a mistake does not mean inevitable damnation. Such an error may need purging, but it is only when one comes to a conscious desire for the way of evil that one is damned.

The concept of freedom in this period of balance in the Middle Ages, then, was one in which all the forces of the culture grouped themselves around the individual to provide support. Yet they did not hamper freedom, individuality, or creativity as long as he or she stayed within the rules of that culture.

This balance, like all others we have seen, was too delicate to last. Within a brief time, the secular forces we saw born during the Middle Ages were to triumph, breaking down the new designs that had been made by St. Thomas, by the architects of the great cathedrals, and by Dante. The fundamental beliefs of the culture were to change in a new epoch, which we call the Renaissance.

Literary Selections

Songs and Poems of the Wandering Scholars

The pull of life was strong in the time when new ideas were breaking down the old medieval walls. And students (even those who were to become learned clergymen) were much the same in those days as they are now.

GAUDEAMUS IGITUR

Let us live, then, and be glad
    While young life's before us!
After youthful pastime had,
After old age, hard and sad,
    Earth will slumber o'er us.

Where are they who in this world
    Ere we kept, were keeping?
Go ye to the gods above;
Go to hell; inquire thereof;
    They are not; they are sleeping.

Brief is life, and brevity
    Briefly shall be ended;
Death comes like a whirlwind strong,
Bears us with his blast along;
    None shall be defended.

Live this university,
    Men that learning nourish;
Live each member of the same,
Long live all that bear its name,
    Let them ever flourish!

Live the commonwealth also,
    And the men that guide it!
Live our town in strength and health,
Founders, patrons, by whose wealth
    We are here provided!

Live all gods! A health to you,
    Melting maids and beauteous;
Live the wives and women too,
Gentle, loving, tender, true,
    Good, industrious, duteous!

Perish cares that pule and pine!
    Perish envious blamers!
Die the Devil, thine and mine!
Die the starch-neck Philistine!
    Scoffers and defamers!

LAURIGER HORATIUS

Horace with your laurel crowned,
Truly have you spoken:
Time, a-rush with leap and bound,
Devours and leaves us broken.

Where are now the flagons, full
Of sweet wine, honey-clear?
Where the smiles and shoves and frowns
Of blushing maiden dear?

Swift the young grape grows and swells;
So do comely lasses!
Lo, on the poet's head, the snows
Of the Time that passes!

What's the good of lasting fame,
If people think it sinful
Here and now to kiss a dame
And drink a jolly skinful!

A GOLIARD'S CREED

A *goliard* is dying; the priest sent for in haste speaks comfortable words; have comfort, good son; let him but recite his Credo.[3]

That I will, Sir, and hear me now.
Credo—in dice I well believe,
That got me often bit and sup,
And many a time hath had me drunk,
And many a time delivered me
From every stich and every penny.

In Deum—never with my will
Gave Him a thought nor ever will.
The other day I took a shirt
From a ribald and I diced it,
And lost, and never gave it back.
If I die, he can have mine.

Put it in writing, 'tis my will,
I would not like it were forgot.

---

3. The Creed being recited is as follows: I believe (credo) in God (in Deum) the Father (Patrem), Omnipotent (Omnipotentem), the Creator (Creatorem) of heaven (coeli) and earth (et terrae) . . . and in the resurrection (et . . . resurrectionem) of the body (corporis) and life everlasting (vitam aeternam). Amen.

Patrem—at St. Denis in France,
Good sir, I had a father once,
Omnipotentem in his having,
Money and horses and fine wearing,
And by the dice that thieveth all things
I lost and gamed it all away. . . .

Creatorem who made all
I've denied—He has His will
Of me now, I know I'm dying,
Nothing here but bone and hide.

Coeli—of Heaven ever think?
Nay, but the wine that I could drink.

Et terrae—there was all my joy. . . .
(The burlesque recitation goes on to the final phrase)

Et corporis—the body's lust
I do perform. Sir Priest, I chafe
At thinking of that other life.
I tell you, 'tis not worth a straw.
And I would pray to the Lord God
That He will in no kind of way

Resurrectionem make of me,
So long as I may drench the place
With good wine where I'll be laid
And so pray I of all my friends
That if I can't, themselves will do't,
And leave me a full pot of wine
Which I may to the Judgment bring.

Vitam aeternam wilt Thou give,
O Lord God? wilt Thou forgive
All my evil, well I know it,

Amen. Priest, I now am through with't.
Through with life. Death hath its pain.
Too much . . . . too much . . . . This agony . . . .
I'm dying. I to God commend you.
I ask it of you—Pray for me."

OUR LADY'S JUGGLER

In this simple story one can see the hold and the
charm of the Cult of the Virgin, especially for the
simple people for whom chivalry and philosophy had
no meaning (fig. 10.2).

In the days of King Louis there lived a poor juggler
by the name of Barnabas, a native of Compiegne, who
wandered from city to city performing tricks of skill and
prowess.

On fair days he would lay down in the public square
a worn and aged carpet, and after having attracted a group
of children and idlers by certain amusing remarks which
he had learned from an old juggler, and which he
invariably repeated in the same fashion without altering a
word, he would assume the strangest postures and
balance a pewter plate on the tip of his nose. At first the
crowd regarded him with indifference, but when, with his
hands and head on the ground he threw into the air and
caught with his feet six copper balls that glittered in the
sunlight, or when, throwing himself back until his neck
touched his heels, he assumed the form of a perfect
wheel and in that position juggled with twelve knives, he
elicited a murmur of admiration from his audience, and
small coins rained on his carpet.

Still, Barnabas of Compiegne, like most of those who
exist by their accomplishments, had a hard time making a
living. Earning his bread by the sweat of his brow, he

Figure 10.2 "King David Playing Harp under the Inspiration of the Holy Ghost, while One Attendant Juggles and
Others Play the Rebec, Trumpet and Oliphant." British Museum, London, eleventh century, English. Reproduced by
the courtesy of the Trustees of the British Museum. This curious juxtaposition of David the Psalm Singer with common
people juggling and playing musical instruments was a
standard medieval practice. At the lower right the ivory oliphant is like the one Roland blew (too late) to summon
Charlemagne to his rescue. Of Arab origin, the rebec was
an early precursor of the violin (see chap. 12).

bore rather more than his share of those miseries we are
all heir to through the fault of our Father Adam.

Besides, he was unable to work as much as he would
have liked, for in order to exhibit his wonderful talents,
he required—like the trees—the warmth of the sun and
the heat of the day. In winter time he was no more than a
tree stripped of its leaves, in fact, half-dead. The frozen
earth was too hard for the juggler. Like the cicada
mentioned by Marie de France, he suffered during the
bad season from hunger and cold. But, since he had a
simple heart, he suffered in silence.

He had never thought much about the origin of
wealth nor about the inequality of human conditions. He
firmly believed that if this world was evil the next could
not but be good, and this faith upheld him. He was not
like the clever fellows who sell their souls to the devil; he
never took the name of God in vain; he lived the life of
an honest man, and though he had no wife of his own, he
did not covet his neighbor's, for woman is the enemy of
strong men, as we learn by the story of Samson which is
written in the Scriptures.

Verily, his mind was not turned in the direction of
carnal desire, and it caused him far greater pain to
renounce drinking than to forgo the pleasure of women.

For, though he was not a drunkard, he enjoyed drinking when the weather was warm. He was a good man, fearing God, and devout in his adoration of the Holy Virgin. When he went into a church he never failed to kneel before the image of the Mother of God and to address her with his prayer:

"My Lady, watch over my life until it shall please God that I die, and when I am dead, see that I have the joys of Paradise."

One evening, after a day of rain, as he walked sad and bent with his juggling balls under his arm and his knives wrapped up in his old carpet seeking some barn where he might go supperless to bed, he saw a monk going in his direction, and respectfully saluted him. As they were both walking at the same pace, they fell into conversation.

"Friend," said the monk, "how does it happen that you are dressed all in green? Are you perchance going to play the part of the fool in some mystery?"[4]

"No, indeed, father," said Barnabas. "My name is Barnabas, and my business is that of juggler. It would be the finest calling in the world if I could eat every day."

"Friend Barnabas," answered the monk, "be careful what you say. There is no finer calling than the monastic. The priest celebrates the praise of God, the Virgin, and the saints; the life of a monk is a perpetual hymn to the Lord."

And Barnabas replied: "Father, I confess I spoke like an ignorant man. My estate cannot be compared to yours, and though there may be some merit in dancing and balancing a stick with a denier[5] on top of it on the end of your nose, it is in no wise comparable to your merit. Father, I wish I might, like you, sing the Office every day, especially the Office of the Very Holy Virgin, to whom I am specially and piously devoted. I would willingly give up the art by which I am known from Soissons to Beauvais, in more than six hundred cities and villages, in order to enter the monastic life."

The monk was touched by the simplicity of the juggler, and as he was not lacking in discernment, he recognized in Barnabas one of those well-disposed men of whom Our Lord has said, "Let peace be with them on earth." And he made answer therefore:

"Friend Barnabas, come with me and I will see that you enter the monastery of which I am the Prior. He who led Mary the Egyptian through the desert put me across your path in order that I might lead you to salvation."

Thus did Barnabas become a monk. In the monastery which he entered, the monks celebrated most magnificently the Cult of the Holy Virgin, each of them bringing to her service all the knowledge and skill which God had given him.

The Prior, for his part, wrote books, setting forth, according to the rules of scholasticism, all the virtues of the Mother of God. Brother Maurice copied these treatises with a cunning hand on pages of parchment, while Brother Alexandre decorated them with delicate miniatures representing the Queen of Heaven seated on the throne of Solomon, with four lions on guard at the foot of it. Around her head, which was encircled by a halo, flew seven doves, the seven gifts of the Holy Spirit: fear, piety, knowledge, power, judgment, intelligence, and wisdom. With her were six golden-haired virgins: Humility, Prudence, Retirement, Respect, Virginity, and

Obedience. At her feet two little figures, shining white and quite naked, stood in suppliant attitudes. They were souls imploring, not in vain, Her all-powerful intercession for their salvation. On another page Brother Alexandre depicted Eve in the presence of Mary, that one might see at the same time sin and its redemption, woman humiliated, and the Virgin exalted. Among the other much prized pictures in his book were the Well of Living Waters, the Fountain, the Lily, the Moon, the Sun, and the Closed Garden, of which much is said in the Canticle; the Gate of Heaven and the City of God. These were all images of the Virgin.

Brother Marbode, too, was one of the cherished children of Mary. He was ever busy cutting images of stone, so that his beard, his eyebrows, and his hair were white with the dust, and his eyes perpetually swollen and full of tears. But he was a hardy and a happy man in his old age, and there was no doubt that the Queen of Paradise watched over the declining days of Her child. Marbode represented Her seated in a pulpit. Her forehead encircled by a halo, with an orb of pearls. He was at great pains to make the folds of Her robe cover the feet of Her of whom the prophet has said, "My beloved is like a closed garden."

At times he represented Her as a graceful child, and Her image seemed to say, "Lord, Thou art My Lord!"

There were also in the monastery poets who composed prose writings in Latin and hymns in honor of the Most Gracious Virgin Mary; there was, indeed, one among them—a Picard—who translated the Miracles of Our Lady into rimed verses in the vulgar tongue.

Perceiving so great a competition in praise and so fine a harvest of good works, Barnabas fell to lamenting his ignorance and simplicity.

"Alas!" he sighed as he walked by himself one day in the little garden shaded by the monastery wall, "I am so unhappy because I cannot, like my brothers, give worthy praise to the Holy Mother of God to whom I have consecrated all the love in my heart. Alas, I am a stupid fellow, without art, and for your service, Madame, I have no edifying sermons, no fine treatises nicely prepared according to the rules, no beautiful paintings, no cunningly carved statues, and no verses counted off by feet and marching in measure! Alas, I have nothing."

Thus did he lament and abandon himself to his misery.

One evening when the monks were talking together by way of diversion, he heard one of them tell of a monk who could not recite anything but the *Ave Maria*. He was scorned for his ignorance, but after he died there sprang from his mouth five roses, in honor of the five letters in the name Maria. Thus was his holiness made manifest.

In listening to this story, Barnabas was conscious once more of the Virgin's beneficence, but he was not consoled by the example of the happy miracle, for his heart was full of zeal and he wanted to celebrate the glory of his Lady in Heaven.

He sought for a way in which to do this, but in vain, and each day brought him greater sorrow, until one morning he sprang joyously from his cot and ran to the chapel, where he remained alone for more than an hour. He returned thither again after dinner, and from that day onward he would go into the chapel every day the moment it was deserted, passing the greater part of the time which the other monks dedicated to the pursuit of the liberal arts and the sciences. He was no longer sad and he sighed no more. But such singular conduct aroused the curiosity of the other monks, and they asked themselves why Brother Barnabas retired alone so often,

---

4. Mystery—one of the religious dramas of the time.
5. Denier—a small coin.

and the Prior, whose business it was to know everything that his monks were doing, determined to observe Barnabas. One day, therefore, when Barnabas was alone in the chapel, the Prior entered in company with two of the oldest brothers, in order to watch, through the bars of the door, what was going on within.

They saw Barnabas before the image of the Holy Virgin, his head on the floor and his feet in the air, juggling with six copper balls and twelve knives. In honor of the Holy Virgin he was performing the tricks which had in former days brought him the greatest fame. Not understanding that he was thus putting his best talents at the service of the Holy Virgin, the aged brothers cried out against such sacrilege. The Prior knew that Barnabas had a simple soul, but he believed that the man had lost his wits. All three set about to remove Barnabas from the chapel, when they saw the Virgin slowly descend from the altar and, with a fold of her blue mantle, wipe the sweat that streamed over the juggler's forehead.

Then the Prior, bowing his head down to the marble floor, repeated these words:

"Blessed are the pure in heart, for they shall see God."

"Amen," echoed the brothers, bowing down to the floor.

The Prolog to THE CANTERBURY TALES
Geoffrey Chaucer (1340?–1400)

Chaucer was exceptionally well read for his time, learned in French, Italian, and Latin literature. Having visited Italy where he acquired a fair knowledge of Italian, he knew the works of Dante but was more influenced by the writings of Boccaccio, especially the *Decameron*. Though he may have been influenced by earlier collections of stories like the *Decameron* and Ovid's *Metamorphoses* (which he also knew well), Chaucer invented the scheme of a pilgrimage as a device to frame his stories and develop the interplay of his characters.

The following excerpt from the "Prolog" (lines 1–18) is given in the original Middle English (*Beowulf* is in Old English), the language in use from early in the twelfth century until late in the fifteenth century, when it was superseded by Early Modern English. For the modern reader, the prime difficulty with Middle English is in the spelling, which can be described as a phonetic system. Therefore, the flavor and some of the meaning of Chaucer's language can be best appreciated by reading these lines aloud, pronouncing each syllable distinctly and with gusto. This version is based on the Hengwrt Manuscript.

Whan that Aprille with his shoures soot
The droghte of Marche hath perced to the roote,
And bathed every veyne in swich licour,
Of which vertu engendred is the flour;
When Zephyrus eek with his swete breeth
Inspired hath in every holt and heeth
The tendre croppes, and the yonge sonne
Hath in the Ram his halfe cours yronne,
And smale fowles maken melodye,
That slepen al the night with open yë,
(So priketh hem Nature in hir corages):
That longen folk to goon on pilgrimages,

(And palmeres for to seken straunge strondes)
To ferne halwes, couthe in sondry londes;
And specially, from every shires ende
Of Engelond, to Caunterbury they wende,
The holy blisful martyr for to seke,
That hem hath holpen, whan that they were seke.

Following now is the complete "Prolog," translated into modern English by Leslie Dae Lindou. Here we are introduced to a fascinating cast of characters representing a panorama of life in the late Middle Ages. Note the shrewdness of Chaucer's descriptions, deft touches that reveal the personality of each individual.

When April with its sweet and welcome showers
The drought of March has pierced, and to the flowers
And every vein of growing things has sent
Life-giving moisture, wholesome nourishment;
When Zephyr,[6] too, has with his own sweet breath
Revived again in every wood and heath
The tender shoots, and when the northering sun
Has half his course into the Ram[7] now run,
And little song-birds make their melody
That sleep all thru the night with open eye
—So Nature urges them with her commands—
Then people long to go in pilgrim bands,
And palmers[8] once again to seek far strands
And distant shrines, well known in many lands:
Especially, from every county's end
Of England, Canterbury-ward they wend,
The holy blessed martyr[9] there to seek
Who was their help when they were ill or weak.

It happened in that season, on a day,
In Southwerk at the Tabard as I lay,
Ready my pilgrimage to undertake
To Canterbury, for my own soul's sake,
At night there came into that hostelry
Some nine-and-twenty in a company
Of various folk, who came by chance to fall
Into one group, and pilgrims were they all;
To Canterbury they all planned to ride.
The chambers and the stables there were wide,
And we were lodged in comfort, with the best.
And very soon—the sun now gone to rest—
So had I spoken with them, every one,
That I was of their fellowship anon,
And planned with them quite early to arise
To take our way, as I shall you advise:

—Nevertheless, while I have time and space,
Before I further in this story pace,
It seems to me both sensible and sound
To tell you in detail of all I found
About each one, just as it seemed to me,
And what they were, and what was their degree,
And tell what kind of costume they were in;
And at a knight, then, will I first begin.

---

6. Zephyr—the west wind: here, the life-giving breath of Spring.

7. Ram—the third sign of the zodiac, which the sun enters ca. March 12 and leaves ca. April 11 to enter Taurus. Chaucer is only saying that April is well advanced; the date is about April 18.

8. Palmers—pilgrims who had visited the Holy Lands bore palms as token of their pilgrimage.

9. Martyr—Thomas à Becket, murdered in the cathedral at Canterbury in 1170, was canonized in 1173. His shrine was the great national shrine, and many stories of miraculous cures were told of it.

Knight

A knight there was, a worthy man,
Who from the time when that he first began
To ride on quests, had well loved chivalry,
Truth and honor, freedom and courtesy.
Full worthy was this man in his lord's war,
And therein had he ridden—none so far—
Thru Christendom, and heathen lands no less,
Always honored for his worthiness.
At Alexandria was he when it was won;
Many a time he had the board begun[10]
Above all other guests, in distant Prussia;
In Latvia[11] he fought, again in Russia,
No Christian man so oft, of his degree.
Against the Moors in Spain he fought, and he
In Africa and Asia Minor warred
Against the infidel; his mighty sword
Found service all about the Inland Sea;
At any noble action, there he'd be.
At mortal battles had he been—fifteen;
And for the faith he fought, at Tramyssene,
In tourney thrice, and each time slew his foe.
And this same worthy knight had been also
At one time with the lord of Palatye
Against another heathen land—Turkey;
And every time he held the topmost prize.
And yet, with all his courage, he was wise—
His conduct, meek as that of any maid.
No villainy had this man ever said
In all his life to any sort of wight.
He was a true, a perfect, gentle knight.
　　　—But, to tell you briefly his array,
His horse was good, but certainly not gay;
He wore a fustian garment (a gypoun)
All rust-and-armor stained (his haubergeon),
For he had just completed the last stage
Of travel, and at once made pilgrimage.

Squire

With him was his son, a fine young Squire,
A lover and a lusty bachelor,
With locks as curly as if laid in press;
Near twenty years of age he was, I guess.
His stature was of ordinary length,
But agile, and revealing a great strength.
And he had ridden in the cavalry
In Flanders, in Artois, and Picardy,
And born him well, within his life's short space,
In hope that he might win his lady's grace.
Fancily clad in fashion's newest whim,
—One thought of flowering fields, on seeing him!—
Singing he was, or whistling, all the day:
He was as fresh as is the month of May.
His gown was short, with sleeves both long and wide;
He knew just how to sit a horse and ride,
To make up songs, and fit the words aright,
To joust, and dance, and draw, and even write.

So hot he loved (at least, so goes the tale)
He slept o'nights less than the nightingale!
Courteous was he, meek, in service able,
And carved before his father at the table.

Yeoman

A yeoman had he—no other servants, tho,
As at that time; it pleased him to ride so—
And he was clad in coat and hood of green.
A sheaf of peacock arrows, bright and keen,
Under his belt he carried, gay but grim;
(He well knew how to keep his gear in trim—
His arrow never drooped with feathers low)
And in his hand he bore a mighty bow.
His head was cropped; his face the sun had burned;
Of woodcraft, every subtle trick he'd learned.
Upon his arm a bracer gay he wore
And by his side a sword and buckler bore,
And on the other side, a dagger gay,
As sharp as point of spear, well sheathed away.
A Christopher medal gleamed upon his breast;
His horn's green sling was hung across his chest.
He must have been a forester, I guess.

Prioress

There was also a nun, a Prioress,
Whose smile was sweetly simple, but coy;[12]
Her greatest oath was but by good St. Loy;
And she was known as Madam Eglantine.
Full well she sang the services divine
Intoning thru her nose right properly.
And French she spoke, both well and carefully,
But Stratford-fashion, if the truth be told;
Parisian French she knew not—hers was old.
Her table-manners were well taught, withal;
She never from her lips let morsels fall,
Nor wet her fingers in the sauce too deep;
She knew just how to lift her food, to keep
A single drop from falling on her breast.
In etiquette she found the greatest zest.
Her upper lip she always wiped so clean
That in her cup there never could be seen
A speck of grease, when she had drunk her fill;
Fine manners at the table were her will.
And truly she was fond of harmless sport,
Pleasant, friendly, and of good report;
She took great pains the court to imitate,
Her manner formal, an affair of state;
For she would have men do her reverence.
But now, to tell about her moral sense,
So kindly was she and so piteous,
She wept, if ever that she saw a mouse
Caught in a trap, if it were dead, or bled.
Some little dogs she had, and these she fed
With roasted meat, or milk and good white bread.
But sore she wept if one of them were dead,
Or if men hit one with a stick, to smart;
And all for her was conscience, tender heart.
Becomingly her wimple fell in pleat;
As blue as glass her eyes, her nose right neat;
Her mouth was very small, and soft, and red;
But certainly she had a fine forehead;
It was almost a span in breadth, I'd say—
She was not under-sized, in any way!
Quite stylish was the cloak the lady wore;
About her arm small coral beads she bore,

---

10. He sat in the seat of honor, at the head of the table: a mark of distinction and worth.

11. Probably he had fought in Latvia or Lithuania, with the Order of Teutonic Knights. Chaucer lists by name other scenes of the Order's exploits: the main point is, they were associated with fighting for the faith rather than for gain. The Knight is very nearly the ideal knight of chivalry.

---

12. In Chaucer's text the word meant "bashful" or "modest."

And they were interspersed with gauds[13] of green,
And therefrom hung a brooch of golden sheen,
Whereon was written first a crowned "A,"
And after, "Amor Vincit Omnia."
She had another nun, for company,
Who was her chaplain; and her priests were three.

Monk

A monk there was—th' administrative sort—
Outrider,—hunting was his favorite sport—
A manly man, to be an abbot able.
Full many a fancy horse he had in stable,
And when he rode, men could his bridle hear
Jingling in the whistling wind as clear
And just as loud as does the chapel bell
Where this good lord was Keeper of the Cell.
The rule of Maurus or St. Benedict[14]
This monk considered old and over-strict.
He'd rather let the old things go their way.
And follow fashions of a newer day.
For texts he didn't give a well-plucked hen
That say that hunters are not holy men,
Nor that a monk, who leaves his cloister's bounds
Is like a fish that's out of water—zounds!
—Why shouldn't monks go out of cloister?
Texts like that aren't worth an oyster!
And I said his views were good thereon.
Why should he study till his wits were gone
Upon a book in cloister, like a clerk,
Or labor with his hands, always at work,
As old St. Austin[15] bids? What good is served?
Let Austin have his work to him reserved!
And so this monk his hunting much preferred.
Greyhounds had he, swift as any bird;
In riding, and in hunting of the hare,
Was his delight—and for no cost he'd spare.
I saw his sleeves were fur-trimmed at the hand,
Expensively, the finest in the land;
And, to fasten up his hood beneath his chin.
He had a rich, elaborate, golden pin;
A love-knot in the larger end there was.
His head was bald, and shone as bright as glass;
As if anointed shone his ruddy face.
He was a lord right fat, and in good case.
His eyes were staring, rolling in his head,
Gleaming like the furnace-fires red.
His boots were supple, and his horse was great;
Now certainly, he was a fine prelate!
He was not pale as some poor starveling ghost.
A fat swan loved he best of any roast.
His palfrey was as brown as any berry.

Friar

A friar there was, a wanton man and merry;
A Limiter,[16] a most impressive one;
Indeed in all four orders there was none
Who knew so much of small talk, fine language;
And he had made right many a marriage
Of young girls at his own expense and hire;

A pillar of his order was this friar!
Familiar and full well beloved was he
With franklins[17] over all in his county,
For as confessor he had won renown
Far more than curates had in their possession
—His order licensed him to hear confession.
His hearing of confession was a pleasure,
His absolution always within measure;
The penance he imposed was never stern—
If something for himself he'd thereby earn!
For when to his poor order gifts were given,
It must be sign the givers were well shriven,
For such gifts, said this friar for his part,
Show clearly that a man is changed at heart.
For many men are hardened, it appears,
So that they find no outlet thru their tears;
Instead of tears and useless weeping, then,
The silver that they give will save such men.
He always kept his tippet[18] stuffed with knives
And pins to give to young attractive wives.
Certainly he had a merry note;
He knew well how to sing, and play a rote,[19]
At song-fests he would win the prize outright.
As any lily flower his neck was white.
And like a champion wrestler he was strong.
All the taverns, as he went along,
And every hostler, and barmaid, he knew,
Better than outcasts and the beggar-crew;
Because, to such a worthy man as he,
It was not fitting, you will all agree,
To have acquaintance with such worthless wretches;
Such contact brings no profit, nothing fetches. . . .
There is no gain in dealing with *canaille*,[20]
But with rich men, of social station high.
And thus, whenever profit would arise,
This friar was humble, courteous, and wise.
So virtuous a man was nowhere found;
And what a beggar, as he made his round!
Why, if a widow had no shoe to show,
So pleasant was his "In principio . . ."[21]
He'd have the widow's mite, before he went!
His income always went beyond his rent.
And he could play around like any whelp;
On love-days[22] he knew how to be of help.
He was not like a needy monk or scholar,
Threadbare, shabby, down to his last dollar;
But he was like a great man or a pope.
Of finest woolen was his semicope,[23]
That rounded like a bell out of its mold.
He lisped a little, if the truth he told,
To make his speech sound sweeter on his tongue;
And in his harping, after he had sung,
His twinkling eyes shone in his head as bright
As do the stars on cold and frosty night.
This worthy Limiter was called Hubert.

---

13. Gauds—the large Paternoster beads marking off the sections of a rosary.

14. St. Benedict and his disciple Maurus, founders of the Benedictine Order; St. Benedict established the famous monastery at Monte Cassino in 529.

15. St. Augustine, Bishop of Hippo, was a great proponent of labor as part of the monastic life.

16. A "Limiter" was a friar licensed to beg within a definite ("limited") region.

17. Franklins were landholders of free, but not of noble, birth; they ranked below the gentry.

18. Tippet—a long scarf; a handy substitute for pockets.

19. Rote—a stringed instrument, sometimes played with a bow, sometimes with a fixed wheel like a hurdy-gurdy. (See fig. 16.3.)

20. Canaille—riff-raff, rabble.

21. "In principio . . ."—the beginning of the Last Gospel. These verses were thought to have supernatural powers, and were used as greeting, blessing, and the like.

22. "Love-days" were days set aside for settlement of disputes by arbitration; the clergy were often the judges.

23. A short cape or cloak.

Merchant

The merchant, next:—with forked beard, and girt
In livery, high on his horse he sat,
Upon his head a Flemish beaver hat;
His boots were clasped up in the latest mode;
He spoke in serious fashion as he rode,
Referring always to his gains in gold.
He wished, he said, to have the sea patrolled
From Middleburgh across to Orewell.[24]
A money-changer, he could buy or sell;
This worthy man knew how his wits to set:
No one ever knew he was in debt,
So well he managed all the deals he made,
His sales and bargains, and his tricks of trade.
He was a worthy man, in every way;
But what his name, I never heard men say!

Clerk

A clerk of Oxford rode with us also,
Who turned to logic-study long ago;
His horse was lean and skinny as a rake,
And he was not so fat, I'll undertake!
But hollow-looking, hungry evermore;
Quite threadbare were the shabby clothes he wore,
For he had found as yet no benefice,
Nor was so worldly as to hold office.
For he had rather have, at his bed's head,
A score of books, all bound in black or red,
Of Aristotle and philosophy
Than rich robes, fiddle, or gay psaltery.
And yet philosophy, if truth be told,
Had brought him in but very little gold,
But all that willing friends to him had lent
On books and learning eagerly he spent;
When friends helped with his schooling, then for those
He'd pray in earnest, for their souls' repose.
Of study he took every care and heed;
Not a word he spoke more than was need;
Then what he said was formal, reverent,
Short and to the point, of high intent;
Pertaining unto virtue was his speech;
And gladly would he learn, and gladly teach.

Sergeant-at-law

A sergeant of the law, who used to go
Full many a time to St. Paul's portico,[25]
There was also, of richest excellence;
Discreet he was and of great reverence.
—At least he seemed so, for his words were wise.
He often sat as justice in assize,[26]
By full commission or in his own right.
His learning and his fame were more than slight,
So he had fees, and robes, abundantly.
Nowhere a greater purchaser[27] than he.

Provisions of the law so well he knew
That none could quibble with the deeds he drew.
But no one does as much as this man does—
And yet, he seemed much busier than he was . . .
From William's day[28] he knew each court decision
In every case, by heart, and with precision.
His documents were drawn up so that none
Could find a fault or loop-hole—not a one;
The Statutes he'd recite, and all by rote,
He rode quite simply in a medley coat,
Girt with a belt of striped silk. No more
I have to tell of what this Sergeant wore.

Franklin

With him a franklin rode, whose beard was white
As any daisy, and his face was bright
And ruddy: sanguine, one would call the man.
He loved a wine-sop as the day began.
He liked to live in comfort and in joy;
Truly, he was Epicurus' boy,
Who stoutly held that comfort—that is, pleasure—
Was of happiness the only measure.
A householder, and a great, was he;
He was St. Julian[29] in his own country.
His bread and ale were uniformly fine;
No man was better stocked than he with wine;
Baked meats were never lacking at his place—
Both fish and flesh—or he'd have felt disgrace!
It snowed in his house both of meat and drink,
Of every good thing that a man can think.
According to the season of the year,
So changed his food, and all his table-cheer;
Fat partridges he kept on his preserve,
And fishponds stocked, his table well to serve.
Woe to the cook, unless his sauce were fine,
And sharp and tasty, and the meal on time!
His covered table was not put away
But stood in readiness the live-long day.
At session,[30] he was lord—no man stood higher—
And many a time he served as Knight-of-Shire.
He wore a knife, and purse—made all of silk—,
Hung from his girdle, white as morning milk.
He'd served as sheriff, and county auditor;
Nowhere was a more worthy vavasour.[31]

The Five Tradesmen

A haberdasher, and a carpenter,
A weaver, dyer, and an arras-maker,
—All these were clad in the same livery
Of one great dignified fraternity;
All fresh and new the gear they wore, it seemed;
Not with brass their knives and trimmings gleamed,
But silver, and fine work in every part;
Their belts and purses were in style, and smart.
Important citizens, enough, were all
These men, to sit on dais in guild-hall,

---

24. The port of Middleburgh, just off the coast of Netherlands, was just opposite the English port of Harwich (then called "Orewell"). The merchant was probably engaged (among other things!) in the wool trade, and desired protection for his shipping.

25. The porch of St. Paul's Cathedral was a traditional meeting-place for lawyers.

26. Assize: session of the court.

27. Purchaser—a buyer of land. Does Chaucer imply that the Sergeant is desirous of becoming a landed gentleman, or that he is a land-speculator?

---

28. The Sergeant knew the law clear back to the conquest—the statutes of William the Conqueror.

29. St. Julian is the patron saint of hospitality.

30. These were probably sessions of the Justices of the Peace, not the big assizes.

31. Vavasour—a substantial landholder.

And anyone of them, it's safe to state,
Was wise enough to be a magistrate;
They certainly had goods enough, and rent;
And, I'm sure, their wives would give assent,
For otherwise they would have been in blame;
It's good to hear a "Madam" with one's name,
And lead the way at church, and to be seen
With mantle borne, as royal as a queen!

Cook

A cook was in their party, to prepare
Their favorite dishes, foods both rich and rare:
Chickens, marrow-bones, and tarts well-flavored.
Many a draught of London ale he'd savored.
He knew how to roast, boil, broil, and fry,
Make soups and sauces hot, and bake a pie.
A pity was it, so it seemed to me,
That on his shin an ulcerous sore had he.
His blanc-mange[32] would be rated with the best.

Shipman

A shipman was there, living far to west
—For all I know he came from Dartmouth town.
He rode as best he could a nag; his gown
Of falding[33] rough hung clear down to his knee;
A dagger hanging on a lace had he
About his neck, beneath his arm and down.
Hot summer suns had made his hue all brown;
A boon companion was this salty tar.
He'd helped himself to many a good wine jar
From Bordeaux, while below his owners slept.
Fine scruple was a thing he never kept.
In sea-fights, if he got the upper hand,
By water he sent them home to every land.
But no man, in his skill to reckon tides,
His streams, his chance and all besides,
His harbors, and his moons, and navigation;
From Hull to Carthage had his reputation.
Bold he was, but wise, in undertaking;
Many a tempest set his beard to shaking!
And he knew all the havens as they were
From Gotland to the Cape of Finisterre,[34]
And every creek in Brittany and Spain.
His barge was called the good ship "Madeleine."

Physician

A doctor of physic, known both far and near,
Was with us; nowhere could you find his peer,
In surgery or physic; what is more,
Well-grounded in astrology's deep lore,
He treated patients for the better part
By horoscope and such-like magic art.
For he knew how to forecast, by his spell,
The ascendant planets that would make them well.
He knew the cause of every malady,
Whether of cold or hot or moist or dry,[35]
Where engendered, from what humor traced;
He was a doctor of much skill and taste.

The cause once known, and of the source once sure,
He quickly brought the sick man to his cure.
And he had ready his apothecaries
To send him potent drugs and lectuaries[36]—
For each assisted other, gold to gain;
Their friendship was no new one, that is plain!
—This doctor knew old Esculapius,
The Greek Deiscorides, and ancient Rufus,
Hippocrates, Galen, Hali the Saracen,
Serapion, and Rhazes, Avicen,
Averroes, Bernard, Constantine,
Gatesden, Gilbert, John the Damascene.[37]
And in his diet temperate was he;
It was not full of superfluity,
But wholesome, one of healthful nourishment.
Bible-study was not this man's bent.
He dressed in costly colors, red and blue,
With taffeta and silken linings, too;
And yet he was a man to hate expense.
He kept what he had earned in pestilence;
And since, in physic, gold's a cordial, he
Found gold was what he loved especially!

Wife of Bath

A goodwife came from Bath, that ancient city,
But she was rather deaf; and that's a pity.
Her skill in making cloth, I hear, was such
That, as they say, she wove "to beat the Dutch."[38]
In all the parish never a woman came
To offering before this worthy dame—
But if there did, so much enraged was she
That she lost all her Christian charity!
Her kerchiefs were of finest weave, and dear;
They must have weighed a full ten pounds, or near,
That on a Sunday covered up her head.
Her hose[39] were fancy-fine, of scarlet red,
And tightly tied, her shoes were soft and new.
Her face was bold, and fair, and red of hue.
She was a worthy woman all her life;
To husbands five this woman had been wife,
Not counting other company in youth;
There's no need now to speak of that, in truth!
Three times to Jerusalem she'd been;
Full many a distant stream her feet were in . . .
To Rome she'd been, and gone to far Boulogne,
In Spain to Santiago, to Cologne;
She knew a lot of wandering by the way.
Gap-toothed this goodwife was, the truth to say.
Easily her ambling horse she sat,
With flowing wimple—on her head a hat
As broad as is a buckler or a shield;
A foot-mantle left her ample hips concealed;
And on her feet she wore well-sharpened spurs.
The gift of laughter and of fun was hers.
Love's remedies she knew, and not by chance;
She knew first-hand the art of that old dance.

---

32. Not like the modern pudding, but a compound of minced capon, almonds, cream, sugar, and flour!

33. Falding—coarse woolen cloth with shaggy nap.

34. That is, from Sweden to the western tip of France.

35. The reference is to the theory of the "bodily humors," or fluids, and their effect on the health and temperament of the person.

36. Lectuaries—more properly, electuaries. Medicine in a sticky or sirupy base, originally meant to be "licked up" by the patient!

37. This impressive list is to indicate that the doctor was thoroughly versed in all the medical authorities, ancient and "modern." It seems curious to a modern reader to find among his qualifications that he is an excellent astrologer.

38. Chaucer says "She passed hem of Ypres and of Gaunt"—the Low Countries were famous for textiles.

39. Not stockings, but gaiters or leggings.

Parson

A good religious man went on this ride,
A parish priest, who served the countryside;
Poor in money, rich in holy work,
A very learned scholar was this clerk.
The gospel of Our Lord he strove to preach,
And tried his poor parishioners to teach.
Benign he was, hard-working, diligent,
In adverse seasons patiently content,
As he had proved on more than one occasion.
He did not threaten excommunication
When poor folk could not pay their tithes; instead,
The little that he had he'd share, his bread
As well as money, with a cheerful heart.
Contentment with a little was his art.
Tho wide his parish, houses far asunder,
He'd not neglect, in spite of rain or thunder,
The afflicted in mind, body, or estate,
The farthest in his parish, small or great;
Staff in hand, he'd visit them, on foot.
This fine example to his flock he put,
That first he acted; afterward he taught.
From out the Gospel these words he had caught.
This figure he had added thereunto:
"If fine gold rust, what shall poor iron do?"
For if the priest be foul, in whom we trust,
No wonder if the ignorant people rust;
A shame it is, and brings the priest to mock—
A shitty shepherd, tending a clean flock!
Rather should a priest example give,
By his clean living, how his sheep should live.
He never set his benefice to hire
And left his sheep encumbered in the mire,
Running up to London, to St. Paul's,
Singing paid requiems within those walls;
Nor in some brotherhood withdrew, alone;
But caring for his flock he stayed at home,
So that no wolf his helpless sheep might harry;
He was a shepherd, not a mercenary.
A virtuous man and holy was he, then,
Not arrogant in scolding sinful men,
Not haughty in his speech, or too divine,
But prudent in his teaching and benign.
To draw the folk to heaven by kindliness
And good example was his business.
But then, if any one were obstinate,
Whoever he was, of high or low estate,
He'd scold him sharply, raise a mighty row;
Nowhere was there a better priest, I vow.
No hankering after pomp and reverence,
No putting on of airs, and no pretence;
The lore of Christ and His apostles true
He taught; but what he preached, he'd do.

Plowman

With him there was a plowman, his own brother,
Who'd loaded many a cart with dung; no other
Was a worker good and true as he,
Living in peace and perfect charity.
God he loved best, with his entire soul,
At all times, whether he knew joy or dole;
And next, as Christ commands, he loved his neighbor.
For he would thresh, or ditch, or dig, and labor
For Jesus' sake, without a thot of pay,
To help poor folk, if in his power it lay.
Cheerfully, in full, his tithes he paid
Both on his goods, and what by work he made.

In tabard clad, he rode an old gray mare.
—(A miller and a reeve were also there,
A summoner, also, and a pardoner,
A manciple and I—that's all there were.)

Miller

The miller was a big and hefty lout,
Brawny, burly, big of bone, and stout.
Against all comers, as events turned out,
He won the ram[40] at every wrestling-bout,
Stocky, broad-shouldered, in build a battering-ram,
There was no door he couldn't tear from jamb
Or break it, running at it with his head.
His beard like any sow or fox was red,
And broad as any spade, and cut off short,
Right atop his nose he had a wart;
In it stood a little tuft of hairs,
Red as the bristles in an old sow's ears.
As for his nostrils, they were black and wide;
A sword and buckler bore he by his side.
His big mouth like a furnace needed stoking:
He was a jesting clown whose bawdy joking
Mostly ran to sin: it wasn't nice.
From the grain he ground he'd steal—and then toll
     thrice;
Good millers have a golden thumb, it's said . . .
A white coat, and a blue hood on his head,
He wore; and with his bagpipe's merry sound
He cheered us as we started, outward-bound.

Manciple

There was a manciple[41] from the Inns of Court[42]
To whom all purchasers could well resort
To learn to buy supplies in large amount;
For whether he bought by cash, or on account,
He watched his dealings with so close an eye
That he came out ahead in every try.
Now is it not indeed by God's own grace
That he, uneducated, could outface
His masters—that heap of learned men?
His employers numbered three times ten,
Legal experts, with good sense endowed:
—There must have been a dozen in the crowd
Worthy to be stewards of rent or land
Of any lord in England, to help him stand
Within his income, if he only would,
In honor, out of debt, all to the good,
Or help him live as sparsely as desired:
Why, they could help a county, as required,
In any kind of case that might befall:—
And yet this manciple could beat them all.

Reeve

The reeve, a scrawny, peevish man was he;
His beard was shaved as close as close could be;
His hair was shorn off short around his ears,
His top docked like a priest's, so it appears.
His legs were very long and very lean,
Thin as a stick; no calf could there be seen.
He managed well the granary and bin;
No auditor could get ahead of him.
And he could estimate, by drought and rain,
The yield he could expect of seed and grain.

---

40. The customary wrestling prize.
41. Steward, or purchasing agent.
42. The lodgings of the lawyers.

His lord's sheep, cows, and other stock,
The swine and horses, and the poultry-flock,
Were wholly in his hands to manage well,
And on his oath the reckoning to tell,
Ever since his lord reached twenty years.
No man could ever find him in arrears.
There was no agent, shepherd, hired hand,
Whose tricks he didn't know or understand;
They feared him, everyone, as they feared death.
His dwelling place stood fair upon the heath,
But sheltered was his place with green trees' shade.
Far better bargains than his lord he made;
Richly he had feathered his own nest.
He knew the way to please his master best,
By giving him, or lending, his own goods,
And getting not mere thanks, but coats and hoods.
In youth, he'd learned a trade—he was a wright;
In carpentry he was a skillful wight.
This reeve's good horse rode at an easy trot;
A dapple-gray he was; his name was Scot.
His long surcoat of Persian blue was made,
And by his side he bore a rusty blade.
Of Norfolk was this reeve of whom I tell,
From just outside a town called Baldeswell.
He tucked up all his garments like a friar,
And rode the hindmost: Such was his desire.

Summoner

A summoner[43] was there with us in that place,
Who had a fire-red cherubic face,
All pimply, full of whelks; his eyes were narrow,
And he was hot and lecherous as a sparrow,
With black and scabby brows, and scanty beard:
His was the sort of face that children feared.
There was no mercury nor brimstone, salve
Of tartar, lead, or borax, that could have
The strength to rid him of the lumps and knobs
Disfiguring his face in ugly gobs;
These acneous pimples covered both his cheeks.
And he was fond of garlic, onions, leeks;
He loved to drink strong wine, as red as blood;
Then spoke and cried as one demented would.
And having drunk his wine, and feeling gay,
Then not a word but Latin would he say;
—He knew a few expressions—two or three—
That he had picked up, out of some decree—
No wonder, for he heard it every day:
And everybody knows that even a jay
Can learn to call out "Wat!" as well as the Pope!
But when he tried with other things to cope,
His slender stock of learning would give out:
"Questio quid juris!"[44] he would shout.
He was a noble rascal, and a kind;
A better fellow would be hard to find.
He would arrange it, for a quart of wine,
For a friend of his to keep a concubine
The whole year thru, and never get in trouble;
Oh, he was very good at dealings double!
And if he liked a person whom he saw,
He'd teach that person not to stand in awe
Nor fear, for what he did, the archdeacon's curse—
Why, does a man's soul live within his purse?

Yet purse alone can suffer penalty:
"Purse is the archdeacon's hell," said he.
(But well I know he lied in saying so;
Such curses ought the guilty men forego.
As absolution saves, so curses slay;
From all *Significavits*,[45] stay away!)
And at his mercy, in his tender charge,
Were young folks of the diocese at large;
He knew their secrets; they were easily led.
He had set a garland on his head
So large it would have served for an ale-stake.[46]
A buckler he had made him of a cake.

Pardoner

With him a noble pardoner rode, his pal
And peer (his patron-house was Ronceval),[47]
Who straight from Rome had come—or so said he—
And loud he sang, "Come hither, love, to me!"
The summoner added, in the bass, a ground:
No trumpet had one half so loud a sound.
The pardoner had yellow hair, like wax,
That hung as limp as does a bunch of flax;
Stringily his locks hung from his head,
So that his shoulders were all overspread.
But thin it lay, in hanks there, one by one.
No hood he wore; he left it off, for fun,
Trussed up in his bag. It seemed to him
That thus he rode in fashion's latest whim,
Uncovered—save for cap—his head all bare.
Staring eyes he had, just like a hare.
A vernicle he'd sewed upon his cap.
His wallet lay before him, in his lap,
Brimful of pardons, hot from Rome, please note!
Small the voice he had, just like a goat.
He had no beard: nor ever would, in truth:
As it were fresh-shaved, his face was smooth;
I think he was a gelding—or a mare.
But of his trade, from Berwyck clear to Ware
Was never such a pardoner as this lad!
In his bag a pillow-case he had
Which—so he claimed—was once Our Lady's veil—
He said he had a fragment of the sail
That once St. Peter used, in days of yore,
Before Our Lord gave him new work, ashore!
He had a cross of latten,[48] set with stones,
And in a glass jar carried some pig's bones.
But with these silly "relics," when he spied
Some simple priest out in the country-side,
On such a day more money would he win
Than in two months the parson could fetch in;
And thus, with flattery and lying mock,
He'd fool the priest and all his simple flock.
But give the devil his due; for, when all's past,
In church he was a great ecclesiast;
Well knew he how to read a Bible story,
But especially well he sang the offertory;
For well he knew that when the song was sung,
He then would preach, and sharpen up his tongue,
To win their money from the gullible crowd;
That's why he sang so merrily and loud.

---

43. Process-server or bailiff for the ecclesiastical court, usually presided over by the archdeacon.

44. "The question is, what part of the law applies?"—a lawyer's technicality.

---

45. *Significavit*—the opening word in a summons to appear before the ecclesiastical court.

46. Ale was advertised by a bunch of greens, hanging on a stake or pole above the door.

47. A London hospital.

48. Cheap metal.

Now I've told you briefly, clause by clause,
The state, the number and array and cause
In which assembled was this company
In Southwerk at this noble hostelry
That's called the Tabard Inn, right near the Bell.

The Reeve's Tale from
THE CANTERBURY TALES
Chaucer

Just as Chaucer gave a very wide view of the population of the people of the late Middle Ages in his
Prolog, in the stories that they tell during the pilgrimage, he presents many of the types of literature
of the time. "The Reeve's Tale," like the preceding
"Miller's Tale," is a *fabliau,* a type of boisterous and
bawdy story popular at the time and, in fact, most any
other time. A manager on a large country estate, Oswald the Reeve is shrewd, cunning, and bad tempered. In his early days he was a carpenter, which
explains why he became incensed by the Miller's version of a foolish old carpenter who was cuckolded by
his young and lively wife. Furthermore, the Reeve was
old and, as he said in his Prologue (not given here),
is now like everyone else who "knows that when a
man no longer has the ability to do a certain thing, he
spends his time talking about it." Prodded by the Host
to cease his sermonizing, the Reeve begins his story,
warning that his language will be just as rough as that
used by the Miller. Not surprisingly, the foolish victim
of the Reeve's tale is a miller. The modern English
translation is by Neville Coghill.

At Trumpington, not far from Cambridge town,
    A bridge goes over where the brook runs down
And by that brook there stands a mill as well.
And it's God's truth that I am going to tell.
    There was a miller lived there many a day
As proud as any peacock and as gay;
He could play bag-pipes too, fish, mend his gear,
And turn a lathe, and wrestle, and poach deer.
And at his belt he carried a long blade,
Trenchant it was as any sword that's made,
And in his pouch a jolly little knife.
No one dared touch him, peril of his life.
He had a Sheffield dagger in his hose.
Round was his face and puggish was his nose;
Bald as an ape he was. To speak more fully,
He was a thorough-going market bully
Whom none dared lay a hand on or come near
Without him swearing that they'd buy it dear.
    He was a thief as well of corn and meal,
And sly at that; his habit was to steal.
Simpkin the Swagger he was called in scorn.
He had a wife and she was nobly born;
Her father was the parson of the town;
A dowery of brass dishes he put down
In order to have Simpkin his relation.
The nuns had given her an education.
Simpkin would take no woman, so he said,
Unless she were a virgin and well-bred,
To save the honour of his yeoman stock;
And she was proud, pert as a magpie cock.

It was a proper sight to see the pair
On holidays, what with him strutting there
In front of her, his hood about his head,
And she behind him all decked out in red,
Like Simpkin's hose, for scarlet-red he had 'em.
No one dared call her anything but 'Madam',
And there was no one bold enough to try
A bit of fun with her or wink an eye,
Unless indeed he wanted Sim the Swagger
To murder him with cutlass, knife or dagger,
For jealous folk are dangerous, you know,
At least they want their wives to think them so.
And then her birth was smirched to say the least;
Being the daughter of a celibate priest
She must maintain her dignity, of which
She had as much as water in a ditch.
She was a sneering woman and she thought
That ladies should respect her, so they ought,
What with her well-connected family,
And education in a nunnery.
    They had a daughter too between them both,
She was a girl of twenty summers' growth;
But that was all except a child they had
Still in the cradle, but a proper lad.
The wench was plump, well-grown enough to pass,
With a snub nose and eyes as grey as glass;
Her rump was broad, her breasts were round and high;
She'd very pretty hair, I will not lie.
The parson of the town, for she was fair,
Intended to appoint the girl as heir
To all his property in house and land
And he was stiff with suitors to her hand.
He purposed to bestow her if he could
Where blood and ancient lineage made it good.
For Holy Church's goods should be expended
On Holy Church's blood, so well-descended,
And holy blood should have what's proper to it
Though Holy Church should be devoured to do it.
    This miller levied toll beyond a doubt
On wheat and malt from all the land about,
Particularly from a large-sized College
In Cambridge, Solar Hall. 'Twas common knowledge
They sent their wheat and malt to him to grind it.
Happened one day the man who ought to mind it,
The college manciple, lay sick in bed,
And some reported him as good as dead.
On hearing which the miller robbed him more
A hundred times than he had robbed before;
For up till then he'd only robbed politely,
But now he stole outrageously, forthrightly.
    The Warden scolded hard and made a scene,
But there! The miller didn't give a bean,
Blustered it out and swore it wasn't so.
    Two poor young Bible-clerks or students, though,
Lived in this College (that of which I spoke).
Headstrong they were and eager for a joke
And simply for the chance of sport and play
They went and plagued the Warden night and day
Just for a little leave to spend the morn
Watching the miller grind their meal and corn,
And each was ready to engage his neck
The miller couldn't rob them half a peck
Of corn by trickery, nor yet by force;
And in the end he gave them leave of course.
    One was called John and Alan was the other,
Both born in the same village, name of Strother,
Far in the north, I cannot tell you where.

Alan collected all his gear with care,
Loaded his corn upon a horse he had,
And off he went with John the other lad,
Each with his sword and buckler by his side.
John knew the way—he didn't need a guide—
Reaches the mill and down the sack he flings.
    Alan spoke first: 'Well, Simon, lad, how's things?
And how's your canny daughter and your wife?'
Says Simpkin, 'Welcome, Alan! Odds my life,
It's John as well! What are you up to here?'
'By God,' said John. 'Needs-must has got no peer,
And it behoves a man that has nie servant
To work, as say the learned and observant.
Wor[49] Manciple is like enough to dee,
Such aches and torments in his teeth has he;
So Alan here and I have brought wor sack
Of corn for grinding and to bring it back.
Help us get home as quickly as ye can.'
'It shall be done,' said he, 'as I'm a man.
What'll you do while I've the job in hand?'
'By God,' said John, 'I have a mind to stand
Right by the hopper here and watch the corn
As it gans in. Never since I was born
Saw I a hopper wagging to and fro.'
    Alan spoke up: 'Eh, John, and will ye so?
Then I shall stand below a short way off
And watch the meal come down into the trough;
I need no more than that by way of sport,
For John, in faith, I'm one of the same sort
And diven't knaa nowt of milling, same as ye.'
    The miller smiled at their simplicity
And thought, 'It's just a trick, what they're about
They think that nobody can catch them out,
But by the Lord I'll blear their eyes a bit
For all their fine philosophy and wit.
The more they try to do me on the deal,
When the time comes, the more I mean to steal.
Instead of flour they shall be given bran.
"The greatest scholar is not the wisest man",
As the wolf said in answer to the mare.
Them and their precious learning! Much I care.'
    And when he saw his chance he sidled out
Into the yard behind and looked about
Without their noticing until at last
He found their horse where they had made him fast
Under an arbour just behind the mill.
    Up to the horse he goes with quiet skill
And strips the bridle off him there and then.
And when the horse was loose, off to the fen
Through thick and thin, and whinneying 'Weehee!'
He raced to join the wild mares running free.
    The miller then went back, and did not say
A word of this, but passed the time of day
With John and Alan till their corn was ground;
And when the meal was fairly sacked and bound,
John wandered out and found their horse was gone.
'Good Lord! Help! Help! Come quickly!' shouted John,
'Wor horse is lost, Alan! The devil's in it!
God's bones, man, use you legs! Come out this minute!
Lord save us all, the Warden's palfrey's lost.'
    Alan forgot his meal and corn and cost,
Abandoning frugality and care.
'What's that?' he shouted, 'Palfrey? Which way? Where?'
    The miller's wife ran clucking like a hen
Towards them, saying, 'Gone off to the fen
To the wild mares as fast as he can go.

---

49. *Wor* means 'our.' John is speaking the north of England
dialect.

Curse on the clumsy hand that tied him so!
Should have known better how to knit the reins.'
John said, 'Bad luck to it. Alan, for Christ's pains,
Put down your sword, man; so will I; let's gan!
We'll rin him like a roe together, man!
God's precious heart! He cannot scape up all!
Why didn't you put the palfrey in the stall?
You must be daft, bad luck to you! Haway!'
And off ran John and Alan in dismay,
Towards the fen as fast as they could go.
    And when the miller saw that this was so,
A good half-bushel of their flour he took
And gave it over to his wife to cook.
'I think,' he said, 'these lads have had a fright.
I'll pluck their beards. Yes, Let 'em read and write,
But none the less a miller is their match.
Look at them now! Like children playing catch.
Won't be an easy job to get him, though!'
    These foolish Bible-clerks ran to and fro
And shouted, 'Woa, lad, stand! . . . Look out behind!
Whistle him up . . . I've got him . . . watch it . . . *mind!*'
But to be brief, it wasn't until night
They caught the palfrey, hunt him as they might
Over the fens, he ran away so fast;
But in a ditch they captured him at last.
    Weary and wet, like cattle in the rain,
Came foolish John and Alan back again.
Said John, 'Alas the day that I was born!
We've earned nowt here but mockery and scorn.
Wor corn is stolen and they'll call us fools,
Warden and all wor meäts in the Schools,
And most of all the miller. What a day!'
    So back they went, John grousing all the way,
Towards the mill and put the horse in byre.
They found the miller sitting by the fire,
For it was night, too late for going home,
And, for the love of God, they begged a room
For shelter and they proffered him their penny.
'A room?' the miller said. 'There isn't any.
There's this, such as it is; we'll share it then.
My house is small, but you are learned men
And by your arguments can make a place
Twenty foot broad as infinite as space.
Take a look round and see if it will do,
Or make it bigger with your parley-voo.'
'Well, Simon, you must have your little joke
And, by St. Cuthbert, that was fairly spoke!
Well, people have a proverb to remind them
To bring their own, or take things as they find them,'
Said John. 'Dear host, do get us out the cup;
A little meat and drink would cheer us up.
We'll give ye the full payment, on my word.
No empty-handed man can catch a bird;
See, here's the silver, ready to be spent.'
    Down into Trumpington the daughter went
For bread and ale; the miller cooked a goose,
And tied their horse up lest it should get loose
Again, and in his chamber made a bed
With clean white sheets and blankets fairly spread,
Ten foot from his, upon a sort of shelf,
His daughter had a bed all by herself
Quite close in the same room; they were to lie
All side by side, no help for it, and why?
Because there was no other in the house.
    They supped and talked and had a fine carouse
And drank a lot of ale, the very best.
Midnight or thereabout they went to rest.

Properly pasted was this miller's head,
Pale-drunk he was, he'd passed the stage of red;
Hiccupping through his nose he talked and trolled
As if he'd asthma or a heavy cold.
To bed he goes, his wife and he together;
She was as jolly as a jay in feather,
Having well wet her whistle from the ladle.
And by her bed she planted down the cradle
To rock the baby or to give it sup.
    When what was in the crock had been drunk up,
To bed went daughter too, and thereupon
To bed went Alan and to bed went John.
That was the lot; no sleeping-draught was needed.
The miller had taken so much booze unheeded,
He snorted like a cart-horse in his sleep
And vented other noises, loud and deep.
His wife joined in the chorus hot and strong;
Two furlongs off you might have heard their song.
The wench was snoring too, for company.
    Alan the clerk in all this melody
Gave John a poke and said, 'Are ye awake?
Did ye ever hear sich sang for guidness sake?
There's family prayers for ye among they noddies!
Wild fire come doon and burn them up, the bodies!
Who ever heard a canny thing like that?
The devil take their souls for what they're at!
All this lang neet I shall na get nie rest.
    'But never ye mind, all shall be for the best;
I tell ye, John, as sure as I'm a man,
I'm going to have that wench there, if I can!
The law grants easement when things gan amiss,
For, John, there is a law that gans like this:
"If in one point a person be aggrieved,
Then in another he shall be relieved."
    'Wor corn is stolen, nivvor doubt of that;
Ill-luck has followed us in all we're at,
And since no compensation has been offered
Against wor loss, I'll take the easement proffered.
God's soul, it shall be so indeed, none other?'
    John whispered back to him, 'Be careful, brother,
The miller is a torble man for slaughter;
If he should wake and find ye with his daughter
He might do injury to you and me.'
'Injury? Him! I coont him nat a flea!'
    Alan rose up; towards the wench he crept.
The wench lay flat upon her back and slept,
And ere she saw him, he had drawn so nigh
It was too late for her to give a cry.
To put it briefly, they were soon at one.
Now, Alan, play! For I will speak of John.
    John lay there still for quite a little while,
Complaining and lamenting in this style:
'A bloody joke . . . Lord, what a chance to miss!
I shall be made a monkey of for this!
My meät has got some comfort for his harms,
He has the miller's daughter in his arms;
He took his chance and now his needs are sped,
I'm but a sack of rubbish here in bed.
And when this jape is told in time to come
They'll say I was a softie and a bum!
I'll get up too and take what chance I may,
For God helps those that help theirsels, they say.'
    He rises, steals towards the cradle, lifts it,
And stepping softly back again, he shifts it
And lays it by his bed upon the floor.

The miller's wife soon after ceased to snore,
Began to wake, rose up, and left the room,
And coming back she groped about in gloom,
Missing the cradle, John had snatched away.
'Lord, Lord,' she said, 'I nearly went astray
And got into the student's bed. . . . How dreadful!
There would have been foul doings. What a bed-ful!'
    At last she gropes to where the cradle stands,
And so by fumbling upwards with her hands
She found the bed and thinking nought but good,
Since she was certain where the cradle stood,
Yet knew not where she was, for it was dark,
She well and fairly crept in with the clerk,
Then lay quite still and tried to go to sleep.
John waited for a while, then gave a leap
And thrust himself upon this worthy wife.
It was the merriest fit in all her life,
For John went deep and thrust away like mad.
It was a jolly life for either lad
Till the third morning cock began to sing.
    Alan grew tired as dawn began to spring;
He had been hard at work the long, long night.
'Bye-bye,' he said, 'sweet Molly. . . . Are ye a'right?
The day has come, I cannot linger here,
But ever mair in life and death, my dear,
I am your own true clerk, or strike me deid!'
'Good-bye, my sweet,' she whispered, 'take good
        heed . . .
But first I'll tell you something, that I will!
When you are riding homewards past the mill
By the main entrance-door, a bit behind it,
There's the half-bushel cake—you're sure to find it—
And it was made out of the very meal
You brought to grind and I helped father steal. . . .
And, dearest heart, God have you in his keeping!'
And with that word she almost burst out weeping.
    Alan got up and thought, 'Dawn's coming on,
Better get back and creep in beside John.'
But there he found the cradle in his way.
'By God,' he thought, 'I nearly went astray!
My heed is tottering with my work to-neet,
That'll be why I cannot gan areet!
This cradle tells me I have lost my tether;
You must be miller and his wife together.'
    And back he went, groping his weary way
And reached the bed in which the miller lay,
And thinking it was John upon the bed
He slid in by the miller's side instead,
Grabbing his neck, and with no more ado
Said, 'Shake yourself, wake up, you pig's-head, you!
For Christ's soul, listen! O such noble games
As I have had! I tell you, by St. James,
Three times the neet, from midnight into morn,
The miller's daughter helped me grind my corn
While you've been lying in your cowardly way . . .'
'You scoundrel!' said the miller, 'What d'you say?
You beast! You treacherous blackguard! Filthy rat!
God's dignity! I'll murder you for that!
How dare you be so bold as to fling mud
Upon my daughter, come of noble blood?'
    He grabbed at Alan by his Adam's apple,
And Alan grabbed him back in furious grapple
And clenched his fist and bashed him on the nose.
Down miller's breast a bloody river flows
Onto the floor, his nose and mouth all broke;
They wallowed like two porkers in a poke,
And up and down and up again they go
Until the miller tripped and stubbed his toe,
Spun round and fell down backwards on his wife.

She had heard nothing of this foolish strife,
For she had fallen asleep with John the clerk,
Weary from all their labours in the dark.
The miller's fall started her out of sleep.
'Help!' she screamed. 'Holly cross of Bromeholme keep
Us! Lord! Into thy hands! To Thee I call!
Simon, wake up! The devil's among us all!
My heart is bursting, help! I'm nearly dead,
One's on my stomach, and another's on my head.
Help, simpkin, help! These nasty clerks are fighting!'

    Up started John, he needed no inciting,
And groped about the chamber to and fro
To find a stick; she too was on the go
And, knowing the corners better than them all,
Was first to find one leaning by the wall;
And by a little shaft of shimmering light
That shone in through a hole—the moon was bright—
Although the room was almost black as pitch
She saw them fight, not knowing which was which;
But there was something white that caught her eye
On seeing which she peered and gave a cry,
Thinking it was the night-cap of the clerk.

    Raising her stick, she crept up in the dark
And, hoping to hit Alan, it was her fate
To smite the miller on his shining pate,
And down he went, shouting, 'O God, I'm dying!'

    The clerks then beat him well and left him lying
And throwing on their clothes they took their horse
And their ground meal and off they went, of course,
And as they passed the mill they took the cake
Made of their meal the girl was told to bake.

    And thus the bumptious miller was well beaten
And done out of the supper they had eaten,
And done out of the money that was due
For grinding Alan's corn, who beat him too.
His wife was plumbed, so was his daughter. Look!
That comes of being a miller and a crook!

    I heard this proverb when I was a kid,
'Do evil and be done by as you did'.
Tricksters will get a tricking, so say I;
And God that sits in majesty on high
Bring all this company, great and small, to Glory!
Thus I've paid out the Miller with my story!

THE ART OF COURTLY LOVE
Andreas Capellanus (fl. 1174–1186)

Countess Marie of Champagne established a Court of
Love at Troyes where Andreas was probably chaplain
to the court, or so he claimed. Andreas was an accomplished writer whose treatise on love provides us with
a vivid and probably accurate picture of courtly life.
Specifically, Andreas intended his manual as a portrayal of the Poitiers court of Marie's mother, Queen
Eleanor of Aquitaine, as it was between 1170 and 1174.

Undoubtedly written by direction of Countess
Marie, the manual is a codification of the etiquette of
love. Andreas combines quotations from classic Latin
writers (mainly Ovid) and the spirit of lyric love poetry by troubadours like Bernart de Ventadorn (see
chap. 12) with his own observation of actual practices, producing a unique work known throughout
Europe in a variety of translations.

Book One
Introduction to the
Treatise on Love

We must first consider what love is, whence it gets its
name, what the effect of love is, between what persons
love may exist, how it may be acquired, retained,
increased, decreased, and ended, what are the signs that
one's love is returned, and what one of the lovers ought
to do if the other is unfaithful.

Chapter I. What Love Is

Love is a certain inborn suffering derived from the sight of
and excessive meditation upon the beauty of the opposite
sex, which causes each one to wish above all things the
embraces of the other and by common desire to carry out
all of love's precepts in the other's embrace.

That love is suffering is easy to see, for before the
love becomes equally balanced on both sides there is no
torment greater, since the lover is always in fear that his
love may not gain its desire and that he is wasting his
efforts. He fears, too, that rumors of it may get abroad, and
he fears everything that might harm it in any way, for
before things are perfected a slight disturbance often
spoils them. If he is a poor man, he also fears that the
woman may scorn his poverty; if he is ugly, he fears that
she may despise his lack of beauty or may give her love to
a more handsome man; if he is rich, he fears that his
parsimony in the past may stand in his way. To tell the
truth, no one can number the fears of one single lover.[50]
This kind of love, then, is a suffering which is felt by only
one of the persons and may be called "single love." But
even after both are in love the fears that arise are just as
great, for each of the lovers fears that what he has
acquired with so much effort may be lost through the
effort of someone else, which is certainly much worse for
a man than if, having no hope, he sees that his efforts are
accomplishing nothing, for it is worse to lose the things
you are seeking than to be deprived of a gain you merely
hope for. The lover fears, too, that he may offend his
loved one in some way; indeed he fears so many things
that it would be difficult to tell them.

That this suffering is inborn I shall show you clearly,
because if you will look at the truth and distinguish
carefully you will see that it does not arise out of any
action; only from the reflection of the mind upon what it
sees does this suffering come. For when a man sees some
woman fit for love and shaped according to his taste, he
begins at once to lust after her in his heart; then the more
he thinks about her the more he burns with love, until he
comes to a fuller meditation. Presently he begins to think
about the fashioning of the woman and to differentiate
her limbs, to think about what she does, and to pry into
the secrets of her body, and he desires to put each part of
it to the fullest use.[51] Then after he has come to this
complete meditation, love cannot hold the reins; but he
proceeds at once to action; straightway he strives to get a
helper and to find an intermediary. He begins to plan how
he may find favor with her, and he begins to seek a place
and a time opportune for talking; he looks upon a brief
hour as a very long year, because he cannot do anything
fast enough to suit his eager mind. It is well known that

---

50. Ovid *Art of Love* II. 517 ff.
51. Compare Ovid *Metamorphoses* VI. 490–93.

many things happen to him in this manner. This inborn suffering comes, therefore, from seeing and meditating. Not every kind of meditation can be the cause of love, an excessive one is required; for a restrained thought does not, as a rule, return to the mind, and so love cannot arise from it.

In Chapter VIII (Book Two), Andreas presents the Rules of Love as the climax of a properly romantic mission. It seems that a knight of Britain cannot win the love of "a certain British lady" until he has brought her the hawk sitting on a golden perch in King Arthur's court. And, he is told,

> you can't get this hawk that you are seeking unless you prove, by a combat in Arthur's palace, that you enjoy the love of a more beautiful lady than any man at Arthur's court has; you can't even enter the palace until you show the guards the hawk's gauntlet, and you can't get this gauntlet except by overcoming two mighty knights in a double combat.

After defeating the pugnacious keeper of a golden bridge, the Briton then vanquishes a giant and rides on to Camelot where he manfully accomplishes the assigned tasks. While seizing the hawk he discovers a written parchment and is told that "This is the parchment on which are written the rules of love which the King of Love . . . pronounced for lovers. You should take it with you and make these rules known to lovers."

These are the rules.
  I. Marriage is no real excuse for not loving.
  II. He who is not jealous cannot love.
  III. No one can be bound by a double love.
  IV. It is well known that love is always increasing or decreasing.
  V. That which a lover takes against the will of his beloved has no relish.
  VI. Boys do not love until they arrive at the age of maturity.
  VII. When one lover dies, a widowhood of two years is required of the survivor.
  VIII. No one should be deprived of love without the very best of reasons.
  IX. No one can love unless he is impelled by the persuasion of love.
  X. Love is always a stranger in the home of avarice.
  XI. It is not proper to love any woman whom one would be ashamed to seek to marry.
  XII. A true lover does not desire to embrace in love anyone except his beloved.
  XIII. When made public love rarely endures.
  XIV. The easy attainment of love makes it of little value; difficulty of attainment makes it prized.
  XV. Every lover regularly turns pale in the presence of his beloved.
  XVI. When a lover suddenly catches sight of his beloved his heart palpitates.
  XVII. A new love puts to flight an old one.[52]
  XVIII. Good character alone makes any man worthy of love.
  XIX. If love diminishes, it quickly fails and rarely revives.
  XX. A man in love is always apprehensive.
  XXI. Real jealousy always increases the feeling of love.
  XXII. Jealousy, and therefore love, are increased when one suspects his beloved.
  XXIII. He whom the thought of love vexes eats and sleeps very little.
  XXIV. Every act of a lover ends in the thought of his beloved.
  XXV. A true lover considers nothing good except what he thinks will please his beloved.
  XXVI. Love can deny nothing to love.
  XXVII. A lover can never have enough of the solaces of his beloved.
  XXVIII. A slight presumption causes a lover to suspect his beloved.
  XXIX. A man who is vexed by too much passion usually does not love.
  XXX. A true lover is constantly and without intermission possessed by the thought of his beloved.
  XXXI. Nothing forbids one woman being loved by two men or one man by two women.

These rules, as I have said, the Briton brought back with him on behalf of the King of Love to the lady for whose sake he endured so many perils when he brought her back the hawk. When she was convinced of the complete faithfulness of this knight and understood better how boldly he had striven, she rewarded him with her love. Then she called together a court of a great many ladies and knights and laid before them these rules of Love, and bade every lover keep them faithfully under threat of punishment by the King of Love. These laws the whole court received in their entirety and promised forever to obey in order to avoid punishment by Love. Every person who had been summoned and had come to the court took home a written copy of the rules and gave them out to all lovers in all parts of the world.

---

52. Compare Cicero *Tusculan Disputations* IV. XXXV.

11
The Medieval Synthesis in Art

Chronological Overview

375–700	Migrations of Germanic and Asiatic tribes[1]
622–732	Islamic conquest of Middle East, western Asia, North Africa, Spain, Portugal
732	Charles Martel turns back Muslims at Poitiers
600–800	Hiberno-Saxon Period; Irish Golden Age
750–900	Carolingian Period
900–1000	Ottonian Period
1000–1150	Romanesque Period in France (until ca. 1200 outside France)
1140–1200	Early Gothic Period
1200–1300	High Gothic Period
1300–1500s	Late Gothic Period; International Style

Islamic Period, 622–

"There is no God but Allah and Mohammed is his prophet." Not a religion of complex beliefs, Islam is based totally on that simple statement; the complexity is in the observance. The Arabic word for submission is *Islam,* the faith; he who submits is a "Muslim," a believer. Submitting unreservedly to an all-powerful God, believers make up a religious community that follows the Koran's detailed rules for every aspect of daily life. Compiled from the writings of the Prophet some twenty years after his death in 632, the Koran is the only authority, the last word in theology, law, and all social institutions. By far the most important textbook in Muslim universities, the Koran may never be translated; the faith has one language and that language is Arabic.

---

1. All dates are approximate except the Charles Martel victory.

Figure 11.1 Koca Sinan, Suleymaniye Camii Mosque, 1550–1557 (foreground); Fatih Camii Mosque, 1463 (background). Istanbul.

Figure 11.2 Ceiling designs, Suleymaniye Camii Mosque

Figure 11.3 Courtyard, El Attarin Medersa, 1323–1325, Fez, Morocco.

Originating in the desert wastes of culturally backward Arabia, a religion as circumscribed as Islam could not have developed a high degree of civilization had it not been for the propagation of the faith by the sword. Unlike most faiths, Islam is a missionary religion (as is Christianity), which launched a *jihad*—a holy war—to conquer half of the known world in a single century. Unified by faith and a common language and immeasurably enriched by contacts with other civilizations, Islam developed and promoted learning and some of the arts from India to the Iberian peninsula.

Strictly limited by the Koran, artistic development was very uneven to put it mildly. Architecture was of paramount importance, particularly in the construction of mosques, but sculpture was, according to Mohammed, idolatrous, a satanic art. Figurative and monumental scale painting were forbidden for similar reasons, leaving only manuscript decoration using organic and geometric designs.

A religion that provides direct access to God through prayers, Islam has no priests, liturgy, or sacraments. Buildings were not needed because praying could be done anywhere, and Mohammed did indeed teach and pray everywhere including his own house. Based on this model, early mosque design evolved into a simple enclosure in which one wall, the *qibla,* faced towards Mecca. A sacred niche, the *mihrab,* was soon added to the qibla, to the right of which was the *minbar,* or pulpit, for readings from the Koran and the Friday sermon. A characteristic feature from the earliest days, the *sahn,* a pool for ritual ablutions, was located in the courtyard. Though *muezzins* (mu–EZ–ins; criers) could call the faithful to prayer from any high place, *minarets,* or tall, slender towers, quickly became standard features of mosque design.

The Fatih Camii Mosque (background, fig. 11.1) was built by Sultan Mehmet II in 1463, ten years after the Ottoman Turks conquered Constantinople. Built on one of the seven hills of Istanbul by Turkey's greatest architect, Koca Sinan, the Suleymaniye Camii Mosque (foreground) honors Sultan Suleyman the

Magnificent. There is no mandatory number of minarets; the only stipulation is that no mosque may have seven minarets like the Great Mosque in Mecca. Patterned after Hagia Sophia (see fig. 8.19), as are most mosques in Istanbul, this massive structure embodies Muslim fascination with complex geometric designs (fig. 11.2). The viewpoint in the illustration is that of a spectator standing on the floor of the mosque and looking straight up at the ceiling. In this view, the central dome is at the bottom and at the top is the half-dome with its circling windows and flanking partial domes. The arches are outlined in red and white stones, and the geometric designs and Arabic calligraphy are brightly lit by the hundreds of windows similar to those in Hagia Sophia (see fig. 8.20).

With the sacred niche—the mihrab—indicating the direction of Mecca, the courtyard of El Attarin Medersa, a Muslim college (fig. 11.3), features the ritual fountain or sahn, panels of glazed faience, and mosaic floors, all with elaborate geometric designs.

Figure 11.4 Interior, The Great Mosque, 785–990, Cordoba, Spain. Now the Cathedral of Cordoba.

Figure 11.5 Portal, Great Mosque, Cordoba

Built by Sultan Abou Said near the end of the golden age of Islamic architecture, El Attarin is an elegant example of delicate, intricate design.

Begun by Caliph Abd al-Rahman in the eighth century, the mosque of the caliphs of Cordoba (fig. 11.4) is so large that a sixteenth-century Christian church was built in its midst. With no axis and thus no focus, the forest of columns—856 in all—symbolizes the worshippers who are as individual as the columns but who are all united in common prayer, part of the great community of believers. The striped

Figure 11.6 Court of the Lions, 1354–1391, The Alhambra, Granada, Spain.

arches are a Muslim invention but the columns were recycled, having been taken from Roman and Christian buildings.

The doorway of the Great Mosque (fig. 11.5) emphasizes the characteristic horseshoe arch of Mozarabic (Spanish Christian) design. Lavishly embellished with mosaics and abstract reliefs, the overall style is best described as Moorish, a synthesis of North African and Spanish styles. One of the glories of Muslim Spain, the Great Mosque was only one of the wonders of Cordoba, itself the most illustrious center of art and learning in all of Europe until its conquest by Christians in 1236.

The ponderous exterior of the palace of the caliphs of Granada, the Alhambra, shields an inner architectural fairyland resonating to the liquid murmer of running water. Because of its desert origins, Islam pictures Hell and Paradise as extensions of the natural environment; Hell is an arid and flaming inferno while Paradise is like an oasis: cool, wet, and lush. Drawing unlimited water from the snows of the Sierra Nevadas, the caliphs built an earthly paradise: delicate, intimate, cooled and soothed by playful fountains and the channels of water coursing throughout the palace, the embodiment of what an Arabian Nights setting should be. A prominent feature of the Alhambra is the Court of the Lions (fig. 11.6) at the center of the most elaborate and ethereal section of the palace. Guarded by rare, for Islam, sculptures of stylized lions, the fountain adds its bubbling sounds to the flowing waters of a fantastic courtyard of delicate columns and arches decorated with tiles and stucco. Lacy arabesques and airy stuccoed ceilings contribute to what is actually a lucid, rhythmic design. Not a single column is both perfectly tapered and precisely vertical, thus symbolizing the imperfections of earthly existence. In other words, even this manufactured Eden is but a defective version of the heavenly paradise to come. The last notable structure built in Moorish Spain, the Alhambra fell to Ferdinand and Isabella in the eventful year of 1492.

Figure 11.7 National Mosque, Kuala Lumpur, Malaysia.

Because they are not bound to a unified liturgy as, for example, Roman Catholic churches are, no two mosques are alike and some, like the Great Mosque at Cordoba, are unique. There are certain distinguishing characteristics, however, that have become conventional. Though a contemporary design in reinforced concrete and marble, the National Mosque (fig. 11.7) is still a recognizable mosque. The dome of the central plan, the freestanding minaret, and the courtyard fountain (not visible here) add up to a modern setting for a very traditional religion.

Hiberno-Saxon Period, ca. 600–800

Though never part of the Roman Empire, Ireland was known by the Latin name *Hibernia,* which later became *Ivernin* in Old Celtic and then *Erin* in Old Irish. Occupied by Celts and Christianized by St. Patrick of Gaul, Ireland was cut off from the continent by the Anglo-Saxon conquest of England. This isolation led to the development of a unique form of Christian monasticism patterned after the solitary hermits of Egypt rather than the urbanized Roman version of Christianity. Founding monasteries in the countryside, Irish monks emphasized a strict ascetic discipline and, unlike the desert saints, a deep devotion to scholarship. Preempting the power of the bishops, Irish monasteries sponsored a remarkable missionary program in England and western Europe which resulted in a spiritual and cultural dominance fittingly called the Irish Golden Age of ca. 600–800.

Manuscripts were produced in abundance to supplement these missionary activities, especially numerous copies of the Bible, all elaborately decorated to signify the supreme importance of the sacred texts. Displaying little interest in the figurative art of Roman Christianity, monks synthesized Celtic and Germanic elements to produce a richly decorated art based on geometric designs and organic abstractions derived from plant and animal forms. Created at a

Figure 11.8 "Cross Page," Bishop Eadfrith (?), *Lindisfarne Gospels,* ca. 698–721. British Museum, London. Reproduced by courtesy of the Trustees of the British Museum.

monastery on the island of Lindisfarne off the east coast of England, the *Lindisfarne Gospels* is a superb example of Hiberno-Saxon decorative art. As meticulous as printed electronic circuitry, the "Cross Page" (fig. 11.8) is a miniature maze of writhing shapes and mirror-image effects highlighted by intertwined dragons and serpents. The Celtic cross spans a page bursting with energy and vitality. With details so fine that they are best studied with a magnifying glass, one wonders how this work was accomplished.

The "X-P (khi-rho) Page" (colorplate 13) is lovely testimony to the masterful use of color to enhance but not compete with either the linear composition or the importance of the gospel text.

The last of the remarkable Hiberno-Saxon illuminated manuscripts, the *Book of Kells* is also the most elaborately decorated. Reduced to the Greek letters XPI (khri), the name of Christ dominates a page swirling with animal and abstract interlaces and geometric decoration (fig. 11.9). Whorls within circles within larger circles dazzle the eye, but closer study reveals two human faces and, on the left vertical of the X, three human figures depicted from the waist up. Near the bottom and to the right of the same vertical is a playful genre scene featuring two cats and four mice.

Figure 11.9 "XPI Page", *Book of Kells,* ca. 760–820. Reproduced by permission of the Board of Trinity College, Dublin.

Figure 11.10 Odo of Metz, Palatine Chapel of Charlemagne, 792–805, Aachen, Germany.

Hiberno-Saxon manuscripts typify the early period of intricate and painstaking Northern craftsmanship, which included weaving, ivory and stone carving, jewelry, and stained glass, a tradition that led to spectacular achievements in the Gothic age and, eventually, to machine design and the industrial revolution. An important factor in the development of Northern crafts may have been climate, for these are mainly indoor activities that could be carried on regardless of the inclement weather of long, dark winters.

Carolingian Art, ca. 750–900

Ruling from 768 to 814 as a Frankish king, Charlemagne saw himself as a successor to the Caesars of Rome, a concept that was reinforced in 800 when the pope crowned him Emperor of the Holy Roman Empire. To his capital at Aachen, Germany, he brought scholars, artists, and craftsmen to help revive classical antiquity. Short-lived but vital for later developments, the Carolingian Renaissance utilized Celtic-Germanic and Mediterranean traditions to produce a Carolingian art that combined classic forms with Christian symbols and subject matter.

Societies tend to develop an architecture based on the availability of building materials, and at that time the vast forests of northern Europe provided an endless supply of wood for the timber-frame construction of private and public buildings. Charlemagne, however, wanted impressive palaces and churches built in the Roman manner, and to do that he had to import southern principles of building in stone. Because there were no local stonemasons, he undoubtedly imported southern masons to work on his buildings and to instruct northern craftsmen, a procedure culminating in the expert stonework of Romanesque and Gothic cathedrals.

One of the few buildings to survive intact from the age of Charlemagne, the chapel of his palace at Aachen (fig. 11.10) is an impressive example of northern stone construction. Designed by Odo of Metz, the first known Northern architect, the chapel is modeled after San Vitale (see colorplate 10), which so impressed Charlemagne during a visit to Ravenna. A revision of San Vitale and not a copy, the chapel is simpler in style but still patterned after the Byzantine central plan. The central octagon is formed by arcades resting on heavy piers. Above this there are tall arches and within them are two levels of decorative columns. As might be expected during the early period of stone construction, the columns and most of the capitals were taken from existing Roman buildings. One would suspect that Charlemagne preferred using columns of the Caesars for his personal chapel.

Figure 11.11 Germigny des Pres, view from the east, 806.

Figure 11.12 Interior, Germigny des Pres

One of the oldest churches in France, Germigny des Pres (fig. 11.11) was erected by Theodolphus, a friend of Charlemagne, and by the emperor's Armenian architect. Taller than the usual Byzantine church, this brick building is topped by a square tower that is capped with a peaked tile roof. Despite destructive attacks by Viking invaders, later called Northmen, and then Normans, the mosaic and much of the structure was preserved and then restored in the nineteenth century. The interior features heavy semicircular arches with a focus from the central altar, which is modern, to the mosaic in the apse (fig. 11.12). Brought back by Charlemagne from Theodoric's palace in Ravenna and composed of 130,000 glass cubes, this is the only Byzantine mosaic in France.

The "Saint Mark" from the *Gospel Book of Archbishop Ebbo of Reimes*, which was painted shortly after Charlemagne's death, derives from a classic model (fig. 11.13). The Hiberno-Saxon influence is discernible in the draperies swirling about the torso in lines as dynamic as those in an Irish manuscript. Rather than a scholar writing a book, Mark is a man inspired by divine guidance, a transmitter of the sacred text. This follows the ancient view that poets, like Homer for example, are divinely inspired and possess superhuman powers.

Influenced possibly by Byzantine decorative arts, Carolingian book covers were made of precious metals and richly ornamented with jewels. Created during the waning influence of the Carolingian dynasty, the "Crucifixion Cover" of the *Lindau Gospels* is of gold, with the figures of Christ and angels delineated in

Figure 11.13 "St. Mark" from the *Gospel Book of Archbishop Ebbo of Reims*, 816–835. Municipal Library, Epernay, France.

Figure 11.14 Interior, St. Martin du Canigou, eleventh century, near Vernet-les-Bains, France.

Figure 11.15 St. Etienne (Abbaye aux Hommes), 1064–1135, Caen, France. View from the southeast.

graceful, sinuous lines (colorplate 14). Outlining the golden Greek cross in gold beads, semi-precious and precious stones, the artist has reinforced the cross motif with jeweled crosses in the four panels and all around the border. Major stones are set away from the gold surface so that reflected light can add to their brilliance. There can be no doubt of the importance of the text within this cover.

After the remarkable reign of Charlemagne (768–814) the Holy Roman Empire declined in power and influence. Nevertheless, the revival of Greek and Roman learning sparked a synthesis of classical civilization and Celtic-Germanic culture, elements of which are still discernible in modern Europe and America.

Romanesque Period, ca. 1000–1150/1200

By about 1000 A.D. virtually all of Europe had been Christianized. After centuries of ferocious attacks, the barbaric Vikings, Magyars, and Slavs had finally been converted to Christianity and assimilated by their victims. Stupendous building programs began all over Europe to replace damaged structures and to construct new churches and monasteries. During the eleventh century the Cluniac Order alone built nearly a thousand monastic churches; every hamlet, village, town, and city had at least one new church. Inevitably architecture and architectural sculpture became the dominant art forms of this vigorous new age.

Located high in the French Pyrenees, the tiny monastic church of St. Martin du Canigou is one of the earliest structures with a complete barrel vault of cut stone (fig. 11.14). Vaulted stone roofs became the

rule for Romanesque churches in place of the wooden truss roofs of earlier buildings; whether accidental or caused by hostile invaders, fire was a constant danger. Stone roofs relieved that difficulty but brought about another: how to support the heavy roof. The solution included thick walls supported by evenly spaced columns alternating with massive piers and connected by semicircular arches. Dimly lit because large windows weaken supporting walls, Romanesque churches are characteristically heavy and solid, giving a feeling of protective walls shutting out a hostile world. Intended for the exclusive use of the religious community, the monastic church shielded the monks from all outside influences.

Christians had been making pilgrimages to scenes of Christ's life since the third century and, during Charlemagne's reign, in ever-increasing numbers. By the tenth century it was commonly believed that viewing sacred relics of Christ and the Saints secured God's pardon for sins, a belief encouraged by pilgrimage churches housing sacred relics.

Begun shortly before the Conqueror sailed for England, St. Etienne was under the personal protection of King William (fig. 11.15). The characteristic twin towers of Norman architecture reach 295' with the aid of spires that were a Gothic addition. The seven towers are a vigorous contribution to the design as well as symbols of the Holy Trinity plus the Four Evangelists. With the Conqueror's tomb before the high altar, St. Etienne still stands as the royal church of the Norman king.

Probably designed by a woman and embroidered on linen by Saxon women, the Bayeux Tapestry is the most precise medieval document which has survived intact, providing daily life scenes and details of clothes, customs, and weapons. In fifty-eight scenes, the rivalry between King Harold of England and William of Normandy is depicted, culminating in the Battle of Hastings (fig. 11.16). In this episode the English, identified by their mustaches, are beginning to succumb to the superior numbers of the French.

Figure 11.16 "The Battle Rages," detail from Bayeux Tapestry, ca. 1070–1080. Wool embroidery on linen. Height ca. 20", entire length 231'. Town Hall, Bayeux, with special authorization of the Village of Bayeux.

The tripartite design features an ornamental band above the violent battle scene and a lower band depicting the casualties. Despite the stylized design, the details are brutally realistic; warriors and horses have died in agony.

The abbey church of Ste.-Madeleine in the village of Vézelay is intimately associated with another kind of warfare: holy war. Originally scheduled for Vézelay, Pope Urban II preached the First Crusade from Clermont in 1095, calling on all Christians to free the Holy Land from the Saracens. In 1146 Vézelay was the site for St. Bernard's Second Crusade and, in 1190, King Richard the Lion-Heart of England and King Phillip Augustus of France departed from Vézelay on the Third Crusade, a disastrous failure, as was every Crusade from the Second in 1146 to the Eighth in 1291. Intended to support and define the Crusades as a second mission to convert the heathen, the _Mission of the Apostles_ tympanum at Vézelay (fig. 11.17) exemplifies the revived relationship of architecture and sculpture in the Romanesque style. Set between the arch and lintel, the tympanum is a compendium of sermons calling on the faithful to emulate the Apostles: save or condemn, preach the gospel, heal the sick, and drive out devils. Following the old convention of relating the size of a figure to its importance, Christ dominates the composition, poised in an almond-shaped frame wearing swirling draperies patterned after Hiberno-Saxon manuscripts. On both sides the Apostles are rising from their seats to commence their evangelical mission. On the archivolts, the relief bands that frame the tympanum, and above the lintel are the benighted people of the world, who in their diseased, crippled, or animalistic condition await the enlightenment. Under the ornamented top archivolt is an inner band of zodiac signs, the seasons, and monthly labors, signifying the year-round Christian mission. In its original condition, complete with bright colors and gold embellishment, the impact of this dynamic work must have been even greater.

Figure 11.17 _Mission of the Apostles,_ tympanum of the central portal of the narthex, ca. 1120–1132, Ste.-Madeleine, Vézelay. _Last judgment_

One of the most distinctive of all Romanesque interiors, the nave of Ste.-Madeleine (fig. 11.18) is high, about 90', with unusual transverse arches of black and white stone, probably inspired by such Islamic buildings as the Great Mosque in Cordoba (see fig. 11.4). The tunnel, or barrel, vault was no longer used because of its inherent drawback: an unbroken series of arches pressed back to back can be lighted or opened only on the opposite ends. Any and every opening in the supporting wall weakens the entire structure. One of the earliest French churches to abandon the barrel vault, Ste.-Madeleine's uses a vault that is intersected at right angles by another vault to form a "groin" or "cross" vault (fig. 11.19). Note that at this high level the groined vaults of Vézelay permit considerable illumination from the clerestory windows. Close study of the interior also reveals that the architect used groin vaults that were too heavy for the exterior wall, vaults so massive that the upper walls are pushed outwards. External flying buttresses (see

Figure 11.18 Nave, Ste.-Madeleine, ca. 1104–1132, Vézelay, France.

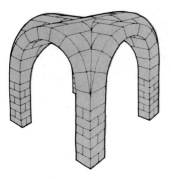

Figure 11.19 Schematic drawing of a cross-vault.

Figure 11.20 Trumeau figure of "The Prophet," Abbey Church of St. Pierre, ca. 1125–1130, Moissac.

an example of the principle in fig. 11.29) had to be added to balance the thrust of the vaults, thus stabilizing this lovely nave.

An outstanding example of architectural sculpture, the strange other-worldly figure of a prophet, possibly Jeremiah, appears on the trumeau, or supporting pier, of a portal of the Abbey Church of St. Pierre at Moissac (MWA–zak; fig. 11.20). The attenuated shape, the long and slender legs, and delicate lines recall Hiberno-Saxon manuscripts. Seemingly too slight to support the mass of masonry, the gentle prophet expresses a spiritual tension and nervous vigor similar to an El Greco painting of four centuries later.

The medieval love of embellishment ranged from manuscripts to stone, including priests' vestments and such ceremonial objects as crosses, chalices, incense burners, candlesticks, and reliquaries. A casket containing a sacred object, a reliquary was invariably made of precious materials and highly decorated. The silver Rhenish reliquary in the shape of a head (colorplate 15) is quite restrained for the period, particularly in the classical details of the hair. Embossed and incised silver figures of the twelve Apostles surround the base of what the twentieth century would label a three-dimensional composite work or "combine." In the twelfth century it was not even regarded as sculpture but as a reliquary, pure and simple.

The linear style of the Ste.-Madeleine tympanum (see fig. 11.17) and "The Prophet" (see fig. 11.20) are also prominent in the *Psalter of St. Swithin* (colorplate 16). In both manuscript scenes elegant arabesques gracefully outline the figures, thus emphasizing the grotesque faces of the brutal soldiers in comparison to the resigned passivity of Christ. Beauty and horror are effectively combined to convey a powerful spiritual message.

The basic Romanesque style of Roman arches and stone vaults supported by compound columns and heavy walls spread throughout western Europe, always displaying, however, certain variations depending on regional conventions and traditions.

Figure 11.21 Busketus, Pisa Cathedral and Campanile, 1063–1272.

Figure 11.22 Pisa Cathedral with Baptistery

Figure 11.23 Benedetto Antelami, *Descent from the Cross,* 1178. Relief, Cathedral of Parma, Italy.

Adhering closely to the basilica plan of Early Christian churches, the buildings of Tuscany also evidenced an increased interest in classical art, a heritage that had never been totally forgotten. The most distinguished complex in the Tuscan Romanesque style is the cathedral group at Pisa (fig. 11.21). Constructed of readily available white marble, the cathedral resembles an Early Christian basilica, but with Romanesque characteristics: the dome over the crossing; the superimposed arcades on the west front; the blind arches encircling the entire building. The extended trancepts with an apse at each end add to the poise and serenity of the design, which makes the famous Leaning Tower, the campanile, all the more striking. Begun in 1174 by Bonanno Pisano on an unstable foundation, the tower began to tilt well before its completion in 1350. Adjusted slightly to the left, the three upper sections were supposed to compensate for the rightward incline. Over 14′ off the perpendicular, the tower, whose bells haven't rung in years, is still moving. Engineering schemes to save the structure are complicated by the stipulation that the tower be stabilized without, however, correcting the tilt of one of Italy's prime tourist attractions.

The view from the top of the campanile clearly shows the cruciform plan of the cathedral with its clerestory windows and upper level of blind arcades (fig. 11.22). The massive baptistery, topped with a dome 115′ in diameter, was built between 1153 and 1278 and later embellished at the upper level with Gothic details, the only discordant note in a grand design.

Contrary to the notion that all medieval art is anonymous, the names of scattered individuals in Italy, France, Belgium, and Holland are known. An early work of the sculptor/architect Antelami, the *Descent from the Cross* (fig. 11.23), somewhat resembles Byzantine ivories but with some classical influence apparent in the delicate scrolls framing the scene.

Figure 11.24 Mont St. Michel, ca. 1017–1144; 1211–1521. Aerial view.

Figure 11.25 Choir and ambulatory, Abbey Church of St. Denis, 1140–1144.

Contrasting sharply with the mourners on the left, the indifferent soldiers are grouped around Christ's robe, symbolizing the secular world. The spiritual world is represented on the left with the expressive curve of Christ's body, the right arm removed from the cross by the angel and extended to the mourners. Damnation is on the right, Salvation on the left.

In all its manifestations, Romanesque art finds its unity in architecture; the church is the Fortress of God where the apocalyptic vision is ever called to mind. Exemplifying this concept, the Abbey of Mont St. Michel in the Sea of Peril (fig. 11.24), rises in awesome majesty off the coast of France. Begun about 1020 by Abbot Hildebert and Richard II of Normandy, grandfather of William the Conqueror, the building

program covered five centuries as abbot succeeded abbot and crusade followed crusade. Mont St. Michel summarizes medieval architecture, a glorious mixture of Norman, Norman Romanesque and Early, High, and Late Gothic styles.

Early Gothic Period, ca. 1140–1200

Erected usually in the countryside as part of monastic communities, Romanesque churches were built by and for "regular" clergy, those who lived under the rule *(regula)* of a religious order. The rise of the great cities of Europe was paralled by the development of the new Gothic style. Staffed by the "secular" clergy, priests who lived "in the world" *(in saecula)*, Gothic churches were urban establishments designed to serve city parishes. Each city's glory and chief community center, the Gothic cathedral was not only the seat *(ex cathedra)* of the bishop but a theatre, classroom, concert hall, court, and general meeting place.

Though the basic structural elements of Gothic architecture were developed and used during the Romanesque period, it remained for an unknown architectural genius to put it all together at St. Denis, just north of Paris (fig. 11.25). Carried out under Abbot Suger who left a detailed account of his administration (1122–1151), the designer supported the weight of the vaults with pointed arches, which are more stable than semicircular arches. The arch principle is one of mutual support; the two halves lean against each other so that the force (gravity) that would cause either to fall actually holds them in place. But, the flatter the arch the greater the lateral thrust at the springline, that is, the outward push where the arch turns upward (fig. 11.26). The lateral thrust is significantly reduced when the pointed arch is used because the springline is angled more nearly downward. Hence, the more pointed the arch the less the tendency to push its supporting pier outwards, thus reducing the need for massive supports.

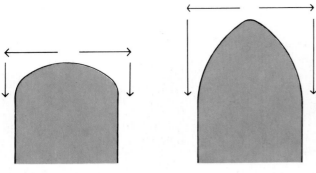

Figure 11.26 Schematic drawings of Romanesque and Gothic arch thrusts.

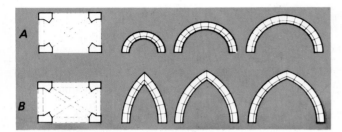

Figure 11.27 (a) Cross vault of semicircular arches over an oblong bay; (b) Cross vault of pointed arches over an oblong bay.

Figure 11.28 West facade, Notre Dame, Paris. Plan, 1163–1250; facade, ca. 1200–1250.

The rounded arch has a fixed diameter because it is always half of a circle. Since it has no unalterable diameter, the pointed arch can rise to almost any height and span any space (fig. 11.27). In the illustration the first rounded arch spans the short side, the second the long side, and the third the diagonal, necessitating piers of different heights. With their identical height, pointed arches simplify the engineering and improve the aesthetic effect with slender columns topped by capitals at a uniform height.

The Gothic vaulting and piers of identical height can be seen at St. Denis (see fig. 11.25). The piers on the right have less masonry to support than the main piers to the left, and are thus considerably slimmer. Still appearing bulky from the back, the primary piers are less massive than Romanesque columns, particularly when viewed from the choir, where the clustered columns now rise gracefully to the high ceiling.

The most striking difference at St. Denis is the marked increase in light. In figure 11.25 one can see, on all three levels, stained glass windows that function as light converters, transforming the interior into a hazy luminosity of shifting colors. The windows are subdivided first by mullions (carved stone posts), by stone tracery to form still smaller glass panels, and by thin lead strips to hold in place the individual pieces of colored glass. The light penetrating the stained glass provides a polychromatic effect, making the glass transparent, while the stone and metal dividers become opaque black lines separating and highlighting the colors. The mystical coloration of Gothic interiors

represents the philosophical idea of light as a Neoplatonic form of ultimate beauty, an earthly manifestation of the divine light of the heavenly kingdom.

On June 11, 1144, Abbot Suger proudly presided at the dedication of the choir of St. Denis in the company of hundreds of priests and laymen, five archbishops, and Louis VII of France and his Queen, Eleanor of Aquitaine. This was a truly momentous occasion, sparking a veritable frenzy of Gothic construction in the Ile de France, the region surrounding Paris. The cathedral at Chartres was begun in 1142, even before the formal dedication at St. Denis, Laon in 1160, Notre Dame of Paris in 1163, Bourges in 1185, and Chartres again in 1194 after a catastrophic fire. These cathedrals, all major enterprises, were followed by hundreds of other churches in a vast building program that, in a single century, included every major city in northern Europe.

The imposing facade of Notre Dame (fig. 11.28) has been justly admired for over seven centuries as a masterpiece of rational design. Solidly buttressed at the corners, the facade rises effortlessly in three levels on which sculptural embellishment is subordinate to the architecture. Unlike the projecting porches of later Gothic cathedrals, the three portals are recessed from the frontal plane and topped by a row of carved saints. The rose window centerpiece is flanked by smaller roses over double windows, above which there is a line of lacy pointed arches. With their subtly embellished cornices and elongated windows, the square towers complete the design with restraint and dignity. This majestic west front is a fitting symbol for the ascendancy of Paris as the cultural and intellectual center of Europe.

The view of the east end of Notre Dame (fig. 11.29) displays in no uncertain terms that critical component of Gothic design, the flying buttress. Springing from heavy piers, two sets of arches curve upwards to support the piers of the exterior walls, providing the counterbalancing force needed to stabilize the structure. It is the flying buttress principle that enabled architects to utilize the curtain walls of

Colorplate 13 Bishop Eadfrith (?), "X–P Page," *Lindisfarne Gospels*. British Library, London. Reproduced by permission of the British Library.

Colorplate 14 "Crucifixion Cover," *Lindau Gospels*, ca. 870, 13¾ × 10½". The Pierpont Morgan Library, New York.

Colorplate 17 High mass, nave of Cathedral of Notre Dame, Coutances, France. Begun 1218.

Colorplate 16 *Psalter of St. Swithin:* "Capture of Christ and the Flagellation," ca. 1250. The British Library, London. Reproduced by permission of the British Library.

Colorplate 18 Southern rose and lancets, Chartres Cathedral

Colorplate 19 Duccio, *The Calling of the Apostles Peter and Andrew,* ca. 1308. Tempera on wood, 17⅛ × 18⅛″. Samuel H. Kress Collection. National Gallery of Art, Washington, D.C.

Colorplate 20 Simone Martini, *Annunciation,* 1333. Tempera on wood, 8′8″ × 10′. (Saints in side panels by Lippo Memmi.) Uffizi Gallery, Florence.

Colorplate 21 Giotto, *Lamentation,* 1305–1306. Fresco, 7'7" × 7'9". Arena Chapel, Padua

Figure 11.29 Apse with flying buttresses, Notre Dame, Paris.

Figure 11.30 West facade, Chartres Cathedral, ca. 1142–1507.

stone pierced by numerous stained glass windows. Also visible in figure 11.29 is the Late Gothic fleche, the slender spire that rises above the crossing. Flying buttresses represent an exposed engineering which provides both the needed physical support and the psychological assurance that the building is totally solid and safe, as indeed it is.

High Gothic Period, ca. 1200–1300

After a disastrous fire in the village of Chartres in 1194, which left intact only the Early Gothic facade of the still unfinished cathedral, the rebuilding of Chartres Cathedral commenced immediately and moved rapidly, with the basic structure completed by 1220. The idea that Gothic cathedrals took decades or even centuries to build is erroneous and probably based on the fact that these buildings were never fully completed; there was always something to be added or elaborated.

The first masterpiece of the mature period, Chartres Cathedral has been called the Queen of Cathedrals, the epitome of Gothic architecture (fig. 11.30). Typically High Gothic but unique to Chartres, the south (right) tower begins with a square base that evolves smoothly into the octagonal shape of the fourth level. From here the graceful spire soars to a height of 344′, the characteristic "finger pointing to God" of the Gothic age. The elaborate north tower, which was not completed until well into the Northern Renaissance, lacks the effortless verticality of the south tower. Verticality was a hallmark of Gothic; cities competed in unspoken contests to erect cathedrals with the highest vaults and the tallest towers. An inspiring House of God was also a symbol of civic achievement. With a facade 157′ wide and measuring 427′ in length, Chartres Cathedral is as prominent a landmark today as when it was built, thanks in part to modern zoning ordinances that control building heights throughout the village.

Incorporated into the facade when the cathedral was rebuilt, the Royal Portal (western doorways) of the earlier church emphasizes the Last Judgment

Figure 11.31 Central doorway, Royal Portal, ca. 1140–1150, Chartres Cathedral.

theme of Romanesque portals but with significant differences (fig. 11.31). Rather than the harsh Damnation of the Last Judgment, the theme is now the Second Coming with its promise of salvation. No longer is there the inventive freedom of the Romanesque; all is unified and controlled. The outer frame is provided by the twenty-four elders of the Apocalypse on the archivolts and the lower row of twelve

Apostles. Surrounded by symbols of the four Evangelists, the now benign figure of Christ raises an arm in benediction in the manner of Caesar Augustus (see fig. 6.5). Beneath the tympanum are the jamb figures, a wholly new idea in architectural sculpture. Conceived and carved in the round, the figures were very likely fashioned after live models rather than copied from manuscripts, a further indication of the emerging this-worldly spirit of the age.

The most significant manifestation of the new age was the dedication of the cathedrals themselves. Named after apostles and saints in previous eras, the new churches were almost invariably dedicated to Our Lady *(Notre Dame).* Mary was Queen of Heaven, interceding for her faithful who, sinners all, wanted mercy, not justice. This was the Cult of the Virgin Mary, the spiritual counterpart of the somewhat improved status of women. The masculine Romanesque was the age of feudalism and conflict; the Gothic was the Age of Chivalry, as derived from courts of love sponsored by powerful women like Eleanor of Aquitaine, Queen of France and then of England. With the development of cathedral schools such as those at Paris and Chartres, Mary was viewed much like Athena, as patroness of arts and science. The right doorway of the Chartres Royal Portal (not illustrated) includes portraits of Aristotle, Cicero, Euclid, Ptolemy, Pythagoras and symbols of the Seven Liberal Arts. The Gothic cathedral represents the medieval synthesis of spiritual and secular life at its best.

Featuring a nave 53′ in width, the most spacious of all Gothic naves, the interior of Notre Dame of Chartres is 130′ in length and 122′ high, the loftiest vault of its day (fig. 11.32). At the rounded end of the choir are the tall pointed arches of the arcade and the triforium gallery of the second level, culminating in the lofty and luminous stained glass windows. At the sides of the illustration can be seen two of the four enormous piers which frame the crossing and which are carved as clustered columns to minimize their bulk. Columns clustered around a central core have the same diameter as a solid pier, but their appearance gives the illusion of lightness and grace.

One of the chief glories of Gothic interiors is the kaleidoscopic color cascading from the mighty stained glass windows. Retaining most of its original windows, Chartres is a treasure house of the art, with clerestory windows 44′ high, all in all some 20,000 square feet of medieval glass. Located at the south end of the transepts, the southern rose is like a gigantic multicolored jewel set above the five figurative lancet windows (colorplate 18). Because it is a southern exposure window, the predominance of color leans towards the warm part of the spectrum from roses to oranges to reds. Its counterpart, the northern rose (not illustrated), transmits the cooler colors, especially many hues of blue. Contrary to what one might expect, direct sunlight on any of the southern windows upsets the chromatic balance of the interior. All of the windows were designed to function best under the even light of the generally grey skies of northern

Figure 11.32 Choir, Notre Dame of Chartres

France, enabling the warm and cool colors to effect a balance of color tones. Surpassing anything up to that time, the craftsmanship and sheer beauty of Gothic stained glass remain incomparable.

As usually seen by tourists, a Gothic cathedral is an enormous empty building, very impressive but more like a museum than a church. Despite the awesome scale of the interior, the cathedral is not at all intimidating in the manner of, say, Egyptian temples. Rather, the church is built for people and when functioning as intended, the interior comes vibrantly alive as an inspirational setting for public worship. Colorplate 17 illustrates an actual high mass in a nave nearly filled with worshippers. A superb example of the Norman High Gothic style, Coutances has a characteristically unadorned and harmonious interior that derives its whole effect from the architecture. Not even the modern dress of the congregation or the speakers on the columns can detract from the timelessness of the setting; the scene is very nearly the same as it has been for over seven centuries.

Designed originally by one of the first known masterbuilders, Robert de Luzarches, the Cathedral of Notre Dame of Amiens marks the culmination of the best ideas of the French Gothic style. Modeled after that of Notre Dame in Paris, the west front (fig. 11.33) is not as controlled and majestic as its model. Its grandeur, however, is overwhelming. Looking like one gigantic and intricate work of sculpture, the facade is dominated by its incomparable portals. The

Figure 11.33 West facade, Cathedral of Notre Dame of Amiens, ca. 1220–1288.

Figure 11.35 Sainte Chapelle, 1245–1248, Paris. View from northeast.

Figure 11.34 Nave, Cathedral of Notre Dame of Amiens

imposing entrances thrusting outward from the facade proclaim the interior in unmistakable terms; the central portal announces the lofty nave and the two flanking doorways the side aisles. In other words, the inner structure is foretold by the exterior design.

Patterned after Chartres, the nave of Amiens is even more integrated, soaring in one breathtaking sweep to 144' above the pavement (fig. 11.34). Unfortunately minus its stained glass, the interior is still the culmination of the High Gothic style: lofty arcades with slender columns rising to the ribbed vaults.

Once thought to have functioned as structural supports for the ceiling, the ribs are actually decorative extensions of columns carrying the design to the pinnacle of the ceiling, which with its groined vaults is completely self-supporting.

Completed in less than thirty-three months for Louis IX of France, later St. Louis, Sainte Chapelle (fig. 11.35) is today a small chapel set in the midst of the Palais de Justice. With virtually no stone walls the structure is a set of piers supporting walls of stained glass. Topped by a spire reaching 246' into the sky, the upper chapel, with its 49' windows, rests on a lower level intended for the use of servants. With almost 7,000 square feet of glass containing 1,134 scenes the upper chapel is a jewelbox of color dominated by brilliant reds and luminous blues (fig. 11.36). Because there are no side aisles, there are no flying buttresses to impede the penetration of light into a building whose walls are about 75 percent glass. Rivaling Chartres in the extent and quality of its original glass, Saint Chapelle managed to survive the Revolution; damaged and neglected, it became a storage area for old government files. Restored in the nineteenth century to an approximation of its original condition, the remarkable fact is that its basic structure is so flawless, so perfectly engineered that it survived completely intact for seven centuries.

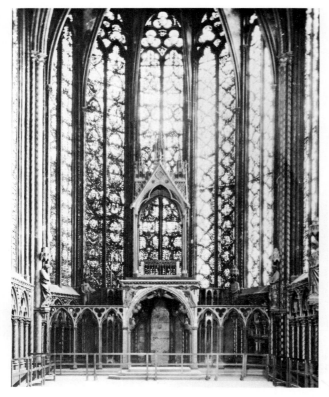

Figure 11.36 Interior, upper chapel, Sainte Chapelle

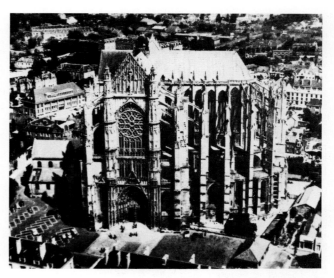

Figure 11.37 Choir of Beauvais Cathedral, France. Aerial view. Begun ca. 1225.

With the cathedral at Beauvais, the competition to build the highest vault came to a crashing end (fig. 11.37). Reaching the incredible height of 157′, the vaulting was a wonderment to all until its collapse in 1284; only the apse was left standing. Rebuilt over a period of forty years, the choir remains today as a testimonial both to Gothic vertical aspirations and the waning of enthusiasm for building enormously expensive churches; the money ran out along with the spirit. Though commonly thought that "tortured stone" could not withstand the lofty vaults of Beauvais, modern engineering research[2] points to a design flaw in an exterior pier, the deterioration of which was not detected. The collapse of 1284 ironically confirmed the nature of Gothic engineering in which the stability of the vaulting depends on the proper functioning of all components. When the single pier failed due to undetected weathering, all the choir vaults came tumbling down. The apse remained standing simply because it was structurally independent. Interestingly enough, the design flaw was corrected during the rebuilding program, meaning that the entire cathedral could then have been completed as originally planned. Today one can look at the choir section and only wonder at what might have been at Beauvais.

2. Robert Mark, *Experiments in Gothic Structure* (Cambridge, Mass.: MIT Press, 1982), pp. 58–77.

Gothic Style outside France

By the second half of the thirteenth century the Gothic style had been accepted throughout Europe, though Italy was less than enthusiastic. Regional variations gave each area its own brand of Gothic. Taking to Gothic as if they had invented it, the English built in the style from the twelfth to the nineteenth centuries. Drawing directly upon the Ile de France style, the English utilized clearly recognizable Gothic characteristics in a manner just as distinctly non-French. The clean lines of French verticality were abandoned at the outset in favor of a multiplicity of verticals topped by veritable forests of ribs that almost obscured the groined vaults, as evidenced in Canterbury Cathedral (fig. 11.38). The nave is not seen as a majestic succession of bays but rather as a steady procession of supports and arches. Because the ribs arch up from the triforium, the clerestory windows are not as prominent in the design as in the French style nor is the stained glass comparable in workmanship or design. A comparison of the interior of Canterbury with those of Chartres (fig. 11.32) and Amiens (fig. 11.34) reveals just how drastic the difference is, which the French are only too willing to point out. The English, on the other hand, view French interiors as cold and impersonal, while English Gothic is warmly intimate, hospitable, and comfortable. Different styles suit different people.

The Italians took up the Gothic style slowly and with many reservations; they were, after all, the ones who had labeled the new style as a barbaric creation of the Goths of the north. Distinctly unclassical, a Gothic cathedral is restless, unsettled, always incomplete, whereas a classical temple is at rest, serenely complete. Nevertheless, the Gothic spirit was on the

Figure 11.38 Nave, Canterbury Cathedral, begun 1174.

Figure 11.39 Giovanni Pisano, Facade, Cathedral of Siena, begun ca. 1285.

move in Italy, becoming part of the classical and Romanesque traditions. For all its Gothic elements, the Cathedral of Siena (fig. 11.39) has square doorways, triangular pediments, and a balanced design reminiscent of the classical and Romanesque traditions. There is a Gothic rose window minus stained glass plus Gothic towers, lacy blind arches, and the three portals. Most of the statuary has been liberated from its architectural bondage and the tympanums feature colorful mosaics. Faced with multicolored marble the facade is an ensemble of Gothic elements mixed with Tuscan Romanesque, all in all a notable example of Italian reaction to the Gothic spirit.

Whatever its regional variations, the Gothic cathedral epitomizes the explosive creativity and intellectual boldness of the Gothic age. Never completely finished, a process rather than an end product, it stood at the center of the storm of changes that would sweep away the medieval synthesis. It represents both the triumphant climax of the Age of Faith and the end of the Middle Ages.

Late Gothic Period, ca. 1300–1500s

An integral part of Gothic architecture, stained glass windows and relief sculpture served the pictorial purposes once provided by mosaics, murals, and frescoes. Virtually nonexistent in the Gothic north, large-scale paintings were still done in Italy, which had maintained its contact with Byzantium. It was Italian painters who synthesized Byzantine and Gothic styles to create new procedures crucial to the future development of Western painting.

Renowned for his skill as a fresco and tempera painter[3], the Florentine Cimabue (chee–ma–BOO–uh; 1240?–1302) introduced features that were incorporated into the developing Italian style. His *Madonna Enthroned* (fig. 11.40) illustrates the new characteristics of strong, forceful figures in an atmosphere of complete serenity. The human scale of the lower figures emphasizes the towering dignity of the Madonna as she holds the mature-looking child. Distinguished from Byzantine icons by its much greater size, the gable shape and solid throne are also Gothic in origin as is the general verticality. The rigid, angular draperies and rather flat body of the Madonna are from the Byzantine tradition, but the softer lines of the angels' faces and their lightly hung draperies were inspired by works from contemporary Constantinople.

Cimabue's naturalistic, monumentally scaled work had a profound influence on his purported pupil Giotto (JOT–toe; ca. 1267–1337), the acknowledged "father of Western painting." Giotto was a one-man revolution in art, who established the illusionary qualities of space, bulk, movement, and human expression, all features of most pictorial art for the next six centuries. His indebtedness to Cimabue is

---

3. Fresco paintings are made on fresh wet plaster with pigments suspended in water; tempera uses pigments mixed with egg yolk and applied, usually, to a panel. Because the drying time for both techniques is very fast, corrections are virtually impossible without redoing entire areas. Therefore, artists had to work rapidly and with precision.

Figure 11.40 Cimabue, *Madonna Enthroned,* ca. 1280–1290. Panel, 12'7½" × 7'4". Uffizi Gallery, Florence.

Figure 11.41 Giotto, *Madonna Enthroned,* ca. 1310. Tempera on panel, 10'8" × 6'8". Uffizi Gallery, Florence.

obvious in his *Madonna Enthroned* (fig. 11.41), but there are significant changes that make it not necessarily better but certainly different. Giotto abandoned the Byzantine tradition and patterned his work after Western models, undoubtedly French cathedral statues. His solid human forms occupy a three-dimensional space surrounded by an architectural framework. His *Madonna Enthroned* is highlighted by the protruding knee of the Madonna, showing that there is a tangible body underneath the robe, a figure of monumental substance. When compared with Cimabue's angels, we see that Giotto's angels, especially the kneeling ones, are placed firmly at the same level on which the base of the Gothic throne rests. The ethereal, floating quality of Byzantine painting has been abandoned in favor of the illusion of tangible space occupied by three-dimensional figures.

Giotto's reputation, already imposing in his own time, rests mainly on his frescoes, most notably the biblical scenes in the Arena Chapel, which are among the most celebrated in the whole history of art. In his *Lamentation* (colorplate 21) the artist has composed a scene in the manner of a Greek tragedy. The mourning tableau is placed in the foreground so that the picture space is at eye level, making us participants in the tragedy, our involvement heightened by the wonderfully expressive backs of the two anonymous mourners. Grief is individualized, with each participant mourning according to his or her personality. The emotional range is vast, from the controlled intensity of the earth-bound figures to the tortured grief of the writhing angels. Giotto's achievements are summarized in this one powerful work: the creation of subtle illusions of tactile qualities; existence and movement in space; a deep psychological understanding of subject and viewer; and the establishment of a continuity of space between viewer and painting. To all of these achievements he brought a profound sense of humanity's awareness of human emotions and of their place in the world. Difficult as it is to realize today, Giotto's contemporaries saw these works as the ultimate reality, so "real" that you could walk into

Figure 11.42. Duccio, *Rucellai Madonna,* 1285. Tempera on wood, 14'9" × 9'6". Uffizi Gallery, Florence.

them. We can give proper credit to this view by comparing Giotto's work with that of his contemporaries and by remembering also that reality, or the illusion of reality, changes from epoch to epoch.

From Siena came two artists whose work was unlike that of either Cimabue or Giotto but who were instrumental in establishing the International Style, the first international movement in Western art. Duccio (DOOT–cho; ca. 1255–1319) painted Byzantine-type faces except for the eyes, but in a style comparable to northern Gothic manuscripts and ivories. The most elegant painter of his time, his *Rucellai Madonna* (fig. 11.42) is highly decorative, with sinuous folds of background drapery and a remarkable delicacy of line for so large a work. Contrasting with the Byzantine-style flatness of the Madonna, the kneeling angels are portrayed much more in the round, combining the Hellenistic-Roman naturalistic tradition with that of French architectural sculpture. This one work is a virtual encyclopedia of the International Style synthesis of Mediterranean and northern cultures.

In his *The Calling of the Apostles Peter and Andrew* (colorplate 19), Duccio depicts a world of golden sky and translucent greenish sea where the commanding but elegant figure of Christ beckons gently to the slightly puzzled fishermen. It is a lovely

creation, the world of Duccio, and this is the style the popes at Avignon and the northern kings and queens admired and called upon their artists to emulate.

Serving the pope's court in Avignon, Duccio's pupil Simone Martini (1284–1344) combined the grace of the Sienese school with the exquisite refinement of Late Gothic architecture. His *Annunciation* (colorplate 20) epitomizes the courtly style. Completely Gothic, the frame is replete with *crockets,* or ornamental leaves and flowers, and *finials,* or carved spires; signifying eternity, the gold-leaf background is Byzantine. Delineated in graceful curved lines, the Angel Gabriel kneels before the Virgin to proclaim "Hail Mary, full of grace. . . ." As the words travel literally from his lips she draws back in apprehension, her body arranged in an elaborate S-curve and covered by a rich blue robe. Between the two figures is an elegant vase containing white lilies symbolic of Mary's purity. As delicately executed as fine jewelry, the artistic conception is aristocratic and courtly, comparable to the polished sonnets of Petrarch, who also served the papal court at Avignon.

With its combined Classical/Byzantine/Gothic attributes, the International Style was promulgated throughout the religious and secular courts of Europe. It found an enthusiastic response wherever wealthy clients prized grace, delicacy, and refinement in art, music, manners, and dress. Aesthetic pleasure was the goal, not spiritual enlightenment.

Summary

While European civilization was descending into the Dark Ages, Islam was assimilating ancient and contemporary cultures, leading to brilliant achievements in medicine, astronomy, mathematics, scholarship, and architecture. Illustrious structures such as the Suleymaniye Mosque in Istanbul, the Great Mosque in Cordoba, and the Alhambra are enduring symbols of Islamic culture.

A curious backwater during Roman times, Christianized Ireland launched missionary activities that led to a golden age highlighted by the production of exquisite manuscripts in the Hiberno-Saxon style. Establishing a tradition of meticulous northern craftsmanship, the *Lindisfarne Gospels* and *Book of Kells* were among the first and best of a long history of illuminated manuscripts.

Charlemagne seized the opportune moment to create the Holy Roman Empire and launch the Carolingian Renaissance. Importing technology and stonemasons from the Mediterranean area, he set in motion the forces that would produce the Romanesque style and climax in the Gothic Age.

The year A.D. 1000 marked the Christianization of virtually all of Europe and the launching of a vast building program of monasteries and churches. Inspired by Roman models, builders constructed stone-vaulted churches such as the pilgrimage church of Ste.-Madeleine. Notable among the numerous monasteries built during the period was Mont St. Michel.

Inspired by the revolutionary design of the choir of St. Denis, French master builders erected some of the most sublime buildings ever conceived by humankind, most notably the Gothic cathedrals of Chartres and Amiens.

Though relatively immune to Gothic architecture, Italian artists synthesized Classical, Byzantine, and Gothic elements to create the first International Style in art. A medieval man like Dante and his friend and fellow Florentine Giotto carried medieval art to its final consummation. Indeed, their work marks the end of the Middle Ages and sets the stage for the Renaissance.

12
Medieval Music: Sacred and Secular

The bountiful storehouse of medieval music marks the first great era of Western music, and yet little of this large repertory is heard by modern audiences. An inseparable part of everyday life, medieval music served the needs of the society: ballads to preserve tales and legends; songs of love and beauty; dances and popular tunes to celebrate the joys of life; dirges and lamentations to express the sorrows; sacred music for praise and worship. This is not the musical art of today's concert halls, but recordings of much of this rich heritage are available in authentic versions.

There is a large body of sacred music but comparatively little secular music prior to the fourteenth century. In common with other nonliterate societies, secular music was passed along to later generations through oral tradition. Music of the church, on the other hand, had a status comparable to the high social position of clerics. As part of the province of the literate and the learned, music was preserved in written form as a link to the eternal. However, the sheer mass of sacred music and secular music (after the thirteenth century) has to be indicative of a comparable amount of secular music, a folk art that was rarely taken seriously and seldom written down. The survival of nearly 1,700 troubadour-trouvère melodies (discussed later in this chapter) attests to the importance of secular music in medieval life.

Sacred Music

The oldest type of music is *monophonic,* or a single melodic line with no other parts or accompaniment. The liturgical (officially authorized) music of the Church of Rome is monophonic in a style called Gregorian chant, or plainsong.

Gregorian Chant

According to legend, Pope Gregory the Great (ruled 590–604; fig. 12.1) ordered a body of liturgical music organized, priests trained in singing the music, and a common liturgy disseminated throughout the Western church. He did reorganize the church, but the chant that bears his name

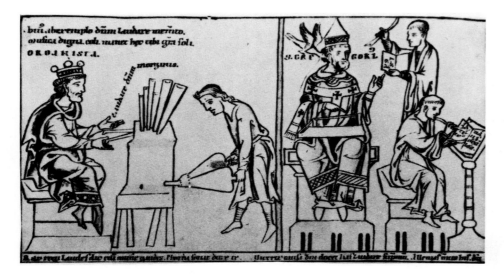

Figure 12.1 "King David as Organist (left) and Pope Gregory the Great," 1241, from Codex Lat. 17403, Bayerische Staatsbibliothek, Munich. Traditionally attributed to David, the Psalms formed a large part of the Gregorian repertory. Inspired by the dove of the Holy Spirit and holding a monochord, Gregory is depicted in his legendary role as codifier of liturgical chant.

Figure 12.2 Guido d'Arezzo, twelfth century manuscript, State Library, Vienna. Seated at the left, Guido is demonstrating on a monochord the two-octave scale (A–B–C–D–E–F–G, etc.), which was converted to neumes and placed on the staff.

church. The texts determine the note values and musical accents; the rhythm of the music follows the rhythm of the words. There is no steady pulsation or beat, no division into regular acccents as there would be in a march or waltz. The undulating melodies flow smoothly, resonating through the cavernous stone churches, weaving a web of sound, and evoking in the worshipers feelings of awe and reverence.

Like secular music, Gregorian chant existed for centuries as an oral tradition. The precise musical notation of the ancient Greeks had been lost, and it was not until the eighth century that a new notational system began to evolve. Symbols for musical pitches, called *neumes,* were at first imprecise as to the actual pitch indicated, leading the monk Guido of Arezzo (ca. 990–1050) to remark that, "In our times, of all men, singers are the most foolish." Blaming the lack of precise musical notation for "losing time enough in singing to have learned thoroughly both sacred and secular letters," Guido invented a four-line musical staff on which neumes could symbolize precise pitches (fig. 12.2). Because of its limited range, chant is still scored on a four-line staff. In the following example the upper staff gives the neumes in Gregorian notation, below which the same melody is scored on the modern five-line staff. The clef sign (upper left) in Gregorian notation is C; the standard staff uses a G clef (see "clef" in the prologue). In both notations the letter-names of the notes are F–G–E–D–F–A–G–A–G, etc.

Gregorian Chant: *Alleluia*

reached its final form during and shortly after the reign of Charlemagne (ruled 768–814). Consisting today of nearly 3,000 melodies, Gregorian chant is a priceless collection of subtle and sophisticated melodies.

Gregorian chant is monophonic, *a cappella* (unaccompanied), and sung by male voices (solo and chorus) in Latin in the musical modes defined by the

Many Gregorian melodies were adapted from Jewish Synagogue chant, especially the Alleluias (Hebrew, *Hallelujah,* praise ye the Lord). The seventh item of the mass (see table 12.1), Alleluias are characteristically *melismatic,* with many notes sung to one syllable. Following is the beginning of an Alleluia from the mass for Epiphany (visit of the Magi). The long and expressive melisma on the final syllable led eventually to innovations in texts and music called *tropes* and *sequences* (see below).

Alleluia, Vidimus stellam

The Mass

The two basic types of Catholic services are the Mass and the Daily Hours of Divine Services, usually called Office Hours. The latter are celebrated eight times daily in religious communities such as monasteries. The Mass, also celebrated daily, is the principal service of the church. Essentially an elaborate reenactment of the Lord's Supper, the central theme is the consecration of the bread and the wine and the partaking of these elements by the congregation. Everything else in the service is either preparation for Communion (the Eucharist, Gk., thanksgiving) or a postscript to this commemorative act.

In a *low* Mass, the words are quietly enunciated by the priest in a low (speaking) voice in front of a silent congregation. In a *high* Mass, the service is recited and sung in a high (singing) voice using either Gregorian chant or a combination of chant and other music.

The Mass consists of the *proper,* in which the texts vary according to the liturgical calendar, and the *ordinary,* which uses the same texts throughout the church year. Both proper and ordinary have texts that are recited or chanted by the celebrants (clergy) or sung by the choir.

The complete Mass is outlined in table 12.1 (italics indicate the sung portions of the text). Although modernization of the Mass permits the incorporation of indigenous modern language, increased layman participation, and congregational singing, the essential structure remains unchanged.

Table 12.1 The Mass

Ordinary (same text)	Proper (changing texts)
	1. *Introit*
2. *Kyrie*	
3. *Gloria*	
	4. Oratio (prayers, collect)
	5. Epistle
	6. Gradual
	7. *Alleluia* (or *Tract* during Lent)
	8. Gospel
9. *Credo*	
	10. *Offertory*
	11. Secret
	12. Preface
13. *Sanctus*	
14. Canon	
15. *Agnus dei*	
	16. *Communion*
	17. Postcommunion
18. *Ite missa est* (or *Benedicamus Domino*)	

Tropes

A *trope* (Latin, *Tropus,* figure of speech) is a textual addition to an authorized text, an interpolation in the chant. Sentences or even whole poems were inserted between words of the original text. Sometimes added words were fitted to preexisting notes; at other times both words and music were injected together into the established text. For example, the chant *Kyrie eleison* (Lord have mercy upon us), with an interpolated trope, would read: Lord, *omnipotent Father, God, Creator of all,* have mercy upon us.

The practice of troping could have resulted from boredom, a desire for creativity, an inability to remember the notes, or varying combinations of all three. The authorized texts had not only remained the same for generations but many of them, particularly the texts of the ordinary, were sung countless times. Thus a need for some variety may have been one of the motivating factors.

More positively, troping permitted exercises in creativity that could enliven the unvarying liturgical music. Of course one wonders, in this connection, how often creative acts are the direct result of trying to cope with monotonous repetition.

A third reason for troping may have been utilitarian. Troping originated during the time (ca. 700) when the musical liturgy was still learned by rote. Many chants had long *melismas,* that is, extended series of notes on a single syllable. (Note: The Alleluia used above as an illustration of chant has an extended melisma on the last syllable.) Attempting to remember all these melismas must have been very trying for singers who already had a large amount of liturgical music crammed into their heads. Textual additions that supplied a syllable for each note of the melisma provided additional reference points for all singers. Tropes, therefore, must have been well received by medieval choirs.

Indeed, tropes became so popular that they threatened to engulf the authorized texts. It was perhaps inevitable that the Council of Trent (1545–1563) finally abolished all tropes.

Sequences

The oldest form of trope was the last syllable, the 'ia' (ja) of the Alleluia (again see the example of the Alleluia given above). Many Alleluias, because of their Oriental origin, ended with an exotic and elaborate melisma on the final syllable. New poetry was added to this melisma and then, in time, the last section was detached from the Alleluia to become a separate composition called a *sequence*—that which follows. After separation had been accomplished, composers felt at liberty to alter the melody line.

The sequence is of special interest because it signaled the beginnings of musical composition for its own sake, a new development that was to lead to the works of composers such as Palestrina, Beethoven, and Stravinsky. The composition of sequences was a first step away from the rigidity of a prescribed musical repertoire. Composers began to explore ever more musical innovations and thus to breech and, ultimately, to break down medieval walls.

A large repertoire of sequences threatened for a time to dominate traditional Gregorian chant. The Council of Trent also tried to abolish sequences, but met with such opposition that four sequences were permitted to remain in the repertoire. Following is the oldest of the surviving sequences, the so-called Easter Sequence by Wipo (Wee-po; ca. 1024–1050), chaplain of Emperor Henry III. This melody also served as the basis for a Lutheran Easter chorale, "Christ Lay in the Bonds of Death" with text by Martin Luther.

Sequence: "Victimae paschali laudes"

Wipo

Vi - cti - mae pa - scha - li lau - des im - mo-lent Chri-sti - a - ni. etc.
(Let Christians dedicate their praises to the Easter victim.)

Liturgical Drama

Religious ceremonies, such as the Mass, extend themselves into the realm of the theatre. The dramatic reenactment of the Last Supper in the Mass led, in time, to the development of medieval drama. The impulse was somewhat similar to that which saw classical Greek drama evolve from the cult of Dionysos. There were notable differences however; Greek tragedy dealt with ethical choices made under stress. The common people of the Middle Ages were not

Figure 12.3 From the *Hortus Deliciarum* by the Abbess Herrad van Landsberg, late twelfth century. Formerly in the town library of Strasbourg, the manuscript was destroyed in the 1870 war. Hanging at the right is a rebec, a bowed string instrument of Arab origin. The female performer holds a harp while, at the left, there hangs a wheel-lyre (organistrum). This instrument has three strings set in motion by a revolving wheel operated by a hand crank, and is an ancestor of the hurdy-gurdy.

nearly as literate as the Greeks. They were more concerned with representations of the Nativity, the Shepherds, the Three Wise Men, and other specific events connected with their religion.

The actors were, in the beginning, priests of the Church and the plays episodes from the life of Christ, particularly the Christmas and Easter stories. During the liturgy, priests interpolated paraphrased dialogues from the Gospels, frequently using tropes. But these miniature dramas were too brief and too abstract for the unlettered congregation. Gradually the actors (clergy) enlarged the Scriptures by using Latin for the formal sections and the vernacular for the dialogues. Eventually whole plays were performed in the native language, which in the early plays was French.

Early liturgical dramas were enacted by the clergy in front of the altar. As the vernacular elements were added, the performances were moved to the church portal and the acting parts taken by laymen who, in time, formed confraternities of actors.

Liturgical dramas were mainly musical plays relying for their effects on singing and on a rich variety of accompanying instruments. Of the dozens of instruments available, favorites included the organ, harp, lyre, horn, trumpet, recorder, rebec (precursor of viols and then violins), drums, and other percussion instruments (fig. 12.3).

The following opening dialogue (sung in Latin) is from *The Play of the Three Kings,* which dates from the late eleventh century. Some of the melodies were borrowed from plainsong, but considerable music was undoubtedly composed for the occasion. This recorded performance is a cappella, but instruments could have been added to underscore the Oriental origins of the Magi.

Conductus: "Song of the Ass,"[1]
The Play of Daniel

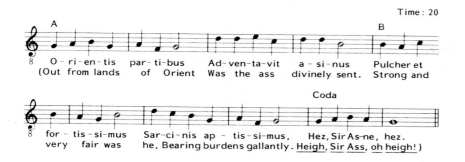

Time: 20

O - ri - en - tis par - ti - bus Ad - ven - ta - vit a - si - nus Pulcher et
(Out from lands of Orient Was the ass divinely sent. Strong and

Coda

for - tis - si - mus Sar - ci - nis ap - tis - si - mus, Hez, Sir As - ne, hez.
very fair was he, Bearing burdens gallantly. Heigh, Sir Ass, oh heigh!)

Liturgical Drama: "Infantem Vidimus"

Shepherds
Infantem vidimus.
(We have seen the Infant.)
Boys
Qui sunt hi, quos stella ducit nos adeuntes, inaudita ferentes?
(Who are those whom the star leads, approaching us and bearing strange things?)
Magi
Nos sumus quos cernites reges Tharsis et Arabum et Saba, dona offerentes Christo Reginato Domino.
(We are those whom you see—the kings of Tharsis, Arabia, and Saba, offering gifts to Christ the King, the new-born Lord.)

The *conductus* was a processional used to "conduct" important characters on and off the stage. One of the most familiar of these was the "Song of the Ass," which was often used to describe Mary's flight into Egypt riding on a donkey. This song is shown as it was used in the twelfth-century *Play of Daniel.* Accompanying the Virgin as she rides into the church on a donkey, the conductus, as befits its function as processional music, is *metrical.* It has four beats to each measure in the manner of a solemn march. Only one of the seven verses is given here.

One of the most influential religious leaders of her time, St. Hildegarde of Bingen (1098–1179) composed chants, songs, and *Play of the Virtues,* a unique liturgical drama treating spiritual material as allegory. Also involved in natural science, medicine, and political and religious debates, the Abbess Hildegarde was appointed prophetess of the Crusades by the pope on the recommendation of Bernard of Clairveaux. Her songs form a link between chant and the minnesinger tradition of Germanic literature.

After the thirteenth-century, liturgical drama developed into mystery plays (from Latin, *ministerium,* service) performed entirely in the vernacular under secular sponsorship. Using music only for processions, fanfares, and dances, these dramatic portrayals of biblical stories (life of Jesus, the Creation, and so forth) eventually evolved into European drama.

Secular Music

Goliards

The goliards of the tenth through thirteenth centuries were wandering students, vagabonds, defrocked priests, minstrels, rascals, artists, and dreamers. They were generally disenchanted with established values and entrenched institutions. They professed to take their name from a "Bishop Golias," whom they claimed as a patron—a very tolerant patron.

Their songs cover many subjects: love songs, drinking songs, spring songs, songs moral and immoral. Their songs were generally light-hearted and frequently obscene and, apparently, so was their conduct.

Though little of their music is extant, considerable poetry has survived. A thirteenth-century manuscript has been published under the title *Carmina Burana.* Selections from this collection have been set to music by the contemporary German composer Carl Orff. (See chapter 26.)

A sampling of the opening lines from poetry in the *Carmina Burana* indicates some basic themes.

"O fortune, variable as the moon"
"I lament fortune's blows"
"Were the world all mine from the sea to the Rhine, I would gladly forsake it all if the Queen of England were in my arms"
"In rage and bitterness I talk to myself"
"I am the Abbot of Cluny, and I spend my time with drinkers"
"When we are in the tavern we don't care who has died"
"The God of Love flies everywhere"
"When a boy and a girl are alone together"
"Sweetest boy I give myself completely to you"

(Note: Three Goliard poems are printed on page 216.)

The vigorous conduct of the goliards and their assault upon established values inevitably led to conflicts with the Church. The movement died out, not because of clerical opposition, but because of the rise of the great medieval universities that replaced wandering students with resident ones.

---

1. G. M. Dreves, *Analecta hymnica* xx, 217, 257; H.C. Greene, *Speculum vi.*

Jongleurs

The *jongleurs* of France (and the *Gauklers,* their German counterparts) were generally not as educated as the goliards. Appearing first during the ninth century, these wandering men—and women—were seldom composers but always entertainers. They played music and sang songs that others had written, did tricks with trained animals, and, in general, helped enliven weddings and other special events. Although some of them were sufficiently talented to be socially acceptable, many were disreputable as far as a despairing clergy was concerned.

Their repertoire included *chansons de geste:* epic chronicles of the valorous deeds of heroes like Charlemagne and Roland. Because the melodies consisted of easily remembered tunes, there was no real need to notate the music and thus very little of it has survived. In a twelfth-century manuscript of the *Chanson de Roland* there are sketches that were apparently used to sing of the exploits of Roland and his horn.

The one authentic *chanson de geste* that has survived appears in the play *Le Jeu de Robin et Marion* by Adam de la Halle.

Chanson de geste: "Audiger dit Raimberge"

Au - di - gier dit Raim - ber - ge Bou - se vous di.

The *chant-fable,* part prose and part verse, was similar to the *chanson de geste* but with a slightly different form. The best-known chant-fable is *Aucassin et Nicolette.*

Troubadours and Trouvères

Coinciding with the flowering of the age of chivalry, the troubadours of Provence and their later followers in northern France, the trouvères, produced the finest repertoire of lyric song of the Middle Ages. Educated aristocrats, both men and women, composed love poetry in the tradition of Ovid, whose love poems and *Art of Love* were undoubtedly known to the cultured nobles of the south of France. The repertoire is large (2,600 troubadour poems, ca. 300 melodies; 4,000 trouvère poems, 1,400 melodies) and covers many subjects: the Crusades, travel, adventure, but mostly romantic love. Despite the relative paucity of surviving melodies, all of the poems were meant to be sung. According to the troubadour Folquet of Marseilles (ca. 1155–1231),"A verse without music is a mill without water."

The earliest known troubadour, Duke William IX of Aquitaine (1071–1126), was a crusader, poet, and performer, whose lusty life and romantic pursuits are reflected in his poetry, of which eleven poems but only one melody have survived. The boldly masculine attitude in the following poem is comparable to Ovid's most aggressive style.

Troubadour Song

Duke William IX of Aquitaine

1. Friends, I'll write a poem that will do:
   But it'll be full of fun
   And not much sense.
   A grab-bag all about love
   And joy and youth.
2. A man's a fool if he doesn't get it
   Or deep down inside won't try
   To learn.
   It's very hard to escape from love
   Once you find you like it.
3. I've got two pretty good fillies in my corral:
   They're ready for any combat—
   They're tough.
   But I can't keep 'em both together:
   Don't get along.
4. If I could tame 'em the way I want,
   I wouldn't have to change
   This set-up,
   For I'd be the best-mounted man
   In all this world.
5. One's the fastest filly up in the hills,
   And she's been fierce and wild
   A long, long time.
   In fact, she's been so fierce and wild,
   Can't stick her in my pen.
6. The other was born here—Confolens way—
   And I never saw a better mare,
   I swear
   But she won't change her wild, wild ways
   For silver or gold.
7. I gave to her master a feeding colt;
   But I kept myself a share
   In the bargain too:
   If he'll keep her one whole year,
   I will a hundred or more.
8. Knights, your advice in this affair!
   I was never so troubled by
   Any business before.
   Which of these nags should I keep:
   Miss Agnes? Miss Arsen?
9. I've got the castle at Gimel under thumb,
   And over at Nieul I strut
   For all the folks to see.
   Both castles are sworn and pledged by oath:
   They belong to *me!*

Considerably more subtle, the next poem is designed to create a romantic, seductive atmosphere.

Troubadour Song

Duke William IX of Aquitaine

1. I'm going to write a brandnew song
   Before the wind and rain start blowing.
   My lady tries and tests me
   To see the way I love her.
   Yet despite the trials that beset me,
   I'd never break loose from her chain.
2. No, I put myself in her bondage,
   Let her write me into her charter.
   And don't think that I'm a drunkard
   If I love my good lady thus,
   For without her I couldn't live.
   I'm so hungry for her love.

3. O, she's whiter than any ivory statue.
   How could I worship any other?
   But if I don't get reinforcements soon
   To help me win my lady's love,
   By the head of St. George, I'll die!—
   Unless we kiss in bower or bed.

4. Pretty lady, what good does it do you
   To cloister up your love?
   Do you want to end up a nun?
   Listen: I love you so much
   I'm afraid that grief will jab me
   If your wrongs don't become the rights I beg.

5. What good will it do if I'm a monk
   And don't come begging round your door?
   Lady, the whole world's joy could be ours,
   If we'd just love each other.
   Over there at my friend Daurostre's
   I'm sending this song to be welcomed and sung.

6. Because of her I shake and tremble,
   Since I love her with the finest love.
   I don't think there's been a woman like her
   In the whole grand line of Lord Adam.

William's son governed the duchy for a few years, followed by his granddaughter, the celebrated Eleanor of Aquitaine (1122–1204), who established a Court of Love in Poitiers and later in Normandy and possibly England. Eleanor sponsored several troubadours and trouvères, the most notable of which was Bernart de Ventadorn (d. 1195). Dante conferred the title of master singer on Arnaut Daniel and consigned another troubadour, Bertran de Born, to Hell (see Canto XXVIII, lines 130–142), but modern critics have ceded the palm to the poet-musician from Ventadorn as the finest lyric poet of the age.

Forty poems, eighteen with music, by Bernart de Ventadorn are known today. Lively, witty, and eminently singable, the subject is always the same: love rewarded, unrequited, noble, sacred, or profane, but always love. In the following *canso* (love song; *chanson* in northern France) the first of six verses is given in both Provençal, the language of the troubadors, and in English.

Troubadour Canso: "Be m'an perdut"[2]

Bernart de Ventadorn (d. 1195)

Musical theme

Be ma'an perdut lai enves Ventadorn tuih meo amic,
(I am indeed lost from the region of Ventadorn/ To all my friends,

pois ma domna no m'ama; et es be dreihz que jamais lai no torn
for my lady loves me not; With reason I turn not back again,

c'a des estai vas me salvatj' egrama.
For she is bitter and ill-disposed toward me.

2. C. Appel, *Bernart von Ventadorn* (Halle, 1915), Plate ix (citing Milan manuscript *Chansonnier* G, folio 14). The form is AAB.

Veus per quem fai semblan irat emorn;
See why she turns a dark and angry countenance to me;

car en s'amor me deleih e'm sojorn!
Because I take joy and pleasure in loving her!

ni de ren als no's rancura ni's clama.
Nor has she ought else with which to charge me.)

After her divorce from the king of France, Eleanor married, in 1152, Henry II, Duke of Normandy and, later, king of England. The next poem implies that Bernart has followed her Court of Love to England and that the haughty highborn lady is either Eleanor herself or a member of her court. Even without the music, the singable quality of the poetry is quite evident.

Lancan Vei per Mei la Landa

Bernart de Ventadorn

1. Whenever I see amid the plain
   The leaves are drifting down from trees
   Before the cold's expansion,
   And the gentle time's in hiding,
   It's good for my song to be heard,
   For I've held back more than two years
   And it's right to make amends.

2. It's hard for me to serve that woman
   Who shows me only her haughty side,
   For if my heart dares make a plea,
   She won't reply with a single word.
   Truly this fool desire is killing me:
   I follow the lovely form of Love,
   Not seeing Love won't attend me.

3. She's mastered cheating, trickery,
   So that always I think she loves me.
   Ah, sweetly she deceives me,
   As her pretty face confounds me!
   Lady, you're gaining absolutely nothing:
   In fact, I'm sure it's toward your loss
   That you treat your man so badly.

4. God, Who nurtures all the world,
   Put it in her heart to take me,
   For I don't want to eat any food
   And of nothing good I have plenty.
   Toward the beautiful one, I'm humble,
   And I render her rightful homage:
   She can keep me, she can sell me.

5. Evil she is if she doesn't call me
   To come where she undresses alone
   So that I can wait at her bidding
   Beside the bed, along the edge,
   Where I can pull off her close-fitting shoes
   Down on my knees, my head bent down:
   If only she'll offer me her foot.

6. This verse has been filled to the brim
   Without a single word that will tumble,
   Beyond the land of the Normans,
   Here across the wild, deep sea.
   [Apparently England.]
   And though I'm kept far from Milordess,
   She draws me toward her like a magnet:
   God, keep that beauty ever safe!

7. If the English king and the Norman duke
   Will it, I'll see her soon
   Before the winter overtakes us.

8. For the king I remain an English-Norman,
   And if there were no Lady Magnet,
   I'd stay here till after Christmas.

A number of female troubadours have been identified (thirteen so far) including Azalais of Porcairagues, Maria of Ventadorn, Lombarda, and the Countess Garsenda of Provence. The most notable poet-musician, whose work is comparable to that of any troubadour, was the Countess of Dia (present day Die), who lived in the Drôme valley in southern France during the twelfth century. Known as Beatritz, her voice is as distinctive as that of Sappho (see chap. 4). In the following dialogue song the lady sweeps aside male rationalizations and exacts a pledge of loyalty, devotion, and a love that was to be shared equally.

Troubadour Song

Beatritz, Countess of Dia

1. Friend, I stand in great distress
   Because of you, and in great pain;
   And I think you don't care one bit
   About the ills that I'm enduring;
   And so, why set yourself as my lover
   Since to me you bequeath all the woe?
   Why can't we share it equally?
2. Lady, love goes about his job
   As he chains two friends together
   So the ills they have and the lightness too
   Are felt by each—in his fashion.
   And I think—and I'm no gabber—
   That all this deepdown, heartstruck woe
   I have in full on my side too.
3. Friend, if you had just one fourth
   Of this aching that afflicts me now,
   I'm sure you'd see my burden of pain;
   But little you care about my grief,
   Since you know I can't break free;
   But to you it's all the same
   Whether good or bad possess me.
4. Lady, because these glozing spies,
   Who have robbed me of my sense and breath,
   Are our most vicious warriors,
   I'm stopping: not because desire dwindles.
   No, I can't be near, for their vicious brays
   Have hedged us in for a deadly game.
   And we can't sport through frolicsome days.
5. Friend, I offer you no thanks
   Because my damnation is not the bit
   That checks those visits I yearn for so.
   And if you set yourself as watchman
   Against my slander without my request,
   Then I'll have to think you're more "true-blue"
   Than those loyal Knights of the Hospital.
6. Lady, my fear is most extreme
   (I'll lose your gold, and you mere sand)
   If through the talk of these scandalmongers
   Our love will turn itself to naught.
   And so I've got to stay on guard
   More than you—by St. Martial I swear!—
   For you're the thing that matters most.
7. Friend, I know you're changeable
   In the way you handle your love,
   And I think that as a chevalier
   You're one of that shifting kind;
   And I'm justified in blaming you,
   For I'm sure other things are on your mind,
   Since I'm no longer the thought that's there.
8. Lady, I'll never carry again
   My falcon, never hunt with a hawk,
   If, now that you've given me joy entire,

I started chasing another girl.
No, I'm not that kind of shyster:
It's envy makes those two-faced talk.
They make up tales and paint me vile.
9. Friend, should I accept your word
   So that I can hold you forever true?
10. Lady, from now on you'll have me true,
    For I'll never think of another.

More direct than most of the poetry of her male counterparts, the following song leaves no doubt about the lady's fiery passion. The slighting reference to the husband may have amused the Count, for this is after all a fictional account of a woman who has much in common with the Wife of Bath in Chaucer's *Canterbury Tales.*

Troubadour Song

Beatritz, Countess of Dia

1. I've suffered great distress
   From a knight whom I once owned.
   Now, for all time, be it known:
   I loved him—yes, to excess.
       His jilting I've regretted,
   Yet his love I never really returned.
   Now for my sin I can only burn:
       Dressed, or in my bed.
2. O, if I had that knight to caress
   Naked all night in my arms,
   He'd be ravished by the charm
   Of using, for cushion, my breast.
       His love I more deeply prize
   Than Floris did Blancheflor's.
   Take that love, my core,
       My sense, my life, my eyes!
3. Lovely lover, gracious, kind,
   When will I overcome your fight?
   O, if I could lie with you one night!
   Feel those loving lips on mine!
       Listen, one thing sets me afire:
   Here in my husband's place I want *you,*
   If you'll just keep your promise true:
       Give me everything I desire.

By the middle of the twelfth century troubadour influences had spread to northern France where notable trouvères included Blondel de Nesles (b. ca. 1155), minstrel to Richard the Lionhearted (ruled 1189–1199 and himself a trouvère); Thibaut IV, King of Navarre (1201–1253); and Adam de la Halle (ca. 1240–1287). Like troubadour cansos, trouvère chansons were monophonic with accompaniment an option depending on available instruments. The following *virelai* is a trouvère form that begins with a refrain that repeats after each verse. Composed by an unknown trouvère, this is a superb example of the sophisticated style of northern France.

Trouvère Virelai: "Or la truix"[3]

Musical theme

---

3. Bodleian Oxford, Douce 308, folio 226 and 237. The form is ABAA.

In 1208 Pope Innocent III preached a crusade against the Albigensian heresy (latter-day Manicheans; see St. Augustine), stating that the church must "use against heretics the spiritual sword of excommunication, and if this does not prove effective, use the material sword." Exploiting the Albigensian Crusade as an excuse to plunder the south of France, nobles and the French Crown totally destroyed the high culture that had fostered the troubadour tradition, chivalry, and the Courts of Love.

Minnesingers and Meistersingers

The *minnesinger* (Ger., *minne*, love) of Germanic literature flourished during the twelfth and thirteenth centuries. Despite the title of "love singer" these poet-musicians were strongly influenced by Christianity and sang spiritual songs of sadness, of tears, and of thoughts of death. The *minnesong* was, in effect, a reconciliation of Christian elements with erotic-secular literature of the troubadour-trouvère tradition.

Meistersingers (master singers) were "prize" singers of the fourteenth through sixteenth centuries. The art of the minnesinger was transformed into a guild of singers who practiced the art and craft of writing and singing songs much as cabinetmakers practiced the art of woodworking. The best-known meistersinger was Hans Sachs, the protagonist of Richard Wagner's opera *Die Meistersinger von Nürnberg*.

Polyphonic Music

The high point of medieval music was the development of polyphony. Polyphony (Gk., *poly-phonos*, many voices) is a style of music in which two or more melodies are played and/or sung together. "Row, Row, Row Your Boat," when sung as a round, is an example of one kind of polyphonic music in which the same melody is sung at different times. "Jesu, Joy of Man's Desiring" by J. S. Bach combines three different melodies.

Related to polyphonic music is a style that evolved several centuries later and is called homophonic (Gk., *homo-phonos*, same voice). Homophonic music consists of a single melody plus accompaniment or, to put it another way, melody and harmony. For example, "The Star Spangled Banner" and "The Battle Hymn of the Republic" are homophonic.

Polyphonic and homophonic are the two aspects of multivoiced music. Neither style exists in a pure form. Music that emphasizes two or more melodies of roughly equal importance is termed polyphonic. Homophonic music emphasizes a predominant melody line accompanied by harmony. The two styles may be illustrated as follows:

Non-Western music (Middle and Far East and Africa) never developed polyphonic or homophonic styles of music. Polyphony was spontaneous rather than planned, the result of accidental conjunctions of melodies rather than a premeditated polyphonic practice such as that developed by Western culture.

Polyphony and harmony (homophony) in Western culture are therefore unique in the world of music. Without the development of polyphonic music during the Middle Ages no subsequent expansion of musical styles could have taken place: no Bach, Beethoven, Beatles, Bob Dylan, or Rolling Stones; no blues, ragtime, jazz, country-western, rock, or pop.

Medieval polyphonic music probably grew out of the monophonic music of the chant. Early attempts at polyphony were quite literal and consisted of adding additional voice parts at fixed distances above and below existing chants. The added voice was referred to as the organizing voice *(vox organalis)* and the whole style of music as *organum*. Two-part music was described as *organum duplum*, three-part as *organum triplum,* and so forth. The original line of chant, now somewhat slower than in monophonic singing, was called the principal voice *(vox principalis)*. Two-part organum can be illustrated as follows:

Eventually the chant melody was moved to the bottom part and referred to as the *cantus firmus* (fixed song). The chant was identified by quoting the initial phrase of the Latin text. The cantus firmus was also called the tenor (Latin, *tenere,* to hold) because it held (retained) the original chant.

All polyphonic compositions of the medieval period used a cantus firmus, usually assigned to the tenor, as a basis for writing music. The practice of using authorized liturgical music (plainsong) as a foundation for composing original music is comparable to basing a sermon on a scriptural quotation. Both procedures quote an approved source as the prerequisite for what was essentially an exercise in creativity.

Polyphonic writing developed rapidly during the twelfth century. The notation of rhythm was improved by composers associated with the cathedral of Notre Dame in Paris as they began writing three-part and even four-part compositions. Borrowing rhythmic modes from poetry (trochaic, iambic, dactylic, etc.), they wrote metrical compositions (music with a regular pulse or beat) with two or three voices above an elongated tenor. The tenor was now so drawn-out that it was usually played by an organ, the only instrument that could sustain the slow-moving notes of the cantus firmus.

Pipe organs were probably introduced into the Western church in the ninth century in response to a need for a greater volume of sound. No other instrument has the inherent ability of an organ to fill a large church with vibrant sound. The room that houses an organ necessarily becomes the sound chamber for the

Polyphonic (3-part)

Melody 1

Melody 2

Melody 3

Homophonic (3-part)

Melody

Harmony

instrument. Thus, the increasingly large naves of Romanesque and, later, Gothic churches supplied huge resonating chambers for the brilliant sound of the king of instruments.

Following is a three-part organum by Perotin, a prominent composer at Notre Dame of Paris. The beginning measures are given in musical notation so that the two-voice lines plus tenor can be seen as well as heard. Any of the melodies can be sung, whistled, or played on an instrument. The complexity of polyphony results from the simultaneity of, in this case, rather uncomplicated melodic lines.

Organum: "Alleluya (Nativitas)"[4]

The *motet,* one of the most important forms of sacred music, was developed in the thirteenth century. In the following example, the text indicates only the source of the borrowed plainsong because an instrument was now used for the cantus firmus. Immediately above the tenor is a composed line with its own set of words, hence the name *motetus* (Fr., *le mot,* the word). The top voice also had its own set of words, which could be a different poem or even a different language. Increasing secularization led to motets, such as the one illustrated, with variations on the same love song sung in French by the *Triplum* and *Motetus.* Titles of early motets were given by indicating the beginning words of all three texts. The opening measures of notation again illustrate the uncomplicated nature of the individual melodies.

"En non Diu! Motet Quant voi;
Eius in Oriente"[5]

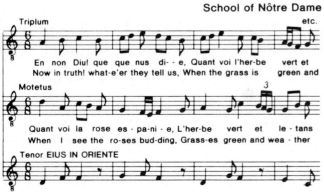

Polyphonic Mass

Musical styles developed very rapidly during the Gothic period (thirteenth and fourteenth centuries) and some composers acquired international reputations. Paradoxically, composers came to be known by name while many of the great master builders of Gothic cathedrals remained anonymous. Guillaume de Machaut, equally proficient as poet and as a composer of both sacred and secular music, was the most acclaimed of the gifted artists of the late Middle Ages (fig. 12.4). He was the first to write a polyphonic setting of all five movements of the ordinary of the Mass, a practice that was subsequently followed by every major composer through the sixteenth century and by many composers up to the present day.

The following portion of the *Agnus Dei* is sung by the upper three voices and accompanied by an instrument on the *contratenor* part, as indicated by the absence of text. The tenor, now the next lowest voice, still sings the cantus firmus. The polyphonic Mass, as distinguished from a motet, uses the Latin text of the monophonic chant. The beginning of the movement is notated in an open score (one staff for each part) so that the more complex movement of the melodies can be compared with the examples previously given of an organum and a motet.

Notre Dame Mass: "Agnus Dei"[6]

Medieval Dance

Sacred Dance

Dancing as a glorification of God was widely accepted in early Christian communities. Especially popular was the "Hymn of Jesus," a round dance (or ring dance) with twelve dancers representing the twelve disciples and the twelve signs of the zodiac. The idea of zodiac dancing in order to restore order to the cosmos can be traced as far back as the ancient Egyptians. However, the most direct influence probably

4. Y. Rokseth, *Polyphonies du XIIIe siècle* (Paris, 1935).
5. Y. Rokseth, *Polyphonies du XIIIe siècle* (Paris, 1935).

6. H. Besseler, *Die Musik des Mittelalters und der Renaissance* (Bucken, *Handbuch der Musikwissenschaft),* Potsdam, 1931, p. 149.

Figure 12.4 "Machaut Receiving Honors of Royalty and Clergy." Miniature by the Master of Bocqueteaux. Biblioteque Nazionale, Paris. This first known portrait of a Western composer is indicative both of Machaut's reputation and the status of a creative artist in Gothic France.

stemmed from the Pythagorean concept of the music of the spheres. This ring dance was also called the Ring Dance of Angels or, simply, Angel Dance.

The *tripudium* dated from early Christianity and was one of the few dance steps to survive into the medieval period. A tripudium was a three-step dance with two steps forward and one step backward. The dance symbolized both the Holy Trinity and, probably, the concept of two (spiritual) steps forward and one (human frailty) step backwards. Beginning as a solemn processional dance, the tripudium later evolved into a lively hopping dance that is still performed in modern Luxembourg in honor of a medieval saint.

"The Way to Jerusalem" was a stately dance that symbolized a pilgrimage to the Holy City. The dance was executed on the design of a labyrinth inlaid in the floor of the church nave. A leader was chosen whose function it was to determine the pace and the steps that matched the pattern of the floor tiles. This was a slow, spiraling dance that coordinated the dance steps with an accompanying chant. In order to make it all the way to Jerusalem, the leader had to arrive at the center of the labyrinth at the precise moment that the final syllable of the chant was sung. The dance was usually performed on a labyrinth modeled after the Cretan version in the palace of King Minos at Knossos. The labyrinth at the Cathedral of Chartres dates from the twelfth century and is forty feet in diameter.

The Dance of Death *(Danse Macabre)* was a phenomenon that appeared during the plague (Black Death), an epidemic that began in Constantinople in 1347 and ravaged all of Europe. The pestilence was virulent and, at the time, inexplicable. An explanation was nevertheless forthcoming: God was punishing the wicked for their sins. The universal hysteria

generated by the plague was fanned by the preaching of the Church, which called upon the sinners to repent.

The peasants, especially, suffering from plague, war, and famine, responded with repentance based on fear: fear of eternal damnation, of the plague, of the dancing ghouls from the graveyard who sought the living for the dance of death. The living, in turn, executed the dance in propitiation of their sins and in hopes of forestalling the Angel of Death.

Choreomania, a kind of dance mania, probably first appeared in England in the twelfth century. It was characterized by group psychosis and frenzied, even demented dancing. During the plague of the Black Death flagellants danced, sang, and vigorously lashed themselves in order to avert the wrath of God. Some participants died while dancing; others were mentally and/or physically crippled for the rest of their lives.

In 1374 a great dance epidemic broke out in most of Europe. Contemporary accounts of this manic behavior were medically farfetched but graphically descriptive of the pervasiveness of this kind of mass hysteria. *Choreomania* has been attributed to many causes, including psychotic reactions to the problems of war, famine, plague, and fear of death.

Secular Dance

Little is known of dancing in the early Middle Ages, but by the eighth or ninth centuries social dancing was a universal activity enjoyed by all persons at all levels of society. The frequent fairs and festivals, with the attendant vigorous dancing, enabled the peasantry to temporarily forget their otherwise bleak and meager existence. Their dances ranged from solo or lusty round dances to gaily executed couple dances.

The milkmaid's dance was an integral part of the May festival, a rite of spring that began on May 29th with a milking festival followed by games and dancing around the fertility symbol of the Maypole. Involving flirtatious milkmaids, garlands of flowers, and virile male pursuit, the milkmaid's dance appears to have been a kind of blindman's bluff set to music.

The country dance (round dance) has been a popular folk form in virtually every society. The lustiness of peasant country dancing is legendary, an exuberance that was tamed by the feudal lords and ladies to become the more genteel contre dance. In the contre dance, there was gradual entrance of couple after couple, which led to a round dance followed by couple dances, all somewhat in the manner of ballroom dancing.

The estampie (Provencal, *estamper,* to stamp) was the most popular dance of the Gothic Age and also one of the oldest forms of instrumental music. Originally a gay open-air dance, it eventually became more compact and, by the fifteenth century was performed indoors. Although it probably began as a round dance, it was the most popular couple dance of the age.

Table 12.2 Development of Medieval Music

	600	700	800	900	1000	1100	1200	1300	1400
Stylistic Periods	Romanesque	→				→ High Romanesque	→ Early Gothic		→ Late Gothic →
General Periods		Monasticism		Feudalism		Crusades / Age of Chivalry			
Musical Periods	Early Middle Ages					School of St. Martial	Sch. of N. Dame	Ars Antiqua → Ars nova →	
Musical Styles — Monophonic Music									
Sacred	Gregorian Chant			Sequences, Tropes		Liturgical Drama (Conductus)			→
Secular				Goliards / Jongleurs		Troubadours / Trouvères	Minnesingers		Meistersingers →
Polyphonic Music				Organum			Motet →	Mass →	
Instrumental Music Dances						Estampie (Ductia)			
Musical Instruments	(aulos) ...					Flageolet		→ Recorder →	
	? ...					(Drum) Tabor →			
						Shawm →			
						Bagpipe →			
						Trumpet →			
							Lute →		
							Gittern →		
	(kithara) ...				Rabab	Rebec →			
								Vielle →	

The music for the estampie was in 3/4 time and consisted of short, rotating phrases that were repeated many times during the course of the dance. To begin the dance, couples stood side by side in a semicircle. The first part of the dance began with both starting on the same foot with a step, close, step, close to first position with heels together. The movements were first to the right, then backward, then forward, then backward once more, and then begin the pattern all over again.

Following is a two-part estampie with the parts labeled simply as Cantus Superior (C.S.) and Cantus Inferior (C.I.). They were to be played by any available instruments. An approximation of the medieval dancing mood can be attained by executing the steps of the estampie to an accompaniment of any two or more different instruments. Percussion instruments such as drum, tambourine, bells, and triangle can and should be added. Liveliness of spirit is far more important than precise execution of dance steps and music.

Estampie: "Instrumental Dance"[7]

13th century

Table 12.2, *Development of Medieval Music,* is an outline and summary of the major developments in music during the Middle Ages. Dotted lines indicate either prior development leading up to a specific musical instrument or, as with monasticism, the waning influence of that way of life. Arrows indicate continuing development or, as with the connection between feudalism and chivalry, one developing out of the other.

The compositional school of Notre Dame was indebted to the School of St. Martial for the latter's development of organum. The Ars Antiqua (Old Art) and Ars Nova (New Art) were theoretical labels for old and new styles of music. Guillaume de Machaut was recognized in his own time as a composer of new music, that is, modern music.

The listing of musical instruments provides only a cross section of the many that were available. Other instruments that could have been listed include the psaltery, harp, rotta (Celtic lyre), fiddle, horn, and a large variety of percussion instruments.

Summary

The history of medieval music is much more than the study of the musical practices of a cultural period. Music of any era, in the playing and the singing, reflects and expresses the hopes, aspirations, frustrations, and despairs of people of all classes and stations in life. Music is still the nearest equivalent to an international language that humanity has yet devised.

Medieval music, when properly performed, can convey to us the *sound* of an era. It can bring alive the vast panorama of medieval life from Gregorian chant to liturgical drama, from troubadour love songs to peasant dances.

The sound of the music has a correlation with the architectural styles of the period. Gregorian chant, for example, was intended for participating worshipers rather than a listening audience. It is, therefore, more effective and persuasive inside the cloistered security of the monastery with its narrow windows, heavy walls, and pervasive quietude.

Polyphonic music, on the other hand, was performance oriented. The greatly expanded interior space of Romanesque churches was a proper area for the new multivoiced style. The arching melodies of organum complemented the rounded arches and high vaulting of the large Romanesque churches.

The dynamic, asymmetrical, complex mass of interreacting tension of stone structure, pointed arches, and soaring vaults that is the Gothic cathedral has its aural counterpart in the dynamic, asymmetrical, complex, and tension-packed art that is Gothic polyphonic music. That the first polyphonic mass was written for performance in the Cathedral of Notre Dame in Paris is more than coincidental. Guillaume de Machaut wrote music, whether consciously or unconsciously, to completely fill the interior of that great cathedral with vigorous and brilliant sound.

---

7. Wooldridge, *Early English Harmony,* London, 1897, pl. 19. Consisting of four variations on the initial section, the form is $AA^1A^2A^3A^4$.

Time Chart for the Middle Ages

Maps Showing a Few Significant Territorial Changes	Important Political, Historical, and Military Events	Philosophical Events	Art, Music, and Literature
	375–500—Great invasions of Roman Empire by northern and eastern tribes. Asiatic Huns harry Germanic peoples	354–430—Augustine formulated doctrine of Church based on Neoplatonism	
	395—Roman Empire split between East (Capital: Constantinople) and West (Capital: Rome or Ravenna)	395—Christianity becomes Roman state religion under Emperor Theodosius	
	410–476—Conventional dates for the fall of Rome. The city captured by tribes of Visigoths and Vandals		
		480–524—Boethius, "Consolations of Philosophy" expresses Roman world-weariness in a Christian-classical synthesis	
	465–511—Clovis established line of Frankish kings and (496) becomes Christian		
	590–604—Pope Gregory defends Rome against invaders—establishes political power of the Church		590–604—Pope Gregory legendary founder of Gregorian chant

The Roman Empire ca. A.D. 300

Invasions of the Roman Empire ca. A.D. 500

Time Chart for the Middle Ages (cont.)

Maps Showing a Few Significant Territorial Changes	Important Political, Historical, and Military Events	Philosophical Events	Art, Music, and Literature
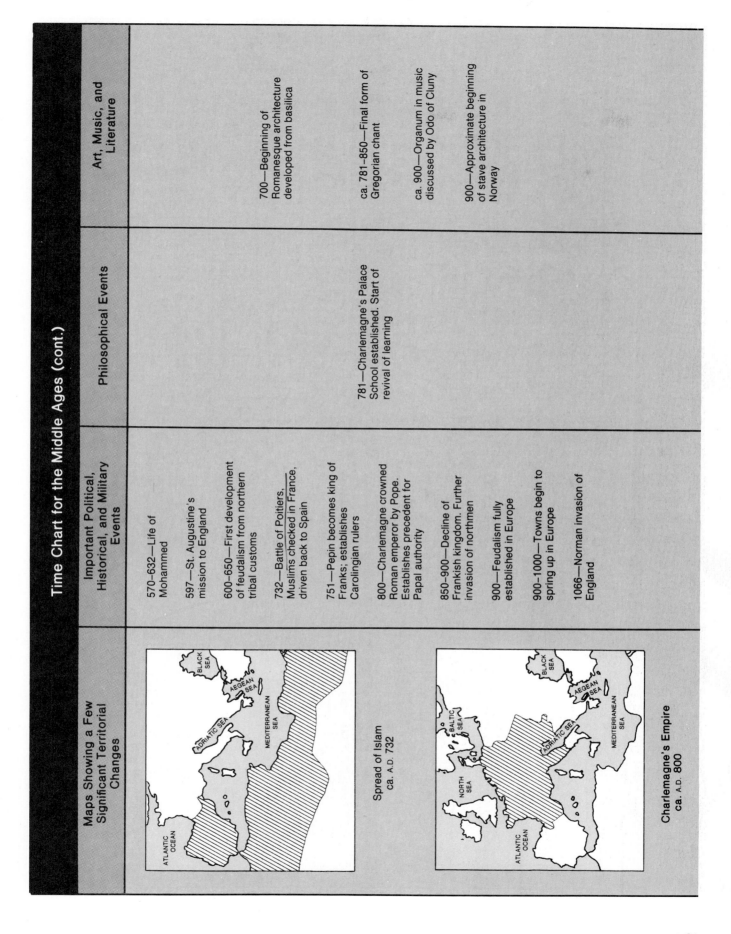	570–632—Life of Mohammed		
	597—St. Augustine's mission to England		700—Beginning of Romanesque architecture developed from basilica
	600–650—First development of feudalism from northern tribal customs		
	732—Battle of Poitiers, Muslims checked in France, driven back to Spain		ca. 781–850—Final form of Gregorian chant
	751—Pepin becomes king of Franks; establishes Carolingian rulers	781—Charlemagne's Palace School established. Start of revival of learning	ca. 900—Organum in music discussed by Odo of Cluny
	800—Charlemagne crowned Roman emperor by Pope. Establishes precedent for Papal authority		900—Approximate beginning of stave architecture in Norway
	850–900—Decline of Frankish kingdom. Further invasion of northmen		
	900—Feudalism fully established in Europe		
	900–1000—Towns begin to spring up in Europe		
	1066—Norman invasion of England		

Spread of Islam
CA. A.D. 732

Charlemagne's Empire
CA. A.D. 800

Time Chart for the Middle Ages (cont.)

Maps Showing a Few Significant Territorial Changes	Important Political, Historical, and Military Events	Philosophical Events	Art, Music, and Literature
	1077—Emperor Henry IV bows to Pope at Canossa	1000–1100—The Battle of Universals; Realist-Nominalist Controversy	1000–1100—Full development of Romanesque architecture
	1100–1300—Main Period of Crusades	1079–1142—Peter Abelard teaches in Paris, *Sic et Non*	1022–1084—Building of Abbey of Mont Saint Michel almost as we know it
	1154–1189—Rule of Henry II in England. Establishment of English common law		1071–1126—First-known troubador—but secular music was already well established
	1150 onwards—Half Spain in Christian hands. Unification of Spain continues		1194—The beginning of building of the present Chartres Cathedral. The height of Gothic style
	1215—Magna Carta—law superior to king	1200—The first trickle of the main body of Aristotle's works enters Europe	1170–1270—In France alone eighty great churches built, almost all devoted to the Virgin. The height of the Cult of the Virgin
	1272—Rudolf of Hapsburg made Austrian king—start of the rise of the House of Hapsburg	1270—Formal founding of University of Paris. For at least 200 years groups of students had collected at Bologna, Salerno, etc.	1240–1302—Cimabue, begins to paint figures naturalistically
	1291—Revolt of Swiss Cantons. Start of democratic Switzerland	1270—Introduction of all of Aristotle's works in Europe	1265–1321—Dante achieves "medieval synthesis" in *The Divine Comedy*
	1295—English parliament established	1214–1294—Roger Bacon bases knowledge on study of physical world	1276–1327—Painter Giotto continues trend toward naturalism
	1302—Estates General founded in France. A hint of democratic government	1225–1274—Thomas Aquinas establishes Church doctrine on Aristotelian principles	1300 onwards—Musical development of counterpoint, polyphony. Improvement of system of musical notation
	1337 to about 1440—Hundred Years War. England loses French lands. Great steps towards unification of both countries		1313–1375—Boccaccio
			1340–1400—Geoffrey Chaucer *The Canterbury Tales*

English and French Territories about 1154

English and French Territories about 1453

Unit 5

The Renaissance, 1350–1600

13

New Ideas and Discoveries Result from a New Way of Looking at the World

The Renaissance (ca. 1350–1600) was a remarkable period of intellectual energy and artistic creativity that ushered out the Middle Ages and set the stage for the emergence of the modern world. *Renaissance,* the French word for *rebirth,* refers not only to the rediscovery of classical Greece and Rome but also, in a larger sense, to fresh ideas about the nature of human beings and their place in the universe. The medieval conception of God as the ultimate reality was superseded by the idea that men and women were unique beings, the noblest creations of God. Everyone had worth and dignity and a free will that made it possible to be and to do, to utilize their God-given capacities to transform the world. They could develop their minds by study and reflection, activities advocated by Cicero as worthy of the "dignity of the human race" (Offices I.30).

The rediscovery of the ancient world originated in Italy, but there were Renaissance stirrings in northern countries that had no classical heritage. Vigorous trade, the beginnings of capitalism, the expansion of trade guilds, growing cities, burgeoning industries, and a spirit of creative enterprise fueled the rebirth of Europe both in the South and in the North.

The Rise of Humanism

On April 8, 1341, Petrarch (Francesco Petrarca; 1304–1374) was crowned with a laurel wreath as the first poet laureate of modern times. Symbolizing an intellectual movement called *humanism* that had begun in Verona and Padua a century earlier, the ceremony honoring the leading humanist took place, fittingly enough, in Rome. Humanism was the rediscovery of the total culture of classical antiquity: literature, history, rhetoric, ethics, and politics. Describing his abandoned law studies at Bologna as "the art of selling justice," Petrarch devoted his life to acquiring what he called the "golden wisdom" of the ancients: the proper conduct of one's private life; the rational governance of the state; the enjoyment of beauty; and the quest for truth. Humanism was a union of love and reason that stressed earthly fulfillment rather than medieval preparations for paradise. The humanists had rediscovered their ancestors, seeing them as real people lending assistance in the restatement of human values. Petrarch wrote letters to Cicero, whom he called his father, and to Virgil, who was, he said, his brother.

There had been earlier stirrings of classical revivals in the ninth-century Carolingian Renaissance and in the twelfth century at the Cathedral School of Chartres and at the Court of Eleanor of Aquitaine, but not until the middle of the fourteenth century did the rediscovery of antiquity become a true cultural movement. Petrarch's friend, the writer Giovanni Boccaccio (bo–KOTCH–yo; 1313–1375), was one of the first Westerners to study Greek, but by 1400 nearly all the Greek authors had been recovered and translated into Latin and Italian: Homer, Herodotos, Thucydides, Aeschylus, Sophokles, Euripides, and all the dialogues of Plato. For the humanists there were three ages of humankind: ancient, middle, and modern. The middle period, the Middle Ages, was seen as a benighted period between the fall of Rome and the rebirth of classical cultures. The men and women of the Renaissance were, in effect, discovering themselves as they recovered the past. They were aware that their age was significantly different from the Middle Ages, that they were the spiritual heirs of a distant past that was being reborn through their own efforts. There was no Latin word for rebirth, but Giorgio Vasari (1511–1574; see chap. 14) invented the word *Renaissance (Rinascita)* in his *Lives of the Most Excellent Italian Architects, Painters, and Sculptors from Cimabue to our own Times* (Florence, 1550). Vasari's term was applied to the fine arts that had developed out of early humanism, but the label now describes an era that consciously freed itself from the bondage of medievalism.

The most influential center of humanistic studies was the Platonic Academy founded at Florence in 1462 by the banker Cosimo de' Medici (1389–1464), the sire of a family that was to control Florence throughout most of the Renaissance. The guiding force of the academy, Marsilio Ficino (fi–CHEE–no; 1433–1499), promoted the study of Platonism through his translations into Latin of Plato, Plotinus, and other philosophers. In his major work, the *Theologia Platonica* (1482), Ficino described a universe presided over by a gracious and loving God who sought to bring humankind to Him through Beauty, one of His attributes. The contemplation of the beauty of nature, of beautiful things, of glorious art became a sort of worship of this God. When beauty was arranged in words or paintings (see colorplate 22), these works of art, too, became a part of the circle of love by which people reached beyond themselves to a loving God. Ficino's theory of "Platonic love," a spiritual bond between lovers of beauty, had strong repercussions in later English, French, and Italian literature.

Pico della Mirandola (PEA–ko della mere–AN–do–luh; 1463–1494) was a friend of Ficino's and a major influence on the humanists of the Forentine academy. His broadly based classical education in Greek and Latin was enriched by studies in Hebrew and Arabic that brought him into contact with Jewish and Arabic philosophy. Pico's attack on astrology impressed even the astronomer Johannes Kepler. More importantly, his conception of the dignity of the human race and the ideal of the unity of truth were significant contributions to Renaissance thought. His *Oration on the Dignity of Man* has been called "The Manifesto of Humanism." The following excerpts from Pico's ringing affirmation of the nobility of humankind epitomize the optimistic Renaissance point of view.

Literary Selection

ORATION ON THE DIGNITY OF MAN
Pico della Mirandola (1463–1494)

I have read in the records of the Arabians, reverend Fathers, that Abdala the Saracen, when questioned as to what on this stage of the world, as it were, could be seen most worthy of wonder, replied: "There is nothing to be seen more wonderful than man." In agreement with this opinion is the saying of Hermes Trismegistus: "A great miracle, Asclepius, is man." But when I weighed the reason for these maxims, the many grounds for the excellence of human nature reported by many men failed to satisfy me—that man is the intermediary between creatures, the intimate of the gods, the king of the lower beings, by the acuteness of his senses, by the discernment of his reason, and by the light of his intelligence the interpreter of nature, the interval between fixed eternity and fleeting time, and (as the Persians say) the bond, nay, rather, the marriage song of the world, on David's testimony but little lower than the angels. Admittedly great though these reasons be, they are not the principal grounds, that is, those which may rightfully claim for themselves the privilege of the highest admiration. For why should we not admire more the angels themselves and the blessed choirs of heaven? At last it seems to me I have come to understand why man is the most fortunate of creatures and consequently worthy of all admiration and what precisely is that rank which is his lot in the universal chain of Being—a rank to be envied not only by brutes but even by the stars and by minds beyond this world. It is a matter past faith and a wondrous one. Why should it not be? For it is on this very account that man is rightly called and judged a great miracle and a wonderful creature indeed.

2. But hear, Fathers, exactly what this rank is and, as friendly auditors, conformably to your kindness, do me this favor. God the Father, the supreme Architect, had already built this cosmic home we behold, the most sacred temple of His godhead, by the laws of His mysterious wisdom. The region above the heavens He had adorned with Intelligences, the heavenly spheres He had quickened with eternal souls, and the excrementary and filthy parts of the lower world He had filled with a multitude of animals of every kind. But, when the work was finished, the Craftsman kept wishing that there were someone to ponder the plan of so great a work, to love its beauty, and to wonder at its vastness. Therefore, when everything was done (as Moses and Timaeus bear witness), He finally took thought concerning the creation of man. But there was not among His archetypes that from which He could fashion a new offspring, nor was there in

His treasurehouses anything which He might bestow on His new son as an inheritance, nor was there in the seats of all the world a place where the latter might sit to contemplate the universe. All was now complete; all things had been assigned to the highest, the middle, and the lowest orders. But in its final creation it was not the part of the Father's power to fail as though exhausted. It was not the part of His wisdom to waver in a needful matter through poverty of counsel. It was not the part of His kindly love that he who was to praise God's divine generosity in regard to others should be compelled to condemn it in regard to himself.

3. At last the best of artisans ordained that that creature to whom He had been able to give nothing proper to himself should have joint possession of whatever had been peculiar to each of the different kinds of being. He therefore took man as a creature of indeterminate nature and, assigning him a place in the middle of the world, addressed him thus: "Neither a fixed abode nor a form that is thine alone nor any function peculiar to thyself have we given thee, Adam, to the end that according to thy longing and according to thy judgment thou mayest have and possess what abode, what form, and what functions thou thyself shalt desire. The nature of all other beings is limited and constrained within the bounds of laws prescribed by Us. Thou, constrained by no limits, in accordance with thine own free will, in whose hand We have placed thee, shalt ordain for thyself the limits of thy nature. We have set thee at the world's center that thou mayest from thence more easily observe whatever is in the world. We have made thee neither of heaven nor of earth, neither mortal nor immortal, so that with freedom of choice and with honor, as though the maker and molder of thyself, thou mayest fashion thyself in whatever shape thou shalt prefer. Thou shalt have the power to degenerate into the lower forms of life, which are brutish. Thou shalt have the power, out of thy soul's judgment, to be reborn into the higher forms, which are divine."

4. O supreme generosity of God the Father, O highest and most marvelous felicity of man! To him it is granted to have whatever he chooses, to be whatever he wills. Beasts as soon as they are born (so says Lucilius) bring with them from their mother's womb all they will ever possess. Spiritual beings, either from the beginning or soon thereafter, become what they are to be for ever and ever. On man when he came into life the Father conferred the seeds of all kinds and the germs of every way of life. Whatever seeds each man cultivates will grow to maturity and bear in him their own fruit. If they be vegetative, he will be like a plant. If sensitive, he will become brutish. If rational, he will grow into a heavenly being. If intellectual, he will be an angel and the son of God. And if, happy in the lot of no created thing, he withdraws into the center of his own unity, his spirit, made one with God, in the solitary darkness of God, who is set above all things, shall surpass them all. Who would not admire this our chameleon? Or who could more greatly admire aught else whatever? It is man who Asclepius of Athens, arguing from his mutability of character and from his self-transforming nature, on just grounds says was symbolized by Proteus in the mysteries. Hence those metamorphoses renowned among the Hebrews and the Pythagoreans.

5. For the occult theology of the Hebrews sometimes transforms the holy Enoch into an angel of divinity whom they call "Mal'akh Adonay Shebaoth," and sometimes transforms others into other divinities. The Pythagoreans degrade impious men into brutes and, if

one is to believe Empedocles, even into plants. Mohammed, in imitation, often had this saying on his tongue: "They who have deviated from divine law become beasts," and surely he spoke justly. For it is not the bark that makes the plant but its senseless and insentient nature; neither is it the hide that makes the beast of burden but its irrational, sensitive soul; neither is it the orbed form that makes the heavens but its undeviating order; nor is it the sundering from body but his spiritual intelligence that makes the angel. For if you see one abandoned to his appetites crawling on the ground, it is a plant and not a man you see; if you see one blinded by the vain illusions of imagery, as it were of Calypso, and softened by their gnawing allurement, delivered over to his senses, it is a beast and not a man you see. If you see a philosopher determining all things by means of right reason, him you shall reverence: he is a heavenly being and not of this earth. If you see a pure contemplator, one unaware of the body and confined to the inner reaches of the mind, he is neither an earthly nor a heavenly being; he is a more reverend divinity vested with human flesh. . . .

6. Let us disdain earthly things, despise heavenly things, and, finally, esteeming less whatever is of the world, hasten to that court which is beyond the world and nearest to the Godhead. There, as the sacred mysteries relate, Seraphim, Cherubim, and Thrones hold the first places; let us, incapable of yielding to them, and intolerant of a lower place, emulate their dignity and their glory. If we have willed it, we shall be second to them in nothing.

Perhaps the greatest teaching of these inspired scholars was that *virtu* was the highest goal of human existence. *Virtu* is not our word *virtue;* it can be defined as "excellence as a person." *Virtu* includes physical courage and daring, a high degree of intelligence, skill in many fields, and, above all, *action* that reveals all these characteristics. The aspiration toward *virtu* led to the "Renaissance man" and "Renaissance woman" of the period, as exemplified by Leonardo da Vinci and Isabella d'Este (see chap. 14).

Renaissance Science: The Secular View of the Universe

The Copernican Revolution

The idea of the universe on which medieval life had been based was that of Ptolemy. The Ptolemaic concept supposed the earth was the center of the universe, with the moon, the planets, and the fixed stars revolving around the earth in more or less fixed spheres (see fig. 13.1). Around the whole lay the crystalline sphere, outside of which lay the realm of God. Throughout the Middle Ages, however, many scientists, particularly the Arabic astronomers, had made observations about the movement of stars and planets that did not readily fit into this scheme and required the addition of more and more spheres. These scientists, working within the limits of Ptolemaic astronomy, also had to postulate certain backward loops of the heavenly bodies to account for variations in their

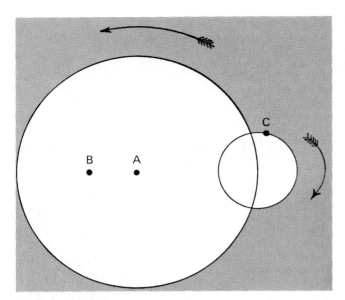

Figure 13.1 The earth in the center of the universe (A), the sun (B), and a heavenly body rotating around the earth (C). Also indicated is its orbit or epicycle (the clockwise arrow orbit). Try to imagine this whole system revolving at once. What figure would it make? If you cannot imagine, see figure 13.2.

periods of rotation. By the time of the Renaissance, the astronomers had built up an enormously complicated system of more than seventy spheres surrounding the earth, with each of the heavenly bodies performing an epicycle, or little backward rotation of its own around a central point on its orbit.

The Ptolemaic system was first questioned by the Polish astronomer and mathematician Nicholas Copernicus, who lived from 1473 to 1543. Copernicus never advanced the theory that the earth was not the center of the universe; he only discovered that mathematical calculations would be simpler if one accepted the sun as a stationary point and based one's calculations upon that. His conclusions were based upon the diagram shown in figure 13.2, which reveals the path a heavenly body performing its grand cycle about the earth (and also its little epicycle) would make.

Copernicus calculated that if we shifted the center of our system of sun and planets from the earth to the sun, we could eliminate the idea of the epicycles, for, as the heavenly body makes its circle around the earth and also makes its little epicyclical journey, it actually describes a new orbit in which the sun is the center. The dotted line in figure 13.2 is the circumference of this circle. Copernicus, as we have said, only suggested this as a method of simplifying the mathematical calculations. Actually he gave an entirely new description of the world, which yielded a new concept of humanity's relation to the universe.

Once one gets the idea of this change in point of view, it seems simple. One wonders how people who had the intelligence to make the complicated calculations concerned with the epicycles could not have gotten this simple idea of changing their perspective. Copernicus could do this because he had the courage to look at the thing *as it was,* uncolored by all the ideas that had been handed down to him. He was willing to junk all of his traditional learning and tell what he really saw. Here, better than any place else, one can see the difference between the Renaissance and the medieval point of view.

The Copernican system, with many modifications, is essentially the concept of our solar system we accept as true today. Some of the modifications of the principle occurred during the Renaissance itself. Tycho Brahe (TIE-ko BRA-hee; 1546–1601) made careful observations of stars and planets that were to serve as factual material for later astronomers' interpretation. Kepler (1571–1630), a German astronomer, refined the calculations of Copernicus, pointing out that the orbits of the planets were ellipses rather than circles and accounting for the fact that the motion of planets was more rapid at some points in their orbits than at others. Galileo (gal–i–LAY–oh; 1564–1642) did more with his telescope than any other person to establish the Copernican system as an astronomical fact, remembering that Copernicus only advanced the idea as a method of simplifying mathematical calculations. Indeed, this phase of Galileo's work was probably as important as any other that he did. While he is best known for his discovery of the laws of motion (one immediately remembers the stories of his experiments in dropping objects from the leaning tower of Pisa), these experiments took place after the Church had banned his further observations with the telescope. (Galileo's work is discussed in greater detail in chap. 17.)

All of these advances in our knowledge about the vast universe of which we are a part were summed up in what is known as the Cartesian revolution, after René Descartes (day–KART; 1596–1650), a French philosopher who formulated the more or less fragmentary evidence into a unified system of scientific philosophy. (Descartes is also discussed in chap. 17.) He reaffirmed the ideas first expressed by the Greek atomist Demokritos that the whole of matter was composed of items of identical substance. All reality for Descartes, then, lay in the motion of this absolute substance through space and time. For him, and the many who followed him, God was reduced to an engineer who had built a very complicated machine and set it in motion. From that time forth, God had no function in the world. By Descartes's division of primary (measurable) qualities and secondary (nonmeasurable) qualities, he brought about a new kind of dualism. Henceforth, the body was the only part of the human that was of real importance; the soul, if it existed at all, belonged to the secondary, the less important group of qualities. From Descartes onward, scientists were only to concern themselves with the question "How does something work?" not "Why does

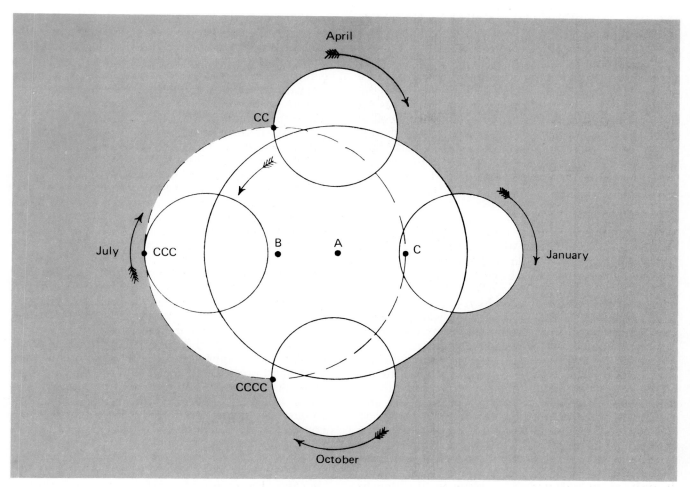

Figure 13.2 The earth (A), the sun (B), and a heavenly body (C) making its epicycle in the same time it makes its orbit around the earth: a full year. Suppose that in January the heavenly body is at point C. Then by April it will have gone a quarter of the way around its orbit with the earth as the center, and it will also have gone a quarter of the way around its epicycle. It will be at point CC. By July it will have gone around another quarter of its circles and will be at point CCC. By October it will be at point CCCC. By January it will be back at its starting point. If we join these points with the line that the planet traveled, we will find its path to be a circle (dotted line), which has the sun at its center.

it work?'' As Randall has summed up the thought of the Cartesian revolution:

> To Descartes thenceforth space or extension became the fundamental reality in the world, motion the source of all change, and mathematics the only relation between its parts. . . . He made of nature a machine and nothing but a machine; purposes and spiritual significance had alike vanished.[1]

We have said many times that one of humankind's great questions was that of our relation to the universe and to God. Henceforth, we must separate the two and ask about our relationship to the universe and our relationship to God. Of the two questions, the world since the scientific revolution has considered the former question the more important. Human institutions, from that day forth, have been built upon the idea of a mathematically ordered universe rather than one actively ruled by God.

1. J. H. Randall Jr., *The Making of the Modern Mind* (New York: Columbia University Press, 1976), pp. 241–42.

Inventions and Discoveries

In China printing was invented in 756, gunpowder in about 1100, and the magnetic compass a decade or two later. All were strictly controlled by the existing social order, enabling the imperial government to maintain control, most of the time, in all of China. There was no central authority in Europe, and so the changes caused by just these three inventions were dramatic. During the 1440s movable type was invented in the Mainz river valley in Germany, possibly by Johannes Gutenberg (1398?–1468). Up to this time learning had been the privilege of the few who could afford to have books copied by hand. The invention of printing made possible the most rapid expansion of knowledge that we have known prior to the proliferation of computers that has occurred in our own time. By 1500 there were over a thousand print shops and millions of volumes in print. Without printing Erasmus of Rotterdam (see chap. 16) would not have achieved his eminence as Europe's foremost man of letters. Printing was a vital factor in the success of the

Protestant Reformation; Martin Luther's tracts attacking the Roman church were rushed into print and spread like wildfire throughout Europe.

The technique of making gunpowder was imported from China and first used during the latter years of the Hundred Years' War (1337–1453) between England and France. Subsequent improvements in firearms and artillery made gunpowder, in effect, a great leveler. One man with a gun was more than a match for a knight on horseback, and even early cannons could bombard medieval castles into submission. The feudal age ended abruptly and, one might say, explosively.

Exploration and Discovery

As mentioned earlier, trade between European cities and those of the Near and Middle East was an important factor in the evolution of the Renaissance, but limited navigational aids forced sailing vessels to generally remain within sight of land. A few intrepid travelers, the most famous of which was the Venetian Marco Polo (1254?–1324?), made their way along the great land routes to India and China. Marco Polo returned to Venice after spending seventeen years in China (1271–1295), but no one at the time believed any of the wonders that he related. Not until the fifteenth century would European sailors have the capability to circumnavigate Africa to reach China, and the driving force behind this exploration was Prince Henry the Navigator (1394–1460), son of King John I of Portugal. Apparently without referring to the Chinese work, a crude magnetic compass had been invented in the twelfth century. Henry improved this crucial device, had accurate maps and tables drawn, improved the design of ships, and reintroduced the use of the astrolabe that had been invented by the Arabs. A ship's latitude (north-south) could be calculated to within about thirty miles by using the astrolabe to determine the angle of the sun above the horizon at noon. This figure was then compared with Henry's tables of the sun's declination at known latitudes for each day of the year.

Navigation could not be made more precise until the marine chronometer was invented in 1760 to determine longitude (east-west). Nevertheless, navigational aids were adequate for voyages of exploration (see fig. 13.3). In 1497, for example, Vasco da Gama (ca. 1469–1524) sailed southwest and then south from Portugal for ninety-seven days before turning east and sailing directly to the known latitude of his African destination, the Cape of Good Hope. He continued around Africa and on to India, returning to Lisbon in 1499 (see fig. 13.3). Prior to da Gama's successful voyage, India had been the destination of Christopher Columbus (ca. 1451–1506), who sailed west rather than south and discovered instead a New World—new to Europeans, that is, with the exception of much earlier Viking voyages. Columbus claimed the land for Spain, which was confirmed when Spain and Portugal drew a vertical line in the Atlantic, with the Americas awarded to Spain and Africa to Portugal. No one knew at the time that the line ran through Brazil,

until it was accidentally discovered by the Portuguese captain Pedro Cabral (1460–ca. 1526), who was blown off course as he sailed down the African coast. A treaty later confirmed Portugal's ownership of Brazil. It apparently occurred to no one that the Americas and Africa were already inhabited by people who were never consulted by their new owners. European colonialism had begun.

Vasco de Balboa (1475–1517) marched across the Isthmus of Panama in 1513 to discover a Pacific Ocean that residents of the Pacific Basin had always known was there. Ferdinand Magellan (1480–1521), a Portuguese in the service of Spain, sailed west in 1519 with five ships to find a passage, now called the Straits of Magellan, around South America and across the Pacific to Asia. He was killed in the Philippines, but his explorations proved empirically that the world was round.

Spain and Portugal intended to divide between them the entire overseas world, but England and France had other ideas. An Italian mariner who the English called John Cabot (1450–1498) was dispatched in 1497 to find a "northwest passage" to the Indies. The passage did not exist, of course, but Cabot's landings somewhere around Labrador and Newfoundland provided England with an opportunity to claim all of North America. The explorations of Jacques Cartier (1494–1553) plus later discoveries by Samuel de Champlain (1567?–1635) gave France competing claims, while the Dutch joined the competition with the explorations of Henry Hudson (?–1611), an Englishman who entered Dutch service in 1609.

Maritime explorers were followed by adventurers like Hernando Cortés (1485–1547) and Francisco Pizarro (1471–1541), who conquered the only two high civilizations of the New World. Cortés took the Aztec empire of Mexico in 1519 with 600 soldiers, and Pizarro conquered the Inca empire of Peru in 1531–1533 with only 180 soldiers.

There was treasure aplenty in the New World, but Europeans found another in their own minds. Accounts of the voyages of explorers seized the Renaissance mind much as the exploration of space engages the minds of our time. Renaissance Europe had opened up new frontiers in art, literature, philosophy, and science, and now there was the lure and challenge of new lands as well. America became, for many Europeans, the literal utopia that Sir Thomas More used as the setting for his fictional *Utopia* (see chap. 16).

The Reformation: New Ideas about God and Humankind

Not only did concepts about the universe and the world change rapidly during the Renaissance, but the Reformation changed the face of Europe. It not only created a major schism in a once monolithic church but also constituted a major social, political, economic, and intellectual revolution. There had been earlier challenges to the authority of the Church of

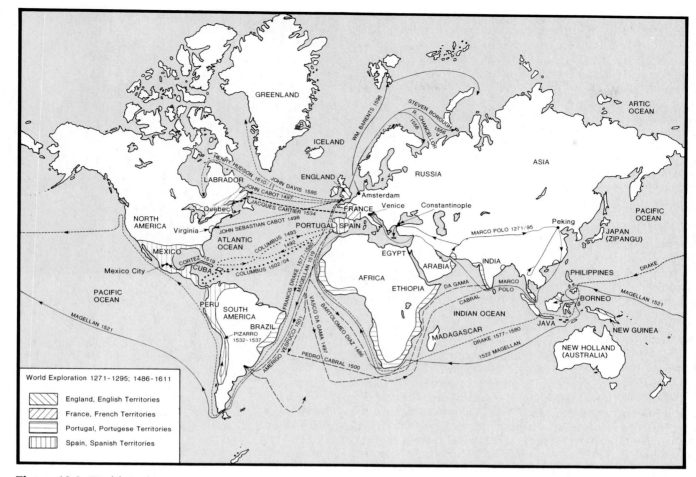

Figure 13.3 World Exploration 1271–1295; 1486–1611.

Rome, but the Reformation started by Martin Luther was the first to succeed on a large scale.

In 1170, for instance, a French merchant named Peter Waldo (d. 1217) founded a puritan sect known as the Waldenses. Preaching apostolic poverty, they rejected Rome and its papal claims. Though excommunicated in 1184 and persecuted for centuries, the sect survives today as the *Vaudois* in the Alps of Italy and France.

In England John Wiclif (or Wycliffe; ca. 1320–1384), an Oxford scholar, revived interest in St. Augustine and openly questioned the need for a priestly hierarchy. Contending that God and the Scriptures were the sole sources of spiritual authority, he translated the Vulgate into English and urged everyone to read it for themselves. He was silenced by the Church, but the Wiclif Bible became important after 1534 when Henry VIII, with his Act of Supremacy, broke away from the Roman Catholic church and confiscated church property.

Jan Hus (or Huss; 1369–1415) was a follower of Wiclif and a priest/professor at Charles University in Prague. His opposition to the sale of indulgences led to charges of the Wiclif heresy, and he was burned at the stake on July 6, 1415. His martyrdom caused bloody riots in Bohemia followed by an evangelical movement of the Unitas Fratrum (Unity of Brethren).

By 1500 the Brethren (later called the Moravian Church), had over 200,000 members in 400 parishes. In 1501 the church published the first hymnal in the vernacular and placed it, along with the Bible, in the hands of the people.

The term *reformation* was used in the late Middle Ages by individuals and groups who protested the secularization of Christianity and the abuses of power and privilege by the church hierarchy from the popes down to parish priests. An unbroken succession of corrupt Renaissance popes from Sixtus IV (1471–1484) to Leo X(1513–1521) fueled the flames of a revolt that was touched off when Martin Luther (1483–1546) posted his ninety-five Theses on the door of the castle church at Wittenberg on October 31, 1517. Luther was incensed at what he called the "sale" of indulgences, particularly the fund-raising activities of a Dominican monk named Tetzel. Operating under papal authority, Tetzel was dealing in indulgences, soliciting contributions to swell the papal treasury (that Leo X had depleted) and to pay for the construction of the new St. Peter's in Rome. Indulgences were the issue and will be discussed later; initially, Luther intended only a clarification of the teachings of the Church. The *origins* of the Reformation are found primarily in Luther's religion.

An Augustinian friar and professor of theology at the University of Wittenberg, Luther had experienced a spiritual crisis. Convinced that he was a lost soul and destined for Hell, Luther took the advice of a confessor and plunged with characteristic fervor into intensive study of the Bible. In the epistles of Paul he rediscovered a faith in salvation by grace. The central doctrines of the early church fathers, especially Augustine, confirmed his belief in the authority of the Word of God: faith alone was sufficient for salvation. Church doctrine stipulated that faith *and* good works were necessary, but Luther stood firm in the conviction that he articulated the true faith of the Church. Faith and the Bible were enough for Luther; the break with Rome was inevitable.

Indulgences were remissions by the Church of temporal punishment either on earth or in purgatory. The Sacrament of Penance of the Roman Catholic church consists of contrition, confession, absolution, and satisfaction on the part of the penitent. The penitent must feel contrition for his or her sins, confess to the priest, and be absolved of guilt. The sinner must satisfy God's justice by working out the penalties assigned by the priest, penalties that could be commuted by the granting of an indulgence. According to the doctrine of *Thesaurus Meritorum,* the Church had a treasury of spiritual merits accumulated from the satisfaction of Christ for the sins of the world and the martyrdom of the Saints. Indulgences transferred spiritual merit from this treasury to the penitent. Too complex for laypersons to understand, many people believed that even sins could be absolved if they could buy enough indulgences, which as Luther observed, "put a grievous instrument in the hands of avarice."

"Therefore those preachers of indulgences err who say that a papal pardon frees a man from all penalty and assures his salvation" was one of Luther's theses, actually statements that he would publicly debate. Arguing some of these points with the theologian John Eck, Luther publicly admitted that his statements really did challenge the authority of the Church. When shown that his position was similar to that of Jan Hus, Luther asserted that the Church was in error in burning Hus. Jan Hus was a condemned heretic, and Luther, basing his defense on the Scriptures, openly challenged the authority of the pope and the councils of the Church.

In 1521 Emperor Charles V convened the estates of the German empire in the town of Worms to force Luther, who had already been excommunicated by the pope, to retract his writings. "I neither can nor will make any retraction, since it is neither safe nor honorable to act against conscience" was his response. Insisting that "the Church universal is the number of the elect," Luther concluded his defense, according to tradition, with the words, "Here I stand. I cannot do otherwise. God help me. Amen." The Diet adopted an edict declaring Luther an outlaw, but the verdict was academic because Luther had many supporters among the German princes (see fig. 13.4). Corruption in the Church and the formation of a new faith helped

Figure 13.4 Lucas Cranach the Younger (1515–1586), *Martin Luther and the Wittenberg Reformers,* ca. 1543. Oil on panel, 27⅝ × 15⅝''. Luther is at the far left and Ulrich Zwingli at the far right. Looming large in the center is John Frederick the Magnanimous, Elector of Saxony and patron of the reformers and the Lutheran Church. The Toledo Museum of Art. Gift of Edward Drummond Libbey.

promote Luther's church, but a rising tide of nationalism and an opportunity to send no more money to Rome were perhaps even more significant in the triumph of the Reformation.

The principles of Lutheranism were later formulated by a Lutheran scholar, Melancthon (1497–1560), who stated them as follows:

1. The only final authority either for conduct or belief is in the Scriptures *(Sola Scriptura).*
2. The one condition of salvation is faith or trust in Divine Love *(Sola Fide).*
3. Faith itself is a gift of God, not an achievement of man *(Sola Gratia).*
4. The community of the faithful is the true church whose only head is Christ. The growth of this church is fostered by preaching the gospel and the observance of two sacraments, Baptism and the Lord's Supper.

The Lutheran belief stresses individuality; salvation and a knowledge of God is a direct process, needing no church or priestly intercessor.

The Reformation in Germany was closely followed by a notable movement in Switzerland, first led by Ulrich Zwingli (1484–1531; see fig. 13.4), who even more than Luther believed in the individuality of worship and the authority of the Scriptures. Later this group was led by John Calvin (1509–1564), a French Protestant who was originally educated for the law as well as theology. When the Protestants were persecuted in France he fled to Geneva, where he lived for the rest of his life. There he established a theocratic republic, that is, a government that was ruled by the elders of the church.

Calvin was a strong believer in predestination, for since God is all-knowing and all-powerful, Calvin reasoned that he must know the fate of every person. In this faith, only a few of the elect were to be saved. The outward sign of salvation was right moral conduct. In 1536 Calvin published *The Institutes of the Christian Religion* (revised into its final form in 1559) in which he stated the philosophy upon which his faith was founded. This includes the unconditional sovereignty of God, which means that whatever happens, happens because God wills it so. He believed in humanity's total depravity and abject helplessness, which makes the help of a Saviour necessary. He stated his belief in a rigorous predestination of all people; some few of the elect will be saved through faith in God, and many will be forever damned. Finally, he stated that the group of the elect constitutes the Church. It is the duty of civil authorities as well as religious authorities to preserve the Church. Therefore an infraction of divine law required civil punishment, and the civil authorities should be under the direction of church authorities. This, as one can see, was a very strict sort of belief, and Calvin forbade many of the ordinary pleasures of life in Geneva and persecuted all those who did not follow his own faith.

Various forms of Calvinism spread throughout Europe. John Knox (1505–1572) founded the Presbyterian church in Scotland and England following the principles laid down by the Swiss leader. The English Puritans who came to America, and whose first colony was a theocracy like that of Geneva, were Calvinists.

The emphasis upon the individual's right to interpret the Scriptures in a personal way, almost the cornerstone of the churches that grew out of the Reformation, quite naturally led to the separation into many sects. Both Lutheranism and Calvinism attracted their members from the rising middle class. Many of the newer sects drew their following from the poorer classes. Among these latter were the Anabaptists, who believed in baptism only when the individual had reached adulthood, and was able to make a free choice. Very strongly present here was the concept of rebirth through baptism. From the Anabaptists came such modern denominations as the Friends (Quakers) and Baptists. The Socinians, who took their name from Faustus Socinus (1539–1604), were antitrinitarians who refused to hold serfs or take part in any war. Persecuted in Poland by the Catholic church led by the Jesuits, they were banished in 1658 on pain of death. The Socinians were the single most important source for the Unitarian church. The Arminian church was led by the Dutch theologian Jacobus Arminius (1560–1609). They were an offshoot of Calvinism, but asserted that each person was free to choose his or her own way of living, thus denying the doctrine of predestination. Their theology was, in essence, accepted in England by the Wesley brothers, who founded the Methodist church.

The English church, known in America as the Episcopal church, came into being during the reign of Henry VIII in England. Although the immediate cause of the break with Rome came when the pope refused to sanction the annulment of Henry's marriage to Catherine of Aragon, the real causes of the break went much deeper than that. In the main, the English monarchs were tired of sending money to Rome, and of seeing much of their land in the possession of the Church. In 1534 the break between England and Rome was completed, and the Act of Supremacy stated that the king of England was the official head of the organization of the English church. At the time, there was little difference in the theology of the English and the Roman churches, and most of the forms of worship, though translated into English, remained the same as they had been in the Roman Catholic church.

The Catholic Reformation, also called the Counter-Reformation, was the papal response to Luther's revolt against Rome. Convened by Pope Paul III (1534–1549), the Council of Trent met from 1545 to 1563 to redefine every phase of Catholic doctrine attacked by the reformers: original sin, grace, redemption, the Sacraments, the Sacrifice of the Mass, and Purgatory. Every violation of discipline was denounced, reforms were enacted, and observance was demanded under pain of censure. The music of the Church was reformed, and there was a strong thrust of Counter-Reformation art and architecture (see chap. 18). The Counter-Reformation was given a mighty assist by the Jesuits (Society of Jesus) founded by Ignatius Loyola in 1534 and formally approved by Pope Paul III in 1540. The Jesuits represented the disciplined drive of the movement, but the popes also revived the Inquisition, an old instrument for the stamping out of heresy. Sitting as medieval courts and using medieval methods of torture, the papal and Spanish Inquisitions were relatively ineffective, however, in stemming the Protestant tide, especially in northern Europe.

How can we sum up the influence of the Reformation upon the lives of people? First, it was a strong prop to nationalism, which was perhaps the greatest single force moving through this whole period of the Renaissance. Second, it had a marked influence on education, in many cases divorcing it from ecclesiastical domination. On the other hand, under the strict influence of the Calvinists in particular, the scope of education was limited largely to the subjects of immediate utilitarian value. As far as the rise of individuality is concerned, the Reformation is almost a declaration of religious independence, for when one admits that the Bible alone is the basis for religious beliefs, one is immediately confronted with the great variety of possible interpretations of that book. As a result, under Protestantism there has risen such a host of sects that the individual can find almost any type of religious belief that appeals to him or her. Finally, Protestantism was a strong influence in the rise of capitalism, for the ideal Calvinist, Methodist or Lutheran took the first psalm strongly to heart:

> Blessed is the man that walketh not in the counsel of the ungodly, nor standeth in the way of sinners, nor sitteth in the seat of the scornful. But his delight is in the law of the Lord; and in his law doth he meditate day and night. And he shall be like a tree planted by the rivers of water, that bringeth forth his fruit in his season; his leaf also shall not wither; and whatsoever he doeth shall prosper.

Clearly this psalm tells us that the good man and good woman shall prosper. In a time when making, saving, and spending money was becoming more and more the sign of success, we come to the conclusion that we can recognize good people because they have prospered in this way. Furthermore, the sober, steady, hard-working way of life advocated by most of the new sects was exactly the sort of life that would promote industrious work and careful spending. And so began the Protestant work ethic, which produces the ideal person for a capitalist system.

The Relation of the Individual to the Group

Capitalism

We have already hinted in the previous paragraph at another of the forces that came into being during the Renaissance: capitalism. This is true. We who live in a capitalist society are prone to take our institutions and arrangements for granted, and assume that they have existed forever. However, until the late Middle Ages, at least, the thing we call capitalism had not existed, and it only came into full flower in the Renaissance. This is another example of the trend toward individualism that moved through this time, for up until now the economic arrangements of life had always been under political and religious domination. Now, exactly as the knowledge of the universe divorced itself from religion, so, too, did economic arrangements become an entirely separate field of human thought and human relationships. Indeed, it appears that much of the strife of our time occurs because of our conscious or unconscious attempts to bring politics and economics together again.

In order to make the distinction clear between the guild system and the capitalist system, it would probably be wise to point out some of the characteristics of the guild system. Under this type of economic organization there was production for human need alone. Furthermore, manufacturing and selling were a part of the same process. For example, a shoemaker made shoes only when someone ordered them. When there were no orders, he made no shoes. His sole purpose in his economic life was to make shoes for people when they wanted them. Furthermore, when the shoemaker died, unless his son inherited the business, the business died with the man. The quality of materials and work and the price of the finished article were rigidly controlled, so that there was no competition in business.

Now, to make the difference clear, let us watch the development of a capitalistic business. Johannes Fugger settled in the city of Augsburg in 1380 where he became a weaver, that is, a member of the leading industry of that town. Soon, however, he began to collect and sell the products of other weavers. Before very long he employed weavers, paying them for their labor, and taking their product for his own. His son, Jacob Fugger I, continued this business, which was expanded under Jacob Fugger II, the leading capitalist of the Renaissance. This member of the family expanded his interests outside of weaving, dealing in metals as well as textiles. He confined his workings largely within the Hapsburg empire, dealing in silver and copper in Austria, and in silver and quicksilver in Spain. He also lent large sums of money to the Hapsburg emperors (they were engaged in at least a half-dozen wars during the Renaissance and were constantly in need of money), in return for which Fugger obtained monopoly rights on the ores of the metals in which he traded. Finally he bought the mines themselves so that he, like many great capitalists in our own time, employed thousands of workmen to whom he paid a wage; he controlled all of his products from raw material to market; there was no supervision over the quality of his products or the price he charged except the amount that the traffic would bear. Finally, he formed a company that existed outside of himself. Fugger had mined silver, copper, and mercury in quantity, with little relation to life-needs. His company piled up "profits," almost a new term, quite aside from the needs of the Fugger family; and these profits were measured in money rather than in lands or goods. From this example, we can, perhaps, discover some of the essential qualities of capitalism.

Perhaps the first characteristic of capitalism is that it creates "companies" that exist quite separately from the people who make them up. That is, the company can be sued, it can contract debts, and it may even do things of which the people who make up the company disapprove.

A second characteristic lies in the fact that the sole purpose of the company is the acquisition of money, and the demand for more money is never satisfied. Again, let us take a modern example: A single capitalist family acquires more money than it can ever spend. They can buy all sorts of luxury items but ride in only one chauffeur-driven limousine (or Lear jet), live in one house at a time, and consume just so much food in a lifetime. There is a physical limit to what can be bought and actually used. However, there is no limit to the amount of money that can be amassed, and the capitalist system assumes that the acquisition of money is the goal of economic activity (see fig. 13.5).

Figure 13.5 Quentin Matsys (1465?–1530), *The Money Lender and His Wife,* 1514. Oil on wood, 28 × 26¾″. Distracted from reading her Bible, the wife is as fascinated as her husband as he lovingly examines his money. The Louvre, Paris.

A third characteristic of capitalism is its rational organization within the "company." The company must plan ahead to assure itself of raw materials in the proper quantity and at the proper time. It must plan ahead to assure itself that it can get rid of the products of its effort. It must utilize the time of its workers and machines to the utmost, which means that there must be an even flow of work throughout the whole concern. The company must know exactly how much of its raw materials, how much of its finished product, and how much money is on hand at any given moment. All this means that it must have a rigid accounting system, both of materials and money, and of human energies as well. Capitalism shapes means to ends, and the end is the making of money profit. It is entirely rational and has no room for emotion in its organization. Any part of the organization that does not make a direct and efficient contribution to the purpose of the company must be cut away.

If the internal organization of the company is marked by this rationality, a fourth characteristic is that the system itself is completely irrational insofar as it is not controlled by government or by agreements within the member-companies of a particular industry. Since each company must grow, the resultant competition is completely ruthless, opportunistic, and irrational. Finally, as one writer points out:

> Profits, no matter how large, can never reach a level sufficiently high to satisfy the economic agent—acquisition therefore becomes unconditional, absolute. Not only does it seize upon all phenomena within the economic realm, but it reaches over into

other cultural fields and develops a tendency to proclaim the supremacy of business interest over all other values.[2]

What were some of the immediate effects of the introduction of this new system of economic endeavor? In the first place, it increased the possibilities for individualism. If people could get to the top of the economic heap, all religious or guild restraints were removed, and they could do exactly what they had the power to do. The only limits on individuals lay in their own imagination, their own ability to plan ahead, their own ability to seize opportunity. A second effect of capitalism was in the increase of goods that were available. Under the handicraft-guild system, goods were available only when people wanted them. Now, capitalists created them and went out to find markets for the products. They made more of everything than was ordered and went out to "sell" these goods to people. In terms of the ownership of material things, capitalism has increased our standard of living manyfold. Not the least of the changes wrought by capitalism was the change in the appearance of cities. Up to this time, stores had not existed except as the booths at fairs could be called stores. Up to this time, the factory—a workshop and living quarters for the craftsman, his apprentices, and his family—had also been the store. The show-windows of today, with their enticing display of goods, the practice of shopping for everything from soup to hats and automobiles: these are the result of the capitalistic system, and the planning of our cities today is a direct result of the new type of merchandising.

One caution must be added. Capitalism did not spring full-fledged into the world. In its first stages during the Renaissance it is called *mercantile capitalism,* in a later stage it is called *industrial capitalism,* recently it has been termed *finance capitalism,* and presently *state capitalism.* In each of these stages its characteristics were somewhat different from those of other stages; each stage had its particular qualities; each stage had its peculiar problems.

The Development of the Sovereign Power

Perhaps the most striking development of the Renaissance was the increase of royal power. We saw the beginning of this movement during the latter part of the Middle Ages, when the inadequacies of feudalism—the lack of a common currency, the blocking of trade by feudal tariff barriers, the inconsistencies in the administration of justice, and the lack of civil servants who were trained for their work—revealed themselves, and the kings drove to new power. Still another force that lent importance to the sovereign was the rich pouring of treasure from the newly discovered lands across the sea. For example, the Spanish monarch claimed a fifth of all treasure brought to Spain by the *conquistadores.* With these funds the kings

---

2. Edwin R. Seligman, ed., "Capitalism," in *Encyclopedia of the Social Sciences,* vol. 3 (New York: Macmillan, 1937), p. 197.

were able to set up brilliant courts that attracted the nobles from their muddy country estates and made these nobles dependent upon the king for their livelihood and for their amusement. Most of the nobility were more than willing to sell out their rural independence for the ritual of seeing the king rise in the morning, or participating, vicariously, at least, in the brilliant art and the sparkling drama with which the kings surrounded themselves, and of taking their part in the great balls and festivals the king provided.

Not only did the nobles give their allegiance to the sovereign, but the common people looked to the throne as the single source of order in a world changing so rapidly that the people could scarcely keep up. "Future shock" was present in the Renaissance as it is today. Order had been the rule of the Middle Ages. Suddenly the authority of the Church was broken in much of northern Europe, the unity of the universe was shattered by the new science, and the economic order that had been controlled by the guilds was shattered by capitalism. People needed some sort of order-giving source to take the place of the shattered systems. The king was the single stabilizing influence in all this chaos. Wherever we turn, we find references to this central position the sovereign held. In Shakespeare's play *Hamlet,* Rosencrantz speaks of the monarch's importance thus:

> The cease of majesty
> Dies not alone, but, like a gulf doth draw
> What's near it with it; it is a massy wheel,
> Fix'd on the summit of the highest mount,
> To whose huge spokes ten thousand lesser things
> Are mortis'd and adjoin'd; which, when it falls,
> Each small annexment, petty consequence,
> Attends the boisterous ruin. Never alone
> Did the king sigh, but with a general groan.

Historically the Renaissance saw the brilliant reigns of the Tudor rulers in England, especially Henry VIII (ruled 1509–1547) and Elizabeth I (ruled 1558–1603). These were two monarchs who understood the rising importance of trade and commerce and the vital role that the middle class played in England's growing prosperity. It was under Elizabeth, too, that the English navy defeated the great Spanish Armada in 1588, making England mistress of the seas until well into the twentieth century.

In France, Francis I (ruled 1515–1547) set a pattern for later kings, such as Louis XIV (ruled 1643–1715), by bringing the best artists to a sumptuously furnished court that became a model for all of Europe. He, too, cemented national feeling by a series of wars fought largely by mercenary soldiers in helpless and divided Italy. France was later bitterly embroiled in a struggle between the Protestant Huguenots, led by the house of Bourbon, and the Catholics, led by the house of Guise. This struggle reached its conclusion in 1598 when Henry of Navarre took the throne as Henry IV, the first Bourbon king (ruled 1598–1610). Henry professed himself a Catholic, but guaranteed certain rights to the Huguenots in selected cities, rights that Louis XIV later cancelled, at which time thousands of Huguenots left the country.

Spain reached its single high point of brilliance at this time, at first under the rule of Ferdinand and Isabella (1474–1504). They and later rulers enjoyed tremendous profits from their conquests in Central and South America. As a matter of fact, the decline of Spain can be attributed to their disinterest in permanent colonies, preferring instead to plunder their holdings. Later, Spain became one of the countries ruled over by the Hapsburgs, for Charles I of Spain (ruled 1519–1556) also held the title of Archduke of Austria. He was, moreover, Charles V, Emperor of the Holy Roman Empire. His holdings included the kingdom of Naples and Sicily plus the Netherlands. The Spanish Hapsburgs became the leading Catholic monarchs in Europe and had the force of the Catholic church as a part of their spiritual and secular power.

In 1566 the Netherlands revolted against the Hapsburg kings, a revolt provoked in large part by the importation of the Inquisition. After a series of bloody wars, Holland became an independent nation, but the area known today as Belgium did not free itself until 1713. Portugal also achieved full independence during the Renaissance, and like Spain, achieved a short-lived glory as a result of the wealth and plunder from its explorers and merchants.

Germany became the battleground of the Thirty Years' War (1618–1648), which began as a conflict between Catholics and Protestants and ended as a political struggle against the Hapsburgs by Holland, France, Sweden, and other nations. Germany was devastated as the largest armies since Roman days surged over the countryside. Sweden alone had over 200,000 men in the field. The ferocity of the struggle prompted the writing of the *Law of War and Peace* (1625) by the Dutch jurist Hugo Grotius. Though he recognized war as "legitimate," he did distinguish between just and unjust conflicts and laid down principles for "humane" warfare. Drawing on actual events of the war, he condemned such acts as poisoning wells, mutilating prisoners, massacring hostages, rape, and pillage. In time the work of Grotius became the basis of the Geneva Conventions. It was this bitter and disastrous war that spurred emigration to America, where there would be a clear separation of church and state and no more religious disagreements fought out on a battlefield.

Italy's fate deserves a special note, for it was in Italy that humanism first appeared, not to mention the inspired creations of artists like Leonardo da Vinci, Michelangelo, and Raphael (see chap. 14). One of the most important stresses in this period was the development of the individual. The Italian cities early fostered ambitious individuals who plied their trade with the cities of the eastern Mediterranean during the late Middle Ages, and had already begun to develop a mercantile capitalism. As a result, a few powerful families rose in Italy, each controlling one of the important cities. The Visconti family ruled in Milan, a council of rich merchants took over the Venetian republic, and the Sforza family was a power in Lombardy and later in Milan. The most notable of the ruling families was the Medici clan in Florence, whose leading member was the famous Lorenzo the Magnificent (1449–1492), a banker, ruler, artist, and patron of the arts. Like the Greek city states of old, however, the rich and powerful cities of Italy could never unite, and they went into decline after 1500, when Italy became a battleground for internal squabbles and rampaging foreign armies that were more efficiently organized under central sovereign powers.

In Summary: A Restatement of the Enduring Questions

There has scarcely been a time, except perhaps our own, when people busied themselves so industriously exploring the dark room of their universe. Wherever they went they turned up new facts that upset any and all old balances and old institutions. Humanism, as one of the instruments of the whole secular spirit, stripped the allegory from all manifestations of nature and aided people in looking at the world as it really was. Humanism also stressed the importance of the individual and the harmonious and complete functioning of the natural person, guided, the humanists hoped, by moderation and good sense, in a rich world. To a certain extent humanism was a revolt against Christian ethics, not only in its turning back to classical sources but also in its insistence on the reasons for leading the good life; it was not in the hope of eternal bliss in heaven, but because the good life was its own reward. At its height humanism was the bridge between medievalism and modernity.

The new science, of which the high points were the heliocentric view of the solar system and the mechanistic theory of the universe, completely shifted the base of all human institutions. Before that time God had been the whole purpose and goal of human life, and it was upon these teleological assumptions that people had based their lives. That basis for human aspirations was swept aside, and men and women saw themselves as inhabitants of a brave new world.

Not only was the theoretical foundation for human values invalidated by scientific discoveries, but the institution that had formerly controlled life's most important functions was questioned and rejected. The keystone of the revolt against the Catholic church was the dazzling realization that people could live in a direct relation to God with no need for an intermediary hierarchy. People who needed religious authority to direct their lives could turn to the Scriptures and read and interpret for themselves. And those who did not need or want religious authority could live their lives without fear.

Vast areas for human endeavor opened at the same time. The idea, as much as the reality, of the New World swept aside musty medieval walls and liberated the European intellect. One tangible reality did come from the New World and that was money. Wealth poured into the countries who sent their buccaneers forth, and the new money bought ease and luxury.

Capitalism offered another marvelously stimulating outlet for individual enterprise. If one were resourceful enough and unscrupulous enough, the sky was the limit.

Each of these freedoms brought with it an undercurrent of doubt and pessimism. If the earth and its inhabitants were no longer the center of God's attention, and God no longer the goal and purpose of men and women, then what were we and what was our purpose, if any, here on earth? If the Bible was to be read and interpreted by each person, where was there any certainty? In a world that ran like a machine, where could people find answers about their relationship to each other and to the Creator of that world? Was the new relationship between people only dog eat dog as the new capitalism suggested? The sole answer the Renaissance could suggest to the necessity for order and stability was that of the absolute monarch. In the seventeenth century these monarchs would claim that they were ordained by God to care for his people. They would, therefore, rule by divine right. As the people observed the actions of their rulers, they had good reason to be uneasy about this new basis for an orderly existence.

Another trend, too small and remote as yet to cause pessimism, but present nevertheless in the intellectual currents of the time deserves mention. Science had discovered a rational world that appeared to operate like a machine, and capitalism, while it guaranteed near freedom for the captains of commerce and industry, operated "rationally," as we have said, within the companies that composed it. This meant that the men and women who worked in capitalistic units were not free. They had cast off their heavenly bondage and guild regulations, but they had gained a new bondage: that of the clock, production quotas, and the account book. The coming Industrial Revolution would exacerbate that bondage.

Renaissance Men and Women: Real and Ideal

> What a piece of work is man! How noble in reason! how infinite in faculty! In form, in moving, how express and admirable! In action how like an Angel! In apprehension, how like a God! The beauty of the world! the paragon of animals! And yet to me what is this quintessence of dust? Man delights not me. . . .
>
> *Hamlet*

When one thinks of the Renaissance, the first thought is usually of the glories of discovery throughout the world or the reforms of Luther, or perhaps one thinks of the prodigious output in the arts. Michelangelo, Shakespeare, Palestrina, Cervantes, Leonardo—the names of the remarkable creators tumble through the mind (see the Time Chart for the Renaissance at the end of this chapter). All of these add up to a picture of the Renaissance as a time of glorious optimism and expansion of the human spirit. It would seem that the possible zones of human action were widened in every respect: geographically, with the new discoveries; spiritually, with the Reformation; economically, with the rise of capitalism. This, of course, is true. But it is only a part of the total picture. Hamlet ends his soliloquy: "What is this quintessence of dust? Man delights not me."

This hints at another aspect of the Renaissance that is as important as the first exuberant picture. Throughout the whole period ran a deep-seated pessimism concerning the nature of human beings. In much of the thought of the time one finds this melancholy strain. What is Hamlet saying? Primarily, that in all appearances, in actions, and in potentialities, men (and women) are great. Yet somehow in reality they fall short of greatness. Such pessimism usually indicates a failure to reach some ideal.

The Renaissance Problem

With the information we now have at hand, we can state the problem that confronted the thinkers of the time. On the one hand they had opportunity unlimited. Wide horizons stretched in all directions. At last it seemed that human beings, with their mighty achievements, could become Godlike creatures.

Yet at the same moment, the very forces that opened these new possibilities undermined the very concept of humans as the special and most loved of all of God's creations. The matters of the soul, of divinity, and even of human emotions were relegated to a secondary position in relation to the physical and quantifiable equalities. Even further, the more purposes and hopes that were held out for humankind, the more did it seem that people's animal nature won ascendancy over their nobler qualities. When the opportunities for advancement opened before them, people seized them savagely and selfishly. Not only did those of low station who had been released by the changing events show themselves unworthy, but even the best and the wisest, the noblest among men and women, saw deeply into their own personalities and found the same base instincts there.

Here, then, is the problem. How can this animal nature of human beings, which now seemed dominant over all other aspects of their character, be dealt with so they could become the noble creatures that, on the surface, they seemed to be? How could the rough, crude, and selfish person be disciplined so that all men and women could proceed in some sort of order to the fulfillment of the total promise of their character and the expanding world in which they lived? Philosophers, theologians, artists, psychologists, and men and women in all walks of life have wrestled with the problem, but the question remains.

Time Chart for the Renaissance

	1350	1400	1450	1500	1550	1600

Art and Music

- Limbourg Bros. fl. 1416
- Brunelleschi 1377–1446
- Donatello 1386–1466
- van Eyck 1390–1441
- Dufay 1400–1474
- van der Weyden 1400–1464
- Masaccio 1401–1429
- Bramante 1444–1510
- Botticelli 1445–1510
- Josquin des Pres 1450–1521
- Bosch 1450–1516
- Grunewald 1470–1528
- Dürer 1471–1528
- Michelangelo 1475–1564
- Raphael 1483–1520
- Titian 1488–1576
- Holbein 1497–1543
- Bruegel the Elder 1525–1569
- Palestrina 1526–1594
- El Greco 1548–1625
- G. Gabrieli 1557–1612

Literary Figures

- Petrarch 1304–1374
- Boccaccio 1313–1375
- Erasmus 1466–1536
- Machiavelli 1469–1527
- Sir Thomas More 1478–1535
- Castiglione 1478–1529
- Rabelais 1494–1553
- Montaigne 1533–1592
- Cervantes 1546–1616
- Spenser 1552–1599
- Shakespeare 1564–1616

Some Important Religious Events

- Wycliffe's English Bible, 1382
- Jan Hus burned at stake, 1415
- Dedication of Florence Cathedral, 1436
- Martin Luther 1483–1546 Started the Reformation
- Posting of 95 Theses, 1517
- Diet of Worms, formal break with church 1521
- Martin Luther's Bible, 1532
- Henry VIII, Act of Supremacy 1534 Church of England
- Society of Jesus received official sanction, 1540
- Calvin's Bible ca. 1547
- Geneva Bible 1560
- Loyola 1491–1556 Founder of Society of Jesus
- John Calvin 1509–1564
- King James Bible 1611

Science and Exploration

Tycho Brahe 1546–1601
Sir Francis Bacon 1561–1626
Galileo 1564–1642
Kepler 1571–1630

Copernicus 1473–1543 Upset Ptolemaic astronomy

Magellan sailed around the world 1519–1522

Balboa discovered Pacific 1500

Da Gama sailed around Africa to India 1497–1499 Vasco

Columbus discovered America 1492

Diaz sailed down Coast of Africa 1486

Political and Economic Events

Lorenzo de' Medici 1449–1492
1453: End of Hundred Years' War; Fall of Constantinople
Rise of capitalist Fugger family
Ferdinand and Isabella of Spain 1474–1516
Henry VIII of England 1509–1547
Francis I of France 1515–1547
Charles I of Spain 1516–1556, as Emperor Charles V 1519–1556
Elizabeth I of England 1558–1603

14

Renaissance Art: A New Golden Age

The Early Renaissance in Fifteenth-Century Italy

Founded by the Romans in the rolling and verdant hills of the Arno River valley, Florence (from *Flora*), the city of flowers, was as early as 1199 a city of bankers and craft guilds. It was destined to become one of the leading financial centers of Europe and the city most closely identified with the Renaissance (fig. 14.1). Intended to symbolize Florentine wealth and influence, the great cathedral Santa Maria del Fiore (St. Mary of the Flower) was begun by Arnolfo di Cambio in 1296. Work slowed down after Arnolfo's death in 1302 and stopped altogether during the terrible days of the Black Death in 1348 and several subsequent years. Like many

Figure 14.1 View of Florence from the Boboli Gardens of the Pitti Palace. Reading from left to right: Giotto's Campanile (see fig. 14.3), the dome of the Florence Cathedral, and the Gothic tower of the Palazzo Vecchio.

cities in Europe, Florence was devastated by the plague, its population falling in just a few summer months from about 130,000 to around 65,000. Recovery was relatively swift, however, and in 1368 the cathedral design was finalized and building resumed, though no one had the faintest idea of how the dome was to be constructed.

In 1417 a special commission announced a competition for the design of the dome, optimistically trusting in Italian genius to solve the problem. The expected genius materialized in the person of Filippo Brunelleschi (broo-nuh-LES-key; ca. 1377–1446), the greatest architect of the Renaissance. His design was selected in 1420 and triumphantly completed about sixteen years later.

On 25 March 1436 all of Florence was bursting with anticipation. Pope Eugene IV, then residing in the Florentine monastery of Sta. Maria Novella, was to preside over the long-awaited consecration of the cathedral. On the day of the Feast of the Annunciation, the pope, accompanied by thirty-seven bishops, seven cardinals, the ruling Signoria, and envoys of foreign powers, began the solemn procession from the doors of the monastery. Moving along the specially constructed passageway (sumptuously carpeted and decorated with tapestries, damask, silk, and fresh flowers), the notables turned into the Via de' Banchi—most fittingly—where the major banking houses were located. Passing through the eleventh-century Baptistery, the dignitaries entered the spacious nave of the cathedral, where a five-hour service celebrated the completion of what was then the largest church in Christendom.

The most famous composer of the time, Guillaume Dufay (doo-FYE; see chap. 15), was present to hear the choir sing his motet *Nuper Rosarum Flores (Flower of Rose)*, commissioned for the occasion by the Florentine Republic. A member of the papal choir, Dufay also represented the Flemish musical tradition of the court of the Dukes of Burgundy, the most elegant and powerful court in northern Europe.

Brunelleschi began his artistic career as a sculptor, but after losing the 1401 competition for the north doors of the Baptistery to Ghiberti he turned his attention to architecture. According to later sources, he made several trips to Rome in the company of the young sculptor Donatello to study and measure the existing buildings of ancient Rome. His design for the largest dome since the Pantheon consisted of eight massive ribs arching upward from an octagonal drum and held in place by a classically inspired lantern (fig. 14.2).

Within the dome a complex web of smaller ribs and horizontal buttresses tied the main ribs firmly together. The design was not only exceptionally stable but was also economical, as it eliminated the need for expensive scaffolding. In addition to designing ribs that could be erected without centering, Brunelleschi invented a hoisting device so practical and simple that city authorities had to issue injunctions forbidding children from riding it to the dome. Averaging

Figure 14.2 Florentine Cathedral Group (aerial view). The Romanesque Baptistery (1060–1150) is at the upper left, partly obscured by Giotto's Campanile (1334–1350s). Cathedral 1296–1436.

Figure 14.3 Giotto, Campanile, 1334–1350s, Florence.

140' in diameter, the dome is 367' high, the dominant feature of the Florentine skyline from that day to this.

The 269' campanile situated at the southwest corner of the 508'-long cathedral was designed by Giotto (see chap. 11) in 1334 and completed by Talenti in the 1350s (fig. 14.3). Though many of the design elements are Gothic, the multicolored marble facing and the lucid proportions of the basically horizontal design reflect Italy's classical heritage.

When Donatello (don-a-TEL-o; 1386?–1466), the greatest of Early Renaissance sculptors, completed his statue of a Biblical prophet (fig. 14.4), he is said to have commanded it to "Speak, speak or the plague take you." The story may be apocryphal, but Renaissance artists did view themselves as creators, not as

Figure 14.4 Donatello, Prophet ("Zuccone"), ca. 1423–1425. Marble, height 6'5". Originally on the campanile, Florence; now in the Museo dell'Opera del Duomo, Florence.

Figure 14.5 Donatello, *David,* ca. 1430–1432 but maybe later. Bronze, height 62". Museo Nazionale del Bargello, Florence.

mere makers of things. With an assurance that the ancient Greeks would have admired, these artists hacked, hewed, painted, and composed as though they partook of the Divine Spirit. Though still regarded by society as craftsmen engaged in manual labor, they repeatedly proclaimed their preeminence as *artists,* an elevated status finally accorded men like Leonardo, Raphael, and Michelangelo in the sixteenth century. Created for a niche in Giotto's campanile, Donatello's Biblical prophet displays the rude power of a zealot, a man of God fiercely denouncing wickedness and vice. Known in Donatello's time as Zuccone ("pumpkin head," i.e., baldy), the figure is classical not in Greek terms but in human terms as an individual. Wearing a cloak thrown hurriedly over his body, the prophet is intent upon his mission: calling down the wrath of God on the faithless.

After a prolonged stay in Rome studying Roman art, Donatello returned in the early 1430s to Florence, where he created the *David* (fig. 14.5), a favorite image of Republican Florence, which saw itself as a latter-day David, champion of liberty. Representing a second stage in the development of Renaissance art, *David* is more classical than the Biblical prophet (see fig. 14.4) standing in a pose reminiscent of the *Hermes* by Praxiteles (see fig. 3.60). While the sinuous grace of the flowing lines and the balance of tension and relaxation is classical, this is the body of an adolescent boy and not that of a Greek athlete or warrior.

The Tuscan shepherd's cap and warrior boots emphasize what is possibly the first life-size freestanding nude since antiquity. The agony evident in the face of the slain Goliath offers a strong contrast to the curiously impassive facial expression of the shepherd boy. The Middle Ages interpreted David's triumph as symbolic of Christ's victory over death, but Donatello's intentions remain a tantalizing mystery.

The intentions of Early Renaissance painters are quite clear, however; they were concerned with creating the illusion of the natural world without regard to metaphysical symbols. Artists studied anatomy to determine how the human body was constructed and how it functioned. By using scientific procedures, they developed linear and aerial perspectives to create the illusion of actual space. They studied optics, light, and color to add the final touches to the illusion of light and personality. Through keen observation they confidently developed new forms for the new age.

Renaissance painting appeared in the 1420s in fully developed form in the work of a single artist. Though only in his mid-twenties, Masaccio (ma-SOT-cho; 1401–1428?) created a fresh repertory of illusionist techniques that were avidly studied by later Renaissance painters, especially Leonardo and Michelangelo. Working with his colleague Masolino, Masaccio painted a series of frescoes in the Brancacci Chapel, of which his *Tribute Money* (fig. 14.6) is the acknowledged masterpiece. The subject is based on

Figure 14.6 Masaccio, *Tribute Money,* ca. 1425. Fresco, 8'4" × 19'8". Brancacci, Chapel, Church of Santa Maria del Carmine, Florence.

Matthew 17:24–27 in which the Roman tax collector, wearing the short tunic, demands his tribute of Peter. Christ instructs Peter to cast a hook and take the first fish caught. In the fish's mouth Peter will find a shekel that he will give to the tax collector "for me and for yourself." Told in continuous narration in the Roman manner (see Trajan's Column, fig. 6.19), Peter appears first in the center, fishing at the left, and finally handing the coin to the tax man at the right. At the time of the painting, Florence was debating a new tax, the *catasto,* based in the modern manner on the ability to pay. Given the outdoor setting of the Arno Valley, rather than the Sea of Galilee, it is possible that the fresco appealed to people to pay their proper earthly taxes, or so the painting was interpreted by a fifteenth-century Florentine archbishop.

Masaccio used three Renaissance illusionist devices in this painting: linear perspective, atmospheric perspective, and chiaroscuro. Apparently developed by Brunelleschi, *linear perspective* is based on the principle of all lines converging on a single vanishing point, located at the head of Christ in this case. Perhaps invented in Italy by Masaccio, *atmospheric perspective* is based on the optical fact that colors become dimmer and outlines hazier as they recede into the distance. Flooding the painting from outside the pictorial space, light strikes the figures at an angle, outlining the bodies in a tangible space, a technique also utilized by the contemporaneous Northern Renaissance painters Robert Campin and Jan van Eyck (see colorplate 24). With light sculpting the bodies in gradations of light and dark, called *chiaroscuro* (key-AR-o-SCOOR-o), the illusion communicates weight, substance, and bulk. In the North, the Boucicaut Master in Paris and van Eyck in Bruges also used atmospheric perspective, indicating that naturalistic painting had become, virtually simultaneously, the goal of a number of widely separated artists.

Figure 14.7 Fra Angelico and Fra Filippo Lippi, *The Adoration of the Magi,* ca. 1445. Tempera on wood, ca. 54" in diameter. Samuel H. Kress Collection. National Gallery of Art, Washington, D.C.

Fra Angelico (ca. 1400–1455) began his career as a painter in the Late Gothic tradition. Entering the Dominican Order in about 1423, Angelico devoted himself to the religious life and to reverential paintings of sacred subjects. He was hailed in his day as one of the two notable Florentine masters after Masaccio (the other was Fra Filippo Lippi), and was a superb painter of landscape and light. His *Adoration of the Magi* (fig. 14.7), completed by his collaborator, Fra Filippo Lippi, was listed in the 1492 Medici inventory as the most valuable piece of a fabulous collection. Apparently designed by Angelico, who probably painted the Holy Family, the work is filled with a multitude of people who have followed the shepherds and magi to celebrate the Advent of the

Figure 14.8 Paolo Uccello, "The Unhorsing of Bernardino della Carda," *Battle of San Romano,* ca. 1455. Tempera on wood, 6′ × 10′5″. Uffizi Gallery, Florence.

Messiah. There is a sense of deep space but no chiaroscuro or atmospheric perspective, even though Lippo supposedly decided to become a painter after viewing Masaccio's frescoes in the Brancacci Chapel. Instead, light is suffused throughout the painting with figures in sharp outlines and with colors remaining vibrant deep into the painting. Symbolism abounds. The dog stands for faithfulness, while the peacock represents resurrection and immortality. The looming mountain probably represents Golgotha, and the ruins could symbolize the classical past. Strikingly representative of the new age was the collaboration of two such disparate personalities. Fra Angelico became prior of the Monastery of San Marco in Florence; Fra Filippo Lippi was eventually defrocked by his order, but not before he sired two children by a nun and otherwise scandalized the church. That Renaissance artists usually portrayed religious subject matter was no sure guide to their spiritual orientation; it was their patrons, rather, who determined the subject matter of works of art.

For an age already using crossbows, gunpowder, and cannons, Renaissance warfare was paradoxical, a cultivated legacy from the Age of Chivalry. Based on soldiering for pay, the so-called *condottiere* (kondot-TYAY-ray; It., one hired as leader) system followed the tradition of medieval lists: armored knights in formal combat complete with code of honor and the pageantry of wheeling and charging with trumpets blowing and banners flying. For the Florentines, the relatively minor fray at San Romano epitomized fifteenth-century concepts of honor and, most especially, *virtu* (It., excellence, manliness). Immortalized by Paolo Uccello (oot-TSCHELL-o; 1397–1475) in three magnificent panels, the *Battle of San Romano* originally hung in the bedchamber of Lorenzo the Magnificent. Now divided among three museums, the left panel (National Gallery, London) depicts the Florentine condottiere Niccolò da Tolentino directing the attack. The right panel (Louvre, Paris) shows a counterattack, while the central panel (Uffizi Gallery, Florence; fig. 14.8) portrays the climax of the battle. One more incident in the wars between Siena and Florence, the Sienese, under Bernardino della Carda, were ravaging the Tuscan countryside until challenged on 1 June 1432 by Florence's military hero Niccolò da Tolentino. After an eight-hour battle capped by the unhorsing of their leader, the Sienese were routed. Uccello was obsessed with the problems of scientific linear perspective and thus more concerned with the patterns of lances, armor, trumpets, and crossbows than with the ferocity of warfare. The result is a stylized composition of a bloodless battle, with horses looking like transplants from a merry-go-round. The work is both a study in perspective and a memorial to military honor, Renaissance style.

Also commemorating a military hero, Donatello's colossal equestrian statue of the Venetian condottiere Gattamelata (fig. 14.9) was commissioned by the general's family, undoubtedly as authorized by the Venetian Senate. Donatello's ten-year sojurn in Padua in effect exported the Florentine Renaissance to

Figure 14.9 Donatello, *Equestrian Monument of Gatta-melata,* 1443–1453. Bronze, height 12′2″. Piazza del Santo, Padua.

Figure 14.10 Leonbattista Alberti (design) and Bernardo Rossellino (architect), Facade, Palazzo Rucellai. Begun 1461, Florence.

northern Italy, spawning a whole school of painting and sculpture influenced by his powerful personality. The statue itself was possibly influenced by the Roman vigor of the equestrian statue of Marcus Aurelius in Rome (see fig. 6.22), then thought to portray Constantine. Donatello's work, however, exceeded the representation of the Roman emperor in the concentrated power of his figure's commanding presence. Apparently guiding his charger by sheer willpower (note the slack reins and spurs), the general is an idealized image of majestic power. Outfitted with a combination of Roman and Venetian armor, the composition of horse and rider is unified by the vigorous diagonals of the general's baton and long sword. Donatello not only solved the technical problems of large-scale bronze casting but created a masterpiece in the process.

During the first half of the fifteenth century, the Roman past was examined by Brunelleschi, Donatello, and others in terms of such classical elements as columns, capitals, and arches. By mid century the whole of antiquity was scrutinized, led by the remarkable humanist Leonbattista Alberti (1404–1472), who adopted the glorious past as a way of life. The first to study in detail the works of the Roman architect Vitruvius (first century B.C.), Alberti wrote enormously influential scientific treatises on painting, architecture, and sculpture. His design for the facade of a wealthy merchant's townhouse was inspired by Roman architecture but, there being no precedents in an ancient society in which rich men lived in country villas, Alberti invented for the Palazzo Rucellai (fig. 14.10) a new architecture based upon his classically derived system of ideal proportions. Divided into three even and clearly articulated stories separated by

friezes and architraves, the structure is faced with rusticated blocks of identical patterns in each bay, changing to related patterns in the upper two stories. Alberti adapted the articulation of superimposed pilasters from the Colosseum (see fig. 6.14), but without the deep spaces of that impressive exterior. He used the Tuscan order for the ground floor and the Corinthian for the top floor. In between he invented his own composite order, a layer of acanthus leaves around a palmette, maintaining that a thorough knowledge of classical designs enabled architects to extend the vocabulary, and then proving his point.

Alberti was responsible for two buildings in Florence, the Palazzo Rucellai and the facade of the Church of Santa Maria Novella, neither of which had any noticeable effect on Florentine artists of the time. Outside of Florence, however, and continuing into the sixteenth century, Alberti's classical designs influenced all Renaissance architects, especially Bramante, Michelangelo, and Palladio. His design for the facade of Santa Maria Novella (fig. 14.11) had to cope with the existing Gothic arches on the ground level, which he accomplished brilliantly by topping them with blind arches and matching their green and white marbles with the corner pilasters and the four pilasters on the second story. His masterstroke was the addition of the volutes on both sides of the narrow upper temple, which solved two problems: (1) it supplied

Figure 14.11 Leonbattista Alberti, Facade, Santa Maria Novella. Completed 1470, Florence.

Figure 14.12 Andrea del Verrocchio, *David*. Bronze, height 49⅝". Museo Nazionale del Bargello, Florence.

needed buttressing for the nave walls and (2) it beautifully filled the space above the side aisles of a basilica-plan church. The harmonious whole of the facade was the result of a rigorous set of proportions. Width and height are identical with a ratio of 1:1. The upper structure can be encased in a square one-fourth the size of the basic square, or a ratio of 1:4. The lower portion is a rectangle of double squares forming a ratio of 1:2. Throughout the facade the proportions can be expressed in whole-number relationships: 1:1, 1:2, 1:3, and so on. Along with Brunelleschi, Alberti was convinced that beauty was inherent in these ratios.

An overriding characteristic of Renaissance artists was their individuality, their need to be uniquely and unmistakably themselves. In three works by Andrea del Verrocchio (veh-ROE-key-o; 1435–1488) we see clear manifestations of this drive for individuality when treating the same subject. Verrocchio's *David* (fig. 14.12) is totally different from Donatello's conception. Donatello's figure is essentially a composition of sinuous and graceful lines; in his young warrior Verrocchio emphasizes texture, a delicate rendering in gleaming bronze of skin, underlying veins, muscle, and bone. These are qualities that, unfortunately, can be best appreciated only when walking around the actual work. The tactile qualities are enhanced by clothing the figure in a skintight short skirt designed to look like leather. That Verrocchio used his pupil Leonardo da Vinci as a model may or may not be true, but Leonardo would have been about the right age.

Donatello's *Equestrian Monument of Gattamelata* (see fig. 14.9) is idealized, but Verrocchio's portrayal of Bartolommea Colleoni (fig. 14.13) is strikingly realistic, with the fiercely scowling general readying his mace as he rides boldly into battle. Twisting in his saddle, the powerful figure seems almost too massive for the sprightly horse to carry. The tensions of horse and rider are portrayed in a dynamic moment in time. The battle is clearly at hand.

Also naturalistic is Verrocchio's portrait bust of Lorenzo the Magnificent (fig. 14.14), banker, poet, patron of the arts, and autocrat of Florence. Any accomplished craftsman can reproduce the crooked ski-slide nose, tight lips, and knitted brow. These are details that assist in the communication of a tangible presence: the overpowering personality of a unique human being. Classical portraiture had been revived and, without question, this is a masterful portrait of one of the dominant figures of the Italian Renaissance.

Three of the leading painters of the last quarter of the century—Botticelli, Ghirlandaio, and Perugino—were all vastly different in temperament and style. Sandro Botticelli (bot-tee-CHEL-lee; 1445–1510), in fact, stands alone as one of the great masters in the use of line. In his *The Adoration of the Magi* (fig. 14.15), Botticelli has painted a circular composition that is opened in the center foreground to admit the spectator. The architectural perspective is tilted upward, inviting the viewer into the work, to complete, as it were, the broken circle of adoration. The shed housing the Nativity group recalls Roman ruins, while the truss roof resembles that of old St. Peter's in Rome. Verrocchio's other famous pupil, Leonardo, claimed that Botticelli's paintings were not "correct" in terms of detail and atmosphere. Botticelli, in fact, deliberately violated the "rules" in this and other paintings; the vanishing point behind the Holy Family differs from the landscape perspective on

Figure 14.13 Andrea del Verrocchio (completed by Leopardi), *Equestrian Monument of Bartolommeo Colleoni,* ca. 1481–1496. Bronze, height ca. 13′. Campo SS Giovanni a Paolo, Venice.

Figure 14.14 Andrea del Verrocchio, *Lorenzo de' Medici,* ca. 1480. Terra-cotta, life size. Samuel H. Kress Collection. National Gallery of Art, Washington, D.C.

Figure 14.15 Sandro Botticelli, *The Adoration of the Magi,* after 1482. Panel, 27⅝ × 41″. Andrew W. Mellon Collection. National Gallery of Art, Washington, D.C.

either side of the Roman-style shed. Conforming to Alberti's doctrine of visual unity in terms of single-point perspective was an option. Renaissance perspective was, after all, only one of several systems for depicting the illusion of depth, an artificial method of representing space and therefore not *the* "correct" method of portraying reality. Botticelli's landscape is not incorrect; it is, in fact, brilliantly conceived for what the artist intends the viewer to experience.

In his celebrated *Birth of Venus* (colorplate 22) Botticelli subordinates perspective and "correct" anatomical proportions and details to the elegant and sensual lines that make his style so delightfully unique. Like many of his generation, especially the elite circle of Lorenzo de' Medici and the "Platonic Academy," Botticelli was fascinated with themes from classical mythology. According to an ancient myth, Venus was born from the sea, a legend interpreted by Ficino as an allegory of the birth of beauty. What the Florentine Neoplatonists actually did believe is still debated. Much of Plato's work had become available but there was also a large body of Neoplatonist writings with Christian elements superimposed on Platonic theories. Whether Botticelli's Venus symbolizes non-Christian or Christian ideas, or both, she is certainly lovely. Possibly inspired by a poem by Poliziano, Botticelli has painted her poised lightly on a conch shell as she is blown gently to shore by two Zephyrs, while one of the Hours hastens to drape her body with a flowered mantle. This is poetry in motion. The sea is flat, marked by upward thrusting V-shaped lines and bound by a stylized shoreline to form a serene setting for the sinuous lines of the moving figures. Probably inspired by classical statues in the Medici collection, the body of the goddess of spiritual and intellectual beauty is elongated and exquisitely curved, proportionately larger than the scale of the landscape. The gold-line shading on the trees is a further indication that Botticelli intended no realistic representation of the landscape. It was, in fact, this sort of stylized treatment of the background that led to Leonardo's comment that Botticelli created landscapes by throwing a sponge at the canvas.

Botticelli was favored by the intellectual elite of Florence, while the style of Domenico del Ghirlandaio (gear-lan-DAH-yo; 1449–1494) was preferred by the merchants and bankers of the city. Not interested in mythological fantasies, Ghirlandaio was a conservative painter for a conservative clientele and, as might be expected, a very successful artist. His *Old Man with a Child* (fig. 14.16), one of his most endearing works, is a compassionate portrayal of an elderly man holding an adoring child who could be his grandson, though the subjects have never been identified. Perhaps influenced by the naturalism of Flemish painting, which was well-known in Italy by this time, the objective treatment of thinning hair and a deformed nose actually adds to the tender scene of familial love. As was customary in Renaissance portraiture, the human subjects totally dominate the composition, reinforced by the lovely and distant landscape.

Until about the middle of the fifteenth century, the Early Renaissance was essentially Florentine; the

Figure 14.16 Domenico del Ghirlandaio, *Old Man with a Child*, ca. 1480. Panel, 24⅜″ × 18′12″. The Louvre, Paris.

second half of the century saw the dissemination of Renaissance techniques throughout Italy, notably by artists like Perugino and Bellini. Though his early training is a mystery, Pietro Vanucci was in Florence by 1472, where he acquired his knowledge of drawing and perspective, possibly from Verrocchio. It was in the Umbrian city of Perugia that he established his reputation and acquired the name by which he is known today: Perugino (pay-roo-GEE-no; ca. 1445–1523), the "Perugian." In his *Crucifixion with Saints* (colorplate 23), Perugino created a masterful pictorial space that is much more open than Florentine landscapes, with a sky stretching to infinity. As polished and cool as the work of the Flemish painter Hans Memling (see fig. 14.23), and probably influenced by his work, the altarpiece shows none of the usual emotions of Florentine crucifixions. Christ is not racked by pain nor do Mary at the left or John at the right display any grief. In the wings St. Jerome and Mary Magdalene stand serenely in counterbalancing poses. In the vast expanse of the natural setting all is quietude. Whether the absence of emotion reflects Vasari's statement (in his *Lives of the Most Eminent Painters, Sculptors, and Architects,* 1550) that Perugino was an atheist may be a moot point. Though religious convictions were important for many people at that time, Renaissance artists were valued chiefly for their skills not their spirits.

Figure 14.17 Giovanni Bellini and Titian, *The Feast of the Gods,* ca. 1514. Oil on canvas, 67 × 74″. Widener Collection. National Gallery of Art, Washington, D.C.

Religious beliefs apparently interfered with some of the work of Giovanni Bellini (ca. 1430–1516), the foremost Venetian painter of the Early Renaissance. *The Feast of the Gods* (fig. 14.17), painted late in his long and productive career, was commissioned by the Duke of Ferrara and intended for the collection of Isabella d'Este, one of the most discerning and demanding patrons of the arts in Renaissance Italy (see chap. 16). Based on a story told by Ovid, the jackass at the left has just brayed, arousing the gods from satiated slumber and saving the wood nymph at the right from the amorous advances of Priapus, Roman god of procreation. Although placed in a glorious Arcadian setting, the nymphs, satyrs, and gods are portrayed more as peasants than as immortals. Bellini may have included portraits of some of his contemporaries; the dreamy goddess in the center (holding a bowl) may be Lucrezia Borgia, daughter of Pope Alexander VI. The lush landscape and pastoral but sensual mood are typical of the Venetian school, of which Bellini was the first master and the probable teacher of Giorgione and Titian. He was among the first to adopt the Flemish invention of oil painting as developed by van Eyck (see fig. 14.19). Because Bellini was too devout for the secular tastes of the Duke and Isabella d'Este, Titian was commissioned to complete the work while converting it into more appropriate pagan terms, which was accomplished by partially disrobing the nymphs and changing some of the gestures to better fit Ovid's story. For the remainder of the Italian Renaissance the Venetian school followed the poetic tradition of vibrant colors depicting the pleasures of men and women, while the Roman and Florentine schools were mainly preoccupied with formal designs and noble themes.

Figure 14.18 The Limbourg Brothers, "February," from the *Très Riches Heures du Duc de Berry,* 1413–1416. Illumination. Musée Condé, Chantilly, France.

The Early Renaissance in the North

The focus of significant new developments in art and music (see chap. 15) was the sumptuous court of the Dukes of Burgundy, from which the dukes governed the most prosperous lands in all of Europe (see the map of Burgundy on page 316). Philip the Bold and his brother, the Duke of Berry, sponsored leading artists like the Limbourg Brothers: Paul, Herman, and Jean (ca. 1385–1416). Their work in manuscript illumination marked the high point of the International Style (Late Gothic), while also moving beyond to a new naturalism. Commissioned by the Duke of Berry, they created for him a personal prayer book, a Book of Hours containing passages of Scripture, prayers, and Office Hours, all lavishly decorated and illustrated with paintings. Of particular interest are the twelve illuminated calendar pages; ten include peasants and aristocrats and two are devoted solely to peasant genre scenes. The month of *February* (fig. 14.18) has, at the top, a zodiac representing the route of the chariot of the sun and including, in this case, the zodiacal signs of Aquarius and Pisces. The scene is an intensely cold, snowy landscape, the first convincing snow scene in Western art. On the upper level a peasant cuts firewood, while another herds a donkey

Figure 14.19 Jan van Eyck, *Ghent Altarpiece* (closed), ca. 1425–1432. St. Bavon, Ghent, Belgium. Copyright A. C. L. Bruxelles.

laden with faggots toward a distant village. In the tiny farmyard snow caps the beehives and covers the roof of the sheep pen except for the unrepaired hole in the roof. At the right a woman blows on her icy hands and stamps her feet to try to restore circulation. With the front wall removed for our benefit, we see a man and a woman seated before the fire with skirts raised high to gather in the welcome warmth. At the doorway, the lady of the house rather more decorously lifts her skirt, while the cat is, of course, cozily warm and comfortable. The perspective that gives the illusion of depth is empirical rather than mathematically precise, the way the artists actually perceived the scene. Marking the beginning of the Northern tradition of naturalistic art, the overriding concern is with the visible world, with loving care devoted to minute details in all their complexity.

The decisive victory of the English king Henry V at Agincourt in 1415 effectively ended, for some forty years, the dominance of the French court and thus royal sponsorship of the courtly International Style. The center for art shifted to the Low Countries, where Philip the Good (ruled 1419–1467) maintained his Burgundian court and negotiated hardheaded trade alliances with England. Artists found in the flourishing cities of Flanders—Bruges, Ghent, Louvain,

Brussels—new patrons in the bankers and merchants who were the true rulers of the wealthiest society in Europe. The society was bourgeois, but cosmopolitan rather than provincial with powerful banking and trade connections throughout Europe. This solid middle class wanted art that pictured the real world and, by a strange coincidence, there were several artists of genius available to help fulfill the passion for naturalism.

The leading painter of the early Flemish school, indeed of any age, Jan van Eyck (Yahn van Ike; ca. 1390–1441) first served the court of John of Bavaria and later at the Burgundian court of Philip the Good. Credited by Vasari with inventing oil painting, it is likely that van Eyck perfected an existing technique. Until the fifteenth century, panel painters worked in tempera, an emulsion of pigment and egg yolk capable of detail and bright color but limited to a narrow range between light and dark. Too dark colors became dead and very light ones became chalklike. Using a technique still not fully understood, van Eyck probably used a *gesso* coating on his panel, a mixture of plaster and water, followed by successive coats of pigments suspended in linseed oil. Applying alternate layers of opaque and translucent color, van Eyck enhanced the brilliance of his colors from the darkest to the lightest with no loss of intensity. With slow-drying oil paints he made infinitely subtle and smooth gradations between color tones, obtaining a jewellike radiance comparable to medieval stained glass. He undoubtedly learned some of his techniques from manuscript painters like the Limbourg Brothers, but it also seems likely that van Eyck was influenced, or possibly inspired, by the stained glass of Gothic churches.

The greatest work of early Flemish painting and a monumental accomplishment in any age, the *Ghent Altarpiece* (fig. 14.19) is a polyptych, a central painting with two hinged wings measuring 11′3″ × 7′2″ when closed and 11′3″ × 14′5″ in the open position. The twenty different panels of the work range from the Annunciation on the outer panels to the Adoration of the Mystic Lamb within. In the lunettes of figure 14.19, the prophet Zechariah (left) with the Erythraean Sibyl, Cumean Sibyl, and prophet Micah symbolize the coming of Christ. The annunciation figures are placed in a contemporary room containing Romanesque and Gothic elements that probably symbolize the Old and New Testaments. In the center panels below, the simulated sculptural figures of St. John the Baptist and St. John the Evangelist are flanked by the donors Jodoc Vyt and his wife.

In the open altarpiece (fig. 14.20) the lower central panel shows the community of saints, come from the four corners of the world to worship at the altar of the Mystic Lamb, from whose heart blood cascades into a chalice. In the foreground the Fountain of Life pours from spigots into an octagonal basin, running toward the observer as the "river of life" (Rev. 22:1). In the left-hand panel, judges and knights ride to the altar, while on the right hermits, pilgrims, and the

Figure 14.20 Jan van Eyck, *Ghent Altarpiece* (open).

giant St. Christopher walk to an altar scene backed by the heavenly Jerusalem in the distance. Forming a continuous view of Paradise, the five lower panels are designed with a rising perspective, another of the innovations of the artist. On the upper level, the Lord has Mary as the Queen of Heaven on his right hand and St. John the Baptist on his left. To either side are choirs of angels with St. Cecelia seated at the portative (portable) organ, flanked by Adam and Eve on the outer panels. The first large nudes in Northern panel painting, the figures of Adam and Eve reveal a keen appreciation of the human body and innovative painting techniques in perspective and lighting. Once bowed by shame, the figures stand erect as the First Man and First Woman. The placement of the altarpiece puts the feet of the two nudes at about eye level, which accounts for the view of the sole of Adam's foot. This bit of naturalism is typical of a visual reality so precise that botanists can identify dozens of flowers and plants in this awesome work.

Probably completed while he was working on the *Ghent Altarpiece,* the *Annunciation* (colorplate 24) is a relatively small work that, with its strong control of space, has a monumental quality. Set in an imaginary church whose mixed Romanesque and Gothic

details probably symbolize the Old and New Testaments, the scene is dominated by an oversized Virgin, portrayed here as the Queen of Heaven. Heavenly light streams in through an upper window, bearing the Dove of the Holy Spirit, its diagonal thrust balanced at the lower right by the lilies of purity. No detail is extraneous; even the designs of the stained glass window and floor tiles foretell the Advent of Christ.

The meticulous details in a van Eyck painting are fascinating, but the whole of a picture—its unity—is greater than the sum of its parts. In a work commissioned by Giovanni Arnolfini, an Italian merchant, he and his bride, Jeanne Cenami, apparently pose for a wedding portrait as a form of wedding certificate, duly witnessed by the artist (seen in the mirror) and notarized on the back wall: "Jan van Eyck was here" (fig. 14.21). In terms of light, space, volume, and the two distinct personalities, all is unified, both visually and psychologically. Patron and artist must have been more than acquaintances; two individuals make up this wedding couple, joined together in a tender moment without the slightest hint of sentimentality. The texture of cloth, glass, metal, wood, and even the furry

Figure 14.21 Jan van Eyck, *Giovanni Arnolfini and His Bride*, 1434. Oil on canvas, 32¼ × 23½". National Gallery, London.

Figure 14.22 Rogier van der Weyden, *Portrait of a Lady*, ca. 1455–1460. Oil on wood, 14½ × 10¾". Andrew W. Mellon Collection. National Gallery of Art, Washington, D.C.

little dog are exquisitely detailed. Though unobtrusive, symbols abound. The single lighted candle is, according to custom, the last to be extinguished on the wedding night, but it may also symbolize Christ as the Light of the World. Carved on the post of a bedside chair is the image of St. Margaret, the patron saint of childbirth. The dog represents fidelity (*fides,* "Fido") and the abandoned slippers are a reminder that the couple is standing on holy ground. Craftsmanship at this level verges on the superhuman; indeed, nothing like this had ever been done before.

Because his paintings were perfect in their own marvelously unique way, van Eyck had many admirers in Northern Europe, Spain, and Italy but no emulators. There were imitators, of course, but no disciples who could even approach his rare gifts. Adopting a more expressive and emotional style than that of van Eyck, Rogier van der Weyden (van dur VYE-den; ca. 1400–1464) was the leading Flemish painter of the next generation, becoming City Painter for Brussels in 1435. When he traveled to Italy for the Holy Year of 1450, he influenced Italian art and was, in turn, impressed by what he saw there, probably including the work of Fra Angelico in Florence and Rome. As technically accomplished as van Eyck, his portraits had a psychological depth then unknown in Flemish painting. *Portrait of a Lady* (fig. 14.22) is a study of

a young woman tentatively identified as Marie de Valengin, the daughter of Philip the Good, Duke of Burgundy. Her forehead and eyebrows are shaved, a fashionable indication of intellectual acumen. Also high fashions, the high-waisted dress and triangular coif focus attention on the exquisite modeling of the face. The portrait is both beautiful and baffling. The impression of an almost ascetic contemplation is contradicted by the sensuality of the full mouth with its ripe underlip. The overall impression is that of an assertive personality, an intelligent, self-confident, and strong-willed young woman. She certainly looks like a princess of the most powerful court in Northern Europe. Contrasting curiously with the broad facial planes, the thin fingers are almost Gothic in style. Bewitching and beguiling, this is a masterful psychological study by one of the first of a long line of Low Country painters leading directly to Hals and Rembrandt.

Hans Memling (ca. 1440–1494) served his apprenticeship in his native Germany but then moved to Flanders where he apparently studied with van der Weyden. A contemporary of Ghirlandaio in Italy, his style is similarly genial and rather naive; it appealed to a large clientele of merchants and led ultimately to a considerable fortune. Utilizing extensive studies of earlier Flemish masters, particularly van Eyck, he developed a somewhat melancholy art of extreme refinement. In *The Presentation in the Temple* (fig.

Figure 14.23 Hans Memling, *The Presentation in the Temple,* ca. 1463. Oil on panel, 23½ × 19″. Samuel H. Kress Collection. National Gallery of Art, Washington, D.C.

Figure 14.24 Hieronymus Bosch, *Death and the Miser,* ca. 1510. Oil on panel, 36⅝ × 12⅛″. Samuel H. Kress Collection. National Gallery of Art, Washington, D.C.

14.23) the figures are immobile, frozen in time, or even outside of time. The light falls on people grouped in harmony with their imaginary setting, which appears to be neither inside nor outside a church. The overall feeling is unworldly and slightly sad.

Memling's work was in tune with a general feeling of pessimism, an erosion of confidence in the moral authority of the church, an almost prophetic feeling of the impending Reformation. In Italy the pessimism was fully warranted, for it was in 1494—the year of Memling's death—that the Medicis were expelled from Florence, coinciding with the invasion of the French armies of Charles VIII, which launched a tumultuous era of warfare in Italy.

This pessimistic age found its supreme artist in the person of Hieronymus Bosch (BOS; ca. 1450–1516), one of history's most enthralling and enigmatic painters. He lived and worked in present-day southern Holland, but little else is known about either his life or his artistic intentions. Art historians have wondered about his bizarre iconography but so have psychiatrists. This was an age obsessed with death and with an almost pathological fear of the devil and his demons. Based on his work, it is plain that Bosch had a pessimistic view of human nature—though some would call his vision realistic—and he certainly raged against sinfulness. In the small panel *Death and the Miser* (fig. 14.24), death waits at the door but the miser cannot decide between the crucifix pointed out by the angel or the bag of gold offered by the demon. At the foot of the bed the miser

appears as greed personified, clutching a rosary with one hand and storing, with the other hand, money in a strongbox held by another demon. The weapons and armor in the foreground probably indicate warfare as an earlier source of wealth. Other figures and objects are also symbolic, probably literal depictions of folk sayings and tales. Within the carefully defined setting we witness life, death, and human nature.

Enormously popular in the sixteenth century, Bosch's paintings typify an age that had a sickening undercurrent of fear of the devil, leading to fierce, misdirected religious zeal. In 1484 Pope Innocent VIII declared witchcraft (possession by the Devil) a prime heresy. During the next two centuries a wave of sadism and misogyny led to the torture, hanging, and burning of more than 100,000 women plus a few children and men who were enveloped in the madness. Two unscrupulous Dominican monks wrote a handbook for witch-hunters, *The Witches Hammer* (1498), a best-seller that went to thirty editions, an ironic testimony to the spread of books following the invention of movable type in the Rhine River valley during the 1430s.

The career of Hieronymus Bosch marked the end of the Early Northern Renaissance and the beginning of a tormented period of warfare in Italy, of corrupt and dissolute Renaissance popes, and of spiritually bankrupt religious orders. One year after Bosch's death Martin Luther published his *Ninety-five Theses* to set in motion the irrepressible Reformation.

The High Renaissance in Italy, ca. 1495–1520

The relatively peaceful and prosperous existence of Florence ended in two rough jolts in the fateful years of 1492 and 1494. Lorenzo the Magnificent, a strong, moderating force in the fortunes of Florence, died in 1492, the same year in which Ferdinand and Isabella captured Cordoba, the last Moorish stronghold in Spain. Columbus, using a map drawn in Florence, discovered the New World and in Rome, Rodrigo Borgia was crowned as Pope Alexander VI, the epitome of a decadent and corrupt Renaissance pontiff and an enemy of the Florentine Republic.

In 1494, concerned about the military support of Lorenzo's dim and feckless son Piero, Ludovico Sforza of Milan encouraged Charles VIII of France to invade Italy. Charles, who was spoiling for a fight, willingly did so. For the next thirty-five years French and Spanish armies, the latter freed by the removal of the Moors, fought the Italian city-states and, for good measure, each other. Always thinking that each invasion was the last, the Italian cities never banded together to expel their foreign tormenters. Paradoxically, it was against this backdrop of almost constant warfare that High Renaissance art flourished. Exploiting and refining Early Renaissance discoveries in Italy and the North, Leonardo da Vinci, Michelangelo, Raphael, and Bramante created masterworks that crowned the Italian Renaissance.

Leonardo da Vinci

The illegitimate son of a peasant girl known only as Caterina and Piero da Vinci, a notary, Leonardo da Vinci (lay-o-NAR-do da VIN-chee; 1452–1519) was the acknowledged universal man of the Renaissance, the most astounding genius in an age of giants. Inventor, civil and military engineer, architect, musician, geologist, botanist, physicist, anatomist, sculptor, and painter, Leonardo left untouched only classical scholarship, poetry, and philosophy. Theology was of no interest to him; he was a lifelong skeptic who recognized no authority higher than the eye, which he called the "window of the soul."

As was customary with bastardy during the Renaissance, Leonardo was acknowledged by his father and, at about age fifteen, was apprenticed to Verrocchio in Florence. Though little else is known about the first thirty years of his life, records indicate that Leonardo, like Masaccio and Botticelli before him, was admitted to the guild as a craftsman in painting. Unlike Early Renaissance masters, however, Leonardo along with Michelangelo launched a successful campaign to raise the status of artists to the highest level of society.

In 1481 Pope Sixtus IV summoned the "best" Tuscan artists to work in the Vatican, including Botticelli, Ghirlandaio, and Perugino, but not Leonardo. Furious at the slight, Leonardo decided to leave Florence, but not before he had completed a commission for the de'Benci family of wealthy bankers. His portrait of Ginevra de'Benci (colorplate 25), the only Leonardo painting in the United States, is an enchanting study of a lovely but strangely tense and wary young woman. She was known to be a very devout person, ill at ease in the fun-loving exuberance of Florence, and sternly disapproving of Lorenzo de' Medici's long-term affair with her aunt. Framing her golden curls in juniper branches (Ginevra means "juniper"), Leonardo has created a melancholy work, the pallid face set against a thinly misted background, with details deliberately softened and blurred. Though not invented by Leonardo, this *sfumato* (sfoo-MAH-toh) technique (literally "smoky") was one of that artist's significant contributions to the art of painting. The twilight atmosphere is another innovation, contrasting sharply with the sunlit paintings of other masters. The painting is minus some six inches at the bottom, which may explain why the lady's hands are not shown, as they are in the *Mona Lisa* and two of Leonardo's other portraits.

Seeking a more appreciative patron than the Medicis or the pope, Leonardo wrote to Ludovico Sforza, Duke of Milan, touting his expertise as a military engineer but mentioning, in just two sentences, that he was also a sculptor and a painter. During his stay in Milan (1482–1499) Leonardo produced *The Last Supper* (fig. 14.25), a treatment of the familiar theme unlike anything done before or since. The High Renaissance begins with this magnificent composition. After suffering the indignities of damp walls, Napoleon's troops, and World War II bombing, the painting has been restored, but only to an approximation of its original condition. The moment of the painting is not the traditional one of the Eucharist but Christ's electrifying statement, "One of you shall betray me." Except for Christ, Leonardo used life models for the disciples, and had difficulty only in finding a suitable Judas. According to Vasari, when the prior of Sta. Maria complained to Sforza that Leonardo was "lazy" in his execution of the painting, Leonardo remarked that locating a Judas was difficult but that the prior would serve nicely. Leonardo's contemporaries would have looked for Judas where other artists had placed him—across the table from Jesus. Instead, we see Judas as part of the first group of three Apostles to the left of Christ, composed in a tight, dark triangle with no light shining on his face. Clutching a bag of money, Judas is in the group but not a part of it. His dark bulk is in sharp contrast to the lighted profile of Peter and the luminous radiance of John. In fact, each Apostle is an individual psychological study, reacting to Christ's startling statement in a manner consistent with his personality.

Figure 14.25 Leonardo da Vinci, *The Last Supper,* ca. 1495–1498. Mural, oil and tempera on plaster, 14'5" × 28'. Refectory of Sta. Maria della Grazie, Milan.

The design of *The Last Supper* has a mathematical unity, with divisions of groups of threes and fours that add up to seven (3 + 4) and multiply into twelve (3 × 4). The three windows place Christ's head in the center window as the second person of the Trinity. The shocked Apostles are grouped into four units of three each, divided in the middle by the isolated triangular (three-sided) design of Christ. Echoing the four groups are the wall panels on either side, and on the ceiling there are seven beams running from both front to back and side to side. Leonardo may have had Christian number symbolism in mind (Holy Trinity, Four Gospels, Seven Cardinal Virtues, Twelve Gates of the New Jerusalem, and so on) but three, four and seven also stand for the Trivium and Quadrivium of the Seven Liberal Arts. Moreover, Pythagorean number symbolism includes the concept of one as unity, three as the most logical number (beginning, middle, end), and four as symbolizing Justice (see chap. 1). Given Leonardo's skepticism and explicit anticlerical feelings, something other than Christian symbolism may be a more appropriate interpretation. There is no question, however, about the picture as a whole. Despite the mathematical precision of the perspective, there is no place from which a spectator can view the perspective "correctly"; it exists as a work apart, on an ideal level beyond everyday experience. As mentioned previously, this is the elevated style of formal design and noble theme that characterizes the High Renaissance.

Leonardo insisted that painters were noble creatures and that painting should be a part of the seven liberal arts. For him, sculptors were craftsmen standing in dust and debris while hammering away at stubborn marble. Michelangelo, on the other hand, claimed that sculpture was as superior to painting as the sun was to the moon.

Michelangelo

Perhaps the greatest artistic genius who ever lived, Michelangelo Buonarroti (me-kell-AHN-djay-lo boo-on-na-ROE-tea; 1475–1564) excelled in four arts: sculpture, painting, architecture, and poetry. A towering figure even in his own time, he was the "Divine Michelangelo." Words and more words have been written trying to account for such a man, but there is no accounting for him. Born of a vain and mean-spirited father and a dimly pathetic mother to whom he never referred, he appeared with prodigious gifts at a time and place seemingly destined to make him divine. He learned painting techniques in Ghirlandaio's studio and sculpting from a pupil of Donatello and from ancient works in the Medici collection. His first masterpiece, the *Pieta* (fig. 14.26), is more fifteenth than sixteenth century in style, with elegant lines reminiscent of Botticelli. The triangular composition is made up of contradictions. Though Christ is dead, the blood pumps through his veins as if he were asleep. The Virgin is portrayed as younger than her son, her lovely face composed rather than distorted by grief; only her left hand indicates her sorrow. The figure of Christ is life size but that of the Virgin is elongated; her head is the same size as Christ's but in proportion she would be about seven feet tall if she were standing. The overall visual effect of these distortions is a super reality beyond earthbound reality.

Figure 14.26 Michelangelo, *Pieta,* 1498–1499/1500. Marble, height 68½". St. Peter's, Rome.

The *Pieta* was a youthful work but the *David* (colorplate 26), started only a year or so later, was the first monumental statue of the High Renaissance, a product of Michelangelo's already mature genius. Though the Palazzo della Signoria already possessed three Davids, two by Donatello (see fig. 14.5) and one by Verrocchio (see fig. 14.12), one more was not too many for a city battling to maintain its power and independence. After the Medicis were expelled in 1494, the crusading monk Savonarola ruled Florence, having had Christ declared King of Florence. Savonarola then legally banned all acts he considered sinful. By 1498 the corrupt but powerful Borgia pope Alexander VI had excommunicated Savonarola. Incredibly, Savonarola excommunicated the pope; following this he was arrested by the Florentine Signory and, with two associates, hanged and then burned. While Michelangelo was working on his David, the dangerous Alexander VI died, in 1503, and shortly thereafter the incompetent Piero de' Medici, known as Piero the Unfortunate, drowned while fighting with the French in an attempt to gain reentry to the city. By 1504 Florence was finally at peace and the prime civic concern was where to place Michelangelo's mighty *David.* The commission to select the site included Leonardo, Botticelli, Perugino, and others, attesting to the status the nearly completed work had already acquired. Originally scheduled to be placed high on Florence Cathedral, *David* was triumphantly set in front of the center of government, the Palazzo Vecchio, where it became the symbol of a republic ready to battle all enemies. (During the nineteenth century the statue was moved indoors to protect it from the weather.)

The Davids of Donatello and Verrocchio were adolescent boys; this is a strapping young man who is standing alert, every muscle vibrant with power. The head might be that of Apollo and the body of Herakles yet this is the portrait of an ideal, a Platonic ideal as well as David the King. His father was both Hebrew and, collectively, Lorenzo, Ficino, and the "Platonic Academy" of Florence.

The fame of the *David* was instant, and Michelangelo had more commissions than he could handle, including one to construct a vast tomb for Pope Julius II. The tomb project was never finished as originally planned, instead, somehow, Michelangelo found himself in 1508 lying on his back atop the scaffolding in the Sistine Chapel. How all this came about has never been satisfactorily explained, but one plausible theory concerns the possible machinations of Bramante, the recently appointed architect of the new St. Peter's. He was known to be concerned about funds for his project and was also intensely jealous of Michelangelo. Julius had lavished enormous sums on his tomb project, money that Bramante needed for his mighty basilica. If the pope could be encouraged to put Michelangelo to work painting the Sistine Chapel ceiling, a monumental undertaking Bramante felt not even Michelangelo could bring off, then he would have no further financial or artistic competition. Whatever transpired behind the scenes, Michelangelo was, in fact, the only artist who was capable of tackling the project.

With a 68' high ceiling that is proportionately too high for its 44 × 132' dimensions, the private chapel of the popes was neither intimate nor monumental; Michelangelo's frescoes *made* it monumental. In only four years, 1508–1512, he filled the entire 700 square yards of barrel-vaulted ceiling with over 300 powerful figures. Relating the Genesis story from the Creation through the Flood, Michelangelo fused Judeo-Christian theology with ancient mythology and Neoplatonic philosophy to create one of the truly awesome works of Western art. In just one detail, the *Creation of Adam* (fig. 14.27), one can perceive some of the majesty of the total work. Embracing an awestruck Eve and with his left hand resting on the shoulder of the Christ Child, God the Father extends his finger and the spark of life to an inert Adam. Against a background of generations waiting to be born, the twisting, dynamic figure is lovingly paternal, imparting to Adam the soul that will actuate his potential nobility. After protesting for four years that he was a sculptor, not a painter, Michelangelo proved that he was both; all of the figures are sculptural forms, conceived in the mind's eye of a sculptor and executed in paint on wet plaster. Totally overwhelming the work of many notable artists on the walls, the ceiling frescoes express the optimism of a supreme artist at the peak of his powers.

Figure 14.27 Michelangelo, *Creation of Adam,* detail of Sistine Chapel Ceiling, 1511. Fresco. Vatican, Rome.

The following sonnet[1] illustrates Michelangelo's personal and agonizingly physical reaction to the task the pope set for him:

SONNET V
To Giovanni da Pistoia
"On the Painting of the Sistine Chapel"
(I' ho gia fatto un gozzo)

I've grown a goitre by dwelling in this den—
    As cats from stagnant streams in Lombardy,
    Or in what other land they hap to be—
    Which drives the belly close beneath the chin:
My beard turns up to heaven; my nape falls in,
    Fixed on my spine: my breast-bone visibly
    Grows like a harp: a rich embroidery
    Bedews my face from brush-drops thick and thin.
My loins into my paunch like levers grind:
    My buttock like a crupper bears my weight;
    My feet unguided wander to and fro;
In front my skin grows loose and long; behind,
    By bending it becomes more taut and strait;
    Crosswise I strain me like a Syrian bow:
      Whence false and quaint, I know,
Must be the fruit of squinting brain and eye;
For ill can aim the gun that bends awry.
      Come then, Giovanni, try
To succour my dead pictures and my fame;
Since foul I fare and painting is my shame.

Bramante

The dominant political figure and artistic patron of the High Renaissance was Pope Julius II (1503–1513), known as the Warrior Pope. Determined to obliterate the awful memories of Alexander VI and the Borgia crimes, he refused to even live in the apartment of his decadent predecessor. Julius II restored order to the city of Rome, reconquered papal provinces with the sword, and proceeded energetically to rebuild his beloved Rome. A fortuitous quirk of history put a dynamic pope in power at precisely the time when he could utilize the mature talents of Michelangelo, Raphael, and Bramante. Donato Bramante of Urbino (1444–1514), the foremost architect of the High Renaissance and a close personal friend of the pope, was entrusted with many building projects, the greatest of which was the construction of a new St. Peter's. Julius II decided, in 1505, that the 1100-year-old Basilica of St. Peter's was to be replaced by a Renaissance structure worthy of the imperial splendor of the new Rome, a project that was not completely finished until 1626 (see fig. 14.33), some 14 architects, 20 popes, and one Reformation later.

Though much of Bramante's design can still be seen in St. Peter's, his architectural genius is better illustrated by a circular structure of only modest size but of immense influence in architectural history. Constructed on the spot where St. Peter was supposedly crucified, the Tempietto (little temple; fig. 14.28) became the prototype of classical domed architecture in Europe and the United States. Placed on a three-step base like a Greek temple, the exquisitely proportioned building was conceived as an articulated work of sculpture in the manner of classical Greek architecture (see chap. 3). Influenced by Leonardo's radial designs, the building is distinguished by the severely Doric colonnade, above which are classical triglyphs and metopes topped by a lightly rhythmical balustrade. The overall effect of majestic serenity in a small building may have been the decisive factor in Bramante's selection as the architect of the pope.

1. John Addington Symonds, trans., *The Sonnets of Michelangelo Buonarotti and Tommaso Campanella* (London: Smith, Elder & Co., 1878), p. 35.

Figure 14.28 Donato Bramante, *Tempietto,* 1502. Height 46′ with external diameter of 29′. S. Pietro in Montorio, Rome.

Figure 14.29 Raphael, *Baldassare Castiglione,* ca. 1515. Oil on canvas, 32¼ × 26½″. The Louvre, Paris.

Raphael

The third artist working in the Vatican, in addition to Bramante and Michelangelo, was Raphael (RAHF-ee-el; 1483–1520), one of the greatest painters in Western art, of whom the English painter Reynolds said, "Of the just hyperbole the perpetual instance is the divine Raphael." Born in Urbino like Bramante, Raphael studied first with Perugino and then, as so many artists had done before him, moved to Florence. Over the four-year period of 1504–1508, he studied the works of Leonardo and Michelangelo and painted many of his famous Madonnas.

The most reproduced painter of the Renaissance, the work of Raphael, especially the Madonnas, is perhaps too familiar. Raphael was an intellectual painter whose works should be studied for both form and content, but viewers tend to see his Madonnas as pretty and sweet, partly because they were intended as sympathetic portrayals of Mother and Child and partly because of countless sentimental imitations of Raphael's style. *The Alba Madonna* (colorplate 27) is a tightly controlled triangular composition derived from Leonardo's style but designed as a *tondo* (circular painting). Unlike Leonardo and other Madonna painters, Raphael used life models, usually in the nude, sketching the basic figure until he had all elements just right. In this work he was concerned with subtly contrasting the humanity of John the Baptist with the divinity of the Christ Child, who is the actual focal point of the painting. The counterbalancing diagonals of the left arm of the Madonna and the back of the kneeling John form the top of the pyramid, while the left leg of Christ echoes the reverse diagonal that extends from the Madonna's left forearm and down her leg. Enclosed within the space between the blue-draped leg and the fur-covered back of John, the figure of the Christ Child is essentially vertical. The one horizontal element in the composition is the right arm of Christ, leading our eye to the slender cross so lightly held. Like so many of Raphael's paintings, this masterpiece suffers perhaps from too much loving care; it has been so vigorously cleaned that the colors are not as vibrant as they undoubtedly once were.

Characterized as Aristotelian in his approach to art, Raphael was a keen observer of nature and of people. His mastery of his craft combined with his perceptive examination of the world about him enabled Raphael to be one of the foremost portrait painters of his age. A member of the circle of Baldassare Castiglione, author of the *Courtier,* a book about courtesy and conduct (see chap. 16), Raphael was described by the writer Aretino as having "every virtue and every grace that is appropriate to a gentleman." It was, in fact, Raphael's social graces and material success that lay at the heart of his cold war with the socially inept Michelangelo. In his portrait of Castiglione (fig. 14.29) Raphael depicts his friend in the cooly composed pose of a Renaissance gentleman. The poise and quiet confidence are emphasized by the restrained elegance of his dress, which exemplifies a cultured society reacting against the flamboyant

Figure 14.30 Giorgione (and Titian?), *Fête Champêtre,* ca. 1505. Oil on canvas, 43¼ × 54¼″. The Louvre, Paris.

dress of the preceding century. With the premature death of the frail Raphael, the High Renaissance in Rome came to an end. By this time the innovations of Leonardo, Michelangelo, Bramante, and Raphael were being studied and applied throughout Italy, especially in Venice, and northward into Germany, France, and the Netherlands (today's Holland and Belgium).

High and Late Renaissance and Mannerism in Sixteenth-Century Italy

The High Renaissance style appeared only in elements of the later work of the long-lived Bellini (see fig. 14.17) but very clearly in the work of a shadowy figure first known as Giorgio and, later, as the famous Giorgione ("big George"; giorge-o-NAY; ca. 1475/77–1510). Very little is known about the man or even his work. He perhaps studied with Bellini and was the teacher of Titian and was, according to Vassari, a humanist, musician, and lover of conversation, parties, nature, and women, probably in reverse order.

Though another hand has added some distant figures in the left landscape, Giorgione's *Adoration of the Shepherds* (colorplate 28) is a superb example of the new pastoral poetic style that Giorgione introduced to painting in general and to the Venetian school in particular. One of the most innovative and influential painters of the Renaissance, Giorgione

used his mastery of light and color to paint magical landscapes in which human figures become part of the Arcadian mood. In fact, in colorplate 28 the landscape is so predominant that the work can be viewed as a landscape with Nativity Scene. The landscape itself is depicted not in naturalistic terms, as in the works of van Eyck or Leonardo, but as nature in the raw as viewed by the eye of the poet. The figures are not drawn but rather formed of contrasting light and shadow, with the body of the child and the heads of the parents radiating a heavenly light against the gloomy recesses of the cave. The high moral tone and noble values of the Florentine/Roman High Renaissance are utterly foreign to this romantic evocation of mood and feeling.

Giorgione died at an early age of the plague, leaving a number of unfinished works. Though it is known that Titian completed some of the paintings, what may never be known is which paintings were involved and what "completed by Titian" really means. In the *Fête Champêtre* (fig. 14.30) we see two opulent nudes painted in the lush Venetian manner; the one on the left is gracefully emptying a crystal pitcher and the other holds a recorder while gazing dreamily into the distance. The fully clothed men are deep in conversation, but only the man casually playing the lute is fashionably dressed. Having been labeled at various times "Pastoral Symphony," "Fountain of Love," or, as here, "Country Festival," the work has even been called an allegory of poetry. In other words, the subject matter may never be known or even be important. The painting exists as an enchanting combination of forms and shapes in a poetic setting, all created by an artist who may have had in mind nothing more than that.

Michelangelo and Mannerism

The art of the remainder of the century can be considered as two basic streams of styles: Mannerism and Late Renaissance. The beauty, harmony, and proportions of the High Renaissance were seen at this time as a golden age, an era in which Leonardo, Michelangelo, and Raphael had convincingly demonstrated that there was nothing an artist could not do.

What was left for later artists? Vasari used the term *maniera,* meaning style, of working "in the manner of" supreme artists like Raphael and Michelangelo. Later artists could either adopt the techniques of the masters or use these techniques as a point of departure, to replace the serenity of the High Renaissance with a Mannerist virtuosity that delighted in twisting, confusing, and distorting human figures. Raphael and Michelangelo studied nature; the Mannerists studied Raphael and Michelangelo, especially Michelangelo.

The so-called Mannerist Crisis may also have been a reaction to the momentous events of the 1520s, some local and others international, that affected the viewpoints and lives of just about everyone.

1. The power of Florence came to an end, as the proud city became a pawn in the hands of the Medici popes Leo X (1513–1521) and Clement VII (1523–1534).
2. During the 1520s Luther's defiance of Pope Leo X led to the dissolution of unified Christianity, followed by over a century of sectarian warfare.
3. In 1526 Suleiman the Turk defeated the Hungarians at Monac and, for decades, continued to menace Christian Europe.
4. In 1527 the political machinations of Clement VII led to the Sack of Rome by the rampaging armies of the Holy Roman Emperor Charles V of Germany.
5. In 1529 Clement VII refused to recognize the marriage of Henry VIII of England and Anne Boleyn, leading to England's break with Rome.

Artistically, the Mannerists were greatly influenced by Michelangelo's sculptures in the Medici Chapel and his *Last Judgment* fresco in the Sistine Chapel. Michelangelo's designs for the New Sacristy of the Medici Chapel were the most nearly complete of his architectural-sculptural conceptions. Signing the contract in 1519, he labored for fifteen years on a mortuary chapel for the tombs of Lorenzo and Giuliano de' Medici (son and grandson of Lorenzo the Magnificent; d. 1516), Lorenzo the Magnificent (d. 1492), and his brother Giuliano de' Medici (murdered in 1478). For most of its construction the project was threatened by exterior forces as outlined above, particularly the humiliation of the papacy

during the 1527 Sack of Rome. By the time the poverty-stricken Clement VII had returned to his burned-out city in 1528, Florence had successfully revolted against the Medici for the third time. However, the 1530 reconquest of the Republic put a Medici governor in charge again, leading to an order for Michelangelo's assassination because he had helped the city fortify itself. Protected by the canon of the Church of San Lorenzo, Michelangelo was pardoned by the Medici pope Clement VII so he could complete the family tomb. With the installation of the pope's illegitimate son, the vicious Alessandro, Duke of Florence, Michelangelo's position was so precarious that when Clement VII died in 1534, he fled to Rome, never again to return to Florence. It is difficult to conceive of a project that was more plagued by violent events or more successful in artistic terms.

During Michelangelo's visit to Rome to obtain Clement VII's pardon, the discussion concerned the Sistine Chapel perhaps even more than the New Sacristy that was destined to remain incomplete. The end wall of the Sistine Chapel contained the *Assumption of the Virgin* by Perugino but Clement proposed to Michelangelo that this be replaced with a Resurrection. By the time the new pope Paul III (1534–1549) had commissioned the artist to paint the entire wall, the subject had become the Last Judgment, though how this came about is unclear. Paul III was a Counter-Reformation pope whose most significant act was the convening of the Council of Trent (1545–1564) to systematically reform the church to counter the challenge of Protestantism. However, nepotism was rampant during Paul's reign and he, along with his sons and daughters, lived the lavish life of a Renaissance pope. Michelangelo, on the other hand, was deeply religious and was, moreover, sixty-one years old when he accepted the commission.

Preoccupied with the fate of humanity and that of his own soul, Michelangelo apparently began *The Last Judgment* (fig. 14.31) with the conviction that the world had gone mad. The ideal beauty and optimism of the chapel ceiling had been superseded by a mood of terror and doom, with the gigantic figure of Christ come to judge the quick and the dead. Based on Matthew 24:30–31, everyone "will see the Son of Man coming on clouds of Heaven with power and great glory," his body twisted and his arm raised in a gesture of damnation. In an energetic clockwise motion, the figures at the bottom rise toward Christ and are either gathered in by waiting angels or pulled by demons down into Hell. The resurrected women (always clothed) and men (generally nude) float into the helping arms of angels, who are unencumbered by wings or halos. The scale of the figures is from small in the region of the Damned, close to eye level, to monumental at the distant top section in the region of the Blessed. The nervous energy and the twisting, writhing, elongated figures are techniques adopted by the Mannerists. In this powerful fresco, however, they are manifestations of the unique artistic vision of a master, a natural evolution, given the subject matter, of his style for the Medici tombs in Florence.

Figure 14.31 Michelangelo, *The Last Judgment,* 1536–1540. Fresco, 48 × 44'. Altar wall of the Sistine Chapel, Vatican, Rome.

Figure 14.32 Michelangelo, *Rondanini Pieta,* ca. 1554–1564. Marble, height 64". Castello Sforza, Milan.

Only a few days before his death, Michelangelo was reworking his *Rondanini Pieta* (fig. 14.32), cutting the head back into the Virgin's shoulder and making the composition a slender, unified work of infinite pathos. Far removed from the High Renaissance style, the elongated figures are reminiscent of the jamb statues of the Royal Portal of Chartres Cathedral (see fig. 11.31), seeming to symbolize the artist's direct appeal to God. His death in his eighty-eighth year, probably of pneumonia, left this sculpture unfinished and his major project, the dome of St. Peter's, still under construction.

Michelangelo's apse and dome of St. Peter's (fig. 14.33) was not a commission but, in his words, done "solely for the love of God." Whether or not Michelangelo's late style can be described as Mannerist, still a moot point, his late architectural style is powerful and confident. The great dome is a huge sculptured shape rising above an apse distinguished by enormous pilasters, Michelangelo's "colossal order," pilasters that are both decorative and structural. The upward thrust of the pilasters is repeated and reinforced by the double columns of the drum, and carried ever upward by the arching ribs to a climax in the lantern. The vertical stress of classic forms, a new Renaissance procedure, is visible proof that classicism can be as emotional and as transcendal as the High Gothic style of Chartres Cathedral (see fig. 11.30).

Colorplate 22 Sandro Botticelli, *Birth of Venus,* after 1482. Tempera on canvas, 5′9″ × 9′½″. Uffizi Gallery, Florence.

Colorplate 23 Perugino, *Crucifixion with Saints,* before 1481. Panel, transferred to canvas: center, 40 × 22¼″; wings, 37¼ × 12″ each. Andrew W. Mellon Collection. National Gallery of Art, Washington, D.C.

Colorplate 24 Jan van Eyck, *Annunciation,* ca. 1430.
Oil on panel, 36½ × 14⅜″. Andrew W. Mellon
Collection. National Gallery of Art, Washington, D.C.

Colorplate 25 Leonardo da Vinci, *Ginevra de'Benci,* ca. 1480/81. Oil and tempera on panel, 15⅛ × 14½″. Ailsa Mellon Bruce Fund. National Gallery of Art, Washington, D.C.

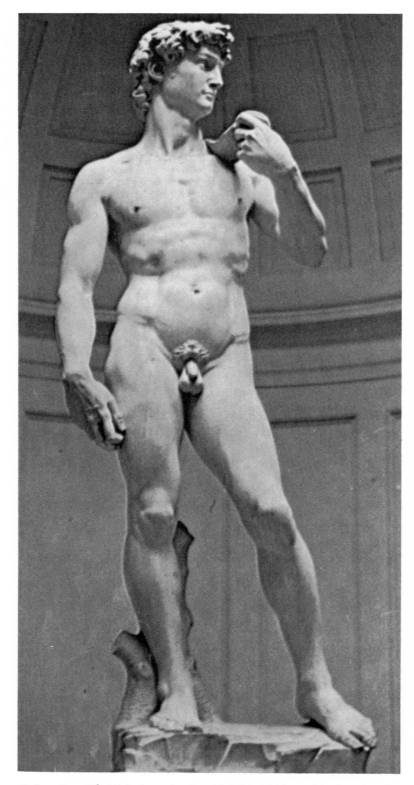

Colorplate 26 Michelangelo, *David*, 1501–1504. Marble, height of figure 14′3″. Academy, Florence.

Colorplate 27 Raphael, *The Alba Madonna,* ca. 1510. Transferred from wood to canvas, diameter of 37¼″. Andrew W. Mellon Collection. National Gallery of Art, Washington, D.C.

Colorplate 28 Giorgione, *Adoration of the Shepherds,* ca. 1505. Oil on panel, 35¾ × 43¼″. Samuel H. Kress Collection. National Gallery of Art, Washington, D.C.

Colorplate 29 Titian, *Venus with a Mirror,* ca. 1555. Oil on canvas, 49 × 41½″. Andrew W. Mellon Collection. National Gallery of Art, Washington, D.C.

Colorplate 30 Tintoretto, *Christ at the Sea of Galilee,* ca. 1555/1575. Oil on canvas, 66¼ × 46″. Samuel H. Kress Collection. National Gallery of Art, Washington, D.C.

Colorplate 31 El Greco, *Laokoön,* ca. 1610–1614. Oil on canvas, 54⅛ × 67⅞″. Samuel H. Kress Collection. National Gallery of Art, Washington, D.C.

Colorplate 32 Matthias Grunewald, *The Small Crucifixion,* ca. 1510. Oil on canvas, 70 × 60″. Samuel H. Kress Collection. National Gallery of Art, Washington, D.C.

Figure 14.33 Michelangelo, Dome of St. Peter's (view from the west), 1546–1564. Height of dome 452'. Completed by della Porta in 1590. Vatican, Rome.

Though the nave was extended far beyond Michelangelo's Greek-cross plan, the dome is still the major landmark of Rome, a fitting symbol for the art and life of Michelangelo.

Unquestionably a Mannerist, Parmigianino (par-me-dja-ah-NEE-no; 1503–1540) painted in an elaborate, tense, elegant, and artificial style in sharp and deliberate contrast to the harmonious naturalism of the High Renaissance. His *Madonna with the Long Neck* (fig. 14.34) is a marvel of decorative beauty. With a swanlike neck, exceptionally long fingers, and cold, ivory-smooth flesh, the Madonna smiles tenderly on a seemingly lifeless Christ Child. The background figure of the biblical prophet is dramatically small, and the rising, uncompleted columns add to the artificiality and strange mood of unreality. Parmigianino planned a complete temple in the background but left it incomplete, further illustrating, perhaps, the perverseness of an artist known to deliberately flaunt social and artistic conventions.

Late Renaissance and Mannerism in Italy and Spain

With an artistic career spanning sixty-eight years, Titian (TISH-n; ca. 1488–1576) was a giant of the High and Late Renaissance, excelling in every aspect of the painter's craft. After Raphael he was the finest portrait artist of the century, courted by the nobles and kings of Europe. Titian achieved the social status advocated by Leonardo, acquiring a towering reputation that led to many honors, the title of count, and a princely life. Repeatedly celebrating the goddess of love, his late painting, *Venus with a Mirror* (colorplate 29) is permeated with a tangible sensuality that is, however, not erotic, expressing instead the natural loveliness of woman. The famous color tones are exceptionally rich

Figure 14.34 Parmigianino, *Madonna with the Long Neck,* 1534–1540. Oil on panel, 7'1" × 4'4". Uffizi Gallery, Florence.

rather than just brilliant, mellowed by layer-upon-layer of glazes. Titian produced several variations upon the Venus-and-mirror theme, but this painting he kept for himself and willed to his son. Perhaps more than any other Renaissance artist, Titian understood the spirit of classical art. Drawing upon the Greeks, he incorporated High Renaissance techniques and some Mannerist devices in what is best described, in this work, as Late Renaissance style.

Titian's Venetian contemporary, Tintoretto (tin-toe-RET-toe; 1518–1594), developed a more fervent style blending Mannerist devices with the drawing technique of Michelangelo. In *Christ at the Sea of Galilee* (colorplate 30) we view a turbulent sea with wave edges as sharp as the blade of a knife, spottily applied white highlights, and deliberately atonal combinations that heighten the emotional content. The curved and elongated figure of Christ dominates an intensely dramatic scene in which the frightened fishermen look to the Savior for deliverance.

A comparison of Tintoretto's *The Last Supper* (fig. 14.35) with that by Leonardo (see fig. 14.25) dramatically illustrates the differences between the High Renaissance and the Mannerist style of the Late Renaissance. In Tintoretto's version the table is sharply angled and placed at the left. The size of the disciples diminishes from foreground to background, with Christ highlighted only by the brilliant glow of his halo. Almost lost in the agitation, Judas, dressed

Figure 14.35 Tintoretto, *The Last Supper,* 1592–1594. Oil on canvas, 12′ × 18′8″. S. Giorgio Maggiore, Venice.

Figure 14.36 Palladio, Villa Rotunda, Vicenza. Begun 1550 and finished by Vencenzo Scamozzi.

like a servant, sits on the opposite side of the table, a pathetic, isolated figure. This is the moment of the Eucharist, the transubstantiation of consecrated bread and wine into the flesh and blood of Christ. The agitated clutter of servants, hovering angels, flaming lamp, and radiant halo combine to express the emotional spirit of the Counter-Reformation.

The intense dramatic style of Tintoretto heralds the coming age of the Baroque, but the architectural designs of Palladio (pah-LAH-djo; 1518–1580) are clearly, lucidly classical. The only North Italian architect comparable to Brunelleschi, Alberti, Bramante, and Michelangelo, Palladio was born Andrea

di Pietro but is known to posterity by a name derived from Pallas Athena, goddess of wisdom. An avid student of classical and Renaissance architecture, Palladio designed churches, public buildings, and private homes. His Villa Rotunda (fig. 14.36), one of nineteen Palladian villas still in existence, was built in the countryside near Venice, much in the manner and style of Roman villas. From a central square identical porticoes thrust out from each side, each with a different view and a slightly variable climate at different hours of the day. Palladian designs became popular for English stately homes, and this particular design became a model for southern plantation homes in the American South, where outdoor living was common for much of the year. In the Villa Rotunda the proportions of length and breadth, height and width, of and between the rooms were based on the Pythagorean ratios of the Greek musical scale (see chap. 1), as in Alberti's proportions for his Church of Santa Maria Novella (see fig. 14.11) but even more rigorously applied.

Paradoxically, only the country villas of Palladio were placed in the natural settings that the Venetian painters Giorgione, Titian, Tintoretto, and Veronese celebrated in their richly colored paintings. Venice itself, except for private gardens, was a congested city of marble, brick, stone, and waterways with few plants, flowers, or trees. The fourth of the great Venetian masters, Paolo Veronese (vair-oh-NAY-se; 1528–1588),

Figure 14.37 Paolo Veronese, *The Finding of Moses*, ca. 1570. Oil on canvas, 22¾ × 17½". Andrew W. Mellon Collection. National Gallery of Art, Washington, D.C.

Figure 14.38 El Greco, *The Penitent St. Peter*, ca. 1598–1600. The San Diego Museum of Art, San Diego, California.

like his contemporaries, glorified nature in his work, but unlike other artists he concentrated on the sumptuous material world. Pleasure-loving Venetians preferred luxurious paintings that dazzled the eye and soothed the conscience. In *The Finding of Moses* (fig. 14.37) Veronese created a cheerful biblical scene redolent with the elegance and luxury that the Venetians themselves enjoyed. The Egyptian princess is richly clothed in Venetian dress, presiding benignly over the rescue of the abandoned child. The composition unwinds from the black page at the lower left up through the lady-in-waiting, who is handing Moses to the Pharaoh's daughter. On the right there is a similar unwinding upward but with a tighter rhythm. The tableau is set in a lush countryside in front of a sturdy Italian bridge and a suitably exotic and fanciful Egyptian city.

Veronese's style is lavishly and opulently Late Renaissance and basically secular, but that of El Greco is mystical, a fervent expression of the Counter-Reformation spirit. The last and possibly the most gifted of the Mannerists, Domenikos Theotokopoulos, known as El Greco (the Greek; 1541–1614), was born in Crete, then a Venetian possession, and trained in Late Byzantine art and Venetian Mannerism before moving to Spain in 1576. Even before the defeat of the Spanish Armada in 1588 Spain was a fading power, artistically provincial and obsessed with the Counter-Reformation, yet it was the proper environment for an artist of El Greco's religious convictions.

Combining the Byzantine tradition with his thorough knowledge of the Venetian masters, El Greco created a passionately religious art that was the embodiment of Spanish mysticism. In his *The Penitent St. Peter* (fig. 14.38) the elongated figure with hands clasped in prayer and anguished eyes turned heavenward in repentance for having denied Christ is set against a dark and mysterious background in which a distant angel is softly illuminated. Although physically tranquil, the scene is turbulent with the emotion of spiritual forces in a triangular composition that directs our eyes to the agonized face. The oft-debated topic of El Greco's astigmatism being responsible for his elongated figures has no basis in fact; the distortions are deliberate and reflect the artist's exposure to Byzantine art and Venetian Mannerism.

Though the subject is secular, El Greco's *Laokoön* (colorplate 31) is equally tormented. Unlike the Hellenistic sculptural version (see fig. 3.69), the Trojan priest and no less than five sons are depicted as attenuated silvery figures, fighting off slender snakes that may be venomous but certainly are not capable of crushing anyone, unlike the powerful sea serpents of the sculptural group. In the background, dramatic clouds hover over the brooding city of Toledo, El Greco's version of Troy before its fall to Agamemnon and his Argive army.

A nation supercharged with religious zeal, Spain formed the spearhead of the Counter-Reformation and was the birthplace of the Society of Jesus (Jesuits) and the stronghold of the Inquisition. El Greco was its peerless master of religious subjects, an artist who, more than any other, made visible the spiritual content of the Catholic faith. Widely admired in his time, El Greco's reputation declined rapidly as Western Europe, but not Spain, plunged enthusiastically into the scientific and intellectual discoveries of the Age of Reason. It was not until the twentieth century that El Greco's unique and intensely personal art received proper recognition.

High and Late Renaissance in the North, ca. 1500–1600

For most of the fifteenth century, Northern artists and some Italians were influenced by the dazzling naturalism of the Flemish masters. Not until the end of the century did Italian influences begin to beguile Northern patrons with their scientific rules and, especially, a literary tradition that included a vocabulary of art criticism. Noble patrons were delighted with classical examples of "good" and "bad" art. Increasingly, this came to mean that art based on models from antiquity was good while the rest, including the entire Flemish tradition was "wrong" or at best "primitive." With remarkable suddenness, Italian artists were busily engaged with important projects for patrons like Henry VII of England and the French royal family, while Northern artists were traveling to Italy to study the masters of the Early and High Renaissance.

During the sixteenth century it became fashionable to view Northern culture as backwards and its artists as inferior, especially those who had not been blessed with Italian instruction in the rules of perspective and proportion. Speaking, in essence, for the Italian Renaissance, Michelangelo remarked to the Portuguese painter Francesco da Hollanda that Flemish landscape paintings were fit only for "young women, nuns, and certain noble persons with no sense of true harmony." "Furthermore," he observed, "their painting is of stuffs, bricks, mortar, the grass of the fields, the shadows of trees and little figures here and there. And all this," said he, "though it may appear good in some eyes, is in truth done without symmetry or proportion." Consigned to the attic of Northern art, the matchless paintings of the Flemish masters were, for over three centuries, derided as primitive or naive. It was not until 1902 that the first international show of fifteenth-century Flemish art was opened in Bruges and only considerably later in this century that the derogatory labels were finally dropped.

For reasons still unknown, Italian art caught on first in Germany, where Albrecht Dürer (DOO-er; 1471–1528) became the founder of the brief but brilliant German High Renaissance. His two trips to Italy (1494–1495 and 1505–1507) exposed him to all of the Italian techniques, but he was never attuned to Italian form, preferring instead the strong lines of the Northern tradition. Though he became a master painter, Dürer's greatest achievements were in the graphic arts of engraving and woodcuts, which were printed in quantity and sold throughout Germany, making the artist a wealthy man.

Figure 14.39 Albrecht Dürer, *The Virgin with the Monkey,* ca. 1498–1499. Engraving, 7¼ × 4¹³⁄₁₆". University Art Collections, Arizona State University, Tempe. Gift of Mr. and Mrs. Read Mullen.

Dürer's *Virgin with a Monkey* (fig. 14.39), one of his many Madonnas, reveals Dürer's own combination of German and Italian styles. Holding a finch, symbol of his passion, the chubby Christ Child looks properly Italian, but the blond Madonna, wearing what appears to be a heavy woolen dress, is clearly Germanic, as is the medieval building in the background. The monkey may have a symbolic meaning or may be included simply to add a touch of exoticism. The fleecy, billowing clouds and meticulous perspective are comparable to Italian art, but the strong details of the dress and the naturalism of the grass and foliage indicate the work of a Northern master.

Dürer was deeply involved in the religious and political movements in Germany and in the Italian humanism that flourished briefly on German soil until the winds of the Reformation blew away what was essentially a Catholic point of view. The leading humanist of sixteenth-century Europe, Erasmus of Rotterdam (1466–1536), influenced many intellectuals of the period including artists like Dürer and Hans Holbein the Younger. In the Erasmus portrait by Dürer (see fig. 16.1) the scholar sits in his study surrounded by books, some presumably his own publications, while he writes a new work. Behind him in Latin is the elaborate title of the print and the name of the artist. At the bottom is Dürer's monogram, above which is the date and above that a Greek inscription that translates as, "His writings portray him even better," meaning that his books were a more accurate

Figure 14.40 Chateau of Azay-le-Rideau, 1518–1529.

Figure 14.41 Chateau of Chambord, north front, begun 1519.

measure of the man than Dürer's reverential portrait. The Northern passion for detail is, to say the least, clearly evident in this print.

Dürer was internationally famous but his worthy contemporary Matthias Grunewald (1483?–1528), though widely known in his own time, was neglected until this century. A highly original artist, Grunewald, whose name was actually Mathis Gothardt Neithardt, was familiar with the work of Dürer and possibly that of Bosch, but there is no evidence of Italian classical influence, as one glance at his *Small Crucifixion* (colorplate 32) will immediately reveal. This is the brutal reality of nailing a man to a cross and leaving him there to die. His body a mass of cuts and suppurating sores, his limbs twisted, his skin grey and speckled with dried blood, Christ is depicted in relentless detail as having died for the sins of all people. The grief of John, Mary, and Mary Magdalene is vibrant with intense pain and sorrow. Grunewald has elevated the horror of the passion to the level of universal tragedy, producing a composition as convincing as anything in Western art.

Fully conversant with all that the Italians had to teach, Hans Holbein the Younger (hol-bine; 1497–1543) was the last of the great painters of the German High Renaissance and one of the finest portrait painters in the history of art. He traveled widely in France, Switzerland, and Italy, then finally settled down in London, where he became the favorite painter of Henry VIII, who furnished a special suite in St. James's Palace for "master Hans." Holbein gained access to the English court through Erasmus of Rotterdam, who provided him with a letter of recommendation to Sir Thomas More. His portrait of More

(see fig. 16.2) is a noble portrayal of the humanist-statesman. Depicted realistically, including a stubble of beard, More wears the luxurious clothes of his rank and the heavy chain of his office as Lord Chancellor of England. With meticulous attention to detail in the manner of van Eyck, Holbein depicts the dignity and determination of a man who will one day be executed for opposing Henry's establishment of the Church of England.

The Italian influence in France is epitomized in the chain of elegant chateaux built throughout the scenic Loire River valley. Combining the French Gothic heritage with Italian details, the Chateau of Azay-le-Rideau (fig. 14.40) has a Gothic silhouette, but the walls and windows are proportioned and decorated in the manner of an Italian palazzo (see fig. 14.10). Entirely surrounded by a wide moat, this tiny jewel of a chateau is harmonious, elegant, and wholly French.

Imposing and elaborate as befits the king of a prosperous nation, the Chateau of Chambord (fig. 14.41) was originally a hunting lodge that was later redesigned for Francis I by an Italian architect who may have been influenced by a nearby resident named Leonardo da Vinci. The huge central block is connected by corridors leading outwards to sets of apartments designed in the modern manner as self-contained units. Anchored at the four corners by large round towers, the entire complex is surrounded by a moat (not visible here). The matching of horizontal and vertical features in windows and moldings is taken directly from the Italian palazzos, but the forest of dormers, chimneys, and lanterns is right out of the Gothic tradition and flamboyantly French.

Most of the Renaissance art of France was courtly but, as mentioned previously, there was a growing middle class of art patrons in the Netherlands, which in the sixteenth century had become a battleground of religious and political strife. Militantly Protestant, particularly in the north (today's Holland), the Netherlands fought a rigid Spanish rule that became even more brutal under the fanatical Philip II and the imported Spanish Inquisition. Nevertheless, the Netherlandish school of painting flourished and produced Pieter Bruegel the Elder (BRU-gul; 1525?–1569), the

Figure 14.42 Pieter Bruegel the Elder, *Landscape with the Fall of Ikarus,* ca. 1558. Oil on canvas, 44⅛ × 29″. Musée Royaux des Beaux Arts, Brussels.

only Northern genius to appear between Dürer and Rubens. A highly educated humanist and philosopher, Bruegel studied in Italy in 1551–1555, returning home with a love of Italian landscapes and a profound knowledge of Italian control of form and space. In *Landscape with the Fall of Ikarus* (fig. 14.42) Bruegel depicts the myth of the reckless one who ignored the advice of his father, Daidalos, and flew so near the sun that the wings fashioned by his father melted, and he plunged to his death in the sea. In the painting Bruegel emphasizes everything but Ikarus, who is just a pair of kicking legs and a splash in the sea in front of the sailing galleon. The plowman and the singing shepherd are oblivious of the fate of a foolish boy who has caused his own destruction. He dies in the sea, but the plowing, the shepherding, the world go serenely on. Bruegel viewed humankind as basically noble, but depicted men and women as faulty individuals who were easily degraded or destroyed by materialism, avarice, or, like Ikarus, just plain folly.

In *The Blind Leading the Blind* (fig. 14.43) Bruegel has drawn upon Matthew 15:12–19 in which Christ warns, "If a blind man leads a blind man, both will fall into a pit." A common moralizing issue of the time, Bosch painted the subject with the two men stipulated by the Bible, but Bruegel increased the number to set up a horizontal composition. With each man suffering from an identifiable eye disease, the design can be followed from the upright man at the left, and then in a descending line dropping to the man who has fallen "into a pit," in this case, a brook. Though this is a strong didactic statement the meaning is not clear. It could be a warning against following false prophets, thus referring to the raging religious controversies of the time. Or the artist may be cautioning against the folly of worldly ambitions that can blind one to the teachings of Christ. The latter interpretation may or may not explain the solid little church in the background, a dignified structure played against six ugly and pathetic individuals reduced to helpless cripples by their own folly. Bruegel seems to be saying that people are free to choose their own fate.

Summary

Symbolized by Brunelleschi's dome and the dedication of Florence Cathedral in 1436, a new age came into being in fifteenth-century Florence, a city of bankers and craftsmen whose self-image was personified by the Davids of Donatello, Verrocchio, and Michelangelo. To create the new style, a fresh repertory of illusionist devices was developed by Masaccio and later utilized by Fra Angelico, Fra Filippo Lippi, and Uccello.

By the second half of the century classical designs had been fully assimilated, leading to the classically based architecture of Alberti and the mythological painting of Botticelli. Florentine innovations spread throughout Italy, promoted by Perugino and by Bellini, the founder of the Venetian school.

The Renaissance in the North took another course. Influenced by the International Style and a long tradition of craftsmanship in manuscript illuminations and stained glass, van Eyck perfected the new technique of oil painting and created matchless works of meticulous naturalism. Rogier van der Weyden and Hans Memling continued in the naturalistic style but, coinciding with the rising pessimism and fear of death and the devil, the bizarre art of Hieronymus Bosch epitomized the religious torment of a society on the brink of the Lutheran Reformation.

Figure 14.43 Pieter Bruegel the Elder, *The Blind Leading the Blind,* 1568. Tempera on canvas, 60 × 34″. National Museum, Naples.

The High Renaissance in Italy was a time of constant warfare highlighted by the incredible achievements of Leonardo in scientific investigation, invention, and painting. Excelling in the arts of sculpture, architecture, painting, and poetry, the "divine Michelangelo" created, among other works, the *Pieta, David,* and the frescoes of the Sistine Chapel ceiling. Raphael achieved a classic balance of form and content that became the hallmark of the High Renaissance, and Bramante, in his Tempietto, designed the prototype of classical domed structures.

In sixteenth-century Venice Giorgione was the first of the Venetian colorists, followed by the assured painting of Titian and the luxuriant style of Veronese. Michelangelo designed the Medici tombs and influenced Mannerist painters like Parmigianino, Tintoretto, and the Spanish painter from Crete called El Greco. During the latter stages of his career Michelangelo painted the awesome *Last Judgment* and designed the apse and dome of St. Peter's. Marking the end of the Renaissance in Italy, Palladio's villas became models for eighteenth- and nineteenth-century domestic architecture in England and the United States.

In sixteenth-century Germany Albrecht Dürer, Matthias Grunewald, and Hans Holbein the Younger were the leading painters of the High Renaissance, while in France, Italian styles influenced French courtly art and contributed to the designs of elegant chateaux in the Loire River valley. Renaissance art in the strife-torn Netherlands culminated in the work of Pieter Bruegel the Elder.

By the end of the sixteenth century the ideals and aspirations of the Renaissance had perished in the wreckage of cultures beset by religious wars with the worst yet to come. Marking the end of an era, the Renaissance set the stage for the emergence of the modern world.

15
Renaissance Music:
Court and Church

The conviction that music was inherently sacred or secular was a medieval idea that ended with the Renaissance. Subject matter was a primary concern, and in the Renaissance, the subject was human life. There were still many threads from the Middle Ages, but the Renaissance flowered and flourished when men and women turned to the physical world of the here and now. Enriched by music, art, and literature, the good life was its own reward and it was attainable on this earth.

Renaissance music dates from about 1420 to 1600. It can be characterized, in large part, as optimistic, lively, and worldly. The once-rigid distinctions between sacred and secular music no longer applied. Sacred music was not always synonymous with devotional, noble, and edifying sounds any more than secular music was necessarily shallow, common, or folksy.

The subject matter rather than the style now determined whether the work was sacred or secular. Renaissance painters used local models for their madonnas, the same models who posed as Aphrodites or nymphs. Composers used melodies where they worked best. The music for Latin poetry, for example, could also be used to accompany a portion of the Mass. Popular songs of the time were sometimes used as a basis for liturgical motets and even for entire masses.

As stated in chapter 13, the Renaissance began around 1350 in Italy and in the North. By the fifteenth century, humanism had spread from Italy to the North, and the work of Flemish painters Jan van Eyck and Rogier van der Weyden (see chap. 14) strongly influenced a number of Italian painters, especially their technique of oil painting. For reasons still not clearly understood, the *musical* Renaissance began in the North—in England, the Low Countries, and in northern France. The most notable of the English composers, John Dunstable (d. 1453) was a contemporary of the early Renaissance composers on the continent and probably influenced them with what his admirers called his "sweet style." On the continent some court and church composers of northern France and the Low Countries (Flanders) formed a group known today as the Franco-Flemish school. True Renaissance artists, they were individualistic, materialistic, and boldly experimental. They had mastered the craft and art of a new style of music, and they delighted in demonstrating their compositional skills with intricate canons and musical puzzles for educated amateurs.

In their quest for new materials and fresh ideas they traveled to Italy, where the simple folk melodies and dance tunes provided further opportunities for polyphonic devices and techniques. Considering the travel hardships then, the mobility of Franco-Flemish composers in the fifteenth century was astounding. The composer Dufay, for example, was discovered at the age of nine in Cambrai in France by talent scouts seeking out precocious young musicians. Before he was twenty-six Dufay had traveled to Italy and then studied in Paris, held a post in northern France, served the court in Bologna, and sung in the papal choir in Rome.

Franco-Flemish composers like Dufay and others dominated Italian musical life in the courts and in the churches for over a century. St. Mark's in Venice, one of the most important musical centers in Europe, employed only Flemish composers until the latter part of the sixteenth century. When Florence decided to dedicate its magnificent cathedral (1436), Dufay was commissioned to write special music for the occasion (see chap. 14).

Music was an integral part of the complex fabric of Renaissance society. A retinue of musicians became a fixture of court life, with the dukes of Burgundy, Philip the Good and Charles the Bold, setting the style. Castiglione (see chap. 14), the chief social arbiter of the Renaissance, thought that his ideal Courtier should be proficient in both vocal and instrumental music:

> I regard as beautiful music, to sing well by note, with ease and beautiful style; but as even far more beautiful, to sing to the accompaniment of the viol, because nearly all the sweetness lies in the solo part, and we note and observe the fine manner and the melody with much greater attention when our ears are not occupied with more than a single voice, and moreover every little fault is more clearly discerned,—which is not the case when several sing together, because each singer helps his neighbor. But above all, singing to the viol by way of recitative seems to me most delightful, which adds to the words a charm and grace that are very admirable.
>
> All keyed instruments also are pleasing to the ear, because they produce very perfect consonances, and upon them one can play many things that fill the mind with musical delight. And not less charming is the music of the stringed quartet, which is most sweet and exquisite. The human voice lends much ornament and grace to all these instruments, with which I would have our Courtier at least to some degree acquainted, albeit the more he excels with them, the better.[1]

---

1. Baldassare Castiglione, *The Book of the Courtier,* trans. Leonard Eckstein Opdycke (New York: Horace Liveright, 1929).

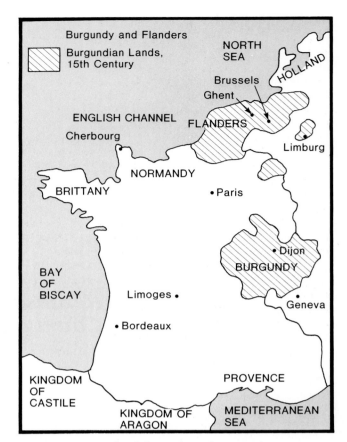

Figure 15.1 Lands of the Dukes of Burgundy

At different times a kingdom, a county, and a duchy, Burgundy became the most powerful and influential political entity in Europe during the fifteenth century. From Philip the Bold in 1336 through John the Fearless and Philip the Good to Charles the Bold (ruled 1467–1477), the rulers of Burgundy made the court in the capital city of Dijon one of the most magnificent in Europe (see fig. 15.1).

The Flemish sculptor Claus Sluter and the painter Jan van Eyck served the "court of plume and panoply" of Philip the Good at the time of its greatest splendor. The court was ostentatious and even flamboyant, but nevertheless according to contemporary accounts, it resembled a sort of fairyland. Women wore hennins, cone-shaped headdresses with long sheer veils hanging from the pointed tops. Their gowns were opulent, frequently decorated with fur and set off by gold throat bands and necklaces. Elaborate furniture and interior designs furnished the proper setting for the elegance of the court.

The court of the dukes of Burgundy set the styles in dress, manners, dancing, music, and the other arts. The principal court dance was the *basse dance,* which was performed with gliding steps, possibly accounting for the designation *basse* (low). The basse dance belonged to a family of related dances: the basse dance proper and the *pas de Brabant* (Italian *saltarello*). It was the custom to follow the dignified basse dance, referred to as the "imperial measure," by the quicker pas de Brabant, thus producing a contrasting pair of slow and fast dance movements, a typical procedure for Renaissance dances. Both used the same basic music; only the rhythms were changed.

Tapestries and miniatures of the period show instrumental ensembles playing for the dancers. The standard group of instruments consisted of two shawms (early oboes) and a slide-trumpet, while the harp, lute, and flute made up the other group. The former group consisted of *hauts* (high, loud) instruments, the latter of *bas* (low, soft) instruments. The hauts instruments were used for festive occasions and were usually played from a balcony or loggia. The bas instruments were used for more intimate dancing and were placed near the dancers.

Court life at Dijon was lively and elegant. In many respects, it was an updated version of the medieval Court of Love with music, both lively and sedate, for dancing and for songs, true French *chansons* extolling love, joy, and beauty. Secular music was in great demand for everything from the intimate rites of courtship to elaborate ceremonial music for the court. There was a remarkable development of sophisticated secular music, but not at the expense of sacred music, which incorporated the techniques and some of the melodies of secular music into a highly refined style.

The Burgundian School

Guillaume Dufay (doo–FYE; ca. 1400–1474) was the most famous composer of the Burgundian school of the Franco-Flemish tradition and one of the greatest of French composers. Following is the beginning of a Dufay mass movement that illustrates the smoother, fuller sounds of Renaissance music. Dufay has broken down the *Kyrie Eleison* into three separate movements: *Kyrie eleison, Christe eleison,* and *Kyrie eleison.* The texture is characteristic of early Renaissance music with mixed vocal and instrumental sounds and with instruments playing the wordless portions of the Mass.

First Kyrie from the Mass
"Se la face ay pale"[2]

Time: 1:40
(Complete)
Guillaume Dufay (ca. 1400–1474)

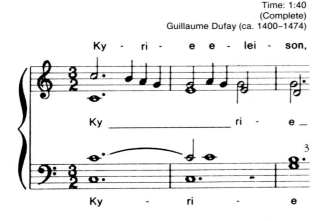

Gilles Binchois (bann–SWAH; ca. 1400–1460) did not have the versatility of Dufay but was a superb composer of French chansons. Some, like the famous "De plus en plus," are as fresh, witty, and bright today as when they were written. Although composed for aristocrats of the court, Binchois's music has a comfortable middle-class air of easy informality. Bourgeois influences had now become significant. Wealthy Flemish merchants were beginning to make their presence felt in the world of art, music, and manners, once the exclusive preserve of aristocracy and clergy.

The Franco-Flemish Tradition

During the latter part of the fifteenth century the center of musical activity gradually shifted from Burgundy to northern France and the Low Countries of Flanders and the Netherlands. The fusion of French elegance, Flemish polyphonic techniques, and Italian vigor led to the highly sophisticated style of the Late Renaissance. Whatever followed from this—even the music of such giants as Palestrina and Lassus—was actually a continuation of northern genius suffused with Italian taste and supported by Italian patronage.

No one person was responsible for the development of the new music. It simply happened that a large group of gifted composers in one geographic area was active at about the same time and that all, at varying times, were involved in Italian musical life. The most important composers were Obrecht and Agricola of the Netherlands; Brumel and de la Rue of northern France; and Isaac, Compère, and Josquin of Flanders. Each was brilliant in his own right, but Josquin outshone them all.

Martin Luther is reported to have said that "Others follow the notes, Josquin makes them do as he wishes." Josquin des Près (ca. 1450–1521), usually referred to as Josquin (JOSS–can), did indeed know what to do with the notes; in his own time he was referred to as the "prince of music." He and his Franco-Flemish contemporaries developed all of the basic features of the Late Renaissance and, in so doing, established music as an international style in western European culture. Josquin was to music what Leonardo, Michelangelo, and Raphael were to the visual arts. A master of compositional techniques, he sometimes invented and consistently refined the methods and materials of Renaissance polyphonic music.

Musical development moved to the north of France and to the Low Countries after the beginning of the slow decline of the Duchy of Burgundy. Both Josquin and the great Orlandus di Lassus were born in Flanders, the latter in 1532. In between these two

2. Smijers, *Algemeene Muziek Geschiedenis,* Utrecht, 1938, p. 101.
3. Musical notation is used on a modest scale throughout this book in order to give brief quotes from works to be studied. These are guides to listening just as literary quotations are guides to reading. Using musical quotes is a necessary, basic procedure that is in no way "technical." Performing music is technical; *reading* music is a simple procedure easily learned by anyone. (See pp. 17–20.)

towering figures there were literally hundreds of excellent composers and performers in the Franco-Flemish school.

While Italy was exporting artists and works of art, it was also importing music and musicians. Western Europeans flowed into Italy to study her literary and visual arts, while musicians from the north moved in to take over most of the major musical positions. Northern dominance was so prevalent that Franco-Flemish music flourished on foreign soil for over a century before Italy was able to produce a Palestrina.

The motet "Ave Maria" by Josquin is an example of the serene lucidity and beauty of music of the High Renaissance. The smoothly flowing lines are woven into an elegant tapestry of luminous sound, a sound somehow comparable to the undulating arches of a Renaissance arcade. Motets are still sacred music, similar to polyphonic masses, but the text is nonscriptural. Instruments are no longer combined or alternated with the voices as in Early Renaissance music; the singing is now consistently unaccompanied (*a cappella*). The vocal texture is continuous with new phrases overlapping preceding phrases to produce an unbroken stream of simultaneous melodies. This ceaseless flow of intricately intertwined melodies is a hallmark of High and Late Renaissance vocal music.

The voices enter one at a time in *imitation;* that is, each of the four voices has essentially the same melodic line when it makes its entrance. Josquin used the text of the "Ave Maria" ("Hail Mary, full of grace . . .") and selected his basic theme from a portion of an "Ave Maria" chant:

Motet: "Ave Maria"[4]

Time: 3:50
Josquin des Près (ca. 1450–1521)

The Flemish composer Orlandus Lassus (1532–1594) was one of the finest composers of a celebrated era, the Golden Age of Polyphony of the sixteenth century. His 1250 compositions were literally international: Latin masses and motets; secular vocal music in French, German, and Italian; and instrumental music in different national styles. Representative of his sacred music, the "Tristis est anima mea" is quoted below in a simplified musical score illustrating the rich and sonorous sound of his music. (See "motet" in the Glossary.)

Motet: "Tristis est anima mea"[5]

Time: 4:00
Orlandus Lassus (1532–1594)

The Italian Style

During the latter part of the sixteenth century, Italian genius manifested itself in the music of native Italians. Italian music had been invigorated by the presence of resident Flemish composers and by the dynamic Counter-Reformation response to Luther's revolt. Flemish composers had fled Spanish tyranny in the Low Countries to pursue their profession in a less hostile setting. There was, moreover, a real need to develop a new style of sacred music because things had gotten out of hand, as Erasmus of Rotterdam cogently pointed out.

> We have introduced an artificial and theatrical music into the church, a bawling and agitation of various voices, such as I believe had never been heard in the theatres of the Greeks and Romans. Horns, trumpets, pipes vie and sound along constantly with the voices. Amorous and lascivious melodies are heard such as elsewhere accompany only the dances of courtesans and clowns.[6]

The Council of Trent (1545–1564) was convened to deal with the abuses pointed out by Luther and other reformers. The problem of music was only incidental to overall concerns, but musical difficulties occupied most of the attention of the Council for over a year. Final recommendations were negative rather than positive. Certain practices were forbidden and certain results were prescribed without, however, specifying the means. The canon finally adopted by the Council in 1562 banned all seductive or impure melodies, whether vocal or instrumental, all vain and worldly texts, all outcries and uproars, that "the House of God may in truth be called a House of prayer."

Shortly after passing the canon against decadent musical practices, the Council took under consideration the possible banning of all polyphonic music, especially polyphonic masses. This ultraconservative movement was countered by Lassus and Palestrina, who, among others, submitted polyphonic music to a special Commission in order to promote a favorable decision. Polyphonic music was preserved when the Council approved, after considerable deliberation, the reformed style of polyphonic music advocated by the composers of the Church.

4. Josquin des Près, *Werke,* Motets, vol. I, Amsterdam, 1935, p. 1.
5. Orlando di Lasso, *Samtliche Werke,* vol. V, Leipzig, 1895, p. 48.
6. Desiderius Erasmus, *Opera Omnia,* VI, 1705, col. 731.

Figure 15.2 St. Mark's Cathedral, begun 1063, Venice. With its five portals and five glittering domes, St. Mark's functioned as a sumptuous backdrop for the elaborate civic ceremonies staged in the great piazza stretched before it. Also see figure 8.22.

Giovanni Pierluigi da Palestrina (1524–1594) was one of the supreme exponents of Catholic polyphonic music of the Renaissance, but his secular music is equally outstanding. Romanticized in the nineteenth century as a lonely and poverty-stricken artist who was wedded to the church, Palestrina was actually a successful professional musician. He briefly considered the priesthood after the death of his first wife, but chose instead to marry a wealthy widow. He was paid well for the music that he wrote for the church and even refused several more lucrative positions rather than leave Rome.

Present-day music students study Palestrina's music for classes in "strict counterpoint," that is, writing polyphonic music in the manner of the sixteenth century with Palestrina as the model composer. Though his compositions serve as a guide to correct contrapuntal writing, Palestrina's music is anything but dogmatic. A model it is but one of clarity, conciseness, and consistency. Using existing plainsong melodies as a point of departure, he wrote in a beautifully balanced style of simultaneous plainsong.

The following plainsong, "Veni sponsa Christi," forms the basis for a Palestrina mass:

Palestrina began with this simple melody, transforming it into a serenely flowing melodic theme:

"Veni sponsa Christi" (named after the plainsong) is a short composition based on this characteristic Palestrina melody. Notice how the smoothly flowing text is fitted to graceful melodic lines.

First Agnus Dei from the Mass:
"Veni sponsa Christi"[7]

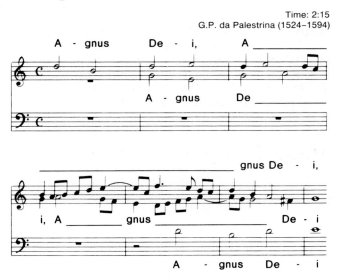

Time: 2:15
G.P. da Palestrina (1524–1594)

Italian Vocal-Instrumental Music

Instrumental music came to the fore during the late Renaissance assisted particularly by the musical directors of the Cathedral of St. Mark's in Venice. St. Mark's Byzantine splendor was typical of the grandiose palaces, churches, ceremonies, and even paintings of that ornate city (see fig. 15.2). As a trading center and crossroads of the world, much of the pomp and pageantry was a deliberate (and successful) attempt to impress visitors with the magnificence of Venice. Grand productions inside the cathedral were also necessary for the desired effect, but the arrangement of the church did not lend itself to large musical groups.

---

7. Ioannis Petraloysii Praenestini, *Opera omnia,* Leipzig, 1886, vol. 18, p. 35.

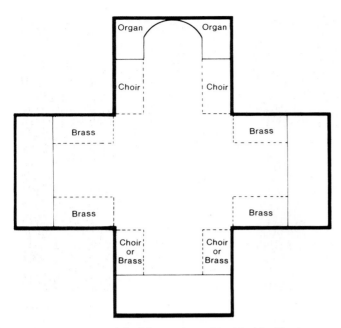

Figure 15.3 Simplified floor plan of St. Mark's, Venice

Figure 15.4 Interior, St. Mark's, Venice. This view is from the west balcony where one organ is located, looking east to the small chancel with the other organ and space for a small choir. Brass choirs were placed at one or more of the four upper corners under massive arches. The conductor stood on the high podium in front of the main-floor choir.

St. Mark's floor plan was that of a Greek cross (fig. 15.3). Following the conventions of the Eastern church, the main floor was reserved for men and the smaller balcony level for women. This design was exploited by creating a new *polychoral* style of *antiphonal* singing, or a procedure whereby the ensemble (chorus with or without orchestra) was divided into several different groups singing and/or playing in *alternation*. Musical productions would include the use of the two organs in their fixed positions plus choirs and brass choirs stationed on several balconies throughout the church. The listener would be overwhelmed with vocal and instrumental music alternating between left and right, front and

rear, etc. Arrangements of choirs and brass choirs could be selected from some of the possibilities indicated in figure 15.3 (also see fig. 15.4).

Following is the motet "In ecclesiis" by G. Gabrieli (1557–1612) for:

Chorus I

Chorus II

Solo voices

Orchestra
> Three cornettos (usually played by trumpets)
> Viola (bowed string instrument in alto register)
> Two trombones
> Pipe organ

The motet consists of five verses and five alleluias and has the following overall structure of text and performing groups (which sing or play from four different locations in the church):

Verse 1.	*In ecclesiis benedicite Domino,* (Praise the Lord in the congregation)	Sopranos (Chorus I) Organ
	Alleluia	Sopranos (Chorus I) Chorus II Organ
Verse 2.	*In omnia loco . . . ,* (In every place of worship praise him)	Tenors (Chorus I) Organ
	Alleluia	Tenors (Chorus I) Chorus II Organ
Sinfonia (orchestral interlude)		
Verse 3.	*In Deo, salutari meo . . . ,* (In God, who is my salvation and glory, is my help, and my hope is in God) .	Altos (Chorus I) Tenors (Chorus I) Orchestra .
	Alleluia	Altos (Chorus I) Tenors (Chorus I) Chorus II Orchestra
Verse 4.	*Deus meus, te invocamus . . . ,* (My God, we invoke thee, we worship thee; deliver us, quicken us)	Sopranos (Chorus I) Tenors (Chorus I) Organ
	Alleluia	Chorus I Chorus II Organ

Verse 5. *Deus, adjutor noster ae-ternam,* Chorus I
Chorus II
Orchestra
(My God, judge us eternally)
Alleluia Chorus I
Chorus II
Orchestra
Organ

Music Printing

Venice was also the setting for the development of printed music. Over nine million books had been printed by the year 1500, but no one had thought of printing music on that scale. A 1457 *Psalterium* that included music had been printed at Mainz and a Roman *Missale* was printed in 1476 in Milan using, for the first time, movable type.

Ottaviano de' Petrucci (peh–TROO–tchee; 1466–1539) used movable type in his printing shop, but he was also an enterprising businessman. On May 25, 1498, he petitioned the Signoria of Venice for a twenty-year license (amounting to a monopoly) to print music to meet a growing demand for domestic music. In 1501 he produced the *Harmonice Musices Odhecaton A (One Hundred Songs of Harmonic Music),* the earliest printed collection of part-music. Rich in Franco-Flemish chansons, this anthology was followed by fifty-eight more volumes of secular and sacred music produced for music-hungry amateurs and an increasing number of professional musicians (see fig. 15.5). An expanding market led, of course, to lower prices and even wider dissemination of music. By the end of the sixteenth century, music publishers were in business throughout Europe.

Instrumental Music

Renaissance instrumental music continued to be primarily functional; that is, it was associated with dances, plays, masquerades, and extravaganzas of noble courts rather than as a performance art with its own special audience.

Dance and music have always been associated and rarely more effectively than in the sixteenth century, which has been called "the century of the dance." The church had long suppressed dancing as both heathenish and lascivious. However, the frantic, compulsive dances of the flagellants of the fourteenth century symbolized a violent reaction against this stifling authority. Simultaneously in the Italian and French courts, men and women joined hands for the first time for folklike round dances and courtly pair dances such as the *danse royale.*

A large variety of dances appeared in the lute, keyboard, and other instrumental music of the sixteenth century. The pair of dances "Der Prinzen-Tanz" and "Proportz" is for the lute, a plucked string instrument with a mellow and resonant tone. This "Prince's Dance" is in slow duple meter (two beats per measure) followed by the same melody "proportionately altered"—designated as "Proportz"—in a

Figure 15.5 *Lady Playing a Dulcimer* from the early sixteenth-century manuscript of the fourteenth-century poem "Les Echecs Amoreux." A few of the many Renaissance instruments are depicted here. The elegantly gowned lady is playing her dulcimer (an instrument still in use) with small hammers. A harp leans against the wall at the left, and a portable organ rests on the floor at the right. In the background are singers and players. Reading from left to right, the instruments are: recorder (still used today and also ancestor of the flute), shawm (ancestor of the oboe), and bagpipes (probably of Asian origin; introduced to Europe by the Romans during the first century A.D.). Biblioteque Nazional fv. 143, Paris.

fast triple meter (three beats per measure). The dance is organized into four short sections, each repeated, which can be labeled *a–b–c–d.* The graph of "Lute Dances" given below is drawn to scale and uses a letter for each section of the music. The numerals indicate the number of measures in each section.[8] Any number of Renaissance dances can be designed and danced to the basic musical structure.

Lute Dances: "Der Prinzen-Tanz; Proportz" (ca.1550)

Scale: ⅛" = 1 measure
Arabic numerals indicate number of measures in each section.

Time: 1:35

Slow (Duple Meter)

ⓐ 4 ⓐ 4 ⓑ 4 ⓑ 4 ⓑ 4 ⓑ 4

Fast (Triple Meter)

ⓒ 8 ⓒ 8 ⓓ (á) 7 ⓓ (á) 8

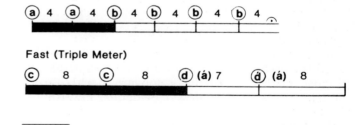

8. If there are four measures they can be counted audibly as 1–2, 2–2, 3–2, 4–2. Four measures of triple meter would count as: 1–2–3, 2–2–3, 3–2–3, 4–2–3.

The chief instrumental rival of the lute was the *harpsichord*—also called cembalo, clavecin, virginal, spinet—the principal keyboard instrument of the sixteenth through the eighteenth centuries. Harpsichords have various shapes, which are generally similar in external appearance to grand, upright, and spinet pianos. The tone is produced by quills plucking the strings and is bright and sharp. Unlike the piano, harpsichords cannot vary their *dynamics* (degrees of loudness or softness) except by using two keyboards, muted strings, or different types of quills. Whole sections are played at one dynamic level; variation is achieved by changing to a louder or softer tone quality in the next section.

In England, the harpsichord was called a *virginal,* supposedly in honor of the "maiden Queen Elizabeth." English music had flourished under Henry VIII, Edward VI, and Mary, and reached, under Elizabeth, a level rarely approached thereafter. English power and wealth, the importation of foreign talent, and increased travel, all combined to make the English assimilation of the Italian Renaissance one of the outstanding periods in Western history. Tudor sacred music was superb, but the secular forms of English music—the madrigals, lute music, virginal music, and fancies for viols—had special importance in the richness of the Elizabethan Age.

The composition "Loth to Depart" for a "pair of virginals"—harpsichord with two keyboards—is by the English composer Giles Farnaby. The piece is written in what had become a common and preferred instrumental form of *theme and variations.* In this case, the theme is in triple meter and is sixteen measures long. After the theme, there is a set of five variations, each patterned after the original theme in structure, melody, and harmony. The formal structure of the piece does not change; the composer achieves variety by making alterations in rhythm, melody, and texture.

Variations for Virginals: "Loth to Depart"[9]

Time: 4:25
Giles Farnaby (ca. 1560–1600)

Theme (beginning)

English Secular Vocal Music

The English madrigal school was inspired by Italian models, but its growth and development has made the English madrigal virtually synonymous with Elizabethan England. A *madrigal,* whether English or Italian, is a secular, unaccompanied part-song, usually in four voices. English madrigals tend toward a balanced texture of polyphonic and homophonic writing and are frequently either merry or melancholy. The outstanding characteristic, however, is the sheer delight in the sounds, rhythms, and meanings of the English language.

The madrigalists are fond of natural word rhythms. They also like to play with onomatopoeia, alliteration, metaphor, and simile and take exceptional pleasure in exploiting double meanings. Word play with triple meanings is even better. Word painting is another notable characteristic whereby composers manipulate the sounds of the music so that they can imitate, imply, or describe the sounds of nature and/or the meaning and sounds of words.

In the following *pastoral madrigal,* the composer quietly poses the question, "Thyrsis? Sleepest thou?" and then continues to press the question until Thyrsis is awakened with some vigorous "hollas." The cuckoo song is imitated, the music "sighs" as the shepherd "sighed as one all undone" and requests to be "let alone alas." The repetitive text of "drive him back to London" pushes the madrigal to an animated conclusion.

Madrigal: "Thyrsis, Sleepest Thou?"[10]

Time: 1:40
John Bennet (ca. 1575–1625)

The *catch* is one of the most interesting and ingenious types of English secular music. Written as a three-part round for male voices, it was designed for double and triple entendre as the texts of the second and third voice parts blended into the gaps in the text of the top voice part. This blending process may be illustrated as follows:

Part 1. Show me now the _____ way _____ .
Part 2.   Lead me to the <u>best</u> man.
Part 3.   Now is the time to ride <u>home</u>.
    (Show me now the <u>best</u> <u>way</u> <u>home</u>.)

The following catches illustrate two characteristic types of humorous songs, which were sung by "gentlemen of quality." These gentlemen had to be good singers so that they could "catch" the melody at the right time.

9. *Fitzwilliam Virginal Book,* vol. II, London, 1899, p. 317.

10. John Bennet, *Madrigals to Four Voices,* London, 1599, no. 8.

Tom the Taylor [11]
Henry Purcell (1659–1695)

Tom making a Mantua [12] for a Lass of pleasure,
Pull'd out, pull'd out, pull'd out his long, his long and
    lawful measure,
But quickly found, tho' woundily streight lac'd Sir
Nine Inches, nine Inches, nine Inches, nine Inches
    would not half surround her wast, Sir.
Three Inches more at length brisk Tom advances,
Yet all, yet all too short, yet all too short, all too short, all
    too short, yet all too short, all too short to reach her
    swinging hances.

A Catch in the Play of the Knight of Malta [13]
Henry Purcell

At the close of the Evening the Watches were set,
The Guards went the Round, and the Ta-ta-ta-too, Ta-ta-ta-
    too, ta-ta-ta-too, ta-ta-ta-too, ta-ta-ta-too, ta-ta-ta-ta-
    ta-too was beat, the ta-ta-ta-ta-ta-ta-too was beat,
But now yonder stars appear in the Sky,
And Ta-ra-ra-ra, Ra-ra-ra-ra, Ra-ra-ra-ra, Ra-ra-ra-ra, Ra-ra-ra-
    ra, Ra-ra-ra-ra, Ra-ra-ra-ra is sounded on high.
We shall soon be reliev'd, then drink, drink away, then
    drink away, then drink, drink, drink away,
Here's to you, and to you, and to you, let us drink, let us
    drink, till 'tis day, let, let us drink till 'tis day.

Summary

The environment of music underwent notable changes during the Renaissance with the inevitable result that the forms of music changed accordingly. The forces of secularization, which were set in motion during the Gothic period, began to rival the power of the church. The expansion of the universities, the development of city centers of trade and commerce, and the rise of a mercantile middle class helped bring about a concurrent development of secular music.

Outdoor concerts using orchestras composed of violins, shawms, trombones, and drums and indoor concerts of recorders, viols, and harpsichord became common. Some of the outdoor performances provided music for dancing, which had changed from improvised music for one or two instruments to composed music for groups of instruments (*consorts*).

The demand for musical instruments for domestic use spurred the development and production of lutes, viols, and especially the instrument that could play both homophonic and polyphonic music, the harpsichord. An even more common household instrument was the *clavichord*. [14]

The newly awakened interest in classical culture, in humanism, and in the creative individual was reflected in the active participation in the arts by educated amateurs. Large and small social gatherings featured performances of solo songs accompanied by lute or harpsichord (or clavichord), a variety of chamber music, and, particularly in England, the singing of part-songs such as madrigals and catches.

The proliferation of secular music did not provoke a decline in sacred music; rather there was a merging of techniques, instruments, and styles. Burgundian composers such as Dufay combined vocal with instrumental music in the Church. Binchois specialized in secular music with particular emphasis upon the special qualities of the French chanson.

Josquin des Près wrote masses and motets, Italian secular music, and French chansons. Lassus wrote 1250 compositions in Latin, French, German, and Italian. Palestrina, serving the church in Rome, wrote mostly sacred music, but did compose a number of Italian madrigals. In Venice, Gabrieli wrote antiphonal, vocal-instrumental music and considerable instrumental music.

The growth of music during the Renaissance was astounding. Within a single century, music changed from an esoteric, church-dominated art form to an international language heard in every court, noble residence, and many middle-class homes throughout Europe.

---

11. *The Catch Club or Merry Companions,* I, Walsh, London, 1762, p. 2.
12. Mantle.
13. *The Catch Club,* p. 38.

14. The tone of the clavichord is produced by depressing the keys so that a metal tangent on the other end of the key would strike the string. The instrument is portable and the tone light and flexible. The principle of striking a string was later, in the eighteenth century, developed into the hammer action of the piano.

16

Shadow and Substance: Literary Insights into the Renaissance

The linguistic dualism of the Renaissance had a very positive effect on the development of literature, philosophy, and science. The Latin that the Church had preserved was the common language of all intellectuals and, moreover, a direct link to the classical past. No wonder Petrarch and other humanists viewed Cicero and Virgil as contemporaries; all wrote in the same language. Developing during the Middle Ages as the spoken languages of the people, the vernaculars became the accepted languages of popular culture. Latin was still viewed as the proper language for scholarly work, but the vernaculars developed during the Renaissance into recognized national languages that became acceptable vehicles for literary expression. Latin provided a kind of intellectual unity; English, French, and Spanish each reinforced a sense of national unity and purpose. Each nation developed its own modern literary tradition, but languages were not isolated by the rise of nationalism. Translations of every language, including Latin, flowed back and forth over national borders, making Renaissance literature as international, in its own way, as art and music.

From the treasure-house of Renaissance literature we can select only a few writers and a variety of literary forms that are realistic, romantic, optimistic, or pessimistic, each mirroring one (or more) of these Renaissance attitudes.

Literary Selections

Though Petrarch intended his epic poem *Africa* to be his major work, his Italian sonnets have been far more influential. His love poetry was inspired by Laura, whom he first saw in the Church of St. Clara of Avignon on April 6, 1327. The following sonnet commemorates that momentous meeting, while also alluding to the day on which Christ supposedly died: April 6.

SONNET III

(Era il giorno ch'al sol si scolarara)
Petrarch (Francesco Petrarca; 1304–1374)

'Twas on the morn when heaven its blessed ray
    In pity to its suffering master veil'd,
    First did I, lady, to your beauty yield,
    Of your victorious eyes th' unguarded prey.
Ah, little reck'd I that, on such a day,
    Needed against Love's arrows any shield;
    And trod, securely trod, the fatal field:
    Whence, with the world's, began my heart's dismay.
On every side Love found his victim bare,
    And through mine eyes transfix'd my throbbing
        heart;
    Those eyes which now with constant sorrows flow:
But poor the triumph of his boasted art,
    Who thus could pierce a naked youth, nor dare
    To you in armor mail'd even to display his bow!

Like Dante's Beatrice, Laura was an ideal, the object throughout Petrarch's life of an unrequited poetic passion. Unlike Beatrice, whom Dante idealized from afar, Laura accepted the poet as a friend—but no more than that. She was married and destined to be the mother of ten children. A sonnet is, by definition, a fourteen-line lyric poem that expresses a single idea or thought, in this case the poet's reaction to Laura's physical beauty.

SONNET LXIX

(Erano i capei d'oro all' aura sparsi)
Petrarch (Francesco Petrarca; 1304–1374)

Her golden tresses were spread loose to air,
    And by the wind in thousand tangles blown,
    And a sweet light beyond all brightness shone
    From those grand eyes, though now of brilliance
        bare;
And did that face a flush of feeling wear?
    I now thought yes, then no, the truth unknown.
    My heart was then for love like tinder grown,
    What wonder if it flamed with sudden flare?
Not like the walk of mortals was her walk,
    But as when angels glide; and seemed her talk
    With other than mere human voice, to flow.
A spirit heavenly, a living sun
    I saw, and if she be no longer so,
    A wound heals not, because the bow's undone.

Petrarch was tormented by his passion, but he was also inspired as a poet because the one-way love affair appealed to his vanity. He was a Renaissance artist, a self-conscious man of letters seeking earthly fame, as the following sonnet clearly reveals.

SONNET XLVII

(Benedetto sia l' giorno e l' mese e l' anno)
Petrarch (Francesco Petrarca; 1304–1374)

Blest be the day, and blest the month, the year,
    The spring, the hour, the very moment blest,
    The lovely scene, the spot, where first oppress'd
    I sunk, of two bright eyes the prisoner:

And blest the first soft pang, to me most dear,
    Which thrill'd my heart, when Love became its guest;
    And blest the bow, the shafts which pierced my
        breast.
    And even the wounds, which bosom'd thence I bear.
Blest too the strains which, pour'd through glade and
       grove,
    Have made the woodlands echo with her name;
    The sighs, the tears, the languishment, the love:
And blest those sonnets, sources of my fame;
    And blest that thought—Oh! never to remove!—
    Which turns to her alone, from her alone which
       came.

Laura died on April 6, 1348, of the Black Death, as did millions of Europeans during that ghastly summer. Petrarch was devastated, as well as transfixed by the date.

SONNET CCXCII

(Gli occhi di ch' io parlai si caldamente)
Petrarch (Francesco Petrarca; 1304–1374)

Those eyes, 'neath which my passionate rapture rose,
    The arms, hands, feet, the beauty that erewhile
    Could my own soul from its own self beguile,
    And in a separate world of dreams enclose,
The hair's bright tresses, full of golden glows,
    And the soft lightning of the angelic smile
    That changed this earth to some celestial isle,—
    Are now but dust, poor dust, that nothing knows.
And yet *I* live! Myself *I* grieve and scorn,
    Left dark without the light I loved in vain,
    Adrift in tempest on a bark forlorn;
Dead is the source of all my amorous strain,
    Dry is the channel of my thoughts outworn,
    And my sad harp can sound but notes of pain.

Throughout the rest of the poet's long life, Laura remained the ideal object, becoming in death the mediator between the penitent and the Divine.

SONNET CCCXIII

(I'vo piangendo i miei passati tempi)
Petrarch (Francesco Petrarca; 1304–1374)

I now am weeping, for the years passed by,
    Wasted in loving but a mortal thing,
    Though I could fly, not rising on the wing,
    To leave some work, perhaps not far from high.
My deeds unworthy, impious, from the sky,
    Thy realm, thou see'st, unseen, immortal King;
    To me, astray and feeble, succour bring,
    And with Thy grace, my soul's defect supply:
So that if tempest-tost, and oft in strife,
    I lived, I yet may die in port, at peace,
    And nobly quit, though spent in vain, my life.
Through my remaining years, so soon to cease,
    Let Thy right hand, my guide, in dying, be
    My stay; Thou know'st I have no hope but Thee.

Exercises

1. In line 11 of Sonnet III, the image of the eyes as a gateway to the heart was a poetic commonplace. Is that image still used today in poetry and songs? Give a few examples.
2. What is the meaning of the image of the "bow" in the last line of sonnets III and LXIX?
3. In the sonnets given here, what are some of the clues that mark these as Renaissance rather than medieval poetry?

Desiderius Erasmus (1466–1536)

Italian humanism had a distinctly pagan flavor, but across the Alps the movement was entirely Christian, with Erasmus (fig. 16.1), the "prince of humanists," in the forefront. He was a true cosmopolitan, making all Europe his home from England to Italy. Although at first well-disposed toward Luther's reforms, he could not accept Luther's denial of free will. "I laid a hen's egg," wrote Erasmus; "Luther hatched a bird of quite another species." With equal clarity he saw the corruption within the Church and the intransigence of Luther and chose to stay aloof. His advice to Pope Adrian VI, a personal friend, was characteristically levelheaded:

> As to writing against Luther, I have not learned enough. . . . One party says I agree with Luther because I do not oppose him. . . . The other finds fault with me because I do oppose him. . . . I did what I could. I advised him to be moderate, and I only made his friends my enemies. . . . They quote this and that to show we are alike. I could find a hundred passages where St. Paul seems to teach the doctrines which they condemn in Luther. I did not anticipate what a time was coming. I did, I admit, help to bring it on; but I was always willing to submit what I wrote to the Church. . . . Those counsel you best who advise gentle measures. . . . For myself, I should say, discover the roots of the disease. Clean out those to begin with. Punish no one. Let what has taken place be regarded as a chastisement sent by Providence, and grant a universal amnesty. If God forgives so many sins, God's vicar may forgive.

Erasmus was a strong supporter of overdue reforms. In his *Colloquies* he wrote that "Luther was guilty of two great crimes—he struck the Pope in his crown, and the monks in their belly." In another vein he sternly admonished his church: "By identifying the new learning with heresy you make orthodoxy synonymous with ignorance." Erasmus preferred a purified church to a divided one.

Erasmus conceived the idea of a satire on just about every aspect of contemporary society during a journey from Italy to England. Written partly during his stay with the English humanist Sir Thomas More and dedicated to More, he called the book *Moria* (the Greek word for Folly) in a punning reference to his

Figure 16.1 Albrecht Dürer (1471–1528), *Erasmus of Rotterdam,* 1526. Engraving, 9¾ × 7½". The Latin inscription states that this was a drawing from life. Metropolitan Museum of Art, New York. Fletcher Fund, 1919.

English friend's name. Appearing in 36 editions in his own lifetime, the *Praise of Folly* was the most widely read book of the century after the Bible. Erasmus had brilliantly reinvented the classical paradoxical encomium in which everyone and everything unworthy of praise are ironically celebrated.

Niccolo Machiavelli (1469–1527)

The thorough humanistic education of Niccolo Machiavelli (MAHK-iya-VEL-lee) and his own political experience helped him to reevaluate the role of the state. For medieval thinkers, the Church looked after the spiritual salvation of its flock, the State attended to their physical well-being, and all operated under Divine Law. Machiavelli observed that the Romans had encouraged civic duties and civic pride, but Christians were supposed to detach themselves from public affairs. The obvious solution was to secularize politics. Make the state preeminent and its own justification, and have it function in accordance with the observable facts of human nature. Machiavelli wrote *The Prince* as a guide for the man he and many Italians fervently longed to see: a ruler who would unite Italy under one jurisdiction. This was a manual for action, the first objective analysis of how political power was obtained and kept. Machiavelli's brilliant analysis is detached, objective, and nonjudgmental. It gave the Renaissance its first candid picture of human nature with all of the idealism, both of medievalism and humanism, stripped away.

> For of men it may generally be affirmed that they are thankless, fickle, false, studious to avoid danger, greedy of gain, devoted to you while you are able to confer benefits upon them, and ready, as I have said before, while danger is distant, to shed their blood, and sacrifice their property, their lives and their

children for you; but in the hour of need they turn against you. . . . Love is held by the tie of obligation, which, because men are a sorry breed, is broken on every whisper of private interest.

Machiavelli's verdict was not simply the opinion of a misanthrope, soured on the world. The author was a social scientist who investigated human affairs with the same cold detachment that Copernicus used to chart the courses of the planets. After considering the fate of governments from that of Athens to all those of his own time, he came to the conclusion that human beings were beasts, at best, and that the successful ruler is the one who treats people accordingly. Though Italy did not achieve unification until the nineteenth century, Machiavelli's theory of absolutism became a model for the rest of Europe.

Literary Selection

THE PRINCE
Niccolo Machiavelli

Men Who Gain a Princedom through Wicked Deeds

In our times, when Alexander VI was reigning, Liverotto of Fermo—who many years before had been left when little without a father—was brought up by his maternal uncle, named Giovanni Fogliani, and in the early years of his youth was placed to serve as a soldier under Paulo Vitelli, in order that, well versed in that profession, he might attain some excellent position in an army. Paulo afterward dying, he served under Vitellozzo his brother; in a very short time, being quickwitted and vigorous in body and mind, he became the first man in his army. But since he thought it servile to be a subordinate, he determined, with the aid of some citizens of Fermo who preferred slavery rather than freedom for their native city, and with the help of the Vitelleschi, to capture Fermo. So he wrote to Giovanni Fogliani that, having been many years away from home, he wished to come to visit him and his native city and also to inspect his inheritance; and—because he had not striven for anything except to gain honor—in order that his fellow citizens might see that he had not spent his time without results, he wished to come with honor escorted by a hundred horsemen from among his friends and servants; and he begged his uncle to be so kind as to arrange that the people of Fermo would receive him honorably. This would bring honor not merely to him but to Giovanni, whose foster child he was. In no way, thereupon, did Giovanni fall short in any duty he owed his nephew, and he had the people of Fermo receive him honorably. Liverotto then took up his lodging in his own mansion. There, having spent some days and carefully made the secret arrangements that his future wickedness required, he gave a splendid banquet, to which he invited Giovanni Fogliani and all the leading men of Fermo. When the meal was finished and all the other matters customary at such banquets, Liverotto, according to plan, started certain serious discourses, talking of Pope Alexander's greatness and of Cesare his son and of their enterprises. After Giovanni and the others had replied to these discourses, he at once rose up, saying these were things to speak of in a place more secret; and he withdrew to a chamber to which Giovanni and all the other citizens followed. No sooner were they seated than, from secret places in the room, out came soldiers who killed Giovanni and all the others. After this slaughter, Liverotto mounted his horse and overran the city and besieged in the Palace the chief magistrates, so that for fear they were compelled to obey him and to confirm a government of which he made himself prince.

[Liverotto's Success]

When all those were dead who, if they had been discontented, could have injured him, he strengthened himself with new dispositions both civil and military in such a way that for a year, during which he held the princedom, not merely was he safe in the city of Fermo, but he had become an object of fear to all his neighbors. His overthrow, indeed, would have been as difficult as that of Agathocles if he had not let Cesare Borgia deceive him at Sinigaglia when, as I said above, the Duke captured the Orsini and Vitelli. There Liverotto too was taken, a year after the parricide he committed, and along with Vitellozzo, who had been his instructor in good and evil, he was strangled.

[Cruelty Prudently Used]

Some may wonder how it came about that Agathocles and others like him, after countless betrayals and cruelties, could for a long time live safely in their native places and defend themselves from foreign enemies, and the citizens never plotted against them; yet many others, even in peaceful times, could not by means of cruelty carry on their governments—and so much the less in the uncertain times of war. I believe this comes from cruelties badly used or well used. *Well used* we call those (if of what is bad we can use the word *well*) that a conqueror carries out at a single stroke, as a result of his need to secure himself, and then does not persist in, but transmutes into the greatest possible benefits to his subjects. *Badly used* are those which, though few in the beginning, rather increase with time than disappear. Princes who follow the first method can, before God and before men, make some improvement in their position, as Agathocles could; the others cannot possibly sustain themselves.

On Taking a State

It is to be noted, that in taking a state the conqueror must arrange to commit all his cruelties at once, so as not to have to recur to them every day, and so as to be able, by not making fresh changes, to reassure people and win them over by benefiting them. Whoever acts otherwise, either through timidity or bad counsels, is always obliged to stand with knife in hand, and can never depend on his subjects, because they, owing to continually fresh injuries, are unable to depend upon him. For injuries should be done all together, so that being less tasted, they will give less offence. Benefits should be granted little by little, so that they may be better enjoyed. And above all, a prince must live with his subjects in such a way that no accident of good or evil fortune can deflect him from his course; for necessity arising in adverse times, severe measures are too late, and the good that you do does not profit, as it is judged to be forced upon you, and you will derive no benefit whatever from it.

Of the Things for Which Men, and Especially Princes, Are Praised or Blamed

It now remains to be seen what are the methods and rules for a prince as regards his subjects and friends. And as I know that many have written of this, I fear that my writing about it may be deemed presumptuous, differing as I do, especially in this matter, from the opinions of others. But my intention being to write something of use to those who understand, it appears to me more proper to go to the real truth of the matter than to its imagination; and many have imagined republics and principalities which have never been seen or known to exist in reality; for how we live is so far removed from how we ought to live, that he who abandons what is done for what ought to be done, will rather learn to bring about his own ruin than his preservation. A man who wishes to make a profession of goodness in everything must necessarily come to grief among so many who are not good. Therefore it is necessary for a prince, who wishes to maintain himself, to learn how not to be good, and to use this knowledge and not use it, according to the necessity of the case.

Leaving on one side, then, those things which concern only an imaginary prince, and speaking of those that are real, I state that all men, and especially princes, who are placed at a greater height, are reputed for certain qualities which bring them either praise or blame. Thus one is considered liberal, another miserly; one a free giver, another rapacious: one cruel, another merciful; one a breaker of his word, another trust-worthy; one effeminate and pusillanimous, another fierce and high-spirited; one humane, another haughty; one lascivious, another chaste; one frank, another astute; one hard, another easy; one serious, another frivolous; one religious, another an unbeliever, and so on. I know that every one will admit that it would be highly praiseworthy in a prince to possess all the above-named qualities that are reputed good, but as they cannot all be possessed or observed, human conditions not permitting of it, it is necessary that he should be prudent enough to avoid the scandal of those vices which would lose him the state, and guard himself if possible against those which will not lose it to him, but if not able to, he can indulge them with less scruple. And yet he must not mind incurring the scandal of those vices, without which it would be difficult to save the state, for if one considers well, it will be found that some things which seem virtues would, if followed, lead to one's ruin, and some others which appear vices result in one's greater security and well-being.

Beginning now with the first qualities above named, I say that it would be well to be considered liberal; nevertheless liberality such as the world understands it will injure you, because if used virtuously and in the proper way, it will not be known, and you will incur the disgrace of the contrary vice. But one who wishes to obtain the reputation of liberality among men, must not omit every kind of sumptuous display, and to such an extent that a prince of this character will consume by such means all his resources, and will be at last compelled, if he wishes to maintain his name for liberality, to impose heavy taxes on his people, become extortionate, and do everything possible to obtain money. This will make his subjects begin to hate him, and he will be little esteemed being poor, so that having by this liberality injured many and benefited but few, he will feel the first little disturbance and be endangered by every peril. If he recognizes this and wishes to change his system, he incurs at once the charge of niggardliness.

A prince, therefore, not being able to exercise this virtue of liberality without risk if it be known, must not, if he be prudent, object to be called miserly. In course of time he will be thought more liberal, when it is seen that by his parsimony his revenue is sufficient, that he can defend himself against those who make war on him, and undertake enterprises without burdening his people, so that he is really liberal to all those from whom he does

not take, who are infinite in number, and niggardly to all to whom he does not give, who are few. In our times we have seen nothing great done except by those who have been esteemed niggardly; the others have all been ruined.

Of Cruelty and Clemency, and Whether It Is Better To Be Loved or Feared

Proceeding to the other qualities before named, I say that every prince must desire to be considered merciful and not cruel. He must, however, take care not to misuse this mercifulness. Cesare Borgia was considered cruel, but his cruelty had brought order to the Romagna, united it, and reduced it to peace and fealty. If this is considered well, it will be seen that he was really much more merciful than the Florentine people, who, to avoid the name of cruelty, allowed Pistoia to be destroyed. A prince, therefore, must not mind incurring the charge of cruelty for the purpose of keeping his subjects united and faithful; for, with a very few examples, he will be more merciful than those, who, from excess of tenderness, allow disorders to arise, from whence spring bloodshed and rapine; for these as a rule injure the whole community, while the executions carried out by the prince injure only individuals. And of all princes, it is impossible for a new prince to escape the reputation of cruelty, new states being always full of dangers.

Nevertheless, he must be cautious in believing and acting, and must not be afraid of his own shadow, and must proceed in a temperate manner with prudence and humanity, so that too much confidence does not render him incautious, and too much diffidence does not render him intolerant.

From this arises the question whether it is better to be loved more than feared, or feared more than loved. The reply is, that one ought to be both feared and loved, but as it is difficult for the two to go together, it is much safer to be feared than loved, if one of the two has to be wanting. For it may be said of men in general that they are ungrateful, voluble, dissemblers, anxious to avoid danger, and covetous of gain; as long as you benefit them, they are entirely yours; they offer you their blood, their goods, their life, and their children, as I have before said, when the necessity is remote; but when it approaches, they revolt. And the prince who has relied solely on their words, without making other preparations, is ruined; for the friendship which is gained by purchase and not through grandeur and nobility of spirit is bought but not secured, and at a pinch is not to be expended in your service. And men have less scruple in offending one who makes himself loved than one who makes himself feared; for love is held by a chain of obligation which, men being selfish, is broken whenever it serves their purpose; but fear is maintained by a dread of punishment which never fails.

In What Way Princes Must Keep Faith

How laudable it is for a prince to keep good faith and live with integrity, and not with astuteness, every one knows. Still the experience of our times shows those princes to have done great things who have had little regard for good faith, and who have been able by astuteness to confuse men's brains, and who have ultimately overcome those who have made loyalty their foundation.

You must know, then, that there are two methods of fighting, the one by law, the other by force: the first method is that of men, the second of beasts; but as the first method is often insufficient, one must have recourse to the second. It is therefore necessary for a prince to know well how to use both the beast and the man.

A prince being thus obligated to know well how to act as a beast must imitate the fox and the lion, for the lion cannot protect himself from traps, and the fox cannot defend himself from wolves. One must therefore be a fox to recognize traps, and a lion to frighten wolves. Those that wish to be only lions do not understand this. Therefore, a prudent ruler ought not to keep faith when by so doing it would be against his interest, and when the reasons which made him bind himself no longer exist. If men were all good, this precept would not be a good one; but as they are bad, and would not observe their faith with you, so you are not bound to keep faith with them. Nor have legitimate grounds ever failed a prince who wished to show tolerable excuse for the non-fulfillment of his promise. Of this one could furnish an infinite number of modern examples, and show how many times peace has been broken, and how many promises rendered worthless, by the faithlessness of princes, and those that have been able to imitate the fox have succeeded best. But it is necessary to be able to disguise this character well, and to be a great feigner and dissembler; and men are so simple and so ready to obey present necessities, that one who deceives will always find those who allow themselves to be deceived.

I will only mention one modern instance. Alexander VI did nothing else but deceive men, he thought of nothing else, and found the occasion for it; no man was ever more able to give assurances, or affirmed things with stronger oaths, and no man observed them less; however, he always succeeded in his deceptions, as he well knew this aspect of things.

It is not, therefore, necessary for a prince to have all the above-named qualities, but it is very necessary to seem to have them. I would even be bold to say that to possess them and always to observe them is dangerous, but to appear to possess them is useful. Thus it is well to seem merciful, faithful, humane, sincere, religious, and also to be so; but you must have the mind so disposed that when it is needful to be otherwise you may be able to change to the opposite qualities. And it must be understood that a prince, and especially a new prince, cannot observe all those things which are considered good in men, being often obliged, in order to maintain the state, to act against faith, against charity, against humanity, and against religion. And, therefore, he must have a mind disposed to adapt itself according to the wind, and as the variations of fortune dictate, and, as I said before, not deviate from what is good, if possible, but be able to do evil if constrained.

A prince must take great care that nothing goes out of his mouth which is not full of the above-named five qualities, and, to see and hear him, he should seem to be all mercy, faith, integrity, humanity, and religion. And nothing is more necessary than to seem to have this last quality, for men in general judge more by the eyes than by the hands, for every one can see, but very few have to feel. Everybody sees what you appear to be, few feel what you are, and those few will not dare to oppose themselves to the many, who have the majesty of the state to defend them; and in the actions of men, and especially of princes, from which there is no appeal, the end justifies the means. Let a prince therefore aim at conquering and maintaining the state, and the means will always be judged honourable and praised by everyone, for the vulgar is always taken by appearances and the issue of the event; and the world consists only of the vulgar, and the few who are not vulgar are isolated when the many have a rallying point in the prince. A certain prince of the present time, whom it is well not to name, never does anything but preach peace and good faith, but he is really a great enemy to both, and either of them, had he observed them, would have lost him state or reputation on many occasions.

Exercises

1. What does Machiavelli mean by cruelty "well used"? Give some contemporary examples of cruelty both "well used" and "badly used." Is Machiavelli correct? Have there been any twentieth-century rulers who were overthrown because of their badly used cruelties? Which ones? Regimes that are headed for destruction?

2. Is it better, according to Machiavelli, for a ruler to be loved or feared? How would the leaders of the U.S.S.R. and the People's Republic of China respond?

3. Machiavelli contends that a ruler does not have to keep good faith. Why not? Under what circumstances? Have any American presidents acted like "a fox and a lion"? Name one or two.

Michelangelo Buonarotti (1475–1564)

The musicality of sonnets by Petrarch and his followers was the accepted style of the Italian Renaissance, but Michelangelo followed his own course in his poetry just as he did in sculpting and painting. His sonnets were, as he himself said, "unprofessional, rude, and rough." Michelangelo did not consider himself a poet in Petrarchian terms but he was praised at the time as a poet in his own right. His sonnets, like the personality of their creator, are powerful and unique and constitute, at their best, the finest lyric Italian poetry of the Renaissance. No knowledge of Michelangelo the sculptor and painter can be complete without knowing the artist as poet. The following two poems were written for Michelangelo's close friend Tommaso de' Cavalieri.

Literary Selections

SONNET XXX

(Veggio co' bei vostri occhi)
Michelangelo Buonarotti

With your fair eyes a charming light I see,
    For which my own blind eyes would peer in vain;
    Stayed by your feet the burden I sustain
    Which my lame feet find all too strong for me;
Wingless upon your pinions forth I fly;
    Heavenward your spirit stirreth me to strain;
    E'en as you will, I blush and blanch again,
    Freeze in the sun, burn 'neath a frosty sky.
Your will includes and is the lord of mine;
    Life to my thoughts within your heart is given;
    My words begin to breathe upon your breath:

Like to the moon am I, that cannot shine
    Alone; for lo! our eyes see nought in heaven
    Save what the living sun illumineth.

SONNET XXXII

(S'un casto amor)

Michelangelo Buonarotti

If love be chaste, if virtue conquer ill,
    If fortune bind both lovers in one bond,
    If either at the other's grief despond,
    If both be governed by one life, one will;
If in two bodies one soul triumph still,
    Raising the twain from earth to heaven beyond,
    If Love with one blow and one golden wand
    Have power both smitten breasts to pierce and thrill;
If each the other love, himself forgoing,
    With such delight, such savour, and so well,
    That both to one sole end their wills combine;
If thousands of these thoughts, all thought outgoing,
    Fail the least part of their firm love to tell:
    Say, can mere angry spite this knot untwine?

Michelangelo met Vittoria Colonna, the marquise of Pescara, while he was working on the Last Judgment (1536–1541; see fig. 14.38) in the Sistine Chapel. Probably the only woman he ever loved, Vittoria was an astute judge of his work, but valued the man even above his creations. Michelangelo viewed her as "God inside a woman." Her death in 1547 was a painful loss for a seventy-two-year-old artist who was already obsessed with the fear of death and hell. Like much of the poetry written for Vittoria, Michelangelo used sculpture as a theme; God had created Adam and that made him a sculptor.

SONNET LXI

(Se'l mie rozzo martello)
After the Death of Vittoria Colonna

Michelangelo Buonarotti

When my rude hammer to the stubborn stone
    Gives human shape, now that, now this, at will,
    Following his hand who wields and guides it still,
    It moves upon another's feet alone:
But that which dwells in heaven, the world doth fill
    With beauty by pure motions of its own;
    And since tools fashion tools which else were none,
    Its life makes all that lives with living skill.
Now, for that every stroke excels the more
    The higher at the forge it doth ascend,
    Her soul that fashioned mine hath sought the skies:
Wherefore unfinished I must meet my end,
    If God, the great artificer, denies
    That aid which was unique on earth before.

Exercise

1. Compare the style of these sonnets with that of Petrarch's poems, granting that all are in English translation. Compare and contrast the vocabulary of the two poets. Petrarch, for example, uses verbs like *shone, flamed, flow,*

Figure 16.2 Hans Holbein the Younger (1497/8–1543). *Sir Thomas More,* ca. 1530. Holbein's superb portrait reveals a visionary and a man of conscience ("a man for all seasons"), who died at the hands of Henry VIII rather than compromise his religious convictions. Copyright the Frick Collection, New York.

beguile, smile, and *rising;* Michelangelo's verbs include *fly, stirreth, strain, bind, conquer, pierce, thrill,* and *spite.* Are there similar parallels in the adjectives and adverbs?

Sir Thomas More (1478–1535)

As discussed previously, Europeans were entranced with the hope and promise of the New World. It was in these newly discovered lands that More (fig. 16.2) placed his *Utopia* (1516). To give his philosophical romance a framework, he relates his conversation with a sailor, Raphael Hythloday, who had sailed with Amerigo Vespucci. Hythloday tells More of a fabulous country that they had discovered named Utopia.

Literary Selection

UTOPIA

Sir Thomas More

More, like Machiavelli, was a realist, but an optimistic realist. He was careful, however, to retain certain checks on human conduct. Like Rabelais, More insists on equality under a representative form of government, much like the system in Switzerland, which he knew. Like Plato, who was his inspiration, he has to resort to a class of slaves to do the dirty work. Warfare, which was incessant during the Renaissance, would be waged outside *Utopia* by mercenaries. (More was also acquainted with Swiss mercenaries.) The limitation of More's thinking is interesting here, for he can extend his ideal state of culture only to the borders of the nation. He was able to place his exploitable savages just beyond the boundaries; yet, in everyday life, they are here and now and with us always.

One characteristic of Renaissance life was particularly revolting to More. This was the religious dissension that split the nations and which was to cost More his life. So in *Utopia,* we find complete religious freedom. Most Utopians adhere to a single faith, but the options are open and protected. Those who seek to impose their beliefs on anyone else will be severely punished.

More did not write a manual for a perfect civilization, and he knew this as well as any modern reader. All of his ideas do, however, merit serious consideration. The world may never be perfect, but we must always aspire to something better.

The island of Utopia containeth in breadth in the middle part of it (for there it is broadest) two hundred miles. Which breadth continueth through the most part of the land, saving that by little and little it cometh in, and waxeth narrower towards both the ends. Which fetching about a circuit or compass of five hundred miles, do fashion the whole island like to the new moon. Between these two corners the sea runneth in, dividing them asunder by the distance of eleven miles or thereabouts, and there surmounteth into a large and wide sea, which by reason that the land on every side compasseth it about, and sheltereth it from the winds, is not rough, nor mounteth not with great waves, but almost floweth quietly, not much unlike a great standing pool: and maketh almost all the space within the belly of the land in manner of a haven: and to the great commodity of the inhabitants receiveth in ships towards every part of the land. The forefronts or frontiers of the two corners, what with fords and shelves, and what with rocks be very jeopardous and dangerous. In the middle distance between them both standeth up above the water a great rock, which therefore is nothing perilous because it is in sight. Upon the top of this rock is a fair and a strong tower builded, which they hold with a garrison of men. Other rocks there be that lie hid under the water, and therefore be dangerous. The channels be known only to themselves. And therefore it seldom chanceth that any stranger unless he be guided by a Utopian can come into this haven. Insomuch that they themselves could scarcely enter without jeopardy, but that their way is directed and ruled by certain landmarks standing on the shore. By turning, translating, and removing these marks into other places they may destroy their enemies' navies, be they never so many. The outside of the land is also full of havens, but the landing is so surely defenced, what by nature, and what by workmanship of man's hand, that a few defenders may drive back many armies.

There be in the island fifty-four large and fair cities, or shire towns, agreeing all together in one tongue, in like manners, institutions and laws. They be all set and situate alike, and in all points fashioned alike, as far forth as the place or plot suffereth.

Of these cities they that be nighest together be twenty-four miles asunder. Again there is none of them distant from the next above one day's journey afoot. There come yearly to Amaurote out of every city three old men wise and well experienced, there to entreat and debate, of the common matters of the land. For this city (because it standeth just in the midst of the island, and is therefore most meet for the ambassadors of all parts of the realm) is taken for the chief and head city. The precincts and bounds of the shires be so commodiously appointed out, and set forth for the cities, that never a one of them all hath of any side less than twenty miles of ground, and of some side also much more, as of that part where the cities be of farther distance asunder. None of the cities desire to enlarge the bounds and limits of their shires. For they count themselves rather the good husbands[1] than the owners of their lands. They have in the country in all parts of the shire houses or farms builded, well appointed and furnished with all sorts of instruments and tools belonging to husbandry. These houses be inhabited of the citizens, which come thither to dwell by course. No household or farm in the country hath fewer than forty persons, men and women, besides two bondmen, which be all under the rule and order of the good man, and the good wife of the house, being both very sage and discreet persons. And every thirty farms or families have one head ruler, which is called a philarch, being as it were a head bailiff. Out of every one of these families or farms cometh every year into the city twenty persons which have continued two years before in the country. In their place so many fresh be sent thither out of the city, which of them that have been there a year already, and be therefore expert and cunning in husbandry, shall be instructed and taught. And they the next year shall teach others. This order is used for fear that either scarceness of victuals, or some other like incommodity should chance, through lack of knowledge, if they should be altogether new, and fresh, and unexpert in husbandry. This manner and fashion of yearly changing and renewing the occupiers of husbandry, though it be solemn and customably used, to the intent that no man shall be constrained against his will to continue long in that hard and sharp kind of life, yet many of them have such a pleasure and delight in husbandry, that they obtain a longer space of years. These husbandmen plough and till the ground, and breed up cattle, and make ready wood, which they carry to the city either by land, or by water, as they may most conveniently. They bring up a great multitude of poultry, and that by a marvellous policy. For the hens do not sit upon the eggs; but by keeping them in a certain equal heat they bring life into them, and hatch them. The chickens, as soon as they come out of the shell, follow men and women instead of the hens. They bring up very few horses: nor none, but very fierce ones: and for none other use or purpose, but only to exercise their youth in riding and feats of arms. For oxen be put to all the labour of ploughing and drawing. Which they grant to be not so good as horses at a sudden brunt, and (as we say) at a dead lift, but yet they hold opinion that they will abide and suffer much more labour and pain than horses will. And they think that they be not in danger and subject unto so many diseases, and that they be kept and maintained with much less cost and charge: and finally that they be good for meat, when they be past

---

1. Husbands—caretakers or farmers.

labour. They sow corn only for bread. For their drink is either wine made of grapes, or else of apples, or pears, or else it is clean water. And many times mead made of honey or liquorice sodden in water, for thereof they have great store. And though they know certainly (for they know it perfectly indeed) how much victuals the city with the whole country or shire round about it doth spend: yet they sow much more corn, and breed up much more cattle, than serveth for their own use, and the over-plus they part among their borderers.[2] Whatsoever necessary things be lacking in the country, all such stuff they fetch out of the city: where without any exchange they easily obtain it of the magistrates of the city. For every month many of them go into the city on the holy day. When their harvest day draweth near and is at hand, then the philarchs, which be the head officers and bailiffs of husbandry, send word to the magistrates of the city what number of harvest men is needful to be sent to them out of the city. The which company of harvest men being there ready at the day appointed, almost in one fair day despatcheth all the harvest work.

Of the Cities, and Namely of Amaurote

As for their cities, he that knoweth one of them, knoweth them all: they be all like one to another, as farforth as the nature of the place permitteth. I will describe therefore to you one or other of them, for it skilleth[3] not greatly which: but which rather than Amaurote? Of them all this is the worthiest and of most dignity. For the residue acknowledge it for the head city, because there is the council house. Nor to me any of them all is better beloved, as wherein I lived five whole years together. The city of Amaurote standeth upon the side of a low hill in fashion almost four square. For the breadth of it beginneth a little beneath the top of the hill, and still continueth by the space of two miles, until it come to the river of Anyder. The length of it, which lieth by the river's side, is somewhat more. The river of Anyder riseth twenty-four miles above Amaurote out of a little spring. But being increased by other small floods and brooks that run into it, and among other two somewhat big ones, before the city it is half a mile broad, and farther broader. And sixty miles beyond the city it falleth into the Ocean sea. By all that space that lieth between the sea and the city, and a good sort of miles also above the city, the water ebbeth and floweth six hours together with a swift tide. When the sea floweth in, for the length of thirty miles it filleth all the Anyder with salt water, and driveth back the fresh water of the river. And somewhat further it changeth the sweetness of the fresh water with saltness. But a little beyond that the river waxeth sweet, and runneth forby the city fresh and pleasant. And when the sea ebbeth, and goeth back again, the fresh water followeth it almost even to the very fall into the sea. There goeth a bridge over the river made not of piles of timber, but of stonework with gorgeous and substantial arches at that part of the city that is farthest from the sea: to the intent that ships may go along forby all the side of the city without let.[4] They have also another river which indeed is not very great. But it runneth gently and pleasantly. For it riseth even out of the same hill that the city standeth upon, and runneth down a slope through the midst of the city into Anyder.

And because it riseth a little without the city, the Amaurotians have inclosed the head spring of it with strong fences and bulwarks, and so have joined it to the city. This is done to the intent that the water should not be stopped nor turned away, or poisoned, if their enemies should chance to come upon them. From thence the water is derived and brought down in canals of brick divers ways into the lower parts of the city. Where that cannot be done, by reason that the place will not suffer it, there they gather the rain water in great cisterns, which doth them as good service. The city is compassed about with a high and thick wall full of turrets and bulwarks. A dry ditch, but deep, and broad, and overgrown with bushes, briers and thorns, goeth about three sides or quarters of the city. To the fourth side the river itself serveth for a ditch. The streets be appointed and set forth very commodious and handsome, both for carriage, and also against the winds. The houses be of fair and gorgeous building, and in the street side they stand joined together in a long row through the whole street without any partition or separation. The streets be twenty feet broad. On the back side of the houses through the whole length of the street, lie large gardens which be closed in round about with the back part of the streets. Every house hath two doors, one into the street, and a postern door on the back side into the garden. These doors be made with two leaves, never locked nor bolted, so easy to be opened, that they will follow the least drawing of a finger, and shut again by themselves. Every man that will, may go in, for there is nothing within the houses that is private, or any man's own. And every tenth year they change their houses by lot. They set great store by their gardens. In them they have vineyards, all manner of fruit, herbs, and flowers, so pleasant, so well furnished and so finely kept, that I never saw thing more fruitful, nor better trimmed in any place. Their study and diligence herein cometh not only of pleasure, but also of a certain strife and contention that is between street and street, concerning the trimming, husbanding, and furnishing of their gardens: every man for his own part. And verily you shall not lightly find in all the city anything that is more commodious, either for the profit of the citizens, or for pleasure.

Of the Magistrates

Every thirty families or farms, choose them yearly an officer, which is called the philarch. Every ten philarchs with all their 300 families be under an officer which is called the chief philarch. Moreover, as concerning the election of the prince, all the philarchs which be in number 200, first be sworn to choose him whom they think most meet and expedient. Then by a secret election, they name prince, one of those four whom the people before named unto them. For out of the four quarters of the city there be four chosen, out of every quarter one, to stand for the election: which be put up to the council. The prince's office continueth all his lifetime, unless he be deposed or put down for suspicion of tyranny. They choose the chief philarchs yearly, but lightly they change them not. All the other offices be but for one year. The chief philarchs every third day, and sometimes, if need be, oftener, come into the council house with the prince. Their council is concerning the commonwealth. If there be any controversies among the commoners, which be very few, they despatch and end them by-and-by. They take ever two philarchs to them in counsel, and every day a new couple. And it is provided that nothing touching the commonwealth shall be confirmed and ratified unless it have been reasoned of

---

2. Borderers—the surrounding countries.

3. Skilleth—matters.

4. Let—hindrance.

and debated three days in the council, before it be decreed. It is death to have any consultation for the commonwealth out of the council, or the place of the common election. This statute, they say, was made to the intent that the prince and chief philarchs might not easily conspire together to oppress the people by tyranny, and to change the state of the weal public. Therefore matters of great weight and importance be brought to the election house of the philarchs, which open the matter to their families. And afterward, when they have consulted among themselves, they show their device to the council. Sometimes the matter is brought before the council of the whole island. Furthermore this custom also the council useth, to dispute or reason of no matter the same day that it is first proposed or put forth, but to defer it to the next sitting of the council. Because that no man when he hath rashly there spoken what cometh first to his tongue's end, shall then afterwards rather study for reasons wherewith to defend and confirm his first foolish sentence, than for the commodity of the commonwealth: as one rather willing the harm or hindrance of the weal public than any loss or diminution of his own existimation. And as one that would not for shame (which is a very foolish shame) be counted anything overseen in the matter at the first. Who at the first ought to have spoken rather wisely, then hastily, or rashly.

Of Sciences, Crafts, and Occupations

Husbandry is a science common to them all in general, both men and women, wherein they be all expert and cunning. In this they be all instruct even from their youth: partly in schools with traditions and precepts, and partly in the country nigh the city, brought up as it were in playing, not only beholding the use of it, but by occasion of exercising their bodies practising it also. Besides husbandry, which (as I said) is common to them all, every one of them learneth one or other several and particular science, as his own proper craft. That is most commonly either clothworking in wool or flax, or masonry, or the smith's craft, or the carpenter's science. For there is none other occupation that any number to speak of doth use there. For their garments, which throughout all the island be of one fashion (saving that there is a difference between the man's garment and the woman's, between the married and the unmarried) and this one continueth for evermore unchanged, seemly and comely to the eye, no let to the moving and wielding of the body, also fit both for winter and summer: as for these garments (I say) every family maketh their own. But of the other foresaid crafts every man learneth one. And not only the men, but also the women. But the women, as the weaker sort, be put to the easier crafts: they work wool and flax. The other more laboursome sciences be committed to the men. For the most part every man is brought up in his father's craft. For most commonly they be naturally thereto bent and inclined. But if a man's mind stand to any other, he is by adoption put into a family of that occupation, which he doth most fantasy.[5] Whom not only his father, but also the magistrates do diligently look to, that he be put to a discreet and an honest householder. Yea, and if any person, when he hath learned one craft, be desirous to learn also another, he is likewise suffered and permitted.

When he hath learned both, he occupieth whether he will: unless the city have more need of the one, than of the other. The chief and almost the only office of the philarchs is, to see and take heed that no man sit idle: but that every one apply his own craft with earnest diligence. And yet for all that, not be wearied from early in the morning, to late in the evening, with continual work, like labouring and toiling beasts.

For this is worse than the miserable and wretched condition of bondmen. Which nevertheless is almost everywhere the life of workmen and artificers, saving in Utopia. For they dividing the day and the night into twenty-four just hours, appoint and assign only six of those hours to work; three before noon, upon the which they go straight to dinner: and after dinner, when they have rested two hours, then they work three and upon that they go to supper. About eight of the clock in the evening (counting one of clock as the first hour after noon) they go to bed: eight hours they give to sleep. All the void time, that is between the hours of work, sleep, and meat, that they be suffered to bestow, every man as he liketh best himself. Not to the intent that they should misspend this time in riot or slothfulness: but being then licensed from the labour of their own occupations, to bestow the time well and thriftly upon some other good science, as shall please them. For it is a solemn custom there, to have lectures daily early in the morning, where to be present they only be constrained that be chosen and appointed to learning. Howbeit a great multitude of every sort of people, both men and women, go to hear lectures, some one and some another, as every man's nature is inclined. Yet, this notwithstanding, if any man had rather bestow this time upon his own occupation (as it chanceth in many, whose minds rise not in the contemplation of any science liberal) he is not letted, nor prohibited, but is also praised and commended, as profitable to the commonwealth. After supper they bestow one hour in play: in summer in their gardens: in winter in their common halls: where they dine and sup. There they exercise themselves in music, or else in honest and wholesome communication. But lest you be deceived, one thing you must look more narrowly upon. For seeing they bestow but six hours in work perchance you may think that the lack of some necessary things hereof may ensue. But this is nothing so. For that small time is not only enough but also too much for the store and abundance of all things that be requisite, either for the necessity, or commodity of life. The which thing you also shall perceive, if you weigh and consider with yourselves how great a part of the people in other countries liveth idle. First almost all women, which be the half of the whole number: or else if the women be anywhere occupied, there most commonly in their stead the men be idle. Beside this how great, and how idle a company is there of priests, and religious men, as they call them? Put thereto all rich men, especially all landed men, which commonly be called gentlemen, and noblemen. Take into this number also their servants: I mean all that flock of stout bragging rush-bucklers. Join to them also sturdy and valiant beggars, cloaking their idle life under the colour of some disease or sickness. And truly you shall find them much fewer than you thought, by whose labour all these things be gotten that men use and live by. Now consider with yourself, of these few that do work, how few be occupied, in necessary works. For where money beareth all the swing, there many vain and superfluous occupations must needs be used, to serve only for riotous superfluity and unhonest pleasure. For the same multitude that now is occupied in work, if they were

---

5. Fantasy—desire or choose.

divided into so few occupations as the necessary use of nature requireth; in so great plenty of things as then of necessity would ensue, doubtless the prices would be too little for the artificers to maintain their livings. But if all these, that be now busied about unprofitable occupations, with all the whole flock of them that live idly and slothfully, which consume and waste every one of them more of these things that come by other men's labour, then two of the workmen themselves do: if all these (I say) were set to profitable occupations, you easily perceive how little time would be enough, yea and too much to store us with all things that may be requisite either for necessity, or for commodity, yea or for pleasure, so that the same pleasure be true and natural. And this in Utopia the thing itself maketh manifest and plain. For there in all the city, with the whole country, or shire adjoining to it scarcely 500 persons of all the whole number of men and women, that be neither too old, nor too weak to work, be licensed from labour. Among them be the philarchs which (though they be by the laws exempt and privileged from labour) yet they exempt not themselves: to the intent they may the rather by their example provoke others to work. The same vacation from labour do they also enjoy, to whom the people persuaded by the commendation of the priests, and secret election of the philarchs, have given a perpetual license from labour to learning. But if any one of them prove not according to the expectation and hope of him conceived, he is forthwith plucked back to the company of artificers. And contrariwise, often it chanceth that a handicraftsman doth so earnestly bestow his vacant and spare hours in learning, and through diligence to profit therein, that he is taken from his handy occupation, and promoted to the company of the learned. Out of this order of the learned be chosen ambassadors, priests, chief philarchs, and finally the prince himself.

Of Warfare

Immediately after that war is once solemnly announced, they procure many proclamations signed with their own common seal to be set up privily at one time in their enemies' land, in places most frequented. In these proclamations they promise great rewards to him that will kill their enemies' prince, and somewhat less gifts, but them very great also, for every head of them, whose names be in the said proclamations contained. They be those whom they count their chief adversaries, next unto the prince. Whatsoever is prescribed unto him that killeth any of the proclaimed persons, that is doubled to him that bringeth any of the same to them alive; yea, and to the proclaimed persons themselves, if they will change their minds and come into them, taking their parts, they proffer the same great rewards with pardon and surety of their lives. Therefore it quickly cometh to pass that they have all other men in suspicion, and be unfaithful and mistrusting among themselves one to another, living in great fear, and in no less jeopardy. For it is well known, that divers times the most part of them (and specially the prince himself) hath been betrayed of them, in whom they put their most hope and trust. So that there is no manner of act nor deed that gifts and rewards do not enforce men unto. And in rewards they keep no measure. But remembering and considering into how great hazard and jeopardy they call them, endeavor themselves to recompense the greatness of the danger with like great benefits. And therefore they promise not only wonderful great abundance of gold, but also lands of great revenues lying in most places among their friends. And their

promises they perform faithfully without any fraud or deceit. This custom of buying and selling adversaries among other people is disallowed, as a cruel act of a base and a cowardish mind. But they in this behalf think themselves much praiseworthy, as who like wise men by this means despatch great wars without any battle or skirmish. Yea they count it also a deed of pity and mercy, because that by the death of a few offenders the lives of a great number of innocents, as well of their own men as also of their enemies, be ransomed and saved, which in fighting should have been slain. For they do no less pity the base and common sort of their enemies' people, than they do their own; knowing that they be driven to war against their wills by the furious madness of their princes and heads. If by none of these means the matter go forward as they would have it, then they procure occasions of debate and dissension to be spread among their enemies. As by causing the prince's brother, or some of the noblemen, to hope to obtain the kingdom. If this way prevail not, then they raise up the people that be next neighbors and borderers to their enemies, and them they set in their necks under the colour of some old title of right, such as kings do never lack. To them they promise their help and aid in their war. And as for money they give them abundance. But of their own citizens they send to them few or none. Whom they make so much of and love so entirely, that they would not be willing to change any of them for their adversary's prince. But their gold and silver, because they keep it all for this only purpose, they lay it out frankly and freely; as who[6] should live even as wealthily, if they had bestowed it every penny. Yea, and besides their riches, which they keep at home, that have also an infinite treasure abroad, by reason that (as I said before) many nations be in their debt. Therefore they hire soldiers out of all countries and send them to battle, but chiefly of the Zapoletes. This people is five hundred miles from Utopia eastward. They be hideous, savage and fierce, dwelling in wild woods and high mountains, where they were bred and brought up. They be of an hard nature, able to abide and sustain heat, cold and labour, abhorring from all delicate dainties, occupying no husbandry nor tillage of the ground, homely and rude both in the building of their houses and in their apparel, given unto no goodness, but only to the breeding and bringing up of cattle. The most part of their living is by hunting and stealing. They be born only to war, which they diligently and earnestly seek for. And when they have gotten it, they be wonders glad thereof. They go forth of their country in great companies together, and whosoever lacketh soldiers, there they proffer their service for small wages. This is only the craft that they have to get their living by. They maintain their life by seeking their death. For them with whom they be in wages they fight hardily, fiercely, and faithfully. But they bind themselves for no certain time. But upon this condition they enter into bonds, that the next day they will take part with the other side for greater wages, and the next day after that, they will be ready to come back again for a little more money. There be few wars thereaway, wherein is not a great number of them in both parties. Therefore it daily chanceth that nigh kinsfolk, which were hired together on one part, and there very friendly and familiarly used themselves one with another,

---

6. "As who should live," etc.: read this "as people who would live just as richly. . ."

shortly after being separate into contrary parts, run one against another enviously and fiercely, and forgetting both kindred and friendship, thrust their swords one in another. And that for none other cause, but that they be hired of contrary princes for a little money. Which they do so highly regard and esteem, that they will easily be provoked to change parts for a halfpenny more wages by the day. So quickly they have taken a smack in covetousness. Which for all that is to them no profit. For that they get by fighting, immediately they spend unthriftily and wretchedly in riot. This people fight for the Utopians against all nations, because they give them greater wages than any other nation will. For the Utopians like as they seek good men to use well, so they seek these evil and vicious men to abuse. Whom, when need requireth, with promises of great rewards, they put forth into great jeopardies. From whence the most part of them never cometh again to ask their rewards. But to them that remain alive they pay that which they promised faithfully, that they may be more willing to put themselves in like dangers another time. Nor the Utopians pass not how many of them they bring to destruction. For they believe that they should do a very good deed for all mankind, if they could rid out of the world all that foul stinking den of that most wicked and cursed people.

Of the Religions in Utopia

There be divers kinds of religion not only in sundry parts of the island, but also in divers places of every city. Some worship for God, the sun; some, the moon; some other of the planets. There be that give worship to a man that was once of excellent virtue or of famous glory, not only as God, but also as the chiefest and highest God. But the most and the wisest part (rejecting all these) believe that there is a certain godly power unknown, everlasting, incomprehensible, inexplicable, far above the capacity and reach of man's wit, dispersed throughout all the world, not in bigness, but in virtue and power. Him they call the father of all. To him alone they attribute the beginnings, the increasings, the proceedings, the changes and the ends of all things. Neither they give divine honours to any other than to him. Yea all the other also, though they be in divers opinions, yet in this point they agree all together with the wisest sort, in believing that there is one chief and principal God, the maker and ruler of the whole world: whom they all commonly in their country language call Mithra. But after they heard us speak of the name of Christ, of his doctrine, laws, miracles, and of the no less wonderful constancy of so many martyrs, whose blood willingly shed brought a great number of nations throughout all parts of the world into their sect; you will not believe with how glad minds, they agreed unto the same: whether it were by the secret inspiration of God, or else for that they thought it next unto that opinion, which among them is counted the chiefest. Howbeit I think this was no small help and furtherance in the matter, that they heard us say, that Christ instituted among his, all things common; and that the same community doth yet remain amongst the rightest Christian companies. Verily howsoever it come to pass, many of them consented together in our religion, and were washed in the holy water of baptism. They also which do not agree to Christ's religion, fear no man from it, nor speak against any man that hath received it. Saving that one of our company in my presence was sharply punished. He as soon as he was baptised began against our wills, with more earnest affection than wisdom, to

reason of Christ's religion; and began to wax so hot in his matter, that he did not only prefer our religion before all other, but also did utterly despise and condemn all other, calling them profane, and the followers of them wicked and devilish and the children of everlasting damnation. When he had thus long reasoned the matter, they laid hold on him, accused him and condemned him into exile, not as a despiser of religion, but as a seditious person and a raiser up of dissension among the people. For this is one of the ancientest laws among them; that no man shall be blamed for reasoning in the maintenance of his own religion. For King Utopus, even at the first beginning, hearing that the inhabitants of the land were, before his coming thither, at continual dissention and strife among themselves for their religions; as soon as he had gotten the victory, first of all he made a decree, that it should be lawful for every man to favour and follow what religion he would, and that he might do the best he could to bring other to this opinion, so that he did it peaceably, gently, quietly, and soberly, without haste and contentious rebuking and inveighing against other. If he could not by fair and gentle speech induce them unto his opinion yet he should use no kind of violence, and refrain from displeasant and seditious words. To him that would vehemently and fervently in this cause strive and contend was decreed banishment or bondage. This law did King Utopus make not only for the maintenance of peace, which he saw through continual contention and mortal hatred utterly extinguished; but also because he thought this decree should make for the furtherance of religion. Whereof he durst define and determine nothing unadvisedly, as doubting whether God desiring manifold and divers sorts of honour, would inspire sundry men with sundry kinds of religion. And this surely he thought a very unmeet and foolish thing, and a point of arrogant presumption, to compel all other by violence and threatenings to agree to the same that thou believest to be true. Furthermore though there be one religion which alone is true, and all other vain and superstitious, yet did he well foresee (so that the matter were handled with reason, and sober modesty) that the truth of its own power would at the last issue out and come to light. But if contention and debate in that behalf should continually be used, as the worst men be most obstinate and stubborn, and in their evil opinion most constant; he perceived that then the best and holiest religion would be trodden underfoot and destroyed by most vain superstitions, even as good corn is by thorns and weeds overgrown and choked. Therefore all this matter he left undiscussed, and gave to every man free liberty and choice to believe what he would.

Exercises

1. Try making a sketch-map or diagram of Amaurote, the Utopian capital. What considerations or specifications does More give that are unnecessary in a modern American city? Are there any specifications that might improve American cities? Such as?
2. The Zapoletes, Utopia's mercenary soldiers, must have presented some problems to their employers. What might these be? Would *you* be willing to serve as a mercenary soldier? Why or why not?

William Shakespeare (1564–1616)

Will Shakespeare was not a classical scholar, having, as he said, "little Latin and less Greek." His formal schooling was limited. His plots were mostly borrowed and his plays intended as box-office hits, which they were. Yet he is the supreme figure of Renaissance literature and the most quoted writer in the English language. How can this be? Critics have said that no human being could have written Mozart's music and the same can be said for the plays of Shakespeare. There is no accounting for genius; we have the music and the plays, and the world is infinitely richer because of them. Shakespeare understood human nature in all its complexity and perversity and was able to translate his perceptions into dramatic speech and action. Whether borrowed, created, or actual historical figures, his characters are unforgettable: Hamlet, King Lear, Falstaff, Macbeth, Romeo, Juliet, Othello, Iago, Portia, Richard III, Cleopatra, and Julius Caesar, to name a few.

The themes in the 37 plays—chronicle-plays, comedies, and tragedies—are timeless, but the flavor of the Renaissance is unmistakable. Like other Renaissance writers, Shakespeare was concerned with the active role of men and women in the lusty and prosperous Elizabethan age: their passions, problems, and aspirations. Like Machiavelli, he saw people as they really were and the vision was, for Shakespeare if not for Machiavelli, profoundly disturbing. Nevertheless, his pessimistic view of the baser instincts of people was tempered by his belief in their ability to achieve, usually through suffering, some measure of dignity and even nobility, as exemplified in *King Lear*.

Summary

Perhaps more than any other period before our own tumultuous century, the Renaissance was lively, disorderly, and exceedingly violent. In an age of contradictions, masterpieces of art, literature, and music were created in the midst of almost continuous strife and commotion. In terms of the culture-epoch theory of history, the Renaissance was the period of chaos during and following the breakdown of the medieval synthesis. The process was terribly painful. Not until the seventeenth century would a new view of reality slowly begin to take shape.

The Time Chart for the Renaissance at the end of chapter 13 should again be consulted for an overview of this tempestuous but dazzling age.

Unit 6

The Early Modern World, 1600–1789

17

Science, Reason, and Absolutism

The Seventeenth Century

Europe emerged from medievalism during the tumultuous Renaissance, but not until 1648 did the passions unleashed by the Reformation and Counter-Reformation gradually subside. Beginning as a conflict between Catholics and Protestants, the Thirty Years' War (1618–1648) evolved into an international war between modern nation-states. The Peace of Westphalia of 1648 that finally ended the slaughter was a landmark in European history, finally laying to rest the last vestiges of medievalism. Once viable values and institutions had completely disappeared. The medieval idea of a unified Christian commonwealth was a relic of the now distant past as were the imperial and papal claims to political power. Adopting the strategies of diplomacy and alliances initiated by Italian city-states, sovereign nations staked out boundaries and competed with each other in the struggle for a new balance of power.

Rapid advances in science and technology revealed vast new horizons, and international trade opened up the whole world to European dominance and, inevitably, European exploitation. The English East Indies Company was founded in 1600, its Dutch counterpart chartered only two years later, followed by the French. With growing power and wealth, the prevailing mood in northern Europe was as positive as the joyful optimism voiced by Miranda in Shakespeare's *The Tempest:*

> O Wonder!
> How many goodly creatures are there here!
> How beauteous mankind is! O brave new world,
> That has such people in't!

Science and Philosophy

Francis Bacon (1561–1626), the English lawyer and statesman, ranks with Descartes and Galileo as one of the founders of modern science and philosophy. He formulated no new scientific hypotheses nor did he make any dramatic discoveries, but he did inquire into the function and ethics of science and scientific research in relation to human life. For Bacon, knowledge was not recognition of any given reality but a search for truth, a journey rather than a destination. Bacon saw clearly that the old culture had come to a dead end and that a new epoch was coming into being. Inventions like gunpowder, the printing press, the compound microscope (ca. 1590), and the telescope (ca. 1608) changed the material world and had to change the ways of thinking about the world. Scientific knowledge and invention, Bacon believed, should be public property to be shared democratically and to be used for the benefit of all people. In his *Novum Organum* (1620) Bacon laid out the logic of scientific inquiry and the principles of the inductive method. Through experiment and observation factual information would be gathered, leading to general statements based only on observable data. For Bacon the principle task of scientific investigation was to remedy the poverty of factual information, a search for knowledge taken for granted in this century but by no means in Bacon's time.

During the sixteenth century the Reformation raised the question of the reliability of religious knowledge, of whether Catholic beliefs were more or less true than Protestant convictions. The rise of science extended the question to the reliability of all knowledge. Skeptics maintained that no certain knowledge was possible, that doubt was always present. Bacon argued that the inductive method augmented by mechanical aids like the compound microscope provided certain knowledge about the world. René Descartes (1596–1650) distrusted sensory evidence, claiming that the senses can deceive us. Well acquainted with skeptics like Montaigne and Mersenne, Descartes followed their arguments to their conclusion, rejecting everything as false. With this process of "Cartesian doubt" he could then, in the depths of uncertainty, find truth and a criterion of truth.

In his *Discourse on Method* (1637) Descartes formulated his "natural method" to accept nothing as true except what was "clearly and distinctly" presented to his mind. It was not until his *Meditations* (1641) that Descartes responded to attacks on all knowledge. Admitting that the senses could not be trusted, Descartes went a step further to postulate an evil demon whose business it was to confuse people about the truth or falsity of anything, even whether or not a square had four sides. The solution is to exorcise the demon by believing in the goodness of the all-powerful God. Descartes doubts not that God exists but how does he know whether or not he himself exists? He finds his answer in the realization that he is a thinking person: *cogito ergo sum,* I think, therefore I am.

Whatever is clearly and distinctly perceived by the *cogito* is true. From this point Descartes proceeded to construct a rational philosophy in which he established the reliability of the senses and proved the existence of the physical world. He believed, further, that God had created two substances, spirit and matter.

The mind was spirit and its essence was consciousness; the essence of the body, or matter, was extension and movement in space. Cartesian dualism thus established a gulf between mind and body that later philosophers removed by proving that mind, body, and nature were all interconnected.

For Descartes mathematics was the "queen of the sciences" and the universe was mechanistic. Applied mathematics would enable scientists to rationally study and understand an orderly cosmos that operated according to natural laws, a position with which Galileo was in complete agreement. Copernicus had proposed the heliocentric theory; Kepler had confirmed it by observation and, with mathematics, determined the three laws of planetary motion:

1. The planets move around the sun in ellipses with the sun at one focus of the ellipse.
2. We can imagine a line joining the sun and a planet. Though the planet's speed varies in its orbit around the sun, yet this imaginary line "sweeps out" equal areas in equal times.
3. The square of the time for one complete revolution of each planet is proportional to the cube of its average distance from the sun.

Professor of mechanics and astronomy at the University of Padua, Galileo Galilei (1564–1642) proved the heliocentric theory empirically with his improved telescope, discovered sun spots and Jupiter's moons, devised two laws of motion, invented the thermometer, improved the compound microscope, investigated the principles of the lever and the pulley, measured air pressure, and investigated the properties of magnetism and sound vibrations. Perhaps even more importantly, he invented the modern method of forming a theory, testing it experimentally, and adjusting the theory to conform to observable results. His two laws of motion are:

1. When a body is once in motion it will remain in motion in a straight line unless acted upon by other forces. One can state this law in another way by saying that a body moving in a vacuum, with no forces acting on it, will continue in motion in a straight line forever.
2. If force is applied to a moving object, the object will change course in the direction of the force that has been applied.

Later in the century, Newton, who will be discussed later, added the third law of motion: for every action there is an equal and opposite reaction. Every time a rocket rises from Cape Canaveral we can see the third law of motion in action.

Galileo had long believed in the Copernican hypothesis but did not become involved in public controversy until his 1613 letter to a friend in which he discussed his telescopic observations. The contents became public knowledge and, after the publication of his *Dialogues Concerning the Two Chief World Systems* (1632), he was charged by the Inquisition with heresy. The Holy Office (Inquisition) claimed that Galileo had agreed, in a signed statement, not to promulgate his views about the heliocentric theory. The statement was a forgery and Galileo was not allowed to appear before the court in his own defense.[1] Nevertheless, he was judged a heretic, forced to recant, and sentenced to lifetime house arrest. The book was first sentenced to public burning but later merely prohibited.

After leaving Rome, Galileo, with the assistance of trusted friends, sent a copy of his book to Switzerland where it was published in Latin. He followed that up with *The New Sciences* (1638), the first great work on modern physics. Prince Mattia de' Medici smuggled the manuscript out of Italy and the work was ultimately published in Holland. Galileo had thus successfully defied Rome but his life was a shambles and Italian science had been set back for generations.

Absolutism

At the beginning of the century both England and France had absolute monarchs who claimed to rule by Divine Right. The thrones of England and Scotland were united by the accession of James I (1603–1625), the son of Mary Stuart, Queen of Scots. His attempts to govern absolutely brought him into conflict with Parliament, and the absolute rule of Charles I (1625–1649) finally led to Civil War (1642–1646) between the king and Parliament. Charles I was tried and executed for treason and the Interregnum began, the Puritan era of the Commonwealth and the Protectorate (1649–1659) under what amounted to the dictatorship of Oliver Cromwell.

It was during the Civil War and for over a century and a half afterwards that the Social Contract theory of government became prominent. In the seventeenth century the idea of a government by consent of the governed did not imply a liberal democracy, but that power was derived from people of the wealthy and influential class as a curb against kingly excesses. It was rarely suggested that working people had any natural rights. Consent did not imply democracy unless that meant consent of *all* the people, and that was an eighteenth-century development that led to the American Revolution. The idea of a Social Contract was a strong current of political thought but there was an important countercurrent. In 1651 Thomas Hobbes (1588–1679) published his *Leviathan* in which he revived the idea of a contract based on subjection to the sovereign power of the monarch. Hobbes justified absolutism but not rule by Divine Right. Convinced that peace and security were prerequisites of society, Hobbes believed that certain individual freedoms had to be sacrificed for the good of the state. A state of nature was anarchy; there had to be a superior power to restore and maintain the stability of society, and that would be the unlimited power of the king. Given the circumstances of the time, the Civil War and the execution of the king, the position of Hobbes is understandable even if not commendable.

Figure 17.1 French school after Gianlorenzo Bernini, *Bust of Louis XIV,* ca. 1665. Bronze, 33½″ high. Versailles was decorated and furnished in the Baroque style represented by this Italian Baroque bust, but the exterior is essentially Neoclassical, the preferred architectural style of Louis XIV. Samuel H. Kress Collection. National Gallery of Art, Washington, D.C.

Upon the death of Cromwell in 1659 Charles II (1660–1685), son of Charles I, was invited to restore the Stuart line. Charles did not openly confront Parliament and managed to go his own way. James II (1685–1688) was not as clever and was forced to abdicate, leaving behind the general conviction that a Catholic king was dangerous to English liberties. Mary, the daughter of James II, was Protestant and married to William of Orange, a Dutch Protestant. Providing they accepted the new Bill of Rights, William and Mary were invited to take the English throne. This was the Glorious Revolution, which, without bloodshed, established a constitutional monarchy. Absolutism was virtually finished in England.

Absolutism in France had a far longer and more violent history. Succeeding to the throne after the assassination of Henry IV, Louis XIII reigned from 1610–1643, but royal power was gradually taken over by his chief minister, Cardinal Richelieu, who operated as a virtual dictator from 1624 to 1642. It was Richelieu who established the French absolutism to which Louis XIV succeeded in 1643 at the age of five under the regency of his mother. During the longest reign of any monarch, Louis XIV (1643–1715) promoted the arts, built the magnificent palace at Versailles (see figs. 18.16, 18.17, and 18.18), and made France the most powerful nation in Europe (fig. 17.1). The nation had, however, an archaic economic system with local customs barriers, tax-farming, and a nobility that paid no taxes at all. Raising revenues simply increased the misery of the people. Further, the king's revocation of the Edict of Nantes that protected the Huguenots from persecution was a disaster. Over 250,000 mostly middle-class craftsmen and their families were forced to flee the country, marking the beginning of the end of Louis's greatness and, ultimately, of the French monarchy itself.

---

1. For further information on the trial and the judicial forgery, see Giorgio de Santillana, *The Crime of Galileo* (New York: Time Incorporated, 1962).

The Enlightenment, ca. 1687–1789

"Enlightenment" and "Age of Reason" are two of several terms that describe the intellectual characteristics of the eighteenth century. The Enlightenment is usually dated from the year in which Newton's epochal *Principia (Mathematical Principles of Natural Philosophy)* appeared (1687) to the beginning of the French Revolution in 1789. An alternate beginning date would be 1688, the year of the Glorious Revolution in England. A difference of a year is insignificant. The *Principia* and the Glorious Revolution were major milestones marking the advance of science, rationalism, and freedom.

The Enlightenment was a self-conscious and extremely articulate movement that was to transform all societies. Europe had experienced some rude shocks, what some writers called the three humiliations. The earth was not at the center of the universe, people were creatures of nature like other animals, and their reason was subject to passions and instincts. For the Enlightenment these new truths represented intellectual advances that enabled people to redefine their responsibilities: discover truth through science; achieve personal happiness in a viable society; explore the full meaning, and limitations, of liberty. The discoveries of Newton provided convincing evidence that the world was orderly and knowable and that, by the same token, human societies could be made orderly and rational through the exercise of enlightened reason.

Science and Philosophy

Sir Isaac Newton (1642–1727) discovered the universal law of gravitation, made important investigations into the nature of light, and invented the branch of mathematics known as the calculus. At this time we are concerned with only the first of these. Newton supposedly remarked, "If I have seen a little farther than others, it is because I have stood on the shoulders of giants." There were many giants, including Copernicus, Brahe, Bruno, Kepler, and Galileo but Newton effected the grand synthesis that explained the operation of the cosmos. First, he refined Galileo's laws of motion:

1. A body remains in a state of rest or of uniform motion in a straight line unless compelled by an external force to change that state. In other words, a body's inertia keeps it in a state of rest or its inertia keeps it moving in a straight line. External force has to be applied to move it from either its state of rest or its straight-line motion.
2. A change in momentum is proportional to the force causing the change and takes place in the direction in which the force is acting. In other words, the increase or decrease in velocity is proportional to the force.
3. To every action there is an equal and opposite reaction.

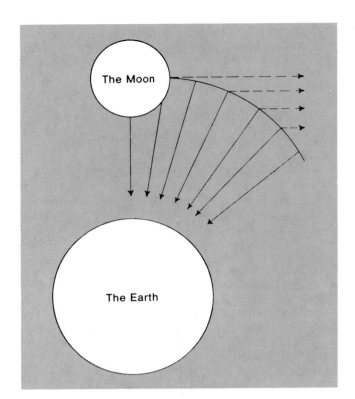

Figure 17.2 Forces acting on the moon to determine its motion.

Galileo had demonstrated the principles of movement of bodies on earth but not the motion of heavenly bodies. Why were their orbits curved? Newton hypothesized that all celestial bodies were mutually attracted to each other. He concentrated his studies on the moon, which he treated as having inertial movement in space and then determined that its orbit was curved because it was continuously falling toward the earth (fig. 17.2). Its inertia would cause it to fly out in a straight line, as shown by the dotted arrows but the gravitational pull of the earth balances the straight-line tendency. Action and reaction are equal and the moon remains in orbit at a standard distance from the earth. Newton calculated the mass of the moon and its distance from the earth and determined that the gravitational pull was inversely proportional to the square of its distance from the earth. Newton also calculated the mass of the sun, the planets and their moons and discovered that each planet would travel according to Kepler's laws only by using the same formula: the gravitational pull of the sun was inversely proportional to the square of a planet's distance from the sun. The mathematical formula was the same whether the object was a terrestrial falling body like an apple or the moon, a law that worked here on earth and far out in space. This was the universal law of gravitation.

Newton (and Edmund Halley) demonstrated that comets obey the same universal principle. He calculated the flattening of the earth at its poles due to its rotation, and proved that the size of a planet determined the length of its day. He showed the effect of latitude on the weight of an object and accounted for the tides as resulting from the combined attraction of the sun and the moon. All of these instances of the operation of gravitation are given here to illustrate some of the different phenomena that can be explained with one law. No wonder Alexander Pope wrote the following couplet:

Nature and nature's laws lay hid in night;
God said, "Let Newton be," and all was light.

The philosophic implications of this unification of scientific principles were astounding. Picture the universe as Newton saw it, a vast and intricate system of whirling bodies in space, a system that was orderly and predictable. Each planet, each moon, each solar system was balanced in the cosmic plan, a balance determined by mechanical forces pulling against each other. Absolute and unvarying, these forces would keep the machine in working order. What, then, was the place of God in this plan? For all practical purposes God was ruled out. Newton was an intensely religious man, however, and he yielded two functions to the Divinity. It was noticed that, over long periods, there were slight irregularities in the motions of the heavenly bodies in terms of Newtonian physics. One function of God was to make certain periodic readjustments. A second function was to maintain an even flow of time and space. In this world picture, then, God became a sort of celestial engineer, turning a wheel here, opening a valve there, keeping an eye on the dials. Even before the close of the eighteenth century, Laplace, a French astronomer, extended the mechanism of gravitation and proved that the irregularities were periodical and subject to a law that kept them within bounds. Many of those who held to the existence of God were deists who looked upon him as the master designer of a perfect world-machine that needed no further tending. In the Declaration of Independence Thomas Jefferson, who was a deist, used the following terminology: laws of nature's God; Creator; Supreme Judge; Divine Providence. Perhaps the most commonly accepted image was that of an "absentee landlord" who had designed the machine and then retired, possibly to a ranch in Mexico.

In these developments we see clearly and distinctly the new reliance upon intellect that characterized the Enlightenment. Human beings using the marvelous mechanisms of their minds could, in time, unlock the most hidden secrets of the universe. And what of human institutions? The cosmos was orderly, rational, and knowable; why couldn't people use their reason to design an orderly and rational society? It was precisely this optimism of the Enlightenment that inspired our Founding Fathers to construct a democracy that would be a model, a beacon of hope for the entire world.

The founders of the Republic had gotten some political ideas from Montesquieu's *Spirit of the Laws* (1748) but they drew mainly from John Locke (1632–1704). Returning from exile after the Glorious Revolution, Locke wrote his *Two Treatises of Government* (1690) to justify constitutional monarchy. In the 15th essay from his *Second Treatise on Civil Government* Locke takes this position:

Now this power, which every man has in the state of Nature, and which he parts with to the society in all such cases where the society can secure him, is to use such means for the preserving of his own property as he thinks good and Nature allows him; and to punish the breach of the law of Nature in others; so as (according to the best of his reason) may most conduce to the preservation of himself and the rest of mankind. So that the end and measure of this power, when in every other man's hands, in the state of Nature, being the preservation of all his society, that is, all mankind in general; it can have no other end or measure, when in the hands of the magistrate, but to preserve the members of that society in their lives, liberties, and possessions.

Locke assumes a natural law that operated in the affairs of human beings much as Newton's world-machine functioned according to natural law, a position also reflected in the opening paragraph of the Declaration of Independence:

When, in the course of human events, it becomes necessary for one people to dissolve the political bands which have connected them with another, and to assume, among the powers of the earth, the separate and equal station to which the laws of nature and of nature's God entitle them, a decent respect to the opinions of mankind requires that they should declare the causes which impel them to the separation.

According to this natural law people had, according to Locke, certain rights which were unalienable, and these were life, liberty, and property. Jefferson substituted for "property" a much more striking and challenging phrase:

We hold these truths to be self-evident, that all men are created equal, that they are endowed by their Creator with certain unalienable Rights, that among these are Life, Liberty, and the pursuit of Happiness. That to secure these rights, Governments are instituted among Men, deriving their just powers from the consent of the governed.

Locke wrote that government existed and had authority only because the people brought it into existence and gave it its authority. If the government violated its trust the people had a right, a natural right, to set up a new government. In short, they had a right to revolt, as Jefferson later stated in the Declaration of Independence.

Economics

Exactly as Locke (and Jefferson) sought natural law as a guide to political affairs and Newton found such a law as the binding force of the universe, so did Adam Smith (1723–1790) seek such a unifying principle for economic affairs. His work, interestingly enough, followed exactly the scientific method which Bacon had established in the previous epoch, for his investigations of the facts of economic life were conducted in a pin factory, and his generalizations were based upon his factual findings.

We are indebted to Smith for the statement of the classical principles of capitalism which were set forth in his volume, *An Inquiry into the Nature and Causes of the Wealth of Nations,* published in 1776. In the time when Smith lived, capitalism had taken the form called *mercantilism,* which was a strictly regulated system of trade, controlled by the government of each nation, and based on the idea that the wealth of a nation depended upon the amount of gold and silver which was held within the nation. In order to achieve a constantly increasing supply of gold and silver, each sought to maintain a favorable balance of trade; that is, each nation tried to keep the value of its yearly exports greater than the value of its yearly imports. With all nations trying to keep such a favorable balance of trade, it is evident that the system is a virtual impossibility, with only one way out. If a nation has colonies, it can make these colonies a source for cheap raw materials and a dumping ground for more expensive manufactured goods. One is reminded of England's policy toward its American colonies. In this way only can the system of mercantilism work, and its faults are obvious: sooner or later the colonies will either develop manufacturing for themselves, or they will be bled white by the mother country. In either case, the system fails.

The first revolt against mercantilism came in France, with a group of economists called the *physiocrats.* They held that the wealth of a nation depended upon the raw materials within the nation rather than the supply of money. They, too, believed that the strict regulation of trade and commerce by a national government was a detriment to economic well-being and progress. Adam Smith studied with this group for a time and mastered their ideas before he worked out his own theories.

Smith's whole effort was to discover a kind of balance in economic affairs that would insure an adequate supply of goods to meet the needs of human beings. He wanted these produced and sold at a fair price so that most people could buy the goods, so that the laborer would receive a fair wage, and so that the manufacturer could receive a fair profit. In order to solve this intricate problem, he proposed a return to nature in economic affairs. That is, he proposed to remove all restrictions of every sort from the manufacturing and sale of goods and from wages. This is the system we recognize as unfettered competition, or *laissez-faire.* How does it work? Perhaps an example will clarify the process.

Smith's first premise is that people are, by nature, acquisitive. They want to pile up as much wealth as possible. So an enterpriser (a person with capital to invest) looks about and sees that people need shoes. This person sets up a shoe factory and charges as much as the traffic will bear for the product. Let us say that the charge is fifty dollars a pair. Immediately other enterprisers will be attracted to the shoe business, since the profits seem very large. As the number of shoes increases, the price will have to drop, if, according to the doctrine of laissez-faire, all people have equal access to raw materials and to markets with no regulation whatever. If such regulation comes into being, of course, the whole process is thrown out of gear. With such freedom, however, the price drops. Finally there are more shoes than can be sold. The inefficient manufacturer can no longer sell the product, and must drop out of the competition. As this happens, slowly the demand catches up with the supply, and the price regulates itself. Finally, the production is adequate for the needs of people; the price is stabilized at a point at which the most efficient producers can make a fair profit. The only thing omitted from the scheme so far is labor.

Labor, said Smith, is a commodity which is for sale just as shoes are. In a new field, wages will be high. Laborers will flock to this work. As labor becomes more plentiful, wages will decline. Finally the labor market in this field will become glutted, and the wages will fall to a point at which the laborers can no longer live. At that point, the inefficient ones will be eliminated and will seek some other form of employment. Eventually the price of labor, like that of shoes, will stabilize itself at a point at which the most efficient laborers in any field are working in that field at a price for their work which affords them a fair living. Others, squeezed out, will find another kind of work in which they are more efficient, and they will be able to make a good living there.

From these examples, it is possible to derive the principles of Smith's laissez-faire economy. First, he said that labor is the source of all wealth within a nation. Second, all people are acquisitive. Third, we must have completely free and unregulated access to raw materials, labor, and markets. Fourth, each person has a natural endowment of skills that should determine the kind of work to be done. Given a free choice of employment the process should lead the worker into the most congenial type of work. Fifth, if all of the conditions above exist, the law of supply and demand will come into operation and solve the problem of adequate goods, fair price, fair profit, and fair wages. Furthermore, each person will be doing what he or she can do best, and consequently the most enjoyable kind of work. Q.E.D.

Or almost Q.E.D. One problem remained, which Smith recognized, and for which he produced a too facile solution. He recognized that monopolies might grow up that might restrict competition. He proposed that governments must limit and control the growth of monopolies so that free competition could continue. He was not able to point to the exact kind of control that would eliminate monopolies, but that in itself would not be a regulation of industry. This problem has plagued all nations who operate with a capitalistic economy ever since.

In summary, however, it can be pointed out that Smith's economic system was exactly the same sort of plan in its sphere of human activity that John Locke's was in its. The first step is a return to nature. Human limitations and human differences in abilities furnish the natural law that is to operate. If this is done, nature will furnish a mechanism for the economic life of people that will regulate itself. The natural forces of supply and demand, like the gravitational pulls of planets and suns upon each other, like the pulls of executive, legislative, and federative branches of government, will form the whole economic structure into a smoothly operating, functional machine. Again, there is hope here. Smith furnished a principle upon which people could reorganize their economic lives. Then, when the initial adjustments were made, we would have a perfect life in the economic sense, and everyone could enjoy a freedom that had never before been known.

Locke and Educational Theory

In keeping with the complete rationalism of the time, John Locke made one other contribution which had great influence upon education and upon the thinking of the social scientists about the nature of human institutions. Locke proposed that the human mind at the moment of birth was a complete blank. It was, he said, a *tabula rasa*, a blank slate. This position directly countered that of the defenders of political and religious absolutism who contended that an inclination to submit to authority was already present in people's minds when they were born. Not so, said Locke. The mind was a blank slate on which would be written all of the experience the individual had throughout life. If good men and women were desired, then the whole job of creating them lay in the necessity of providing wholesome experience for them. Providing good experiences become the function of education and of human institutions in general, for it is within these institutions that the personality is shaped.

This, one sees immediately, becomes a machine-like process. One starts with the human mind as raw material. One molds it by good experience and the finished product is, at least theoretically, a good person. The process can, of course, work in the opposite direction, for bad experiences could produce a bad person. It is from this basic idea that most of our ideas of universal education, and most of our effort to provide a healthy environment come. Along with Sokrates, men and women of the Enlightenment tended to believe that virtue was knowledge and that ignorance was vice. An educated mind was its own reward. It still is.

David Hume (1711–1776)

Locke's theories of mind and understanding revealed some inconsistencies that were later filled in by the Scottish philosopher David Hume, a sane and urbane man who epitomized the enlightened thinker. Beginning with Locke's empiricist theory of knowledge, Hume went on to prove that there were limits to human reason. Anticipating a great public outcry, he published, in three volumes, *A Treatise of Human Nature being an Attempt to Introduce the Experimental Method of Reasoning into Moral Subjects* (1739–1740). Instead, no one noticed the book at the

time; as Hume sadly said: "it fell dead-born from the press." It could not, however, be ignored for long. In volume one Hume granted certain knowledge only to arithmetic and algebra, and to geometry providing the maxims are true. Beyond that, he said, there is only probable knowledge, thus anticipating modern scientific thought.

Hume's principle concern was with cause and effect, or causality. If we observe that a certain event A is always followed by B then we assume that A causes B. If, for example, we hold a match to a piece of paper and see the paper burn, we connect the two events and say that the flaming match caused the paper to burn. Not so, says Hume. That paper always burns when a match is held to it is a *belief* that is developed through *custom,* that is, experience. We have seen this happen so often we assume that it *must* happen every time and therein lies the rub. Since A (the match) does not *cause* B (paper) to burn we cannot assume that paper is *certain* to burn. It is probable but not certain. The paper, for example, could have been soaked in a chemical that no amount of flame would set afire. Further, we cannot bite into an apple with the certainty that it will taste like an apple; it could taste like roast pork. We assume that the sun will rise tomorrow but it is impossible to establish that it must necessarily rise. Newton's law of universal gravitation is therefore probable and not necessarily universal. As American space vehicles have probed ever deeper into the cosmos scientists have watched with extreme curiosity to see if Newton's law remains valid. There have been no inconsistencies to date but no scientist would be willing to predict what the situation might be a thousand light years away. As Hume says, there are limits to human reason. He accepted a world based on probability rather than certainty. Through observation and reasoning we can determine, short of certainty, only *how* nature operates but not *why*.

Hume's skepticism also applied to religion and religious beliefs, and followed a long history of skeptical doubts about the truths of Judeo-Christianity. In the sixteenth century a Portuguese Jewish refugee in Holland, Uriel Da Costa, started out questioning the truth of orthodox Judaism and ended up stating that all religions were made by human beings. The French skeptic Isaac La Peyrère wrote *Man Before Adam* (1656) in which he claimed that there were people all over the world before Adam; the Bible cannot therefore be an accurate account of human history. La Peyrère's work led two Biblical scholars, Baruch de Spinoza (1632–1677) and Father Richard Simon (1638–1712), to reexamine religious knowledge. Spinoza concluded that the Bible was not divine revelation but merely a history of Jewish activities and superstitions. He proposed instead a religious pantheism in which all existence was embraced in one substance (God or Nature), a position of great appeal for the coming Romantic movement. The greatest Biblical scholar of his age, Father Simon set out to prove that scholars could never find an accurate text of the Bible nor discover what it meant. Unlike Spinoza, Simon was convinced that there was a Biblical message and tried, through critical scholarship, to determine what the message was.

The most famous of the French skeptics, Pierre Bayle (1647–1706), wrote his *Historical and Critical Dictionary* (1697–1702), in which he undermined the metaphysical theories of Descartes, Spinoza, Locke, and Leibniz; attacked all existing theologies; ridiculed the heroes of the Old Testament; and challenged all rational knowledge. He advocated abandoning reason in favor of blind faith, but there was little left but doubt about understanding anything at all except by describing everything in historical terms. Voltaire called Bayle's *Dictionary* the "Arsenal of the Enlightenment."

An avid reader of Bayle, Hume saw, as apparently no other Enlightenment thinker did, the plight of human beings if Bayle's doubts could not be answered. Hume never doubted that people could be certain about the evils of murder, stealing, and the like nor should they be uncertain about Newton's laws. Uncertainty belonged in the philosopher's study. People, through a study of human history, had to recognize different kinds of knowledge and live their lives as sane and civilized human beings. There were no absolute truths and one should not believe anything absolutely. He was particularly concerned about religious conflicts. "Errors in religion," he wrote, "are dangerous; those in philosophy only ridiculous." He believed, in the final analysis, that people could lead their lives as he did his, exercising their natural passions and common sense as they cheerfully enjoyed the uncertainties of everyday life.

Immanual Kant (1724–1804)

The leading thinker of the German Enlightenment, Kant responded to Hume's skepticism with the famous remark that he had been "awakened from his dogmatic slumbers." In his three *Critiques (Pure Reason,* 1781; *Practical Reason,* 1788; *Judgement,* 1793) Kant laid out a complete philosophical system. He showed that knowledge *a priori* was possible because people could perceive the world of space, forms, and causality and, because of the intrinsic nature of the human mind, understand phenomena. As he said, we can know only appearances like colors, shapes, and sounds but never the thing-in-itself; true knowledge cannot transcend experience. But, we can have reliable knowledge because all minds function the same way.

In ethics Kant stated that good actions must be done from a sense of duty and that moral law was derived from his categorical imperative: "act only according to the maxim which you at the same time will to be a universal law." People, he said, were independent moral agents with the freedom to choose right actions. As practical necessities Kant postulated the existence of God to insure that virtue was crowned with happiness and immortality so that the pursuit of moral perfection could continue in the afterlife.

Kant was the founder of German idealism. His philosophy appealed to the heart as opposed to the coldness of theoretical reason. This had enormous appeal for the German Romantic movement. In terms of the Enlightenment, his principle that every person was to be considered as an end in herself or himself is a form of the doctrine of the Rights of Man. Kant coined the prevailing motto for the Enlightenment: "Dare to Know!"

The Philosophes

Called *Les Philosophes* (the philosophers) or *Encyclopedistes* because most of them wrote articles for Diderot's monumental *Encyclopedia,* the philosophes were not all philosophers but included writers, poets, artists, mathematicians, dramatists, and scientists. One of the leading philosophes, Denis Diderot (dee-duh-RO; 1713–1784) was editor-in-chief of the *Encyclopedia* (1747–1772). Published in twenty-eight volumes but suppressed in 1759 by the government and thereafter printed clandestinely, the work was a summary of all human knowledge. Its prevailing spirit was scorn for the past and for organized religion, and glorification of reason, the arts, the experimental sciences, and industry. The *Encyclopedia* assumed that religious toleration and freedom of thought would win out and implied throughout that the condition of the common people should be the main concern of the government. A call to arms in twenty-eight volumes, the *Encyclopedia* was perhaps the key influence that led to the French Revolution.

In his *Persian Letters* (published anonymously in 1721) Montesquieu (mon-tes-KYO; 1689–1755) satirized European, especially French, society, leaving no phase of human activity untouched by its devastating wit and irony. His most influential book, *The Spirit of the Laws* (1748), was a scientific study of comparative government whose theories of checks and balances found their way into the United States Constitution.

Diderot, Voltaire, and Rousseau were the most influential of the French philosophes but the latter two will not be considered at this point. Voltaire and his satirical novel *Candide* are considered near the end of this chapter. A kind of reverse image of Voltaire the rationalist, Rousseau was a powerful influence on the Romantic movement and is discussed in chapter 20.

Absolutism and the Enlightenment

Louis XIV was a despot but he could, with some justification, be called an enlightened monarch. The same cannot be said for the next two kings. Louis XV, great grandson of Louis XIV, ruled ineptly but luxuriously from 1715–1774 and his weak and vascillating grandson, Louis XVI (1774–1793) went to the guillotine.

A rival state, the kingdom of Brandenburg-Prussia, rose to power during the decline of French power and influence. Frederick I was crowned the first king of

Prussia in 1701, followed by Frederick William I (1713–1740), who began Prussian expansion. Frederick the Great (1740–1786) excelled at waging war and made Prussia the dominant military power in Europe. Known as a "benevolent despot," he promoted social and legal reforms and established a glittering court with musical performances by Johann Sebastian Bach and by Frederick himself. But the king did remark that "my people say what they please and I do as I please." Enlightenment had a way to go.

The founder of the modern Russian state, Peter the Great (1682–1725) mercilessly "Westernized" his country and savagely destroyed his enemies. He was admittedly a genius and he was undoubtedly more than a bit mad. To this day he has been admired as an enlightened leader and viewed with horror as a sadistic monster. Catherine the Great (1762–1791) was of German birth but she became thoroughly Russianized. Influenced by the Enlightenment, she planned vast reforms, but a peasant revolt in 1773–1775 and the French Revolution caused her to reverse course and, among other actions, enslave the serfs.

Only in Britain was there any real political freedom. Under the Hanoverian kings George I (1714–1727) and George II (1727–1760), Robert Walpole became, in fact, if not in name, the prime minister (1721–1742). William Pitt (1757–1761) was a strong prime minister but resigned when the next king, George III (1760–1820), decided he wanted to direct policy. Lord North was an acquiescent prime minister and, between king and prime minister, they inadvertently brought a new democratic republic into being. Absolutism during the Enlightenment was anything but enlightened.

Literature, 1600–1789

John Donne (1573–1631)

Though the seventeenth century is often referred to as the Baroque era, the term is more appropriate for art and music (see chaps. 18 and 19) than it generally is for literature. Donne's poetry does display some of the opulence and splendor associated with the Baroque but Donne has, instead, been characterized as the leader of the Metaphysical school, referring, in general, to the powerful intellectual content of his work, his concentrated images, and his remarkable ability to range between the intensely personal and the cosmic. Poets like Andrew Marvell and others were influenced by Donne, but they formed no organized school nor would they have endorsed the Metaphysical school label that John Dryden and Samuel Johnson affixed to the poetry of Donne and Marvell.

Poet, prose stylist, and preacher, John Donne was an experienced man of the world who spoke with great intellectual vigor in his love poems and in his Holy Sonnets. Neglected for three centuries after his death, he is now recognized as one of the finest poets in the English language, perhaps second only to Shakespeare.

In the following song Donne uses six different vivid images to express the impossibility, as he saw it, of woman's constancy.

Literary Selections

SONG
John Donne

Go and catch a falling star,
    Get with child a mandrake root,
Tell me where all past years are,
    Or who cleft the devil's foot,
Teach me to hear mermaids singing,
Or to keep off envy's stinging,
      And find
      What wind
Serves to advance an honest mind.

If thou be'st born to strange sights,
    Things invisible to see,
Ride ten thousand days and nights,
    Till age snow white hairs on thee;
Thou, when thou return'st, wilt tell me
All strange wonders that befell thee,
      And swear,
      Nowhere
Lives a woman true and fair.

If thou find'st one, let me know;
    Such a pilgrimage were sweet;
Yet do not: I would not go,
    Though at next door we might meet;
Though she were true when you met her,
And last till you write your letter,
      Yet she
      Will be
False, ere I come, to two or three.

The following poem uses unique images that reflect Donne's secret marriage to his patron's niece, a happy union but one that clouded the rest of the poet's life. Only John Donne could effectively express life, love, and loving in terms of a flea.

THE FLEA
John Donne

Mark but this flea, and mark in this,
How little that which thou deniest me is;
It sucked me first, and now sucks thee,
And in this flea our two bloods mingled be;
Thou know'st that this cannot be said
A sin, nor shame, nor loss of maidenhead,
    Yet this enjoys before it woo,
    And pampered swells with one blood made of two,
    And this, alas! is more than we would do.

Oh stay, three lives in one flea spare,
Where we almost, yea, more than married are.
This flea is you and I, and this
Our marriage-bed and marriage-temple is;
Though parents grudge, and you, we 're met
And cloistered in these living walls of jet.
    Though use make you apt to kill me,
    Let not, to that, self-murder added be,
    And sacrilege, three sins in killing three.

"The Good-Morrow" exemplifies Donne's ability to vastly extend personal experience; what lovers discover in their intimacy is raised to the universal and the immortal.

THE GOOD-MORROW
John Donne

I wonder, by my troth, what thou and I
Did till we loved; were we not weaned till then,
But sucked on country pleasures childishly?
Or snorted we in the Seven Sleepers' den?
'T was so; but this, all pleasures fancies be:
If ever any beauty I did see
Which I desired and got, 't was but a dream of thee.

And now good-morrow to our waking souls,
Which watch not one another out of fear;
For love all love of other sights controls,
And makes one little room an everywhere.
Let sea-discoverers to new worlds have gone,
Let maps to other, worlds on worlds have shown,
Let us possess one world; each hath one, and is one.

My face in thine eye, thine in mine appears,
And true plain hearts do in the faces rest;
Where can we find two better hemispheres
Without sharp north, without declining west?
Whatever dies, was not mixed equally;
If our two loves be one, or thou and I
Love so alike that none do slacken, none can die.

Near the end of his career Donne became obsessed with the thought of death. In the following Holy Sonnet he uses intense language and images to try to put death in perspective.

HOLY SONNET X
John Donne

Death, be not proud, though some have callèd thee
Mighty and dreadful, for thou art not so;
For those whom thou think'st thou dost overthrow
Die not, poor Death, nor yet canst thou kill me.
From rest and sleep, which but thy pictures be,
Much pleasure, then from thee much more must flow;
And soonest our best men with thee do go,
Rest of their bones, and soul's delivery.
Thou art slave to Fate, chance, kings, and desperate men,
And dost with poison, war, and sickness dwell,
And poppy or charms can make us sleep as well
And better than thy stroke; why swell'st thou then?
One short sleep past, we wake eternally
And Death shall be no more; Death, thou shalt die.

Exercises

1. Donne's poetry has been aptly called "strong-lined" because of his powerful images and sharp changes in rhythm. Try reading his "Song" aloud, listening for the abrupt change in rhythm of *And find/What wind* plus similar changes in the second and third stanzas. How much do these contribute to "strong-lined" poetry?

2. Identify the three stages in "The Flea": the moral the poet draws from the flea; when the woman proposes to kill it; when she actually does so.

3. Compare, in "The Good-Morrow," personal images with those that are much larger. Consider, for example, *one little room* and *every where, sea-discovers, worlds on worlds.* Look also at verbs like *loved, sucked,* and *snorted.*

4. In the "Holy Sonnet" Donne equates death with extended, restful sleep. Is his point of view convincing? Would it persuade an atheist?

Andrew Marvell (1621–1678)

Late in his career Marvell wrote stinging political satires, but he is best known today for his classically inspired lyric poetry about love and nature. "To his Coy Mistress" is a seduction poem in the tradition of Catullus and other classical writers in which the theme is the fleeting moment and the tone is urgent. We must seize the moment and make love now. Though the theme is serious the style is both graceful and playful and, withal, sophisticated.

Literary Selection

TO HIS COY MISTRESS
Andrew Marvell

Had we but World enough, and Time,
This coyness Lady were no crime.
We would sit down, and think which way
To walk, and pass our long Loves Day.
Thou by the *Indian Ganges* side
Should'st Rubies find: I by the Tide
Of *Humber* would complain. I would
Love you ten years before the Flood:
And you should if you please refuse
Till the Conversion of the *Jews*.   10
My vegetable Love should grow
Vaster than Empires, and more slow.
An hundred years should go to praise
Thine Eyes, and on thy Forehead Gaze.
Two hundred to adore each Breast:
But thirty thousand to the rest.
An Age at least to every part,
And the last Age should show your Heart.
For Lady you deserve this State;
Nor would I love at lower rate.   20
   But at my back I alwaies hear
Times winged Charriot hurrying near:
And yonder all before us lye
Desarts of vast Eternity.
Thy Beauty shall no more be found;
Nor, in thy marble Vault, shall sound
My ecchoing Song: then Worms shall try
That long preserv'd Virginity:
And your quaint Honour turn to dust;
And into ashes all my Lust.   30
The Grave's a fine and private place,
But none I think do there embrace.

Now therefore, while the youthful hew
Sits on thy skin like morning dew,
And while thy willing Soul transpires
At every pore with instant Fires,
Now let us sport us while we may;
And now, like am'rous birds of prey,
Rather at once our Time devour,
Than languish in his slow-chapt pow'r.   40
Let us roll all our Strength, and all
Our sweetness, up into one Ball:
And tear our Pleasures with rough strife,
Thorough the Iron gates of Life.
Thus, though we cannot make our Sun
Stand still, yet we will make him run.

Exercise

1. Did the Coy Mistress acquiesce? Look again at
   the first and last lines, at the progression from
   not having enough time to the illusion of time
   flying by.

John Milton (1608–1674)

An ardent supporter of the Puritan cause, Milton became Latin secretary in Cromwell's government and,
in several important tracts, one of its principle defenders. Upon the Restoration of the Stuart line with
Charles II (1660) Milton was fined and forcibly retired, after which he dictated his epic poems *Paradise Lost* (1667) and *Paradise Regained* (1671). One
of the world's great epic poems, *Paradise Lost* relates
the story of Satan's rebellion against God and the Fall
of Man. Milton's intention was, as he said, to "justify
the ways of God to man."

The epic poems were among the first to use blank
verse (unrhymed iambic pentameter), but Milton also
wrote some notable sonnets. Considered to be among
his finest work in small form, the two sonnets given
below are in the standard form of 14 lines in rhymed
iambic pentameter.

On Easter Sunday (1655) in the Piedmont region
of northwestern Italy, the Duke of Savoy slaughtered
about 1,700 members of the Protestant Waldensian
sect that dated back to 1170 (see Reformation in chap.
13). Protestant Europe was horrified; Milton's response was a sonnet tense with low-keyed fury. The
"martyred blood" refers to Tertullian's statement that
"the blood of the martyrs is the seed of the Church."
The "Triple tyrant" is the pope, whose tiara has three
crowns, and "Babylonian woe" is a reference to Revelation 18 in which the obliteration of the city of
luxury and vice is described. Along with many Protestants, especially Puritans, Milton saw the destruction of Babylon as an allegory of the ultimate fate of
the Catholic Church.

Literary Selections

ON THE LATE MASSACRE IN PIEDMONT (1655)
John Milton

Avenge, O Lord, thy slaughtered Saints, whose bones
          Lie scattered on the Alpine mountains cold;
          Even them who kept thy truth so pure of old,
When all our fathers worshiped stocks and stones,
Forget not: in thy book record their groans
          Who were thy sheep, and in their ancient fold
          Slain by the bloody Piemontese, that rolled
Mother with infant down the rocks. Their moans
The vales redoubled to the hills, and they
          To heaven. Their martyred blood and ashes sow
O'er all the Italian fields, where still doth sway
          The triple Tyrant; that from these may grow
A hundredfold, who, having learnt thy way,
          Early may fly the Babylonian woe.

Because of overwork Milton's eyesight had become impaired as early as 1644, and by 1652 he was
totally blind. The first of two sonnets about his blindness, the following poem signals the poet's submission to fate though he had not yet found his way to
using, in darkness, "that one talent which is death to
hide."

ON HIS BLINDNESS (1655)
John Milton

When I consider how my light is spent
          Ere half my days in this dark world and wide,
          And that one Talent which is death to hide
Lodged with me useless, though my soul more bent
To serve therewith my Maker, and present
          My true account, lest He returning chide,
          "Doth God exact day-labour, light denied?"
I fondly ask. But Patience, to prevent
That murmur, soon replies, "God doth not need
          Either man's work or his own gifts.
               Who best
          Bear his mild yoke, they serve him best.
               His state
Is kingly: thousands at his bidding speed,
          And post o'er land and ocean without rest;
          They also serve who only stand and wait."

Exercise

1. Milton seethes with indignation over the fate of
   the slaughtered saints in Italy but not over the
   loss of his sight. What are some of the words
   that convey this mood of resignation? Consider,
   for example, words like *spent, bent, mild,* and
   murmur.

Alexander Pope (1688–1744)

Milton's poetry can be reasonably described as Baroque; that of Pope is even more clearly Neoclassic. In *The Essay on Criticism* he formulated an aesthetics of poetry, emphasizing the necessity for precise language, logical order, and clear form. Pope's own poetry was didactic, witty, satiric, technically superb; it epitomized the Neoclassic style of eighteenth-century England. Pope, in fact, expressed his goal in his own verse:

> True wit is nature to advantage dressed,
> What oft was thought, but ne'er so well expressed.

His *Essay on Man* (1733–1734) optimistically summarizes eighteenth-century views on the rational universe, reasonable behavior, and deism. The poem is not profound in philosophic terms but rather admired for its skillful craftsmanship and sparkling wit. Pope's optimism was rejected by Voltaire in *Candide,* as discussed a bit later.

Literary Selection
ESSAY ON MAN
Alexander Pope

Epistle I

Awake, my St. John! leave all meaner things
To low ambition and the pride of kings.
Let us, since life can little more supply
Than just to look about us and to die,
Expatiate free o'er all this scene of man;
A mighty maze! but not without a plan;
A wild, where weeds and flowers promiscuous shoot;
Or garden, tempting with forbidden fruit.
Together let us beat this ample field,
Try what the open, what the covert yield;
The latent tracts, the giddy heights, explore,
Of all who blindly creep, or sightless soar;
Eye Nature's walks, shoot Folly as it flies,
And catch the manners living as they rise;
Laugh where we must, be candid where we can;
But vindicate the ways of God to man.

I

Say first, of God above or man below,
What can we reason but from what we know?
Of man, what see we but his station here,
From which to reason, or to which refer?
Through worlds unnumber'd though the God be known,
'Tis ours to trace him only in our own.
He, who through vast immensity can pierce,
See worlds on worlds compose one universe,
Observe how system into system runs,
What other planets circle other suns,
What varied being peoples every star,
May tell why Heav'n has made us as we are.
But of this frame, the bearings and the ties,
The strong connections, nice dependencies,
Gradations just, has thy pervading soul
Looked through, or can a part contain the whole?
Is the great chain that draws all to agree,
And drawn supports, upheld by God or thee?

II

Presumptuous man! the reason wouldst thou find,
Why form'd so weak, so little, and so blind?
First, if thou canst, the harder reason guess,
Why form'd no weaker, blinder, and no less?
Ask of thy mother earth, why oaks are made
Taller or stronger than the weeds they shade!
Or ask of yonder argent fields above
Why Jove's satellites are less than Jove!
  Of systems possible, if 't is confest
That wisdom infinite must form the best,
Where all must full or not coherent be,
And all that rises rise in due degree,
Then, in the scale of reas'ning life, 't is plain
There must be somewhere such a rank as Man:
And all the question (wrangle e'er so long)
Is only this, if God has placed him wrong?
  Respecting Man, whatever wrong we call,
May, must be right, as relative to all.
In human works, though labor'd on with pain,
A thousand movements scarce one purpose gain;
In God's, one single can its end produce;
Yet serves to second too some other use.
So Man, who here seems principal alone,
Perhaps acts second to some sphere unknown,
Touches some wheel, or verges to some goal;
'Tis but a part we see, and not a whole.
When the proud steed shall know why man restrains
His fiery course, or drives him o'er the plains;
When the dull ox, why now he breaks the clod,
Is now a victim, and now Egypt's god;
Then shall man's pride and dullness comprehend
His actions', passions', being's, use and end;
Why doing, suff'ring, check'd, impell'd; and why
This hour a slave, the next a deity.
  Then say not man's imperfect, Heav'n in fault;
Say rather man's as perfect as he ought:
His knowledge measur'd to his state and place,
His time a moment, and a point his space.
If to be perfect in a certain sphere,
What matter soon or late, or here or there?
The blest today is as completely so,
As who began a thousand years ago.

III

Heav'n from all creatures hides the book of Fate,
All but the page prescrib'd, their present state:
From brutes what men, from men what spirits know:
Or who could suffer Being here below?
The lamb thy riot dooms to bleed today,
Had he thy reason, would he skip and play?
Pleas'd to the last, he crops the flow'ry food,
And licks the hand just rais'd to shed his blood.
Oh blindness to the future! kindly giv'n,
That each may fill the circle mark'd by Heav'n:
Who sees with equal eye, as God of all,
A hero perish, or a sparrow fall,
Atoms or systems into ruin hurl'd,
And now a bubble burst, and now a world.
  Hope humbly then; with trembling pinions soar;
Wait the great teacher Death, and God adore!
What future bliss he gives not thee to know,
But gives that hope to be thy blessing now.
Hope springs eternal in the human breast;
Man never is, but always to be blest.
The soul, uneasy, and confin'd from home,
Rests and expatiates in a life to come.

Lo! the poor Indian, whose untutor'd mind
Sees God in clouds, or hears him in the wind;
His soul proud Science never taught to stray
Far as the solar walk or milky way;
Yet simple Nature to his hope has giv'n,
Behind the cloud-topt hill, an humbler heav'n;
Some safer world in depth of woods embrac'd,
Some happier island in the watery waste,
Where slaves once more their native land behold,
No fiends torment, no Christians thirst for gold!
To be, contents his natural desire;
He asks no angel's wing, no seraph's fire;
But thinks, admitted to that equal sky,
His faithful dog shall bear him company.

IV

Go, wiser thou! and in thy scale of sense,
Weigh thy opinion against Providence;
Call imperfection what thou fancy'st such,
Say, Here he gives too little, there too much!
Destroy all creatures for thy sport or gust,
Yet cry, If man's unhappy, God's unjust;
If man alone engross not Heav'n's high care,
Alone made perfect here, immortal there:
Snatch from his hand the balance and the rod,
Rejudge his justice, be the God of God!
In pride, in reas'ning pride, our error lies;
All quit their sphere and rush into the skies.
Pride still is aiming at the blest abodes,
Men would be angels, angels would be gods.
Aspiring to be gods if angels fell,
Aspiring to be angels, men rebel:
And who but wishes to invert the laws
Of order, sins against the Eternal Cause.

V

Ask for what end the heav'nly bodies shine,
Earth for whose use? Pride answers, " 'Tis for mine!
For me kind Nature wakes her genial pow'r,
Suckles each herb, and spreads out ev'ry flow'r;
Annual for me, the grape, the rose renew
The juice nectareous and the balmy dew;
For me the mine a thousand treasures brings;
For me health gushes from a thousand springs;
Seas roll to waft me, suns to light me rise;
My footstool earth, my canopy the skies."
But errs not Nature from this gracious end,
From burning suns when livid deaths descend,
When earthquakes swallow, or when tempests sweep
Towns to one grave, whole nations to the deep?
"No," 't is reply'd, "the first Almighty Cause
Acts not by partial but by gen'ral laws:
Th' exceptions few; some change since all began;
And what created perfect?"—Why then man?
If the great end be human happiness,
Then Nature deviates; and can man do less?
As much that end a constant course requires
Of show'rs and sunshine, as of man's desires:
As much eternal springs and cloudless skies,
As men forever temp'rate, calm, and wise.
If plagues or earthquakes break not Heav'n's design,
Why then a Borgia or a Catiline?
Who knows but he, whose hand the lightning forms,
Why heaves old ocean, and who wings the storms,
Pours fierce ambition in a Caesar's mind,
Or turns young Ammon loose to scourge mankind?

From pride, from pride our very reas'ning springs;
Account for moral, as for natural things:
Why charge we Heav'n in those, in these acquit?
In both, to reason right is to submit.
Better for us, perhaps, it might appear,
Were there all harmony, all virtue here;
That never air or ocean felt the wind;
That never passion discompos'd the mind.
But all subsists by elemental strife;
And passions are the elements of life.
The gen'ral order, since the whole began,
Is kept in Nature, and is kept in man.

VI

What would this man? Now upward will he soar,
And little less than angel, would be more!
Now looking downwards, just as griev'd appears
To want the strength of bulls, the fur of bears.
Made for his use all creatures if he call,
Say what their use, had he the pow'rs of all?
Nature to these, without profusion, kind,
The proper organs, proper pow'rs assign'd;
Each seeming want compensated of course,
Here with degrees of swiftness, there of force:
All in exact proportion to the state;
Nothing to add, and nothing to abate;
Each beast, each insect happy in its own:
Is Heav'n unkind to man, and man alone?
Shall he alone, whom rational we call,
Be pleas'd with nothing, if not bless'd with all?
The bliss of man (could pride that blessing find),
Is not to act or think beyond mankind;
No powers of body or of soul to share,
But what his nature and his state can bear.
Why has not man a microscopic eye?
For this plain reason, man is not a fly.
Say what the use, were finer optics giv'n,
To inspect a mite, not comprehend the heav'n?
Or touch, if tremblingly alive all o'er,
To smart and agonize at every pore?
Or quick effluvia darting through the brain,
Die of a rose in aromatic pain?
If Nature thunder'd in his opening ears,
And stunn'd him with the music of the spheres,
How would he wish that Heav'n had left him still
The whisp'ring zephyr and the purling rill?
Who finds not Providence all good and wise,
Alike in what it gives, and what denies?

VII

Far as creation's ample range extends,
The scale of sensual, mental powers ascends.
Mark how it mounts to man's imperial race,
From the green myriads in the peopled grass;
What modes of sight betwixt each wide extreme,
The mole's dim curtain, and the lynx's beam:
Of smell, the headlong lioness between,
And hound sagacious on the tainted green:
Of hearing, from the life that fills the flood,
To that which warbles through the vernal wood:
The spider's touch how exquisitely fine!
Feels at each thread, and lives along the line:
In the nice bee, what sense so subtly true
From pois'nous herbs extracts the healing dew?
How instinct varies in the grov'ling swine,
Compar'd, half-reas'ning elephant, with thine!
'Twixt that and reason, what a nice barrier;
Forever sep'rate, yet forever near!

Remembrance and reflection, how ally'd;
What thin partitions sense from thought divide;
And middle natures, how they long to join,
Yet never pass th' insuperable line!
Without this just gradation, could they be
Subjected, these to those, or all to thee?
The pow'rs of all subdu'd by thee alone,
Is not thy reason all these pow'rs in one?
See, through this air, this ocean, and this earth,
All matter quick, and bursting into birth.
Above, how high progressive life may go!
Around, how wide! how deep extend below!
Vast Chain of Being! which from God began,
Natures ethereal, human, angel, man,
Beast, bird, fish, insect, what no eye can see,
No glass can reach; from infinite to thee,
From thee to nothing. On superior pow'rs
Were we to press, inferior might on ours:
Or in the full creation leave a void,
Where, one step broken, the great scale's destroy'd:
From Nature's chain whatever link you strike,
Tenth or ten thousandth, breaks the chain alike.

　　　And if each system in gradation roll
Alike essential to the amazing Whole,
The least confusion but in one, not all
That system only, but the Whole must fall.
Let earth unbalanc'd from her orbit fly,
Planets and suns run lawless through the sky;
Let ruling angels from their spheres be hurl'd,
Being on being wreck'd, and world on world;
Heav'n's whole foundations to their centre nod,
And Nature tremble to the throne of God!
All this dread Order break—for whom? for thee?
Vile worm!—Oh! madness! pride! impiety!

IX

What if the foot, ordain'd the dust to tread,
Or hand, to toil, aspir'd to be the head?
What if the head, the eye, or ear repin'd
To serve mere engines to the ruling Mind?
Just as absurd for any part to claim
To be another in this gen'ral frame;
Just as absurd to mourn the tasks or pains
The great directing Mind of All ordains.

　　　All are but parts of one stupendous whole,
Whose body Nature is, and God the soul;
That, chang'd through all, and yet in all the same,
Great in the earth, as in th' ethereal frame,
Warms in the sun, refreshes in the breeze,
Glows in the stars, and blossoms in the trees,
Lives through all life, extends through all extent,
Spreads undivided, operates unspent;
Breathes in our soul, informs our mortal part,
As full, as perfect in a hair as heart;
As full, as perfect in vile man that mourns,
As the rapt seraph that adores and burns:
To him no high, no low, no great, no small;
He fills, he bounds, connects, and equals all.

X

Cease then, nor Order imperfection name:
Our proper bliss depends on what we blame.
Know thy own point: this kind, this due degree
Of blindness, weakness, Heav'n bestows on thee.
Submit: in this or any other sphere,
Secure to be as blest as thou canst bear;
Safe in the hand of one disposing Pow'r
Or in the natal, or the mortal hour.

All Nature is but art unknown to thee;
All chance, direction which thou canst not see;
All discord, harmony not understood;
All partial evil, universal good;
And, spite of pride, in erring reason's spite,
One truth is clear, *whatever is, is right.*

Epistle II
I

Know then thyself, presume not God to scan:
The proper study of mankind is Man.
Plac'd on this isthmus of a middle state,
A being darkly wise and rudely great:
With too much knowledge for the skeptic side,
With too much weakness for the Stoic's pride,
He hangs between; in doubt to act, or rest;
In doubt to deem himself a god or beast;
In doubt his mind or body to prefer;
Born but to die, and reas'ning but to err;
Alike in ignorance, his reason such,
Whether he thinks too little or too much:
Chaos of thought and passion, all confus'd;
Still by himself abus'd, or disabus'd;
Created half to rise, and half to fall;
Great lord of all things, yet a prey to all;
Sole judge of truth, in endless error hurl'd:
The glory, jest, and riddle of the world!

II

Two principles in human nature reign;
Self-love to urge, and reason to restrain;
Nor this a good, nor that a bad we call,
Each works its end to move or govern all:
And to their proper operation still
Ascribe all good; to their improper, ill.

　　　Self-love, the spring of motion, acts the soul;
Reason's comparing balance rules the whole.
Man, but for that, no action could attend,
And, but for this, were active to no end:
Fix'd like a plant on his peculiar spot,
To draw nutrition, propagate, and rot;
Or, meteor-like, flame lawless thro' the void,
Destroying others, by himself destroyed.

　　　Most strength the moving principle requires;
Active its task, it prompts, impels, inspires.
Sedate and quiet, the comparing lies,
Form'd but to check, deliberate, and advise.
Self-love still stronger, as its objects nigh;
Reason's at distance and in prospect lie:
That sees immediate good by present sense;
Reason, the future and the consequence.
Thicker than arguments, temptations throng,
At best more watchful this, but that more strong.
The action of the stronger to suspend,
Reason still use, to reason still attend.
Attention, habit and experience gains;
Each strengthens reason, and self-love restrains . . .

V

Vice is a monster of so frightful mien,
As to be hated needs but to be seen;
Yet seen too oft, familiar with her face,
We first endure, then pity, then embrace:
But where the extreme of vice was ne'er agreed:
Ask where's the north? at York, 'tis on the Tweed;
In Scotland, at the Orcades; and there,
At Greenland, Zembla, or the Lord knows where.

No creature owns it in the first degree,
But thinks his neighbor farther gone than he;
Even those who dwell beneath its very zone,
Or never feel the rage, or never own;
What happier natures shrink at with affright
The hard inhabitant contends is right.

    Virtuous and vicious every man must be;
Few in the extreme, but all in the degree:
The rogue and fool by fits is fair and wise;
And ev'n the best, by fits, what they despise.
'T is but by parts we follow good or ill;
For, vice or virtue, self directs it still;
Each individual seeks a sev'ral goal;
But Heav'n's great view is one, and that the whole . . .

Epistle III
I

Here then we rest: "The Universal Cause
Acts to one end, but acts by various laws."
In all the madness of superfluous health,
The trim of pride, the impudence of wealth,
Let this great truth be present night and day:
But most be present, if we preach or pray.

    Look round our world, behold the chain of love
Combining all below and all above.
See plastic Nature working to this end:
The single atoms each to other tend;
Attract, attracted to, the next in place
Form'd and impell'd its neighbor to embrace.
See matter next with various life endu'd,
Press to one centre still, the gen'ral good.
See dying vegetables life sustain,
See life dissolving vegetate again:
All forms that perish other forms supply,
(By turns we catch the vital breath, and die,)
Like bubbles on the sea of matter borne,
They rise, they break, and to that sea return.
Nothing is foreign; parts relate to whole;
One all-extending, all-preserving soul
Connects each being, greatest with the least;
Made beast in aid of man, and man of beast;
All serv'd, all serving: nothing stands alone;
The chain holds on, and where it ends, unknown . . .

Exercises

1. In the first section of Epistle I is Pope a "rationalist"—one who believes that the human mind can find answers to all his questions? Why do you answer as you do?
2. In Epistle I:VII Pope refers to the "Vast chain of being." What does he mean by this?
3. Pope speaks of man as the *glory,* the *jest,* and the *riddle* of the world. In what sense does he use each term? Name three men or women, or one person in three different situations that would explain Pope's meaning.
4. In your estimation, what is the point of the brief selection from Epistle III: inescapable Law; constant Change; Continuity and Interdependence; inevitable Death and Decay; the Separateness of all things; or some other idea?

5. Who would have given the more favorable review on the *Essay on Man* (if he could have read it!): Newton or Rousseau? Dante or Machiavelli? Shakespeare or Donne? Why do you think so?

Jonathan Swift (1667–1745)

Born in Ireland of English parents, Jonathan Swift is identified with Ireland and its political troubles and yet, for most of his life, he tried to break away from Ireland. His dream of becoming an English bishop failed; instead he was given the deanship of St. Patrick's Cathedral in Dublin. At first feeling exiled in Ireland he later became closely identified with its poverty and political privation.

A master of language used in a lucid and forceful style, Swift was the greatest English satirist in an age of satire, perhaps because he was more detached, viewing English life and customs from his vantage point in Ireland. His masterpiece, *Gulliver's Travels* (1726), savagely exposed and attacked every human weakness and vice over there in Britain. His brilliant pamphlet, "A Modest Proposal," was written in the white heat of indignation. Ireland's poverty and misery, in his own words, did "tear his heart." His proposal is all the more horrendous in its reasoned logic as he ironically suggests a practical, rational solution to Irish destitution and privation.

Literary Selection
A MODEST PROPOSAL

for Preventing the Children of Poor People in Ireland from Being a Burden to Their Parents or Country, and for Making Them Beneficial to the Public.
1729
Jonathan Swift

It is a melancholy object to those who walk through this great town, or travel in the country, when they see the streets, the roads, and cabin-doors, crowded with beggars of the female sex, followed by three, four, or six children, all in rags, and importuning every passenger for an alms. These mothers, instead of being able to work for their honest livelihood, are forced to employ all their time in strolling to beg sustenance for their helpless infants: who, as they grow up, either turn thieves for want of work, or leave their dear native country to fight for the Pretender in Spain, or sell themselves to the Barbadoes.

I think it is agreed by all parties, that this prodigious number of children in the arms, or on the backs, or at the heels of their mothers, and frequently of their fathers, is, in the present deplorable state of the kingdom, a very great additional grievance; and, therefore, whoever could find out a fair, cheap, and easy method of making these children sound, useful members of the commonwealth, would deserve so well of the public, as to have his statue set up for a preserver of the nation.

But my intention is very far from being confined to provide only for the children of professed beggars; it is of a much greater extent, and shall take in the whole number of infants at a certain age, who are born of parents in effect as little able to support them, as those who demand our charity in the streets.

As to my own part, having turned my thoughts for many years upon this important subject, and maturely weighed the several schemes of our projectors, I have always found them grossly mistaken in their computation. It is true, a child, just born, may be supported by its mother's milk for a solar year, with little other nourishment; at most, not above the value of two shillings, which the mother may certainly get, or the value in scraps, by her lawful occupation of begging; and it is exactly at one year old that I propose to provide for them in such a manner, as, instead of being a charge upon their parents, or the parish, or wanting food and raiment for the rest of their lives, they shall, on the contrary, contribute to the feeding, and partly to the clothing, of many thousands.

There is likewise another great advantage in my scheme, that it will prevent those voluntary abortions, and that horrid practice of women murdering their bastard children, alas, too frequent among us! sacrificing the poor innocent babes, I doubt more to avoid the expense than the shame, which would move tears and pity in the most savage and inhuman breast.

The number of souls in this kingdom being usually reckoned one million and a half, of these I calculate there may be about two hundred thousand couple whose wives are breeders; from which number I subtract thirty thousand couple, who are able to maintain their own children, (although I apprehend there cannot be so many, under the present distresses of the kingdom;) but this being granted, there will remain a hundred and seventy thousand breeders. I again subtract fifty thousand, for those women who miscarry, or whose children die by accident or disease within the year. There only remain a hundred and twenty thousand children of poor parents annually born. The question therefore is, How this number shall be reared and provided for? which, as I have already said, under the present situation of affairs, is utterly impossible by all the methods hitherto proposed. For we can neither employ them in handicraft or agriculture; we neither build houses (I mean in the country,) nor cultivate land: they can very seldom pick up a livelihood by stealing, till they arrive at six years old, except where they are of towardly parts; although I confess they learn the rudiments much earlier; during which time they can, however, be properly looked upon only as probationers; as I have been informed by a principal gentleman in the county of Cavan, who protested to me, that he never knew above one or two instances under the age of six, even in a part of the kingdom so renowned for the quickest proficiency in that art.

I am assured by our merchants, that a boy or a girl before twelve years old is no saleable commodity; and even when they come to this age they will not yield above three pounds or three pounds and half-a-crown at most, on the exchange; which cannot turn to account either to the parents or kingdom, the charge of nutriment and rags having been at least four times that value.

I shall now, therefore, humbly propose my own thoughts, which I hope will not be liable to the least objection.

I have been assured by a very knowing American of my acquaintance in London, that a young healthy child, well nursed, is, at a year old, a most delicious, nourishing, and wholesome food, whether stewed, roasted, baked, or boiled; and I make no doubt that it will equally serve in a fricassee or a ragout.

I do therefore humbly offer it to public consideration, that of the hundred and twenty thousand children already computed, twenty thousand may be reserved for breed, whereof only one-fourth part to be males; which is more than we allow to sheep, black-cattle, or swine; and my reason is, that these children are seldom the fruits of marriage, a circumstance not much regarded by our savages, therefore one male will be sufficient for four females. That the remaining hundred thousand may, at a year old, be offered in sale to the persons of quality and fortune through the kingdom; always advising the mother to let them suck plentifully in the last month, so as to render them plump and fat for a good table. A child will make two dishes at an entertainment for friends; and when the family dines alone, the fore or hind quarter will make a reasonable dish, and, seasoned with a little pepper or salt, will be very good boiled on the fourth day, especially in winter.

I have reckoned, upon a medium, that a child just born will weigh twelve pounds, and in a solar year, if tolerably nursed, will increase to twenty-eight pounds.

I grant this food will be somewhat dear, and therefore very proper for landlords, who, as they have already devoured most of the parents, seem to have the best title to the children.

Infants' flesh will be in season throughout the year, but more plentifully in March, and a little before and after: for we are told by a grave author, an eminent French physician, that fish being a prolific diet, there are more children born in Roman Catholic countries about nine months after Lent, than at any other season; therefore, reckoning a year after Lent, the markets will be more glutted than usual, because the number of Popish infants is at least three to one in this kingdom; and therefore it will have one other collateral advantage, by lessening the number of Papists among us.

I have already computed the charge of nursing a beggar's child (in which list I reckon all cottagers, labourers, and four-fifths of the farmers) to be about two shillings per annum, rags included; and I believe no gentleman would repine to give ten shillings for the carcass of a good fat child, which, as I have said, will make four dishes of excellent nutritive meat, when he has only some particular friend, or his own family, to dine with him. Thus the squire will learn to be a good landlord, and grow popular among his tenants; the mother will have eight shillings net profit, and be fit for work till she produces another child.

Those who are more thrifty (as I must confess the times require) may flay the carcass; the skin of which, artificially dressed, will make admirable gloves for ladies, and summer-boots for fine gentlemen.

As to our city of Dublin, shambles may be appointed for this purpose in the most convenient parts of it, and butchers we may be assured will not be wanting; although I rather recommend buying the children alive, then dressing them hot from the knife, as we do roasting pigs.

A very worthy person, a true lover of his country, and whose virtues I highly esteem, was lately pleased, in discoursing on this matter, to offer a refinement upon my scheme. He said, that many gentlemen of this kingdom, having of late destroyed their deer, he conceived that the want of venison might be well supplied by the bodies of young lads and maidens, not exceeding fourteen years of age, nor under twelve; so great a number of both sexes in every country being now ready to starve for want of work and service; and these to be disposed of by their parents, if alive, or otherwise by their nearest relations. But, with due deference to so excellent a friend, and so deserving a patriot, I cannot be altogether in his sentiments; for as to the males, my American acquaintance assured me, from frequent experience, that their flesh was generally tough and lean, like that of our schoolboys, by continual exercise, and their taste disagreeable; and to fatten them would not answer the charge. Then as to the females, it would, I think, with humble submission, be a loss to the public, because they soon would become breeders themselves: and besides, it is not improbable that some scrupulous people might be apt to censure such a practice, (although indeed very unjustly,) as a little bordering upon cruelty; which, I confess, has always been with me the strongest objection against any project, how well soever intended.

But in order to justify my friend, he confessed that this expedient was put into his head by the famous Psalmanazar, a native of the island Formosa, who came from thence to London above twenty years ago; and in conversation told my friend, that in his country, when any young person happened to be put to death, the executioner sold the carcass to persons of quality as a prime dainty; and that in his time the body of a plump girl of fifteen, who was crucified for an attempt to poison the emperor, was sold to his imperial majesty's prime minister of state, and other great mandarins of the court, in joints from the gibbet, at four hundred crowns. Neither indeed can I deny, that if the same use were made of several plump young girls in this town, who, without one single groat to their fortunes, cannot stir abroad without a chair, and appear at playhouse and assemblies in foreign fineries which they never will pay for, the kingdom would not be the worse.

Some persons of a desponding spirit are in great concern about that vast number of poor people, who are aged, diseased, or maimed; and I have been desired to employ my thoughts, what course may be taken to ease the nation of so grievous an encumbrance. But I am not in the least pain upon that matter, because it is very well known, that they are every day dying, and rotting, by cold and famine, and filth and vermin, as fast as can be reasonably expected. And as to the young labourers, they are now in almost as hopeful a condition: they cannot get work, and consequently pine away for want of nourishment, to a degree, that if at any time they are accidentally hired to common labour, they have not strength to perform it; and thus the country and themselves are happily delivered from the evils to come.

I have too long digressed, and therefore shall return to my subject. I think the advantages by the proposal which I have made, are obvious and many, as well as of the highest importance.

For first, as I have already observed, it would greatly lessen the number of Papists, with whom we are yearly over-run, being the principal breeders of the nation, as well as our most dangerous enemies; and who stay at home on purpose to deliver the kingdom to the Pretender, hoping to take their advantage by the absence of so many good Protestants, who have chosen rather to leave their country, than stay at home and pay tithes against their conscience to an Episcopal curate.

Secondly, The poorer tenants will have something valuable of their own, which by law may be made liable to distress, and help to pay their landlord's rent; their corn and cattle being already seized, and money a thing unknown.

Thirdly, Whereas the maintenance of a hundred thousand children, from two years old and upward, cannot be computed at less than ten shillings a piece per annum, the nation's stock will be thereby increased fifty thousand pounds per annum, beside the profit of a new dish introduced to the tables of all gentlemen of fortune in the kingdom, who have any refinement in taste. And the money will circulate among ourselves, the goods being entirely of our own growth and manufacture.

Fourthly, The constant breeders, beside the gain of eight shillings sterling per annum by the sale of their children, will be rid of the charge of maintaining them after the first year.

Fifthly, This food would likewise bring great custom to taverns; where the vintners will certainly be so prudent as to procure the best receipts for dressing it to perfection, and, consequently, have their houses frequented by all the fine gentlemen, who justly value themselves upon their knowledge in good eating: and a skilful cook, who understands how to oblige his guests, will contrive to make it as expensive as they please.

Sixthly, This would be a great inducement to marriage, which all wise nations have either encouraged by rewards, or enforced by laws and penalties. It would increase the care and tenderness of mothers toward their children, when they were sure of a settlement for life to the poor babes, provided in some sort by the public, to their annual profit or expense. We should see an honest emulation among the married women, which of them could bring the fattest child to the market. Men would become as fond of their wives during the time of their pregnancy, as they are now of their mares in foal, their cows in calf, their sows when they are ready to farrow; nor offer to beat or kick them (as is too frequent a practice) for fear of a miscarriage.

Many other advantages might be enumerated. For instance, the addition of some thousand carcasses in our exportation of barrelled beef; the propagation of swine's flesh, and improvement in the art of making good bacon, so much wanted among us by the great destruction of pigs, too frequent at our table; which are no way comparable in taste or magnificence to a well-grown, fat, yearling child, which, roasted whole, will make a considerable figure at a lord mayor's feast, or any other public entertainment. But this, and many others, I omit, being studious of brevity.

Supposing that one thousand families in this city would be constant customers for infants' flesh, beside others who might have it at merry-meetings, particularly at weddings and christenings, I compute that Dublin would take off annually about twenty thousand carcasses; and the rest of the kingdom (where probably they will be sold somewhat cheaper) the remaining eighty thousand.

I can think of no one objection, that will possibly be raised against this proposal, unless it should be urged, that the number of people will be thereby much lessened in the kingdom. This I freely own, and it was indeed one principal design in offering it to the world. I desire the reader will observe, that I calculate my remedy for this one individual kingdom of Ireland, and for no other that ever was, is, or I think ever can be, upon earth. Therefore let no man talk to me of other expedients: of taxing our absentees at five shillings a pound: of using neither clothes, nor household-furniture, except what is our own growth and manufacture: of utterly rejecting the materials and instruments that promote foreign luxury: of curing the expensiveness of pride, vanity, idleness, and gaming in our women; of introducing a vein of parsimony, prudence, and temperance: of learning to love our country, in the want of which we differ even from LAPLANDERS, and the inhabitants of TOPINAMBOO: of quitting our animosities and factions, nor acting any longer like the Jews, who were murdering one another at the very moment their city was taken: of being a little cautious not to sell our country and conscience for nothing: of teaching landlords to have at least one degree of mercy toward their tenants: lastly, of putting a spirit of honesty, industry, and skill into our shopkeepers; who, if a resolution could now be taken to buy only our native goods, would immediately unite to cheat and exact upon us in the price, the measure, and the goodness, nor could ever yet be brought to make one fair proposal of just dealing, though often and earnestly invited to it.

Therefore I repeat, let no man talk to me of these and the like expedients, till he has at least some glimpse of hope, that there will be ever some hearty and sincere attempt to put them in practice.

But, as to myself, having been wearied out for many years with offering vain, idle, visionary thoughts, and at length utterly despairing of success, I fortunately fell upon this proposal; which, as it is wholly new, so it has something solid and real, of no expense and little trouble, full in our own power, and whereby we can incur no danger in disobliging ENGLAND. For this kind of commodity will not bear exportation, the flesh being of too tender a consistence to admit a long continuance in salt, although perhaps I could name a country, which would be glad to eat up our whole nation without it.

After all, I am not so violently bent upon my own opinion as to reject any offer proposed by wise men, which shall be found equally innocent, cheap, easy, and effectual. But before something of that kind shall be advanced in contradiction to my scheme, and offering a better, I desire the author, or authors, will be pleased maturely to consider two points. First, as things now stand, how they will be able to find food and raiment for a hundred thousand useless mouths and backs. And, secondly, there being a round million of creatures in human figure throughout this kingdom, whose whole subsistence put into a common stock would leave them in debt two millions of pounds sterling, adding those who are beggars by profession, to the bulk of farmers, cottagers, and labourers, with the wives and children who are beggars in effect; I desire those politicians who dislike my overture, and may perhaps be so bold as to attempt an answer, that they will first ask the parents of these mortals, whether they would not at this day think it a great happiness to have been sold for food at a year old, in the manner I prescribe, and thereby have avoided such a perpetual scene of misfortunes, as they have since gone through, by the oppression of landlords, the impossibility of paying rent without money or trade, the want of common sustenance, with neither house nor clothes to cover them from the inclemencies of the weather, and the most inevitable prospect of entailing the like, or greater miseries, upon their breed for ever.

I profess, in the sincerity of my heart, that I have not the least personal interest in endeavouring to promote this necessary work, having no other motive than the public good of my country, by advancing our trade, providing for infants, relieving the poor, and giving some pleasure to the rich. I have no children by which I can propose to get a single penny; the youngest being nine years old, and my wife past child-bearing.

Exercise

1. The Irish complained that "the English are devouring the Irish." Swift turned the metaphor into "A Modest Proposal." Forgetting the actual subject matter for the moment, is this proposal rational and practical? Will it help relieve poverty by reducing the population while increasing family incomes? If you answered these questions in the affirmative you are beginning to appreciate the intellectual nature of satire, for satire must be logical and persuasive if it is to accomplish its purpose. The plan is made all the more horrible by Swift's dispassionate tone and flawless logic.

Thomas Gray (1716–1771)

A quiet and solitary professor of modern history at Cambridge, Thomas Gray was a thorough scholar in the classics, old Welsh and Norse literature, and even read Shakespeare, though many classicists at the time regarded the Bard as half barbaric. An expert literary critic, Gray seemed to have criticized his poetry before he wrote it and therefore wrote little. By far his best-known work, his *Elegy* is loved by unsophisticated readers the world over and, paradoxically, is admired by literary critics. It is a classic poem in the classical style: artfully subtle, with a firm control of imagery, cadence, and mood.

Literary Selection

ELEGY WRITTEN IN A COUNTRY CHURCHYARD
Thomas Gray

The curfew tolls the knell of parting day,
    The lowing herd wind slowly o'er the lea,
The plowman homeward plods his weary way,
    And leaves the world to darkness and to me.

Now fades the glimmering landscape on the sight,   5
    And all the air a solemn stillness holds,
Save where the beetle wheels his droning flight,
    And drowsy tinklings lull the distant folds;

Save that from yonder ivy-mantled tow'r,
    The moping owl does to the moon complain   10
Of such as, wand'ring near her secret bow'r,
    Molest her ancient solitary reign.

Beneath those rugged elms, that yew-tree's shade,
    Where heaves the turf in many a mould'ring heap,   15
Each in his narrow cell forever laid,
    The rude forefathers of the hamlet sleep.

The breezy call of incense-breathing Morn,
    The swallow twitt'ring from the straw-built shed,
The cock's shrill clarion, or the echoing horn,
    No more shall rouse them from their lowly bed.   20

For them no more the blazing hearth shall burn,
   Or busy housewife ply her evening care;
No children run to lisp their sire's return,
   Or climb his knees the envied kiss to share.

Oft did the harvest to their sickle yield,   25
   Their furrow oft the stubborn glebe has broke;
How jocund did they drive their team afield!
   How bow'd the woods beneath their sturdy stroke!

Let not Ambition mock their useful toil,
   Their homely joys, and destiny obscure;   30
Nor Grandeur hear with a disdainful smile
   The short and simple annals of the poor.

The boast of heraldry, the pomp of pow'r,
   And all that beauty, all that wealth e'er gave,
Await alike th' inevitable hour.   35
   The paths of glory lead but to the grave.

Nor you, ye proud, impute to these the fault,
   If Mem'ry o'er their tomb no trophies raise,
Where thro' the long-drawn aisle and fretted vault
   The pealing anthem swells the note of praise.   40

Can storied urn, or animated bust,
   Back to its mansion call the fleeting breath?
Can Honour's voice provoke the silent dust,
   Or Flatt'ry soothe the dull cold ear of death?

Perhaps in this neglected spot is laid   45
   Some heart once pregnant with celestial fire,
Hands, that the rod of empire might have sway'd,
   Or wak'd to ecstasy the living lyre.

But Knowledge to their eyes her ample page
   Rich with the spoils of time did ne'er unroll;   50
Chill Penury repress'd their noble rage,
   And froze the genial current of the soul.

Full many a gem of purest ray serene
   The dark unfathom'd caves of ocean bear;
Full many a flower is born to blush unseen,   55
   And waste its sweetness on the desert air.

Some village Hampden, that with dauntless breast
   The little Tyrant of his fields withstood,
Some mute inglorious Milton here may rest,
   Some Cromwell guiltless of his country's blood.   60

Th' applause of list'ning senates to command,
   The threats of pain and ruin to despise,
To scatter plenty o'er a smiling land,
   And read their hist'ry in a nation's eyes,

Their lot forbade: nor circumscrib'd alone   65
   Their growing virtues, but their crimes confin'd;
Forbade to wade thro' slaughter to a throne,
   And shut the gates of mercy on mankind;

The struggling pangs of conscious truth to hide,
   To quench the blushes of ingenuous shame,   70
Or heap the shrine of Luxury and Pride
   With incense kindled at the Muse's flame.

Far from the madding crowd's ignoble strife,
   Their sober wishes never learn'd to stray;
Along the cool sequester'd vale of life   75
   They kept the noiseless tenor of their way.

Yet ev'n these bones from insult to protect
   Some frail memorial still erected nigh,
With uncouth rhymes and shapeless sculpture deck'd
   Implores the passing tribute of a sigh.   80

Their name, their years, spelt by th' unletter'd Muse,
   The place of fame and elegy supply;
And many a holy text around she strews,
   That teach the rustic moralist to die.

For who, to dumb Forgetfulness a prey,   85
   This pleasing anxious being e'er resign'd,

Left the warm precincts of the cheerful day,
   Nor cast one longing, ling'ring look behind?

On some fond breast the parting soul relies,
   Some pious drops the closing eye requires;   90
Ev'n from the tomb the voice of Nature cries,
   Ev'n in our ashes live their wonted fires.

For thee, who, mindful of th' unhonour'd dead,
   Dost in these lines their artless tale relate;
If chance, by lonely Contemplation led,   95
   Some kindred spirit shall enquire thy fate,—

Haply some hoary-headed swain may say,
   "Oft have we seen him at the peep of dawn
Brushing with hasty steps the dews away,
   To meet the sun upon the upland lawn: 100

"There at the foot of yonder nodding beech,
   That wreathes its old fantastic roots so high,
His listless length at noontide would he stretch,
   And pore upon the brook that babbles by.

"Hard by yon wood, now smiling as in scorn,   105
   Mutt'ring his wayward fancies he would rove;
Now drooping, woeful-wan, like one forlorn,
   Or craz'd with care, or cross'd in hopeless love.

"One morn I miss'd him on the custom'd hill,
   Along the heath, and near his fav'rite tree;   110
Another came; nor yet beside the rill,
   Nor up the lawn, nor at the wood was he;

"The next, with dirges due in sad array,
   Slow through the church-way path we saw him
      borne:—
Approach and read (for thou canst read) the lay   115
   Grav'd on the stone beneath yon aged thorn."

THE EPITAPH

Here rests his head upon the lap of Earth,
   A youth, to Fortune and to Fame unknown:
Fair Science frown'd not on his humble birth,
   And Melancholy mark'd him for her own.   120

Large was his bounty, and his soul sincere,
   Heav'n did a recompense as largely send:
He gave to Mis'ry all he had, a tear,
   He gain'd from Heav'n ('t was all he wish'd)
      a friend.

No farther seek his merits to disclose,   125
   Or draw his frailties from their dread abode,
(There they alike in trembling hope repose,)
   The bosom of his Father and his God.

Exercises

1. Notice at the beginning of the poem some of
   the words used to establish the melancholy
   mood: *parting, lowing, slowly, weary, darkness.*
   What are some of the other words and images?
2. Does the poem prefer obscurity and ignorance
   to wealth and knowledge? Why?
3. What is the central argument of the poem?
   Consider the type of poem being written and
   where it is composed.
4. The poem is gently melancholy but is it
   pessimistic? Is it, in other words, despairing or
   plaintive?

Voltaire (François Marie de Arouet; 1694–1778)

As philosopher, critic, and writer, Voltaire was the leading intellectual figure of the Enlightenment. A tireless opponent of the Church and the *ancien regime* of the Bourbon kings, he was twice imprisoned in the Bastille (1717, 1726) and exiled in 1726. His studies in England of Newton and Locke reinforced his hatred of absolutism and heightened his admiration of English liberalism. Upon his return to France he published a veritable torrent of works that criticized all of the existing conditions. Whereas Pope had written, "Whatever is, is right," Voltaire's motto might well have been, "Whatever is, is wrong." Particularly did he think that everything was wrong in France.

Voltaire sought his freedom at first in Berlin at the court of Frederick the Great, where he lived for three years, but he could not get along with the German king any better than he had with the French king. So he established himself near Geneva, where he spent most of the last quarter century of his life. One may well question Voltaire's sincerity, for he was always concerned with his personal comfort and wealth; he certainly could not have been too much concerned with the cause of universal freedom when he went to Berlin and sought to make his permanent home under the protection of Frederick. But whatever one may say of his personal life, his doubting and skeptical works found a wide audience. Of all of his writing, and there is an incredible amount of it, *Candide* is probably the best-known work.

The tone of *Candide* is as important as anything Voltaire has to say, for he holds up to ridicule everything which the Europe of the time held dear. By his very tone, Voltaire shows himself to be the debunker of his time. The trouble with Voltaire is the trouble with all debunkers: he has little better to offer. As he looks at his world, everything seems futile and silly: the glories of war; the church, either Catholic or Protestant; even nature itself. They are all senseless and unreasonable. When it is all over, the best that he can suggest is retirement to the farm, where at least one can cultivate one's garden. One may remark in passing that this is far from a complete answer in the face of chaotic conditions; but, lacking such a complete answer, it is much better than none. The development of one's own life and the minding of one's own business may be better than mistaken activity.

Most of Voltaire's values are negative, and he did much to contribute to the confusion of his time, for he brought the faults of his age into sharp focus. That, however, was of value in itself, for he helped in bringing about the revolutions which upset the old order of absolutism. Perhaps the painter Jacques Louis David best summed up Voltaire's legacy to his country. During the ceremony of July 10, 1791, when Voltaire's body was transferred to an honored place in the Pantheon, David said, simply: "He taught us to be free."

Thomas Jefferson (1743–1826)

The American Revolution (1775–1783) was hailed throughout the world as the first significant triumph of rationalism. The causes of the uprising were certainly as much economic as ideological yet liberal, rational beliefs were expressed in this war against absolutism and the imposition of authority upon people who had little voice in their own government. One of the clearest voices of the new nation was that of Thomas Jefferson, author of the Declaration of Independence, third president of the United States, and the founder of the University of Virginia, the last being, for Jefferson, his most significant achievement. Jefferson's address upon first assuming the presidency is a masterful speech that effectively summarizes the ideals of the Enlightenment.

Literary Selection

FIRST INAUGURAL ADDRESS
Thomas Jefferson

During the contest of opinion through which we have passed, the animation of discussions and of exertions has sometimes worn an aspect which might impose on strangers unused to think freely and to speak and to write what they think; but this being now decided by the voice of the nation, announced according to the rules of the constitution, all will, of course, arrange themselves under the will of the law, and unite in common efforts for the common good. All, too, will bear in mind this sacred principle, that though the will of the majority is in all cases to prevail, that will, to be rightful, must be reasonable; that the minority possess their equal rights, which equal laws must protect, and to violate which would be oppression. Let us, then, fellow citizens, unite with one heart and one mind. Let us restore to social intercourse that harmony and affection without which liberty and even life itself are but dreary things. And let us reflect that having banished from our land that religious intolerance under which mankind so long bled and suffered, we have yet gained little if we countenance a political intolerance as despotic, as wicked, and capable of as bitter and bloody persecutions. During the throes and convulsions of the ancient world, during the agonizing spasms of infuriated men, seeking through blood and slaughter his long-lost liberty, it was not wonderful that the agitation of the billows should reach even this distant and peaceful shore; that this should be more felt and feared by some and less by others; that this should divide opinions as to measures of safety. But every difference of opinion is not a difference of principle. We have called by different names brethren of the same principle. We are all republicans—we are all federalists. If there be any among us who would wish to dissolve this Union or to change its republican form, let them stand undisturbed as monuments of the safety with which error of opinion may be tolerated where reason is left free to combat it. I know, indeed, that some honest men fear that a republican government cannot be strong; that this government is not strong enough. But would the honest patriot, in the full tide of successful experiment, abandon a government which has so far kept us free and firm, on the theoretic and visionary fear that this government, the world's best hope, may by possibility want energy to preserve itself? I trust not. I believe this, on the contrary, the strongest government on earth. I believe it is the only one where every man, at the call of the law, would fly to the standard of the law, and would meet invasions of the public order as his own personal concern. Sometimes it is said that man cannot be trusted with the government of himself. Can he, then, be trusted with the government of others? Or have we found angels in the form of kings to govern him? Let history answer this question.

Let us, then, with courage and confidence pursue our own federal and republican principles, our attachment to our union and representative government. Kindly separated by nature and a wide ocean from the exterminating havoc of one quarter of the globe; too high-minded to endure the degradations of the others; possessing a chosen country, with room enough for our descendants to the hundredth and thousandth generation; entertaining a due sense of our equal right to the use of our own faculties, to the acquisitions of our own industry, to honor and confidence from our fellow citizens, resulting not from birth but from our actions and their sense of them; enlightened by a benign religion, professed, indeed, and practiced in various forms, yet all of them inculcating honesty, truth, temperance, gratitude, and the love of man; acknowledging and adoring an overruling Providence, which by all its dispensations proves that it delights in the happiness of man here and his greater happiness hereafter; with all these blessings, what more is necessary to make us a happy and a prosperous people? Still one thing more, fellow citizens—a wise and frugal government, which shall restrain men from injuring one another, shall leave them otherwise free to regulate their own pursuits of industry and improvement, and shall not take from the mouth of labor the bread it has earned. This is the sum of good government, and this is necessary to close the circle of our felicities.

About to enter, fellow citizens, on the exercise of duties which comprehend everything dear and valuable to you, it is proper that you should understand what I deem the essential principles of our government, and consequently those which ought to shape its administration. I will compress them within the narrowest compass they will bear, stating the general principle, but not all its limitations. Equal and exact justice to all men, of whatever state or persuasion, religious or political; peace, commerce, and honest friendship, with all nations—entangling alliances with none; the support of the state governments in all their rights, as the most competent administrations for our domestic concerns and the surest bulwarks against anti-republican tendencies; the preservation of the general government in its whole constitutional vigor, as the sheet anchor of our peace at home and safety abroad; a jealous care of the right of election by the people—a mild and safe corrective of abuses which are lopped by the sword of revolution

where peaceable remedies are unprovided; absolute acquiescence in the decisions of the majority—the vital principle of republics, from which is no appeal but to force, the vital principles and immediate parent of despotism; a well-disciplined militia—our best reliance in peace and for the first moments of war, till regulars may relieve them; the supremacy of the civil over the military authority; economy in the public expense, that labor may be lightly burdened; the honest payment of our debts and sacred preservation of the public faith; encouragement of agriculture, and of commerce as its handmaid: the diffusion of information and arraignment of all abuses at the bar of public reason; freedom of religion; freedom of the press; and freedom of person under the protection of the *habeas corpus;* and trial by juries impartially selected—these principles form the bright constellation which has gone before us, and guided our steps through an age of revolution and reformation. The wisdom of our sages and the blood of our heroes have been devoted to their attainment. They should be the creed of our political faith—the text of civil instruction—the touchstone by which to try the services of these we trust; and should we wander from them in moments of error or alarm, let us hasten to retrace our steps and to regain the road which alone leads to peace, liberty, and safety.

I repair, then, fellow citizens, to the post you have assigned me. With experience enough in subordinate offices to have seen the difficulties of this, the greatest of all, I have learned to expect that it will rarely fall to the lot of imperfect man to retire from this station with the reputation and the favor which bring him to it. Without pretentions to that high confidence you reposed in our first and great revolutionary character, whose preeminent services had entitled him to the first place in his country's love, and destined for him the fairest page in the volume of faithful history, I ask so much confidence only as may give firmness and effect to the legal administration of your affairs. I shall often go wrong through defect of judgment. When right, I shall often be thought wrong by those whose positions will not command a view of the whole ground. I ask your indulgence for my own errors, which will never be intentional; and your support against the errors of others, who may condemn what they would not if seen in all its parts. The approbation implied by your suffrage is a consolation to me for the past; and my future solicitude will be to retain the good opinion of those who have bestowed it in advance, to conciliate that of others by doing them all the good in my power and to be instrumental to the happiness and freedom of all.

Relying, then, on the patronage of your good will, I advance with obedience to the work, ready to retire from it whenever you become sensible how much better choice it is in your power to make. And may that Infinite Power which rules the destinies of the universe, lead our councils to what is best, and give them a favorable issue for your peace and prosperity.

Time Chart for the Early Modern World, 1600–1789

	1600	1650	1700	1750	1800

Artists and Musicians

Inigo Jones 1573–1652
Caravaggio 1573–1610
Rubens 1577–1640
Hals 1580/85–1666
Poussin 1594–1665
Bernini 1598–1680
Zurburan 1598–1640
Velasquez 1599–1660
Borromini 1599–1644
van Dyck 1599–1641
Rembrandt 1606–1669
Leyster 1609–1660
Ruisdael 1628–1682
Vermeer 1632–1675
Wren 1632–1723
Mansart 1646–1708
Corelli 1653–1713
Couperin 1668–1733
Watteau 1684–1721
Bach 1685–1750
Vivaldi 1685–1743
Chardin 1699–1779
Boucher 1703–1770
Gainsborough 1727–1788
Fragonard 1732–1806
Haydn 1732–1809
Houdon 1741–1828
Jefferson 1743–1826
David 1748–1825
Stuart 1755–1828
Mozart 1756–1791
Canova 1757–1822
Beethoven 1770–1827

Literary Figures

Donne 1573–1631
Milton 1608–1674
Marvell 1621–1678
Swift 1667–1745
Pope 1688–1744
Montesquieu 1689–1755
Voltaire 1694–1778
Diderot 1713–1784
Gray 1716–1771
Rousseau 1718–1778

Philosophers and Scientists

- Bacon 1561–1626
- Galileo 1564–1642
- Hobbes 1588–1679
- Descartes 1596–1650
- Locke 1632–1704
- Spinoza 1632–1677
- Newton 1641–1727
- Halley 1656–1742
- Hume 1711–1776
- Kant 1724–1804

Rulers

England
- James I 1603–1625
- Charles I 1625–1649
- Cromwell 1649–1659
- Charles II 1660–1685
- James II 1685–1688
- William & Mary 1688–1702
- Anne 1702–1714
- George I 1714–1727
- George II 1727–1760
- George III 1760–1820

France
- Louis XIV 1643–1715
- Louis XV 1715–1774
- Louis XVI 1774–1793

Prussia
- Frederick I 1701–1713
- Frederick William I 1713–1740
- Frederick the Great 1740–1786

Russia
- Peter the Great 1682–1725
- Catherine the Great 1762–1791

Events

- Founding of English East India Co. 1600
- Netherlands revolt from Spain 1609
- Thirty Years War 1618–1648
- Galileo condemned by Inquisition 1632
- Revocation of Edict of Nantes 1685
- *Principia* by Newton 1687
- England's Glorious Revolution 1688
- Diderot's *Encyclopedia* 1747–1772
- Watt's improved steam engine 1775
- American revolution 1775–1783
- *Wealth of Nations* 1776
- French revolution 1789–1815

18

Art: Baroque, Rococo, and Neoclassic

The Baroque Age, ca. 1580–1700

An age of expansion following the Renaissance era of discovery, the Baroque was a time of conflicts and contradictions that encompassed extremes: Louis XIV and Rembrandt; Bernini and Descartes; Milton and Bach. In architecture and the visual arts the Baroque began in the last quarter of the sixteenth century and extended into the eighteenth, culminating in the supreme expression of the Baroque: the music of Bach and Handel (see chap. 19).

The characteristics of Baroque art are movement, intensity, tension, and energy, traits that are perhaps more natural to music than to the more static arts of painting, sculpture, and architecture. Nevertheless, revolutionary innovations in all of the arts produced a Baroque style that can be extravagant, excessive, or even grotesque. Baroque art has a fascination all its own, particularly when it is not judged by such other standards as, for example, the classical canons of balance, restraint, and control of the High Renaissance style.

The sometimes contradictory variations of the Baroque style can be studied in terms of three broad categories of patrons: the Counter-Reformation Church of Rome; the aristocratic courts of Louis XIV of France and the Stuarts of England; and the bourgeois merchants of Holland. Though drive, intensity, and contrast are common characteristics of all Baroque art, the style will be considered here as reactions to the needs of these patrons and labeled Counter-Reformation, Aristocratic, and Bourgeois Baroque art.

Counter-Reformation Baroque

Founded in 1534 by Ignatius of Loyola, the Society of Jesus (Jesuits) formed the spearhead of the Counter-Reformation. The mother church of the order, Il Gesu (Church of Jesus) was the first building in the new style, becoming a model for church design throughout the Catholic world,

Figure 18.1 G. B. Vignola (plan) and G. C. della Porta (facade), Il Gesu, 1568–1584, Rome.

especially in Latin America (fig. 18.1). The four pairs of pilasters on each level visually stabilize the facade and add a rhythmic punctuation that the evenly spaced columns of the classical style do not have (see fig. 3.44). Baroque architecture, from its very beginning, is characterized by the strong accents of paired columns or pilasters. The dramatic effect of paired pilaster and column framing a central portal under a double cornice exemplifies the theatricality of the Baroque style, making the entrance seem like an invitation to hurry into the church. The proportions of the two stories and the framing volutes are derived from Alberti's Santa Maria Novella (see fig. 14.11), while the classical pediment is reminiscent of Alberti and Palladio (see fig. 14.36). Il Gesu is not a wholly new design but rather a skillful synthesis of existing elements into a new and dramatic style.

In the interior (fig. 18.2), chapels recessed in the walls replace side aisles, making the richly decorated central space a theatre for the enactment of the Lord's Supper. Light pours through the dome windows and upon the high altar in this architectural embodiment of the militant and mystical Society of Jesus.

The twin towers of the Cathedral of Salzburg (fig. 18.3) characterize a style of Baroque architecture prevalent north of the Alps, in Latin America, and in the Western United States. When covered with stucco whitewashed a gleaming white, this style of Baroque became California Mission architecture. Anchored by paired pilasters on both sides, the facade is set back from the bold towers framing a two-level front that climaxes in an elaborately designed pediment embellished with sculptures. The large flat surface areas of this Early Baroque church will, in later buildings, be filled with niches and sculpture to create a more elaborate and restless facade (see fig. 18.9).

The Baroque style of painting appeared abruptly in the person of the northern Italian artist called Caravaggio (ca-ra-VOD-jo; 1573–1610), perhaps the first artist to deliberately shock not only the public but also his fellow artists. The most important Italian painter

Figure 18.2 Interior, Il Gesu

Figure 18.3 Solari, Cathedral of Salzburg, 1614, Austria.

of the seventeenth century, Caravaggio was militantly opposed to classical concepts like clarity and restraint. Using chiaroscuro and nonrealistic dramatic lighting, his paintings had an intense psychological impact that profoundly influenced most Baroque artists, including Rembrandt and Velasquez. In his *Crucifixion of St. Peter* (fig. 18.4), Caravaggio placed his

Figure 18.4 Caravaggio, *Crucifixion of St. Peter,* 1601. Oil on canvas, 90 × 69″. Santa Maria del Popolo, Rome.

figures in the immediate foreground, starkly outlined against an indeterminate background. Sentenced by the Romans to die on the cross, Peter insisted that he, unlike his Master, must be crucified upside down and we, viewing the agonizing scene at eye level, are drawn inexorably into the violence of the tragedy. The details are realistic, from the dirty feet of one executioner to the nail-pierced feet of Peter. The composition is designed for maximum impact. In the complex interplay of the slashing diagonals the figure of Peter is completely depicted, while the three executioners are shown only partially. The lighting is theatrical, intensifying a dramatic effect made more vivid by Caravaggio's innovative use of chiaroscuro.

Caravaggio's life was as dramatic as his art. A man of violent passions, he killed another man in a fight and, badly wounded, fled Rome for Naples. Later thrown into prison, he violated his oath of obedience and escaped to Sicily, but later returned to Naples where he was nearly fatally wounded in another fight. Destitute and ill with malaria, he died during a violent rage over a misunderstanding on the very day that his papal pardon was announced. In sharp contrast to his turbulent life, his *Supper at Emmaus* (fig. 18.5) is a low-keyed, personal drama. As recounted in Luke 24: 28–31, Christ was invited to supper by two of his disciples who, at the moment that he raised his hand to bless the food, recognized their risen Lord. The disciple on the left raises his hands in astonishment, while the other clutches the corner of the table. Unaware of the import of the discovery, the two servants

Figure 18.5 Caravaggio, *Supper at Emmaus,* ca. 1600. Oil on canvas, 69 × 55½″. (Brera Museum, Milan.)

Figure 18.6 Gianlorenzo Bernini, *David,* 1623. Marble, life size. Borghese Gallery, Rome.

are puzzled but dutiful. Set against a dark background, the eye-level composition invites the viewer to participate, to sit at the table between the two disciples.

In his life and in his art Caravaggio was at odds with his time, but Gianlorenzo Bernini (bear-NEE-nee; 1598–1680) was the Counter-Reformation personified. A superbly gifted sculptor/architect with a virtuosity comparable to that of Michelangelo, Bernini was regarded in his own century as not only its best artist but also its greatest man. He himself saw that his renown would decline with the waning of Counter-Reformation energy, but his emotional art has now regained some of its luster. His *David* (fig. 18.6) is a young warrior tensely poised over his discarded armor and harp, every muscle strained to hurl the fatal stone at an unseen Goliath, who seems to be approaching from behind and above the level of the viewer. When compared with Michelangelo's *David* (see colorplate 26) we experience the intense energy of the Baroque, so much so that there is an impulse to leap out of the way of the stone missile. The bit lip is Bernini's own expression as copied from a mirror, and realism is further heightened by the grip of David's foot on the actual base of the statue.

Rome was Bernini's city and he left his stamp on it literally everywhere, but nowhere so effectively as in his enhancement of St. Peter's (fig. 18.7). The oval piazza, together with the embracing arms of the colossal colonnade, form a spectacular entrance to the

Figure 18.7 St. Peter's Basilica, Rome. Apse and dome by Michelangelo (1547–1564); nave and facade by Carlo Maderno (1607–1626); Colonnade and piazza by Gianlorenzo Bernini (1617–1667).

largest church in Christendom. The 284 massive Doric columns are 39′ high and are topped with 15′ statues of 96 saints, demarcating a piazza that can accommodate about 250,000 people. Bernini used the pavement design, the Egyptian obelisk, and the two fountains to unify the piazza and give it human scale.

Once in the awesome nave of the church, the visitor is surrounded by other manifestations of Bernini's genius: monumental sculptures, the Throne of St. Peter, elegant relief carvings, even the patterned marble floor. Under Michelangelo's soaring dome stands the Baldacchino (ball-da-KEY-no; fig. 18.8), an 85′-high canopy over the tomb of St. Peter. The title is derived from the Italian: *baldacco* is a silk cloth draped as a canopy over important people or places. In this case, the drapery is bronze as is the entire canopy, including the intricate designs covering the four columns. The Baldacchino was commissioned by the Barberini pope Urban VIII, who ordered the bronze plates removed from the dome of the Pantheon (see colorplate 8) and melted down, prompting the pope's physician to remark that, "What the barbarians didn't do the Barberini did." Bernini patterned the serpentine column design after the twisted marble columns saved from Old St. Peter's, which were thought by Constantine to have survived from King Solomon's Temple. Some critics refer to the Baldacchino as architecture and others as sculpture; in either case, it is an artistic triumph under difficult circumstances. It had to be large enough to be significant under Michelangelo's enormous dome but not disproportionate to the size of the nave. Bernini himself called the solution one that "came out well by luck."

Bernini was Pope Urban VIII's favorite, but by no means the only artist supported by the lavish building program that drained the Vatican treasury. One of Bernini's severest critics was the rival architect Francesco Borromini (BOR-o-ME-nee; 1599–1644), a brooding and introspective genius who resented Bernini's favored status and grand reputation. Rejecting Bernini's predilection for rich marbles and lavishly painted stucco, Borromini concentrated on the interplay of elaborate curves and lines. In the small monastic Church of S. Carlo alle Quattro Fontane (fig. 18.9), Borromini used a series of intersecting ellipses in an undulating facade richly embellished with columns, sculpture, plaques, and scrolls, all in stone and relying for their effect on design rather than on opulent materials. The impression of restless, mystical passion must have had great appeal, for this small Baroque church was emulated throughout southern Europe.

The appeal of Bernini's *Ecstasy of St. Theresa* (fig. 18.10) is emotional, mystical, spiritual, and, withal, palpably sensual. Based on the writings of St. Theresa, the Spanish mystic, the saint is depicted in the throes of rapture as the angel is about to pierce her with the golden arrow of Divine Love. Epitomizing the Roman High Baroque, the altarpiece has become a stage for a theatrical work of intense religiosity, a visual counterpart of the *Spiritual Exercises* of Ignatius of Loyola that Bernini himself practiced every day.

Figure 18.8 Gianlorenzo Bernini, Baldacchino, 1624–1633. St. Peter's Basilica, Rome.

Figure 18.9 Francesco Borromini, S. Carlo alle Quattro Fontane, begun 1638. Rome.

Figure 18.10 Gianlorenzo Bernini, *Ecstasy of St. Theresa,*
1645–1652. Marble and gilt, life size. Cornaro Chapel, Sta.
Maria della Vittoria, Rome.

Figure 18.11 Baldassare Longhena, Sta. Maria della Salute,
1631–1687, Venice.

Figure 18.12 A. Tremignon and E. Meyring, Church of San
Moise, on the Grand Canal, Venice.

The Roman Baroque style, with regional variations, became dominant throughout Catholic Europe.
In Venice, Baldassare Longhena's (1598–1682)
Church of Sta. Maria della Salute (fig. 18.11) was built
at the entrance to the Grand Canal, becoming one of
the landmarks of that opulent city. Truly Baroque
mainly in its multiplicity of shapes and forms, the
church also reflects local Byzantine and Renaissance
principles, even including a Roman triumphal arch for
the main facade at the right. The lofty dome is supported by eighteen huge spiral buttresses that appear
to be derived from the modest volutes of Il Gesu (see
fig. 18.1).

With all its splendor, complexity, and opulence,
the Baroque became the reigning style throughout the
Catholic world. That does not mean, however, that
every Baroque church was well designed. Lesser architects adopted elements of the style, but failed to
achieve the artistic effect of, say, a Borromini design.
The Church of San Moise (fig. 18.12) is a case in point;
Baroque has run amok. The facade is a compendium
of every Baroque characteristic and device of the time,
designed to be "Baroque." The intention was earnest
but the effect is stultifying, a kind of negative testimony to the architectural genius of artists like Bernini
and Borromini.

The fervent mysticism of Counter-Reformation
Spain was expressed in the Mannerism of El Greco
(see chap. 14) and, in the seventeenth century, in the
art of Francisco de Zurbarán (zoor-ba-RAHN;
1598–1664). Influenced by Caravaggio though he

never studied in Italy, Zurbarán translates spiritual
ideas into poetic visual reality. His *Agnus Dei* (fig.
18.13) presents the Lamb of God as a symbol of Christ
the perpetual sacrifice. With loving attention to detail
he contrasts the delicate curls with the altar cloth,
emphasizing the serenity of the sacrifice and the severity of the site. Reflecting the tenets of the Qui-
etists, the most mystical of Spanish sects, the mood
encompasses passivity, spiritual solitude, faith, and
silence in the presence of God.

Unlike his Spanish contemporaries, Diego Velasquez (ve-LASS-kis; 1599–1660) was not interested in
religious subjects. Allegorical figures, swirling clouds,
and rhapsodic faces were never a part of a unique style
that was concerned with nature and the optical effects
of light. During his studies in Italy he became fascinated with the paintings of Titian and Tintoretto, but
cared not at all for the style of Raphael, nor was he

Figure 18.13 Francisco de Zurbarán, *Agnus Dei*, 1635–1640. Oil on canvas, 20½ × 13¼″. The San Diego Museum of Art. San Diego, California.

Figure 18.14 Diego Velasquez, *Maids of Honor (Las Meninas)*, 1656. Oil on canvas, 10′5″ × 9′. Prado Museum, Madrid.

influenced by Rubens even though the latter was a personal friend. A court painter to King Philip IV for thirty years, Velasquez worked with the effects of light on objects and colors, producing candid portraits that never descended to the level of common courtly pictures. His *Maids of Honor* (fig. 18.14) is his acknowledged masterpiece and one of the most celebrated works of the century. The painting is a symphony of deep pictorial space, light, and images of reality, from what we actually see in the room to the implied presence of the king and queen, whose images are reflected in the mirror. The painter himself looks back at us as he works on a painting that is probably the one at which we are looking. At the front of the picture plane, light falls on the dog with the child's foot placed on its back, on the court dwarf, and, in the near foreground, on the Infanta Margarita and her two attendants. Standing behind a lady-in-waiting and wearing the cross of the Order of Santiago, the artist pauses with paintbrush poised; slightly deeper in the middle ground we see a couple engaged in conversation. The mirror on the back wall reveals the presence of the artist's patrons and, behind the courtier in the open doorway, space recedes to infinity. What looks at first like a genre scene in the artist's studio is actually a stunning spacial composition of five or six receding planes. As it is usually displayed in the Prado Museum, the painting faces a mirror on the opposite wall in which the spectator sees an electrifying image of receding space, an illusion that further confuses reality because the mirror includes the viewer as part of the painting. Space was a major preoccupation of the Baroque from the large interior space of Baroque churches to the great piazza fronting St. Peter's and the fascinating illusion of deep space in the *Maids of Honor.*

Aristocratic Baroque

Peter Paul Rubens (1577–1640) lived during an age marked by extremes. Galileo, Kepler, and Descartes were helping shape a new vision of the world, but there was also the dark and bloody side of witchcraft

trials, the Inquisition, and the ferocious Thirty Years' War. Throughout his entire lifetime Rubens's own country, the Netherlands, was engaged in a struggle for independence from Spain, and yet Rubens painted works that jubilantly praised the human spirit and celebrated the beauty of the natural world. He was not indifferent to human suffering—far from it—but his temperament was wholly sunny and positive. He possessed a rare combination of good health, good looks, good sense, a talent for business, phenomenal artistic ability, and a remarkable intellect. He was fluent in six modern languages and classical Latin, and was reputed to be capable of listening to a learned lecture while painting, conversing, and dictating letters. One of the most gifted and accomplished painters who ever lived, Rubens amassed a fortune and enjoyed it all.

In only eight years of study in Italy, Rubens mastered the classical style of ancient Rome plus those of the High and Late Renaissance. Upon completing a series of paintings for Marie de' Medici, the Dowager Queen of France, he established his reputation as the preeminent painter for kings, nobles, and princes of the church. His *Assumption of the Virgin* (colorplate 33), though considerably smaller than his many giant works, is filled with the boundless energy that characterizes all his work. The diametric opposite of Caravaggio's stark realism, the figures are richly and colorfully garbed, with pink and chubby cherubs and solicitous angels effortlessly wafting the Virgin into heaven. The rich sensual quality of Rubens's work was prized by aristocratic patrons and by the church; glamour, splendor, and glory gave favorable answers to the doubts and questions of the faithful, assuring them that heaven and earth alike were equally beautiful.

In his large-scale *Rape of the Daughters of Leucippus* (colorplate 34), Rubens depicts Castor and Pollux, the sons of Jupiter, abducting two mortal maidens with whom they have fallen in love. In a design like an ascending spiral, Rubens has built his colors up in rich, contrasting textures: the luminous flesh of the opulent bodies; the deeply tanned, muscular gods; sparkling armor; and shimmering horse-flesh. The low horizon increases the illusion of the ascension to the realm of the gods and adds to the buoyancy of a composition that is explosive with energy. Only the passive cupid is isolated from the intense action. The nudes are designed to complement each other, adding to the balance of the composition; what is concealed in one is revealed in the other.

No one knows how many assistants Rubens employed in his huge studio in Antwerp. As a court painter he paid no guild tax and therefore kept no records of the people who copied popular works or roughed out canvases that the master would complete and sell at a price based on the square footage and the personal contribution of Rubens. Of the few assistants who were successful in their own right, Anthony van Dyck (1599–1641) is by far the most notable. Unable to develop his talents in the overpowering presence of his teacher, van Dyck left to seek his fortune, which he found in abundance at the court of Charles I of England. With his aristocratic and refined style, van Dyck became the century's foremost portrait painter for court and church, producing elegant portrayals that always improved on the appearance of the model. While working in Genoa before settling down in the English court, van Dyck painted a portrait of the *Marchesa Elena Grimaldi* (fig. 18.15). A model of the art of portraiture in the grand manner, van Dyck designed the angled parasol to balance the dark mass at the bottom. Contributing to the illusion of the Marchesa's regal height, the classical columns add just the right touch of aristocratic confidence and dignity. Van Dyck had a unique ability to portray his subjects as they wished to appear without, however, stepping over the line to mere sycophancy.

Throughout his mature career Nicolas Poussin (poo-SAN; 1594–1665) painted in the grand manner but in a style entirely different from van Dyck and, especially, Rubens. Emphasizing line, lucidity, and control, Poussin chose only lofty subject matter drawn from ancient history, mythology, and biblical stories. He was an elitist, an aristocrat of paint and canvas, a French Classicist in an age of Romantic exuberance. Religious subject matter was treated, he thought, in a base and vulgar manner in most of the works by Caravaggio and his followers. Poussin's Baroque Classical style attracted followers just as did the quite different Baroque style of Rubens, touching off a controversy between "Rubenists" and "Poussinists" that may never be resolved. The basic disagreement was between color and line. Line and drawing were absolute values in representing things according to the Poussinists,

Figure 18.15 Anthony van Dyck, *Marchesa Elena Grimaldi,* ca. 1623. Oil on canvas, 97 × 68″. Widener Collection. National Gallery of Art, Washington, D.C.

and color was merely accidental because it depended on light. Color was, of course, what fascinated Rubens and his followers, who painted the colorful world as they perceived it, while the Poussinists constructed idealized forms of the world as it should be. Actually, the conflict was not just Rubenists versus Poussinists but the eternally opposing views of artists who were, in general, inclined towards romanticism as opposed to artists who were classically oriented. Romanticism in the nineteenth century is a stylistic period and is not to be confused with romantic or classical tendencies of artists in any period. When considered in very broad terms, the Renaissance was classically oriented, while the Baroque was inclined towards romanticism except, of course, for Poussin. Classicists emphasize objectivity, rationality, balance, and control; Romanticists stress subjectivity, nonrationality, and the restless expression of emotion. Leonardo, Raphael, Poussin, Haydn, and Mozart are classicists; Tintoretto, the later Michelangelo, El Greco, Rubens, Verdi, Tchaikovsky, and Delacroix are romanticists.

In *Holy Family on the Steps* (colorplate 35) Poussin has designed an upward-angled perspective that is enforced by the steps across the bottom of the painting. Reminiscent of Raphael's style that Poussin studied so assiduously, the triangular composition is slightly off center, putting the head of Christ almost precisely in the mathematical center of the painting.

Figure 18.16 Louis le Vau and Jules Hardouin Mansart, Palace of Versailles, 1669–1685.

Figure 18.17 East front, Palace of Versailles

From vases to temples the setting is Roman and the mode is derived, according to Poussin, from the *ethos* of the Greek musical scales (see chap. 4), which in this case may be the sweetly lyrical quality of the Ionic scale. Appearing at first to be starkly geometric, the drama and classical beauty of the work are apparent in the balance of solids and voids, cylinders and cubes, and in the balanced contrast of hard stone and soft foliage, drapery, and cooly supple flesh. To compare this work with *The Assumption of the Virgin* (see colorplate 33) is to perceive and to understand the difference between Classicism and Romanticism in the broad sense in which these terms are used here.

French tastes were attuned to a rationalized version of the Baroque as represented in the work of Poussin and, on a grand scale, in the royal palace at Versailles. Soon after Louis XIV assumed full control of the government (ca. 1661), French classicism was deliberately used to create a "royal style" that reinforced and enhanced the absolute rule of the king of France. Classical architecture has, since that time, been used by banks to indicate their financial stability and by rulers and dictators from Napoleon to Hitler, Mussolini, and Stalin to symbolize authority, control, and power.

Originally a hunting lodge for Louis XIII, the Palace at Versailles was rebuilt and vastly enlarged for Louis XIV, the self-styled Sun King whose power was so immense that he supposedly declared that *"L'etat, c'est moi"* (I am the state). He certainly said, "It is legal because I wish it." Designed initially by Louis le Vau (luh-VO; 1612–1670) and completed by Jules Hardouin Mansart (man-SAR; 1646–1708), the Palace was oriented along an east-west axis with the western front facing the extensive gardens (fig. 18.16). Far too large to photograph in its entirety, the view shown is of the southwest wing of the three-wing Garden Front. The design is basically classical, with three floors and windows equally spaced and lined up above each other in diminishing size from ground-level French doors to the square top windows. The paired Ionic columns on the two projecting fronts are Baroque and intended to enliven an exterior that would otherwise be bland and boring.

Facing squarely into the morning sun, the east front has three courts (fig. 18.17). The vast outer court extends from the ornamental outer gates (not shown) up to the pair of elevated classical temple fronts and was intended for court functionaries. Restricted to the

Figure 18.18 Marble Court, Palace of Versailles

nobility, the second court begins at the corner of the temple fronts and ends at the outer limit of the inner Marble Court (fig. 18.18). Used only by the royal family, this court faced the Royal Apartments, located on the top floor where the morning sun could greet the Sun King—and vice versa. Indeed, the "rising" *(levée)* was a major daily ritual attended by members of the court selected for the honor. The facade of the king's wing rises from Baroque paired columns on the ground floor through French doors above, and on up to the Royal Apartment on the top floor, surmounted by an elaborate sunburst, the latter a characteristic Baroque device possibly invented by Bernini for his Throne of St. Peter.

The vastness of the palace can be overpowering except when viewed as intended, as the principle structure set within the spacious formal gardens designed by André le Nôtre (lu NO-truh; 1613–1700), which are classical in every way except for Baroque scale and extension of space. Every flower, shrub, hedge, and tree is set precisely in place and enlivened by reflecting pools and 1,200 fountains, a superb setting for a king who imposed his will even upon nature. Since the king's minister of finance concealed the costs, there are no reliable figures on what it cost to build and maintain Versailles, but today the French government can afford to operate the fountains just during the summer tourist months, and then only on Sunday evenings.

Bourgeois Baroque

Dutch art flourished in an environment utterly unlike the regal splendor of France or the flamboyant Baroque of the southern Catholic countries. Freed at last from the Spanish yoke, Holland became a prosperous trading nation: Protestant, hardworking, and predominantly middle class. Calvinism opposed images in churches, and there was no royal court or hereditary nobility, meaning that there were no traditional patrons of the arts. The new patrons were private collectors and there were many. Just about everyone in the nation of nearly two million inhabitants wanted

Figure 18.19 Frans Hals, *Portrait of an Officer,* ca. 1640. Oil on canvas, 33¾ × 27". Andrew W. Mellon Collection. National Gallery of Art, Washington, D.C.

paintings for their living rooms, and schools at Amsterdam, Haarlem, Delft, and Utrecht labored to supply a demand somewhat comparable to the Golden Age of Greece or fifteenth-century Florence.

The first of the great Dutch masters, Frans Hals (1580/85–1666) was one of history's most brilliant portraitists. There is no precedent for the liveliness of his canvases or the spontaneous brilliance of his brushwork. In *Portrait of an Officer* (fig. 18.19), a portly gentleman with hand on hip, his head jauntily tilted, stares at the viewer. Large surfaces are treated casually but the lacework is delicately precise. Not a deep character study, this is a portrait of a passing acquaintance captured in a brief moment but rendered as a momentary but uncompromising truth.

Judith Leyster (LIE-ster; 1609–1660) specialized in genre paintings, especially of musicians, and was one of the few artists prior to this century who could suggest musical performance through form, line, and color. In *Self-Portrait* (fig. 18.20) Leyster portrays herself in formal dress but in a relaxed and casual pose that echoes, in a lower key, the laughing violinist on her canvas who is playing the instrument rather than just holding it. Influenced by the Utrecht school of Caravaggio disciples and her teacher, Frans Hals, her style is clearly her own. However, it was not until this century that "Leyster" replaced "Hals" on several paintings that she had completed during her late teens or early twenties. Dutch artists were proud of their craft, and this attitude is reflected in the jaunty ease and confident self-assertion of the artist. Italian artists of the High Renaissance promoted the idea of the

Figure 18.20 Judith Leyster, *Self-Portrait,* ca. 1635. Oil on canvas, 29⅜ × 25⅝″. Gift of Mr. and Mrs. Robert Woods Bliss. National Gallery of Art, Washington, D.C.

Figure 18.21 Rembrandt van Rijn, *The Apostle Bartholomew,* 1657. Oil on canvas, 64¾ × 55¾″. Timkin Gallery, San Diego Museum of Art, San Diego, California.

artist as a noble creator, but in bourgeois Holland, superlative skills in the crafts were valued on their own merits.

Some Dutch artists like Hals specialized in portraits, while Leyster painted genre scenes, and others concentrated on history or landscapes. Rembrandt van Rijn (van rhine; 1606–1669), however, worked with consummate ease in all areas. He is, in fact, one of a handful of supreme masters of the entire European tradition. Calvinism frowned on religious images, which may explain why sculpture was not popular, but on the other hand, the Reformed Church rejected all authority except individual conscience. This meant, in effect, that artists could study the Bible and create sacred images as they personally envisioned them, which is precisely what Rembrandt did. He could not accept the stern God of the Calvinists and he never painted a Last Judgment. He was concerned instead with the human drama of the Old Testament, the loving and forgiving God of the New Testament, and the life and Passion of Christ. In *The Descent from the Cross* (colorplate 37) the two main focal points of the drama are the body of Christ and the face of his fainting mother. Eliminating all superfluous details with his characteristic dark background, the artist conveys the tenderness with which the broken body is being lowered from the cross. The composition is extremely tight, concentrating our attention on the key figures and, through the skillful use of chiaroscuro, flooding the canvas with the most profound grief. Not even Rembrandt himself surpassed the expressive combination of space and light.

Rembrandt's portrayal of *The Apostle Bartholomew* (fig. 18.21) is a powerful study of Christ's disciple, who was flayed alive while on a preaching mission in Armenia. During the Middle Ages he was sometimes portrayed holding some of his own flesh in his hands, but Rembrandt creates instead a resurrected disciple holding the knife that symbolizes his martyrdom. That Rembrandt chose to depict this lesser-known apostle is curious and may refer to the Massacre of St. Bartholomew. The largely middle-class Huguenots (French Protestants) were opposed to both the pope and the king. On 24 August 1572 (St. Bartholomew's Day) more than 30,000 Huguenots were massacred by fanatical followers of Catherine de' Medici, the regent, and her son, King Charles IX. Pope Gregory XIII (1572–1585) celebrated the occasion by singing a *Te Deum* and having a medal struck to memorialize the event, but throughout Protestant Europe, reaction to the slaughter was intensely bitter and long-lasting. A devout Protestant who followed only his own conscience, Rembrandt was opposed to the authority of Calvin, not to mention a pope or a king. His monumental study of the martyred apostle could therefore symbolize the martyrdom of the Huguenots who died on the saint's day.

Jan Vermeer (yahn ver-MEER; 1632–1675) did not paint monumental subject matter with the passion of Rembrandt, but he did have a special magic that transmuted everyday reality into eternal symbols. Fewer than forty paintings survive, and all but three are of sparsely furnished interiors of modest size. Vermeer has, in fact, done for ordinary rooms what High

Renaissance artists did for ordinary human bodies: elevated them to the level of universals. With an eye for detail comparable to van Eyck's, Vermeer's speciality is light, natural light streaming into the interior, usually from the left, filling a space punctuated by objects and figures seemingly suspended in light. In *Woman Holding a Balance* (fig. 18.22) Vermeer has created an apparently simple scene of a woman, probably his wife Catharina in one of her eleven pregnancies, holding an empty balance. With jewelry on the table and a painting of the Last Judgment on the wall, there is a temptation to assume that this is a moral analogy, a weighing of worldly possessions against a background of divine judgment. Dutch Calvinists would not have had a Last Judgment anywhere in the house, but this may be Catharina's room and she, unlike her husband, was Catholic. Nevertheless, the mood is introspective and her expression serene. Married to a painter who in his lifetime never sold a painting, a man of extravagant tastes with a host of creditors, this painting may represent nothing more nor less than a woman contentedly contemplating jewelry received from a loving husband. The highest level of art may not be to encourage laughter, passion, or tears but to invoke dreams, and dreams are perhaps best left unexplained.

After his premature death, Vermeer's paintings were used to satisfy creditors who undoubtedly had no more appreciation of his worth than a society that had ignored him. Not rediscovered until the 1860s, his use of color and light was a revelation to the Impressionists, who thought themselves the first to discover that shadows were not black but also had color. In *The Girl with a Red Hat* (colorplate 38), there is a technical mastery that, in combination with Vermeer's scientific study of light, makes this one of the finest works of the artist's brief mature period. Here, as if they were visualized molecules, we see floating globules of colored light. Light glints from an eye, an earring, and the lips of a young woman unexpectedly caught in a soft-focus candid "photograph." Under the spectacular hat, light and shadow are painted in subtle gradations of color emphasized by the gleaming white ruff. Vermeer applied paint to canvas with a dexterity and charm that has never been equaled.

Vermeer exploited color and light, while Jacob van Ruisdael (ROIS-dale; 1628–1682) specialized in space. The finest Dutch landscape painter and one of the greatest in Western art, Ruisdael painted the immensity of space from memory and imagination. In *Wheatfields* (colorplate 36) the vast and brooding sky, forecasting a coming storm, takes up two-thirds of the canvas. Ruisdael's landscapes are frequently devoid of people, and when they are present, as here, they are inconsequential figures compared with the magnificence of nature. The atmospheric perspective encourages the illusion that we are looking into space so deep that it verges on infinity.

Seventeenth century Dutch burghers are justly famed for their support of the art of painting, and Dutch museums are today filled to overflowing with "Dutch masters" and "little Dutch masters." Many

Figure 18.22 Jan Vermeer, *Woman Holding a Balance,* ca. 1657. Oil on canvas, 16¾ × 15". Andrew W. Mellon Collection. National Gallery of Art, Washington, D.C.

painters of that golden age acquired wealth and fame, but for whatever reason, Rembrandt, Hals, and Vermeer, the greatest of the Dutch school, all died in poverty.

Rococo Art, ca. 1715–1789

With the death of Louis XIV in 1715, the academic classical art of the Baroque had lost its chief patron. It was with great relief that the French court abandoned the Palace and the Baroque, moving back to Paris and to a new way of life in their elegant townhouses, where manners and charm were far more interesting than grandeur and geometric order. This was the Age of Enlightenment and of the Rococo style of art, contradictory but not mutually exclusive. In fact, the Enlightenment and the American and French revolutions cannot be fully understood without knowing what the Rococo was all about. That Rococo is merely Baroque made small or Baroque made light are bromides that do have a certain element of truth, but Rococo is also a style in its own right. Royalty and nobility became obsolete during the Enlightenment, and Rococo art illustrates with astonishing accuracy the superficial values of an aristocracy whose days were numbered. The imposing Baroque forms were reduced to depictions of the pursuit of pleasure and escape from boredom. Rococo art was not decadent but the society that it portrayed most certainly was.

Jean Antoine Watteau (vah-TOE; 1684–1721), the first and greatest French Rococo artist, was born of Flemish parents in Valenciennes, a city that had been French for only six years. Yet, he transformed French

Figure 18.23 Antoine Watteau, *A Pilgrimage to Cythera*, 1717. Oil on canvas, 76½ × 51″. The Louvre, Paris.

art from the classicism of Poussin into a new style of gaiety and tenderness, casual but elegant, that even today is recognized as Parisian in the sophisticated tradition later reinforced by artists like Renoir and Degas. Watteau's *A Pilgrimage to Cythera* (fig. 18.23), an early Rococo work, is also the most important. Cythera was the legendary island of love of Venus, whose statue at the right presides over the amorous festivities. Grouped couple by couple, the elegantly garbed party is preparing to board a fanciful boat attended by cherubs, but not without a wistful backward glance at the pleasures enjoyed on the isle of love. Characteristic of Rococo design is the reverse C (Ɔ) that can be traced from the heads at the lower left, curves past the couple on the hillock, and turns back to the left along the delicate tips of the tree branches. Though it is a large painting, the scene is remarkably intimate. Each couple is totally preoccupied with each other and forms a distinct unit as they talk, smile, whisper, or touch. Beneath the frivolity and charm there is a warm feeling of good people and good times. Watteau has transformed the amorous dalliances of an idle and privileged class into lyric poetry.

Venus was queen of the Rococo at its height in the 1750s, and François Boucher (boo-SHAY; 1703–1770) was her most talented interpreter. The protégé of Madame de Pompadour, mistress of Louis XV and arbiter of Rococo style, Boucher was a master of the sensual and frequently erotic art of the period. With astounding energy and great virtuosity he produced paintings, designed tapestries, decorated porcelain, and created opera and ballet settings. With his

many students and widely circulated engravings, he became the most influential artist in Europe. His *Venus Consoling Love* (colorplate 39) depicts a slim and delicate beauty who would be more comfortable at the French court than on Mount Olympos. She was, in fact, at the French court, for this is one of Boucher's many portraits of Mme. de Pompadour, to whom the painting belonged. Here are the characteristic ivory, pink, blue, silver, and gold colors of the Rococo, all elegantly detailed by one of the great virtuosos of the painter's brush. The painting is frankly pretty, and meant to be, but its design, though very subtle, is a carefully controlled interplay of sinuous curves. Nowhere is there a straight line. A study of the apparent diagonals of the goddess's body discloses a series of curves, flattering curves of supple and creamy flesh. This is an idealized version of Pompadour, totally different from other Boucher paintings that reveal the intellectual brilliance of an enlightened woman who assisted in the publication of Diderot's *Encyclopedia*. Her physician, Dr. Quesway, quoted her foreboding remark, *"Apres moi le deluge!"* (After me the flood!, i.e., disaster), and Voltaire wrote, on the occasion of her death in 1764, that he would miss her because "She was one of us; she protected Letters to the best of her power."

The most eminent pupil of Boucher and Chardin and the last of the great Rococo artists, Jean-Honoré Fragonard (frah-go-NAR; 1732–1806) lived to see the revolution destroy the Rococo age and all it represented. A master of the elegantly erotic paintings that

Figure 18.24 Jean-Honore Fragonard, *A Young Girl Reading,* ca. 1776. Oil on canvas, 32 × 25½''. Gift of Mrs. Mellon Bruce in memory of her father Andrew W. Mellon, 1961. National Gallery of Art, Washington, D.C.

Figure 18.26 Jean-Baptiste-Simeon Chardin, *The Kitchen Maid.* 1738. Oil on canvas, 18½ × 14¾''. Samuel H. Kress Collection. National Gallery of Art, Washington, D.C.

Figure 18.25 Étienne Falconet, *Madame de Pompadour as the Venus of the Doves.* Samuel H. Kress Collection. National Gallery of Art, Washington, D.C.

delighted his patrons, Fragonard also had a technical skill and an eye for composition that enabled him to distill the essence of a personal and warmly intimate scene, such as *A Young Girl Reading* (fig. 18.24).

The spirit of the age in three-dimensional form is represented by Etienne Falconet (fal-ca-NAY; 1716–1791) in his harmonious sculptural group entitled *Madame de Pompadour as the Venus of the Doves* (fig. 18.25). The coquettish eroticism that delighted this decadent society is clearly evident in this lighthearted work, so typical of the figures that decorated Sèvres porcelain, music boxes, snuff boxes, and other accoutrements of the good life of idleness and luxury.

But there was another current, one that celebrated the sober virtues of the middle class. Jean-Baptiste-Simeon Chardin (shar-DAN; 1699–1779) sought the underlying nobility that could be found in scenes of daily life. Nothing was so humble but that his brush could reveal its charm. His depiction of *The Kitchen Maid* (fig. 18.26) has a natural dignity in sharp contrast to the artificiality of the courtly Rococo style. Chardin painted what he saw, which was, essentially, light falling on pleasing shapes: face, apron, basin, turnips. The result is a quietly beautiful composition by the finest still-life painter of the eighteenth century.

Rococo architecture is charming and beguiling in small structures and, when tastefully done, even in

Figure 18.27 Johann Michael Fischer, Church of Ottobeuren, begun ca. 1720. Bavaria.

Figure 18.28 Interior, Ottobeuren

Figure 18.29 Cherubs, Ottobeuren

Figure 18.30 Thomas Gainsborough, *Mrs. Richard Brinsley Sheridan*, ca. 1783. Oil on canvas, 66½ × 60½". Andrew W. Mellon Collection. National Gallery of Art, Washington, D.C.

large buildings. The Benedictine Church of Ottobeuren (fig. 18.27) has twin towers derived from Baroque designs but unified with superimposed pilasters punctuated with decorative windows. The outward-thrusting middle section is characteristic of the Rococo, both assertive and inviting.

The interior of the church (fig. 18.28) is a celestial symphony of white stucco, gold gilt, and profuse decoration set off to best advantage by the north-south orientation of the building and the large clear-glass windows. All of the elegantly textured decorations are carved wood, and the "marble" columns are actually wood painted to look like marble. The spritely Rococo cherubs (fig. 18.29) and even the dangling tassel are painted wood. The virtuosity of the wood-carvers of Bavaria is magnificently celebrated in Ottobeuren.

Neither the artificial elegance of the French Rococo nor the exuberance of Bavarian Rococo had a place in an English society that was generally more sober than the French and, unlike Catholic Bavaria, solidly Protestant. In both subject matter and style, Thomas Gainsborough's (1727–1788) portrait of *Mrs. Richard Brinsley Sheridan* (fig. 18.30) symbolizes the

Figure 18.31 Inigo Jones, Queen's House, north facade, 1610–1618. Greenwich.

Figure 18.32 Inigo Jones, Palladian Bridge, 1647–1653. Wilton House, Wiltshire.

dashing, worldly taste of English high society. This is the beautiful singer who married Sheridan, the wit, brilliant member of Parliament, and writer of plays like *School for Scandal* and *The Rivals*. Here nature is artificial, arranged as a proper background to highlight the natural beauty and unpretentious air of the sitter. In contrast to the sprightly sophistication of Boucher's women, Mrs. Sheridan is the very picture of the tasteful elegance so admired by British society.

Neoclassic Art

The visual arts of the Renaissance and the Baroque made little impact on English culture. Apparently preoccupied with their justly celebrated achievements in dramatic literature, poetry, and music, the English continued to build in the Gothic and Tudor styles and to import painters like Holbein, Rubens, and van Dyck. After the visit to Italy of Inigo Jones (1573–1652), the king's surveyor (architect), a revolution began in English architecture. Jones's middle-class British sensibilities were offended by the extravagance of Michelangelo's style, but he was profoundly impressed with Palladio's architectural designs. Jones did not copy Palladian buildings, but instead selected classical characteristics as a basis for his own architectural style. His Queen's House (fig. 18.31) is the first English building designed in the Neoclassic style that would become so prominent in England and North America. Chaste and clean with the poise of pure Roman classicism, the house has slight rustication on the ground floor derived from an early Renaissance style long since abandoned by the Italians (see fig. 14.10). With simple window openings and matching lower and upper balustrades, the curving double stairway adds a discreet touch of dignity and grace.

Along with his design for the stately home called Wilton House, Jones included the so-called Palladian Bridge (fig. 18.32), an influential concept that combined Roman triumphal arches with an Ionic colonnade. The arches were transformed with simple classical pediments instead of Roman squared-off tops.

The entire structure is lighter and more graceful because the columns are proportionately taller than their classical models.

English architecture was influenced by Palladian and Baroque characteristics more rapidly than anyone might have anticipated. In 1666 King Charles II commissioned Christopher Wren (1632–1723) to design a new dome for the Gothic Cathedral of St. Paul's, a design that Wren planned in the "Roman manner." A professor of astronomy at Oxford and an amateur architect, Wren soon had more than he bargained for; the Great Fire of 1666 destroyed most of London, necessitating a major rebuilding program with Wren as the chief architect. Of the more than fifty churches that Wren designed, the most important project was the new St. Paul's, an eclectic design influenced by Jones, Palladio, and the French and Italian Baroque, and masterfully synthesized by Wren (fig. 18.33). St. Paul's is one of a limited number of English buildings with Baroque characteristics, but overall the design is dominated by the classical dome that is reminiscent, on a massive scale, of Bramante's Tempietto (see fig. 14.28). Punctuated by paired Corinthian columns in the Baroque manner, the facade is basically classical, but the ornate twin towers are similar to Borromini's curvilinear style (see fig. 18.9). None of Wren's London churches is quite like any other, though most are classical; some have towers, others steeples, and a few domes.

The Church of St. Martin-in-the-Fields (fig. 18.34) was designed by James Gibbs (1682–1754) as influenced by Wren, with whom he studied. Essentially a Roman temple with a classical steeple, this is a prototype of similar churches constructed throughout the United States, especially in New England. Usually of wood frame and clapboard construction and painted white, these classical buildings became one of the most familiar church designs in nineteenth century America.

In France the Rococo style was deemed too frivolous for public buildings and the Baroque style too elaborate, leaving the way open for a French version of Neoclassicism. Ange-Jacques Gabriel (1698–1782), court architect for Louis XV, made his reputation with

Figure 18.33 Christopher Wren, St. Paul's Cathedral, 1675–1710, west facade, London.

Figure 18.34 James Gibbs, St. Martin-in-the-Fields, 1721–1726, Tralfager Square, London.

his design for the Petit Trianon on the grounds of Versailles. Restrained, symmetrical, and exquisitely proportioned, the diminutive palace was contructed by and for Mme. de Pompadour who was, in effect, the ruler of France in place of the weak and inept Louis XV. Clearly reflecting her classical architectural tastes, the Petit Trianon is in the austere Augustan style of Republican Rome, a style that became dominant in Paris and other French cities during the second half of the eighteenth century.

The philosophes of the Enlightenment were, as might be expected, hostile to the Rococo style. Their attitude accounts for the sudden fame of Jean-Baptiste Greuze (grooz; 1725–1805), who was praised by Diderot and other philosophes for paintings depicting bourgeois life. Diderot thought that paintings such as *The Village Bride* (fig. 18.35) celebrated the virtues of the simple life and the sterling moral values of the sober and sedate middle class. Greuze's work did please, but not the middle class; rather, it appealed to the philosophes who, along with the upper middle class and aristocracy, lived a life depicted more accurately by Boucher. The charming rusticity of Greuze's painting with a gentle patriarch, blushing bride, gawky bridegroom, and chickens pecking on the floor was sentimental, as phony and romanticized as Rococo paintings with their idyllic landscapes and the elite playing at being gods, goddesses, shepherds, and shepherdesses. Worse yet, they were hypocritical. Greuze's rural maidens, wide-eyed in their simpering innocence, are painted with sly sensual touches and erotic undertones that make the frankly amoral paintings of Boucher look positively poetic and moral.

The gap between the aristocracy and the middle class was possibly no greater than it had been for generations, but by the last quarter of the century it became far more noticeable. The philosophes expounded on the gap along with revolutionary political and economic ideas that were no longer theories but active principles in England's American colonies. When it became apparent that the art of Greuze and his imitators did not truly reflect their revolutionary fervor, the philosophes turned to Neoclassic art. Excavations at Pompeii and Herculaneum, begun in 1748 under the aegis of King Charles of Bourbon, were bringing to light a new chapter from the history of ancient Rome, sparking a renewed interest in antiquity that was not confined to the arts. Political theorists who were advocating democratic equality, fervent patriotism, and the rule of reason thought they had found all this in Republican Rome.

A far more gifted artist than Greuze, Jacques Louis David (da-VEED; 1748–1825) developed his Neoclassic style during his studies in Rome (1775–1781). Refusing to merely copy Roman statues and paintings, to become an antiquarian, he chose instead to be a propagandist, to place his talent at the service of revolutionary ideals. David used the forms of ancient art to extol the virtues of patriotism and democracy.

Figure 18.35 Jean-Baptiste Greuze, *The Village Bride,* 1761. Oil on canvas, 46½ × 36″. The Louvre, Paris.

Painted shortly before the French Revolution, *The Death of Sokrates* (fig. 18.36) became one of the most popular paintings of the century and set the tone for didactic art of the highest quality. Sokrates the Greek philosopher is depicted here as the apostle of reason, the patron saint of Roman Stoics like Epictetus and Marcus Aurelius. With the body of a young athlete and the face of a benign sage, Sokrates dominates a sharply focused composition similar to the dramatic chiaroscuro of Caravaggio. The figures of the twelve disciples, no coincidence, are rendered as precisely as marble statues, precision of detail being a David trademark. David's message is unmistakable: men of principle should be willing to die in defense of their ideals. Nobles and tradesmen, philosophers and priests, seemingly everyone bought engravings of the painting, including Louis XVI, who admired its noble sentiments.

David's works, with their detailed, meticulous realism and appeal to reason, were conceived and executed as cries for revolution. During the revolution itself David was a member of the Convention that sentenced Louis XVI and Marie Antoinette to death. For twenty-five years he was a virtual dictator of the arts

in France. Following his dicta, Rococo salons were stripped of their sensuous paintings and curvaceous furnishings, remodeled in Neoclassic style, and equipped with furniture patterned after Greek vase paintings and Pompeiian murals. Fashionable men and women adopted Roman names such as Portia and Brutus, styled their hair in the antique manner, and even costumed themselves in classical togas. Madame Tallien (fig. 18.37), a leading figure in revolutionary salons, is shown in the approved new look of the revolution as painted by an unknown artist in the style of David.

David was a highly successful artist with many students and, of course, numerous imitators. As with any well-known artist, paintings were sometimes attributed to him so that they would fetch a higher price, which is what happened with the portrait of *Mlle. du Val d'Ognes* (fig. 18.38). Purchased in 1917 as a David for $200,000, the painting has since been attributed by some critics to Constance Marie Charpentier (1767–1849), a Parisian artist who studied with David and several other noted painters. Winner of a gold medal and an exhibitor in ten salons, her work appears to be hidden away either in private collections or behind the names of more famous artists. That the

Figure 18.36 Jacques Louis David, *The Death of Sokrates,* 1787. Oil on canvas, 78 × 59″. The Metropolitan Museum of Art, New York. Wolfe Fund, 1931.

Figure 18.37 School of David, *Portrait of Madame Tallien.* San Diego Museum of Art, San Diego, California.

Figure 18.38 Unknown French Artist, *Mlle. du Val d'Ognes,* ca. 1800. Oil on canvas, height 63½″. Metropolitan Museum; of Art, New York. Bequest of Isaac D. Fletcher.

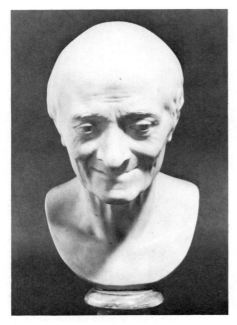

Figure 18.39 Jean Antoine Houdon, *Voltaire,* ca. 1775. Chester Dale Collection. National Gallery of Art, Washington, D.C.

Figure 18.40 Antonio Canova, *Pauline Borghese as Venus,* 1805. Marble, life size. Borghese Gallery, Rome.

painting could ever have been attributed to David is very odd. While the style is Neoclassic, the brushwork firm and lucid, and the garb elegantly classical, the mood is totally alien to David's style. Strangely haunting, there is a brooding and unreal quality about the work that prompted critics to use terms like "merciless portrait," "unforgettable," and "mysterious masterpiece." These remarks were made while the painting still bore the name of David, but they are no less appropriate even if the artist's name might be Charpentier.

Figure 18.41 Gilbert Stuart, *Mrs. Richard Yates,* 1793. Oil on canvas, 30¼ × 25″. Andrew W. Mellon Collection. National Gallery of Art, Washington, D.C.

Portrait sculpture, as might be expected, was a natural for the Neoclassic style, but there were no sculptors comparable to David. Jean Antoine Houdon (ooh-DON; 1741–1828), the finest French sculptor of the age, was admired by the philosophes, many of whom he portrayed with great accuracy. His portrait of Voltaire (fig. 18.39) is a realistic depiction of the aging philosopher, clearly communicating his personality with twinkling eyes and wry and cynical smile.

Houdon was friendly with other revolutionaries, like George Washington and Benjamin Franklin, and created a portrait of Franklin and two statues of Washington. Despite his revolutionary background and realistic portraits, Houdon could win only reluctant acceptance from Napoleon, who much preferred the Neoclassic style of Italian sculptor Antonio Canova (ka-NO-va; 1757–1822), whose art along with that of David became propaganda tools for the Empire. Canova's lovely study of *Pauline Borghese as Venus* (fig. 18.40) is an idealized version of feminine charm, a very sensual portrait of Napoleon's sister and, though classical, an evocation of imperial luxury rather than the noble dignity of Republican Rome.

The Neoclassic style found a home in the new republic of the New World. The leading American painter, Gilbert Stuart (1755–1828), painted many founding fathers, particularly George Washington, whose portrait on the dollar bill is from Gilbert Stuart. In his portraits Stuart displayed a mastery of flesh tones, having discovered, like the Impressionists, that flesh coloration was a combination of colors. His portrait of *Mrs. Richard Yates* (fig. 18.41) is typical of the

Figure 18.42 Thomas Jefferson, State Capitol, 1785–1789, Richmond, Virginia.

Neoclassic style in a new democracy in which neither dress nor background gives a clue to the social status of the sitter. European portraiture customarily added a proper setting and adornment indicating a regal or noble subject. In this portrait of the wife of a New York importer we see a cooly poised and confident woman. Her strongly featured face with the raised eyebrows and slightly drooping eyelids is faintly skeptical, the face of a shrewd and capable Yankee.

As U.S. minister to France, Thomas Jefferson (1743–1826) had an opportunity to study French Neoclassic architecture and, especially, Roman architecture in France and Italy. He was fascinated by the Maison Carrée (see fig. 6.7) in southern France and was determined to introduce Roman architecture into the United States. Jefferson's design of the Capitol of Virginia (fig. 18.42) was patterned after the Maison Carrée, but with Ionic capitals and constructed of wood painted gleaming white. Larger than the Roman temple, the Virginia Capitol building has an aura of noble dignity precisely as intended by its designer.

Neoclassicism is popular because it is easily comprehended. Political themes and purposes aside, the classical impulse is towards physical and intellectual perfection as embodied in buildings that express the essence of poised, serene beauty. The Greeks not only invented the style but perfected it, and for twenty-five centuries the Western world has copied it.

Summary

The word *Baroque* was coined by eighteenth century classicists as a disdainful term denoting the art of an extravagant, disorderly, contradictory, and sometimes bizarre age. Powerful forces that were to shape the modern world were reflected in the Counter-Reformation style promoted by the Church of Rome, the Aristocratic style of absolute monarchs, and the Bourgeois style of the Protestant middle class of Holland.

The mother church of the Jesuits, Il Gesu, was the first church of a style that reached its apogee in the art of Bernini. The dramatic chiaroscuro and gritty realism of Caravaggio influenced every painting school in Europe including the Spanish mystic Zurbarán and Velasquez, the master of pictorial space.

The expressive and exuberant style of Rubens made him the top court painter of the century, while van Dyck painted courtly portraits of aristocratic patrons. The first and foremost of the Baroque Classicists, Poussin emphasized drawing and design over Rubenesque color and emotion, setting off a conflict between Poussinists and Rubenists that defined and illustrated the contradictory forces of the seventeenth century. Aristocratic art dominated the age as it dominated no other, as symbolized by the magnificent palace of Louis XIV at Versailles. Representing the divine right monarchy of Louis XIV, Versailles also connoted the emergence of France as the most influential and powerful nation in Europe.

With no princely or priestly patrons, the artists of Calvinist Holland produced works commissioned by a prosperous middle class that had an apparently insatiable taste for paintings. Although they were artistically the most successful, Hals, Rembrandt, and Vermeer fared less well financially than many lesser artists.

The decorative and delightfully erotic Rococo style was as much a part of the Enlightenment as the learned speculation of the philosophes. The art of Watteau, Boucher, Fragonard, and Falconet mirrored the elegance, idleness, and artificiality of the French nobility, while Chardin concentrated on painting objects and scenes of everyday life. In Austria and in Bavaria, churches like Ottobeuren represented a festive Catholic Rococo style, while in England the style was manifested in a more restrained British manner, as seen in the art of Gainsborough.

Almost entirely immune to Renaissance and Baroque styles, England responded enthusiastically to the Palladian-inspired architecture of Inigo Jones and the essentially Neoclassic designs of Christopher Wren and James Gibbs. Sponsored in France by Mme. de Pompadour, the Neoclassic style dominated the vast building program of the second half of the eighteenth century. Prerevolutionary classicism found its strongest expression in the art of David and Houdon, and found a home in America as represented in the work of Gilbert Stuart and Thomas Jefferson.

Neoclassicism spanned the eighteenth and nineteenth centuries as a prerevolutionary and then a postrevolutionary style. It served the needs of a society struggling to free itself from oppression and, paradoxically, a Napoleonic age that utilized Neoclassicism as a symbol of law, order, and authority.

Colorplate 33 Peter Paul Rubens, *The Assumption of the Virgin,* ca. 1626. Oil on panel, 49⅜ × 37⅛″. Samuel H. Kress Collection. National Gallery of Art, Washington, D.C.

Colorplate 34 Peter Paul Rubens, *Rape of the Daughters of Leucippus,* ca. 1618. Oil on canvas, 7′3″ × 6′10″. Alte Pinakothek, Munich.

Colorplate 35 Nicolas Poussin, *Holy Family on the Steps,* 1648. Oil on canvas, 38¼ × 27″.
Samuel H. Kress Collection. National Gallery of Art, Washington, D.C.

Colorplate 36 Jacob van Ruisdael, *Wheatfields*. Oil on canvas, 51¼ × 39⅜. Metropolitan Museum of Art, New York. Bequest of Bejamin Altman, 1913.

Colorplate 37 Rembrandt van Rijn, *The Descent from the Cross,* 1653. Oil on canvas, 56¼ × 43¾″. Widener Collection. National Gallery of Art, Washington, D.C.

Colorplate 38 Jan Vermeer, *The Girl with a Red Hat,* ca. 1660. Oil on wood, 9⅛ × 7⅛″. Andrew W. Mellon Collection. National Gallery of Art, Washington, D.C.

Colorplate 39 François Boucher, *Venus Consoling Love,* 1751. Oil on canvas, 42⅛ × 33⅜″. Gift of Chester Dale. National Gallery of Art, Washington, D.C.

19

Music: Baroque, Rococo, and Classical

Baroque Music (1600–1750)

Modern music, music as we know it, began sometime around the year 1600 as the Renaissance waned and the new Age of Reason began to take shape. The unbroken line of development leading from early organum to the smoothly flowing symmetry of the a cappella vocal music of the Golden Age of Polyphony came to an end. The old world of *private* music for the church, the courts, and a cultural elite steadily declined in influence and importance. The modern world in which music became a *public* art was taking shape amidst the intellectual, political, and social ferment of the seventeenth century.

Stimulated by exploration, scientific discovery, the emergence of capitalism, the middle class, and the modern state, and the continuing conflict between Reformation and Counter-Reformation, *audiences* of the common man were created. Churches could no longer take the piety of their communicants for granted; they were obliged to build structures with a maximum of floor space, structures that resembled theatres more than they did Gothic or Renaissance churches. In a setting bursting with agitated forms and twisting, curving shapes with elaborate decorative details, these audiences were preached to, firmly and fervently.

This new *Baroque* style was applied to all public buildings whether they were churches, concert halls, or opera houses. Even the Baroque palaces (such as Versailles) of ruling heads of state assumed a quasi-public character in their dual roles as royal residences and showcases of national prestige and power.

There was a consistent dualism in the Baroque era, a sometimes precarious balance of opposing forces: church and state, aristocracy and affluent middle class. Baroque architecture achieved a sculptured effect by balancing the massiveness of its basic structure with elaborate decoration and exploitation of three-dimensional effects. Even the cylindrical columns of the facades were grouped in pairs.

Baroque music displayed the same dualism with balanced vocal-instrumental groups, consistent use of two-part (binary) forms and the reduction of the church modes to only two modes: major and minor.

The emergence of instrumental music to a position of equal importance with vocal music practically eliminated the a cappella style. All Baroque vocal music had an instrumental accompaniment whether it was a mass, motet, oratorio, passion, cantata, or opera. Purely instrumental music established new forms such as the balanced participation of small and large groups in the concerto grosso and the pieces for two solo instruments with keyboard accompaniment (called trio sonatas). Even the dynamics were dualistic, with consistent use of alternating loud and soft passages.

Keyboard Music

Harpsichord

Dance Suite Dancing has been a fundamental activity since the dim dawn of the human race—dances to appease the gods, exorcise evil spirits, invoke fertility—and for the sheer exhilaration of physical and emotional release. Dancing attained a new prestige during the seventeenth-century Age of Kings, with magnificent balls in the great courts. The lords and ladies refined lusty and sometimes crude peasant dances into a social art of grace and charm without, however, discarding the omnipresent eroticism of social dancing.

During the early Baroque period short instrumental pieces were composed in the manner and style of various popular dances. The exotic and erotic Sarabande, for example, was transformed into a stylized and sophisticated art form that sometimes subtly implied what the original boldly proclaimed. Later on, a similar process changed the waltz from an "indecent" dance into a popular social dance, leading finally to an art form; for example, "The Blue Danube" by Johann Strauss, Jr. Late twentieth-century composers are more than likely to accord similar treatment to dances of the 1980s.

During the seventeenth century these stylized dances were combined in collections of chamber music called *dance suites* and played by harpsichords, other solo instruments, and various instrumental ensembles. There are usually five or six dances (or movements) in a suite, each a different type of dance with a standard sequence, which can be described as A–C–S–O–G: Allemande, Courante, Sarabande, Optional dance(s), Gigue. The dance suite was truly international in character; the original folk dances were, respectively, German, French, Spanish, and English (jig). Each dance suite had, however, a basic unity; that is, *each dance was in the same key.*

"Each dance was in the same *key*"—a significant statement about this period and one that goes beyond the mere technicalities of music. The new "key" to reality was the rational world of Descartes and, later, the mechanistic world of Newton. After Descartes, philosophers and scientists of the Enlightenment unlocked the door leading to a new world in which, they

thought, they could begin to examine and to comprehend a rational universe of order and logic. The single key of Baroque compositions can be compared, in function, with Newton's law of universal gravitation; music and physics attempt to explain motion in the simplest possible terms.

For the first time in history music acquired what was considered to be a firm and rational foundation: a key. Many centuries before, the multitudinous modes of the Greeks were reduced to the eight church modes that formed the musical material of everything from plainsong through Renaissance polyphonic music. The Baroque saw the emergence of two new concepts: (1) all music written in a consistent pitch relationship called a key, with a choice of either major or minor mode, and (2) a temporary disenchantment with the complexities of polyphonic music in favor of blocks of sound called chords or harmony.

By exploiting homophonic music (one sound, i.e., one block of harmony following another) and a fixed pitch relationship, composers were merely reflecting the new view of reality. The "old music" was gradually replaced by less complicated music which was considered to be lucid and rational, though of course always expressive. This is not to say that this was a conscious decision by anyone or that there was instant recognition of the drastic changes that had taken place. Rather, musicians, like all artists, reacted to the new view of reality with a combination of old and new techniques that gave a new sound to a new age.

This new sound, as in the music of Johann Sebastian Bach (1685–1750), can be considered the beginning of modern music. Compositions by twentieth-century composers such as Stravinsky, Prokofiev, and Bartók are more closely related to the music of Bach than Bach's work relates, in turn, to the Renaissance. Palestrina, Lassus, and other Renaissance musicians were writing for the Church and for an educated aristocracy. Bach, though sometimes serving as a court composer, also performed routine services which ranged from conducting choir rehearsals to composing music for next Sunday's worship service.

The music of Bach is admired for its artistry and for its superb craftsmanship. In his own day, however, Bach composed much of his music in response to specific demands. Many of his organ works were written and performed for church services and for special programs. His sacred cantatas, written for particular Sundays of the liturgical year, were normally performed only once. Having served their purpose, they were consigned to storage where, many years later, a young Mozart could discover them and exclaim, "Now here is a man from whom I can learn," or words to that effect.

Much of Bach's output was intended for performance by amateur musicians and, more importantly, to be listened to by audiences composed essentially of the middle-class burghers of Germany. This middle class, of increasing influence and affluence, was becoming the primary audience of not only that period but of all subsequent periods. Today's mass audience is a logical development of the processes that began during the eighteenth century.

The following dance suite for harpsichord is typical of solo keyboard music of the Baroque. The setting for a performance could be as simple as an amateur performing in the parlor of a middle-class home or as elaborate as a professional performance on a gold-encrusted harpsichord at a royal court.

The dance suite was based on actual dances from the past, dances that were codified, stylized, and refined into a succession of dance movements for a listening rather than a dancing audience. Following are only the titles and major themes of the suite.

French Suite no. 1 in d Minor

J. S. Bach (1685–1750)
Total Time: 12:30

Allemande (Fr., *German,* **i.e., a German dance)**

Courante (Fr., *courir,* **to run, a running dance)**

Sarabande (from Spain)

Minuet I (French dance of rustic origin)

Minuet II

Gigue (from sixteenth-century English or Irish jig)

Organ

Fugue Intellectuals of the Age of Enlightenment believed that there was a basic explanation for the rational order of the universe—and the discoveries of Isaac Newton seemed (at that time) to support this point of view. Composers of the era mirrored this view with their consistent use of a single musical concept called, variously, *motive, theme, subject, melody,* or *tune.* They wrote *monothematic* (one theme) compositions and depended upon their craftsmanship, intellectual agility, and musical sensitivity to keep their one-theme compositions from becoming exercises in monotony. Not all Baroque composers succeeded and not even the best composers consistently won this game of intellectual musicianship.

The musical rules for writing monothematic dance suites, fugues, inventions, preludes, passacaglias, and so forth were well established by the eighteenth century; even children could follow the rules for writing a fugue with all of the clever devices for making something interesting out of a single musical idea—but the result was frequently dull, duller, or dullest. Those who emerged victorious in the contest were great craftsmen such as J. S. Bach, who added the vital spark of creative genius: men who could take a single theme and spin a web of glorious sound. Bach brought fugue writing to its highest point of artist perfection; his *Art of Fugue,* written for a keyboard instrument, is considered the epitome of the art and the craft.

The prime instrument for the performance of fugues and other monothematic styles was the pipe organ. Baroque organs were the only solo instruments capable of filling Baroque churches and concert halls with a variety and volume of sound unequaled by any other instrument. The clarity and grandeur of these magnificent instruments has never been surpassed. The proof of this statement can still be heard throughout Europe; many of the original instruments have never ceased pouring forth the unique color and brilliance of the Baroque (fig. 19.1).

Two of the most challenging of all Baroque musical forms were the fugue and the passacaglia. The Baroque period became a veritable wasteland of bad fugues but, as usual, the good ones survived. The passacaglia (even an unsuccessful one) was a comparative rarity because only a minority of brave souls tackled its formidable musical-intellectual challenge (an example of a supremely successful passacaglia follows the fugue outlined below).

A fugue has been called the strictest free form in music *and* the freest strict form in music. Both statements happen to be true, because the composer is limited to a theme which must occur throughout the composition in essentially its original form. However, there is no prescribed length for the composition nor any standard methods of achieving variety amidst the almost constant restatement of the theme in one voice or another. Writing a fugue is a thoroughly rational procedure that tests the composer's craft: making musical sense out of what is essentially a mathematical exercise. And now to the rules of the game.

A *fugue* is an exercise in ingenuity. The composer uses a single theme (called *subject*) which is played (or sung) several times by each voice throughout a composition, for example, four voices in a four-part fugue. Fugues have staggered entries (begin with one voice, add a second voice, third voice, etc.) exactly like the imitative entries of Renaissance choral music. In fugue, however, there is only the single subject, with variety provided in part by *episodes*, or sections in which none of the voices have the subject.

After the first voice has sounded the subject, a second voice answers (starts the subject) while the first voice moves into a *counter subject*, which is a secondary theme used against (counter to) the subject. There may be two or even three counter subjects, and they may be used every time the subject appears. A typical opening fugal pattern would look like this:

Following is an organ fugue by J. S. Bach. The long subject is given in its entirety, for it is typical of Bach's strong, rhythmical themes. The fugue is referred to as "Little" because Bach wrote another, more elaborate fugue in the same key of g minor, referred to as "Great."

Figure 19.1 Baroque pipe organ, dating from the fifteenth century with eighteenth-century casework, Grote Kerk, Haarlem, Holland. Organ designers were as concerned with the exterior design of the case as with the tone quality of the pipes.

Organ Fugue in g Minor ("Little")

J. S. Bach
Time: 4:00

Subject

Passacaglia A *passacaglia*, like the fugue, is a polyphonic form using a single basic theme. The resemblance ends there, however, because the passacaglia theme is played over and over in the same key, usually in the lowest voice, while the composer devises *variations* of rhythm, melody, and (sometimes) harmony in the upper voices. This was a challenging form for gifted composers because of the problems posed by what could be the monotonous repetition of a single theme.

Based as it is on an old dance form, the Baroque passacaglia is moderately slow in tempo and is in triple meter. The theme usually begins on the third beat of the measure, with a *pickup*. The form is sometimes described as *variations on a ground* (ground = bass).

The following passacaglia uses an eight-measure theme, plus twenty variations of eight measures each. In other words, there is a new variation every twenty-four beats. Although never stopping its forward motion the piece is divided into four distinct sections:

I. Variations 1–8: gradual buildup in texture and volume
II. Variations 9–13: reduction to somewhat lighter texture followed by a gradual increase in volume and texture
III. Variations 14–15: sharp reduction to very light texture
IV. Variations 16–20: strong buildup to thick texture and forceful climax in final variation

The passacaglia moves directly into a fugue based on the first portion of the theme.

J. S. Bach
Time: 7:20

Instrumental

Trio Sonata

Baroque music was particularly notable for the wide-spread development of private music-making by zealous performers who played or sang for the sheer joy of making their own music. Not all of them were as skilled as professionals, but self-expression was more important than technical proficiency. These multitudes of musicians whose personal pleasure was more than sufficient payment for performance were *amateurs:* true lovers of music in the best meaning of the term.

Musical instruments became necessary functional furniture for a burgeoning middle class that was becoming ever more affluent. Baroque music was, in many respects, ready-made for amateur performances (or vice versa?), because composers never indicated the exact speed or tempo of their compositions nor did they do more than provide occasional directions regarding dynamics (relative loudness or softness). These procedures gave amateurs considerable margin for error. Moreover, specific directions as to which instruments were to be used were frequently left to the discretion (and resources) of the performers.

The ubiquitous trio sonata (see detailed description below) provided ideal material for amateurs because it was written in the conventional form of two melodic lines plus generalized directions for keyboard accompaniment. The two melodies could be performed by any two available instruments and the accompaniment by any keyboard instrument (clavichord, harpsichord, or pipe organ). The pivotal figure in trio sonatas (and large compositions) was the keyboard performer; it was assumed that he or she was the most competent musician, which was usually the case. He provided the foundation for the *continuation* of the piece, which led to the adoption of the Italian word *continuo* to describe the function of the keyboard musician. It was up to him to fill in the harmony and to cover up the blank spots whenever the possibly less-expert musicians played wrong notes, lost their place, or otherwise strayed from grace.

Baroque chamber music (but also including operatic arias) was highly improvisational inasmuch as performers were expected to add their personal touches to a given melodic line. Compositions were "personalized" in terms of available instruments, the expertise and imagination of performers, and, most importantly, the musical challenge presented by the composer. Not until jazz appeared on the scene during the latter part of the nineteenth century did performers again have the individual freedom that was accorded amateur and professional musicians of the Baroque period.

The typical trio sonata was performed by four instruments: two violins, harpsichord, and cello. There were, however, three lines of music: one for each violin and a bass line for cello and harpsichord which included a musical shorthand (called *figured bass*) for the chords to be played on the harpsichord. The harpsichordist was free to fill in the harmonies as necessary since the function was to improvise a suitable accompaniment.

Trio sonatas usually had a four-movement sequence of slow–fast–slow–fast. By the early part of the seventeenth century the familiar Italian words used to indicate approximate tempos were in common use, namely, *allegro, adagio, andante, presto,* and the like. The two violins would be used in imitation throughout each movement. In slow movements the second violin would follow closely after the first violin. In fast movements, however, the second entrance would be delayed until the first violin had played a complete theme.

The following trio sonata is entitled *Sonata da chiesa,* which is a generic term for a church sonata of a more profound nature than a *sonata da camera* (chamber sonata), such as a dance suite.

Sonata da chiesa in e Minor, opus 3, no. 7[1]

Arcangelo Corelli (1653–1713)
Total Time: 6:20

I (First Movement)

Theme a
Grave (very slow)

II

Theme a
Allegro (fast)

III

Theme a
Adagio (slow)

---

1. "Opus 3" means this is the third large collection of trio sonatas by the composer (*opus* = work). That this is the seventh trio sonata in the collection is indicated by "no. 7."

Theme a
Allegro

repeated
many
times

Concerto

The classic Baroque concerto was the *concerto grosso* in which a small group of soloists *(concertino)* performed in conjunction with a full orchestra *(tutti* or *concerto grosso)*. Bach, Handel, and Vivaldi did write *solo concertos* for single instruments but Baroque composers preferred the sonority of the concertino as it blended and contrasted with the full orchestra.[2] Baroque concerto grossos usually have the following characteristics:

Three movements: fast–slow–fast
Tuttis (Italian, *all*): soloist(s) and orchestra play
    together
Solo passages with orchestral accompaniment
Orchestral interludes
Echo effects: *forte* (loud) passages followed
    immediately by *piano* (soft) passages

One of the inimitable sounds of the period was that of the Baroque trumpet. Formerly limited to use in warfare and at royal courts, the trumpet became a favorite instrument because of its bright tone quality and its rich, full sound.

The following concerto for two trumpets and orchestra exploits many of the capabilities of high-pitched Baroque trumpets. The contrasts between light and dark are highlighted by the contrasts between the glittering tones of the trumpets and the sonorous sounds of the strings.

Concerto in C Major for Two Trumpets and Orchestra

Antonio Vivaldi (1685–1743)
Total Time: 8:10

I

The first movement has a main section that is played three times and is connected by variations of three melodic ideas.

Allegro

Theme a

II

The slow movement (*largo*) is only six measures in length and amounts to a soft orchestral interlude between fast movements.

_____
2. A composition for solo instrument and keyboard accompaniment is a *sonata*.

There are three main themes, usually started by Trumpet I and imitated by Trumpet II.

Allegre moderato (moderately fast)

Theme a

f (forte)

Theme b

Theme c

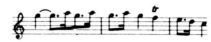

Vocal-Instrumental

Chorale

When Martin Luther failed to convince Rome that the Church was long overdue for internal reform he was, in effect, forced into an external reformation. Among his basic ideas was his concern for congregational participation in the service of worship. Congregational singing was of special importance to Luther because it tended to bind the congregation and the clergy together in a common endeavor. Also, music had, in Luther's opinion, a spiritual, transcendental quality that enriched and elevated the worship service. Unlike John Calvin, Luther, once a priest of the Church of Rome, culled the rich musical heritage of the Church, selecting and adapting plainsong to the needs and capabilities of Protestant congregations. For the first time in many centuries common people once again took an active part in worship as they raised their voices in song.

By definition, a *chorale* is a hymn tune of the German Protestant church. The tempo is usually slow and the musical form is A–A–B (bar form). Bar form has a repeated phrase of A followed by a new phrase identified as B. The following chorale is derived from the Easter sequence *Victimae paschali laudes*.

The typical Lutheran service of the eighteenth century began at 7:00 A.M. and concluded at noon. In the larger churches professional musicians (such as Bach) were expected to teach school during the week, maintain the organ, train a volunteer choir, compose special instrumental and vocal music for each Sunday of the year, and play the organ and direct the choir during the Sunday service. Each Sunday occupied a special place in the liturgical year, with special emphasis upon Christmas, the Epiphany, Easter, and Pentecost. The music for each Sunday of the liturgical calendar had to correspond with the special meaning of that Sunday from opening chorale prelude through the hymns, the cantata, and the concluding postlude.

Chorale: *Christ lag in Todesbanden*
(Christ Lay in Death's Dark Prison)

Text by Martin Luther
(total of seven verses)

Harmonized by J. S. Bach
Time: 1:35

7. We cel-e-brate this Ho-ly Feast in rev-er-ence u-nit-ed. Christ Him-self the
The e-vil leav-en works no more, Thy Word its curse has right-ed.

Feast will be and nour-ish our souls that we by Faith may gain sal-va-tion. Hal-le-lu-jah!

Chorale Prelude: *Christ lag in Todesbanden*

J. S. Bach
Time: 1:35

Chorale Prelude

An organ composition consisting of variations on a chorale melody is called a *chorale prelude.* The variations are to be played *before* the congregation sings the chorale, hence the term *prelude.* The intention of the organist is to set the general mood of the chorale so the congregation can sing it with more understanding.

The above chorale prelude is based on the melody *Christ lag in Todesbanden.* The tempo is now slower because Bach has added a descending, undulating accompaniment pattern. This constant downward movement is a bit of characteristic tone painting and represents the body of Christ buried in the tomb.

Cantata

A *cantata* (Italian, *cantare,*[3] to sing) is a set of movements for soloist(s), chorus (usually), and instrumental accompaniment based on a continuous narrative text. The text may be either secular or sacred, but the latter form is more familiar, primarily due to the large output of sacred cantatas by Johann Sebastian Bach.[4]

The following cantata is based entirely on the chorale illustrated in the two versions outlined above. The seven verses by Martin Luther are separated into seven different movements preceded by a brief instrumental introduction. Because the melody is present in some form in each verse the piece is called a *chorale cantata.*

Cantata no. 4: *Christ lag in Todesbanden*

J. S. Bach
Time: 22:10 (complete)

Sinfonia (orchestra prelude)[5]

Verse I—four-part chorus (SATB) and orchestra
Chorale melody (A–A–B): sung by sopranos in *augmentation* (each note twice as long as in original melody)

Text:
Christ lay by death enshrouded, *from* mortal sin to save us.
He is again arisen, *eternal* life He gave us.
So now let us be joyful, and *magnify* Him thankfully
And *singing Hallelujah, Hallelujah!*

The singing of a new line of text is indicated with the italicized words above.

---

3. As compared with *sonata* (Italian, *sonare,* to sound). A "sounding piece" is one played by instruments.
4. Bach, however, also wrote a cantata extolling the virtues of a new beverage introduced in Europe: "The Coffee Cantata."

5. Orchestra composed of two flutes, three oboes, four trumpets, two timpani, violins I and II, violas, continuo (harpsichord or organ and cello).

Verse II—soprano, alto, and orchestra
Chorale melody divided between two voices
Striding bass figure used throughout:

Text:
O Death, none could lay thee low, no child of man subdue thee.
Our sin brought all this to pass, for there is no health in us.
Therefore soon came Death, Ah soon, and threw over us his net,
To hold us captive fast imprisoned, Hallelujah!

Verse III—Tenors and orchestra
Chorale melody with embellishments for the Hallelujah's
Orchestral figure used throughout:

Text:
Jesus Christ, our God's own son, for us to earth descended.
And all our sin has He atoned, and so Death's rule has ended.
All Death's power here below is now a vain, an empty show;
His sting is lost forever, Hallelujah!

Verse IV—four-part chorus and orchestra
Chorale melody sung by altos; other parts based on the melody and used in imitation

Text:
It was a wonderful array, with Life and Death embattled,
For Life is victor over Death, Death is swallowed up in victory.
So the saying comes to pass, Death swallowed up in victory.
O Grave, where is thy victory? Hallelujah.

Verse V—basses and orchestra
Chorale melody in triple meter with embellishments, especially with the concluding Hallelujah's; chorale melody also in orchestra

Text:
For us the Easter lamb was slain, God's promised boon bestowing.
High hung He there upon the Cross, with Love supernal glowing.
His Blood sprinkled on our door, with Faith bade Death to pass o'er.
The Slayer can no more harm us. Hallelujah!

Verse VI—sopranos, tenors, and orchestra
Chorale melody: both voices in imitation
Jumping bass figure throughout:

Text:
So let us keep this Holy Feast, with glad and gay rejoicing
For us the Sun is shining bright, our Lord Himself is risen.
Lighted by His glowing Grace, our radiant Hearts are glorified.
The Night of Sin is now over. Hallelujah!

Verse VII—four-part chorus and orchestra
Exactly the same form as the original chorale given on page 393

Opera

Opera (Italian, from Latin *opera,* work) is generally considered to be the most "Baroque" of all of the artistic media of the age. Opera began as a "reform" movement in the late sixteenth century as an attempt to return to what was mistakenly thought to be the proper combination of words and music used by the ancient Greeks. Text was all-important, vocal lines were sparse, and accompaniment minimal. However, within a remarkably short period of time opera developed into a full-blown music drama with elaborate sets, costumes, and choruses. Despite various regional differences in style between Florence, Rome, Venice, Vienna, Paris, and London, opera became the most spectacular and popular art form of the period.

"Art form" may not be the proper term for some purists, because opera was a collage of the arts and crafts of music, poetry, acting, dance, set design, costuming, lighting, and so forth. Elaborate opera houses were built all over Europe for an art form which, in a manner of speaking, put the vitality of an era on stage for all to see and hear.

Italian operas became the favorite artistic import for most of the nations of western Europe. French nationalism, however, strongly resisted the dominance of Italian music. Critics lambasted Italian operas as being too long, monotonous, too arty, archaic in language, and with flamboyant singing that obscured the sound and the sense of the words, thus leaving no appeal to the logical French mind. Additionally, the male sopranos and altos—the *castrati*—were said to horrify the women and to cause the men to snicker.

But the most important reasons why the French resisted Italian opera were probably because of drama and the dance. As drama, Italian opera was not in the same league with the theatre of Corneille, Racine, and Molière. Dance—French ballet—was central to the French musical stage but only minimal in Italian opera.

The struggle between French and Italian music finally became an actual confrontation when the noted Italian opera composer, Cavalli, was commissioned to write a festive opera for the wedding of Louis XIV. It was at this point that the director of the king's music, Jean Baptiste Lully (1632–1687)—born Gianbattista Lulli in Florence—turned the occasion to his advantage. The opera was indeed performed in 1662 for the king's wedding and it was monumental, lasting some six hours. However, each act concluded with one of Lully's large-scale ballets. The French reaction to this spectacle was interesting: the entire production was seen, not as a music drama with interpolated dances, but as a gigantic ballet with operatic interludes. Cavalli returned to Italy, vowing never to write another opera while Lully continued his intrigues becoming, in time, as absolute a sovereign in music as Louis XIV was in affairs of state. Capping a highly successful career, Lully died with one of the greatest fortunes ever amassed by a musician.

Italian opera did prevail in England where all attempts at establishing English opera were ultimately futile. The German-born George Frederick Handel (1685–1759) dominated the London theatrical scene with forty operas in thirty years, all Italian. Despite the consistently high quality of his music, Handel's operas were, in the long run, financial failures. London nobility was too weak to support opera and the court was not interested. The middle class was definitely not interested in musical entertainment designed for the nobility and sung in a foreign language.

The enormous success of *The Beggar's Opera* (1728) by John Gay and Johann Pepusch served to highlight the precarious state of opera in London. Called a "Newgate Pastoral" by Jonathan Swift, this ballad opera combined political satire with parodies of Italian opera. A twentieth-century version of this perennial musical play by Bertolt Brecht and Kurt Weill is entitled *Threepenny Opera,* "because beggars can pay only three-pence admission."

In the latter part of his career Handel turned from composing operas for the nobility to writing oratorios for the middle class. He had written Anglican church music and oratorios since he first settled in London, but he did not concentrate on oratorios until after his operatic period. His most celebrated work, the *Messiah* (1741), receives many performances today, while his other oratorios and his operas are less in demand.

Rococo (1725–1775)

The last stage of the Baroque period is characterized by an even more ornate style called *Rococo* (from the French, *rocaille,* rock, and *coquilles,* shells). The Baroque principles of design were applied to surfaces rather than to outlines. The grandeur of the Baroque was scaled down to an emphasis on interior design and decorative scroll and shell work, resulting in a sort of domesticated, sometimes decadent, Baroque.

In music, *rococo* is the "gallant style," a highly refined art of elegant pleasantness suitable for intimate social gatherings in fashionable salons. Among the chief exponents were François Couperin and Domenico Scarlatti with Rococo styles comparable to the painting of Watteau, Boucher, and Fragonard, the sculpture of Falconet, and the designs of Cuvilliés.

The Amalienburg lodge (fig. 19.2), located on the grounds of Nymphenburg Palace near Munich, represents the epitome of Rococo refinement, grace, and elegance: opulence on a small scale. The central mirror in figure 19.2 reflects an outside window, indicating a room large enough for masked balls but small enough to be intimate. Approximately thirty

Figure 19.2 François Cuvilliés, Hall of Mirrors, The Amalienburg, Nymphenburg Palace, Munich, 1734–1739.

couples could dance to a small chamber orchestra or listen to a harpsichord recital.

The room is a compendium of Rococo characteristics: white plaster ceiling with lacy silver tendrils, lavish use of mirrors, all with curvilinear frames, light blue walls with silver insets and shell-like decoration, parquet floor, elaborately carved furniture in silver with cabriole legs and, highlighting the room, an array of exquisite chandeliers.

The following harpsichord composition is as representative of Rococo music as the Hall of Mirrors is of Rococo decoration. The texture of the piece is light and airy, and the melodic line is replete with curving embellishments.

Piece for Clavecin: *La Galante*

François Couperin (1668–1733)
Time: 2:10

The principal theme is used throughout in imitation. The form or structure of the piece is still two-part, called binary and described as A–B. Even with the Rococo title the piece is in fact a *gigue.*

Theme

Key: E Major

Classicism in Music (1760–1827)

The Classical period in music dates from about 1760, the beginning of Haydn's mature style, to about 1827, the year of Beethoven's death. Haydn, Mozart, and Beethoven were musical giants in what has been called the Golden Age of Music, an era of extraordinary musical achievements. Other eras have perhaps been as musically productive but none have become so mutually identifiable as the Classical period, the Golden Age, and the musical output of Haydn, Mozart, and Beethoven.

Table 19.1 Comparison of Stylistic Periods of the Arts

		Approximate Dates	Important Individuals
Period: Baroque		1600–1700	Descartes, Galileo, Kepler, Bacon, Spinoza
Artistic Style:	**Baroque**		
	Architecture	1575–1740	Bernini, Wren, Mansart, Perrault, LeVau
	Music	1600–1750	Corelli, Lully, Vivaldi, Handel, Bach, Purcell
	Painting	1600–1720	Rubens, Rembrandt, Steen, Hals, Vermeer, Van Dyck, Velasquez
	Sculpture	1600–1720	Bernini
Period: The Enlightenment		1687–1789	Newton, Voltaire, Diderot, Locke, Hume, Kant, Rousseau, Frederick II, Jefferson, Franklin
Artistic Style:	**Rococo**		
	Architecture	1715–1760	Erlach, Hildebrandt, Asam, Cuvilliés, Fischer
	Music	1725–1775	Couperin, some of Haydn and Mozart
	Painting	1720–1789	Watteau, Chardin, Boucher, Fragonard
	Sculpture	1770–1825	Clodion, Falconet
Artistic Style:	**Neoclassic**		
	Architecture	1750–1830	Chalgrin, Vignon, Fontaine
	Music (Classicism)	1760–1827	Haydn, Mozart, Beethoven, Gluck
	Painting	1780–1850	David, Ingres
	Sculpture	1800–1840	Canova, Thorwalden, Houdon

The basic homophonic style of Classicism has many antecedents in several earlier periods of music. It is therefore appropriate to briefly review these earlier periods.

Music in the Renaissance was primarily polyphonic and written in the old liturgical modes. Some Renaissance music, English madrigals in particular, was quite homophonic and was, moreover, tonal; that is, it was written in either a major or a minor key rather than in a liturgical mode. The music of Gabrielli in Venice was also strongly homophonic with a preference for sonorous harmonies rather than the multiple melody lines used by Renaissance composers like Josquin, Lassus, and Palestrina.

At the beginning of the seventeenth century there was a relatively brief period of strongly homophonic music as composers attempted to recreate what they thought was the text-oriented musical style of the ancient Greeks. These experiments in words and music led to the development of the new style of music called opera. Opera, the epitome of the new Baroque style, quickly became elaborate and ornate and combined homophonic and polyphonic music. The vocal-instrumental music of the age developed a new and complex style of polyphony, culminating in the music of Handel and Bach.

The Rococo style used Baroque ornamentation, but the style was much more homophonic, less profound, and more stylishly elegant. Some of the characteristics of the Rococo, notably less complex homophonic techniques, were incorporated into a new style called *Classicism, Neoclassicism,* or *Viennese Classicism* (Haydn, Mozart, Beethoven). Classicism is the preferred term for music of the period while Neoclassicism is generally applied to the sister arts.

At no time are the stylistic periods of the arts precisely synchronized. Careful study of the comparative outline given (table 19.1) will indicate that the prevailing world views of the periods since the Renaissance are reflected in the arts at different points in time. Any number of inferences can be drawn regarding the influence of an era on the arts and the arts on each other. It is important to remember, however, that the artistic production of specific individuals is of paramount concern. The uniqueness of the works of art reflects the uniqueness of the individual, the artist who creates these works.

The Classical period of music might also be called the Advanced Age of the Amateur Musician. Baroque music, with its figured bass accompaniments and demands for improvisation, was partially the province of the professional but with real possibilities for gifted amateurs. On the other hand, the latter part of the eighteenth century featured modern notation, with every note written down plus indications for interpretation (tempo, dynamics, etc.), thus providing a better opportunity for music-making by middle- and upper-class amateurs.

The vastly increased demand for music for all occasions resulted in a flood of new compositions (mostly instrumental). There were serenades for outdoor parties, chamber music for indoor gatherings, symphonies for the newly established symphony orchestras, and operas for the increasing number of private and public opera houses. The newly invented piano (ca. 1710 by Cristofori), with its ability to play soft and loud (full name, *pianoforte*) on the single keyboard, rapidly replaced harpsichord and clavichord as the standard home instrument for amateur performance. Amateur chamber music societies were organized for the presentation of programs ranging from sonatas to duets, trios, and so forth, for the various instruments, including the quartets for a homogeneous group of string instruments called, naturally enough, string quartets.

All of this musical activity was of little benefit to those who tried to earn a living with their music. Eighteenth-century musicians were, on the whole, accorded a rather lowly position on the social scale. Typically, composers like Franz Joseph Haydn worked for a noble family like the Esterhazy, wore servant's livery, and sat "below the salt" at the dinner table. Not until the latter part of his life did Haydn achieve any financial independence, and he had to go to the London concert scene to do it. Ironically, the descendants of the once powerful Esterhazy family are notable today only to the extent that some of Haydn's unpublished music may still be in their possession.

Haydn

The professional life of Franz Joseph Haydn (1732–1809) was quite typical of the vicissitudes of a musical career, and yet, Haydn fared a bit better than many of his contemporaries. In a short sketch that he contributed to a 1776 yearbook, Haydn wrote that he sang at court in Vienna and in St. Stephen's Cathedral until his services were terminated at the latter. His services were eminently satisfactory but his voice changed and he was summarily dismissed.

> When my voice finally changed I barely managed to stay alive by giving music lessons to children for about eight years. In this way many talented people are ruined: they have to earn a miserable living and have no time to study.

There were numerous musical opportunities for a musician in Vienna, and most of them paid very little. Musicians were forced to hold down a number of positions in order to survive. Haydn had as many as three jobs on a Sunday morning: playing violin at one church, the organ at another, and singing in the choir at a third. When he finally achieved full employment with the Esterhazy family, he was quite willing, at that time, to relinquish a certain amount of personal freedom.

Haydn, as the first of the composers in the Classical style, led the way in establishing some basic instrumental ensembles like the symphony orchestra and the string quartet. Large enough to produce a rich, full tone but small enough to be intimate and to leave room for personal expression, the string quartet was the preferred classical musical group. Consisting of first and second violin, viola, and cello, corresponding to the SATB division of voices in choral music, the three members of the violin family can achieve a fine balance of unified tone.

The following string quartet by Haydn was composed early in his career and has both Rococo and Classical characteristics. The forms are classical and the melodies quite Rococo in their lightness, clarity, and elegance. The first, second, and last movements

use *sonata form,* an important invention of the period. Classical composers had tired of the late Baroque proclivity for ever more elaborate and sometimes ponderous polyphony. A simpler homophonic style began to emerge and to gradually replace the polyphonic manipulation of a single musical theme. By abandoning the polyphonic, vocal-instrumental style, composers were faced with a dilemma: how to develop a coherent style of purely instrumental music. A certain unity was inherent in vocal music because of the text. Without a text, composers were faced with the possibility of a chaotic mass of instrumental sounds.

Sonata form[6] was an eighteenth-century solution to the problem of the design of instrumental music. In a very real sense, the invention of sonata form reflected the Enlightenment ideals of a structure that was lucid, logical, and symmetrical.

The technical term *sonata form* is a label for a procedure that uses a *dual subject* rather than the single subject of the Baroque style. The first of these two subjects is usually vigorous and dynamic while the second is generally quieter and more lyrical. The two subjects should be, musically speaking, logical parts of the whole; the second subject should somehow complement and balance the first.

In the first movement of the Haydn quartet given below *theme a* is straightforward and vigorous; *theme b* is smoother and more lyrical and with the stipulation that it be played "sweetly." The two subjects (themes) of sonata form are connected by a *bridge,* a transitional passage, which leads smoothly from *theme a* to *theme b.* Following *theme b* there is a closing section called a *codetta.* The complete unit of two themes with connecting transition and closing section contains all the thematic material which has been presented or to which the ear has been *exposed.* This unit is called an *exposition* and can be outlined as indicated below. During the Classical period expositions were normally repeated, as indicated by the sets of double dots.

Exposition

‖: *Theme a* Bridge *Theme b* Codetta :‖

After the basic material has been presented in the exposition, the composer then proceeds to manipulate and exploit selected thematic material in the *development* section. Any and all material may be subjected to a variety of treatment.

Near the end of the development section, the composer usually introduces the *return,* a transitional section which prepares the way for a *recapitulation* of the material from the exposition. The recapitulation does repeat, more or less, the material from the exposition, but there are subtle variances that help avoid monotony.

---

6. Sonata form was not limited to sonatas which are compositions for solo instruments plus accompaniment. The form was also used for trios, quartets, concertos, and symphonies.

After the codetta of the recapitulation, the composer may add a final *coda* if it is felt that something is needed to bring the movement to a satisfactory conclusion.

A complete sonata form can be outlined as follows:

Exposition   Development   Recapitulation

‖: *a* bridge *b* codetta :‖ ‖: return   *a* bridge *b* codetta (coda):‖

String Quartet in F Major, opus 3, no. 5

Franz Joseph Haydn (1732–1809)
Total Time: 13:20

I

Theme a

p   *f*

Theme b

p Dolce (sweetly)

II

This is the famous Serenade movement. The first violin plays *con sordino* (with mute) accompanied by the other instruments playing *pizzicato* (plucking the strings). The effect is like an outdoor serenade for violin and guitar.

Theme a

Dolce

Theme b

III

Theme a

F:

Theme a (Trio)

B♭:

IV

Theme a

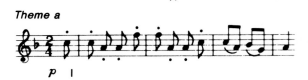

p I

Theme b

p V

Mozart

The nature of musical genius has been a subject of considerable interest to twentieth-century psychologists. The exact nature of the qualities that can be labeled "genius" remains tantalizingly elusive. Thus, the accomplishments of Wolfgang Amadeus Mozart (1756–1791), possibly the greatest musical genius who ever lived, are both awesome and inexplicable.

Mozart devoted virtually his entire life to the composition and performance of music. Like Haydn, he had to endure the slights of a society as yet unready and unwilling to recognize, let alone support, his incredible gifts. Unlike Haydn, he never found a noble patron. His brief, poverty-stricken life and eventual burial in an unmarked grave testify eloquently to the status of a musician in Vienna during the Golden Age of Music.

There are many accounts of Mozart's precocity but none more typical of his manner of composition—and life-style—than the occasion of the premiere of his opera, *Don Giovanni*. The opera was complete except for the overture which was, according to the composer, "finished." On the day of the premiere, Mozart was busily engaged in shooting billiards, one of his favorite occupations. In reply to urgent questioning, he reiterated that he had completed the overture. Upon being pressed to produce a musical score he finally admitted that the piece was indeed completed—in his head—and that he had not gotten around to writing it down. Many cups of coffee later, the complete parts, still dripping with wet ink, were rushed to the opera house where the orchestra, with no time left for rehearsing, sight-read the music. Characteristically, the thousands of musical notes which Mozart had mentally arranged added up to a masterpiece in the field of operatic overtures.

The following symphony by Mozart was probably not written down as hastily as the operatic overture but, stylistically, the similarities are many for only several years separated the two works. The symphony is supremely concise and lucid, stylish and elegant, and powerful but always lyrical. In Mozart's hands, the symphony orchestra sings like one instrument.

Symphony no. 40 in g Minor (1788)

Wolfgang Amadeus Mozart (1756–1791)
Total time: 27:20
(complete symphony)

The modern symphony orchestra was developed during the Classical period. Standard components were a nucleus of a full body of strings plus woodwinds and sometimes trumpets and timpani. Mozart's Symphony no. 40 used the following instrumentation: flute, two oboes, two clarinets, two bassoons, two French horns, violin I, violin II, viola, cello, bass.

A *symphony* may be defined as a sonata for orchestra, just as the quartet by Haydn was a sonata for string quartet. The first, second, and last movements are in sonata form. The form of the third movement can be described as Minuet–Trio–Minuet. As with the Haydn quartet, only the basic themes are given.

A summary of Mozart's musical compositions is given below. The list indicates at least three things: (1) the breadth of Mozart's musical interests; (2) the kinds of music required of Mozart (most of his work was commissioned); and (3) the incredible productivity of a sometimes destitute young musician who died in his thirty-sixth year.

Vocal

Secular

  57 Arias
  24 Operas and other stage works
  19 Duets and trios
  37 Songs
Many cadenzas

Sacred

   8 Cantatas
  37 Kyries and other works
   7 Litanies and vespers
  19 Masses
  17 Church sonatas (organ)
   4 Oratorio arrangements

Instrumental

Piano

- 10 Piano duets
- 35 Minuets and variations
- 12 Trios, quartets, quintets
- 33 Sonatas and fantasias
- 30 Piano concertos
- 9 Miscellaneous compositions

Many cadenzas

Violin, Strings, Orchestra

- 40 Violin sonatas
- 11 Violin concertos
- 5 String duets and trios
- 25 String quartets
- 6 String quintets
- 13 Miscellaneous chamber works
- 13 Miscellaneous concertos
- 52 Symphonies
- 101 Serenades, divertimenti, cassations, etc.

Beethoven

Ludwig van Beethoven (1770–1827), unlike Haydn and Mozart, forged a place for himself as an economically independent musician. He was not above selling the same composition to different publishers and, in fact, did so quite often. He reasoned that the publishers had cheated composers long enough; he was merely collecting retribution for a long chain of abuses.

Beethoven's finances were generally sound though somewhat chaotic. His health, on the other hand, was another matter. He began to notice a hearing loss at an early age, a loss that gradually evolved into total deafness. This deafness became, at times, almost more than a musician could bear.

The fact that some of Beethoven's greatest music was composed while he was completely deaf is a testament to his genius and to his unconquerable spirit. He himself conducted the premiere of his Ninth Symphony, that powerful and imposing work dedicated to the exalted ideal of the Brotherhood of Man. At the conclusion of the symphony he remained facing the orchestra, solitary in his silence, and thinking that the work had failed. Finally, someone turned him about to face the thunderous applause of an audience that was both inspired and deeply moved.

Beethoven's Third Symphony, the *Eroica,* was originally dedicated to Napoleon, whom Beethoven regarded as a true Faustian man (see chap. 20). There were many victims of Napoleon's march to power— "while man's desires and aspirations stir, he cannot choose but err"—but it appeared that he was using his energy to make the world a better place in which people could work out their freedom. However, Napoleon declared himself emperor, and Beethoven furiously erased his name from the dedicatory page of the *Eroica,* leaving the work implicitly dedicated to the heroic impulses of a Faustian man or, simply, to an unknown hero.

Beethoven poured the very essence of classical symphonic music into his Fifth Symphony, a work which has often been cited as the perfect symphony. Though sometimes threatening to break the bounds of classical form, Beethoven, in the Fifth, channeled his titanic energy into the driving rhythms of this mighty work. The Fifth Symphony is a summary of many aspects of Beethoven's genius: the terse, surging energy of the first movement, the moving and mellow lyricism of the second movement, the exuberant vitality of the scherzo, and the sheer drive of the finale.

The orchestra as Beethoven knew it was simply not large and expressive enough for this symphony. He enlarged his tonal palette by adding instruments at both ends of the spectrum and then adding trombones in the middle to obtain the full and rich sound that he had to have. Following is the instrumentation for the enlarged orchestra needed to perform Beethoven's Fifth Symphony: piccolo, two flutes, two oboes, two clarinets, two bassoons, contra-bassoon, two French horns, two trumpets, three trombones, two timpani, sixteen violin I, fourteen violin II, ten viola, eight cello, six bass. (The number of strings can vary; these are approximations.)

The first movement is in sonata form. The second movement is a theme and variations. The theme is stated and then followed by a series of increasingly elaborate variations. Rather than a minuet, Beethoven uses a scherzo for the third movement, which is faster and more dynamic. For the fourth movement Beethoven uses sonata form with a very long coda.

The Fifth Symphony achieves a maximum effect with the utmost economy of musical materials. Essentially, the entire symphony is built out of one musical interval and one rhythmic pattern:

Interval of 3rd plus pattern of

This *motive* is so brief that it is referred to as a *germ motive* from which the entire symphony is germinated.

The Fifth Symphony is a prime example of the Classical style: logical, direct, and to the point, objective, controlled, achieving maximum effect with a minimum of means (use of the germ motive). Beethoven is considered by some to be a pivotal figure in musical styles standing midway between classicism and the dawning Age of Romanticism; however, his heroic style and even his introspective later works all testify to his fundamental classical outlook, namely, his rational control of his own destiny. Beethoven's music served *him;* he was the master who, with disciplined creativity, molded (and sometimes hammered) his musical materials into the structured sounds of the Classical style.

Symphony no. 5 in c Minor, opus 67 (1808)

Ludwig van Beethoven (1770–1827)
Total Time: 30:45

I

Theme a

Bridge

Horns

Theme b

II

Theme and variations: Theme, four variations, restatement of theme and coda

Theme a   violas cellos

p Dolce

III

Scherzo: form is Scherzo-Trio-Scherzo (A-B-A)
Note: Scherzo is similar in form to the minuet but faster and more vigorous.

Scherzo:
Theme a

pp low strings

violins

Theme b (Derived from *Germ Motive*)

Horns

Trio

Theme a

f low strings (cellos, basses)

Transition directly to 4th movement

50

4th movement

pp   sempre *pp*

Violin I's gradually rising in pitch. Instruments added, full orchestra reached four measures from end.

IV

Sonata form (in march style)

Theme a

tutti

Theme b

Summary

From about 1600 to 1750, the Baroque style built a new kind of music on the classical foundations of the Renaissance. The flexible modal system of the past was narrowed down to a single tonal center, or *key,* with the modal possibilities reduced to two: major or minor. Compensating for the limiting of tonal materials to a single major or minor key were the new possibilities for building compositions in terms of contrasting keys and modulating from one key to another.

Baroque *dance suites,* based in a single key, combined stylized dance types of three or four national origins into a coherent sequence of contrasting movements (A–C–S–O–G) in binary form.

With the establishment of a tonal center, the *fugue* became one of the basic monothematic styles of the Baroque. Composers could manipulate both the fugal subject and various major and minor key relations. The *passacaglia,* on the other hand, remained in the same key throughout, with variations built out of varying textures and rhythmic patterns.

The ubiquitous *trio sonata* was perhaps most representative of Baroque music-making because of the emphasis on instrumental music with improvised accompaniment in the *continuo* part. *Concertos* were more formal because of the larger number of instrumentalists involved, but the continuo still played an important accompanying part for orchestra and soloist(s).

Following the Reformation, the German sacred songs called *chorales* assumed an important place in congregational singing and in organ literature in the form of *chorale preludes. Cantatas, oratorios,* and *operas* were the most important vocal forms of the Baroque although there was still a tradition of composing masses and motets.

The surface elements of the ornate Baroque style assumed a primary emphasis in the style called Rococo. The Rococo, or ''gallant style'' of music (1725–1775), with its light, airy texture and elegant ornamentation served as a bridge between the sumptuous Baroque and the gracefully refined style of the Classical period.

During the Classical period (1760–1827), instrumental musicians, whether professional or amateur, came into their own. The improvement in musical instruments and the great interest in amateur performance encouraged the composition of chamber music *(sonatas, string quartets,* etc.) and orchestral music ranging from *serenades* for soirees to *symphonies* for the growing number of concert halls. Monothematic polyphony was replaced by a dual-subject (bi-thematic) structure called *sonata form* in which composers could combine two contrasting subjects into an expressive and balanced whole.

The Classical period, coinciding with the height of the Age of Enlightenment, created chamber music and the symphony orchestra virtually as they are known today. Even more important, music progressed from a more or less private concern of the aristocracy or the church to a public art available to all.

Unit 7

The Middle Modern World, 1789–1914

20

Revolution, Romanticism, Realism

Power and Politics

With the advantage of 20–20 hindsight we can see the rise of nationalism, colonialism, and imperialism to an inexorable climax in the Great War that was supposed to end all wars. Catchwords along the way were national honor, fame, and glory but the brutal realities were envy, greed, destruction, and death. Amidst the thunder of the Guns of August the Romantic Century was laid to rest on the static battlefields of Europe, along with half a generation of young men.

Revolution to Waterloo

By 1792 the French Revolution was faltering. There had been a noble "Declaration of the Rights of Man and the Citizen," feudalism had been abolished, the monastic orders suppressed and church properties confiscated, but the enemies of France were assaulting the borders and internal disorder was increasing. The execution of Robespierre in 1794 ended the Terror but it took the establishment of the Directory in 1795 to temporarily stabilize the state. Composed of men of conspicuous wealth, the Directory ruled from 1795 to 1799 with the assistance of the military, most notably the Corsican general Napoleon Buonaparte (1769–1821). Under the guise of saving the revolution Napoleon seized power in a coup d'état in 1799 and declared himself First Consul. Proclaiming himself emperor in 1804, Napoleon launched a course of conquest that engulfed much of Europe and part of Africa. Waterloo (June 18, 1815) was an anticlimax to the fall of a conqueror who lost his entire Grand Army of 500,000 men on the scorched steppes of Russia.

Napoleon saw himself as the enlightened, benevolent despot who had saved the revolution (fig. 20.1), but he had to maintain order with the army and, especially, his secret police. He did establish the Code of Napoleon, a model of modern civil laws that buried the inequities of the *ancien regime* and set the stage for the rise of the middle class. The Napoleonic legend of the military and political genius who fostered liberalism and nationalism contains, therefore, elements of truth. The ideals

405

Figure 20.1 Jacques Louis David, *Napoleon in His Study,* 1812. Oil on canvas, 80½ × 49¼″. Wearing the Legion of Honor, Napoleon is pictured by his court painter as a conscientious ruler who has stayed up until 4:12 A.M. working for his subjects. Samuel H. Kress Collection. National Gallery of Art, Washington, D.C.

of the French Revolution did, in time, inspire the spread of democracy throughout the Western world. The other side of the coin was dark and bloody; the Napoleonic wars caused enormous destruction of lives and property.

The French were fascinated by Napoleon as leader and legend but the rest of Europe viewed him much as did Lord Byron, who wrote his "Ode to Napoleon Buonaparte" upon learning of the Emperor's abdication and banishment to Elba in 1814. Following are the first and last stanzas of a vitriolic nineteen-stanza poem exulting in the downfall of a tyrant who could have been the equal, according to Byron, of an American general.

Literary Selection
ODE TO NAPOLEON BUONAPARTE
Lord Byron

'T is done—but yesterday a King!
　　And arm'd with Kings to strive—
And now thou art a nameless thing:
　　So abject—yet alive!
Is this the man of thousand thrones,
Who strew'd our earth with hostile bones,
　　And can he thus survive?
Since he, miscall'd the Morning Star,
Nor man nor fiend hath fallen so far.

Where may the wearied eye repose,
　　When gazing on the Great;
Where neither guilty glory glows,
　　Nor despicable state?
Yes—one—the first—the last—the best—
The Cincinnatus of the West,
　　Whom envy dared not hate,
Bequeath'd the name of Washington,
To make man blush there was but one!

April 10, 1814

Napoleon's conquerors were deep in deliberations at the Congress of Vienna when he escaped from Elba and rallied his still loyal armies for a Hundred Days campaign that ended, once and for all, on the field of Waterloo. Final banishment to the remote island of St. Helena and a heavy guard assured the allies of a peace on their terms.

Called the "peace concert of Europe," the Congress of Vienna involved Austria, Prussia, Russia, and England, but its guiding spirit was Prince Clemens von Metternich (MEH–ter–NIKH; 1773–1859), the chief minister of Austria. A reactionary and arch defender of the old order, Metternich sought and achieved a balance of power that favored Austria and reinforced established monarchies at the expense of all liberal movements, marking the period of 1815–1848 as the Age of Metternich. Napoleon's foreign minister, Prince Charles Maurice de Talleyrand (1754–1838), betrayed Napoleon, won easier peace terms for his country, and effected the restoration of the Bourbon kings with Louis XVIII (1814–1824), the brother of Louis XVI.

The Revolutions of 1830 and 1848

The heavy-handed, reactionary rule of Charles X (1824–1830), who succeeded Louis XVIII, led to the July Revolution of 1830 in which the workers of Paris challenged the government. When the troops and police refused to fire on the rioters, the king quickly abdicated, delighting the liberals who, with visions of major social improvements, saw a possibility of relieving the misery of the workers who were oppressed by the monarchy and the Industrial Revolution. Upon invitation of the Chamber of Deputies, Louis Philippe (1830–1848) assumed rule of a "bourgeois monarchy," which catered to the wealthy middle class and ignored the industrial workers. The brief July Revolution sparked violence in Germany, Italy, Spain, Portugal, Poland, and Belgium, all of which was put down by force except in Belgium which, in 1831, won its independence from Holland.

A wave of revolutions swept Europe in 1848, the year in which Marx and Engels published *The Communist Manifesto.* The suppressed forces of liberalism erupted in France, Prussia, Austria, Hungary, Bohemia, Croatia, and the Italian possessions of the Hapsburgs. Repression was even more severe than in 1830 but, as Marx had written, "The specter of Communism" was haunting Europe.

The Industrial Revolution

Between 1750 and 1850 there were, in England, striking changes in the economic structure as the nation moved from an agrarian society to modern industrialism. The change had been astonishingly rapid because so many important factors already existed: capitalism, international trade, mercantilism, colonialism, the Protestant work ethic. England already had hand-operated domestic (cottage) industries; what was needed was power to drive the machinery and this became available when, in 1769, James Watt patented an improved version of the steam engine that Thomas Newcomen had invented in ca. 1700 to pump water out of mine shafts.[1]

Why was England the original home of the Industrial Revolution rather than prosperous Holland or rich and powerful France? American economic historian W. W. Rostow suggests that national pride and confidence were buoyed by a series of English military victories but, more importantly, that the mix of needed resources was best in England:

> Britain, with more basic industrial resources than the Netherlands; more nonconformists, and more ships than France; with its political, social, and religious revolution fought out by 1688—Britain alone was in a position to weave together cotton manufacture, coal and iron technology, the steam-engine and ample foreign trade to pull it off.[2]

With its head start England became the textile center of the world but, after 1850, Belgium, France, Germany, and the United States were also involved not only in industrialization but in dramatic changes in communications, agricultural chemistry, machinery, and transportation. Railroads and steamships helped turn northern Europe and North America into an energetic and highly competitive complex that, in effect, functioned like an economic community.

Development of the Western Nations

Only in France did the 1848 revolution succeed and then just briefly. The Second Republic lasted from 1848 to 1852, followed by the Second Empire of Napoleon III (1852–1870). Deliberately provoked by Bismarck, the Franco-Prussian War (1870–1871) toppled the inept emperor and humiliated the nation. The Third Republic of 1871 finally exorcised absolutism in France but the Dreyfus Affair (1894–1906) nearly ripped the nation asunder. Falsely accused of treason, Captain Alfred Dreyfus (dry–fus; 1859–1935)

was cashiered from the army and given a life sentence on Devil's Island. Generally speaking, anti-Semites, royalists, militarists, and Catholics backed the army while republicans, socialists, intellectuals, and anti-clericals supported Dreyfus. Emile Zola, for example, was jailed for his inflammatory newspaper article: *"J'Accuse"* (1898). It took a civil court to exonerate Dreyfus and reinstate him in the army as a major. Monarchists and Catholics were discredited, paving the way for the separation of Church and State.

Otto Fürst von Bismarck (1815–1898), the premier of Prussia (1862–1890), personally created the German Empire in 1871 when he had William I of Prussia proclaimed emperor (1871–1888). Consolidating his gains after the Danish War (1864), Austro-Prussian War (1866), and Franco-Prussian War (1870–1871), the "iron chancellor" made a unified Germany the new power in Europe. William II (1888–1918), the grandson of Queen Victoria, had his own ideas about royal power and dismissed his chancellor in 1890. Bismarck criticized the Kaiser unceasingly as the emperor armed his nation for the conflict that erupted in 1914. William II abdicated in 1918.

Under the reign of Francis II (1792–1835) Austria was defeated on four different occasions by the French. Ferdinand (1835–1848) had frequent fits of insanity, which left Metternich free to govern in his name. The 1848 revolution drove Ferdinand from the throne and Metternich from power but the monarchy continued under the ill-fated Francis Joseph (1848–1916), Emperor of Austria and King of Hungary (1867–1916). The emperor's brother, Maximilian I, was installed by Napoleon III as Emperor of Mexico (1864–1867) but executed by the revolutionary forces of Juarez after the French emperor withdrew his troops. Elizabeth, the wife of Francis Joseph, was assassinated in 1898 by an Italian anarchist and his only son, Archduke Rudolf, was found dead along with his mistress Baroness Maria Vetsera at Mayerling. Thought to possibly be a double suicide, the tragedy remains a mystery. Heir-apparent to Francis Joseph, his grandnephew Archduke Francis Ferdinand (1863–1914) and his wife were assassinated on June 28, 1914, by a Serbian nationalist at Sarajevo, leading to the ultimate tragedy of World War I.

Ruled by the Turks since 1456, Greece finally began, in 1821, a rebellion that engaged the romantic imagination of the Western world. Ancient Greece was the birthplace of democracy and of Western culture, and Philhellenic (pro-Greek) committees in Europe and America sent supplies and money while demanding that civilized nations intervene directly, which, eventually, England, France, and Russia did. The war was ferocious with Greek peasants slaughtering every Turk in sight and the Turks retaliating, for example, by killing or selling into slavery all 30,000 residents of the island of Chios, which inspired Delacroix's painting of *Massacre at Chios*. Lord Byron could not resist the siren call of Greek independence and died there in 1824. By 1832 independence had been achieved but Greek nationalism was not fully victorious until after World War II.

---

1. Reinvented would be a more appropriate word. The ancient Greeks were apparently the first to invent the steam engine. Judging by the drawings of Heron (or Hero) of Alexandria (ca. second century A.D.), steam power was used in toy gadgets that caused birds to sing and Tritons to blow their horns. See Brumbaugh, Robert S. *Ancient Greek Gadgets and Machines.* Westport, Conn.: Greenwood Press, 1975.
2. W. W. Rostow, *The Stages of Economic Growth* (New York: Cambridge University Press, 1960), p. 33.

Early in the nineteenth century Italy was temporarily unified under Napoleon, but the Congress of Vienna again reduced it to petty states. After abortive revolts in 1821, 1830, and 1848, Giuseppe Garibaldi (1807–1882) spearheaded the Risorgimento (rie–sor–jie–MEN–toe; resurgence) which, by 1861, established Italy as the first political entity since the demise of the Roman Empire. Victor Emmanuel II (1861–1878) was supported by Garibaldi and Camillo Benzo Cavour (1810–1861) as the first monarch of the Kingdom of Italy. By 1870 the Papal States had been incorporated into the kingdom but not until 1929 was Vatican City established as a separate sovereign state of 108 acres.

Plagued by Czarist repression and widespread corruption, poverty, and ignorance, Russia was the most backward country in Europe. Czar Alexander I (1801–1825) attempted some reforms but, under the influence of Metternich, he became a reactionary and his successor, Nicholas I (1825–1855), was even more rigid. The campaign of Nicholas to dominate southeast Europe led to the Crimean War (1853–1856) in which the allied powers of Turkey, England, France, and Sardinia stopped, for a time, Russian expansionism. The main campaign was the siege of the Russian Naval Base at Sevastopol but the war itself was notorious for the appalling neglect of wounded soldiers and general incompetence of command. Florence Nightingale organized field hospitals but nothing could save the troops from tragic blunders epitomized by the futile gallantry of the Light Brigade. Tennyson's poem typifies the romantic fantasies about honor and glory that were later to end in the Great War.

Literary Selection

THE CHARGE OF THE LIGHT BRIGADE
Alfred, Lord Tennyson

I

Half a league, half a league,
    Half a league onward,
All in the valley of Death
    Rode the six hundred.
'Forward, the Light Brigade!
Charge for the guns!' he said:
Into the valley of Death
    Rode the six hundred.

II

'Forward, the Light Brigade!'
Was there a man dismay'd?
Not tho' the soldier knew
    Some one had blunder'd:
Their's not to make reply,
Their's not to reason why,
Their's but to do and die:
Into the valley of Death
    Rode the six hundred.

III

Cannon to right of them,
Cannon to left of them,
Cannon in front of them
    Volley'd and thunder'd;
Storm'd at with shot and shell,
Boldly they rode and well,
Into the jaws of Death,
Into the mouth of Hell
    Rode the six hundred.

IV

Flash'd all their sabres bare,
Flash'd as they turn'd in air
Sabring the gunners there,
Charging an army, while
    All the world wonder'd:
Plunged in the battery-smoke
Right thro' the line they broke;
Cossack and Russian
Reel'd from the sabre-stroke
    Shatter'd and sunder'd.
Then they rode back, but not
    Not the six hundred.

V

Cannon to right of them,
Cannon to left of them,
Cannon behind them
    Volley'd and thunder'd;
Storm'd at with shot and shell,
While horse and hero fell,
They that had fought so well
Came thro' the jaws of Death,
Back from the mouth of Hell,
All that was left of them,
    Left of six hundred.

VI

When can their glory fade?
O the wild charge they made!
    All the world wonder'd.
Honour the charge they made!
Honour the Light Brigade,
    Noble six hundred!

The reign of Alexander II (1855–1881) was about as authoritarian as that of Nicholas I but he did belatedly liberate about forty million serfs with his 1861 Emancipation Act. The assassination of Alexander II led to the brutally oppressive regime of Alexander III (1881–1894) and the inept but equally oppressive reign of Nicholas II (1894–1917), the last of the czars.

The long reign of England's George III (1760–1820) actually ended in 1811 when the king became totally insane. Functioning as Prince Regent (1811–1820) and then king, George IV (1820–1830) led a wildly profligate life that earned the hatred of his subjects. William IV (1830–1837) agreed to the Reform Bill of 1832 that extended suffrage to property-owning subjects, thus still excluding the great mass of workers. His niece, Victoria (1837–1901), re-established the prestige of the crown while presiding over the enormous expansion of the British Empire, symbolized by her crowning as Empress of India in 1876. Though the English monarchy was largely decorative, Victoria determinedly took her role seriously, presiding over the conversion of the country into a political democracy with humanitarian reforms and a measure of social and economic democracy. The British developed a liberal democracy at home while pursuing aggressive imperialism abroad.

Several decades before Victoria's death Victorian earnestness and sobriety had become, for many writers and artists, increasingly boring. Many were ready for a new era and certainly Edward VII (1901–1910) was ready to rule, having been Prince of Wales for sixty years. The Edwardian Age was as flashy and flamboyant as the king himself. Frivolity and high living were eminently fashionable for those who could afford to live in the grand manner. The accession of George V (1910–1936) restored some measure of decorum but all that ended in the late summer of 1914.

Inspired in part by the doctrine of Manifest Destiny, the United States tripled its size during the nineteenth century and increased its population nearly twentyfold. Even more remarkable was the fact that the nation could expand so enormously and still maintain its union. The Civil War (1861–1865) was a cruel test sufficient to destroy perhaps any other nation. Though slavery was an inflammatory issue the conflict was between widely divergent ways of life and different economic structures. Mainly industrial, the North was vigorous and aggressive in the spirit of Calvinism while the South was primarily agricultural with a relaxed and cavalier life-style. Despite the ferocious fighting, the constant threats of wholesale reprisals and other vengeful measures were never realized. Jefferson Davis did spend two years in prison but this was followed by thirty years of peaceful existence. Just as remarkable, Lee surrendered to Grant at Appomattox, the war was over, and that fact was accepted by the South as the final end of a rebellion that would never again be seriously considered. Reconstruction might have proceeded less radically had Lincoln not been assassinated but, nevertheless, his views seemed to temper northern radicals and encourage the moderates. In his memorable Second Inaugural Address, given just five weeks before the end of the war, Lincoln set the tone of what would ultimately prove to be the sanest and wisest attitude in the aftermath of the nation's internal agony.

Literary Selection

SECOND INAUGURAL ADDRESS

March 4, 1865
Abraham Lincoln

Fellow-countrymen: At this second appearing to take the oath of the presidential office, there is less occasion for an extended address than there was at the first. Then a statement, somewhat in detail, of a course to be pursued, seemed fitting and proper. Now, at the expiration of four years, during which public declarations have been constantly called forth on every point and phase of the great contest which still absorbs the attention and engrosses the energies of the nation, little that is new could be presented. The progress of our arms, upon which all else chiefly depends, is as well known to the public as to myself; and it is, I trust, reasonably satisfactory and encouraging to all. With high hope for the future, no prediction in regard to it is ventured.

On the occasion corresponding to this four years ago, all thoughts were anxiously directed to an impending civil war. All dreaded it—all sought to avert it. While the inaugural address was being delivered from this place, devoted altogether to saving the Union without war, insurgent agents were in the city seeking to destroy it without war—seeking to dissolve the Union, and divide effects, by negotiation. Both parties deprecated war; but one of them would make war rather than let the nation survive; and the other would accept war rather than let it perish. And the war came.

One-eighth of the whole population were colored slaves, not distributed generally over the Union, but localized in the Southern part of it. These slaves constituted a peculiar and powerful interest. All knew that this interest was, somehow, the cause of the war. To strengthen, perpetuate, and extend this interest was the object for which the insurgents would rend the Union, even by war; while the government claimed no right to do more than to restrict the territorial enlargement of it.

Neither party expected for the war the magnitude or the duration which it has already attained. Neither anticipated that the cause of the conflict might cease with, or even before, the conflict itself should cease. Each looked for an easier triumph, and a result less fundamental and astounding. Both read the same Bible, and pray to the same God; and each invokes his aid against the other. It may seem strange that any men should dare to ask a just God's assistance in wringing their bread from the sweat of other men's faces; but let us judge not, that we be not judged. The prayers of both could not be answered—that of neither has been answered fully.

The Almighty has his own purposes. "Woe unto the world because of offenses! for it must needs be that offenses come; but woe to that man by whom the offense cometh." If we shall suppose that American slavery is one of those offenses which, in the providence of God, must needs come, but which, having continued through his appointed time, he now wills to remove, and that he gives to both North and South this terrible war, as the woe due to those by whom the offense came, shall we discern therein any departure from those divine attributes which the believers in a living God always ascribe to him? Fondly do we hope—fervently do we pray—that this mighty scourge of war may speedily pass away. Yet, if God wills that it continue until all the wealth piled by the bondman's two hundred and fifty years of unrequited toil shall be sunk, and until every drop of blood drawn with the lash shall be paid by another drawn with the sword, as was said three thousand years ago, so still it must be said, "The judgments of the Lord are true and righteous altogether."

With malice toward none; with charity for all; with firmness in the right, as God gives us to see the right, let us strive on to finish the work we are in; to bind up the nation's wounds; to care for him who shall have borne the battle, and for his widow, and his orphan—to do all which may achieve and cherish a just and lasting peace among ourselves, and with all nations.

The End of an Era

The Industrial Revolution was a major factor in the complex chain of events leading to the "Great War." Germany, England, France, and Russia were competing in the quality and price of industrial products while also searching for new colonial markets that would absorb some of their booming production. In Europe, after the unification of Germany and Italy, there was very little territory "available" for annexation. There were, in other words, more predatory nations than there were suitable victims. In order to protect what they had and hoped to acquire, nations enlarged their armies and navies and equipped them with the latest technology in munitions and weaponry.

Another crucial factor leading to war was the issue of national identity. As late as the 1860s citizens of Florence generally saw themselves as Florentines or Tuscans; residents of Normandy were Norman rather than French; the population of Munich was Bavarian first and German second, and so on. The physical unification of Germany and Italy stimulated a sense of national identity symbolized by the powerful image of Great Britain as a sovereign nation, with national pride fueled by feelings of national superiority. When James Thomson wrote,

The nations not so blest as thee,
    Must in their turn, to tyrants fall;
Whilst thou shalt flourish great and free,
    The dread and envy of them all.
        Rule Britannia! Britannia rules the waves!
        Britons will never be slaves.

he had no idea of sharing the waves or anything else with other nations.

The Romantic idea of the sovereign individual was enlarged to include each citizen as a critical component in the noble and heroic image of the sovereign state. There was for the Romantic no true identity separate from the homeland, as Sir Walter Scott emphasized.

Literary Selection
BREATHES THERE THE MAN
Sir Walter Scott

Breathes there the man with soul so dead
Who never to himself hath said,
    This is my own, my native land!
Whose heart hath ne'er within him burned,
As home his footsteps he hath turned
    From wandering on a foreign strand!
If such there breathe, go, mark him well;
For him no minstrel raptures swell;
High though his titles, proud his name,
Boundless his wealth as wish can claim,
Despite those titles, power, and pelf,
The wretch, concentred all in self,
Living, shall forfeit fair renown,

And, doubly dying, shall go down
To the vile dust from whence he sprung,
Unwept, unhonored, and unsung.

In their efforts to avoid open warfare, the major nations made alliances that attempted to maintain a balance of power. To guard against French power Bismarck effected a Triple Alliance (1882) of Germany, Austria-Hungary, and Italy. France and Russia countered in 1894 with a Dual Alliance that made Germany uneasy about a two-front war and, in 1907, England joined the two nations in what was called a "close understanding" (Triple Entente). The tinderbox was the Balkans where nationalist ambitions were continually clashing. Russia wanted to make the Black Sea a Slavic lake but Britain saw a Russian thrust as a threat to the empire. By this time Turkey, the "sick man of Europe," was virtually powerless, newly independent Serbia was a threat to the Austro-Hungarian Empire, and Germany had her eye on Balkan conquests. The high level of international tension was extremely dangerous because all nations were armed to the teeth.

Nationalist activities touched a spark to the Balkan tinder and nationalist stubbornness, duty, and honor provoked a war that many diplomats and statesmen believed was a better alternative than seeing their nation humiliated by loss of face. On June 28, 1914, a Serbian nationalist assassinated the Austrian Archduke Francis Ferdinand and his wife. After obtaining Germany's backing for whatever Austria proposed to do about Serbia, a true "blank check," Austria issued an ultimatum that the Serbs could not wholly accept. Because it was inconsistent with "national honor," Austria turned down a British proposal for a compromise conference and declared war on Serbia on July 28, 1914, despite German attempts to withdraw the blank check. Russia began to mobilize but slowed things down as Germany insisted that the Austrians could be made to compromise. Fearing that her enemies would quickly overwhelm her, the Russian government again ordered full mobilization and Germany responded with an ultimatum to cease mobilizing or face a fight. With no Russian response Germany began mobilizing on August 1 and declared war on Russia the same day, which says something about German preparedness. French mobilization also began on August 1 and Germany declared war on Russia's ally on August 3. Britain dithered and delayed until Germany announced her intention to violate Belgium's neutrality as established in 1839; when Britain declared war on August 4 the German chancellor sneeringly remarked that the English had gone to war over a "scrap of paper." Actually, as pointed out by Barbara Tuchman,[3] the German Staff had laid plans years before the war to violate Belgium's neutrality. The "scrap of paper" remark inflamed world

---

3. Barbara Tuchman, *The Guns of August* (New York: Macmillan, 1962).

and British public opinion, which solidly backed a government that had honored its treaty and thus the nation. The response was typified by Thomas Hardy's poem, "Cry of the Homeless."

Literary Selection
CRY OF THE HOMELESS

After the Prussian Invasion of Belgium
Thomas Hardy

"Instigator of the ruin—
    Whichsoever thou mayst be
Of the masterful of Europe
    That contrived our misery—
Hear the wormwood-worded greeting
    From each city, shore, and lea
      Of thy victims:
      "Conqueror, all hail to thee!"

"Yea: 'All hail!' we grimly shout thee
    That wast author, fount, and head
Of these wounds, whoever proven
    When our times are throughly read.
'May thy loved be slighted, blighted,
    And forsaken,' be it said
      By thy victims,
      'And thy children beg their bread!'

"Nay: a richer malediction!—
    Rather let this thing befall
In time's hurling and unfurling
    On the night when comes thy call;
That compassion dew thy pillow
    And bedrench thy senses all
      For thy victims,
      Till death dark thee with his pall."

August 1915

Generally speaking, the war was fought with twentieth-century weapons (machine guns, tanks, poison gas, artillery) and nineteenth-century tactics (mass frontal assaults, artillery duels, use of cavalry). There were many theatres of action but the 300–mile Western Front was the main meat grinder with mass charges launched between trenches into point-blank machine gun fire. In four years sixteen nations had casualties (killed, died, wounded, missing) of nearly 40 million. One example will suffice to illustrate the extent of the slaughter. In the center of the French village of Sully-sur-Loire there stands a war memorial designed as a tall obelisk. On one side are listed, in categories, those from the village who died in World War II. The categories themselves communicate much about the conflict with Nazi Germany: "Killed in Action," "Murdered by the Gestapo," "Died in Concentration Camp," and "Missing." Eight names are engraved on the World War II side. On the opposite side the single category is "Killed in Action": There are ninety-six names.

As some historians have noted, World War I began as the most popular war in history. Just about everyone was spoiling for a fight, a chance to demonstrate the great fighting spirit of their country, to prove their valor and nobility, to honor their country. All these Romantic notions died in the trenches and are buried from Flanders Fields to Verdun. Throughout Western history no event has ended an era with such finality as did the Great War.

Literature, Philosophy, and Science

A maze of conflicting ideas and contentious national identities, the nineteenth century produced an exceptional number of gifted writers, thinkers, and scientists, with some of the more important figures considered here. Included are representative persons and representative works in sufficient detail to adequately survey the period.

Romanticism

More an attitude to be explored than a term to be defined, Romanticism began around 1780 as a reaction against the Enlightenment. The Romantic Movement itself lasted from about 1780 to about 1830 but Romantic ideas and issues were present in a variety of forms right up to 1914.

In its initial stages Romanticism was mainly a German movement but the inspiration came from Jean Jacques Rousseau (1712–1778). Rousseau began his *Social Contract* (1762) with a ringing declamation: "Man is born free and everywhere he is in chains." According to Rousseau, the source of the trouble was too much education and of the wrong kind at that. Self-forged chains could not be thrown off with more "progress"; instead, people must emulate the Noble Savage by returning to a state of innocence in nature. Civilization had corrupted us, claimed Rousseau, but a return to nature was the proper antidote. More a call to action than a coherent program, just what Rousseau meant by "back to nature" has been debated for centuries. Some idea of his attitude can be obtained from Rousseau's analysis of the "wrong kind of education":

> Astronomy was born of superstition, eloquence of ambition, hatred, falsehood, and flattery; geometry of avarice; physics of an idle curiosity; and even moral philosophy of human pride. Thus the arts and sciences owe their birth to our vices; and we should be less doubtful of their advantages, if they had sprung from our virtues.
>
> Their evil origin is, indeed, but too plainly reproduced in their objects. What would become of the arts were they not cherished by luxury? If men were not unjust, of what use were jurisprudence? What would become of history if there were no tyrants, wars, or conspiracies? In a word, who would pass his life in barren speculations if everybody, attentive only to the obligations of humanity and the necessities of nature, spent his whole life in serving his country, obliging his friends, and relieving the unhappy?
>
> from *Discourse on the Arts and Sciences,* 1749, by Jean Jacques Rousseau

Literary Selection

ÉMILE

Jean Jacques Rousseau (1712-1778)

Rousseau presented his ideas about the proper education of children in the form of a novel. In the two brief selections given here we see first an opening essay on the nature of education, and, second, an example of the proper education of the pupil Emile.

Book I

Everything is good as it comes from the hand of the Author of things; everything degenerates in the hand of man. He forces a piece of ground to nourish harvests alien to it, a tree to bear fruit not its own; he mingles and confounds climates, elements, seasons; he mutilates his dog, his horse, his slave; he turns everything upside down, he disfigures everything; he loves deformity and monsters. He does not want anything to be as nature made it, not even man; it must be groomed for him, like a riding-school horse; it must conform to his whim like a tree in his garden. . . .

It is you I address, gentle and far-seeing mother, who know that you must withdraw yourself from the established highway and protect the tender sapling from the shock of human opinion! Cultivate, water the young plant before it dies; its fruits will one day be your greatest joy. Build early a protecting wall about the soul of your child; another may mark out the boundary, but you alone must erect the barrier.

Plants are formed by cultivation and men by education. If a man were born tall and strong, his height and strength would be worthless to him until he had learned to make use of them; both could be harmful to him, in keeping others from thinking he needed help; left to himself, he could die of misery before he understood his own needs. We pity the childish state; we do not see that the human race would have perished if man had not started out as a child.

We are born feeble, we need strength; we are born deprived of everything, we need help; we are born stupid, we need judgment. Everything we lack at our birth, but need when we are grown, is given by our education.

This education comes to us from nature, from men, or from things. The internal development of our faculties and organs is the education of nature; the use we learn to make of this development is the education of men; and the acquisition of our own experience from the objects which affect us is the education of things.

Each one of us, then, is fashioned by three sorts of teachers. The pupil in whom their various teachings clash is badly educated, and will never be at peace with himself; the one in whom they all emphasize the same purpose and tend towards the same ends, goes straight to his goal and lives harmoniously. Such an one is well educated.

Now, of these three different educations, that of nature is the only one that does not depend on us at all; that of things depends on man only in certain respects. That of man is the only one of which we are truly the masters: even here we are in control only theoretically; for who can hope to direct completely the discourse and actions of all those surrounding a child?

Since, then, education is an art, it is almost impossible that it should be successful, for the circumstances necessary to its success are determined by no one person. All that one can do with the greatest care is, more or less, to approach the goal, but one needs good luck to reach it.

What is this goal? It is the very same as nature's; that has just been proved. Since the combination of these educations is necessary for their perfecting, it is toward the one over which we have no control that we must direct the other two. But perhaps this word nature is too vague a term; we must try here to define it.

Nature, we are told, is only habit. What does that mean? Are there not habits which are developed only with effort, and which never stifle nature? Such is, for example, the habit of plants, the vertical direction of which is interfered with. Once the restraints are removed, the plant retains the inclination which it has been forced to take; but even so the sap has not changed its primitive direction, and, if the plant continues to thrive, its growth will return to the vertical. It is the same with the tendencies of man. As long as we stay in one situation, we keep those which are the result of custom and which are the least natural to us; but as soon as the situation changes the learned habit stops and the natural returns. Education is certainly a habit. Now are there not people who forget and lose their education and others who retain it? From whence comes this difference? If we limit the meaning of nature to the habits which conform to the natural, we may spare ourselves this nonsense.

We are born sensitive, and from our birth we are affected in diverse ways by the objects which surround us. As soon as we have, so to speak, the consciousness of our sensations, we are disposed to seek out or to flee from the objects which produce them, first according as to whether they are agreeable or displeasing to us, then according to the harmony or discord which we find between ourselves and these objects, and finally according to the judgments which we form concerning the idea of happiness and perfection which our reason gives us. These judgments are extended and strengthened in accordance with our becoming more sensitive and more enlightened; but limited by our habits, they are changed more or less by our opinions. Before this change, they are what I call nature in us.

It is to these primitive urges, then, that we must relate everything; and this could be done if our three educations were merely different; but what is to be done when they are opposed?—when, instead of educating a man for himself, we wish to educate him for others, then harmony is impossible. Forced to combat nature or social institutions, we must choose between making a man or a citizen; for one cannot do both at the same time.

All small societies, when confined and close-knit, draw away from the world at large. Every patriot is intolerant of foreigners; they are mere men, they have no worth to him. This difficulty is inevitable but it is a slight one. It is essential to be kind to the people with whom one lives. Outside, the Spartan was ambitious, miserly, unrighteous; but disinterestedness, justice, and concord reigned within his walls. Beware of those citizens of the world who study their books for dutiful acts which they disdain to carry out at home. This kind of philosopher loves the barbarian in order to be free from loving his neighbor.

The natural man is all for himself; he is a numerical unity, the absolute entity, in harmony only with himself or his equals. The civil man (the man in society) is but a fractional unit belonging to the denominator whose sole value is in relation to the whole, which is the social body. Good social institutions are those that know best how to strip man of his nature, to take from him his real existence and give him one which is only relative, and to add his personality to the common unity; to the end that each individual will no longer think of himself as one, but as a part of the whole, no longer a thinking being except in the group. A Roman citizen was neither a Caius nor a Lucius: he was a Roman. . . .

A woman of Sparta had five sons in the army and awaited news of the battle. A helot arrived and she asked for news, trembling. "Your five sons have been killed." "Ignoble slave, did I ask you that?" "We are victorious!" The mother ran to the temple and gave thank-offerings to the gods. There is your citizen.

One who, in civilized society, hopes to maintain the pre-eminence of the natural does not know what he asks. Always at odds with himself, forever vacillating between his inclinations and his duty, he will never be either man or citizen; he will be no good to himself or others. He will be one of those contemporary men, a Frenchman, an Englishman, a citizen. He will be a nonentity.

To be something, to be himself and always whole, a man must act as he speaks, he must be sure always of the road he must take, take it resolutely and follow it always. I am waiting for someone to show me such a prodigy to know if he is man or citizen, or how he undertakes to be both at the same time.

From these necessarily opposed aims come two forms of contrary institutions: the one held in common and public, the other individual and private.

If you want to get an idea of public education, read Plato's *Republic*. It is not at all a political work, as those who judge a book only by its title believe it to be: it is the finest treatise on education that anyone ever wrote.

When people want to return to a never-never land, they think of Plato's institution: if Lycurgus[4] had done no more than put his in writing, I should find it much more fanciful. Plato simply purified the heart of man: Lycurgus denaturalized it.

That public system exists no longer, and can exist no longer, because where there is no nation there can be no citizen. These two words *Nation* and *Citizen* should be removed from modern languages. I know quite well the reason for this, but I do not want to discuss it: it has nothing to do with my subject.

Those laughable institutions they call "colleges" I do not think of in connection with public education. Neither do I count the education of the world, because this education leads toward two contrary goals, and misses both of them; it is useful only to produce two-faced men, who seem always to defer to others but who are really interested only in pleasing themselves. Now this behavior, being common to all, deceives no one in particular. It is so much wasted effort.

From these contradictions arises the one which we feel constantly within ourselves. Pulled by nature and by man in opposite directions; forced to divide ourselves among these different compulsions, we make compromises which lead neither to one goal nor the other. Thus besieged and vacillating during the whole course of our life, we end it without having found peace within ourselves and without having been any good to ourselves or others.

---

4. Lycurgus, the Spartan king, did not write about education; he established the actual system of training in Sparta to which Rousseau refers.

There remains finally private education, or that of nature, but what can a man mean to others if he is educated only for himself. If perhaps the proposed double object could be resolved into one, by removing the contradictions of man we could remove a great obstacle to his happiness. To make a judgment, we must see the finished man; we must have observed his tendencies, seen his progress, followed his advance; in a word, we must know the natural man. I believe you will have taken some steps (made some progress) in our research after having read this discussion.

What must we do to fashion this rare being?—much, without doubt: that is, prevent anything from being done. When it is only a question of sailing against the wind, we tack; but if the sea is high and we want to stay in one place, we must drop anchor. Take care, young pilot, that your cable does not slip or your anchor drag, and that your vessel does not drift without your noticing it.

In the social order where every place is allocated, each one must be educated for his niche. If a man leaves the place for which he was prepared, he no longer fits anywhere. Education is useful to the extent that destiny harmonizes it with the vocation of the parents; in all other instances, it is harmful to the student, if only for the prejudices it gives him. In Egypt, where the son was obliged to step into his father's place, education at least had an assured purpose: but among us where only classes remain, and where men change from one to the other constantly, no one knows whether, in educating his son to take his place, a father may be working against the son's best interests.

In the natural order, since men are equal, their common calling is man's estate, and whoever is well educated for this, cannot fill unworthily any position which relates to it. Whether I destine my pupil for the army, the church, the bar, is of little importance. No matter what the calling of his parents, nature calls him to human life. Living is the trade I should like to teach him. Leaving my hands, he will not be, I admit, magistrate, soldier, or priest; he will be first of all a man: everything that a man should be, he will know how to be, when called on, as well as any man; and in vain will fortune change his place, for he will always be at home. . . .

* * *

. . . For a time we had noticed, my pupil and I, that amber, glass, wax, different substances when they were rubbed would attract straws, and that others did not attract them. By chance we discovered one which had a still stranger attribute, which was to attract from quite a distance and without being rubbed, filings and other bits of iron. How long this quality amused us without our being able to perceive anything beyond it! Finally we found that this characteristic was communicated to the iron even magnetized in a certain sense. One day we went to the fair; a juggler attracted with a piece of bread a wax duck floating on a basin of water. Very much astonished, we did not call him a sorcerer, however, for we did not know what a sorcerer was. Continually struck with effects of which we did not know the causes, we were in no hurry to make judgments, and remained quietly ignorant until we found the answer.

On returning to our lodging, as a result of talking about the duck at the fair we began to try to imitate it. We took a well-magnetized needle, covered it with white wax which we shaped like a duck as best we could, in such a way that the needle traversed the body and the eye formed the beak. We placed the duck on the water and brought near the beak a key, and we saw, with what joy you may imagine, that our duck followed the piece of bread. To observe in what direction the duck faced when left quiet on the water was something for us to do another time. As for the present, full of our plans, we asked for nothing more.

The same evening we returned to the fair with some prepared bread in our pockets and as soon as the magician performed his trick, our little savant, who could hardly contain himself, said that this trick was not difficult and that he could do as well himself. He was taken at his word and at once took from his pocket the bread containing the bit of iron. As he approached the table his heart was pounding, and, almost trembling, he held out the bread. The duck came and followed it; the child cried out and quivered with joy. As people clapped and the assembly acclaimed him, his head was completely turned and he was beside himself. The juggler, overwhelmed, came, nevertheless to embrace and congratulate him and to request the honor of his presence the next day, adding that we would take pains to assemble a still larger crowd to applaud his cleverness. My proud little naturalist wanted to make a speech, but I shut him up at once and took him away, overwhelmed with praise.

The child with evident excitement counted the minutes the next day. He invited everyone he met; he wanted the whole human race to witness his glory. He could hardly wait for the time to come, he was ready ahead of time, we flew to the meeting place; the room was already full. As he entered, his young heart swelled. Other tricks had to come first; the juggler surpassed himself and did astonishing things. The child saw nothing of all this; he was agitated, he perspired, his breathing was labored. He spent the time fingering the bread in his pocket with a hand trembling with impatience. At last it was his turn; the master announced him ceremoniously. He approached a little ashamedly, he brought out the bread. New vicissitude of human things!—the duck, so tame the day before, had become wild today. Instead of presenting its beak, it turned tail and fled; it avoided the bread and the hand which held it with the same care with which it had formerly followed them. After a thousand useless attempts, each one jeered at, the child whined, said that he was being duped, that this was another duck substituted for the first one, and defied the juggler to attract it.

The juggler, without replying, took a piece of bread and held it out to the duck; which at once followed the bread and came to the hand which held it. The child took the same piece of bread, but far from succeeding better than before, he saw the duck make fun of him and do pirouettes all around the basin; he went off at last, quite upset, and did not dare expose himself to catcalls.

Then the juggler took the bread that the child had brought and made use of it as successfully as with his own: he drew out the iron (magnet) before the people, more laughter at our expense: then with the bread thus emptied he attracted the duck as before. He did the same thing with another piece, cut by a third person, he did the same with his glove, with the end of his finger; finally he went off to the center of the room and in an emphatic tone such as show people use, declaring that the duck would obey his voice no less than his gesture, he spoke and the duck obeyed: he told it to go to the right and it turned right; to come back, and it came; to turn and it turned; the movement followed close upon the order.

The redoubled applause was a still greater insult to us. We slipped out without being noticed, and shut ourselves up in our room, without going about to tell everyone of our prowess, as we had planned to do.

The next morning there was a knock at the door, I opened it; there stood the juggler. He mildly objected to our behaviour. What had he done to us that we would undertake to discredit his tricks and deprive him of a livelihood? What is so marvelous after all about drawing along a wax duck to cause us to purchase that ability at the expense of the living of an honest man? "By my faith, gentlemen, if I had some other talent by which to earn my living, I should hardly take pride in this one. You ought to know that a man who has spent his life continually practicing this miserable trade would know more about it than you who have spent only a few minutes on it. If I did not show you my finest tricks at once, it was because a man must not be in a hurry to display foolishly all he knows. I always take care to keep my best tricks for a great occasion, and beyond that I have still greater ones to halt young upstarts. Also, gentlemen, I come in goodwill to disclose the secret which embarrassed you so much, requesting that you will not make use of it to harm me, and that you will be more restrained another time."

Then he showed us his apparatus, and we saw with the utmost surprise that it was nothing but a strong, well mounted magnet which a child hidden under the table moved about without our realizing it.

The man put away his apparatus and after we had expressed our thanks and our apologies, we wanted to give him a present; he refused it. "No, gentlemen, I am not pleased enough with you to accept your gift; I leave you in my debt in spite of yourselves; this is my only revenge. Learn that there is generosity in all classes; I get paid for my tricks but not for my lessons."

Exercises

1. What are the three aspects of education according to Rousseau? What should be the aim of the two aspects that people can do anything about?
2. What distinction does Rousseau make between the *person* and the *citizen?* What is his opinion of the citizen?
3. Some of today's educators claim that vocational training is of little value because job requirements are changing so rapidly. What would Rousseau say about this problem?
4. In terms of the person and the citizen what sort of education would Rousseau advocate, then, to accomplish his purpose?

Johann Gottfried von Herder (1744–1803) was the leader of the precursor of Romanticism, the *sturm und drang* (SHTOORM oont DRAHNG) movement in German literature, a term derived from Klinger's novel *Die Wirrwarr; oder Sturm und Drang* ("Chaos; or storm and stress"). A passionate opponent of French rationalism of the Enlightenment, Herder emphasized the *Volksgeist* (spirit of the people) in Germany, claiming that each *volk* found its *geist* in its language, literature, and religion. This was, in effect, a cultural nationalism that became the basis of later German nationalism.

In his early writings Johann Wolfgang von Goethe (GUHR–tuh; 1749–1832) was one of the leading exponents of the movement. Written after an unhappy love affair, his *The Sorrows of Young Werther* (1774) was a morbidly sensitive tale full of sentiment and gloomy feelings that culminated in the suicide of the tragic Werther. Though Goethe was later to regret the storm and stress of his little book, it made him an instant celebrity.

The philosopher Friedrich William Joseph von Schilling (1775–1854) contributed to the Romantic Movement with his theory that nature and mind were inseparable and differed only in degree rather than in kind. For Schilling the creative artist was the "ideal Romantic man," a genius who presented his work as instinctively created apart from any conscious effort. From this Nietzsche was to evolve his idea of the creative genius as a "superman" who was "beyond good and evil."

Second only to Goethe in German literature, Friedrich von Schiller (1759–1805) was influenced by Kant and, in turn, was a major influence on modern German literature. An idealist who hated tyranny, Schilling had a vision of the universal fellowship of all humankind. It was his poem "An die Freude" (to joy) that Beethoven used as the "Ode to Joy" in the final movement of his mighty Ninth Symphony.

Arthur Schopenhauer (1788–1860) also contributed to the Romantic Movement with his generally pessimistic theories. According to Schopenhauer, reality is a blind driving force manifested in individuals as Will. Individual wills inevitably clash, causing strife and pain, from which there is no escape except by a negation of the will. Temporary escape is possible, however, through creative acts in art and science.

According to Schopenhauer and other romantics, creativity emerges from the unconscious but there are also instinctual drives that conflict with the creative impulses. In other words, the unconscious cuts both ways and the Romantics were vividly aware of the "night-side" that could release demonic destruction, as Schopenhauer pointed out in *The World of Will and Idea* (1818). Blind human will achieves only unhappiness or, as Goya said, "The sleep of reason produces monsters" (see chap. 22). Schopenhauer concluded that reason had to permit the release of creativity while simultaneously controlling the passions, but he was not optimistic about the results.

To summarize the Romantic Movement is difficult if we consider only what these individual writers and philosophers advocated. What most Romantics were opposed to gives a clearer picture, and the Enlightenment was their main target. Geometric thinking, empiricism, Neoclassicism, all were areas subject to reason and, said the Romantics, all had become mechanized and dehumanized. The great Newton had become only a materialist and a narrow materialist at that.

All Romantics emphasized individuality, the irrational component of the human personality and a sense of the infinite, a search for religious reality beyond sensible experience to find God in nature and within the human heart. Far from a return to orthodoxy, the impulse to recreate wonder in the world by finding God in nature was common to many Romantics except for poets like Byron and Shelley, who sought no God at all. The closest thing to a Romantic consensus lay in the emphasis on the primacy of humane concerns, the celebration of the emotional nature of human beings, and the necessity for creative activity through the exercise of an unfettered imagination.

Romanticism in England

Romanticism was effectively expressed in nineteenth-century art and music, in historical novels, Gothic tales, and romantic stories of love and adventure. In no one medium is the Romantic mood better expressed, for an English-speaking audience, than in the work of the English poets.

William Blake (1757–1827)

A self-proclaimed mystic with minimal formal schooling, Blake was a fundamentalist Protestant who believed that the Bible was the sole source of religious knowledge. Very much an individualist, he detested institutionalized religion, claiming that the human imagination was the sole means of expressing the Eternal. Blake referred to people as the Divine Image, the possessors of the humane virtues of mercy, pity, peace, and love. Equally gifted as an artist, Blake illustrated all but one of his volumes of poetry plus the Book of Job, Dante, and the poems of Thomas Gray.

From the collection called the *Songs of Innocence,* the following two poems celebrate the joy of the simple pastoral life and that of the Christian life. Written in 1789, they coincide with the beginning of the French Revolution that, for Blake, held so much promise of a better life for all people.

Literary Selections
INTRODUCTION
William Blake

Piping down the valleys wild,
Piping songs of pleasant glee,
On a cloud I saw a child,
And he laughing said to me:

'Pipe a song about a Lamb!'   5
So I piped with merry cheer.
'Piper, pipe that song again;'
So I piped: he wept to hear.
'Drop thy pipe, thy happy pipe;
Sing thy songs of happy cheer:'   10
So I sang the same again,
While he wept with joy to hear.

'Piper, sit thee down and write
In a book, that all may read.'
So he vanish'd from my sight,   15
And I pluck'd a hollow reed,

And I made a rural pen,
And I stain'd the water clear,
And I wrote my happy songs
Every child may joy to hear.   20

THE LAMB
William Blake

    Little Lamb, who made thee?
    Dost thou know who made thee?
Gave thee life, and bid thee feed,
By the stream and o'er the mead;
Gave thee clothing of delight,   5
Softest clothing, woolly, bright;
Gave thee such a tender voice,
Making all the vales rejoice!
    Little Lamb, who made thee?
    Dost thou know who made thee?   10

    Little Lamb, I'll tell thee,
    Little Lamb, I'll tell thee:
He is called by thy name,
For He calls Himself a Lamb.
He is meek, and He is mild;   15
He became a little child.
I a child, and thou a lamb,
We are called by His name.
    Little Lamb, God bless thee!
    Little Lamb, God bless thee!   20

Blake's *Songs of Experience* are concerned with the sick and corrupt world in which good and evil co-exist. In "The Tiger" Blake asks the age-old question: did the good God create evil?

THE TIGER
William Blake

Tiger! Tiger! burning bright
In the forests of the night,
What immortal hand or eye
Could frame thy fearful symmetry?

In what distant deeps or skies   5
Burnt the fire of thine eyes?
On what wings dare he aspire?
What the hand dare seize the fire?

And what shoulder, and what art,
Could twist the sinews of thy heart?   10
And when thy heart began to beat,
What dread hand? and what dread feet?

What the hammer? what the chain?
In what furnace was thy brain?
What the anvil? what dread grasp   15
Dare its deadly terrors clasp?

When the stars threw down their spears,
And water'd heaven with their tears,
Did he smile his work to see?
Did he who made the Lamb make thee?   20

Tiger! Tiger! burning bright
In the forests of the night,
What immortal hand or eye,
Dare frame thy fearful symmetry?

Exercise

1. In his *The Marriage of Heaven and Hell* Blake wrote that "Attraction and Repulsion, Reason and Energy, Love and Hate are necessary to Human Existence." Is this attitude reflected in the poems about the lamb and the tiger? Is the tiger, in other words, wholly evil or a symbol of necessary vigor and energy?

William Wordsworth (1770–1850)

The greatest of the English nature poets, Wordsworth was influenced by Rousseau and the spirit of the French Revolution. Strongly opposed to the flowery artificiality of Neoclassic poetry, Wordsworth and Samuel Taylor Coleridge published *Lyrical Ballads* (1798), which contained a new poetic manifesto. Wordsworth referred to his poetry as "emotion re-collected in tranquility" but, as he stated in his manifesto, he deliberately chose to write in "the language of conversation in the middle and lower classes of society." Indicating that "Tintern Abbey" was in a new style, Wordsworth chose the simple title of "Lines" to evoke a world soul that, for him, was present in all nature. The poem is divided into four sections. In the first section (11. 1–23) the poet sets a meditative scene; in the second scene (11. 23–58) are the poet's thoughts about the significance of the landscape. In the heart of the poem, the third section (11. 59–112), Wordsworth reviews the meanings the landscape had for him at different stages of his life. The Friend in the final section (11. 112–160) is the poet's sister, Dorothy, whom he tries to convince that the land-scape will restore her tranquility.

Literary Selections

LINES

Composed a Few Miles above Tintern Abbey, on Revisiting the Banks of the Wye During a Tour
July 13, 1798
William Wordsworth

Five years have past; five summers, with the length
Of five long winters! and again I hear
These waters, rolling from their mountain-springs
With a sweet inland murmur.—Once again
Do I behold these steep and lofty cliffs,
That on a wild secluded scene impress
Thoughts of more deep seclusion; and connect
The landscape with the quiet of the sky.
The day is come when I again repose
Here, under this dark sycamore, and view   10
These plots of cottage-ground, these orchard-tufts,
Which at this season, with their unripe fruits,
Are clad in one green hue, and lose themselves
Among the woods and copses, nor disturb
The wild green landscape. Once again I see
These hedgerows, hardly hedgerows, little lines

Of sportive wood run wild: these pastoral farms,
Green to the very door; and wreaths of smoke
Sent up, in silence, from among the trees!
With some uncertain notice, as might seem   20
Of vagrant dwellers in the houseless woods,
Or of some Hermit's cave, where by his fire
The Hermit sits alone.
                              These beauteous Forms,
Through a long absence, have not been to me
As is a landscape to a blind man's eye:
But oft, in lonely rooms, and 'mid the din
Of towns and cities, I have owed to them,
In hours of weariness, sensations sweet,
Felt in the blood, and felt along the heart;
And passing even into my purer mind,   30
With tranquil restoration:—feelings too
Of unremembered pleasure: such, perhaps,
As have no slight or trivial influence
On that best portion of a good man's life,
His little, nameless, unremembered acts
Of kindness and of love. Nor less, I trust,
To them I may have owed another gift,
Of aspect more sublime; that blessed mood,
In which the burthen of the mystery,
In which the heavy and the weary weight   40
Of all this unintelligible world,
Is lightened:—that serene and blessed mood,
In which the affections gently lead us on,—
Until, the breath of this corporeal frame
And even the motion of our human blood
Almost suspended, we are laid asleep
In body, and become a living soul:
While with an eye made quiet by the power
Of harmony, and the deep power of joy,
We see into the life of things.
                                          If this   50
Be but a vain belief, yet, oh! how oft,
In darkness, and amid the many shapes
Of joyless daylight; when the fretful stir
Unprofitable, and the fever of the world,
Have hung upon the beatings of my heart,
How oft, in spirit, have I turned to thee,
O sylvan Wye! Thou wanderer thro' the woods,
How often has my spirit turned to thee!

     And now, with gleams of half-extinguished
          thought,
With many recognitions dim and faint,   60
And somewhat of a sad perplexity,
The picture of the mind revives again:
While here I stand, not only with the sense
Of present pleasure, but with pleasing thoughts
That in this moment there is life and food
For future years. And so I dare to hope,
Though changed, no doubt, from what I was when
          first
I came among these hills; when like a roe
I bounded o'er the mountains, by the sides
Of the deep rivers, and the lonely streams,   70
Wherever nature led: more like a man
Flying from something that he dreads, than one
Who sought the thing he loved. For nature then
(The coarser pleasures of my boyish days,
And their glad animal movements all gone by)
To me was all in all.—I cannot paint
What then I was. The sounding cataract
Haunted me like a passion: the tall rock,
The mountain, and the deep and gloomy wood,

Their colours and their forms, were then to me   80
An appetite; a feeling and a love,
That had no need of a remoter charm,
By thought supplied, or any interest
Unborrowed from the eye.—That time is past,
And all its aching joys are now no more,
And all its dizzy raptures. Not for this
Faint I, nor mourn nor murmur; other gifts
Have followed, for such loss, I would believe,
Abundant recompence. For I have learned
To look on nature, not as in the hour   90
Of thoughtless youth; but hearing oftentimes
The still, sad music of humanity,
Nor harsh nor grating, though of ample power
To chasten and subdue. And I have felt
A presence that disturbs me with the joy
Of elevated thoughts: a sense sublime
Of something far more deeply interfused,
Whose dwelling is the light of setting suns,
And the round ocean and the living air,
And the blue sky, and in the mind of man: 100
A motion and a spirit, that impels
All thinking things, all objects of all thought,
And rolls through all things. Therefore am I still
A lover of the meadows and the woods,
And mountains; and of all that we behold
From this green earth; of all the mighty world
Of eye and ear, both what they half create,
And what perceive; well pleased to recognise
In nature and the language of the sense,
The anchor of my purest thoughts, the nurse,   110
The guide, the guardian of my heart, and soul
Of all my moral being.
                              Nor perchance,
If I were not thus taught, should I the more
Suffer my genial spirits to decay:
For thou art with me, here, upon the banks
Of this fair river; thou, my dearest Friend,
My dear, dear Friend, and in thy voice I catch
The language of my former heart, and read
My former pleasures in the shooting lights
Of thy wild eyes. Oh! yet a little while   120
May I behold in thee what I was once,
My dear, dear Sister! and this prayer I make,
Knowing that Nature never did betray
The heart that loved her; 'tis her privilege,
Through all the years of this our life, to lead
From joy to joy: for she can so inform
The mind that is within us, so impress
With quietness and beauty, and so feed
With lofty thoughts, that neither evil tongues,
Rash judgments, nor the sneers of selfish men,   130
Nor greetings where no kindness is, nor all
The dreary intercourse of daily life,
Shall e'er prevail against us, or disturb
Our cheerful faith, that all which we behold
Is full of blessings. Therefore let the moon
Shine on thee in thy solitary walk;
And let the misty mountain winds be free
To blow against thee: and in after years,
When these wild ecstasies shall be matured
Into a sober pleasure, when thy mind   140
Shall be a mansion for all lovely forms,
Thy memory be as a dwelling-place
For all sweet sounds and harmonies; oh! then,
If solitude, or fear, or pain, or grief,
Should be thy portion, with what healing thoughts
Of tender joy wilt thou remember me,
And these my exhortations! Nor, perchance

If I should be where I no more can hear
Thy voice, nor catch from thy wild eyes these gleams
Of past existence, wilt thou then forget   150
That on the banks of this delightful stream
We stood together; and that I, so long
A worshipper of Nature, hither came
Unwearied in that service: rather say
With warmer love, oh! with far deeper zeal
Of holier love. Nor wilt thou then forget,
That after many wanderings, many years
Of absence, these steep woods and lofty cliffs,
And this green pastoral landscape, were to me
More dear, both for themselves and for thy sake!   160

The following sonnet mourns a world so overwhelmed with materialism that it may lose its spiritual qualities. Proteus and Triton are from Greek mythology and symbolize the poet's conviction that the wonders of nature that delighted the ancients cannot, in the long run, be destroyed by the Industrial Age. Wordsworth was a Romantic optimist.

THE WORLD IS TOO MUCH WITH US
William Wordsworth

The world is too much with us; late and soon,
Getting and spending, we lay waste our powers;
Little we see in Nature that is ours;
We have given our hearts away, a sordid boon!
This Sea that bares her bosom to the moon,
The winds that will be howling at all hours,
And are up-gathered now like sleeping flowers,
For this, for everything, we are out of tune;
It moves us not.—Great God! I'd rather be
A Pagan suckled in a creed outworn;
So might I, standing on this pleasant lea,
Have glimpses that would make me less forlorn;
Have sight of Proteus rising from the sea;
Or hear old Triton blow his wreathéd horn.

Exercises

1. In his "Lines" Wordsworth describes two memorable periods in his life (11. 65–83 and 83–111). How are these periods characterized? Changes have taken place since the poet's first visit to this almost magical place. Has the scene changed, the poet himself, or both?
2. If Wordsworth were to write "The World Is Too Much With Us" today would he be as optimistic about the survival of nature's wonders? Why or why not?

Samuel Taylor Coleridge (1772–1834)

Though he did not consider himself a Romantic poet, Coleridge did make a classic Romantic statement: "Each man is meant to represent humanity in his own way, combining its elements uniquely." Coleridge set great store on imagination over fancy, claiming that fancy was only the ability to copy or elaborate on previous examples; imagination was the ability to create new worlds. "Kubla Khan" is a notable example of an inspired vision whether or not, as Coleridge claimed, the poem was composed during an opium reverie and later written down. Coleridge and many other Romantics were fascinated with the exotic Orient. The grandson of Mongol conqueror Genghis Khan, Kubla Khan (1215?–1294) founded the Yuan dynasty of China and sponsored Marco Polo as his agent to the West.

Literary Selection
KUBLA KHAN
Samuel Taylor Coleridge

In Xanadu did Kubla Khan
　　A stately pleasure-dome decree:
Where Alph, the sacred river, ran
Through caverns measureless to man
　　Down to a sunless sea.
So twice five miles of fertile ground
With walls and towers were girdled round:
And here were gardens bright with sinuous rills,
Where blossomed many an incense-bearing tree
And here were forests ancient as the hills,   10
Enfolding sunny spots of greenery.
But oh! that deep romantic chasm which slanted
Down the green hill athwart a cedarn cover!
A savage place! as holy and enchanted
As e'er beneath a waning moon was haunted
By woman wailing for her demon-lover!
And from this chasm, with ceaseless turmoil seething,
As if this earth in fast thick pants were breathing,
A mighty fountain momently was forced,
Amid whose swift half-intermitted burst   20
Huge fragments vaulted like rebounding hail,
Or chaffy grain beneath the thresher's flail:
And 'mid these dancing rocks at once and ever
It flung up momently the sacred river.
Five miles meandering with a mazy motion
Through wood and dale the sacred river ran,
Then reached the caverns measureless to man,
And sank in tumult to a lifeless ocean:
And 'mid this tumult Kubla heard from far
Ancestral voices prophesying war!   30
　　The shadow of the dome of pleasure
　　Floated midway on the waves;
　　Where was heard the mingled measure
　　From the fountain and the caves.
It was a miracle of rare device,
A sunny pleasure-dome with caves of ice!
　　A damsel with a dulcimer
　　In a vision once I saw:
　　It was an Abyssinian maid,
　　And on her dulcimer she played,   40
　　Singing of Mount Abora.
　　Could I revive within me
　　Her symphony and song,
　　To such a deep delight 'twould win me,
That with music loud and long,
I would build that dome in air,
That sunny dome! those caves of ice!
And all who heard should see them there,
And all should cry, Beware! Beware!
His flashing eyes, his floating hair!   50
Weave a circle round him thrice,
And close your eyes with holy dread,
For he on honey-dew hath fed,
And drunk the milk of Paradise.

　　　　　　　　　　　　　　　　　　　　　　1797

Exercise

1. Coleridge claimed that "Kubla Khan" appeared to him in a dream and that what he later wrote down was "a fragment." But, is the poem incomplete? Could it be that the first thirty-six lines are an exercise in creative imagination and the remainder a lament over the loss of poetic power? In these terms is the poem complete or incomplete?

George Noel Gordon, Lord Byron (1788–1824)

The most flamboyant and controversial personality of the age, Lord Byron epitomizes the Romantic hero. With his egotism and superhuman vigor he gloried in physical and mental license, learning relatively late and only in part the virtue of moderation. He wrote his words, he said, "as a tiger leaps" and aimed many of them at conventional social behaviour, cant, and hypocrisy. Much of his poetry was prosaic when compared with the iridescent style of Shelley and Keats but, as he said, his genius was eloquent rather than poetical. His reputation was early and firmly established with *Childe Harold's Pilgrimage,* a poetic travelogue, but his masterpiece is *Don Juan,* a work full of irony and pathos of which Byron wrote in the Dedication:

I want a hero: an uncommon want,
. . .
But can't find any in the present age
Fit for my poem (that is, for my new one):
So, as I said, I'll take my friend Don Juan.

Literary Selections

The lovely lyric that follows was inspired by Lady Wilmot Horton, whom Byron had seen in a ballroom wearing a mourning dress decorated, strangely enough, with numerous spangles.

SHE WALKS IN BEAUTY
Lord Byron

She walks in beauty, like the night
    Of cloudless climes and starry skies;
And all that 's best of dark and bright
    Meet in her aspect and her eyes:
Thus mellow'd to that tender light
    Which heaven to gaudy day denies.

One shade the more, one ray the less,
    Had half impair'd the nameless grace
Which waves in every raven tress,
    Or softly lightens o'er her face;
Where thoughts serenely sweet express
    How pure, how dear their dwelling-place.

And on that cheek, and o'er that brow,
    So soft, so calm, yet eloquent,
The smiles that win, the tints that glow,
    But tell of days in goodness spent,
A mind at peace with all below,
    A heart whose love is innocent!

June 12, 1814

Byron was a revolutionary in spirit but his inspiration was based upon classical art and its emphasis upon emotion controlled by the intellect. The Greek revolt against the Turks provided Byron with the opportunity to become a revolutionary Graecophile. Several years before sailing for Greece on July 14, 1823 (Bastille Day), he wrote the following ironic lines:

WHEN A MAN HATH NO FREEDOM TO FIGHT FOR AT HOME
Lord Byron

When a man hath no freedom to fight for at home,
    Let him combat for that of his neighbours;
Let him think of the glories of Greece and of Rome,
    And get knock'd on the head for his labours.

To do good to mankind is the chivalrous plan,
    And is always as nobly requited;
Then battle for freedom wherever you can,
    And, if not shot or hang'd, you'll get knighted.

Almost to the day of his premature death Byron was torn between the heroic defiance of Prometheus and the worldly, cynical defiance of Don Juan. In the end, he chose the Promethean way and died during the Greek struggle for independence.

PROMETHEUS
Lord Byron

Titan! to whose immortal eyes
    The sufferings of mortality,
    Seen in their sad reality,
Were not as things that gods despise;
What was thy pity's recompense?
A silent suffering, and intense;
The rock, the vulture, and the chain,
All that the proud can feel of pain,
The agony they do not show,
The suffocating sense of woe,   10
    Which speaks but in its loneliness,
And then is jealous lest the sky
Should have a listener, nor will sigh
    Until its voice is echoless.

Titan! to thee the strife was given
    Between the suffering and the will,
    Which torture where they cannot kill;
And the inexorable Heaven,
And the deaf tyranny of Fate,
The ruling principle of Hate,   20
Which for its pleasure doth create
The things it may annihilate,
Refused thee even the boon to die:
The wretched gift eternity
Was thine—and thou hast borne it well.
All that the Thunderer wrung from thee
Was but the menace which flung back
On him the torments of thy rack;
The fate thou didst so well foresee,
But would not to appease him tell;   30
And in thy Silence was his Sentence,
And in his Soul a vain repentance,
And evil dread so ill dissembled,
That in his hand the lightnings trembled.
Thy Godlike crime was to be kind,
    To render with thy precepts less
    The sum of human wretchedness,

And strengthen Man with his own mind;
But baffled as thou wert from high,
Still in thy patient energy,   40
In the endurance, and repulse
    Of thine impenetrable Spirit,
Which Earth and Heaven could not convulse,
    A mighty lesson we inherit:
Thou art a symbol and a sign
    To Mortals of their fate and force;
Like thee, Man is in part divine,
    A troubled stream from a pure source;
And Man in portions can foresee
His own funereal destiny,   50
His wretchedness, and his resistance,
And his sad unallied existence:
To which his Spirit may oppose
Itself—and equal to all woes,
    And a firm will, and a deep sense,
Which even in torture can descry
    Its own concenter'd recompense,
Triumphant where it dares defy,
And making Death a Victory.

                          Diodati, July, 1816

Though unable to moderate his course, Byron was fully aware of the causes of his self-destruction, as revealed in several lines from his poignant "Epistle to Augusta:"

I have been cunning in mine overthrow,
    The careful pilot of my proper woe.
Mine were my faults, and mine be their reward.
    My whole life was a contest, since the day
That gave me being, gave me that which marr'd
    The gift,—a fate, or will, that walk'd astray.

Exercises

1. Two contrary aspects of Byron's personality are evidenced in "She Walks in Beauty" and "When a Man Hath No Freedom." How would you describe these very different aspects?
2. Prometheus was the Titan who stole fire from Mount Olympos and gave it to humankind. Zeus, the Thunderer in the poem, had him chained to a rock where a vulture perpetually tears out his liver. What does Prometheus symbolize for Byron? Greece under Turkish tyranny? Himself? Both?

Percy Bysshe Shelley (1792–1822)

Shelley and his friend John Keats established romantic verse as the prime poetic tradition of the period; to this day "Shelley and Keats" and "Romantic poetry" are virtually synonymous. A lifelong heretic who was expelled from Oxford because of his pamphlet *The Necessity of Atheism,* Shelley saw all humankind as the Divine Image to whom poets spoke as the "unacknowledged legislators of the world" (*A Defense of Poetry).* His masterpiece is *Prometheus Unbound,* a lyrical drama in four acts in which he gave full expression to his "passion for reforming the world." Also composed at Leghorn, Italy, and published with *Prometheus Unbound* was "To a Skylark," the composition of which was described by Mrs. Shelley:

> It was on a beautiful summer evening while wandering among the lanes, whose myrtle hedges were the bowers of the fireflies, that we heard the caroling of the skylark, which inspired one of the most beautiful of his poems.

Literary Selections

TO A SKYLARK
Percy Bysshe Shelley

Hail to thee, blithe spirit!
    Bird thou never wert,
That from heaven, or near it,
    Pourest thy full heart
In profuse strains of unpremeditated art.   5
    Higher still and higher
        From the earth thou springest
    Like a cloud of fire;
        The blue deep thou wingest,
And singing still dost soar, and soaring ever singest.   10
    In the golden lightning
        Of the sunken sun,
    O'er which clouds are brightning,
        Thou dost float and run;
Like an unbodied joy whose race is just begun.   15
    The pale purple even
        Melts around thy flight;
    Like a star of heaven,
        In the broad day-light
Thou art unseen, but yet I hear thy shrill delight,   20
    Keen as are the arrows
        Of that silver sphere,
    Whose intense lamp narrows
        In the white dawn clear,
Until we hardly see, we feel that it is there.   25
    All the earth and air
        With thy voice is loud,
    As, when night is bare,
        From one lonely cloud
The moon rains out her beams, and heaven is overflowed.   30
    What thou art we know not;
        What is most like thee?
    From rainbow clouds there flow not
        Drops so bright to see,
As from thy presence showers a rain of melody.   35
    Like a poet hidden
        In the light of thought,
    Singing hymns unbidden,
        Till the world is wrought
To sympathy with hopes and fears it heeded not: 40
    Like a high-born maiden
        In a palace tower,
    Soothing her love-laden
        Soul in secret hour
With music sweet as love, which overflows her bower: 45
    Like a glow-worm golden
        In a dell of dew,
    Scattering unbeholden
        Its aërial hue

Among the flowers and grass, which screen it from
    the view: 50
        Like a rose embowered
           In its own green leaves,
        By warm winds deflowered,
           Till the scent it gives
Makes faint with too much sweet these heavy-winged
    thieves: 55
        Sound of vernal showers
           On the twinkling grass,
        Rain-awakened flowers,
           All that ever was
Joyous, and clear, and fresh, thy music doth surpass: 60

        Teach us, sprite or bird,
           What sweet thoughts are thine:
        I have never heard
           Praise of love or wine
That panted forth a flood of rapture so divine.   65

        Chorus Hymenæal,
           Or triumphal chaunt,
        Matched with thine would be all
           But an empty vaunt,
A thing wherein we feel there is some hidden want.   70

        What objects are the fountains
           Of thy happy strain?
        What fields, or waves, or mountains?
           What shapes of sky or plain?
What love of thine own kind? what ignorance of pain?   75

        With thy clear keen joyance
           Languor cannot be:
        Shadow of annoyance
           Never came near thee:
Thou lovest; but ne'er knew love's sad satiety.   80

        Waking or asleep,
           Thou of death must deem
        Things more true and deep
           Than we mortals dream,
Or how could thy notes flow in such a crystal stream?   85

        We look before and after,
           And pine for what is not:
        Our sincerest laughter
           With some pain is fraught;
Our sweetest songs are those that tell of saddest
    thought.   90

        Yet if we could scorn
           Hate, and pride, and fear;
        If we were things born
           Not to shed a tear,
I know not how thy joy we ever should come near.   95

        Better than all measures
           Of delightful sound,
        Better than all treasures
           That in books are found,
Thy skill to poet were, thou scorner of the ground!   100

        Teach me half the gladness
           That thy brain must know,
        Such harmonious madness
           From my lips would flow,
The world should listen then, as I am listening now.   105

"Ode to a West Wind" was, according to Shelley:

. . . conceived and chiefly written in a wood that skirts the Arno near Florence, and on a day when that tempestuous wind, whose temperature is at once mild and animating, was collecting the vapours which pour down the autumnal rains. They began, as I foresaw, at sunset with a violent tempest of hail and rain, attended by that magnificent thunder and lightning peculiar to the Cisalpine regions.

ODE TO THE WEST WIND
Percy Bysshe Shelley

I

O, wild West Wind, thou breath of Autumn's being,
Thou, from whose unseen presence the leaves dead
Are driven, like ghosts from an enchanter fleeing,

Yellow, and black, and pale, and hectic red,
Pestilence-stricken multitudes: O, thou,   5
Who chariotest to their dark wintry bed

The wingèd seeds, where they lie cold and low,
Each like a corpse within its grave, until
Thine azure sister of the spring shall blow

Her clarion o'er the dreaming earth, and fill   10
(Driving sweet buds like flocks to feed in air)
With living hues and odours plain and hill:

Wild Spirit, which art moving every where;
Destroyer and preserver; hear, O, hear!

II

Thou on whose stream, 'mid the steep sky's
    commotion,   15
Loose clouds like earth's decaying leaves are shed,
Shook from the tangled boughs of Heaven and Ocean,

Angels of rain and lightning: there are spread
On the blue surface of thine airy surge,
Like the bright hair uplifted from the head   20
Of some fierce Mænad, even from the dim verge
Of the horizon to the zenith's height
The locks of the approaching storm. Thou dirge

Of the dying year, to which this closing night
Will be the dome of a vast sepulchre,   25
Vaulted with all thy congregated might

Of vapours, from whose solid atmosphere
Black rain, and fire, and hail will burst: O, hear!

III

Thou who didst waken from his summer dreams
The blue Mediterranean, where he lay,   30
Lulled by the coil of his crystàlline streams,

Beside a pumice isle in Baiæ's bay,
And saw in sleep old palaces and towers
Quivering within the wave's intenser day,

All overgrown with azure moss and flowers   35
So sweet, the sense faints picturing them! Thou
For whose path the Atlantic's level powers

Cleave themselves into chasms, while far below
The sea-blooms and the oozy woods which wear
The sapless foliage of the ocean, know   40

Thy voice, and suddenly grow grey with fear,
And tremble and despoil themselves: O, hear!

IV

If I were a dead leaf thou mightest bear;
If I were a swift cloud to fly with thee;
A wave to pant beneath thy power, and share   45

The impulse of thy strength, only less free
Than thou, O, uncontrollable! If even
I were as in my boyhood, and could be

The comrade of thy wanderings over heaven,
As then, when to outstrip thy skiey speed   50
Scarce seemed a vision; I would ne'er have striven

As thus with thee in prayer in my sore need.
Oh! lift me as a wave, a leaf, a cloud!
I fall upon the thorns of life! I bleed!

A heavy weight of hours has chained and bowed   55
One too like thee: tameless, and swift, and proud.

V

Make me thy lyre, even as the forest is:
What if my leaves are falling like its own!
The tumult of thy mighty harmonies

Will take from both a deep, autumnal tone,   60
Sweet though in sadness. Be thou, spirit fierce,
My spirit! Be thou me, impetuous one!

Drive my dead thoughts over the universe
Like withered leaves to quicken a new birth!
And, by the incantation of this verse,   65

Scatter, as from an unextinguished hearth
Ashes and sparks, my words among mankind!
Be through my lips to unawakened earth

The trumpet of a prophecy! O, wind,
If Winter comes, can Spring be far behind?   70

Exercises

1. How does Shelley achieve the seemingly effortless buoyancy of "To a Skylark"? Consider the rhythm and the use of words like *blithe, springest, soar, float,* and many others.
2. The central image in the "Ode to the West Wind" is, of course, the wind itself. What does the wind represent? Consider the fact that in Latin and Greek, the words for wind, breath, soul, and inspiration are identical or interrelated. Could the wind symbolize a quickening of the inner spirit in response to the exterior movement? What is the significance of an *Autumn* wind? How many images are there of the cycle of life and death?

Mary Wollstonecraft Godwin Shelley (1797–1851)

Though not a poet, Mary Shelley deserves special mention here. She was the daughter of noted feminist Mary Wollstonecraft (1759–1797), author of *Vindication of the Rights of Women* (1792), and the equally notable social reformer William Godwin (1756–1836), a disciple of Jeremy Bentham and a man who strongly influenced Shelley's reforming zeal. Shelley had left Harriet, his wife, for Mary and moved to the continent where he later married her. While reading ghost stories one evening, Lord Byron suggested that each should write a tale of the supernatural. Mary Shelley's contribution was *Frankenstein; or, The Modern Prometheus* (1818). Using the central themes of Faustian ambition and Promethean creativity, Mary told the story of the scientist Frankenstein who dared to create life itself and, in so doing, dehumanized himself and brought destruction on all those he loved. Frankenstein's creation needed love and sympathy but was greeted instead with disgust and revulsion. Symbolizing Romantic ideas of isolation and alienation, Frankenstein's creation turned from a search for love to hatred of all humankind and murderous destruction. Mary Shelley's story is even more influential today as a modern myth about the horrifying potential of human creativity like, for example, nuclear weapons, when divorced from ethical considerations.

John Keats (1795–1821)

Generally speaking, the verse of both Keats and Shelley have a musicality that sets their work apart from all other Romantic poetry. Though trained as an apothecary and not even thinking of becoming a poet until he was eighteen, Keats began writing poetry with a sense of urgency and forebodings of an early death (his mother and, later, his brother died of the disease that was to carry him off: tuberculosis). Keats was the first to admit that his first volume of poetry had many flaws but not that it was "alternately florid and arid," as one critic bitingly observed. Keats's own reaction to a barrage of criticism was quite relaxed: "About a twelvemonth since, I published a little book of verses; it was read by some dozen of my friends, who lik'd it; and some dozen whom I was unacquainted with, who did not."

Keats is the only Romantic poet whose sonnets have been compared with those by Shakespeare, which he studied in depth and concluded that "He has left nothing to say about nothing or anything." Nevertheless, when the British Museum acquired the Elgin marbles that Lord Elgin had taken from the Parthenon in Athens (see chap. 3), Keats's reaction was a sonnet memorable for its subtle imagery and mixed feelings of personal mortality and artistic immortality.

Literary Selections

ON THE ELGIN MARBLES
John Keats

My spirit is too weak; mortality
    Weighs heavily on me like unwilling sleep,
    And each imagined pinnacle and steep
Of godlike hardship tells me I must die
Like a sick eagle looking at the sky.
    Yet 'tis a gentle luxury to weep,
    That I have not the cloudy winds to keep
Fresh for the opening of the morning's eye.
Such dim-conceived glories of the brain,
    Bring round the heart an indescribable feud;
So do these wonders a most dizzy pain,
    That mingles Grecian grandeur with the rude
Wasting of old Time—with a billowy main
    A sun, a shadow of a magnitude.

Keats generally obeyed his own rule of stopping his writing when the poetry ceased to come "as easily as leaves upon a tree," which accounts, at least in part, for the seemingly effortless style of his poetry. In his contemplation of a Grecian urn (see, for example, fig. 3.56) Keats succeeds in fusing his personality with the urn, partaking, as he said, of "fellowship with essence."

ODE ON A GRECIAN URN
John Keats

I

Thou still unravished bride of quietness,
    Thou foster-child of silence and slow time,
Sylvan historian, who canst thus express
    A flowery tale more sweetly than our rhyme:
What leaf-fringed legend haunts about thy shape   5
    Of deities or mortals, or of both,
        In Tempe or the dales of Arcady?
        What men or gods are these? What maidens loath?
What mad pursuit? What struggle to escape?
        What pipes and timbrels? What wild ecstacy?   10

II

Heard melodies are sweet, but those unheard
    Are sweeter; therefore, ye soft pipes, play on;
Not to the sensual ear, but, more endeared,
    Pipe to the spirit ditties of no tone.
Fair youth, beneath the trees, thou canst not leave   15
    Thy song, nor ever can those trees be bare;
        Bold lover, never, never canst thou kiss,
Though winning near the goal—yet, do not grieve;
    She cannot fade, though thou hast not thy bliss,
        For ever wilt thou love, and she be fair!   20

III

Ah, happy, happy boughs! that cannot shed
    Your leaves, nor ever bid the spring adieu;
And, happy melodist, unwearied,
    For ever piping songs for ever new;
More happy love! more happy, happy love!   25
    For ever warm and still to be enjoyed,
        For ever panting, and for ever young;
All breathing human passion far above,
    That leaves a heart high-sorrowful and cloyed,
        A burning forehead, and a parching tongue.   30

IV

Who are these coming to the sacrifice?
    To what green altar, O mysterious priest,
Leadest thou that heifer lowing at the skies,
    And all her silken flanks with garlands drest?
What little town by river or sea-shore,   35
    Or mountain-built with peaceful citadel,
        Is emptied of this folk, this pious morn?
And, little town, thy streets for evermore
    Will silent be; and not a soul to tell
        Why thou art desolate, can e'er return.   40

V

O Attic shape! Fair attitude! with brede
    Of marble men and maidens overwrought,
With forest branches and the trodden weed;
    Thou, silent form, dost tease us out of thought
As doth eternity: Cold Pastoral!   45

When old age shall this generation waste,
    Thou shalt remain, in midst of other woe
Than ours, a friend to man, to whom thou sayest,
"Beauty is truth, truth beauty,"—that is all
    Ye know on earth, and all ye need to know.   50

Most Romantics adored what they imagined the Middle Ages to have been; none would have tolerated for a moment the reality of the medieval world. "La Belle Dame sans Merci" ("The Lovely Lady without Pity") is perhaps the finest example of Romantic medievalism. Though the title is taken from a medieval poem by Alain Chartier, the ballad is the poet's own magical version of the ageless myth of the hapless mortal who succumbed to the irresistable charms of a supernatural and pitiless seductress. The first three stanzas are addressed to the distraught knight by an unknown questioner; the balance of the poem forms his anguished reply.

LA BELLE DAME SANS MERCI
John Keats

O what can ail thee, knight-at-arms,
    Alone and palely loitering?
The sedge has withered from the lake,
    And no birds sing.

O what can ail thee, knight-at-arms,
    So haggard and so woe-begone?
The squirrel's granary is full,
    And the harvest's done.

I see a lily on thy brow,
    With anguish moist and fever dew;
And on thy cheek a fading rose
    Fast withereth too.

I met a lady in the meads,
    Full beautiful—a faery's child;
Her hair was long, her foot was light,
    And her eyes were wild.

I set her on my pacing steed,
    And nothing else saw all day long;
For sidelong would she bend, and sing
    A faery's song.

I made a garland for her head,
    And bracelets too, and fragrant zone;
She looked at me as she did love,
    And made sweet moan.

She found me roots of relish sweet,
    And honey wild, and manna-dew;
And sure in language strange she said,
    "I love thee true."

She took me to her elfin grot,
    And there she wept and sighed full sore:
And there I shut her wild, wild eyes
    With kisses four.

And there she lulled me asleep,
    And there I dreamed—Ah! woe betide!
The latest dream I ever dreamed,
    On the cold hill-side.

I saw pale kings and princes too,
    Pale warriors—death-pale were they all;
Who cried, "La Belle Dame Sans Merci
    Hath thee in thrall!"

I saw their starved lips in the gloam,
    With horrid warning gaped wide;
And I awoke, and found me here
    On the cold hill's side.
And this is why I sojourn here,
    Alone and palely loitering;
Though the sedge is withered from the lake,
    And no birds sing.

Exercises

1. In "To the Elgin Marbles" what does the poet mean by *shadow* and by *magnitude?* Consider the fact that the Elgin Marbles were fragments of some of the finest sculptures on the Parthenon. The Parthenon itself was, and is, the most beautiful temple in Greece but it was, 2,500 years ago, only one of many lovely Greek temples.

2. Who or what speaks the final two lines of "Ode on a Grecian Urn"? Also, what does *Beauty is truth, truth beauty* really mean? If this statement refers to everyday life it doesn't make much sense. Suppose, instead, that the reference is to great art. Do sublime works of art like a Grecian urn crystalize truth and that's why beauty is truth?

3. How does Keats maintain the medieval mood in "La Belle Dame sans Merci"? Look, for example, at obvious words like *thee, knight-at-arms,* and *dancing steed* and subtle words like *meads, garland,* and *elfin.*

Johann Wolfgang von Goethe
(GUHR–tu; 1749–1832)

Germany's greatest writer achieved instant fame with the publication of *The Sorrows of Young Werther* (1774), a morbid tale that captured the imagination of all Europe. Werther's hopeless longing for his best friend's wife was autobiographical, but Werther's subsequent suicide was merely in the tradition of romantic despair, emulated, tragically, by a number of young men who died of a bullet in the brain while holding a copy of the novel. Calling Romanticism "a sickness," Goethe proceeded to write novels and plays in the Neoclassic style. A "Renaissance man" rather than a "Romantic hero," Goethe made important contributions to botany, the theory of evolution, physics, and devoted much of the rest of his life to the retelling of the legend of Dr. Johannes Faustus (ca. 1480–1540), who supposedly sold his soul to the Devil (Mephistopheles) in exchange for youth, knowledge, and power. Goethe's *Faust* (1808–1832) became the mythic symbol for the restless search for the meaning of life, and the will to wrest the fullest possibilities from a lifetime of titanic deeds. In his relentless drive to enlarge the meaning of life the "Faustian man" is Romantic, but his will to power and knowledge was always and inevitably doomed to failure. In the final analysis, Faust's salvation lay in his heroic self-regeneration and his acceptance of his own mortality.

Late in his long career Goethe again became a romantic poet but, as usual, in his own original fashion. Long attracted to poetry of the Middle East, Goethe published his *West-Eastern Divan* (1819), his last important body of lyric poetry, in which he sought wisdom, piety, and peace through a central motif of love. Inspired by a translation of the *Divan* of Hafiz, a fourteenth-century Persian poet, Goethe wrote twelve books of mostly love poetry. One book was devoted to the conquests of Timur (Tamerlane), the Mongol conqueror of Hafiz's homeland. In Goethe's mind Timur's ravages were paralleled by Napoleon's Russian campaign of 1812, including the scorched-earth policy of the Russian defenders that sealed the fate of the Grand Army. Goethe's thesis was that love and peace were not possible until after Napoleon had been eliminated.

Literary Selection
VII. BOOK OF TIMUR
Johann Wolfgang von Goethe

I

The Winter and Timur

So around them closed the winter
With resistless fury. Scattering
Midst them all his icy breathings.
Winds he lashed from every quarter
As a hostile troop against them;
Over them gave power tyrannic
To his frost-fanged storm and tempest.
Down he came to Timur's council,
Shrilled his threat and spake on this wise:
"Slack and slow, O man forbidden,
Be thy march, unrighteous tyrant!
Longer yet shall hearts be wasted,
Scorching in thy flames and burning?
Art thou of the damnèd spirits
One? Behold, I am the other.
Hoar of head art thou; I likewise;
Stark we make the land and mortals.

Mars thou art; I am Saturnus,
Stars that strike with baneful influence,
Dreadfullest in their conjunction.
Souls thou slayest; airs of heaven
Dost thou freeze; my airs are colder
Than thou e'er canst be. Thy savage
Host, they martyrize the faithful
With a thousand several tortures.
Well, in these my days, God grant it,
Direr ill shall be discovered.
I, by God, in nought will spare thee!
Let God hear what gift I proffer!
Ay, by God, from death's cold shudder
Nought, O greybeard, shall defend thee,
Not the broad hearth's glow of fuel,
Not the flame-leaps of December."

Goethe's idealized lovers were Hatem (Goethe) and Zuleika (Marianne von Willemer).

III

Hatem

Now that Zuleika is thy name
I should also named be.
When thy beloved thou dost acclaim
Hatem—that the name shall be.
'Tis but to have me known aright,
And no presumption shall there be;
Who names himself St George's Knight
Pretends not like St George to be.
Not Hatem Thai, who every gift could give,
I, in my poverty, can be;
Not Hatem Zograi, wealthiest that did live
Of all the poets, might I be;

Yet up to both mine eyes to lift—
That shall not wholly blameful be;
To take bliss and to give the gift,
Will ever noble joyance be.
Self-love in joy's exchange—sweet thrift—
Rapture of Paradise shall be!

IV

Hatem

It is not Opportunity
    Makes thieves, herself she heads the roll;
For from my heart, its treasury,
    All that was left of love she stole.

To thee the spoil she has consigned,
    The sum of all my life had won;
So now, made poor, I look to find
    My very life from thee alone.

But even already pity charms
    Those lustrous eyes to which I sued,
And I may welcome in thine arms
    The fortune of my life renewed.

V

Zuleika

Since of my joys your love is chief,
    I chide not Opportunity;
For if with you she played the thief,
    How has her booty gladdened me.

But wherefore "theft"? Of free choice give
    Yourself to me! though for my part
Too willingly would I believe—
    Yes, I am she who stole your heart.

What you have given thus freely brings
    Noble return, to match your stake—
My rest, my opulent life; these things
    I joy to give; 'tis yours to take!

Mock not! No word of being "made poor!"
    Are we not rich, of love possessed?
I hold you in my arms, and sure
    Such fortune reckons with the best.

IX

Hatem

Interpret this! In truth I can:
    Have I not often by your side
Told how the Doge Venetian
    Maketh the sea his bride?
The ring in the Euphrates fell
    From off your finger even so.

Ah! thousand songs celestial,
    Sweet dreams, from thee shall flow!
But I, from farthest Hindustan,
    Made for Damascus, hoping there
With the next starting caravan,
    Toward the Red Sea to fare.

Your stream, the grove, the terrace, this,
    Has bound me to, as wedded mate;
Here shall my spirit, till love's last kiss,
    To you be dedicate.

X

Zuleika

Skilled am I to read men's glances;
One says—"Ah, I love, I suffer!
Live in longing, live despairing!"
And what more a maiden knoweth.
All such speech can nought avail me,
All such speech unmoved must leave me;
But, my Hatem, these your glances
Give the day its gleam and glory.
For they say, "She yonder glads me,
As nought else on earth can gladden;
Lo, I look on roses, lilies,
Pomp and wealth of every garden,
Look on cypress, myrtle, violets,
Sprung to adorn the world with beauty,
And adorned she stands a marvel,
Compassing us with sweet surprises,
Quickening us, restoring, blessing,
So that health returns upon us,
And we sigh again for sickness."
Then you looked upon Zuleika,
And in sickness found a healing,
In your healing found a sickness,
Smiled and turned your eyes upon her,
As you never smiled on others.
And Zuleika felt the glance's
Ever-living speech—"She glads me
As nought else on earth has gladdened."

Exercise

1. Compare the language of the five love poems with that of "The Winter and Timur." In the latter, phrases like *resistless fury, icy breathings,* and *frost-fanged storm* are fierce in meaning and in sound. Look for other phrases that have the same quality. Try reading the Timur poem aloud and then one of the love poems. How do the rhythms and sounds differ?

Hegel and Marx

The most important German philosopher after Kant, Georg Wilhelm Hegel (HAY-gul; 1770–1831) influenced European and American philosophers, historians, theologians, and political theorists. Described by Bertrand Russell as "the hardest to understand of all the great philosophers," the discussion of Hegel will be limited here to those doctrines that influenced Karl Marx. Hegel believed in an all-encompassing Absolute, a world Spirit that expressed itself in the historical process. Basing his logic on the "triadic dialectic," Hegel stated that for every concept (thesis) there was its opposite idea (antithesis). Out of the dynamic interaction between the two extremes would emerge a synthesis which, in turn, would become a new and presumably higher thesis. Absolute Being, for example, is a thesis while Absolute Unbeing is its antithesis. The synthesis is Absolute Becoming, meaning that the universe is eternally recreating itself.

The notable cultures of the past were, according to Hegel, stages in the evolutionary development of the world Spirit toward perfection and freedom. Human beings and their institutions must inevitably clash because all are subject to error but, nevertheless, they must act and, through striving, find the "path of righteousness." Essentially Faustian in the conviction that perfectability was attainable only through continuous activity and unavoidable conflict, Hegel's philosophy of history was evolutionary. Not only all humankind but the world itself was progressing ever upward, away from imperfection and toward the Absolute.

By mid-century the horrible working conditions and dismal lives of factory workers concerned social reformers thoughout Europe. Many spoke out against the exploitation of the working class but none so dramatically as the Communists.

Literary Selection

MANIFESTO OF THE COMMUNIST PARTY

Karl Marx and *Friedrich Engels*

A specter is haunting Europe—the specter of communism. All the powers of old Europe have entered into a holy alliance to exorcise this specter: Pope and Czar, Metternich and Guizot, French Radicals and German police spies.

Where is the party in opposition that has not been decried as communistic by its opponents in power? Where is the Opposition that has not hurled back the branding reproach of communism, against the more advanced opposition parties, as well as against its reactionary adversaries?

Two things result from this fact:

I. Communism is already acknowledged by all European powers to be itself a power.

II. It is high time that Communists should openly, in the face of the whole world, publish their views, their aims, their tendencies, and meet this nursery tale of the specter of communism with a manifesto of the party itself.

To this end, Communists of various nationalities have assembled in London, and sketched the following manifesto, to be published in the English, French, German, Italian, Flemish, and Danish languages.

I

Bourgeois and Proletarians

The history of all hitherto existing society is the history of class struggles.

Freeman and slave, patrician and plebeian, lord and serf, guildmaster and journeyman, in a word, oppressor and oppressed, stood in constant opposition to one another, carried on an uninterrupted, now hidden, now open fight, a fight that each time ended, either in a revolutionary reconstitution of society at large, or in the common ruin of the contending classes.

In the earlier epochs of history, we find almost everywhere a complicated arrangement of society into various orders, a manifold gradation of social rank. In ancient Rome we have patricians, knights, plebeians, slaves; in the Middle Ages, feudal lords, vassals, guildmasters, journeymen, apprentices, serfs; in almost all of these classes, again, subordinate gradations.

The modern bourgeois society that has sprouted from the ruins of feudal society, has not done away with class antagonisms. It has but established new classes, new conditions of oppression, new forms of struggle in place of the old ones.

Our epoch, the epoch of the bourgeoisie, possesses, however, this distinctive feature: It has simplified the class antagonisms. Society as a whole is more and more splitting up into two great classes directly facing each other—bourgeoisie and proletariat. . . .

The Communists disdain to conceal their views and aims. They openly declare that their ends can be attained only by the forcible overthrow of all existing social conditions. Let the ruling classes tremble at a Communist revolution. The proletarians have nothing to lose but their chains. They have a world to win.

Workingmen of all countries, unite!

Because he believed in the basic goodness of human beings, Karl Marx (1818–1883), along with his collaborator Friedrich Engels (1820–1895), formulated a doctrine of inevitable progress that would lead to the perfect classless society in which private property and the profit motive would be relics of the imperfect past. From Hegel he took the dialectic, not as world Spirit but as material forces, a concept espoused by the German philosopher Ludwig Feuerbach (1804–1872). In effect, Marx turned Hegel's dialectic upside down, contending that it was not consciousness that determined human existence but the social existence of people that defined their consciousness.

For Marx, the way people made a living, their "means of production," determined their beliefs and institutions. To demonstrate the working out of dialectical materialism Marx concentrated on the feudal society of the Middle Ages. The ruling class consisted of the nobility and clergy as the thesis. With the development of trade an increasingly affluent middle class, the bourgeoisie, rose as the antithesis in the class struggle. Following the American and French revolutions the bourgeois class merged with the vanquished nobility as the synthesis. Traders, bankers, and factory owners made up the ruling class of capitalists, the new thesis, while the oppressed workers, the proletariat, were the antithesis. The final class struggle between capitalists and workers would, according to Marx, inevitably result in victory for the proletariat, who would take over the means of production. Under the "dictatorship of the proletariat" the entire capitalist apparatus would be collectivized. With only one class remaining the class struggle would cease. The state, according to Marx, with its laws, courts, and police served only to oppress the proletariat and thus would no longer be necessary and would therefore "wither away."

The inevitable march of history to a classless society did not happen, of course, as Marx had predicted. In order to better protect the working class democratic governments have had to regulate industry and adopt various degrees of "state socialism." The theoretical dictatorship of the proletariat still functions in the U.S.S.R. with no signs of withering away of the state in Russia or in any country controlled by Marxist-Leninist ideology. Hard-core Marxists still contend that the revolution will have to be worldwide before the withering away can take place.[5]

Charles Darwin (1809–1882)

Anaximander of Miletus (610–ca. 547 B.C.) postulated an elementary theory of evolution, but it was not until the nineteenth century that the theories of Erasmus Darwin, Jean-Baptiste de Lamarch, Thomas Malthus, and the detailed naturalistic observations of Charles Darwin finally led to Darwin's publication of *On the Origin of Species by Means of Natural Selection* (1859). After serving as naturalist on the surveying ship *Beagle* (1831–1836) Darwin read in Thomas Malthus's *On Population* (1798) the thesis that population increased by geometric ratio (1, 2, 4, 16, etc.), while the food supply increased arithmetically (1, 3, 5, 7, 9, etc.). The limited food supply, Malthus observed, naturally checked unlimited population increases. Darwin wrote:

> It at once struck me that under the circumstances favorable variations would tend to be preserved and unfavorable ones destroyed. The result of this would be the formation of a new species. Here then I had a theory by which to work.

This is the doctrine of natural selection, the result of chance permitting the survival of the fittest.

Darwin proceeded from three facts to his deductions:

Fact 1. All organisms tend to increase geometrically.

Fact 2. The population of a given species remains more or less constant.

Fact 3. Within any species there is considerable variation.

Deduction 1. With more young produced than can survive there must be competition for survival.

Deduction 2. The variations within a species means that a higher percentage of those with favorable variations will survive and, conversely, a higher percentage of those with unfavorable variations will die or fail to reproduce. This is natural selection. Furthermore, the favorable variations are generally transmitted by heredity, meaning that natural selection will tend to maintain and act to improve the ability of the species to survive.

Modern evolution theory confirms Darwin's facts and deductions as outlined above, but adds some significant variations in terms of modifications, mutations, and recombinations. Modification is a variation due to external or internal factors and is not the result of inheritance. Take, for example, two brothers, one leading an active and healthy life and the other immersed in alcoholism. The odds on survival are not difficult to predict.

The copying of genes in the process of reproduction is not always precise. A copy that differs slightly from the original is a mutation and the mutated gene will continue to reproduce itself unless the mutation results in an unfavorable variation that increases the chances against survival. Mutations tend, on the whole, to result in unfavorable variations.

Darwin was not aware of the full implications of Gregor Mendel's (1822–1884) experiments in genetics, specifically the fact that sexual reproduction results in a recombination of existing genetic units that may produce or modify inheritable combinations. Take, for example, twelve children born of the same parents. Though there is generally a familial resemblance, each child will be distinctly different because of the different recombination of genes.

Darwin was reluctant to publish his theories until he learned that Alfred Russel Wallace (1823–1913) had independently developed a theory of evolution. Both men submitted a paper to the Linnean Society on the theory of natural selection; both papers were read on July 1, 1858, and later published. Even when Darwin published his *Origin of Species* the following year he considered his work a brief abstract of twenty-five years of detailed studies.

Darwin's work provoked a great controversy, of course, because it denied supernatural intervention in the functioning of the universe. He could and did ride out the theological storm but not the attacks of naturalists who claimed a special place for *homo sapiens* separate from other species. In the introduction to his *The Descent of Man* (1871) Darwin noted that he had many notes on the origin or descent of man but that he was determined "not to publish, as I thought that I should thus only add to the prejudices against my views." Indeed, his *Origin of Species* implied "that man must be included with other organic beings in any general conclusion respecting his manner of appearance on this earth." *The Descent of Man* is therefore a response to hostile naturalists and a sequel to the *Origin of Species* in which Darwin discussed the evolution of *homo sapiens* from lower

---

5. For a detailed analysis of current Soviet problems see Marshall I. Goldman, *USSR in Crisis: The Failure of an Economic System* (New York: W. W. Norton and Company, 1983).

forms of life. The conclusion of this work reveals Darwin as a realist and as an optimist.

Literary Selection

THE DESCENT OF MAN
Charles Darwin

The main conclusion arrived at in this work, namely, that man is descended from some lowly organised form, will, I regret to think, be highly distasteful to many. But there can hardly be a doubt that we are descended from barbarians. The astonishment which I felt on first seeing a party of Fuegians on a wild and broken shore will never be forgotten by me, for the reflection at once rushed into my mind—such were our ancestors. These men were absolutely naked and bedaubed with paint, their long hair was tangled, their mouths, frothed with excitement, and their expression was wild, startled, and distrustful. They possessed hardly any arts, and like wild animals lived on what they could catch; they had no government, and were merciless to every one not of their own small tribe. He who has seen a savage in his native land will not feel much shame, if forced to acknowledge that the blood of some more humble creature flows in his veins. For my own part I would as soon be descended from that heroic little monkey, who braved his dreaded enemy in order to save the life of his keeper, or from that old baboon,who descending from the mountains, carried away in triumph his young comrade from a crowd of astonished dogs—as from a savage who delights to torture his enemies, offers up bloody sacrifices, practices infanticide without remorse, treats his wives like slaves, knows no decency, and is haunted by the grossest superstitions.

Man may be excused for feeling some pride at having risen, though not through his own exertions, to the very summit of the organic scale; and the fact of his having thus risen, instead of having been aboriginally placed there, may give him hope for a still higher destiny in the distant future. But we are not here concerned with hopes or fears, only with the truth as far as our reason permits us to discover it; and I have given the evidence to the best of my ability. We must, however, acknowledge, as it seems to me, that man with all his noble qualities, with sympathy which feels for the most debased, with benevolence which extends not only to other men but to the humblest living creature, with his god-like intellect which has penetrated into the movements and constitution of the solar system—with all these exalted powers—Man still bears in his bodily frame the indelible stamp of his lowly origin.

What is the status of Darwinism today? Is the theory of evolution simply a theory, a kind of glorified hypothesis that may be knocked down by contradictory scientific evidence or because someone comes up with a better theory? In *Nature,* a leading British scientific journal, a lead editorial states:

> The first requirement of any theory, good or bad, is that it should be consistent with such phenomena as there are, and logically consistent. Darwinism is consistent with the data to which Darwin had access more than a century ago. One of the remarkable

features of the theory is that it remains consistent with the vastly greater body of data now available.

On the grounds of internal consistency, Darwinism has also triumphed quite remarkably. Today's molecular biology has provided an independent (and potentially extremely powerful) method of telling the relationships between species and groups of species, many of them only distantly related to each other. The result is a striking confirmation of the general character of the relationships suggested by Darwin and his contemporaries. To be sure, it is not possible to tell from a comparison of the structures of proteins found in primates whether people are more closely related to gorillas or chimpanzees, but that only goes to fill out Darwin's notion of divergent evolution from some common stock. At the same time, however, the quite remarkable constancy of some materials, the histone proteins for example, is vividly suggestive of the common origin of all living things, and of their persistence over time. The way in which the theory of evolution has been able to survive such a long succession of discoveries bearing on the mechanism of inheritance—the rediscovery of Mendelism, the discovery of chromosomes, the recognition of what genes are and the recognition that genes are usually pieces of double-stranded DNA—is striking evidence of its overwhelming consistency. No theory of such a grand scale in the physical sciences has done as well in the past century.[6]

Social Darwinism

Herbert Spencer (1820–1903) was an English philosopher and an advocate not only of evolution in nature but in human institutions as well. "Survival of the fittest," the phrase coined by Spencer, meant, claimed the Social Darwinists, that the rich were better adapted to the rigors of competitive life; they were, in short, more fit to survive than the poor. Opposed to governmental intervention in economic affairs, trade unions, and socialist ideas like welfare, powerful capitalists like John D. Rockefeller and Andrew Carnegie claimed that unrestrained competition had a scientific basis comparable to evolution in nature. This position was, of course, an attempt to justify laissez-faire capitalism.

On a larger scale, Social Darwinism helped reinforce the idea that some nations were more fit than rival nations and defeating a rival in warfare would demonstrate that superiority. Indeed, it became almost a moral duty, in evolutionary terms, to conquer an inferior people and populate their lands with fitter human beings. Late nineteenth-century imperialism thus had an ideal social philosophy to justify the growth of empire. Cecil Rhodes, the British imperialist, even held the view that a world of Anglo-Saxons was the best of all possible worlds, thus adding racism to the social evolution theory. In 1845 a journalist and diplomat named John Louis O'Sullivan coined the

---

6. "How true is the theory of evolution?" *Nature* 290 (12 March 1981): 75–76.

term *manifest destiny* which, when reinforced by social evolution, provided the justification of American imperialism.

In the fullness of time Darwinian ideas spread into every corner of the intellectual domain: anthropology, sociology, history, literature, art, music, legal and political institutions. Just about everything was investigated in terms of origin, development, and survival or disappearance.

There is no denying the enormous influence of evolutionary theory in all of these areas, but great care has to be taken when applying a scientific theory to nonscientific areas. "Natural selection," for scientists, means the way things work in nature and no more than that. Social Darwinists used evolutionary theory to justify individuality and unfettered competition as if the marketplace were a scientific laboratory. Scientific terminology was selected to undergird the way things were supposed to be. "Survival of the fittest" was intended to prove that the wealthy and powerful were fit and no one else. As a matter of fact, the most fit in Darwin's natural world were those who left, over a period of time, the most dependents who could survive natural selection. Not necessarily the smartest, biggest, or strongest, just survivors.

Furthermore, the same conservative Social Darwinists who claimed that a capitalistic economy was a struggle for existence with only the fittest surviving refused, for the most part, to compete in a free market. They wanted high tariffs to protect them from foreign competition and would tolerate no competition for improved wages and working conditions on the part of organized labor. Those who argued so persuasively for competition, like Rockefeller and Carnegie, effectively eliminated almost all competition so that they could enjoy their virtual monopolies in steel and oil. In the final analysis, Social Darwinism is a misnomer in terms of using Darwin's name. The true social philosophy of America's Robber Barons at the height of laissez-faire capitalism can best be summed up in the memorable statement of Cornelius Vanderbilt: "The public be damned!"

It was only in nature that ruthless competition was natural. Competition in business, however ruthless, appears to be practical and efficient providing no one is cheating. In terms of human nature, however, neither natural nor business competition seems to present an acceptable pattern for human behavior. Ethical and humane considerations must be applied to human beings.

Liberalism

Jeremy Bentham (1748–1832) was the founder of the rationalist philosophy of utilitarianism, a doctrine whose central idea is that actions are not right or wrong in themselves; they can be judged only by their consequences. Utilitarianism is based on the assumption that all human beings pursue happiness and that they do this by seeking pleasure and avoiding pain. The criterion of the value of deeds is their utility, that is, whether or not they lead to the greatest happiness of the greatest number. Bentham's ethics are, in effect, an inversion of those of Kant. Kant calls for action as a duty and on principle; Bentham's values are based on the consequences of actions.

Bentham believed, along with classical (laissez-faire) economists, that government governs best when it governs least, and that it should be relatively passive in social affairs. He was, however, an ardent reformer and his detailed studies of English institutions convinced him that the pleasure derived by some in the pursuit of self-interest caused pain for others, sometimes many, many others. He and his followers, the Philosophic Radicals, came to believe that the state should intervene to help provide the greatest happiness for the greatest number. Their influence helped bring about considerable administrative, legal, and economic reforms that broadened, in the twentieth century, into the concept of the welfare state.

James Mill was a disciple of Bentham and the director of a rigorous "educational experiment" for his son, John Stuart Mill (1806–1873). At the age of three, young Mill had learned Greek and, at seven, was reading Plato's dialogues. During the following year he taught Latin to his sister. By the time John Stuart Mill started college, he had what he called a twenty-five-year headstart on his classmates. There were drawbacks, however. "I grew up," Mill wrote in his celebrated *Autobiography* (1873) "in the absence of love and in the presence of fear." Referring to himself as a "reasoning machine," Mill had a breakdown at twenty from which he recovered by turning to music and the Romantic poets, especially Coleridge and Wordsworth. It was also during this period of crisis that Mill met Harriet Taylor, the wife of a London merchant. A woman of remarkable intellect comparable to that of Mill, Harriet was his intense Platonic love and intellectual companion until 1851, when her husband died and they were finally married. The belated education in music and art plus the association with Harriet, whom Mill credited with much assistance in his writing, helped make Mill the foremost humanitarian liberal of the century.

Mill adopted utilitarianism at an early age but distinguished pleasures by qualities rather than mere quantities as Bentham had done. For Mill the greatest pleasures were intellectal, ranking far above sensual pleasures. As he said, he would "rather be Sokrates dissatisfied than a fool satisfied." Mill's position was comparable to that of the Epicureans when he said that "human beings have faculties more elevated than the animal appetites, and when once conscious of them, do not regard anything as happiness which does not include their gratification." Among the greatest pleasures for Mill were freedom of thought, speech, and action, but only up to the point where this freedom might impinge upon that of another individual. His famous political essay *On Liberty* (1859) explores the "nature and limits of power which can be legitimately exercised over the individual." His arguments in defense of free speech in a democratic society are just as convincing today, and his warning against "the tyranny of the majority" is equally apropos for our own age.

In order to help secure the greatest good for the greatest number, Mill was an extremely active reformer, pressing for extended suffrage, measures to protect children and actions to improve the lot of the poor. Virtually alone among intellectuals of his time, Mill was convinced that women were the intellectual equals of men. Vigorously opposed to the inferior status of women, he wrote the *Subjection of Women* (1869), a strongly worded book that was responsible for some changed laws and a number of changes in opinions. Though he did not reject classical economics, Mill did see that modifications were necessary and, moreover, long overdue. In the midst of self-righteous, materialistic Victorians, Mill's sane and sophisticated voice was like a liberal breath of fresh air.

Victorian Poets

By the late Victorian period England was a bustling and prosperous country. Mechanized, industrialized, and urbanized, it was also a tiny island on whose flag the sun never set, the most powerful and far-flung empire the world had ever known. Early Romantics had envisioned a new society flourishing in a golden age, but late Victorians witnessed endless colonial wars, smoke blanketing the countryside from hundreds of belching smokestacks, and miles of dreary row houses inhabited by overworked and underpaid factory workers. The Industrial Revolution had defiled nature but, after Darwin, there was no solace in a nature "red with tooth and claw." What, then, was the role of the poet?

Alfred, Lord Tennyson (1809–1892)

The most representative poet of the late Victorian era, Tennyson reflected the mood of the period in poetry that was contemplative, sad, quiet, melancholy, sometimes wistful, and often pessimistic. The old optimism of the Early Romantics was gone.

Literary Selections

In the following poem Mariana, from Shakespeare's *Measure for Measure,* waits in the "moated grange" (farmhouse complex) for the lover who has deserted her. The scene painting is remarkably consistent with the dark and hopeless feelings of the abandoned Mariana and is, in fact, the embodiment of her feelings.

MARIANA
Alfred, Lord Tennyson

"Mariana in the moated grange."
Measure for Measure

With blackest moss the flower plots
    Were thickly crusted, one and all;
The rusted nails fell from the knots
    That held the pear to the gable wall.
The broken sheds looked sad and strange: 5
    Unlifted was the clinking latch;
    Weeded and worn the ancient thatch

Upon the lonely moated grange.
    She only said, "My life is dreary,
        He cometh not," she said;   10
    She said, "I am aweary, aweary,
        I would that I were dead!"
Her tears fell with the dews at even;
    Her tears fell ere the dews were dried;
She could not look on the sweet heaven,   15
    Either at morn or eventide.
After the flitting of the bats,
    When thickest dark did trance the sky,
    She drew her casement curtain by,
And glanced athwart the glooming flats.   20
    She only said, "The night is dreary,
        He cometh not," she said;
    She said, "I am aweary, aweary,
        I would that I were dead!"
Upon the middle of the night,   25
    Waking she heard the nightfowl crow;
The cock sung out an hour ere light;
    From the dark fen the oxen's low
Came to her; without hope of change,
    In sleep she seemed to walk forlorn,   30
    Till cold winds woke the gray-eyed morn
About the lonely moated grange.
    She only said, "The day is dreary,
        He cometh not," she said;
    She said, "I am aweary, aweary,   35
        I would that I were dead!"
About a stonecast from the wall
    A sluice with blackened waters slept,
And o'er it many, round and small,
    The clustered marish-mosses crept.   40
Hard by a poplar shook alway,
    All silver-green with gnarlèd bark:
    For leagues no other tree did mark
The level waste, the rounding gray.
    She only said, "My life is dreary,   45
        He cometh not," she said;
    She said, "I am aweary, aweary,
        I would that I were dead!"
And ever when the moon was low,
    And the shrill winds were up and away,   50
In the white curtain, to and fro,
    She saw the gusty shadows sway.
But when the moon was very low,
    And wild winds bound within their cell,
    The shadow of the poplar fell   55
Upon her bed, across her brow.
    She only said, "The night is dreary,
        He cometh not," she said;
    She said, "I am aweary, aweary,
        I would that I were dead!"   60
All day within the dreamy house,
    The doors upon their hinges creaked;
The blue fly sung in the pane; the mouse
    Behind the moldering wainscot shrieked,
Or from the crevice peered about.   65
    Old faces glimmered through the doors,
    Old footsteps trod the upper floors,
Old voices called her from without.
    She only said, "My life is dreary,
        He cometh not," she said;   70
    She said, "I am aweary, aweary,
        I would that I were dead!"

The sparrow's chirrup on the roof,
   The slow clock ticking, and the sound
Which to the wooing wind aloof   75
   The poplar made, did all confound
Her sense; but most she loathed the hour
   When the thick-moted sunbeam lay
   Athwart the chambers, and the day
Was sloping toward his western bower.   80
     Then, said she, "I am very dreary,
      He will not come," she said;
     She wept, "I am aweary, aweary,
      Oh God, that I were dead!"

Tennyson wrote often about contemporary events such as "The Charge of the Light Brigade," but his best poetry is about the past, particularly the classical past. In "Ulysses" the Greek hero has returned, after twenty years, to Penelope, his "aged wife," and Telemachus, a dutiful son who is content to stay at home and "make mild a rugged people." Ulysses is always the man of action, the embodiment of the Faustian man, whose mission in life is succinctly stated in the last line of the poem.

ULYSSES
Alfred, Lord Tennyson

It little profits that an idle king,
By this still hearth, among these barren crags,
Matched with an aged wife, I mete and dole
Unequal laws unto a savage race,
That hoard, and sleep, and feed, and know not me.
I cannot rest from travel: I will drink
Life to the lees: all times I have enjoyed
Greatly, have suffered greatly, both with those
That loved me, and alone; on shore, and when
Through scudding drifts the rainy Hyades   10
Vext the dim sea. I am become a name;
For always roaming with a hungry heart
Much have I seen and known: cities of men
And manners, climates, councils, governments,
Myself not least, but honored of them all,—
And drunk delight of battle with my peers,
Far on the ringing plains of windy Troy.
I am a part of all that I have met;
Yet all experience is an arch wherethrough
Gleams that untraveled world, whose margin fades 20
For ever and for ever when I move.
How dull it is to pause, to make an end,
To rust unburnished, not to shine in use!
As though to breathe were life! Life piled on life
Were all too little, and of one to me
Little remains: but every hour is saved
From that eternal silence, something more,
A bringer of new things; and vile it were
For some three suns to store and hoard myself,
And this gray spirit yearning in desire   30
To follow knowledge, like a sinking star,
Beyond the utmost bound of human thought.
   This is my son, mine own Telemachus,
To whom I leave the scepter and the isle—
Well-loved of me, discerning to fulfill
This labor, by slow prudence to make mild
A rugged people, and through soft degrees
Subdue them to the useful and the good.
Most blameless is he, centered in the sphere
Of common duties, decent not to fail   40

In offices of tenderness, and pay
Meet adoration to my household gods,
When I am gone. He works his work, I mine.
   There lies the port: the vessel puffs her sail:
There gloom the dark broad seas. My mariners,
Souls that have toiled, and wrought, and thought with
    me—
That ever with a frolic welcome took
The thunder and the sunshine, and opposed
Free hearts, free foreheads—you and I are old;
Old age hath yet his honor and his toil;   50
Death closes all: but something ere the end,
Some work of noble note, may yet be done,
Not unbecoming men that strove with Gods.
The lights begin to twinkle from the rocks:
The long day wanes: the slow moon climbs: the deep
Moans round with many voices. Come, my friends,
'Tis not too late to seek a newer world.
Push off, and sitting well in order smite
The sounding furrows; for my purpose holds
To sail beyond the sunset, and the baths   60
Of all the western stars, until I die.
It may be that the gulfs will wash us down:
It may be we shall touch the Happy Isles,
And see the great Achilles, whom we knew.
Though much is taken, much abides; and though
We are not now that strength which in old days
Moved earth and heaven, that which we are, we
    are,—
One equal temper of heroic hearts,
Made weak by time and fate, but strong in will
To strive, to seek, to find, and not to yield.   70

Exercise

1. In Tennyson's version is Ulysses a noble hero who refuses to submit meekly to old age and death or is he an arrogant, self-centered old man with little concern for his family? Why shouldn't he be "Matched with an aged wife"? Penelope is younger than Ulysses and she did wait twenty faithful years for her husband to return from his Odyssey. Whatever your opinion, is he believeable as a human being?

Matthew Arnold (1822–1888)

As a poet and literary critic Arnold was as pessimistic about human beings and their institutions as were his colleagues, but through sheer force of will he created a cheerful demeanor and purposive character for himself. Possibly the most anti-Victorian figure in Victorian England, Arnold was an apostle of high culture and a lifelong enemy of Puritanism, the "Barbarians" (the aristocracy), and the "Philistines" (the middle class). His melancholic and despairing view of human alienation in a hostile universe is memorably expressed in "Dover Beach." When the poet says to his female companion, "Ah love, let us be true to one another!" the objective is not love but survival. Arnold was a realist, not a romantic.

DOVER BEACH
Matthew Arnold

[First published 1867.]

The sea is calm to-night,
The tide is full, the moon lies fair
Upon the Straits;—on the French coast, the light
Gleams, and is gone; the cliffs of England stand,
Glimmering and vast, out in the tranquil bay.
Come to the window, sweet is the night air!
Only, from the long line of spray
Where the ebb meets the moon-blanch'd sand,
Listen! you hear the grating roar
Of pebbles which the waves suck back, and fling, 10
At their return, up the high strand,
Begin, and cease, and then again begin,
With tremulous cadence slow, and bring
The eternal note of sadness in.

  Sophocles long ago
Heard it on the Aegaean, and it brought
Into his mind the turbid ebb and flow
Of human misery; we
Find also in the sound a thought,
Hearing it by this distant northern sea. 20

The sea of faith
Was once, too, at the full, and round earth's shore
Lay like the folds of a bright girdle furl'd;
But now I only hear
Its melancholy, long, withdrawing roar,
Retreating to the breath
Of the night-wind down the vast edges drear
And naked shingles of the world.

Ah, love, let us be true
To one another! for the world, which seems 30
To lie before us like a land of dreams,
So various, so beautiful, so new,
Hath really neither joy, nor love, nor light,
Nor certitude, nor peace, nor help for pain;
And we are here as on a darkling plain
Swept with confused alarms of struggles and flight,
Where ignorant armies clash by night.

Exercises

1. Compare the liquid and nasal sounds of lines 1–8 with the much harsher sounds of lines 9–14. Notice, also, that the opening lines describe a lovely seascape, with a discordant tone entering at line 9 in both sounds and sense.

2. What was it that Sophocles heard long ago and far away?

3. What happened to the "sea of faith"? Why?

4. The verbs in lines 1–8 are positive but, in lines 30–31, the world *seems* like a land of dreams. What is the world really like?

5. What are the many implications inherent in the last line? Consider the levels of meaning in each of the key words—*ignorant, armies, clash, night*—and then reflect on the entire line. How far have we come from the opening lines?

Thomas Hardy (1840–1928)

Though he denied being a pessimist, the novels, short stories, and poems of Thomas Hardy reveal a pessimism every bit as profound as that of Matthew Arnold. Like Arnold, Hardy was a realist. He claimed that human effort could make the world a better place, but his prose and poetry are brimming over with sadness over the waste and frustration of life. Though he outlived the Victorian Age, Hardy's output typifies the late Victorian mood of ironic sadness as, for example, in "Neutral Tones" in which the imagery is consistent and convincing.

NEUTRAL TONES
Thomas Hardy

We stood by a pond that winter day,
And the sun was white, as though chidden of God,
And a few leaves lay on the starving sod;
  —They had fallen from an ash, and were gray.

Your eyes on me were as eyes that rove 5
Over tedious riddles of years ago;
And some words played between us to and fro
  On which lost the more by our love.

The smile on your mouth was the deadest thing
Alive enough to have strength to die; 10
And a grin of bitterness swept thereby
  Like an ominous bird a-wing. . . .

Since then, keen lessons that love deceives,
And wrings with wrong, have shaped to me
Your face, and the God-cursed sun, and a tree, 15
  And a pond edged with grayish leaves.

1898

One of the last and probably the most unpopular of England's colonial wars, the Boer War (1899–1902) was a brutal struggle that forced the South Africans (Afrikaaners) to submit to British domination. "Drummer Hodge" is a lament for an English soldier buried where a "kopje-crest" (Afrikaans, small hill) breaks the veldt (Afrikaans, prairie), a stranger to this part of the world who did not know the meaning of a dry tableland region called "the broad Karoo."

DRUMMER HODGE
Thomas Hardy

They throw in Drummer Hodge, to rest
  Uncoffined—just as found:
His landmark is a kopje-crest
  That breaks the veldt around;
And foreign constellations west 5
  Each night above his mound.

Young Hodge the Drummer never knew—
  Fresh from his Wessex home—
The meaning of the broad Karoo,
  The Bush, the dusty loam, 10
And why uprose to nightly view
  Strange stars amid the gloam.

Yet portion of that unknown plain
  Will Hodge forever be;

His homely Northern breast and brain 15
　　Grow to some Southern tree,
And strange-eyed constellations reign
　　His stars eternally.

1902

Written on the last day of the nineteenth century, "The Darkling Thrush" morosely defines a century that ends, for Hardy, with a whimper, and anticipates a new hundred years that seems to offer little hope of anything better.

THE DARKLING THRUSH
Thomas Hardy

I leant upon a coppice gate
　　When Frost was specter-gray,
And Winter's dregs made desolate
　　The weakening eye of day.
The tangled bine-stems scored the sky 5
　　Like strings of broken lyres,
And all mankind that haunted nigh
　　Had sought their household fires.

The land's sharp features seemed to be
　　The Century's corpse outleant, 10
His crypt the cloudy canopy,
　　The wind his death-lament.
The ancient pulse of germ and birth
　　Was shrunken hard and dry,
And every spirit upon earth 15
　　Seemed fervorless as I.

At once a voice arose among
　　The bleak twigs overhead
In a fullhearted evensong
　　Of joy illimited; 20
An aged thrush, frail, gaunt, and small,
　　In blast-beruffled plume,
Had chosen thus to fling his soul
　　Upon the growing gloom.

So little cause for carolings 25
　　Of such ecstatic sound
Was written on terrestrial things
　　Afar or nigh around,
That I could think there trembled through
　　His happy good-night air 30
Some blessed Hope, whereof he knew
　　And I was unaware.

1902

Hardy wrote the following poem in April 1914 to describe, with foreboding, gunnery practice in the English Channel. The war began four months later.

CHANNEL FIRING
Thomas Hardy

That night your great guns, unawares,
Shook all our coffins as we lay,
And broke the chancel window-squares,
We thought it was the Judgment Day
And sat upright. While drearisome 5
Arose the howl of wakened hounds:
The mouse let fall the altar-crumb,
The worms drew back into the mounds,

The glebe cow drooled. Till God called, "No;
It's gunnery practice out at sea 10
Just as before you went below;
The world is as it used to be:

"All nations striving strong to make
Red war yet redder. Mad as hatters
They do no more for Christés sake 15
Than you who are helpless in such matters.

"That this is not the judgment hour
For some of them's a blessed thing,
For if it were they'd have to scour
Hell's floor for so much threatening. . . . 20

"Ha, ha. It will be warmer when
I blow the trumpet (if indeed
I ever do; for you are men,
And rest eternal sorely need)."

So down we lay again. "I wonder, 25
Will the world ever saner be,"
Said one, "than when He sent us under
In our indifferent century!"

And many a skeleton shook his head.
"Instead of preaching forty year," 30
My neighbor Parson Thirdly said,
"I wish I had stuck to pipes and beer."

Again the guns disturbed the hour,
Roaring their readiness to avenge,
As far inland as Stourton Tower, 35
And Camelot, and starlit Stonehenge.

1914

Exercises

1. Why are the stars *strange* in "Drummer Hodge"? How was he buried? What does this imply about the treatment of living soldiers?
2. In "The Darkling Thrush" Hardy uses words gloomy in sense and sound such as *spectre-gray, dregs, desolate,* and *broken.* What are some of the other depressing words? Why does Hardy choose the image of a joyfully singing thrush? What effect does this have on the generally morbid tone of the poem?
3. In "Channel Firing" why does the poet select the names Stourton Tower, Camelot, and Stonehenge? Consider the following facts: Stourton Tower was built in the eighteenth century to commemorate King Alfred's ninth-century victory over the Danes, Camelot was the fabled sixth-century home of King Arthur, and Stonehenge is a mysterious circle of enormous stones dating from about 1800 B.C.

Romanticism and Realism in America

For the United States the nineteenth century was the great age of expansion, from thirteen colonies to forty-five states, three territories, Alaska, Hawaii, the Philippines, Puerto Rico, Guam, and American Samoa. The vast physical growth and economic development was not paralleled, however, by significant developments in the fine and literary arts—not for some time. Early in the century writers were still intimidated by British letters but seeking ways to declare their literary independence. The emergence of Romanticism in England struck a responsive spark in America, and writers like Washington Irving (1783–1859), William Cullen Bryant (1794–1878), and James Fenimore Cooper (1789–1851) produced romantic works in a new American style. Because of limited space we will begin with the next generation of writers and trace the development of American literature from Romanticism to Realism with selected poetry and a short story by representative American authors.

Edgar Allen Poe (1809–1849)

One of the few literary figures with an international reputation that this nation has produced, Poe was a brilliant literary critic, poet, and writer of highly imaginative short stories. Among the first to condemn crass American materialism, Poe devoted himself wholly to his art, becoming the first American to live his life entirely as an artist. Poe defined poetry as "the creation of beauty" and contended that all poetry should appeal equally to reason and emotion. Poe felt that all poetry should be composed in terms of beauty, restraint, and unity of effect and, indeed, his poetry is the embodiment of his theory of art. Inspired by the loss of a beautiful woman, "Annabel Lee" is a lyric masterpiece in a lucid and musical style.

Literary Selections
ANNABEL LEE
Edgar Allen Poe

It was many and many a year ago,
　In a kingdom by the sea,
That a maiden there lived whom you may know
　By the name of Annabel Lee;
And this maiden she lived with no other thought
　Than to love and be loved by me.

I was a child and she was a child,
　In this kingdom by the sea,
But we loved with a love that was more than love,
　I and my Annabel Lee;
With a love that the wingèd seraphs of heaven
　Coveted her and me.

And this was the reason that, long ago,
　In this kingdom by the sea,
A wind blew out of a cloud, chilling
　My beautiful Annabel Lee;
So that her highborn kinsmen came
　And bore her away from me,
To shut her up in a sepulchre
　In this kingdom by the sea.

The angels, not half so happy in heaven,
　Went envying her and me;
Yes! that was the reason (as all men know,
　In this kingdom by the sea)
That the wind came out of the cloud by night,
　Chilling and killing my Annabel Lee.

But our love it was stronger by far than the love
　Of those who were older than we,
　Of many far wiser than we;
And neither the angels in heaven above,
　Nor the demons down under the sea,
Can ever dissever my soul from the soul
　Of the beautiful Annabel Lee:

For the moon never beams, without bringing me dreams
　Of the beautiful Annabel Lee;
And the stars never rise, but I feel the bright eyes
　Of the beautiful Annabel Lee;
And so, all the night-tide, I lie down by the side
Of my darling—my darling—my life and my bride,
　　In her sepulchre there by the sea,
　　In her tomb by the sounding sea.

Exercise

1. This is one of the most musical of all Poe's poems. How does he achieve this effect? Consider the rhythm and the word selection, particularly the use of repeated words and phrases.

Ralph Waldo Emerson (1803–1882)

Poe was a conscious representative of a Southern tradition in literature, that of a romantic Virginia Cavalier. Just as consciously, Emerson and his colleagues were New England Romantics who reconciled romantic abstractions with the hardheaded realities of Yankee individualism. The creed of Emerson, Thoreau, Margaret Fuller, and others was transcendentalism, a belief that human beings and the universe were in perfect harmony and moving in a Hegelian manner toward perfection. High-minded and highly individualistic, transcendentalism stressed the individual's conscience as the sole judge in spiritual matters, total self-reliance in all matters, and the necessity for social reforms.

For Poe poetry was beauty but Emerson viewed it as a necessary function for the individual who was seeking truth. Emerson wrote his essays but, in a sense, he thought that his poems wrote him. Many of Emerson's poems are the result of the poet's attempts to perceive the deeper meaning of nature, such as "The Rhodora," which was emblematic of the beauty bestowed by spirit on the world and implanted in human beings.

Literary Selections
THE RHODORA

On Being Asked, Whence is the Flower?
Ralph Waldo Emerson

In May, when sea-winds pierce our solitudes,
I found the fresh Rhodora in the woods,
Spreading its leafless blooms in a damp nook,
To please the desert and the sluggish brook.
The purple petals, fallen in the pool,
Made the black water with their beauty gay;
Here might the red-bird come his plumes to cool,
And court the flower that cheapens his array.
Rhodora! if the sages ask thee why
This charm is wasted on the earth and sky,
Tell them, dear, that if eyes were made for seeing,

Then Beauty is its own excuse for being:
Why thou wert there, O rival of the rose!
I never thought to ask, I never knew:
But, in my simple ignorance, suppose
The self-same Power that brought me there brought you.

Like many other romantics, particularly Hegel, Emerson was influenced by Oriental philosophy and religion. His "Brahma" is a tightly constructed parable about the unity that underlies the world and all that is in it.

BRAHMA

Ralph Waldo Emerson

If the red slayer think he slays,
    Or if the slain think he is slain,
They know not well the subtle ways
    I keep, and pass, and turn again.

Far or forgot to me is near;
    Shadow and sunlight are the same;
The vanished gods to me appear;
    And one to me are shame and fame.

They reckon ill who leave me out;
    When me they fly, I am the wings;
I am the doubter and the doubt,
    And I the hymn the Brahmin sings.

The strong gods pine for my abode,
    And pine in vain the sacred Seven;
But thou, meek lover of the good!
    Find me, and turn thy back on heaven.

Emerson's most famous poem is the "Concord Hymn" that memorialized the first battle of the Revolutionary War.

CONCORD HYMN

Sung at the Completion of the Battle Monument, July 4, 1837

Ralph Waldo Emerson

By the rude bridge that arched the flood,
    Their flag to April's breeze unfurled,
Here once the embattled farmers stood
    And fired the shot heard round the world.

The foe long since in silence slept;
    Alike the conqueror silent sleeps;
And Time the ruined bridge has swept
    Down the dark stream which seaward creeps.

On this green bank, by this soft stream,
    We set to-day a votive stone;
That memory may their deed redeem,
    When, like our sires, our sons are gone.

Spirit, that made those heroes dare
    To die, and leave their children free,
Bid Time and Nature gently spare
    The shaft we raise to them and thee.

Exercises

1. In "The Rhodora" Emerson says *that if eyes were made for seeing,/Then beauty is its own excuse for being*. What does this mean? That beauty is as necessary as sight? In "Grecian Urn" Keats wrote that *beauty is truth, truth beauty*. Was Emerson thinking along the same lines or was he referring to nature rather than art?
2. "Brahma" contains a number of paradoxes like *shadow and sunlight are the same*. What are the other paradoxes and what do these imply?

Henry David Thoreau (1817–1862)

Emerson and Thoreau were close friends all their lives but no two people were less alike personally or more alike in their transcendentalist conviction that individuals should lead active and responsible lives. Thoreau felt that most people lived lives of "quiet desperation" and made his point at Walden Pond by coexisting for two years in harmony with nature. His account of his experiences in *Walden* (1854) was his masterwork, but his thoughtful essay on "Civil Disobedience" was largely unread in his own day. Inspired probably by a night in jail because of his refusal, on principle, to pay a poll tax, "Civil Disobedience" was a major influence on Mahatma Gandhi and, later, on Martin Luther King, Jr.

Walt Whitman (1819–1892)

In his essay on "The Poet" Emerson wrote that the poet has a special mission because "the experience of each new age requires a new confession, and the world seems always waiting for its poet." It was the age of affirmation of American aspirations and the exuberant voice of American democracy was that of Walt Whitman, which Emerson himself immediately recognized. Upon receiving the first edition of *Leaves of Grass* (1855), Emerson wrote Whitman that this was "the most extraordinary piece of wit and wisdom that America has yet contributed" and greeted the poet "at the beginning of a great career." Few writers, not to mention an indifferent general public, were as perceptive as Emerson and even he later advised Whitman to go easy on the erotic poetry, advice which Whitman consistently ignored. *Leaves of Grass* was to be the poet's only book. Through nine editions (1855–1892) it grew with his life and, in effect, became his life. "This is no book," wrote Whitman, "who touches this touches a man."

A poet of many voices, Whitman rejected the genteel tradition and what he called "book-words," selecting instead the language of the common people, a unique blend of journalistic jargon, everyday speech, and a great variety of foreign words and phrases. A pantheist, mystic, and ardent patriot, Whitman advocated humanity, brotherhood, and freedom, not only in the United States but throughout the world.

The following chantlike poem is in Whitman's "catalog style" and illustrates his lusty mode as the "bard of democracy."

Literary Selections
I HEAR AMERICA SINGING
Walt Whitman

I hear America singing, the varied carols I hear,
Those of mechanics, each one singing his as it should be
    blithe and strong,
The carpenter singing his as he measures his plank or
    beam,
The mason singing his as he makes ready for work, or
    leaves off work,
The boatman singing what belongs to him in his boat, the
    deck-hand singing on the steamboat deck,
The shoemaker singing as he sits on his bench, the hatter
    singing as he stands,
The wood-cutter's song, the ploughboy's on his way in
    the morning, or at noon intermission or at sundown,
The delicious singing of the mother, or of the young wife
    at work, or of the girl sewing or washing,
Each singing what belongs to him or her and to none
    else,
The day what belongs to the day—at night the party of
    young fellows, robust, friendly,
Singing with open mouths their strong melodious songs.

Always an ardent supporter of the Union, Whitman was so distressed about the "peculiar institution" of slavery that he became an active Abolitionist. His involvement in the Civil War became personal when he began caring for his wounded brother George in an Army hospital, and stayed on to nurse others stricken by the war. The following poem is from *Drum-Taps,* which was added to *Leaves of Grass* in 1865.

BY THE BIVOUAC'S FITFUL FLAME
Walt Whitman

By the bivouac's fitful flame,
A procession winding around me, solemn and sweet and
    slow—but first I note,
The tents of the sleeping army, the fields' and woods' dim
    outline,
The darkness lit by spots of kindled fire, the silence,
Like a phantom far or near an occasional figure moving,
The shrubs and trees, (as I lift my eyes they seem to be
    stealthily watching me,)
While wind in procession thoughts, O tender and
    wondrous thoughts,
Of life and death, of home and the past and loved, and of
    those that are far away;
A solemn and slow procession there as I sit on the
    ground,
By the bivouac's fitful flame.

Whitman found in the tragic death of Abraham Lincoln the symbol for all the men and women who had suffered and died in America's most terrible war. His poem "When Lilacs Last in the Dooryard Bloom'd" is both a magnificent elegy for a fallen leader and a profound statement of Whitman's love and compassion for all humankind.

Exercises

1. "I Hear America Singing" clearly represents Whitman as the poet of democracy. What are the uniquely American aspects of this poem? Is there, for example, any hint of a hierarchy?
2. What is the mood of "By the Bivouvac's Fitful Flame" and how is this accomplished? Consider rhythm, word choice, and, especially, the use of *and*.

Herman Melville (1819–1891)

Born in the same year as Whitman and also influenced by Emerson, Melville had not one but two literary careers. Like Whitman, Melville was fascinated by the sea and images of the sea, but Whitman's vision was essentially positive while Melville's was ironic and tragic, the viewpoint of a realist as opposed to Whitman the romantic. Several years after publishing his greatest novel, *Moby-Dick* (1851), Melville turned, for reasons still unknown, to an exclusive preoccupation with poetry. (He did leave at his death the manuscript of *Billy Budd* but with no clues as to when it was written.) Melville's ten-year career as a prose writer and thirty-year sequel as a poet were as unnoticed by the general public of the time as was the poetry of Whitman.

Deeply disturbed over the coming war, Melville followed the self-appointed mission of the Abolitionist John Brown who, in his zeal to free the slaves, had secured support from Emerson, Thoreau, and many others. Brown's capture of the U.S. Arsenal at Harper's Ferry was a major step in his campaign, but the government recaptured the Arsenal and hanged John Brown. Melville's brooding poem uses the image of the dead Abolitionist as a prologue to war.

Literary Selections
THE PORTENT
Herman Melville

Hanging from the beam,
    Slowly swaying (such the law),
Gaunt the shadow on your green,
    Shenandoah!
The cut is on the crown
(Lo, John Brown),
And the stabs shall heal no more.

Hidden in the cap
    Is the anguish none can draw;
So your future veils its face,
    Shenandoah!
But the streaming beard is shown
(Weird John Brown),
The meteor of the war.

1859

One of the bloodiest conflicts of the Civil War, the Battle of Shiloh (April 6–7, 1862) cost the lives of thousands of soldiers, and forecast both the terrible battles to come and the inevitable defeat of the Confederacy. No one, not even Whitman, wrote more eloquently and sadly about the war than did Herman Melville.

SHILOH

A Requiem
(April, 1862)
Herman Melville

Skimming lightly, wheeling still,
   The swallows fly low
Over the field in clouded days,
   The forest-field of Shiloh—
Over the field where April rain
Solaced the parched ones stretched in pain
Through the pause of night
That followed the Sunday fight
   Around the church of Shiloh—
The church so lone, the log-built one,
That echoed to many a parting groan And natural prayer
   Of dying foemen mingled there—
Foemen at morn, but friends at eve—
   Fame or country least their care:
(What like a bullet can undeceive!)
   But now they lie low,
While over them the swallows skim,
   And all is hushed at Shiloh.

Though Melville's sympathies lay with the North, he saw the war as equally tragic for North and South with neither side wholly right or wholly wrong.

ON THE SLAIN COLLEGIANS
Herman Melville

Youth is the time when hearts are large,
   And stirring wars
Appeal to the spirit which appeals in turn
   To the blade it draws.
If woman incite, and duty show
   (Though made the mask of Cain),
Or whether it be Truth's sacred cause,
   Who can aloof remain
That shares youth's ardor, uncooled by the snow
   Of wisdom or sordid gain?

The liberal arts and nurture sweet
Which give his gentleness to man—
   Train him to honor, lend him grace
Through bright examples meet—
That culture which makes never wan
With underminings deep, but holds
   The surface still, its fitting place,
   And so gives sunniness to the face
And bravery to the heart; what troops
   Of generous boys in happiness thus bred—
   Saturnians through life's Tempe led,
Went from the North and came from the South,
With golden mottoes in the mouth,
   To lie down midway on a bloody bed.

Woe for the homes of the North,
And woe for the seats of the South:
All who felt life's spring in prime,
And were swept by the wind of their place and time—
   All lavish hearts, on whichever side,

Of birth urbane or courage high,
Armed them for the stirring wars—
Armed them—some to die.
   Apollo-like in pride,
Each would slay his Python—caught
The maxims in his temple taught—
   Aflame with sympathies whose blaze
Perforce enwrapped him—social laws,
   Friendship and kin, and by-gone days—
Vows, kisses—every heart unmoors,
And launches into the seas of wars.
What could they else—North or South?
Each went forth with blessings given
By priests and mothers in the name of Heaven;
   And honor in all was chief.
Warred one for Right, and one for Wrong?
So put it; but they both were young—
Each grape to his cluster clung,
All their elegies are sung.

The anguish of maternal hearts
   Must search for balm divine;
But well the striplings bore their fated parts
   (The heavens all parts assign)—
Never felt life's care or cloy.
Each bloomed and died an unabated Boy;
Nor dreamed what death was—thought it mere
Sliding into some vernal sphere.
They knew the joy, but leaped the grief,
Like plants that flower ere comes the leaf—
Which storms lay low in kindly doom,
And kill them in their flush of bloom.

The naval battle between the ironclads *Merrimac* and *Monitor* (March 9, 1862) symbolized for Melville the inhuman mechanization of war. He was a realist, the first poet to describe *modern* warfare for what it really was: killing people by means of advanced technology.

A UTILITARIAN VIEW OF THE MONITOR'S FIGHT
Herman Melville

Plain be the phrase, yet apt the verse,
   More ponderous than nimble;
For since grimed War here laid aside
His painted pomp, 'twould ill befit
   Overmuch to ply
   The rhyme's barbaric cymbal.

Hail to victory without the gaud
   Of glory; zeal that needs no fans
Of banners; plain mechanic power
Plied cogently in War now placed—
   Where War belongs—
   Among the trades and artisans.

Yet this was battle, and intense—
   Beyond the strife of fleets heroic;
Deadlier, closer, calm 'mid storm;
No passion; all went on by crank,
   Pivot, and screw,
   And calculations of caloric.

Needless to dwell; the story's known.
   The ringing of those plates on plates
Still ringeth round the world—
The clangor of that blacksmith's fray.
   The anvil-din
   Resounds this message from the Fates:

War shall yet be, and to the end;
    But war-paint shows the streaks of weather;
War yet shall be, but warriors
Are now but operatives; War's made
        Less grand than Peace,
    And a singe runs through lace and feather.

Melville's ambivalent feelings about the sea are summed up in "Pebbles." The sea was a cruel and lonely world, inhuman and dangerous but, at the same time, Melville felt that it had restorative powers that could purify the spirit. Nevertheless, man "sails on sufferance there."

PEBBLES
Herman Melville

I

Though the Clerk of the Weather insist,
    And lay down the weather-law,
Pintado and gannet they wist
That the winds blow whither they list
    In tempest or flaw.

II

Old are the creeds, but stale the schools,
    Revamped as the mode may veer,
But Orm from the schools to the beaches strays,
And, finding a Conch hoar with time, he delays
    And reverent lifts it to ear.
That Voice, pitched in far monotone,
    Shall it swerve? Shall it deviate ever?
The Seas have inspired it, and Truth—
    Truth, varying from sameness never.

III

In hollows of the liquid hills
    Where the long Blue Ridges run,
The flattery of no echo thrills,
    For echo the seas have none;
Nor aught that gives man back man's strain—
The hope of his heart, the dream in his brain.

IV

On ocean where the embattled fleets repair,
Man, suffering inflictor, sails on sufferance there.

V

Implacable I, the old implacable Sea:
    Implacable most when most I smile serene—
Pleased, not appeased, by myriad wrecks in me.

VI

Curled in the comb of yon billow Andean,
    Is it the Dragon's heaven-challenging crest?
Elemental mad ramping of ravening waters—
    Yet Christ on the Mount, and the dove in her nest!

VII

Healed of my hurt, I laud the inhuman Sea—
Yea, bless the Angels Four that there convene;
For healed I am even by their pitiless breath
Distilled in wholesome dew named rosmarine.

Exercises

1. In "The Portent" what is the effect of the words *Shenandoah* and *Weird?* What vistas are opened up? What feelings?
2. During the Battle of Shiloh the Union lost over 13,000 men and the Confederacy nearly 11,000, but the latter was hailed as the "victor." Consider the paradoxes in the situation and in the poem like, for example, the church at the center of the conflict and the strange mixture of friend and foe.
3. In "On the Slain Collegians" does Melville view the Civil War as necessary?
4. Compare the word choice in the "Collegians" with those describing the *Monitor's* fight. Notice in both poems how sound and sense tend to be synonymous, which is, of course, a characteristic of good poetry. Try reading both poems aloud.
5. Melville's ambivalence about the sea is reflected in almost every line of "Pebbles." Consider words and phrases like *reverent, implacable, I smile serenely, ravening waters,* and many more.

Mark Twain (1835–1910)

The second half of the century saw the emergence of realism in American literature and throughout the Western world. There was a new interest in common people and everyday facts of life. Among the new realists were Dickens, Thackeray, and George Eliot in England, Zola and Balzac in France, and William Dean Howells (1837–1921) in the United States. As editor-in-chief of the influential *Atlantic Monthly,* Howells advocated realism and supported regional writers. Mark Twain (pseudonym of Samuel Langhorne Clemens) was, however, the only major writer to emerge from what can be called the grass-roots movement.

The first important author to be born west of the Mississippi, Mark Twain, more than any other writer of his time, symbolized the power and exuberance of the expansive American spirit that blossomed after the Civil War. Twain spoke and wrote in the voice of the people in celebration of the winning of the west. (The later, darker Twain will not be considered here.) His major works include *Innocents Abroad* (1869) and *Roughing It* (1872) but his masterwork can be considered as a kind of trilogy: *The Adventures of Tom Sawyer* (1876); *Life on the Mississippi* (1883); and *The Adventures of Huckleberry Finn* (1885). Perhaps his best short story, "The Notorious Jumping Frog of Calaveras County" was an oft-told tale but it took a Mark Twain to give it form and style. The story is reprinted below but in actuality, this is only the first of a three-part exercise by the inimitable Twain. Upon learning that a French critic had called it a good story that, however, was not funny, Twain translated the tale into French and then translated *that* version into English. Twain concluded that the original was funny but that the French-into-English version was awkward and unfunny. The point is, of course, that Twain's American English was so idiomatic that it was untranslatable.

Literary Selection

THE NOTORIOUS JUMPING FROG OF CALAVERAS COUNTY
Mark Twain

In compliance with the request of a friend of mine, who wrote me from the East, I called on good-natured, garrulous old Simon Wheeler, and inquired after my friend's friend, Leonidas W. Smiley, as requested to do, and I hereunto append the result. I have a lurking suspicion that *Leonidas W.* Smiley is a myth; that my friend never knew such a personage; and that he only conjectured that if I asked old Wheeler about him, it would remind him of his infamous *Jim* Smiley, and he would go to work and bore me to death with some exasperating reminiscence of him as long and as tedious as it should be useless to me. If that was the design, it succeeded.

I found Simon Wheeler dozing comfortably by the bar-room stove of the dilapidated tavern in the decayed mining camp of Angel's, and I noticed that he was fat and bald-headed, and had an expression of winning gentleness and simplicity upon his tranquil countenance. He roused up, and gave me good day. I told him that a friend of mine had commissioned me to make some inquiries about a cherished companion of his boyhood named *Leonidas W.* Smiley—*Rev. Leonidas W.* Smiley, a young minister of the Gospel, who he had heard was at one time a resident of Angel's Camp. I added that if Mr. Wheeler could tell me anything about this Rev. Leonidas W. Smiley, I would feel under many obligations to him.

Simon Wheeler backed me into a corner and blockaded me there with his chair, and then sat down and reeled off the monotonous narrative which follows this paragraph. He never smiled, he never frowned, he never changed his voice from the gentle-flowing key to which he tuned his initial sentence, he never betrayed the slightest suspicion of enthusiasm; but all through the interminable narrative there ran a vein of impressive earnestness and sincerity, which showed me plainly that, so far from his imagining that there was anything ridiculous or funny about his story, he regarded it as a really important matter, and admired its two heroes as men of transcendent genius in *finesse*. I let him go on in his own way, and never interrupted him once.

"Rev. Leonidas W. H'm, Reverend Le—well, there was a feller here once by the name of *Jim* Smiley, in the winter of '49—or maybe it was the spring of '50—I don't recollect exactly, somehow, though what makes me think it was one or the other is because I remember the big flume warn't finished when he first come to the camp; but anyway, he was the curiousest man about always betting on anything that turned up you ever see, if he could get anybody to bet on the other side; and if he couldn't he'd change sides. Any way that suited the other man would suit *him*—any way just so's he got a bet, *he* was satisfied. But still he was lucky, uncommon lucky; he most always come out winner. He was always ready and laying for a chance; there couldn't be no solit'ry thing mentioned but that feller'd offer to bet on it, and take ary side you please, as I was just telling you. If there was a horse-race, you'd find him flush or you'd find him busted at the end of it; if there was a dog-fight, he'd bet on it; if there was a cat-fight, he'd bet on it; if there was a chicken-fight, he'd bet on it; why, if there was two birds setting on a fence, he would bet you which one would fly first; or if there was a camp-meeting, he would be there reg'lar to bet on Parson Walker, which he judged to be the best exhorter about here, and so he was too, and a good man. If he even see a straddle-bug start to go anywheres, he would bet you how long it would take him to get to—to wherever he was going to, and if you took him up, he would foller that straddle-bug to Mexico but what he would find out where he was bound for and how long he was on the road. Lots of the boys here has seen that Smiley, and can tell you about him. Why, it never made no difference to *him*—he'd bet on *any* thing—the dangdest feller. Parson Walker's wife laid very sick once, for a good while, and it seemed as they warn't going to save her; but one morning he come in, and Smiley up and asked him how she was, and he said she was considerable better—thank the Lord for his inf'nite mercy—and coming on so smart that with the blessing of Prov'dence she'd get well yet; and Smiley, before he thought, says, 'Well, I'll resk two-and-a-half she don't anyway.'

"Thish-yer Smiley had a mare—the boys called her the fifteen-minute nag, but that was only in fun, you know, because of course she was faster than that—and he used to win money on that horse, for all she was so slow and always had the asthma, or the distemper, or the consumption, or something of that kind. They used to give her two or three hundred yards' start, and then pass her under way; but always at the fag end of the race she'd get excited and desperate like, and come cavorting and straddling up, and scattering her legs around limber, sometimes in the air, and sometimes out to one side among the fences, and kicking up m-o-r-e dust and raising m-o-r-e racket with her coughing and sneezing and blowing her nose—and *always* fetch up at the stand just about a neck ahead, as near as you could cipher it down.

"And he had a little small bull-pup, that to look at him you'd think he warn't worth a cent but to set around and look ornery and lay for a chance to steal something. But as soon as money was up on him he was a different dog; his under-jaw'd begin to stick out like the fo'castle of a steamboat, and his teeth would uncover and shine like the furnaces. And a dog might tackle him and bully-rag him, and bite him, and throw him over his shoulder two or three times, and Andrew Jackson—which was the name of the pup—Andrew Jackson would never let on but what *he* was satisfied, and hadn't expected nothing else—and the bets being doubled and doubled on the other side all the time, till the money was all up; and then all of a sudden he would grab that other dog jest by the j'int of his hind leg and freeze to it—not chaw, you understand, but only just grip and hang on till they throwed up the sponge, if it was a year. Smiley always come out winner on that pup, till he harnessed a dog once that didn't have no hind legs, because they'd been sawed off in a circular saw, and when the thing had gone along far enough, and the money was all up, and he come to make a snatch for his pet holt, he see in a minute how he'd been imposed on, and how the other dog had him in the door, so to speak, and he 'peared surprised, and then he looked sorter discouraged-like, and didn't try no more to win the fight, and so he got shucked out bad. He give Smiley a look, as much as to say his heart was broke, and it was *his* fault, for putting up a dog that hadn't no hind legs for him to take holt of, which was his main dependence in a fight, and then he limped off a piece and laid down and died. It was a good pup, was that Andrew Jackson, and would have made a name for hisself if he'd lived, for the stuff was in him and he had genius—I know it, because he hadn't no opportunities to speak of, and it don't stand to reason that a dog could make such a fight as he could under them circumstances if he hadn't no talent. It always makes me feel sorry when I think of that last fight of his'n, and the way it turned out.

"Well, thish-yer Smiley had rat-tarriers, and chicken cocks, and tomcats and all them kind of things, till you couldn't rest, and you couldn't fetch nothing for him to bet on but he'd match you. He ketched a frog one day, and took him home, and said he cal'lated to educate him; and so he never done nothing for three months but set in his back yard and learn that frog to jump. And you bet you he *did* learn him, too. He'd give him a little punch behind, and the next minute you'd see that frog whirling in the air like a doughnut—see him turn one summerset, or maybe a couple, if he got a good start, and come down flat-footed and all right, like a cat. He got him up so in the matter of ketching flies, and kep' him in practice so constant, that he'd nail a fly every time as fur as he could see him. Smiley said all a frog wanted was education, and he could do 'most anything—and I believe him. Why, I've seen him set Dan'l Webster down here on this floor—Dan'l Webster was the name of the frog—and sing out, 'Flies, Dan'l, flies!' and quicker'n you could wink he'd spring straight up and snake a fly off'n the counter there, and flop down on the floor ag'in as solid as a gob of mud, and fall to scratching the side of his head with his hind foot as indifferent as if he hadn't no idea he'd been doin' any more'n any frog might do. You never see a frog so modest and straight-for'ard as he was, for all he was so gifted. And when it come to fair and square jumping on a dead level, he could get over more ground at one straddle than any animal of his breed you ever see. Jumping on a dead level was his strong suit, you understand; and when it come to that, Smiley would ante up money on him as long as he had a red. Smiley was monstrous proud of his frog, and well he might be, for fellers that had traveled and been everywheres all said he laid over any frog that ever *they* see.

"Well, Smiley kep' the beast in a little lattice box, and he used to fetch him down-town sometimes and lay for a bet. One day a feller—a stranger in the camp, he was—come acrost him with his box, and says:

" 'What might it be that you've got in the box?'

"And Smiley says, sorter indifferent-like, 'It might be a parrot, or it might be a canary, maybe, but it ain't—it's only just a frog.'

"And the feller took it, and looked at it careful, and turned it round this way and that, and says, 'H'm—so 'tis. Well, what's *he* good for?'

" 'Well,' Smiley says, easy and careless, 'he's good enough for *one* thing, I should judge—he can outjump any frog in Calaveras County.'

"The feller took the box again, and took another long, particular look, and give it back to Smiley, and says, very deliberate, 'Well,' he says, 'I don't see no p'ints about that frog that's any better'n any other frog.'

" 'Maybe you don't,' Smiley says. 'Maybe you understand frogs and maybe you don't understand 'em; maybe you've had experience, and maybe you ain't only a amature, as it were. Anyways, I've got *my* opinion, and I'll resk forty dollars that he can outjump any frog in Calaveras County.'

"And the feller studied a minute, and then says, kinder sadlike, 'Well, I'm only a stranger here, and I ain't got no frog; but if I had a frog, I'd bet you.'

"And then Smiley says, 'That's all right—that's all right—if you'll hold my box a minute, I'll go and get you a frog.' And so the feller took the box, and put up his forty dollars along with Smiley's, and set down to wait.

"So he set there a good while thinking and thinking to himself, and then he got the frog out and prized his mouth open and took a teaspoon and filled him full of quail-shot—filled him pretty near up to his chin—and set him on the floor. Smiley he went to the swamp and slopped around in the mud for a long time, and finally he ketched a frog, and fetched him in, and give him to this feller, and says:

" 'Now, if you're ready, set him alongside of Dan'l, with his fore paws just even with Dan'l's, and I'll give the word.' Then he says, 'One—two—three—*git!*' and him and the feller touched up the frogs from behind, and the new frog hopped off lively, but Dan'l give a heave, and hysted up his shoulders—so—like a Frenchman, but it warn't no use—he couldn't budge; he was planted as solid as a church, and he couldn't no more stir than if he was anchored out. Smiley was a good deal surprised, and he was disgusted too, but he didn't have no idea what the matter was, of course.

"The feller took the money and started away; and when he was going out at the door, he sorter jerked his thumb over his shoulder—so—at Dan'l, and says again, very deliberate, 'Well,' he says, '*I* don't see no p'ints about that frog that's any better'n any other frog.'

"Smiley he stood scratching his head and looking down at Dan'l a long time, and at last he says, 'I do wonder what in the nation that frog throw'd off for—I wonder if there ain't something the matter with him—he 'pears to look mighty baggy, somehow.' And he ketched Dan'l by the nap of the neck, and hefted him, and says, 'Why blame my cats if he don't weigh five pound!' and turned him upside down and he belched out a double handful of shot. And then he see how it was, and he was the maddest man—he set the frog down and took out after that feller, but he never ketched him. And—"

[Here Simon Wheeler heard his name called from the front yard, and got up to see what was wanted.] And turning to me as he moved away, he said: "Just set where you are, stranger, and rest easy—I ain't going to be gone a second."

But, by your leave, I did not think that a continuation of the history of the enterprising vagabond *Jim* Smiley would be likely to afford me much information concerning the Rev. *Leonidas W.* Smiley, and so I started away.

At the door I met the sociable Wheeler returning, and he buttonholed me and recommenced:

"Well, thish-yer Smiley had a yaller one-eyed cow that didn't have no tail, only just a short stump like a bannanner, and—"

However, lacking both time and inclination, I did not wait to hear about the afflicted cow, but took my leave.

Exercise

1. This tale became a humorous classic because it is a virtual compendium of comic elements and devices. Almost immediately we are told that Simon Wheeler was an old windbag who launches right into a "monotonous narration." This is a story within a story highlighted by the comic character and folksy dialect of bald-headed Simon. The other major character, Jim Smiley, will bet on anything, even whether or not Parson Walker's wife will live or die. The imagery is graphic, there's lots of local color, and the "tables turned" theme provides the proper comic twist. Identify some of the images, elements of local color, and exaggerations like the mare called the "fifteen-minute nag." Do not overlook the bull pup named Andrew Jackson. In short, just how complex is this story?

Emily Dickinson (1830–1886)

The poetry of the "recluse of Amherst" is also realistic. Twain's universe was the exterior world; Dickinson's was that of the inner world of her own psyche. Published years after her death, her 1,775 poems were written as if they were entries in a diary, the private thoughts of a private person who took just a little from society and shut out all the rest. Her gemlike, frequently cryptic verses are unique, unlike poetry of any writer of any age.

Literary Selections

X
IN A LIBRARY
Emily Dickinson

A precious, mouldering pleasure 't is
To meet an antique book,
In just the dress his century wore;
A privilege, I think,

His venerable hand to take,
And warming in our own,
A passage back, or two, to make
To times when he was young.

His quaint opinions to inspect,
His knowledge to unfold
On what concerns our mutual mind,
The literature of old;

What interested scholars most,
What competitions ran
When Plato was a certainty,
And Sophocles a man;

When Sappho was a living girl,
And Beatrice wore
The gown that Dante deified.
Facts, centuries before,

He traverses familiar,
As one should come to town
And tell you all your dreams were true:
He lived where dreams were sown.

His presence is enchantment,
You beg him not to go;
Old volumes shake their vellum heads
And tantalize, just so.

XXII
Emily Dickinson

I had no time to hate, because
The grave would hinder me,
And life was not so ample I
Could finish enmity.

Nor had I time to love; but since
Some industry must be,
The little toil of love, I thought,
Was large enough for me.

VI
A SERVICE OF SONG
Emily Dickinson

Some keep the Sabbath going to church;
I keep it staying at home,
With a bobolink for a chorister,
And an orchard for a dome.

Some keep the Sabbath in surplice;
I just wear my wings,
And instead of tolling the bell for church,
Our little sexton sings.

God preaches,—a noted clergyman,—
And the sermon is never long;
So instead of getting to heaven at last,
I'm going all along!

XLVI
DYING
Emily Dickinson

I heard a fly buzz when I died;
    The stillness round my form
Was like the stillness in the air
    Between the heaves of storm.

The eyes beside had wrung them dry,
    And breaths were gathering sure
For that last onset, when the king
    Be witnessed in his power.

I willed my keepsakes, signed away
    What portion of me I
Could make assignable,—and then
    There interposed a fly,

With blue, uncertain, stumbling buzz,
    Between the light and me;
And then the windows failed, and then
    I could not see to see.

XVII
Emily Dickinson

I never saw a moor,
I never saw the sea;
Yet know I how the heather looks.
And what a wave must be.

I never spoke with God,
Nor visited in heaven;
Yet certain am I of the spot
As if the chart were given.

X

Emily Dickinson

I died for beauty, but was scarce
Adjusted in the tomb,
When one who died for truth was lain
In an adjoining room.

He questioned softly why I failed?
"For beauty," I replied.
"And I for truth,—the two are one;
We brethren are," he said.

And so, as kinsmen met a night,
We talked between the rooms,
Until the moss had reached our lips,
And covered up our names.

XI

Emily Dickinson

Much madness is divinest sense
To a discerning eye;
Much sense the starkest madness.
'T is the majority
In this, as all, prevails.
Assent, and you are sane;
Demur,—you're straightway dangerous,
And handled with a chain.

XXVII
THE CHARIOT

Emily Dickinson

Because I could not stop for Death,
He kindly stopped for me;
The carriage held but just ourselves
And Immortality.

We slowly drove, he knew no haste,
And I had put away
My labor, and my leisure too,
For his civility.

We passed the school where children played,
Their lessons scarcely done;
We passed the fields of gazing grain,
We passed the setting sun.

We paused before a house that seemed
A swelling of the ground;
The roof was scarcely visible,
The cornice but a mound.

Since then 't is centuries; but each
Feels shorter than the day
I first surmised the horses' heads
Were toward eternity.

Exercises

1. How, in Poem X, does the poet feel about books and how does she convey that feeling?
2. Why is hate, in Poem XXII, greater than love?
3. Would you call Poem VI pantheistic? Is it opposed to conventional religion or merely indifferent?

4. Is the fly in Poem XLVI metaphorical or real? Why did you answer as you did? Why did she use legal terms in stanza 3?
5. Compare *beauty* and *truth* in Poem X with Keats's statement about beauty and truth in "Grecian Urn." Are the two versions similar? Identical?
6. Is the divine madness in Poem XI like that of the Fool in *King Lear?* Explain your answer.
7. Poem XXVII contains many of the unusual metaphors for which Dickinson is famous. What are some of them? How effective are they?

Paul Laurence Dunbar (1872–1906)

Emancipation had released the slaves from bondage only to suspend Black Americans somewhere between African cultures to which they could not return and an American culture that refused to admit them. The first black poet to reach a national audience, Dunbar wrote a poignant poem about the situation, a poem that is still quoted today.

Literary Selection

SYMPATHY

Paul Laurence Dunbar

I know what the caged bird feels, alas!
    When the sun is bright on the upland slopes;
When the wind stirs soft through the springing grass,
And the river flows like a stream of glass;
    When the first bird sings and the first bud opes,
And the faint perfume from its chalice steals—
I know what the caged bird feels!

I know why the caged bird beats his wing
    Till its blood is red on the cruel bars;
For he must fly back to his perch and cling
When he fain would be on the bough a-swing;
    And a pain still throbs in the old, old scars
And they pulse again with a keener sting—
I know why he beats his wing!

I know why the caged bird sings, ah me,
    When his wing is bruised and his bosom sore,—
When he beats his bars and he would be free;
It is not a carol of joy or glee,
    But a prayer that he sends from his heart's deep core,
But a plea, that upward to Heaven he flings—
I know why the caged bird sings!

Exercises

1. The *caged bird* is a metaphor for what? Is it a multiple metaphor? Please explain.
2. What is implied by the peaceful images in stanza 1? The violent images in stanza 2?
3. Who or what will free the caged bird?

Stephen Crane (1871–1900)

Though sometimes identified as a writer in the realistic style called naturalism, Crane was actually influenced by Monet, Renoir, and other Impressionists. A journalist by profession and a war correspondent, Crane used word-painting in a manner comparable to the Impressionists' use of color. His *The Red Badge of Courage* (1895) is perhaps the finest short novel in the English language and "The Open Boat" and "The Blue Hotel" rank at the top of American short stories. Of Crane's poems, the following two seem most appropriate to conclude this survey of nineteenth-century life and literature.

Literary Selections

WAR IS KIND
Stephen Crane

Do not weep, maiden, for war is kind.
Because your lover threw wild hands toward the sky
And the affrighted steed ran on alone,
Do not weep.
War is kind.

    Hoarse, booming drums of the regiment,
    Little souls who thirst for fight
    These men were born to drill and die.
    The unexplained glory flies above them,
    Great is the battle-god, great, and his kingdom—
    A field where a thousand corpses lie.

Do not weep, babe, for war is kind.
Because your father tumbled in the yellow trenches,
Raged at his breast, gulped and died,
Do not weep.
War is kind.

    Swift blazing flag of the regiment,
    Eagle with crest of red and gold,
    These men were born to drill and die.
    Point for them the virtue of slaughter,
    Make plain to them the excellence of killing
    And a field where a thousand corpses lie.

Mother whose heart hung humble as a button
on the bright splendid shroud of your son,
Do not weep.
War is kind.

A MAN SAID TO THE UNIVERSE
Stephen Crane

A man said to the universe:
"Sir, I exist!"
"However," replied the universe,
"The fact has not created in me
A sense of obligation."

Time Chart for the Middle Modern World, 1789–1914

	1800	1825	1850	1875	1900	1925

Artists

Goya 1746–1828
Constable 1776–1837
Ingres 1780–1867
Gericault 1791–1824
Corot 1796–1875
Delacroix 1799–1863
Daumier 1808–1879
Millet 1814–1875
Courbet 1819–1877
Manet 1832–1883
Degas 1834–1917
Whistler 1834–1903
Homer 1836–1910
Cézanne 1839–1906
Rodin 1840–1917
Monet 1840–1926
Renoir 1841–1919
Morisot 1841–1895
Cassatt 1844–1926
Rousseau 1844–1910
van Gogh 1853–1890
Seurat 1859–1891
Toulouse-Lautrec 1864–1901
Munch 1864–1944

Musicians

Schubert 1797–1828
Berlioz 1803–1869
Mendelssohn 1809–1847
Chopin 1810–1849
Liszt 1811–1886
Brahms 1833–1897
Tchaikovsky 1840–1893
Puccini 1858–1924
Debussy 1862–1918
Strauss 1864–1949

Literary Figures

Rousseau 1718–1778
Goethe 1749–1832
Schiller 1759–1805
Blake 1757–1827
Wordsworth 1770–1850
Coleridge 1772–1834
Byron 1788–1824
Shelley 1792–1822
Mary Shelley 1797–1851
Keats 1795–1821
Emerson 1803–1882
Tennyson 1809–1892
Poe 1809–1849
Thoreau 1817–1860
Whitman 1819–1892
Melville 1819–1891
Arnold 1822–1888
Dickinson 1830–1886
Twain 1835–1910
Hardy 1840–1928
Crane 1871–1900
Dunbar 1872–1906

Government

England
George III 1760–1820
George IV 1820–1830
William IV 1830–1837
Victoria 1837–1901
Edward VII 1901–1910
George V 1910–1936

France
Napoleon 1804–1812
Louis XVIII 1814–1824
Charles X 1824–1830
Louis Philippe 1830–1848
Second Republic 1848–1852
Napoleon III 1852–1870
Third Republic 1871–

Germany
William I 1871–1888
William II 1888–1918

Russia
Alexander I 1801–1825
Nicholas I 1825–1855
Alexander II 1855–1881
Alexander III 1881–1894
Nicholas II 1894–1918

Italy
Victor Emmanuel II 1861–1878
Humbert I 1878–1900
Victor Emmanuel III 1900–1946

Time Chart for the Middle Modern World, 1789–1914 (cont.)

	1800	1825	1850	1875	1900	1925

Events

- Congress of Vienna 1815
- Age of Metternich 1815–1848
- French July revolution 1830
- Wave of revolutions 1848
- *Communist Manifesto*
- Crimean War 1853–1856
- *Origin of Species* 1859
- American Civil War 1861–1865
- Liberation of Russian serfs 1861
- Lincoln's Emancipation Proclamation 1863
- Franco-Prussian War 1870–1871
- Dreyfuss Affair 1894–1906
- World War I 1914–1918

21

Romanticism in Music

The ever-changing sequence of artistic styles can be seen in broad per-spective as a constant back and forth movement between two extremes. In painting, these outer boundaries are represented by the Rubenists, who emphasized color, and Poussinists, who advocated line and drawing. In nineteenth-century painting Delacroix was a Rubenist; Ingres and David were the Poussinists. These extremes are referred to, in music, as *romanticism* and *classicism*. As in painting, the emphasis of romantic music is on color and that of classical music is on the primacy of line and design. Music is a different medium, of course, and perhaps more abstract than painting; the distinctions and parallels are therefore less finely drawn. As an exercise in extremes, the opposing concepts can be stated in many different ways:

Classicism	Romanticism
intellectual	emotional
objective	subjective
rational	nonrational
tranquil	restless
simple	ornate
Apollonian	Dionysian

At no time can an artistic style be classified as wholly classic or wholly romantic. An inclination in favor of either extreme results in a classifica-tion of the style *as* that extreme, a process that can be compared to a seesaw touching ground at one end because of a slight shift of balance. Although it is manifestly foolish to consider all of Mozart's music, for example, as intellectual but not emotional, tranquil, and simple rather than ornate and restless, the fact remains that Mozart's music is essentially classic in its meticulous detail, restraint, and clarity of design.

Nineteenth-century music generally follows the romantic mode and is concerned primarily with either miniature or large-scale works, with comparatively little in between. There are intimate art songs for solo voice and piano and single-movement piano pieces at one extreme, and large symphonic works and even larger vocal-instrumental works at the other. The emphasis is on tone color (or sound), that fourth element of music (melody, harmony, rhythm, tone color). Piano pieces are "characteristic" compositions written specifically for that instrument; songs are written for specific voice types; symphonies are scored for a greater range of instrumental tone color and a greater volume of sound. The international aspects of seventeenth- and eighteenth-century music are replaced by highly individualistic styles of writing and strong nationalistic expression. The "Austrian" quality of the classical music of Haydn and Mozart is not germane to any study of their compositions. During the romantic period the "German" characteristics of Wagner, Schubert, and Schumann and the "Italian" qualities of Verdi, Rossini, and Donizetti are part of the stylistic picture. In other words, nineteenth-century music reflects the rise of nationalism.

German Lieder

An important aspect of the Romantic movement was the inauguration of a new style, the setting of preexisting poetry—almost always Romantic poetry—to music in an artful matching of mood and meaning. Nationalism was again a prominent characteristic, for the new style was keyed to the meticulous setting of poetry in the original language, and the language was German.

In 1814, the Viennese composer Franz Schubert (1797–1828) set to music the poem "Gretchen am Spinnrade" from Goethe's *Faust*. The resultant combination was a new artistic medium called a *lied* (Ger., song); the German art song movement or style was referred to as *lieder* (songs). The generic term *lieder* is applied to the German Romantic songs of Schubert, Schumann, Brahms, and others, though *lied* is the word Germans also use when they refer to just any song.

Composers had written songs, in all languages, before Schubert wrote the first lied. Lieder are not just songs, however, for composers displayed a remarkable unity of purpose—the recreation of a poem in musical terms—along with a typically Romantic range of personal styles. Schubert wrote lieder and Brahms wrote lieder; both were adept at the art of merging poetry and music, but Brahms does not sound like Schubert. The Romantic movement was notable for the personal touch, for individuality at all costs. Romantic artists sought personalized expression in a variety of contrasting and even paradoxical procedures: large-scale works coexisting with miniatures, Neo-Gothic (new-old styles were in) with Neo-Classic, Neo-Baroque with Neo-Romanesque, and quite logically, somehow, Mary Shelley's *Frankenstein* with Goethe's *Faust*.

Art songs, or lieder, were important miniatures in an era that indulged itself with the grandiose or doted on the diminutive. There was remarkably little middle ground, for the Romantic sought the heights and the depths and had little patience with the ordinary. Complexity was preferred; simplicity was abhorred. If one art form was good then two art forms were even better. Art songs represented the essence of Romanticism for they combined the arts of poetry and music into a new and rarefied style.

First came the poem and then the song, which attempts to capture the feelings, the mood, indeed the essence of what the poet is trying to communicate. The rhythm, inflection, sound, and meaning of the language are corroborated and heightened by the composer's own personal language of melody, harmony, rhythm, and tone color.

Following is a lied by Schubert based on a poem from *Faust* by Goethe. German art songs are not translated because translations spoil the interrelation of words and music. The German text with English translation is provided so that the listener can follow one and understand the other. The song is made up of ten verses, as indicated by the numbers in the text.

Gretchen am Spinnrade (1814)
(Margaret at the Spinning Wheel)

Franz Schubert (1797–1828)
Poem by Goethe (from *Faust*)

Synopsis: Margaret sits in her room at the spinning wheel and sings of her love for Faust, knowing that this love will prove fatal. The scene occurs near the end of Part I of *Faust*.

Accompaniment pattern in the piano

sempre legato—"always smooth," imitating the whirring of the spinning wheel.

sempre staccato—"always staccato," imitating the working of the treadle.

1. Mei-ne Ruh' ist hin, mein Herz ist schwer;
   ich fin-de, ich fin-de sie nim-mer und nim-mer-
   mehr.
   (My peace is gone, My heart is sore:
   I shall find it never And never more.)
2. Wo ich ihn nicht hab', ist mir das Grab,
   die gan-ze Welt ist mir ver-gällt.
   (He has left my room An empty tomb
   He has gone and all My world is gall.)
3. Mein ar-mer Kopf ist mir ver-rückt,
   mein ar-mer Sinn ist mir zer-stückt.
   (My poor head Is all astray,
   My poor mind Fallen away.)
4. Mei-ne Ruh' ist hin, mein Herz ist schwer;
   ich fin-de, ich fin-de sie nim-mer und nim-mer-
   mehr.
   (My peace is gone, My heart is sore;
   I shall find it never And never more.)
5. Nach ihm nur schau' ich zum Fen-ster hin-aus,
   (Tis he that I look through The window to see
   He that I open The door for—he!)
6. nach ihm nur geh' ich aus dem Haus.
   Sein ho-her Gang, sein' ed-le Ge-stalt,
   sei-nes Mun-des Lä-cheln, sei-ner Au-gen Ge-
   walt,
   (His gait, his figure, So grand, so high,
   The smile of his mouth, The power of his eye.)
7. und sei-ner Re-de Zau-ber-fluss,
   sein Hän-de-druck und ach, sein Kuss! (Piano)
   (And the magic stream Of his words—what
   bliss
   The clasp of his hand And, ah, his kiss!)
8. Mei-ne Ruh' ist hin, mein Herz ist schwer;
   ich fin-de, ich fin-de sie nim-mer und nim-mer-
   mehr.
   (My peace is gone, My heart is sore:
   I shall find it never And never more.)
9. Mein Bu-sen drängt sich nach ihm hin.
   Ach, dürft' ich fas-sen und hal-ten ihn!
   (My heart's desire Is so strong, so vast;
   Ah, could I seize him And hold him fast.)
10. und küs-sen ihn, so wie ich wollt'
    an sei-nen Küs-sen ver-ge-hen sollt',
    O köont' ich ihn küs-sen, so wie ich wollt',
    an sei-nen Küs-sen ver-ge-hen sollt',
    an sei-nen Küssen ver-ge-hen sollt'!
    Mei-ne Ruh' ist hin, mein Herz ist schwer'.
    (Piano)
    (And kiss him forever Night and day,
    And on his kisses Pass away!)

Piano Music

The Romantic emphasis upon the uniqueness of the individual was symbolized by the dominance of the piano as the single most popular musical instrument, as typical of the Romantic era as the guitar is of contemporary life. The piano was ubiquitous because it could accompany lieder, blend into a chamber music ensemble or, in a piano concerto, dominate a symphony orchestra. Its prime attraction, however, was its independence, for it was a superb solo instrument.

Figure 21.1 Eugene Delacroix, *Frédéric Chopin*, 1838. Oil on canvas, 18 × 15″. Delacroix (see chap. 22) seldom painted portraits on commission; instead, he depicted some of his personal friends, the victims, like himself, of what he and other artists called the "Romantic agony." The Louvre, Paris.

Eighteenth-century pianos were relatively small with a clear and delicate tone. Nineteenth-century pianos were larger, more sonorous than clear, and loud enough to fill the largest concert hall. The range of tone was representative of the Romantic propensity for extremes. Whether playing the tender "Lullaby" by Brahms or the thunderous "Revolutionary Etude" by Chopin, the pianist was a commanding figure throughout the entire Romantic period. The pianist continues to dominate today's concert world, possibly because of the uninterrupted popularity of the Romantic repertoire.

The nineteenth century was an age of virtuosos. Franz Liszt and Frédéric Chopin were spectacular performers on the piano and, equally remarkable, was Niccolo Paganini, the virtuoso of the violin. Virtuosity and showmanship were so widely admired that, for example, Paganini would conclude a concert with a razor blade hidden in his right hand. Near the end of an already sensational performance he would deftly cut the violin strings, one by one, until he could triumphantly conclude on the last remaining string.

Franz Liszt was fond of planting a female admirer in the front row of the concert hall. At the most dramatic moment the young lady, obviously overcome by the beauty and power of Liszt's playing, would rise slowly to her feet and ecstatically faint away. The master would rush to her side, carry her on stage and, holding her artistically draped body over one arm, triumphantly conclude the composition with one hand.

Frédéric Chopin (sho–pan; 1810–1849) was a fine concert pianist but he did not confuse virtuoso performance with the circus showmanship of Liszt and Paganini (fig. 21.1). Although he was successful in the concert hall he gave fewer than seventy-five public concerts in his entire career. In terms of temperament and style, he was much more at home in the fashionable salons of Paris. The so-called poet of the keyboard developed a highly personal style that represents the epitome of the Romantic spirit. Chopin's music can be heard as a kind of musical poetry not unlike the blending of words and music in German art songs. The formal designs of his music— sonata form, binary and ternary forms—are quite traditional but the content is unique. Some of the range of Chopin's piano style can be appreciated by considering three representative pieces: a ballade, an étude, and a prelude (see p. 451).

Ballade in g Minor is loosely related to the medieval French verse in which the refrain comes at the end of the stanza. In this dramatic and rhapsodic composition Chopin uses sonata form and reverses themes *a* and *b* in the recapitulation, after which he brings the work to a vigorous close with a brilliant coda.

Ballade in g Minor, op. 23

Form: Modified Sonata

Frédéric Chopin (1810–1849)
Time: 7:00

Chopin wrote a number of *études*, compositions for concentrated study of technical problems in piano playing. That these studies are more than mere exercises is typical of Chopin's unique musicality. The E-Major Étude is a study in piano touch. The right hand must bring out the songlike melody but subordinate the undulating accompanying figure even though the two elements are played by the same hand. The contrasting middle section, for all its brilliance, is probably less difficult technically than the delicate handling of the main theme.

Étude in E Major, op. 10, no. 3

Form: Ternary (A–B–A)

Chopin
Time: 3:45

Chopin wrote twenty-four *preludes* in opus 28, each in a different key. The last prelude in the series is one of his most unusual and powerful compositions. As befits a prelude, which for Chopin is a short piano piece in one movement, there is only one subject. In the d-minor Prelude, the subject is limited almost entirely to a d-minor chord (d–f–a); in fact, the left hand plays the same d-minor chord for the first ten measures, and over one-third of the piece is devoted to this single chord. From the unchanging harmony of the opening section through the five statements of the theme to the final three low d's on the keyboard the accumulative effect is almost hypnotic.

Prelude in d Minor, op. 28, no. 24

Form: Single Subject

Table 21.1 Comparative Sizes of Orchestras

	Mozart (1788)	Beethoven (1808)	Strauss (1895)
Woodwinds	flute 2 oboes 2 clarinets 2 bassoons	piccolo 2 flutes 2 oboes 2 clarinets 2 bassoons	piccolo 3 flutes 3 oboes English horn 3 clarinets bass clarinet 3 bassoons contrabassoon
Brass	2 French horns	2 French horns 2 trumpets 3 trombones	8 French horns 6 trumpets 3 trombones tuba
Percussion		timpani	timpani, snare drum, bass drum, cymbals, triangle
Strings	violin I violin II viola cello bass	violin I violin II viola cello bass	violin I violin II viola cello bass

The Symphony

The symphony was one of the primary forms of the nineteenth century but not all composers chose to follow the symphonic tradition. Those who did write symphonies sometimes adopted classical practices, altered them to suit their purposes, or simply rejected them completely. In order to achieve an overview of the remarkable variety of orchestral music, we will consider a symphonic work by each of six different composers: Felix Mendelssohn, Hector Berlioz, Franz Liszt, Richard Strauss, Peter I. Tchaikovsky, and Johannes Brahms. However, before taking up the Romantic tradition in symphonic literature it is necessary to consider the development of the orchestra itself.

The greatly augmented symphony orchestra with its strong brass and percussion sections and enlarged body of woodwinds provided a particularly effective medium for Romantic music. The classic orchestra had a nucleus of strings plus a small woodwind section and just a few brass and percussion instruments. The nineteenth-century orchestra added full sections of woodwinds and brass which could play as independent sections as well as filling in the ensemble. The comparative size of the orchestra over a period of a single century is illustrated in table 21.1.

Orchestra size grew even beyond the enormous ensemble specified by Strauss before being reduced to an average-sized modern orchestra that could play most symphonic music and still meet a sizable payroll. The additional instrumentalists needed for works by Strauss and others are now hired especially for the occasion. Figure 21.2 is a seating plan observed in principle by most modern orchestras. Because of their limited volume the strings are seated in front and the woodwinds in the center; brass, bass instruments, and percussion bring up the rear (also see fig. 21.3).

Felix Mendelssohn (1809–1847) was the grandson of the great Jewish philosopher Moses Mendelssohn. His father was a wealthy banker and his mother a woman with an exceptional cultural background. In addition to his superior intellect and rarefied socio-economic background, Mendelssohn was endowed with a wealth of musical talent.

Mendelssohn admired classical forms and followed them closely. However, the classical spirit was acquired rather than assimilated and the classical forms that he used became more like noble gestures rather than natural expressions. Because of the clarity of his writing and his control of the emotional content Mendelssohn is best described as a classical Romanticist.

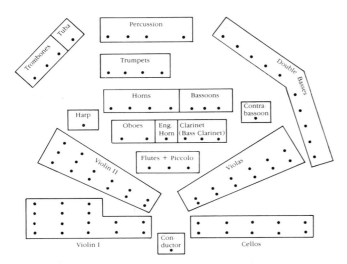

Figure 21.2 Typical seating plan of a modern symphony orchestra.

Figure 21.3 A modern symphony orchestra

The Fourth Symphony was written during an extended sojourn in Italy. The symphony is called "Italian," probably because of the sunny first theme of the opening movement and the brilliant *Saltarello* which forms the last movement and which was probably inspired by a carnival in Rome that the composer had observed. Mendelssohn characteristically avoided anything that was overdone or in bad taste. The orchestra, therefore, was virtually the same size as that used by Mozart.

Symphony no. 4 in A Major, op. 90 (1833)

"Italian"
Felix Mendelssohn (1809–1847)
Total Time: 30:00

I

Form: Sonata

Theme a

Theme b

II

Form: Ternary (A–B–A)

Principal theme

III

Form: Minuet–Trio–Minuet

Minuet   Trio

IV

Form: Modified theme and variations

Theme

Hector Berlioz (bear–lee–OS; 1803–1869) was a red-headed Romantic from the south of France, a revolutionary artist whose only personal instrument was the guitar but whose preferred instrument was the entire symphony orchestra. Despite his flamboyance—his lifetime dream was hearing ten thousand trumpets from a mountaintop—he was a solid musician and an orchestral innovator who strongly influenced Liszt, Wagner, Tchaikovsky, and Strauss.

One of Berlioz's most successful and most controversial works was his *Symphonie Fantastique* which he completed in 1830, only three years after the death of Beethoven. Berlioz had been influenced by the popular *Confessions of an English Opium Eater* (1821) by Thomas de Quincey and contemplated using the idea of an opium dream in conjunction with his music. He also fell madly in love with a Shakespearean actress named Harriet Smithson. It is now impossible to tell what the components were of this frenzied, desperate love affair which, strangely enough, led to marriage, a union which was both short-lived and disastrous.

Berlioz was completely entranced with what he saw as the Romantic elements in Shakespeare's plays. He was therefore as stagestruck by the Shakespearean women played by Miss Smithson as he was infatuated with the actress herself. In the midst of their stormy marriage, Berlioz combined his conception of Shakespeare's women, his passion for Miss Smithson, and his interest in opium into the fanciful story line (program) that led to the creation of the *Symphonie Fantastique*.

Symphonie Fantastique, op. 14 (1830)
(Épisode de la vie d'un artiste)

Hector Berlioz
Total Time: 48:00

I (Daydreams—Passions)

Idée fixe

II (A ball)

Principal theme (following Intro.)

III (Scene in the country)

Principal theme (following Intro.)

IV (March to the scaffold)

Theme a (following Intro.)

Theme b

V (Dream of a Witches' Sabbath)

Dies irae

Berlioz considered classical forms as merely empty shells. Instead he concentrated on an *idée fixe,* a single theme that would be the common thread for each of the five movements of his daring new symphony. The idée fixe was a kind of *leit motif*—a procedure that Wagner was to exploit—that represented both the ideal of perfect love and the artist's idealized version of Harriet Smithson.

Following are the titles of the five movements plus a brief explanation of what the composer apparently had in mind when he wrote the music.

I. *Rêveries—Passions* (Daydreams—Passions). The artist, despairing of ever possessing his beloved, attempts to poison himself with opium. What follows in this and in the other movements are a series of opium-induced dreams, fantasies, and nightmares. This first movement is a frequently euphoric reverie about the artist's passion for his beloved.

II. *Un bal* (A ball). There is a fancy ball at which the beloved appears, slipping in and out of the dancers. The idée fixe, representing the beloved, is heard as she appears among the dancers.

III. *Scène aux champs* (Scene in the country). An idyllic scene of calm serenity in the bucolic countryside.

IV. *Marche au supplice* (March to the scaffold). In his delirium, the artist imagines he has killed his beloved and that he is being taken on a tumbrel to the guillotine.

V. *Songe d'une nuit de Sabbat* (Dream of a Witches' Sabbath). Following his execution the artist dreams that he is present at a gruesome Witches' Sabbath complete with a parody of the *Dies irae* (Day of Judgment) as a part of a Black Mass. The idée fixe is also parodied as his beloved appears as a debased prostitute.

Franz Liszt (1811–1886) felt that it was possible to create organized musical compositions without forcing the ideas into the traditional forms of the Classical period. He used programs for much of his music—hence the term *program music*—but operated from a different point of view than did Berlioz.

Liszt was dedicated to the Romantic ideal of uniting the various arts. He respected the uniqueness of the musical language but he advocated the addition of extramusical concepts that would "humanize" the music and make it more meaningful to the listener.

> The musician who is inspired by nature exhales in tones nature's most tender secrets without copying them. . . . Since his language is more arbitrary and more uncertain than any other . . . and lends itself to the most varied interpretations, it is not without value . . . for the composer to give in a few lines the spiritual sketch of his work and . . . convey the idea which served as the basis for his composition. . . .

This will prevent faulty elucidations, hazardous interpretations, idle quarrels with intentions the composer never had, and endless commentaries which rest on nothing.[1]

Franz Liszt was perhaps the only composer of program music to understand the real meaning of Beethoven's preface to his Sixth Symphony: "More the expression of sentiment than painting." Richard Strauss contended that a tone poem could, for example, "describe a teaspoon" so that all listeners could envision a similar image. Liszt denied the capability of music to be this literal and to be this limited. Instead, he created the symphonic poem, a new art form that followed the dictates of Beethoven. He stated broad concepts for his programs and then dissolved these concepts into the wonderfully abstract language of music.

Les Preludes, the most famous of Liszt's twelve symphonic poems, was inspired by a *meditation poetique* by the mystical French poet Alphonse de Lamartine. The musical score is prefaced by a quotation from Lamartine that expresses a favorite Romantic theme—man pitted against Fate:

> What is our life but a series of preludes to that unknown song whose first solemn note is tolled by Death? Love is the enchanted dawn of every existence, but where is the life in which the first enjoyment of bliss is not dispelled by some tempest? Yet no man is content to resign himself for long to the benificent charms of Nature; when the trumpet sounds, he hastens to danger's post, so that in the struggle he may regain full consciousness of himself, and the possession of all his powers.

Liszt uses a germ motive that, unlike Berlioz's idée fixe, ties the work together in a process of continuous transformation. Constructed in six sections, the piece begins with the germ motive, followed by section 1 in which the motive becomes majestic. In section 2 the motive turns into a love song in a pastoral mood, followed by a new, tender love theme in section 3. The pace quickens dramatically in section 4 and then relaxes into a bucolic mood in section 5. In section 6 the two love themes are transformed into rousing battle calls and the piece concludes triumphantly in a typically romantic burst of exaltation.

1. Franz Liszt, *Gesammelte Schriften,* Leipzig, 1881–1910, p. 104.

Les Preludes (1854)
Symphonic Poem

Franz Liszt (1811–1886)

Richard Strauss (1864–1949) exploited the large symphony orchestra in a manner very similar to Liszt's treatment of the piano and Paganini's performances on the violin. The orchestra became, in his hands, an enormous virtuoso instrument. One of the great orchestrators, Strauss expanded to an unprecedented degree the techniques of individual musicians and the capabilities of the orchestra as a whole.

Notoriously reluctant to try new ideas, symphonic musicians bristled and balked whenever a new Strauss composition was placed on their music stands. Strauss was asking them to play sequences of notes that they had never played before and sometimes to play in a manner that had never occurred to them. Certain patterns of notes were so new that musicians deemed them impossible to play. More, perhaps, than any composer of his time, Strauss was responsible for the increased playing skills of symphonic musicians. Even today the music of Strauss is considered difficult to play. The designation of "impossible" is reserved for later composers who continue to confront and to challenge the orchestral musicians.

The *tone poem* (or *symphonic poem*) was the favorite form of program music for the large orchestra. Originated by Franz Liszt and developed by Richard Strauss, the tone poem generally utilized a dramatic narrative as the basis for an extended one-movement composition. The music would attempt to describe such grandiose conceptions as *A Hero's Life, Death and Transfiguration,* the affairs of a lover (*Don Juan*), and the adventures of a practical joker (*Till Eulenspiegel's Merry Pranks*). The tone poem about the practical joker is one of the most successful ventures in this genre, principally because of the vivid, dramatic music and tightly-knit construction. The story is by no means the only one that can be associated with the music but, nevertheless, it is the story that the composer had in mind when he wrote the music.

Till Eulenspiegel's Merry Pranks (1895)

Richard Strauss (1864–1949)
Total Time: 14:00

Form: Through-composed. Because of the sequence of events in the dramatic narrative, there is no repetition of thematic material as there would be in absolute music.

There are two themes (*a* and *b*) which are used throughout the piece and which represent Till himself:

Till Eulenspiegel was an actual fourteenth-century character who achieved considerable notoriety as a sometimes likable rogue, swindler, prankster, and scoundrel. The Strauss tone poem is built around a selection of Till's adventures, including the final adventure of being brought to justice for his many offenses.

There are six scenes and an epilogue. There is a primary theme in each section and repeated material in the epilogue.

1. *Till in the Marketplace*
2. *Till the Priest*
3. *Till in Love*
4. *Till and the Philistines*
5. *To Be or Not to Be Himself*
6. *Till's Sad End*

Following is a brief synopsis of the events in each section:

Introduction
The two Till themes (*a* and *b*) are presented.

1. *Till in the Marketplace*
After a pause, the 'a' theme is heard and we have a typical market scene with much bustling activity, women gossiping in their stalls and so forth. Till slips into the square, mounts a horse and careens through the square, making a shambles of it. Leaving consternation in his wake, he rides out of sight.

2. *Till the Priest*
Till appears as a caricature of a priest, dripping unction and morality. He is not really comfortable in the role and abandons it quickly when a pretty girl walks by.

3. *Till in Love*
A short violin solo signals this latest adventure as Till follows the girl, catches up with her and does his best to make a good impression. His advances are repulsed and he storms off swearing vengeance on all humankind.

4. *Till and the Philistines*
The hopping theme announces the arrival of some musty professors and doctors. Till falls in with them and amazes all and sundry with his brilliance as he propounds one ridiculous notion after another. Quickly becoming bored with such stodgy scholars, Till leaves them behind in a state of shocked amazement.

5. *To Be or Not to Be Himself*
In the longest section of the piece Till wrestles with his conscience, such as it is. The question is whether he should continue in his erratic, exciting, and sometimes scandalous life or reform and settle down with the good burghers who have been the butt of so many of his pranks. After considerable indecision he finally decides to remain true to his real nature and continue as the scoundrel he has always been. This decision is announced by a jubilant orchestra.

6. *Till's Sad End*
At almost the very moment he decides to be himself the snare drum roll announces that Till has been dragged off to face the stern justice of the court. The low, threatening chords hurl the charges at Till, who answers impudently the first two times (solo clarinet). The answer to the third volley of charges is an anguished squeal from the clarinet and Till is marched to the scaffold. An ominous drop in pitch (interval of a M7) portrays the dropping of the trap

door. His soul takes flight to the accompaniment of fluttering clarinet and flute and the mortal Till is no more. A short pizzicato string passage leads to the Epilogue.

7. *Epilogue*
The 'a' theme is heard for the last time. In retrospect Till becomes an amusing devil and immortal rogue, as indicated by the triumphant close for full orchestra.

Peter Ilich Tchaikovsky (chy–KOF–skee; 1840–1893) seldom succeeded in mastering musical forms, but he was remarkably skillful in his handling of the symphonic orchestra. The lush sounds of Tchaikovsky's orchestra have become a kind of hallmark for the dramatic intensity and emotional extremes of the Romantic movement.

Tchaikovsky's orchestral music ranges from ponderous melodrama to vapid sentimentality and yet, at his best, he has created enormously popular works for ballet—*Swan Lake, The Nutcracker, Sleeping Beauty*—and three successful symphonies, the Fourth, the Fifth, and the Sixth. His symphonies are cast in Classical forms but there is little concern with the development of thematic ideas in the Classical sense. Rather there are broadly sweeping melodies or powerful dramatic themes that are developed, in a manner of speaking, through the exploitation of the orchestral colors of the symphonic ensemble itself. The Russian preference for variations on a theme and for bold color changes is never heard to better advantage than in the symphonic music of Tchaikovsky.

Symphony no. 5 in e Minor, op. 64 (1888)

Peter I. Tchaikovsky (1840–1893)
Total Time: 53:00

I

Introduction
Theme (Motto theme used in all four movements)

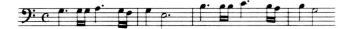

Theme a

ii

Theme a

Theme b

III

Waltz in Scherzo form

Theme a   *Trio*

IV

Sonata form

Theme a   *Theme b*

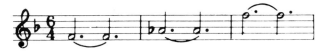

The Romantic affinity for lush lyricism, storm and stress, grandiose display, and programmatic music was reflected in varying degrees in the music of all the nineteenth-century composers. *Johannes Brahms* (1833–1897), however, was supremely conscious of the heritage of Classical music and particularly the monumental contributions of Beethoven. He waited until rather late in his career to write his first symphony; critics were quick to label this powerful work "the Beethoven Tenth."

Brahms made deliberate attempts to exert some sort of control over his inherent Romantic tendencies. In his four symphonies, as in most of his music, Brahms utilized Baroque and Classical models but exploited them in a personal style that is a unique combination of Classical and Romantic traits.

Considered in his own time as something of a reactionary, the composer "born too late," Brahms actually helped pave the way for the swing of the pendulum back to Classic concepts that have been prominent in much of the music of the twentieth century. Among the many unusual circumstances in the development of artistic styles, nothing is more ironic than the appearance of Brahms in the avant-garde of modern music while his contemporaries, the self-styled modernists Liszt, Strauss, and Wagner, are now seen as archetypes of nineteenth-century Romanticism.

In his Third Symphony, Brahms turns a typically frugal amount of musical material into a major symphonic work. He builds the entire composition out of a three-note *motto*:

The notes F–A–F are derived from the words *frei aber froh* (free but happy) which was supposedly the motto that Brahms used to indicate his life-style. Unlike the motto in Tchaikovsky's Fifth Symphony, which is a complete, self-contained melody, this pattern is a motive from which Brahms generates a variety of musical ideas.

Symphony no. 3 in F Major, op. 90 (1883)

Form: Sonata   Johannes Brahms (1833–1897)
                             Total Time: 31:40

I

Form: Sonata

Theme a   *Theme b*

II

Form: Sonata

Theme a: clarinets, bassoons

Theme b

III

Form: Ternary

Theme a

Theme b

IV

Form: Sonata, with delayed Development coming between *a* and *b* in the Recapitulation. Also uses the motto of the first movement and the *b* theme of the second movement.

Theme a

Theme b

Opera

Opera underwent drastic changes in style and intent during the nineteenth century. Early in the century, Beethoven's *Fidelio* (1805) represented what might be called international opera. With the emergence of Romanticism there was a corresponding rise in national schools of opera with Italy dominating the European (and American) scene.

Italian opera, as typified by Verdi's *Rigoletto* (1851), was a mélange of melodramatic plots, popular-type melodies, and "effective" solos and ensembles. There was more emphasis upon *bel canto* (beautiful singing) than upon logical development of plot and character. Later operas, Verdi's *Aïda* (1871) for example, evidenced an ever-increasing concern with dramatic values culminating, perhaps inevitably, in the complex music dramas of Richard Wagner. Wagner conceived of opera, his *Tristan und Isolde* (1859) for example, as a super art form, a viewpoint roughly comparable to Byron's conception of himself as a super hero and Nietzsche's theory of a superman.

Wagner's insistence upon the musical-literary totality of his myth-based music dramas provoked strong reactions in favor of so-called realism in subject matter and a new simplicity in musical treatment. A similar reaction against academic painting led to the emergence of such Romantic Realists as Millet and Corot of the Barbizon School and, especially, the Realists Daumier and Courbet. A comparable movement in literature, called Naturalism, was led by Emile Zola.

Giacomo Puccini (poo–CHEE–nee; 1858–1924) was perhaps the leading Realist in operatic literature. His tragic operas, *La Bohème, Madame Butterfly,* and *Tosca,* are among the most popular works in the standard repertoire of leading opera companies. *La Bohème* is the opera selected for inclusion here because with it one can perhaps best persuade a neophyte that a theatrical work in which everything is sung is actually a viable means of expressive communication. The field of opera has suffered for far too long from the misguided notion that it is esoteric and "highbrow" and thus not fit for middle-class consumption.

The text of *La Bohème* was drawn from Henri Murger's *Scenes de la Vie en Bohème,* the time is 1830, and the setting is an artist's garret in the Bohemian section of the Latin Quarter of Paris. The characters in order of appearance are: Marcello, a painter, *baritone;* Rodolfo, a poet, *tenor;* Colline, a philosopher, *bass;* Schaunard, a musician, *baritone;* Benoit, a landlord, *bass;* Mimi, an embroiderer, *soprano;* Parpignol, a toy vendor, *tenor;* Musetta, a shop girl, *soprano;* Alcindoro, a councilor of state, *bass;* Customhouse sergeant, *bass;* Students, working girls, citizens, shopkeepers, street vendors, soldiers, waiters, boys and girls, etc. Following is a brief summary of the plot.

La Bohème (1896)

Giacomo Puccini (1858–1924)

Act I

Scene: In the Attic   Time: 35:00

Four struggling young artists, Rodolfo, Marcello, Colline, and Schaunard are living together in the garret. Mimi timidly knocks at the door and asks Rodolfo to light her candle. It is love at first sight, to coin a phrase, and they eventually exit upstage center, singing a love duet.

Act II

Scene: In the Latin Quarter   Time: 17:00

The four artists and Mimi convene at a cafe. Musetta, Marcello's former girlfriend, appears on the arm of Alcindoro, her current admirer. Musetta uses her considerable charms to rekindle Marcello's interest in her and all march offstage behind a passing military band.

Act III

Scene: A toll gate at an entrance to Paris   Time: 24:00

Musetta and Marcello can be heard in the tavern in the background. Mimi appears and asks Marcello to help her separate from Rodolfo. As Rodolfo comes out of the tavern he exclaims that he has decided to leave Mimi. She then tells him that she must return to another lover but they cling together knowing that they must part when spring comes.

Act IV

Scene: In the Attic   Time: 28:00

The four bachelors and Musetta are in the apartment when Mimi appears, desperately ill. The friends rush out seeking food, medicine, and a doctor, leaving Mimi and Rodolfo alone. They return in time to witness Mimi's death.

The plot of *La Bohème* is commonplace. The characterization is fixed from the outset rather than developed. The mutual attraction of the young lovers is instant and total without any attempt at verisimilitude. The stormy romance of Musetta and Marcello remains at that entry level. *La Bohème* reads, on paper, like a third-rate soap opera.

Then why has this opera been so enormously popular for almost a century? Surely it is not because of the plot, the characterization, the pathos of the tragic love affair. Perhaps it is because Rodolfo and Mimi represent some profound truths about life, suffering, love, and death. Hardly.

In the parlance of the theatre, *La Bohème* is effective when placed "on the boards" because "it plays." It is believable because it sings and sings gloriously. From the vivacious opening measures audiences willingly, even eagerly, suspend their disbelief.

Mimi then sings "I am Mimi" and Rodolfo is enchanted.

Rodolfo sings to Mimi of his hopes and aspirations as a poet.

For the conclusion of Act I Puccini uses Rodolfo's melody in a soaring love duet. The musical language of love has rarely sounded better.

In order to learn how to listen to an opera, one should listen to an opera: *La Bohème* in this case. The preceding remark is not facetious or condescending. The obvious is sometimes obscured by an academic fog of talking rather than doing. Listen to the opera all the way through with nothing more in mind than enjoying Puccini's singable melodies. Listen again with the idea of identifying the different characters by voice register (soprano, baritone, etc.) and by characterization; for example, Musetta's melodies tend to be flamboyant while Mimi's melodies are gentle and very lyrical.

Check the plot using liner notes, one of the many opera guides, or even the musical score, which has interesting stage directions and an English translation. All current recordings are in Italian but, after all, music is the closest thing we have to an international language.

Listen again to each act as you identify the interplay of personalities and ideas. Listen again to each act while visualizing, in your mind's eye, sets, costumes, Mimi, Rodolfo, Musetta, Marcello, and the others. Finally, put aside all details, settle back and listen to Puccini's melodies work their magic. Ultimately you will want to see the opera on the stage, where it belongs. If at all possible do not settle for a second-rate production. Puccini deserves better.

Impressionism in Music

By the end of the nineteenth century the main stream of Romanticism had about run its course. The decline was marked by the appearance of what was thought to be the *new* style of *Impressionism.* Just as the Renaissance had faded into Mannerism and the Baroque into Rococo, the refined essence of Romanticism was distilled into a final stage named after the painting style of Monet, Degas, Renoir, and others.

The so-called Impressionistic music of Debussy and Ravel—Debussy detested the term *Impressionism*—spearheaded a French revolt against the domination of German Romanticism and particularly the overwhelming exuberance of Wagner. The competition of German and French nationalism was a major factor in the Impressionist movement. Debussy cultivated an art that was subtle, delicate, and discreet, an art that was a sensuous rather than an emotional experience. For Debussy, German Romanticism was ponderous and tedious while French music possessed the Gallic spirit of elegance and refinement.

Many similarities exist between the painting of the Impressionists and the sophisticated music of Debussy and Ravel. The Impressionists tried to capture the play of color and light; favorite images included dappled sunlight through leaves and the play of light on water, fields, flowers, and buildings. The musicians dealt with an art of movement that attempted to translate this interplay of color and light into shimmering and sensual sounds.

Closely related to Impressionism in painting and music was the Symbolism of Mallarmé, Verlaine, and Baudelaire. They achieved an indefiniteness with words that had been the privilege of music alone. They likened their poetry to music and sought tone color in word sounds and symbolic meanings of words rather than any definite meaning. Word plays, as with the tonal play of Impressionistic music, was, according to Verlaine, "the gray song where the indefinite meets the precise."

The effects that musical Impressionism achieved were the result of a number of innovations and extensions of musical resources.

Modes   The old church modes came into favor again during late Romanticism and were exploited further by the Impressionists. The effects they sought were counter to the clear tonality of the major-minor system. The modes, among other scales, provided a wider range of colors and the desirable vagueness of tonality.

Other Scales   The strong Oriental influence was reflected in the use of the *pentatonic scale* (five-tone scale), that is the basis for the folk music of Bali, China, and other Oriental cultures.

pentatonic scales[2]

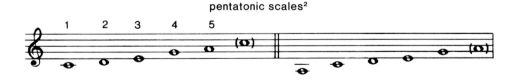

2. These scales can be played using only the black keys of the piano. Pentatonic scales are commonly used in many cultures outside the Orient; for example, Scotland, American Indian, American folk songs.

Particularly appropriate for the vague tonalities and drifting harmonies of Impressionism was the *whole-tone scale.* This was a six-tone scale with a whole step between each pitch. With all tones equidistant, there was no clear tonal center. In fact, there were only two whole-tone scales possible: one starting on a white note and ending on a black note, and the other starting on a black note and ending on a white note.

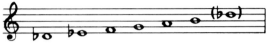

Form   Classical forms were generally abandoned in favor of the vague outlines, drifting quality, and dreamlike effects so basic to the style. This is not to say that the music is formless—there is a beginning, middle, and end—but rather that the forms are subtle and dictated by the effects of impressions sought by the composer.

Orchestration   The massed woodwind and/or brass sounds of the orchestras of Brahms, Strauss, Wagner, and so forth, were anathema to the Impressionists. They replaced the dark and ponderous sound of the Germanic orchestras with a much lighter, shimmering effect and much more individualistic use of instruments. They delighted in the exotic sounds of the English horn and the flutes and clarinets in the low register. Violins frequently played in extremely high registers and were often muted. Trumpets and horns were frequently muted. The characteristic sounds of the orchestra were supplemented by the harp, triangle, lightly brushed cymbals, and the bell tones of the small keyboard instrument called the *celeste.* The treatment of the pure sounds of the individual instruments was very much like the use of tiny brushstrokes of pure colors by the painters.

The piano remained a favorite instrument for the Impressionists, but the sounds had little in common with the style, for example, of Chopin. The emphasis was on coloration, sensation, subtle harmonic effects, a great delicacy of tone. Everything was programmatic, whether a tonal description of a specific event or the evocation of a general idea, image, or sensation.

In the following piano composition, Debussy describes the Breton legend of the sunken cathedral of Ys which, on certain mornings, rises out of the misty sea with its bells tolling and with monks intoning their prayers and singing Gregorian chant. After a brief moment the cathedral sinks again below the surface, and rippling waters gradually close over its lofty towers. Because of its detailed program, this composition is Romantic in style. The other two compositions by Debussy (*Sails* and *Prelude to the Afternoon of a Faun*) are less explicit and are therefore more in the style of Impressionism.

La Cathédrale Engloutie, Preludes, vol. I, no. X (1910) *(The Engulfed Cathedral)*

Form: a–b–á–c–b–c̀–a²
Three-note motive throughout plus the three themes

Claude Debussy (1862–1918)

Theme a   Theme b   Theme c

Another composition from the same set of preludes bears only the symbolic title of *Voiles* (*Sails;* p. 461). The listener is free to make any association in keeping with the music and the one-word clue that the composer has placed at the *end* of the composition. The musical techniques that make the piece *sound* the way it does can of course be studied and analyzed. It would not be proper, however, to inform the listener which sensations or images should be called to mind. The title and the music are quite sufficient; the listener can take it from there.

The piece uses the whole-tone scale throughout, except for a brief section on the pentatonic scale.

Voiles, Preludes, vol. I, no. II (1910) (*Sails*)

Form: Ternary
(more or less)

Claude Debussy

Theme a

Whole-tone scale

Pentatonic scale

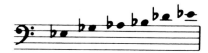

The delicate subtleties and discreet coloration of Impressionism appear to best effect in the carefully chosen palette of the orchestra. For his *Prelude to the Afternoon of a Faun*, Debussy used the following instrumentation:

3 flutes	Antique cymbals
2 oboes	(small, tuned cymbals)
English horn	violin I
2 clarinets	violin II
2 bassoons	viola
4 French horns	cello
2 harps	bass

Debussy's music was inspired by a study of the poem "Ecologue" by Stéphane Mallarmé. All poetry is difficult to translate and that of the Symbolists is impossible. The general feeling of the mood that Debussy attempted to portray can be better understood by reading the following paraphrase of Mallarmé's poem:

A faun—a simple, sensuous, passionate being—wakens in the forest at daybreak and tries to recall his experience of the previous afternoon. Was he the fortunate recipient of an actual visit from nymphs, white or golden goddesses, divinely tender and indulgent? Or is the memory he seems to retain nothing but the shadows of a vision, no more substantial than the arid rain of notes from his own flute? He cannot tell. Yet surely there was, surely there is, an animal whiteness among the brown reeds of the lake that shines out yonder? Were they, are they, swans? No! But Naiads plunging? Perhaps!

Vaguer and vaguer grows the impression of this delicious experience. He would resign his woodland godship to retain it. A garden of lilies, golden-headed, white-stalked, behind the trellis of red roses? Ah! the effort is too great for his poor brain. Perhaps if he selects one lily from the garth of lilies, one benign and beneficent yielder of her cup to thirsty lips, the memory, the ever-receding memory, may be forced back. So, when he has glutted upon a branch of grapes, he is wont to toss the empty skins into the air and blow them out in a visionary greediness. But no, the delicious hour grows vaguer; experience or dreams, he will now never know which it was. The sun is warm, the grasses yielding; and he curls himself up again, after worshipping the efficacious star of wine, that he may pursue the dubious ecstasy into the more helpful boskages of sleep.[3]

Prélude à l'Après-midi d'un Faune (1895)

Claude Debussy

Form: Ternary. The piece is built on one main theme (*a*) which goes through a series of transformations before returning in its original form. There are four other themes that appear at least twice and that should be identified (themes *b, c, d,* and *e*).

Theme a
flute

Theme b	Theme c	Theme d	Theme e
clarinet	oboe	woodwinds	oboe

Summary

Some of the elements of nineteenth-century Romanticism were present in the later works of Beethoven, but the lyric strains of full-blown Romanticism were paramount in the vocal and instrumental works of Franz Schubert. The characteristic style of German art songs (*lieder*) was created by the composer from Vienna and further developed by the German composers Schumann, Brahms, and Wolf. Frédéric Chopin made the piano his personal instrument with his unique style, and the very nature of Romanticism reinforced this individuality of personal expression. The music of Liszt, Strauss, Tchaikovsky, Verdi, and most emphatically, Richard Wagner reflected this intensely subjective approach to artistic experience. They, like Rousseau, if not better than other men, were "at least different."

---

3. Edmund Gosse, "French Profiles," *The Collected Essays of Edmund Gosse,* William Heinemann, Ltd., London, 1905. Needless to say the "faun" of this fantasy is in no way related to a "fawn."

The decline of absolute music in favor of a full range of miniature to grandiose program music was probably the most significant musical characteristic of the century. The abstract titles of the eighteenth century (sonata, serenade, symphony) were, to a considerable extent, abandoned for descriptive or poetic titles. In addition, there were dreamy *nocturnes,* cute *capriccios,* and dashing *rhapsodies* distinguished more by sound and fury than by strong intrinsic design. Filled with emotion for its own sake and thus unabashedly sentimental, and lacking also the disciplined energy of the pre-Napoleonic era, Romantic music provided the sounding board of the age.

The creation of the tone poem seemed to be the inevitable result of a Romantic propensity for reinforcing music with the literary arts. Two arts seemed to be better than one. By the same token, six trumpets were better than two and a hundred-piece orchestra superior to a sixty-piece orchestra. If the trend to monumental Napoleonic ideas had continued, the French Romantic, Hector Berlioz might have eventually recruited the ten thousand trumpets playing from a mountaintop that he so ardently longed to hear.

The latter part of the century saw a gradual leveling off in the growth of the symphony orchestra. The tone poems of Strauss and the huge vocal-instrumental works of Mahler and Bruckner represented a point of no return, a stage reached after a reaction against the grandiloquence had already set in. Brahms reacted against the extravagant use of musical materials and orchestral sounds by deliberately returning to the more disciplined practices of an earlier age. Debussy, Ravel, and other Impressionists also reacted negatively by sharply reducing the orchestra in order to concentrate on the pure tone colors of individual instruments. However, they did continue in the Romantic tradition of program music, carrying it to its ultimate conclusion with techniques similar to the symbolism of Mallarmé and Verlaine. The transition from nineteenth-century Romanticism to the so-called New Music of the twentieth century was accomplished in large part by the Impressionists, who inaugurated many of the materials of modern music while writing the final chapter of Romantic music.

22

Nineteenth-Century Art: Conflict and Diversity

The Romantic Movement and the Neoclassic Style

The Romantic movement first manifested itself in literature and music: the poetry of Wordsworth and Coleridge, the songs of Schubert, and the operas of Carl Maria von Weber. The visual arts were, however, in thrall to David, Napoleon's court painter, and to Napoleon's determination to confirm the legitimacy of his empire with the classical architecture of Imperial Rome. In 1806 Napoleon commissioned Jean Francis Chalgrin (shal–GREN; 1739–1811) to construct a mighty arch to honor the victories of the French fighting forces (fig. 22.1). Placed in the center of twelve radiating avenues, the arch is 164′ high and 148′ wide, larger than the triumphal arch of any Caesar. It stands today at the climax of the Avenue des Champs Elysées over the tomb of the Unknown Soldier, commemorating French imperial glory and the military triumphs of an emperor who did not live to see its completion.

The Church of St. Mary Magdalen, known as The Madeleine (fig. 22.2), was originally begun in 1764 and later razed to be replaced with a building modeled after the Pantheon in Rome. Napoleon ordered that structure replaced by a new temple, a massive building dedicated to the glory of the Grand Army. The Madeleine has fifty-two majestic Corinthian columns running completely around the building, each 66′ tall. The eight-column front and complete peristyle are reminiscent of the Parthenon (see fig. 3.44) but the 23′ high podium is of Roman origin and similar to the Maison Carrée (see fig. 6.7). Napoleon's Temple of Glory is a skillful synthesis of Graeco-Roman elements into a unified and imposing design.

Jean-Auguste-Dominique Ingres (ang'r; 1780–1867) was only nine years old when the revolution began and was never an enthusiastic supporter of Napoleon's self-proclaimed revolutionary ideals. Ingres was, however, David's most talented pupil and an advocate of a Neoclassic style that had evolved from revolutionary art into state-endorsed dogma. Contending that David's style was too heavily incised, Ingres developed a fluid drawing technique influenced by Pompeiian frescoes and patterned after elegant linear figures of Greek vase paintings (see fig. 3.56). His *Grand*

Figure 22.1 Jean François Chalgrin (and others), Arch of Triumph, 1806–1836. Place Charles de Gaulle, Paris.

Figure 22.2 Pierre Vignon, The Madeleine, 1806–1842, Paris.

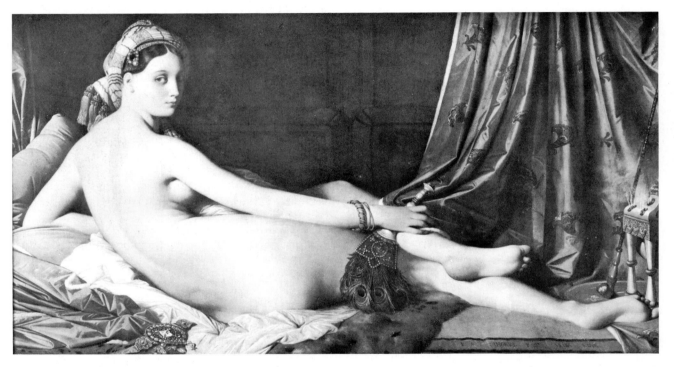

Figure 22.3 Jean-Auguste-Dominique Ingres, *Grand Odalisque,* 1814. Oil on canvas, 35¼ × 63¾". The Louvre, Paris.

Odalisque (fig. 22.3) is not a classical version of feminine beauty, however, but a superb example of the artist's unique mix of Neoclassic and Romantic ideas. The reclining-nude pose can be traced to Titian and the smoothly-flowing contours of the sculpturesque body are cooly Classical; but, the subject is an odalisque, a harem slave girl who represents an exotic concept dear to the Romantics. The small head, elongated limbs, and languid pose are very mannered in the decorative style of Parmigianino (see fig. 14.34).

The first of the illustrious painters of the Romantic era, Francisco de Goya (GO–ya; 1746–1828) was unique even in a time of remarkably individualistic artists. A contemporary of David, with whom he had nothing in common, Goya was influenced by Velasquez and Rembrandt but not at all by antiquity or the Renaissance. Appointed painter to the court of Spain in 1799, Goya created many acutely candid studies of a royal family that presided over a corrupt and decadent administration. His portrait of *Carlos IV of Spain as Huntsman* (fig. 22.4) is a devastating study of an arrogant and pompous monarch. Possibly symbolizing the plight of the Spanish people, the dog sits humbly and meekly at the feet of a vacant-faced king whom Goya has posed as if he were a mighty hunter.

The portrait of *Maria Luisa, Queen of Spain* (fig. 22.5) reveals an equally arrogant personality. Elegantly gowned and wearing pointed slippers on her tiny feet, the queen towers over a muted landscape.

Figure 22.4 Francisco de Goya, *Carlos IV of Spain as Huntsman,* ca. 1799. Oil on canvas, 18¼ × 11¾". Andrew W. Mellon Collection. National Gallery of Art, Washington, D.C.

Figure 22.5 Francisco de Goya, *Maria Luisa, Queen of Spain,* ca. 1799. Oil on canvas, 18¼ × 11¾". Andrew W. Mellon Collection. National Gallery of Art, Washington, D.C.

Goya has vividly captured the malicious glint in her eyes and the cruelty implicit in her tight mouth. The monarchs are not only portrayed as insolent but there is also an aura of evil. If these characteristics are so evident, why did the royal family retain Goya as their court painter? They may have been dazzled by the artist's skillful painting of their splendid costumes but they were, in fact, too stupid to view themselves as Goya, and posterity, see them.

Goya extended his critical appraisal of the royal family to a general view of human folly, vice, and stupidity as depicted in a series of paintings and engravings called *The Caprices.* Then, Napoleon's 1808 occupation of Spain provided the artist with a powerful new subject: the bestiality and utter futility of war. Goya and many of his countrymen had hoped for French reforms of the debased Spanish court; instead, the merciless brutality of French soldiers provoked an equally savage resistance. In a series of unforgettable etchings called *The Disasters of War,* Goya brilliantly depicted the sordid consequences of warfare. His *Grande hazaña! Con muertos!* (Great exploit! In casualties!; fig. 22.6) conveys the horror of mutilation

Figure 22.6 Francisco de Goya, *Grande hazaña! Con muertos!,* from *The Disasters of War,* ca. 1814. Etching, edition of 1863. Private collector.

Figure 22.7 Théodore Gericault, *The Raft of the Medusa,* 1818–1819. Oil on canvas, ca. 16′ × 23′. The Louvre, Paris.

and violent death with a startling economy of means. Euripides and Goya stand virtually alone in their convincing portrayals of the senselessness of warfare.

Goya's art was intensely personal and impossible to classify. He was a true Romantic, however, in his concern about placing too much faith in the primacy of reason, that goddess of an Enlightenment that led to a violent revolution, the Reign of Terror, and, ultimately, to Napoleon. In an etching entitled ''The Sleep of Reason Produces Monsters,'' Goya illustrated the primitive, bestial instincts that were unleashed whenever reason was not eternally vigilant. Goya left Spain in 1824 during another period of repression and died in exile in France. His art was not known outside Spain until late in the Romantic movement.

The most talented French painter of early Romanticism, Théodore Gericault (ZHAY–ree–ko; 1791–1824), won artistic immortality with his painting of *The Raft of the Medusa* (fig. 22.7). Like other Romantic artists, Gericault seized upon a contemporary event (in 1816), in this case a tragedy that caused a national scandal. Jammed with colonists bound for French West Africa, the *Medusa* ran aground off the African coast because of the incompetence of the ship's captain, who then filled the *Medusa's* six boats with his own party and sailed to shore. About 150 men and one woman were left to shift for themselves.[1] In the painting, the few remaining survivors on their makeshift raft have just sighted a rescue ship on the horizon and are frantically signaling for help. Gericault researched the tragedy like an investigative reporter, interviewing survivors, studying corpses in the morgue, even building a raft in his studio. The result is not just a realistic reporting of the event but a drama of heroic proportions of men against the sea. The slashing diagonals and vivid chiaroscuro lead our eye to the triangle formed by the extended arms, with the waving figure at the apex; all movement is projected forward toward the distant sail. Gericault's graphic realism was characteristic of the Romantic intent to shock the sensibilities of the viewer and evoke an emotional response. Government attempts to cover up the errors of a French naval officer stirred the public to a frenzy and focused attention on the painting as a political statement, much to the artist's dismay, rather than as a compelling work of art.

Following Gericault's early death as a result of a riding accident, Eugène Delacroix (de–la–KWRAH; 1799–1863), a peerless colorist, became the leading Romantic artist. The first major French artist to visit Islamic countries, Delacroix was fascinated with the colorful vitality of North African cultures. In *Arabs Skirmishing in the Mountains* (colorplate 40) he demonstrates a vibrant range of intense hues and strong contrasts of light and dark. As the artist wrote in one of his journals, ''the more the contrast the greater the force.'' His ability to capture the illusion of movement makes the dramatic impact of the pitched battle all the more convincing. Continuing the

---

1. For details of the century's worst French scandal prior to the Dreyfus Case see Alexander McKee's *Death Raft: The Human Drama of the Medusa Shipwreck* (New York: Warner Books, Inc., 1977).

Colorplate 40 Eugene Delacroix, *Arabs Skirmishing in the Mountains,* 1863. Oil on canvas, 36⅜ × 29⅜″. Chester Dale Fund, 1966. National Gallery of Art, Washington, D.C.

Colorplate 41 John Constable, *Wivenhoe Park, Essex,* 1816. Oil on canvas, 22⅛ × 39⅞″. (Widener Collection. National Gallery of Art, Washington, D.C.)

Colorplate 42 Winslow Homer, *Breezing Up*, 1876. Oil on canvas, 24⅛ × 38⅛″. Gift of the W. L. and May T. Mellon Foundation, 1943. National Gallery of Art, Washington, D.C.

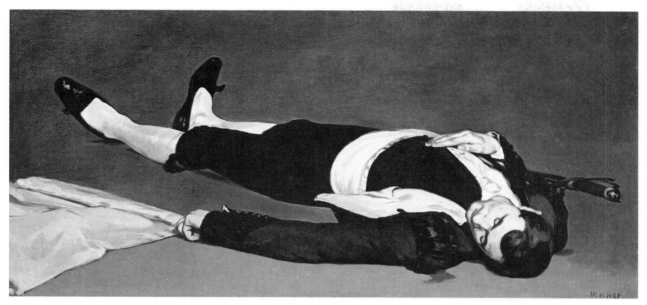

Colorplate 43 Edouard Manet, *The Dead Toreador,* 1864. Oil on canvas, 29⅞ × 60⅜″. Widener Collection. National Gallery of Art, Washington, D.C.

Colorplate 44 Edgar Degas, *Four Dancers,* ca. 1899. Oil on canvas, 59¼ × 71¼″. Chester Dale Collection, 1962. National Gallery of Art, Washington, D.C.

Colorplate 45 Claude Monet, *Rouen Cathedral, West Façade Sunlight,* 1894. Oil on canvas, 39½ × 26″. Chester Dale Collection, 1962. National Gallery of Art, Washington, D.C.

Colorplate 46 Auguste Renoir, *Girl with a Watering Can,* 1876. Oil on canvas, 39½ × 28¾″. Chester Dale Collection, 1962. National Gallery of Art, Washington, D.C.

Colorplate 47 Paul Cézanne, *Le Château Noir,* ca. 1904. Oil on canvas, 29 × 38″. Gift of Eugene and Agnes Meyer, 1958. National Gallery of Art, Washington, D.C.

Colorplate 48 Paul Gauguin, *Self-Portrait,* 1889. Oil on wood, 31¼ × 20¼″. Chester Dale Collection, 1962. National Gallery of Art, Washington, D.C.

Colorplate 49 Georges Seurat, *Sunday Afternoon on the Island of La Grande Jatte*, 1884–1886. Oil on canvas, 10'6" × 69''. Courtesy the Art Institute of Chicago.

Colorplate 50 Henri Matisse, *The Blue Window,* 1911, Autumn. Oil on canvas 51½ × 35⅜″. Collection, The Museum of Modern Art, New York. Abby Aldrich Rockefeller Fund.

Colorplate 51 Pablo Picasso, *Still Life,* 1918. Oil on canvas, 54¼ × 38¼″. Chester Dale Collection, 1962. National Gallery of Art, Washington, D.C.

Figure 22.8 François Rude, *La Marseillaise (The Departure of the Volunteers in 1792)*, 1833–1836. Stone, ca. 42 × 26'. Arch of Triumph, Paris.

squabble between color and line (Romanticism vs. Classicism), Delacroix was the Rubenist and his rival, Ingres (see fig. 22.3), the Poussinist of the nineteenth century. For a colorist like Delacroix the perfect style, as he said, was a combination of Michelangelo and Goya, whose works were then being rediscovered.

Romantic painters were enamored with the sister arts: the plays of Shakespeare, medieval romances, English romantic poetry, and, especially, music. Delacroix preferred, surprisingly, the classical style of Mozart to the flamboyant romanticism of his French contemporary Hector Berlioz (see chap. 21) but was a personal friend of Frédéric Chopin, whose poetic piano music had a special appeal, not only for Delacroix, but also for many writers and artists of the time. His portrait of Chopin (see fig. 21.1) epitomizes the melancholy suffering of the Romantic genius.

Though there were no Romantic sculptors the caliber of Goya and Delacroix, François Rude (1784–1855) did design a notable work for the Arch of Triumph. His *La Marseillaise* (fig. 22.8), the only distinguished sculpture on the Arch, is a dramatic patriotic work depicting citizen-soldiers leaving to defend the borders of the new republic against foreign invaders. Done in very high relief and dressed in

Roman armor, when they are dressed, the volunteers are urged on by Bellona, the Roman war goddess, portrayed here as a Goddess of Victory singing the stirring call to arms of the French National Anthem: *La Marseillaise.*

In England, Romantic art responded more to Rousseau's back-to-nature movement than it did to the ideological drive of the revolution and subsequent Napoleonic wars; England had already had a revolution. English Romantic poets—Wordsworth, Coleridge, Shelley, Keats—described the beauties of nature in highly personal terms. Landscape was prominent in their poetry but not as description for its own sake; rather, poets responded to aspects of the natural scene that stimulated their thinking, leading to meditations on nature that, as Wordsworth observed, involved the "Mind of Man." On the other hand, nature was frequently the subject matter for Romantic painters. John Constable (1776–1837), one of the finest of all English painters, studied landscapes with a scientific objectivity. Rather than simply recording tangible objects he sought the intangible qualities of atmosphere, light, and, especially, the sky. The justly-famed "Constable sky" is the dominating element in his poetic response to the peaceful scene at *Wivenhoe Park, Essex* (colorplate 41). Sunlight shining on the wind-driven clouds and the effect of sunshine on fields and water have a luminosity rivaling even the Dutch masters, and the entire canvas has a freshness never before achieved in painting. The lustrous sky is the crowning glory of the picture, triumphantly confirming the artist's claim that this area was the "principle instrument for expressing sentiment." After his first exposure to Constable's work, Delacroix repainted the sky of an already completed work, and the Impressionists were no less dazzled by the skies of Constable.

Many Romantic writers and architects were antiquarians, researching history for authentic details of the glorious past. Sir Walter Scott wrote what he called romances, historical novels like *Ivanhoe* that were set in medieval England. Scott's obsession with the past led him to the construction of an elaborate country estate resembling a medieval castle that he named Abbotsford, after a river crossing used by medieval abbots (fig. 22.9). The medieval tower is a decorative appendage to a baronial mansion of gables, clustered chimney pots, Neoclassic windows, and elaborate gardens in the casual English manner. Scott's vision of himself as the lord of a manor led to a prodigious production of novels just to make the payments on his romantic dream house.

Typical of the concern with the medieval past, the Museum of Natural History (fig. 22.10) was patterned after Italian Romanesque church designs. The elaborate arches, columns, and other details are now placed on the exterior of a secular public building. Romanesque churches were built by skilled stonemasons but Neoromanesque buildings of the Victorian Age used cast-iron skeletons covered with mass-produced elements of Romanesque details.

Figure 22.9 Abbotsford, home of Sir Walter Scott, on the Tweed River, Scotland. Begun ca. 1820.

Figure 22.10 Alfred Waterhouse, Museum of Natural History, 1873–1879, London.

The largest and most successful architectural recollection of the past were the Houses of Parliament, designed by Sir Charles Barry (1795–1860) with the assistance of Gothic scholar Augustus Welby Pugin (1812–1852; fig. 22.11). The English felt, as did the French and Germans, that the Gothic style was the perfect expression of the national past, a heritage both noble and Christian. The Parliamentary Commission specified that the design for the new seat of government be either Gothic or Elizabethan and nothing else. Barry favored the Neoclassic style but Pugin convinced him that the English Late Gothic style was the proper glorification of the British spirit and a celebration of medieval craftsmanship in the face of mass-produced items of the Industrial Age. Actually, the body of the building is symmetrical in the Palladian manner surmounted by a Gothic fantasy of turrets, towers, and battlements.

Inspired by the design of Parliament, the Gothic Revival style of about 1855–1885 was enthusiastically adopted by English and American architects. Constructed during the height of the Revival by a timber contractor, the Victorian Gothic mansion in California (fig. 22.12) is a wooden frame structure with an incredible variety of surface decoration and detail. "More is better" was a Victorian preference that is exuberantly realized in this prize example of American Gothic.

Realism

Countering the Romantic fantasies of their literary and artistic contemporaries, the Realists concentrated on the real world as they perceived it, with an objective matter-of-factness that alienated the followers of Gericault and Delacroix. Settling near the village of Barbizon in the Forest of Fontainebleau south of Paris,

Figure 22.11 Barry and Pugin, The Houses of Parliament, London.

Figure 22.12 Victorian Gothic mansion, ca. 1885, Eureka, California.

painters of the Barbizon School imitated Rousseau's back-to-nature movement while simultaneously escaping the disorder and confusion of the 1848 Revolution. Rousseau's "noble savage" was interpreted by Barbizon associate François Millet (me–YAY; 1814–1875) as a heroic peasant who exemplified the dignity of working the land. In *The Sower* (fig. 22.13) Millet's peasant has the monumentality of Michelangelo and an earthy quality comparable to the bourgeois Dutch tradition. Himself the son of peasants, Millet chose to live the life of a peasant, sympathetically depicting his protagonists as actors in a kind of divine drama in a style antithetic to the French academic tradition.[2]

2. Disdained since about 1860 as artistically inferior, French academic art has, since about 1965, experienced a rebirth. See, for example, *The Encyclopedia of World Art,* vol. XVI (New York: McGraw-Hill Book Company, 1983), pp. 230–231.

Though he did not consider himself a member of the Barbizon School, Jean-Baptiste-Camille Corot (ko–ROW; 1796–1875) lived in the area and shared their strong commitment to direct visual experience. In the *Forest of Fontainebleau* (fig. 22.14) Corot painted the full range of light and dark values, depicting visual reality at a single moment in time. Working very quickly, Corot sought the underlying rhythm of nature, composing his landscapes so that the magic moment of truth would be revealed to all. One of the finest Western landscape painters, Corot became as the poet Baudelaire said he would, "the master of an entire younger generation."

Corot, Millet, and the Barbizon School can be described as Romantic Realists for there is an element of escapism in their work. In Paris, however, the realities of political and social unrest before and after the

Figure 22.13 François Millet, *The Sower,* ca. 1850. Oil on canvas, 39¾ × 32½″. Shaw Collection. Museum of Fine Arts, Boston.

Figure 22.14 Jean-Baptiste-Camille Corot, *Forest of Fontainebleau,* ca. 1830. Oil on canvas, 69⅛ × 95¼″. Chester Dale Collection, 1962. National Gallery of Art, Washington, D.C.

Figure 22.15 Honoré Daumier, *Le Ventre Legislatif,* 1834. Lithograph. The Arizona State University Art Collections, Arizona State University. Gift of Oliver B. James.

1848 Revolution were of far greater concern to a hard-bitten Realist like Honoré Daumier (doe–me–AY; 1808–1879). Known to his contemporaries as a caricaturist, Daumier created over 4,000 lithographs[3] satirizing the major and minor foibles of the day. In his caricature of *Le Ventre Legislatif* ("The Legislative Belly"; fig. 22.15) Daumier depicted the venality, pomposity, and stupidity of the collective "Legislative Belly," i.e., "Body." With devastating candor Daumier gives us a cast of politicians all too well known in the body politic of democratic societies.

Daumier's political caricatures once landed him in jail but that did not curtail his acid pen; in a series of lithographs called *Ancient History* the artist lambasted the Neoclassicists. *Pygmalion* (fig. 22.16) is a comical rendering of the classical myth about the sculptor who fell in love with his beautiful creation and invited her to come to life. Daumier pictured the sculptor as a journeyman stone hacker astonished by the flirtatious response of a dumpy, unattractive Galatea.

Daumier was just as forceful a contemporary social critic in oils as he was in his lithographs, claiming that scenes of contemporary everyday life had to be painted because "one must be of one's own time."

---

3. One of the graphic arts, lithography is a printmaking process that was widely popular in the nineteenth century for newspaper and magazine illustrations. In lithography (Gk., "writing on stone") the design is drawn on stone or a metal plate with a greasy printing ink and then reproduced by the standard printing process.

In *The Washerwoman* (fig. 22.17) he used a strong chiaroscuro in the manner of Rembrandt, whom he greatly admired, to depict the weariness of a mother who is tenderly assisting her child up the steps. Looming large against the vague urban background, the figure has a monumental nobility that is comparable, though on a much smaller scale, with Michelangelo's grandiose figures on the Sistine Chapel ceiling.

Realism in art was given a name and a leader in the person of Gustave Courbet (koor–BAY; 1819–1877), who even took the time to issue a "Manifesto of Realism." At the Andler Keller, one of the first Parisian beer halls, the swaggering, flamboyant Courbet held forth as the apostle of the physical world of visible objects. "Show me an angel," he once remarked, "and I will paint you an angel." Courbet found his natural subjects in the common people of his home village of Ornans in eastern France. As he said, "to paint a bit of country, one must know it. I know my country." *Burial at Ornans* (fig. 22.18) depicts a rural

Figure 22.16 Honoré Daumier, *Pygmalion,* from the series *Histoire Ancienne.* Private collection.

Figure 22.17 Honoré Daumier, *The Washerwoman,* ca. 1863. Oil on panel, 19¼ × 13″. The Louvre, Paris.

Figure 22.18 Gustave Courbet, *Burial at Ornans,* 1849–1850. Oil on canvas, ca. 10′3″ × 21′9″. The Louvre, Paris.

Figure 22.19 Joseph Paxton, Crystal Palace, 1850–1851, London.

scene on a monumental scale normally reserved for epic historical events. Much to the consternation of the critics, Courbet turned the somber reality of this simple country funeral into a noble occasion that he called "true history." Combining religious symbolism with realism, Courbet included the dog as it was depicted in the Office of the Dead in medieval manuscripts; the people were all painted from life in innumerable sittings demanded by the artist. Composed on a horizontal S-curve, the figures of clergy, pall-bearers, friends, and relatives stand in poses ranging from indifference to composed grief. The staff with the crucifix is positioned to give the illusion of Christ's actual death on Golgotha. This and other paintings were rejected by the Universal Exposition, leading to the construction of a shed, called by Courbet "The Pavilion of Realism," for the exhibition of his uncompromising works.

Realism spread throughout Europe as artists were attracted to the style but it was especially popular in the United States, where pragmatism and realism were characteristics of the American way of life. Beginning his career as an illustrator for *Harper's Weekly,* Winslow Homer (1836–1910) was influenced by Corot and Courbet, but not at the expense of his American point of view. Homer lived during what Mark Twain had called the Gilded Age, a grossly materialistic era of pretentious opulence, but his style was firmly fixed in genre paintings in the mode of American realism. In *Breezing Up* (colorplate 42) Homer celebrated his lifelong love affair with the sea in a joyous composition of wind, salt air, and sparkling sea. Fatigued but happy with the day's catch, the fisherman and boys are returning home. With the catboat placed at eye level and slanting away from the viewer, we are drawn into an illusion of movement and the feeling of a job well done. Exemplifying Homer's statement, "When I have selected a thing carefully, I paint it exactly as it appears," the details are finely drawn: wrinkled clothes, light sparkling from metal fittings, a lighthouse at the lower left, a wheeling gull at the upper

right. Homer's ability to give the illusion of light emanating from his canvases paralleled the development of French Impressionism across the ocean from his native New England.

Homer's career was remarkably divergent from that of his older contemporary, author Herman Melville. Both were New Englanders and fascinated by the sea but Homer's vision was generally positive while Melville's was darkly ambiguous. Homer covered the Civil War as an illustrator for *Harper's Weekly;* Melville wrote two volumes of war poems that were totally unknown at the time. Homer was a highly successful and popular painter; Melville was not recognized as one of America's greatest writers until many years after his obscure death. Ironically, both were Realists (see chap. 20 for some of Melville's poetry).

Realism in painting can be compared, to some extent, with the development of late nineteenth-century architecture. Abandoning copies of older styles, architects turned to modern building materials to design functional structures serving specific purposes. Epitomizing the new attitude toward utilitarian design, the Crystal Palace (fig. 22.19) was constructed of 5,000 prefabricated iron columns and girders and nearly 300,000 panes of glass. A greenhouse designer by profession, Sir Joseph Paxton (1801–1865) oversaw the construction of an immense structure that covered nineteen acres in Hyde Park and contained almost a million square feet of floor space. Assembled in only four months, the Crystal Palace housed London's "Great Exhibition of the Works of All Nations," a triumphant display of the miracles wrought by the Industrial Revolution. The theme of the exhibition was "Progress" as represented by the mechanized marvels within the glittering structure, itself a symbol of the "Age of Progress." The first of many similar buildings, the Crystal Palace was dismantled after the exhibition and reassembled south of London where, in 1936, it was destroyed by fire. Though cast-iron structures were vulnerable to fire, the Crystal Palace

Figure 22.20 Gustave Eiffel, Eiffel Tower, 1889, Paris

did establish the practicality of metal as a building material. With the 1856 invention of the Bessemer process of making steel the technology was already available for the construction of twentieth-century high-rise buildings.

The first high-rise structure in the world was designed by an engineer, Gustave Eiffel (I-fel; 1832–1923), for the Paris Exhibition of 1889, another celebration of technological advances. Rising to an imposing height of 984', the Eiffel Tower (fig. 22.20) symbolized the Age of Progress in modern France. Like a giant erector set, it was assembled on the site; prefabricated and prepunched girders were bolted together in a masterful demonstration of precision design and production. Though denounced from the outset by purists who objected to the violation of the Parisian skyline, the tower stands today as the enduring symbol of the City of Light.

Impressionism

In one respect Impressionism was an outgrowth of Realism but in another it was a revolutionary artistic movement almost as profound in its effect as the Early Renaissance in Italy. Impressionists saw themselves as the ultimate Realists whose main concern was the perception of optical sensations of light and color. Whether or not the Impressionists were consciously aware of photographic techniques, scientific research

in optics, or the physiology of the eye is not important; they painted as if the world were not matter in space but a source of sensations of light and color. Objects were perceived as agents for the absorption and reflection of light; there were no sharp edges, indeed, no lines in nature. In nature, form and space were implied by infinitely varied intensities of color and light, and shadows were not black but colored in relation to the objects casting the shadows. This is Impressionist theory in essence but the individual artists developed styles, of course, that sometimes contradicted the theories.

A major innovator in Western painting, Edouard Manet (ma–NAY; 1832–1883) was not an Impressionist but his influence on the movement was critical. Realizing that modeled transitions did not exist in nature, he worked instead in planes. Also one of the first artists to paint with pure colors, eliminating dark shadows that had been used for centuries, Manet was a pioneer in the use of light as his subject; light was the actual subject matter of the painting that he submitted in 1863 to the jury of the Paris Salon. An unconventional painting with a conventional title, *Déjeuner sur l'herbe* (*Luncheon on the Grass;* fig. 22.21) was refused by the jury but exhibited in a special Salon des Refusés, where it caused a storm of controversy. Though the ostensible subject matter was possibly derived from Giorgione's *Fête Champêtre* (see fig. 14.30), the contemporary dress of the men in combination with the unconcerned nakedness of the woman deeply shocked the public; even Courbet, who did not object to the nude, criticized the work as flat and formless. Manet had almost totally abandoned Renaissance perspective, accepting the canvas for what it really was: a two-dimensional surface. The hue and cry over the work bewildered the artist; the subject, after all was *light* as clustered around the nude, the background figure, the still life in the left foreground. The grouping of the dark areas further emphasized the harsh light of day, giving the painting a powerful visual impact. For Manet and the Impressionists the objects and figures in their paintings were sometimes treated impersonally, as opportunities to depict light sensations. Frequently detached and nonjudgmental, Manet and the Impressionists, except for Renoir, were often more entranced with optical sensations than with humanity.

The public, however, was not detached and it was very judgmental. The reaction to Manet's *Olympia* (fig. 22.22) that he exhibited at the 1865 Salon caused one of the greatest scandals in art history. Critics called Manet "a buffoon" and the nude a "female gorilla" and "yellow-bellied odalisque," while boisterous crowds flocked to see a work that another critic advised pregnant women and proper young ladies to avoid at all costs. Manet had painted his model, Victorine Meurend (who also posed for the Déjeuner), as an elegant and worldly-weary lady of the evening. With an orchid in her hair and wearing only a black ribbon around her neck, she stares disdainfully at the viewer while ignoring the bouquet proferred by her

Figure 22.21 Edouard Manet, *Dejeuner sur l'herbe,* 1863. Oil on canvas, 7' × 8'10". The Jeu de Paume, Paris.

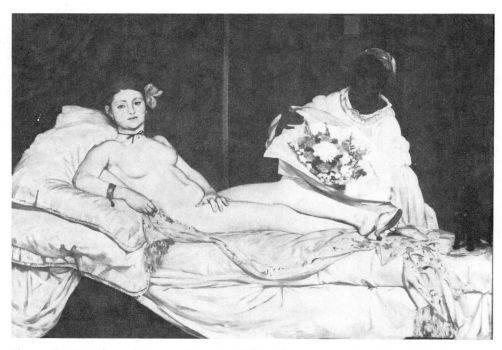

Figure 22.22 Edouard Manet, *Olympia.* 1863. Oil on canvas, 51¼ × 74¾". The Jeu de Paume, Paris.

Figure 22.23 Berthe Morisot, *In the Dining Room,* 1881–1883. Oil on canvas, 24½ × 19¾″. Chester Dale Collection, 1962. National Gallery of Art, Washington, D.C.

maid. Critics were no more incensed about the flagrant nakedness than with the black-on-black coloration of the maid's face against the background, not to mention the black cat at the foot of the suggestively rumpled bed, also painted against a black background. The picture became a *cause célèbre,* pitting modernists against traditionalists. In his novel *Of Human Bondage* Somerset Maugham gleefully described the Latin Quarter in which reproductions of *Olympia* were prominent in virtually every student room, bar, and sidewalk cafe. Even today the picture is distinctly modern. Manet forces his viewers to look *at* his flat picture rather than *into* it. The traditional boxlike space behind the frontal picture plane has been eliminated, presenting a situation that leaves much to the imagination. A comparison of *Olympia* and the *Odalisque* of Ingres (see fig. 22.3) reveals the difference, at that time, between acceptable nudity and the disagreeable reality of a naked prostitute.

Manet was the first Western artist to reject Renaissance perspective as fraudulent, as basically contrary to the reality of an arrangement of colors and shapes on a flat surface. In *The Dead Toreador* (colorplate 43) he continued to antagonize a public that expected to see a dramatic depiction of a bullfighter fatally gored in the ring. Again, this is not a narrative but a striking arrangement of white, olive, pink, and black against a neutral background. Manet, like many of his contemporaries, was influenced by the newly popular Japanese prints in which two-dimensionality, line, and flat color planes were basic components of the style.

Following the innovations of Manet, who went on to experiment in other directions, the Impressionists developed a definite system with its own aesthetic principles. For centuries artists had been painting what they knew but the Impressionists were more interested in painting what they saw. The recent development of paint tubes and canisters liberated artists from the messy and time-consuming process of mixing pigments; more importantly, portable paints freed artists from their studios, enabling them to roam the countryside and paint *en plein air* (in open air). To see and capture the wondrous glories of nature and revel in the evanescent effects of sunlight became the new aesthetic.

The spokesman and chief painter of the Impressionist style was Claude Monet (mo–NAY; 1840–1926), who throughout his long and productive career relied wholly upon his visual perceptions. For him, especially, there were no objects like trees, houses, or figures but some green here, a patch of blue there, a bit of yellow over here, and so on. Monet was "only an eye" said his contemporary, Paul Cézanne, "but what an eye!" The mechanics of vision were a major concern of Monet and the other Impressionists. To achieve intensity of color, pigments were not combined on the palette but laid on the canvas in primary hues so that the eye could do the mixing. A dab of yellow, for example, placed next to one of blue is perceived, from a distance, as green, a brilliant green because the eye accomplishes the optical recomposition. Further, each color leaves behind a visual sensation which is its afterimage or complementary color. The afterimage of red is blue-green and that of green is the color red. The adjacent placement of red and green reinforces each color through its afterimage, making both red and green more brilliant. Impressionists generally painted with pure pigments in the colors of the spectrum; conspicuously absent from the spectrum and thus from Impressionist canvases was black, a favorite of academic painters. Monet contended that black was not a color and he was scientifically correct; black is the absence of color. This, of course, did not keep artists like Degas and Manet (*The Dead Toreador*) from using black with dramatic effect.

Portable paints in the open sunlight and color perception were two components of Impressionist technique. The third component was speed. Making natural light explode on canvas necessitated quick brushstrokes that captured a momentary impression of reflected light, a reflection that changed from minute to minute. Monet's procedure was to paint furiously for seven or eight minutes and then move quickly to another canvas to capture a different light. Should a painting require additional effort he would return to the same spot the following day at precisely the same time, a procedure he followed in his many paintings of Rouen Cathedral done at different times of day. Early in the morning the elaborate Gothic facade would appear to be quite solid but later in the day, as in *Rouen Cathedral, West Facade Sunlight* (colorplate 45), the stonework has dissolved into a luminous haze of warm colors. *Impressionism* is a term used derisively by a critic who, upon seeing Monet's 1872 painting entitled *Impression, Sunrise,* remarked that it was "only an impression." That the term is generally apropos is apparent in Monet's impression of sunlight on medieval stonework.

Monet was a magnificent "eye" whose achievements are far more appreciated today than in his own time. On the other hand, the work of his celebrated contemporary, Auguste Renoir (ren-o'AR; 1841–1919), has always had great appeal, possibly because Renoir portrayed people rather than buildings, landscapes, or lily ponds. The finest painter of luscious nudes since Rubens, Renoir had a unique ability to create the illusion of soft and glowing human flesh. He painted females of all ages, once exclaiming that if "God had not created woman I don't know whether I would have become a painter!" *Girl with a Watering Can* (colorplate 46) is a marvel of iridescent color. Renoir's associates were astonished by his carefree approach to painting but, "if painting weren't fun," protested the artist, "you may be sure that I wouldn't do it." That joyous attitude is readily apparent in this luminous evocation of happy innocence.

Edgar Degas (DAY–gah; 1834–1917) also specialized in women, but mainly women in their casual but graceful roles as ballet dancers. Delighting in studying forms in motion, he drew dancers and race horses and, in so doing, gained a remarkable vitality in his work. *Four Dancers* (colorplate 44) was one of his last large oil paintings but it also shows the influence of the pastel medium that he used in most of his later works. Of all the Impressionists, Degas was most interested in photography, both in taking pictures and in basing some of his works on photographs. This off-stage ballet scene has the appearance of a candid snapshot of dancers limbering up and checking their costumes before going on stage. Actually, Degas posed dancers in his studio to orchestrate the illusion of spontaneity that he wanted. It should be noted that Degas's concern with composition and his use of black make his style less impressionistic than the style of Monet.

The Impressionists were a cohesive group of avant-garde artists that revolved around the central personality of Manet. The regular meeting place of Manet's "school" was the Café Guerbois, where Manet, Monet, Renoir, Degas, Whistler, the photographer Nadar, Émile Zola, Baudelaire, and others congregated to argue passionately about the role of the modern artist. Berthe Morisot (more–uh–so; 1841–1895) was a member of the group but, as a proper young woman, she was denied the opportunity to socialize at the cafe with her colleagues. A student of both Corot and Manet, she had the unusual distinction of having her work accepted by both the Impressionists and the Salon. In her *In the Dining Room* (fig. 22.23) she depicted her maid and little white dog in a setting in which the forms are silhouetted as elements in a design literally flooded with

Figure 22.24 Mary Cassatt, *The Bath,* ca. 1891–1892. Oil on canvas, 39¼ × 26″. Courtesy, The Art Institute of Chicago.

light. An enthusiastic admirer of her art, the Symbolist poet Stéphane Mallarmé, wrote in his catalog for an exhibition of her work: "To make poetry in the plastic arts demands that the artist portray on the surface the luminous secret of things, simply, directly, without extraneous detail." And so she did.

Both of the American painters who exhibited with the Impressionists, Cassatt and Whistler, drew their inspiration from their techniques but each developed a different and very personal style. Mary Cassatt (1844–1926) was American by birth and training and, though she lived in France for much of her life, is considered by the French to be the best artist America has yet produced. The influence of two-dimensional Japanese woodcuts is apparent in *The Bath* (fig. 22.24) but the extraordinary quality of the lines is uniquely her own. Both decorative and functional, the fluid lines enclose what seems at first to be a simple domestic scene. But, this is a highly stylized composition that we look down upon, an intimate and tender moment presented in a closed form that shuts out the viewer, and the world. We experience the rich warmth of the scene but we are not a part of it.

James McNeill Whistler (1834–1903), like Henry James, considered American civilization, such as it was, an embarrassment. Like James, Whistler became an expatriate, even denying that he was born in Lowell, Massachusetts: "I shall be born when and where I want, and I do not choose to be born in Lowell."

Figure 22.25 James McNeill Whistler, *Arrangement in Gray and Black, No. 1,* ca. 1877. Oil on canvas, 57 × 64½". The Louvre, Paris.

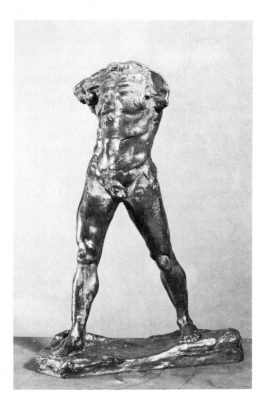

Figure 22.26 Auguste Rodin, *The Walking Man,* 1877–1878. Gift of Mrs. John W. Simpson. National Gallery of Art, Washington, D.C.

Whistler was highly critical, naturally, of American realists like Winslow Homer (see colorplate 42), advocating instead "art for art's sake." The Impressionists were sufficiently artistic for his tastes and he adapted some of their modern techniques to his uniquely personal style. Subject matter, he felt, was of no importance; in his *Arrangement in Gray and Black, No. 1* (fig. 22.25) Whistler contended that no one could possibly be interested in the artist's mother. The lasting popularity of "Whistler's Mother" contradicts his thesis, for there is a very personal feeling here. Color, line, pattern, and composition communicate a serenity that is both a portrait and an abstract composition.

During the eighteenth and nineteenth centuries sculpture failed to keep pace with painting and architecture. The work of Houdon (see fig. 18.39) was significant but the sculptures of Daumier and Degas were scarcely known at the time. And then there was Auguste Rodin (ro–DAN; 1840–1917), the greatest sculptor since Bernini, a dynamo of a man who captured the spontaneity and immediacy of Impressionism in three-dimensional form. Like Renoir and Degas, Rodin was concerned with the human figure but, totally unlike any Impressionist, his figures are depicted in moments of stress or tension. Intended originally as a study for *St. John the Baptist Preaching, The Walking Man* (fig. 22.26) is a study in motion and motion is all that we sense. Headless and armless,

Figure 22.27 Auguste Rodin, *The Thinker,* 1879–1889. Gift of Mrs. John W. Simpson. National Gallery of Art, Washington, D.C.

Figure 22.28 Vincent van Gogh, *La Mousmé,* 1888. Oil on canvas, 28⅞ × 22¾″. Chester Dale Collection, 1942. National Gallery of Art, Washington, D.C.

there is no expression or gesture to distract our attention from the strongly striding torso moving its muscular legs in long steps. The surface shimmers with light, shaped by the artist to further heighten the illusion of motion.

Rodin's commission for *The Gates of Hell* produced a number of figures extracted from a monumental work that was never completely finished. Sitting atop the Gates and brooding over Rodin's conception of Dante's *Inferno, The Thinker* (fig. 22.27) is a prodigious work of tension in repose. Similar to Michelangelo's superhuman forms that Rodin studied in detail, the figure is sunk in deep thought. What is he thinking of? Rodin said at one time that it was Dante contemplating his poem and another time that this was a dreamer and then a creator. Whether writer, dreamer, or creator, *The Thinker* remains a fascinating enigma.

Post-Impressionism

Post-Impressionism is a catchall term for some highly individual artists who reacted against the purely visual emphasis of Impressionism. The first and foremost of the Post-Impressionists, Paul Cézanne (say–ZAN; 1839–1906) was, in fact, one of the giants of European painting. His art lay somewhere between representation and abstraction, an intellectualized approach to applying paint to canvas. For Cézanne the whole purpose of painting was to express the emotion that the forms and colors of the natural world evoked in the artist. His landscapes look like his native Provence but not literally; everything has been clarified and concentrated. Cézanne took liberties

with ordinary visual experience that challenge our perceptions and force us to view the world in a new way, in Cézanne's way. In *Le Chateau Noir* (colorplate 47) Cézanne gave the building a brooding air of mystery in keeping with the local legend that it was haunted by the ghost of an alchemist. In common with his other landscapes, there are no living creatures and the forms of the dense forest and the arcane building on its rocky spur are synthesized with the artist's characteristically muted blue-green and orange hues. The Impressionists used color to dissolve form and space; Cézanne did precisely the opposite by using color to define form in a very tangible space. Cézanne constructed his paintings slowly, methodically, with an intellectual control comparable to the art of Poussin. *Le Chateau Noir* has what he called a "durable museum quality" because Cézanne painted not just what he saw but what he knew.

Cézanne sold some of his paintings for as little as nine dollars but the Dutch artist, Vincent van Gogh (van–GO; 1853–1890), sold only one painting during his ten-year career, depending entirely on his brother for support. Van Gogh began as an Impressionist but changed his style drastically after studying Japanese prints, which he found "extremely clear, never tedious, as simple as breathing." Though van Gogh never attained this degree of facility he did learn to treat the picture surface as an area to be decorated in masses of flat or slightly broken color. In *La Mousmé* (fig. 22.28) he painted a young girl from Provence, to

Figure 22.29 Vincent van Gogh, *The Olive Orchard*, 1889. Oil on canvas, 28¾ × 36¼". Chester Dale Collection, 1962. National Gallery of Art, Washington, D.C.

which he had moved in 1888 to capture in the brilliant sunlight some of the beauty that he imagined existed in Japan. The word *mousmé* was taken from a contemporary romantic novel in which it was used to characterize the innocent charm of youthful Japanese teahouse attendants. Poised motionless against a neutral background and holding some oleander flowers, the thirteen-year-old peasant girl seems totally removed from everyday experience. She represents the artist's aim "to paint men and women with that quality of the eternal which used to be suggested by the halo."

Twice confined to a hospital in Arles after a mental breakdown in 1889, van Gogh resumed painting and continued to produce during his subsequent year-long confinement in a mental asylum at St. Remy. Though sometimes permitted to paint outdoors when accompanied by a guard, *The Olive Orchard* (fig. 22.29) was painted "from memory," as he wrote his brother Theo. In late works such as this, van Gogh was intent on getting large quantities of paint onto the canvas, squeezing colors directly from the tube and then working them with brush and palette knife. The result was a very thick impasto that makes the paintings three-dimensional in the manner of topographical models. The flamelike cypress and writhing olive trees of Provence fascinated the artist. In this decorative and swirling composition the olive pickers are seemingly suspended in space as part of the design.

Painted in a field near the asylum, *The Starry Night* (see colorplate 4) is an ecstatic vision of the power and glory of the universe. A tall cypress flames toward the whirling and exploding stars of a cosmic drama unknown to the inhabitants of the peaceful village below. This expressive work represents the artist's reverent celebration of the wonders of nature and is not, as some have contended, symptomatic of his illness.

Moving northwest of Paris to the village of Auvers-sur-Oise after his release from the asylum, van Gogh completed about sixty paintings during the last two months of his tragic life. There has never been an acceptable explanation for his fits of madness nor why he chose to commit suicide at age thirty-seven. In none of his work, however, is there even a hint of madness. At his funeral his friend and physician, Dr. Paul Gachet, said, "He was an honest man and a great artist. He had only two aims: humanity and art. It was the art that . . . will insure his survival."

Van Gogh's onetime friend, Paul Gauguin (go–GAN; 1848–1903) has been a kind of folk hero for desk-bound romantics who dream of dropping out of the rat race to pursue their artistic muse. The reality of Gauguin's life and career is, however, not the stuff of dreams. An amateur painter for many years, Gauguin had naively assumed that he would be as successful as a full-time painter as he had been as a stockbroker. Within three years after giving up his career in 1883, everything was gone: wife, family, money; he found himself living on borrowed funds at a run-down country inn in Brittany. Fascinated by the peasant costumes and deep piety of Breton women, Gauguin painted *Vision after the Sermon (Jacob Wrestling with the Angel)* (fig. 22.30) as a symbolic religious drama. The peasant women have just left the church after perhaps hearing a sermon by the priest (at the far right) about Jacob's bout with the angel, at which they are staring. Painted in flat, boldly outlined colors, the picture reveals Gauguin's keen perception of the power of belief and imagination in the almost medieval world of the Breton peasant.

A rebel at odds with conventional behavior and society in general, Gauguin was seldom bothered with self-doubt. Writing to his absent wife, he proclaimed that "I am a great artist and I know it." Probably inspired by Japanese prints, as was much of his work, his *Self-Portrait* (colorplate 48) includes a slight oriental cast to the eyes in this strikingly off-centered composition. Presenting himself with an ironic halo, his temptations are symbolized by the sharply outlined apples and the snake that he holds like a cigarette. Painted in the manner of a cloisonné enamel, the vivid colors are divided by incised lines, with everything flattened except the arrogant but sadly reflective face of a man who once wrote that he felt "like a brigand, which, for that matter, I am to many people."

Forever restless, Gauguin was drawn to the warm climate of Provence where he roomed briefly, and quarreled, with van Gogh, and then drifted to tropical climates: Panama, Martinique, Tahiti, and the Marquesas, where he died. In Tahiti Gauguin found, he thought, an antidote to the sickness of European civilization, a "primitive life" that would nurture his style. Actually, the Society Islands were governed by the French and Gauguin had evolved his tropical style before settling down in Polynesia. Gauguin's dream of "solitude under the tropical sun" was compromised by illness, poverty, and harassment by French authorities but, nevertheless, his work acquired a new

Figure 22.30 Paul Gauguin, *Vision after the Sermon (Jacob Wrestling with the Angel),* 1888. Oil on canvas, 36¼ × 28¾". National Galleries, Edinburgh. Courtesy National Galleries of Scotland.

Figure 22.31 Paul Gauguin, *Fatata te Miti (By the Sea),* 1892. Oil on canvas, 26¾ × 36". Chester Dale Collection, 1942. National Gallery of Art, Washington, D.C.

vigor. *Fatata te Miti* (fig. 22.31) is a masterful evocation of sun, sea, and Polynesian beauties in a decorative composition that illustrates the artist's theories about resemblances between abstract patterns and music. It may have been this painting (or the one discussed below) that the Symbolist poet Mallarmé called a "musical poem that needs no libretto."

Critics of the time found Gauguin's colors bizarre and his drawing crude but the public accepted the content of his paintings as actual illustrations of Tahitian life and customs. Though Gauguin admitted that his Tahiti was a subjective interpretation of what was "vaguest and most universal in nature," we still have a romantic image of Tahiti in Gauguin's mode. In *Where Do We Come From? What Are We? Where*

Are We Going? (see colorplate 1) Gauguin executed what he called his "spiritual testament," completed shortly before his abortive suicide attempt. Stating that "I will never do anything better or even like it," Gauguin painted this as a voyage of discovery, not as a statement of his rather confused ideas about birth, life, and death. The painting is a fusion of antitheses: sunlight and moonlight; night and day; the warmness of life and the coldness of death. The cycle of life can be read from childhood on the right to the old woman waiting for death at the left. Ultimately, this work attests, as Gauguin said, to "the futility of words," not to mention the futility of life.

Causing nearly as much controversy as works by Manet, Georges Seurat (sue–RAH; 1859–1891) exhibited *Sunday Afternoon on the Island of La Grande*

Figure 22.32 Henri de Toulouse-Lautrec, *Quadrille at the Moulin Rouge,* 1892. Gouache on cardboard, 31½ × 23¾". Chester Dale Collection, 1942, National Gallery of Art, Washington, D.C.

Figure 22.33 Henri Rousseau, *The Equatorial Jungle,* 1909. Oil on canvas, 55¼ × 51". Chester Dale Collection, 1942. National Gallery of Art, Washington, D.C.

Jatte (colorplate 49) at the eighth and final Impressionist show of 1886. Critics had a field day lambasting the dots of color, the "procession of pharaohs," and a "clearance sale of Nuremberg toys." Favorable critics, and there were some, labeled the new style Neoimpressionism or Divisionalism, while Paris wits chose the word "confettism." Seurat himself used the term "chromo-luminarium" to describe a method of painting with tiny dots using the colors of the spectrum. Aspiring to paint in a scientific manner based on the optical theories of Helmholtz and others, Seurat used his *petit points,* his dots, to construct a monumental composition of "museum quality," as advocated by Cézanne. The scene is a popular summer resort near Paris where middle-class city dwellers could bathe, picnic, and promenade. Though the dots of pure color were supposed to fuse in the eye this does not happen, save in the luminosity of the river. Instead, the spectator is conscious of the myriads of dots that, in a nonchromatic way, contribute as units of scale to the grandeur that Seurat achieved; his optical theories were, in practice, more artistic than scientific. In addition, he developed a control of line, proportions, and masses of light and shade that make this a classical composition in the manner of Poussin and David. In its psychological impact the work is curiously modern. People, animals, hats, and parasols are structural and decorative elements, as isolated from each other as they are from the viewer. A typical Impressionist genre scene has become a melancholic comment on alienation and isolation in late Victorian society, symbolizing the underlying pessimism of the age.

The bawdy night life of Parisian society was vividly depicted by Henri de Toulouse-Lautrec (tu–LOSE–la–TREK; 1864–1901), who delighted in portraying people at cabarets, theatres, the races, and brothels. He especially enjoyed the tawdry gaiety of Montmartre's most colorful music hall, the Moulin Rouge. In *Quadrille at the Moulin Rouge* (fig. 22.32) he portrayed the earthy vitality of the dancer Gabrielle as she hikes her skirts to begin the quadrille, a dance that grew out of the high-kicking cancan. Confronted by the professional dancer is an elegant and refined patron of the establishment, who reaches obediently for her skirt to begin the dance. Far more concerned with the human comedy than most Impressionists were, Toulouse-Lautrec, like Daumier, has given us, in his paintings and inimitable posters, vivid pictures of the Gilded Age.

The most influential of the Post-Impressionists were Cézanne and an obscure toll collector named Henri Rousseau (1844–1910). An isolated and enigmatic genius who began painting late in life, Rousseau taught himself to paint "alone," as he said, "and without any master but nature." His naive ideal was what he called the "truth" of the camera; he was actually convinced that his paintings were as "realistic" as a photograph. His jungle landscapes were painted with a startling directness of vision that influenced Picasso and others, but, these were tropics of the mind produced by the magical vision of a simple man who, apparently, never left France. Nothing in *The Equatorial Jungle* (fig. 22.33) is identifiable in botanical

Figure 22.34 Edvard Munch, *The Scream,* 1893. Oil on canvas, 36 × 29". Nationalgallereit, Oslo.

Held in the studio of Picasso in 1908, three years after the revolutionary show of the Fauves (see chap. 25), the guest of honor was Henri Rousseau, nearing the end of his career and still unrecognized by the public. Guests included artists Georges Braque and Marie Laurecin, writers Apollinaire, Max Jacob, Gertrude Stein, and other luminaries of the new epoch. Picasso had ordered the food for the wrong day but there was ample wine and abundant good spirits, with violin entertainment provided by the guest of honor. The only real tribute the unassuming little toll collector cum painter ever received prompted him to whisper confidentially to Picasso that, "after all, you and I are both great painters: I in the Modern style and you in the Egyptian." Though Picasso's "Egyptian" style was actually his African mask period, Henri Rousseau's remark turned out be correct on both counts.

terms. What we see is a brooding and sinister jungle inhabited by a mysterious bird (a vulture?) and two strange-looking animals. There is an eerie and timeless stillness about this exotic, compelling scene that communicates the wonder that the artist must have felt as he painted his visions, images so real that, as he told his colleagues, they actually terrified the painter.

Van Gogh, Gauguin, Seurat, and Rousseau were critical of the disease of civilization but their pervasive pessimism was not limited to French urban culture. The Norwegian painter Edvard Munch (MOONK; 1864–1944), manipulated themes of evil, terror, and death to depict the plight, as he saw it, of *fin de siècle* European civilization, themes similar to those of the English poets Matthew Arnold and Thomas Hardy (see chap. 20). In *The Scream* (fig. 22.34) Munch portrayed a terror-stricken person whose sexual and facial identity has been obliterated by a piercing scream that is echoed in undulating lines of the landscape. Like his friend and associate, Henrik Ibsen, Munch dealt with the unbearable tensions of the modern world that led to anxiety, alienation, and, as here, terror. Though his iconography was intensely personal, Munch's pessimistic vision strongly influenced the later German Expressionist movement (see chap. 25).

A rather impromptu special event, the *banquet Rousseau,* symbolically marks the end of the old era and the advent of the twentieth-century avant-garde.

Summary

Romanticism was a reaction in all the arts against the Enlightenment. For a time, however, the visual arts in France were in the service of Napoleon and David, his court painter. The Arch of Triumph and Church of the Madeleine made significant contributions to the Neoclassic face of Paris and the paintings of Ingres established an academic style against which later artists were to rebel.

Painting in a style uniquely his own, Goya was one of the most important painters of the century. The French Romantic style was established by the dramatic work of Gericault and continued by the peerless colorist Delacroix. John Constable was the leading Romantic landscape painter in England while Romantic architecture was revivalist, as manifested in the Gothic Revival Houses of Parliament.

By the second half of the century Realists like Millet, Corot, Daumier, and Courbet dominated the Parisian art scene while, in America, Winslow Homer was a leading artist in the ongoing tradition of American realism. Imaginative uses of industrial technology saw the construction of prefabricated structures like the Crystal Palace and the Eiffel Tower.

Led by the innovations of Manet, the Impressionist movement became the avant-garde of European art. Considering themselves the ultimate Realists, Monet, Renoir, Degas, Morisot, Cassatt, and others helped establish Impressionism as one of the most influential of all artistic styles. Whistler did his own personal version of modern art and, in Paris, Rodin produced the most dramatic and expressive sculpture since the High Renaissance.

Reacting against the visual emphasis of Impressionism in very personal terms, the Post-Impressionists included Cézanne, who distilled on canvas the forms and colors of the natural world, and Seurat, who used a similar approach but with dots of color. Van Gogh and Gauguin used vivid colors to create very expressive works while Toulouse-Lautrec portrayed the high life and low life of his age. Rousseau created works from his private dream world that were a revelation to Picasso and others of the new avant-garde. Like many artists and writers of the late Victorian era, Munch reacted against modern urban society with themes of alienation and terror. It can be said that a century which began with the Arch of Triumph ended with *The Scream.*

Unit **8**

The Twentieth Century

23

Things Fall Apart: The Center Cannot Hold

Historical Overview, 1918–1939

World War I can be viewed as Act 2 in a drama that began in 1871 with Bismarck's formation of the German Empire and concluded with World War II as Act 3 in a tragedy that engulfed most of the world. The period of 1918–1939 can be seen, in retrospect, as an entr'acte that set the stage for the last act.

When the Armistice between the Allies and Germany and her allies was agreed upon for November 11, 1918, the stated intent was to stop the fighting and arrange for a just peace. The Treaty of Versailles that was signed on June 28, 1919, was, however, harshly punitive. Germany and her allies were forced to accept the "war guilt" clause and, further, to accept *all* responsibility for causing the war. War reparations were to be paid to all 32 allies; Germany lost virtually her entire armed services, overseas colonies, and portions of her land area, including the critical Polish Corridor that divided Germany and gave Poland a passage to the sea. Woodrow Wilson's attempts to curb the nationalistic zeal of Britain's Lloyd George and France's Clemenceau were essentially futile. Even Wilson's prize project, the League of Nations that was part of the Peace of Versailles, ended, finally, in failure caused, in part, by the refusal of the United States to join this valiant, doomed attempt to civilize the conduct of nations. The League of Nations did settle a few disputes but was powerless to prevent Japan's invasion of Manchuria in 1931, Mussolini's invasion of Ethiopia in 1935, and Germany's withdrawal from the League to rearm.

The Allies had led the Germans to believe that Kaiser Wilhelm II and his imperial government were primarily responsible for the war. But it was the new Weimar Republic that signed the dictated peace and it was, therefore, the Republic that bore the onus of German humiliation at the conference table. Moreover, the Treaty of Versailles made no provision for the economic rehabilitation of Europe nor were there any assurances for the futures of new nations like Czechoslovakia and Yugoslavia, which had been carved out of the dismembered Austro-Hungarian empire. The Treaty of Versailles caused more discontent and unrest than even the 1815 Congress that had ended the Napoleonic wars.

The March 1917 revolution in Russia had disposed of the czar but the new Provisional government, despite rising unrest, continued to pursue the war. V. I. Lenin (1870–1924) capitalized on new defeats at the front to seize the government and establish the All-Russian Congress of the Soviets. Concluding a separate disastrous peace with Germany, Lenin established a dictatorship of the Communist party that barely survived the ferocious Civil War of 1917–1920. Under Leon Trotsky (1877–1940) a new Red Army destroyed the rebel White armies and then helped Lenin solidify his hold on the government. Following Lenin's death in 1924, a power struggle between Trotsky and Joseph Stalin (1879–1953) saw Stalin emerge, in 1927, as the absolute dictator of the Soviet Union. Stalin's agents assassinated Trotsky in Mexico in 1940.

The new democracies were beset by economic difficulties in the 1920s and assaulted by Communists on the left and hardcore nationalists on the right. Benito Mussolini (1883–1945) marched on Rome in 1922 and assumed full dictatorial powers by 1926. Designed to produce a corporate totalitarian state, the doctrines of Italian fascism stressed the dominance of the state and the subordination of the individual, the desirability of war, and the Social Darwinian "right" of Italy to expand at the expense of "inferior" nations.

The initial successes of Italian fascism impressed not only the older Western democracies but also many malcontents in Germany, who bitterly resented the war guilt clause of the Treaty of Versailles. Compounding the discontent, the German military clique fostered the belief that Germany had never been defeated on the field of battle; she had been betrayed at home, said the military, by pacifist liberals. Following the disastrous inflation of 1923 the National Socialist German Workers Party (Nazis) launched a propaganda campaign that capitalized on German belief in the sellout at Versailles; coupled with the barrage was a virulent anti-Semitism that blamed the Jews for many of Germany's postwar problems while proclaiming the absolute supremacy of the Aryan master race. Led by Adolf Hitler (1889–1945), a spellbinding political orator, the Nazis achieved their first significant power when, in 1933, President von Hindenburg appointed Hitler as Chancellor of the Republic. Utilizing the emergency powers of Article 48 of the constitution, Hitler eradicated all opposition with his bloody purge of 1934. He was now absolute ruler of a Third Reich that was to last for "a thousand years."

The direct road to World War II began, probably, with the Japanese seizure of Manchuria in 1931, followed by her withdrawal from the League of Nations in 1933, and her invasion of China in 1937.

Germany withdrew from the League in 1933 to begin arming for war, which was also the year in which Dachau, the first concentration camp, was opened. In 1936 Hitler occupied the Rhineland in defiance of the Treaty of Versailles, a step that is now seen as the last opportunity for England and France to avert war in Europe.

Italy challenged the League of Nations by invading Ethiopia in 1935. The League's feeble response was to vote economic sanctions that failed miserably. No longer a member of the League, Germany supplied arms and supplies for her future ally.

The Spanish Civil War of 1936–1939 had the effect of polarizing world opinion between the fascists and monarchists of "loyalist" Francisco Franco (1892–1975) and rebel factions led by socialists, communists, and an assortment of liberals. Hitler backed Franco, using the opportunity to field-test his new war machines. It was German bombers that attacked the undefended Basque town of Guernica, an atrocity immortalized by Picasso in his *Guernica* (see fig. 25.11).

After signing a Rome-Berlin treaty with Mussolini in 1936, Hitler launched his campaign for a union (*anschluss*) with German-speaking Austria, which he occupied in early 1938. The next target was the German-speaking Sudeten area of Czechoslovakia. After working up a full-scale crisis with his oratory, Hitler agreed to a four-power conference at Munich on September 29, 1938. Hitler, Mussolini, British Prime Minister Neville Chamberlain and Premier Edouard Daladier of France conferred in an atmosphere of conciliation artfully orchestrated by Hitler. Chamberlain returned to England proclaiming "peace in our time" but, actually, England and France had helped dismember hapless Czechoslovakia. Hitler acquired the Sudetenland at Munich and all of Czechoslovakia by the following spring.

The final step was Poland, which was fated to be divided between Germany and Russia. On August 23, 1939, Germany and Russia signed a nonagression pact that relieved Hitler of his concerns about waging a two-front war. On September 1, 1939, the German armies rolled into Poland and, on September 3, 1939, England and France honored their commitment to Poland by declaring war on Germany. The Peace of Versailles that was supposed to confirm the Great War as the "war to end all wars" had lasted a scant twenty years.

The Culture-Epoch Theory and the Twentieth Century

Our distance from past ages enables us to perceive the periods when a culture was balanced, when the balance tipped into chaos, when the adjustment began that led to a new period of balance, and so on. Analyzing our own age is far more difficult, perhaps impossible, yet as thinking beings, we try to understand where we are and where we might be going. First, let us review the culture-epoch theory.

Philosophers of history have found many patterns that seem to account for the growth, flowering, and decay of civilizations. In this book we are using a modified and simplified form of the *culture-epoch theory* as a framework upon which to arrange our materials. This theory is neither more nor less "true" than any of a half-dozen other theories that attempt to account for changes throughout the recorded story of humankind.

According to the culture-epoch theory, a culture is founded upon whatever conception of reality is held by the great majority of people over a considerable period of time. This is true even though the majority may not be aware of any concept of reality or, more probably take it so much for granted that they are not aware it is simply a human idea, held on faith. Thus, for most people at the time this is written, a typewriter is real, a physical tree is real, and all things which can be seen, heard, smelled, felt, or tasted are real.

As a matter of fact, a number of scientists, philosophers, and religious thinkers have given us different concepts of reality, which have also been widely held. These thinkers have contemplated the millions of forms of life, many of them bearing resemblances to others, yet each one different; they have examined the forms of earth, air, fire, and water; they have wondered about the processes of change by which a tree today may, at some time in the future, disintegrate into earth and reappear in some totally alien form. They have watched such nontangible things as sunlight and air becoming leaf and branch. Pondering these things, they come inevitably to the ultimate question: "What is the nature of reality?"

To reach an answer, they usually focus on a few profound inquiries, some of which may be given here. For example, they might say, "We see change all around us. We see grass eaten and turn into cow. We see cow eaten and turn into man. We see man disintegrate and turn into earth. If all these changes can take place, what are the universal elements of which all things are composed?" Or they might say, "We see an individual human, John Doe, as baby, as youth, as adult, as senile old man, as corpse. From one moment to the next, he is never the same. Yet he is always the same, John Doe, a distinct being. Can it be that nothing is permanent, that reality is a process rather than a thing or group of things? If we have change, then, how does the process take place? And more important, we know that we live in a world of constant change, but what force directs the process?"

"Nonsense," retorts another group of thinkers. "That which is in a constant state of flow cannot be real. Only that which is permanent and unchanging can be real. What, then, in the universe is permanent, unchanging in itself, yet is able to transform itself, manifest itself, or produce from itself the countless forms which we see around us?"

These are some of the basic questions the pure thinker contemplates. The answers are various concepts of reality.

Based upon the idea of reality accepted as "true," specialized thinkers build different thought-structures that underlie visible institutions. These include a philosophy of justice from which particular forms of law and government spring; a philosophy of education which dictates the nature of our schools and the material taught in them; a religious philosophy that becomes apparent in churches and creeds; and an economic philosophy that yields its particular ways of producing and distributing goods and services, including the token-systems used as money. Other philosophies and institutions could be named, but these are some that greatly affect our daily living.

When these are formed, we have a complete culture, but always by the time such a pattern is established, we have forces at work which tend to destroy it. The destroyers are new pure thinkers who note inconsistencies within the idea of reality itself, and who question postulates or find contradictions.

From these new thinkers (philosophers, scientists, theologians) comes a new idea of reality so convincing it cannot be brushed aside. It must be accepted. Suddenly the whole structure of the culture finds itself without foundation. The justice and the law appropriate in the old culture no longer fit on the new foundation; the old education is no longer appropriate; old religious beliefs no longer describe our position in relation to God; old ways of making things and distributing them no longer suffice.

At this time people are plunged into a *period of chaos,* the first step in the formation of a new epoch.

The symptoms of the period of chaos lie around us now in such profusion that they scarcely need description. In the latter part of the twentieth century this is where we live. New and shocking ideas, moralities, and beliefs are introduced and discarded; terrorists attack established governments; civil strife and wars of conquest rage; everyone damages the environment; over everything looms the menace of nuclear obliteration. At the mercy of events beyond their control, some people try to turn back the clock to better, more peaceful days; others seek refuge and security in fundamentalist beliefs; still others retreat to paramilitary armed camps; many just mindlessly camp in front of their television sets, hoping, perhaps, that all the problems will somehow vanish. In other words, we see in the late twentieth century a period of chaos that may or may not be giving evidence of resolution, but more on that later.

Out of the turmoil and confusion of chaotic periods of past cultures there emerges the *period of adjustment.* At this point notable artists, whether painters, writers, sculptors, composers, or creators in some other medium, make their important contributions to society. Pheidias and Sokrates of ancient Athens, the master builders of Gothic cathedrals, Michelangelo, Beethoven, Goethe, Picasso, Sartre, Stravinsky, these innovators suggest the new line, shape, and pattern for a new culture, a new period of balance.

What is the role of the artist in the development of a cultural pattern? The artist does not necessarily know all about new ideas of reality. The artist in our time, for example, need not know all about Einstein's Special and General theories of Relativity (which are discussed below). The artist is simply a person of greater sensitivity than others, and with fine skills in one medium. As a sensitive person, the artist feels perhaps more keenly than the rest of us the tensions of the time—the pulls of this belief and the pulls of a contradictory one. An artist will not rest until he or she has explored this confusing experience and discovered some meaning, some significance therein. The great artist is always the composer (whether musician, writer, painter, architect, sculptor, choreographer, movie director), the person who puts things together in new relationships and finds new meanings for experience.

It comes down to this: styles in beauty change as the basic characteristics of people change. Or perhaps it works the other way; perhaps as new glimpses of beauty are caught by the artists, people themselves change to conform to the new beauty.

However it may happen, the artist, especially in the period of chaos and early in the period of adjustment within a culture-epoch, personally feels the stresses, tensions, and turmoil of the period. The artist explores conflicts within, which are the conflicts of the general population as well, and creates new structures, new designs, to synthesize the elements of conflict and give new meaning to experience. Some works of art, probably depending upon the individual artist's breadth of vision and ability to compose insight into significance, are seized upon as symbols of new pattern and new truth in society. They express the new idea of beauty and truth.

At this point another element of the population—we may call them the *intellectuals*—enters the picture. They are people like ourselves, college students and faculty members, government officials, ministers, business executives, and many others who think seriously about things and who, like the artists, have been troubled by the conflict of their times. They still are working within the period of adjustment in an epoch. They become aware of new meanings and patterns produced by the artists, and they start reshaping these designs into new philosophies of justice, of economics, of religion, and the like, and begin to build concrete institutions out of the philosophies that they have created. Through their work, order slowly emerges out of chaos.

When their work is finished, we come to the third period within a culture-epoch, the *period of balance.* At this point, the idea of reality, the philosophies which underlie our basic institutions, and the institutions themselves are all in harmony. Early in a period of balance, life must be very satisfying; everyone must know the reason for getting up in the morning to face the day. But if balance lasts too long, life begins to get dull. The big jobs seem to be done, and decadence, boredom, and deterioration may set in. The long and painful decline of the Roman Empire was just such a period.

But change comes inevitably. At the beginning of the twentieth century physicists were assuring young scientists that the great discoveries in physics had all been made and that only little tidying-up jobs remained. At the same time, Einstein was beginning his work, which was to supersede all our knowledge in physics. Just when people have been certain of everything in their periods of balance, new pure thinkers come along to upset the whole apple cart into a new epoch.

The last period of cultural balance extended from about 1600 to about 1918, though forces were already in motion in the late nineteenth and early twentieth centuries that were to destroy the old order. From before 1918 to the dawn of the nuclear age in the 1950s there was certainly a period of chaos. Are we now in a period of adjustment? Are we moving to a new age and, if so, what will be the new realities?

During the past several decades new attitudes have become increasingly important. We know through evolutionary studies, for example, that all living things are evolving (everything in the cosmos, in fact) and that all are interrelated. On our own tiny world homo sapiens does not have dominion over the world or over so-called lower forms of life. The balance of life in our world is precarious; we know, or should know, that we cannot alter our environment without worldwide repercussions and we cannot damage our environment without ultimately harming ourselves.

This holistic view of living things expands to include our concept of the cosmos as expressed by Einstein and others, and applies to the inner world of the human personality as expressed by Freud and other psychologists. Contemporary holistic views of evolving personality, society, the environment, and the cosmos suggest a coming new age that may be called a world in process, a world in which everything is in a continual stage of becoming. Goal-oriented cultures of the past may be replaced by change-oriented cultures of the future. Once people begin viewing their cultural identities as journeys rather than as destinations, the new age may have begun.

In this and the following chapters we will consider the contributions of Einstein and Freud, the Electronic Age, the Global Village, and the reactions of many artists to the chaos, adjustment, and new directions of the twentieth century.

Einstein and Relativity

The old social order had ended in 1918 but the predictable world-machine described by Newtonian science had ended even earlier. In 1900 Max Planck (1858–1947) took a major step away from visible perceptions of the physical world to a theory that described the microcosmos by using mathematical abstractions. While studying the radiant energy given off by heated bodies, Planck discovered that energy radiated not in unbroken streams but in discontinuous bits or portions that he called *quanta*. In terms of both emission and absorption of atomic and subatomic particles, Planck hypothesized that the energy transfer was discontinuous and involved a unit of energy (quantum) that could be calculated using what is called Planck's Constant. He concluded that the energy in each quantum could be computed by using the equation $E = hv$, in which v is the frequency of the radiation and h is Planck's Constant. Roughly a decimal point followed by 26 zeroes and ending in 6624, this miniscule number remains one of nature's most fundamental constants.

In conjunction with Quantum Theory, Werner Heisenberg (1901–1976) developed, in 1927, his "Principle of Uncertainty," which states, in effect, that theory can accurately predict the behavior of statistically large numbers of particles but not the behavior of individual particles. Using principles now known to science, it is impossible to simultaneously determine the position and velocity of, for example, an electron. If the position is observed, that act of observing will alter its velocity and, conversely, the more accurate the determination of its velocity the more indefinite is the position of the electron. The old science relied on a study of cause and effect (or causality and determinism) but the Principle of Uncertainty undermined these formerly sturdy pillars. In philosophy, the uncertainty of cause and effect in the physical world led to renewed arguments for the existence of free will. If physical events cannot be determined precisely and cannot be predicted, then perhaps the still relatively unknown capabilities of the human intellect might be a decisive factor in the destiny of humankind.

Albert Einstein (1879–1955) postulated that light photons were also quanta and went on to develop his Special Theory of Relativity (1905). In essence, his Special Theory rests on the hypothesis that neither space nor time has an objective reality. Space is an arrangement of perceived objects and time has no independent existence apart from our measurements of a sequence of events. Our clocks are geared to our solar system. What we call an hour is actually a measurement of an arc of 15 degrees in space based on the apparent movement of the sun. A year is, therefore, the time it takes the earth to orbit the sun, which is 365¼ days. Mercury has an 88-day year and other planets have their own time frame. As Einstein said, time is subjective and based on how people remember events as a sequence of "earlier" and "later," associating a greater number with the later event, an association that is defined by means of a clock.

In particular, Einstein's Special Theory stipulates that the velocity of light is constant for all uniformly moving systems anywhere in the universe. There is neither absolute space nor absolute time but the velocity of light is the absolute speed limit of the universe. There can be no fixed interval of time independent of the system to which it is referred nor can there be simultaneity independent of an established reference. Einstein assumes, for example, that there is an observer seated beside a railroad track who sees a bolt of lightning at the far left (bolt A) and another at the far right (bolt B). Assuming that the observer is positioned precisely between A and B, the bolts will be perceived as simultaneous because all events have the same frame of reference. Now, assume that a train is moving along the track from right to left at the brisk speed of light (186,284 miles/second) and that another observer (2) is riding on the top of the train. Assume, further, that observer 2 is exactly opposite observer 1 at the precise moment that bolts A and B strike. Observer 2 will perceive bolt A

but not bolt B. The train is moving away from bolt B at the speed of light, meaning that the light waves of bolt B will never catch up with the train. Observer 2 is in a different frame of reference than is observer 1.

Based on his Special Theory, Einstein determined that with an increase in velocity, the mass of an object will also increase relative to an observer. Because motion is a form of kinetic energy, the increase in motion that leads to an increase in mass means that the mass has increased in energy. Einstein computed the value of the equivalent mass (m) in any unit of energy (e), leading to the equation that mass is equal to its energy over the square of the speed of light (c^2), or $m = e/c^2$. The remaining algebraic step results in the equation $e = mc^2$, the most famous equation of our age. As Einstein demonstrated mathematically, mass and energy were equivalent. What we normally call mass is concentrated energy that, with the proper trigger, can be released. The detonation of the first atomic device at Alamogordo, New Mexico, on July 16, 1945, demonstrated the transmutation of matter into energy in the forms of light, heat, sound, and motion.

Newton's laws still satisfactorily explain phenomena based on human experiences but they are too limited for modern physics. Einstein's laws of motion are based on the relativity of distance, time, and mass, what he called the "four-dimensional space-time continuum," that is, three dimensions of space and one of time. Relativity thus gives scientists the means to accurately and completely describe the workings of nature.

Einstein later expanded his system into the General Theory of Relativity in which he examined what it is that guides all moving systems. His Special Theory had stated that the velocity of light was constant for all uniformly moving systems. His General Theory is broader and states that the laws of nature are the same for all systems regardless of their states of motion. The basic premise of his Special Theory held true, that all motion, uniform or nonuniform, had to be judged within some system of reference because absolute motion did not exist. He could not, however, distinguish between the motion caused by inertial forces (acceleration, centrifugal forces, etc.) and motion caused by gravitation. This led to his Principle of the Equivalence of Gravitation and Inertia, a new theory of gravitation more accurate and complete than Newton's Law of Universal Gravitation. Newton had postulated gravitation as a force or attraction but Einstein's Law of Gravitation simply describes the behavior of objects in a gravitational field by describing the paths they follow.

Gravitation, for Einstein, was a form of inertia, leading him to conclude that light, like any material body, was subject to gravitation when passing through a very strong gravitational field. He then proved that light travels in a predictable curve given sufficient gravitational pull. Einstein's universe has no straight lines. Euclidian geometry defines a straight line as the shortest distance between two points but, in space, there are only vast circles delineating all of space that, though it is finite, is unbounded.

As Einstein observed, Relativity defined the outer limits of our knowledge and Quantum Theory defined the inner limits. What bothered him was that the two systems are unrelated to each other: "The idea that there are two structures of space independent of each other, the metric-gravitational and the electromagnetic is intolerable to the theoretical spirit." A persistent believer in the fundamental uniformity and harmony of nature, Einstein devoted the latter part of his career to a search for a Unified Field Theory that would construct a bridge between Relativity and Quantum Mechanics. The search continues.

Freud and the Inner World

Though he had written his celebrated *The Interpretation of Dreams* in 1900 and *The Psychopathology of Everyday Life* in 1904, the psychological theories of Sigmund Freud (1856–1939) did not become influential until after World War I. A rational social and humanitarian scientist, Freud developed cogent theories of the role of the unconscious in human actions and the irrational aspects of human behavior. Though there have been subsequent modifications of some of his theories, Freudian psychology remains one of the dominant systems of the century.

Freud evolved a theory of the tripartite personality consisting of the id, ego, and superego. There are no clear boundaries between these concepts but each can be described in isolation. Representing our biological endowment, the id (Latin, "it") resides in our unconscious as an amalgam of our drives and instincts. Hunger, thirst, elimination, and sex are some of the drives that compel us to avoid pain and to seek pleasure through gratification. Either through action or wish fulfillment pentup energy is discharged and tension relieved. Freud considered life and love as positive life forces (libido or Eros) and aggressiveness, destruction, and the death wish as negative forces.

The ego is the reality principle, the thinking, conscious self that interacts with objective reality. The well-developed ego controls the id, determining when and how instinctive drives are satisfied.

The superego is a combination of the moral code of the parents and the person, a kind of conscience that is a product of socialization and cultural traditions. Motivated by fear of punishment and desire for approval, the superego can be perhaps best described as a synthesis of the ego-ideal and conscience. The psychological rewards for the superego are feelings of pride and accomplishment; psychological punishment causes feelings of guilt and inferiority.

The well-balanced personality has a strong ego generally in control of the id and superego, restraining the id while recognizing the censorship of the superego. A neurotic person has lost some control, for whatever reason, over conscious actions, giving in to aggressive instincts from the id, or succumbing to feelings of guilt and inferiority exacted by the superego. Psychosis is a serious mental illness in which the patient has lost all touch with reality.

Freud invented what he called psychoanalysis, a systematic therapy for the treatment of neurosis. The task of the analyst was to help the patient uncover repressed matter, mainly through free association and the interpretation of dreams. Essentially, the analyst assisted the patient in understanding the reasons for abnormal behavior; once the patient uncovered the repressions that caused undesirable actions, the ego could consciously deal with the problem. Recognition of the basic problem(s) would help restore emotional balance.

Partly because he treated mostly neurotic patients, and partly because any new idea is likely to carry its originator to extremes, Freud rode his interpretations very hard in one particular direction. For him, practically all of the mental disorders that he treated were ultimately traceable to one basic frustration: the denial of the life force, the libido—that is, the sexual drive. All symbols were apparently, for him, reducible to sexual symbols. Freud's discovery that sexuality goes far back into childhood, even infancy, was a radical departure from the views of his day. It is, therefore, quite understandable that the sexual factor should loom so large in his investigations, for there is no one of the human drives that is so hedged about with all sorts of taboos. Even in our own time, which is supposedly sexually liberated, there are a variety of sexual mores, both in the ways one should act and the ways in which one should not.

Later psychologists have pointed out that human beings are motivated by, in addition to sex, social and cultural factors and their interpersonal relationship with their analyst. Freud, however, has not been entirely superseded; we have derived many benefits from his work. He challenged the mechanistic view of human personality by insisting that human beings were complex individuals and not simply power switchboards; by so doing he opened the way for later humanistic psychology. Freud also brought the whole problem of mental and emotional well-being or illness to the attention of society. Even in his time mental illness was frequently regarded as possession of the mind by evil spirits or, at best, a disgraceful condition that should be hidden away or locked up in a madhouse. Mental patients were treated like lepers, shut away and forgotten. Freud changed all that by demonstrating that emotionally disturbed individuals were truly ill and that their illness could be treated. Though his intimate knowledge of human nature made him critical and pessimistic he was convinced, nevertheless, that knowledge gained through scientific investigation was the best way to understand and deal with the human condition.

Literary Selection

CIVILIZATION AND ITS DISCONTENTS
Sigmund Freud (1856–1939)

Freud had long been disturbed about negative aspects of the sex drive such, for example, as sadism. For him love did indeed "make the world go around" while sadism, though it was related to Eros, was aggressively destructive. How can the goodness of Eros be reconciled with the cruelty of sadism? The answer, as Freud points out in the following selection, is that life-enhancing Eros has an antithesis that seeks to destroy life. He calls the latter an instinct for death, a death wish that is forever locked in combat with the positive life-force of Eros. Sadism is therefore a manifestation of the aggressiveness of the death wish, a perversion of Eros, erotic but destructive. Furthermore, Freud points out, there are nonerotic aggressive instincts that threaten the stability of the individual and even that of society itself. His view of the aggressive, destructive instinct as a threat to civilization underscores the pervasive pessimism of the period between world wars, not to mention our own age.

VI

Never before in any of my previous writings have I had the feeling so strongly as I have now that what I am describing is common knowledge . . . that I am using up paper and ink to expound things which are self-evident. If it should appear that the recognition of a special independent instinct of aggression would entail a modification of the psycho-analytical theory of instincts, I should be glad to seize upon the idea.

We shall see that this is not so, that it is merely a matter of coming to grips with a conclusion to which we long ago committed ourselves, following it to its logical consequences. Analytic theory has evolved gradually enough, but the theory of instincts has groped its way forward. And yet that theory was so indispensable that something had to be put in its place. In my perplexity I made my starting point Schiller's aphorism that hunger and love make the world go around. Hunger represents the instinct for self-preservation while love strives after objects; its chief function is preservation of the species. Thus first arose the contrast between ego instincts and object instincts. To denote the energy of the latter I introduced the term "libido." An antithesis was thus formed between the ego instincts and the libidinal instincts directed towards objects, i.e., love in its widest sense. One of these object instincts, the sadistic, stood out in that its aim was so very unloving; moreover, it clearly allied itself with the ego instincts, and its kinship with instincts of mastery without libidinal purpose could not be concealed. Nevertheless, sadism plainly belonged to sexual life—the game of cruelty could take the place of the game of love. Neurosis appeared as the outcome of a struggle between self-preservation and libido, a conflict in which the ego was victorious but at the price of great suffering.

Modifications in this theory became essential as our inquiries advanced from the repressed to the repressing forces, from the object instincts to the ego. The decisive step was the introduction of the concept of narcissism, i.e., the discovery that the ego is cathected with libido, that the ego is the libido's original home and, to some extent, its headquarters. This narcissistic libido turns towards objects, becoming object libido, and can change back into narcissistic libido. The concept of narcissism made possible an analytic understanding of the traumatic neuroses as well as many diseases bordering on the psychoses. It was not necessary to abandon the view that the transference-neuroses are attempts of the ego to guard itself against sexuality but the concept of the libido was jeopardized. Since the ego instincts, too, were libidinal, it seemed inevitable that we should make libido coincide with instinctual energy in general, as Jung had already advocated. Yet I retained a groundless conviction that the instincts could not all be of the same kind. It was in *Beyond the Pleasure Principle* (1920) that the repetition-compulsion and the conservative character of instinctual life first struck me. While speculating on the origin of life and of biological parallels, I concluded that, beside the instinct preserving the organic substance and binding it into ever larger units, there must exist an antithesis, which would seek to dissolve these units and reinstate their antecedent inorganic state; that is, a death instinct as well as Eros. The phenomena of life would be explicable from the interplay and counteracting effects of the two. Demonstrating the working of this hypothetical death instinct was not easy. Manifestations of Eros were conspicuous enough; one might assume that the death instinct worked within the organism towards its disintegration but that was no proof. A more fruitful idea was that part of the instinct is diverted towards the external world and surfaces as an instinct of aggressiveness and destructiveness. In this way the instinct could serve Eros in that the organism was destroying something other than itself. One can suspect that the two kinds of instinct seldom—perhaps never—appear in isolation from each other, but are alloyed with each other in varying and very different proportions. In sadism, long known to us as a component instinct of sexuality, we observe a particularly strong alloy between trends of love and the destructive instinct; while its counterpart, masochism, would be a union between destructiveness directed inwards and sexuality.

The assumption of the existence of an instinct of death or destruction has met with resistance even in analytic circles; I am aware that there is a frequent inclination rather to ascribe whatever is dangerous and hostile in love to an original bipolarity in its own nature. To begin with it was only tentatively that I put forth the views I have developed here, but in the course of time they have gained such a hold upon me that I can no longer think in any other way. To my mind, they are far more serviceable from a theoretical viewpoint than any other possible ones; they provide that simplification, without either ignoring or doing violence to the facts, for which we strive in scientific work. I know that in sadism and masochism we have always seen before us manifestations of the destructive instinct (directed outwards and inwards), strongly alloyed with erotism; but I can no longer understand how we can have overlooked the ubiquity of non-erotic aggressivity and destructiveness and can have failed to give it its due place in our interpretation of life. I remember my own defensive attitude when the idea of an instinct of destruction first emerged in psycho-analytic literature, and how long it took before I became receptive to it. That others should have shown, and still show, the same attitude of rejection surprises me less. For "little children do not like it" when there is talk of the inborn human inclination to "badness," to aggressiveness and destructiveness, and so to cruelty as well. God has made them in the image of His own perfection; nobody wants to be reminded how hard it is to reconcile the undeniable existence of evil—despite the protestations of Christian Science—with His all-powerfulness or His all-goodness.

The name "libido" can once more be used to denote the manifestations of the power of Eros in order to distinguish them from the energy of the death instinct. It must be confessed that we have much greater difficulty in grasping that instinct; we can only suspect it, as it were, as something in the background behind Eros, and it escapes detection unless its presence is betrayed by its being alloyed with Eros. It is in sadism, where the death instinct twists the erotic in its own sense and yet at the same time fully satisfies the erotic urge, that we succeed in obtaining the clearest insight into its nature and its relation to Eros. But even where it emerges without any sexual purpose, in the blindest fury of destructiveness, we cannot fail to recognize that the satisfaction of the instinct is accompanied by an extraordinarily high degree of narcissistic enjoyment, owing to its presenting the ego with a fulfillment of the latter's old wishes for omnipotence. The instinct of destruction, moderated and tamed, and, as it were, inhibited in its aim, must, when it is directed towards objects, provide the ego with the satisfaction of its vital needs and with control over nature. This is how things appear to us now; future research and reflection will no doubt bring further light which will decide the matter.

In all that follows I adopt the viewpoint, therefore, that the inclination to aggression is an original, self-subsisting instinctual disposition in man, and that it constitutes the greatest impediment to civilization. At one point I was led to the idea that civilization was a special process in the service of Eros, whose purpose is to combine single human individuals, and after that families, then races, peoples and nations, into one great unity, the unity of mankind. Why this has to happen, we do not know; the work of Eros is precisely this. These collections of men are to be libidinally bound to one another. Necessity alone, the advantages of work in common, will not hold them together. But man's aggressive instinct, the hostility of each against all and of all against each, opposes this programme of civilization. This aggressive instinct is the derivative and the main representative of the death instinct which we have found alongside of Eros and which shares world-dominion with it. And now, I think, the meaning of the evolution of civilization is no longer obscure to us. It must present the struggle between Eros and Death, between the instinct of life and the instinct of destruction as it works itself out in the human species.

Exercises

1. Discuss the difference between ego instincts and object instincts.
2. How does Freud explain sadism and masochism?
3. Try explaining the strains of contemporary society in terms of the struggle between Eros and Death.

Whatever illusions the nineteenth century may have preserved about the perfectability of human behavior and human institutions perished during the four dreadful years of World War I. Much of the art and literature of the postwar period reflected a profound pessimism, a feeling that Western civilization carried the seeds of its own destruction. (See the Dada art movement in chap. 25.) The following poems and essays express some of the prevailing sentiments, some of the loneliness, alienation, and despair experienced by the postwar generation. And little did anyone know that within less than a generation, the Great War was to receive a number.

Literary Selections

THE LOVE SONG OF J. ALFRED PRUFROCK
Thomas Stearns Eliot (1888–1965)

Written in England around the beginning of World War I, *Prufrock* is a dramatic monologue of a middle-aged and frustrated social misfit who is vainly trying to adjust to a petty and superficial society. The larger perspective is that of bankrupt idealism, a decaying of nations, societies, and religious institutions. With juxtaposed images enlarged by dramatic echoes of Hesiod, Dante, and Shakespeare, Eliot builds a mood of futility and despair.

S'io credesse che mia risposta fosse
A persona che mai tornasse al mondo,
Questa fiamma staria senza piu scosse.
Ma perciocche giammai di questo fondo
Non torno vivo alcun s'i'odo il vero,
Senza tema d'infamia ti rispondo.[1]

Let us go then, you and I,
When the evening is spread out against the sky
Like a patient etherized upon a table;
Let us go, through certain half-deserted streets,
The muttering retreats
Of restless nights in one-night cheap hotels
And sawdust restaurants with oyster-shells:
Streets that follow like a tedious argument
Of insidious intent
To lead you to an overwhelming question . . .   10
Oh, do not ask, 'What is it?'
Let us go and make our visit.

In the room the women come and go
Talking of Michelangelo.

The yellow fog that rubs its back upon the window-panes,
The yellow smoke that rubs its muzzle on the window-
     panes
Licked its tongue into the corners of the evening,
Lingered upon the pools that stand in drains,
Let fall upon its back the soot that falls from chimneys,
Slipped by the terrace, made a sudden leap,   20
And seeing that it was a soft October night,
Curled once about the house, and fell asleep.

---

1. "If I thought I were making answer to one that might return to view the world, this flame should evermore cease shaking. But since from the abyss, if I hear true, none ever came alive, I have no fear of infamy, but give thee answer due." The speaker is Guido da Montefeltro, who was condemned to Hell as a Counsellor of Fraud (Dante, *Inferno,* XXVII, 61–66). Dante had asked him why he was being punished and Guido, still fearful of what might be said about him, answers truthfully because he thinks Dante is also dead. Prufrock, like Guido, is fearful of society's judgment.

And indeed there will be time
For the yellow smoke that slides along the street,
Rubbing its back upon the window-panes;
There will be time, there will be time
To prepare a face to meet the faces that you meet;
There will be time to murder and create,
And time for all the works and days of hands²
That lift and drop a question on your plate;   30
Time for you and time for me,
And time yet for a hundred indecisions,
And for a hundred visions and revisions,
Before the taking of a toast and tea.

In the room the women come and go
Talking of Michelangelo.

And indeed there will be time
To wonder, 'Do I dare?' and, 'Do I dare?'
Time to turn back and descend the stair,
With a bald spot in the middle of my hair—   40
(They will say: 'How his hair is growing thin!')
My morning coat, my collar mounting firmly to the chin,
My necktie rich and modest, but asserted by a simple
        pin—
(They will say: 'But how his arms and legs are thin!')
Do I dare
Disturb the universe?
In a minute there is time
For decisions and revisions which a minute will reverse.

For I have known them all already, known them all:—
Have known the evenings, mornings, afternoons,   50
I have measured out my life with coffee spoons;
I know the voices dying with a dying fall
Beneath the music from a farther room.
        So how should I presume?

And I have known the eyes already, known them all—
The eyes that fix you in a formulated phrase,
And when I am formulated, sprawling on a pin,
When I am pinned and wriggling on the wall,
Then how should I begin
To spit out all the butt-ends of my days and ways?   60
        And how should I presume?

And I have known the arms already, known them all—
Arms that are braceleted and white and bare
(But in the lamplight, downed with light brown hair!)
Is it perfume from a dress
That makes me so digress?
Arms that lie along a table, or wrap about a shawl.
        And should I then presume?
        And how should I begin?

        . . . . .

Shall I say, I have gone at dusk through narrow
        streets   70
And watched the smoke that rises from the pipes
Of lonely men in shirt-sleeves, leaning out of
        windows? . . .

I should have been a pair of ragged claws
Scuttling across the floors of silent seas.

        . . . . .

And the afternoon, the evening, sleeps so peacefully!
Smoothed by long fingers,
Asleep . . . tired . . . or it malingers,
Stretched on the floor, here beside you and me.

---

2. *Works and days* recalls Hesiod's poem entitled *Works and Days* (ca. 750 B.C.). Ironically contrasting with Prufrock's frivolous world, Hesiod's poem extols the virtues of hard labor on the land.

Should I, after tea and cakes and ices,
Have the strength to force the moment to its crisis?   80
But though I have wept and fasted, wept and prayed,
Though I have seen my head (grown slightly bald)
        brought in upon a platter,
I am no prophet—and here's no great matter;³
I have seen the moment of my greatness flicker,
And I have seen the eternal Footman hold my coat, and
        snicker,
And in short, I was afraid.

And would it have been worth it, after all,
After the cups, the marmalade, the tea,
Among the porcelain, among some talk of you and me,
Would it have been worth while,   90
To have bitten off the matter with a smile,
To have squeezed the universe into a ball⁴
To roll it toward some overwhelming question,
To say: 'I am Lazarus, come from the dead,⁵
Come back to tell you all, I shall tell you all'—
If one, settling a pillow by her head,
        Should say: That is not what I meant at all,
        That is not it, at all.

        . . . . .

And would it have been worth it, after all,
Would it have been worth while,   100
After the sunsets and the dooryards and the sprinkled
        streets,
After the novels, after the teacups, after the skirts that trail
        along the floor—
And this, and so much more?—
It is impossible to say just what I mean!
But as if a magic lantern threw the nerves in patterns on a
        screen:
Would it have been worth while
If one, settling a pillow or throwing off a shawl,
And turning toward the window, should say:
        'That is not it at all,
        That is not what I meant, at all.'   110

        . . . . .

No! I am not Prince Hamlet, nor was meant to be;
Am an attendant lord, one that will do
To swell a progress, start a scene or two,
Advise the prince; no doubt, an easy tool,⁶
Deferential, glad to be of use,
Politic, cautious, and meticulous;
Full of high sentence, but a bit obtuse;
At times, indeed, almost ridiculous—
Almost, at times, the Fool.
I grow old . . . I grow old . . .   120
I shall wear the bottoms of my trousers rolled.⁷

---

3. *I am no prophet,* i.e., no John the Baptist, who was beheaded by Herod and his head brought in on a tray to please Salome, Herod's stepdaughter (Matthew 14: 3–11). Prufrock views himself as a sacrificial victim but he is neither saint nor martyr.
4. *Universe into a ball* recalls "Let us roll all our strength and all our sweetness up into a ball" from the poem "To a Coy Mistress" by Andrew Marvell (see chap. 17). Prufrock's attempt to raise the conversation to a cosmic level with an allusion to a love poem is doubly ironic; the imaginary lady casually brings the discussion back to trivialities (11. 96–98).
5. *Lazarus* was raised from the grave by Christ (John 11:1–44). Can this society be brought back from the dead?
6. *Advise the prince* apparently refers to Polonius, the king's adviser in *Hamlet.* The cross-reference is to Guido da Montefeltro, also a false counsellor.
7. Cuffed (rolled) trousers were stylish at the time. Middle-aged and socially inept, Prufrock tries to appear young and fashionable.

Shall I part my hair behind? Do I dare to eat a peach?
I shall wear white flannel trousers, and walk upon the
    beach.
I have heard the mermaids singing, each to each.

I do not think that they will sing to me.

I have seen them riding seaward on the waves
Combing the white hair of the waves blown back
When the wind blows the water white and black.

We have lingered in the chambers of the sea
By sea-girls wreathed with seaweed red and brown   130
Till human voices wake us, and we drown.

Exercises

1. What kind of a society is implied in which "the women come and go Talking of Michelangelo" (11. 13–14)?
2. Compare Eliot's references to time in lines 23–26 with the first line of Marvell's "To his Coy Mistress" in chapter 17. How do the meanings differ?
3. What is implied in line 32 by "time yet for a hundred indecisions"?
4. What kind of life has Prufrock led that can be measured "with coffee spoons" (line 51)?
5. Describe, in your own words, Prufrock's physical appearance, personality, and social conduct.

THE SECOND COMING
William Butler Yeats (1865–1939)

This poem, written by Yeats in 1920, conveys a sense of the dissolution of civilization. His image of the cycle of history is a "gyre" (a spiral turning, pronounced with a hard *g*). Imagine a falconer losing control of his falcon as the bird soars in widening circles and eventually breaks away. Lines 4–8 refer to the Russian Revolution of 1917 but they can also be taken as a portent of the rise of fascism in the twenties and thirties. *Spiritus Mundi* is the soul of the universe which connects all human souls in what Yeats calls the "Great Memory," or universal subconscious.

Turning and turning in the widening gyre
The falcon cannot hear the falconer;
Things fall apart: the center cannot hold;
Mere anarchy is loosed upon the world,
The blood-dimmed tide is loosed, and everywhere
The ceremony of innocence is drowned;
The best lack all conviction, while the worst
Are full of passionate intensity.

Surely some revelation is at hand:
Surely the Second Coming is at hand.
The Second Coming! Hardly are those words out
When a vast image out of the *Spiritus Mundi*
Troubles my sight: somewhere in the sands of the desert
A shape with lion body and the head of a man,
A gaze blank and pitiless as the sun,
Is moving its slow thighs, while all about it
Reel shadows of the indignant desert birds.

The darkness drops again; but now I know
That twenty centuries of stony sleep
Were vexed to nightmare by a rocking cradle,
And what rough beast, its hour come round at last,
Slouches towards Bethlehem to be born?

Exercises

1. What does the poet mean, in lines 7 and 8, by the "best" and the "worst"?
2. There is a name for a shape with the head of a man and the body of a lion. What is it and why does Yeats evoke this image?
3. What is the implication of the "rocking cradle"?
4. Describe the feeling aroused by the last two lines of the poem.

DULCE ET DECORUM EST
Wilfred Owen (1893–1918)

Perhaps the most promising English poet to die in the war, Wilfred Owen, unlike most of his contemporaries, saw no honor or glory in a conflict that he referred to as "this deflowering of Europe." The closing quotation of this somber poem is from the poet Horace: "It is sweet and fitting to die for one's country." Owen apparently hoped that this "old lie" would never again lead nations to war. He was killed in action on November 4, 1918, one week before the Armistice that ended the fighting.

Bent double, like old beggars under sacks,
Knock-kneed, coughing like hags, we cursed through
    sludge,
Till on the haunting flares we turned our backs
And towards our distant rest began to trudge.
Men marched asleep. Many had lost their boots   5
But limped on, blood-shod. All went lame; all blind;
Drunk with fatigue; deaf even to the hoots
Of tired, outstripped Five-Nines that dropped behind.

Gas! Gas! Quick, boys!—An ecstasy of fumbling,
Fitting the clumsy helmets just in time;   10
But someone still was yelling out and stumbling
And flound'ring like a man in fire or lime . . .
Dim, through the misty panes and thick green light,
As under a green sea, I saw him drowning.
In all my dreams, before my helpless sight,   15
He plunges at me, guttering, choking, drowning.

If in some smothering dreams you too could pace
Behind the wagon that we flung him in,
And watch the white eyes writhing in his face,
His hanging face, like a devil's sick of sin;   20
If you could hear, at every jolt, the blood
Come gargling from the froth-corrupted lungs,
Obscene as cancer, bitter as the cud
Of vile, incurable sores on innocent tongues,—
My friend, you would not tell with such high zest   25
To children ardent for some desperate glory,
The old Lie: Dulce et decorum est
Pro patria mori.

Exercises

1. Notice the many participles in lines 2 and 3. Is their effect active or passive?
2. Read line 6 aloud while listening to the sounds. How many weak syllables are there? Strong syllables? What is the effect?

SHINE, PERISHING REPUBLIC
Robinson Jeffers (1887–1962)

Postwar America was a world power but Jeffers saw the darker side, a crass and materialistic nation mired "in the mould of its vulgarity." The reader can determine whether the poem, written in 1924, is still apropos.

While this America settles in the mould of its vulgarity,
    heavily thickening to empire.
And protest, only a bubble in the molten mass, pops and
    sighs out, and the mass hardens.
I sadly smiling remember that the flower fades to make
    fruit, the fruit rots to make earth.
Out of the mother; and through the spring exultances,
    ripeness and decadence; and home to the mother.
You making haste haste on decay: not blameworthy; life is
    good, be it stubbornly long or suddenly
A mortal splendor: meteors are not needed less than
    mountains: shine perishing republic.
But for my children, I would have them keep their
    distance from the thickening center: corruption
Never has been compulsory, when the cities lie at the
    monster's feet there are left the mountains.
And boys, be in nothing so moderate as in love of man, a
    clever servant, insufferable master.
There is the trap that catches noblest spirits, that
    caught—they say—God, when he walked on earth.

Exercises

1. Identify the images that refer to the cycle of life and death.
2. What is implied by "meteors are not needed less than mountains"?
3. Jeffers wrote in 1924 that "corruption Never has been compulsory." Does this still apply in the 1980s? Consider, for example, air, water, and noise pollution, especially acid rain. Can we avoid this pollution? Stop it? How?

YET DO I MARVEL
Countee Cullen (1903–1946)

One of the leaders of a 1920s literary movement called the Harlem Renaissance, Cullen can be seen, at first glance, as a voice of moderation compared with black protests since World War II. Cullen's references are from the Western literary tradition (Greek mythology, Dante) and the form is that of a sonnet, but line 12 is derived from the last two lines of "The Tiger" by William Blake: "What immortal hand or eye/Dare frame thy fearful symmetry?" (see chap. 20). Blake asks how a good God can put evil in the world; Cullen ponders a similar question about the evil of racism. The tone is moderate, the sentiment is not.

I doubt not God is good, well-meaning, kind,
And did He stoop to quibble could tell why
The little buried mole continues blind,
Why flesh that mirrors Him must some day die,
Make plain the reason tortured Tantalus   5
Is baited by the fickle fruit, declare
If merely brute caprice dooms Sisyphus
To struggle up a never-ending stair.
Inscrutable His ways are, and immune
To catechism by a mind too strewn   10
With petty cares to slightly understand
What awful brain compels His awful hand.
Yet do I marvel at this curious thing:
To make a poet black, and bid him sing!

                                    1924, 1925

Exercises

1. How many images are there of the way things are? Consider, for example, blind moles, Tantalus, and Sisyphus. (Tantalus was condemned by Zeus to stand up to his chin in water that receded everytime he tried to drink. Above his head hung fruit that the wind kept perpetually out of his reach. His name has given us the verb *tantalize*. The Myth of Sisyphus may be found in chap. 24.)
2. The last line implies that people who can write poetry *must* write poetry. Why is this so? Does the same compulsion hold true for painters, composers, and sculptors? Give some examples.

THE ETHICS OF LIVING JIM CROW, 1937
An Autobiographical Sketch
Richard Wright (1908–1960)

Raised in poverty in Mississippi, Richard Wright became a powerful spokesman for human rights and human dignity at a time when black artists and writers were finally being taken seriously. *Native Son* (1940) is his finest novel, followed by *Black Boy* (1945) and numerous books dealing with America's race problems. Before World War II few white Americans were aware of the effects of Jim Crow laws and customs in the North and, especially, in the South. Though such practices are no longer legal or condoned by responsible citizens, Jim Crow attitudes, both Black and White, persist as a disturbing reality in the long struggle for equal opportunity for all Americans. Neither polemical nor didactic, Wright's reflective essay is an artist's statement about how Jim Crow affected his life.

I

My first lesson in how to live as a Negro came when I was quite small. We were living in Arkansas. Our house stood behind the railroad tracks. Its skimpy yard was paved with black cinders. Nothing green ever grew in that yard. The only touch of green we could see was far away, beyond the tracks, over where the white folks lived. But cinders were good enough for me and I never missed the green growing things. And anyhow cinders were fine weapons. You could always have a nice hot war with huge black cinders. All you had to do was crouch behind the brick pillars of a house with your hands full of gritty ammunition. And the first woolly black head you saw pop out from behind another row of pillars was your target. You tried your very best to knock it off. It was great fun.

I never fully realized the appalling disadvantages of a cinder environment till one day the gang to which I belonged found itself engaged in a war with the white boys who lived beyond the tracks. As usual we laid down our cinder barrage, thinking that this would wipe the white boys out. But they replied with a steady bombardment of broken bottles. We doubled our cinder barrage, but they hid behind trees, hedges, and the sloping embankment of their lawns. Having no such fortifications, we retreated to the brick pillars of our homes. During the retreat a broken milk bottle caught me behind the ear, opening a deep gash which bled profusely. The sight of blood pouring over my face completely demoralized our ranks. My fellow-combatants left me standing paralyzed in the center of the yard, and scurried for their homes. A kind neighbor saw me, and rushed me to a doctor, who took three stitches in my neck.

I sat brooding on my front steps, nursing my wound and waiting for my mother to come from work. I felt that a grave injustice had been done me. It was all right to throw cinders. The greatest harm a cinder could do was leave a bruise. But broken bottles were dangerous; they left you cut, bleeding, and helpless.

When night fell, my mother came from the white folks' kitchen. I raced down the street to meet her. I could just feel in my bones that she would understand. I knew she would tell me exactly what to do next time. I grabbed her hand and babbled out the whole story. She examined my wound, then slapped me.

"How come yuh didn't hide?" she asked me. "How come yuh awways fightin'?"

I was outraged, and bawled. Between sobs I told her that I didn't have any trees or hedges to hide behind. There wasn't a thing I could have used as a trench. And you couldn't throw very far when you were hiding behind the brick pillars of a house. She grabbed a barrel stave, dragged me home, stripped me naked, and beat me till I had a fever of one hundred and two. She would smack my rump with the stave, and, while the skin was still smarting impart to me gems of Jim Crow wisdom. I was never to throw cinders any more. I was never to fight any more wars. I was never, never, under any conditions, to fight white folks again. And they were absolutely right in clouting me with the broken milk bottle. Didn't I know she was working hard every day in the hot kitchens of the white folks to make money to take care of me? When was I ever going to learn to be a good boy? She couldn't be bothered with my fights. She finished by telling me that I ought to be thankful to God as long as I lived that they didn't kill me.

All that night I was delirious and could not sleep. Each time I closed my eyes I saw monstrous white faces suspended from the ceiling, leering at me.

From that time on, the charm of my cinder yard was gone. The green trees, the trimmed hedges, the cropped lawns grew very meaningful, became a symbol. Even today when I think of white folks, the hard, sharp outlines of white houses surrounded by trees, lawns, and hedges are present somewhere in the background of my mind. Through the years they grew into an overreaching symbol of fear.

It was a long time before I came in close contact with white folks again. We moved from Arkansas to Mississippi. Here we had the good fortune not to live behind the railroad tracks, or close to white neighborhoods. We lived in the very heart of the local Black Belt. There were black churches and black preachers; there were black schools and black teachers; black groceries and black clerks. In fact, everything was so solidly black that for a long time I did not even think of white folks, save in remote and vague terms. But this could not last forever. As one grows older one eats more. One's clothing costs more. When I finished grammar school I had to go to work. My mother could no longer feed and clothe me on her cooking job.

There is but one place where a black boy who knows no trade can get a job, and that's where the houses and faces are white, where the trees, lawns, and hedges are green. My first job was with an optical company in Jackson, Mississippi. The morning I applied I stood straight and neat before the boss, answering all his questions with sharp yessirs and nosirs. I was very careful to pronounce my *sirs* distinctly, in order that he might know that I was polite, that I knew where I was, and that I knew he was a *white* man. I wanted that job badly.

He looked me over as though he were examining a prize poodle. He questioned me closely about my schooling, being particularly insistent about how much mathematics I had had. He seemed very pleased when I told him I had had two years of algebra.

"Boy, how would you like to try to learn something around here?" he asked me.

"I'd like it fine, sir," I said, happy. I had visions of "working my way up." Even Negroes have those visions.

"All right," he said. "Come on."

I followed him to the small factory.

"Pease," he said to a white man of about thirty-five, "this is Richard. He's going to work for us."

Pease looked at me and nodded.

I was then taken to a white boy of about seventeen.

"Morrie, this is Richard, who's going to work for us."

"Whut yuh sayin' there, boy!" Morrie boomed at me.

"Fine!" I answered.

The boss instructed these two to help me, teach me, give me jobs to do, and let me learn what I could in my spare time.

My wages were five dollars a week.

I worked hard, trying to please. For the first month I got along O.K. Both Pease and Morrie seemed to like me. But one thing was missing. And I kept thinking about it. I was not learning anything and nobody was volunteering to help me. Thinking they had forgotten that I was to learn something about the mechanics of grinding lenses, I asked Morrie one day to tell me about the work. He grew red.

"Whut yuh tryin 't' do, nigger, get smart?" he asked.

"Naw; I ain' tryin' t' git smart," I said.

"Well, don't, if yuh know whut's good for yuh!"

I was puzzled. Maybe he just doesn't want to help me, I thought. I went to Pease.

"Say, are yuh crazy, you black bastard?" Pease asked me, his gray eyes growing hard.

I spoke out, reminding him that the boss had said I was to be given a chance to learn something.

"Nigger, you think you're *white,* don't you?"

"Naw, sir!"

"Well, you're acting mighty like it!"

"But, Mr. Pease, the boss said . . ."

Pease shook his fist in my face.

"This is a *white* man's work around here, and you better watch yourself!"

From then on they changed toward me. They said good-morning no more. When I was just a bit slow in performing some duty, I was called a lazy black son-of-a-bitch.

Once I thought of reporting all this to the boss. But the mere idea of what would happen to me if Pease and Morrie should learn that I had "snitched" stopped me. And after all the boss was a white man, too. What was the use?

The climax came at noon one summer day. Pease called me to his workbench. To get to him I had to go between two narrow benches and stand with my back against a wall.

"Yes sir," I said.

"Richard, I want to ask you something," Pease began pleasantly, not looking up from his work.

"Yes, sir," I said again.

Morrie came over, blocking the narrow passage between the benches. He folded his arms, staring at me solemnly.

I looked from one to the other, sensing that something was coming.

"Yes, sir," I said for the third time.

Pease looked up and spoke very slowly.

"Richard, *Mr.* Morrie here tells me you called me *Pease.*"

I stiffened. A void seemed to open up in me. I knew this was the showdown.

He meant that I had failed to call him Mr. Pease. I looked at Morrie. He was gripping a steel bar in his hands. I opened my mouth to speak, to protest, to assure Pease that I had never called him simply *Pease,* and that I had never had any intentions of doing so, when Morrie grabbed me by the collar, ramming my head against the wall.

"Now be careful, nigger!" snarled Morrie, baring his teeth. "*I* heard yuh call 'im *Pease!* 'N' if yuh say yuh didn't, yuh're callin' me a *lie,* see?" He waved the steel bar threateningly.

If I had said: No, sir, Mr. Pease, I never called you *Pease* I would have been automatically calling Morrie a liar. And if I had said: Yes, sir, Mr. Pease, I called you *Pease,* I would have been pleading guilty to having uttered the worst insult that a Negro can utter to a southern white man. I stood hesitating, trying to frame a neutral reply.

"Richard, I asked you a question!" said Pease. Anger was creeping into his voice.

"I don't remember calling you *Pease,* Mr. Pease," I said cautiously. "And if I did, I sure didn't mean . . ."

"You black son-of-a-bitch! You called me *Pease,* then!" he spat, slapping me till I bent sideways over a bench. Morrie was on top of me, demanding:

"Didn't you call 'im *Pease?* If yuh say yuh didn't, I'll rip yo' gut string loose with this bar, yuh black granny

dodger! Yuh can't call a white man a lie 'n' git erway with it, you black son-of-a-bitch!"

I wilted. I begged them not to bother me. I knew what they wanted. They wanted me to leave.

"I'll leave," I promised. "I'll leave right *now.*"

They gave me a minute to get out of the factory. I was warned not to show up again, or tell the boss.

I went.

When I told the folks at home what had happened, they called me a fool. They told me that I must never again attempt to exceed my boundaries. When you are working for white folks, they said, you got to "stay in your place" if you want to keep working.

II

My Jim Crow education continued on my next job, which was portering in a clothing store. One morning, while polishing brass out front, the boss and his twenty-year-old son got out of their car and half dragged and half kicked a Negro woman into the store. A policeman standing at the corner looked on, twirling his nightstick. I watched out of the corner of my eye, never slackening the strokes of my chamois upon the brass. After a few minutes, I heard shrill screams coming from the rear of the store. Later the woman stumbled out, bleeding, crying, and holding her stomach. When she reached the end of the block, the policeman grabbed her and accused her of being drunk. Silently, I watched him throw her into a patrol wagon.

When I went to the rear of the store, the boss and his son were washing their hands at the sink. They were chuckling. The floor was bloody and strewn with wisps of hair and clothing. No doubt I must have appeared pretty shocked, for the boss slapped me reassuringly on the back.

"Boy, that's what we do to niggers when they don't want to pay their bills," he said, laughing.

His son looked at me and grinned.

"Here, hava cigarette," he said.

Not knowing what to do, I took it. He lit his and held the match for me. This was a gesture of kindness, indicating that even if they had beaten the poor old woman, they would not beat me if I knew enough to keep my mouth shut.

"Yes, sir," I said, and asked no questions.

After they had gone, I sat on the edge of a packing box and stared at the bloody floor till the cigarette went out.

That day at noon, while eating in a hamburger joint, I told my fellow Negro porters what had happened. No one seemed surprised. One fellow, after swallowing a huge bite, turned to me and asked:

"Huh! Is tha' all they did t' her?"

"Yeah. Wasn't tha' enough?" I asked.

"Shucks! Man, she's a lucky bitch!" he said, burying his lips deep into a juicy hamburger. "Hell, it's a wonder they didn't lay her when they got through."

III

I was learning fast, but not quite fast enough. One day, while I was delivering packages in the suburbs, my bicycle tire was punctured. I walked along the hot, dusty road, sweating and leading my bicycle by the handlebars. A car slowed at my side.

"What's the matter, boy?" a white man called.

I told him my bicycle was broken and I was walking back to town.

"That's too bad," he said. "Hop on the running board."

He stopped the car. I clutched hard at my bicycle with one hand and clung to the side of the car with the other.

"All set?"

"Yes, sir," I answered. The car started.

It was full of young white men. They were drinking. I watched the flask pass from mouth to mouth.

"Wanna drink, boy?" one asked.

I laughed as the wind whipped my face. Instinctively obeying the freshly planted precepts of my mother, I said:

"Oh, no!"

The words were hardly out of my mouth before I felt something hard and cold smash me between the eyes. It was an empty whisky bottle. I saw stars, and fell backwards from the speeding car into the dust of the road, my feet becoming entangled in the steel spokes of my bicycle. The white men piled out and stood over me.

"Nigger, ain' yuh learned no better sense'n tha' yet?" asked the man who hit me. "Ain' yuh learned t' say *sir* t' a white man yet?"

Dazed, I pulled to my feet. My elbows and legs were bleeding. Fists doubled, the white man advanced, kicking my bicycle out of the way.

"Aw, leave the bastard alone. He's got enough," said one.

They stood looking at me. I rubbed my shins, trying to stop the flow of blood. No doubt they felt a sort of contemptuous pity, for one asked:

"Yuh wanna ride t' town now, nigger? Yuh reckon yuh know enough t' ride now?"

"I wanna walk," I said, simply.

Maybe it sounded funny. They laughed.

"Well, walk, yuh black son-of-a-bitch!"

When they left they comforted me with:

"Nigger, yuh sho better be dawn glad it wuz us yuh talked t' tha' way. Yuh're a lucky bastard, 'cause if yuh'd said tha' t' somebody else, yuh might've been a dead nigger now."

IV

Negroes who have lived South know the dread of being caught alone upon the streets in white neighborhoods after the sun has set. In such a simple situation as this the plight of the Negro in America is graphically symbolized. While white strangers may be in these neighborhoods trying to get home, they can pass unmolested. But the color of a Negro's skin makes him easily recognizable, makes him suspect, converts him into a defenseless target.

Late one Saturday night I made some deliveries in a white neighborhood. I was pedaling my bicycle back to the store as fast as I could, when a police car, swerving toward me, jammed me into the curbing.

"Get down and put up your hands!" the policemen ordered.

I did. They climbed out of the car, guns drawn, faces set, and advanced slowly.

"Keep still!" they ordered.

I reached my hands higher. They searched my pockets and packages. They seemed dissatisfied when they could find nothing incriminating. Finally, one of them said:

"Boy, tell your boss not to send you out in white neighborhoods after sundown."

As usual, I said:

"Yes, sir."

V

My next job was as hall-boy in a hotel. Here my Jim Crow education broadened and deepened. When the bell-boys were busy, I was often called to assist them. As many of the rooms in the hotel were occupied by prostitutes, I was constantly called to carry them liquor and cigarettes. These women were nude most of the time. They did not bother about clothing, even for bell-boys. When you went into their rooms, you were supposed to take their nakedness for granted, as though it startled you no more than a blue vase or a red rug. Your presence awoke in them no sense of shame, for you were not regarded as human. If they were alone, you could steal side-long glimpses at them. But if they were receiving men, not a flicker of your eyelids could show. I remember one incident vividly. A new woman, a huge, snowy-skinned blonde, took a room on my floor. I was sent to wait upon her. She was in bed with a thick-set man; both were nude and uncovered. She said she wanted some liquor and slid out of bed and waddled across the floor to get her money from a dresser drawer. I watched her.

"Nigger, what in hell you looking at?" the white man asked me, raising himself upon his elbows.

"Nothing," I answered, looking miles deep into the blank wall of the room.

"Keep your eyes where they belong, if you want to be healthy!" he said.

"Yes, sir."

VI

One of the bell-boys I knew in this hotel was keeping steady company with one of the Negro maids. Out of a clear sky the police descended upon his home and arrested him, accusing him of bastardy. The poor boy swore he had had no intimate relations with the girl. Nevertheless, they forced him to marry her. When the child arrived, it was found to be much lighter in complexion than either of the two supposedly legal parents. The white men around the hotel made a great joke of it. They spread the rumor that some white cow must have scared the poor girl while she was carrying the baby. If you were in their presence when this explanation was offered, you were supposed to laugh.

VII

One of the bell-boys was caught in bed with a white prostitute. He was castrated and run out of town. Immediately after this all the bell-boys and hall-boys were called together and warned. We were given to understand that the boy who had been castrated was a "mighty, mighty lucky bastard." We were impressed with the fact that next time the management of the hotel would not be responsible for the lives of "trouble-makin' niggers." We were silent.

VIII

One night, just as I was about to go home, I met one of the Negro maids. She lived in my direction, and we fell in to walk part of the way home together. As we passed the white night-watchman, he slapped the maid on her buttock. I turned around, amazed. The watchman looked at me with a long, hard, fixed-under stare. Suddenly, he pulled his gun and asked:

"Nigger, don't yuh like it?"

I hesitated.

"I asked yuh don't yuh like it?" he asked again, stepping forward.

"Yes, sir," I mumbled.

"Talk like it, then!"

"Oh, yes, sir!" I said with as much heartiness as I could muster.

Outside, I walked ahead of the girl, ashamed to face her. She caught up with me and said:

"Don't be a fool! Yuh couldn't help it!"

This watchman boasted of having killed two Negroes in self-defense.

Yet, in spite of all this, the life of the hotel ran with an amazing smoothness. It would have been impossible for a stranger to detect anything. The maids, the hall-boys, and the bell-boys were all smiles. They had to be.

IX

I had learned my Jim Crow lessons so thoroughly that I kept the hotel job till I left Jackson for Memphis. It so happened that while in Memphis I applied for a job at a branch of the optical company. I was hired. And for some reason, as long as I worked there, they never brought my past against me.

Here my Jim Crow education assumed quite a different form. It was no longer brutally cruel, but subtly cruel. Here I learned to lie, to steal, to dissemble. I learned to play that dual role which every Negro must play if he wants to eat and live.

For example, it was almost impossible to get a book to read. It was assumed that after a Negro had imbibed what scanty schooling the state furnished he had no further need for books. I was always borrowing books from men on the job. One day I mustered enough courage to ask one of the men to let me get books from the library in his name. Surprisingly, he consented. I cannot help but think that he consented because he was a Roman Catholic and felt a vague sympathy for Negroes, being himself an object of hatred. Armed with a library card, I obtained books in the following manner: I would write a note to the librarian, saying: "Please let this nigger boy have the following books." I would then sign it with the white man's name.

When I went to the library, I would stand at the desk, hat in hand, looking as unbookish as possible. When I received the books desired I would take them home. If the books listed in the note happened to be out, I would sneak into the lobby and forge a new one. I never took any chances guessing with the white librarian about what the fictitious white man would want to read. No doubt if any of the white patrons had suspected that some of the volumes they enjoyed had been in the home of a Negro, they would not have tolerated it for an instant.

The factory force of the optical company in Memphis was much larger than that in Jackson, and more urbanized. At least they liked to talk, and would engage the Negro help in conversation whenever possible. By this means I found that many subjects were taboo from the white man's point of view. Among the topics they did not like to discuss with Negroes were the following: American white women; the Ku Klux Klan; France, and how Negro soldiers fared while there; French women; Jack Johnson; the entire northern part of the United States; the Civil War; Abraham Lincoln; U.S. Grant; General Sherman; Catholics; the Pope; Jews; the Republican Party; slavery; social equality; Communism; Socialism; the 13th and 14th Amendments to the Constitution; or any topic calling for positive knowledge or manly self-assertion on the part of the Negro. The most accepted topics were sex and religion.

There were many times when I had to exercise a great deal of ingenuity to keep out of trouble. It is a southern custom that all men must take off their hats when they enter an elevator. And especially did this apply to us blacks with rigid force. One day I stepped into an elevator with my arms full of packages. I was forced to ride with my hat on. Two white men stared at me coldly. Then one of them very kindly lifted my hat and placed it upon my armful of packages. Now the most accepted response for a Negro to make under such circumstances is to look at the white man out of the corner of his eye and grin. To have said: "Thank you!" would have made the white man *think* that you *thought* you were receiving from him a personal service. For such an act I have seen Negroes take a blow in the mouth. Finding the first alternative distasteful, and the second dangerous, I hit upon an acceptable course of action which fell safely between these two poles. I immediately—no sooner than my hat was lifted—pretended that my packages were about to spill, and appeared deeply distressed with keeping them in my arms. In this fashion I evaded having to acknowledge his service, and, in spite of adverse circumstance, salvaged a single shred of personal pride.

How do Negroes feel about the way they have to live? How do they discuss it when alone among themselves? I think this question can be answered in a single sentence. A friend of mine who ran an elevator once told me:

"Lawd, man! Ef it wuzn't fer them polices 'n' them ol' lynchmobs, there wouldn't be nothin' but uproar down here!"

Exercises

Near the end of this essay the author lists, as of 1937, the following topics that "were taboo from the white man's point of view": "American white women; the Ku Klux Klan; France, and how Negro soldiers fared while there; French women; Jack Johnson; the entire northern part of the United States; the Civil War; Abraham Lincoln; U. S. Grant; General Sherman; Catholics; the Pope; Jews; the Republican Party; slavery; social equality; Communism; Socialism; the 13th and 14th Amendments to the Constitution."

1. Is this true today and, if so, to what extent?
2. Are some topics no longer applicable and, if so, which ones? Why?
3. Are there any new topics?
4. In your conversations with another person who differs from you—race, religion, sex, nationality—do you find yourself avoiding certain topics? Which topics? Why?

24

Ideas and Conflicts That Motivate the Twentieth Century

Historical Overview, 1939–1980s

The Great Depression following the breakdown of economic systems was "cured" by the escalating production of weapons for war. England and France frantically, and belatedly, prepared for the resumption of hostilities with Germany in a war notably different from any other in mankind's interminable history of violence.

Soldiers fought in fields and pastures in the nineteenth century, in the trenches in 1914–1918, but in 1939–1945 the furious new battlefield described in the poem given below was the air itself. The bomber was the cost-efficient delivery system of World War II; targets included not only opposing armies but myriads of cities and their millions of inhabitants. Whether blasting Berlin and London, fire-bombing Dresden and Tokyo, or nuking Hiroshima and Nagasaki, civilian casualties vastly outnumbered those of the military, and warfare was total. The conflict between Eros and man's aggressive instincts, as described by Freud, seems canted towards the death wish. Mankind appears capable of limitless destruction until there is nothing left to destroy.

THE FURY OF AERIAL BOMBARDMENT
Richard Eberhart (1904–1984)

You would think the fury of aerial bombardment
Would rouse God to relent; the infinite spaces
Are still silent. He then looks on shock-pried faces
History, even, does not know what is meant.

You would feel that after so many centuries
God would give man to repent; yet he can kill
As Cain could, but with multitudinous will,
No farther advanced than in his ancient furies.

Was man made stupid to see his own stupidity?
Is God by definition indifferent, beyond us all?
Is the eternal truth man's fighting soul
Wherein the Beast ravens in its own avidity?

Of Van Wettering I speak, and Averill,
Names on a list, whose faces I do not recall
But they are gone to early death, who late in school
Distinguished the belt feed lever from the belt holding
pawl.

World War II ended on August 14, 1945, with the Japanese surrender, and the whole world expected a new era of peace and stability. The United States, with its nuclear monopoly and enormous industrial capacity, emerged as an unrivaled superpower; having learned some bitter lessons from the League of Nations, the United Nations began to function as the first real consortium of nations; with the assistance of the Marshall Plan, war-ravaged nations launched recovery programs that, in some cases, verged on the miraculous. The new era of peace and stability lasted four years, from 1945 to Russia's detonation of its own atomic bomb in 1949. The sharply reduced power of the Western European nations and the shambles of the old colonial order left a vacuum that was filled by the United States and Russia, now two superpowers who were engaged in a continued struggle for world dominance. Mutual nuclear deterrence, a "balance of terror," has kept nuclear weapons in their silos but so-called conventional wars abounded. If a major war is defined as one in which there are more than a thousand combatants, there have been about 100 major wars since 1945. African and Asian nationalism, endless Middle East crises, the wars in Korea and Vietnam, OPEC, the looming shadow of the People's Republic of China, the litany of the trials and tribulations of our era is endless and yet, somehow, the world blunders on short of Armageddon.

Since World War II the United States has become more democratic, but it hasn't been easy. The so-called Second Reconstruction in American history began in the late 1940s with presidential decrees that banned discrimination in federal jobs and ordered desegregation of the armed forces. The target of the first stage of the civil rights movement, segregation in public education was struck down by the landmark Supreme Court decision of 1954. Despite sometimes violent opposition the nation's schools were gradually integrated while, at the same time, other forms of discrimination were challenged with boycotts, sit-ins, and "freedom rides." Congress enacted, in 1957, the first civil rights legislation since 1865, followed by voting legislation in 1960, and, in 1964, by a comprehensive Civil Rights Act that banned discrimination on the basis of race, sex, nationality, or religion in public places, employment, and unions.

By 1965 the attack on segregation was essentially completed and stage two of the civil rights movement had begun. The rising demand was for equal opportunity, not only for jobs but in every area in American life. Mounting dissatisfaction with ghetto life, *de facto* segregation, and deteriorating urban environments fueled frustrations that writers like Langston Hughes early saw as unbearable. Hughes, the leading writer of the Harlem Renaissance, summed up the smoldering situation in 1951 with a prophetic eleven-line poem:

HARLEM
Langston Hughes (1902–1967)

What happens to a dream deferred?

    Does it dry up
    like a raisin in the sun?
    Or fester like a sore—
    And then run?   5
    Does it stink like rotten meat?
    Or crust and sugar over—
    like a syrupy sweet?

    Maybe it just sags
    like a heavy load.   10

    Or *does it explode?*

Harlem, Detroit, Watts, and other urban centers erupted in the 1960s and extreme violence did not subside until after 1969. Equal opportunity for many Blacks, Hispanics, Native Americans, and other minorities remains a "dream deferred."

During the two decades of civil rights activism other fundamental changes were beginning to quietly transform American life. Once a nation of farmers, the Industrial Revolution made laborers the dominant work force. By the mid 1950s, however, white-collar workers outnumbered blue-collar laborers and, by the early 1980s, the manufacturing work force had dwindled to about 13 percent and farmers to 3 percent of the working population. The United States had shifted from an industrial society to an information society based on high technology; computers, communication satellites, robots, and other electronic hardware and software herald what has been called the Age of Information, the Computer Age, the Communications Age. According to John Naisbitt[1] 75 percent of all jobs will involve computers in some way by about 1985. Smokestack industries like steel, textiles, and shipbuilding will continue to decline in the Western world as heavy industry expands in Third World countries. Alvin Toffler[2] predicts individualized entertainment and information services that will become available to everyone, and a whole new range of social, political, psychological, and religious adaptions throughout the Western world and around the Pacific Basin (Japan, Hong Kong, Singapore, Korea, Taiwan, Australia).

Developing technology tends to follow a line of least resistance. The first book printed with movable type, the Gutenberg Bible, looked like a handwritten manuscript. The first automobiles were called "horseless carriages" because they were indeed carriages with motors. Computer technology first followed two general lines of development: nonthreatening games that tend to make computers "user friendly" and improvements in existing technology like, for example,

---

1. John Naisbitt, *Megatrends: Ten New Directions Transforming Our Lives* (New York: Warner Books, Inc., 1982).
2. Alvin Toffler, *The Third Wave* (New York: William Morrow and Co., 1980).

the word processor. Still to come is a third line of development. No one can really predict the different directions that computers will take except to say that, inevitably, there will be startling new applications of computer technology.

Einstein gave us new conceptions of space, and the age of computers and telecommunications has forced us to recognize space as a concept connected by electronics and not just as a physical reality connected by interstate highways. Telecommunication conferences with participants sitting at video consoles in London, Paris, Rome, and New York are old hat and this is only the beginning. The world has shrunk to a global village. No one can say what the globalization of culture will lead to but the prognosis can be optimistic. The possibility of instantaneous close contact with people and their institutions can lead to closer human ties than at any time in human history.

Philosophy

Probably every philosophical system ever invented has surfaced at one time or another during this troubled century. One of the most influential of these philosophies, existentialism, is more of a mood or attitude than a complete philosophical system. Formulated during World War II by French writer Jean Paul Sartre during his years with the French Resistance, existentialism had an immediate appeal for a desperate world. Actually, the roots of the movement go back to several disparate personalities of the nineteenth century, particularly Kierkegaard, a Danish anticlerical theologian, and Nietzsche, a German atheist.

Friedrich Nietzsche (NEE–chuh; 1844–1900) stressed the absurdity of human existence and the inability of our reason to understand the world. Himself a passionate individualist, Nietzsche proclaimed the will to power as the only value in the face of a meaningless world. He rejected any ideas or system that would limit the freedom of the individual, particularly Christianity, which taught, he contended, a "slave morality" of sympathy, kindness, humility, and pity, qualities beneficial only to the weak and the helpless. His "noble" man was a superman, an incarnate will to power, who would rise above the herd, the "bungled and the botched," to establish a "master morality" of aristocratic qualities like strength, nobility, pride, and power. "God is dead," Nietzsche proclaimed, meaning that all absolute systems from Plato onwards had died with the God of the Judeo-Christian tradition.

A fervent admirer of the culture of ancient Greece, Nietzsche evolved an influential aesthetic theory of the Apollonian and Dionysian modes. The Apollonian mode is intellectual. It draws an aesthetic veil over reality, creating an ideal world of form and beauty. The Apollonian found expression in Greek mythology, in Homer's epic poems, in sculpture, painting, architecture, and Greek vases.

The Dionysian, somewhat like Freud's id, is the dark, turgid, and formless torrent of instinct, impulse, and passion that tends to sweep aside everything in its path. Tragedy and music are typical Dionysian art forms that transmute existence into aesthetic phenomena without, however, drawing a veil over authentic existence. The Dionysian represents existence in aesthetic form and affirms this, says Nietzsche, in the human condition. True culture, for Nietzsche, was a unity of life forces, the dark Dionysian element combined with the love of form and beauty that characterizes the Apollonian. The highest product of this balanced culture is the creative genius, the superman.

Adolf Hitler drew on Nietzsche's purported work, *The Will to Power,* for key ideas about German superiority, the Master Race (Nietzsche's superman), and anti-Semitism. Scholars finally proved, by 1958, that Nietzsche did not write *The Will to Power.* After his death, Nietzsche's proto-Nazi sister combined his notebook jottings with thirty forged letters and other fabrications to publish the volume in her brother's name. Actually, Nietzsche was more anti- than pro-German, referring to Germans as "blond beasts of prey" and casting scorn on "their repulsive habit of stimulating themselves with alcohol." Far from a racist, Nietzsche saw all the races on the globe blending into a uniform color of beige and he called anti-Semites "another name for failures."

The basic theme of Nietzsche's life and thought was the antipolitical individual who sought self-perfection far from the modern world. His desire was "to live for one's education free from politics, nationality, and newspapers." For him, knowledge was power and the will to power was the use of education for the betterment of humankind. "Above all," he said, "become who you are!"

A melancholy and lonely Dane, Soren Kierkegaard (KEER–kuh–gard; 1813–1855) was almost totally unnoticed in his own time, even more so than Nietzsche. Kierkegaard's concern, like that of Nietzsche, was with the individual, whom he saw as an actor on the stage of life. For each individual there was, according to Kierkegaard, the possibility of three ascending levels of existence along life's way: aesthetic, ethical, and religious. The aesthetic level was that of the pleasure seeker, and the only goals were newer pleasant sensations. Eventually, the futile pursuit of pleasure ends in despair and life is absurd. The only way to rise above the aesthetic level is to recognize the reality of choice.

The second level is that of the ethical, which does not eliminate the aesthetic mode but rises above it. The ethical life is not, however, the same as advocating abstract ethical theories; one can know about ethical theories and still be an unethical slob. The ethical person, for Kierkegaard, is actively committed to long-range purposes, dedicated to the continuity of life, free to choose and be bound to a commitment. Choice is a necessity in the ethical life and, Kierkegaard says, the only absolutely ethical choice is between good and evil. But, this is not enough. We are virtually helpless in facing the evils and injustices of everyday life; these evils can be overcome only by an outpouring of love and generosity beyond human justice and human powers. Such love and generosity is possible only if something transcending us breaks into history and works in our lives. Kierkegaard believed that the breakthrough of the eternal into history had happened with the birth of Christ.

To recapitulate: after the vain pursuit of pleasure we feel despair; through choice we can raise ourselves to the ethical level and become committed to our responsibilities but this eventually proves insufficient, we become a "knight of infinite resignation." At this point we can choose to leap beyond reason to the religious mode of existence using the passion called faith ("where reason ends there begins faith").

Faith, for Kierkegaard, means total commitment to the inner personality of God. We cannot cleverly argue our way to God; we either accept God completely or reject Him completely. The second and final leap of faith is into the arms of Jesus. However, Kierkegaard says, this leap to the God-man of Christian history is conceptually absurd. The intensity of the leap of faith to God is vastly increased by the second venture to the level of Christianity, which is unintelligible. As Kierkegaard wrote, "In an unpermissible and unlawful way people have become *knowing* about Christ, for the only permissible way is to be *believing.*"

These absolute ventures are total personal decisions taken in absolute loneliness with the utmost responsibility. The isolation of the individual in such a decision is absolute and this, says Kierkegaard, is what it means to be a human being. These leaps of faith make an existing individual. Speculative philosophy, according to Kierkegaard, plus the Christian establishment and the press had confused basic facts: "Christendom has done away with Christianity without being quite aware of it."

Values, for Kierkegaard, were not esoteric essences: "Good and evil are ways of existing and the human good is to exist authentically." Conversely, evil is an unauthentic, ungenuine existence. Authentic existence is a matter of choice and the existing person knows the risk and feels the dread of individual responsibility. But, as Kierkegaard observed, "dread is the possibility of freedom" and "man is condemned to freedom."

Kierkegaard was a theistic existentialist; Jean Paul Sartre (SAR–truh; 1905–1980) was an atheistic existentialist. Kierkegaard made two leaps of faith: to God and then to the God-man of Christian history. Sartre, on the other hand, contended that the idea of God was self-contradictory, that the man called Christ could not be both divine and human because the terms are mutually exclusive. In other words, said Sartre, divine means nonhuman and human means that which is not divine. You cannot draw a circular square or a square circle. And, if there is no God, there are no fixed values, no absolute right or wrong or good or bad. In *The Brothers Karamazov* Dostoevsky has one of his characters say, "But you see, if there were

no God, everything would be possible." And that is precisely Sartre's point, that human beings are the sole source of values and anything is possible.

Sartre's basic premise was that existence precedes essence. First, a person *is*; what he or she becomes is settled in the course of existence. For the existentialist things in the world just *are*; only human beings can create themselves. Liberty is unrestricted, our capacity for choice is unrestricted, and making choices is what makes us human. The only meaning that life has is in the meaning of the values that we choose. Values are not waiting to be discovered; we invent values. To the question "What meaning is there in life?" the existentialist replies, "only what you put into life." But, as Sartre warns, the exercise of freedom is inseparably linked with responsibility:

> Man is condemned to be free; because once thrown into the world, man is responsible for everything he does.

You can never choose anything, wrote Sartre, without realizing that this is the choice you wish all humankind to make. If you choose truth then you want everyone to be truthful; if you choose to steal then you are willing that everyone should be a thief. In every choice you have chosen for all humankind, a crushing responsibility, a condition that Sartre calls *anguish.*

What are the values for which the existentialist is willing to assume responsibility? The answer has a curiously old-fashioned ring: the values are those of individualism; value is *in* the individual; value *is* the individual. The supreme virtue is responsible choice, what we call integrity, and the ultimate vice is self-deception. The Greeks said that we should "know thyself" and the existentialist fervently agrees. What you choose determines what you will become but, Sartre emphasizes, you can change, you can redirect your steps. What gives meaning to life is not what *happens* to us but what we ourselves *do*. We are actors on the stage of life. As Sartre said: "Man is encompassed by his own existence and there is no exit." In 1947 Sartre wrote in *Existentialism:*

> Existentialism is nothing less than an attempt to draw all the consequences of a coherent atheistic position. It isn't trying to plunge man into despair at all. But if one calls every attitude of unbelief despair, like the Christian, then the word is not being used in its original sense. Existentialism isn't so atheistic that it wears itself out showing that God doesn't exist. Rather, it declares that even if God did exist, that would change nothing. There you've got our point of view. Not that we believe that God exists, but we think the problem of his existence is not the issue. In this sense existentialism is optimistic, a doctrine of action, and it is plain dishonesty for Christians to make no distinction between their own despair and ours and then to call us despairing.

Existentialism owes its popularity in no small part to repeated failures in politics, economics, and social organizations that have scarred our century. Whatever shortcomings the movement may have, it is not just a body of philosophical speculations but an attitude that helps a great many people in this muddled world to pursue a personal freedom, a way of life that seeks quality rather than quantity.

Literary Selections

The following works highlight just a few of the problems of our troubled century.

THE WALL

Jean Paul Sartre (1905–1980)

In this classic existential short story Sartre stresses the following themes: mindless brutality (representing the indifferent universe), the absence of values or meaning (life has only as much meaning as we ourselves choose to provide), and loneliness (we lead a solitary existence and we die alone). Life is depicted as meaningless and absurd throughout the story, climaxing in the ultimate absurdity on the last page. That the protagonist is a Communist and that the setting is the Spanish Civil War is incidental; the narrator could be on either side of any war.

They pushed us into a big white room and I began to blink because the light hurt my eyes. Then I saw a table and four men behind the table, civilians, looking over the papers. They had bunched another group of prisoners in the back and we had to cross the whole room to join them. There were several I knew and some others who must have been foreigners. The two in front of me were blond with round skulls; they looked alike. I supposed they were French. The smaller one kept hitching up his pants; nerves.

It lasted about three hours; I was dizzy and my head was empty; but the room was well heated and I found that pleasant enough: for the past 24 hours we hadn't stopped shivering. The guards brought the prisoners up to the table, one after the other. The four men asked each one his name and occupation. Most of the time they didn't go any further—or they would simply ask a question here and there: "Did you have anything to do with the sabotage of munitions?" Or "Where were you the morning of the 9th and what were you doing?" They didn't listen to the answers or at least didn't seem to. They were quiet for a moment and then looking straight in front of them began to write. They asked Tom if it were true he was in the International Brigade; Tom couldn't tell them otherwise because of the papers they found in his coat. They didn't ask Juan anything but they wrote for a long time after he told them his name.

"My brother José is the anarchist," Juan said, "you know he isn't here any more. I don't belong to any party, I never had anything to do with politics."

They didn't answer. Juan went on, "I haven't done anything. I don't want to pay for somebody else."

His lips trembled. A guard shut him up and took him away. It was my turn.

"Your name is Pablo Ibbieta?"

"Yes."

The man looked at the papers and asked me, "Where's Ramon Gris?"

"I don't know."

"You hid him in your house from the 6th to the 19th."

"No."

They wrote for a minute and then the guards took me out. In the corridor Tom and Juan were waiting between two guards. We started walking. Tom asked one of the guards, "So?"

"So what?" the guard said.

"Was that the cross-examination or the sentence?"

"Sentence," the guard said.

"What are they going to do with us?"

The guard answered dryly, "Sentence will be read in your cell."

As a matter of fact, our cell was one of the hospital cellars. It was terrifically cold there because of the drafts. We shivered all night and it wasn't much better during the day. I had spent the previous five days in a cell in a monastery, a sort of hole in the wall that must have dated from the middle ages: since there were a lot of prisoners and not much room, they locked us up anywhere. I didn't miss my cell; I hadn't suffered too much from the cold but I was alone; after a long time it gets irritating. In the cellar I had company. Juan hardly ever spoke: he was afraid and he was too young to have anything to say. But Tom was a good talker and he knew Spanish well.

There was a bench in the cellar and four mats. When they took us back we sat and waited in silence. After a long moment, Tom said, "We're screwed."

"I think so too," I said, "but I don't think they'll do anything to the kid."

"They don't have a thing against him," said Tom. "He's the brother of a militiaman and that's all."

I looked at Juan: he didn't seem to hear. Tom went on, "You know what they do in Saragossa? They lay the men down on the road and run over them with trucks. A Moroccan deserter told us that. They said it was to save ammunition."

"It doesn't save gas," I said.

I was annoyed at Tom: he shouldn't have said that.

"Then there's officers walking along the road," he went on, "supervising it all. They stick their hands in their pockets and smoke cigarettes. You think they finish off the guys? Hell no. They let them scream. Sometimes for an hour. The Moroccan said he damned near puked the first time."

"I don't believe they'll do that here," I said. "Unless they're really short on ammunition."

Day was coming in through four airholes and a round opening they had made in the ceiling on the left, and you could see the sky through it. Through this hole, usually closed by a trap, they unloaded coal into the cellar. Just below the hole there was a big pile of coal dust; it had been used to heat the hospital, but since the beginning of the war the patients were evacuated and the coal stayed there, unused; sometimes it even got rained on because they had forgotten to close the trap.

Tom began to shiver. "Good Jesus Christ, I'm cold," he said. "Here it goes again."

He got up and began to do exercises. At each movement his shirt opened on his chest, white and hairy. He lay on his back, raised his legs in the air and bicycled. I saw his great rump trembling. Tom was husky but he had too much fat. I thought how rifle bullets or the sharp points of bayonets would soon be sunk into this mass of tender flesh as in a lump of butter. It wouldn't have made me feel like that if he'd been thin.

I wasn't exactly cold, but I couldn't feel my arms and shoulders any more. Sometimes I had the impression I was missing something and began to look around for my coat and then suddenly remembered they hadn't given me a coat. It was rather uncomfortable. They took our clothes and gave them to their soldiers leaving us only our shirts—and those canvas pants that hospital patients wear in the middle of summer. After a while Tom got up and sat next to me, breathing heavily.

"Warmer?"

"Good Christ, no. But I'm out of wind."

Around eight o'clock in the evening a major came in with two *falangistas.* He had a sheet of paper in his hand. He asked the guard, "What are the names of those three?"

"Steinbock, Ibbieta and Mirbal," the guard said.

The major put on his eyeglasses and scanned the list: "Steinbock . . . Steinbock . . . Oh yes . . . You are sentenced to death. You will be shot tomorrow morning." He went on looking. "The other two as well."

"That's not possible," Juan said. "Not me."

The major looked at him amazed. "What's your name?"

"Juan Mirbal," he said.

"Well, your name is there," said the major. "You're sentenced."

"I didn't do anything," Juan said.

The major shrugged his shoulders and turned to Tom and me.

"You're Basque?"

"Nobody is Basque."

He looked annoyed. "They told me there were three Basques. I'm not going to waste my time running after them. Then naturally you don't want a priest?"

We didn't even answer.

He said, "A Belgian doctor is coming shortly. He is authorized to spend the night with you." He made a military salute and left.

"What did I tell you," Tom said. "We get it."

"Yes," I said, "it's a rotten deal for the kid."

I said that to be decent but I didn't like the kid. His face was too thin and fear and suffering had disfigured it, twisting all his features. Three days before he was a smart sort of kid, not too bad; but now he looked like an old fairy and I thought how he'd never be young again, even if they were to let him go. It wouldn't have been too hard to have a little pity for him but pity disgusts me, or rather it horrifies me. He hadn't said anything more but he had turned grey; his face and hands were both grey. He sat down again and looked at the ground with round eyes. Tom was good hearted, he wanted to take his arm, but the kid tore himself away violently and made a face.

"Let him alone," I said in a low voice, "you can see he's going to blubber."

Tom obeyed regretfully; he would have liked to comfort the kid, it would have passed his time and he wouldn't have been tempted to think about himself. But it annoyed me: I'd never thought about death because I never had any reason to, but now the reason was here and there was nothing to do but think about it.

Tom began to talk. "So you think you've knocked guys off, do you?" he asked me. I didn't answer. He began explaining to me that he had knocked off six since the beginning of August; he didn't realize the situation and I could tell he didn't *want* to realize it. I hadn't quite realized it myself, I wondered if it hurt much, I thought of bullets, I imagined their burning hail through my body. All that was beside the real question; but I was calm: we had all night to understand. After a while Tom stopped talking and I watched him out of the corner of my eye; I saw he too had turned grey and he looked

rotten; I told myself "Now it starts." It was almost dark, a dim glow filtered through the airholes and the pile of coal and made a big stain beneath the spot of sky; I could already see a star through the hole in the ceiling: the night would be pure and icy.

The door opened and two guards came in, followed by a blonde man in a tan uniform. He saluted us. "I am the doctor," he said. "I have authorization to help you in these trying hours."

He had an agreeable and distinguished voice. I said, "What do you want here?"

"I am at your disposal. I shall do all I can to make your last moments less difficult."

"What did you come here for? There are others, the hospital's full of them."

"I was sent here," he answered with a vague look. "Ah! Would you like to smoke?" he added hurriedly, "I have cigarettes and even cigars."

He offered us English cigarettes and *puros,* but we refused. I looked him in the eyes and he seemed irritated. I said to him, "You aren't here on an errand of mercy. Besides, I know you. I saw you with the fascists in the barracks yard the day I was arrested."

I was going to continue, but something surprising suddenly happened to me; the presence of this doctor no longer interested me. Generally when I'm on somebody I don't let go. But the desire to talk left me completely; I shrugged and turned my eyes away. A little later I raised my head; he was watching me curiously. The guards were sitting on a mat. Pedro, the tall thin one, was twiddling his thumbs, the other shook his head from time to time to keep from falling asleep.

"Do you want a light?" Pedro suddenly asked the doctor. The other nodded "Yes": I think he was about as smart as a log, but he surely wasn't bad. Looking in his cold blue eyes it seemed to me that his only sin was lack of imagination. Pedro went out and came back with an oil lamp which he set on the corner of the bench. It gave a bad light but it was better than nothing: they had left us in the dark the night before. For a long time I watched the circle of light the lamp made on the ceiling. I was fascinated. Then suddenly I woke up, the circle of light disappeared and I felt myself crushed under an enormous weight. It was not the thought of death, or fear; it was nameless. My cheeks burned and my head ached.

I shook myself and looked at my two friends. Tom had hidden his face in his hands. I could only see the fat white nape of his neck. Little Juan was the worst, his mouth was open and his nostrils trembled. The doctor went to him and put his hand on his shoulder to comfort him: but his eyes stayed cold. Then I saw the Belgian's hand drop stealthily along Juan's arm, down to the wrist. Juan paid no attention. The Belgian took his wrist between three fingers, distractedly, the same time drawing back a little and turning his back to me. But I leaned backward and saw him take a watch from his pocket and look at it for a moment, never letting go of the wrist. After a minute he let the hand fall inert and went and leaned his back against the wall, then, as if he suddenly remembered something very important which had to be jotted down on the spot, he took a notebook from his pocket and wrote a few lines. "Bastard," I thought angrily, "let him come and take my pulse. I'll shove my fist in his rotten face."

He didn't come but I felt him watching me. I raised my head and returned his look. Impersonally, he said to me, "Doesn't it seem cold to you here?" He looked cold, he was blue.

"I'm not cold," I told him.

He never took his hard eyes off me. Suddenly I understood and my hands went to my face: I was drenched in sweat. In this cellar, in the midst of winter, in the midst of drafts, I was sweating. I ran my hands through my hair, gummed together with perspiration; at the same time I saw my shirt was damp and sticking to my skin: I had been dripping for an hour and hadn't felt it. But that swine of a Belgian hadn't missed a thing; he had seen the drops rolling down my cheeks and thought: this is the manifestation of an almost pathological state of terror; and he had felt normal and proud of being alive because he was cold. I wanted to stand up and smash his face but no sooner had I made the slightest gesture than my rage and shame were wiped out; I fell back on the bench with indifference.

I satisfied myself by rubbing my neck with my handkerchief because now I felt the sweat dropping from my hair onto my neck and it was unpleasant. I soon gave up rubbing, it was useless; my handkerchief was already soaked and I was still sweating. My buttocks were sweating too and my damp trousers were glued to the bench.

Suddenly Juan spoke. "You're a doctor?"

"Yes," the Belgian said.

"Does it hurt . . . very long?"

"Huh? When . . . ? Oh, no," the Belgian said paternally. "Not at all. It's over quickly." He acted as though he were calming a cash customer.

"But I . . . they told me . . . sometimes they have to fire twice."

"Sometimes," the Belgian said, nodding. "It may happen that the first volley reaches no vital organs."

"Then they have to reload their rifles and aim all over again?" He thought for a moment and then added hoarsely, "That takes time!"

He had a terrible fear of suffering, it was all he thought about: it was his age. I never thought much about it and it wasn't fear of suffering that made me sweat.

I got up and walked to the pile of coal dust. Tom jumped up and threw me a hateful look: I had annoyed him because my shoes squeaked. I wondered if my face looked as frightened as his: I saw he was sweating too. The sky was superb, no light filtered into the dark corner and I had only to raise my head to see the Big Dipper. But it wasn't like it had been: the night before I could see a great piece of sky from my monastery cell and each hour of the day brought me a different memory. Morning, when the sky was a hard, light blue, I thought of beaches on the Atlantic; at noon I saw the sun and I remembered a bar in Seville where I drank *manzanilla* and ate olives and anchovies; afternoons I was in the shade and I thought of the deep shadow which spreads over half a bull-ring leaving the other half shimmering in sunlight; it was really hard to see the whole world reflected in the sky like that. But now I could watch the sky as much as I pleased, it no longer evoked anything in me. I liked that better. I came back and sat near Tom. A long moment passed.

Tom began speaking in a low voice. He had to talk, without that he wouldn't have been able to recognize himself in his own mind. I thought he was talking to me but he wasn't looking at me. He was undoubtedly afraid to see me as I was, grey and sweating: we were alike and worse than mirrors of each other. He watched the Belgian, the living.

"Do you understand?" he said. "I don't understand."

I began to speak in a low voice too. I watched the Belgian. "Why? What's the matter?"

"Something is going to happen to us that I can't understand."

There was a strange smell about Tom. It seemed to me I was more sensitive than usual to odors. I grinned. "You'll understand in a while."

"It isn't clear," he said obstinately. "I want to be brave but first I have to know. . . . Listen, they're going to take us into the courtyard. Good. They're going to stand up in front of us. How many?"

"I don't know. Five or eight. Not more."

"All right. There'll be eight. Someone'll holler 'aim!' and I'll see eight rifles looking at me. I'll think how I'd like to get inside the wall, I'll push against it with my back . . . with every ounce of strength I have, but the wall will stay, like in a nightmare. I can imagine all that. If you only knew how well I can imagine it."

"All right, all right!" I said, "I can imagine it too."

"It must hurt like hell. You know, they aim at the eyes and the mouth to disfigure you," he added mechanically. "I can feel the wounds already; I've had pains in my head and in my neck for the past hour. Not real pains. Worse. This is what I'm going to feel tomorrow morning. And then what?"

I well understood what he meant but I didn't want to act as if I did. I had pains too, pains in my body like a crowd of tiny scars. I couldn't get used to it. But I was like him, I attached no importance to it. "After," I said, "you'll be pushing up daisies."

He began to talk to himself: he never stopped watching the Belgian. The Belgian didn't seem to be listening. I knew what he had come to do; he wasn't interested in what we thought; he came to watch our bodies, bodies dying in agony while yet alive.

"It's like a nightmare," Tom was saying. "You want to think something, you always have the impression that it's all right, that you're going to understand and then it slips, it escapes you and fades away. I tell myself there will be nothing afterwards. But I don't understand what it means. Sometimes I almost can . . . and then it fades away and I start thinking about the pains again, bullets, explosions. I'm a materialist, I swear it to you; I'm not going crazy. But something's the matter. I see my corpse; that's not hard but *I'm* the one who sees it, with *my* eyes. I've got to think . . . think that I won't see anything anymore and the world will go on for the others. We aren't made to think that, Pablo. Believe me: I've already stayed up a whole night waiting for something. But this isn't the same: this will creep up behind us, Pablo, and we won't be able to prepare for it."

"Shut up," I said, "Do you want me to call a priest?"

He didn't answer. I had already noticed he had the tendency to act like a prophet and call me Pablo, speaking in a toneless voice. I didn't like that: but it seems all the Irish are that way. I had the vague impression he smelled of urine. Fundamentally, I hadn't much sympathy for Tom and I didn't see why, under the pretext of dying together, I should have any more. It would have been different with some others. With Ramon Gris, for example. But I felt alone between Tom and Juan. I liked that better, anyhow: with Ramon I might have been more deeply moved. But I was terribly hard just then and I wanted to stay hard.

He kept on chewing his words, with something like distraction. He certainly talked to keep himself from thinking. He smelled of urine like an old prostate case. Naturally, I agreed with him, I could have said everything he said: it isn't *natural* to die. And since I was going to die, nothing seemed natural to me, not this pile of coal dust, or the bench, or Pedro's ugly face. Only it didn't please me to think the same things as Tom. And I knew that, all through the night, every five minutes, we would keep on thinking things at the same time. I looked at him sideways and for the first time he seemed strange to me: he wore death on his face. My pride was wounded: for the past 24 hours I had lived next to Tom, I had listened to him, I had spoken to him and I knew we had nothing in common. And now we looked as much alike as twin brothers, simply because we were going to die together. Tom took my hand without looking at me.

"Pablo, I wonder . . . I wonder if it's really true that everything ends."

I took my hand away and said, "Look between your feet, you pig."

There was a big puddle between his feet and drops fell from his pants-leg.

"What is it," he asked, frightened.

"You're pissing in your pants," I told him.

"It isn't true," he said furiously. "I'm not pissing. I don't feel anything."

The Belgian approached us. He asked with false solicitude. "Do you feel ill?"

Tom did not answer. The Belgian looked at the puddle and said nothing.

"I don't know what it is," Tom said ferociously. "But I'm not afraid. I swear I'm not afraid."

The Belgian did not answer. Tom got up and went to piss in a corner. He came back buttoning his fly, and sat down without a word. The Belgian was taking notes.

All three of us watched him because he was alive. He had the motions of a living human being, the cares of a living human being; he shivered in the cellar the way the living are supposed to shiver; he had an obedient, well-fed body. The rest of us hardly felt ours—not in the same way anyhow. I wanted to feel my pants between my legs but I didn't dare; I watched the Belgian, balancing on his legs, master of his muscles, someone who could think about tomorrow. There we were, three bloodless shadows; we watched him and we sucked his life like vampires.

Finally he went over to little Juan. Did he want to feel his neck for some professional motive or was he obeying an impulse of charity? If he was acting by charity it was the only time during the whole night.

He caressed Juan's head and neck. The kid let himself be handled, his eyes never leaving him, then suddenly, he seized the hand and looked at it strangely. He held the Belgian's hand between his own two hands and there was nothing pleasant about them, two grey pincers gripping this fat and reddish hand. I suspected what was going to happen and Tom must have suspected it too: but the Belgian didn't see a thing, he smiled paternally. After a moment the kid brought the fat red hand to his mouth and tried to bite it. The Belgian pulled away quickly and stumbled back against the wall. For a second he looked at us with horror, he must have suddenly understood that we were not men like him. I began to laugh and one of the guards jumped up. The other was asleep, his wide open eyes were blank.

I felt relaxed and over-excited at the same time. I didn't want to think any more about what would happen at dawn, at death. It made no sense. I only found words or emptiness. But as soon as I tried to think of anything else I saw rifle barrels pointing at me. Perhaps I lived through my execution twenty times; once I even thought it was for good: I must have slept a minute. They were dragging me to the wall and I was struggling; I was asking for mercy. I woke up with a start and looked at the Belgian: I was afraid I might have cried out in my sleep. But he was stroking his moustache, he hadn't noticed anything. If I had wanted to, I think I could have slept a while; I had been awake for 48 hours. I was at the end of my rope. But I didn't want to lose two hours of life: they would come to wake me up at dawn, I would follow them, stupefied with sleep and I would have croaked without so much as an "Oof!"; I didn't want that, I didn't want to die like an animal, I wanted to understand. Then I was afraid of having nightmares. I got up, walked back and forth, and, to change my ideas, I began to think about my past life. A crowd of memories came back to me pell-mell. There were good and bad ones—or at least I called them that *before.* There were faces and incidents. I saw the face of a little *novillero* who was gored in Valencia during the *Feria,* the face of one of my uncles, the face of Ramon Gris. I remembered my whole life: how I was out of work for three months in 1926, how I almost starved to death. I remembered a night I spent on a bench in Granada: I hadn't eaten for three days. I was angry, I didn't want to die. That made me smile. How madly I ran after happiness, after women, after liberty. Why? I wanted to free Spain, I admired Pi y Margall, I joined the anarchist movement, I spoke in public meetings: I took everything as seriously as if I were immortal.

At that moment I felt that I had my whole life in front of me and I thought, "It's a damned lie." It was worth nothing because it was finished. I wondered how I'd been able to walk, to laugh with the girls: I wouldn't have moved so much as my little finger if I had only imagined I would die like this. My life was in front of me, shut, closed, like a bag and yet everything inside of it was unfinished. For an instant I tried to judge it. I wanted to tell myself, this is a beautiful life. But I couldn't pass judgment on it; it was only a sketch; I had spent my time counterfeiting eternity, I had understood nothing. I missed nothing: there were so many things I could have missed, the taste of *manzanilla* or the baths I took in summer in a little creek near Cadiz; but death had disenchanted everything.

The Belgian suddenly had a bright idea. "My friends," he told us, "I will undertake—if the military administration will allow it—to send a message for you, a souvenir to those who love you. . . ."

Tom mumbled, "I don't have anybody."

I said nothing. Tom waited an instant then looked at me with curiosity. "You don't have anything to say to Concha?"

"No."

I hated this tender complicity: it was my own fault, I had talked about Concha the night before. I should have controlled myself. I was with her for a year. Last night I would have given an arm to see her again for five minutes. That was why I talked about her, it was stronger than I was. Now I had no more desire to see her, I had nothing more to say to her. I would not even have wanted to hold her in my arms: my body filled me with horror because it was grey and sweating—and I wasn't sure that her body didn't fill me with horror. Concha would cry when she found out I was dead, she would have no taste for life for months afterward. But I was still the one who was going to die. I thought of her soft, beautiful eyes. When she looked at me something passed from her to me. But I knew it was over: if she looked at me *now* the look would stay in her eyes, it wouldn't reach me. I was alone.

Tom was alone too but not in the same way. Sitting cross-legged, he had begun to stare at the bench with a sort of smile, he looked amazed. He put out his hand and touched the wood cautiously as if he were afraid of breaking something, then drew back his hand quickly and shuddered. If I had been Tom I wouldn't have amused myself by touching the bench; this was some more Irish nonsense, but I too found that objects had a funny look: they were more obliterated, less dense than usual. It was enough for me to look at the bench, the lamp, the pile of coal dust, to feel that I was going to die. Naturally I couldn't think clearly about my death but I saw it everywhere, on things, in the way things fell back and kept their distance, discreetly, as people who speak quietly at the bedside of a dying man. It was *his* death which Tom had just touched on the bench.

In the state I was in, if someone had come and told me I could go home quietly, that they would leave me my life whole, it would have left me cold: several hours or several years of waiting is all the same when you have lost the illusion of being eternal. I clung to nothing, in a way I was calm. But it was a horrible calm—because of my body; my body, I saw with its eyes, I heard with its ears, but it was no longer me; it sweated and trembled by itself and I didn't recognize it any more. I had to touch it and look at it to find out what was happening, as if it were the body of someone else. At times I could still feel it, I felt sinkings, and fallings, as when you're in a plane taking a nosedive, or I felt my heart beating. But that didn't reassure me. Everything that came from my body was all cockeyed. Most of the time it was quiet and I felt no more than a sort of weight, a filthy presence against me; I had the impression of being tied to an enormous vermin. Once I felt my pants and I felt they were damp; I didn't know whether it was sweat or urine, but I went to piss on the coal pile as a precaution.

The Belgian took out his watch, looked at it. He said, "It is three-thirty."

Bastard! He must have done it on purpose. Tom jumped; we hadn't noticed time was running out; night surrounded us like a shapeless, somber mass, I couldn't even remember that it had begun.

Little Juan began to cry. He wrung his hands, pleaded, "I don't want to die. I don't want to die."

He ran across the whole cellar waving his arms in the air then fell sobbing on one of the mats. Tom watched him with mournful eyes, without the slightest desire to console him. Because it wasn't worth the trouble: the kid made more noise than we did, but he was less touched: he was like a sick man who defends himself against his illness by fever. It's much more serious when there isn't any fever.

He wept: I could clearly see he was pitying himself; he wasn't thinking about death. For one second, one single second, I wanted to weep myself, to weep with pity for myself. But the opposite happened: I glanced at the kid, I saw his thin sobbing shoulders and I felt inhuman: I could pity neither the others nor myself. I said to myself, "I want to die cleanly."

Tom had gotten up, he placed himself just under the round opening and began to watch for daylight. I was determined to die cleanly and I only thought of that. But ever since the doctor told us the time, I felt time flying, flowing away drop by drop.

It was still dark when I heard Tom's voice: "Do you hear them?"

Men were marching in the courtyard.

"Yes."

"What the hell are they doing? They can't shoot in the dark."

After a while we heard no more. I said to Tom, "It's day."

Pedro got up, yawning, and came to blow out the lamp. He said to his buddy, "Cold as hell."

The cellar was all grey. We heard shots in the distance.

"It's starting," I told Tom. "They must do it in the court in the rear."

Tom asked the doctor for a cigarette. I didn't want one; I didn't want cigarettes or alcohol. From that moment on they didn't stop firing.

"Do you realize what's happening," Tom said.

He wanted to add something but kept quiet, watching the door. The door opened and a lieutenant came in with four soldiers. Tom dropped his cigarette.

"Steinbock?"

Tom didn't answer. Pedro pointed him out.

"Juan Mirbal?"

"On the mat."

"Get up," the lieutenant said.

Juan did not move. Two soldiers took him under the arms and set him on his feet. But he fell as soon as they released him.

The soldiers hesitated.

"He's not the first sick one," said the lieutenant. "You two carry him; they'll fix it up down there."

He turned to Tom. "Let's go."

Tom went out between two soldiers. Two others followed, carrying the kid by the armpits. He hadn't fainted; his eyes were wide open and tears ran down his cheeks. When I wanted to go out the lieutenant stopped me.

"You Ibbieta?"

"Yes."

"You wait here; they'll come for you later."

They left. The Belgian and the two jailers left too, I was alone. I did not understand what was happening to me but I would have liked it better if they had gotten it over with right away. I heard shots at almost regular intervals; I shook with each one of them. I wanted to scream and tear out my hair. But I gritted my teeth and pushed my hands in my pockets because I wanted to stay clean.

After an hour they came to get me and led me to the first floor, to a small room that smelt of cigars and where the heat was stifling. There were two officers sitting smoking in the armchairs, papers on their knees.

"You're Ibbieta?"

"Yes."

"Where is Ramon Gris?"

"I don't know."

The one questioning me was short and fat. His eyes were hard behind his glasses. He said to me, "Come here."

I went to him. He got up and took my arms, staring at me with a look that should have pushed me into the earth. At the same time he pinched my biceps with all his might. It wasn't to hurt me, it was only a game: he wanted to dominate me. He also thought he had to blow his stinking breath square in my face. We stayed for a moment like that, and I almost felt like laughing. It takes a lot to intimidate a man who is going to die; it didn't work. He pushed me back violently and sat down again. He said, "It's his life against yours. You can have yours if you tell us where he is."

These men dolled up with their riding crops and boots were still going to die. A little later than I, but not too much. They busied themselves looking for names in their crumpled papers, they ran after other men to imprison or suppress them; they had opinions on the future of Spain and on other subjects. Their little activities seemed shocking and burlesqued to me; I couldn't put myself in their place, I thought they were insane. The little man was still looking at me, whipping his boots with the riding crop. All his gestures were calculated to give him the look of a live and ferocious beast.

"So? You understand?"

"I don't know where Gris is," I answered. "I thought he was in Madrid."

The other officer raised his pale hand indolently. This indolence was also calculated. I saw through all their little schemes and I was stupefied to find there were men who amused themselves that way.

"You have a quarter of an hour to think it over," he said slowly. "Take him to the laundry, bring him back in fifteen minutes. If he still refuses he will be executed on the spot."

They knew what they were doing: I had passed the night in waiting; then they had made me wait an hour in the cellar while they shot Tom and Juan and now they were locking me up in the laundry; they must have prepared their game the night before. They told themselves that nerves eventually wear out and they hoped to get me that way.

They were badly mistaken. In the laundry I sat on a stool because I felt very weak and I began to think. But not about their proposition. Of course I knew where Gris was; he was hiding with his cousins, four kilometers from the city. I also knew that I would not reveal his hiding place unless they tortured me (but they didn't seem to be thinking about that). All that was perfectly regulated, definite and in no way interested me. Only I would have liked to understand the reasons for my conduct. I would rather die than give up Gris. Why? I didn't like Ramon Gris any more. My friendship for him had died a little while before dawn at the same time as my love for Concha, at the same time as my desire to live. Undoubtedly I thought highly of him: he was tough. But it was not for this reason that I consented to die in his place; his life had no more value than mine; no life had value. They were going to slap a man up against a wall and shoot at him till he died, whether it was I or Gris or somebody else made no difference. I knew he was more useful than I to the cause of Spain but I thought to hell with Spain and anarchy; nothing was important. Yet I was there, I could save my skin and give up Gris and I refused to do it. I found that somehow comic; it was obstinacy. I thought, "I must be stubborn!" And a droll sort of gaiety spread over me.

They came for me and brought me back to the two officers. A rat ran out from under my feet and that amused me. I turned to one of the *falangistas* and said, "Did you see the rat?"

He didn't answer. He was very sober, he took himself seriously. I wanted to laugh but I held myself back because I was afraid that once I got started I wouldn't be able to stop. The *falangista* had a moustache. I said to

him again, "You ought to shave off your moustache, idiot." I thought it funny that he would let the hairs of his living being invade his face. He kicked me without great conviction and I kept quiet.

"Well," said the fat officer, "have you thought about it?"

I looked at them with curiosity, as insects of a very rare species. I told them, "I know where he is. He is hidden in the cemetery. In a vault or in the gravediggers' shack."

It was a farce. I wanted to see them stand up, buckle their belts and give orders busily.

They jumped to their feet. "Let's go. Molés, go get fifteen men from Lieutenant Lopez. You," the fat man said, "I'll let you off if you're telling the truth, but it'll cost you plenty if you're making monkeys out of us."

They left in a great clatter and I waited peacefully under the guard of *falangistas*. From time to time I smiled, thinking about the spectacle they would make. I felt stunned and malicious. I imagined them lifting up tombstones, opening the doors of the vaults one by one. I represented this situation to myself as if I had been someone else: this prisoner obstinately playing the hero, these grim *falangistas* with their moustaches and their men in uniform running among the graves; it was irresistibly funny. After half an hour the little fat man came back alone. I thought he had come to give the orders to execute me. The others must have stayed in the cemetery.

The officer looked at me. He didn't look at all sheepish. "Take him into the big courtyard with the others," he said. "After the military operations a regular court will decide what happens to him."

"Then they're not . . . not going to shoot me? . . ."

"Not now, anyway. What happens afterwards is none of my business."

I still didn't understand. I asked, "But why . . . ?"

He shrugged his shoulders without answering and the soldiers took me away. In the big courtyard there were about a hundred prisoners, women, children and a few old men. I began walking around the central grass-plot, I was stupefied. At noon they let us eat in the mess hall. Two or three people questioned me. I must have known them, but I didn't answer: I didn't even know where I was.

Around evening they pushed about ten new prisoners into the court. I recognized Garcia, the baker. He said, "What damned luck you have! I didn't think I'd see you alive."

"They sentenced me to death," I said, "and then they changed their minds. I don't know why."

"They arrested me at two o'clock," Garcia said.

"Why?" Garcia had nothing to do with politics.

"I don't know," he said. "They arrest everybody who doesn't think the way they do. He lowered his voice. "They got Gris."

I began to tremble. "When?"

"This morning. He messed it up. He left his cousin's on Tuesday because they had an argument. There were plenty of people to hide him but he didn't want to owe anything to anybody. He said, 'I'd go and hide in Ibbieta's place, but they got him, so I'll go hide in the cemetery.'"

"In the cemetery?"

"Yes. What a fool. Of course they went by there this morning, that was sure to happen. They found him in the gravediggers' shack. He shot at them and they got him."

"In the cemetery!"

Everything began to spin and I found myself sitting on the ground: I laughed so hard I cried.

Exercises

1. Why was there no real connection between the information the prisoners supplied at the interrogation and their death sentences? Why was the sentence read to them in their cell rather than in the interrogation room?
2. What significance is there in the narrator being held in a hospital cellar after spending several days in the cell of a medieval monastery?
3. What is the significance of running trucks over prisoners rather than shooting them? Does it save ammunition (while using gas) or does it make any difference?
4. Juan Mirbal contends that he did not do anything, that there is no reason for him to die. If, as appears likely, he was accidentally caught up in events, what is implied here in terms of Existential themes?
5. What is the significance of the major's assumption that the prisoners do not want a priest?
6. What characteristics of Existential belief are symbolized by the Belgian doctor? You should consider the various words used to describe the doctor and his actions.
7. Why does Tom feel impelled to "understand" what is going to happen to him? Why does the narrator feel that this is irrelevant?
8. The narrator contemplates "the pretext of dying together." What does this imply? Look also at other references to dying.
9. What attitudes do the prisoners have about a possible life after death?
10. What does the narrator mean by the statement "I had spent my time counterfeiting eternity"?
11. Why does the narrator have no desire to see Concha? What does this signify?
12. Consider the words "alone" and "lonely." How are they used?
13. Why is the narrator locked in the laundry after his interrogation about Ramon Gris?
14. Why did it, as the narrator said, make no difference whether he or Ramon Gris was shot?
15. Why, at the end, did the narrator laugh so hard that he cried?

THE MYTH OF SISYPHUS
Albert Camus (1913–1966)

Both Sartre and Albert Camus were active in the French Resistance and both won the Nobel Prize for literature. Camus's brilliant novel, *The Stranger,* superbly delineates the existential themes of absurdity, anguish, despair, and alienation but Camus always denied that he was an existentialist. He claimed instead that the world was so absurd that the philosopher should logically contemplate suicide. The alternative, for Camus, was to dismiss the world and lead an active, heroic life. The hero of ordinary life is the person who resolutely shoulders the responsibilities that life imposes, knowing full well that all is futile and meaningless, an attitude that is exemplified in the essay "The Myth of Sisyphus." In Greek mythology Sisyphus was a rogue-hero who delighted in tricking the gods. When death (Thanatos) came for him Sisyphus tied him up and no one died until Zeus intervened. Sisyphus was then taken to Hades but won a temporary leave so that he could return to the world to punish his wife for not giving him a proper burial. Actually, Sisyphus had instructed her to throw his body in the street so that he had an excuse for returning. Once free of Hades he refused to return and finally died of old age. The gods were so furious that, through all eternity, they required Sisyphus to roll a huge stone up a hill only to have it plunge back down once it reached the crest. The divine plan was to keep Sisyphus too busy to plan another escape but, as Camus concludes, "One must imagine Sisyphus happy" in the act of doing.

The gods had condemned Sisyphus to ceaselessly rolling a rock to the top of a mountain, whence the stone would fall back of its own weight. They had thought with some reason that there is no more dreadful punishment than futile and hopeless labor.

If one believes Homer, Sisyphus was the wisest and most prudent of mortals. According to another tradition, however, he was disposed to practice the profession of highwayman. I see no contradiction in this. Opinions differ as to the reasons why he became the futile laborer of the underworld. To begin with, he is accused of a certain levity in regard to the gods. He stole their secrets. Ægina, the daughter of Æsopus, was carried off by Jupiter. The father was shocked by that disappearance and complained to Sisyphus. He, who knew of the abduction, offered to tell about it on condition that Æsopus would give water to the citadel of Corinth. To the celestial thunderbolts he preferred the benediction of water. He was punished for this in the underworld. Homer tells us also that Sisyphus had put Death in chains. Pluto could not endure the sight of his deserted, silent empire. He dispatched the god of war, who liberated Death from the hands of her conqueror.

It is said also that Sisyphus, being near to death, rashly wanted to test his wife's love. He ordered her to cast his unburied body into the middle of the public square. Sisyphus woke up in the underworld. And there, annoyed by an obedience so contrary to human love, he obtained from Pluto permission to return to earth in order to chastise his wife. But when he had seen again the face of this world, enjoyed water and sun, warm stones and the sea, he no longer wanted to go back to the infernal darkness. Recalls, signs of anger, warnings were of no avail. Many years more he lived facing the curve of the gulf, the sparkling sea, and the smiles of earth. A decree of the gods was necessary. Mercury came and seized the impudent man by the collar and, snatching him from his joys, led him forcibly back to the underworld, where his rock was ready for him.

You have already grasped that Sisyphus is the absurd hero. He *is,* as much through his passions as through his torture. His scorn of the gods, his hatred of death, and his passion for life won him that unspeakable penalty in which the whole being is exerted toward accomplishing nothing. This is the price that must be paid for the passions of this earth. Nothing is told us about Sisyphus in the underworld. Myths are made for the imagination to breathe life into them. As for this myth, one sees merely the whole effort of a body straining to raise the huge stone, to roll it and push it up a slope a hundred times over; one sees the face screwed up, the cheek tight against the stone, the shoulder bracing the clay-covered mass, the foot wedging it, the fresh start with arms outstretched, the wholly human security of two earth-clotted hands. At the very end of his long effort measured by skyless space and time without depth, the purpose is achieved. Then Sisyphus watches the stone rush down in a few moments toward that lower world whence he will have to push it up again toward the summit. He goes back down to the plain.

It is during that return, that pause, that Sisyphus interests me. A face that toils so close to stones is already stone itself! I see that man going back down with a heavy yet measured step toward the torment of which he will never know the end. That hour like a breathing-space which returns as surely as his suffering, that is the hour of consciousness. At each of those moments when he leaves the heights and gradually sinks toward the lairs of the gods, he is superior to his fate. He is stronger than his rock.

If this myth is tragic, that is because its hero is conscious. Where would his torture be, indeed, if at every step the hope of succeeding upheld him? The workman of today works every day in his life at the same tasks, and this fate is no less absurd. But it is tragic only at the rare moments when it becomes conscious. Sisyphus, proletarian of the gods, powerless and rebellious, knows the whole extent of his wretched condition: it is what he thinks of during his descent. The lucidity that was to constitute his torture at the same time crowns his victory. There is no fate that cannot be surmounted by scorn.

If the descent is thus sometimes performed in sorrow, it can also take place in joy. This word is not too much. Again I fancy Sisyphus returning toward his rock, and the sorrow was in the beginning. When the images of earth cling too tightly to memory, when the call of happiness becomes too insistent, it happens that melancholy rises in man's heart: this is the rock's victory, this is the rock itself. The boundless grief is too heavy to bear. These are our nights of Gethsemane. But crushing truths perish from being acknowledged. Thus, Œdipus at the outset obeys fate without knowing it. But from the moment he knows, his tragedy begins. Yet at the same moment, blind and desperate, he realizes that the only bond linking him to the world is the cool hand of a girl. Then a tremendous remark rings out: "Despite so many ordeals, my advanced age and the nobility of my soul make me conclude that all is well." Sophocles' Œdipus, like Dostoevsky's Kirilov, thus gives the recipe for the absurd victory. Ancient wisdom confirms modern heroism.

One does not discover the absurd without being tempted to write a manual of happiness. "What! by such narrow ways—?" There is but one world, however. Happiness and the absurd are two sons of the same earth. They are inseparable. It would be a mistake to say that happiness necessarily springs from the absurd discovery. It happens as well that the feeling of the absurd springs from happiness. "I conclude that all is well," says Œdipus, and that remark is sacred. It echoes in the wild and limited universe of man. It teaches that all is not, has not been, exhausted. It drives out of this world a god who

had come into it with dissatisfaction and a preference for futile sufferings. It makes of fate a human matter, which must be settled among men.

All Sisyphus' silent joy is contained therein. His fate belongs to him. His rock is his thing. Likewise, the absurd man, when he contemplates his torment, silences all the idols. In the universe suddenly restored to its silence, the myriad wondering little voices of the earth rise up. Unconscious, secret calls, invitations from all the faces, they are the necessary reverse and price of victory. There is no sun without shadow, and it is essential to know the night. The absurd man says yes and his effort will henceforth be unceasing. If there is a personal fate, there is no higher destiny, or at least there is but one which he concludes is inevitable and despicable. For the rest, he knows himself to be the master of his days. At that subtle moment when man glances backward over his life, Sisyphus returning toward his rock, in that slight pivoting he contemplates that series of unrelated actions which becomes his fate, created by him, combined under his memory's eye and soon sealed by his death. Thus, convinced of the wholly human origin of all that is human, a blind man eager to see who knows that the night has no end, he is still on the go. The rock is still rolling.

I leave Sisyphus at the foot of the mountain! One always finds one's burden again. But Sisyphus teaches the higher fidelity that negates the gods and raises rocks. He too concludes that all is well. This universe henceforth without a master seems to him neither sterile nor futile. Each atom of that stone, each mineral flake of that night-filled mountain, in itself forms a world. The struggle itself toward the heights is enough to fill a man's heart. One must imagine Sisyphus happy.

Exercises

1. Imagine several children on a sandy beach busily constructing a large sand castle. A passerby maliciously stomping on a tower leads to a brief but violent confrontation. Finally the builders complete their elaborate fairy-tale structure just as the encroaching tide tentatively laps at the outer walls. The construction crew observes attentively as the noble turrets subside into the swirling water and then, losing interest, pick up their things and set off for the beach house. Why was there a fight over the mutilated tower but only calm acceptance of the watery demise of the castle? How is all of this analogous to Sisyphus and his rock?

2. Consider now the millionaire who feels that he must aim for a hundred million, then a billion, or more. How much money will be enough, or is money even the main focus? How does this relate to Sisyphus?

3. Let us say that the gods have relented and that, as Sisyphus muscles the rock into place, it teeters for a moment and then remains firmly in place. Describe Sisyphus's feelings. Have the gods indeed relented or have they devised a more fiendish form of punishment?

Existentialism: Postscript

The same type of character as Sisyphus is found in Camus's novel *The Plague* (written, one recognizes, after Camus had split from Existentialism but maintaining the same attitude toward the hero) in Monsieur Grand, who does his daily duties as a clerk in the city government; in his spare time he carefully tabulates the number of dead in the plague; and he vainly tries to communicate with the world through his novel—which never gets written beyond the first sentence.

Beyond this everyday sort of hero, some Existentialists, particularly the Christian Existentialists, imagine that a person can become a sort of superhero when he or she infuses pointless life with meaning, and thereby creates meaning in the universe. Some of the Christian Existentialists believe that Christ was such a figure; and that, if the actuality for such Being exists within one individual, then it is also a potentiality for all humanity.

A large number of philosophers and Christian theologians have advanced and developed this Christian Existentialist point of view. Among them are Ernst Block and the Dutch Roman Catholic theologian, E. Schillebeeckx. Oversimplifying greatly, they view God as the Creative Purpose of the World; the End toward which the world is moving. Block has referred to Him as "the God who is not yet"; Schillebeeckx as the God who is "wholly new." This concept is a far cry from the standard view of a God who was complete and whole from the beginning of time, and who rules the world either as loving Father or as Great Engineer. Instead, He is constantly inventing Himself or being invented here on earth, exactly as the Existentialist person, moment by moment, invents himself or herself.

Literary Selections

On the Road, from THE WHITE ALBUM
Joan Didion (b. 1934)

A sense of loss of national purpose brooded over the land. Where is America heading? Joan Didion, in the selection given below, replies, "nowhere." She does, however, describe, in devastating detail, where we are now. Her impressionistic picture of a puzzled nation depicts transcience, superficiality, and boredom. Values are skewed and mobility is an illusion: "Time was money. Money was progress. Decisions were snap." A self-indulgent, business-oriented nation rethinks the sixties, the fifties. Where did we go wrong?

Where are we heading, they asked in all the television and radio studios. They asked it in New York and Los Angeles and they asked it in Boston and Washington and they asked it in Dallas and Houston and Chicago and San Francisco. Sometimes they made eye contact as they asked it. Sometimes they closed their eyes as they asked it. Quite often they wondered not just where we were heading but where we were heading "as Americans," or "as concerned Americans," or "as American women," or, on one occasion, "as the American guy and the American

woman." I never learned the answer, nor did the answer matter, for one of the eerie and liberating aspects of broadcast discourse is that nothing one says will alter in the slightest either the form or the length of the conversation. Our voices in the studios were those of manic actors assigned to do three-minute, four-minute, seven-minute improvs. Our faces on the monitors were those of concerned Americans. On my way to one of those studios in Boston I had seen the magnolias bursting white down Marlborough Street. On my way to another in Dallas I had watched the highway lights blazing and dimming pink against the big dawn sky. Outside one studio in Houston the afternoon heat was sinking into the deep primeval green of the place and outside the next, that night in Chicago, snow fell and glittered in the lights along the lake. Outside all these studios America lay in all its exhilaratingly volatile weather and eccentricity and specificity, but inside the studios we shed the specific and rocketed on to the general, for they were The Interviewers and I was The Author and the single question we seemed able to address together was *where are we heading.*

> "8:30 A.M. to 9:30 A.M.: LIVE on WFSB TV/THIS MORNING.
> "10 A.M. to 10:30 A.M.: LIVE on WINF AM/THE WORLD TODAY.
> "10:45 A.M. to 11:45 A.M.: PRESS INTERVIEW with HARTFORD COURANT.
> "12 noon to 1:30 P.M.: AUTOGRAPHING at BARNES AND NOBLE.
> "2 P.M. to 2:30 P.M.: TAPE at WDRC AM/FM.
> "3 P.M. to 3:30 P.M.: PRESS INTERVIEW with THE HILL INK.
> "7:30 P.M. to 9 P.M.: TAPE at WHNB TV/WHAT ABOUT WOMEN."

From 12 noon to 1:30 P.M., that first day in Hartford, I talked to a man who had cut a picture of me from a magazine in 1970 and had come round to Barnes and Noble to see what I looked like in 1977. From 2 P.M. to 2:30 P.M., that first day in Hartford, I listened to the receptionists at WDRC AM/FM talk about the new records and I watched snow drop from the pine boughs in the cemetery across the street. The name of the cemetery was Mt. St. Benedict and my husband's father had been buried there. "Any Steely Dan come in?" the receptionists kept asking. From 8:30 A.M. until 9 P.M., that first day in Hartford, I neglected to mention the name of the book I was supposed to be promoting. It was my fourth book but I had never before done what is called in the trade a book tour. I was not sure what I was doing or why I was doing it. I had left California equipped with two "good" suits, a box of unanswered mail, Elizabeth Hardwick's *Seduction and Betrayal,* Edmund Wilson's *To the Finland Station,* six Judy Blume books and my eleven-year-old daughter. The Judy Blume books were along to divert my daughter. My daughter was along to divert me. Three days into the tour I sent home the box of unanswered mail to make room for a packet of Simon and Schuster press releases describing me in favorable terms. Four days into the tour I sent home *Seduction and Betrayal* and *To the Finland Station* to make room for a thousand-watt hair blower. By the time I reached Boston, ten days into the tour, I knew that I had never before heard and would possibly never again hear America singing at precisely this pitch: ethereal, speedy, an angel choir on Dexamyl.

Where were we heading. The set for this discussion was always the same: a cozy oasis of wicker and ferns in the wilderness of cables and cameras and Styrofoam coffee cups that was the actual studio. On wicker settees across the nation I expressed my conviction that we were heading "into an era" of whatever the clock seemed to demand. In green rooms across the nation I listened to other people talk about where we were heading, and also about their vocations, avocations, and secret interests. I discussed L-dopa and biorhythm with a woman whose father invented prayer breakfasts. I exchanged makeup tips with a former Mouseketeer. I stopped reading newspapers and started relying on bulletins from limo drivers, from Mouseketeers, from the callers-in on call-in shows and from the closed-circuit screens in airports that flashed random stories off the wire ("CARTER URGES BARBITURATE BAN" is one that got my attention at La Guardia) between advertisements for *Shenandoah.* I gravitated to the random. I swung with the nonsequential.

I began to see America as my own, a child's map over which my child and I could skim and light at will. We spoke not of cities but of airports. If rain fell at Logan we could find sun at Dulles. Bags lost at O'Hare could be found at Dallas/Fort Worth. In the first-class cabins of the planes on which we traveled we were often, my child and I, the only female passengers, and I apprehended for the first time those particular illusions of mobility which power American business. Time was money. Motion was progress. Decisions were snap and the ministrations of other people were constant. Room service, for example, assumed paramount importance. We needed, my eleven-year-old and I, instant but erratically timed infusions of consommé, oatmeal, crab salad and asparagus vinaigrette. We needed Perrier water and tea to drink when we were working. We needed bourbon on the rocks and Shirley Temples to drink when we were not. A kind of irritable panic came over us when room service went off, and also when no one answered in the housekeeping department. In short we had fallen into the peculiar hormonal momentum of business travel, and I had begun to understand the habituation many men and a few women have to planes and telephones and schedules. I had begun to regard my own schedule—a sheaf of thick cream-colored pages printed with the words "SIMON & SCHUSTER/A DIVISION OF GULF & WESTERN CORPORATION"—with a reverence approaching the mystical. We wanted 24-hour room service. We wanted direct-dial telephones. We wanted to stay on the road forever.

WE SAW AIR AS OUR ELEMENT. In Houston the air was warm and rich and suggestive of fossil fuel and we pretended we owned a house in River Oaks. In Chicago the air was brilliant and thin and we pretended we owned the 27th floor of the Ritz. In New York the air was charged and crackling and shorting out with opinions, and we pretended we had some. Everyone in New York had opinions. Opinions were demanded in return. The absence of opinion was construed as opinion. Even my daughter was developing opinions. "Had an interesting talk with Carl Bernstein," she noted in the log she had been assigned to keep for her fifth-grade teacher in Malibu, California. Many of these New York opinions seemed intended as tonic revisions, bold corrections to opinions in vogue during the previous week, but since I had just dropped from the sky it was difficult for me to distinguish those opinions which were "bold" and "revisionist" from those which were merely "weary" and "rote." At the time I left New York many people were expressing a bold belief in "joy"—joy in children, joy in wedlock, joy in the dailiness of life—but joy was trickling down fast to show-business personalities. Mike Nichols,

for example, was expressing his joy in the pages of *Newsweek,* and also his weariness with "lapidary bleakness." Lapidary bleakness was definitely rote.

We were rethinking the Sixties that week, or Morris Dickstein was.

We were taking another look at the Fifties that week, or Hilton Kramer was.

I agreed passionately. I disagreed passionately. I called room service on one phone and listened attentively on the other to people who seemed convinced that the "texture" of their lives had been agreeably or adversely affected by conversion to the politics of joy, by regression to lapidary bleakness, by the Sixties, by the Fifties, by the recent change in administrations and by the sale of *The Thorn Birds* to paper for one-million-nine.

I lost track of information.

I was blitzed by opinion.

I began to see opinions arcing in the air, intersecting flight patterns. The Eastern shuttle was cleared for landing and so was lapidary bleakness. John Leonard and joy were on converging vectors. I began to see the country itself as a projection on air, a kind of hologram, an invisible grid of image and opinion and electronic impulse. There were opinions in the air and there were planes in the air and there were even people in the air: one afternoon in New York my husband saw a man jump from a window and fall to the sidewalk outside the Yale Club. I mentioned this to a *Daily News* photographer who was taking my picture. "You have to catch a jumper in the act to make the paper," he advised me. He had caught two in the act but only the first had made the paper. The second was a better picture but coincided with the crash of a DC–10 at Orly. "They're all over town," the photographer said. "Jumpers. A lot of them aren't even jumpers. They're window washers. Who fall."

What does that say about us as a nation. I was asked the next day when I mentioned the jumpers and window washers on the air. *Where are we headed.* On the 27th floor of the Ritz in Chicago my daughter and I sat frozen at the breakfast table until the window washers glided safely out of sight. At a call-in station in Los Angeles I was told by the guard that there would be a delay because they had a jumper on the line. "I say let him jump," the guard said to me. I imagined a sky dense with jumpers and fallers and DC–10s. I held my daughter's hand at takeoff and landing and watched for antennae on the drive into town. The big antennae with the pulsing red lights had been for a month our landmarks. The big antennae with the pulsing red lights had in fact been for a month our destinations. "Out I–10 to the antenna" was the kind of direction we had come to understand, for we were on the road, on the grid, on the air and also in it. *Where were we heading.* I don't know where you're heading, I said in the studio attached to the last of these antennae, my eyes fixed on still another of the neon FLEETWOOD MAC signs that flickered that spring in radio stations from coast to coast, but I'm heading home.

Exercises

Replete with vivid images, this selection is a mine of metaphors and pungent phrases. The following questions should be only the beginning of your explorations into deeper meanings.

1. Consider "manic actors assigned to do three-minute improvs." What does this tell you about our life-style? About TV?

2. What is the face of a "concerned American"? How often have you seen politicians wearing this face?

3. What is implied by "I never learned the answer nor did the answer matter"? Consider the basic question, "where are we going as Americans?"

4. The author first praised America's eccentricity and specificity but added, "inside the studios we shed the specific and rocketed on to the general." What is implied? Mediocrity?

5. What does the absence of similes do for the style?

6. At one point the question, "where are we heading" is followed by a typed schedule of appointments. What is implied about our day-to-day lives?

7. Ostensibly the writer is describing a book promotional tour. What are the deeper implications? Why is there no mention of the book in question, not even the title? Is this country promoting things of intrinsic or extrinsic value?

8. Consider the setting for the panel discussions which "was always the same: a cozy oasis of wicker and ferns in the wilderness of cables and cameras and Styrofoam cups." An oasis in what? Who really uses wicker furniture? Are the ferns real? And what about the ubiquitous Styrofoam cups? Add up the scene and what do you have?

9. Describe the implications of "the peculiar hormonal momentum of business travel." Words like "momentum," "planes," "telephones," and "schedules" are used but there is no mention of destinations or accomplishments. Is this another elaborate metaphor for self-delusion or false values? The lack of a national purpose? How many metaphors can you find which communicate these general ideas?

TENEBRAE
Denise Levertov (b. 1923)

No other war in American history has had the impact of Vietnam. Conflicting postmortems are still appearing and the spectre of Agent Orange shadows the lives of many Vietnam veterans. Written in 1967 during the protest march on the Pentagon, Levertov's poem, "Tenebrae,"[3] remains as an indictment and an elegy.

Heavy, heavy, heavy, hand and heart.
We are at war,
bitterly, bitterly at war.

And the buying and selling
buzzes at our heads, a swarm   5
of busy flies, a kind of innocence.

---

3. Tenebrae (Latin, darkness), are church services for the last three days of Holy Week that commemorate the suffering and death of Christ. The candles that are lighted at the beginning of the service are extinguished one by one after each Psalm is sung or read, symbolizing the darkness that fell on the land at the time of the crucifixion.

Gowns of gold sequins are fitted,
sharp-glinting. What harsh rustlings
of silver moiré there are,
to remind me of shrapnel splinters.   10

And weddings are held in full solemnity
not of desire but of etiquette,
the nuptial pomp of starched lace;
a grim innocence.

And picnic parties return from the beaches   15
burning with stored sun in the dusk;
children promised a TV show when they get home
fall asleep in the backs of a million station wagons,
sand in their hair, the sound of waves
quietly persistent at their ears.   20
They are not listening.

Their parents at night
dream and forget their dreams.
They wake in the dark
and make plans. Their sequin plans   25
glitter into tomorrow.
They buy, they sell.

They fill freezers with food.
Neon signs flash their intentions
into the years ahead.   30

And at their ears the sound
of the war. They are
not listening, not listening.

Exercises

1. Compare the contrasting words and images between rampant materialism and the reality of warfare.

2. What turned *a kind of innocence* into *a grim innocence?*

3. What intentions do neon signs flash?

4. Are they *not listening* because they cannot hear, or will not hear?

A SOLDIER'S EMBRACE
Nadine Gordimer (b. 1923)

In her novels and short stories South Africa's Nadine Gordimer is primarily concerned with the apartheid policies of the Afrikaaner government. In her novel *July's People* (1981), for example, the black revolution, which Gordimer and other white liberals feel is inevitable, has already happened and South Africans, black and white, are trying to adjust to the new order. In "A Soldier's Embrace" the revolution has also succeeded but Gordimer's poignant story of the strange ambivalence of race relations has no geographical boundaries. Her setting is Africa but winning freedom from oppression could take place anywhere in the world.

The day the cease-fire was signed she was caught in a crowd. Peasant boys from Europe who had made up the colonial army and freedom fighters whose column had marched into town were staggering about together outside the barracks, not three blocks from her house in whose rooms, for ten years, she had heard the blurred parade-ground bellow of colonial troops being trained to kill and be killed.

The men weren't drunk. They linked and swayed across the street; because all that had come to a stop, everything *had* to come to a stop: they surrounded cars, bicycles, vans, nannies with children, women with loaves of bread or basins of mangoes on their heads, a road gang with picks and shovels, a Coca-Cola truck, an old man with a barrow who bought bottles and bones. They were grinning and laughing amazement. That it could be: there they were, bumping into each other's bodies in joy, looking into each other's rough faces, all eyes crescent-shaped, brimming greeting. The words were in languages not mutually comprehensible, but the cries were new, a whooping and crowing all understood. She was bumped and jostled and she let go, stopped trying to move in any self-determined direction. There were two soldiers in front of her, blocking her off by their clumsy embrace (how do you do it, how do you do what you've never done before) and the embrace opened like a door and took her in—a pink hand with bitten nails grasping her right arm, a black hand with a big-dialled watch and thong bracelet pulling at her left elbow. Their three heads collided gaily, musk of sweat and tang of strong sweet soap clapped a mask to her nose and mouth. They all gasped with delicious shock. They were saying things to each other. She put up an arm round each neck, the rough pile of an army haircut on one side, the soft negro hair on the other, and kissed them both on the cheek. The embrace broke. The crowd wove her away behind backs, arms, jogging heads; she was returned to and took up the will of her direction again—she was walking home from the post office, where she had just sent a telegram to relatives abroad: ALL CALM DON'T WORRY.

The lawyer came back early from his offices because the courts were not sitting although the official celebration holiday was not until next day. He described to his wife the rally before the Town Hall, which he had watched from the office-building balcony. One of the guerilla leaders (not the most important; he on whose head the biggest price had been laid would not venture so soon and deep into the territory so newly won) had spoken for two hours from the balcony of the Town Hall. 'Brilliant. Their jaws dropped. Brilliant. They've never heard anything on that level: precise, reasoned—none of them would ever have believed it possible, out of the bush. You should have seen de Poorteer's face. He'd like to be able to get up and open his mouth like that. And be listened to like that. . .' The Governor's handicap did not even bring the sympathy accorded to a stammer; he paused and gulped between words. The blacks had always used a portmanteau name for him that meant the-crane-who-is-trying-to-swallow-the-bullfrog.

One of the members of the black underground organization that could now come out in brass-band support of the freedom fighters had recognized the lawyer across from the official balcony and given him the freedom fighters' salute. The lawyer joked about it, miming, full of pride. 'You should have been there—should have seen him, up there in the official party. I told you—really—you ought to have come to town with me this morning.'

'And what did you do?' She wanted to assemble all details.

'Oh I gave the salute in return, chaps in the street saluted *me* . . . everybody was doing it. *It was marvellous.* And the police standing by; just to think, last month—only last week—you'd have been arrested.'

'Like thumbing your nose at them,' she said, smiling.

'Did anything go on around here?'

'Muchanga was afraid to go out all day. He wouldn't even run up to the post office for me!' Their servant had come to them many years ago, from service in the house of her father, a colonial official in the Treasury.

'But there was no excitement?'

She told him: 'The soldiers and some freedom fighters mingled outside the barracks. I got caught for a minute or two. They were dancing about; you couldn't get through. All very good-natured.—Oh, I sent the cable.'

An accolade, one side a white cheek, the other a black. The white one she kissed on the left cheek, the black one on the right cheek, as if these were two sides of one face.

That vision, version, was like a poster; the sort of thing that was soon peeling off dirty shopfronts and bus shelters while the months of wrangling talks preliminary to the take-over by the black government went by.

To begin with, the cheek was not white but pale or rather sallow, the poor boy's pallor of winter in Europe (that draft must have only just arrived and not yet seen service) with homesick pimples sliced off by the discipline of an army razor. And the cheek was not black but opaque peat-dark, waxed with sweat round the plump contours of the nostril. As if she could return to the moment again, she saw what she had not consciously noted: there had been a narrow pink strip in the darkness near the ear, the sort of tender stripe of healed flesh revealed when a scab is nicked off a little before it is ripe. The scab must have come away that morning: the young man picked at it in the troop carrier or truck (whatever it was the freedom fighters had; the colony had been told for years that they were supplied by the Chinese and Russians indiscriminately) on the way to enter the capital in triumph.

According to newspaper reports, the day would have ended for the two young soldiers in drunkenness and whoring. She was, apparently, not yet too old to belong to the soldier's embrace of all that a land-mine in the bush might have exploded for ever. That was one version of the incident. Another: the opportunity taken by a woman not young enough to be clasped in the arms of the one who (same newspaper, while the war was on, expressing the fears of the colonists for their women) would be expected to rape her.

She considered this version.

She had not kissed on the mouth, she had not sought anonymous lips and tongues in the licence of festival. Yet she had kissed. Watching herself again, she knew that. She had—god knows why—kissed them on either cheek, his left, his right. It was deliberate, if a swift impulse: she had distinctly made the move.

She did not tell what happened not because her husband would suspect licence in her, but because he would see her—born and brought up in the country as the daughter of an enlightened white colonial official, married to a white liberal lawyer well known for his defence of blacks in political trials—as giving free expression to liberal principles.

She had not told, she did not know what had happened.

She thought of a time long ago when a school camp had gone to the sea and immediately on arrival everyone had run down to the beach from the train, tripping and tearing over sand dunes of wild fig, aghast with ecstatic shock at the meeting with the water.

De Poorteer was recalled and the lawyer remarked to one of their black friends, 'The crane has choked on the bullfrog. I hear that's what they're saying in the Quarter.'

The priest who came from the black slum that had always been known simply by that anonymous term did not respond with any sort of glee. His reserve implied it was easy to celebrate; there were people who 'shouted freedom too loud all of a sudden.'

The lawyer and his wife understood: Father Mulumbua was one who had shouted freedom when it was dangerous to do so, and gone to prison several times for it, while certain people, now on the Interim Council set up to run the country until the new government took over, had kept silent. He named a few, but reluctantly. Enough to confirm their own suspicions—men who perhaps had made some deal with the colonial power to place its interests first, no matter what sort of government might emerge from the new constitution? Yet when the couple plunged into discussion their friend left them talking to each other while he drank his beer and gazed, frowning as if at a headache or because the sunset light hurt his eyes behind his spectacles, round her huge-leaved tropical plants that bowered the terrace in cool humidity.

They had always been rather proud of their friendship with him, this man in a cassock who wore a clenched fist carved of local ebony as well as a silver cross round his neck. His black face was habitually stern—a high seriousness balanced by sudden splurting laughter when they used to tease him over the fist—but never inattentively ill-at-ease.

'What was the matter?' She answered herself; 'I had the feeling he didn't want to come here.' She was using a paper handkerchief dipped in gin to wipe greenfly off the back of a pale new leaf that had shaken itself from its folds like a cut-out paper lantern.

'Good lord, he's been here hundreds of times.'
'—Before, yes.'

What things were they saying?

With the shouting in the street and the swaying of the crowd, the sweet powerful presence that confused the senses so that sound, sight, stink (sweat, cheap soap) ran into one tremendous sensation, she could not make out words that came so easily.

Not even what she herself must have said.

A few wealthy white men who had been boastful in their support of the colonial war and knew they would be marked down by the blacks as arch exploiters, left at once. Good riddance, as the lawyer and his wife remarked. Many ordinary white people who had lived contentedly, without questioning its actions, under the colonial government, now expressed an enthusiastic intention to help build a nation, as the newspapers put it. The lawyer's wife's neighbourhood butcher was one. 'I don't mind blacks.' He was expansive with her, in his shop that he had occupied for twelve years on a licence available only to white people. 'Makes no difference to me who you are so long as you're honest.' Next to a chart showing a beast mapped according to the cuts of meat it provided, he had hung a picture of the most important leader of the freedom fighters, expected to be first

President. People like the butcher turned out with their babies clutching pennants when the leader drove through the town from the airport.

There were incidents (newspaper euphemism again) in the Quarter. It was to be expected. Political factions, tribally based, who had not fought the war, wanted to share power with the freedom fighters' Party. Muchanga no longer went down to the Quarter on his day off. His friends came to see him and sat privately on their hunkers near the garden compost heap. The ugly mansions of the rich who had fled stood empty on the bluff above the sea, but it was said they would make money out of them yet—they would be bought as ambassadorial residences when independence came, and with it many black and yellow diplomats. Zealots who claimed they belonged to the Party burned shops and houses of the poorer whites who lived, as the lawyer said, 'in the inevitable echelon of colonial society', closest to the Quarter. A house in the lawyer's street was noticed by his wife to be accommodating what was certainly one of those families, in the outhouses; green nylon curtains had appeared at the garage window, she reported. The suburb was pleasantly overgrown and well-to-do; no one rich, just white professional people and professors from the university. The barracks was empty now, except for an old man with a stump and a police uniform stripped of insignia, a friend of Muchanga, it turned out, who sat on a beer-crate at the gates. He had lost his job as night-watchman when one of the rich people went away, and was glad to have work.

The street had been perfectly quiet; except for that first day.

The fingernails she sometimes still saw clearly were bitten down until embedded in a thin line of dirt all round, in the pink blunt fingers. The thumb and thick fingertips were turned back coarsely even while grasping her. Such hands had never been allowed to take possession. They were permanently raw, so young, from unloading coal, digging potatoes from the frozen Northern Hemisphere, washing hotel dishes. He had not been killed, and now that day of the cease-fire was over he would be delivered back across the sea to the docks, the stony farm, the scullery of the grand hotel. He would have to do anything he could get. There was unemployment in Europe where he had returned, the army didn't need all the young men any more.

A great friend of the lawyer and his wife, Chipande, was coming home from exile. They heard over the radio he was expected, accompanying the future President as confidential secretary, and they waited to hear from him.

The lawyer put up his feet on the empty chair where the priest had sat, shifting it to a comfortable position by hooking his toes, free in sandals, through the slats. 'Imagine, Chipande!' Chipande had been almost a protégé—but they didn't like the term, it smacked of patronage. Tall, cocky, casual Chipande, a boy from the slummiest part of the Quarter, was recommended by the White Fathers' Mission (was it by Father Mulumbua himself?—the lawyer thought so, his wife was not sure they remembered correctly) as a bright kid who wanted to be articled to a lawyer. That was asking a lot, in those days—nine years ago. He never finished his apprenticeship because while he and his employer were soon close friends, and the kid picked up political theories from the books in the house he made free of, he became so involved in politics that he had to skip the country one jump ahead of a detention order signed by the crane-who-was-trying-to-swallow-the-bullfrog.

After two weeks, the lawyer phoned the offices the guerilla-movement-become-Party had set up openly in the town but apparently Chipande had an office in the former colonial secretariat. There he had a secretary of his own; he wasn't easy to reach. The lawyer left a message. The lawyer and his wife saw from the newspaper pictures he hadn't changed much: he had a beard and had adopted the Muslim cap favoured by political circles in exile on the East Coast.

He did come to the house eventually. He had the distracted, insistent friendliness of one who has no time to re-establish intimacy; it must be taken as read. And it must not be displayed. When he remarked on a shortage of accommodation for exiles now become officials, and the lawyer said the house was far too big for two people, he was welcome to move in and regard a self-contained part of it as his private living quarters, he did not answer but went on talking generalities. The lawyer's wife mentioned Father Mulumbua, whom they had not seen since just after the cease-fire. The lawyer added, 'There's obviously some sort of big struggle going on, he's fighting for his political life there in the Quarter.' 'Again,' she said, drawing them into a reminder of what had only just become their past.

But Chipande was restlessly following with his gaze the movements of old Muchanga, dragging the hose from plant to plant, careless of the spray; 'You remember who this is, Muchanga?' she had said when the visitor arrived, yet although the old man had given, in their own language, the sort of respectful greeting even an elder gives a young man whose clothes and bearing denote rank and authority, he was not in any way overwhelmed nor enthusiastic—perhaps he secretly supported one of the rival factions?

The lawyer spoke of the latest whites to leave the country—people who had got themselves quickly involved in the sort of currency swindle that draws more outrage than any other kind of crime, in a new state fearing the flight of capital: 'Let them go, let them go. Good riddance.' And he turned to talk of other things—there were so many more important questions to occupy the attention of the three old friends.

But Chipande couldn't stay. Chipande could not stay for supper; his beautiful long velvety black hands with their pale lining (as she thought of the palms) hung impatiently between his knees while he sat forward in the chair, explaining, adamant against persuasion. He should not have been there, even now; he had official business waiting, sometimes he drafted correspondence until one or two in the morning. The lawyer remarked how there hadn't been a proper chance to talk; he wanted to discuss those fellows in the Interim Council Mulumbua was so warily distrustful of—what did Chipande know?

Chipande, already on his feet, said something dismissing and very slightly disparaging, not about the Council members but of Mulumbua—a reference to his connection with the Jesuit missionaries as an influence that 'comes through'. 'But I must make a note to see him sometime.'

It seemed that even black men who presented a threat to the Party could be discussed only among black men themselves, now. Chipande put an arm round each of his friends as for the brief official moment of a photograph, left them; he who used to sprawl on the couch arguing half the night before dossing down in the lawyer's pyjamas. 'As soon as I'm settled I'll contact you. You'll be around, ay?'

'Oh, we'll be around.' The lawyer laughed, referring, for his part, to those who were no longer. 'Glad to see you're not driving a Mercedes!' he called with reassured affection at the sight of Chipande getting into a modest car. How many times, in the old days, had they agreed on the necessity for African leaders to live simply when they came to power!

On the terrace to which he turned back, Muchanga was doing something extraordinary—wetting a dirty rag with Gilbey's. It was supposed to be his day off, anyway; why was he messing about with the plants when one wanted peace to talk undisturbed?

'Is those thing again, those thing is killing the leaves.'

'For heaven's sake, he could use methylated for that! Any kind of alcohol will do! Why don't you get him some?'

There were shortages of one kind and another in the country, and gin happened to be something in short supply.

Whatever the hand had done in the bush had not coarsened it. It, too, was suede-black, and elegant. The pale lining was hidden against her own skin where the hand grasped her left elbow. Strangely, black does not show toil—she remarked this as one remarks the quality of a fabric. The hand was not as long but as distinguished by beauty as Chipande's. The watch a fine piece of equipment for a fighter. There was something next to it, in fact looped over the strap by the angle of the wrist as the hand grasped. A bit of thong with a few beads knotted where it was joined as a bracelet. Or amulet. Their babies wore such things; often their first and only garment. Grandmothers or mothers attached it as protection. It had worked; he was alive at cease-fire. Some had been too deep in the bush to know, and had been killed after the fighting was over. He had pumped his head wildly and laughingly at whatever it was she—they—had been babbling.

The lawyer had more free time than he'd ever remembered. So many of his clients had left; he was deputed to collect their rents and pay their taxes for them, in the hope that their property wasn't going to be confiscated—there had been alarmist rumours among such people since the day of the cease-fire. But without the rich whites there was little litigation over possessions, whether in the form of the children of dissolved marriages or the houses and cars claimed by divorced wives. The Africans had their own ways of resolving such redistribution of goods. And a gathering of elders under a tree was sufficient to settle a dispute over boundaries or argue for and against the guilt of a woman accused of adultery. He had had a message, in a round-about way, that he might be asked to be consultant on constitutional law to the Party, but nothing seemed to come of it. He took home with him the proposals for the draft constitution he had managed to get hold of. He spent whole afternoons in his study making notes for counter or improved proposals he thought he would send to Chipande or one of the other people he knew in high positions: every time he glanced up, there through his open windows was Muchanga's little company at the bottom of the garden. Once, when he saw they had straggled off, he wandered down himself to clear his head (he got drowsy, as he never did when he used to work twelve hours a day at the office). They ate dried shrimps, from the market: that's what they were doing! The ground was full of bitten-off heads and black eyes on stalks. His wife smiled. 'They bring them. Muchanga won't go near the market since the riot.' 'It's ridiculous. Who's going to harm him?'

There was even a suggestion that the lawyer might apply for a professorship at the university. The chair of the Faculty of Law was vacant, since the students had demanded the expulsion of certain professors engaged during the colonial regime—in particular of the fuddy-duddy (good riddance) who had gathered dust in the Law chair, and the quite decent young man (pity about him) who had had Political Science. But what professor of Political Science could expect to survive both a colonial regime and the revolutionary regime that defeated it? The lawyer and his wife decided that since he might still be appointed in some consultative capacity to the new government it would be better to keep out of the university context, where the students were shouting for Africanization, and even an appointee with his credentials as a fighter of legal battles for blacks against the colonial regime in the past might not escape their ire.

Newspapers sent by friends from over the border gave statistics for the number of what they termed 'refugees' who were entering the neighbouring country. The papers from outside also featured sensationally the inevitable mistakes and misunderstandings, in a new administration, that led to several foreign businessmen being held for investigation by the new regime. For the last fifteen years of colonial rule, Gulf had been drilling for oil in the territory, and just as inevitably it was certain that all sorts of questionable people, from the point of view of the regime's determination not to be exploited preferentially, below the open market for the highest bidder in ideological as well as economic terms, would try to gain concessions.

His wife said, 'The butcher's gone.'

He was home, reading at his desk; he could spend the day more usefully there than at the office, most of the time. She had left after breakfast with her fisherman's basket that she liked to use for shopping, she wasn't away twenty minutes. 'You mean the shop's closed?' There was nothing in the basket. She must have turned and come straight home.

'Gone. It's empty. He's cleared out over the weekend.'

She sat down suddenly on the edge of the desk; and after a moment of silence, both laughed shortly, a strange, secret, complicit laugh. 'Why, do you think?' 'Can't say. He certainly charged, if you wanted a decent cut. But meat's so hard to get, now; I thought it was worth it—justified.'

The lawyer raised his eyebrows and pulled down his mouth: 'Exactly.' They understood; the man probably knew he was marked to run into trouble for profiteering—he must have been paying through the nose for his supplies on the black market, anyway, didn't have much choice.

Shops were being looted by the unemployed and loafers (there had always been a lot of unemployed hanging around for the pickings of the town) who felt the new regime should entitle them to take what they dared not before. Radio and television shops were the most favoured objective for gangs who adopted the freedom fighters' slogans. Transistor radios were the portable luxuries of street life; the new regime issued solemn warnings, over those same radios, that looting and violence would be firmly dealt with but it was difficult for the police to be everywhere at once. Sometimes their actions became street battles, since the struggle with the looters changed character as supporters of the Party's rival political factions joined in with the thieves against the police. It was necessary to be ready to reverse direction, quickly turning down a side street in detour if one encountered such disturbances while driving around town. There were bodies sometimes; both husband and wife had been fortunate enough not to see any close up, so far. A company of the freedom fighters' army was brought down from the north and installed in the barracks to supplement the police force; they patrolled the Quarter, mainly. Muchanga's friend kept his job as gatekeeper although there were armed sentries on guard: the lawyer's wife found that a light touch to mention in letters to relatives in Europe.

'Where'll you go now?'

She slid off the desk and picked up her basket. 'Supermarket, I suppose. Or turn vegetarian.' He knew that she left the room quickly, smiling, because she didn't want him to suggest Muchanga ought to be sent to look for fish in the markets along the wharf in the Quarter. Muchanga was being allowed to indulge in all manner of eccentric refusals; for no reason, unless out of some curious sentiment about her father?

She avoided walking past the barracks because of the machine guns the young sentries had in place of rifles. Rifles pointed into the air but machine guns pointed to the street at the level of different parts of people's bodies, short and tall, the backsides of babies slung on mothers' backs, the round heads of children, her fisherman's basket—she knew she was getting like the others: what she felt was afraid. She wondered what the butcher and his wife had said to each other. Because he was at least one whom she had known. He had sold the meat she had bought that these women and their babies passing her in the street didn't have the money to buy.

It was something quite unexpected and outside their own efforts that decided it. A friend over the border telephoned and offered a place in a lawyers' firm of highest repute there, and some prestige in the world at large, since the team had defended individuals fighting for freedom of the press and militant churchmen upholding freedom of conscience on political issues. A telephone call; as simple as that. The friend said (and the lawyer did not repeat this even to his wife) they would be proud to have a man of his courage and convictions in the firm. He could be satisfied he would be able to uphold the liberal principles everyone knew he had always stood for; there were many whites, in that country still ruled by a white minority, who deplored the injustices under which their black population suffered etc. and believed you couldn't ignore the need for peaceful change etc.

His offices presented no problem; something called Africa Seabeds (Formosan Chinese who had gained a concession to ship seaweed and dried shrimps in exchange for rice) took over the lease and the typists. The senior clerks and the current articled clerk (the lawyer had always given a chance to young blacks, long before other people had come round to it—it wasn't only the secretary to the President who owed his start to him) he managed to get employed by the new Trades Union Council; he still knew a few blacks who remembered the times he had acted for black workers in disputes with the colonial government. The house would just have to stand empty, for the time being. It wasn't imposing enough to attract an embassy but maybe it would do for a Charge d'Affaires—it was left in the hands of a half-caste letting agent who was likely to stay put: only whites were allowed in, at the country over the border. Getting money out was going to be much more difficult than disposing of the house. The lawyer would have to keep coming back, so long as this remained practicable, hoping to find a loophole in exchange control regulations.

She was deputed to engage the movers. In their innocence, they had thought it as easy as that! Every large vehicle, let alone a pantechnicon, was commandeered for months ahead. She had no choice but to grease a palm, although it went against her principles, it was condoning a practice they believed a young black state must stamp out before corruption took hold. He would take his entire legal library, for a start; that was the most important possession, to him. Neither was particularly attached to furniture. She did not know what there was she felt she really could not do without. Except the plants. And that was out of the question. She could not even mention it. She did not want to leave her towering plants, mostly natives of South America and not Africa, she supposed, whose aerial tubes pushed along the terrace brick erect tips extending hourly in the growth of the rainy season, whose great leaves turned shields to the spatter of Muchanga's hose glancing off in a shower of harmless arrows, whose two-hand-span trunks were smooth and grooved in one sculptural sweep down their length, or carved by the drop of each dead leaf-stem with concave medallions marking the place and building a pattern at once bold and exquisite. Such things would not travel; they were too big to give away.

The evening she was beginning to pack the books, the telephone rang in the study. Chipande—and he called her by her name, urgently, commandingly—'What is this all about? Is it true, what I hear? Let me just talk to him—'

'Our friend,' she said, making a long arm, receiver at the end of it, towards her husband.

'But you can't leave!' Chipande shouted down the phone. 'You can't go! I'm coming round. Now.'

She went on packing the legal books while Chipande and her husband were shut up together in the living-room.

'He cried. You know, he actually cried.' Her husband stood in the doorway, alone.

'I know—that's what I've always liked so much about them, whatever they do. They feel.'

The lawyer made a face: there it is, it happened; hard to believe.

'Rushing in here, after nearly a year! I said, but we haven't seen you, all this time . . . he took no notice. Suddenly he starts pressing me to take the university job, raising all sorts of objections, why not this . . . that. And then he really wept, for a moment.'

They got on with packing books like builder and mate deftly handling and catching bricks.

And the morning they were to leave it was all done; twenty-one years of life in that house gone quite easily into one pantechnicon. They were quiet with each other, perhaps out of apprehension of the tedious search of their possessions that would take place at the border; it was said that if you struck over-conscientious or officious freedom fighter patrols they would even make you unload a piano, a refrigerator or washing machine. She had bought Muchanga a hawker's licence, a hand-cart, and stocks of small commodities. Now that many small shops owned by white shopkeepers had disappeared, there was an opportunity for humble itinerant black traders. Muchanga had lost his fear of the town. He was proud of what she had done for him and she knew he saw himself as a rich merchant; this was the only sort of freedom he understood, after so many years as a servant. But she also knew, and the lawyer sitting beside her in the car knew she knew, that the shortages of the goods Muchanga could sell from his cart, the sugar and soap and matches and pomade and sunglasses, would soon put him out of business. He promised to come back to the house and look after the plants every week; and he stood waving, as he had done every year when they set off on holiday. She did not know what to call out to him as they drove away. The right words would not come again; whatever they were, she left them behind.

Exercises

1. What was symbolized by the embrace of a white European soldier, a black African freedom fighter, and a white woman? What went wrong after that? Why did it go wrong?

2. Consider the role of the black priest who did not want to come to the lawyer's home *after* freedom.

3. Muchanga, the old black servant, is a key figure in the story. At first he wasn't enthusiastic about greeting the returned black leader. Later, he stays with the lawyer and his wife but refuses to take orders from them. What happened to change his attitude? Does he represent the great mass of people who used to work for white families?

4. What was the significance of the African amulet worn next to a fine (European) watch?

5. Perhaps the most important statement was made by the lawyer's wife when she said, about Chipande, "I know—that's what I've always liked so much about them, whatever they do. They feel." What is implied?

6. What were the "right words" that were left behind?

25

Art in the Twentieth Century: Shock Waves and Reactions

Art is either a plagiarist or a revolutionist.
Paul Gauguin

Would you realize what Revolution is, call it Progress; and would you realize what Progress is, call it Tomorrow.
Victor Hugo

Prelude

The beginnings of contemporary art can be traced back to the revolutionary innovations of Edouard Manet, especially as exemplified in his *Olympia* (see fig. 22.22). Manet had insisted that the actual subject matter was "light" but the new conception was even more fundamental than that; the artist's response to the rapidly changing world about him was, in effect, visible on the canvas. *Olympia* was a naked prostitute from Manet's contemporary world. She gazed unconcernedly at a shocked public that still expected art to be an academic enterprise, art that drew its subject matter from myths and legends and instructed the viewer in the beauty of color and line. This was, however, the Age of Progress, the industrial era of cities, factories, slums, trains, Marx, Darwin, and Bismarck. The Renaissance tradition was no longer adequate or even appropriate. The Impressionists did paint from nature but Monet also painted, many times, a Parisian train station crowded with powerful locomotives emitting clouds of steam. Gauguin fled to Polynesia to escape a civilization that he saw as corrupt and diseased. Cézanne's sources were nature, people, and objects of the world in which he lived, not stories and myths of the past. The contemporary world was the basis for the new reality of painting. The stage was set for the advent of modernism.

Artistic Styles to 1945

Painting and Sculpture

Fauvism and Expressionism   Modern art was in the air in 1905, especially in Collioure, a fishing port on the French Mediterranean coast a few miles from the Spanish border. Summering there with his family and a fellow artist, Henri Matisse (ma–TEESS; 1869–1954) saw some Tahitian paintings by Gauguin and was forcibly reminded of Gauguin's contention that color was whatever the artist perceived it to be. Still searching for a style, Matisse had become dissatisfied with copying nature as an Impressionist and he refused to even consider the dots-of-color technique of Seurat. At age thirty-six he found his style in Collioure. In the sparkling southern light he began painting in bold colors with broad and exuberant brushstrokes; he would delight in color for the rest of a long and marvelously productive career. When he displayed some of his Collioure pictures in Paris at the 1905 Salon d'Automne critics were outraged, claiming that the "blotches of barbaric color" bore no relationship to real painting. There was, in fact, a whole roomful of wildly colorful paintings by Matisse, his Collioure colleague André Derain, and other French artists. Perhaps seeking to localize the repercussions, the judges assigned all of their paintings to Room VII, leading the horrified public to believe that this was an organized school with Matisse, the eldest, as its leader. A critic's remark about a roomful of Fauves (foves, "wild beasts")[1] gave the group a name, and critical and public hostility helped create a movement. For a public still unfamiliar with the works of van Gogh and Gauguin, Fauve paintings were shocking. Color was, after all, *true;* apples were red and trees were green. In *The Blue Window* (colorplate 50) Matisse has painted a landscape that is also a still life. The lampshade is green but the beautifully rounded trees in the background are blue. They are, nevertheless, still perceived as trees in an elegantly cool and decorative composition of curving shapes within a series of carefully proportioned rectangles. Color has been freed to become whatever the artist wants it to be.

In an earlier work, *La Coiffure* (fig. 25.1), Matisse reveals the influence of Japanese prints, works similar to those that so affected the styles of van Gogh and Gauguin. Matisse was not, however, a tortured creator like the two lonely Post-Impressionists. Throughout his sixty-year career he was a hard-working but consistently cheerful painter and sculptor who seemingly paid not the slightest attention to the woes of the world, not even the two terrible wars that his country had endured. He was neither insensitive nor indifferent; his concern was with the creation of beauty in a world that had become most unbeautiful.

---

1. Though commonly translated as "wild beasts," *fauves* actually means deer; the French call wild beasts *les grands fauves.*

Figure 25.1 Henri Matisse, *La Coiffure,* 1901. Oil on canvas, 37¼ × 31¼". Chester Dale Collection, 1962. National Gallery of Art, Washington, D.C.

Georges Rouault (roo–OH; 1871–1958) was, on the other hand, obsessed with the plight of humankind in the twentieth century. Deeply religious, unlike most modern artists, he was unable to accept the joyful hedonism of Matisse or even the relaxed styles of other Fauves. His sympathies lay with clowns and other circus performers, whom he saw as symbols for the tragic victims of society; he was extremely hostile toward corrupt judges and the demimonde of criminals and prostitutes. *Nude with Upraised Arms* (fig. 25.2) is a tortuous study of agitated lines and crude, fleshy form. Clearly judgmental about the woman's ancient profession, the painting has, nevertheless, a ripe sensuality that contrasts sharply with the gracefully decorative nude by Matisse.

Beginning about the same time as Fauvism, German Expressionism was influenced by the French movement and by the anguished work of Edvard Munch (see fig. 22.34). The leading Expressionist sculptor, Ernst Barlach (1870–1938), displays a medieval, craftsmanlike quality in his work. Even though the medium is bronze his *Shivering Woman* (fig. 25.3) has the appearance of a wood carving. Monumental in mass despite its small scale, the huddled figure is a powerful study of concentrated misery. The art of the German avant-garde has an intense emotional content reminiscent of the work of Grünewald (see colorplate 32).

German artists were more concerned with political and social conditions before and after World War I than were the French, and none more so than

Figure 25.2 Georges Rouault, *Nude with Upraised Arms,* 1906. Oil on canvas, 24¾ × 18¾". Chester Dale Collection, 1962. National Gallery of Art, Washington, D.C.

Figure 25.3 Ernst Barlach, *Shivering Woman.* Bronze, height 10", width 6". The University Art Collections, Arizona State University, Tempe. Gift of Oliver B. James.

Käthe Kollwitz (1867–1945). Both a sculptor and a graphic artist, Kollwitz became, in 1919, the first female member of the Prussian Academy. A Socialist and a feminist, she concentrated on themes of poverty and injustice, and the problem of being a woman and mother in militaristic Prussia. In *The Only Good Thing About It* (fig. 25.4) the exhausted mother stares numbly at the viewer, her newborn baby on her chest, her other child nestled down in the bed. The baby is presumably a girl. When first published the print had a caption that read: "If they are not used as soldiers they at least deserve to be treated as children." Kollwitz's lifelong campaign against German militarism began even before her personal tragedies. Her only son was killed in combat in World War I and her only grandson met the same fate in World War II.

With his satirical drawings George Grosz (1893–1959) became a prominent spokesman for the antiwar movement in Germany during the 1920s. At first identified with the Berlin Dadists (see Dada below), Grosz developed a pessimistic Expressionist style influenced by the powerful imagery of Grünewald and Bosch (see fig. 14.24). His opposition to the Nazi movement forced him to flee Germany in 1932 for the United States, where he realized his dream of becoming an American citizen. Painted during the horror of a war that he, among many, had forseen, *I Am Glad I Came Back* (fig. 25.5) depicts a grinning

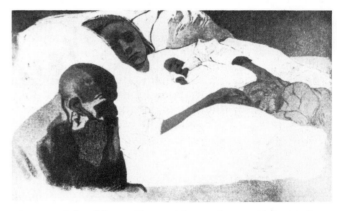

Figure 25.4 Käthe Kollwitz, *The Only Good Thing About It,* 1909. Print. Kunstbibliothek, West Berlin.

skeleton peering through parted draperies at the holocaust of World War II. Symbolically, the work is a vision of the rebirth of the Four Horsemen of the Apocalypse: War, Famine, Pestilence, and Death.

The expressive qualities of strong color impressed some Russian artists also, especially Wassily Kandinsky (1866–1944). Paradoxically, Russia had a long history of strong colors derived from its Byzantine tradition, which Kandinsky came to realize as he

Figure 25.5 George Grosz, *I Am Glad I Came Back,* 1943. Oil on masonite, 28 × 20″. The University Art Collections, Arizona State University, Tempe. Gift of Oliver B. James.

Figure 25.6 Pablo Picasso, *The Tragedy,* 1903. Oil on wood, 41½ × 27⅛″. Chester Dale Collection, 1962. National Gallery of Art, Washington, D.C.

studied the intense colors of richly ornamented peasant houses, furniture, and clothing. Moving to Munich to study the movement, he began painting in the German Expressionist style. It was not until about 1908 that he discovered, apparently accidentally, that color could operate independently of subjects. Red, for example, need not be on an apple nor green on a tree; colors could function in expressive compositions without representing specific objects. Called the first Abstract Expressionist as early as 1919, Kandinsky developed theories about the spiritual qualities of colors and the interrelationship of music and art. In *Panel 3* (also known as *Summer;* colorplate 5) he created what can be described as "visual poetry" or "visual music," a celebration of the warmth and brightness of summer.

Cubism and Other Abstractions   The most famous and successful artist of this century, Pablo Picasso (1881–1973), was a one-man art movement whose innovations throughout a long and enormously productive career make him impossible to classify or categorize. He is discussed under this heading because he, along with Georges Braque (bra'ak; 1882–1963), invented Cubism. Working in his native Spain after a discouraging first attempt at a career in Paris, Picasso painted *The Tragedy* (fig. 25.6) as a

somber monochromatic study, in blue, of sorrowing figures in a timeless setting by an unknown sea. There have been numerous explanations for the artist's brief Blue Period (ca. 1903–1904) but the likeliest appears to be his prolonged melancholy at this stage of his career.

After deciding, in 1904, to live in Paris permanently, Picasso was still poverty-stricken, but his first mistress helped brighten his life and his style. The last of the circus-theme paintings of his Rose Period (ca. 1904–1905), the *Family of Saltimbanques* (fig. 25.7) was his first large painting, a kind of summary that concluded the period. The Jester stands between Harlequin at the left along with two boy acrobats. Like objects in a still life, the figures are expressionless and motionless. As was his custom, Picasso has portrayed some members of his "gang," including himself as Harlequin, but there is no explanation for the isolated woman at the right.

Picasso could have painted in the lyrical Rose Period style indefinitely. By 1906 his works were selling so well that he had become, next to Matisse, perhaps the best-known painter in Paris. And so, having mastered the style, he moved on to a new style. His studies of ancient Iberian sculptures and African masks and figures like the *Dogon Ancestor Figure* (fig. 25.8) led him to produce a painting of five nude women that astonished and horrified art dealers, and even his

Figure 25.7 Pablo Picasso, *Family of Saltimbanques,* 1905. Oil on canvas, 90⅜ × 83¾″. Chester Dale Collection, 1962. National Gallery of Art, Washington, D.C.

Figure 25.8 African, *Dogon Ancestor Figure* (2 views). Wood, 8⅝ × 2¼ × 2″. The University Art Collections, Arizona State University, Tempe. Gift of Dr. and Mrs. Richard Bessom.

friends. Unlike anything ever seen in art, *Les Demoiselles d'Avignon* (fig. 25.9) represented a breakthrough as epochal as Masaccio's *The Tribute Money* (see fig. 14.6) at the beginning of the Italian Renaissance. Masaccio established Renaissance perspective; with this painting Picasso destroyed it. Just about all the rules were broken: flat picture plane with no one-point perspective; angular and fragmented bodies; distorted faces with enormous eyes; two figures wearing grotesque Africanlike masks. With a remarkable economy of means Picasso created tense and massive figures whose heads and facial features are seen simultaneously in full face and profile, marking a great step forward in the evolution of Cubism. A friend of the artist added the title later, a reference to a brothel on Avignon Street in Barcelona.

Picasso and Braque took Cubism through several phases, from a faceting of three-dimensional figures to flattened images and rearranged forms. In *Still Life* (colorplate 51) Picasso uses forms from the "real" world to confuse reality and illusion. All is two-dimensional but shadows cast by objects on the tilted tabletop further add to the confusion. What is reality here? Actually, colors and forms on canvas. Inspired in part by Cézanne's compressed forms (see colorplate 47), Cubism was a refutation of our Mediterranean classical heritage as the sole criteria for creating and viewing art. Though Picasso did not forsake Cubism, his studies in Rome of ancient and Renaissance art led to Neoclassic works like *The Lovers* (fig. 25.10). Recalling both classical sculpture and the style of Raphael, the two figures are conceived with bulk and monumentality but outlined with sure, delicate lines.

Figure 25.9 Pablo Picasso, *Les Demoiselles d'Avignon,* 1907. Oil on canvas, 8′ × 7′8″. Collection, The Museum of Modern Art, New York.

Figure 25.10 Pablo Picasso, *The Lovers,* 1923. Oil on canvas, 51¼ × 38¼". Chester Dale Collection, 1962. National Gallery of Art, Washington, D.C.

Inspired by a new German mistress with blond hair and high-bridged nose, Picasso painted her in a number of colorful works, of which his personal favorite was *Girl Before a Mirror* (see colorplate 7). Standing nude before a mirror, she is young and innocent but the mirror image is older and darker, mysterious and sultry. The wide range of vivid colors set off by heavy dark lines is reminiscent of medieval stained glass, perhaps indicating that Picasso had in mind Eve the Temptress or even a modern-day version of the Madonna.

During the afternoon of April 26, 1937, the Spanish Civil War came home to the Spanish artist living in Paris. German bombers virtually destroyed the Basque town of Guernica and, 25 sketches and one month later, Picasso had completed his anguished protest against the brutal destruction of a defenseless town (fig. 25.11). The central figure is a wounded horse that, according to the artist, represents the people, while the bull symbolizes not Fascism but brutality and darkness. Possibly representing the threatened Light of Reason, a light bulb is superimposed on the blazing sun. Painted on an enormous scale in a stark black, white, and gray, the work is a monumental protest against the impersonal brutality of modern warfare. At the bottom center is one small symbol of life: a fragile flower above the broken sword.

Picasso decreed that the work would remain on loan to the Museum of Modern Art in New York until democracy was restored in Spain, a condition that was deemed satisfied in 1982.

In the United States, Georgia O'Keeffe (b. 1887), whose training was entirely American, applied abstract concepts to American themes. Her *Horse's Skull on Blue* (fig. 25.12) evokes the mood of the Southwest, to which she moved permanently after the death of her husband, the celebrated photographer Alfred Stieglitz (1864–1946). Together they had operated the Little Gallery of the Photo-Secession that Stieglitz had earlier opened at 291 Fifth Avenue in New York. At "291," as the art world called it, they had shown, for the first time in America, works by Cézanne, Picasso, Toulouse-Lautrec, Rodin, Matisse, Brancusi, and Henri Rousseau.

American abstract artists, like their European counterparts, had to combat the hostility of a public accustomed to representational art and the resistance of both academicians and the Ash Can school (discussed below under Realism). The modernists of "291" ended the internecine warfare by inducing academicians and Ash Can artists to form, in 1911, the Association of American Artists and Painters. An exhibition of contemporary American art was to be the first project, but the end result was the epochal New York Armory Show of 1913, still the most controversial exhibition ever staged in this country. Convinced that the public was ready for new ideas, the organizers included European modernists in what was officially called the International Exhibition of Modern Art. Works by Cézanne, Rousseau, Gauguin, van Gogh, Matisse, Duchamp, and Picasso astounded and infuriated artists, critics, and, most of all, the public. The shocked organizers dismissed the public reaction as militant ignorance, which it was, but American modernists were dismayed to see how far behind they themselves were. The Armory Show was "the greatest single influence that I have experienced" said Stuart Davis (1894–1964) as he altered his style and, like many American artists, sailed to Paris. His cubistic *Radio Tubes* (fig. 25.13) is a characteristically whimsical celebration of American technology at a time when advanced technology was naively thought to be uniquely American. Contending that the camera was the proper instrument for recording facts, Davis believed, as did most modernists, that his function was to make new statements. Though influenced by European Cubism, *Radio Tubes* is, in its own way, as American as the work of Georgia O'Keeffe.

Though he was attracted to the work of the French Cubists, the Dutch artist Piet Mondrian (1872–1944) felt that their art did not express what he called "pure reality." He sought "plastic expression" in a basic reality made up solely of colors and forms. *Composition in White, Black, and Red* (colorplate 52) is a precisely balanced work in a style generally called Geometric Abstraction. Of the sixteen rectangles no two are of the same size or shape nor are all the heavy black lines the same width. The poised serenity of Mondrian's "compositions" is as classical as a Greek

Figure 25.11 Pablo Picasso, *Guernica,* 1937. Oil on canvas, 25' 5¾" × 11'5½". The Prado Museum, Madrid.

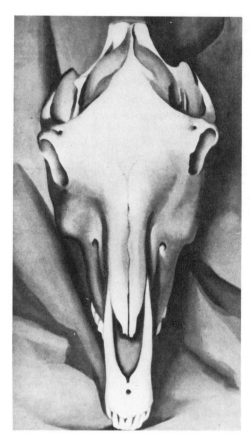

Figure 25.12 Georgia O'Keeffe, *Horse's Skull on Blue,* 1930. Oil on canvas, 30 × 16". The University Art Collections, Arizona State University, Tempe. Gift of Oliver B. James.

Figure 25.13 Stuart Davis, *Radio Tubes,* 1940. Gouache, 22 × 14". The University Art Collections, Arizona State University, Tempe. Gift of Oliver B. James.

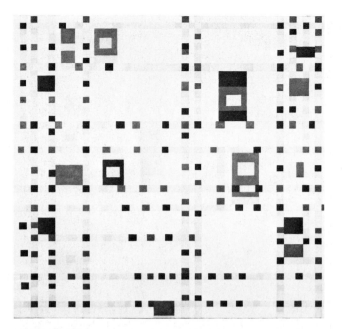

Figure 25.14 Piet Mondrian, *Broadway Boogie Woogie,* 1942–1943. Oil on canvas, 50 × 50". Collection, The Museum of Modern Art, New York. Given anonymously.

Figure 25.15 Constantin Brancusi, *The Kiss,* 1908. Limestone, height 23". The Philadelphia Museum of Art. Louise and Walter Arensberg Collection.

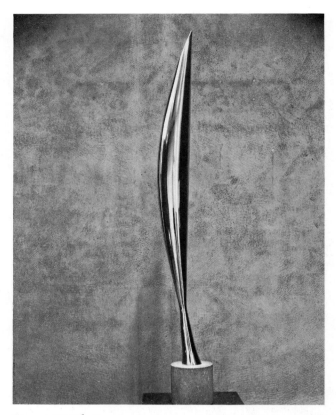

Figure 25.16 Constantin Brancusi, *Bird in Space,* ca. 1928. Polished bronze, unique cast, ca. 54" high. Collection, The Museum of Modern Art, New York.

temple. Mondrian's ideas influenced many artists but they have also been popularized, in simplified and sometimes distorted versions, in fashion, interior, and advertising design.

Both Mondrian and Kandinsky produced nonrepresentational art and both believed that their paintings were analogous to music. Though this analogy may not be apparent in colorplate 52, unless in conjunction with the music of Mozart, Mondrian's *Broadway Boogie Woogie* (fig. 25.14) is different; it pulses with the rhythm and vitality of New York's Great White Way. Along with European artists Marc Chagall, Max Ernst, Yves Tanguy, Thomas Mann, Bertolt Brecht, and others, Mondrian lived in New York as a refugee from Hitler and the German armies. Though he did not live to see the defeat of Nazi Germany, this work and a companion piece called *Victory Boogie Woogie* embodied the artist's admiration for America.

The Roumanian sculptor Constantin Brancusi (bran-KOOSH; 1876–1957) was first influenced by Rodin when studying in Paris but developed an abstract style that was to influence many artists. An ancestor of cubist sculture, the amusing *The Kiss* (fig. 25.15) reduces this kind of personal interaction to its essentials, to a meaningful minimum. His *Bird in Space* (fig. 25.16) conveys, in an elegantly swelling shape, the soaring spirit of flight. It is a magnificent work of transcendental beauty that epitomizes the sculptor's statement: "I bring you pure joy."

Figure 25.17 Marc Chagall, *I and the Village,* 1911. Oil on canvas, 75⅝ × 59⅝″. Collection, The Museum of Modern Art, New York. Mrs. Simon Guggenheim Fund.

Fantasy, Dada, and Surrealism Fantasy plays a large part in twentieth-century art, and the Russian artist Marc Chagall (shah–GALL; b. 1889) has been a leading exponent. Chagall combines Fauve color and Cubist forms with a personal vision of his early life in a Russian village. In *I and the Village* (fig. 25.17) cow and peasant speak to each other; a peasant marches up the street after his wife, who floats upside down; and a magic tree grows out of a hand. Chagall's paintings are meant to be enjoyed as pictorial arrangements of images that fascinated the artist and enchant the viewer.

The German-Swiss artist Paul Klee (klay; 1879–1940) was a master of fantasy. Through his teaching at the Bauhaus (see fig. 25.29) and his painting, Klee was one of the most influential artists of the century. Rejecting illusionistic art as obsolete, he turned to the art of children and primitives as inspirations for his paintings. *Fish Magic* (colorplate 58) is a whimsical fantasy of disparate objects placed, with infinite care, in harmonious relationships. Nothing in this work is invented. As a shrewd observer of nature and people, Klee coded his findings and arranged them on canvas. Everything is from the real world but transformed into a magical composition.

The fantasies of Giorgio de Chirico (day KEE–re–ko; 1888–1979) were as subjective as those of Chagall but infused with pessimism and melancholy. Born in Greece of Italian parents, de Chirico first studied in Athens but, like many artists of the time,

Figure 25.18 Giorgio de Chirico, *The Nostalgia of the Infinite,* ca. 1913–1914, dated 1911 on the painting. Oil on canvas, 53¼ × 25½″. Collection, The Museum of Modern Art, New York. Purchase.

wound up in Paris where he studied the Old Masters in the Louvre. Strongly influenced by the German philosopher Nietzsche (see chap. 24), de Chirico looked upon himself as a metaphysical painter who explored the mysteries of life. In *The Nostalgia of the Infinite* (fig. 25.18) he used a distorted Renaissance perspective in a characteristic dreamlike cityscape in which everything is real, except that it isn't. Pennants are flying vigorously from a sinister and threatening tower in front of which two miniscule figures cast disproportionately long shadows. Like most of his images, this building actually exists in Turin but the strange juxtaposition creates another reality that is not of the waking world.

As early as 1914 it had become obvious to some artists that World War I marked the low point of a bankrupt Western culture. By 1916, exiles from the war that was consuming Europe had formed, in neutral Switzerland, the Cabinet Voltaire, a loose-knit and contentious group devoted to attacking everything that Western civilization held dear. For whatever reason, these writers, artists, musicians, and poets chose the word *Dada* to identify their iconoclastic movement. Dada was an idea whose time had come, for it happened even earlier in New York with the arrival, in 1915, of Marcel Duchamp (due–SHAWM; 1887–1968). Duchamp was always the greatest exponent of the "anti-art" movement known as Dada, having already turned "found" objects into art by, for example, hanging a snow shovel on a gallery wall and labelling it *In Advance of a Broken Arm.* He made the first mobile in 1913 by fastening an inverted bicycle wheel to the top of a stool and presenting it as a sculpture with moving parts. Typical of his assault on the citadel of formal art was the reproduction of the *Mona Lisa* to which he added a moustache and a goatee and the title of *L.H.O.O.Q.* which, when pronounced letter by letter in French means "She's got a hot ass."

Duchamp found a congenial home in Stieglitz's "291" and began work on his Dada masterpiece enigmatically titled *The Bride Stripped Bare by Her Bachelors, Even,* more commonly referred to as *The Large Glass* (colorplate 53). The following analysis is based on Duchamp's notes which, given the artist's proclivity for paradox and irony, may be accepted, modified, or rejected. According to Duchamp, this is the story of a bride, located in the upper section and symbolized by an internal combustion engine with a reservoir of love gasoline and a magneto of desire. She is lusted after by the nine bachelors in the left lower section: the reddish-brown molds resembling chessmen. Each bachelor is a stereotype of what were, at the time, masculine occupations: priest, delivery boy, policeman, warrior, gendarme, undertaker's assistant, busboy, stationmaster, and flunky. Capillary tubes carry gas from each bachelor mold to the center of the glass and to one of seven funnels, where the gas solidifies into large needles. These needles, in turn, break into spangles of frosty gas and then into liquid drops of semen that splash into the bride's domain. At the moment depicted in the glass the bride is stripped but she remains undefiled; bride and bachelors are caught between desire and possession/surrender. Duchamp intended the work to be humorous and sexual, satirizing machines, people, and social conventions. He succeeded on all counts.

Figure 25.19 Kurt Schwitters, *Sichtbar,* 1923. Collage, ca. 7 × 5″. Estate of Kurt Schwitters. Courtesy Marlborough Gallery, New York.

The leading German Dadaist, Kurt Schwitters (1887–1948), collected trash from wastebaskets and gutters to compose collages of the detritus of civilization. When once asked what art was, Schwitters responded with, "What isn't?" *Sichtbar* (fig. 25.19), meaning "visible," proves that an artist can arrange the unlikeliest materials into a meaningful statement. Like so many of his constructions, this work visualizes the modern city as a compressor and energizer of life, constantly changing, leaving behind the rubbish of yesterday.

Though Schwitters continued to collect and arrange his Dada collages, completely filling several three-story houses in the process, the movement was generally absorbed by the Surrealists, who coalesced around the Manifesto of Surrealism issued in 1924 by the writer André Breton, a disciple of Sigmund Freud (see chap. 23). Surrealism in art is, briefly stated, the theory that dreams, and those waking moments when subconscious images overwhelm our intellect, furnish us with material far more relevant to our lives than traditional subject matter. The world of psychic experience, as explored by Freud and others, was to be combined with consciousness to create a super-reality *(surréalité)* called Surrealism.

Surrealism was an organized movement in revolt against conventional art and society but there was no single style. Artists like Joan Miro (ME–row; 1893–1983) drew upon their personal dream world.

Colorplate 52 Piet Mondrian, *Composition in White, Black, and Red,* 1936. Oil on canvas, 41 × 40¼". Collection, The Museum of Modern Art, New York. Gift of the Advisory Committee.

Colorplate 53 Marcel Duchamp, *The Bride Stripped Bare by Her Bachelors, Even,* 1915–1923. Oil, lead wire and foil, and dust and varnish on plate glass (in two parts), 9′ 1¼″ × 5′ 9⅛″. Philadelphia Museum of Art. Bequest of Katherine S. Dreier.

Colorplate 54 Joan Miro, *Person Throwing a Stone at a Bird,* 1926. Oil on canvas, 36¼ × 29″. Collection, The Museum of Modern Art, New York. Acquired through the Lillie P. Bliss Bequest.

Colorplate 55 Jackson Pollack, *Number 1,* 1948. Oil on canvas, 9′8″ × 5′8″. Collection, The Museum of Modern Art, New York. Purchase.

Colorplate 56 Willem de Kooning, *Woman I,*
1950–1952. Oil on canvas, 75⅞ × 58″. Collection, The
Museum of Modern Art, New York. Purchase.

Colorplate 57 Mark Rothko, *Number 10,* 1950. Oil on
canvas, 90⅜ × 57⅛″. Collection, The Museum of
Modern Art, New York. Gift of Philip Johnson.

Colorplate 58 Paul Klee, *Fish Magic,* 1925. Oil and watercolor, varnished, 38⅝ × 30¼″. Philadelphia Museum of Art. Louise and Walter Arensberg Collection.

Colorplate 59 Otto Duecker, *Russell, Terry, J. T., and a Levi Jacket,* 1979. Oil on masonite cutouts. Courtesy, The Elaine Horwitch Galleries, Scottsdale.

Figure 25.20 Salvador Dali, *The Persistence of Memory,* 1931. Oil on canvas, 13 × 9¼″. Collection, The Museum of Modern Art, New York. Given anonymously.

Figure 25.21 Meret Oppenheim, *Luncheon in Fur,* 1936. Fur-covered cup, saucer, and spoon. Collection, The Museum of Modern Art, New York.

In *Person Throwing a Stone at a Bird* (colorplate 54) Miro does not abstract the human image but seems, instead, to humanize abstractions. In a witty and humorous style, sometimes called Biomorphic Abstraction, he creates an amoebic person with one huge foot, bulbous body, and orange and yellow eye. This being seems to fall back in wonder as an oblong stone falls in a delineated trajectory toward an appealing bird with a crescent torso from which a longline neck projects to a lavendar head topped by a flaming cock's comb. This is super-reality. "Everything in my pictures exists," stated Miro; "there is nothing abstract in my pictures."

Still the professed spokesman of the movement, Salvador Dali (DAH–lee; b. 1904) stresses paradox, disease, decay, and eroticism. *The Persistence of Memory* (fig. 25.20) is a tiny painting of a vast landscape in which watches hang limply and dejectedly. A strange chinless creature with protruding tongue (alive? dead?) lies in the foreground of a Renaissance perspective construction lit by an eerie glow. A dead tree grows out of a table (?) on which the only flat watch lies, a metal timepiece infested with sinister-looking bugs. Anything is possible in dreams.

Startling distortions or juxtapositions are basic to Surrealism as Meret Oppenheim's (b. 1913) surrealistic object *Luncheon in Fur* (fig. 25.21) demonstrates. The absurdity of a fur-lined teacup has become a symbol of Surrealism. Her now familiar but bizarre ensemble is typical of the push-pull effect of many Surrealist works. Our intellect is titillated but our senses of touch and taste are outraged.

With the exception of one artist there has been little significant surrealist sculpture. Surrealists believed in automatism, in just letting a painting happen, and shaping solid objects is too painstaking an endeavor to be directed by the subconscious. Only Alberto Giacometti (zhak–ko–MET–ti; 1901–1966) succeeded in creating three-dimensional equivalents of surrealist pictures. *The Palace at 4* A.M. (fig. 25.22) is an airy cage with a skeletal backbone in a smaller

Figure 25.22 Alberto Giacometti, *The Palace at 4* A.M., 1932–1933. Wood, glass, wire, and string, 25 × 28 × 15¾″. Collection, The Museum of Modern Art, New York. Purchase.

cage at the right and the figure of a woman on the left, the latter possibly representing the artist's mother. In the center is a spoon shape with which the artist said he identified and, at the upper right, the skeleton of a prehistoric bird that supposedly greets the dawn at 4 A.M. The air of dreamlike mystery is all pervasive.

Dreams can also be nightmares. In *The Blue Doll* (fig. 25.23) the American Surrealist Alton Pickens (b. 1917) depicts the murder of a doll, or perhaps two dolls. The distorted and brutal figures dominate an eerie and terrifying scene that is the stuff of nightmares.

Figure 25.23 Alton Pickens, *The Blue Doll,* 1942. Oil on canvas, 42⅞ × 35″. Collection, The Museum of Modern Art, New York. James Thrall Soby Fund.

Figure 25.24 Yves Tanguy, *The Stone in the Tree,* 1942. Oil on canvas, 24 × 18″. The University Art Collections, Arizona State University, Tempe. Gift of Oliver B. James.

Figure 25.25 John Sloan, *Roof Gossips,* ca. 1912. Oil on canvas, 24 × 20″. The University Art Collections, Arizona State University, Tempe. Gift of Oliver B. James.

Yves Tanguy (tawn–geay; 1900–1955) was a member of the original Surrealist group in Paris. After his escape from the Nazis in 1939 he was associated with the New York group of emigrées and later became an American citizen. He was, like Rousseau, an untrained artist. Throughout his career he painted vast and desolate landscapes inhabited by strange, haunting objects. *The Stone in the Tree* (fig. 25.24) depicts an endless space with no reference points. The eerie objects are not totally lifeless, seeming to possess a flicker of life left over from a destroyed universe. The artist appears to be portraying (in 1942!) our world after the ultimate nightmare of a nuclear holocaust.

Realism in America   From the early days of the Republic there has always been a strain of Realism on the American scene, a tradition separate from European Realists like Courbet and Millet. While European artists were experimenting with Impressionism, Americans like Thomas Eakins (1844–1916) and Winslow Homer (see colorplate 42) continued to paint reality as they perceived it. At the beginning of this century Robert Henri (hen–RYE; 1865–1929) founded a new school of realism called The Eight. Working almost entirely in New York, the followers of Henri painted city scenes of tenement life and everyday activities of, mainly, the working class. A derogatory remark by a critic gave still another new style a label. After the caustic comment that they "even painted ash cans," The Eight became known as the

Ash Can school. John Sloan (1871–1951), a leading artist of the school, painted *Roof Gossips* (fig. 25.25) as if the three women on the tenement roof were the subject of a casual snapshot. Actually, the work is an artful composition of lines and forms. Reminiscent of the high viewpoint of Mary Cassatt's *The Bath* (see fig. 22.24), we witness an intimate and relaxed scene but are not a part of it. Academicians were critical of the gritty realism of Sloan and the Ash Can school but did join with them and the avant-garde of "291" to present the Armory Show the year after this work was painted.

A student of Henri's in the early 1900s, Edward Hopper (1882–1967) was more concerned with formal design than were his Ash Can colleagues. He did not paint people in everyday life but sought subjects like old houses and buildings along the coast of Maine and on Cape Cod. His *Cottage, Cape Cod* (fig. 25.26), like most of his paintings, rests on a solid horizontal base

Figure 25.26 Edward Hopper, *Cottage, Cape Cod,* 1942. Oil on canvas, 27 × 19". The University Art Collections, Arizona State University, Tempe. Gift of Oliver B. James.

Figure 25.27 Diego Rivera, *Niña Parada,* 1937. Oil on canvas, 31½ × 23½". The University Art Collections, Arizona State University, Tempe. Gift of Oliver B. James.

from which the rising verticals and slanting diagonals outline a house "with sunlight on the side" as Hopper preferred to paint. The broad, uncluttered planes, sunlight, and shadows give the house a brooding air of loneliness and melancholy.

Best described as Social Realists, Diego Rivera, José Orozco, and David Siqueiros were the most important Mexican mural painters of the century. Diego

Figure 25.28 Antonio Gaudi, Church of the Holy Family, 1883–1926. Barcelona.

Rivera (1886–1957), though he lived and studied in Europe for many years, disavowed modernism in his zeal to create a distinctly Mexican style in the Socialist spirit of the protracted Mexican revolution (1910–1940). Like most of his subjects, *Niña Parada* (fig. 25.27) is one of the common people, a stocky child with a heavy body and broad, impassive face. Despite her obvious youth she looks considerably older. Weary and endlessly patient, she represents a class that for centuries had been downtrodden and exploited.

Architecture

Art Nouveau was a turn-of-the-century style that grew out of an English Arts and Crafts movement to revive medieval craftsmanship. Determined to raise interior and decorative design to the eminence enjoyed by painting and sculpture, Art Nouveau artists and craftsmen developed an elaborate curvilinear style that assiduously avoided straight lines and right angles. Line drawings by Aubrey Beardsley (1872–1898) and multicolored lamps by Louis Comfort Tiffany (1848–1933) were Art Nouveau, as was the basic style of the Spanish architect Antonio Gaudi (gow–D; 1852–1926). In his Church of the Holy Family (fig. 25.28) Gaudi went beyond the Art Nouveau style to architectural innovations never seen before or since. Working with a church that had already been started as a Gothic revival structure, Gaudi added four bottle-shaped spires pierced by innumerable holes and topped by glittering crystal decorations. Although the enormous building is primarily of cut stone, it looks eroded and dessicated, organic rather than man-made. Much of the exterior is studded with bright ceramic decorations, with more scheduled to be added if and when the building is completed.

Art Nouveau tried, unsuccessfully, to deny the Industrial Age but the work of the design school called Bauhaus (BOUGH–house) exploited modern technology. As director of Bauhaus, Walter Gropius (1883–1969) promoted instruction in not only painting, sculpture, and architecture, but also in the crafts, with everything oriented toward the latest in technology and industrial design. The workshop (fig. 25.29) is a four-story box with an interior steel skeleton enclosed by window walls of glass, the latter a

Gropius invention. The design established the principles of the International Style that was to dominate architectural design into the 1970s. Expensive to heat and to cool, not to mention washing the windows, International Style buildings appear as anomalies in the energy-conscious 1980s. For half a century, however, they were the essence of modernity.

The International Style was brilliantly developed by the Swiss painter-architect Charles-Edouard Jeanneret known as Le Corbusier (luh core–BOOS–iay; 1887–1965). For Le Corbusier, houses were "machines for living," as efficient as airplanes were for flying. Totally devoid of ornament, his Villa Savoye (fig. 25.30) is partially supported by the slender columns but rests mostly on a recessed unit containing service functions, servants quarters, entrance hall, and staircase to the living quarters on the second level. The living room is separated from an open interior terrace by floor-to-ceiling panes of glass, making the terrace a basic part of living arrangements.

International Style buildings are, in effect, disdainful of their environment, thrusting away from the earth to create their own internal space. America's greatest architect, Frank Lloyd Wright (1867–1959), disagreed totally with this concept. Wright's buildings are generally organic, seemingly a natural consequence of their environment. One of his most imaginative designs is the Kaufmann House (fig. 25.31). Built on a site that would challenge any architect and which obviously inspired Wright, the house is situated on a steep and rocky hillside over a waterfall. Combining native rock construction with daring cantilevers colored beige to blend with the environment, the structure cannot even be imagined on any other site. The Villa Savoye and Falling Water represent, between them, opposite theories of modern design; subsequent developments tended to fall somewhere between the two extremes.

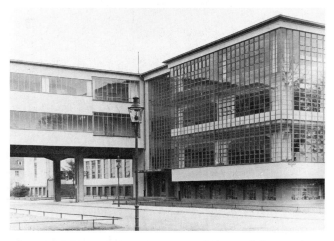

Figure 25.29 Walter Gropius, Workshop of the Bauhaus, 1925–1926. Dessau, Germany.

Figure 25.30 Le Corbusier, Villa Savoye, 1929. Poissy-sur-Seine, France.

Figure 25.31 Frank Lloyd Wright, Kaufmann House ("Falling Water"), 1936. Bear Run, Pennsylvania.

Artistic Styles Since 1945

Painting and Sculpture

Action Painting: Abstract Expressionism   After World War II, New York replaced Paris as the artistic capital of the Western world. The acknowledged leader of a new artistic movement was Jackson Pollock (1912–1956), who was once a Social Realist. Pollock's personal style of Abstract Expressionism began to bloom when he quit easel painting and, instead, tacked a large, unstretched canvas to the floor. Walking all around the canvas he became completely absorbed as he dropped, dripped, poured, and spattered paint on the canvas. Though he had no preconceived ideas when he began a canvas he could, as he said, "control the flow of the paint," and he did complete works with brushstrokes as needed. His *Number 1* (colorplate 55) is an intricate and complex interplay of curvilinear lines and controlled spatters illustrating, as he remarked, "energy made visible." Pollock's energetic involvement in the act of painting led to the term Action Painting as a general descriptor of the movement.

Pollock's style of Abstract Expressionism totally abandoned all recognizable forms and shapes, a remarkable achievement in itself. His *Galaxy* (fig. 25.32) has both lines and shapes; forms rest upon forms that cover still other forms. As our eyes move endlessly over the vitalized canvas we seem to perceive distant, indistinct solar systems through a blizzard of molecular dots that themselves appear to be faraway stars.

The Dutch-American artist Willem de Kooning (b. 1904) works in violent motions using a brush heavy with paint. His favorite theme is that of the eternal woman: earth mother and goddess of fertility. *Woman I* (colorplate 56) is a giant, earthy figure of a woman

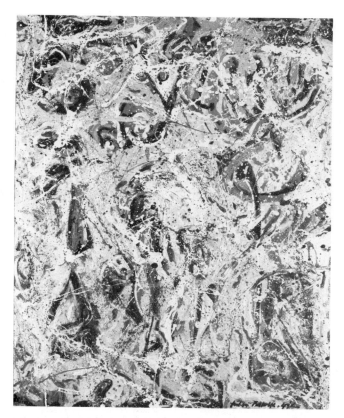

Figure 25.32 Jackson Pollock, *Galaxy,* 1946. Joslyn Art Museum, Omaha, Nebraska. Gift of Miss Peggy Guggenheim.

painted in slashing brushstrokes. An energetic portrayal of a goddess cum movie queen and sex symbol, this is one man's view of the other half of the human race.

In his mature style Mark Rothko (1903–1970) covered large canvases with luminous, softly bleeding rectangles of color. *Number 10* (colorplate 57) is an extremely subtle combination of softly glowing colors separated by ragged, foggy edges. Compared with the dynamics of Pollock and de Kooning, this is Abstract Expressionism in a gentle and meditative mood in a style frequently called Color Field.

Reaction against Action: Pop Art   The emotional fervor of Abstract Expressionism burned itself out in about fifteen years, to be superseded by a Dada-type reaction. The self-confidence of America after World War II had been jolted by the Korean conflict, the Cold War, and the buildup in Vietnam. A new breed of artists was skeptical of American accomplishments and chose the banalities of American life to satirize the superficiality of American culture. First called Neo-Dadaists, these artists used recognizable subject matter from American popular culture: soup cans, comic strips, road signs, and cult figures from Rock music and commercial Hollywood movies.

Figure 25.33 Robert Rauschenberg, *Bed,* 1955. Combine painting, 74 × 31″. Leo Castelli, New York.

The movement was labeled Pop Art when it burst on the national scene in 1962, but Robert Rauschenberg (b. 1925) had been working his way from Abstract Expressionism to Pop Art since the mid 50s. His *Bed* (fig. 25.33) includes a pillow and quilt over which he has splashed paint. Real objects have been combined with paint, destroying their original, familiar meaning so that they become part of a composition with an independent existence. Neither sculpture nor painting, this is, as the artist says, a combine that unites two-dimensional and three-dimensional art.

Figure 25.34 Robert Rauschenberg, *Monogram,* 1959. Construction, 48 × 72 × 72″. Moderna Museet, Stockholm, Sweden.

There are recognizable objects in Rauschenberg's *Monogram* (fig. 25.34) like the old tire, stuffed Angora goat, and pieces of stenciled signs. The goat and tire were once waste that has been recycled, so to speak. Paradoxically, they are still distasteful objects, retaining their identity and creating a tension between themselves and the total work. They should not be there but they are, undeniably, there, forever and ever. Rauschenberg has stated that painting is related to art and to life and that his function is to "act in the gap between the two."

Another early leader of the Pop movement, Jasper Johns (b. 1930), painted familiar images like flags, targets, maps, and numbers. Commenting that they were so common that they had become almost invisible, Johns felt that everyday images could be known in their own right. Numerals, for example, can be given identities (fig. 25.35). *Figure 6* is as delicate as a subtle tracery; *Figure 7* is soft and lacking in clarity, as enigmatic as the *Mona Lisa* that peers at us; *Figure 8* is reminiscent of the chiaroscuro in Rembrandt's late etchings; and *Figure 9* is bold and assertive. The tension between the two-dimensionality of the numerals and their psychological depth is striking.

Rauschenberg and Johns generally retain the painterly quality of Abstract Expressionism, but Roy Lichtenstein (b. 1923) adopted the mechanical techniques and imagery of comic strips, including the Benday dots used in newspaper reproductions of the comics. He also used the hard lines of comic strips but his paintings are monumental in scale. His cold and impersonal portrayal of a *Drowning Girl* (fig. 25.36) was an indictment of the casual and callous attitudes of many Americans toward violence in comic strips, in the streets, in Vietnam. The technique is that of the "low art" of the comics but the result is a potent artistic statement. Lichtenstein, for obvious reasons, selected nothing from comic strips like *Peanuts.*

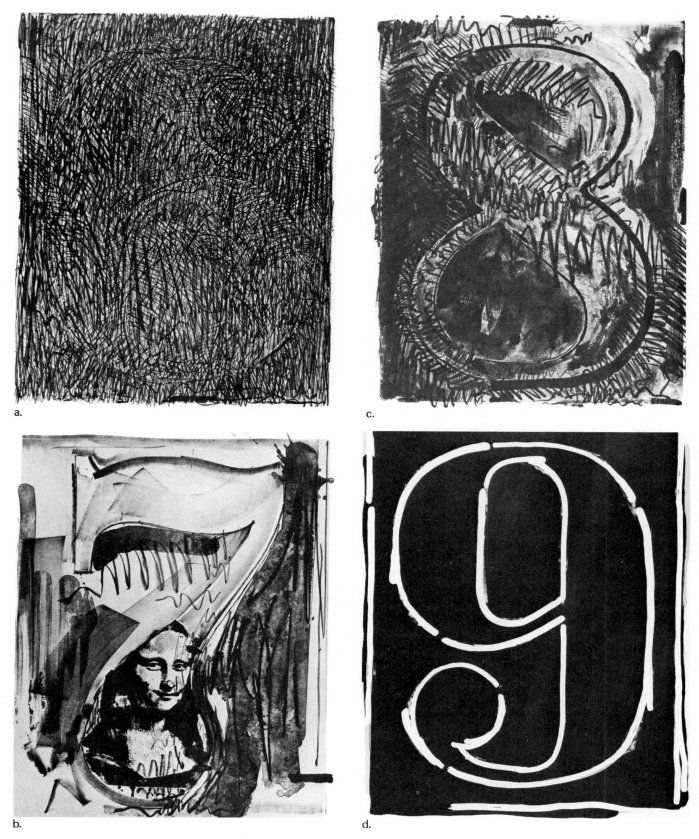

Figure 25.35 Jasper Johns, *Black Numerals,* 1966. a. *Figure 6,* b. *Figure 7,* c. *Figure 8,* d. *Figure 9,* 1968. Lithographs, 37 × 30″ each. Copyright Gemini G. E. L., 1968.

Figure 25.36 Roy Lichtenstein, *Drowning Girl,* 1963. Oil and synthetic polymer paint on canvas, 67⅝ × 66¾". Collection, The Museum of Modern Art, New York. Gift of Philip Johnson and Mr. and Mrs. Bagley.

Andy Warhol (b. 1925) began his career as a commercial artist, working with images and methods that provided a whole vocabulary of banality. His Campbell's Soup cans, Coca-Cola bottles, and multiple portraits of celebrities have made him the best known of Pop artists. *The American Man (Portrait of Watson Powell)* (fig. 25.37) is the first known portrait by a Pop artist to be commissioned by a businessman for a corporate collection. This multi-portrait suggests the continuity of filmstrips except that the thirty-two images vary only in the subtle changes of light and dark. With his serialized multi-images Warhol establishes a boredom that can become hypnotic.

EAT, SLEEP, LOVE are some of the words that Robert Indiana (b. Robert Clark of Indiana in 1928) extracts from signs to treat as subject matter. LOVE, as in the reiterated "make love not war" slogan of antiwar protestors of the 60s, is the subject of Indiana's jewelry designs, painting, sculpture, and printing. *The Black and White Love* (fig. 25.38) is a complex design that resonates with multiple meanings. Is this the word that makes the world go round? Indiana's handcut aluminum sculpture of *Love* (fig. 25.39) is boldly provocative, forcing the viewer to wonder why the "O" can't stand upright. Is LOVE askew or is it the society that uses the word so readily?

Early in the Pop movement Claes Oldenburg (b. 1929) specialized in creating sculptures like his classic six-foot hamburger. Later he turned to soft vinyl sculptures of everyday objects: shirts, ties, electrical outlets, and the like, all ten or twenty times actual size. Oldenburg's capacity for innovation is astounding,

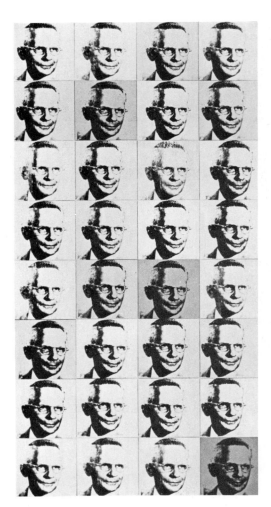

Figure 25.37 Andy Warhol, *The American Man (Portrait of Watson Powell),* 1964. Silkscreen ink and acrylic on canvas, 10'8⅞" × 5'4⅜". Courtesy, The American Republic Insurance Company, Des Moines, Iowa.

sometimes amusing, like his 4' clothespins, sometimes frightening, like his proposal for a park monument in the shape of an H-bomb mushroom cloud. His *Proposal for a Giant Balloon in the Form of a Typewriter Eraser* (fig. 25.40) is monumental even in the structural model and the mind boggles at the thought of the eraser soaring through the sky.

The sculptures of Edward Kienholz (b. 1927) have been called Pop but his work is also expressionistic and surreal. He combines painting, sculpture, collage, and the stage to depict the shabbiness, stupidity, and cruelty of modern urban life: an abandoned patient in a desolate mental ward; patrons in a seedy cafe; lovers on the back seat of a decrepit car. In a satirical vein, *The Friendly Grey Computer—Star Gauge Model #54* (fig. 25.41) appears, at first, to be "user friendly." A second look shows, however, a human being who has turned into a mechanized contraption that clanks and whirrs. Or has Model #54 swallowed the user?

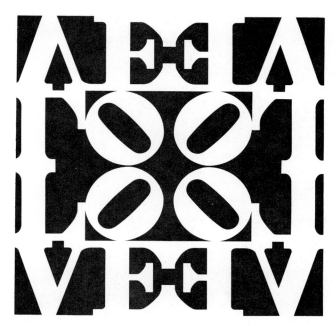

Figure 25.38 Robert Indiana, *The Black and White Love,* ca. 1966. Silkscreen. Printed by Multiples, New York.

Figure 25.39 Robert Indiana, *Love,* 1960. Aluminum, 12 × 12 × 6″. Published by Multiples, New York. Edition of six.

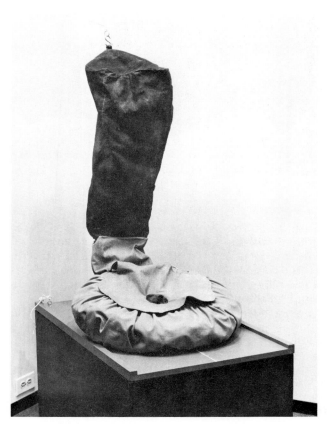

Figure 25.40 Claes Oldenburg, *Proposal for a Giant Balloon in the Form of a Typewriter Eraser—Structural Model,* 1970. Painted canvas, spray enamel, liquitex, and shredded foam rubber, 58″ high. Collection of the High Museum, Atlanta, Georgia. Courtesy of the Margo Leavin Gallery, Los Angeles.

Figure 25.41 Edward Kienholz, *The Friendly Grey Computer—Star Gauge Model #54,* 1965. Motorized assemblage, 40 × 39⅛ × 24½″. Collection, The Museum of Modern Art, New York. Gift of Jean and Howard Lipman.

Figure 25.42 Josef Albers, *Homage to the Square: Ascending*, 1953. Oil on composition board, 43½" square. Whitney Museum of American Art, New York.

Figure 25.43 Kenneth Noland, *Cirium of 1964*. Arcylic on canvas, 18' × 8'9". Joslyn Art Museum, Omaha, Nebraska.

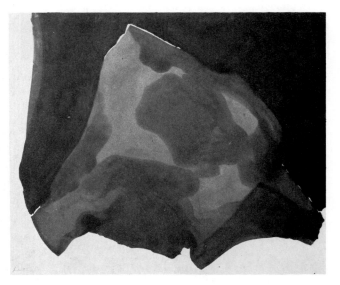

Figure 25.44 Helen Frankenthaler, *Monoscape,* 1969. Joslyn Art Museum, Omaha Nebraska.

Color, Geometry, and Optics   One of the first graduates of the Bauhaus, Josef Albers (1888–1976) emigrated to the United States in 1933, where his work influenced the development of abstract geometric painting and Op art. His *Homage to the Square* paintings were a serialization similar to Monet's paintings of haystacks and lily ponds, a process, not a solution. Working with three or four squares of different colors, Albers explored, in hundreds of paintings, the interaction of colors and straight lines. *Homage to a Square: Ascending* (fig. 25.42) has a yellow square surrounded by white, surrounded in turn by grey, and framed by powder blue. The overall effect of this particular scheme is a remarkable serenity quite unlike Rothko's glowing colors and fuzzy lines (see colorplate 57).

Kenneth Noland (b. 1924) was influenced by Albers and Mondrian but chose abstract images painted boldly and with immaculate precision. Sometimes called a "hard-edge" painter, Noland is known for his immense paintings of chevron or wedge shapes. *Cirium of 1964* (fig. 25.43) is simple, bold, and enormous.

Working against the currents of Abstract Expressionism and Geometric Abstraction, Helen Frankenthaler (b. 1928) stained the raw canvas to achieve a limpid freshness quite unlike the work of other artists. In *Monoscape* (fig. 25.44) large amorphous forms seem to float like pools of mercury. The tension is heightened by the interplay of the unstable shapes and the flat, pristine background.

The assemblage of sculptures of Louise Nevelson (b. 1900) reflect the geometric forms of pre-Columbian sculpture, but her overriding interest in working with wood can be traced to her father's career as a cabinetmaker and her involvement with the wood in his shop. *Illumination—Dark* (fig. 25.45) is a large wooden wall on which the artist has arranged selected pieces of wood culled from old houses to form a three-dimensional geometric abstraction. With bronze-painted shapes against the flat black background of the wall, the piece resembles both a cupboard and a cityscape like the artist's native New York. As Nevelson has said, she "putters endlessly" with the design until she gets it right. The result here is a subtle blend of delicacy, mystery, and strength.

American painters like Albers and Noland were concerned with straight lines but the British artist Bridget Riley (b. 1931) worked with the possibilities inherent in curved lines. *Current* (fig. 25.46) is a terse composition that communicates directly with the eye and the optic nerve. Though she has been called an Op artist (from Optical art), Riley's style goes beyond merely confusing or tricking the eye. What we have here is a new way of perceiving and experiencing motion.

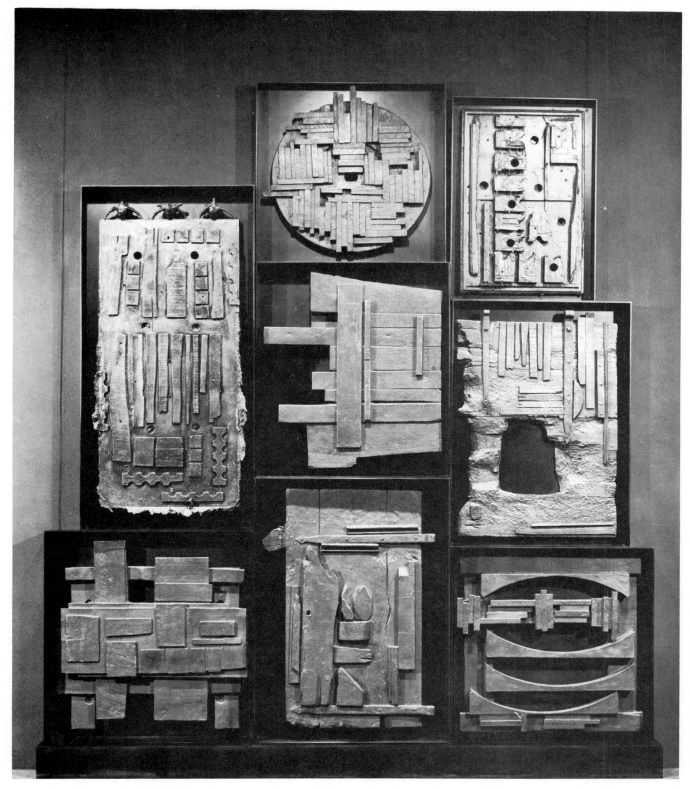

Figure 25.45 Louise Nevelson, *Illumination—Dark,* 1961. Wood and bronze reliefs, 10′5″ × 9½″ × 5″ deep. Whitney Museum of American Art, New York.

Figure 25.46 Bridget Riley, *Current,* 1964. Synthetic-resin paint on composition board, ca. 58⅞ × 53⅜". Collection, The Museum of Modern Art, New York. Philip Johnson Fund.

Figure 25.47 Jean Dubuffet, *Portrait of Henri Michaux,* 1947. Oil and other substances on canvas, 51½ × 38⅜". The Sidney and Harriet Janis Collection. Gift of the Museum of Modern Art, New York.

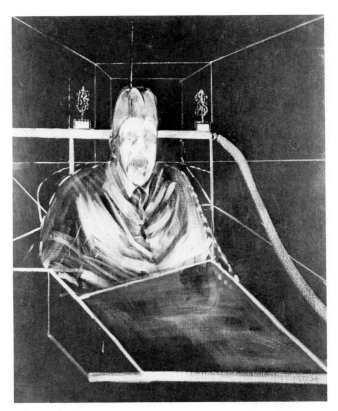

Figure 25.48 Francis Bacon, *Number VII from Eight Studies for a Portrait,* 1953. Oil on canvas, 60 × 46⅛". Collection, The Museum of Modern Art, New York. Gift of Mr. and Mrs. William A. M. Burden.

Fantasy, Expressionism, and Surrealism Jean Dubuffet (due–boo–FAY; b. 1901), the most notable French artist since World War II, found his inspiration in strangely different areas: art of the insane, children's art, and graffiti. Dubuffet painted intuitively, somewhat like the Abstract Expressionists, but his subjects were fantastic figures and landscapes. He combined pigments with different mixtures of plaster, sand, or twigs to make a thick impasto that he scratched and scored to make grotesque figures like his *Portrait of Henri Michaux* (fig. 25.47). The artist referred to this style as *art brut,* which can be translated as brutal art or ugly art; both are apropos. Whatever the label, this attack on conventional artistic standards, even in the twentieth century, has a powerful primordial quality that both attracts and repels.

The Irish-born Francis Bacon (b. 1901) paints tormented visions distorted to the point of insanity. Preoccupied with deformity and disease, he selects works by Old Masters and restates them as anguished symbols of contemporary life. *Number VII from Eight Studies for a Portrait* (fig. 25.48) is based on the portrait of Pope Innocent X (1644–1655) by Velasquez, who depicted the pope as a powerful, intelligent, and cooly confident pontiff. Bacon uses Renaissance perspective but places the pope in an isolation booth where his anguished screams tear his head asunder.

Figure 25.49 Leonel Gongora, *Velasquez Painting Gongora,* 1961. Oil on canvas, ca. 50 × 36″. The University Art Collections, Arizona State University, Tempe.

Figure 25.50 Roy de Forest, *Inside the Bull,* 1973. Polymer on canvas, 72¾ × 66¾″. American Art Heritage Fund. Arizona State University Art Collections, Tempe.

Figure 25.51 Fritz Scholder, *Waiting Indian No. 4,* 1970. Oil on canvas, 70 × 64″. The University Art Collections, Arizona State University, Tempe.

Velasquez also costars in a fantasy work by Leonel Gongora (GONG–go–ra; b. 1932), a Colombian painter who was educated in the United States. Both a tribute to the Spanish tradition and a fanciful manipulation of reality, *Velasquez Painting Gongora* (fig. 25.49) depicts the youthful artist in seventeenth-century garb standing before a portrait of Velasquez. The reference is to the *Maids of Honor* by Velasquez (see fig. 18.14) in which Velasquez looks directly at the viewer as Gongora does in this painting. The mirror that reflects the images of the king and queen in *Maids of Honor* has become the portrait of an older Velasquez, creating the illusion that the portrait is a reflection of the Spanish artist as he paints Gongora. Reality is adroitly confused and extended in both space and time.

Fantasy becomes light-hearted in the work of the innovative California painter and sculptor Roy de Forest (b. 1930), who delights in exploring states beyond seriousness. *Inside the Bull* (fig. 25.50) depicts a cruise ship sailing by a tropical isle with one palm tree and a candy-eyed native. The gentle bull stands calmly over a white Spitz dog with fiery red eyes. Fanciful, delightful, semipsychedelic, and replete with incongruities, this style can be described as "funk art" in the manner of the funky sounds of Soul Jazz (see chap. 26).

The best-known American Indian artist, Fritz Scholder (b. 1937), shows the influence of Expressionism and Pop Art but his subject matter sets him apart from both styles. Scholder uses serialism to portray the paradoxical position of Native Americans in American life. With a poignant irony he has depicted stereotypes: a Super Chief eating an ice cream cone; a drunken Indian clutching a can of beer like a tomahawk; a Hollywood Indian and his captive Anglo maiden. Scholder's work is satirical and searching, depicting the degradation and basic nobility of his people. *Waiting Indian No. 4* (fig. 25.51) stands majestically in a barren landscape. In his awesome dignity he refuses to accept any part of a stereotype in the Anglo world.

Philip Curtis (b. 1907) combines a remarkable gift for fantasy with classical techniques of the Renaissance tradition. *Farewell* (fig. 25.52) pictures a family waving good-bye to a little girl who frantically returns

Figure 25.52 Philip Curtis, *Farewell,* 1961. Collection of Edward Jacobson, Phoenix, Arizona.

Figure 25.53 Alexander Calder, *Many Pierced Discs,* 65 × 49″. The University Art Collections, Arizona State University, Tempe.

their gestures from the caboose of a train. Belatedly, we realize that the child and the parting train are part of a billboard and our senses reel with the enigma. Curtis steadfastly maintains that he is not a Surrealist but critics are unconvinced. There are no apparent Freudian undertones but this is a super-reality beyond everyday experience.

For centuries sculptors have labored to give their works the illusion of movement. Alexander Calder (1898–1976) invented abstract works that actually moved. Influenced by Surrealism and geometric abstractions, Calder created the true mobile. *Many Pierced Discs* (fig. 25.53) is a fantasy of abstract shapes wired together and delicately balanced so that it can respond to the slightest breeze. An indoor rather than an outdoor mobile that is activated by the wind, this work rests on its pedestal in an art gallery where it can gently gyrate and bow to museum visitors.

Mark di Suvero's (b. 1933) *Side Frames* (fig. 25.54) is a giant outdoor mobile, an abstract fantasy on a grand scale. A large pendant is held, seemingly tenuously, by a cable attached to a long balanced beam. Despite the work's monumental size the pendant is completely free to sway or twist in the wind. Di Suvero's works are energy structures, metallic lyrics of action and reaction.

Henry Moore (b. 1898) is the most important English artist in any medium. Like Calder, he was influenced by Surrealism but went on to develop his unique abstract figural style. In *Girl Seated Against a Square Wall* (fig. 25.55) the figure is abstracted into a depersonalized version of the female concept. The attenuated legs, arms, neck, and the tiny head recall the Mannerist emotionalism of El Greco. The arms encapsulate and press space to the torso, just as the girl's legs and the bench's supports emphasize and contrast space and bulk. Space, for Moore, is as important as solids; this figure is surrounded by a much larger space as suggested by the floor and square wall.

Minimal Art Minimal Art began in the 1960s as a movement to reduce art to basics: one shape or one color or one idea. Also called Primary Structures or Primary Art, the style is easier to observe than to discuss. *Sentaro* (fig. 25.56) by Tony DeLap (b. 1927) is a sculpture/painting reduced to a basic shape and a single color. This is a beautiful hunk of a bright red rectangular box that seemingly floats within its plastic case. DeLap used commercial staining and spraying techniques so that the saturated painting/sculpture is a solid color field with no trace of brushwork or other manipulation by the artist. The vitality and spontaneity of Abstract Expressionism has given way to a laidback restraint comparable to Cool Jazz (see chap. 26).

American sculptor David Smith (1906–1965) applied his experience of working in an automotive plant and locomotive factory to sculpting with steel which, as he said, "had little art history." His *Cubi XV* (fig. 25.57) is a gravity-defying combination of simple geometric components that set up a lively interplay of forms and space. The stainless steel is highly polished, with controlled light patterns that make the metal surface as sensual as works by Brancusi (see fig. 25.16) or Verrocchio (see fig. 14.12).

Figure 25.54 Mark di Suvero, *Side Frames,* 1979. Steel, 24′ long × 12′ wide × 16′ high. Courtesy of ConStruct, Chicago.

Figure 25.55 Henry Moore, *Girl Seated Against a Square Wall,* 1958–1959. Bronze, 41¾ × 33⁷⁄₁₆″. Museum of Art, The University of Arizona. Gift of Edward J. Gallagher, Jr.

Figure 25.56 Tony DeLap, *Sentaro,* 1967. Aluminum, wood, plexiglass, and lacquer, 16 × 16 × 5″ deep. American Art Heritage Fund. Arizona State University Art Collections, Tempe.

Figure 25.57 David Smith, *Cubi XV*. Steel, 10'5⅛" × 4'10½". The San Diego Museum of Art, San Diego, California.

Figure 25.58 Ronald Bladen, *X*, 1967. Wood, 22'8" × 24'6". Courtesy Fishback Gallery, New York.

For an exhibition in Washington's Corcoran Gallery, Ronald Bladen (b. 1918) created a giant *X* of painted wood (fig. 25.58) that virtually filled a classical two-story hall. The spectator can not only walk around the sculpture but through it as well. Large-scale Minimalist works such as this offer valid alternatives to representational public monuments which, more often than not, are forgettable clichés. The understated elegance and enormous power of the Washington Memorial to the veterans of the Vietnam War is a case in point.

Varieties of Realism Though never absent from the American scene, Realism has again become a major factor in a variety of styles called New Realism, Magic Realism, or Photorealism. The sculptor Duane Hanson (b. 1925) makes casts of living people and paints the resulting figures to look completely lifelike, including real clothing and accessories. Richard Estes (b. 1936) projects a slide directly on canvas and makes a precise copy with an airbrush. Hanson selects subjects like gaudily-dressed tourists, junkies, and overweight shoppers, while Estes paints banal cityscapes totally devoid of people. In their subject matter Hanson and Estes follow the orientation of Pop Art but other artists use photorealism in a more positive vein. In *The Glass Table* (fig. 25.59) John Moore (b. 1941) uses a superb technique to depict the light and airy corner of a room. The table waits invitingly for someone to walk in and sit down.

Ben Schonzeit (b. 1942) reveals an apparent fidelity to photographic reality in his *Tools* (fig. 25.60) but close observation discloses crisp tactile details on the right and soft focus on the left. To see a 2'-tall nib of an ink pen and brushheads almost as large is disconcerting, perhaps more so than some Surrealist anomalies. With his enormous *Tools* Schonzeit transforms his viewers into, in effect, a Lilliputian-sized audience. On the other hand, gargantuan movie screens and the sight of 6"-high football players racing about a TV screen may have innoculated the public against size-shock.

Our society has apparently learned to accept many real/unreal mystifications of the everyday world. Indeed, when Otto Duecker (b. 1948) paints larger-than-life-sized figures, cuts them out, and arranges them in galleries, homes, and warehouses, we are inclined to accept them as "real." In *Russell, Terry, J.T., and a Levi Jacket* (colorplate 59) we see the artist posed in front of his four cutouts and appearing, in this photograph, somehow less real than his creations.

Figure 25.59 John Moore, *The Glass Table,* 1975. Acrylic on canvas, 90 × 75″. The University Art Collections, Arizona State University, Tempe. Gift of the Childe Hassam Fund, 1975.

Figure 25.61 James Havard, *Cane Garden,* 1979. Courtesy, The Elaine Horwitch Galleries, Scottsdale.

Figure 25.60 Ben Schonzeit, *Tools,* 1974. Acrylic on canvas, 60 × 44″. Courtesy, Ponderosa System, Inc., Dayton, Ohio.

James Havard (b. 1937) is a leading artist in a new generation of American abstract painters. He challenges one's concept of reality by creating illusionistic nonobjective paintings in a style called Abstract Illusionism. His *Cane Garden* (fig. 25.61) deliberately violates the unity of canvas and what is painted on it. Havard gives every stroke of paint a texture, bulk, even shadows, all of which seem to rest upon, but not

become a part of, a solid-colored canvas. In fact, Havard's work is a painting of a nonobjective painting. What is real? Earlier, it was stated that each generation develops its own concepts of reality. For the present century, frequently called the Age of Uncertainty, it might be more accurate to point out that several concepts of reality are acceptable or, possibly, tolerable.

Hispanic and Black Artists

Contemporary artists of Hispanic or African heritages are just as involved with mainstream art as their colleagues; artists are, after all, contributing members of the international community of artists, more involved with breaking down national or ethnic barriers than erecting them. An overview of past and present developments by Hispanic and black artists is given here because American society has, primarily in the past, had barriers that excluded minorities from the mainstream of American life, barriers that, in effect, created a history of Hispanic and black art and artists. Moreover, when minority artists worked in prevailing styles their art was frequently downgraded as "imitative." When their work expressed their ethnic heritage it was all too often criticized because it did not conform to establishment attitudes about what art should be, a no-win situation that is finally largely in the past.

There are no typical Hispanic (or Mexican American or Chicano) artists nor are there any styles that are clearly Hispanic. The most common attribute of Hispanic artists is that they, in general, live in the American Southwest in areas formerly belonging to Mexico. Some are influenced by the pre-Columbian past while others deny it. The European tradition that

Spain brought to Mexico influences some artists and repels others. They are bilingual, their roots are in pre-Columbian times, followed by three centuries of Spanish rule and a century and a half of American culture. Their culture is complex, their tradition rich, and their search for identity as Americans is what much of their art, and culture, is all about.

The most important influences early in the century were those of Mexican muralists José Orozco (1883–1949) and Rufino Tamayo (b. 1899), both of whom executed major works while living in this country. Antonio García (b. 1901) and Porfirio Salinas (b. 1912) are leading artists of the first generation of Hispanic painters. Both are realists with García specializing in portraiture and Salinas in landscapes of his native Texas. In the second generation Edward Chávez (b. 1917) and Michael Ponce de León (b. 1922) have gained national prominence. Chávez is an abstractionist in the cubist mode while de León is a printmaker who specializes in bas-relief prints. Influenced by Pop Art, Melesio Casas (b. 1929) has done a series of paintings based on movies and TV advertising that he calls "Humanscapes." Sculptor Manuel Neri (b. 1930) is influenced by pre-Columbian art and Orozco and paints sculptures that he has hacked out of plaster. Ralph Ortiz (b. 1934) is a Destructive artist. For his Piano Destruction Concert Ortiz attacks with an ax an upright piano that has plastic bags of animal blood suspended inside. The resulting mess of blood-stained keys, splinters, and strings is, according to Ortiz, an artistic realization of violence that symbolizes the violence and destruction of the real world. Luis Jimenez (b. 1940) creates polychromed sculptures made of epoxy and fiberglass. Influenced by Pop Art and popular culture, Jimenez's works are lusty, humorous, and charged with explosive energy, particularly works like *Rodeo Queen* and *California Chick,* not to mention his show that he called *Texas Sweet Funk.*

American artists of African ancestry have contributed to the arts in America since Jamestown was founded in 1619. Joshua Johnson (1765–1830), the most celebrated of Black artisan-painters, painted family portraits, some of which are in the National Gallery, though most have been retained by descendents of the original families. His *The Westwood Children* (fig. 25.62) has a charming modern appeal with its artful asymmetrical arrangement of the children, the dog, and the tree outside. The children are dressed in identical outfits but each is distinguished by hair style, placement of the feet, and the held objects.

Influenced by the mysticism of the Hudson River School, Robert S. Duncanson (1817–1872) was recognized in his own time as an outstanding landscape painter. His *Blue Hole, Flood Waters, Little Miami River* is one of the finest works in the romantic style of the Hudson River tradition. Artist Edward M. Bannister (1828–1901) was described by a friend as impelled to pursue an artistic career after reading in a New York newspaper that "while the Negro may harbor an appreciation of art, he is unable to produce it." Refusing to accept patronage for the usual study

Figure 25.62 Joshua Johnson, *The Westwood Children,* ca. 1807. Oil on canvas, 41⅛ × 46″. Gift of Edgar William and Bernice Chrysler Garbisch, 1959. National Gallery of Art, Washington, D.C.

in Europe, Bannister developed a landscape style in the Hudson River tradition that, in 1876, became nationally recognized when he won a gold medal at the Philadelphia Centennial Exposition.

Sculptor Edmonia Lewis (1843–ca. 1900) also won an award at the Philadelphia Exposition but her career was very different from that of Bannister. Bannister avoided racial themes; Lewis exploited racial issues. Created in the Neoclassic style, her sculpture *Forever Free* celebrated the thirteenth amendment to the constitution that prohibited slavery.

A student of Thomas Eakins at the Pennsylvania Academy of Art, Henry O. Tanner (1859–1937) was the first black American artist to achieve an international reputation with his election to the French Academy. Like many other artists whose ethnic background placed them in a minority population, Tanner rejected the label, at the time, of Negro artist. Whether black, Hispanic, Indian, or even American, American artists like Tanner insisted upon recognition in their own right without stereotypical labels. Tanner did not disavow his heritage but he did insist that he was an artist who happened to be black and who happened to be an American. Not surprisingly, a dichotomy still exists among some black artists who seek acceptance as mainstream artists but who are proud of their heritage.

A notable artist in the manner of colonial artisan-painters, Horace Pippin (1888–1946) was a self-taught painter whose style can be described as modernized abstractions of folk art traditions. Unlike the French primitive Henri Rousseau, Pippin's work was acclaimed in his lifetime and acquired by major American museums.

Hale Woodruff's (b. 1900) most notable work is the three-panel series, *The Amistad Murals,* at Talladega College in Alabama. The subject is the 1839 revolt of Africans aboard the Spanish slave ship who,

Figure 25.63 Jacob Lawrence, *Daybreak—A Time to Rest,* 1967. Tempera on masonite, 30 × 24″. Gift of an anonymous donor, 1973. National Gallery of Art, Washington, D.C.

after seizing the ship, were captured by an American ship and tried in New Haven for mutiny. With the assistance of John Quincy Adams and other Abolitionists, the Africans were finally returned to their homeland.

Richmond Barthé (b. 1901) is one of the most prolific and successful American sculptors. Notable among his creations are the *African Dancer* and *The Blackberry Woman,* which were acquired by the Whitney Museum of American Art. Long a notable and influential art teacher at Howard University, Lois Maillol Jones (b. 1905) is an accomplished textile designer and painter of cityscapes and landscapes in the spirit of Cézanne. Particularly outstanding are her Haitian paintings and her *Africa* series of 1971.

Romare Beardon (b. 1914) began his career as a cartoonist. After studying with George Grosz he developed a painting style based on Cubist techniques. His mature works are powerful collages of the black experience, but genre art rather than propaganda. Juxtaposing African motifs and contemporary black figures, Beardon redefines the human image "in terms of the Negro experience I know best."

One of the most celebrated artists at mid-century was Jacob Lawrence (b. 1917), who uses vigorous silhouetted patterns and narrative subject matter. Deeply committed to black history in America, Lawrence is perhaps best known for the series *The Migration of the Negro* (1940–1941) and his *Harlem* series of 1943. *Daybreak—A Time to Rest* (fig. 25.63) is related, like much of his work, to the life of a black hero: Harriet

Tubman, a famed conductor on the Underground Railway, in a children's book entitled *Harriet and the Promised Land,* which he illustrated. The work is balanced between a dream world and reality, an artful juxtaposition of identifiable images and abstractions. The huge feet are pointed north but even when traveling the route to freedom, there must be a time to rest and to dream of the promised land.

Charles White (b. 1918), like Hale Woodruff and Jacob Lawrence, was employed during the Depression by the W.P.A. Art Project. In a style influenced by Mexican muralists Diego Rivera and David Siqueiros, White completed powerful murals like, for example, *The Contribution of the Negro to American Democracy* (1943) at Hampton Institute. White later specialized in lithographs and charcoal and ink drawings because he felt that he could communicate better with his intended audience of black Americans. Always a strong social critic, White's later works, such as his *Wanted Poster* series of the turbulent 1960s, reveal a lot of anger. Admittedly propaganda pieces, this series is, nevertheless, artistically eloquent.

Norma Morgan (b. 1928) divides her time between England and the United States, considering herself an artist born in America, and not necessarily a black artist. Noted for her "magic-realist" etchings and copper engravings, her *David in the Wilderness* is owned by the Museum of Modern Art. Norma Morgan is considered a mainstream artist but there is a movement called Blackstream of which Benny Andrews (b. 1930) is a leading member. His *Trash* (1972) is a large and powerful work that attacks American junk culture while, at the same time, depicting Andrews's consistent theme that black artists are creating art as uniquely American as jazz.

Benny Andrews and other Blackstream artists like Milton Johnson, Joe Everstreet, Raymond Saunders, and Malcolm Bailey all depict the strength of black people under adverse conditions. Each of them has contributed to American art the vitality and uniqueness of the black experience, qualities that are not derived from European cultures. The current generation of black artists is, in effect, breaking down ethnic and national barriers. First and foremost, they are artists successfully reinforcing the cultural pluralism that is the real strength of this complex nation.

Art in the 1980s

Contemporary artistic styles are wildly pluralistic with no one style predominating. A renewed interest in figural painting called, for want of a better term, "New Painting," is significant but some older styles persist and innovations abound. Art in the 80s is, in general, no longer a Bohemian activity and New York is no longer the primary center of artistic activity. Artists like Julian Schnabel, David Salle, and Laurie Anderson are making a living out of art by promoting a "fast track" art market rivaling the hyped success of Rock stars and soap-opera personalities. The marketing of art and "art stars" has become another American enterprise with the implication that "success" is more important than aesthetics. Where this will lead is anybody's guess but

Figure 25.64 Wallace K. Harrison, Le Corbusier, and others, Secretariat Building of the United Nations, 1947–1950. New York.

just a listing of contemporary styles, attitudes, and movements will indicate the range of artistic activity in the current decade.

New Painting	Primitivism
French Nouveau Realisme	Naïves
Italian Arte Povera	Abstractionists
Pop and Post-Pop	Nul/Zero
Fluxus	Environmental Art
Conceptual Art	Performance Art
Minimalism	Body Art
German-Italian	Noise or Sound Art
"transavantgarde"	Vague Art
Earth Art	

Whether any one style will predominate in the manner of Impressionism or Cubism is unlikely, given the rapid interactions of our Global Village in the Communications Age. Artistic influences are international but artists are always individuals. They will pursue their own goals, creating artworks faster than critics can conjure up labels and this is as it should be. Works of art are always best judged on their own merits regardless of style, school, or movement.

Architecture

Before World War II skyscraper designs were generally eclectic, clothing steel skeletons with older styles. The innovations of Louis Sullivan (1856–1924) and Frank Lloyd Wright were more influential in Europe than at home and the International Style had yet to make much of an impression outside of Europe. Until the 1950s New York skyscrapers were circumscribed by the demands of clients and rigid zoning restrictions. Buildings had to occupy every square foot of expensive real estate but zoning ordinances required that some sunlight had to fall into manmade canyons. The result was the so-called ziggurat, a setback design with upper floors terraced back from the street.

What was to become an international Renaissance in architecture, mainly International Style, was

Figure 25.65 Gio Ponti, Pier Luigi Nervi, and Arturo Danosso, Pirelli Tower, 1956–1959. Milan, Italy.

launched with the design of the United Nations complex in New York. Because modern buildings were so complicated most were designed by a group of architects and engineers. Wallace K. Harrison (b. 1895) headed an international team that designed the Secretariat Building (fig. 25.64) in the shape of a giant slab, as suggested by Le Corbusier. Clothed on the sides in glass and on the ends in marble, the structure was the first American building to embody the Bauhaus tradition. Because it occupied only a portion of the riverfront site, it avoided the setback restrictions that can be seen in the Empire State Building (on the left) and Chrysler Building (on the right).

The Pirelli Tower in Milan (fig. 25.65) represents an imaginative variation on the International Style. Gio Ponti designed the sleek and subtly proportioned facade while the innovative structural design was by Nervi, the self-styled "architectural engineer." Though it has thirty-three floors and is 416' high, the entire building is suspended from two giant transverse spines 79' apart. The floors are cantilevered from the pylons, making the columnless office space within totally open and thus completely flexible.

The German architect Ludwig Mies van der Rohe (1886–1969) was initially influenced by Gropius but developed his own Minimalist version of International Style. Illustrating his motto that "less is more,"

Figure 25.66 Ludwig Mies van der Rohe, Gallery of the Twentieth Century, 1962–1968. West Berlin.

his art museum in West Berlin (fig. 25.66) is classically simple, refined, and elegant.

Though he was an influential pioneer of the International Style, Le Corbusier later abandoned his boxes on stilts (see fig. 25.30) for a more sculptural style. His design for the pilgrimage chapel of Notre-Dame-du-Haut (fig. 25.67) was revolutionary, unlike any other building. The plan is irregular in every respect. Thick, curving white walls are topped by a heavy overhanging roof and flanked by a tall white tower on the left and a shorter tower on the right. The towers are decorative but they also transmit natural light to the two altars within. Window openings are cut through the massive walls to make tunnels of light (fig. 25.68). Randomly placed, the windows are of different sizes and cut through the walls in a variety of angles. Stained glass is used but each window has a different design and color scheme. The overall effect is intimate and magical.

Figure 25.67 Le Corbusier, Notre-Dame-du-Haut, 1950–1955. Ronchamp, France.

Figure 25.68 Interior, Notre-Dame-du-Haut.

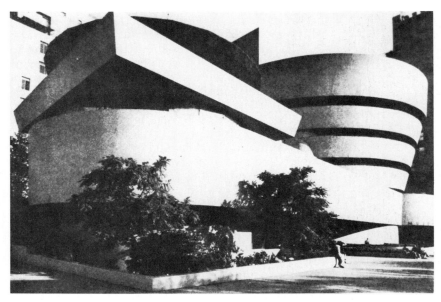

Figure 25.69 Frank Lloyd Wright, The Solomon R. Guggenheim Museum, 1943–1959. New York.

Figure 25.70 Interior, Solomon R. Guggenheim Museum

Figure 25.71 Eero Saarinen, TWA Terminal. 1956–1962. JFK International Airport, New York.

Frank Lloyd Wright designed many buildings based on the circle but none as dramatic as the Solomon R. Guggenheim Museum in New York (fig. 25.69). The front circle is the administrative unit with the gallery behind. The structure is essentially a cylinder rising in expanding circles. This is the antithesis, in every respect, of the International Style. Inside the building (fig. 25.70) a circular ramp rises to the top in six complete turns around a 90′ well that climaxes in a skylight dome. Visitors are taken to the top in an elevator, permitting them to walk on a continuous downhill grade while inspecting artworks placed on the outside wall. The design necessarily limits how art is displayed but the interior of the Guggenheim is one of Wright's boldest and most successful concepts.

New York's JFK International Airport is an uninspired collection of architectural clichés with the sole exception of the TWA Terminal (fig. 25.71). Designed by Eero Saarinen (1910–1961), the structure is a triumph, a curvilinear enclosure of space that actually looks like an air terminal. Built of reinforced concrete, the continuously curving surfaces symbolize flight in a manner reminiscent of Brancusi's *Bird in Space* (see fig. 25.16). The interior of the terminal (fig. 25.72) reveals a graceful interplay of flowing curves with a minimum of vertical supports.

Figure 25.72 Interior, TWA Terminal

Figure 25.73 R. Buckminster Fuller, American Pavilion, EXPO 67. Montreal, Canada.

Figure 25.74 Moshe Safdie and associates, Habitat, EXPO 67. Montreal, Canada.

Functional as well as aesthetically appealing, the design effectively guides passengers to and from the aircraft.

R. Buckminster Fuller (1895–1983) was an unconventional architect-engineer who, among other things, invented the geodesic dome. Composed of mutually sustaining tetrahedrons and octahedrons, these spheroids can be constructed almost anywhere, out of virtually any material, and at very low cost. Used at first for greenhouses and temporary structures, the first large geodesic dome appeared at EXPO 67 as the American Pavilion (fig. 25.73). Because the design is eminently practical on any scale, Fuller even envisioned cities under geodesic domes with full control of the climate. Air and noise pollution may, of course, present a problem or two.

At the same exposition, Moshe Safdie (b. 1945) presented a new concept in urban habitation called Habitat (fig. 25.74). Various sized housing units, each

a complete apartment, are attached to a zigzag concrete framework. Each Habitat can be extended in any direction and assembled in a variety of heights, giving the occupants a diversified range of views and perspectives. When compared with sterile high-rise apartment buildings with every floor the same size, the Habitat concept offers a practical and aesthetic form of multiple dwellings for people who like living in clustered units.

The design competition for the new opera house in Sydney, Australia, was won by Danish architect Joern Utzon (b. 1918) in 1956, but it took thirteen years and several more architects and engineers to figure out how to build the unique concept (fig. 25.75). A cultural center that includes opera house, exhibition hall, theatre, and other facilities, the soaring gull-wing design faced with brilliant white ceramic tiles is a visual triumph, thanks in part to its location on one of the world's great harbors.

Figure 25.75 Utzon, Hall, Todd, and Littleton, Sydney Opera House, 1959–1972. Bennelong Point, Sydney, Australia.

Figure 25.76 Renzo Piano and Richard Rogers, Georges Pompidou National Center for Art and Culture (Beaubourg), 1977. Paris. View of east side.

Even before its dedication the Pompidou National Center for Arts and Culture (fig. 25.76) provoked a storm of controversy. The building is, in effect, turned inside out. Brilliantly painted structural supports, heating and cooling ducts, elevators, and staircases form the exterior, leaving the interior open to

Figure 25.77 Philip Johnson, Model for Chippendale skyscraper. New York.

any arrangement by using movable partitions. Designed as a center for art, music, drama, film, and industrial arts, the structure also contains a Public Information Center (media library) and a variety of bars and restaurants. A prime tourist attraction and beehive of cultural activities, the building is perhaps more detested by many Parisians than even the Eiffel Tower. Sobriquets are legion: *art brut,* boiler room, factory, kinetic architecture, honest architecture, indecent architecture, science fiction architecture, and so on and on. Set in the midst of historical Paris, the Pompidou is, to say the least, quite noticeable.

Outside of a few well-proportioned International Style buildings, rectangular glass boxes have become three-dimensional platitudes: sterile, inefficient, and boring. Some recent designs are more energy-efficient and, whether Romantic or Classical, deliberately antithetical to outdated modernism in the mode of the International Style. Philip Johnson's (b. 1906) classical design for his so-called Chippendale skyscraper (fig. 25.77) has an entrance reminiscent of Brunelleschi's Pazzi Chapel. The pediment is similar to eighteenth-century furniture designed in England by Thomas Chippendale (1718–1779). Between entrance and pediment the building (currently under construction for AT&T) is still a straight-line high-rise minus windows.

Summary

The multiplicity of styles and innumerable artists of the present century cannot be adequately covered in a chapter or even in a set of books. The discussion of most major styles and some of the important artists should be considered as a preamble to continuing studies of what today's artists are creating. Twentieth-century art is as accessible in this country as Renaissance art is in Italy and can be viewed in any good-sized American city. Most of the illustrations for this chapter, for example, were drawn from the collections of fourteen American museums and galleries from New York to the West Coast. Following is a summary in outline form, providing both a review of the chapter and a framework for personal initiative.

I. Artistic Styles to 1945
  A. Painting and Sculpture
    1. Prelude
      a) Edouard Manet
      b) Impressionism: Monet et al
      c) Post-Impressionism: Cézanne et al
    2. Fauvism
      a) Henri Matisse
      b) Georges Rouault
    3. Expressionism
      a) Wassily Kandinsky (Abstract Expressionism)
      b) Ernst Barlach
      c) Käthe Kollwitz
      d) George Grosz
    4. Cubism
      a) Pablo Picasso (including Blue and Rose Periods and Neoclassicism)
      b) Stuart Davis
    5. Abstractionists
      a) Georgia O'Keeffe
      b) Piet Mondrian (geometric, plasticism)
      c) Constantin Brancusi
    6. Fantasy
      a) Marc Chagall
      b) Paul Klee
      c) Giorgio de Chirico (metaphysical)
    7. Dada
      a) Marcel Duchamp
      b) Kurt Schwitters
    8. Surrealism
      a) Joan Miro
      b) Salvador Dali
      c) Meret Oppenheim
      d) Alberto Giacometti
      e) Alton Pickens
      f) Yves Tanguy
    9. Realism in America
      a) John Sloan (Ash Can school)
      b) Edward Hopper
      c) Diego Rivera (Social Realism)
  B. Architecture
    1. Antonio Gaudi (Art Noveau and Expressionism)
    2. Walter Gropius (International Style)
    3. Le Corbusier (International Style)
    4. Frank Lloyd Wright (Organic architecture)
II. Artistic Styles since 1945
  A. Painting and Sculpture
    1. Abstract Expressionism
      a) Jackson Pollock
      b) Willem de Kooning
      c) Mark Rothko (Color Field)
    2. Pop Art
      a) Robert Rauschenberg
      b) Jasper Johns
      c) Roy Lichtenstein
      d) Andy Warhol
      e) Robert Indiana
      f) Claes Oldenburg
      g) Edward Kienholz
    3. Color, Geometry, and Optics
      a) Josef Albers (geometric)
      b) Kenneth Noland (hard-edge)
      c) Helen Frankenthaler (abstract color)
      d) Louise Nevelson (geometric abstraction)
      e) Bridget Riley (curved lines, optics)
    4. Fantasy, Expressionism, and Surrealism
      a) Jean Dubuffet (*art brut*)
      b) Francis Bacon (fantasy/ expressionism)
      c) Leonel Gongora (fantasy/ expressionism)
      d) Roy de Forest (fantasy/funk)
      e) Fritz Scholder (Pop/Expressionism)
      f) Philip Curtis (Surrealism)
      g) Alexander Calder (abstract fantasy/ kinetic)
      h) Mark di Suvero (abstract fantasy/ kinetic)
      i) Henry Moore (abstract figural)
    5. Minimal Art
      a) Tony DeLap
      b) David Smith
      c) Ronald Bladen
    6. Varieties of Realism
      a) John Moore (New Realism)
      b) Ben Schonzeit (altered Photorealism)
      c) Otto Duecker (Photorealism Cutouts)
      d) James Havard (Abstract Illusionism)
    7. Hispanic and Black Artists (overview)
      a) Joshua Johnson (artisan-painter)
      b) Jacob Lawrence (image/abstraction)

B. Architecture
    1. Wallace Harrison (International Style)
    2. Ponti and Nervi (International Style)
    3. Ludwig Mies van der Rohe (Minimalist International Style)
    4. Le Corbusier (sculptural architecture)
    5. Frank Lloyd Wright (functional/organic)
    6. Eero Saarinen (functional/expressionism)
    7. R. Buckminster Fuller (geodesic dome)
    8. Moshe Safdie (Habitat)
    9. Joern Utzon (Expressionism)
    10. Piano and Rogers (*art brut*/kinetic architecture)
    11. Philip Johnson (Neoclassicism)

WARNING!: The above outline with artists placed neatly in pigeonholes is a generalized approximation and guide and only that. Artists, as stated before, are individuals and their works are unique. Treat the text and outline as points of departure, keeping in mind that artists do change their styles and that, art critics notwithstanding, we are still too close in time to many styles to make valid judgments. Mozart, for example, had no idea that he was a Classical composer; he was criticized in his day as an avant-garde composer.

Finally, consider art as what anyone elects to present to us as art, as evidence of human creativity. If we do not like an artwork perhaps it communicates something we already know but refuse to acknowledge. Paradoxically, a work of art that tells us something we know and understand can leave us dissatisfied. We do want the artist to challenge our emotions, our intellect, our knowledge. The more we study art the more likely we are to respond to and to seek out challenges.

26
Modern Music

Twentieth-century music has developed in what are essentially two phases. Phase one is a continuation and development of instruments, forms, and styles inherited from the rich tradition of Bach, Beethoven, and Brahms. Phase two began in the 1950s with the electronic age. Though the past is still influential, this is essentially a new world of music using an incredible variety of electronic sounds, instruments, synthesizers, computer composition and computer performance, and the innovations continue to proliferate.

In terms of our musical heritage Igor Stravinsky (1882–1971) is perhaps the one contemporary composer whose career best summarizes the ceaseless experimentation and multiplicity of styles of the first three-quarters of this century. He exploited all the "neo" styles from Neo-Gothic to Neo-Romantic, pausing along the way to try his hand, unsuccessfully, at modern jazz. Thoroughly grounded in the music of the past—he admired the music of Bach above all—he was a superb musical craftsman as well as a bold and daring innovator. Always associated with the European avant-garde, he influenced Diaghilev, Cocteau, Picasso, and Matisse and was, in turn, influenced by all of them.

The first and perhaps strongest impetus came from Diaghilev, who commissioned several ballet scores for the Ballet Russe de Monte Carlo of which the first was *The Firebird.* Following the successful *Firebird,* Stravinsky produced the popular *Petrouchka* ballet score and then turned his attention to the ballet *The Rite of Spring.*

Success was not immediate for this daringly original work. The 1913 premiere in Paris set off a full-scale riot between Stravinsky's avant-garde partisans and his far more numerous detractors. The audience was restless before the music even began; the two camps of "liberal artist" and "conservative establishment" had, in effect, already chosen up sides. The liberals were as determined to like the work as the conservatives were bent on open hostility.

The high register bassoon solo at the very beginning of the piece provoked some sneers and even some audible laughs from the conservative camp and the situation went downhill from there. Things had gotten totally out of hand by the time the police arrived, with the consequence that the premiere performance was never completed. On a special television program aired many years later Stravinsky sat in that Parisian hall in the same seat which he had occupied in 1913. When asked what he did during the riot, Stravinsky replied, "I just stood up, told all of them to go to hell and walked out."

The Rite of Spring, subtitled Pictures of Pagan Russia, exploits a very large symphonic orchestra and uses many unique instrumental effects to portray the primitive ceremonies.

2 Piccolos	4 Tubas
2 Flutes	Small Timpani
Alto Flute	4 Timpani
4 Oboes	Bass Drum
English Horn	Other Percussion: Triangle,
E♭ Clarinet	Cymbals, Antique
3 B♭ Clarinets	Cymbals, Tam Tam
Bass Clarinet	(gong), Snare Drum,
3 Bassoons	Tambourine, Guiro
Contrabassoon	(serrated gourd with
8 French Horns	stick)
D Trumpet	Violin I
4 C Trumpets	Violin II
Bass Trumpet	Viola
3 Trombones	Cello
	Bass

The ballet is built around the spring fertility rites of ancient Russia. The scenes include the invocation of the coming of spring, various spring dances, games of the rival tribes, the selection of the sacrificial virgin, and finally, her sacrificial dance of death. The music is divided into two main parts with eight sections to Part I and six sections to Part II. In general, the music is *through-composed,* because each section is a specific scene in a dramatic sequence. Parts I and II are separate, but there are no breaks between sections.

Le Sacre du Printemps (1913)
(The Rite of Spring)

Igor Stravinsky (1882–1971)
Total Time: 32:25

Part I: The Adoration of the Earth

Section A. Introduction (Adoration of the Earth)
Meter: Many but principally *duple*
    The invocation of the birth of spring. On stage a group of girls is seen sitting before the sacred mound, each girl holding a long garland. The tribal sage appears and leads them towards the mound.
Theme One: Bassoon (Phrygian mode)
Theme Two: English horn (Pentatonic)

Section B. Dance of the Youths and Maidens
Meter: Duple, with strong syncopations
Theme One: Strings (rhythmic patterns)
Theme Two: Bassoons
Theme Three: French horn

Section C. Dance of Abduction
Meter: Constantly changing
Theme One: Trumpet, piccolo, flutes in Fanfare style (Dorian mode)

Section D. Spring Rounds
    There are four couples left on stage. Each man lifts a girl on his back and, with a solemn and measured tread, begins making the Rounds of Spring.
Theme One: Soprano and bass clarinets (Pentatonic)
Theme Two: Flutes, violins (Dorian)

Section E. Games of the Rival Cities
    The young warriors of the rival tribes display their prowess. Near the end of the section the sage pushes his way through the crowd.
Theme One: Muted trumpet, horns (Aeolian)
Theme Two: Muted trumpets (Mixolydian)
The two themes, representing the rival tribes, alternate throughout.

Section F. Entrance of the Sage
    After making his entrance near the end of the preceding scene the village wise man (portrayed by four tubas) assumes direction of the proceedings.

Section G. Adoration of the Earth
    The dancers prostrate themselves in adoration of the mystic powers of the earth. This section is only *four measures* long and features bassoons, timpani, and string bass and closes with a very soft, dissonant chord in the strings.

Section H. Dance of the Earth
    An exuberant dance in praise of the fertility of the earth.

Part II: The Sacrifice

Section A. Introduction (Pagan Night)
    The sage and the girls sit motionless around the fire in front of the sacred mound. They must choose the girl who is to be sacrificed to ensure the earth's fertility.

Section B. Mystic Circles of the Adolescents
    The girls dance the mystic circles until one stands suddenly transfixed as she realizes that she is the chosen one.

Section C. Dance to the Glorified One
    In honor of the sacrificial victim there is a vigorous dance which builds up to a frenzied climax.

Section D. Evocation of the Ancestors
    Strong rhythmic and dance patterns to invoke the blessings of the ancestors.

Section E. Ritual Performance of the Ancestors
    Undulating, pulsating rhythmic patterns to which the village elders perform a shuffling, swaying dance.

Section F. Sacrificial Dance
    The chosen one begins a frenzied dance and continues until she collapses and dies. The men carry her body to the foot of the sacred mound as an offering to the gods of fertility.

Atonality

Atonality was a musical idea whose time had come. Strictly speaking, atonality is a twentieth-century technique which arbitrarily declares the twelve different notes in an octave to be created free and equal. No one tone would predominate; there would be no tonal center, no tonic, no tonality. Curiously symptomatic of the twentieth century, the new system was associated with mathematics and, by coincidence, the system demanded true equality of *black* notes with *white* notes.

Modern science depends on highly sophisticated mathematics and, quite naturally, modern musicians developed their system of what might be called mathematical music. Atonal composers used no more than simple arithmetic, but this was quite sufficient for their manipulations of notes, rhythm, texture, and so forth. Following is a brief description of the process of change from tonal to atonal music, a development which, in retrospect, appears to have been inevitable. Also included are some games that people can play with twelve-tone arithmetic.

Tonal music, which had superseded the modes during the seventeenth century, was based on the idea that the seven tones of a diatonic scale belonged to a key and that the other five tones were outside the key. Composers relied more and more on the five tones outside the key to give color and variety to their music. By the end of the nineteenth century musicians such as Wagner and Brahms were regularly using all of the tones as a twelve-tone system of tonality revolving around a central pitch called tonic, or tonal center.

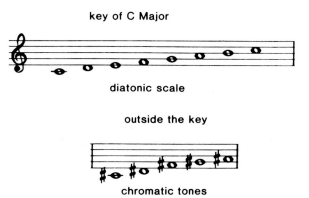

key of C Major

diatonic scale

outside the key

chromatic tones

After World War I, Arnold Schoenberg (SHURN-burg; 1874–1951) developed a system in which all twelve tones were considered to be exactly equal and therefore with no tonal center. There would be no dissonance or consonance as such because all the pitches could be used in any combination and without reference to the predominance of any single pitch. This system of twelve equal musical pitches is called *atonality,* or the *dodecaphonic (twelve-tone) system.*

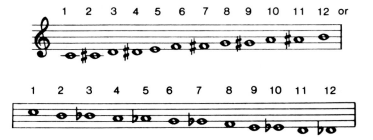

Without a tonic pitch to give the music some sort of unity, it was necessary to devise another kind of unifying system. This new device was called a *tone row,* or *basic set.* Composers invented melodic sequences of the twelve tones, using each tone only once and refraining from using any sequence of notes which would imply a key (tonality). Since it is neither necessary nor desirable to limit the twelve different tones to one octave, a basic set (tone row) could look like this:

Basically, the twelve-tone system lends itself to polyphonic rather than homophonic writing. Almost anyone can devise and use a mixture of polyphonic and homophonic techniques. Because of the infinite possibilities of manipulating the row, the problem becomes one of *selectivity,* selecting those possibilities which make sense musically.

Twelve-tone composition is not solely a musical process but partly a mathematical and/or mechanical procedure. The finished composition might be very different and original in sound (and it might not). Whether it is good or bad music (or something in between) still remains the province of the composer, who makes up one or more tone rows, manipulating, selecting, and modifying until he gets the *musical results* he wants. Twelve-tone technique is neither a virtue nor a vice; it is merely a means to an end. It may assist the composer in discovering new melodic, rhythmic, and harmonic ideas and different combinations of these ideas. It will not do a thing for the finished product; that rests within the sphere of the creative individual.

Alban Berg (1885–1935) was one of the most musically creative of the twelve-tone composers. His style is also notable for clear, clean orchestral writing. For his Violin Concerto he used a small, versatile orchestra with a delicate contrapuntal texture. Following is the instrumentation for the Violin Concerto (the instruments in parentheses are doubled by the same instrumentalists):

2 Flutes (2 Piccolos)
  Alto Saxophone
  (clarinet)
  Bass Clarinet
  Contrabassoon
2 Trumpets
  Tuba
  Strings

2 Oboes (2 English
  Horns)
2 Clarinets
2 Bassoons
4 Horns
2 Trombones
  Timpani, Bass Drum,
  Cymbals, Snare
  Drum, Tam Tam,
  Triangle

His tone row for the Violin Concerto was not a mechanical contrivance but a point of departure for pure music making. He deliberately chose a row which had clear tonal implications, a mixture of *g minor* (the primary tonality), *a minor,* and a portion of the whole-tone scale. The following is the tone row for the Violin Concerto:

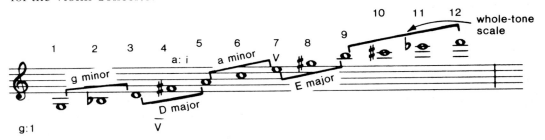

Violin Concerto (1935)

Alban Berg (1885–1935)
Total Time: 25:15

There are two separate movements, each divided into two distinct sections:

I Andante; Allegretto
II Allegro; Adagio

I Andante

Form: Ternary (103 measures)
Tempo: Andante   Time: 4:00

Theme a (Row)
solo violin

Theme b
solo violin

Form: Ternary, i.e., Scherzo— — — — — — Trio — — —
— — — Scherzo
Tempo: Allegretto

Theme a
solo violin

Theme b
solo violin

Trio I (*Theme a*)
strings

Trio II (*Theme b*)
flute

Coda (Carinthian folk tune) (*Theme c*)
horn

II Allegro

Form: Ternary

Tempo: Allegro ("But always rubato, free as in a cadenza")

The movement is one long violin cadenza which is played in a rhapsodic manner as specified in the composer's tempo indication. This particular cadenza is no mere display of virtuosity but a unified movement featuring brilliant solo work and orchestral accompaniment. Theme b dominates the movement.

Theme a: Tutti
Theme b: Horn
Theme c: Solo Violin

II Adagio (Continued)

Form: Variations on the chorale *Oh, Eternity, Thou Word of Thunder* from Bach's Cantata no. 60, *It is Enough! So Take My Spirit Lord* (95 measures)

Tempo: Adagio

Theme (harmonization by J. S. Bach, melody in Lydian mode)

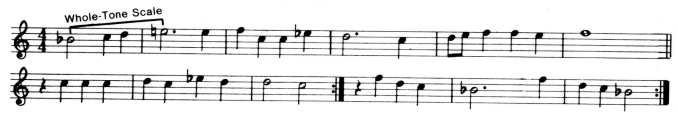

The styles of twentieth-century music are many and varied, as befits a dynamic art in a rapidly changing age. The vogue of neoprimitivism *(The Rite of Spring* and other similar compositions) had its day; Romanticism, whether called Neo-Romantic or Post-Romantic, continues to have some influence; nationalism is once again a characteristic of the works of some composers. One trend has been toward Classicism, as in the works of the twelve-tone school and, among many others, the music of the Russian composer Serge Prokofiev (1891–1953).

Prokofiev went through a primitive phase, and his music does have certain nationalistic characteristics. He has had exceptional success with descriptive music, as attested to by his motion-picture scores and the universally popular *Peter and the Wolf.* The bulk of his writing, however, has a classical orientation and deals mainly with the abstract forms of sonata, concerto, and symphony. His Fifth Symphony is written for the large orchestra in which Russian composers take particular delight. The musical content is rich, expressive, and often highly dramatic. The form is lucidly classical, logical, and controlled.

Symphony no. 5 in B♭ Major, op. 100 (1944)

Serge Prokofiev (1891–1953)
Total Time: 44:00

I

Form: Sonata

Tempo: Andante

II
Form: Ternary (Scherzo-Trio-Scherzo)
Tempo: Allegro marcato

Trio
Theme a

Theme b

III
Form: Ternary
Tempo: Adagio

Theme a

Theme b

Theme c

IV
Form: Rondo (Primary theme *a* alternating with secondary themes *b, c,* and so forth to give A–B–A–C–A–B–A).The introduction uses material from the first movement.
Tempo: Allegro giocoso

Theme a

Theme b

Theme c

Béla Bartók (1881–1945) was one of the outstanding composers of the century. Born in Hungary, he escaped the Nazi terror and settled in New York City where he made a meager living as a piano teacher and as a concert pianist. Only after his death was there any significant recognition of the consistently high quality of his music. The shy, soft-spoken Hungarian refugee has written some powerful music characterized by great intensity and depth of feeling, music which sings and plays without becoming flippant, music which is sometimes somber and occasionally tragic in tone but which is not dejected or self-pitying. His work consistently manifests an affirmative life-force which epitomizes the man and his music.

Béla Bartók's style was an amalgam of Hungarian folk music, great rhythmic ingenuity, and a fundamental allegiance to Classical forms. He delighted in the folk music of southeastern Europe because it helped free him from the tyranny of the major-minor system; moreover, many of his rhythmic conceptions were derived from folk dances of the same area. His preoccupation with formal unity and coherence led him to a unique style of *continuous variations,* a dynamic and thoroughly modern style of relentless tension and growth.

His Concerto for Orchestra, which sounds like a contradiction in terms, is an orchestral piece in which nearly all of the instruments are treated in a soloistic manner. The virtuoso in this case is the entire orchestra. There are five movements, each very different in content, but all a part of the dynamic drive which culminates in the fifth and last movement. His sonata form is called "modified sonata form" because of his consistent application of the continuous variation principle. In other words, his recapitulations are never simple restatements of expositions but variations on those statements. The traditional ternary form is used for the second movement but even here the return to the A section is a varied rather than a literal one. The third and fourth movements exploit the *arch form* which is so much of a part of Bartók's style: A–B–C–B–A. Bartók's continuous variations, however, modify this form to A–B–C–B'–A'.

Concerto for Orchestra (1943)

Béla Bartók (1881–1945)
Total Time: 37:00

I
Form: Modified sonata form
Tempo: Andante non troppo
Allegro vivace

Introduction
Theme One
low strings

Theme Two
tpt.

II "Game of Pairs"
Form: Ternary (All material varied in the closing section)
Tempo: Allegretto scherzando

This movement is in the nature of an exercise for a succession of pairs of instruments. The movement begins with a snare drum solo followed by two bassoons a *sixth* apart. The bassoons remain a sixth apart throughout their solo section; no other harmonic interval is used. The bassoons are followed by two oboes a *third* apart, a pair of clarinets a *seventh* apart, two flutes a *fifth* apart, and two muted trumpets in *seconds.* Bartók deliberately imposed on his own creativity a problem of trying to write in a rigorously predetermined pattern and still maintain interest and musical value, a typical exercise in ingenuity which artists seem to delight in inflicting on themselves.

Exposition Allegro vivace

Theme a
violins

Theme b
oboe

Section A
Introduction: Snare drum

Theme One: Bassoons in sixths (m6)

Theme Two: Oboes in thirds (m3)

Theme Three: Clarinets in sevenths (m7)

Theme Four: Flutes in fifths (p5)

Theme Five: Muted trumpets in seconds (m2)

Section B
Theme a (Chorale theme)
Brass Choir

III "Elegia"
Form: Arch (A–B–C–B′–A′)
Tempo: Andante non troppo

Introduction

string basses

Section A
Theme a

oboe

Section B
Theme b

Violins, cl.

Section C
Theme c

violas

IV "Intermezzo Interrotto" (Interrupted Intermezzo)
Theme c is a parody of material from Dmitri Shostakovitch's Seventh (Leningrad) Symphony. The listener can form his own judgment as to Bartók's opinion of the symphony.
Form: Arch (A–B–C–B′–A′)
Tempo: Allegretto

Section A
Theme a

oboe

Section B
Theme b

violas

Section C
Theme c

clarinet *accellerando*

V "Finale"
Form: Modified sonata form
Tempo: Presto

Introduction

Pesante   horn

Theme a
Presto   violins

pp

Theme b
bassoon

Theme c
trumpet

f

Some contemporary composers have reacted against the prevailing Classical concepts of the twentieth century as well as against the innovations of composers who are experimenting with computer compositions and the manipulation of electronic tapes. These modern-day Neo-Romantics are still primarily interested in program music, major-minor tonality, tertiary harmony, and large vocal and instrumental ensembles. They have adopted some modern techniques but have incorporated them into what is essentially a nineteenth-century framework.

Carl Orff, in his cantata *Carmina Burana* (see chapter 12 on medieval music), used the poetry of the medieval goliards to write what he calls a "dramatic cantata." The wandering scholars, defrocked monks, vagabonds, minstrels, rascals, artists, and dreamers who were known as goliards rebelled against the strictures of society and protested the rule of the establishment, in this case the Church and the aristocracy.

The text of Orff's cantata was selected from the thirteenth-century collection of goliard poems which was discovered in Bavaria in the Benedictine monastery of Benediktbeuren, hence the name *Carmina Burana (Songs of Beuren)*. These *cantiones profanae* (secular songs) were written in a mixture of Latin, French, and German. They sing of nature and the joys of love, the tavern, and the free life. There is a strong undercurrent of protest against the cruel fate of those who do not conform to the conventions of society.

Carmina Burana is a concert piece for soloists, boy's chorus, small chorus, large chorus, and a large orchestra augmented by two pianos, five timpani, and a large percussion section (glockenspiel, xylophone, castanets, drums, ancient cymbals, etc.). Orff selected twenty-four verses and divided them into four sections:

Introduction—1,2

In the Spring—3–10

In the Tavern—11–14

The Court of Love—15–25 (verse 25 is a repeat of the opening verse)

There is no thematic development. The music consists of a series of clear-cut stanzas, many of which are repeated with a change of dynamics, orchestration, and the like.

Carmina Burana; Cantiones Profanae (1936)

Carl Orff (1895–1982)
Total Time: 50:40

Introduction

1. "O fortune variable as the moon." Large chorus and orchestra.
2. "I lament fortune's blows." Men's chorus, piano, bassoons.

In the Spring

3. "The bright face of spring shows itself to the world." (Imitation of Gregorian chant.) Small chorus, woodwinds, pianos.
4. "The sun, pure and fine, tempers all." Baritone solo, strings.
5. "Behold the spring, welcome and long awaited." Chorus, orchestra.
6. *On the lawn.* Dance, orchestral.
7. "The noble wood is filled with buds and leaves. Where is my love?" Large chorus, small chorus, orchestra.
8. "Shopkeeper, give me color to paint my cheeks, so that the young men will not resist my charm." Sopranos, large chorus, small chorus, orchestra.
9. *Round dance* in three sections for orchestra. Large chorus; small chorus.
10. "Were the world all mine from the sea to the Rhine, I would gladly forsake it all if the Queen of England were in my arms." Large chorus, orchestra.

In the Tavern

11. "In rage and bitterness I talk to myself." Baritone solo.
12. "The roasted swan sings 'Once I dwelt in the lake and was a beautiful swan. O miserable me! Now I am roasted black!'" Tenor solo (falsetto) and orchestra.
13. "I am the Abbot of Cluny, and I spend my time with drinkers." Baritone solo and men's chorus.
14. "When we are in the tavern we don't care who has died." Male chorus, orchestra.

The Court of Love

15. "The God of Love flies everywhere." Boys' choir, orchestra.
16. "Day and night and all the world against me." Baritone solo, orchestra.
17. "There stood a maid in a red tunic." Soprano solo, orchestra.
18. "My heart is filled with sighing." Baritone solo, chorus, orchestra.
19. "When a boy and a girl are alone together, happy is their union." Male sextet.
20. "Come, come, do not let me die." Double chorus, orchestra.
21. "My mind is torn between opposites; between love's desire and chastity." Soprano solo, orchestra.
22. "Pleasant is the season, O maidens, so rejoice you lads!" Baritone, soprano, boys' choir, chorus, orchestra.
23. "Sweetest boy, I give myself completely to you!" Soprano solo.
24. "Hail to thee most beautiful." Chorus and orchestra.
25. "O fortune, variable as the moon." (Repeat of opening chorus.)

Music of Today

The musical selections presented so far represent a cross section of established classics of the first half of the century. There has been an explosive growth of movements and styles since World War II which includes pre-World War II composers (and their techniques) who still exert a powerful influence and, in addition, a growing number of post-war avant-garde composers.

The Futurists gave concerts of noises before World War I with imaginative use of explosions, snorts, hisses, murmurs, screams, howls, laughter, sobs, and sighs, for example, which influenced the Dadaists and the music of Varèse. With their insistence upon songs of factories, warships, cars, and planes and exploitation of machine and electrical power they also influenced such artists as Leger. Although they were outside the mainstream of traditional European music and few of their works survived, they opened the door to post-World War II exploitation of the world of acoustic phenomena.

Next to the development of new ideas in European music, some of the most important experimental work was taking place in the United States. What had been a more or less transplanted European tradition led to a distinctive American sound in the development of jazz (to be discussed later) and the startling innovations of Charles Ives (1874–1954). Ives was a one-man movement who anticipated just about every important musical development of the past half century: serial and aleatory music,[1] mixed meters and tempos, blocks of sound, free forms, the possibilities of accidental or chance acoustical experiences, assemblages, collages, and even early manifestations of Pop art. However, despite an impressive array of avant-garde techniques, Ives was still a traditional New Englander who wanted to maintain his philosophical

---

1. Aleatory (AY–lee–uh–TORE–e) or chance music.

relationship with the recent literary past. His important *Concord Sonata* for piano has the four movements named after the Transcendentalists: Emerson, Hawthorne, the Alcotts, and Thoreau.

To understand what Ives is getting at in his music it is necessary to recognize the music that he quotes, the church hymns, dance music, and military band music. These quotes are comments on life in the small towns and rural areas of America. His nostalgic *Three Places in New England,* for orchestra, is replete with quotes from Americana and illustrates a concern for his American heritage as profound as that of Walt Whitman.

Three Places in New England (1903–1911)

Charles Ives (1874–1954)

I *The "St. Gaudens" in Boston Common: Col. Shaw and His Colored Regiment.*
Following are the opening lines of a poem which Ives wrote into the score:
Moving,—Marching—Faces of Souls!
Marked with generations of pain,
Part-freers of a Destiny,
Slowly restlessly—swaying us on with you
Towards other Freedom!

II *Putnam's Camp, Redding, Connecticut.*
Ives wrote: "Near Redding Center is a small park preserved as a Revolutionary Memorial; for here General Israel Putnam's soldiers had their winter quarters in 1778–1779. Long rows of stone camp fireplaces still remain to stir a child's imagination. The scene is a "4th of July" picnic held under the auspices of the First Church and the Village Cornet Band. The child wanders into the woods and dreams of the old soldiers, of the hardships they endured, their desire to break camp and abandon their cause, and of how they returned when Putnam came over the hills to lead them. The little boy awakes, he hears the children's songs and runs down past the monument to "listen to the band" and join in the games and dances.

III *The Housatonic at Stockbridge.*
Ives quotes the poem of that name by Robert Underwood Johnson:

Contented river! in thy dreamy realm—
The cloudy willow and the plumy elm . . .
Thou hast grown human laboring with men
At wheel and spindle; sorrow thou dost ken . . .
Wouldst thou away!
I also of much resting have a fear;
Let me thy companion be
By fall and shallow to the adventurous sea!

The twelve-tone composition of the Viennese School of Schoenberg, Berg, and Webern (VAY–burn) went into temporary decline with the growing power of fascist dictatorships in the thirties and war in the forties. Many composers fled for their lives from totalitarian states which demanded simplistic music in a national style in conformance with the military monoliths which the arts were commanded to serve. Schoenberg emigrated to the United States, Berg died

Symphony for Small Orchestra, op. 21 (1928)

Anton Webern (1883–1945)

in 1935, but Webern stayed on in Vienna quietly creating rigorous twelve-tone music which was to captivate post-war composers. Ironically Webern survived tyranny and the war only to be accidentally killed by an American soldier shortly after the end of the war.

The music of Anton Webern (1883–1945) is difficult to characterize apart from the sound: a kind of cubistic pointillism with meaningful breathing space. He has written some of the most beautiful rests in music—the sounds of silence. He uses few notes in a short space of time, manipulating isolated, contrasted tone colors in a space-time continuum. All is rigorous, precise, twelve-tone mathematics, but the result combines the isolation of single tones with the disassociation of sequential events which somehow make up a total musical interrelationship. Although half of his limited production was devoted to vocal music, his mature style is fully illustrated in two instrumental pieces: Symphony, op. 21 (1928) and Variations for Orchestra, op. 30 (1940).

The opening measures of Webern's Symphony, opus 21, are given above as a visual illustration of the restraint and precision of his music.

Partly because of the presence of Schoenberg, twelve-tone composition in the United States flourished during the war, and later reoccupied most of Europe, with the exception of Iron Curtain countries, which continued to condemn its dissonant complexities as "bourgeois decadence." The American composer Milton Babbitt (b. 1916), among others, expanded twelve-tone writing from a method into an elaborate system called *serial technique* or *serial composition*. Although the old method was never a matter of simply arranging the twelve pitches into a row, the new procedure systematized other elements of music such as rhythm, harmony, tempo, dynamics,

timbre, and so forth. For example, a serial composition could contain mathematical permutations of twelve pitches, a sixteen-unit rhythmic organization, a sequence of twenty-nine chords, and fourteen timbres (tone colors). When one considers the fact that there are approximately half a billion ways of arranging just the twelve pitches, the mathematical possibilities of serial technique systems approach infinity. Whether or not these combined mathematical procedures produce music worth listening to is strictly up to a composer who has to choose from an infinitely greater range of possibilities than ever confronted Stravinsky, not to mention Bach or Beethoven.

Following are examples of serial techniques using six notes in a horizontal (melodic) pattern, vertical (harmonic) pattern, and in a rhythmic pattern:

In the fifties Babbitt began working in electronic music with the R.C.A. Electronic Sound Synthesizer. Electronic music uses artificial tones produced by electronic means as, for example, in the earlier and far simpler instrument called the Hammond organ.

Babbitt's experience with synthesized music affected such nonelectronic works as *All Set* for jazz ensemble and *Sounds and Words* for soprano with piano accompaniment. He went on to juxtapose the two types of music in a work combining voice and synthesizer in a setting of Dylan Thomas's *Vision and Prayer*.

Olivier Messiaen (mes–YAYN; b. 1908) is a leading proponent of European serial composition and also the teacher of Stockhausen and Boulez, two of the most important avant-garde composers. As an expert ornithologist and student of Eastern music, Messiaen utilizes authentic bird calls and Hindu *talas* and *ragas* within a highly original serial system. Examples of his work include many organ compositions plus such representative orchestral works as *Oiseaux exotiques* (1956) and *Chronochromie* (1960).

After the war a new program of studies was inaugurated in Darmstadt, Germany to help German (and other European) composers catch up on artistic developments, particularly in the United States, which had been blacked out by the Nazi nightmare. Leading figures in the movement were Stockhausen and especially Pierre Boulez (boo–LESZ; b. 1925), a French composer whose professed musical influences were Debussy, Stravinsky, and Webern. However, in line with the classic French approach to artistic theory, Boulez has related his musical work to the literary production of Mallarmé, James Joyce, and the diaries of Paul Klee. Characteristic works include a setting of Surrealist poems entitled *Le Marteau sans maître* and his Third Piano Sonata.

While the serialists pursue the manifold possibilities of their systems, other composers have concentrated on the exploitation of noise and timbre first introduced by the pre-World War I Futurists. Traditionally, tone color has been more ornamental than essential to Western music and the incorporation of "noise" was unthinkable. But musical sounds as such are only a miniscule part of the modern world of acoustical phenomena. We are surrounded and often engulfed by noise which ranges from city traffic, electrical appliances, and factory din to the "noises" of nature: sounds of the animal world, thunder, rain, hail, seasounds, windsounds, and so forth.

Previous Western cultures have tended to rank "musical" sounds (simple acoustical events with regular pitch vibrations) above "noise" (a complex mixture of regular and irregular vibrations). Some modern composers have attempted to express the sounds of nature in traditional musical terms while at the same time incorporating "noise-making" instruments of the percussion section such as drums, rattles, gourds, and cymbals. Because of the ever-growing interest in different cultures, non-Western percussion instruments were introduced in the nineteenth century and extensively used in the twentieth century. Traditionalists scorned these intruders as nonpitched and therefore antimusical, but innovative composers enthusiastically employed the possibilities of combining timbre and noise into a new musical fabric which violated virtually every precept of conventional melody and harmony.

Webern was the first modern composer to emphasize tone color as a musical idea in its own right, but Edgard Varèse (1883–1965) was the first outstanding composer to write a major work—*Ionisation* (1931) for thirteen percussionists and forty instruments—based on a new musical conception utilizing noise and timbre. Although critics vigorously attacked Varèse throughout his long career for his "insane barbarous and atrocious" treatment of music, *Ionisation* has become a classic work—and it has yet to be determined where music leaves off and sheer, unadulterated noise begins. During the war years Varèse's influence waned but returned with full force when he turned his talents to the *musique concrète* which was developed in the late forties by technicians at the French National Radio. Musique concrète uses preexisting recorded sounds (tones and noises), thus establishing the important idea that all aural impressions are available as raw material for creative composers. Varèse provided what are probably the two most significant compositions in this genre with *Deserts* (1954) for tape and instrumental ensemble and *Poème Electronique*, commissioned to be played by over four hundred spinning loudspeakers at the 1958 Brussels World's Fair.

As indicated above in the work of Babbitt, the Darmstadt school, Varèse, and the Paris school, many roads of contemporary music lead to several varieties of electronic music. In fact, electronic music appears to be a natural consequence in the evolution of Western music. In the early predominantly vocal era, the singer was his own instrument. During the Baroque period there was a general parity between vocal and instrumental music, after which instrumental music clearly dominated vocal music. The musician now used what amounted to a mechanical extension for his music making, with varying degrees of disassociation between performer and instrument; for example, wind players are in close contact with their instruments, string players have some direct control, but keyboard instruments, especially the pipe organ, are quite mechanical. The evolution from a personal instrument (the voice) to an instrument once removed (e.g., the trumpet) has now reached a twice-removed instrument which is wholly the product of technology and which is entirely removed from direct human contact.

This instrumental evolution seems to reflect the condition of contemporary culture in which so many activities are carried on untouched by human hands. Computers are talking to computers while many people find it ever more difficult to communicate with each other. One might argue that the exclusion of human beings from the production of musical sounds spells the death of art and the triumph of technology. On the other hand, there is some evidence that the new possibilities in the manipulation of sound can open up a whole new era of musical forms while simultaneously stimulating new vitality in vocal and instrumental music. If this optimistic view proves to be the correct one, it will bear out the thesis emphasized throughout this book: the ferment and rapid change in contemporary life is apparently a necessary prelude to a more humane society which may already be taking form. In any event, the work in electronic music is basically a reflection of the current crisis-dilemma-opportunity situation now operative in contemporary life, and electronic music, along with all our highly developed technology, is here to stay. What happens with machines is still the prerogative of those who build the machines.

Over thirty years ago—in 1951—the electronic studio of Cologne Radio was put into operation, thus semi-officially launching the age of electronic music. Other studios were subsequently opened in Paris, Milan, Tokyo, and at Columbia University and the Bell Laboratories in the United States—and many more are now in operation. Karlheinz Stockhausen (b. 1928) of the Cologne Studio has been a leader in a medium which has particular importance in his work: he could create new forms out of his basic idea of serial control of transformation and thus break down conventional distinctions between clarity and complexity and, most especially, between noise and pitch. Representative compositions include Op. 1970 and Solo for Electronic Instrument with Reverberation.

After the mid-fifties, the nature of avant-garde music began to change, due largely to the leadership of Stockhausen. Total serialism grew into new materials based on the many ways of transforming textures, colors, and sound densities. From the earlier "controlled chance" compositions, with some options controlled by the composer and others by the performer, the movement has shifted to multiple forms of control and chance and so-called "open forms" with chance the major factor. Aleatory music (Latin, *alea:* dice) is a general term describing various kinds of music in which chance, unpredictability, ambiguity, and even sheer chaos is realized in performance. If strict serial music represents a kind of Newtonian, mathematical determinism, then aleatory music represents its exact opposite: a symbolic rolling of musical dice just to see what will happen.

This conflict between determined calculation and chance is a musical equivalent to the current situation in science. The precision of the Newtonian world-machine has been supplanted by a modern science which is forced to settle for contingent proofs, complementary truths, and/or mathematical concepts of uncertainty. Quantum mechanics recognizes the element of chance and its language has even been carried over, however ineffectively, into aesthetic theories. Strict mathematical concepts (except for "pure" mathematics), whether in science or art, can lead only to dead ends: scientific "truths" which are jarred by further gains in knowledge and strict mathematics in music which lead to the sterility of nonart. Chance music is therefore a corollary of modern science, and especially of both the profundity and absurdity of contemporary life.

The American composer John Cage (b. 1912) was among the first to experiment with chance music. In the late thirties he worked with a "prepared piano" which was designed to produce percussive sounds and noises that were unrelated to its traditional sound. Since the early fifties he has produced works of indeterminate length, of chance operations, of chance media (a concert of a group of radios tuned to different stations), and similar techniques. One of his most widely discussed compositions is a piano solo titled *4'33"* during which the pianist merely sits quietly at the piano for this period of time, after which he bows and leaves the stage. Obviously the composition "sounds" different at each performance because of the variance in noise from the audience. This composition would have to be considered the ultimate in Minimal art as well as an achievement somewhat comparable in everyday life to the "non-wheat" which a farmer produces in exchange for government money. Carrying this idea to its logical conclusion would have the government paying artists for non-poetry, nonnovels, and nonpaintings. The ultimate absurdity would seem to have been reached and Dada would reign supreme.

And Dada is related to chance music, or vice versa, just as are Cage's ideas of the Chinese chance technique of coin throwing from the *I Ching* and his fascination with Zen Buddhism. Chance music concerts may include instructions on manuscripts such as: "Start when you like and repeat as often as necessary," "Hold this note as long as you like and then go on to the next one," "Wait till the spirit moves you and then make up your own piece," and so forth. Performers are also instructed to destroy their instruments, stare at the audience, propel vehicles about the stage, blow sirens, flash lights, and perform other stimulating activities. The end result might be called Aimless Theatre rather than theatre of the absurd, although there appear to be common elements. For an encore there may or may not be a full-blown Happening followed by the ultimate absurdity—leaving the concert hall to return to "real" life.

Pierre Boulez has done extensive work with aleatory music but his work is not at the mercy of blind chance as in the case with Cage, or myopic chance as with Stockhausen. Boulez himself states that chance is guided; the work leaves much to the discretion of the performer and can thus be seen from several angles, something like the mobiles of Calder.

Contemporary music contains perhaps more than its fair share of politically motivated music. Soviet composers like Dmitri Shostakovitch (1906–1975) were expected to follow the party line and supposedly his well-known Fifth Symphony did so. In his *Memoirs* (smuggled out of Russia and published in 1979) Shostakovitch revealed some startlingly different ideas. According to him the Fifth Symphony was meant to describe Stalin's Great Terror of 1936–1937. The Seventh Symphony, called the Leningrad, was actually planned before the war; the so-called invasion theme, with its fearsomely swelling fortissimo, had nothing to do with the Nazi attack. "I was thinking," wrote Shostakovitch, "of other enemies of humanity [namely Stalin and his killers] when I composed the theme." "The majority of my symphonies are tombstones," stated Shostakovitch. "Too many of our people died and were buried in places unknown to anyone. . . . I'm willing to write a composition for each of the victims, but that's impossible, and that's why I dedicate my music to them all."

During the thirties many artists, in a quest for Utopia, moved over to the party line but most moved back again after Utopia was more clearly seen as Shostakovitch had experienced it first-hand, a brutal totalitarian empire. In the fifties the themes changed to pacifism, antiwar and individual freedom. Britain's Benjamin Britten (1913–1979) wrote his notable *War Requiem* for the rededication of Coventry Cathedral after its destruction by German bombers during the war. In Italy, Dallapiccola (b. 1904) has become a persuasive artist dedicated to universal humanism. His techniques follow Schoenberg and Berg but his humanistic philosophy is expressed in works such as *Canti di Prigionia (Songs of Imprisonment)* and the opera *Il prigioniero (The Prisoner)*.

Not all contemporary music is of the avant-garde variety. Paul Hindemith (1895–1963) was a Neoclassicist in his retention of tonal writing and his devotion to the style of J. S. Bach. He also advocated *Gebrauchmusik* (useful music) and wrote music for all ages and degrees of musical skills and for numerous special events which called for appropriate music. One of his best works is the symphonic version of *Mathis der Maler,* a moving depiction in sound of the *Isenheim Altarpiece* by Matthias Grünewald (1480–1528). Kurt Weill (1900–1950), after he met the playwright Bertolt Brecht, deliberately rejected the complexities of modern music. In conjunction with Brecht he wrote *The Threepenny Opera* and *The Fall of the House of Mahagony.* These two operas were partly responsible for the renaissance of musical theatre in America which began with Rodgers and Hammerstein's *Oklahoma!* and continued through their *South Pacific, Carousel,* and *The Sound of Music.* Bernstein's *West Side Story,* Lerner and Loewe's *My Fair Lady* and *Camelot,* and Newley's *The Roar of the Greasepaint; The Smell of the Crowd* are notable contributions to the musical theatre. The finest talent in contemporary music theatre is unquestionably Stephen Sondheim, who writes both words and music. His musicals include *West Side Story* (lyrics), *A Funny Thing Happened on the Way to the Forum, A Little Night Music, Pacific Overtures,* and *Sweeney Todd.*

George Gershwin (1898–1937) may be one of America's best composers. Criticized by musical snobs as being "popular" and thus, for some strange reason, beyond the pale, his music has endured and much of it has become a part of the standard repertory. The *Rhapsody in Blue, An American in Paris,* and the Concerto in F have all become known throughout the world as truly representative of American music. *Of Thee I Sing* is now recognized as musical theatre at its satirical best and *Porgy and Bess*—a smash hit at La Scala in Milan—is perhaps America's finest opera.

Following are brief descriptions of additional major American composers along with one or more representative compositions by each.

Earle Browne (b. 1926) wrote *Available Forms II for Large Orchestra, Four Hands* for two conductors who choose from among thirty-eight "sound events."

Elliott Carter's (b. 1908) Concerto for Orchestra was commissioned for the 125th anniversary of the New York Philharmonic Society. It is a major work by a superb craftsman in the Post-Renaissance tradition.

Aaron Copland's (b. 1900) Suite from the Ballet *Appalachian Spring* and the ballet score *Rodeo* have become modern classics.

George Crumb (b. 1929) wrote *Echoes of Time and the River: Four Processionals for Orchestra* (cf. Thomas Wolfe) using all titles as poetic metaphors rather than for specific meanings.

Time Cycle, Four Songs for Soprano and Orchestra by Lukas Foss (b. 1922) uses a literary "time-motive" with each poem referring to time, clocks, or bells.

Symphony no. 3 by Roy Harris (1898–1979) was the first symphony by an American composer to achieve worldwide acclaim.

Carl Ruggles (1876–1971) took the title of his orchestral work *Sun-Treader* from Robert Browning's tribute to Shelley.

Symphony no. 6 by William Schuman (b. 1910) was commissioned by the Dallas Symphony Orchestra.

As with so many important orchestral works, the Symphony no. 3 by Roger Sessions (b. 1896) was commissioned by a symphony orchestra, in this case the Boston Symphony.

Samuel Barber (1910–1981) based his *Knoxville: Summer of 1915* on a fragment by the writer James Agee.

Windows by Jacob Druckman (b. 1928) won the Pulitzer Prize for 1972, a fitting recognition for a major work.

Synchrony was a collaborative effort between Henry Cowell (1897–1965) and Martha Graham.

Lou Harrison's (b. 1917) Symphony on G is serially based on twelve tones while literally basing itself on the note "G."

Mysterious Mountain by Alan Hovhaness (b. 1911) is written in the manner of a romantic symphony but with a variety of modern techniques.

Wallingford Riegger's (1885–1961) Symphony no. 3 is a blending of traditional and twelve-tone techniques.

George Rochberg (b. 1918) uses two six-note groups derived from a single twelve-tone row for his Symphony no. 2.

Gunther Schuller (b. 1925) composed his tonal impressions of visual art with his *Seven Studies on Themes of Paul Klee.* Schuller has been a leader in the movement known as "third-stream jazz" which attempts to combine jazz with chamber and/or symphonic music.

The Plow that Broke the Plains by Virgil Thomson (b. 1896) is an orchestral suite extracted from the score of a documentary film about the drought of the 1930s.

Charles Wuorinen (b. 1938) wrote his Concerto for Amplified Violin and Orchestra after winning a Pulitzer Prize in 1970 for an electronic composition.

Following are brief descriptions of additional major European composers—by country—with representative compositions.

Austria

Ernst Krenek (b. 1900) has written a jazz opera entitled *Jonny spielt auf.* Perhaps his most important work is the opera *Karl V,* a prophetic piece predating the rise of Hitler.

Egon Wellesz (1885–1974) has been almost equally famous as a composer and as a musicologist. His finest stage work is the *Bakchantinnen,* based on Euripides' *The Bacchae.*

One of the most curious figures in twentieth-century music is Joseph Mathias Hauer (1883–1959), an inventor of a twelve-tone system. Unlike Schoenberg, who refused to violate his twelve-tone row, Hauer contended, among other things, that there were 479,001,600 possible combinations of twelve notes. His theories may be more interesting than his music.

Hans Erich Apostel (b. 1901) has been strangely neglected, possibly because his music is starkly austere, conceived as an architectonic act with a minimum of romantic accoutrements.

Czechoslovakia

Vieteslav Nóvak (1870–1949) was strongly influenced by the more flamboyant qualities of Slovak folksong. *The Storm,* a symphony-like cantata, is his best dramatic work.

Leoś Janácek (1854–1928) was perhaps the most important Czech composer of this century. Major works include: *Diary of a Young Man Who Disappeared, Concertino* for seven instruments, Quartet no. 2, *Sinfonietta,* and the *Glagolitic Mass.*

One of the more strikingly original composers is Alois Hába (1893–1973) who developed a technique of microtones which includes quarter-tone, sixth-tone, and twelfth-tone scales.

The work of Bohuslav Martinu (1890–1959) is the most cosmopolitan in outlook. Perhaps his long residence in France, Switzerland, and the United States accounts for this, and yet his music remains Czech to the core. His compositions include four symphonies and two piano concertos.

Eugen Suchon (b. 1908) is a Slovak composer whose sociological-psychological drama *Krutnava* is the first Slovak national opera.

Petr Eben (b. 1929) is a traditionalist who draws as much from Gregorian chant as he does from contemporary techniques. His compositions include the large-scale orchestral work *Vox clamantis.*

England

William Walton (1929–1982) achieved early fame with his *Facade,* a setting for a series of "nonsense" poems by Edith Sitwell. His dramatic cantata *Belshazzar's Feast* is one of the great choral works of the century.

Michael Tippett (b. 1905) produced nothing of any lasting value before his mid-thirties. *The Midsummer Marriage, King Priam,* and *The Knot Garden* are his three operas, all of which have aroused considerable controversy. Critical opinion ranges from condemnation to acclaim with very little in a moderated middle ground. All three works are actually very significant contributions to the operatic stage and any or all of them may find a permanent place in the opera house. His oratorio, *A Child of Our Time,* transforms a Nazi pogrom against the Jews into a formidable image of terrible reality.

Maxwell Davies (b. 1930) is possibly the leading British composer of the younger generation. He is both a modernist and a traditionalist in works such as *L'Homme armé* (based on the fifteenth-century mass) and *Revelation and Fall.*

France

Darius Milhaud (1892–1974) was one of the most prolific composers of the century. His music for Cocteau's pantomime, *Le Boeuf sur le Toit,* set the standard for a chic, hard, chrome-plated music. His later works include the operas *Bolivar* and *David* and the suite *Opus Americanum.*

Arthur Honegger (1892–1955) made his reputation with *Le Roi David,* a biblical drama for chorus and orchestra. Perhaps his most significant works are his dramatic oratorios *Amphion* and *Jeanne d'Arc au bûcher.*

Francis Poulenc (1899–1963) channeled his enormous talent into two disparate directions, an ultra-Parisian side of music halls, circus bands, and street-corner ensembles along with a devotion to serious sacred music. He set Cocteau's *Cocardes* to the sounds of a street-corner ensemble. For Diaghilev, he wrote a brilliant score for the ballet *Les Biches.* During World War II, he played a prominent part in the "musical resistance" movement and wrote one of his finest works during the German occupation, the cantata *Figure humaine* which ends with a hymn to Liberté. His choral works are monumental: Mass in G, *Litanies à la Vierge noire de Rocamadour, Stabat Mater, Gloria,* and *Sept repons des tenebras.* The role of Francis Poulenc in twentieth-century music is unique because of the unabashed pleasure-giving quality of his music. Even his religious works are never morbid or sentimental for he wore his religion happily. Even when he was at his witty, Parisian best he was never banal, trivial, or superficial. Above all, he staunchly refused to take anything seriously, which may be the most eloquent testimony of all to this musical blithe spirit.

Germany

Hans Werne Henze (b. 1926) has precocious talents which, after early success in Germany, he moved to Italy where he indulged himself in Italian romanticism—a Rimbaud cantata *Being Beauteous* and *Nocturnes and Arias*. By 1970, his Italian dream had ended as he faced a mind-blowing Rolling Stones concert in Rome and the attempted assassination of a students' revolutionary leader. His angry protest piece *Versuch uber Schweine* was one result of his politicalization. Henze's conversion to Marxism was also marked by his controversial *Raft of the Medusa*.

Gyorgy Ligeti (b. 1923) worked with Stockhausen at the electronic studios in Cologne. His technique is exemplified in his *Aventures* and *Nouvelles Aventures* in which the "language" used is limited to phonetic sounds with no meaning. His most notable pieces to date are the *Requiem* and the *Lux Aeterna*.

Mauricio Kagel (b. 1931) of Buenos Aires worked in the electronic studios at Cologne and taught at the Darmstadt electronic complex. His music can be said to eternally rejuvenate itself and, at each moment of performance, to produce new sounds and other surprises. His *Transicion,* written for piano, percussion, and two tape recorders, uses a pianist playing in the traditional manner, a percussionist striking various parts of the piano, these sounds recorded—and distorted—on the first tape recorder, and the whole concert hall scene recorded by the second tape recorder and played back during the performance.

Greece

Iannis Xenakis (b. 1922) has emerged as an important avant-garde composer. He collaborated with Le Corbusier in designing the Philips Pavilion for the Brussels World's Fair and wrote music for it. His *Strategie* for two orchestras and two conductors is a contest between the two instrumental ensembles in which the conductors are given certain specifications about the nineteen sections of the composition and, at the conclusion of the battle, the applause of the audience determines the winner.

Holland

Peter Schat (b. 1935) has studied with Pierre Boulez and figures prominently in many avant-garde programs as a serial composer with aleatory and improvisational passages in the manner of John Cage.

Italy

Luciano Berio (b. 1925) achieved prominence with his pioneering of the Milan Radio electronic music studio. He has the ability to write music ideally suited to the nature of individual instruments, such as his *Sequenzas*. Probably his best and most original work is *Circles,* written to poems by e e cummings.

Poland

Witold Lutoslawski (b. 1913) strives to extend the frontiers of music while remaining within the bounds of the Post-Renaissance tradition. In *Trois poèmes d'Henri Michaux,* he uses various methods of producing sound—exclusive of singing—varying between quiet whispers and violent calls, cries, and screams.

Russia

Nikolai Myaskovsky (1881–1950) is representative of the neutral, easily forgotten artisan-composers which the Soviet Union has vigorously promoted.

Aram Khachaturian (1903–1978) reflects vivid Armenian folksongs in works like the Piano Concerto, Violin Concerto, and his very popular ballets.

Scandinavia

Bengt Hambraeus (b. 1928) was the first Scandinavian composer to write an electronic piece, albeit in Cologne, with his *Doppelrohr II*.

Bo Nilsson (b. 1937) explores unusual and striking sonorities, as in the *Brief an Gosta Oswald* for three sound groups.

Spain

Joaquin Turina (1882–1949) had a vast output including, for example, forty-nine different series of piano music. He is at his best in orchestral works such as *La Procesión del Rocio* and *Danzas Fantásticas*.

Manuel de Falla (1876–1946) was one of the notable composers of the century. His contributions to the repertoire include *Love the Sorcerer, The Three-Cornered Hat, Nights in the Gardens of Spain*, the *Retalbo,* and the Harpsichord Concerto.

Oscar Esplá (1886–1971) is the third of the Spanish masters of the twentieth century. His best works include *El Sueno de Eros, La Nochebuena del Diablo,* and *Don Quijote valando las armas*.

Switzerland

Frank Martin (1890–1974) based his major work, *Le vin herbe,* on the Tristan legend. His *In terra pax* was written for the end of World War II.

Rolf Lieberman (b. 1910) has also made a name for himself as an operatic director in Germany. His best-known work is his Concerto for Jazzband and Symphony Orchestra.

Summary

Twentieth-century music, like the music of every age, effectively mirrors the prevailing patterns of the century. The impending catastrophe of World War I was forecast in the primitive barbarity of Stravinsky's *The Rite of Spring.* Reflecting the rational, intellectual aspects of the Age of Analysis were the serial techniques of Alban Berg as he exploited the self-imposed discipline of the tone row to achieve the musical results of the Violin Concerto.

Prokofiev's Neoclassical Fifth Symphony displayed another kind of discipline, that of casting modern tonal materials in classical forms and making the forms serve the music. Orff's *Carmina Burana* gives some indication of the persistence of the Romantic tradition in a century which seems to have little time for sentiment. Bartók's Concerto for Orchestra, with its continuous variation technique, seems to epitomize the age, the restless, ever-changing forms of contemporary life.

The pre-World War I Futurists began the exploration of the musical possibilities of noise and timbre which Varèse later developed into a uniquely modern musical style. Charles Ives anticipated many of the innovations of avant-garde twelve-tone composers such as Schoenberg, Berg, and Webern and, after World War II, the avant-garde developed the twelve-tone method into complete serial systems.

Electronic music in various forms (*musique concrète* and synthesizers) exerted an ever-growing influence as reflected in much or all of the work of Babbitt, Messiaen, Boulez, Stockhausen, Varèse, and Cage. Aleatory music, with or without electronic assistance, is not dominating the musical scene but it is certainly making strong waves.

Britten, Shostakovich, and Dallapiccola, among others, have used a variety of styles to convey sociopolitical viewpoints, while Hindemith concentrated on expanding the resources of tonal music and Weill deliberately rejected the complexities of contemporary music in favor of a synthesis of traditional styles (including jazz) which influenced the development of modern musical theatre.

American composers have made important contributions to the international scene. Gershwin, Copland, Harris, Sessions, and Barber, among others, have contributed a variety of significant contemporary music. European composers continue to dominate Western music though not as exclusively as they have in the past. Krenek, Janacek, Martinu, Walton, Tippett, Milhaud, and Honegger have continued the Post-Renaissance tradition; Ligeti, Kagel, Xenakis, Berio, and Nilsson have been leaders in experimental music utilizing electronic resources.

The essence of much of the music of this century can be summarized in the phrase "Things fall apart: the center cannot hold." The old musical centers of clear-cut keys, major-minor tonality, and traditional musical instruments are no longer apropos. Composers have been trying to find and/or establish new centers, new ways of relating to a rapidly changing world.

The search for new musical values has utilized mathematics (twelve-tone and serial techniques), technology (electronic media), the sounds of people, and the sounds of nature. Traditional music has been bent, borrowed, violated, and ignored. The search goes on and, probably, only the next century can look back and describe where the search has led us and what twentieth-century music was all about.

Jazz in America

Jazz is a uniquely different style of music, the result of a fusion—collision might be a better word—of certain elements of African and American musical cultures. Aside from the music of the American Indian, music in the United States was of European origin and under the influence of European musical styles. This influence extended to both North and South America.

Given the broad influence of European civilization and the presence of African slaves and freedmen throughout the United States, the islands of the Caribbean, Central and South America, the singular and significant fact remains that jazz is a style of music that originated solely in the United States. By the turn of the century, Negro spirituals, ragtime, blues, and jazz were established types or styles of music. None of these styles, however, existed at this time anywhere else in the Western Hemisphere.

The French, Spanish, Portuguese, and even English cultures of the West Indies, Central and South America seemed to have provided a climate in which African arts, crafts, customs, and religious beliefs could coexist with their European counterparts: a climate in which transplanted Africans could maintain a considerable portion of their customs mixed, of course, with many elements of Western culture, Christianity in particular. For whatever reasons, and there appear to be many, the dominant white culture of the American South was not as tolerant of African customs as were the transplanted European cultures south of the United States. There existed a strong conflict between white and black Americans in almost every area of life: religion, folklore, music, art, dance, and social and political customs. This continuing cultural conflict, it should be pointed out, is only one complex area amidst the persistent problems of race relations and need not be equated with strife in areas such as civil liberties, equality of educational, housing, and job opportunities. Fundamental differences in the ways of living built up by a group of human beings, namely *culture,* may very well lie at the heart of some of the problems, but those considerations lie outside the scope of this book.

In summary, jazz is a musical style that evolved out of a three-century history of cultural and racial conflict, a clash between an inflexible dominant culture and a powerful and persistent subculture with its own age-old beliefs and customs.

The elements of jazz are those of any music: melody, harmony, rhythm, and tone color. It is the Afro-American mixture, however, that makes the difference. The development of any style of music normally follows an evolutionary process *within* a single culture. Outside influences, when they appear, tend to be transformed and absorbed into the stylistic development. For example, the Viennese waltz is a modified, speeded-up version of an old Austrian folk dance called the *ländler.* The ländler was Austrian; the changes were compatible with Austrian concepts of melody, harmony, rhythm, and tone color. The finished product was in all respects a result of Austrian culture and the musical genius of one Johann Strauss, Jr. It would be ludicrous to remove the Strauss melody and insert a Russian boat song, an Irish jig, or an American Indian rain dance. Scale, harmony, rhythm, and tone color would be all wrong because an incompatible melody was introduced into a foreign context.

In a manner of speaking, jazz sounds the way it does because it *is* a compound of several different and even opposing concepts of melody, rhythm, and tone color. In very general terms, jazz can be defined as a style of music that consists of Afro-European melody, European harmony, African rhythm, and Afro-European tone color. A built-in conflict of musical styles lies at the root of jazz and probably accounts, at least in part, for the feelings of dislocation and sometimes anguish and even pain on the part of performers and listeners.

The fundamental conflict in the materials of jazz occurs in *scale* and *tuning*. Equal temperament, with its twelve equal semitones in each octave, is the tuning standard for Western music. On the other hand, African melody was and is based on the tones present in the overtone series. The distances between pitches range from whole steps and half steps, similar to those in the tempered scale, to other intervals *between* half steps, including *quarter tones* (tones approximately midway between, say, C♯ and D♭). African harmony is quite rudimentary; melody, rhythm, and tone color are far more important.

African melodies, with their different-sized intervals, were sung in a culture that did not use such a variety of intervals, that built musical instruments in equal temperament, a culture in which African songs were often characterized as out of tune, primitive, and/or a poor imitation of "proper" singing.

The Elements of Jazz

Scale The combining of African scales with the European diatonic scale produced a hybrid called the *blues scale*.[2] In terms of the equal-tempered piano the blues scale can be described as a diatonic scale plus three *blue notes*: flatted 3rd, 5th, and 7th scale degrees.

In a single melody line there can be a mixture of diatonic notes and blue notes:

In actual performance the blues scale might be described as a pentatonic scale plus flatted 5th (g♭ or f♯):

blues scale on C

The blues scale on C can be used *against* the three primary triads in several different ways:

Blues scales all based on C
x = blue notes

Blues scales based on chord roots, C, F, G:
x = blue notes

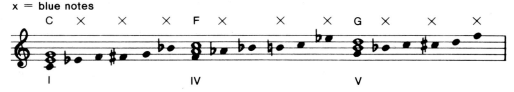

---

2. The blues scale is not African in itself although its origins necessarily lie in African music. Rather it is an Afro-American scale, and it is the elemental component out of which jazz is made.

A simple melodic line using only the blues scale on C would sound like this when played against the primary diatonic chords (the name of the chord is given in parentheses):

I (C6)   IV(F6)   V7 (G7)   I (C6)

A melody such as the one above would be written the same way whether played on the piano, on another instrument, or sung; however, the melody would be performed in equal temperament only on the piano. In any other medium (vocal or instrumental) the flatted 3rd might be the same pitch as the piano Eb or several other slightly higher pitches *between* Eb and Eᵍ (there is no commonly used notational system which can accurately indicate these pitches):

The vocalist or instrumentalist can produce any of the preceding pitches, slide from one to another or play with or "worry" the notes. The best that the pianist can do is strike Eb and Eᵍ together as a substitute for the note in between.

Rhythm   Rhythm is the main ingredient in African music: highly developed, intricate, complex, as sophisticated in its own way as the harmonic system of Western culture. The African rhythms which have crossed over into jazz and into much of our modern concert music are but a relatively simple portion of a whole world of elaborate percussion music. Compare, for example, the single rhythmic pattern of an

Indian dance

or that of a waltz

with the simultaneous rhythms of a quartet of African percussionists:

Guiro (scratched gourd)

High Drum   Right Hand / Left Hand

Middle Drum

Low Drum

There are two interrelated fundamental characteristics of African rhythm: *beat* and *syncopation.* Emerging from the simultaneous rhythm patterns is a *subjective beat,* a rhythmic pulsation which is not necessarily played by any one drummer but which results from the combination of the whole. The beat is implicit. This beat (whether explicit or implicit) is so

much a part of jazz that it can be called its *heartbeat* or *pulse.* Jazz can thus be defined as the "beauty of the beat."

Syncopation is a displacement or shifting of accents so they disagree with natural metrical accents.

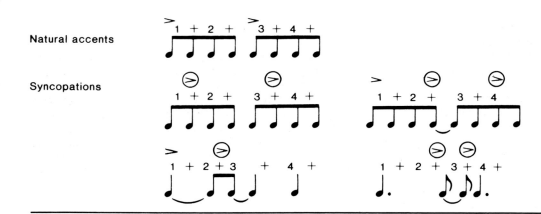

Syncopation has the effect of tugging at the beat, a process that emphasizes the existence of the basic pulse by setting up a conflict with that pulse. The pull of syncopation on the ongoing beat gives a kind of *swing* to the music, a buoyant resiliency which is a fundamental characteristic of jazz.

Tone Color   The story is told of the World War II air base in Africa which stockpiled aviation gasoline in steel drums. The drums were unloaded and stacked by native laborers, one of whom accidentally dropped a drum and noticed a booming, reverberant tone as the heavy drum hit the hard ground. His neighbor immediately dropped his drum in order to discover its tone color. Within a very few minutes, in their delight at discovering new tone colors, the entire crew was enthusiastically engaged in dropping, hitting, and scraping gasoline drums.

Beating on logs, sticks, bones, metal, or drums, scratching gourds, shaking rattles, all are activities designed to exploit tone colors within a rhythmic framework. An African drummer can obtain several dozen different timbres as he uses his thumbs, fingers, flat of the hand, or fist on various areas of a drumhead. All that is necessary for a percussion instrument is a distinctive tone color with virtually no limit to the number and variety of possible tone colors.

Distinctive tone color in jazz is not confined to the drums. It extends to the colors obtained by using mutes, hats, plungers, handkerchiefs, or anything else that will give variety to the timbre of instruments such as trumpet and trombone. Instrumentalists also use growls, slurs, slides, and so forth in what is basically an attempt to give an expressive range and personal quality to their music. The colors may be cool or hot or anything in between; in any event, jazz musicians are concerned with their sound, the distinctive coloration of their performance.

Harmony   Harmony is one of the most highly developed elements of Western culture but of only slight importance in African music. Consequently, the fusion of African and American music was essentially a combining of African melody, rhythm, and tone color with an established harmonic system. The result, as stated before, was a synthesis of conflicting stylistic elements and the beginning of a new style of music called jazz.

Primary Origins of Jazz

Jazz probably came into existence at one or more places in the American South some time between the end of the Civil War and the last decade of the nineteenth century (ca. 1890). The precise date may never be pinpointed because jazz was a compound of preexisting music.

There are many types of black music, some probably dating back to the arrival of the first slaves in the early part of the seventeenth century and others gradually developing in response to, or despite, the American environment. The African vocal tradition survived and adjusted to the new conditions and the new religion (Christianity). The instrumental tradition, however, was generally repressed by the planters who suspected, and rightly so, that African drums could communicate such matters as possible slave rebellion. The planters were also concerned about breaking up tribal units and traditions, little suspecting that tribal histories were perpetuated by the drummers and the language of the drum script.[3] The banjo (African, *banjar*) did survive but European instruments were gradually taken up by black musicians. The outline below specifies the various types of vocal music, ceremonies, instrumental styles and ensembles, dances, and stage presentations which lie, in varying degrees, at the roots of jazz.

Black Music in America

Vocal Music (with and without accompaniment)	**Instrumental Music** Creole music (dances, woodwind instruments)

---

3. Some African languages, especially the varieties of Bantu, used different pitch levels of vowel sounds for different word meanings. Tribal historians were highly select drummers who were trained to play the *talking drum* by beating out the word rhythms while at the same time varying the pitch by means of a stretched membrane. Thus, the drum script was almost a vocal sound which could be transmitted over considerable distances with the use of relay drummers.

Secular	Sacred
Work songs	Spirituals
Hollers	Ring shouts
Street cries	Gospel songs
Ballads	Jubilees
Blues	Song-sermon
Marches	(semivocal)
Brass bands	Voodoo ceremonies
Ragtime	(dances, singing,
Minstrel shows (vocal	percussion)
and instrumental)	

The sound of the music is the only practical way for gaining an understanding of any music, and particularly the many styles of black folk music. Following are pre-jazz styles (as outlined above), including specific examples, their background, and characteristics.

African Music

1. "Dundun Drums" (talking drums). In *Dances of the Yoruba of Nigeria.* Folkways FE 4441.
2. "Religious Drumming to the Deity Orishania," The Yoruba, Nigeria. In *African and Afro-American Drums.* Folkways FE 4502.

Pre-Jazz Styles (Black Folk Music)

Work Song

Background and Characteristics　Directly and closely related to African work songs. Strong, regular beat, blues scale, syncopations,[4] usually unaccompanied solo song but may use guitar or banjo accompaniment. Associated with manual labor that tends to a rhythmic regularity, such as rowing a boat, driving railroad spikes, and chopping wood.

Examples
1. Leadbelly. "Juliana Johnson." In *Jazz,* Vol. I. Folkways FV 2801.
2. Leadbelly. "Looky Yonder Where de Sun Done Gone." In *Last Session,* Vol. I. Folkways 2941.

Holler (Field Holler)

Background and Characteristics　Sung to non-rhythmic fieldwork such as picking cotton or hoeing corn. Unaccompanied, irregular beat, narrative or singsong text, varied repetition of words and phrases, some prolonged syllables with elaborated melodic line.

Examples
1. "Old Hannah." In *Jazz,* Vol. I. Folkways FV 2801.
2. Leadbelly. "Bring Me Li'l' Water, Silvey." *Take This Hammer.* Verve, Folkways 9001; S9001.

---

4. All these styles use blue notes and syncopations unless otherwise specified.

Street Cry

Background and Characteristics　Song to accompany the selling of fruits, vegetables, fish, and so forth in the streets of a city or village. Unaccompanied, constant repetition of the name of the product with varying inflections on the words, including changes in pitch and tone quality. Conversion of words to consistent rhythmic patterns, a prevailing characteristic of most black music. The ends of phrases frequently use a *falsetto break* in which the voice slides up an octave or so in pitch and abruptly breaks off.

Examples
1. "Strawberry Woman" and "Crab Man." In *Porgy and Bess: Original Sound Track Recording.* Columbia OL—5410; OS—2016.
2. Van Wey, Adelaide. "Sweet Oranges" and "Blue Berries." *New Orleans Creole Songs and Cries,* 10″. Folkways 2202.

Ballad

Background and Characteristics　Narrative song in numerous verses. African heroic songs of kings, hunters, and warriors are translated into ballads about folk heroes such as John Henry, the steel-driving man.

Example
1. Leadbelly. "John Henry." In *Jazz,* Vol. I. Folkways FV 2801.

Blues

Background and Characteristics　The most important single influence in the development of jazz. There are two kinds of blues: folk (rural blues) and urban (true jazz blues). Only the folk blues will be considered here. (See page 580 for Urban Blues.)

The blues reflect African customs and musical traditions, but they are native to America. The blues are personal, subjective, introspective, a way of protesting misfortune and identifying trouble. Singing the blues is a survival technique for counteracting bad times, loneliness, and despair.

Blues lyrics usually consist of three lines of poetry. The first line is repeated (possibly with a slight variation) followed by a third line which completes the thought. Because blues are usually improvised, the repeating of the second line gives the singer a better chance to make up the last line. There may be only one verse or there may be many verses in a narrative blues. Favorite subjects are love, traveling, and trouble, but almost anything makes a fit subject, as shown by the following blues poems.

Love:

Love is like a faucet, you can turn it off or on (twice)
But when you think you've got it, it's done turned off and gone.

Traveling:

I went to the deepot, an' looked upon de boa'd. (twice)
It say: dere's good times here, dey's better down de road.

Proverbs:

My momma tole me, my daddy tole me too: (twice)
Everybody grin in yo' face, ain't no friend to you.

Images:

Ef blues was whiskey, I'd stay drunk all de time. (twice)
Blues ain't nothin' but a po'man's heart disease.

Comedy:

Want to lay my head on de railroad line, (twice)
Let the train come along and pacify my mind.

Tragedy:

(one line images)
Got the blues but too dam mean to cry.
Standin' here lookin' one thousand miles away.
I hate to see the evenin' sun go down.
Been down so long, Lawd, down don't worry me.

The music of the blues is quadruple meter and is eight, twelve, sixteen, and sometimes twenty bars in length. The *twelve-bar blues* is the most common of all patterns. It accompanies the three-phrase rhymed couplet in the most popular poetic meter of iambic pentameter. The harmony is limited to the primary triads.

Chilly Winds

Examples

1. "Careless Love." Brownie McGhee. *Blues.* Folkways 3557; or: *Wilbur de Paris Plays, Jimmy Witherspoon Sings, New Orleans Blues.* Atlantic 1266.
2. "Every Night When the Sun Goes Down." Elizabeth Knight. *Hootenanny Tonight.* Folkways 2511.
3. "Joe Turner Blues." Big Bill Broonzy. *Sings Country Blues.* Folkways 2326; or: *Louis Armstrong Plays W. C. Handy.* Columbia CL—591.

Spiritual

Background and Characteristics Many derived from Protestant hymns but with significant changes in melody and rhythm. Usually improvised, especially during church services or prayer meetings. Most common pattern is solo verse with group refrain. Call and response patterns (song leader alternating with group response) also quite common. The texts are variations of existing hymns, paraphrases of biblical passages, or sometimes wholly original. They are notable for vividness of imagery, the relating of biblical stories with direct and telling simplicity, and a strong concern for the sounds and rhythms of words.

Examples

1. "Didn't It Rain." Mahalia Jackson. *Newport 1958: Mahalia Jackson.* Columbia CL—1244.
2. "Michael Row the Boat Ashore." *We Shall Overcome: Songs of the Freedom Riders.* Folkways FH 5591.
3. "Down by the Riverside." *Pete Seeger at Carnegie Hall.* Folkways 2412; or: Mahalia Jackson. *Bless This House.* Columbia CL—899; CS—8761.
4. "Every Time I Feel the Spirit." Josh White. *Chain Gang Songs.* Elektra 158; 7158; or: Marian Anderson. *Spirituals.* RCA Victor, LM 2032.

Ring Shout

Background and Characteristics   Similar to an African circle dance in form and character. Usually performed outdoors after a service. A ring would be formed and a spiritual sung to start it moving, accompanied by hand claps and foot stomping. The same spiritual would be sung over and over, usually with added verses until the cumulative effect would be hypnotic.

Example
1. "Come an' Go with Me." Odetta. *Odetta Sings Ballads and Blues.* Tradition 1010; or *Guy Carawan Sings,* Vol. II. Folkways 3548; or Hally Wood. *Hootenanny at Carnegie Hall.* Folkways 2512.

Gospel Song

Background and Characteristics   Many derived from Protestant gospel songs. They differ from hymns and spirituals mostly in the texts, which are more personal and subjective. "I," "me," "my" (sometimes "we") are the key words in songs that tend to reduce the religious experience to a personal viewpoint. Melody and harmony are generally simpler than in spirituals.

Examples
1. "My God Is Real." Mahalia Jackson. *Newport 1958: Mahalia Jackson.* Columbia CL—1244.
2. "We Shall Overcome." *We Shall Overcome: Songs of the Freedom Riders.* Folkways FH 5591.

Jubilee

Background and Characteristics   A type of spiritual which sings jubilantly of the Year of Jubilee "When the Saints Go Marching In."

Example
1. "When the Saints Go Marching In." Many jazz recordings available

Song-Sermon

Background and Characteristics   Delivered from the pulpit and usually beginning with a scriptural quotation. The vocal delivery of the minister proceeds from the spoken word to a kind of intoned chant and culminating in ringing declamation and vocalized phrases on higher and higher pitches. The African custom of responding verbally to the utterance of important personages such as a tribal chieftan is reflected in the congregational response to the song-sermon. There are shouts of "amen," "yes sir," "hallelujah," and impromptu wordless crooning.

Examples
1. "Dry Bones." *Jazz,* Vol. I. Folkways VB 2801.
2. "It Ain't Necessarily So." *Porgy and Bess.* Columbia OL—5410.

Voodoo (Vodun)

Background and Characteristics   Voodoo is the name given to the combination of African and Catholic religious rites and beliefs which was developed in Haiti by the Dahomeans of West Africa and which still exists in the West Indies and portions of the United States. Voodoo rites took place in Congo Square in New Orleans before being driven underground. Voodoo helped perpetuate African customs and music and probably made a significant contribution to Afro-American music and to the development of jazz.

Examples
1. *Drums of Haiti.* Folkways 4403.
2. *Cuba: Cult Music.* Folkways 4410.
3. *Jamaica: Cult Rhythms.* Folkways 4461.

Minstrel Show

Background and Characteristics   Dating from about mid-nineteenth century, minstrel shows were generally sentimentalized "scenes of plantation life" performed by an all-male, all-white cast. Characteristic black elements were present in some of the group dances, the use of rhythmic "bones," tambourine, and banjo, the soft shoe dances and the cakewalk finale (see "Ragtime"). The romantic ballads, basso profundo, silver-voiced tenor, sliding trombones, and southland chorus were, at best, distantly related to black music. Stephen Collins Foster's songs (many of them based on black folk music) were a popular staple. Minstrelsy dealt with stereotypes which no longer exist, if they ever did, but it can be credited with disseminating a portion of black musical culture throughout the United States and Europe and preparing the way for the more authentic music of a later period.

Example

1. *A Complete Authentic Minstrel Show.* Somerset SF—1600.

Ragtime

Background and Characteristics   A written-down style of music originally composed for the piano and featuring syncopated rhythmic patterns over a regular left-hand accompaniment in duple meter. The essentials of ragtime probably were in existence prior to the Civil War although Scott Joplin is formally credited as the first to write ragtime in the mid-1890s.

Blacks in their slave quarters liked to imitate the fancy balls in the plantation house by staging a cakewalking contest. The highest-stepping couple "took the cake." The basic cakewalk patterns consisted of duple meter plus two kinds of melodic syncopations:

There is a considerable body of ragtime piano literature, most of which is too difficult for the average pianist to play. Consequently, there is much watered-down semi-ragtime popular music from the period 1900–1920. Almost any piece of music can be "ragged" by changing the meter to duple, if necessary, and converting the rhythms into ragtime patterns. In developed ragtime these syncopations would include the two patterns illustrated above plus the more difficult pattern of four-note groups in which every third note is accented:

Examples

1. "Original Rags." Scott Joplin. *Ragtime: Piano Roll Classics*. Riverside RLP 12—126.
2. Joseph Lamb. *Classic Ragtime*. Folkways 3562.
3. *Reunion in Ragtime*. Stereoddities S 1900.
4. "Golliwog's Cake Walk" from the *Children's Corner Suite* by Claude Debussy. Angel 35067; or: Columbia ML—4539; or: Columbia ML—5967; MS—6567.
5. Scott Joplin. *Ragtime Songs (for piano)*. Nonesuch 71248.

The Styles of Jazz

New Orleans Style

Background and Characteristics   New Orleans style jazz probably began in the 1890s as brass band performances of spirituals and gospel songs, and ragtime versions of standard band marches. This is the so-called *traditional jazz* which, in a more discreet version played by white musicians, became known as Dixieland jazz. The original New Orleans style, however, still exists and is normally referred to as such.

Brass bands secured many of their instruments from the pawn shops of the South where they had been deposited after the Civil War by returning military bandsmen. The instrumentation was fairly typical of marching bands: trumpets, trombones, tuba, snare drum, bass drum, and usually one clarinet. The bands played and paraded for all special functions but especially for the funeral processions. According to a long-standing tradition the bands played spirituals and dirges on the way to the cemetery and some of the same music in a jazz idiom on the way back from the cemetery.

New Orleans jazz is ensemble jazz; everyone plays all the time. In general, the first trumpet has the melody, the clarinet a moving obbligato above the trumpet, and the trombone a contrapuntal bass below the lead trumpet. The material is normally gospel songs, spirituals, and marches, and the meter invariably duple. ("In the churches they sang the spirituals. In the bright New Orleans sun, marching down the street, they played them.") Needless to say, all the music was played by ear and everyone was free to improvise a suitable part for himself. ("You play your part and I play mine. You don't tell me what you want and I don't tell you. We will all variate on the theme.") The texture was polyphonic, a crude but dynamic grouping of musical voices improvising simultaneously on the melodic and harmonic framework of preexisting music. One word can describe New Orleans jazz: *exuberant.*

Examples

1. "Medley of Hymns."*Jazz Begins*. Atlantic 1297.
2. "Just a Closer Walk with Thee." Young Tuxedo Jazz Band. *Jazz Begins*. Atlantic 1297.
3. "High Society." Sweet Emma Barrett and her Dixieland Boys. *New Orleans: The Living Legends,* 2 Volumes. Riverside 356—7.

Urban Blues

Background and Characteristics   Urban blues are the heart of the true jazz idiom. The accompaniment has changed from the folk (or country) blues guitar to piano or jazz band. The subject matter revolves around the problems of urban (ghetto) life. The feeling is still bittersweet, and the form has crystallized into the classic twelve-bar blues accompanying the rhymed couplet in iambic pentameter. The blues may be sung or played by any instrument. The urban blues appeared as a recognizable style in the 1920s (on records).

Examples

1. "Mean Old Bed Bug Blues." Bessie Smith. *Jazz,* Vol. 2. Folkways FJ 2802.
2. "How Long Blues." *Jazz,* Vol. 2. Folkways FJ 2802.
3. "Back Water Blues." Dinah Washington. *Newport '58: Dinah Washington.* Mercury MG 36141.
4. *What is Jazz.* Leonard Bernstein. Columbia CL—919. Illustrations of jazz styles using "Empty Bed Blues"; topics include blues scale, a Swahili song, blue notes, rhythm, beat, syncopation, tone color, harmony, form, and a "Macbeth Blues"

Chicago Style

Background and Characteristics With the closing of Storyville, New Orleans's legal red-light district (1897–1917), jazz musicians began moving North in increasing numbers. Prohibition and the resultant practice of bootlegging helped make the Roaring Twenties city of Chicago the host for unemployed musicians playing the new and exciting sounds of jazz. Briefly stated, Chicago jazz is New Orleans jazz moved indoors. The ensemble used on the march in the New Orleans sun now played in crowded speakeasies for dances like the Fox Trot, Shimmy, Black Bottom, and Charleston.

Some of the simultaneous improvising remains, but the bands are playing many popular songs in a more homophonic but still lively and swinging style. The meter is mostly duple, but the instrumentation has changed. The piano, a newcomer to jazz, furnishes the rhythmic harmonic background; drums, guitar or banjo, tuba, or string bass, the rhythm. Varying combinations of trumpet, clarinet, trombone, and saxophone (another newcomer) play the melody and harmony. March tempos have been superseded by a range of tempos suitable for the various dances. The one word for Chicago style would be *frenetic.*

Examples

1. "Black Bottom Stomp." Jelly Roll Morton's Hot Peppers. *Jazz,* Vol. 5. Folkways FJ 2805.
2. "Somebody Stole My Gal." Bix Beiderbecke. *Jazz,* Vol. 6. Folkways FJ 2806.
3. "Margie." Bix Beiderbecke. *Jazz,* Vol. 6. Folkways FJ 2806.
4. "China Boy." Eddie Condon. *Chicago Jazz Album.* Decca 8029.

Swing (ca. 1935–1945)

Background and Characteristics The swing period of jazz began in the Depression years, the so-called Dancing Thirties. After the repeal of Prohibition in 1933 the speakeasies closed down and jazz musicians were again out of work. The migration turned in the direction of New York with its radio stations and large ballrooms, and the crowds of young dancers seeking evenings of economical entertainment.

The six- or eight-piece bands of the Chicago era were large enough for the tiny speakeasies but too small for spacious ballrooms. More musicians had to be added and stylistic changes made to accommodate them. The individuality of New Orleans and Chicago styles was subordinated to ensemble playing mixed with solo performances. The solution for handling larger numbers of players was the harmonized lead: brass sections of two trumpets and two trombones played as a unit with the first trumpet playing lead (melody) while the remaining instruments supplied the harmony. A saxophone section of three or four instruments also operated as a unit.

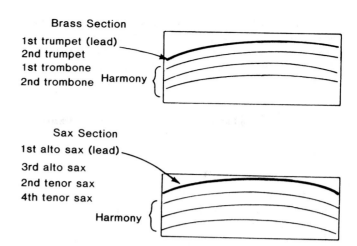

A rhythm section of piano, drums, guitar, and string bass supplied a solid four beats to a bar (quadruple meter) for the brass and sax sections, which played as independent units or as a full ensemble.

Stylistic Characteristics of Swing

1. Four heavy beats to a bar.
2. Three units: brass, saxes, rhythm.
3. Harmonized lead: brass and saxes.
4. Repertoire of popular songs in swing style plus a few jazz compositions from the preswing era. Little or no blues.
5. Extensive use of *riffs,* short rhythmic phrases or figures repeated a number of times. Riffs were used to give unity to the music, to help build up tension through constant repetition and to serve as contrasting and/or filling material against the harmonized lead in another section. Riffs were played by brass and saxes, separately or with two different figures simultaneously.

Examples

1. "A Tisket a Tasket." Ella Fitzgerald. *Original Hit Performances: The Late 30's.* Decca DL 4000.
2. "Don't Be That Way." Benny Goodman. *Carnegie Hall Jazz Concert,* Vol. I. Columbia CL—814.
3. "One O'Clock Jump." Benny Goodman. *Carnegie Hall Jazz Concert,* Vol. I. Columbia CL—814.
4. *Bei mir bist du schoen.* Benny Goodman. *Carnegie Hall Jazz Concert,* Vol. 3. Columbia CL—816.

Kansas City Jump (ca. 1935–1945)

Background and Characteristics There are many similarities between the Kansas City, or jump style and swing, sometimes called stomp style. Swing was mainly the province of white bands while Kansas City was the preferred style for many black bands. There is little difference in the instrumentation; both used the four-beat style and both used riffs, especially Kansas City, which preferred saxes in unison for riffs.

However, Kansas City was blues-based rather than oriented toward popular songs. The harmonic progression of the twelve-bar blues furnished the framework for many compositions. Swing was generally written-down or arranged jazz; Kansas City used written arrangements and considerable group improvisation. Both styles used improvised solos. Kansas City avoided the heavy sound of swing meter by using four, even, rather light beats to a bar. The piano was much more prominent, both as a solo instrument and as the dominant instrument of the rhythm section.

Examples

1. "627 Stomp." Pete Johnson. *Kansas City Jazz.* Decca DL 3044.
2. "Piney Brown Blues." Joe Turner. Decca DL 8044.
3. "Doggin' Around." Count Basie. Decca DL 8044.
4. "One O'Clock Jump." *Original Hit Performances: The Late 30's.* Decca DL 4000.
5. "Woodchopper's Ball." Woody Herman. *Original Hit Performances: Into the 40's.* Decca DL 4001.

Boogie-Woogie

Background and Characteristics Boogie-woogie became popular during the thirties but apparently had been in existence long before then. Called Texas bass, or Texas walking bass, it probably originated in the southwestern United States as a piano style. Boogie-woogie uses a *basso ostinato* in the left hand and a variety of figures in the right hand, all within the framework of the twelve-bar blues. The left hand plays the same pattern in the "obstinate bass," changing to different notes only when the harmony changes. Eight notes to the bar is the most typical rhythmic pattern.

The combination of strong beat, boogie-woogie bass, twelve-bar blues, and vocal solo became popular in the thirties as Rhythm and Blues (in the black communities). In the fifties the style changed to the amplified "big beat" of rock 'n' roll.

Examples

1. "Slow Boogie." Jack Dupre. *Jazz,* Vol. 1. Folkways FV 2801.
2. "Honky Tonk Train Blues." Meade Lux Lewis. *Jazz,* Vol. 10. Folkways 2810.

Boogie-Woogie Bass Patterns

walking bass

New Orleans Revival (1939–   )

Background and Characteristics Big band jazz of the swing era put the finishing touches on the fading fortunes of the old, free-swinging New Orleans style. A group of white San Francisco musicians took the first steps, in 1939, toward a revival of traditional jazz. Old jazzmen were brought out of retirement and old records studied. The end result was the development of a variety of approaches to traditional jazz under the general heading of New Orleans Revival. Some Revivalists used the ragtime piano (or no piano), banjo, tuba, clarinet, trumpet, trombone, and drums in the authentic two-beat New Orleans style. Many others mixed New Orleans with the four-beat characteristics of swing to achieve the style called Dixieland. Typical Dixieland jazz uses the "front line" of obbligato clarinet, lead trumpet, and fluid trombone (tailgate trombone) backed by drums, bass, and piano.

Examples

1. "Original Dixieland One-Step." Eddie Condon. *Jazz Omnibus.* Columbia CL—1020.
2. "Maryland My Maryland." Turk Murphy. Columbia CL—1020.
3. "Washington and Lee Swing." Mound City Six. *Dixieland from St. Louis.* Everest LPBR—5002.
4. *Come On and Hear.* Dukes of Dixieland. Decca 4708; 74708.
5. Pete Fountain. *Standing Room Only.* Coral 57474; 757474.

The Bop Revolution (ca. 1944–1950)

Background and Characteristics During the long musician's recording and broadcasting strike midway through World War II, an entirely new style of jazz was being developed. Upon the resumption of broadcasting and recording the unsuspecting public heard for the first time, in the style known as bop (or rebop or bebop), the startling sounds of the beginning of modern jazz.

The increasingly regimented big band swing and the by-now monotonous repetition of riffs had stifled most individual creativity. Bop took musical control away from the arranger and returned it to the performing musician.

Stylistic Characteristics of Bop

1. The heavy four-beat pattern employed by the full-rhythm section of the swing band was taken over by the *string bass,* giving a much lighter sound to the basic beat.
2. The drummer, freed from the necessity of maintaining the basic "four," kept the beat on the *cymbal,* reserving the *snare drum* for accompanying patterns and coordinated effects with the soloists. The *bass drum* was played intermittently for special effects, a practice called "bomb dropping."
3. The *piano* was also liberated from the tyranny of the basic four. The pianist accompanied, complimented, and augmented the soloists, a process known as "comping."
4. The *guitar* abandoned the regular strumming of chords and began to function as a melodic as well as a rhythmic instrument.
5. The bop style usually featured the unison playing of *trumpet* and *alto saxophone* in highly elaborated melodic and rhythmic patterns.
6. Quadruple meter was maintained, but riffs were abandoned completely. The band was reduced to a small ensemble of six or seven instruments (combo). Harmony was modernized with much use made of the "flatted fifth" of the blues scale.
7. The conventional pattern of paraphrasing an existing melody and "playing the changes," for instance, improvising upon the changes of harmony of a piece of music, became subordinated to the bop practice of adding new melodies to the existing harmonic patterns of standard songs. For example, the addition of a new melody to the chords of the old popular song "Whispering," produced a new composition entitled "Groovin' High."

Examples

1. "Groovin' High." Gillespie, Parker. *Groovin' High with Dizzy Gillespie.* Savoy MG—12020.
2. "Hot House." Gillespie, Parker. *Groovin' High with Dizzy Gillespie.* Savoy MG—12020.
3. "Salt Peanuts." Gillespie, Parker. *Groovin' High with Dizzy Gillespie.* Savoy MG—12020.
4. "52nd Street Theme." *The Amazing Bud Powell,* Vol. 1. Blue Note BLP—1503.
5. Charlie Parker. *Greatest Recording Session.* Savoy 12079.

Cool Jazz (ca. 1946–   )

Background and Characteristics   Derived from bop and originally known as "cool bop." Deliberate cooling off of the hot jazz of the bop style.

Stylistic Characteristics

1. Instrumentation oriented toward the cool sounds of flute, guitar (acoustic), Chinese cymbals, muted trumpet. Use of straight tone (without vibrato).
2. Emphasis on homophonic texture. Strong influence of the impressionists Debussy and Ravel.
3. Usually based on popular songs.
4. A soft, sometimes dreamy, lag-a-long, behind-the-beat style.

Examples

1. "Moon Dreams." Miles Davis. *Birth of the Cool.* Capitol TT—1974.
2. "September in the Rain." George Shearing. *The Very Best of George Shearing.* MGM 4169; S 4169.
3. "Lullaby of Birdland." George Shearing. MGM 4169.
4. "My Reverie." Barney Kessel. *Music to Listen to Barney Kessel By.* Contemporary 3521; 7521.
5. "Indian Summer." Barney Kessel. *Music to Listen to Barney Kessel By.* Contemporary 3521; 7521.
6. *Lee Konitz.* Pacific Jazz 38.
7. Miles Davis. *Original Quintet.* Prestige 7254; S—7254.

Progressive Jazz (ca. 1946–   )

Background and Characteristics   *Progressive* is the term sometimes used to encompass the whole field of modern jazz. The term was originally employed in the belief that *progress* could be made in the art of jazz. *Progress* is a term, however, more applicable to technology than to the arts; better television sets can undoubtedly be built, but more artistic television programs are by no means a concomitant development. The term *progressive jazz* will be used here to describe modern big band jazz.

Stylistic Characteristics

1. An amalgamation of the elements of swing, bop, and symphonic orchestra techniques and instrumentation.
2. Large ensembles characterized by the increased range and versatility of traditional jazz instruments plus the addition of symphonic instruments such as flute, oboe, English horn, bassoon, French horn, fluegelhorn, celeste, chimes, cello, violins, harp, harpsichord.
3. Influenced by twentieth-century composers such as Stravinsky, Bartók, Prokofiev, Schoenberg.

4. Heavy use of quartal harmony (chords built in fourths), polychords (superimposed tertiary chords), dissonance, and some twelve-tone techniques.
5. Exploitation of a variety of meters in addition to the traditional quadruple meter. Use of polymeters (simultaneous use of different meters).

Examples

1. "Misty." Stan Kenton. *Adventures in Jazz.* Capitol T—1796; ST—1796.
2. "Limehouse Blues." Stan Kenton. *Adventures in Jazz.* Capitol T—1796; ST—1796.
3. Stan Kenton. *Conducts L.A. Neophonic Orchestra.* Capitol MAS—2424; SMAS—2424.
4. Stan Kenton. *Greatest Hits.* Capitol T—2327; ST—2327.
5. "That's Where It Is." Woody Herman. *Encore: Woody Herman.* Philips 200092; 600092.
6. "Better Get It in Your Soul." Woody Herman. *Encore: Woody Herman.* Philips 200092.
7. Woody Herman. *Greatest Hits.* Columbia CL—2491; CS—9291.
8. Count Basie. *Big Band Scene '65.* Roulette 52117; S—52117.

Latin (Afro-Cuban, Afro-Brazilian; ca. 1946–   )

Background and Characteristics   The Latin style of jazz is based on the reservoir of Afro-American dance rhythms of the West Indies, Central and South America. Among the many dances of African origin are the Rhumba, Conga, Samba, Mambo, Afro, Bolero, Tango, Cha Cha, Meringue, Calinda, Bamboula, and Guaracha. Combining African rhythms and jazz produced the jazz samba (bossa nova); many more similar combinations will apparently be forthcoming. For example, the combination of Mexican mariachi music with elements of rock 'n' roll and jazz has produced the peripheral jazz sound of the Tijuana Brass.

Stylistic Characteristics   The use of Latin instruments is the hallmark of Latin Jazz:

Maracas—gourd rattles
Guiro—serrated gourd with scraper
Claves—percussion sticks
Conga drum—large single-skin drum
Bongo drums—pair of small, single-skin drums
Marimba—large xylophone with metal resonators
Cowbell, tambourine, snare drum and bass drum

The other basic characteristic of Latin-styled jazz is, of course, the use of continuous syncopated rhythms, with percussion instruments using the same patterns throughout a composition.

In many cases the Latin influence is used in combination with other jazz styles.

Examples

1. "The Girl from Ipanema." Stan Getz. *Getz-Gilberto.* Verve 8545; 68545.
2. "Bim Bom." Stan Getz. *Big Band Bossa Nova: Stan Getz.* Verve 8494; 68494.
3. "Morning of the Carnival." *New Wave: Dizzy Gillespie.* Philips 200070; 600070.
4. "Days of Wine and Roses." *Kessel/Jazz: Contemporary Latin Rhythms.* Reprise 6073; 9—6073.

Mainstream Jazz (ca. 1946–   )

Background and Characteristics   Mainstream is a continuation and updating of the swing tradition but without the stereotyped riffs and cumbersome written arrangements. Swing, the so-called classical period of jazz, has continued as a mainstream, middle-of-the-road style of jazz. As such it is not particularly concerned with exotic instrumentation or experimentation but rather with a communicable, emotional expression and the requirement that the music must always swing. There is no set instrumentation, but the quadruple meter of swing is standard.

Examples

1. *Mainstream, 1958.* Savoy 12127.
2. Benny Goodman. *Together Again!* Victor LPM—2698; LSP—2698.
3. Benny Goodman. *Greatest Hits.* Columbia CL—2483; CS—2983.
4. Lionel Hampton. *Taste of Hamp.* Glad–Hamp 1009; S—1009.

Hard Bop (1958–   )

Background and Characteristics   Hard bop is modern bop with the same uncompromising drive of the earlier style: dynamic melody line in unison and explosive attack and figuration in the various instruments, especially percussion. The instrumentation tends to remain with the five-piece ensemble: trumpet, alto sax, piano, drums, bass. The so-called East Coast school of jazz is oriented toward the hard bop sound mixed with soul jazz (see following).

Examples

1. "Room 608." *Horace Silver and the Jazz Messengers.* Blue Note 1518.
2. *The Jazz Messengers.* Savoy 12171.

Soul Jazz (ca. 1960–   )

Background and Characteristics   One of the strongest movements in recent years, soul jazz is a return to the church music ("soul music") roots of jazz. Soul emphasizes an emotional depth of communication and scorns the intellectual pretensions ("wigging") of white musicians in general and West Coast musicians in particular. "Soul" indicates more of an approach to jazz performance than any particular style, but there are certain characteristics that all "soul" tends to have in common.

Stylistic Characteristics

1. Heavy use of the "amen cadence," for example, subdominant chord moving to tonic chord to end a phrase (IV–I).
2. Preponderance of subdominant and dominant chords (IV and V).
3. Many open sounds of the perfect fifth and fourth and considerable use of the tritone (three whole steps or D5 or A4).
4. Considerable use of triple meter.
5. Exploitation of "funky" sounds such as tone colors, melodies, and rhythms derived from old work songs, folk blues, hollers, gospel songs. Also the use of "funky" rhythm (duple).

Examples

1. "Filet of Soul." Les McCann. *Shampoo*. Pacific Jazz 63; S-63.
2. "This Here." Cannonball Adderly. *Quintet in San Francisco*. Riverside 311; 1157.
3. Cannonball Adderly. *Them Dirty Blues*. Riverside 322; 1170.
4. Les McCann. *Soul Hits*. Pacific Jazz 78; S—78.
5. Grant Green. *His Majesty King Funk*. Verve 8627; 68627.
6. Ramsey Lewis. *Down to Earth*. Mercury 20536; 60536.
7. Bobby Timmons. *Workin' Out*. Prestige 7387; S—7387.

West Coast Jazz (ca. 1960–   )

Background and Characteristics Jazzmen have been known to remark that East Coast jazz is jazz that is played on the East Coast and that, by the same token, West Coast musicians are playing West Coast jazz. The differences, however, encompass more than a New York or California locale. Many West Coast musicians have been preoccupied with polyphonic devices, 3/4, 5/4, 7/4, and mixed time signatures, classical forms (sonata, rondo, fugue), and various exotic sounds (oriental, Arabic, Hindu, etc.). Their East Coast critics contend that they have emphasized techniques at the expense of the swinging sound which is fundamental to all jazz styles.

Examples

1. "Blue Rondo a la Turk." Dave Brubeck. *Time Out*. Columbia CL—1397; CS—8192.
2. "Take Five." Dave Brubeck. *Time Out*. Columbia CL—1397; CS—8192.
3. Dave Brubeck. *Impressions of Japan*. Columbia CL—2212; CS—9012.
4. Dave Brubeck. *Time In*. Columbia CL—2512; CS—9312.

5. "The Fakir." Cal Tjader. *Several Shades of Jade*. Verve 8507; 68507.
6. "Cherry Blossoms." Cal Tjader. *Several Shades of Jade*. Verve 8507; 68507.
7. Cal Tjader. *Breeze from the East*. Verve 8575; 68575.
8. Shelly Mann. *West Coast*. Contemporary 3507.

Third-Stream Jazz (ca. 1960–   )

Background and Characteristics Third-Stream jazz runs between the twin streams of classical music and jazz, borrowing techniques from both but attempting to stay in the jazz idiom. There had been earlier confrontations with classical music in the eras of ragtime ("ragging the classics") and swing ("swinging the classics"). Later jazz movements borrowed instrumental, melodic, harmonic techniques and musical forms from contemporary concert music. Third Stream went one step further with attempts to combine jazz quartets with string quartets and jazz combos with symphony orchestras, the latter in the manner of Baroque concerto grossos.

Some critics have contended that jazz and classical music are basically incompatible and others that Third-Stream music features fair to good jazz improvisation in a context of bad to mediocre string quartet or symphony orchestra writing. The experiments continue and the issue has yet to be resolved.

Examples

1. "Fugue in D Major." Swingle Singers. *Bach's Greatest Hits*. Philips 200097; 600097.
2. "Fugue in C Minor." Swingle Singers. *Bach's Greatest Hits*. Philips 200097; 600097.
3. "Largo." Swingle Singers. *Going Baroque*. Philips 200126; 600126.

Note: The preceding three examples are note-for-note performances of Bach's music. Originally written for harpsichord and/or orchestral instruments the music is here performed vocally with rhythmic syllables and accompanied by drums. No other changes have been made.

4. "Sketch." Modern Jazz and Beaux Arts Quartets. *Third Stream Music*. Atlantic 1345; S—1345.
5. "Allegro-Blues." From "Dialogues for Jazz Combo and Orchestra." Dave Brubeck. *The Dave Brubeck Quartet*. Columbia CL—1466; CS—8257.

Free Form Jazz (The "New Thing") (ca. 1960–   )

Background and Characteristics The constant experimentation in all fields of twentieth-century music has, to a limited extent, carried over into jazz. A small but persistent vanguard of young musicians has been concentrating on the possibilities of free improvisation. In free improvisation there are no preexisting chord changes on which to improvise, no set patterns, no arbitrary limitations of any kind. Musicians are encouraged to a free self-expression which is responsible only to its own inner world of discipline and logic.

The results to date of free improvisation, simply called the New Thing, have caused considerable debate. Questions have been raised about the difference between freedom and license and about the problem of anarchy and sheer chaos when no one musician knows what his colleagues are doing. Communication between performers and the listening public is also a considerable problem which is far from resolution. Free Form jazz may indeed revitalize the whole field of modern jazz, or it may degenerate into the other extreme in which only the emancipated soloist knows what he is doing—if indeed he does know what he is doing.

Examples

1. "W.R.U." Ornette Coleman. *Ornette!* Atlantic 1378; S—1378.
2. Ornette Coleman. *Free Jazz/Collective Improvisation.* Atlantic 1364; S—1364.
3. "Pithecanthropus Erectus." Charlie Mingus. *Giant Steps.* Atlantic 1237.
4. Charlie Mingus. *Tonight at Noon.* Atlantic 1416; S—1416.
5. John Coltrane. *New Thing at Newport.* Impulse 94; S—94.
6. Ornette Coleman. *Town Hall Concert.* ESP Disc 1006; S—1006.

Liturgical Jazz (ca. 1960–   )

Background and Characteristics   A comparatively recent movement to incorporate jazz into church worship services has opened up an outlet for jazz which it had long been denied. Jazz has become a fixture in concert halls, in regional and international jazz festivals, in government-sponsored goodwill tours, and as the subject of scholarly conferences, learned treatises, and doctoral dissertations. Its return to its original association with religious practices appears to be a natural consequence of its acceptance as an independent art form. The early spirituals, ring shouts, jubilees, and gospel songs have come full circle as the jazz idiom to which they contributed so much has found a place in modern worship.

The use of jazz and jazz instruments has been a long-accepted practice in many black revivals, "storefront" churches, and tent meetings. The acceptance of jazz as another valid mode of musical expression has taken place in the prescribed formal patterns of some of the churches in the major Protestant denominations and a few Catholic churches. The prime moving force has been the attempt to update the liturgy by using some contemporary modes of thought and musical expression. Much of the liturgical music now in use dates from the Romantic period and appears out of place in the late twentieth century. Some

of the sentimental Romantic period music used to accompany hymns, chants, and responses is being replaced by older music (medieval, Renaissance, Baroque) as well as by twentieth-century music.

The practice of using contemporary modes of thought and artistic expression was a natural part of church practices in past centuries. In the Gothic era, for example, the Gothic church was a *modern* church, with sculptures and stained glass by modern artists and music by modern composers. The Gothic cathedral in all its parts was a new church for a new age. The same procedures held true for Renaissance and Baroque churches. Bach and his contemporaries were expected to write new music for almost every Sunday. On the other hand, the eclectic nineteenth century with its Neo-Gothic cathedrals, Neo-medieval country houses, Neo-Baroque opera houses, French Provincial and Renaissance mansions, Neo-Roman train stations, and Neo-Classic government buildings was preoccupied with the past; it failed to develop its own mode of expression. The artistic sterility of the Romantic century carried over into the present century, which had to make a special effort to break away from the borrowed past.

The modes of expression of a bygone era have tended to linger on in the formal religious practices of the twentieth century. The updating of these practices is a task to which many churches have dedicated themselves. The appearance (reappearance is probably a better word) of contemporary words, ideas, musical instruments, musical styles, dance, and drama within the churches is evidence of the impulse toward a more relevant church in contemporary life. The process of modernizing the musical language has even gone to the extreme of including "hootenanny masses" and rock 'n' roll services.

The resistance to liturgical jazz has come from a variety of sources for a variety of reasons. Some have mistakenly confused jazz with popular music. Others have reasoned that a music which was formerly associated with New Orleans bordellos, Chicago speakeasies, dance halls, and night clubs is obviously not good enough for church. This argument overlooks the fact that much of the music presently used in the church had similar humble origins. Moreover, there is no such category as "sacred music"; there is only music which is used in connection with sacred services.

Examples

1. "Introit." *20th Century Folk Mass.* Fiesta 2500.
2. "Kyrie." *20th Century Folk Mass.* Fiesta 2500.

Beaumont's so-called folk mass was a pioneer effort in the attempt to use contemporary music in the church. Referred to, unfortunately, as the Jazz Mass it is a prime example of what not to do. The piece is only distantly related to jazz, being an amalgam of warmed-over swing combined with a sentimental and pretentious Hollywood style. Its only virtue is a demonstration of the fact that the ancient texts of the church tend to shine forth with new vigor when set to newer musical ideas. The *20th Century Folk Mass* provides a pertinent reminder for all who attempt to use liturgical jazz, namely, that there is no substitute for quality. Bad to mediocre jazz badly performed has no place in church or concert hall.

The following examples of Paul Horn and Duke Ellington are of far better quality and demonstrate some of the possibilities of good liturgical jazz.

3. "Kyrie Eleison." *Jazz Suite on the Mass Texts.* Victor LPM—3414; LSP—3414.
4. "Credo in unum Deum." *Jazz Suite on the Mass Texts.* Victor LPM—3414; LSP—3414.

The Kyrie combines some elements of chant and medieval music with jazz scoring and improvisation. The Credo is an experiment in congregational participation and improvisation backed up by improvised commentary by Horn's alto sax.

5. "In the Beginning." Duke Ellington. *Concert of Sacred Music.* Victor LPM—3582; LSP—3582.
6. *Psalmkonzert* by Heinz Werner Zimmermann, Cantata 640 229; available from Barenreiter & Neuwerk, Sortiment, 35 Kassel-Wilhelmshöhe, Heinrich-Schutz-Allee 35, Fernruf 30011—16.

The *Psalmkonzert* uses five-part mixed choir (SSATB), children's choir, three trumpets, string bass, and vibraphone. The style is a blend of jazz techniques with classical polyphonic practices. The resources used are within the reach of a good church music program without the necessity of having to go outside the church for a professional ensemble.

7. "Gloria in Excelsis Deo." *Vince Guaraldi at Grace Cathedral.* Fantasy 3367; 8367.
8. Joe Masters. *The Jazz Mass.* Columbia CL—2598; CS—9398.

The Evolution of Jazz

The evolution of jazz can best be summarized by providing a chart outlining the various periods, dates, styles, major centers, and major figures (see page 588). It is interesting to note that jazz has undergone approximately the same pattern of evolution in its single century of existence as has the music of Western civilization since the fall of Rome. For this reason the chart includes some major periods of Western culture as they are roughly approximated by the sequence of jazz styles. The outline should be considered as a very generalized overview of the evolution of the elusive art known as jazz.

Eclectic, Crossover, and Fusion

The heading of this section indicates a greater mixing of musical styles than ever before. The sounds of the seventies and eighties are compounded of many stylistic elements. Artificial barriers are coming down and "interdisciplinary" music appears to be increasingly important in our everyday musical life, not only in America but all around the globe.

Popular music (whatever *that* means) includes everything from a "top 40" rock performance with guitars at one hundred decibels to amalgams of folk-rock, jazz-rock, blues-rock and a combination or synthesis of any and all of these elements, including significant traces of classical, oriental, electronic, and country-and-western influences. The simplistic rock 'n' roll of the mid-fifties has been replaced by a far more sophisticated music utilizing whatever musical instruments, styles, and resources best serve the purposes of the performers.

Big band music of the World War II era is back on the jazz scene. Retrospective recordings of the half-century career of Duke Ellington top the jazz charts but Woody Herman, Bob Crosby, and others are in there swinging. The revival of the "classical" style of jazz (see the Outline of the Evolution of Jazz on page 588 has been explained as evidence of nostalgia for the days when issues were simpler, the good guys won, and energy was something a breakfast cereal provided. This may be so, at least in part, but the mindless and monotonous sounds of disco seem to have fostered a countermovement of real dance music. After all, the swing style was primarily a superb form of dance music, the very essence of the Dancing Thirties and Forties.

Current jazz styles range from traditional jazz in the New Orleans manner to Ragtime, Dixieland, Chicago, Bop, Mainstream, Free Jazz, and, as mentioned above, Big Band Swing. Added to this twentieth-century melange are the eclectic styles called *fusion* and *crossover*. Fusion dates from the early sixties as jazz-rock, now musically defined by *Downbeat* magazine as "an agreement between jazz, rock and funk." "Crossover," according to *Downbeat*, "downplays the rocking aspects, adding a recognizable dose of popular melody, sometimes transmitted vocally."

Practitioners of fusion include Miles Davis (later style), Tony Williams's Lifetime, John McLaughlin's Mahavishnu Orchestra, and the groups Return to Forever and Weather Report. Crossover musicians include Chuck Mangione, Bob James, and Grover Washington, Jr. Groups which are best described as fusion/crossover include Spyro Gyra, Seawind, Auracle, and Caldera.

Crossover groups are written off by regular jazz musicians as merely pop-type performers, and certainly there are some huge record sales which confirm this judgment. Fusion, however, is another matter. The central argument is purist versus fusion; pure jazz as opposed to jazz corrupted by undesirable elements; Mainstream against the Philistines. The intensity of the conflict between jazz purists and the fusion forces simply highlights the assurance that contemporary jazz is dynamic, vital, and flourishing; the swinging beat goes on—all over the globe.

Outline: The Evolution of Jazz

Western Culture	Jazz	Dates	Primary and Secondary Styles and Characteristics	Major Centers or Areas	Major Figures
Dark Ages	Folk Origins	Pre-Civil War	Work Songs, Hollers, Street Cries, Ballads, Blues, Spirituals, Ring Shouts, Gospel Songs, Jubilees, Song-sermons, Voodoo, Creole Music	Old South	unknown
		1840–1900	Minstrel Shows (Cakewalk)	U.S. and Europe	Stephen Collins Foster, E.P. Christy, Dan Emmett
Middle Ages	Traditional	1890–1918	Ragtime, Brass Bands: Spirituals, Gospel Songs, Jubilees, Blues and Ragtime Marches	New Orleans	Buddy Bolden, Bunk Johnson
Baroque	Pre-Classical	1918–1929	Advanced New Orleans Style	South, Midwest	King Oliver, Jelly Roll Morton, Louis Armstrong, Sidney Bechet, Kid Ory, Original Dixieland Jazz Band
			Chicago (Modified New Orleans Style)	Chicago	Bix Beiderbecke, Eddie Condon
			Beginning Big Band; Piano	New York	Fletcher Henderson, James P. Johnson, Fats Waller
	Transitional	1929–1934	Transition to Big Band Styles	New York	Fletcher Henderson, Duke Ellington
				Kansas City	Bennie Moten
Classical	Classical	1935–1945	Swing	New York (nationwide)	Fletcher Henderson, Benny Goodman, Coleman Hawkins, Teddy Wilson, Lionel Hampton, Art Tatum, Chick Webb, Roy Eldridge, Casa Loma
			Kansas City Jump	Kansas City	Count Basie, Lester Young, Woody Herman
			Boogie-Woogie	Midwest	Meade Lux Lewis, Pete Johnson, Albert Ammons
		1939–	New Orleans Revival, Dixieland	West Coast	Lu Watters, Turk Murphy, Bob Scobey, Bunk Johnson
Modern	Modern	1944–	Bop	New York	Charlie Parker, Dizzy Gillespie, Bud Powell
		1946–	Cool (Impressionism)	New York, West Coast	Miles Davis, Lee Konitz, George Shearing
			Progressive	West Coast	Stan Kenton, Woody Herman
			Latin	New York Los Angeles	Chano Pozo, Tito Puente, Machito, Gilberto, Schifrin
			Mainstream		Benny Goodman, Lionel Hampton, Count Basie
		1958–	Hard Bop	East Coast Detroit	Jazz Messengers
		1960–	Soul	East Coast	Cannonball Adderly, Les McCann, Ramsey Lewis, Bobby Timmons
			West Coast	West Coast	Dave Brubeck, Cal Tjader
			Third Stream	East and West Coast	Gunther Schuller, Modern Jazz Quartet, Brubeck
			Free Form (The New Thing)	New York	Ornette Coleman, John Coltrane, Charlie Mingus
			Liturgical		Paul Horn, Lalo Schifrin, Duke Ellington, Vince Guaraldi
		1970s and 1980s	Mainstream Fusion Crossover	International	Most jazz musicians. Miles Davis, Tony Williams, John McLaughlin, Chuck Mangione, Bob James, Grover Washington, Jr.

27 Twentieth-Century Literature

Nowhere does our analogy of the broken center fit more exactly than in the field of contemporary literature. Amid the wreckage of old values, modern authors search for new meanings, new forms, and a new sense of personal identity and community.

One can propose almost any thesis about contemporary literature and support it with a large body of writing, for the wide experimentation of today has produced many types, moods, and themes. Perhaps the only defensible approach to "contemporary" literature is to make a few very wide and controversial generalizations about modern writing, and then to comment on a few specific literary works which seem to embody various trends and which are anthologized at the end of the chapter so that the student may read them and agree or disagree with the critical comments expressed here.

Perhaps the first of the generalizations that can be made is that the far-out writers of the latter part of our century have abandoned most of the restrictions on form and idea which were characteristic of a great deal of nineteenth-century writing. It is possible to find in our century at least two "literatures of the twentieth century," almost chronological and sequential, with the obvious break following World War II. The two types are related in that both are in revolt against the literary tradition of the nineteenth century and against the rigid structure of Victorian mores. The difference lies in the recognition of the early twentieth-century writers that a common core existed against which they might voice their protest; the writers since World War II are cast adrift, with little unifying force and few webs of connection, and with the urge, almost the necessity, to create anew the meanings and values of life and the consciousness of the race.

During the first part of the century, we witnessed the almost "conventional" revolt of which John Livingston Lowes wrote, "The ceaseless swing of the artistic pendulum is from the convention of a former age to the revolt of a new day, which in its turn becomes a convention from which still newer artists will in their turn revolt."[1]

---

1. John Livingston Lowes, *Convention and Revolt in Poetry,* New York, Gordon Press, n.d.

The poetic convention of the nineteenth century generally favored the tight-knit structure of recognizable stanzaic form: blank verse or couplet, tercet or quatrain, or other nameable unit. Exceptions are of course to be found, but in general a poem *looked* like a poem, because that was the way poems looked! The order and pattern and design appealed to an audience that liked design, approved of pattern, and believed in order.

But, about 1914, with such a group as the Imagist poets, the convention was challenged with "vers libre" ("free verse")—lines unrhymed and unmetrical. Not only is the form of Eliot's poem, *The Waste Land,* different from that of the past, but the meaning of his poem represents a revolt against the predominate optimism (or even the pessimism) of the nineteenth century. Yet with all the innovation of form and meaning, Eliot recognizes and works within the recognizable tradition. In the first place, the poem is not only to be felt and experienced, it must be thought out; it is an extremely intellectual poem within the rational tradition. Second, Eliot expects his reader to share a common background of meanings and knowledge.

At about the same time that Eliot was composing *The Waste Land,* Aldous Huxley was writing *Brave New World,* a novel that pictures a society pursuing our present value-system until it has killed nearly all human values. The novel attacked entrenched and accepted values, but it followed the patterned, chronologically structured form of the plotted novel, and made certain assumptions about the common center of meanings which were held by both the author and the reader. For instance, Huxley assumes a knowledge of Shakespeare, and, even more, he assumes that the reader shares with him a value system which says that Shakespeare is *good;* better than the Huxleyan depicted "feelies" (an extension of the movies) or a trip with mind-altering drugs.

The great body of "high-brow" literature since World War II and Existentialism cannot make these assumptions.

What has happened? Because World War II involved the obvious choice between freedom or submitting to an inhuman system, operated by a small group of power-mad men, all the rituals and emotions of patriotism seemed appropriate. Yet, when the conflict ended, the world went back to its old ways; the victors seemed to take more of a beating than the vanquished. Particularly in the United States, a period of introspection set in which allowed us to see our own guilts and the hollowness of much of our way of life. The old materialistic standards, as opposed to standards dealing with the quality of life itself, seemed no longer appropriate. The wars in Korea and especially Vietnam challenged much of the exuberance for the "rightness" of our value system.

At the same time, all over the Western world, we were introduced to philosophies of Existentialism which denied inherent intelligence and purpose in the universe, or inherent meaning to individual life.

Since that general philosophy has been introduced earlier, we need not repeat that discussion. The effect on an ever-growing number of intelligent, creative persons, however, has been to destroy the old center of certainty; to force them to peer over the brink of life and discover nothing but senseless void beyond. For many in this group of people, old value systems have been seriously questioned or destroyed completely. One may take courage in the increasingly large number of people, young and old, and certainly among most artists and writers, who have faced the problem of constantly "inventing" themselves and who have begun to suggest new meanings for life which are flexible and relative.

In all of this discussion, it must be borne in mind that these developments in literature are not entirely "new." Pessimism was not invented in the twentieth century; Existentialism had its immediate source in Kierkegaard in the nineteenth century and can be traced as far back as the Greek philosopher, Demokritos; new forms for literature (even Black Humor) have many antecedents; particularly the darkly humorous novel has a great-grandfather in Sterne's *Tristram Shandy.* Science fiction has a long history before our time. It would seem, instead, that the small, isolated, and relatively unknown trickles of thought and form in past centuries have flowed together to become the mainstream of literary creation.

Even the most superficial look at contemporary literature reveals at least three sets of taboos which have been swept away, and whose vanishing has had a profound effect on present-day writing.

The first of these is the loosening of social taboos on morality in general and sexual morality in particular. Not long ago it was almost impossible to buy a copy of Henry Miller's novels or D.H. Lawrence's *Lady Chatterly's Lover* in the United States, since they shocked our mass-sense of morality and were officially banned. Now social restrictions have become so relaxed that these particular books are not even very exciting in terms of raw sex. Almost all of the bare and athletic manifestations of love, as ends in themselves, have become rather dreary commonplaces. This trend toward complete sexual freedom has gone so far that it threatens to become self-defeating. One can scarcely say that when you've seen one nude, you've seen them all, but at least the element of shock has largely vanished.

A second aspect of this loss of what was once called "morality" is the change in our generally accepted ideas of *good* and *bad;* in a great deal of early contemporary writing, goodness seems to be a combination of luck and the functioning of the endocrine glands, or perhaps more simply, Not Being Caught. Examples of this—the antihero—are not hard to find. Saul Bellow's fine novel, *Seize the Day,* has Tommy Wilhelm as its protagonist, certainly one of the dirtiest slobs in literature, whose one redeeming feature is a response to humanity in the midst of a cold and negative environment. Even in such popular fiction as John Le Carré's *The Spy Who Came in from the Cold,* the hero is one who has no sense of honor or patriotism (in an establishment which is equally amoral, although it is on "our side") until his personality finally warms to the plight of a single human being in an act of personal loyalty, not in terms of any generalization like patriotism or democracy. In much of our early recent fiction the terms *goodness* and *badness* have little meaning in their old contexts.

Herein lies one of the hopeful examples of new growth and new value systems. The completely negative antihero seems to have run his course, and a new picture of the hero has begun to emerge. The *old* hero was one who went forth in the world to do battle against enemies who were quite obviously bad guys. This hero clothed himself in noble generalities such as patriotism, honor, or love for the damsel-in-distress. Time after time he met the enemy, often suffering temporary defeat, but finally good triumphed, and the hero rode off into the sunset with the girl as prize. Except in highly commercial writing, this hero is dead. Then came the complete antihero who had few if any redeeming features. But in the two novels mentioned above, *Seize the Day* and *The Spy Who Came in from the Cold,* or McMurphy in Ken Kesey's *One Flew Over the Cuckoo's Nest,* we have the hero who accepts none of the glorious generalizations, whose shining armor may be a set of rags and a three-day growth of beard; but a hero who has faced the truth of the existential human condition and whose final heroism lies in an act of faith for human life, human dignity, and human love. This position is magnificently explained in the long conversation between Tarrou and Dr. Rieux in Camus's novel, *The Plague,* and it is exemplified very briefly in Hemingway's story, *A Clean, Well-lighted Place.* In these instances and many others, we see the discarding of old systems of value, but in the very rubble that they have created artists suggest new views of life and new values that promise fertility and growth both for now and the future.

There are, moreover, new heroes, some of them tragic, in recent fiction, but these protagonists are heroines. In Judith Rossner's *Looking for Mr. Goodbar* schoolteacher Theresa Dunn is a tragic victim of male-oriented society. Anne Tyler's *Dinner at the Homesick Restaurant* is concerned with the pain and destruction inflicted on a family by, initially, the desertion of the father. On the other hand, Isadore Wing in Erica Jong's *Fear of Flying* has been compared with no less than the irrepressible Wife of Bath. Based on John Cleland's eighteenth-century novel *Fanny Hill,* Jong's *Fanny* is an exuberant and triumphant feminist. Gail Godwin's *A Mother and Two Daughters* is a celebration of American life in feminine terms and a solid statement of faith in human capacity for good. Included in this chapter is Godwin's "A Sorrowful Woman," a somber story of a woman victimized by enforced domesticity.

A second taboo which has been removed from literary creation is the restriction to "polite" language; no English word is outside the pale for use in literature. Written language formerly reserved for the walls of restrooms now appears regularly in our "better" magazines—in fiction, poetry, and nonfiction. No moral judgment needs to be made of this new

freedom. Certainly by the time any boy or girl has come to junior high school age, he or she is familiar with all the four-letter words; and, intrinsically, the word "excrement" is neither better nor worse than its four-letter synonym. One may wonder if this new freedom, like the freedom to disrobe, may soon become worn thin and lose its shock value. Writers who are now forced by the new convention to use the short Anglo-Saxon word may find a true freedom by choosing whatever language is best suited to the purpose of their artwork from the entire range of language.

A third restriction which has been removed from all writing is the necessity for rational or chronological structure in prose, for traditional "sense" in poetry. The old requirement that a literary work have a beginning, a middle, and an end is removed except for the requirements imposed by the printed page. For present-day writers the necessity for "plot" is no longer present. Plot may be defined as the working out of a theme, usually clearly stated, which is developed in chronological order by the confrontation of two "sides" in opposition, with the ultimate victory of one side over the other. Until the last quarter of a century (with notable exceptions, of course) this has been the standard structure for most fiction and drama. It is still used in most mass-appeal literature and in much artistic (as different from purely commercial) writing. But it is not necessary, and much of the important contemporary writing has discarded the usual flow-of-time convention as well as that of two forces in opposition. Except for the big Broadway shows, most theatre has discarded logical development in an attempt to achieve immediate and direct feeling which does not fit Aristotelian concepts of either thought or dramatic art. With the old structures no longer required, writers are now free to seek truth in many different ways. Experimentalism in form, sometimes successful, sometimes merely confusing, has become a commonplace in the writers' art.

Within its internal structure, one of the most noticeable characteristics of artistic literature in our time is its symbolic nature, for in much of the newer writing the authors use visible and tangible objects to represent some meaning which lies beyond words. The device is nothing new: Melville's *Moby Dick* is certainly something more than a mere white whale, and Sophokles' portrayal of the blindness of Tiresias or the self-blinding of Oedipus is a way of representing the gaining of spiritual sight as well as the purely physical fact of blindness. But modern literature abounds in symbolism to the point where the reading of a contemporary story or novel or poem frequently becomes the solving of a jigsaw puzzle in which one attempts to fit together all of the symbols into a pattern or patterns of significance.

Freudian symbols were once the most frequently encountered, but now one finds patterns of color symbolism; Christian symbolism abounds almost *ad nauseam;* symbols dealing with primitive initiation rites and fertility are very common. Another sort of symbol makes a parable of the entire work. William Carlos

Williams's story, "The Use of Force," is an instance; the surface story of the doctor who tries to force a little girl to open her mouth, for purposes of diagnosis, becomes a cosmic situation that reveals all the violence and force in the world of men. The difference from the past lies perhaps in the degree of sophistication with which the modern writer employs such a device: the taste of the time delights in ingenuity, the intellectual delight of recognizing and following the hints and clues of the skillfully contrived tale, rather than the simple acceptance of face values. Here may be found one reason that plot is of less importance with many fiction writers than it has been in the past; they delight in taking a small surface incident and exploring it, probing down and down through various levels of meaning—sociological, psychological, philosophical, even mythical. It must be stated again that the device is not new in itself; great literature has always had different levels of significance; but it has become a very conscious method of writing in much of the fiction of the present century.

With these general remarks, we might turn to a few observations about the specific forms of writing of our time.

Poetry

The poetry of the present day is such an enormous and varied field that one could find illustration for any thesis he chose to propound. In this chapter are a number of poems illustrating ideas here dealt with; the selection is, necessarily, arbitrary. All one can say is, "Here is the evidence; does it ring true?"

The experimentalism characteristic of twentieth-century literature may, in the poetry of the time, be considered under three aspects: experiments in form, in subject, and in language. In a good poem, these aspects are so closely united as to be inseparable in their total effect, but it is sometimes rewarding to arbitrarily look at them separately.

We have already commented on the innovations in form which came into vogue with the "New Poets" about the time of World War I, and of which Eliot's *The Waste Land* and *The Love Song of J. Alfred Prufrock* (see chap. 23) are excellent examples. Robinson Jeffers's "Shine Perishing Republic" (see chap. 23) is another instance of free verse, with his characteristic long, flowing line. It is interesting to note the rhythmic effect of the poem, the phrasing often indicated by punctuation, but rhythm is not meter.

Perhaps the most strikingly different experiment is e. e. cumming's "anyone lived in a pretty how town" (included in this chapter). The poet delights in typographical eccentricity: lack of capitals or punctuation, frequent parentheses; the example quoted is mild in comparison with others among his poems. It is interesting to note his use, avoidance, and distortion of rhyme: *town-down, winter-did, same-rain.*

Innovation in subject-matter and form almost necessarily demands a difference in language. This does not simply mean that the modern poet talks about the artifacts of our culture—airplanes, or space travel, for example—but that he or she uses a deliberately distorted grammar, syntax, and logic. What will one say of cummings's "anyone lived in a pretty how town"? One must untangle the phrase, to find in it perhaps a sardonic amusement at a gushing cliché—"How pretty this little town is!" When this poet wishes to point out the passage of time, he does not say "time after time, as trees come out leaf by leaf"; he telescopes it to "when by now and tree by leaf," and the apparent nonsense suddenly becomes new sense.

Perhaps a longer look at a specific poem might clarify this insistence upon the difference in language. Dylan Thomas's "When All My Five and Country Senses" (included in this chapter) may seem pretty baffling at first reading. How can *fingers* forget *green thumbs* and what is the half-moon's *vegetable eye*? Certainly the poet is not talking with simple directness; his words do not "mean" with a single, unchanging meaning, but seem to move in several directions at once. Suppose we try to paraphrase in this fashion: "If all my five natural senses could perceive clearly, see—like my eyes—then even the sense of touch, that helped love grow, would 'see' with the passage of time how love grows old and is laid by, like fruit after harvest; the sense of hearing would 'see' love finished, driven away, ending in discord; the tongue, which is both taste and talk, would 'see' love's pains reluctantly ended; the sense of smell would 'see' love consumed as in a fire. But my heart has other means of perception of love, and these will go on beyond the decaying senses, so that my heart will still know love."

Or suppose that a conventional poet had tried to deal with the same idea in a conventional fashion:

Were all my wits perceptive as my eye
Each would tell the same sad tale of waste;
That Love, to which they witness, will go by
And pass beyond them without hope or haste—
Will vanish like a leaf, a smoke, a cry,
As fleeting as a sound or smell or taste.
This I know; but more than this I know:
Still will my heart love on, tho this sense be gone:
Let hand or nostril, eye, ear, tongue, all go:
In other senses will my heart love on.

But paraphrase in prose or verse cannot convey the excitement and vitality of the original poem, with all its startling and centrifugal pulls. Here is not orderly sequence of thought, clearly conveyed; the mind leaps from "fingers" to "green thumbs" to the fertility-and-time association with "half-moon" and its "vegetable" (crescent? growing?) eye. It is not logical (neither is love!), but it is provocative and stimulating; not the mind alone, but the imagination, is stirred. One need not *like* the poem to be aware that here is something intensely alive and interesting, however unpredictable. The ambiguity is part of the effect; why is the "lynx tongue" "lashed to syllables"? Does "lashed" mean *bound, tied, confined,* or *whipped, stirred, driven?* The meanings are different to the point of contradiction, yet both may be appropriate. So, too, someone looking at the paraphrases above may exclaim, "Oh no! that's not it at all!"

Obviously the few poems included in this chapter cannot do justice to the range and variety of contemporary poetry; but there is enough to find illustration of the ideas presented here. Modern poetry (like that of any other period!) is not all incomprehensible nor gloomy; some of it is very much alive, and speaks our language. Further acquaintance with these and others like them will serve not merely as a comment on the times, but as enjoyment in the poems themselves, for their own sake.

Drama

For a number of reasons, modern drama has come very close to death and has had to resurrect itself in forms which are even stranger than are the forms for other types of literature. The reasons for its moribund state are easy to see: rising costs of production made big box-office necessary—therefore only those productions with a wide and not very subtle appeal could be produced. One answer to this problem has been the big musical show: *Oklahoma!, Camelot, West Side Story, Hello Dolly,* and many others. Revivals of time-tested and mass-approved dramatists have been another answer to the pressing financial problems which beset the legitimate theatre. Another factor which posed a threat to the live stage has been the usurpation by movies and television of the standard-brand, situation drama. Because of the width of the camera-eye, the possibility for an infinite number of settings, and because TV audiences numbering in the millions do not mind being interrupted every few minutes with a commercial, TV and film can present mass entertainment much more lavishly than live theatre.

While the bread and butter of the legitimate stage was being taken away from it in the early part of the century, all sorts of experimental theatres were springing up all over the world. In these, production costs were kept at a minimum—bare stages lacking any scenery grew commonplace; the "star" system was replaced by the use of good, young, and unknown actors who worked for Equity minimum wages—so that mass audiences were no longer necessary. With small, avant-garde audiences, dramatists were freed to try all sorts of experiments which would never be acceptable in the more tradition-bound Broadway theatre.

One of the first innovations was the attempt to bring the members of the audience into the play with mechanical innovations like the theatre-in-the-round. More recently an actor or several actors have simply stopped the rehearsed drama for a time to sit on the edge of the stage and talk to any members of the audience who have the courage to enter into the conversation. Then, the conversation period ended, the actors step back into their formal roles.

In no realm of literature has the Dionysiac, antirational abandonment found expression so much as in the theatre. Such dramas have become fairly commonplace; moving away from the usual concept of a play, they revert to the unplanned and unpredictable "Happening" as they consciously attempt to break down the logical, intellectualized part of human understanding and the barriers which it creates between people.

One of the significant directions in drama was the emergence of the Theatre of the Absurd, based, as the name implies, on the Existentialist concept of a meaningless universe. Probably the best-known play of this genre is Samuel Beckett's (b. 1906) *Waiting for Godot* (1952), which exhibits most of the qualities of the type. The drama takes place, not in sequential time, but in a timeless present. The characters wait for their own identity, but since in such a universe the individual must create himself, identity is never achieved. Such drama substitutes "tension" for what has traditionally been thought of as "conflict," but with the tension in the mind and emotions of the spectator. Since the tension is often left unresolved, as different from the neatly tied endings of the conventional play, the theatre-goer is left with tremendous questions in his mind which he must resolve for himself. Theatre which, in itself, seems to be nonlogical turns out to pose the greatest intellectual questions at exactly the point where they should be raised—in the mind of the individual. A questioning of values is left instead of the catharsis of the old Aristotelian definition. Indeed, Euripides anticipated this type of drama in the choral speeches with which he completes both *The Bacchae* and *Alcestis:*

Gods manifest themselves in many forms,
Bring many matters to surprising ends;
The things we thought would happen do not happen;
The unexpected, God makes possible:
And that is what has happened here today.

More recently Sam Shepard (b. 1943) has emerged as America's leading playwright. Shepard writes in a hyperrealistic mode comparable to the Photorealism (New Realism, Magic Realism) of artists like Richard Estes and Duane Hanson (see chap. 25). But, like abstract illusionist James Havard (see p. 547), Shepard's realism is illusory; the facts are there, it seems, but where reality begins and ends borders on a fifth dimension. Like his *Buried Child* (1979 Pulitzer prize) and *Curse of the Starving Class,* Shepard's *Fool for Love* (1983) is a lower middle-class family drama, in this case an elegaic myth of doomed incestuous love. Shepard's symbols are derived from junk food data and movie, TV, and auto mystiques that represent all that is tawdry and tacky in American life. In *True West* (1980) Shepard extols the mythic West, the Old West that is fast succumbing to cement mixers and bulldozers. In this and many other of his forty plus plays Shepard poses a basic question: must this New World become like the Old World just because so much of the Old World is becoming like us?

Modern Prose Fiction

Everything that has been said previously about literature in the twentieth century applies to the short story and the novel. As in poetry, one of the important concerns of the prose writer is to develop new forms, new methods of penetrating into the truths of human experience. Hitherto *plot* has been one of the chief methods by which fiction writers made their explorations. Many contemporary writers have abandoned this method of telling their story, with the result that form has become almost completely free.

Two forms of fiction, either new or renovated, have come into prominence in our century: black humor and science fiction. Of the first of these, Heller's novel *Catch 22* is the best known, and one of the best examples. Black humor *is* funny, but with a bitterness that stings. Basically it is satire against all the established ways of thought and action, but a satire which uses surrealistic techniques to achieve its purposes. The typical novel of this sort uses scenes which are sharply etched, with almost photographic naturalism. Yet the scenes and events exist in a crazy juxtaposition—as in a Dali painting—so that all ordinary sense is lost, and the mind which is accustomed to see logical relationships is utterly confounded. The reader is left with the sense of living through a funny nightmare in which time is compressed or expanded, in which space is purely relative and may change without warning to the intellect. The total impact of such a novel is that it is a crazy world, and if one were insane one would find it amusing—and then the reversal: maybe the world of the novel is sane and our conventional, Aristotelian minds are really the crazy part.

A brief discussion of *Catch 22* may serve to clarify the points we are making. The central object of ridicule throughout the novel is our rational thought which goes around in a circle until it ends in total absurdity. The novel takes place on an Air Force base off the coast of Italy and seems to satirize military life, but a closer scrutiny reveals that it is a bitter attack against much of twentieth-century society and its values. The "Catch" is first revealed when Yossarian, a bombardier and the protagonist of the novel, objects to flying more missions and goes to the medical officer, pleading insanity, in order to get sent home. The doctor explains to him that a man who expresses fear in a dangerous situation is necessarily sane, and therefore cannot be released. Yossarian asks about the men who are flying missions without protest. The doctor's explanation is simple: Those men are insane, but since they aren't asking to be relieved of duty he can't send them home. If they asked, they, like Yossarian, would show that they were sane and therefore be returned to duty. This is "Catch 22"; perfectly logical, totally absurd, and allowing no hope. Time after time, in many different situations throughout the early sections of the book, this same roundabout logic is revealed to establish an atmosphere of almost complete hopelessness.

Many other of the fallacies of our present way of life are satirized as well. One of these is our dependence upon paperwork rather than facts in making judgments; indeed ex-P.F.C. Wintergreen, a mail clerk, directs the actions of the military more completely than the generals through the handling and scrambling of messages. Another case in point concerns the suicidal mission to bomb the city of Bologna, when Yossarian sneaks down to the central map at headquarters and moves the ribbon which shows the Allied ground position above the city. This is discovered the next morning and word is transmitted from one level of command to the next that Bologna has been taken and the bombing mission is therefore unnecessary. For days this is believed until finally the true word gets through and the mission is rescheduled.

Perhaps the most bitter of attacks is made against the profit system as represented by the supply officer, Milo Minderbinder and his M and M Enterprises. Starting with the simple trading for supplies, he finally deals with both the enemy and his own side; at one point he directs the enemy bombing of his own airbase, at another he arranges a total battle, having charge of both sides. All this is with an enormous profit to himself, though he constantly reminds each person that the person "has a share" in M and M Enterprises. "Having a share" is certainly one of the great double-meanings of the book.

The first two-thirds of the book are timeless, shifting from one incident to another with no regard to chronology. For Yossarian, however, the central incident is probably the death of his crewmate, Snowden. Snowden has been wounded by antiaircraft fire, and Yossarian is in the rear of the plane treating the obvious wound. Then he opens Snowden's flak suit and discovers the real and mortal wound as Snowden's guts spill out of the body. At this point Yossarian realizes that the world, friend or enemy, is really divided into two groups, the killers and the victims, and that he, as bombardier, has been one of the killers. He refuses this role and for a time goes naked (even when the general is pinning a medal on him) rather than wear the military uniform. The Snowden incident is referred to many times throughout the early part of the novel and is fully explained about two-thirds of the way through at a point when the story begins to exist in chronological time. This is the incident which leads to the first explanation of *Catch 22* and the hopelessness of the situation.

One pilot, Yossarian's tentmate, Orr, has seemed more insane than the rest throughout most of the book. His planes keep having engine trouble or are shot down over the sea. Orr always crash-lands his craft in the water, from which the crew is rescued as they work with the survival gear in the plane. Finally Orr lands in the sea, and all of the crew but he are rescued. It appears that he has drowned.

The novel ends with a scene in the hospital with Yossarian and other officers complaining that there is no hope, no hope at all. Then they receive word that Orr has successfully paddled his inflated life raft to neutral Sweden and is alive. The mood changes. Yossarian runs away to Rome with the promise that he, too, somehow, will reach Sweden. The other men, bound by various obligations, will not run for it, but the fact remains that hope remains. Man may not conquer, but he can refuse to be conquered. In spite of *Catch 22,* the individual can assert himself.

Science fiction as a type is not really new, for most utopian literature shares in its fantasy. Jules Verne and H.G. Wells wrote science fiction before our century. What is really new about it is its reacceptance as a serious genre. What had degenerated into comic strip stuff in the 1930s, somewhat below the level of serious thought, is now widely accepted. The difference lies in the reasons for writing science fiction. The utopians used it to show that things could be better. Jules Verne wrote high-quality, highly popular adventure literature. At the present time Sci-fi's purpose is to unchain the mind from its ordinary channels. As we move through "time-warps," we begin to live in a world in which A may not be A; in which not-A can very well be A. Serious science fiction is now one of the mind-expanding tools which opens new dimensions of thought and life for its devotees.

One of the most usual techniques for the fiction writer of this century is to take a relatively simple action or pattern of action and explore it in its depth, rather than running its length as the plot-story does. In such a case we usually have a surface action, with one or more levels of meaning revealed beneath that surface. It is often possible to distinguish sociological levels, philosophic or psychological levels, and mythical levels of significance. To reach these levels the author frequently uses the types of symbols which have been mentioned previously, and which very often yield meanings that are more felt than stated in words. At the moment it is interesting to compare some outstanding aspects of meaning which concern many writers of short stories and novels. These may be called the pessimism of modern fiction and its optimism.

Although one recognizes that some of the great writers of the nineteenth century were pessimistic, in that century and early in the present one, optimism was the dominant mood of most fiction, for goodness and virtue were, in the main, triumphant. About the time of the First World War, however, we find a very considerable change in the mood of the writers. Starting about that time we have the proletarian writers and the naturalistic writers who thought that society stifled the individual and turned life to tragedy or pathos or despair. Most of these novels are revolts against the materialistic goals which society has imposed upon people, which the individual persons accept, and which finally betray the individual. Theodore Dreiser's *An American Tragedy,* John Dos Passos's *Manhattan Transfer,* and even Aldous Huxley's *Brave New World* can be read as examples of this trend.

That these views of life are pessimistic there can be little doubt but they are not total, for they place the blame on forces external to man. If we could reform society, they seem to say, then the spirit of man could be liberated. Even in the bitter irony of *Brave New World* we have Helmholtz Watson who dreams beyond the bondages of his culture and who welcomes exile as a chance to create.

This mood of social criticism continued approximately from the end of the First World War, 1918, through the depression, and to the beginning of the Second World War. Steinbeck's *Grapes of Wrath* remains as one of the most notable products of the time, for below the surface story of the Joads during the depression (a social problem which has been almost completely forgotten) lie strong political and religious levels of significance which have enduring value.

One could cite many examples of pessimism expressed as social criticism, but, as we have said, such despair is not total. Hope remains that society itself may be reformed and with it may come the regeneration of the human spirit. To oversimplify, this is a pessimism which is still rooted in our present materialistic value system.

Very early, however, appeared another thought: that the universe itself was accidental and without purpose, that the conditions which support life on a mediocre planet arose as a part of the cosmic accident, and that the life or death of any man or group of men is completely insignificant. Such a point of view, expressed early in the century in Somerset Maugham's *Of Human Bondage,* makes any human plan or purpose or striving completely pointless. All forms of society become nothing more than traps to snare the individual into a senseless conformity. This type of pessimism might be called "proto-Existentialism."

Later such an American writer as William Faulkner explored the depths of pessimism in his series of novels dealing with Yoknapatawpha County, Mississippi. In these novels, using symbols of violence, rape, incest, fire, and insanity, Faulkner depicts the complete degeneracy of the aristocratic or commercial white man. In his Nobel Prize acceptance speech Faulkner stated his optimistic belief that man will not only endure, he will prevail. In the literary works themselves, however, one can still find only the expression of the lost and displaced nature of man in a universe that lacks pattern or purpose.

To conclude this discussion of the literature of our century, one sees first a welter of experimentation in forms and meanings, some successful, others not. The purpose of all the experimentation, however, is to free our minds; to take them out of old bondages which have hampered their search for truth. New meanings have required new forms, new language, new exploration in the realms of time, space, and consciousness. Throughout the century, doomsayers have predicted the demise of the novel as a literary form; literature in the 1980s proves them wrong. When Colombian novelist Gabriel García-Márquez received the 1982 Nobel Prize for Literature, the international literary world was reminded that there are many active world-class novelists, some of which are: Saul Bellow and John Updike (U.S.); Doris Lessing (U.K.); Jorge Luis Borges (Argentina); Gunter Grass (West Germany); Nadine Gordimer (South Africa; see "A Soldier's Embrace" in chap. 24); Yokio Mishima age when print media are supposedly succumbing to the relentless onslaught of computer technology, more books (poetry, short stories, novels, biographies, drama, essays) are being published than at any time in history. No one can reasonably predict what the coming century holds but the literary arts are currently flourishing as perhaps never before.

Literary Selections

anyone lived in a pretty how town
e e cummings (1894–1962)

Playful syntax and novel versification, among other things, characterize the poetry of e e cummings. The line in the following poem about the growing up process is a case in point: "down they forgot as up they grew."

anyone lived in a pretty how town
(with up so floating many bells down)
spring summer autumn winter
he sang his didn't he danced his did.

Women and men (both little and small)
cared for anyone not at all
they sowed their isn't they reaped their same
sun moon stars rain

children guessed (but only a few
and down they forgot as up they grew
autumn winter spring summer)
that no one loved him more by more

when by now and tree by leaf
she laughed his joy she cried his grief
bird by snow and stir by still
anyone's any was all to her

someones married their everyones
laughed their cryings and did their dance
(sleep wake hope and then) they
said their nevers they slept their dream

stars rain sun moon
(and only the snow can begin to explain
how children are apt to forget to remember
with up so floating many bells down)

one day anyone died i guess
(and noone stooped to kiss his face)
busy folk buried them side by side
little by little and was by was

all by all and deep by deep
and more by more they dream their sleep
noone and anyone earth by april
wish by spirit and if by yes.

Women and men (both dong and ding)
summer autumn winter spring
reaped their sowing and went their came
sun moon stars rain

Exercises

1. Much of the poetry of cummings is very rhythmic with considerable use of what is called the "variable foot." In stanza 1, for example, the variation occurs in the third line.

Try reading the poem aloud to hear how the variations set off the nimble words in the other lines.

2. Many of the phrases are disassociated from expected relationships. Try rephrasing some of these to see what happens to the rhythm. Do the conventional versions become rather commonplace?

WHEN ALL MY FIVE AND COUNTRY SENSES SEE
Dylan Thomas (1914–1953)

The carefully crafted work of Welsh poet Dylan Thomas consistently deals with the unity and process of life. Earlier in this chapter the following poem was analyzed but the essence of this poetry is primarily an aural experience. It should, therefore, be read aloud, and many times.

When all my five and country senses see,
The fingers will forget green thumbs and mark
How, through the halfmoon's vegetable eye,
Husk of young stars and handful zodiac,
Love in the frost is pared and wintered by.
The whispering ears will watch love drummed away
Down breeze and shell to a discordant beach,
And, lashed to syllables, the lynx tongue cry
That her fond wounds are mended bitterly,
My nostrils see her breath burn like a bush.
My one and noble heart has witnesses
In all love's countries, that will grope awake:
And when blind sleep drops on the spying senses,
The heart is sensual, though five eyes break.

Chapter 1 from INVISIBLE MAN
Ralph Ellison (b. 1914)

A searing novel about black America and white America, Ralph Ellison's *Invisible Man,* winner of the 1952 National Book Award, is both a folk novel and a polished work in the American literary tradition. Opening with a bizarre boxing match in a white man's "smoker" and culminating in an explosive race riot, this is the epic tale of one man's voyage to self-discovery, a man who is "invisible simply because people refuse to see me." Appearing originally as a short story and then as chapter 1, the following selection gives something of the flavor of a book which should be read in its entirety.

It goes a long way back, some twenty years. All my life I had been looking for something, and everywhere I turned someone tried to tell me what it was. I accepted their answers too, though they were often in contradiction and even self-contradictory. I was naïve. I was looking for myself and asking everyone except myself questions which I, and only I, could answer. It took me a long time and much painful boomeranging of my expectations to achieve a realization everyone else appears to have been born with: That I am nobody but myself. But first I had to discover that I am an invisible man!

And yet I am no freak of nature, nor of history. I was in the cards, other things having been equal (or unequal) eighty-five years ago. I am not ashamed of my grandparents for having been slaves. I am only ashamed of myself for having at one time been ashamed. About eighty-five years ago they were told that they were free, united with others of our country in everything pertaining to the common good, and, in everything social, separate like the fingers of the hand. And they believed it. They exulted in it. They stayed in their place, worked hard, and brought up my father to do the same. But my grandfather is the one. He was an odd old guy, my grandfather, and I am told I take after him. It was he who caused the trouble. On his deathbed he called my father to him and said, "Son, after I'm gone I want you to keep up the good fight. I never told you, but our life is a war and I have been a traitor all my born days, a spy in the enemy's country ever since I give up my gun back in the Reconstruction. Live with your head in the lion's mouth. I want you to overcome 'em with yeses, undermine 'em with grins, agree 'em to death and destruction, let 'em swoller you till they vomit or bust wide open." They thought the old man had gone out of his mind. He had been the meekest of men. The younger children were rushed from the room, the shades drawn and the flame of the lamp turned so low that it sputtered on the wick like the old man's breathing. "Learn it to the younguns," he whispered fiercely; then he died.

But my folks were more alarmed over his last words than over his dying. It was as though he had not died at all, his words caused so much anxiety. I was warned emphatically to forget what he had said and, indeed, this is the first time it has been mentioned outside the family circle. It had a tremendous effect upon me, however. I could never be sure of what he meant. Grandfather had been a quiet old man who never made any trouble, yet on his deathbed he had called himself a traitor and a spy, and he had spoken of his meekness as a dangerous activity. It became a constant puzzle which lay unanswered in the back of my mind. And whenever things went well for me I remembered my grandfather and felt guilty and uncomfortable. It was as though I was carrying out his advice in spite of myself. And to make it worse, everyone loved me for it. I was praised by the most lily-white men of the town. I was considered an example of desirable conduct—just as my grandfather had been. And what puzzled me was that the old man had defined it as *treachery*. When I was praised for my conduct I felt a guilt that in some way I was doing something that was really against the wishes of the white folks, that if they had understood they would have desired me to act just the opposite, that I should have been sulky and mean, and that that really would have been what they wanted, even though they were fooled and thought they wanted me to act as I did. It made me afraid that some day they would look upon me as a traitor and I would be lost. Still I was more afraid to act any other way because they didn't like that at all. The old man's words were like a curse. On my graduation day I delivered an oration in which I showed that humility was the secret, indeed, the very essence of progress. (Not that I believed this—how could I, remembering my grandfather?—I only believed that it worked.) It was a great success. Everyone praised me and I was invited to give the speech at a gathering of the town's leading white citizens. It was a triumph for our whole community.

It was in the main ballroom of the leading hotel. When I got there I discovered that it was on the occasion of a smoker, and I was told that since I was to be there anyway I might as well take part in the battle royal to be fought by some of my schoolmates as part of the entertainment. The battle royal came first.

All of the town's big shots were there in their tuxedoes, wolfing down the buffet foods, drinking beer and whiskey and smoking black cigars. It was a large room with a high ceiling. Chairs were arranged in neat rows around three sides of a portable boxing ring. The fourth side was clear, revealing a gleaming space of polished floor. I had some misgivings over the battle royal, by the way. Not from a distaste for fighting, but because I didn't care too much for the other fellows who were to take part. They were tough guys who seemed to have no grandfather's curse worrying their minds. No one could mistake their toughness. And besides, I suspected that fighting a battle royal might detract from the dignity of my speech. In those pre-invisible days I visualized myself as a potential Booker T. Washington. But the other fellows didn't care too much for me either, and there were nine of them. I felt superior to them in my way, and I didn't like the manner in which we were all crowded together into the servants' elevator. Nor did they like my being there. In fact, as the warmly lighted floors flashed past the elevator we had words over the fact that I, by taking part in the fight, had knocked one of their friends out of a night's work.

We were led out of the elevator through a rococo hall into an anteroom and told to get into our fighting togs. Each of us was issued a pair of boxing gloves and ushered out into the big mirrored hall, which we entered looking cautiously about us and whispering, lest we might accidentally be heard above the noise of the room. It was foggy with cigar smoke. And already the whiskey was taking effect. I was shocked to see some of the most important men of the town quite tipsy. They were all there—bankers, lawyers, judges, doctors, fire chiefs, teachers, merchants. Even one of the more fashionable pastors. Something we could not see was going on up front. A clarinet was vibrating sensuously and the men were standing up and moving eagerly forward. We were a small tight group, clustered together, our bare upper bodies touching and shining with anticipatory sweat; while up front the big shots were becoming increasingly excited over something we still could not see. Suddenly I heard the school superintendent, who had told me to come, yell, "Bring up the shines, gentlemen! Bring up the little shines!"

We were rushed up to the front of the ballroom, where it smelled even more strongly of tobacco and whiskey. Then we were pushed into place. I almost wet my pants. A sea of faces, some hostile, some amused, ringed around us, and in the center, facing us, stood a magnificent blonde—stark naked. There was dead silence. I felt a blast of cold air chill me. I tried to back away, but they were behind me and around me. Some of the boys stood with lowered heads, trembling. I felt a wave of irrational guilt and fear. My teeth chattered, my skin turned to goose flesh, my knees knocked. Yet I was strongly attracted and looked in spite of myself. Had the price of looking been blindness, I would have looked. The hair was yellow like that of a circus kewpie doll, the face heavily powdered and rouged, as though to form an abstract mask, the eyes hollow and smeared a cool blue, the color of a baboon's butt. I felt a desire to spit upon her as my eyes brushed slowly over her body. Her breasts were firm and round as the domes of East Indian temples, and I stood so close as to see the fine skin texture and beads of pearly perspiration glistening like dew around the pink and erected buds of her nipples. I wanted at one and the same time to run from the room, to sink through the floor, or go to her and cover her from my eyes and the eyes of the others with my body; to feel the soft thighs, to caress her and destroy her, to love her and murder her, to hide from her, and yet to stroke where below the small American flag tattooed upon her belly her thighs formed a capital V. I had a notion that of all in the room she saw only me with her impersonal eyes.

And then she began to dance, a slow senuous movement; the smoke of a hundred cigars clinging to her like the thinnest of veils. She seemed like a fair bird-girl girdled in veils calling to me from the angry surface of some gray and threatening sea. I was transported. Then I became aware of the clarinet playing and the big shots yelling at us. Some threatened us if we looked and others if we did not. On my right I saw one boy faint. And now a man grabbed a silver pitcher from a table and stepped close as he dashed ice water upon him and stood him up and forced two of us to support him as his head hung and moans issued from his thick bluish lips. Another boy began to plead to go home. He was the largest of the group, wearing dark red fighting trunks much too small to conceal the erection which projected from him as though in answer to the insinuating low-registered moaning of the clarinet. He tried to hide himself with his boxing gloves.

And all the while the blonde continued dancing, smiling faintly at the big shots who watched her with fascination, and faintly smiling at our fear. I noticed a certain merchant who followed her hungrily, his lips loose and drooling. He was a large man who wore diamond studs in a shirtfront which swelled with the ample paunch underneath, and each time the blonde swayed her undulating hips he ran his hand through the thin hair of his bald head and, with his arms upheld, his posture clumsy like that of an intoxicated panda, wound his belly in a slow and obscene grind. This creature was completely hypnotized. The music had quickened. As the dancer flung herself about with a detached expression on her face, the men began reaching out to touch her. I could see their beefy fingers sink into the soft flesh. Some of the others tried to stop them and she began to move around the floor in graceful circles, as they gave chase, slipping and sliding over the polished floor. It was mad. Chairs went crashing, drinks were spilt, as they ran laughing and howling after her. They caught her just as she reached a door, raised her from the floor, and tossed her as college boys are tossed at a hazing, and above her red, fixed-smiling lips I saw the terror and disgust in her eyes, almost like my own terror and that which I saw in some of the other boys. As I watched, they tossed her twice and her soft breasts seemed to flatten against the air and her legs flung wildly as she spun. Some of the more sober ones helped her to escape. And I started off the floor, heading for the anteroom with the rest of the boys.

Some were still crying and in hysteria. But as we tried to leave we were stopped and ordered to get into the ring. There was nothing to do but what we were told. All ten of us climbed under the ropes and allowed ourselves to be blindfolded with broad bands of white cloth. One of the men seemed to feel a bit sympathetic and tried to cheer us up as we stood with our backs against the ropes. Some of us tried to grin. "See that boy over there?" one of the men said. "I want you to run across at the bell and give it to him right in the belly. If you don't get him, I'm going to get you. I don't like his looks." Each of us was told the same. The blindfolds were put on. Yet even then I had been going over my speech. In my mind each word was as bright as flame. I felt the cloth pressed into place, and frowned so that it would be loosened when I relaxed.

But now I felt a sudden fit of blind terror. I was unused to darkness. It was as though I had suddenly found myself in a dark room filled with poisonous cottonmouths. I could hear the bleary voices yelling insistently for the battle royal to begin.

"Get going in there!"

"Let me at that big nigger!"

I strained to pick up the school superintendent's voice, as though to squeeze some security out of that slightly more familiar sound.

"Let me at those black sonsabitches!" someone yelled.

"No, Jackson, no!" another voice yelled. "Here, somebody, help me hold Jack."

"I want to get at that ginger-colored nigger. Tear him limb from limb," the first voice yelled.

I stood against the ropes trembling. For in those days I was what they called ginger-colored, and he sounded as though he might crunch me between his teeth like a crisp ginger cookie.

Quite a struggle was going on. Chairs were being kicked about and I could hear voices grunting as with a terrific effort. I wanted to see, to see more desperately than ever before. But the blindfold was tight as a thick skin-puckering scab and when I raised my gloved hands to push the layers of white aside a voice yelled, "Oh, no you don't, black bastard! Leave that alone!"

"Ring the bell before Jackson kills him a coon!" someone boomed in the sudden silence. And I heard the bell clang and the sound of the feet scuffling forward.

A glove smacked against my head. I pivoted, striking out stiffly as someone went past, and felt the jar ripple along the length of my arm to my shoulder. Then it seemed as though all nine of the boys had turned upon me at once. Blows pounded me from all sides while I struck out as best I could. So many blows landed upon me that I wondered if I were not the only blindfolded fighter in the ring, or if the man called Jackson hadn't succeeded in getting me after all.

Blindfolded, I could no longer control my motions. I had no dignity. I stumbled about like a baby or a drunken man. The smoke had become thicker and with each new blow it seemed to sear and further restrict my lungs. My saliva became like hot bitter glue. A glove connected with my head, filling my mouth with warm blood. It was everywhere. I could not tell if the moisture I felt upon my body was sweat or blood. A blow landed hard against the nape of my neck. I felt myself going over, my head hitting the floor. Streaks of blue light filled the black world behind the blindfold. I lay prone, pretending that I was knocked out, but felt myself seized by hands and yanked to my feet. "Get going, black boy! Mix it up!" My arms were like lead, my head smarting from blows. I managed to feel my way to the ropes and held on, trying to catch my breath. A glove landed in my mid-section and I went over again, feeling as though the smoke had become a knife jabbed into my guts. Pushed this way and that by the legs milling around me, I finally pulled erect and discovered that I could see the black, sweat-washed forms weaving in the smoky-blue atmosphere like drunken dancers weaving to the rapid drum-like thuds of blows.

Everyone fought hysterically. It was complete anarchy. Everybody fought everybody else. No group fought together for long. Two, three, four, fought one, then turned to fight each other, were themselves attacked. Blows landed below the belt and in the kidney, with the gloves open as well as closed, and with my eye partly opened now there was not so much terror. I moved carefully, avoiding blows, although not too many to attract attention, fighting from group to group. The boys groped about like blind, cautious crabs crouching to protect their mid-sections, their heads pulled in short against their shoulders, their arms stretched nervously before them, with their fists testing the smoke-filled air like the knobbed feelers of hypersensitive snails. In one corner I glimpsed a boy violently punching the air and heard him scream in pain as he smashed his hand against a ring post. For a second I saw him bent over holding his hand, then going down as a blow caught his unprotected head. I played one group against the other, slipping in and throwing a punch then stepping out of range while pushing the others into the melee to take the blows blindly aimed at me. The smoke was agonizing and there were no rounds, no bells at three minute intervals to relieve our exhaustion. The room spun round me, a swirl of lights, smoke, sweating bodies surrounded by tense white faces. I bled from both nose and mouth, the blood spattering upon my chest.

The men kept yelling, "Slug him, black boy! Knock his guts out!"

"Uppercut him! Kill him! Kill that big boy!"

Taking a fake fall, I saw a boy going down heavily beside me as though we were felled by a single blow, saw a sneaker-clad foot shoot into his groin as the two who had knocked him down stumbled upon him. I rolled out of range, feeling a twinge of nausea.

The harder we fought the more threatening the men became. And yet, I had begun to worry about my speech again. How would it go? Would they recognize my ability? What would they give me?

I was fighting automatically when suddenly I noticed that one after another of the boys was leaving the ring. I was surprised, filled with panic, as though I had been left alone with an unknown danger. Then I understood. The boys had arranged it among themselves. It was the custom for the two men left in the ring to slug it out for the winner's place. I discovered this too late. When the bell sounded two men in tuxedoes leaped into the ring and removed the blindfold. I found myself facing Tatlock, the biggest of the gang. I felt sick at my stomach. Hardly had the bell stopped ringing in my ears than it clanged again and I saw him moving swiftly toward me. Thinking of nothing else to do I hit him smash on the nose. He kept coming, bringing the rank sharp violence of stale sweat. His face was a black blank of a face, only his eyes alive— with hate of me and aglow with a feverish terror from what had happened to us all. I became anxious. I wanted to deliver my speech and he came at me as though he meant to beat it out of me. I smashed him again and again, taking his blows as they came. Then on a sudden impulse I struck him lightly and as we clinched, I whispered, "Fake like I knocked you out, you can have the prize."

"I'll break your behind," he whispered hoarsely.

"For *them*?"

"For *me*, sonofabitch!"

They were yelling for us to break it up and Tatlock spun me half around with a blow, and as a joggled camera sweeps in a reeling scene, I saw the howling red faces crouching tense beneath the cloud of blue-gray smoke.

For a moment the world wavered, unraveled, flowed, then my head cleared and Tatlock bounced before me. That fluttering shadow before my eyes was his jabbing left hand. Then falling forward, my head against his damp shoulder, I whispered,

"I'll make it five dollars more."

"Go to hell!"

But his muscles relaxed a trifle beneath my pressure and I breathed, "Seven?"

"Give it to your ma," he said, ripping me beneath the heart.

And while I still held him I butted him and moved away. I felt myself bombarded with punches. I fought back with hopeless desperation. I wanted to deliver my speech more than anything else in the world, because I felt that only these men could judge truly my ability, and now this stupid clown was ruining my chances. I began fighting carefully now, moving in to punch him and out again with my greater speed. A lucky blow to his chin and I had him going too—until I heard a loud voice yell, "I got my money on the big boy."

Hearing this, I almost dropped my guard. I was confused: Should I try to win against the voice out there? Would not this go against my speech, and was not this a moment for humility, for nonresistance? A blow to my head as I danced about sent my right eye popping like a jack-in-the-box and settled my dilemma. The room went red as I fell. It was a dream fall, my body languid and fastidious as to where to land, until the floor became impatient and smashed up to meet me. A moment later I came to. An hypnotic voice said FIVE emphatically. And I lay there, hazily watching a dark red spot of my own blood shaping itself into a butterfly, glistening and soaking into the soiled gray world of the canvas.

When the voice drawled TEN I was lifted up and dragged to a chair. I sat dazed. My eye pained and swelled with each throb of my pounding heart and I wondered if now I would be allowed to speak. I was wringing wet, my mouth still bleeding. We were grouped along the wall now. The other boys ignored me as they congratulated Tatlock and speculated as to how much they would be paid. One boy whimpered over his smashed hand. Looking up front, I saw attendants in white jackets rolling the portable ring away and placing a small square rug in the vacant space surrounded by chairs. Perhaps, I thought, I will stand on the rug to deliver my speech.

Then the M.C. called us, "Come on up here boys and get your money."

We ran forward to where the men laughed and talked in their chairs, waiting. Everyone seemed friendly now.

"There it is on the rug," the man said. I saw the rug covered with coins of all dimensions and a few crumpled bills. But what excited me, scattered here and there, were the gold pieces.

"Boys, it's all yours," the man said. "You get all you grab."

"That's right, Sambo," a blond man said, winking at me confidentially.

I trembled with excitement, forgetting my pain. I would get the gold and the bills, I thought. I would use both hands. I would throw my body against the boys nearest me to block them from the gold.

"Get down around the rug now," the man commanded, "and don't anyone touch it until I give the signal."

"This ought to be good," I heard.

As told, we got around the square rug on our knees. Slowly the man raised his freckled hand as we followed it upward with our eyes.

I heard, "These niggers look like they're about to pray!"

Then, "Ready," the man said. "Go!"

I lunged for a yellow coin lying on the blue design of the carpet, touching it and sending a surprised shriek to join those rising around me. I tried frantically to remove my hand but could not let go. A hot, violent force tore through my body, shaking me like a wet rat. The rug was electrified. The hair bristled up on my head as I shook myself free. My muscles jumped, my nerves jangled, writhed. But I saw that this was not stopping the other boys. Laughing in fear and embarrassment, some were holding back and scooping up the coins knocked off by the painful contortions of the others. The men roared above us as we struggled.

"Pick it up, goddamnit, pick it up!" someone called like a bass-voiced parrot. "Go on, get it!"

I crawled rapidly around the floor, picking up the coins, trying to avoid the coppers and to get greenbacks and the gold. Ignoring the shock by laughing, as I brushed the coins off quickly, I discovered that I could contain the electricity—a contradiction, but it works. Then the men began to push us onto the rug. Laughing embarrassedly, we struggled out of their hands and kept after the coins. We were all wet and slippery and hard to hold. Suddenly I saw a boy lifted into the air, glistening with sweat like a circus seal, and dropped, his wet back landing flush upon the charged rug, heard him yell and saw him literally dance upon his back, his elbows beating a frenzied tattoo upon the floor, his muscles twitching like the flesh of a horse stung by many flies. When he finally rolled off, his face was gray and no one stopped him when he ran from the floor amid booming laughter.

"Get the money," the M.C. called. "That's good hard American cash!"

And we snatched and grabbed, snatched and grabbed. I was careful not to come too close to the rug now, and when I felt the hot whiskey breath descend upon me like a cloud of foul air I reached out and grabbed the leg of a chair. It was occupied and I held on desperately.

"Leggo, nigger! Leggo!"

The huge face wavered down to mine as he tried to push me free. But my body was slippery and he was too drunk. It was Mr. Colcord, who owned a chain of movie houses and "entertainment palaces." Each time he grabbed me I slipped out of his hands. It became a real struggle. I feared the rug more than I did the drunk, so I held on, surprising myself for a moment by trying to topple *him* upon the rug. It was such an enormous idea that I found myself actually carrying it out. I tried not to be obvious, yet when I grabbed his leg, trying to tumble him out of the chair, he raised up roaring with laughter, and, looking at me with soberness dead in the eye, kicked me viciously in the chest. The chair leg flew out of my hand and I felt myself going and rolled. It was as though I had rolled through a bed of hot coals. It seemed a whole century would pass before I would roll free, a century in which I was seared through the deepest levels of my body to the fearful breath within me and the breath seared and heated to the point of explosion. It'll all be over in a flash, I thought as I rolled clear. It'll all be over in a flash.

But not yet, the men on the other side were waiting, red faces swollen as though from apoplexy as they bent forward in their chairs. Seeing their fingers coming toward me I rolled away as a fumbled football rolls off the receiver's fingertips, back into the coals. That time I luckily sent the rug sliding out of place and heard the coins ringing against the floor and the boys scuffling to pick them up and the M.C. calling, "All right, boys, that's all. Go get dressed and get your money."

I was limp as a dish rag. My back felt as though it had been beaten with wires.

When we had dressed the M.C. came in and gave us each five dollars, except Tatlock, who got ten for being last in the ring. Then he told us to leave. I was not to get a chance to deliver my speech, I thought. I was going out into the dim alley in despair when I was stopped and told to go back. I returned to the ballroom, where the men were pushing back their chairs and gathering in groups to talk.

The M.C. knocked on a table for quiet. "Gentlemen," he said "we almost forgot an important part of the program. A most serious part, gentlemen. This boy was brought here to deliver a speech which he made at his graduation yesterday. . . ."

"Bravo!"

"I'm told that he is the smartest boy we've got out there in Greenwood. I'm told that he knows more big words than a pocket-sized dictionary."

Much applause and laughter.

"So now, gentlemen, I want you to give him your attention."

There was still laughter as I faced them, my mouth dry, my eye throbbing. I began slowly, but evidently my throat was tense, because they began shouting, "Louder! Louder!"

"We of the younger generation extol the wisdom of that great leader and educator," I shouted, "who first spoke these flaming words of wisdom: 'A ship lost at sea for many days suddenly sighted a friendly vessel. From the mast of the unfortunate vessel was seen a signal: "Water, water; we die of thirst!" The answer from the friendly vessel came back: "Cast down your bucket where you are." The captain of the distressed vessel, at last heeding the injunction, cast down his bucket, and it came up full of fresh sparkling water from the mouth of the Amazon River.' And like him I say, and in his words, 'To those of my race who depend upon bettering their condition in a foreign land, or who underestimate the importance of cultivating friendly relations with the Southern white man, who is his next-door neighbor, I would say: "Cast down your bucket where you are"—cast it down in making friends in every manly way of the people of all races by whom we are surrounded. . . .' "

I spoke automatically and with such fervor that I did not realize that the men were still talking and laughing until my dry mouth, filling up with blood from the cut, almost strangled me. I coughed, wanted to stop and go to one of the tall brass, sand-filled spittoons to relieve myself, but a few of the men, especially the superintendent, were listening and I was afraid. So I gulped it down, blood, saliva and all, and continued. (What powers of endurance I had during those days! What enthusiasm! What a belief in the rightness of things!) I spoke even louder in spite of the pain. But still they talked and still they laughed, as though deaf with cotton in dirty ears. So I spoke with greater emotional emphasis.

I closed my ears and swallowed blood until I was nauseated. The speech seemed a hundred times as long as before, but I could not leave out a single word. All had to be said, each memorized nuance considered, rendered. Nor was that all. Whenever I uttered a word of three or more syllables a group of voices would yell for me to repeat it. I used the phrase "social responsibility" and they yelled:

"What's that word you say, boy?"

"Social responsibility," I said.

"What?"

"Social . . ."

"Louder."

". . . responsibility."

"More!"

"Respon—"

"Repeat!"

"—sibility."

The room filled with the uproar of laughter until, no doubt, distracted by having to gulp down my blood, I made a mistake and yelled a phrase I had often seen denounced in newspaper editorials, heard debated in private.

"Social. . ."

"What?" they yelled.

". . . equality—"

The laughter hung smokelike in the sudden stillness. I opened my eyes, puzzled. Sounds of displeasure filled the room. The M.C. rushed forward. They shouted hostile phrases at me. But I did not understand.

A small dry mustached man in the front row blared out, "Say that slowly, son!"

"What, sir?"

"What you just said!"

"Social responsibility, sir," I said.

"You weren't being smart, were you, boy?" he said, not unkindly.

"No, sir!"

"You sure that about 'equality' was a mistake?"

"Oh, yes, sir," I said. "I was swallowing blood."

"Well, you had better speak more slowly so we can understand. We mean to do right by you, but you've got to know your place at all times. All right, now, go on with your speech."

I was afraid. I wanted to leave but I wanted also to speak and I was afraid they'd snatch me down.

"Thank you, sir," I said, beginning where I had left off, and having them ignore me as before.

Yet when I finished there was a thunderous applause. I was surprised to see the superintendent come forth with a package wrapped in white tissue paper, and, gesturing for quiet, address the men.

"Gentlemen, you see that I did not overpraise this boy. He makes a good speech and some day he'll lead his people in the proper paths. And I don't have to tell you that this is important in these days and times. This is a good, smart boy, and so to encourage him in the right direction, in the name of the Board of Education I wish to present him a prize in the form of this. . . ."

He paused, removing the tissue paper and revealing a gleaming calfskin brief case.

". . . in the form of this first-class article from Shad Witmore's shop."

"Boy," he said, addressing me, "take this prize and keep it well. Consider it a badge of office. Prize it. Keep developing as you are and some day it will be filled with important papers that will help shape the destiny of your people."

I was so moved that I could hardly express my thanks. A rope of bloody saliva forming a shape like an undiscovered continent drooled upon the leather and I wiped it quickly away. I felt an importance that I had never dreamed.

"Open it and see what's inside," I was told.

My fingers a-tremble, I complied, smelling the fresh leather and finding an official-looking document inside. It was a scholarship to the state college for Negroes. My eyes filled with tears and I ran awkwardly off the floor.

I was overjoyed; I did not even mind when I discovered that the gold pieces I had scrambled for were brass pocket tokens advertising a certain make of automobile.

When I reached home everyone was excited. Next day the neighbors came to congratulate me. I even felt safe from grandfather, whose deathbed curse usually spoiled my triumphs. I stood beneath his photograph with my brief case in hand and smiled triumphantly into his stolid black peasant's face. It was a face that fascinated me. The eyes seemed to follow everywhere I went.

That night I dreamed I was at a circus with him and that he refused to laugh at the clowns no matter what they did. Then later he told me to open my brief case and read what was inside and I did, finding an official envelope stamped with the state seal; and inside the envelope I found another and another, endlessly, and I thought I would fall of weariness. "Them's years," he said. "Now open that one." And I did and in it I found an engraved document containing a short message in letters of gold. "Read it," my grandfather said. "Out loud!"

"To Whom It May Concern," I intoned. "Keep This Nigger-Boy Running."

I awoke with the old man's laughter ringing in my ears.

(It was a dream I was to remember and dream again for many years after. But at that time I had no insight into its meaning. First I had to attend college.)

Exercises

1. Why did the protagonist say that his grandfather's dying words "acted like a curse"?
2. Was the true function of the "battle royal" solely entertainment? Explain your answer.
3. What was implied in the way white males treated the naked blonde dancer? Was this at all comparable to the attitude toward blacks? In what ways?
4. The electrified rug was a metaphor for what?
5. Do you feel that the all-pervasive brutality in this story was exaggerated? If your answer was "yes" you might want to look much deeper into the history of race relations in this country and then examine your own attitude.

LIFE, FRIENDS, IS BORING. WE MUST NOT SAY SO

John Berryman (1914–1972)

Berryman, like many other artists, saw the middle years of the century as a dreary procession of wars and other calamities. With his formally designed poetry he tried to relieve some of his personal anguish while making some kind of order in a disorderly world, a world that was worse than absurd; it was boring. Only three years after a critic had observed that Berryman "had come to poetic terms with the wreck of the modern world," the poet leaped to his death from a bridge in Minneapolis.

Life, friends, is boring. We must not say so.
After all, the sky flashes, the great sea yearns,
we ourselves flash and yearn,
and moreover my mother told me as a boy
(repeatedly) "Ever to confess you're bored
means you have no

Inner Resources." I conclude now I have no
inner resources, because I am heavy bored.
Peoples bore me,
literature bores me, especially great literature,
Henry bores me, with his plights & gripes
as bad as achilles,

who loves people and valiant art, which bores me.
And the tranquil hills, & gin, look like a drag
and somehow a dog
has taken itself & its tail considerably away
into mountains or sea or sky, leaving
behind: me, wag.

Exercises

1. Describe the missing "Inner Resources."
2. Why is great literature more boring than everyday literature?
3. Why the juxtaposition of "tranquil hills" and "gin"?

DEER IN THE WORKS

Kurt Vonnegut (b. 1922)

Mindless, destructive progress is the theme of the following satirical short story by Kurt Vonnegut. As part of a corporate entity with "federal" and "apparatus" in its title, the "Ilium Works" (Ilium is another name for ancient Troy), whose claim to fame is size ("second-largest industrial plant in America") makes unspecified things to meet "armament contracts." Pitted against a plant which "spewed acid fumes and soot" is a young journalist who has to settle for a job in promotion and publicity. Much like the naive journalist, a deer wanders into the "works," upsetting the routine and inviting the destruction accorded the environment. A deer is impeding progress? Shoot the deer!

The big black stacks of the Ilium Works of the Federal Apparatus Corporation spewed acid fumes and soot over the hundreds of men and women who were lined up before the red-brick employment office. It was summer. The Ilium Works, already the second-largest industrial plant in America, was increasing its staff by one third in order to meet armament contracts. Every ten minutes or so, a company policeman opened the employment-office door, letting out a chilly gust from the air-conditioned interior and admitting three more applicants.

"Next three," said the policeman.

A middle-sized man in his late twenties, his young face camouflaged with a mustache and spectacles, was admitted after a four-hour wait. His spirits and the new suit he'd bought for the occasion were wilted by the fumes and the August sun, and he'd given up lunch in order to keep his place in line. But his bearing remained jaunty. He was the last, in his group of three, to face the receptionist.

"Screw-machine operator, ma'am," said the first man.

"See Mr. Cormody in booth seven," said the receptionist.

"Plastic extrusion, miss," said the next man.

"See Mr. Hoyt in booth two," she said. "Skill?" she asked the urbane young man in the wilted suit. "Milling machine? Jig borer?"

"Writing," he said. "Any kind of writing."

"You mean advertising and sales promotion?"

"Yes—that's what I mean."

She looked doubtful. "Well, I don't know. We didn't put out a call for that sort of people. You can't run a machine, can you?"

"Typewriter," he said jokingly.

The receptionist was a sober young woman. "The company does not use male stenographers," she said. "See Mr. Dilling in booth twenty-six. He just might know of some advertising-and-sales-promotion-type job."

He straightened his tie and coat, forced a smile that implied he was looking into jobs at the Works as sort of a lark. He walked into booth twenty-six and extended his hand to Mr. Dilling, a man of his own age. "Mr. Dilling, my name is David Potter. I was curious to know what openings you might have in advertising and sales promotion, and thought I'd drop in for a talk."

Mr. Dilling, an old hand at facing young men who tried to hide their eagerness for a job, was polite but outwardly unimpressed. "Well, you came at a bad time, I'm afraid, Mr. Potter. The competition for that kind of job is pretty stiff, as you perhaps know, and there isn't much of anything open just now."

David nodded. "I see." He had had no experience in asking for a job with a big organization, and Mr. Dilling was making him aware of what a fine art it was—if you couldn't run a machine. A duel was under way.

"But have a seat anyway, Mr. Potter."

"Thank you." He looked at his watch. "I really ought to be getting back to my paper soon."

"You work on a paper around here?"

"Yes, I own a weekly paper in Dorset, about ten miles from Ilium."

"Oh—you don't say. Lovely little village. Thinking of giving up the paper, are you?"

"Well, no—not exactly. It's a possibility. I bought the paper soon after the war, so I've been with it for eight years, and I don't want to go stale. I might be wise to move on. It all depends on what opens up."

"You have a family?" said Mr. Dilling pleasantly.

"Yes. My wife, and two boys and two girls."

"A nice, big, well-balanced family," said Mr. Dilling. "And you're so young, too."

"Twenty-nine," said David. He smiled. "We didn't plan it to be quite that big. It's run to twins. The boys are twins, and then, several days ago, the girls came."

"You don't say!" said Mr. Dilling. He winked. "That would certainly start a young man thinking about getting a little security, eh, with a family like that?"

Both of them treated the remark casually, as though it were no more than a pleasantry between two family men. "It's what we wanted, actually, two boys, two girls," said David. "We didn't expect to get them this quickly, but we're glad now. As far as security goes—well, maybe I flatter myself, but I think the administrative and writing experience I've had running the paper would be worth a good bit to the right people, if something happened to the paper."

"One of the big shortages in this country," said Dilling philosophically, concentrating on lighting a cigarette, "is men who know how to do things, and know how to take responsibility and get things done. I only wish there were better openings in advertising and sales promotion than the ones we've got. They're important, interesting jobs, understand, but I don't know how you'd feel about the starting salary."

"Well, I'm just trying to get the lay of the land, now—to see how things are. I have no idea what salary industry might pay a man like me, with my experience."

"The question experienced men like yourself usually ask is: how high can I go and how fast? And the answer to that is that the sky is the limit for a man with drive and creative ambition. And he can go up fast or slow, depending on what he's willing to do and capable of putting into the job. We might start out a man like you at, oh, say, a hundred dollars a week, but that isn't to say you'd be stuck at that level for two years or even two months."

"I suppose a man could keep a family on that until he got rolling," said David.

"You'd find the work in the publicity end just about the same as what you're doing now. Our publicity people have high standards for writing and editing and reporting, and our publicity releases don't wind up in newspaper editors' wastebaskets. Our people do a professional job, and are well-respected as journalists." He stood. "I've got a little matter to attend to—take me about ten minutes. Could you possibly stick around? I'm enjoying our talk."

David looked at his watch. "Oh—guess I could spare another ten or fifteen minutes."

Dilling was back in his booth in three minutes, chuckling over some private joke. "Just talking on the phone with Lou Flammer, the publicity supervisor. Needs a new stenographer. Lou's a card. Everybody here is crazy about Lou. Old weekly man himself, and I guess that's where he learned to be so easy to get along with. Just to feel him out for the hell of it, I told him about you. I didn't commit you to anything—just said what you told me, that you were keeping your eyes open. And guess what Lou said?"

"Guess what, Nan," said David Potter to his wife on the telephone. He was wearing only his shorts, and was phoning from the company hospital. "When you come home from the hospital tomorrow, you'll be coming home to a solid citizen who pulls down a hundred and ten dollars a week, *every* week. I just got my badge and passed my physical!"

"Oh?" said Nan, startled. "It happened awfully fast, didn't it? I didn't think you were going to plunge right in."

"What's there to wait for?"

"Well—I don't know. I mean, how do you know what you're getting into? You've never worked for anybody but yourself, and don't know anything about getting along in a huge organization. I knew you were going to talk to the Ilium people about a job, but I thought you planned to stick with the paper another year, anyway."

"In another year I'll be thirty, Nan."

"Well?"

"That's pretty old to be starting a career in industry. There are guys my age here who've been working their way up for ten years. That's pretty stiff competition, and it'll be that much stiffer a year from now. And how do we know Jason will still want to buy the paper a year from now?" Ed Jason was David's assistant, a recent college graduate whose father wanted to buy the paper for him. "And this job that opened up today in publicity won't be open a year from now, Nan. Now was the time to switch—this afternoon!"

Nan sighed. "I suppose. But it doesn't seem like you. The Works are fine for some people; they seem to thrive on that life. But you've always been so free. And you love the paper—you know you do."

"I do," said David, "and it'll break my heart to let it go. It was a swell thing to do when we had no kids, but it's a shaky living now—with the kids to educate and all."

"But, hon," said Nan, "the paper is making money."

"It could fold like that," said David, snapping his fingers. "A daily could come in with a one-page insert of Dorset news,

or—"

"Dorset likes its little paper too much to let that happen. They like you and the job you're doing too much."

David nodded. "What about ten years from now?"

"What about ten years from now in the Works? What about ten years from now anywhere?"

"It's a better bet that the Works will still be here. I haven't got the right to take long chances any more, Nan, not with a big family counting on me."

"It won't be a very happy big family, darling, if you're not doing what you want to do. I want you to go on being happy the way you have been—driving around the countryside, getting news and talking and selling ads; coming home and writing what you want to write, what you believe in. You in the Works!"

"It's what I've got to do."

"All right, if you say so. I've had my say."

"It's still journalism, high-grade journalism," said David.

"Just don't sell the paper to Jason right away. Put him in charge, but let's wait a month or so, please?"

"No sense in waiting, but if you really want to, all right." David held up a brochure he'd been handed after his physical examination was completed. "Listen to this, Nan: under the company Security Package, I get ten dollars a day for hospital expenses in case of illness, full pay for twenty-six weeks, a hundred dollars for special hospital expenses. I get life insurance for about half what it would cost on the outside. For whatever I put into government bonds under the payroll-savings plan, the company will give me a five per cent bonus in company stock—twelve years from now. I get two weeks' vacation with pay each year, and after fifteen years, I get three weeks. Get free membership in the company country club. After twenty-five years, I'll be eligible for a pension of at least a hundred and twenty-five dollars a month, and much more if I rise in the organization and stick with it for more than twenty-five years!"

"Good heavens!" said Nan.

"I'd be a damn fool to pass that up, Nan."

"I still wish you'd waited until the little girls and I were home and settled, and you got used to them. I feel you were panicked into this."

"No, no—this is it, Nan. Give the little girls a kiss apiece for me. I've got to go now, and report to my new supervisor."

"Your what?"

"Supervisor."

"Oh. I thought that's what you said, but I couldn't be sure."

"Good-by, Nan."

"Good-by, David."

David clipped his badge to his lapel, and stepped out of the hospital and onto the hot asphalt floor of the world within the fences of the Works. Dull thunder came from the buildings around him, a truck honked at him, and a cinder blew in his eye. He dabbed at the cinder with a corner of his handkerchief and finally got it out. When his vision was restored, he looked about himself for Building 31, where his new office and supervisor were. Four busy streets fanned out from where he stood, and each stretched seemingly to infinity.

He stopped a passerby who was in less of a desperate hurry than the rest. "Could you tell me, please, how to find Building 31, Mr. Flammer's office?"

The man he asked was old and bright-eyed, apparently getting as much pleasure from the clangor and smells and nervous activity of the Works as David would have gotten from April in Paris. He squinted at David's badge and then at his face. "Just starting out, are you?"

"Yes sir. My first day."

"What do you know about that?" The old man shook his head wonderingly, and winked. "Just starting out. Building 31? Well, sir, when I first came to work here in 1899, you could see Building 31 from here, with nothing between us and it but mud. Now it's all built up. See that water tank up there, about a quarter of a mile? Well, Avenue 17 branches off there, and you follow that almost to the end, then cut across the tracks, and—Just starting out, eh? Well, I'd better walk you up there. Came here for just a minute to talk to the pension folks, but that can wait. I'd enjoy the walk."

"Thank you."

"Fifty-year man, I was," he said proudly, and he led David up avenues and alleys, across tracks, over ramps and through tunnels, through buildings filled with spitting, whining, grumbling machinery, and down corridors with green walls and numbered black doors.

"Can't be a fifty-year man no more," said the old man pityingly. "Can't come to work until you're eighteen nowadays, and you got to retire when you're sixty-five." He poked his thumb under his lapel to make a small gold button protrude. On it was the number "50" superimposed on the company trademark. "Something none of you youngsters can look forward to wearing some day, no matter how much you want one."

"Very nice button," said David.

The old man pointed out a door. "Here's Flammer's office. Keep your mouth shut till you find out who's who and what *they* think. Good luck."

Lou Flammer's secretary was not at her desk, so David walked to the door of the inner office and knocked.

"Yes?" said a man's voice sweetly. "Please come in."

David opened the door. "Mr. Flammer?"

Lou Flammer was a short, fat man in his early thirties. He beamed at David. "What can I do to help you?"

"I'm David Potter, Mr. Flammer."

Flammer's Santa-Claus-like demeanor decayed. He leaned back, propped his feet on his desk top, and stuffed a cigar, which he'd concealed in his cupped hand, into his large mouth. "Hell—thought you were a scoutmaster." He looked at his desk clock, which was mounted in a miniature of the company's newest automatic dishwasher. "Boy scouts touring the Works. Supposed to stop in here fifteen minutes ago for me to give 'em a talk on scouting and industry. Fifty-six per cent of Federal Apparatus' executives were eagle scouts."

David started to laugh, but found himself doing it all alone, and he stopped. "Amazing figure," he said.

"It *is*," said Flammer judiciously. "Says something for scouting and something for industry. Now, before I tell you where your desk is, I'm supposed to explain the rating-sheet system. That's what the Manuals say. Dilling tell you about that?"

"Not that I recall. There was an awful lot of information all at once."

"Well, there's nothing much to it," said Flammer. "Every six months a rating sheet is made out on you, to let you and to let us know just where you stand, and what sort of progress you've been making. Three people who've been close to your work make out independent ratings on you, and then all the information is brought together on a master copy—with carbons for you, me, and Personnel, and the original for the head of the Advertising and Sales Promotion Division. It's very helpful for everybody, you most of all, if you take it the right way." He waved a rating sheet before David. "See? Blanks for appearance, loyalty, promptness, initiative, cooperativeness—things like that. You'll make out rating sheets on other people, too, and whoever does the rating is anonymous."

"I see." David felt himself reddening with resentment. He fought the emotion, telling himself his reaction was a small-town man's—and that it would do him good to learn to think as a member of a great, efficient team.

"Now about pay, Potter," said Flammer, "there'll never be any point in coming in to ask me for a raise. That's all done on the basis of the rating sheets and the salary curve." He rummaged through his drawers and found a graph, which he spread out on his desk. "Here— now you see this curve? Well, it's the average salary curve for men with college educations in the company. See— you can follow it on up. At thirty, the average man makes this much; at forty, this much—and so on. Now, this curve above it shows what men with real growth potential can make. See? It's a little higher and curves upward a little faster. You're how old?"

"Twenty-nine," said David, trying to see what the salary figures were that ran along one side of the graph. Flammer saw him doing it, and pointedly kept them hidden with his forearm.

"Uh-huh." Flammer wet the tip of a pencil with his tongue, and drew a small "x" on the graph, squarely astride the average man's curve. "There *you* are!"

David looked at the mark, and then followed the curve with his eyes across the paper, over little bumps, up gentle slopes, along desolate plateaus, until it died abruptly at the margin which represented age sixty-five.

The graph left no questions to be asked and was deaf to argument. David looked from it to the human being he would also be dealing with. "You had a weekly once, did you, Mr. Flammer?"

Flammer laughed. "In my naive, idealistic youth, Potter, I sold ads to feed stores, gathered gossip, set type, and wrote editorials that were going to save the world, by God."

David smiled admiringly, "What a circus, eh?"

"Circus?" said Flammer. "Freak show, maybe. It's a good way to grow up fast. Took me about six months to find out I was killing myself for peanuts, that a little guy couldn't even save a village three blocks long, and that the world wasn't worth saving anyway. So I started looking out for Number One. Sold out to a chain, came down here, and here I am."

The telephone rang. "Yes?" said Flammer sweetly. "Puh-*bliss*-itee." His benign smile faded. "No. You're kidding, aren't you? Where? Really—this is no gag? All right, Lord! What a time for this to happen. I haven't got anybody here, and I can't get away on account of the goddam boy scouts." He hung up. "Potter—you've got your first assignment. There's a deer loose in the Works!"

"Deer?"

"Don't know how he got in, but he's in. Plumber went to fix a drinking fountain out at the softball diamond across from Building 217, and flushed a deer out from under the bleachers. Now they got him cornered up around the metallurgy lab." He stood and hammered on his desk. "Murder! The story will go all over the country, Potter. Talk about human interest. Front page! Of all the times for Al Tappin to be out at the Ashtabula Works, taking pictures of a new viscometer they cooked up out there! All right—I'll call up a hack photographer downtown, Potter, and get him to meet you out by the metallurgy lab. You get the story and see that he gets the right shots. Okay?"

He led David into the hallway. "Just go back the way you came, turn left instead of right at fractional horsepower motors, cut through hydraulic engineering, catch bus eleven on Avenue 9, and it'll take you right there. After you get the story and pictures, we'll get them cleared by the law division, the plant security officer, our department head and buildings and grounds, and shoot them right out. Now get going. That deer isn't on the payroll—he isn't going to wait for you. Come to work today—tomorrow your work will be on every front page in the country, if we can get it approved. The name of the photographer you're going to meet is McGarvey. Got it? You're in the big time now, Potter. We'll all be watching." He shut the door behind David.

David found himself trotting down the hall, down a stairway, and into an alley, brushing roughly past persons in a race against time. Many turned to watch the purposeful young man with admiration.

On and on he strode, his mind seething with information: *Flammer, Building 31; deer, metallurgy lab; photographer. Al Tappin. No. Al Tappin in Ashtabula. Flenny the hack photographer. No. McCammer. No. McCammer is new supervisor. Fifty-six per cent eagle scouts. Deer by viscometer laboratory. No. Viscometer in Ashtabula. Call Danner, new supervisor, and get instructions right. Three weeks' vacation after fifteen years. Danner not new supervisor. Anyway, new supervisor in Building 319. No. Fanner in Building 39981983319.*

David stopped, blocked by a grimy window at the end of a blind alley. All he knew was that he'd never been there before, that his memory had blown a gasket, and that the deer was not on the payroll. The air in the alley was thick with tango music and the stench of scorched insulation. David scrubbed away some of the crust on the window with his handkerchief, praying for a glimpse of something that made sense.

Inside were ranks of women at benches, rocking their heads in time to the music, and dipping soldering irons into great nests of colored wires that crept past them on endless belts. One of them looked up and saw David, and winked in tango rhythm. David fled.

At the mouth of the alley, he stopped a man and asked him if he'd heard anything about a deer in the Works. The man shook his head and looked at David oddly, making David aware of how frantic he must look. "I heard it was out by the lab," David said more calmly.

"Which lab?" said the man.

"That's what I'm not sure of," said David. "There's more than one?"

"Chemical lab?" said the man. "Materials testing lab? Print lab? Insulation lab?"

"No—I don't think it's any of those," said David.

"Well, I could stand here all afternoon naming labs, and probably not hit the right one. Sorry, I've got to go. You don't know what building they've got the differential analyzer in, do you?"

"Sorry," said David. He stopped several other people, none of whom knew anything about the deer, and he tried to retrace his steps to the office of his supervisor, whatever his name was. He was swept this way and that by the currents of the Works, stranded in backwaters, sucked back into the main stream, and his mind was more and more numbed, and the mere reflexes of self-preservation were more and more in charge.

He chose a building at random, and walked inside for a momentary respite from the summer heat, and was deafened by the clangor of steel sheets being cut and punched, being smashed into strange shapes by great hammers that dropped out of the smoke and dust overhead. A hairy, heavily muscled man was seated near the door on a wooden stool, watching a giant lathe turn a bar of steel the size of a silo.

David now had the idea of going through a company phone directory until he recognized his supervisor's name. He called to the machinist from a few feet away, but his voice was lost in the din. He tapped the man's shoulder. "Telephone around here?"

The man nodded. He cupped his hands around David's ear, and shouted. "Up that, and through the—" Down crashed a hammer. "Turn left and keep going until you—" An overhead crane dropped a stack of steel plates. "Four doors down from there is it. Can't miss it."

David, his ears ringing and his head aching, walked into the street again and chose another door. Here was peace and air conditioning. He was in the lobby of an auditorium, where a group of men were examining a box studded with dials and switches that was spotlighted and mounted on a revolving platform.

"Please, miss," he said to a receptionist by the door, "could you tell me where I could find a telephone?"

"It's right around the corner, sir," she said. "But I'm afraid no one is permitted here today but the crystallographers. Are you with them?"

"Yes," said David.

"Oh—well, come right in. Name?"

He told her, and a man sitting next to her lettered it on a badge. The badge was hung on his chest, and David headed for the telephone. A grinning, bald, big-toothed man, wearing a badge that said, "Stan Dunkel, Sales," caught him and steered him to the display.

"Dr. Potter," said Dunkel, "I ask you: is that the way to build a X-ray spectrogoniometer, or is that the way to build an X-ray spectrogoniometer?"

"Yes," said David. "That's the way, all right."

"Martini, Dr. Potter?" said a maid, offering a tray.

David emptied a Martini in one gloriously hot, stinging gulp.

"What features do you want in an X-ray spectrogoniometer, Doctor?" said Dunkel.

"It should be sturdy, Mr. Dunkel," said David, and he left Dunkel there, pledging his reputation that there wasn't a sturdier one on earth.

In the phone booth, David had barely got through the telephone directory's A's before the name of the supervisor miraculously returned to his consciousness: *Flammer!* He found the number and dialed.

"Mr. Flammer's office," said a woman.

"Could I speak to him, please? This is David Potter."

"Oh—Mr. Potter. Well, Mr. Flammer is somewhere out in the Works now, but he left a message for you. He said there's an added twist on the deer story. When they catch the deer, the venison is going to be used at the Quarter-Century Club picnic."

"Quarter-Century Club?" said David.

"Oh, that's really something, Mr. Potter. It's for people who've been with the company twenty-five years or more. Free drinks and cigars, and just the best of everything. They have a wonderful time."

"Anything else about the deer?"

"Nothing he hasn't already told you," she said, and she hung up.

David Potter, with a third Martini in his otherwise empty stomach, stood in front of the auditorium and looked both ways for a deer.

"But our X-ray spectogoniometer *is* sturdy, Dr. Potter," Stan Dunkel called to him from the auditorium steps.

Across the street was a patch of green, bordered by hedges. David pushed through the hedges into the outfield of a softball diamond. He crossed it and went behind the bleachers, where there was cool shade, and he sat down with his back to a wiremesh fence which separated one end of the Works from a deep pine woods. There were two gates in the fence, but both were wired shut.

David was going to sit there for just a moment, long enough to get his nerve back, to take bearings. Maybe he could leave a message for Flammer, saying he'd suddenly fallen ill, which was essentially true, or—

"There he goes!" cried somebody from the other side of the diamond. There were gleeful cries, shouted orders, the sounds of men running.

A deer with broken antlers dashed under the bleachers, saw David, and ran frantically into the open again along the fence. He ran with a limp, and his reddish-brown coat was streaked with soot and grease.

"Easy now! Don't rush him! Just keep him there. Shoot into the woods, not the Works."

David came out from under the bleachers to see a great semicircle of men, several ranks deep, closing in slowly on the corner of fence in which the deer was at bay. In the front rank were a dozen company policemen with drawn pistols. Other members of the posse carried sticks and rocks and lariats hastily fashioned from wire.

The deer pawed the grass, and bucked, and jerked its broken antlers in the direction of the crowd.

"Hold it!" shouted a familiar voice. A company limousine rumbled across the diamond to the back of the crowd. Leaning out of a window was Lou Flammer, David's supervisor. "Don't shoot until we get a picture of him alive," commanded Flammer. He pulled a photographer out of the limousine, and pushed him into the front rank.

Flammer saw David standing alone by the fence, his back to a gate. "Good boy, Potter," called Flammer. "Right on the ball! Photographer got lost, and I had to bring him here myself."

The photographer fired his flash bulbs. The deer bucked and sprinted along the fence toward David. David unwired the gate, opened it wide. A second later the deer's white tail was flashing through the woods and gone.

The profound silence was broken first by the whistling of a switch engine and then by the click of a latch as David stepped into the woods and closed the gate behind him. He didn't look back.

Exercises

1. Why is the protagonist named David?
2. Compare the company benefits with those David might have as the publisher of a small-town newspaper. What point is the author making about American life and private enterprise?
3. What was the significance of meeting a "fifty-year man"?
4. What is implied by Mr. Flammer's statement that 56 percent of the executives were Eagle scouts?
5. What are the implications of the categories on the rating sheets?
6. Review the different activities encountered by David as he looks for the deer. In which place would you like to work? Why or why not?
7. What will the firm do with the deer after it is killed? What does this imply?
8. Consider the significance of the scene with pursuers in full cry after the wounded deer. Is a deer a dangerous animal?
9. Would *you* let the deer go? Why or why not?

Flight on the Wind
from HOUSE MADE OF DAWN
N. Scott Momaday (b. 1934)

In *House Made of Dawn,* winner of the Pulitzer Prize in 1969, young Abel returns to tribal life, wondering if he can resume the ancient ways after living like an Anglo in the Army. The seemingly endless conflict of Anglo and Indian ways is symbolized by the excerpt given below in which the captured, shivering eagle represents an Indian view of life in America.

He had seen a strange thing, an eagle overhead with its talons closed upon a snake. It was an awful, holy sight, full of magic and meaning.

The Eagle Watchers Society was the sixth to go into the kiva at the summer and autumn rain retreats. It was an important society, and it stood apart from the others in a certain way. This difference—this superiority—had come about a long time ago. Before the middle of the last century there was received into the population of the town a small group of immigrants from the Tanoan city of Bahkyula, a distance of seventy or eighty miles to the east. These immigrants were a wretched people, for they had experienced great suffering. Their land bordered upon the Southern Plains, and for many years they had been an easy mark for marauding bands of buffalo hunters and thieves. They had endured every kind of persecution until one day they could stand no more and their spirit broke. They gave themselves up to despair and were then at the mercy of the first alien wind. But it was not a human enemy that overcame them at last; it was a plague. They were struck down by so deadly a disease that, when the epidemic abated, there were fewer than twenty survivors in all. And this remainder, too, should surely have perished among the ruins of Bahkyula had it not been for these *patrones,* these distant relatives who took them in at the certain risk of their own lives and the lives of their children and grandchildren. It is said that the cacique himself went out to welcome and escort the visitors in. The people of the town must have looked narrowly at those stricken souls who walked slowly towards them, wild in their eyes with grief and desperation. The Bahkyush immigrants brought with them little more than the clothes on their backs, but even in this moment of deep hurt and humiliation, they thought of themselves as a people. They carried three things that should serve thereafter to signal who they were: a sacred flute; the bull mask of Pecos; and the little wooden statue of their patroness *Maria de los Angeles,* whom they called Porcingula. Now, after the intervening years and generations, the ancient blood of this forgotten tribe still ran in the veins of men.

The Eagle Watchers Society was the principal ceremonial organization of the Bahkyush. Its chief, Patiestewa, and all its members were direct descendants of those old men and women who had made that journey along the edge of oblivion. There was a look about these men, even now. It was as if, conscious of having come so close to extinction, they had got a keener sense of humility than their benefactors, and paradoxically a greater sense of pride. Both attributes could be seen in such a man as old Patiestewa. He was hard, and he appeared to have seen more of life than had other men. In their uttermost peril long ago, the Bahkyush had been fashioned into seers and soothsayers. They had acquired a tragic sense, which gave to them as a race so much dignity and bearing. They were medicine men; they were rainmakers and eagle hunters.

He was not thinking of the eagles. He had been walking since daybreak down from the mountain where that year he had broken a horse for the rancher John Raymond. By the middle of the morning he was on the rim of the Valle Grande, a great volcanic crater that lay high up on the western slope of the range. It was the right eye of the earth, held open to the sun. Of all the places that he knew, this valley alone could reflect the great spatial majesty of the sky. It was scooped out of the dark peaks like the well of a great, gathering storm, deep umber and blue and smoke-colored. The view across the diameter was magnificent; it was an unbelievably great expanse. As many times as he had been there in the past, each first new sight of it always brought him up short, and he had to catch his breath. Just there, it seemed, a strange and brilliant light lay upon the world, and all the objects in the landscape were washed clean and set away in the distance. In the morning sunlight the Valle Grande was dappled with the shadows of clouds and vibrant with rolling winter grass. The clouds were always there, huge, sharply described, and shining in the pure air. But the great feature of the valley was its size. It was too great for the eye to hold, strangely beautiful and full of distance. Such vastness makes for illusion, a kind of illusion that comprehends reality, and where it exists there is always wonder and exhilaration. He looked at the facets of a boulder that lay balanced on the edge of the land, and the first thing beyond, the vague, misty field out of which it stood, was the floor of the valley itself, pale and blue-green, miles away. He shifted the focus of his gaze, and he could just make out the clusters of dots that were cattle grazing along the river in the faraway plain.

Then he saw the eagles across the distance, two of them, riding low in the depths and rising diagonally towards him. He did not know what they were at first, and he stood watching them, their far, silent flight erratic and wild in the bright morning. They rose and swung across the skyline, veering close at last, and he knelt down behind the rock, dumb with pleasure and excitement, holding on to them with his eyes.

They were golden eagles, a male and a female, in their mating flight. They were cavorting, spinning and spiralling on the cold, clear columns of air, and they were beautiful. They swooped and hovered, leaning on the air, and swung close together, feinting and screaming with delight. The female was full-grown, and the span of her broad wings was greater than any man's height. There was a fine flourish to her motion: she was deceptively, incredibly fast, and her pivots and wheels were wide and full-blown. But her great weight was streamlined, perfectly controlled. She carried a rattlesnake; it hung shining from her feet, limp and curving out in the trail of her flight. Suddenly her wings and tail fanned, catching full on the wind, and for an instant she was still, widespread and spectral in the blue, while her mate flared past and away, turning round in the distance to look for her. Then she began to beat upward at an angle from the rim until she was small in the sky, and she let go of the snake. It fell, slowly, writhing and rolling, floating out like a bit of silver thread against the wide backdrop of the land. She held still above, buoyed up on the cold current, her crop and hackles gleaming like copper in the sun. The male swerved and sailed. He was younger than she and a little more than half as large. He was quicker, tighter in his moves. He let the carrion drift by; then suddenly he gathered himself and stooped, sliding down in a blur of motion to the strike. He hit the snake in the head, with not the slightest deflection of his course or speed, cracking its long body like a whip. Then he rolled and swung upward in a great pendulum arc, riding out his momentum. At the top of his glide he let go of the snake in turn, but the female did not go for it. Instead she soared out over the plain, nearly out of sight, like a mote receding into the haze of the far mountain. The male followed, and he watched them go, straining to see, saw them veer once, dip and disappear.

Now there was the business of the society. It was getting on towards the end of November, and the eagle hunters were getting ready to set forth to the mountains. He brooded for a time, full of a strange longing; then one day he went to old Patiestewa and told him of what he had seen. "I think you had better let me go," he said. The old chief closed his eyes and thought about it for a long time. Then he answered: "Yes, I had better let you go."

The next day the Bahkyush eagle watchers started out on foot he among them, northward through the canyon and into the high timber beyond. They were gone for days, holding up here and there at the holy places where they must pray and make their offerings. Early in the morning they came out of the trees on the edge of the Valle Grande. The land fell and reached away in the early light as far as the eye could see, the hills folding together and the gray grass rolling in the plain, and they began the descent. At midmorning they came to the lower meadows in the basin. It was clear and cold, and the air was thin and sharp like a shard of glass. They needed bait, and they circled out and apart, forming a ring. When the circle was formed, they converged slowly towards the center, clapping and calling out in a high, flat voice that carried only a little way. And as they closed, rabbits began to jump up from the grass and bound. They got away at first, many of them, while the men were still a distance apart, but gradually the ring grew small and the rabbits crept to the center and hid away in the brush. Now and then one of them tried to break away, and the nearest man threw his stick after it. These weapons were small curved clubs, and they were thrown with deadly accuracy by the eagle hunters, so that when the ring was of a certain size and the men only a few feet apart, very few of the animals got away.

He bent close to the ground, his arm cocked and shaking with tension. A great jackrabbit buck bounded from the grass, straight past him. It struck the ground beyond and sprang again, nearly thirty feet through the air. He spun round and hurled the stick. It struck the jackrabbit a glancing blow just as it bounded again, and it slumped in the air and fell heavily to the ground.

The clapping and calling had stopped. He could feel his heart beating and the sweat growing cold on his skin. There was something like remorse or disappointment now that the rabbits were still and strewn about on the ground. He picked one of the dead animals from the brush—it was warm and soft, its eyes shining like porcelain, full of the dull lustre of death—then the great buck, which was not dead but only stunned and frozen with fear. He felt the warm living weight of it in his hands; it was brittle with life, taut with hard, sinewy strength.

When he had bound the bait together and placed it in the sack, he gathered bunches of tall grass and cut a number of evergreen boughs from a thicket in the plain; these he tied in a bundle and carried in a sling on his back. He went to the river and washed his head in order to purify himself. When all was ready, he waved to the others and started off alone to the cliffs. When he came to the first plateau he rested and looked across the valley. The sun was high, and all around there was a pale, dry uniformity of light, a winter glare on the clouds and peaks. He could see a crow circling low in the distance. Higher on the land, where a great slab of white rock protruded from the mountain, he saw the eagle-hunt house; he headed for it. The house was a small tower of stone, built round a pit, hollow and open at the top. Near it was a shrine, a stone shelf in which there was a slight depression. There he placed a prayer offering. He got into the house, and with boughs he made a latticework of beams across the top and covered it with grass. When it was finished there was a small opening at the center. Through it he raised the rabbits and laid them down on the boughs. He could see here and there through the screen, but his line of vision was vertical, or nearly so, and his quarry would come from the sun. He began to sing, now and then calling out, low in his throat.

The eagles soared southward, high above the Valle Grande. They were almost too high to be seen. From their vantage point the land below reached away on either side to the long, crooked tributaries of the range; down the great open corridor to the south were the wooded slopes and the canyon, the desert and the far end of the earth bending on the sky. They caught sight of the rabbits and were deflected. They veered and banked, lowering themselves into the crater, gathering speed. By the time he knew of their presence, they were low and coming fast on either side of the pit, swooping with blinding speed. The male caught hold of the air and fell off, touching upon the face of the cliff in order to flush the rabbits, while the female hurtled in to take her prey on the run. Nothing happened; the rabbits did not move. She overshot the trap and screamed. She was enraged and she hurled herself around in the air. She swung back with a great clamor of her wings and fell with fury on the bait. He saw her the instant she struck. Her foot flashed out and one of her talons laid the jackrabbit open the length of its body. It stiffened and jerked, and her other foot took hold of its skull and crushed it. In that split second when the center of her weight touched down upon the trap he reached for her. His hands closed upon her legs and he drew her down with all of his strength. For one instant only did she recoil, splashing her great wings down upon the beams and boughs—and she very nearly broke from his grasp; but then she was down in the darkness of the well, hooded, and she was still.

At dusk he met with the other hunters in the plain. San Juanito, too, had got an eagle, but it was an aged male and poor by comparison. They gathered round the old eagle and spoke to it, bidding it return with their good will and sorrow to the eagles of the crags. They fixed a prayer plume to its leg and let it go. He watched it back away and crouch on the ground, glaring, full of fear and suspicion. Then it took leave of the ground and beat upward, clattering through the still shadows of the valley. It gathered speed, driving higher and higher until it reached the shafts of reddish-gold final light that lay like bars across the crater. The light caught it up and set a dark blaze upon it. It levelled off and sailed. Then it was gone from sight, but he looked after it for a time. He could see it still in the mind's eye and hear in his memory the awful whisper of its flight on the wind. He felt the great weight of the bird which he held in the sack. The dusk was fading quickly into night, and the others could not see that his eyes were filled with tears.

That night, while the others ate by the fire, he stole away to look at the great bird. He drew the sack open; the bird shivered, he thought, and drew itself up. Bound and helpless, his eagle seemed drab and shapeless in the moonlight, too large and ungainly for flight. The sight of it filled him with shame and disgust. He took hold of its throat in the darkness and cut off its breath.

Exercises

1. What is symbolized by the image of an eagle holding a snake?
2. Consider the first full paragraph. Could this be a capsule history of what happened to Native Americans?
3. What kinds of feelings are invoked by the descriptions of the land? Can cities be described in this general manner?
4. Consider the mating flight of the two eagles and what this symbolizes.
5. Why was the old eagle freed? Why was the female killed?

A SORROWFUL WOMAN
Gail Godwin (b. 1937)

The following short story is a study of the gradual disintegration of a human personality. In keeping with the "once upon a time" lead, the style is similar to a fairy tale except that "happily ever after" does not happen. The reader should consider the monotonously repetitive tasks taken over by the husband and later shared with the live-in girl and compare these with the usual tasks of men in their jobs at the office or wherever. Then, consider how all of this relates to the final "legacy" of food, laundry, and sonnets.

Once upon a time there was a wife and mother one too many times

One winter evening she looked at them: the husband durable, receptive, gentle; the child a tender golden three. The sight of them made her so sad and sick she did not want to see them ever again.

She told the husband these thoughts. He was attuned to her; he understood such things. He said he understood. What would she like him to do? "If you could put the boy to bed and read him the story about the monkey who ate too many bananas, I would be grateful." "Of course," he said. "Why, that's a pleasure." And he sent her off to bed.

The next night it happened again. Putting the warm dishes away in the cupboard, she turned and saw the child's grey eyes approving her movements. In the next room was the man, his chin sunk in the open collar of his favorite wool shirt. He was dozing after her good supper. The shirt was the grey of the child's trusting gaze. She began yelping without tears, retching in between. The man woke in alarm and carried her in his arms to bed. The boy followed them up the stairs, saying, "It's all right, Mommy," but this made her scream. "Mommy is sick," the father said, "go and wait for me in your room."

The husband undressed her, abandoning her only long enough to root beneath the eiderdown for her flannel gown. She stood naked except for her bra, which hung by one strap down the side of her body; she had not the impetus to shrug it off. She looked down at the right nipple, shriveled with chill, and thought, How absurd, a vertical bra. "If only there were instant sleep," she said, hiccuping, and the husband bundled her into the gown and went out and came back with a sleeping draught

guaranteed swift. She was to drink a little glass of cognac followed by a big glass of dark liquid and afterwards there was just time to say Thank you and could you get him a clean pair of pajamas out of the laundry, it came back today.

The next day was Sunday and the husband brought her breakfast in bed and let her sleep until it grew dark again. He took the child for a walk, and when they returned, red-cheeked and boisterous, the father made supper. She heard them laughing in the kitchen. He brought her up a tray of buttered toast, celery sticks and black bean soup. "I am the luckiest woman," she said, crying real tears. "Nonsense," he said. "You need a rest from us," and went to prepare the sleeping draught, find the child's pajamas, select the story for the night.

She got up on Monday and moved about the house till noon. The boy, delighted to have her back, pretended he was a vicious tiger and followed her from room to room, growling and scratching. Whenever she came close, he would growl and scratch at her. One of his sharp little claws ripped her flesh, just above the wrist, and together they paused to watch a thin red line materialize on the inside of her pale arm and spill over in little beads. "Go away," she said. She got herself upstairs and locked the door. She called the husband's office and said, "I've locked myself away from him. I'm afraid." The husband told her in his richest voice to lie down, take it easy, and he was already on the phone to call one of the babysitters they often employed. Shortly after, she heard the girl let herself in, heard the girl coaxing the frightened child to come and play.

After supper several nights later, she hit the child. She had known she was going to do it when the father would see. "I'm sorry," she said, collapsing on the floor. The weeping child had run to hide. "What has happened to me, I'm not myself anymore." The man picked her tenderly from the floor and looked at her with much concern. "Would it help if we got, you know, a girl in? We could fix the room downstairs. I want you to feel freer," he said, understanding these things. "We have the money for a girl. I want you to think about it."

And now the sleeping draught was a nightly thing, she did not have to ask. He went down to the kitchen to mix it, he set it nightly beside her bed. The little glass and the big one, amber and deep rich brown, the flannel gown and the eiderdown.

The man put out the word and found the perfect girl. She was young, dynamic and not pretty. "Don't bother with the room, I'll fix it up myself." Laughing, she employed her thousand energies. She painted the room white, fed the child lunch, read edifying books, raced the boy to the mailbox, hung her own watercolors on the fresh-painted walls, made spinach soufflé, cleaned a spot from the mother's coat, made them all laugh, danced in stocking feet to music in the white room after reading the child to sleep. She knitted dresses for herself and played chess with the husband. She washed and set the mother's soft ash-blonde hair and gave her neck rubs, offered to.

The woman now spent her winter afternoons in the big bedroom. She made a fire in the hearth and put on slacks and an old sweater she had loved at school, and sat in the big chair and stared out the window at snow-ridden branches, or went away into long novels about other people moving through other winters.

The girl brought the child in twice a day, once in the later afternoon when he would tell of his day, all of it tumbling out quickly because there was not much time, and before he went to bed. Often now, the man took his wife to dinner. He made a courtship ceremony of it, inviting her beforehand so she could get used to the idea. They dressed and were beautiful together again and went out into the frosty night. Over candlelight he would say, "I think you are better, you know." "Perhaps I am," she would murmur. "You look . . . like a cloistered queen," he said once, his voice breaking curiously.

One afternoon the girl brought the child into the bedroom. "We've been out playing in the park. He found something he wants to give you, a surprise." The little boy approached her, smiling mysteriously. He placed his cupped hands in hers and left a live dry thing that spat brown juice in her palm and leapt away. She screamed and wrung her hands to be rid of the brown juice. "Oh, it was only a grasshopper," said the girl. Nimbly she crept to the edge of a curtain, did a quick knee bend and reclaimed the creature, led the boy competently from the room.

So the husband came alone. "I have explained to the boy," he said. "And we are doing fine. We are managing." He squeezed his wife's pale arm and put the two glasses on her table. After he had gone, she sat looking at the arm.

"I'm afraid it's come to that," she said. "Just push the notes under the door; I'll read them. And don't forget to leave the draught outside."

The man sat for a long time with his head in his hands. Then he rose and went away from her. She heard him in the kitchen where he mixed the draught in batches now to last a week at a time, storing it in a corner of the cupboard. She heard him come back, leave the big glass and the little one outside on the floor.

Outside her window the snow was melting from the branches, there were more people on the streets. She brushed her hair a lot and seldom read anymore. She sat in her window and brushed her hair for hours, and saw a boy fall off his new bicycle again and again, a dog chasing a squirrel, an old woman peek slyly over her shoulder and then extract a parcel from a garbage can.

In the evening she read the notes they slipped under her door. The child could not write, so he drew and sometimes painted his. The notes were painstaking at first; the man and boy offering the final strength of their day to her. But sometimes, when they seemed to have had a bad day, there were only hurried scrawls.

One night, when the husband's note had been extremely short, loving but short, and there had been nothing from the boy, she stole out of her room as she often did to get more supplies, but crept upstairs instead and stood outside their doors, listening to the regular breathing of the man and boy asleep. She hurried back to her room and drank the draught.

She woke earlier now. It was spring, there were birds. She listened for sounds of the man and the boy eating breakfast; she listened for the roar of the motor when they drove away. One beautiful noon, she went out to look at her kitchen in the daylight. Things were changed. He had bought some new dish towels. Had the old ones worn out? The canisters seemed closer to the sink. She inspected the cupboard and saw new things among the old. She got out flour, baking powder, salt, milk (he bought a different brand of butter), and baked a loaf of bread and left it cooling on the table.

The force of the two joyful notes slipped under her door that evening pressed her into the corner of the little room; she had hardly space to breathe. As soon as possible, she drank the draught.

Now the days were too short. She was always busy. She woke with the first bird. Worked till the sun set. No time for hair brushing. Her fingers raced the hours.

Finally, in the nick of time, it was finished one late afternoon. Her veins pumped and her forehead sparkled. She went to the cupboard, took what was hers, closed herself into the little white room and brushed her hair for a while.

"The girl upsets me," said the woman to her husband. He sat frowning on the side of the bed he had not entered for so long. "I'm sorry, but there it is." The husband stroked his creased brow and said he was sorry too. He really did not know what they would do without that treasure of a girl. "Why don't you stay here with me in bed," the woman said.

Next morning she fired the girl who cried and said, "I loved the little boy, what will become of him now?" But the mother turned away her face and the girl took down the watercolors from the walls, sheathed the records she had danced to and went away.

"I don't know what we'll do. It's all my fault, I know. I'm such a burden, I know that."

"Let me think. I'll think of something." (Still understanding these things.)

"I know you will. You always do," she said.

With great care he rearranged his life. He got up hours early, did the shopping, cooked the breakfast, took the boy to nursery school. "We will manage," he said, "until you're better, however long that is." He did his work, collected the boy from the school, came home and made the supper, washed the dishes, got the child to bed. He managed everything. One evening, just as she was on the verge of swallowing her draught, there was a timid knock on her door. The little boy came in wearing his pajamas. "Daddy has fallen asleep on my bed and I can't get in. There's not room."

Very sedately she left her bed and went to the child's room. Things were much changed. Books were rearranged, toys. He'd done some new drawings. She came as a visitor to her son's room, wakened the father and helped him to bed. "Ah, he shouldn't have bothered you," said the man, leaning on his wife. "I've told him not to." He dropped into his own bed and fell asleep with a moan. Meticulously she undressed him. She folded and hung his clothes. She covered his body with the bedclothes. She flicked off the light that shone in his face.

The next day she moved her things into the girl's white room. She put her hairbrush on the dresser; she put a note pad and pen beside the bed. She stocked the little room with cigarettes, books, bread and cheese. She didn't need much.

At first the husband was dismayed. But he was receptive to her needs. He understood these things. "Perhaps the best thing is for you to follow it through," he said. "I want to be big enough to contain whatever you must do."

All day long she stayed in the white room. She was a young queen, a virgin in a tower; she was the previous inhabitant, the girl with all the energies. She tried these personalities on like costumes, then discarded them. The room had a new view of streets she'd never seen that way before. The sun hit the room in late afternoon and she took to brushing her hair in the sun. One day she decided to write a poem. "Perhaps a sonnet." She took up her pen and pad and began working from words that had lately lain in her mind. She had choices for the sonnet, ABAB or ABBA for a start. She pondered these possibilities until she tottered into a larger choice: she did not have to write a sonnet. Her poem could be six, eight, ten, thirteen lines, it could be any number of lines, and it did not even have to rhyme.

She put down the pen on top of the pad.

In the evenings, very briefly, she saw the two of them. They knocked on her door, a big knock and a little, and she would call Come in, and the husband would smile though he looked a bit tired, yet somehow this tiredness suited him. He would put her sleeping draught on the bedside table and say, "The boy and I have done all right today," and the child would kiss her. One night she tasted for the first time the power of his baby spit.

"I don't think I can see him anymore," she whispered sadly to the man. And the husband turned away, but recovered admirably and said, "Of course, I see."

The man and boy came home and found: five loaves of warm bread, a roast stuffed turkey, a glazed ham, three pies of different fillings, eight molds of the boy's favorite custard, two weeks' supply of fresh-laundered sheets and shirts and towels, two hand-knitted sweaters (both of the same grey color), a sheaf of marvelous watercolor beasts accompanied by mad and fanciful stories nobody could ever make up again, and a tablet full of love sonnets addressed to the man. The house smelled redolently of renewal and spring. The man ran to the little room, could not contain himself to knock, flung back the door.

"Look, Mommy is sleeping," said the boy. "She's tired from doing all our things again." He dawdled in a stream of the last sun for that day and watched his father roll tenderly back her eyelids, lay his ear softly to her breast, test the delicate bones of her wrist. The father put down his face into her fresh-washed hair.

"Can we eat the turkey for supper?" the boy asked.

Exercises

1. Itemize the steps in the "abnormal" behavior of the wife from the opening paragraph on. Does this progression appear to be inevitable? What might the husband have done to stop this deterioration?
2. Consider the husband's solution of a live-in girl. What does this tell us about the husband and about his attitude toward his wife?
3. What is the significance of each of the gifts that the wife left for her son and her husband?
4. Why was it necessary for the child to be a boy? Why not a girl? Consider the implications of the final sentence.

MAN THINKING ABOUT WOMAN
Don L. Lee (b. 1942)

The first work is a love poem that should, like all poetry, be read aloud, taking care to pause at the caesuras (blank spots) but not between lines. The pauses add even more tenderness to what is already a gentle, lyric love song.

some thing is lost in me,
like
the way you lose old thoughts   that
somehow seemed unlost at the right time.
i've not known it or you many days;   5
we met as friends with an absence of strangeness.
it was the month
that my lines got longer & my metaphors softer.
it was the week   that
i felt the city's narrow breezes rush about   10
me
looking for a place to disappear
as   i walked the clearway,
sure footed in used sandals screaming to be replaced
your empty shoes (except for used stockings)   15
partially hidden beneath the dresser
looked at me,
as i sat thoughtlessly   waiting
for your touch.
that day,   20
as your body rested upon my chest
i saw the shadow of the
window blinds   beam
across the unpainted ceiling
going somewhere   25
like the somewhere i was going
when
the clearness of yr/teeth,
& the scars on yr/legs stopped me.
your beauty: un-noticed by regular eyes   is   30
like   a blackbird resting
on a telephone wire   that moves
quietly with the wind.
a southwind.

In the second poem Don Lee speaks as a black poet in a manner comparable to the Blackstream artists discussed in chapter 25. "Burned out hair" refers to hair straightened by a hot comb while "nappy-headed" is natural hair. The first reference implies denial of a heritage and the second a violent activism that seems equally unpalatable. The use of lowercase letters possibly reflects the influence of writer Imamu Amiri Baraka (formerly LeRoi Jones), not e e cummings. It is here an effective way to maintain a murmering, low-keyed mood that actually underscores the tension.

MIXED SKETCHES
Don L. Lee (b. 1942)

u feel that way sometimes
wondering:
as a nine year old sister
with burned out hair oddly
smiles at you and sweetly calls you   5
brother.
u feel that way sometimes
wondering:
as a blackwoman & her 6 children
are burned out of their apartment with no place   10
to go & a nappy-headed nigger comes running thru
our neighborhood with a match in his hand cryin
revolution.
u feel that way sometimes
wondering: 15
seeing sisters in two hundred dollar wigs & suits
fastmoving in black clubs in late surroundings   talking
about the late thoughts in late language waiting for late
          men
that come in with, "i don't want to hear bout nothing   20
black tonight."
u feel that way sometimes
wondering:
while eating on newspaper tablecloths
& sleeping on clean bed sheets that couldn't   25
stop bed bugs   as black children watch their
mothers leave the special buses returning from
special neighborhoods
to clean their "own" unspecial homes.
u feel that way sometimes   30
wondering:
wondering, how did we survive?

Exercises

1. In "Man Thinking about Woman" what is
   implied by the progression of the words *days,
   month, week,* and *that day?* What is a *narrow
   breeze?* What were the actual circumstances of
   this encounter?
2. Why is the second poem titled "Mixed
   Sketches"? The poem implies that there are
   three responses to racism. What are they?

NIKKI-ROSA
Nikki Giovanni (b. 1943)

The following poem is autobiographical and the poet
did indeed become "famous or something." The
poem was written in 1968 during the latter days of violent protests but it is a proud, clear statement of
identity. Don Lee asks "how did we survive?" Nikki
Giovanni provides one cogent answer. Woodlawn, in
the poem, was a black suburb of Cincinnati, Ohio.

childhood remembrances are always a drag
if you're Black
you always remember things like living in Woodlawn
with no inside toilet

and if you become famous or something   5
they never talk about how happy you were to have your
          mother
all to your self and
how good the water felt when you got your bath from one
          of those
big tubs that folk in chicago barbecue in
and somehow when you talk about home   10
it never gets across how much you
understood their feelings
as the whole family attended meetings about Hollydale
and even though you remember
your biographers never understand   15
your father's pain as he sells his stock
and another dream goes
and though your're poor it isn't poverty that
concerns you
and though they fought a lot   20
it isn't your father's drinking that makes any difference
but only that everybody is together and you
and your sister have happy birthdays and very good
          christmasses
and I really hope no white person ever has cause to write
          about me
because they never understand Black love is Black
          wealth and they'll   25
probably talk about my hard childhood and never
          understand that
all the while I was quite happy.

Exercise

1. Are childhood remembrances "always a drag" if
   you are poor, white, and live in a slum, even if
   the slum is not a ghetto? How does black love
   differ from white love? In other words, is this a
   poem about racism or is it more about a loving
   family that produced a very fine American poet?

Summary

Time Chart for the Twentieth Century at the end of this
chapter provides an overview of our bewildering century of
violence and invention. The century has been one of interminable warfare, including the two most destructive wars
in human history, but there have also been remarkable
technological developments. Consider transportation, for
example. The Wright brothers flew the first heavier-than-air
flying machine in 1903. Thirty-one years later the jet engine
was invented and, eighteen years after that, commercial jets
were making the world much smaller. Goddard invented
the liquid fuel rocket in 1926, the Russians put Sputnik into
orbit twenty-one years later and, twelve years after that, an
American astronaut walked on the moon.

Communications technology also developed in a rush.
Twelve years after the beginning of commercial television
transcontinental television became a reality; a decade later
communication satellites were starting to beam television
to the entire world. We do indeed live in a Global Community with the possibility, no mattter how faint, of evolving
into a peaceful community in which human values will be
more important than material possessions and national ri-
valries. High tech makes this possible but only human
beings can make it a reality.

The Literature of Moving Images

Film can and should be studied as an art form but it is a medium that must be experienced, preferably in a theatre with an audience. With very few exceptions movies are made to make money in public showings before a mass audience. "Motion picture industry" is the term generally used to describe corporate enterprises that use a large number of highly skilled people: screenwriter, director, actors, cinematographer, film editor, film scorer, set and costume designers, and many others. Unlike a novel, say, by Albert Camus, a film cannot be credited to a single creator. Critics tend to lavish credit on the director as the person in charge but this is only a convention that tends to slight everyone else. One cannot, for example, think of director Elia Kazan's *On the Waterfront* without recalling Marlon Brando's masterful performance. In the final analysis no film is better than its literary base, the screenplay itself, for this is where virtually all movies begin.

Movies are a prime mass entertainment medium the world over and, as commercial enterprises, about 99 percent of them are eminently forgettable. But from the beginning of motion pictures, there have been exceptions, movies that have made an artistic impact and that have withstood the test of time. Usually referred to as film classics, these are masterpieces that have effectively synthesized the efforts of many creators. Following is a list of movies that are generally regarded as true classics. Some, perhaps, are not to everyone's taste but all are notable works of art and all should be seen, preferably more than once. They are among the best of a new literature that began in this century. Following the standard procedure, credit for the movies is assigned to the directors but, in every case, the viewer should give due credit to all participants, both on and off camera.

Antonioni, Michelangelo. *L'Avventura.* Italy, 1959.
Bergman, Ingmar. *The Seventh Seal.* Sweden, 1956.
———. *Wild Strawberries.* Sweden, 1957.
Buñuel, Luis. *Belle de Jour.* France, 1968.
Chaplin, Charles. *The Gold Rush.* U.S., 1925.
Cocteau, Jean. *Beauty and the Beast.* France, 1947.
DeSica, Vittorio, *The Bicycle Thief.* Italy, 1948.
Eisenstein, Serge. *Potemkin.* Russia, 1925.
Fellini, Federico. *La Strada.* Italy, 1954.
———. *La Dolce Vita.* Italy, 1959.
Gance, Abel. *Napoleon.* France, 1925, 1982.
Griffith, David W. *Intolerance.* U.S., 1916.
Hitchcock, Alfred. *Vertigo.* U.S., 1958.
Kazan, Elia. *On the Waterfront.* U.S., 1954.
Kurosawa, Akira. *Roshomon.* Japan, 1950.
———. *Ikiru.* Japan, 1952.
———. *Seven Samurai.* Japan, 1954.
Lang, Fritz. *M.* Germany, 1931.
Penn, Arthur. *Bonnie and Clyde.* U.S., 1967.
Renoir, Jean. *La Grande Illusion.* France, 1938.
———. *Rules of the Game.* France, 1939, 1965.
Truffaut, Francois. *The 400 Blows.* France, 1959.
———. *Jules and Jim.* France, 1961.
Welles, Orson. *Citizen Kane.* U.S., 1941.
Wiene, Robert. *The Cabinet of Dr. Caligari.* Germany, 1919.
Wilder, Billy. *Some Like It Hot.* U.S., 1959.

1900–1980s

1900 Freud, *The Interpretation of Dreams;* quantum theory; beginnings of jazz in American South

1901 First transatlantic radio telegraphic transmission

1902 First phonograph recordings

1903 Flight of Wright brothers; Picasso's Blue Period

1905 Einstein's Special Theory of Relativity; first moving pictures by Edison; Fauves in Paris

1906 San Francisco earthquake

1907 Picasso, *Les Demoiselles d'Avignon*

1909 F. L. Wright, Robie House; founding of NAACP; Diaghilev unveils Ballet Russe in Paris

1911 Chagall, *I and the Village;* Matisse, *The Blue Window*

1912 Kandinsky, *Concerning the Spiritual in Art*

1913 Stravinsky, *Rite of Spring;* Armory Show in New York

1914 World War I (to 1918)

1915 Dada movement begins

1916 Einstein's General Theory of Relativity

1917 Lenin triumphs in Russia

1918 Worldwide influenza epidemic kills ca. 20 million

1919 Treaty of Versailles; Bauhaus founded

1920 Women win vote in U.S.; prohibition in U.S. (to 1933)

1920s Chicago style jazz; The Jazz Age

1921 Major powers meet in Limitation of Armaments Conference

1922 Fascists seize power in Italy; Eliot, *The Wasteland;* radar invented

1924 Breton, *First Surrealist Manifesto;* death of Lenin

1925 Brancusi, *Bird in Space;* Gropius, Workshop of Bauhaus

1926 First television transmission; first liquid fuel rocket

1927 Stalin dictator in Russia; Lindbergh's flight to Paris

1928 First sound movie; Weill, *Threepenny Opera*

1929 Wall Street panic; beginning of Great Depression; Corbusier, Villa Savoye

1930 Sinclair Lewis wins Nobel Prize for Literature; big band jazz flourishes (into 40s)

1931 Sino-Japanese war (to 1945); Dali, *The Persistence of Memory*

1932 Huxley, *Brave New World*

1933 Hitler chancellor of Germany; Roosevelt begins New Deal

1934 Discovery of antibiotics;

1935 WPA Art Project (to 1940); Congress passes Social Security Act

1936 F. L. Wright, Kaufmann House; Spanish Civil War (to 1939)

1937 Picasso, *Guernica*

1938 Germany annexes Austria; Czechoslovakia dismembered

1939 World War II (to 1945); first commercial television; invention of jet aircraft engine; automatic sequence computer developed

1940 Richard Wright, *Native Son;* first successful plutonium fission

1941 Pearl Harbor bombed

1942 Uranium fission, atomic reactor

1943 Pollock's first exhibition; race riots in Detroit and New York

1944 Beginnings of Bop (Modern) jazz

1945 Atomic bomb on Hiroshima; New York becomes new international art center

1946 Camus, *The Stranger;* Orwell, *1984;* Philippines win independence from U.S.

1947 Beginning of Marshall Plan for Europe; transistor invented; United Nations Building

1948 Israel becomes independent state; LP recordings marketed

1949 Russia acquires atomic weapons; China goes Communist

1950 Korean War (to 1953); U.S. military advisers sent to Vietnam

1950s Beginnings of electronic music; art "happenings"; "beat" generation

1951 Transcontinental television inaugurated

1952 Hydrogen bomb exploded by U.S. in South Pacific

1953 Death of Stalin; Beckett, *Waiting for Godot*

1954 U.S. Supreme Court disallows segregation; DeGaulle returns to power

1955 Rauschenberg, *Bed;* beginning of Civil Rights movement in South

1956 Interstate highway system inaugurated; first transatlantic telephone cable

1957 Russia launches Sputnik; Congress passes first Civil Rights legislation since reconstruction

1958 Beginning of jet airline passenger service; LASAR beam invented

1959 Rauschenberg, *Monogram;* Wright's Guggenheim Museum completed

1960s Pop Art flourishes; Hippies, Yippies, protestors

1961 First manned orbital flight (Russia)
1962 Rachel Carson's *Silent Spring* launches environmentalist movement; Saarinen, TWA Terminal
1963 John F. Kennedy assassinated; quasars discovered
1964 Kubrick movie *Dr. Strangelove;* China explodes atom bomb
1965 Height of Beatlemania; foundation of the National Organization for Women
1966 Indiana, *The Black and White Love*
1967 First human heart transplant; Safdie, Habitat and Fuller, American Pavilion, EXPO 67
1968 Assassination of Martin Luther King and Robert Kennedy
1969 American moon walk; Rock Festival at Woodstock; race riots in Watts, Detroit, New York
1970 Toffler, *Future Shock*
1970s New Realism in art; art and technology; rapid advances in computors and robotics
1971 Shostakovitch, *Symphony No. 15*
1972 UN Conference on the Human Environment to study pollution
1973 First orbital laboratory (Skylab)
1974 First energy crisis; Nixon resigns presidency
1975 American withdrawal from Vietnam
1976 Moratorium lifted on Recombinant DNA technology (genetic engineering)
1977 Piano and Rogers, Pompidou Center, Paris
1978 Sadat of Egypt and Begin of Israel share Nobel Peace Prize; first ''test-tube baby delivered in England
1979 Nobel Prize in Medicine awarded for invention of computed axial tomography (CAT scan); Iran takes Americans hostage at U.S. Embassy
1980s Age of Information and Communication; rapid developments in High Tech

Glossary

Pronunciation: Approximations are given where necessary. The syllables are to be read as English words and with the capital letters accented.

Abbreviations: L., Latin; F., French; G., German; Gk., Greek; I., Italian; v., Vide (see).

Asterisks: An asterisk preceding a word or phrase indicates that a definition and/or illustration can be found under that heading.

Abbreviations: The musical abbreviations used are included here under one heading for easy reference.

Accel.   *accelerando* (ah–chel–er–AHN–doe), becoming faster.

Br.   bridge, connecting section between themes.

Bsn., Bssn.   bassoon.

C.b.   contra bass, that is, string bass.

Cl., clar.   clarinet.

Cresc.   *crescendo* (cray–SHEN–doe), becoming louder.

D.C.   *da capo* (dah–KAH–po), repeat from the beginning.

D.S.   *dal segno* (dahl–SEHN–yo), repeat from the sign.

Dim.   *diminuendo,* becoming softer.

Eng. hn.   English horn, alto oboe.

f   *forte* (FORE–tay), loud.

ff   *fortissimo,* very loud.

fff   *fortississimo,* very, very loud.

Fl.   flute.

fp   *forte piano,* loud and immediately soft.

Hn., Fr. hn.   French horn.

Low br.,   low brass, trombones and tubas (sometimes French horns).

Low stgs.   low strings, that is, cello, string bass.

Low w.w.'s   low woodwinds, that is, bass clarinet, bassoon, contra bassoon.

mf   mezzo forte (MEH–dso), half loud (medium loud).

mp   mezzo piano, half soft (medium soft).

Ob.   oboe.

Picc.   piccolo.

Pizz.   *pizzicato,* strings plucked with the fingers.

p   *piano* (pea–AHN–no), soft.

pp   *pianissimo,* very soft.

ppp   *pianississimo,* very, very soft.

Reeds   clarinet, oboe, bassoon, bass clarinet, etc.

R.h., l.h.   right hand, left hand (keyboard instruments).

Rit.   *ritardando,* become slower.

SATB   soprano, alto, tenor, bass (usually applied to vocal ensemble).

sf, sff, sfz   *sforzando* (sfor–TSAHND–o), strongly accented.

Sn. drum   snare drum, side drum.

Stgs.   strings, that is, the string section of the orchestra (violin, viola, cello, bass).

Tpt.   trumpet.

Tr.   trill.

Trans.   transition.

Trom.   trombone.

Vla.   viola.

Vlc.   violoncello, cello.

Vln.   violin.

W.w.'s   woodwinds (flute, oboe, clarinet, bassoon).

A

Abacus The flat slab on top of a *capital.

Acanthus A plant whose thick leaves are reproduced in stylized form on *Corinthian capitals. (See fig. 6.8.)

A cappella (ah ka–PELL–ah; L.) Originally unaccompanied music sung "in the chapel." Term now applies to choral music without instrumental accompaniment.

Accent In music, stress or emphasis on a tone or chord. Regular accents are assumed in metrical music. Special accent marks are used as necessary:> ∧ sfz (sforzando), etc.

Accidental In music a sign used to add or cancel chromatic alterations, for example, ♯ (raise a semitone), ♭ (lower a semitone), x (raise a whole tone), ♭♭ (lower a whole tone), ♮ (cancel previous sharps or flats).

Acoustics The science of sound.

Aerial perspective See perspective.

Agnosticism (Gk., *agnostos,* unknowing) The impossibility of obtaining knowledge of certain subjects; assertion that people cannot obtain knowledge of God.

Agnus Dei (L., Lamb of God) Last item of the *Ordinary of the *Mass.

Agora In ancient Greece, a marketplace/public square.

Allegory A literary mode with a literal level of meanings plus a set of meanings above and beyond themselves. This second level may be religious, social, political, or philosophical, e.g., *The Faerie Queen* by Spenser is an allegory about Christian virtues.

Alleluia Latinization for the Hebrew *Halleluyah* ("praise ye the Lord"). Third item of the *proper of the *Mass.

Alto, Contralto The second highest part in choral music, that is, S <u>A</u> T B.

Ambulatory A passageway around the *apse of a church. (See fig. 11.25.)

Amphora Greek vase, usually quite large, with two handles and used to store food staples. (See fig. 3.23.)

Apocalypse Prophetic revelation; the Book of Revelation in the New Testament.

A posteriori (a–pos–TEER–e–or–e; L., following after) Reasoning from observed facts to conclusions; inductive; empirical.

A priori (a–pree–OAR–e) Reasoning from general propositions to particular conclusions; deductive; nonempirical.

Apse A recess, usually semicircular, in the east wall of a Christian church or, in a Roman *basilica, at the wall opposite to the general entrance way.

Arabesque ·Literally Arablike. Elaborate designs of intertwined flowers, foliage, and geometric patterns used in Islamic architecture. (See fig. 11.6.)

Arcade A series of connected *arches resting on columns. (See fig. 6.9.)

Arch A curved structure (semicircular or pointed) spanning a space, usually made of wedge-shaped blocks. Known to the Greeks, who preferred a *post and lintel system, but exploited by the Romans.

Archetype (Gk. *arche,* first; *typos,* form) The original pattern of forms of which things in this world are copies.

Architrave The lowest part of an *entablature, a horizontal beam or lintel directly above the *capital. (See figs. 3.38 and 14.10.)

Aria (I., AHR–yah; F., air) Solo song (sometimes duet) in *operas, *oratorios, *cantatas.

Arpeggio (ahr–PEJ–o; I., harplike) In music the playing of a *chord with the notes sounding in quick succession rather than simultaneously.

Ars antiqua (L., old art) Music of the late twelfth and thirteenth centuries.

Ars nova (L., new art) Music of the fourteenth century. Outstanding composers were Machaut (France) and Landini (Italy).

Art Nouveau A style of architecture, crafts, and design of the 1890s and a bit later characterized by curvilinear patterns. Examples include Tiffany lamps and the work of Beardsley and Klimt.

Art song Song intending an artistic combination of words and music, as distinct from popular song or folk song. (See chap. 21.)

Atheism (Gk., *a,* no; *theos,* god) The belief that there is no God; also means "not theistic" when applied to those who do not believe in a personal God.

Atonality A type of music in which there is no tonal center, no key note. v. Twelve-tone technique and serial composition. (See chap. 26.)

Atrium The court of a Roman house, roofless, and near the entrance. Also the open, colonnaded court attached to the front of early Christian churches. (See fig. 6.3.)

Aulos (OW–los) A shrill sounding oboelike instrument associated with the Dionysian rites of the ancient Greeks. Double-reed instrument normally played in pairs by one performer. (See fig. 4.2.)

Avant-garde (a–vahn–GARD) A French term meaning, literally, advanced guard, and used to designate innovators and experimentalists in the various arts.

B

Bagpipe A reed instrument with several pipes attached to a bag (skin reservoir). One or two pipes *(chanters)* have tone holes and are used for the melody. The longer pipes *(drones)* sustain the same notes throughout. Probably of Asiatic origin and imported by the Romans in first century, A.D.

Baldachino (ball–da–KEEN–o) A canopy over a tomb or altar of which the most famous is that over the tomb of St. Peter in St. Peter's in Rome; designed by Bernini. (See fig. 18.8.)

Ballad (L., *ballare,* to dance) Originally a dancing song. A narrative song, usually folk song but term also applied to popular songs.

Ballade Medieval *trouvère song. In the nineteenth and twentieth centuries dramatic piano pieces, frequently inspired by romantic poetry.

Balustrade A railing plus a supporting row of posts.

Banjo *Guitar family instrument, probably introduced into Africa by Arab traders and brought to America on the slave ships. The body consists of a shallow, hollow metal drum with a drumhead on top and open at the bottom. It has four or more strings and is played with fingers or plectrum.

Bar In music notation originally vertical lines through the staff (which are now called bar lines). Bar is synonymous with *measure.

Bar form Originated with German *minnesinger-*meistersinger tradition. A form of music with the first *phrase repeated followed by a different phrase, for example, A–A–B. Also see Form.

Bar Line   v. Bar.

Barrel vault   v. Vault.

Basilica   In Roman architecture, a rectangular public building used for business or as a tribunal. (See fig. 8.9.) Christian churches that use a *cruciform plan are patterned after Roman basilicas. Though basilica is an architectural style, the Roman church calls a church a basilica if it contains the bones of a saint.

Bass   "Low" musical voice as opposed to "high." Used in the following special ways: (1) lowest adult male voice; (2) bass clef has F on the fourth line; (3) short for bass viol., bass fiddle, double bass (string bass) in the orchestra; (4) prefixed to the name of an instrument to indicate the largest (and lowest) member of an instrumental family, for example, bass clarinet, bass trombone, etc.

Bass clef   v. Bass (2).

Bay   In Romanesque and Gothic churches the area between the columns.

Behaviorism   School of psychology that restricts both animal and human psychology to the study of behavior; stress on the role of the environment and on conditioned responses to exterior stimuli.

Blank verse   Unrhymed *iambic pentameter* (v. meter) in the English language, much used in Elizabethan drama.

Bourgeoisie   The middle class; in Marxist theory the capitalist class, which is opposed to the proletariat, the lower or industrial working class.

Brass instruments   Instruments of metal that produce a tone by vibrating the lips in a cup- or funnel-shaped mouthpiece. They include: (from high pitch to low) *trumpet, cornet, fluegelhorn, *French horn, baritone horn (euphonium), *trombone, *tuba.

Buttress   Exterior support used to counter the lateral thrust of an *arch or *vault. A *pier buttress* is a solid mass of masonry added to the wall; a *flying buttress* is typically a pier standing away from the wall and from which an arch "flies" from the pier to connect with the wall at the point of outward thrust. (See fig. 11.29.)

C

Cadence   Term in music applied to the concluding portion of a phrase (temporary cadence) or composition (permanent cadence).

Campanile   Italian for bell tower, usually freestanding. The Leaning Tower of Pisa is a campanile. (See fig. 11.21.)

Canon   (Gk., law, rule) A contrapuntal device in music in which one or more melodies strictly imitates an opening melody throughout its entire length. A canon is the strictest type of imitative *counterpoint. Canons that have no specified way to end but which keep going around are called "rounds," for example, "Three Blind Mice."

Canso   A *troubadour song in *"bar form," for example, A–A–B.

Cantata   (I., *cantare,* to sing) A "sung" piece as opposed to a "sound" (instrumental) piece, for example, sonata. The term is now generally used for secular or sacred choral works with orchestral accompaniment, which are on a smaller scale than *oratorios.

Cantilever   A self-supporting projection which needs no exterior bracing; e.g., a balcony or porch can be cantilevered. (See fig. 25.31.)

Cantus firmus   (L., fixed song) A preexisting melody used as the foundation for a *polyphonic composition. *Plainsong melodies were used for this purpose, but other sources included secular songs, Lutheran chorales, and scales. Any preexisting melody may serve as a cantus firmus.

Capital   The top or crown of a column.

Cartoon   A full-size preliminary drawing for a pictorial work, usually a large work such as a *mural, *fresco, or *tapestry. Also a humorous drawing.

Caryatid   (care–ee–AT–id) A female figure that functions as a supporting column; male figures that function in a like manner are called *atlantes* (at–LAN–tees; plural of Atlas). (See fig. 3.53.)

Catharsis   (Gk., *katharsis,* purge, purify) Purification, purging of emotions effected by tragedy (Aristotle).

Cella   The enclosed chamber in a classical temple that contained the cult statue of the god or goddess after whom the temple was named.

Chamber music   Term now restricted to instrumental music written for a limited number of players in which there is only one player to each part, as opposed to orchestral music, which has two or more players to some parts, for example, sixteen players on the first violin part. True chamber music emphasizes ensemble rather than solo playing.

Chanson   (F., song) A major part of the *troubadour-*trouvère tradition, dating from the eleventh through the fourteenth centuries. Generic term for the general song production to a French text.

Chevet   (sheh–VAY; F., pillow) The eastern end of a church, including *choir, *ambulatory, and *apse.

Chiaroscuro   (kee–AR–oh–SKOOR–oh; I., light-dark) In the visual arts the use of gradations of light and dark to represent natural light and shadows.

Chinoiserie   (she–nwaz–eh–REE; F.) Chinese motifs as decorative elements for craft objects, screens, wallpaper, and furniture; prominent in eighteenth-century Rococo style.

Choir   That part of the church where the singers and clergy are normally accommodated; usually between the *transept and the *apse; also called chancel. (See fig. 11.32.)

Chorale   A hymn tune of the German Protestant (Lutheran) church.

Chord   In music the simultaneous sounding of three or more tones.

Chromatic   (Gk., *chroma,* color) The use of notes that are foreign to the musical scale and have to be indicated by a sharp, flat, natural, etc. The *chromatic scale* is involved in these alterations. It consists of twelve tones to an octave, each a semitone apart.

Chromatic scale   v. Chromatic.

Church modes   In music the medieval scale system of four basic modes (Dorian, Phrygian, Lydian, Mixolydian) and four related modes (Hypodorian, Hypophrygian, Hypolydian, Hypomixolydian). May also include Ionian and Aeolian, which are somewhat comparable to the *major-minor system.

Cire perdue   (seer pair–DUE; F., lost wax) A metal casting method in which the original figure is modeled in wax and encased in a mold; as the mold is baked the wax melts and runs out, after which the molten metal is poured into the mold.

Clavichord The earliest type of stringed keyboard instrument (twelfth century). Probably developed from the *monochord. It is a 2′ × 4′ oblong box with a keyboard of about three octaves. The strings run parallel to the keyboard, as opposed to harpsichords and pianos, in which the strings run at right angles to the keyboard. The keys are struck from below by metal tangents fastened to the opposite ends of elongated keys. The tone is light and delicate but very expressive because the performer can control the loudness of each note. It was sometimes called a "table *clavier" because it was portable.

Clavier Generic term for any instrument of the stringed keyboard family: clavichord, harpsichord, and piano.

Clef (F., key) In music a symbol placed on the staff to indicate the pitches of the lines and spaces. There are three clefs in use today: G, F, and C. The G clef is used to indicate that the note on the second line is G (treble clef). The F clef is usually used to indicate that F is on the fourth line (bass clef).

Treble Clef

Bass Clef

The C clef places middle C on either the third line (alto clef) or fourth line (tenor clef).

Alto Clef

Tenor Clef

Clerestory In a basilica or church, the second level, the wall that rises above the roof of the other parts and has numerous windows. (See fig. 8.11.)

Cloister An inner court bounded by covered walks; a standard feature of monastery architecture.

Collage (F., pasting) Paper and other materials pasted on a two-dimensional surface.

Colonnade A series of spaced columns, usually connected by lintels. (See fig. 8.11.)

Column A vertical support, usually circular, which has a base (except in *Doric style), shaft, and *capital. (See fig. 3.39.)

Comedy A play or other literary work in which all ends well, properly, or happily. Opposite of *tragedy.

Con (I., with) For example, *con moto* (with motion).

Concerto (con-CHAIR-toe; I.) A musical work for one or more solo voices with orchestral accompaniment.

Conductus In music a twelfth- or thirteenth-century metrical (as opposed to nonmetrical plainsong) song for one or more voices in a sacred or secular style. A conductus may be *monophonic or *polyphonic.

Contrapposto (I., set against). Figural sculpture in which parts of the body (usually hips and legs, arms and shoulders) are set against each other along a central axis, setting up an alternation of tension and relaxation.

Contrapuntal In the style of *counterpoint.

Corinthian The most ornate style of Greek architecture, little used by the Greeks but preferred by the Romans; tall, slender, channeled columns topped by an elaborate capital decorated with stylized acanthus leaves. (See fig. 6.8.)

Cornice The horizontal, projecting member crowning an *entablature.

Cosmology Philosophic study of the origin and nature of the universe.

Counterpoint The musical craft or technique of combining two or more melodies, of writing note against note *(punctus contra punctum)*. Music which consists of simultaneous melodies (two or more) is called *contrapuntal music or *polyphonic (many voiced) music.

Couplet In poetry two successive rhymed lines in the same meter.

Credo (L., I believe) Third item of the *Ordinary of the *Mass.

Crescendo, Decrescendo (cray-SHEN-doe, day-cray-SHEN-doe; I.) Standard musical terminology for increasing or decreasing loudness. Also indicated by abbreviations *cresc.* and *decresc.,* or signs < and >.

Crocket In Gothic architecture an ornamental device shaped like a curling leaf and placed on the outer angles of *gables and pinnacles. (See colorplate 20.)

Crossing In a church, the space formed by the interception of the *nave and the *transepts.

Cruciform The floor plan of a church in the shape of a Latin cross.

D

Daguerrotype After L. J. M. Daguerre (1789–1851) the inventor. Photograph made on a silver-coated glass plate.

Determinism (L., *de* + *terminus,* end) The doctrine that all events are conditioned by their causes and that people are mechanical expressions of heredity and environment; in short, we are at the mercy of blind, unknowing natural laws; the universe could care less.

Deus ex machina (DAY-oos ex ma-KEE-na; L.) In Greek and Roman drama a deity who was brought in by stage machinery to resolve a difficult situation; any unexpected or bizarre device or event introduced to untangle a plot.

Dialectic Associated with Plato as the art of debate by question and answer. Also dialectical reasoning using *syllogisms (Aristotle) or, according to Hegel, the distinctive characteristic of speculative thought.

Diatonic (Gk., through the tones) Applied to musical scales in which each letter name is used once only, for example, c–d–e–f–g–a–b–(c), c–d–e♭–f–g–a♭–b♭–c, etc.

Dome A hemispherical vault; may be viewed as an arch rotated on its vertical axis.

Doric The oldest of Greek temple styles, characterized by sturdy *columns with no base and an unornamented cushionlike *capital. (See figs. 3.39 and 14.28.)

Drum The circular sections that make up the shaft of a *column; also the circular wall on which a *dome is placed. (See fig. 3.40.)

Drums Percussion musical instruments having a skin stretched over one or both ends of a frame.

1. *Timpani* (kettledrums) The skin is stretched over a metal half-sphere. They can be tuned to definite pitch.
2. *Side drum* (snare drum) Shallow drum with metal snares (taut wire coils) on the bottom drumhead. The tone is dry and crisp.
3. *Tenor drum* A larger and deeper version of the snare drum. The tone is similar to that of a tom-tom. It does not use snares.
4. *Bass drum* The largest drum used in the orchestra. The tone is rather booming.
5. *Conga drum* One head stretched over the top of a long cylinder.
6. *Bongo drums* Small pair of single-headed drums.
7. *Tambourine* A small single-headed drum with metal discs set around the frame.

Dualism In metaphysics, a theory that admits two independent substances, e.g., Plato's dualism of the sensible and intelligible worlds, Cartesian dualism of thinking and extended subjects, Kant's dualism of the noumenal and the phenomenal.

Dynamic marks Words or symbols indicating the relative degrees of loudness or softness in a musical performance. Some of the more important markings are summarized as follows:

Term	Symbol	Meaning
pianissimo (pea-uh-NEES-see-mo)	pp	very soft
piano (pea-AHN-no)	p	soft
mezzo piano (MEH-dso)	mp	half soft
mezzo forte (FORE-tay)	mf	half loud
forte	f	loud
fortissimo	ff	very loud
forte piano	fp	loud and immediately soft
sforzando (sforr-TSAHND-o)	sfz	strongly accented
also: *crescendo, *decrescendo		

E

Elegy A meditative poem dealing with the idea of death.

Elevation The vertical arrangements of the elements of an architectural design; vertical projection.

Empiricism A proposition that the sole source of knowledge is experience, that no knowledge is possible independent of experience.

Engaged column A nonfunctional form projecting from the surface of a wall; used for visual articulation. (See fig. 6.7.)

Engraving The process of using a sharp instrument to cut a design into a metal plate, usually copper; also the print that is made from the plate after ink has been added.

Entablature That part of a building of post and lintel construction between the capitals and the roof. In classical architecture this includes the *architrave, *frieze, and *cornice. (See fig. 3.38.)

Entasis (EN-ta-sis) A slight convex swelling in the shaft of a *column.

Epic A lengthy narrative poem dealing with protagonists of heroic proportions and issues of universal significance, e.g., Homer's *Iliad*.

Epicurean One who believes that pleasure, especially that of the mind, is the highest good.

Epistemology A branch of philosophy that studies the origin, validity, and processes of knowledge.

Eschatology (Gk., *ta eschata,* death) That part of theology dealing with last things: death, judgment, heaven, hell.

Estampie (es-TAHM-pea) A dance form popular during the twelfth to fourteenth centuries. Consists of a series of repeated sections, for example, aa, bb, cc, etc.

Etching A kind of *engraving in which the design is incised into a wax-covered metal plate, after which the exposed metal is etched by a corrosive acid; the print made from the plate is also called an etching.

Ethos In ancient Greek music the "ethical" character attributed to the various modes. The Dorian was considered strong and manly; the Phrygian, ecstatic and passionate; the Lydian, feminine, decadent, and lascivious; the Mixolydian, mournful and gloomy.

Euphemism An innocuous term substituted for one considered to be offensive or socially unacceptable, e.g., "passing away" for "dying."

F

Façade One of the exterior walls of a building, usually the one containing the main entrance.

Fenestration The arrangement of windows or other openings in the walls of a building.

Fiddle Colloquialism for the violin. Also used to designate the bowed ancestors of the violin, particularly the medieval instrument used to accompany dances.

Finial In Gothic architecture an ornament fitted to the peak of an *arch; any ornamental terminating point, such as the screw-top of a lamp. (See colorplate 20.)

Flageolet (flaj-o-LET; F.) A small wind instrument, a forerunner of the *recorder.

Flamboyant Late Gothic architecture of the fifteenth or sixteenth centuries, which featured wavy lines and flamelike forms.

Flat v. Accidental.

Fleche (flesh; F., arrow) In architecture a slender spire above the intersection of the *nave and *transepts. (See fig. 11.29.)

Flute A *woodwind instrument made of wood (originally), silver, gold, or preferably platinum. It is essentially a straight pipe with keys, is held horizontally and played by blowing across a mouth (blow) hole located near one end. The tone is mellow in the bottom octave, becoming thinner and brighter up to the top of the range. Though many thousands of years old, the flute was not used in instrumental ensembles until the early eighteenth century, when it began to replace the *recorder.

Fluting The vertical grooves, usually semicircular, in the shaft of a *column or *pilaster.

Folk song   A song of unknown (usually) authorship preserved by means of an oral tradition. A folk song is never composed by "folk" (or a committee); it is the creation of one or two individuals (words and/or music) and tends to be remembered and transmitted because the words and music are somehow pertinent to the environment in which it was created. Folk songs about special situations (labor unions, strikes, political causes, and movements, etc.) tend to fade away in time. Folk songs having something to do with the human condition may last indefinitely.

Foot   A metrical unit in poetry such as the iamb ⌣/. Also see meter.

Foreshortening   Creating the illusion in painting or drawing that the subject is projecting out of or into the frontal plane of a two-dimensional surface.

Form, Musical form   Musical form is an intelligible structure that distinguishes music from haphazard sounds or noises. Since music is an intelligible ordering of tones all music has "form," that is, it has a beginning, middle, and end; it exists in time. "Form" is therefore any organization or structuring of any combination, or all of the four elements of music (melody, harmony, rhythm, tone color). In general, music is ordered (formed) in such a manner as to possess enough unity to achieve coherence or continuity and sufficient variety to avoid monotony (short of chaos). All musical forms consist of varying relationships of unity and variety. There are many ways of organizing musical structure; following are a few of the more important forms.

   I. Single forms (pieces or single movements).
     A. Sectional (with clearly defined [more or less] interior divisions).
     B. Continuous.
       1. Through composed (no repetition). *Organum, some medieval *motets.
       2. Imitative (contrapuntal forms): *passacaglia, *fugue, Renaissance *masses, and *motets.
   II. Composite forms are simply compositions with two or more movements, for example, *symphony, *cantata, etc.

Free verse   A verse that uses devices other than meter and rhyme.

Fresco   (I., fresh) Painting on plaster, usually wet plaster on which the colors are painted, sinking in as the plaster dries and the fresco becomes part of the wall. (See fig. 14.31.)

Frets   Thin strips of wood or metal fastened to the fingerboard of string instruments like the *viol and *guitar (but *not* members of the violin family). The frets are placed to mark specific notes.

Frieze   In architecture decorated horizontal band, often embellished with carved figures and molding; the portion of an *entablature between the *architrave and the *cornice above.

Fugue   *Polyphonic musical composition in which a single theme is developed by the different musical voices in succession. A favorite style of Baroque composers like Bach and Handel.

Fundamental   In musical acoustics the lowest note of the overtone series. The generating tone for the series.

G

Gable   In architecture the triangular section at the end of a pitched roof, frequently with a window below. (See fig. 18.12.)

Genre   (ZHAN–re) In the pictorial arts a depiction of scenes of everyday life. (See fig. 18.26.)

Gittern   English name for the medieval *guitar.

Glockenspiel   A percussion instrument with rectangular metal bars laid out in a keyboard pattern. It is played with two mallets and has a sharp, bright tone.

Goliards   Wandering Bohemians of the tenth through the thirteenth centuries: students, young ecclesiastics, dreamers, and the disenchanted.

Gospels   In the Bible, New Testament accounts (Matthew, Mark, Luke, John) of the life and teachings of Christ.

Gouache   (goo–AHSH; F.) Watercolor made opaque by adding zinc white.

Graphic arts   Visual arts that are linear in character: drawing, engraving, printing, printmaking, typographic, and advertising design.

Greek cross   A cross in which the four arms are of equal length.

Gregorian chant   v. Plainsong.

Groin   In architecture the edge (groin) formed by the intersection of two *vaults. (See figs. 11.18 and 11.19.)

Guitar   A plucked string instrument with a flat body and six strings (modern guitar). Brought into Europe during the Middle Ages by the Moorish conquest of Spain.

H

Harmony   In music the vertical (simultaneous) sound of two or more pitches. Harmonic development is a major achievement of Western music while remaining secondary in the rest of the world's music.

Harp   A stringed instrument with a large triangular frame and about forty-five strings. In the modern harp the seven pedals change the pitches of the strings so that the harp can play chromatically, i.e., all twelve tones of the octave. The harp has been mentioned in recorded history since the days of the Babylonian Empire.

Harpsichord   Actually a harp turned on its side and played by means of quills or leather tongues operated by a keyboard. It was the most common keyboard instrument of the sixteenth to eighteenth centuries and is again being built today in increasing numbers.

Hatching   A series of closely spaced parallel lines in a drawing or print giving the effect of shading.

Hedonism   The doctrine that pleasure or pleasant consciousness are intrinsically good; that pleasure is the proper—and the actual—motive for every choice.

Heroic couplet   Two successive lines of rhymed iambic pentameter, e.g., Pope's *Essay on Man.*

Hieratic   (HYE–uh–RAT–ik) Of or used by priests; priestly.

Hieroglyphic   Symbols or pictures standing for a word, syllable, or sound; writing system of ancient Egyptians.

Homophonic   (Gk., same sound) Music in which a single melodic line is supported by chords or other subordinate material (percussion instruments).

Horn The modern orchestral instrument, the French horn, is frequently referred to as a horn. Also, a generic designation for any instrument that has a mouthpiece through which the performer blows.

Hubris (HU–bris) *Tragic flaw,* i.e., excessive pride or arrogance that injures other people (not physically) and brings about the downfall of the person with the flaw.

Hue The name of a color. The chief colors of the spectrum are: red, yellow, blue (primary); green, orange, violet (secondary).

Hydraulis Ancient Greek pipe organ, probably invented in the Middle East 300–200 B.C. Air for the pipes was provided by hydraulic pressure and the pipes activated by a keyboard. Originally the tone was delicate and clear, but the Romans converted it into a noisy outdoor instrument by a large increase in air pressure.

Hymn A poem of praise. Usually, but not necessarily, sacred. The music accompanying a hymn is called the hymn tune.

I

Icon (EYE–kon; Gk., image) Two-dimensional representation of a holy person; in the Greek church a panel painting of a sacred personage.

Iconography Visual imagery used to convey concepts in the visual arts; the study of symbolic meanings in the pictorial arts.

Illumination Decorative illustrations or designs, associated primarily with medieval illuminated manuscripts.

Impasto (I., paste) A painting style in which the pigment is laid on thickly, as in many of van Gogh's paintings. (See figs. 22.28 and 22.29.)

Intaglio (in–TAL–yo) A graphic technique in which the design is incised; used on seals, gems, and dies for coins and also for the kinds of printing and printmaking that have a depressed ink-bearing surface.

Ionic A style of Greek classical architecture using slender, *fluted *columns and *capitals decorated with scrolls and volutes. (See fig. 3.52.)

Isocepholy (I–so–SEPH–uh–ly) In the visual arts a convention that arranges figures so that the heads are at the same height. (See figs. 3.49 and 3.59.)

J

Jamb figure Sculpted figure flanking the portal of a Gothic church. (See fig. 11.31.)

Jongleur (zhon–GLEUR) French professional musicians (minstrels) of the twelfth and thirteenth centuries who served the *troubadours and *trouvères.

K

Keystone The central wedge-shaped stone in an arch; the last stone put in place and which makes the arch stable. (See fig. 11.27.)

Kithara (KITH–a–ra) The principal stringed instrument of the ancient Greeks. Essentially a larger version of the *lyre, it has a U-shaped form and usually seven to eleven strings running vertically from the cross arm down to the sound box at the base of the instrument. The legendary instrument of Apollo. (See fig. 4.3.)

Kyrie eleison (Gk., Lord have mercy) The first item of the *Ordinary of the *Mass.

L

Lantern In architecture a small decorative structure that crowns a *dome or roof. (See fig. 14.33.)

Latin cross A cross in which the vertical member is longer than the horizontal arm it bisects.

Legato (leh-GAH-toe; I.) Musical term meaning smooth, moving smoothly from note to note. Opposite of *staccato.

Libretto (I., little book) The text or words of an *opera, *oratorio, or other extended choral work.

Lied, Lieder (leet, LEE–der; G., song, songs). Term usually applied to the German romantic *art songs of Schubert, Schumann, Brahms, Wolf, and others. Also used for medieval songs, that is, *minnesinger and *meistersinger.

Lintel In architecture a horizontal crosspiece over an open space, which carries the weight of some of the superstructure. (See fig. 3.36.)

Lithography A printmaking process that uses a polished stone (or metal plate) on which the design is drawn with a crayon or greasy ink. Ink is chemically attracted only to the lines of the drawing, with a print made by applying paper to the inked stone. (See fig. 22.15.)

Liturgical Pertaining to public worship, specifically to the organized worship patterns of the Christian churches.

Liturgical drama Twelfth- and thirteenth-century enactments of biblical stories, frequently with music. Developed into the "mystery plays" of the fourteenth through sixteenth centuries.

Lituus (L.) Bronze trumpet used by the Roman armies. Shaped like the letter J.

Lost wax process v. *cire perdue.*

Lute Plucked stringed instrument with a pear-shaped body and a fingerboard with *frets. It had eleven strings tuned to six notes (five sets of double strings plus a single string for the highest note). It was the most popular instrument of the sixteenth century and was used into the eighteenth century. Lutes are again being made, mainly for present-day performances of Renaissance music.

Lyre (or Lyra) Ancient Greek instrument, a simpler form of the *kithara. The sound box was often made of a tortoise shell. Used mainly by amateurs. The larger kithara was used by professional musicians. (See fig. 4.1.)

Lyric Poetry sung to the accompaniment of a lyre (Greek); troubadour and trouvère poetry intended to be sung; short poems with musical elements. (See fig. 4.1.)

M

Madrigal Name of uncertain origin that refers to fourteenth-century vocal music or, usually, to the popular sixteenth-century type. Renaissance madrigals were free-form vocal pieces (usually set to love lyrics) in a *polyphonic style with intermixed *homophonic sections. Flemish, Italian, and English composers brought the madrigal to a high level of expressiveness in word painting and imagery. Madrigals were sometimes accompanied but mostly *a cappella. (See chap. 15.)

March Music for a parade or procession. The *meter is usually duple (simple or compound) but is sometimes quadruple.

Mass The central service of public worship of some Christian churches, principally the Roman Catholic church. The musical portions are indicated below.

Ordinary (same text)	Proper (text varies by the liturgical calendar)
Kyrie Eleison	Introit
Gloria in Excelsis Deo	Gradual
Credo in Unum Deum	Alleluia
Sanctus	Offertory
Agnus Dei	Communion

Materialism The doctrine that the only reality is matter; that the universe is not governed by intelligence or purpose but only by mechanical cause and effect.

Measure In music a group of beats set off by bar lines.

Meistersinger (G., mastersinger) The highest level in the music-poetry guilds of Germany in the fifteenth and sixteenth centuries. Succeeding the earlier *minnesinger tradition the guilds held song schools and awarded prizes, with top prizes for creating new songs going to the "mastersingers."

Melisma A melodic unit sung to one syllable; plainsong has frequent *melismatic* passages.

Melody A succession of musical sounds, that is, the horizontal organization of music as compared with harmony, which is a vertical organization of tones. Melody is inseparable from rhythm because it has an up and down motion of pitches and, simply stated, long and short durations of rhythm.

Metaphor A common form of figurative language that compares two dissimilar objects by stating that the two are identical, e.g., "the moon is blue."

Metaphysics Philosophic inquiry into the ultimate and fundamental reality; "the science of being as such."

Meter In music a grouping of beats into patterns of two, three, or four beats or combinations thereof; in English poetry the basic rhythmic pattern of stressed (—) and unstressed (ᴗ) syllables. Metrical patterns include: *iambic* (ᴗ —), *trochaic* (— ᴗ), *anapestic* (ᴗ ᴗ —), and *dactylic* (— ᴗ ᴗ).

Metope (MET–o–pay) In classical architecture the panel between two *triglyphs in a *Doric *frieze; may be plain or carved. The Parthenon metopes are all carved. (See fig. 3.50.)

Minnesinger (G., from *minne,* love) German poet-musicians of noble birth of the thirteenth to fifteenth centuries (leading to the *meistersingers) who were influenced by the *troubadour-trouvère tradition of the age of chivalry. They composed *monophonic songs, usually in *bar form.

Minstrel v. Jongleur.

Modes, rhythmic A thirteenth-century system of music rhythmic notation based on the patterns of poetic meter. Rhythmic modes give the characteristic flavor to thirteenth-century *organum and *motets because of the constant repetition of the same rhythmic patterns. All modes were performed in so-called "perfect" meter, that is, triple.

Rhythmic Mode	Poetic Meter	Accent Pattern	Performed
I	Trochaic	— ᴗ	♩ ♪♩ ♪
II	Iambic	ᴗ —	♪♩ ♪♩
III	Dactylic	— ᴗ ᴗ	♩. ♪♩
IV	Anapaestic	ᴗ ᴗ —	♪♩ ♩.
V	Spondiac	— —	♩. ♩.
VI	Tribrachic	ᴗ ᴗ ᴗ	♪♪♪ ♪♪♪

Monism (Gk., *mones,* single) The philosophical position that there is but one fundamental reality. The classical advocate of extreme monism was Parmenides of Elea; Spinoza is a modern exponent.

Monochord A device consisting of a single string stretched over a soundboard with a movable bridge. Used to demonstrate the laws of acoustics, especially the relationships between intervals and string lengths and the tuning of scales. (See fig. 12.2.)

Monophonic (Gk., one sound) A single line of music without accompaniment or additional parts, as in *plainsong, *troubadour-trouvère-minnesinger songs, and some *folk songs, hollers, street cries, and blues.

Montage (moan–TAHZH) A composition made of existing photographs, paintings, or drawings; in cinematography the effects achieved by superimposing images or using rapid sequences.

Mosaic The technique of embedding bits of stone, colored glass, or marble in wet concrete to make designs or pictures for walls or floors. To achieve a complex interplay of light and shadows, the bits are set in the holding material with minute differences in the angles, as in the mosaics of San Vitale in Ravenna. (See colorplates 11 and 12.)

Motet (from F., *mot,* word) The most important form of early *polyphonic music (ca. thirteenth to seventeenth centuries).

1. *Medieval motet* (thirteenth–fourteenth centuries). Usually 3 parts (triplum, motetus, tenor). The tenor "holds" to a *cantus firmus and the upper two voices sing different texts (sacred and/or secular).

2. *Renaissance* motet (fifteenth–sixteenth centuries). A four- or five-part composition, a cappella, generally polyphonic, with a single Latin text. A serious vocal piece intended for use in sacred services.

There are also Baroque motets (by J. S. Bach) for mixed chorus and orchestra (German text) and some Romantic motets (Brahms), again in the *a cappella style.

Motive   The smallest musical idea, usually part of a theme, which is used in various ways to give unity to musical expressions. Motives may be melodic (and rhythmic), purely rhythmic, harmonic or different combinations of these elements. Motives can be considered as building blocks of music or as a glue that holds music together.

Mullion   A vertical member that divides a window into sections; also used to support the glass in stained-glass windows.

Mural   A painting on a wall; a *fresco is a type of mural.

Myth   Stories explaining natural phenomena, customs, institutions, religious beliefs, and so forth of a people. Usually concerned with the supernatural, gods, goddesses, heroic exploits, and the like.

N

Narthex   A porch or vestibule of a church through which one passes to enter the *nave.

Natural   In music the sign ♮ used to cancel a previous sharp or flat. Also see accidentals.

Naturalism   The view that the universe requires no supernatural cause or government, that it is self-existent, self-explanatory, self-operating, and self-directing, that the universe is purposeless, deterministic, and only incidentally productive of man. In relation to literature sometimes defined as "realism on all fours." The dominant traits of literary naturalism are biological determinism (people are what they must be because of their genes) and environmental determinism (people are what they are because of where they were nurtured). It all comes out to nature versus nurture.

Nave   The main central space of a church running from the entrance to the *crossing of the *transepts; typically flanked by one or two side aisles. Name derived from *naval* because the barrel *vault ceiling has the appearance of the inside hull of a ship.

Nomos, Nome   (Gk., law, rule) In the Homeric tradition in ancient Greece the term is used to refer to the traditional phrases and melodies singers used to recite the epics and odes.

Notation   A set, any set, of symbols used to put music into written form. It should be pointed out that musical notation (even modern notation) can only approximate the sounds the composer wants. Actual performance practices must be based not only on a reading knowledge of music but also on an awareness of performance practices and the conventions of particular periods of music. Size of audience, acoustics of a room, and capabilities of the performer also affect the conversion of musical notation into actual music.

Notes and rest values   Modern musical system based on the whole and fractional divisions of a whole note, for example:

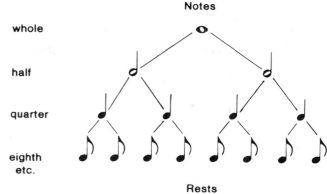

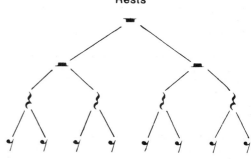

Notre Dame school   The composers of the twelfth- and thirteenth-century cathedral school at Notre Dame of Paris, most notably Leonin and Perotin. The Notre Dame school probably invented rhythmic notation for *polyphonic music.

O

Oboe   (from F., "high wind," that is, high-pitched instrument) A double-reed, soprano-range instrument with a conical bore (slightly expanding diameter from reed to bell). It has a nasal but mellow and poignant tone.

Odalisque   (oh–de–LISK) French word for a harem slave or concubine but used more broadly to refer to a reclining female figure, a favorite subject of painters like Ingres and Matisse. (See fig. 22.3.)

Ode   A formal lyric on a usually dignified theme, in exalted language, e.g., works by Horace.

Office hours   In the Roman Catholic church the services (usually observed only in monastic churches) that take place eight times a day (every three hours): Matins, Lauds, Prime, Terce, Sext, None, Vespers, and Compline. Musically the important services are Matins, Vespers, and Compline.

Ontology   (Gk., *on,* being + *logos,* logic) Philosophic inquiry into the ultimate nature of things, what it means to be.

Opera (from I., *opera in musica,* work in music) A play in which the text is generally sung throughout to the accompaniment of an orchestra. Modern opera had its beginnings in Florence in the late sixteenth century when some musicians, poets, and scholars attempted a revival of Greek drama, which they assumed to have been sung throughout. Opera depends for its effect on communicating through song rather than other theatrical conventions such as blank verse. It is a complex synthesis of various arts: music, poetry, scenery, stagecraft, costume design, and acting. Because it is so complex it is expensive to produce (and attend) and therefore has a certain association with "society" as a prestige symbol. However, when a well-written opera is effectively staged, acted, and sung (in the language of the audience) the effect is not that of an esoteric status symbol but rather an overwhelming musical-theatrical-artistic experience.

Opus (L., work) Abbreviated as op., it generally indicates the chronological order of "works" of music. When the designation is, for example, op. 2 no. 4, the work is the fourth part or portion of a composer's second major work. This designation is usually used for a related series of short compositions, for example, twenty-four *Preludes* by Chopin in his Opus 28.

Oratorio A musical setting of a religious or epic theme for performance by soloists, chorus, and orchestra in a church or concert hall. Originally (early seventeenth century) they were similar to operas (sacred operas) with staging, costumes, and scenery. They are now usually presented in concert form, for example, *The Messiah,* by G. F. Handel.

Orchestra (from Gk., *orcheisthai,* to dance) In ancient Greek theatres the circular or semicircular space in front of the stage used by the chorus; group of instrumentalists performing ensemble music, e.g. symphony orchestra.

Ordinary of the Mass v. Mass.

Organ, Pipe organ An instrument (see Hydraulis) of ancient origin consisting of from two to seven keyboards (manuals) and a set of pedals (usually thirty-two notes) for the feet. Organs have anywhere from a few hundred up to ten thousand individual pipes, a mechanical wind supply (electric blower), and a keyboard action that is either mechanical (directly connected to pipes with wooden "trackers"), pneumatic, or electric (opening the pipes with air or with electrical action). Some modern organs are so complex that they have built-in computers to assist with "registration," that is, the selection of which ranks (or sets) of pipes to use. Many pipe organ manufacturers are operating around the clock in an effort to keep up with the demand for what has been called the king of instruments. The pipe organ is not to be confused with the numerous electronic imitations, which attempt to reproduce the sound of real pipes.

Organum (OR–ga–num; L.) The name given to the earliest types of *polyphonic music. Beginning with about the ninth century, organum was first strict, then parallel, free (contrary motion), and *melismatic. See (in the text) the section on medieval music for description and illustrations of the stages of organum.

Overture Musical introduction to an *opera, *oratorio, or other large work; an independent orchestral work in one movement.

P

Pantheism (Gk., *pan,* all, + *theos,* god) As a religious concept, the doctrine that God is immanent in all things.

Pediment In classic architecture a triangular space at the end of a building framed by the *cornice and the ends of the sloping roof (*raking cornices). (See fig. 3.38.)

Pendentive In architecture a concave triangular piece of masonry, four of which form a transition from a square base to support the circular rim of a *dome. (See fig. 8.20.)

Percussion Instruments that are played by striking, shaking, scraping, etc. See separate articles for more detailed descriptions of individual instruments. Percussion instruments can be divided into two groups:

Instruments of definite pitch
Timpani
Glockenspiel or Bells
Celesta
Xylophone
Marimba
Chimes
Vibraphone

Instruments of indefinite pitch
Snare drum (side drum)
Tenor drum
Bass drum
Tambourine
Triangle
Cymbals
Tam-Tam (gong)
Castanets
Guiro
Maracas

Period An inner division of music usually consisting of two or three *phrases.

Peristyle A series of columns that surround the exterior of a building or the interior of a court, e.g., the Parthenon has a peristyle. (See figs. 3.44 and 22.2.)

Perspective The illusion of a three-dimensional world on a two-dimensional surface. *Linear perspective* uses lines of projection converging on a vanishing point and with objects appearing smaller the further from the viewer. *Aerial (atmospheric) perspective* uses diminished color intensity and blurred contours for objects apparently deeper in space.

Phrase A division of music larger than a *motive but smaller than a *period. It is a unit of melody (harmony and rhythm) of no specific length that expresses at least a comprehensible portion of a musical idea. It might be compared with a phrase of speech.

Pier A mass of masonry, usually large, used to support arches or lintels; more massive than a *column and with a shape other than circular. (See fig. 15.10.)

Pieta (pyay–TA; I., pity, compassion) Representations of the Virgin mourning the body of her Son. (See fig. 14.26.)

Pilaster A flat vertical column projecting from the wall of a building; usually furnished with a base and capital in the manner of an *engaged column, which is rounded rather than rectangular like the pilaster.

Plainsong   The term generally used for the large body of nonmetrical, *monophonic, *liturgical music of the Roman Catholic church. Also called Gregorian chant.

Polyphony   (po-LIF-o-nee) *Polyphonic* (pol-ly-PHON-ik) "Many-voiced" music, that is, melodic interest in two or more simultaneous melodic lines. Examples of polyphonic music would be *canons and *rounds.

Positivism   Philosophic inquiry limited to problems open to scientific investigation. Traditional subjects such as aesthetics and metaphysics are dismissed as "meaningless" because their content cannot be subjected to verification.

Post and lintel   A structural system in which vertical supports or columns support horizontal beams. The lintel can span only a relatively short space because the weight of the superstructure centers on the mid-point of the horizontal beam. In a structural system using *arches the thrust is distributed to the columns supporting the bases of the arches, thus allowing for a greater span. The lintel is also called an *architrave. (See fig. 3.36.)

Pragmatism   (Gk., *pragma,* things done) Philosophic doctrine that the meaning of a proposition or course of action lies in its observable consequences and that its meaning is the sum of its consequences. In everyday life the favoring of practical means over theory; if something works it's good; if not, it's bad.

Primary colors   The *hues of red, yellow, and blue with which the colors of the spectrum can be produced. Primary colors cannot be produced by mixing.

Program music   Music intended to depict ideas, scenes, or other extramusical concepts. (See chap. 21.)

Proper of the Mass   v. Mass.

Proscenium   (Gk., *pro,* before; *skene,* stage) In traditional theatres the framework of the stage opening.

Psalm   A sacred song, poem, or hymn; the songs in the Old Testament book of The Psalms.

Psalter   Vernacular name for the book of The Psalms. v. Psalm.

Psaltery   Ancient or medieval instrument consisting of a flat soundboard over which a number of strings are stretched. A psaltery is plucked with the fingers. A similar instrument, the dulcimer, is played by striking the strings with hammers. The *harpsichord is a keyed psaltery. (See fig. 10.1.)

Putto   (I., plural *putti,* boy) The cherubs in Italian Renaissance painting and in rococo painting of the eighteenth century. (See colorplate 39.)

Q

Quatrain   A stanza of four lines, either rhymed or unrhymed.

R

Raking cornice   The end (cornice) on the sloping sides of a triangular *pediment.

Rebec   A small bowed medieval string instrument adapted from the Arabian *rebab.* It was one of the instruments from which the violin developed during the sixteenth century. (See fig. 12.3.)

Recorder   A straight, end-blown *flute, as distinct from the modern side-blown (transverse) flute. It was used from the Middle Ages until the eighteenth century and has been revived in the twentieth century.

Refrain   Recurring section of text (and usually music), e.g., verse-refrain.

Relief   In sculpture, carvings projecting from a background that is a part of the whole. Reliefs may be high (almost disengaged from the background) or low (*bas relief,* slightly raised above the background).

Reliquary   (F., remains) A receptacle for storing or displaying holy relics. (See colorplate 15.)

Rhythm   The temporal organization of music, for example, anything and everything that has to do with the motion of music, with the movement of sound in time. Rhythm is involved with pulsations (beats) that are either played or implied but it should not be confused with *meter, which is a regular pattern of beats or pulsations.

Rondo   A musical form with a primary theme alternating with several contrasting themes, e.g., ABACA.

Rotta   A medieval harp, probably originating with the Celts of western Europe. Also called a Celtic harp.

Round   In music a commonly used name for a circle *canon. At the conclusion of a melody the singer returns to the beginning, repeating the melody as often as desired. Examples: "Brother James," "Dona Nobis Pacem," and "Row, Row Your Boat."

S

Sanctuary   A sacred or holy place set aside for the worship of a god or gods; a place of refuge or protection.

Sanctus   (L., Holy) The fourth item in the *Ordinary of the *Mass.

Sarcophagus   A stone coffin. (See fig. 8.8.)

Satire   An indictment of human foibles using humor as a weapon, e.g., "A Modest Proposal" by Swift (chap. 17).

Scale   (L., ladder) The tonal material of music arranged in a series of rising or falling pitches. Because of the variety in the world's music there are many different scales. The basic scale of European music is the diatonic scale (C–D–E–F–G–A–B–C), i.e., the white keys of the piano. This arrangement of tones is also called a major scale or, more properly, a C major scale. Other commonly used scales are:

Minor	C–D–E♭–F–G–A♭–B♭–C
Whole tone	C–D–E–F♯–G♯–A♯–C
Pentatonic	C–D–F–G–A–C
Dorian mode	C–D–E♭–F–G–A–B♭–C
Phrygian mode	C–D♭–E♭–F–G–A♭–B♭–C

Scholasticism   The philosophy and method of medieval theologians in which speculation was separated from observation and practice, revelation was regarded as both the norm and an aid to reason, reason respected authority, and scientific inquiry was controlled by theology.

Secondary colors   Those *hues located between the *primary hues on a traditional color wheel: orange, green, and violet.

Semitone The smallest standard interval in Western music; half of a whole tone, for example, from C to C♯ on the piano keyboard.

Sempre (SEM–pra; I., Always).

Sequence A type of chant developed in the early Middle Ages in which a freely poetic text was added to the long *melisma at the end of the Alleluias. Subsequently separated from the Alleluias, the sequences became independent syllabic chants. The composition of many original sequences finally led to the banning of all but five sequences by the Council of Trent (1545–1563).

Serial composition A general term applied to twentieth-century music that uses a tone row (v. twelve-tone technique), but which also serializes other elements of music, such as *rhythm, *dynamics, and *timbre.

Sfumato (sfoo–MAH–toe) A hazy, smoky blending of color tones in a painting to create ambiguities of line and shape, as in Leonardo's *Ginevra de'Benci.* (See colorplate 25.)

Sharp v. Accidental.

Shawm A double-reed instrument that preceded the *oboe.

Simile A comparison between two quite different things, usually using "like" or "as."

Snare drum v. Drum.

Sonata (I., *sonare,* to sound) An instrumental (sounding) piece which, in the seventeenth century, denoted a composition for a single instrument. Since about 1750 the term has come to mean a composition in several movements for a keyboard instrument or for solo instrument with keyboard accompaniment. "Duet sonatas" (solo instrument plus keyboard) usually have three movements (fast-slow-fast), while solo sonatas usually have four movements (fast-slow-moderate-fast).

Sonata form A term used for a structural design in which two contrasting themes appear in an initial exposure (exposition), after which one or both are altered, fragmented, and otherwise exploited (development). The form concludes with a return to the initial material (recapitulation) followed by a concluding section (coda) when necessary. Sonata form differs from other musical forms in that it is a dual thematic form with the two themes of approximately equal importance.

Sonnet A fourteen-line poem in iambic pentameter. Petrarch, the fourteenth-century Italian poet, used a rhyming scheme of *abbaabba* followed by *cde cde* or variants thereof. Shakespeare used a rhyming scheme of *abab cdcd efef gg,* or four *quatrains followed by a *rhymed couplet. (See chap. 16.)

Soprano The highest female singing voice, that is, <u>S</u> A T B. The term is also applied to the highest pitched instruments in a family of instruments, for example, soprano saxophones.

Spinet Originally a name for small *harpsichords with only one manual (keyboard). The term is used today for small upright pianos.

Squinch In architecture a device to effect a transition from a polygonal base to a circular dome. (See fig. 8.17 and accompanying explanation.)

Staff (musical) A set of five horizontal lines on which music is written. *Plainsong still uses a four-line staff.

Stele (STEE-lee) A carved slab of stone or pillar used especially by the Greeks as a grave marker. (See fig. 3.59.)

Still life In pictorial arts inanimate objects used as subject matter.

Stringed instruments Instruments in which the sound is produced by a stretched string. They may be divided into four main groups (see individual definitions for descriptions):

Stretched strings on a frame.
Plucked: zither.
Plucked, with keyboard: harpsichord, virginal, spinet.
Struck by hammer: dulcimer.
Struck by hammer, with keyboard: piano.
Strings touched by tangents: clavichord.

Instruments having a body and a neck.
Plucked: lute family (round back), guitar family (flat back).
Bowed: violin family, viols, vielle, rebec.

Instruments with projecting arms and crossbar: lyre, kithara.

Instrument with vertical strings: harp.

String quartet The standard chamber music ensemble of violin I and II, viola, cello. String quartets date from about 1750. In effect they are *sonatas for four instrumentalists.

Strophic A song in which the same music is used for all stanzas. When new music is used for each stanza the song is through-composed.

Stylobate The third of three steps of a Greek temple on which the *columns rest; essentially the platform on which the *cella and *peristyle are erected. (See fig. 3.38.)

Syllogism A form of deductive reasoning consisting of a major premise, minor premise, and a conclusion. Example: all men are mortal; Socrates is a man; therefore Socrates is mortal.

Symphony Since the classic era (1760–1827) the term stands for a *sonata for orchestra. Symphonies are played, naturally enough, by symphony orchestras and are usually (but not always) in a four-movement form.

Syncopation Stressing a beat or portion of a beat that is usually weak or unaccented. Most commonly used in jazz.

T

Tabor A medieval drum shaped like a long cylinder. Played with one stick to accompany a small *recorder, hence the standard combination of pipe and tabor.

Teleology (Gk., *telos,* end, completion) The theory of purpose, ends, goals, final cause; opposite of materialism.

Tempera A painting technique using pigment suspended in egg yolk.

Tempo   The pace or speed of a musical composition. Since the seventeenth century, Italian terms have been used to give an approximation of the desired tempo. The invention of the metronome provides a more precise indication of a specific tempo. However, the size of an audience, the acoustics of a hall, and many other factors make the matter of tempo subject to a variety of interpretations. Some of the more common Italian tempo markings are given below, reading from slow tempo to progressively faster tempos:

Largo   Slow, broad.

Grave   (GRAH–vay) Slow, solemn.

Lento   Slow.

Adagio   (uh–DAH–jo) "At ease," slow.

Andante   (ahn–DAHN–tay) "Walking tempo," that is, moderate.

Andante cantabile   (kahn–TAH–bi–lay) In a singing manner.

Andante con moto   Andante "with motion."

Andantino   Slightly faster than andante.

Allegretto   (ahl–luh–GRET–toe) Moderately lively.

Allegro   (ahl–LEH–gro) "Cheerful," that is, fast.

Allegro appassionato   With passion.

Allegro giocoso   (joe–KO–so) Merrily.

Allegro marcato   Emphatic.

Allegro moderato   Moderately fast.

Allegro non troppo   Fast but "not too fast."

Molto allegro   "Much" fast, that is, very fast.

Vivace   (vee–VAH–chay) Very fast.

Presto   Very fast.

Presto con fuoco   Very fast, "with fire."

Prestissimo   Very, very fast.

Tenor   (L., *tenere,* to hold) (1) Originally the part that "held" the melody on which early sacred polyphonic music was based. (2) The highest male voice (S A T̲ B). (3) Prefix to the name of an instrument, for example, tenor saxophone.

Terra-cotta   (I., baked earth) A baked clay used in ceramics and sculptures; a reddish color.

Tesserae   (TESS–er–ee) Bits of stone and colored glass used in *mosaics.

Tetrachord   In ancient Greek music a succession of four descending notes (a–g–f–e), which formed the nucleus of Greek music theory. Now loosely applied to any four-note segment of a scale.

Texture   The melodic (horizontal) and harmonic (vertical) fabric of music, comparable to the horizontal and vertical aspects (warp and woof) of woven fabrics. There are three basic textures: *monophonic, *homophonic, *polyphonic. All music (except monophonic music) consists of a varying combination of vertical and horizontal relationships. A polyphonic texture with two distinct melodies still has a vertical aspect brought about by the harmonic intervals formed by the two melodies. A texture with two clearly defined melodies is necessarily described as polyphonic, providing there is also a realization of the harmonic implications of simultaneous melodies.

Thrust   The outward force caused by the weight and design of an *arch or *vault, a thrust that must be countered by a *buttress. (See fig. 11.26.)

Timbre   (tambr; F., tone color) Also used in English as a term referring to the coloration of musical tones, that is, the quality that enables a listener to distinguish, for example, between a flute, an oboe, and a clarinet. Tone color is the result of the relative strengths and weakness of the tones (partials) in the overtone series. In practical terms tone color is dependent on how a tone is produced (blowing, striking, bowing, etc.), the material used (wood, silver, platinum, etc.), and the abilities of individual performers. Two different trumpet players, for example, would produce a slightly different tone color when alternating on the same instrument.

Tone   (1) In music a sound of well-defined pitch, as distinct from noise. (2) The distance of a whole step (two semitones).

Tone color   v. Timbre.

Tragedy   A serious play or other literary work with an unhappy or disastrous ending caused, in Greek drama, by *hubris on the part of the protagonist.

Transcendental   Beyond the realm of the senses; rising above common thought or ideas; exalted.

Transept   That part of a *cruciform-plan church whose axis intersects at right angles the long axis of the cross running from the entrance through the *nave to the *apse; the cross-arm of the cross.

Treble clef   v. Clef.

Triforium   In a Gothic cathedral, the gallery between the *nave arcades and the *clerestory; the triforium gallery opens on the nave with an *arcade. (See fig. 11.34.)

Triglyph   Projecting block with vertical channels that alternates with *metopes in a *Dorian *frieze of a Greek temple. The ends of the marble beams are stylized versions of the wooden beams used in early temples.

Trombone   A tenor-baritone-range brass instrument with a cylindrical bore, played with a cup-shaped mouthpiece and a movable slide. The slide is the oldest method (fifteenth century) of changing the length of air column in a brass instrument, making the trombone the oldest member of the modern brass family.

Trompe-l'oeil   (trohmp LUH–yuh; F.) Illusionistic painting designed to convince the observer that what is seen is an actual three-dimensional object rather than a two-dimensional surface; literally, "eye fooling."

Trope   Additional text and/or music added to a preexisting *plainsong. The earliest tropes were *sequences. Troping became so widespread that it was banned by the Council of Trent. *Liturgical drama was a direct outgrowth of the trope.

Troubadour   Poet-musicians, mostly of aristocratic birth, of southern France (Provence) who, during the period ca. 1100–1300, cultivated the arts of poetry and music in chivalrous service to romantic love. Their music was *monophonic in style and popular in flavor but exerted considerable influence on the development of *polyphonic music.

Trouvère Poet-musicians of central and northern France from ca. 1150–1300. Their music developed from the *troubadours and showed the same general characteristics except for the change in language from that of the south (Provençal) to the medieval forerunner of modern French.

Trumeau A pillar or column placed in the center of a portal to help support the *lintel. (See fig. 11.20.)

Trumpet A soprano-range brass instrument with basically a cylindrical bore and a cup mouthpiece. The modern trumpet lengthens the air column by using valves. The trumpet is the standard orchestral instrument and should not be confused with the instrument of shorter length and similar shape used frequently in military bands, namely, the *cornet*. The cornet has basically a conical bore and a milder and more mellow tone.

Tuba The bass instrument of the brass family with conical bore, three to five valves, and played with a cup mouthpiece.

Twelve-tone technique A twentieth-century procedure developed by Schoenberg and based on the equal tonal value of the twelve different notes within one octave. Basic to this system of *atonality is the tone row in which the twelve different notes are arranged in a nontonal pattern and used repeatedly with only mathematical variations: reverse order, change of octave, and so forth.

Tympanum The space, usually elaborately carved, enclosed by the lintel and arch of a doorway; also, the space within the horizontal and *raking cornices of a *pediment. (See fig. 11.17.)

V

Vanishing point In linear *perspective the point at which parallel lines converge on the horizon.

Vault A masonry ceiling constructed on the principle of the arch. A *barrel vault* is an uninterrupted series of arches amounting to a very deep arch. (See fig. 11.14.)

Vibrato (I., shaken) In music rapid but minute fluctuations of pitch that add a certain expressive quality to the pitch. Vocalists and string players traditionally use a vibrato on every note but other performers may or may not, depending on the circumstances.

Vielle Medieval stringed instrument (twelfth to fifteenth centuries), succeeded by the *viol (sixteenth century), which in turn was replaced by the *violin family.

Viol (VIE–ul) A family of bowed stringed instruments that were popular during the Renaissance and early Baroque periods and are being made again today. Three sizes were normally used, all with flat backs and sloping shoulders, and played sitting down with the instrument held between the knees. The string bass (bass viol) is the sole survivor of the viol family in the modern orchestra.

Viola The alto-tenor member of the violin family. Slightly larger than the violin but with a rather muffled tone, the viola has been a regular member of the orchestra since the seventeenth century.

Violin The violin emerged from the various bowed string instruments around 1600 and, with its brighter and more brilliant tone, replaced the *viols during the seventeenth century. As distinguished from the viol, it has a slightly rounded back and round shoulders. The best violins ever made were built in and around Cremona, Italy, from ca. 1600–1750 by the families Amati, Guarnierius, and Stradivarius.

Virelai A form of medieval French poetry with a refrain before and after each stanza. Virelais were used by *trouvères and exploited during the Gothic period by Machaut and others.

Virginal A *harpsichord used mainly in England and supposedly played by young ladies. The shape was frequently rectangular. When built in the standard two-keyboard form it was called a "pair of virginals."

Volute The spiral scrolls of an *Ionian *capital.

Voussoir (voo–SWAHR; F.) The wedge-shaped blocks of stone used to construct *arches and *vaults. (See fig. 11.27.)

W

Whole tone scale v. Scales.

Woodcut A wood block that has been carved so that the design stands out slightly from the block, comparable to printing type.

Woodwinds A group of instruments most of which were, at one time, built of wood. There are three general types (see separate definitions for more detailed information):

Tube open at both ends
Piccolo
Flute
Alto flute

Double-reed instruments
Oboe
English horn
Bassoon
Contra bassoon

Single-reed instruments
Clarinet
Bass clarinet
Contra bass clarinet
Saxophone family

X

Xylophone (Gk., wood sound) A percussion instrument consisting of a "keyboard" of hardwood bars and played with mallets. The tone is dry, brittle, and penetrating.

Credits

Photographs

Figure 18.14   Alinari/Art Resource.
Figure 18.21   Timkin Gallery, San Diego Museum of Art, San Diego, California.
Figure 18.22   Andrew W. Mellon Collection. National Gallery of Art, Washington, D.C.
Figure 18.23   Alinari/Art Resource.
Figure 18.24   Gift of Mrs. Mellon Bruce in memory of her father Andrew W. Mellon, 1961. National Gallery of Art, Washington, D.C.
Figure 18.25   Samuel H. Kress Collection. National Gallery of Art, Washington, D.C.
Figure 18.26   Samuel H. Kress Collection. National Gallery of Art, Washington, D.C.
Figure 18.35   Alinari/Art Resource.
Figure 18.36   The Metropolitan Museum of Art. Wolfe Fund, 1931.
Figure 18.37   San Diego Museum of Art, San Diego, California.
Figure 18.38   Metropolitan Museum of Art, New York. Bequest of Isaac D. Fletcher.
Figure 18.39   Chester Dale Collection. National Gallery of Art, Washington, D.C.
Figure 22.3   Alinari/Art Resource.
Figure 22.4   Andrew W. Mellon Collection. National Gallery of Art, Washington, D.C.
Figure 22.5   Andrew W. Mellon Collection. National Gallery of Art, Washington, D.C.
Figure 22.7   Alinari/Art Resource.
Figure 22.8   Art Reference Bureau.
Figure 22.13   Shaw Collection. Museum of Fine Arts, Boston.
Figure 22.15   The Arizona State University Art Collections, Arizona State University. Gift of Oliver B. James.
Figure 22.17   Art Reference Bureau.
Figure 22.18   Art Reference Bureau.
Figure 22.21   Art Reference Bureau.
Figure 22.22   Art Reference Bureau.
Figure 22.25   Art Reference Bureau.
Figure 22.26   Gift of Mrs. John W. Simpson. National Gallery of Art, Washington, D.C.
Figure 22.30   National Galleries, Edinburgh. National Galleries of Scotland.
Figure 22.34   Art Reference Bureau.
Figure 25.1   National Gallery of Art, Washington, D.C.
Figure 25.2   Chester Dale Collection, 1962. National Gallery of Art, Washington, D.C.
Figure 25.6   National Gallery of Art, Washington, D.C.
Figure 25.8   The University Art Collections, Arizona State University, Tempe. Gift of Dr. and Mrs. Richard Besson.
Figure 25.9   Collection, The Museum of Modern Art, New York.
Figure 25.10   Chester Dale Collection, 1962. National Gallery of Art, Washington, D.C.
Figure 25.11   The Prado Museum, Madrid.
Figure 25.14   Collection, The Museum of Modern Art, New York. Given anonymously.
Figure 25.15   The Philadelphia Museum of Art. Louise and Walter Arensberg Collection.
Figure 25.16   Collection, The Museum of Modern Art, New York.
Figure 25.17   Collection, The Museum of Modern Art, New York. Mrs. Simon Guggenheim Fund.
Figure 25.18   Collection, The Museum of Modern Art, New York.
Figure 25.19   Courtesy Marlborough Gallery, New York.
Figure 25.20   Collection, The Museum of Modern Art, New York. Given anonymously.
Figure 25.22   Collection, The Museum of Modern Art, New York.
Figure 25.23   The Museum of Modern Art, New York. James Thrall Soby Fund.
Figure 25.27   The University Art Collections, Arizona State University, Tempe.
Figure 25.31   Art Reference Bureau.
Figure 25.32   Joslyn Art Museum, Omaha, Nebraska.
Figure 25.33   Leo Castelli, New York.
Figure 25.34   Moderna Museet, Stockholm, Sweden.
Figure 25.35   Copyright Gemini G. E. L., 1968.
Figure 25.36   Collection, The Museum of Modern Art, New York.
Figure 25.37   Courtesy, The American Republic Insurance Company, Des Moines, Iowa
Figure 25.38   Multiples, New York.
Figure 25.39   Multiples, New York.
Figure 25.40   Collection of the High Museum, Atlanta, Georgia. Courtesy of the Margo Leavin Gallery, Los Angeles.
Figure 25.41   Collection, The Museum of Modern Art, New York.
Figure 25.42   Whitney Museum of American Art, New York.
Figure 25.43   Joslyn Art Museum, Omaha, Nebraska.
Figure 25.44   Joslyn Art Museum, Omaha, Nebraska.
Figure 25.45   Whitney Museum of American Art, New York.
Figure 25.46   Collection, The Museum of Modern Art, New York.
Figure 25.47   Collection, The Museum of Modern Art, New York.
Figure 25.48   Collection, The Museum of Modern Art, New York.
Figure 25.49   The University Art Collections, Arizona State University, Tempe.
Figure 25.50   American Art Heritage Fund. Arizona State University Art Collections, Tempe.
Figure 25.51   The University Art Collections, Arizona State University, Tempe.
Figure 25.52   Collection of Edward Jacobson, Phoenix, Arizona.
Figure 25.53   The University Art Collections, Arizona State University, Tempe.
Figure 25.54   Courtesy of ConStruct, Chicago.
Figure 25.55   Museum of Art, The University of Arizona.

Figure 25.56   American Art Heritage Fund. Arizona State University Art Collections, Tempe.
Figure 25.57   The San Diego Museum of Art, San Diego, California.
Figure 25.58   Courtesy Fishback Gallery, New York.
Figure 25.59   The University Art Collections, Arizona State University, Tempe.
Figure 25.60   Courtesy, Ponderosa System, Inc., Dayton, Ohio.
Figure 25.61   Courtesy, The Elaine Horwitch Galleries, Scottsdale.

Literary Selections

The Bobbs-Merrill Company, Inc., for permission to reprint "Apology," from *Euthyphro Apology & Crito,* translated by F. J. Church and R. D. Cumming, Copyright © 1959, by the Bobbs-Merrill Co., Inc. Reprinted by permission of the publisher. For permission to reprint "On the Dedication of the Colosseum in Rome," from *Martial: Selected Epigrams,* translated by Ralph Marcellino, © 1968, by the Bobbs-Merrill Co., Inc. Reprinted by permission of the publisher.

Boosey and Hawkes, Inc., for selections from Bartok's Concerto for Orchestra. Copyright © 1946 by Hawkes & Son (London) Ltd. Renewed 1973. Reprinted by permission of Boosey and Hawkes, Inc.

Broadside Press Publications for "Nikki-Rosa" from *Black Judgment.* Copyright © 1968 by Nikki Giovanni. Reprinted by permission of Broadside Press. And for "Man Thinking About Woman" and "Mixed Sketches" from *Directionscore,* © 1971 by Don L. Lee. Reprinted by permission of Broadside Press.

Delacorte Press for "Deer in the Works" excerpted from the book *Welcome to the Monkey House* by Kurt Vonnegut, Jr. Copyright © 1955 by Kurt Vonnegut, Jr. Originally published in *Esquire.* Used by permission of Delacorte Press/Seymour Lawrence.

Duke University Press for selections from *The Prince.* Published in *Machiavelli: The Chief Works and Others,* vol. 1, translated and edited by Allan H. Gilbert. By permission of Duke University Press. Copyright © 1965, Duke University Press (Durham, N.C.).

Farrar, Straus & Giroux, Inc., for "Life, friends, is boring" from *77 Dream Songs* by John Berryman. Copyright © 1959, 1962, 1963, 1964 by John Berryman. Reprinted by permission of Farrar, Straus & Giroux, Inc.

Harcourt Brace Jovanovich, Inc., for "The Love Song of J. Alfred Prufrock" from *Collected Poems 1909–1962* by T. S. Eliot, copyright 1936 by Harcourt Brace Jovanovich, Inc.; copyright © 1963, 1964 by T. S. Eliot. Reprinted by permission of the publisher. And for "anyone lived in a pretty how town" from *Poems 1923–1954* by e e cummings; copyright 1940 by e e cummings; renewed by Marion Morehouse Cummings. Reprinted by permission of Harcourt Brace Jovanovich, Inc.

Harper & Row, Publishers, Inc., for "Yet Do I Marvel" from *On These I Stand* by Countee Cullen. Copyright 1925 by Harper & Row Publishers, Inc.; renewed 1953 by Ida M. Cullen. By permission of Harper & Row, Publishers, Inc. And for "Flight on the Wind" from *House Made of Dawn* by N. Scott Momaday. Copyright © 1966, 1967, 1968 by N. Scott Momaday. By permission of Harper & Row, Publishers, Inc. And for "The Ethics of Living Jim Crow" from *Uncle Tom's Children* by Richard Wright. Copyright 1937 by Richard Wright. By permission of Harper & Row, Publishers, Inc.

Holt, Rinehart and Winston, Inc., for A. E. Housman's "With rue my heart is laden," from "A Shropshire Lad," Authorized Edition from *The Collected Poems of A. E. Housman,* Copyright 1939, 1940, © 1965 by Holt, Rinehart and Winston. Copyright © 1967, 1968 by Robert E. Symons. Reprinted by permission of Holt, Rinehart and Winston, Publishers.

Loeb Classical Library of the Harvard University Press for the selection from *Arrian's Discourses of Epictetus,* translated by W. A. Oldfather. Reprinted by permission.

Macmillan Publishing Co., Inc., for "The Second Coming" from *Collected Poems* by William Butler Yeats. Copyright 1924 by Macmillan Publishing Co., Inc., renewed 1952 by Bertha Georgie Yeats. Reprinted with permission of Macmillan Publishing Company.

Mason and Lipscom for permission to reprint some poems from *Selected Poems of Catullus,* translated by Carl Sesar, © 1974.

The National Council of Churches of Christ in the U.S.A. The Scripture Quotations in this publication are from the Revised Standard Version of the Bible, copyrighted 1946, 1952, © 1971, 1973 by the Division of Christian Education of the National Council of Churches of Christ in the U.S.A., and used by permission.

Nature for "How True is the Theory of Evolution" by Charles Darwin. Reprinted by permission from *Nature,* Vol. 290, No. 11, pp. 75–76. Copyright © 1981 Macmillan Journals Limited.

Index

All B.C. dates are specified. Titles of works are set in italics with the artist's name in parentheses. Descriptive titles of art and titles of essays, short stories, and poems are enclosed in quotation marks. Titles of literary selections and excerpts are set in boldface type. Page numbers of black-and-white illustrations are in boldface type; colorplates are specifically so designated. See the Glossary for definitions of technical terms.

A

Aachen (Aix-la-Chapelle), Germany, 190, 235
Abacus, 86
Abbotsford, 467, **468**
Abelard, Peter, French philosopher/ teacher (1079–1142), 208–9
Abelard and Heloise (Dronke), 208
Abraham, father of Judaism, 156, 172, **176**
Abraham and the Celestial Visitors, Church of Santa Maria Maggiore, Rome, 176, **176**
Absolutism, 280, 281, 328, 343, 348–49, 360, 373–74
Abstract Expressionism, 524, 535, 536, 540, 542, 544
Academy of Plato, 47, 122, 210
A cappella, 252, 387, 388
Acoustics, 37–38, 99, 106
Actium, Battle of, 115
Act of Supremacy, 275, 277
Adam, 159, 172, 213, 296
Adams, Henry, American author (1838–1918), 206, 207 (quotation), 209
Adoration of the Magi (Fra Angelico and Fra Filippo Lippi), **288,** 288–89
Adoration of the Magi, The (Botticelli), 291, **292,** 293
Adoration of the Shepherds (Giorgione), 304, colorplate 28
Adrian VI, Pope (1459–1523), 327
Adventures of Huckleberry Finn, The (Twain), 438
Adventures of Tom Sawyer, The (Twain), 438
Aegean Sea, 26, **27,** 28, 31, 34, 73
Aeneas, 97, 111–12, 119, 126–27, 142
Aeneid (Virgil), 111–12, 125–27
Aeschylus, Greek dramatist (525–456 B.C.), 42–46, 47, 51, 52, 57, 82, 105, 119, 270
Africa, 573, 574, 575, 576–78, 579, 584
Africa (Jones), 549
Africa (Petrarch), 325
African Dancer (Barthé), 549
Agamemnon, King of Mycenae (ca. 1200 B.C.), 28, 31, 43 (box), 44, 75, 112, 126, 309
Agamemnon (Aeschylus), 43–45, 52, 105
Agaue, 48 (box), 50
Age of Progress, 472, 473, 521
Age of Reason, 119, 344, 387
Agnus Dei (Palestrina), 319 (music)
Agnus Dei (Zurbarán), 370, **371**
Agora, Athens, 47, 57

Agricola, Alexander, Flemish composer (1446–1506), 317
Aida (Verdi), 458
Aigisthos, 43 (box), 44
Aigues-Mortes, France, 189, **189**
Akhilleus, 28, 31, 79, 82, 91, 125, 127
"Akhilleus Bandaging Patroklos's Wound," 82, **82**
"Akhilleus Slaying Penthesilea" (Exekias), 79, **79**
Akropolis, Athens, 45, 46, 47, 84, 86, 87, **87,** 90, 119. *See also* Erechtheion; Parthenon; Propylaia; Temple of Athena Nike
Akrotiri, Thera (Santorini), 27, 28
Alba Madonna, The (Raphael), 303, colorplate 27
Albers, Josef, American artist (1888–1976), 540, **540**
Alberti, Leonbattista, Florentine humanist and architect (1404–1472), 290, **290, 291,** 308, 366
Albigensian
crusade, 259
"heresy," 259
Alcestis (Euripides), 593
Alcuin, English churchman and scholar (735?–804), 190
Alexander I, Czar of Russia (1777–1825), 408
Alexander II, Czar of Russia (1818–1881), 408
Alexander III, Czar of Russia (1845–1894), 408
Alexander VI (Rodrigo Borgia), Pope (1431?–1503), 294, 299, 301, 302
Alexander the Great, King of Macedonia (356–323 B.C.), 53–54, **54,** 56, 57, 70, 92, 94, 120, 145
Alexandria, Egypt, 53–54, 57, 159, 186
Alhambra, The, Granada, Spain, 233
Alkaios, Greek poet-musician, 102, **103**
"Alkaios and Sappho with Lyres," 103, **103**
Alkibiades, Athenian general, 50
Allah, 231
Alleluias, 252, **252,** 253, **253,** 254
Alleluya (Nativitas) (Perotin), 260, 260 (music)
All Set (Babbitt), 568
Altar of Zeus, Pergamon, 95, 96, **96**
Amalienburg lodge, Munich (Cuvilliés), 395, **395**
Ambrose, St., Bishop of Milan (340?–397), 126 (overview), 186
Amenhotep III, Egyptian pharaoh of New Kingdom, 71
American in Paris, An (Gershwin), 570

American Man, The (Portrait of Watson Powell) (Warhol), 538, **538**
American Pavilion, EXPO 67 (Fuller), 553, **553**
American Tragedy, An (Dreiser), 595
Amiens Cathedral, France, 244–45, **245,** 246, 249
Amistad Murals, The (Woodruff), 548–49
Amos, Book of (Bible), 5:11–15; 6:4–8, 157 (text)
Amos, Hebrew prophet (8th c. B.C.), 157
Amphion, Greek musician, 100
Amphion (Honegger), 571
Amphitheatres, Roman, in,
Arles, 146, **146**
Nîmes, 146
Pompeii, 146
Rome, 118–19, 124, 125, 145, 146, 150, 290
Verona, 146
Amphora of the Dipylon, 76, **76**
Anabaptists, 277
Anagram: "Jesus Christ, the Son of God, Savior," 171, **171**
Anakreon, Greek poet-musician (fl. 6th c. B.C.), 33, 102
Anavyssos Kouros, 80, 81, **81**
Anaximandvos, Ionian philosopher (ca. 610–547 B.C.) 35–36, 427
Ancient History (Daumier), 470
Anderson, Laurie, American artist (b. 1937), 549
Andreas Capellanus, court chaplain and writer (fl. 1174–1186), 229–30
Andrews, Benny, American artist (b. 1930), 549
Angel Dance, 261
Angelico, Fra, Florentine painter (1400–1455), 288–89, 297
"Annabel Lee" (Poe), 434 (text)
Annunciation (Martini), 249, colorplate 20
Annunciation (van Eyck), 296, colorplate 24
Anouilh, Jean, French playwright (b. 1910), 7 (quotation)
Anselm of Canterbury, prelate and philosopher (1033–1109), 208
Antelami, Benedetto, Italian sculptor and architect (late 12th, early 13th c.), 240–41
Antonine emperors, 116 (box), 149, 151
Antoninus Pius, Roman emperor (86–161), 116 (box), 147, 151
"anyone lived in a pretty how town" (cummings), 592, 596 (text)
Aphrodite, 29, 30 (box), **89,** 119, 171, 315

Aphrodite of Knidos (Praxiteles), **93,** 93–94
Aphrodite of Melos, 96, **96**
Apocalypse, 166, 243, 523
Apollinaire, Guillaume, French poet and critic (1880–1918), 482
Apollo, 29, 30 (box), 44, 45, 73, 100, 101, 102, 105, 301
    cult of, 100, 105
Apollo and Marsyas (Greek), 101, **101**
Apollonian mode (Nietzsche), 503
Apology (Plato), 51, 53n, 57–67 (text)
Apostel, Hans Erich, Austrian composer (b. 1901), 571
Apostle Bartholomew, The (Rembrandt), 375, **375**
Apostles, 159, 162, 164, 175, 181, 187, 238, 239, 300 in art, 244
Apoxyomenos (Lysippos), 94, **94**
Appalachian Spring (Copland), 570
Apuleius, Lucius, Latin writer (fl. 2d c.), 126 (overview)
Aqueducts, Roman, 118, 140, 143–44, 145
Aquinas, St. Thomas, theologian and philosopher (1225–1274), 209, 211–12, 213, 214, 215, 216
Arabesques, 191, 233, 239
Arabic, 209, 232, 270
Arabs, 190, 191, 232, 271, 274
Arabs Skirmishing in the Mountains (Delacroix), 466, colorplate 40
Arch and vault construction, 143, **143,** 144, 146, 147, 239, 241–42
Arches, Roman triumphal, 143, 146–47, 149–50
Archilochos, Greek musician (fl. ca. 660 B.C.), 102
Architecture
    Art Nouveau, 533–34
    Baroque, 365–66, 368–71, 373–74, 586
    Byzantine, 178–81
    California Mission, 366
    Carolingian, 189, 235, 236
    early Christian, 169, 173–75, 240
    Egyptian, 6, 70–73, 89, 91, 175
    Gothic, 181, 211, 212, 213, 215, 237, 240, 241–49
    Greek, 6, 47, 76, 80, 84–91, 96, 145
    Greek archaic, 79
    Greek classical, 84–91, 302
    Greek geometric, 76
    Hellenistic, 96
    International Style, 534, 550–51
    Islamic, 231–34
    late nineteenth century, 472–73
    Minoan, 73–74
    Mycenaean, 75
    Neoclassic, 384–85
    Neogothic, 468, 469
    Neoromanesque, 467, **468**
    Norman, 237, 241
    organic, 534, **535**
    Renaissance, 285–86, 290–91, 302, 306–7, 308, 311
    Rococo, 395
    Roman, 141, 142–44, 145–50, 290
    Romanesque, 237, 238–39, 240, 241
    twentieth century, 533–34, **535,** 550–54
    Victorian, 468, **469**

Architrave, 85, 87, 90
Arch of
    Constantine, 149–50, **150**
    Septimus Severus, 149
    Titus, 143, 146–47, **147**
Arena Chapel. *See* Giotto
Areopagus, Athens, 45
Arete, 123, 124
Argos, 28, 43, 45, 50
Arian heresy, 169 (overview), 177, 186
Aristophanes, Athenian dramatist (Old Comedy) (ca. 448–380 B.C.), 51
Aristotle, Greek philosopher (384–322 B.C.), 7 (quotation), 49, 53, 56–57, 79, 105, 155, 159, 191, 208, 209, 211, 212, 213, 244, 303
Aristoxenus of Tarentum, Greek music theorist and philosopher (fl. 4th c. B.C.), 105
Armory Show (1913), 526, 532
Army, Roman, 113, 114, 115, 117, 148, 151, 185
Arnold, Matthew, English poet (1822–1888), 431, 432, 482
Arrangement in Gray and Black, No. 1 (Whistler), 477, **477**
Arrian of Nicomedia (Flavius Arrianus), Greek historian and philosopher (ca. 100–170), 135–36
Ars Antiqua (Old Art), 263
Ars Nova (New Art), 263
Art
    Abstract, 13–14, 524–30
    Abstract Expressionism, 535
    aesthetics of, 9, 12
    Baroque, 365–74
        Aristocratic, 371–74
        Bourgeois, 374–76
        Counter-Reformation, 365–71
    basis for understanding, 12–15
    Blackstream, 549, 611
    Byzantine, 14, 150, 178, 180, 181
    Carolingian, 236–37
    Classicism, 91, 463–64
    Cubism, 524–27
    Cycladic, 73
    Dada, 530
    early Christian, 150, 169–81 (chap. 8)
    Egyptian, 13, 70–73, 75, 77, 78, 82, 84
    Etruscan, 139–40
    Expressionism, 522–23
    Fantasy, 529–30
    Fauvism, 522–23
    Flemish, 13, 294–99
    Gothic, 241–42, 247–49
    Greek, 69–97 (chap. 3), 139, 140, 141, 145, 170, 171
    Greek archaic, 77–82
    Greek classical, 82–94, 180, 181, 463
    Greek geometric, 14, 76–77
    Hellenistic, 94–97
    Hiberno-Saxon, 234–35
    Hispanic, 547–48
    Impressionism, 473–78
    Islamic, 231–33
    Mannerism, 305–10
    Medieval, 231–50 (chap. 11)
    Minimal, 544–46
    Minoan, 73–75

Mycenaean, 75
Neoclassic, 380–85
nineteenth century, 463–82 (chap. 22)
nonobjective, 12, 14, 540–42
Op, 540, 542
Paleolithic, 3–4
Photorealism, 546–47
Pop, 535–39
Post-Impressionism, 478–82
Realism, 468–73, 532–33, 546–47
Renaissance, 285–313 (chap. 14)
    Early, 285–99
    High, 299–305, 310–11
    Late, 305–10, 311–12
Rococo, 376–80
Roman, 140–51
Romanesque, 237, 238, 240–41
Romanticism, 464–68
Surrealism, 530–32, 543–44
twentieth century, 521–56 (chap. 25)
Artemis, 29, 30 (box), 43, 73, **88**
Arthur, King, legendary British king, 230
Art Nouveau, 533, 534
Art of Courtly Love, The (Capellanus), 195n, 229–30 (text)
Art of Love (Ovid), 256
Ash Can school, 526, 532
Askanius (Ilus, Iulus), 126
Aspasia, consort of Perikles (470?–410 B.C.), 51–52
Association of American Artists and Painters, 526
Assumption of the Virgin (Rubens), 371–72, 373, colorplate 33
Astrodome, Houston, 150
Astrolabe, 274
Astrology, 120
Athanasius, Bishop of Alexandria (293?–373), 186
Athena, 6, 28, 29, 30 (box), 45, 46, 47, 86, **88,** 89, 90, 101, 119, 308
Athena Nike, Temple of (Kallikrates), 86, **90,** 90–91
Athens, 4, 6, 25, 26, 32, 34, 41–58, 71, 80, 82, 86, 87, 90, 91, 92, 99, 102, 105, 113, 119, 120, 121, 122, 125, 177, 328. *See also* Attica
Atlantis, 28
Atomic theory, Greek, 42
Atonality (twelve-tone system), 558–61, 567–68
Atreus, 43 (box), 44
Atrium, 174
    early Christian, 174
    Roman, 141, **141**
Attalos I, King of Pergamon (fl. 200 B.C.), 95, 96
Attica, 34, 35, 46, 50. *See also* Athens
Attila the Hun, invader of Europe (ca. 406–453), 192, 193
Aucassin et Nicolette, 256
Audiger dit Raimberge (de la Halle), 256 (music)
Augustine, St., Bishop of Hippo, Christian theologian and philosopher (354–430), 55, 122, 126 (overview), 186–88, 194, 207, 208, 212, 259, 275, 276

Augustus (Gaius Julius Caesar), Roman emperor (63 B.C.–A.D. 14), 115, 115 (quotation), 116 (box), 117, 119, 120, 125, 142, **142**, 143, 144, 148, 244

Augustus of Primaporta (Roman), 142, **142**, 148, 150, 151

Aulos, 100, **100**, 101, 101 (box), **101**, 102, 104, 105, 151

Aulos Player of the Ludovisi Throne, **100**

Ausonius, 112 (quotation)

Autobiography (Mill), 429

Available Forms II for Large Orchestra, Four Hands (Browne), 570

Ave Maria (Josquin), 318 (music)

Azay-le-Rideau, Château, 311, **311**

Aztec empire, 274

B

Babbitt, Milton, American composer (b. 1916), 567–68

Babylon, 35, 120

Babylonian Captivity, 156, 157, 161

Bacchae, The (Euripides), 50, 571, 593

Bach, Johann Sebastian, German composer (1685–1750), 10, 15, 20, 259, 349, 365, 388, 389, 390, 391, 392, 393, 396, 557, 567, 585, 586

Bacon, Francis, English-Irish painter (b. 1901), 542

Bacon, Francis, English scientist and philosopher (1561–1626), 341–42, 345

Bagpipe, 262 (table), **321**

Bailey, Malcolm, American artist (b. 1947), 549

Bakchantinnen (Wellesz), 571

Balboa, Vasco Núñez de, Portuguese explorer (1475–1517), 274

Baldacchino (Bernini), 369, **369**

Baldassare Castiglione (Raphael), 303, **303**

Ballade in G minor (Chopin), 450 (music)

Ballet Russe de Monte Carlo, 557

Balzac, Honoré de, French writer (1799–1850), 438

Bannister, Edward M., American painter (1828–1901), 548

Banquet Rousseau, The, 482

Baptism, 181, 186, 187

Baptists, 277

Barber, Samuel, American composer (1910–1981), 570

Barbizon School, 468–69

Barlach, Ernst, German sculptor (1870–1938), 522

Baroque style, 308, 352, 376, 457, 459
in architecture, 365–66, 368–70, 373–74
in art, 349, 366–68, 370–73, 374–76
in music, 349, 387–95, 586

Barry, Sir Charles, English architect (1795–1860), 468

Barthé, Richmond, American sculptor (b. 1901), 549

Bartók, Béla, Hungarian composer (1881–1945), 388, 562–65, 583

Basilica, 143, 150, 177, 178, 179, 240

Basilica (Roman), Volubilis, Morocco, 174, **174**

Basse dance, 316

Bath, England, 118

Bath, The (Cassatt), 476, **476,** 532

Baths, Roman, 118, **118,** 141, 143, 145

Baths of
Caracalla, 118n
Trajan, 145, **145**

Battle Hymn of the Republic, The, 259

Battle of
Actium, 115
Hastings, 237–38
Marathon, 34, 43, 47
Plataea, 35
Roncevaux, 193, 206
Salamis, 35, 78, 82, 91
Thermopylai, 34–35
Universals, 205, 208–9, 211

"Battle Rages, The" *Bayeux Tapestry,* 237–38, **238**

Baudelaire, Charles, French poet (1821–1867), 459, 469, 476

Bauhaus, 529, 534, 540, 550

Bayeux Tapestry, 237–38, **238**

Bayle, Pierre, French skeptic (1647–1706), 348

Beardsley, Aubrey, English artist (1872–1898), 533

Beardon, Romare, American painter (b. 1914), 549

Beatles, 259

Beatritz, Countess of Dia, French troubadour (12th century), 258

Beauvais Cathedral, France, 246, **246**

Beckett, Samuel, French novelist and playwright (b. 1906), 593

Bed (Rauschenberg), 536, **536**

Beethoven, Ludwig van, German composer (1770–1827), 6, 8, 16, 17, 254, 259, 395, 396, 400–401, 452, 454, 457, 557, 567

Beggar's Opera, The (Gay and Pepusch), 395

Being Beauteous (Henze), 572

Bellini, Giovanni, Italian painter (ca. 1430?–1516), 293, 294, 304

Bellow, Saul, American writer (b. 1915), 590, 595

Belshazzar's Feast (Walton), 571

Be m'an perdut (Bernart de Ventadorn), 257 (text)

Bentham, Jeremy, English political philosopher (1748–1832), 422, 429

Beowulf, 191, 192, 193, 194, 195–96 (text), 219

Berg, Alban, Austrian composer (1885–1935), 559–61, 566

Berio, Luciano, Italian composer (b. 1925), 572

Berlioz, Hector, French composer (1803–1869), 451, 452–53, 454, 467

Bernard of Clairvaux, French monk, Saint (1090–1153), 255

Bernart de Ventadorn, French troubadour (d. 1195), 229, 257 (text)

Bernini, Gianlorenzo, Italian architect and sculptor (1598–1680), 365, 368–70, 374, 477

Bernstein, Leonard, American composer and conductor (b. 1918), 570

Berryman, John, American poet (1914–1972), 602

Bible, 29, 160, 208, 209, 212, 234, 275, 276, 277, 281, 327, 347, 348, 415
Amos 5:11–15; 6:4–8, 157 (text)
Ecclesiastes 3:1–22, 162 (text)
Ezekiel 18:25–32, 158 (text)
I Corinthians 13:1–13, 164 (text)
Five Parables, 164–65 (text)
Isaiah 9:6; 11:1–9, 157 (text)
Job, 160–61
John 1:1–5, 159 (text)
Matthew 5–7 (Sermon on the Mount), 162–64 (text)
Psalms 24; 137; 150, 161 (text)
Revelation 6:1–8; 21:1–4, 166–67 (text)
Second Isaiah 40:1–9; 53:3–6, 158 (text)

Biches, Les (Poulenc), 571

"Big Blonde" (Parker), 8

Billy Budd (Melville), 436

Binchois, Gilles, Burgundian composer (ca. 1400–1460), 317

Bird in Space (Brancusi), 528, **528,** 552

Birth of Venus (Botticelli), 293, colorplate 22

"Bishop Golias," 255

Bismarck, Otto Fürst von, German statesman (1815–1898), 407, 410, 521

Black and White Love, The (Indiana), 538, **539**

Blackberry Woman, The (Barthé), 549

Black Death, 261, 285

Black humor, 594–95

Black Numerals (Johns), 536, **537**

Blackstream art, 549, 611

Bladen, Ronald, American sculptor (b. 1918), 546

Blake, William, English artist, poet, and mystic (1757–1827), 415–16

Blind Leading the Blind, The (Bruegel), 312, **313**

Block, Ernst, Christian existentialist, 513

Blondel de Nesles, French trouvère (b. ca. 1155), 258

Blue Danube, The (Strauss, Jr.), 388

Blue Doll, The (Pickens), 531, **532**

Blue Hole, Flood Waters, Little Miami River (Duncanson), 548

"Blue Hotel, The" (Crane), 443

Blues, 573, 577–78, 580–81, 582, 585

Blue Window, The (Matisse), 522, colorplate 50

Boccaccio, Giovanni, Italian poet and humanist (1313–1375), 219, 270

Boethius (Anicius Manlius Severinus), Roman consul and philosopher (ca. 475–524), 126 (overview), 150, 185, 192

Boeuf sur le Toit, Le (Milhaud), 571

Bohème, La (Puccini), 458–59

Bolivar (Milhaud), 571

Boogie-Woogie, 582

Boogie-Woogie Bass Patterns, 582 (music)

Book of Kells (Hiberno-Saxon), 14, 234, **235**
Book of Timur (Goethe), 424–25 (text)
Bop style jazz, 582–83, 584, 587
Borges, Jorge Luis, Argentinian author (b. 1899), 595–96
Borgia
    Lucrezia (1480–1519), 294
    Rodrigo. *See* Alexander VI, Pope
Borromini, Francesco, Italian architect (1599–1667), 369, 370, 380
Bosch, Hieronymus, Flemish painter (ca. 1450–1516), 298, 299, 311, 312, 523
Botticelli, Sandro, Florentine painter (1445–1510), 291, 293, 299, 300, 301
Boucher, François, French artist (1703–1770), 377, 381, 395
Boulez, Pierre, French composer (b. 1925), 568, 572
Bourges Cathedral, France, 242
Brahe, Tycho, Danish astronomer (1546–1601), 272, 344
"Brahma" (Emerson), 435 (text)
Brahms, Johannes, German composer (1833–1897), 448, 449, 451, 457, 460, 557, 559
Bramante, Donato d'Agnolo, Milanese architect (1444–1514), 290, 299, 301, 302, 303, 304, 308, 380
Brancacci Chapel, Florence, 287–88, 289
Brancusi, Constantin, Roumanian sculptor (1876–1957), 526, 528, 544, 552
Braque, Georges, French painter (1882–1963), 482, 524, 525
Brave New World (Huxley), 590, 595
"Bread and Circuses" (Rome), 113, 124
"Breathes There the Man" (Scott), 410 (text)
Brecht, Bertolt, German playwright (1898–1956), 395, 528, 570
Breezing Up (Homer), 472, colorplate 42
Breton, André, French writer (1896–1966), 530
Bride Stripped Bare by Her Bachelors, Even, The (Duchamp), 530, colorplate 53
Brief an Gosta Oswald (Nilsson), 572
Britten, Benjamin, English composer (1913–1979), 570
Broadway Boogie Woogie (Mondrian), 528, **528**
Brothers Karamazov, The (Dostoevsky), 504
Brown, John, abolitionist (1800–1859), 436
Browne, Earle, American composer (b. 1926), 570
Browning, Robert, English poet (1812–1889), 570
Bruegel the Elder, Pieter, Flemish painter (1525?–1569), 13, 14, 311–12
Brumel, Antoine, Flemish composer (ca. 1480–1520), 317
Brunelleschi, Filippo, Florentine architect (1377–1446), 286, 288, 291, 308, 554

Bryant, William Cullen, American poet (1794–1878), 434
Buccina (Roman trumpet), 152
Buddha (Siddhãrtha Gautama), founder of Buddhism (ca. 563–ca. 483 B.C.), 29
Bull, ceiling painting (Lascaux), 4, **4**
Bull from the Sea, The (Renault), 27
Burgundy, Dukes of, 286, 294, 297, 317
Burial at Ornans (Courbet), 470, **471**, 472
Buried Child (Shepard), 593
Byron, (George Noel Gordon), Lord, English poet (1788–1824), 406, 407, 415, 419–20, 422, 458
"By the Bivouac's Fitful Flame" (Whitman), 436 (text)
Byzantine, 176, 180, 190, 235, 236, 247, 250, 309, 319, 370, 523
    churches, 178–81, 236
    culture, 206, 210
    Empire, 176, 177–81
    mosaics, 178, 179, 181
Byzantium, 26, 32, 79, 117, 180, 185, 190, 247. *See also* Constantinople and Istanbul

C

Cabinet Voltaire, 530
Cabot, John, English explorer from Italy (fl. 1450–1498), 274
Caesar, Gaius Julius, Roman general, statesman, and historian (100–44 B.C.), 6, 114–15, 115 (quotation), 116 (box), 126 (overview), 141, **142**, 146
Cage, John, American composer (b. 1912), 569, 572
Calder, Alexander, American sculptor (1896–1976), 544, 569
Calf-Bearer (Greek), 78, **79**, 170, 171
California Chick (Jimenez), 548
California Mission architecture, 366
Caligula (Gaius Caesar Germanicus), Roman emporer (12–41), 115, 116 (box), 146
Calling of the Apostles Peter and Andrew, The (Duccio), 249, colorplate 19
Calvin, John, French Protestant reformer (1509–1564), 188, 276, 277, 375, 392
Calvinism, 277, 278, 374, 375, 409
Camelot, legendary location of King Arthur's court, 230
Camelot (Lerner and Loewe), 570, 593
Campanile (Giotto), 285, **285**, 286, **286**, 287
Campin, Robert, Flemish painter (ca. 1378–1444), 288
Camus, Albert, French novelist and essayist (1913–1960), 511–12, 513, 591
Candide (Voltaire), 348, 352, 360
Cane Garden (Havard), 547, **547**
Canon of
    architecture (Greek), 76
    sculpture, Greek (Polykleitos), 84, **84**, 94
Canova, Antonio, Italian sculptor (1757–1822), 384

Canterbury Cathedral, England, 246, **247**
Canterbury Tales (Chaucer), 258
Canti di Prigionia (Dallapiccola), 570
Cantus firmus, 259, 260
Capitalism, 269, 278–79, 280, 281, 282, 387, 407, 427, 428, 429
Capitoline She-Wolf, The (Roman), **112**
Caprices, The (Goya), 465
Caracalla (Marcus Aurelius Antoninus), Roman emperor (188–217), 115, 116 (box), 151
Caravaggio (Michelangelo Merisi), Milanese painter (1573–1610), 366–67, 368, 370, 371, 372, 374, 382
Carcassonne, France, **189**
Carlos IV of Spain as Huntsman (Goya), 464, **465**
Carmina Burana (Orff), 255, 565–66 (text)
Carnegie, Andrew, American industrialist (1835–1919), 428, 429
Carolingian
    architecture, 190, 235, 236
    art, 236–37
    mosaic, 236
    period, 231 (overview)
    Renaissance, 189–90, 235–37, 249, 270
Carousel (Rodgers and Hammerstein), 570
Carter, Elliott, American composer (b. 1908), 570
Cartesian revolution, 273
Carthage, 112, 113, 114, 124, 126, 127, 140 (overview), 186
Cartier, Jacques, French explorer (1494–1553), 274
Caryatids, 90, **90**
Casas, Melesio, American painter (b. 1929), 548
Cassatt, Mary, American painter (1844–1926), 476, 532
Castiglione, Baldassare, Count, Italian writer (1478–1529), 303, 316
Catacombs, Rome, 170–71
Catacombs of St. Callixtus, Rome, **170**
Catacombs of St. Priscilla, Rome, **170**
Catch, in music, 322–23
Catch in the Play of the Knight of Malta, A (Purcell), 323 (text)
Catch 22 (Heller), 594–95
Cathédrale, Engloutie, La (Debussy), 460
Cathedrals, 207, 212, 213, 215, 235, 240
    Gothic, 211, 212, 213, 215, 235, 242–47, 260
    Romanesque, 235, 240, 241, 260
Catherine of Aragon, Queen of England (1485–1536), 277
Catherine the Great, Czarina of Russia (1729–1796), 349
Catholic Church, 281, 350
Catholicism, 342, 360
Cato, Marcus Porcius, the Elder, Roman consul and censor (234–149 B.C.), 114, 155
Catullus, Gaius Valerius, Latin poet (84–54 B.C.), 103, 125, 126 (overview), 132–33
Cavalli, Pietro Francesco, Italian opera composer (1602–1676), 394, 395

Cavour, Camillo Benzo, Italian statesman (1810–1861), 408
Cella, 85, 87, 89, 91, 142
Celto-Germanic culture, 191–93, 194, 211, 234, 235, 237
Censor, Roman, 113, 114
Central-plan churches, 178, 179, 180, 235
Cervantes, Saavedra, Miguel de, Spanish writer (1547–1616), 281
Cerveteri, Etruscan city, 139
Cézanne, Paul, French painter (1839–1906), 475, 478, 481, 521, 525, 526, 549
Chagall, Marc, Russian painter (b. 1887), 528, 529
Chalgrin, Jean Francis, French architect (1739–1811), 463, 464
Chamberlain, Neville, English statesman (1869–1940), 486
Chambord, Château of, 311, **311**
Champlain, Samuel de, French explorer (1567–1635), 274
"Channel Firing" (Hardy), 433 (text)
Chanson de Roland, 256. *See also* Song of Roland
Chansons de geste, 256
Chant-fable, 256
Chardin, Jean-Baptiste, French painter (1699–1779), 377
"Charge of the Light Brigade" (Tennyson), 408 (text), 431
"Chariot, The" (Dickinson), 442 (text)
Chariot racing, 179
    Greek, 83, 123
    Roman, 124, 145, 151
Charlemagne, Holy Roman Emperor (742–814), 189–90, 191, 193, 194, 217, 235–37, 252, 256
Charles I, King of England (1600–1649), 343, 372
Charles II, King of England (1630–1685), 343, 351, 380
Charles V, Holy Roman Emperor (1500–1558), 276, 280, 305
Charles VIII, King of France (1470–1498), 298, 299
Charles IX, King of France (1550–1574), 375
Charles X, King of France (1757–1836), 406
Charles the Bold, Duke of Burgundy (1433–1477), 316
Charpentier, Constance Marie, French artist (1767–1849), 382–84
Chartres Cathedral, France, 160, 211, 213, 215, 242, **243,** 243–44, **244,** 245, 246, 261, 306
    School of, 270
Château Noir, Le (Cézanne), 478, colorplate 47
Chaucer, Geoffrey, English poet (ca. 1340–1400), 127, 160, 210–11, 219–29, 258
Chávez, Edward, American painter (b. 1917), 548
Chekhov, Anton Pavlovich, Russian writer and physician (1860–1904), 8
Chiaroscuro, 288, 289, 375, 470, 536
Chicago style jazz, 581, 587

Childe Harold's Pilgrimage (Byron), 419
Child of Our Time, A (Tippett), 571
Child with a Goose, 95
Chilly Winds, 578 (music)
Chippendale, Thomas, English furniture designer (1718–1779), 554
"Chippendale" skyscraper (Johnson), 554, **554**
Chirico, Giorgio de, Italian painter (1888–1980), 529–30
Chivalry, 195n, 205, 206, 207, 210, 244, 259, 263, 289
Chopin, Frédéric, Franco-Polish composer (1810–1849), 16, 449–51, 467
Choreomania, 261
Chorus, Greek drama, 43–45, 104–5, 151–52
Christ, Jesus, founder of Christianity (ca. 4 B.C.–A.D. 29), 7, 11, 29, 142, 158–60, 162, 166, 169, 170, 171, 172, 175, 177, 186, 188, 234, 237, 239, 254, 255, 287, 288, 299, 301, 325, 367, 370, 375, 504, 513
    in art, 170, 171, 172, 177, 178, 179, 180, 237, 238, 240, 241, 293, 299, 300, 303, 307, 308, 309, 310, 311, 367, 372
Christ at the Sea of Galilee (Tintoretto), 307, colorplate 30
Christendom, 158, 174, 178, 286, 369
Christ Enthroned (Roman), 171, **172**
Christianity, 7, 55, 56, 57, 117, 120, 122, 124, 125, 149, 151, 152, 156, 159, 160, 164, 166, 170–81 (chap. 8), 186, 187, 188, 191, 193, 194, 232, 233, 234, 235, 237, 238, 261, 275, 305, 573, 576
Christ lag in Todesbanden
    cantata, 393–94
    chorale, 393
    chorale prelude, 393
Christ Lay in the Bonds of Death (Luther), 254
Christ Pantocrater, St. Irene, Constantinople (Istanbul), 178, **179**
Christ Teaching the Apostles in the Heavenly Jerusalem, Santa Pudenziana, Rome, 175–76, **176**
Chronochromie (Messiaen), 568
Chrysler Building, New York, 550, **550**
Church, Christian
    early, 148, 169–76
    medieval, 185–88
    Roman Empire, in, 117, 119, 122, 169–76, 185–86
Churches. *See* Architecture; *names of specific churches*
Church Fathers, 208, 209
Church of Rome, 119, 148, 185, 186, 188, 189, 194, 208–10, 211, 212, 214, 234, 272, 274, 275, 276, 365, 392
Church of the Holy Family (Gaudi), Barcelona, **533,** 533–34
Cicero, Marcus Tullius, Roman statesman and orator (106–43 B.C.), 112 (quotation), 114, 117 (quotations), 121, 125, 126 (overview), 151, 244, 269, 270, 325

Cimabue, Giovanni, Italian painter (1240–1302), 247, 248
Cimon, Athenian statesman and general (510–499 B.C.), 46
Circles (Berio), 572
Circus Maximus, Rome, 124, 145, **145**
Cirium of 1964 (Noland), 540, **540**
Cities, rise of, 205–6, 210, 241
City of God, The (Augustine), 122, 186, 187
City-states
    Etruscan, 140 (overview)
    Greek, 26, 31, 32, 42, 45, 47, 50, 53, 56, 80, 104, 119, 139, 145, 281
"Civil Disobedience" (Thoreau), 435
Civilization and Its Discontents
    (Freud), 490–92 (text)
Civil rights, 502
Civil War
    American, 436, 437, 438, 439, 472, 576, 579, 580
    English, 343
    Russian, 486, 494
    Spanish, 486, 505, 526
Classicism, 372, 373, 447
Claudius (Tiberius Claudius Drusus Nero Germanicus), Roman emperor (10 B.C.–A.D. 54), 116 (box)
Clavichord, 391, 396
Clean, Well-lighted Place, A (Hemingway), 591
Cleland, John, English writer (1709–1789), 591
Clemenceau, Georges, French premier (1841–1929), 485
Clemens, Samuel Langhorne (pseud. Mark Twain), American writer (1835–1910), 438–40, 441, 472
Clement VII, Medici pope (ca. 1478–1534), 305
Cleopatra VII, Queen of Egypt (69–30 B.C.), 115
Clerestory, 174, 238, 240, 244, 246
Clergy
    regular, 188, 241
    secular, 188, 241
Clodia (Lesbia), 132
Clouds, The (Aristophanes), 51
Cluniac Order, 237
Cocardes (Poulenc), 571
Cocteau, Jean, French poet (1889–1963), 9 (quotation), 557
Cogito ergo sum (Descartes), 342
Coiffure, La (Matisse), 522, **522**
Coins
    Greek, 47
    Roman, 142
Coleridge, Samuel Taylor, English poet (1772–1834), 416, 418, 429, 463, 467
Colloquies (Erasmus), 327
Colosseum, Rome, **112,** 118–19, 124, 125, 135, 141, **145,** 145–46, **146,** 147, 150, 290
Colossi of Memnon, 70, **70**
Columbus, Christopher, Italian explorer (1451–1506), 274, 299

Columns
  Carolingian, 235
  Gothic, 242
  Greek, 85, **85, 86,** 86–87
  Islamic, 232–33
  Romanesque, 237
Combat between a Lapith and a Centaur
  (Greek), 88, **89**
Comedy, Greek
  New, 119
  Old, 51
Comitatus, 191
Commentaries on the Gallic Wars
  (Caesar), 114, 115
Commodus (Lucius Aelius Aurelius),
  Roman emperor (161–192), 115,
  117, 149n, 273, 274
Communism, 406, 426
Communist Manifesto, The (Marx and
  Engels), 406, 426 (text)
Compère, Loyset, Flemish composer
  (d. 1518), 317
Composition in White, Black, and Red
  (Mondrian), 526, 528
Conceptualism, 209–11
Concertino (Janáček), 571
Concerto for Amplified Violin and
  Orchestra (Wuorinen), 571
Concerto for Jazz Band and Symphony
  Orchestra (Lieberman), 572
Concerto for Orchestra (Bartók), 563–65
  (music)
Concerto for Orchestra (Carter), 570
Concerto grosso, 388, 392
Concerto in C major for Two Trumpets
  and Orchestra (Vivaldi), 392
  (music)
Concerto in F (Gershwin), 570
"Concord Hymn" (Emerson), 435 (text)
Concord Sonata (Ives), 566
Conductus, 255, 255 (music)
Confessions, The (St. Augustine), 186
Confessions of an English Opium Eater
  (de Quincey), 452
Congress of Vienna, 406, 408
Consolation of Philosophy (Boethius),
  150, 185, 192 (text)
Constable, John, English painter
  (1776–1837), 467
Constantine I, the Great, Roman emperor
  (272–337), 116 (box), 117, 140
  (overview), 149, 150, 173, 177, 178,
  186, 290
Constantinople, 117, 140 (overview), 169
  (overview), 177–80, 181, 191, 206,
  232, 247, 369. *See also* Byzantium;
  Istanbul
Constitution, United States, 348
Consul, Roman, 113, 114, 150, 185
*Contribution of the Negro to American
  Democracy, The* (White), 549
Cool style jazz, 544, 583
Cooper, James Fenimore, American author
  (1789–1851), 434
Copernican system, 272
Copernicus, Nicholaus, Polish astronomer
  and mathematician (1473–1543),
  272, 328, 342, 344

Copland, Aaron, American composer
  (b. 1900), 570
Corbusier, Le (Charles-Édouard
  Jeanneret), Swiss architect
  (1887–1965), 534, 550, 551, 572
Corelli, Arcangelo, Italian composer
  (1653–1713), 391–92
Corinth, 48, 49, 53, 114, 123n, 124
Corinthian architectural order, 85, **85,** 86,
  96, **96,** 119, 142, 144, 146, 148, 174,
  290, 380, 463
Corneille, Pierre, French playwright
  (1606–1684), 394
Corot, Jean-Baptiste-Camille, French
  landscape painter (1796–1875),
  458, 469, 472, 476
Cortés, Hernando, Spanish conquistador
  (1485–1547), 274
Cossutius, Italian architect (fl. A.D. 131),
  96
Costa, Uriel da, Portuguese-Jewish
  theologian (ca. 1591–1647), 347
Cottage, Cape Cod (Hopper), 532–33, **533**
Council of
  Five Hundred (Athens), 34
  Nicea, 169 (overview), 177, 186
  Trent, 277, 305, 318
Counter-Reformation, 277, 305, 308, 309,
  318, 341, 365, 368, 370, 387
Couperin, François, French composer
  (1668–1733), 395
Courbet, Gustave, French painter
  (1819–1877), 458, 470–72, 473, 532
Courtier, The (Castiglione), 303
Court of the Lions, The, Alhambra,
  Granada, Spain, 233, **233**
Courts of Love, 206, 210, 229, 244, 257,
  259, 317
Coutances Cathedral, France, 244,
  colorplate 17
Cowell, Henry, American composer
  (1897–1965), 570
Cranach the Younger, Lucas, German
  painter (1515–1586), 276
Crane, Stephen, American writer
  (1871–1900), 443
Crassus, Marcus Licinius, Roman
  statesman (ca. 115–53 B.C.), 114,
  115
Creation of Adam, Sistine Chapel
  (Michelangelo), 301, **302**
Crete, 25n, 26, 27, 28, 29, 48 (box), 73, 75,
  76, 100, 309
Critique (Kant)
  of Judgement, 348
  of Practical Reason, 348
  of Pure Reason, 348
Cromwell, Oliver, Puritan leader and Lord
  Protector of the Commonwealth
  (1599–1658), 343, 351
Crossover, in music, 587
Cross Page, *Lindisfarne Gospels* (Hiberno-
  Saxon), 234, **234**
Cross plan
  Greek, 180, 181
  Latin, 174
Crucifixion, 171
Crucifixion, Church of Santa Sabina,
  Rome, 171, **171**

Crucifixion, Monastery Church, Daphne,
  Greece, 181, **181**
Crucifixion Cover, *Lindau Gospels,*
  236–37, colorplate 14
Crucifixion of St. Peter (Caravaggio),
  366–67, **367**
Crucifixion with Saints (Perugino), 293,
  colorplate 23
Cruciform plan (or shape), 174, 215, 240
Crumb, George, American composer
  (b. 1929), 570
Crusades, 191, 193, 205, 206, 238, 241,
  255, 256
"Cry of the Homeless" (Hardy), 411
  (text)
Crystal Palace (Paxton), **472,** 472–73
Cubi XV (Smith), 544, **546**
Cubism, 524–28
Cullen, Countee, American poet
  (1903–1946), 495
Culture-epoch theory, 5, 6, 486, 488
cummings, e e, American poet
  (1894–1962), 572, 592, 596, 611
Current (Riley), 540, 542
Curse of the Starving Class (Shepard), 593
Curtis, Philip, American painter (b. 1907),
  543–44
Cuvilliés, François de, French architect
  (1731–1777), 395
Cybele, 119, 120
Cycladic culture, 70, 73
Cycladic head, 73, **73**
Cyrus the Great, Persian king (d. 529 B.C.),
  156

D

Dada, 523, 530–32, 535, 566, 569
Daidalos, 69, 312
Daladier, Édouard, French premier
  (1884–1970), 486
Dali, Salvador, Spanish artist (b. 1904),
  531
Dallapiccola, Luigi, Italian composer
  (b. 1904), 570
Dance
  Burgundian, 316–17
  eighteenth century, 388
  Greek, 104
  medieval, 251, 260–61, 263
  Renaissance, 321
  seventeenth century, 388, 389, 390,
    394–95
  twentieth century, 579, 581, 584
Dance of Death (*Danse Macabre*), 261
Dance suite, 388, 389, 391
Daniel, Book of (Bible), 166
Dante Alighieri, Florentine poet
  (1265–1321), 127, 211, 213, 214,
  215, 219, 257, 415, 478, 492, 495
Danzas Fantásticas (Turina), 572
Darius I, King of Persia (ca. 558–486 B.C.),
  34
"Darkling Thrush, The" (Hardy), 433
  (text)
"Darling, The" (Chekhov), 8
Darwin, Charles, English naturalist
  (1809–1882), 427–29, 430, 521
Darwin, Erasmus, physician and
  grandfather of Charles Darwin
  (1731–1802), 427

Daumier, Honoré, French artist (1808–1879), 458, 470, 477, 481

David, Jacques Louis, French painter (1748–1825), 360, 381–82, 383, 384, 463, 464, 481

David, King of Palestine, 156, 170, 207, 301

David (Bernini), 368, **368**

David (Donatello), 287, **287**, 301

David (Michelangelo), 5, 301, 368, colorplate 26

David (Milhaud), 571

David (Verrocchio), 291, **291**, 301

David in the Wilderness (Morgan), 549

Davies, Maxwell, English composer (b. 1930), 571

da Vinci. *See* Leonardo da Vinci

Davis, Jefferson, American statesman, president of the Confederacy (1808–1889), 409

Davis, Stuart, American artist (1894–1964), 526, 527

Daybreak—A Time to Rest (Lawrence), 549, **549**

Dead Toreador, The (Manet), 475, colorplate 43

Death and the Miser (Bosch), 298, **298**

Death and Transfiguration (Strauss), 455

Death of Sokrates, The (David), 382, **383**

Debussy, Claude, French composer (1862–1918), 459, 461, 568, 583

Decameron (Boccaccio), 219

Decathlon, 123n

de Chirico. *See* Chirico

Declaration of Independence (Jefferson), 345 (quotation), 360

"Deer in the Works" (Vonnegut), 602–6 (text)

de Falla. *See* Falla

Defense of Poetry, A (Shelley), 420

de Forest, Roy, American artist (b. 1930), 543

Degas, Hilaire Germain Edgar, French artist (1834–1917), 377, 459, 476, 477

Déjeuner sur l'herbe (Manet), 473, **474**

de Kooning, Willem, Dutch-American artist (b. 1904), 535

Delacroix, Eugène, French painter (1798–1863), 372, 407, 447, 466–67, 468

De Lap, Tony, American painter (b. 1927), 544

Delian
    League, 47
    Treasury, 47, 87

Delos, 47, 73, 97, 100, 125

Delphi, 31, 34, 45, 100, 102, 123, 123n, 125

Delphi, Stadium at, 123, **123**

Delphi Charioteer, 83, **83**

Delphic oracle, 31, 48, 48 (box), 102, 119

Demeter, 29, 30 (box)

Demoiselles d'Avignon, Les (Picasso), 524–25, **525**

Demokritos, Greek philosopher (460?–362? B.C.), 42, 47, 159, 272, 590

Demosthenes, Athenian orator (384–322 B.C.), 53, **53**

de Quincey, Thomas, English essayist (1785–1859), 452

Derain, André, French painter (1880–1954), 522

Descartes, René, French philosopher and mathematician (1596–1650), 272, 273, 341, 342, 348, 365, 371, 388

Descent from the Cross (Antelami), **240,** 240–41

Descent from the Cross, The (Rembrandt), 375, colorplate 37

Descent of Man, The (Darwin), 427–28 (text)

Deserts (Varèse), 568

Deus ex machina, 42

Development of Medieval Music, 262 (table), 263

Diaghilev, Sergei Pavlovich, Russian ballet producer (1872–1929), 557, 571

Dialogues Concerning the Two Chief World Systems (Galileo), 342

Diary of a Young Man Who Disappeared (Janáček), 571

Diaspora, 156

Dickens, Charles, English novelist (1812–1870), 438

Dickinson, Emily, American poet (1830–1886), 441–42

Diderot, Denis, French philosopher and encyclopedist (1713–1784), 348, 377, 381

Didion, Joan, American writer (b. 1934), 513–14

Dido, Queen of Carthage, 112, 126

Dinner at the Homesick Restaurant (Tyler), 591

Diocletian (Gaius Aurelius Valerius Diocletianus), Roman emperor (245–313), 116 (box), 117, 149, 173

Dionysian mode (Nietzsche), 503

Dionysius II, tyrant of Syracuse (c. 430–367 B.C.), 57

Dionysos, 30 (box), 42, 48 (box), 50, 88, **88**, 89, **89**, 106

Dionysos, cult of, 100, 104, 105

Diptych of Consul Boethius (Roman), 150, **151**

Disasters of War, The (Goya), 465

Discobolus (Myron), 84, **84**

Discourse on Method (Descartes), 342

Discourse on the Arts and Sciences (Rousseau), 411 (quotation)

"Discourses of Epictetus" (Arrian), 135–36 (text)

Divine Comedy, The (Dante), 5, 193, 211, 213, 215

Dixieland jazz, 580, 582, 587

Dogon Ancestor Figure, 524–25, **525**

Domitian (Titus Flavius Domitianus), Roman emperor (51–96), 116 (box), 146, 147, 166

Donatello (Donato di Niccolo di' Betto Bardi), Florentine sculptor (1386?–1466), 286, 289–90, 291, 300

Donatist heresy, 186

Donatus, Bishop of Carthage (4th c.), 186

Don Giovanni (Mozart), 398

Donizetti, Gaetano, Italian composer (1797–1848), 448

Don Juan (Byron), 419

Don Juan (Strauss), 455

Donne, John, English poet and preacher (1573–1631), 349–50

"Do Not Weep, Maiden, for War Is Kind" (Crane), 443 (text)

Don Quijote valando las armas (Esplá), 572

Doppelrohr II (Hambraeus), 572

Dorian, 31, 76, 100, 103
    city, 80
    clothing, 80

Dorian mode, 100, 100n, 105

Doric architectural order, 85, **85,** 86, 87, 91, 102, 141, 146, 302, 369

Doryphoros (Polykleitos), 84, **84,** 93, 96, 142, 145

Dos Passos, John, American novelist (1896–1970), 595

Dostoevsky, Feodor Mikhailovich, Russian novelist (1821–1881), 504

"Dover Beach" (Arnold), 432 (text)

Drachma, Athenian, **47**

Draco, Athenian lawgiver (fl. 621 B.C.), 33, 113

Drama. *See names of individual dramas and dramatists*
    Greek, 42–46, 48–50, 89, 104–5
    liturgical, 197, 254–55, 263
    medieval, 42, 197–204, 210, 213, 254–55
    modern, 593
    Roman, 126 (overview), 151

Dreiser, Theodore, American novelist (1871–1945), 595

Dreyfus, Captain Alfred, French officer (1859–1935), 407

Dreyfus Affair, 407

Drowning Girl (Lichtenstein), **536,** 538

Druckman, Jacob, American composer (b. 1928), 570

"Drummer Hodge" (Hardy), 432–33 (text)

Dryden, John, English poet and critic (1631–1700), 349

Duccio di Buoninsegna, Sienese painter (1255–1319), 249

Duchamp, Marcel, French-American artist (1887–1968), 526, 530

Duecker, Otto, American artist (b. 1948), 546, 547

Dufay, Guillaume, Burgundian composer (1400–1474), 286, 316, 317

"Dulce et Decorum Est" (Owen), 494 (text)

Dulcimer, **321**

Dunbar, Paul Laurence, American poet (1872–1906), 442

Duncanson, Robert S., American painter (1817–1872), 548

Dunstable, John, English composer (d. 1453), 315

Dürer, Albrecht, German painter and engraver (1471–1528), 310–11, 312

Durrell, Lawrence, English author (b. 1912), 90n
"Dying" (Dickinson), 441 (text)
Dying Gaul, The (Greek), 94–95, **95**
Dylan, Bob, American musician (b. 1941), 259

E

Eakins, Thomas, American artist (1844–1916), 532, 548
Easter Sequence (Wipo), 254, **254**
Eben, Petr, Czech composer (b. 1929), 571
Eberhart, Richard, American poet (1904–1984), 501–2
Ecclesiastes (Bible), 3:1–22, 162 (text)
Echoes of Time and the River: Four Processionals for Orchestra (Crumb), 570
"Ecologue" (Mallarmé), 461 (text)
Economics, 278–80, 281. *See also* Capitalism
   Enlightenment, 345–47
   Renaissance, 278–80
   Social Darwinism, 428–29
Ecstasy of St. Theresa (Bernini), 369, **370**
Edict of
   Milan (Constantine), 117, 173
   Nantes, 343
Education
   Greek, 55, 99, 105, 106
   Locke, John, 347
   medieval, 189, 209–10, 212
   Roman, 114, 119
Edward VI, King of England (1537–1553), 322
Edward VII, King of England (1841–1910), 409
Egypt, 27, 28, 34, 35, 53, 70, 71, 72, 75, 115, 119, 150, 156, 191, 234
Egyptian culture, 6, 31, 70–73, 77, 78, 82, 89, 91, 260
Eiffel, Gustave, French engineer (1832–1923), 473
Eiffel Tower (Eiffel), 473, **473**, 554
Ein feste Burg (Luther), 12 (music)
Einstein, Albert, German-American physicist (1879–1955), 6, 7, 15, 208, 487, 488–90, 503
El Attarin Medersa, Fez, Morocco, **232**, 232–33
Eleanor of Aquitaine, Queen of France and then of England (1122–1204), 206, 229, 242, 244, 257, 270
Eleatic philosophy, 41–42
"Elegy Written in a Country Churchyard" (Gray), 358–59 (text)
Elektra, 43 (box), 49–50
Elektra (Aeschylus), 49
Elektra (Euripides), 49–50
Elektra (Sophokles), 49
Eleusian mysteries, 30 (box), 54, 56, 79, 120
Elgin, Thomas Bruce, 7th earl of, (1766–1841), 90
Eliot, George (Marian Evans), English novelist (1819–1880), 438

Eliot, T(homas) S(tearns), American poet and playwright (1888–1965), 492–94, 590, 592
Elizabeth I, Queen of England (1533–1603), 197, 280, 332
Ellington, Edward Kennedy (Duke), American jazz musician and composer (1899–1974), 587
Ellison, Ralph, American writer (b. 1914), 596–601
Emerson, Ralph Waldo, American essayist and poet (1803–1882), 8 (quotation), 117 (quotation), 434–35, 436, 566
Émile (Rousseau), 412–14 (text)
Empedokles, Greek philosopher (495–ca. 435 B.C.), 79
Emperor Justinian and His Courtiers, San Vitale, Ravenna, 178, colorplate 11
Emperors
   Byzantine, 169 (overview), 177–80
   Holy Roman, 189–90, 235, 237
   Roman, 115, 116 (box), 117, 118, 119, 120, 121, 122, 123, 124, 125, 142, 143, 144, 145, 146, 147, 148, 149, 150, 176
Empire State Building, 550, **550**
Empress Theodora and Retinue, San Vitale, Ravenna, 178, colorplate 12
Encyclopedia (Diderot), 348, 377
Encyclopedists. See Philosophes
Engels, Friedrich, German socialist writer (1820–1895), 426
Engineering
   Gothic, 243, 245, 246
   Roman, 118, 143–44, 146
Enlightenment, The, 344–49, 360, 376, 388, 389, 397, 411, 414, 415, 466
En non Diu! (School of Notre Dame, Paris), 260 (music)
Enteleche theory (Aristotle), 56, 57, 213
Ephialtes, Athenian statesman (d. 461 B.C.), 46
Epictetus, Stoic philosopher (60–110), 121–22, 126 (overview), 135–36, 382
Epicureanism, 120, 121, 130, 155, 429
Epicurus, Greek philosopher (ca. 342–270 B.C.), **120**, 120–21, 130
Epidauros, theatre of (Polykleitos the Younger), 42, **104**, 125
Episcopal church, 277
"Epistle to Augusta" (Byron), 420 (text)
Equatorial Jungle, The (H. Rousseau), **481**, 481–82
Equestrian Monument of Bartolommeo Colleoni (Verrocchio), 291, **292**
Equestrian Monument of Gattamelata (Donatello), 289–90, **290**, 291
Equestrian Statue of Marcus Aurelius (Roman), 149, **149**, 290
Erasmus, Desiderius, Dutch humanist (ca. 1466–1536), 273, 310–11, 318
Erasmus of Rotterdam (Dürer), **327**
Eratosthenes, Greek mathematician and astronomer (3rd. c. B.C.), 117
Erechtheion (Mnesikles), Athens, 86, 90, **90**

Erigena, John Scotus, Irish scholar (fl. 845–867), 208
Ernst, Max, German-American artist (1891–1976), 528
Esplá, Oscar, Spanish composer (1886–1971), 572
Essay in Criticism (Pope), 352
Essay on Man (Pope), 352–55 (text)
Estampie, 261, 263
Este, Isabella d', Italian patron of the arts (1474–1539), 271, 294
Estes, Richard, American painter (b. 1936), 546, 593
Ethics of Living Jim Crow, 1937 (Wright), 495–99 (text)
Ethos, doctrine of, 99, 101 (box), 105, 273
Etruscan culture, 112, 113, 139–40, 141, 151
Etruscan sarcophagus, 139–40, **140**
Étude in E major, op. 10, no. 3 (Chopin), 450 (music)
Eucharist, 169, 171, 181, 253, 299, 308
Euclid, Greek mathematician (fl. 300 B.C.), 244
Eumenides (Aeschylus), 43, 45–46, 52
Euripides, Greek dramatist (480–406 B.C.), 48, **49**, 49–50, 51, 92, 105, 270, 466, 571, 593
Evans, Sir Arthur, English archeologist (1851–1941), 26, 73
Eve, 172, 207, 213, 526
   in art, 296, 301
Everyman, 194, 197, 197–204 (text), 210, 213
Evolution, 427–28
Evolution of Jazz, 588 (outline)
Exekias, Greek vase painter and potter (fl. 500 B.C.), 78–79, 82
Existentialism, 503–13, 590, 593
   Christian, 503–4, 513
Existentialism (Sartre), 504 (quotation)
Expressionism, in art, 522–24
Ezekiel, Book of (Bible), 18:25–32, 158 (text)
Ezekiel, Hebrew prophet (fl. 592–570 B.C.), 157–58

F

Façade (Walton), 571
Falconet, Étienne, French sculptor (1716–1791), 378, **378**
Falla, Manuel de, Spanish composer (1876–1946), 572
Fall of the House of Mahagony (Brecht and Weill), 570
Family of Saltimbanques (Picasso), 524, **525**
Fanny (Jong), 591
Fanny Hill (Cleland), 591
Fantasy, in art, 529–30, 543
Farewell (Curtis), 543–44, **544**
Farmers
   Greek, 31–33
   medieval, 189
   Roman, 113, 119
Fatata te Miti (Gauguin), 480, **480**
Fatih Camii Mosque, Istanbul, 232, **232**

Faulkner, William, American novelist (1897–1962), 595
Faust (Goethe), 448–49
Faustian man, 400, 424, 431
Fauvism, 522
Fear of Flying (Jong), 591
Feast of the Gods, The (Bellini and Titian), 294, **294**
"February," *Très Riches Heures du Duc de Berry* (Limbourg Brothers), 294, **294**
Ferdinand V, King of Spain (1452–1516), 233, 280, 299
Fête Champêtre (Giorgione), **304**, 304–5, 473
Feudalism, 188, 193, 194, 205, 206, 210, 212, 244, 263, 279, 405
Feuerbach, Ludwig, German philosopher (1804–1872), 426
Ficino, Marsilio, Florentine humanist (1433–1499), 270, 293, 301
Fidelio (Beethoven), 457
Figure humaine (Poulenc), 571
Film. *See* Motion pictures
Finding of Moses, The (Veronese), 309, **309**
Firebird, The (Stravinsky), 557
First Corinthians (Bible), 13:1–13, 164 (text)
"First Inaugural Address" (Jefferson), 360–61 (text)
Fish Magic (Klee), 529, colorplate 58
Fitzgerald, Robert, American writer and translator of Greek and Latin (b. 1910), 25n
Flavian emperors, 145, 146, 147
Flavian Woman, 147, **147**
"Flea, The" (Donne), 349 (text)
"Flight on the Wind," *House Made of Dawn* (Momaday), 606–8 (text)
Florence, Italy, 4, 270, 281, 285, 286, 287, 289, 290, 291, 293, 297, 298, 299, 303, 305, 316, 374
Florence Cathedral, 148, 285, **285**, 286, **286**, 301
Flying buttress, 238, 242, 243, **243**, 245
Folquet of Marseilles, French troubadour (d. 1231), 256 (quotation)
Fool for Love (Shepard), 593
Forest of Fountainbleau (Corot), 469, **470**
Forever Free (Lewis), 548
Form
    in art, 13–14
    in music, 11–12, 20–22, 397–98
Forum, Pompeii, 141, **141**
Forums, Roman, 118, 141, 145, 146, 149
Foss, Lukas, American composer (b. 1922), 570
Foster, Stephen Collins, American composer (1826–1864), 579
Four Dancers (Degas), 476, colorplate 44
4'33" (Cage), 569
Four Horsemen of the Apocalypse, 166
Fourth Eclogue (Virgil), 125
Fourth Horseman of the Apocalypse, **166**
Fragonard, Jean-Honoré, French painter (1732–1806), 377–78, 395
Francis I, King of France (1494–1547), 280, 311

Francis Joseph, Emperor of Austria and King of Hungary (1830–1916), 407
Franco, Francisco (1892–1975), 486
Franco-Flemish school, 315–16, 317, 318, 321
Franco-Prussian War, 407
Frankenstein (Mary Shelley), 422, 448
Frankenthaler, Helen, American artist (b. 1928), 540
Franklin, Benjamin, American statesman, scientist, and writer (1706–1790), 384
Frederick I, King of Prussia (1657–1713), 348
Frederick II, the Great, King of Prussia (1712–1786), 349, 360
Frederick William I, King of Prussia (1688–1740), 349
Free Form jazz, 585–86, 587
Free will, 187, 192, 213, 214, 215, 327
French Revolution, 348, 349, 376, 379, 382, 405, 406, 415, 416, 426
French Suite No. 1 in D minor (Bach), 389 (music)
Frescoes, 119, 247, 301, 305
Freud, Sigmund, Austrian psychoanalyst (1856–1939), 208, 488, 490–92, 503, 530
Friendly Grey Computer—Star Gauge Model #54 (Kienholz), 538, **539**
Frieze, 86, 87, 89, 95
Frogs, The (Aristophanes), 51
Fugger,
    Jacob I, German merchant (d. 1469), 278
    Jacob II, German merchant prince (1459–1525), 278
    Johannes, German textile merchant (1348–1409), 278
Fuller, Margaret, American author and lecturer (1810–1850), 434
Fuller, R. Buckminster, American architect and engineer (1895–1983), 553
Funny Thing Happened on the Way to the Forum, A (Sondheim), 570
Furies, the (the Erinyes), 29, 44, 45, 46
"Fury of Aerial Bombardment, The" (Eberhart), 501–2 (text)
Fusion, in jazz, 587
Futurists, in music, 566, 568

G

Gabriel, Ange-Jacques, French architect (1698–1782), 380–81
Gabrieli, Giovanni, Italian composer (ca. 1557–1612), 320, 396
Gachet, Dr. Paul, friend of Vincent van Gogh, 479 (quotation)
Galante, La (Couperin), 395 (music)
Galaxy (Pollock), 535, **535**
Galileo (Galileo Galilei) Italian astronomer (1564–1642), 272, 341, 342–43, 344, 371
Gallery of the Twentieth Century (Mies van der Rohe), 550–51, **551**
Gama, Vasco da, Portuguese explorer (ca. 1469–1524), 274
Games
    Greek, 122–24
    Roman, 124–25

Gandhi, Mahatma, Indian leader (1869–1948), 435
Garcia, Antonio, American painter (b. 1901), 548
García-Márquez, Gabriel, Colombian writer (b. 1928), 595
Garibaldi, Giuseppe, Italian patriot and soldier (1807–1882), 408
Gates of Hell, The (Rodin), 478
Gaudeamus Igitur, 216 (text)
Gaudi, Antonio, Spanish architect (1852–1926), 533–34
Gauguin, Paul, French artist (1848–1903), 12–13, 479–80, 482, 521 (quotation), 522, 526
Gay, John, English poet and playwright (1685–1732), 395
Geneva Conventions, 280
George I, King of England (1660–1727), 349
George II, King of England (1683–1760), 349
George III, King of England (1738–1820), 349, 408
George IV, King of England (1762–1830), 408
George V, King of England (1865–1936), 409
Gericault, Théodore, French painter (1791–1824), 466, 468
Germigny des Pres, France, 236, **236**
Gershwin, George, American composer (1898–1937), 570
Gesu, Il (da Vignola and della Porta), 365–66, **366,** 370
Ghent Altarpiece (van Eyck), 295, **295,** 296, **296**
Ghiberti, Lorenzo, Florentine sculptor (ca. 1378–1455), 286
Ghirlandaio, Domenico del, Florentine painter (1449–1494), 293, 299, 300
Giacometti, Alberto, Italian sculptor (1901–1966), 531
Gibbs, James, English architect (1682–1754), 380
Ginevra de'Benci (Leonardo), 299, colorplate 25
Giorgione (Giorgio Barbarelli), Venetian painter (1477–1510), 294, 304–5, 308, 473
Giotto, Florentine painter (1267–1337), 177, 247–48, 249, 250, 286, 287
Giovanni, Nikki, American poet (b. 1943), 612
Giovanni Arnolfino and His Bride (van Eyck), 296–97, **297**
Girl Before a Mirror (Picasso), 15, 526, colorplate 7
Girl Seated Against a Square Wall (Moore), 544, **545**
Girl with a Red Hat (Vermeer), 376, colorplate 38
Girl with a Watering Can (Renoir), 476, colorplate 46
Gladiatorial combat, 112, 119, 122, 124–25, 151
Glagolitic Mass (Janáček), 571
Glass Table, The (Moore), 546, **547**
Global Village, 488, 503, 550

Gloria (Poulenc), 571
Glorious Revolution, 343, 344
Gods. *See individual names*
   Greek, 29–31, 44, 45, 47, 55, 56–57, 81,
      88, 89, 92, 93, 95, 96, 124. *See*
      also Drama
   Norse, 191
   Roman, 119–22, 124, 155
Godwin, Gail, American writer (b. 1937),
      591, 609–11
Godwin, William, English political
      philosopher (1756–1836), 422
Goethe, Johann Wolfgang von, German
      poet and dramatist (1749–1832), 6,
      415, 424–25, 448–49
Golden Age
   Athens, of, 41, 82, 84, 86, 91, 92, 97,
      124, 145
   Augustan, 126 (overview), 140
      (overview)
   Byzantine
      First, 169 (overview), 178–80
      Second, 169 (overview), 180–81
   Greece, 374
   Irish, 131 (overview), 234, 235, 249
Golden Mean, 56, 57
Goliards, 211, 216–17, 255, 256, 565
Goliard's Creed, A, 216–17 (text)
"Good-Morrow, The" (Donne), 350
   (text)
Good Shepherd (Roman), 171, **172**
Good Shepherd, The, Mausoleum of
      Empress Galla Placidia, Ravenna,
      Italy, 177, **177**
Good Shepherd, The (Roman), Catacombs
      of St. Callixtus, Rome, 170, **170**
Gordimer, Nadine, South African writer
      (b. 1923), 515–20, 596
Gospel song, 579, 580, 585, 586
Gothic, 6, 215, 235, 241–50, 263, 286, 288,
      290, 297, 311, 380
   architecture, 181, 211, 212, 213, 215,
      237, 240, 241–47, 295, 306, 387,
      586
   music, 260–63, 586
   painting, 247–49, 294
Goya, y Lucientes, Francisco José de,
      Spanish painter (1746–1828), 415
      (quotation), 464–66, 467
Gracchus, Gaius Sempronius, Roman
      statesman (153–121 B.C.), 114
Gracchus, Tiberius Sempronius, Roman
      statesman (163–133 B.C.), 114
Graeco-Roman civilization, 144, 156, 185,
      188, 191, 192, 194, 211
Graham, Martha, American dancer and
      choreographer (b. ca. 1894), 570
Grand Central Station, New York, 118
Grande hazaña! Con muertos! (Goya),
      465, 465–66
Grand Odalisque (Ingres), 463–64, **464**
Grant, Ulysses S(impson), general and
      United States president
      (1822–1885), 409
Grapes of Wrath, The (Steinbeck), 595
Grass, Günter, German writer and artist
      (b. 1927), 596
Graves, Robert, English writer and critic
      (b. 1895), 27

Gray, Thomas, English poet (1716–1771),
      358–59
Great Mosque, Cordoba, Spain, 233, **233,**
      238, 249
Great War, The. *See* World War I
Greco, El (Doménikos Theotokópoulos),
      Greek painter (1541–1614), 239,
      309–10, 370, 372, 544
Greece, 4, 25–108 (unit 1), 115, 117, 119,
      120, 121, 122–24, 148, 150, 156,
      190, 192, 206, 269, 503. *See also*
      Athens; Minoan culture;
      Mycenaean culture; Sparta
   ancient (map), 27
   climate, 26
   geography, 26
   history (chronological)
      Cycladic (Aegean; ca. 3000–2000
         B.C.), 70, 73
      Minoan (ca. 2600–1125 B.C.), 26, 27,
         28, 73–75
      Mycenaean (ca. 1599–1100 B.C.),
         27–28, 31, 32, 75
      Geometric period (ca. 1100–700
         B.C.), 75–77
      Archaic period (ca. 750–500 B.C.),
         31–35, 77–82
      Classical period (Hellenic Athens;
         ca. 500–323 B.C.), 41–57 (chap. 2),
         82–94
      Hellenistic period (ca. 323–30 B.C.),
         94–97
   Greek
      alphabet, 101, 112, 171, 234
      democracy, 33–34, 35, 46, 52, 53n, 71,
         77
      language, 41, 145, 159, 160, 209, 270
      music, 99–106 (chap. 4)
      musical notation, 101, 105
      Pantheon, 28, 30, 119
      religion, 29–31, 35, 39, 119
      science, 81, 99
      spelling, 35n
Greek Experience, The (Bowra), 46
      (quotation)
Greek Orthodox Church, Naxos, 180, **180**
Greeks, 6, 25–108 (unit 1), 112, 113, 114,
      117, 119, 120, 121, 122–24, 125,
      127, 142, 144, 145, 149, 155, 156,
      159, 160, 161, 162, 169, 188, 237,
      254, 287, 307, 382, 385, 388, 394,
      396, 504
Greek temple
   facade, **85**
   floor plan, **85**
Gregorian
   chant, 10, 17, 251–52, 253, 254, 263,
      460
   notation, 252
Gregory I, the Great, Saint, Pope
      (540–604), 171 (quotation), 188,
      251–52
Gretchen am Spinnrade (Schubert),
      448–49 (text)
Greuze, Jean-Baptiste, French painter
      (1725–1805), 381, 382
Gropius, Walter, German-American
      architect (1883–1969), 534, 550

Grosz, George, German-American artist
      (1893–1959), 523, 524, 549
Grotius, Hugo, Dutch jurist (1583–1645),
      280
Grünewald, Matthias (Mathis Gothart
      Nithart), German painter
      (1455–1528), 311, 522, 523, 570
Guernica (Picasso), 526, **527**
Guggenheim Museum (Wright), 552, **552**
Guido d'Arezzo, music theorist and
      teacher (10th c.), **252,** 252
      (quotation)
Guilds, 197, 206, 210, 215, 269, 278, 280,
      282
Gulliver's Travels (Swift), 355
Gunpowder, 273, 274, 289, 342
Gutenberg, Johannes, German printer
      (1400–1468), 273
Gutenberg Bible, 502
Gymnastics, Greek, 47, 99, 105, 106

H

Haba, Alois, Czech composer
      (1893–1973), 571
Habitat (Safdie), 553, **553**
Hadrian (Publius Aelius Hadrianus),
      Roman emperor (76–138), 96, 116
      (box), 145, 147, 148, 149, 150, 151
Hagia Sophia, Istanbul (Anthemius of
      Tralles and Isodorus of Miletos),
      179, **179,** 180, 232
Halle, Adam de la, French trouvère
      (1230–ca. 1288), 256, 258
Halley, Edmund, English astronomer
      (1656–1742), 344
Hals, Frans, Dutch painter (1580–1666),
      297, 374, 375, 376
Hambraeus, Bengt, Scandinavian
      composer (b. 1928), 572
Hamilton, Edith, English classical scholar
      (1867–1963), 35, 43
Hamlet (Shakespeare), 8, 9, 280
      (quotation), 281 (quotation), 282
      (quotation)
Hammerstein II, Oscar, American lyricist
      (1895–1960), 570
Handel, George Frederick, German
      composer (1685–1759), 8, 20, 365,
      392, 395, 396
Hannibal, Carthaginian general (247–ca.
      183 B.C.), 113, 119, 127
Hanson, Duane, American sculptor
      (b. 1925), 546, 593
Hapsburgs, 278, 280, 406
Hard Bop jazz, 584
Hardy, Thomas, English novelist and poet
      (1840–1928), 411, 432–33, 482
"Harlem" (Hughes), 502 (text)
Harlem (Lawrence), 549
Harlem Renaissance, 495, 502
Harmonice Musices Odhecaton A
      (Petrucci), 321
Harold, King of England (1022?–1066),
      237
Harp, 254, **254,** 263, 317, **321**
Harpsichord, 322, 388, 389, 391, 395, 396
Harpsichord Concerto (de Falla), 572
Harris, Roy, American composer
      (1898–1979), 570

Harrison, Lou, American composer
(b. 1917), 570
Harrison, Wallace K., American architect
(b. 1895), 550
Hastings, Battle of, 237–38, **238**
Hauer, Joseph Mathias, Austrian composer
(1883–1959), 571
Havard, James, American painter
(b. 1937), 547, 593
Hawthorne, Nathaniel, American novelist
(1804–1864), 566
Haydn, Franz Joseph, Austrian composer
(1732–1809), 372, 395, 396,
397–98, 399, 400, 448
Head of a Bearded Man (Roman), 149,
149
Heaven (Dante), 214
Hebrews, 156, 159, 160, 161, 188
Hegel, Georg Wilhelm, German
philosopher (1770–1831), 425–26,
435
Heisenberg, Werner, German physicist
(1901–1976), 489
Hektor, 28, 125, 127
Helen of Troy, 25n, 31, 43 (box)
Hell (Dante), 127, 214
Hell (Islamic), 233
Heller, Joseph, American novelist
(b. 1923), 594–95
Hello Dolly! (Herman), 593
Helmholtz, Herman Ludwig Ferdinand
von, German scientist
(1821–1894), 481
Hemingway, Ernest, American writer
(1899–1961), 591
Henri, Robert, American artist
(1865–1929), 532
Henry IV (Henry of Navarre), King of
France (1553–1610), 280, 343
Henry V, King of England (1387–1422),
295
Henry VII, King of England (1457–1509),
310
Henry VIII, King of England (1491–1547),
275, 277, 280, 305, 311
Henry the Navigator, Prince of Portugal
(1394–1460), 274
Henze, Hans Werner, German composer
(b. 1926), 572
Herakleitos, Ionian philosopher
(ca. 535–475 B.C.), 36, 41, 159
Herakles, 125, 301
*Herakles Discovering the Infant Telephos
in Arcadia* (Roman), **144**, 144–45
Hera of Samos, 78, **79**
Herculaneum, 144, 151, 381
Herder, Johann Gottfried von, German
philosopher and poet (1744–1803),
414–15
Herman, Woodrow Charles (Woody),
American jazz musician (b. 1913),
587
Hermes with the Infant Dionysos
(Praxiteles), 92–93, **93**, 287
Herodotos, Greek historian (ca. 484–425
B.C.), 34, 70, 71 (quotation), 112,
270
Hero's Life, A (Strauss), 455
Hesiod, Greek poet (fl. 8th c. B.C.), 29, 31,
32, 33, 119, 492

Hestia, 29, **89**
Hiberno-Saxon art, 234–35, 236, 238, 239
Hildegarde of Bingen, German abbess,
Saint (1098–1179), 255
Hindemith, Paul, German-American
composer (1895–1963), 570
Hippokrates, Greek physician (460–377
B.C.), 81
Historical and Critical Dictionary
(Bayle), 348
Histories (Herodotos), 71
Hitler, Adolph, German dictator
(1889–1945), 373, 486, 503, 528,
571
Hobbema, Meindert, Dutch painter
(1639–1709), 13
Hobbes, Thomas, English philosopher
(1588–1679), 343
Holbein the Younger, Hans, German
painter (1497–1543), 310, 380
Holler (Field Holler), 577, 585
Holy Family on the Steps (Poussin),
372–73, colorplate 35
Holy Land, 206, 238
"Holy Sonnet X" (Donne), 350 (text)
Homage to the Square: Ascending
(Albers), 540, **540**
Homer, Greek epic poet-musician
(fl. 9th c. B.C.), 25n, 28, 31, 32, **32,**
33, 34, 39, 75, 76, 77, 100, 102, 119,
125, 126, 236, 270, 503
Homer, Winslow, American painter
(1836–1910), 472, 477, 532
Honegger, Arthur, French composer
(1892–1955), 571
Honorius, Flavius, Roman emperor
(384–423), 116 (box), 117, 177
Hopper, Edward, American artist
(1882–1967), 532–33, **533**
Horace (Quintus Horatius Flaccus), Latin
poet (65–8 B.C.), 117n (quotation),
118 (quotation), 119 (quotation),
121, 125 (quotation), 126
(overview), 494
Horizon Book of Ancient Rome (Payne),
119n (quotation)
Horsemen, Parthenon, 89, **89**
Horse's Skull on Blue (O'Keeffe), 526,
527
Hortus Deliciarum (Abbess Herrad van
Landsberg), **254**
Houdon, Jean Antoine, French sculptor
(1741–1828), 384, 477
Housman, A. E., English poet
(1859–1936), 10–11
Hovhaness, Alan, American composer
(b. 1911), 570
Howells, William Dean, American novelist
and critic (1837–1920), 438
Hubris, 43 (box), 69, 101
Hudson, Henry, Dutch explorer from
England (d. 1611), 274
Hudson River School, 548
Hughes, Langston, American poet
(1902–1967), 502
Hugo, Victor Marie, French poet,
dramatist, and critic (1802–1885),
521 (quotation)
Huguenots, 280, 343, 375

Humanism
Greek, 119
Renaissance, 269, 270, 280, 281, 290,
310, 312, 315, 327
Hume, David, Scottish philosopher
(1711–1776), 347–48
Hundred Years' War, 274
Hus, Jan, Czech religious reformer and
martyr (ca. 1369–1415), 275, 276
Huxley, Aldous Leonard, English novelist
(1894–1963), 590, 595
Hydraulis, 151, 151n
Hymn of Jesus, sacred dance, 260

I

I Am Glad I Came Back (Grosz), 523, **524**
I and the Village (Chagall), 529, **529**
Ibsen, Henrik, Norwegian dramatist
(1828–1906), 482
Iconoclastic Controversy, 169 (overview),
178, 180
Idée fixe, 453, 454
"I Died for Beauty" (Dickinson), 442
(text)
Ignatius of Loyola, Saint, Spanish founder
of Jesuits (1491–1556), 277, 365,
369
"I Had No Time to Hate" (Dickinson),
441 (text)
"I Hear America Singing" (Whitman),
436 (text)
Ikarus, 69, 125, 312
Iktinus, Greek architect (fl. 5th c. B.C.), 87
Iliad (Homer), Greek epic poem, 28, 32,
75, 76, 77, 125, 127
Illumination—Dark (Nevelson), 540, **541**
Impression—Sunrise (Monet), 476
Impressionism
in art, 376, 384, 443, 467, 472, 473–77,
522, 532
in music, 459–61
Post-, 478–82
In Advance of a Broken Arm (Duchamp),
530
"In a Library" (Dickinson), 441 (text)
Inca empire, 274
India, 35, 53, 191, 232, 274
Indiana, Robert (Robert Clark), American
artist (b. 1928), 538, 539
Indulgences, sale of, 275, 276
Industrial Revolution, 281, 406, 407, 410,
430, 472, 502
In Ecclesis (Gabrieli), 320–21 (text)
"I Never Saw a Moor" (Dickinson), 441
(text)
Infantem Vidimus, 255 (music)
Inferno (Dante), 478
Ingres, Jean-Auguste-Dominique, French
painter (1780–1867), 447, 463–64,
475
Innocent III, Pope (1160?–1216), 259
(quotation)
Innocent VIII, Pope (1432–1492), 298
Innocents Abroad (Twain), 438
*Inquiry into the Nature and Causes of the
Wealth of Nations, An* (Smith), 346
Inquisition, 160, 277, 280, 309, 311, 342,
371
Inside the Bull (de Forest), 543, **543**

Institutes of the Christian Religion
(Calvin), 277
Instruments, musical. *See also names of
individual instruments*
  Baroque, 389, 390, 391
  Classical, 396, 397, 399
  electronic, 567–69, 572
  Greek, 100–102, 103, 104, 105, 106,
    151–52
  Impressionism, 459–61
  in jazz, 576, 577, 579, 580, 581–84
  Latin, 584
  medieval, **207, 252,** 254, **254,** 259, 263
  Rococo, 395
  Romantic, 449–50, 451, 452, 455
International style
  architecture, 534, 550, 551, 552, 554
  painting, 231 (overview), 249, 250,
    294, 295
Interpretation of Dreams, The (Freud),
  490
In terra pax (Martin), 572
In the Dining Room (Morisot), **475,** 476
In the Gloaming, 21 (music), 22
"Introduction" (Blake), 415–16 (text)
Invisible Man (Ellison), 596–601 (text)
Ionian, 100, 103
  cities, 35, 80
  clothing, 78, 80, 92
  coast, 31, 36
  music, 100
  philosophy, 35–39, 41, 56
  sculpture, 78, 95
Ionic architectural order, 85, **85,** 86, 90,
  95, **96,** 141, 146, 373, 380, 395
Ionisation (Varèse), 568
Iphigeneia, 43, 43 (box)
Ireland, 190, 234, 249, 355
Irish Golden Age, 231 (overview), 234,
  235, 249
Irving, Washington, American author
  (1783–1859), 434
Isaac, Heinrich, Flemish composer
  (ca. 1450–1517), 317
Isabella I, Queen of Spain (1451–1504),
  233, 280, 299
**Isaiah, Book of (Bible), 9:6; 11:1–9;
  53:3–6,** 157–58 (text)
Isaiah, Hebrew prophet (fl. 740 B.C.), 157
Isenheim Altarpiece (Grünewald), 570
Islam, 191, 231, 232, 249, 466
Islamic
  architecture, 232–34, 249
  art, 232
  astronomy, 249
  culture, 190, 191, 205, 206, 210, 232–34
  mathematics, 206, 249
  medicine, 206, 249
  religion, 231–32
  scholarship, 249
  science, 206
Isocephalic convention, 92
Isokrates, Athenian orator (436–338 B.C.),
  53 (quotation)
Israel, 156, 160, 161
Istanbul, 26, 180. *See also* Constantinople
Ivanhoe (Scott), 467
Ives, Charles, American composer
  (1874–1954), 566

J

J'Accuse (Zola), 407
James, Henry, American novelist
  (1843–1916), 476
James I, King of England (1566–1625),
  343
James II, King of England (1633–1701),
  343
Janáček, Leoš, Czech composer
  (1854–1928), 571
Jazz, 10, 16, 391, 544, 549, 566, 573, 588.
  See also names of individual styles
  elements, 573–76
  evolution, 588
  origins, 576–77
  pre-jazz styles, 577–80
  styles, 580–87
Jeanne d'Arc au bûcher (Honegger), 571
Jeffers, Robinson, American poet
  (1887–1962), 495, 592
Jefferson, Thomas, American statesman
  and president (1743–1826), 143,
  345 (quotation), 360–61, 385
Jefferson Memorial, Washington, D.C.,
  142–43
Jerome, St., Christian scholar, Church
  father (ca. 340–420?), 126
  (overview)
Jerusalem, 146, 156, 158, 161, 166, 172,
  175, 261, 300
Jesu, Joy of Man's Desiring (Bach), 259
Jesuits (Society of Jesus), 277, 309
Jesus. *See* Christ
Jeu de Robin et Marion, Le (de la Halle),
  256
Jews, 147, 157, 159, 160, 161, 191
Jimenez, Luis, American sculptor
  (b. 1940), 548
Job, 160, 161, 172
Job, Book of (Bible), 160, 415
Jocasta, 48, 48 (box), 49
John, Gospel of (Bible), 36, 1:1–5, 159
  (text), 162
John, Saint, Apostle and evangelist
  (d. ca. 100), 36, 159, 175
John of Patmos, Christian visionary
  (1st c. A.D.), 166–67 (text)
Johns, Jasper, American artist
  (b. 1930), 536
Johnson, Joshua, American artist
  (1765–1830), 548
Johnson, Milton, American artist
  (b. 1932), 549
Johnson, Phillip, American architect
  (b. 1906), 554
Johnson, Samuel, English author
  (1709–1784), 349
Jonah, 171, 172, 173
Jonah Sarcophagus (Roman), 172, **173**
Jones, Inigo, English architect
  (1573–1652), 380
Jones, Lois Maillol, American artist
  (b. 1905), 549
Jong, Erica (Mann), American writer
  (b. 1942), 591
Jongleurs, 256
Jonny spielt auf (Krenek), 571

Joplin, Scott, American composer
  (1868–1917), 579
Josquin des Pres, Flemish composer
  (1450–1521), 317, 318, 396
Joyce, James, Irish author (1882–1941)
"Joy to the World," 19 (music)
Jubilee, 579, 586
Judaeus, Philo, of Alexandria, Hellenistic-
  Judaic philosopher (ca. 30 B.C.–A.D.
  50), 159
Judaism, 57, 156–62, 347
Judeo-Christian tradition, 190, 504
Julian the Apostate, Roman emperor
  (331?–363), 116 (box)
Julius Caesar. *See* Caesar, Gaius Julius
Julius II (Giuliano della Rovere), Pope
  (1443–1513), 301, 302
Jupiter, 30 (box), 119, 120, 121, 126, 372
Justinian I, the Great, Byzantine emperor
  (483–565), 169 (overview),
  177–80, 190, colorplate 11
Juvenal (Decimus Junius Juvenalis), Latin
  satiric poet (60–140), 117
  (quotation), 126 (overview)

K

Kagel, Mauricio, German-Brazilian
  composer (b. 1931), 572
Kallikrates, Greek architect (fl. 5th c. B.C.),
  87, 90–91
Kalos k'agathos, 123, 124
Kandinsky, Wassily, Russian artist
  (1866–1944), 12, 14, 523–24, 528
Kansas City Jump style jazz, 581–82
Kant, Immanuel, German philosopher
  (1724–1804), 348, 415, 425, 426,
  429
Karl V (Krenek), 571
Kaufmann House (Wright), 534, **535**
Kazan, Elia, American stage and film
  director (b. 1909), 613
Keats, John, English poet (1795–1821),
  420, 422–24, 467
Kepler, Johannes, German astronomer
  (1571–1630), 270, 272, 342, 344,
  371
Kesey, Ken, American writer (b. 1935),
  591
Khachaturian, Aram, Russian composer
  (1903–1978), 572
Kienholz, Edward, American sculptor
  (b. 1927), 538, 539
Kierkegaard, Sören Aabye, Danish
  philosopher (1813–1855), 503–4,
  590
King, Martin Luther, Jr., American civil
  rights leader (1929–1968), 435
*King David as Organist and Pope Gregory
  the Great,* 252, **252**
*King David Playing Harp under the
  Inspiration of the Holy Ghost, while
  One Attendant Juggles and Others
  Play the Rebec, Trumpet, and
  Oliphant,* **217**
King Must Die, The (Renault), 27
King Priam (Tippett), 571
Kiss, The (Brancusi), 528, **528**
Kitchen Maid, The (Chardin), 378, **378**

Kithara, 91, 100, 101 (box), 106, 151
Klee, Paul, Swiss painter (1879–1940), 529, 568
Kleisthenes, Athenian reformer (fl. 507 B.C.), 33, 34, 46
Klytaimestra, 43, 43 (box), 44, 45, 46
Knossos, Palace of (Minoan), 26, 73, **73**, 74, **74**, 261. *See also* Crete; Minoan culture
Knot Garden, The (Tippett), 571
Knox, John, Scottish founder of the Presbyterian Church (ca. 1505–1572), 277
Knoxville: Summer of 1915 (Barber), 570
Kollwitz, Käthe, German artist (1867–1945), 523
Koran, 29, 231, 232
Kore, 77–78, 80–82
Kore (La Delicata), 81–82, 81
Korean War, 502, 535, 590
Kore from Chios, 80, **80**
Kore in Dorian Peplos, 80, **80**
Kore of Auxerre, 77, **78**, 80
Kouros, 77–78, 80–81, 123
Kouros of Sounion, 77, 78, **78**, 80
Křenek, Ernst, Austrian composer (b. 1900), 571
Kritios Boy, 82, **82**
Krutnava (Suchon), 571
Kubla Khan, 418
"Kubla Khan" (Coleridge), 418 (text)
Kyrie Eleison (Dufay), 317 (music)

L

"La Belle Dame sans Merci" (Keats), 423–24 (text)
Lady Chatterly's Lover (Lawrence), 590
Lady Playing a Dulcimer, **321**
Laissez-faire, 346, 428, 429
Lamarck, Jean-Baptiste de, French naturalist (1744–1829), 427
Lamartine, Alphonse de, French poet (1790–1869), 454
"Lamb, The" (Blake), 416 (text)
Lamentation (Giotto), 248, colorplate 21
"Lancan Vei per Mei la Landa" (Bernart de Ventadorn), 257 (text)
Lancelot, Knight of the Round Table, 206, 207
Landscape with the Fall of Ikarus (Bruegel), 312, **312**
Lands of the Dukes of Burgandy (map), 316
Laokoön (El Greco), 309, colorplate 31
Laokoön and His Sons (Hagesandros, Polydoros, and Athenodoros of Rhodes), 94, 97, **97**
Laon Cathedral, France, 242
Laplace, Pierre Simon, Marquis de, French astronomer (1749–1827), 345
Large Glass, The (The Bride Stripped Bare by Her Bachelors, Even) (Duchamp), 530, colorplate 53
Lascaux, caves of, 3–4
Lassus, Roland de, Flemish composer (1532–1594), 317, 318, 388, 396
Last Judgement, 166, 167, 188, 375, 376
Last Judgement (Michelangelo), Sistine Chapel, 142, 305–6, **306**

Last Supper, 171
Last Supper, The (Leonardo), 299–300, **300**
Last Supper, The (Tintoretto), 307–8, **308**
Latin Style jazz, 584
Lauriger Horatius, 216 (text)
Law, Roman, 114, 117, 119, 122, 160, 170
Law of War and Peace (Grotius), 280
Lawrence, D(avid) H(erbert), English novelist (1885–1930), 590
Lawrence, Jacob, American artist (b. 1917), 549
Laws (Plato), 70 (quotation), 102
League of Nations, 485, 502
Lear, King (Shakespeare), 337
Leaves of Grass (Whitman), 435, 436
LeCarré, John (David John Moore Cornwell), English novelist (b. 1931), 590
Lee, Don L., American poet (b. 1942), 611–12
Lee, Robert E(dward), Confederate general (1807–1870), 409
Léger, Fernand, French artist (1881–1955), 566
Leibniz, Gottfried Wilhelm, Baron von, German philosopher (1646–1716), 348
Lenin, Nikolai (Vladimir Ilyich Ulyanov), Russian revolutionary (1870–1924), 486
Le Nôtre, André, French landscape designer (1613–1700), 374
Leo X, Medici Pope (1475–1521), 275, 305
Leonardo da Vinci, Florentine artist (1452–1519), 271, 280, 281, 287, 291, 293, 299–300, 301, 302, 303, 305, 307, 311, 317, 372
Leonidas, King of Sparta (d. 480 B.C.), 34
Lerner, Alan Jay, American author and lyricist (b. 1918), 570
Lessing, Doris, English novelist (b. 1919), 595
Leucippus, Greek philosopher (5th c. B.C.), 42
Le Vau, Louis, French architect (1612–1670), 373
Levertov, Denise, American poet (b. 1923), 515
Lewis, Edmonia, American sculptor (1843–ca. 1900), 548
Leyster, Judith, Dutch painter (1609–1660), 374, 375, **375**
L'Homme armé (Davies), 571
Libation Bearers (Aeschylus), 43, 44–45
Lichtenstein, Roy, American artist (b. 1923), 536, 538
Lieberman, Rolf, Swiss composer (b. 1910), 572
"Life, Friends, Is Boring. We Must Not Say So" (Berryman), 602 (text)
Life on the Mississippi (Twain), 438
Ligeti, Gyorgy, German composer (b. 1923), 572
Limbourg brothers, Pol, Jan, and Herman, Flemish painters (fl. 1380–1416), 294–95
Lincoln, Abraham, 16th president of the United States (1809–1865), 160, 409, 436

Lindau Gospels (Carolingian), 236–37, colorplate 14
Lindisfarne Gospels (Hiberno-Saxon), 234, **234**, colorplate 13
Lindisfarne Monastery, England, 234
Linear A writing (Minoan), 26
Linear B writing (Minoan), 28
"Lines Composed a Few Miles above Tintern Abbey" (Wordsworth), 416–18 (text)
Lion Gate, Mycenae, 75, **75**
Lippi, Fra Filippo, Florentine painter (ca. 1406–1469), 288–89
Liszt, Franz, Hungarian composer (1811–1886), 449, 451, 452, 453–55, 457
Litanies à la Vierge noire de Rocamadour (Poulenc), 571
Literary selections (listed chronologically)
  Greek, 51–53, 57–67
  Roman, 118–19, 127–37
  Bible, 157–58, 161–67
  medieval, 195–96, 197–204, 216–30
  Renaissance, 270–71, 326, 328–36
  seventeenth century, 349–51
  eighteenth century, 352–61
  nineteenth century, 406, 408, 409, 410, 411, 412–14, 415–25, 426, 428, 430–43
  twentieth century, 491–99, 501, 502, 505–12, 513–20, 596–612
Literature. *See also names of individual authors and works*
  basis for understanding, 10–11
  Bible, 29, 160, 208, 209, 212, 234, 275, 276, 277, 281, 312, 327, 347, 348, 415
  drama, 42–46, 48–50, 197
  eighteenth century, 352, 360
  Greek, 42–46, 48–50, 51, 145
  medieval, 192–94, 210–11, 213–15, 216
  nineteenth century, 411, 424, 434, 435, 438–39
  poetry, 102–3, 193–94, 210–11, 255, 256, 330, 349, 351, 352, 415, 416, 419, 420, 422, 424, 430, 434, 435, 592–93
  Renaissance, 325
  Roman, 125–27
  seventeenth century, 349
  twentieth century, 588–96
Little Night Music, A (Sondheim), 570
Liturgical drama, 254–55
Liturgical jazz, 586–87
Lives of the Most Excellent Italian Architects, Painters, and Sculptors from Cimabue to Our Own Times (Vasari), 270, 293
Livy (Titus Livius), Roman historian (59 B.C.–A.D. 17), 126 (overview)
Lloyd George, David, British statesman (1863–1945), 485
"Loath to Depart" (Farnaby), 322 (music)
Locke, John, English political philosopher (1632–1704), 345 (quotation), 346, 348, 364
Logos, 36, 135, 159
Longhena, Baldassare, Venetian architect (1598–1682), 370

Looking for Mr. Goodbar (Rossner), 591
Lorenzo de'Medici (Verrocchio), **292**
Louis VII, King of France (ca. 1121–1180), 206, 242
Louis IX, King of France, Saint (1214–1270), 245
Louis XIII, King of France (1601–1643), 343, 373
Louis XIV (Sun King), King of France (1638–1715), 15, 280, 343, 348, 365, 373–74, 376, 394, 395
Louis XIV (Rigaud), 15, colorplate 6
Louis XIV, Bust of (School of Bernini), **343**
Louis XV, King of France (1710–1774), 348, 377, 380, 381
Louis XVI, King of France (1754–1793), 348, 382, 406
Louis XVIII, King of France (1755–1824), 406
Louis Philippe, King of France (1773–1850), 406
Love (Indiana), 538, **539**
Lovers, The (Picasso), 525, **526**
"Love Song of J. Alfred Prufrock, The" (Eliot), 492–94 (text), 592
Love the Sorcerer (de Falla), 572
Loyola. *See* Ignatius of Loyola
Lucan (Marcus Annaeus Lucanus), Latin poet (39–65), 115
Lucian (Lucianus), Greek prose writer (ca. 125–ca. 180), 126 (overview)
Lucretius, Latin poet and philosopher (96–55 B.C.), 121, 126 (overview), 130–32
Luke, Gospel of (Bible), 159, 162
Luke, Saint, Apostle, 175
Lullaby (Brahms), 449
Lully, Jean Baptiste, Italian composer in France (1632–1687), 394, 395
Luncheon in Fur (Oppenheim), 531, **531**
Lute, 317, 321, 322
Luther, Martin, German leader of the Reformation (1483–1546), 275–76, 281, 299, 305, 317, 318, 327, 392, 393. *See also* Reformation
Lutheranism, 276, 277, 278
Lutoslawski, Witold, Polish composer (b. 1913), 572
Lux Aeterna (Ligeti), 572
Lyceum of Aristotle, 47, 56
Lyre, 100, **100**, 101 (box), 102, 104, 105, 254
Lyre Player "The Boston Throne" (Greek), **100**
Lyrical Ballads (Wordsworth and Coleridge), 416
Lysippos of Sikyon (fl. 4th c. B.C.), 94
Lysistrata (Aristophanes), 51

M

Machaut, Guillaume de, French composer and poet (1300–1377), 260, 261
Machaut Receiving Honors of Royalty and Clergy, **261**
Machiavelli, Niccolo, Florentine diplomat, novelist, and philosopher (1469–1527), 327–30, 337

Madame Butterfly (Puccini), 458
Madame de Pompadour as the Venus of the Doves (Falconet), 378, **378**
Madame Tallien (School of David), 382, **383**
Madeleine, The (Vignon), 463, **464**
Mlle. du Val d'Ognes (unknown French artist), 382, **383**, 384
Madonna Enthroned (Cimabue), 247, **248**
Madonna Enthroned (Giotto), 248, **248**
Madonna with the Long Neck (Parmigianino), 307, **307**
Madrigals, 322, 396
Magellan, Ferdinand (Fernas de Magalkaes), Portuguese explorer (1480–1521), 274
Magna Graecia, 79, 80, 112, 140
Maids of Honor (Las Meninas) (Velasquez), 371, **371**, 543
Mainstream jazz, 584, 587
Maison Carrée, Nîmes, France, 142–43, **143**, 385, 463
Major Emperors of Rome, 116 (box)
Mallarmé, Stéphane, French poet (1842–1898), 459, 461, 476, 480, 568
Mallia, Palace of (Minoan), 26
Malthus, Thomas, English economist (1766–1834), 427
Manet, Édouard, French painter (1832–1883), 473–74, 476, 521
Manhattan Transfer (Dos Passos), 595
Manichaeans, 186, 259
Manifest Destiny, 409, 429
Manifesto of
   Humanism, 270
   Realism (Courbet), 470
   Surrealism (Breton), 530
Mann, Thomas, German writer (1875–1955), 528
Mannerism, in art, 304, 305–8, 459
Manorialism, 188, 189, 194, 210
"Man Said to the Universe, A" (Crane), 443 (text)
Mansart, Jules Hardouin, French architect (1646–1708), 373
"Man Thinking about Woman" (Lee), 611 (text)
Manuscripts
   Carolingian, 236, 239
   Gothic, 249, 252, 261
   Hiberno-Saxon, 234–35, 236, 238, 249
   Islamic, 232
   Romanesque, 252, 254
Many Pierced Discs (Calder), 544, **544**
Marathon, Battle of, 34, 43, 47
Marcel, Gabriel, French philosopher (1889–1973), 8 (quotation)
Marchesa Elena Grimaldi (van Dyck), 372, **372**
Marco Polo, 418
Marcus Aurelius Antoninus, Roman emperor (121–180), 115, 116 (box), 117, 121, 122, 126 (overview), 130, 136–37 (text), 147, 149, **149**, 150, 382
Maria Luisà, Queen of Spain (Goya), 464–65, **465**
"Mariana" (Tennyson), 430–31 (text)

Marie Antoinette, Queen of France (1755–1793), 382
Marie of Champagne, French countess (12th c.), 206, 229
Marinatos, Spyridon, Greek archeologist (1901–1974), 26, 27
Mark, Gospel of (Bible), 159, 162
Mark, Saint, Apostle, 175
Mark Antony (Marcus Antonius), Roman general (83–30 B.C.), 115
Marlowe, Christopher, English dramatist (1564–1593), 197
Marseillaise, La (Rude), 467, **467**
Marteau sans maître, Le (Boulez), 568
Martel, Charles, leader of the Franks (689–741), 191, 231 (overview)
Martial (Marcus Valerius Martialis), Latin epigramist (40–104), 126 (overview), 134–35
Martin, Frank, Swiss composer (1890–1974), 572
Martini, Simone, Sienese painter (1284–1344), 249
Martin Luther and the Wittenberg Reformers (Cranach the Younger), **276**
Martinu, Bohuslav, Czech composer (1890–1959), 571
Marvell, Andrew, English poet (1621–1678), 349, 350–51
Marx, Karl, German writer on economics and socialism (1818–1883), 406, 426–27, 521
Masaccio (Guidi de San Giovanni), Tommaso, Florentine painter (1401–1428), 287–88, 289, 299, 525
Mask from Mycenae, 75, **75**
Massacre at Chios (Delacroix), 407
Mass in G (Poulenc), 571
Mathematics, 36–39, 99
Mathis der Maler (Hindemith), 570
Matisse, Henri, French artist (1869–1954), 522, 524, 526, 557
Matsys (Massys), Quentin, Flemish painter (ca. 1465?–1530), 279
Matthew, Gospel of (Bible), 159, 162, 162–65 (text)
Matthew, Saint, Disciple, 175
Maugham, William Somerset, English novelist and playwright (1874–1965), 475, 595
Mausoleum (Cenotaph) (Roman), 144, **144**
Mecca, 190, 232
Medea (Euripides), 50
Medici, Cosimo de', Florentine banker (1389–1464), 270
Medici, Lorenzo de', Florentine ruler and patron of arts and letters (1449–1492), 281, 289, 291, **292**, 293, 299, 301, 305
Medici, Marie de', Queen of France (1573–1642), 371
Medici Chapel, 305
Medici family, 281, 288, 293, 298, 299, 301, 305
Meditations (Descartes), 342
Meditations, Book II (Marcus Aurelius), 136–37 (text)

Meistersingers, 259
Meistersinger von Nürnberg, Die
    (Wagner), 259
Melancthon, Philipp, Lutheran scholar
    (1497–1560), 276
Melville, Herman, American novelist and
    poet (1819–1891), 436–38, 472,
    591
Memling, Hans, Flemish painter
    (ca. 1430–1494), 293, 297–98
Memorial Oration (Perikles), 51–52,
    52–53 (text)
Menander, Greek New Comedy dramatist
    (342?–291? B.C.), 119
Mendel, Gregor, Austrian geneticist
    (1822–1884), 427
Mendelssohn, Felix, German composer
    (1809–1847), 451–52
Messiaen, Olivier, French composer
    (b. 1908), 568
Messiah, The (Handel), 395
Metamorphoses (Ovid), 219
Metaphysics (Aristotle), 57n
Methodist church, 277
Metopes, 85, 86, 87, 302
Metternich, Clemens Fürst von, Austrian
    statesman (1773–1859), 406, 408
Michelangelo Buonarotti, Italian artist
    (1475–1564), 4, 6, 14, 97, 142, 280,
    281, 287, 290, 299, 300–302, 303,
    304, 305–7, 308, 310, 317, 330–31,
    368, 369, 372, 380, 467, 469, 470,
    478
Middle Ages, 7, 119, 125, 127, 148,
    185–266 (unit 4), 269, 270, 271,
    275, 278, 279, 280, 287, 315, 325,
    375, 427
    architecture, 181, 211, 212, 213, 215
    art, 231–50 (chap. 11)
    drama, 42, 197–204, 210, 213
    history, 185–94, 205–16
    literary selections, 195–204, 216–30
    music, 251–61 (chap. 12)
    painting, 170, 171, 172, 175, 247–49
    poetry, 256–58
Midsummer Marriage, The (Tippett), 571
Mies van der Rohe, Ludwig, German
    architect (1886–1969), 550–51
Migration of the Negro, The (Lawrence),
    549
Milhaud, Darius, French composer
    (1892–1974), 571
Mill, James, English philosopher
    (1773–1836), 429
Mill, John Stuart, English philosopher
    (1806–1873), 429–30
Miller, Henry, American writer
    (1891–1980), 4 (quotation), 590
Millet, Jean François, French painter
    (1814–1875), 458, 469, 532
Miltiades, Athenian general (d. 489 B.C.), 34
Milton, John, English poet (1608–1674), 351,
    352, 365
Minimal art, 544–46
Minnesingers, 259
Minoan culture, 26, 27, 28, 69, 70, 73–76,
    77, 261
Minos, King of Crete (Minoans), 26, 48
    (box), 73, 261

Minotaur, 69, 73, 91
Minstrel Show, 579
Mirandola. *See* Pico
Miro, Joan, Spanish painter (1893–1983),
    530–31
Mishima, Yokio, Japanese author
    (1925–1972), 596
Mission of the Apostles, Ste.-Madeleine,
    Vézelay, France, 238, **238**
"Mixed Sketches" (Lee), 612 (text)
Mnesekles, Greek architect (fl. 437 B.C.), 90
Moby Dick (Melville), 436, 591
Modest Proposal, A (Swift), 355–58 (text)
Mohammed (Mahomet), Islamic prophet
    (570?–632), 29, 190, 231, 232
Molière (Jean Baptiste Poquelin), French
    actor and playwright (1622–1673),
    394
Momaday, N. Scott, American writer
    (b. 1934), 606–8
Mona Lisa (Leonardo), 8, 299, 530, 536
Mona Lisa L.H.O.O.Q. (Duchamp), 530
Monasteries, 180, 188, 234, 237, 249, 253
Mondrian, Piet, Dutch painter (1872–1944),
    14, 526, 528, 540
Monet, Claude, French painter (1840–1926),
    443, 459, 475–76, 521, 540
Money Lender and His Wife, The (Matsys),
    279
Monogram (Rauschenberg), 536, **536**
Monoscape (Frankenthaler), 540, **540**
Monotheism, 156, 157, 158
Montaigne, Michel de, French essayist and
    philosopher (1533–1592), 342
Montesquieu, Charles Louis de Secondat,
    Baron de la Brède et de, French jurist
    and political philosopher
    (1689–1755), 345, 348
Monticello, Virginia (Jefferson), 143
Mont-St. Michel, France, 241, **241**
Mont-St. Michel and Chartres (H. Adams),
    209
Moore, Henry, English sculptor (b. 1898),
    544, 545
Moore, John, American painter (b. 1941),
    546, 547
Moravian Church, 275
More, Sir Thomas, English statesman and
    author (1478–1535), 274, 311, 327,
    331–36
Morgan, Norma, American artist (b. 1928),
    549
Morisot, Berthe, French painter
    (1841–1895), 475, 476
Mosaics
    Byzantine, 178, 179, 181, 190, 236
    Carolingian, 236
    early Christian, 175–76, 177
    Gothic, 247
    Hellenistic, 175
    Mozarabic, 233
    Roman, 119, 175
Moses, Hebrew lawgiver (fl. 13th c. B.C.),
    111, 156, 162, 171
Mosque, 72, **72**, 179, 180, 232–33, 234
Motet, 260, 318, 320
Mother and Two Daughters, A (Godwin),
    591
Motion pictures, 613

Mousmé, La (van Gogh), **478**, 478–79
Mozart, Wolfgang Amadeus, Austrian
    composer (1756–1791), 10, 16,
    337, 372, 388, 395, 396, 398–99,
    400, 447, 467, 528
Mrs. Richard Brinsley Sheridan
    (Gainsborough), **379**, 379–80
Mrs. Richard Yates (Stuart), **384**, 384
"Much Madness is Divinest Sense"
    (Dickinson), 442 (text)
Mumford, Lewis, American philosopher
    (b. 1895), 3 (quotation), 191
    (quotation)
Munch, Edvard, Norwegian painter
    (1864–1944), 482, 522
Murger, Henri, French writer
    (1822–1861), 458
"Muse on Mount Helicon" (Akhilleus
    Painter), 91–92, **91**
Muses, The, 30 (box), 91, 99, 102
Museum of Natural History (Waterhouse),
    467, **468**
Music
    aleatory, 566, 569
    atonal, 558–61
    Baroque, 349, 387–95
    basis for understanding, 11–12
    Burgundian school, 316–17
    cantata, 393–94, 565–66
    chorale, 392–93
    chorale prelude, 393
    Classical period, 395–401
    concertos, 392, 559–61, 562–65
    Development of Medieval Music, 262
        (table)
    electronic, 567–69, 572
    elements of, 16–17, 102
    English madrigal school, 322–23
    ethos, 99, 101, 105, 106, 373
    Etruscan, 151
    form, 10, 11–12, 20–22, 397–98
    Franco-Flemish, 315–18
    fugue, 389–90
    fundamentals of, 18–22
    Futurists, 568
    German lieder, 448–49
    Greek, 99–106 (chap. 4), 151, 252, 308
    Greek drama, in, 104–5
    Greek games, in, 102
    Gregorian chant, 10, 17, 251–54, 259,
        263
    harmony, 17
    Hebrew, 253
    homophonic, 20, 159, 259
    Impressionism, 459–61
    Italian style, 318–19
    jazz, 10, 16, 391, 573–88
    listening to, 11–12, 16–18, 22
    literacy, 11, 17–18
    medieval, 251–61 (chap. 12)
    melody, 17
    meter, 17
    modern, 557–72 (chap. 26)
    monophonic, 20, 251, 252, 259
    motet, 260
    musicals, 16, 570
    "Music of the spheres," 38, 99
    nationalism, 448
    Neo-Romantic, 565–66

notation of, 18–20, 101, 105, 106, 252
opera, 394–95, 317n, 457–59
passacaglia, 390–91
polyphonic, 20, 259–60, 263
printing, 321
Pythagoras, 37–38, 99, 261
Renaissance, 315–23 (chap. 15)
response to, 10, 16
rhythm, 16–17, 252, 259, 575–76
Rococo period, 395
Roman, 146, 151–52
Romanticism, 447–61 (chap. 21)
scales, 19, 252, 574–75
serial composition, 566, 567, 569, 572
symphony, 398–401, 451–55, 456–57, 561–62, 566–67
time signatures, 17
tone color, 17
tone poem, 455–56
trio sonata, 391–92
"Music and Her Attendants," **207**
"Music of the Spheres," 38, 99
Muslim, 185, 189–191, 206, 209, 231, 233
Mussolini, Benito, Italian dictator (1883–1945), 373, 485, 486
Myaskovsky, Nikolai, Russian composer (1881–1950), 572
Mycenaean culture, 27–28, 31, 70, 73, 75–77
Mycerinus and His Queen, 70, **70**
My Fair Lady (Lerner and Loewe), 570
Myron, Greek sculptor (480–407 B.C.), 84
Mysterious Mountain (Hovhaness), 570
Myth of Er, *Republic* (Plato), 127
"Myth of Sisyphus, The" (Camus), 511–12 (text)

N

Nadar (Félix Tournachon), French photographer (1820–1910), 476
Napoléon Buonaparte (or Bonaparte), General and emperor of France (1769–1821), 124, 145, 299, 373, 384, 400, 405–6, **406,** 407, 408, 424, 463, 466
Napoléon in His Study (David), **406**
Napoléon III (Louis Napoléon Bonaparte), Emperor of the French (1808–1873), 407
Narration
   continuous (Roman), 148, 172, 288
   simultaneous (Greek), 89, 148
National Mosque, Kuala Lumpur, Malaysia, 234, **234**
Natural selection, 427–28
Nave, 174, 177, 178, 238, 239, 244, 245, 247, 369
Nazi Party, 486, 523, 528, 532, 562, 568, 571
Necessity of Atheism, The (Shelley), 420
Neoclassic style, 352
   in architecture, 380–81, 385
   in art, 381–85
Neoplatonism, 122, 186, 187, 208, 242, 293, 301
Neri, Manuel, American sculptor (b. 1930), 548

Nero (Claudius Caesar Drusus Germanicus), Roman emperor (37–68), 115, 116 (box), 121–22, 124, 146, 151
Nervi, Pier Luigi, Italian architectural engineer (1891–1979), 550
"Neutral Tones" (Hardy), 432 (text)
Nevelson, Louise, American sculptor (b. 1900), 540, 541
Newcomen, Thomas, English inventor (1663–1729), 407
Newley, Anthony, English actor and composer (b. 1931), 570
New Orleans Revival style jazz, 582
New Orleans style jazz, 580, 581, 582
New Sciences, The (Galileo), 343
New Testament (Bible), 159, 160, 162, 166, 172, 173, 295, 296, 375
Newton, Sir Isaac, English scientist and mathematician (1642–1727), 342, 344–45, 347, 348, 360, 388, 389, 415, 489
New World, 274, 281, 299, 384
Nicholas I, Czar of Russia (1796–1855), 408
Nicholas II, Czar of Russia (1868–1918), 408
Niebelungenlied (*Volsunga saga*), 192, 193
Nietzsche, Friedrich Wilhelm, German philosopher (1844–1900), 415, 458, 503, 529
Nightingale, Florence, English nurse (1820–1910), 408
Nights in the Gardens of Spain (de Falla), 572
Nike (Paionios), 92, **92**
Nike of Samothrace (Pythokritos of Rhodes), 95, **95**
"Nikki-Rosa" (Giovanni), 612 (text)
Nilsson, Bo, Scandinavian composer (b. 1937), 572
Niña Parada (Rivera), 533, **533**
Nochebuena del Diablo, La (Esplá), 572
Nocturnes and Arias (Henze), 572
Noland, Kenneth, American artist (b. 1924), 540
Nominalism, 208–9
Nomos Pythikos (Sakadas of Argos), 102
Norsemen, 190, 191, 193, 236
Nostalgia of the Infinite, The (de Chirico), **529,** 529–30
"Notorious Jumping Frog of Calaveras County, The" (Twain), 438, 439–40
Notre Dame Cathedral, Paris, **242,** 242–43, **243,** 244, 259, 260, 263
Notre-Dame-du-Haut (Corbusier), 551, **551**
Notre Dame Mass: Agnus Dei (Machaut), 260, 260(music)
Nóvak, Vieteslav, Czech composer (1870–1949), 571
Novum Organum (Bacon), 342
Nude with Upraised Arms (Rouault), 522, **523**
Number 1 (Pollock), 535, colorplate 55

Number VII from Eight Studies for a Portrait (Bacon), 542, **542**
Number 10 (Rothko), 535, colorplate 57
Nuper Rosarum Flores (Flower of Rose) (Dufay), 286
Nutcracker, The (Tchaikovsky), 456

O

Obrecht, Jacob, Flemish composer (ca. 1430–1505), 317
Octavian, 115. *See also* Augustus
Odalisque (Ingres), 475
"Ode on a Grecian Urn" (Keats), 423 (text)
"Ode to Joy," Ninth Symphony (Beethoven), 415
Ode to Joy (Beethoven), 21 (music)
Ode to Joy (Schiller), 415
"Ode to Napoleon Buonaparte" (Byron), 406 (text)
"Ode to the West Wind" (Shelley), 421–22 (text)
Odysseus, 28, 29, 31, 34, 125
Odyssey (Homer), 32, 77, 125
Oedipus, 48, 48 (box), 49
Oedipus the King (Sophokles), 31, 48–49, 100, 161
Offering Bearers (Egyptian), 71, **71**
Of Human Bondage (Maugham), 475, 595
Of Thee I Sing (Gershwin), 570
Oiseaux exotiques (Messiaen), 568
O'Keeffe, Georgia, American painter (b. 1887), 526, 527
Oklahoma! (Rodgers and Hammerstein), 570, 593
Old Comedy, Greek, 51
Oldenburg, Claes, American artist (b. 1929), 538, 539
Old Man with a Child (Ghirlandaio), 293, **293**
Old Testament (Bible), 160, 162, 173, 177, 295, 296, 348, 375
Oliphant, 193, **217**
Olive Orchard, The (Van Gogh), 470, **479**
Olympia, 92, 102, 122, 123, 124
Olympia (Manet), 473, **474,** 475, 521
Olympiad, 122, 123, 124
Olympian Zeus, Temple of the (Cossutius), 96, **96**
Olympic games, 76, 84, 102, 122–24
Olympics, modern, 123, 123n
Olympos, 102
Olympos the Phrygian, Greek musician, 100, 101
One Flew Over the Cuckoo's Nest (Kesey), 591
"On His Blindness" (Milton), 351 (text)
On Liberty (Mill), 429
Only Good Thing About It, The (Kollwitz), 522–23, **523**
On Population (Malthus), 427
On the Dedication of the Colosseum in Rome (Martial), 135 (text)
"On the Elgin Marbles" (Keats), 422 (text)
"On the Late Massacre in Piedmont" (Milton), 351 (text)

On the Nature of Things (Lucretius), 121, 130–32 (text)

On the Origin of Species by Means of Natural Selection (Darwin), 427

"On the Painting of the Sistine Chapel" (Michelangelo), 302 (text)

On the Republic (Cicero), 127

"On the Road", *The White Album* (Didion), 513–14 (text)

"On the Slain Collegians" (Melville), 437 (text)

On the Waterfront (Kazan), 613

"Open Boat, The" (Crane), 443

Opera, 388, 394–95, 396, 457–59

Oppenheim, Meret, American artist (b. 1913), 531

Opus Americanum (Milhaud), 571

Op. 1970 (Stockhausen), 569

Orant, Catacombs of St. Priscilla, 170, **170**

Oration of the Dignity of Man (Pico), 270–71 (text)

Oresteia (Aeschylus), 43–46

Orestes, 43, 43 (box), 44, 45, 49–50

Orff, Carl, German composer (1895–1980), 255, 565–66

Organ, pipe, 151n, **207, 252,** 254, 259–60, **321,** 389, 390, **390,** 391–93

Organum, 259, 260, 263, 387

Or La Truix (trouvère song), **258**

Orozco, José, Mexican painter (1883–1949), 533, 548

Orpheus, Greek musician, 100, 101

"Orpheus Among the Thracians" (Orpheus Painter), **102**

Ortiz, Ralph, American artist (b. 1934), 548

Osiris, 119, 120

Ostrogoths, 192
  Kingdom of, 169 (overview), 177, 185

Ottobeuren (Fischer), Benedictine Church of, Bavaria, 379, **379**

"Our Lady's Juggler," 208, 216, 217–19 (text)

Ovid (Publius Ovidius Naso), Latin poet (43 B.C.–A.D. 18), 111 (quotation), 114 (quotation), 117 (quotation), 119 (quotation), 126 (overview), 219, 229, 256, 294

Owen, Wilfred, English poet (1893–1918), 494

"Owls of Athena," 47, 117

P

Pacific Overtures (Sondheim), 570

Paganini, Niccolò, Italian violinist and composer (1782–1840), 449, 455

Painting. *See* Art; *and the names of individual artists*

Paionios, Greek sculptor (fl. 421 B.C.), 92

Palace at 4 A.M., The (Giacometti), 531, **531**

Palatine Chapel of Charlemagne (Odo of Metz), Aachen, Germany, **190,** 235, **235**

Palatine School (Charlemagne), 190

Palazzo Rucellai (Alberti), Florence, 290, **290**

Palestine, 11, 103, 156, 170

Palestrina, Giovanni Pierluigi da, Italian composer (1524–1594), 254, 281, 317, 318, 319, 388, 396

Palladian Bridge (Jones), 380, **380**

Palladio, Andrea di Pietro, Italian architect (1518–1580), 290, 308, 366, 380

Panel 3 (Kandinsky), 14, 524, colorplate 5

Panini, Giovanni, Italian painter (ca. 1691–1765), 149

Pantheon, Greek, 29

Pantheon, Rome, 118, 119, **148,** 148–49, 151, 286, 369, 463

Parables, Five (Bible), Matthew 18:23–35; 20:1–16; 25:14–30 and **Luke 10:30–37; 15:4–32,** 164–65 (text)

Paradise (Islamic), 233

Paradise Lost (Milton), 351

Paradise Regained (Milton), 351

Parker, Dorothy, American writer (1893–1967), 8

Parliament, Houses of (Barry and Pugin), 468, **469**

Parmenides of Elea, Greek philosopher (514–? B.C.), 41, 42, 79

Parmigianino (Francesco Mazzuoli), Italian painter (1503–1540), 307, 464

Parthenon (Iktinus and Kallikrates) Athens, 5, 6, 47, 80, 86, 87, **87,** 88, 89, 90, 91, 92, 95, 96, 148, 422, 463
  frieze, 89, 92, 95
  pediment, 88, 96
  schematic drawing, 88
  stereobate and stylobate, 87, **88**

Passacaglia, 389, 390

Passacaglia in C minor (Bach), 390–91 (music)

Paul (Saul of Tarsus), Saint, Apostle (ca. 10–64), 159, 164, 166, 172, 186

Paul III, Pope (1468–1549), 277, 305

Pauline Borghese as Venus (Canova), 384, **384**

Pax Romana (Roman peace), 115, 140 (overview)

Paxton, Sir Joseph, English architect (1801–1865), 472

Pazzi Chapel (Brunelleschi), 554

"Pebbles" (Melville), 438 (text)

Peloponnesian War, 50, 51, 53, 54

Penitent St. Peter, The (El Greco), 309, **309**

Pentathlon, 123

Penthesilea, Queen of the Amazons, 79, **79**

Pentheus, King of Thebes, 48, 50

Pepusch, Johann, German-English composer (1667–1752), 395

Perikles, Athenian statesman (ca. 495–429), 25, **46,** 46–47, 50, 51–52, 52–53 (text), 54, 57, 84, 86, 87, 91, 92, 106, 124

Pérotin, French composer (fl. 1200), 260

Persia, 31, 50, 53, 120, 191

Persian Empire, 34, 53

Persian Letters (Montesquieu), 348

Persians, 31, 34, 35, 39, 51, 53, 78, 82, 91, 190

Persian Wars, 34, 42, 53

Persistence of Memory, The (Dali), 531, **531**

Person Throwing a Stone at a Bird (Miro), 531, colorplate 54

Perspective, in art, 288, 289, 291, 293, 295, 300

Perugino (Pietro Vannucci), Italian painter (1445–1523), 293, 299, 301, 303

Peter (Simon Peter), Saint, Apostle (d. 64?), 14, **147,** 148, 159, 172, 177, 188, 366–67, **367**

Peter and the Wolf (Prokofiev), 561

Peter the Great, Czar of Russia (1672–1725), 349

Petit Trianon (Gabriel), 381

Petrarch, Francesco, Italian humanist poet (1304–1374), 250, 269, 270, 325–27

Petronius Arbiter, Gaius, Latin writer (d. 66), 126 (overview)

Petrouchka (Stravinsky), 557

Petrucci, Ottaviano de', Venetian music printer (1466–1539), 321

Phaistos, Palace of, Crete (Minoan), 26

Pharaohs, 71, 77, 78

Pheidias, Greek sculptor (490–432 B.C.), 6, 8, 86, 87, 88

Philip the Bold, Duke of Burgundy (1342–1404), 294

Philip the Good, Duke of Burgundy (1396–1467), 295, 316

Philip II, King of Macedonia (382–336 B.C.), 53, 56

Philip IV, King of Spain (1605–1665), 371

Philoktetes (Sophokles), 29

Philosophes, Les, 348, 381, 384

Philosophy. *See also names of individual philosophers*
  Abelard, 208–9, 210 (quotation)
  absolutism (Hobbes), 343
  Anaximandros, 35, 36
  Aristotle, 7 (quotation), 49, 53, 56–57, 79, 105, 155, 159, 191, 208, 209, 211, 212, 213, 244, 303
  Atomist, 42
  Augustine, St., 55, 122, 126 (overview), 186–88, 194, 207, 208
  Battle of Universals, 205, 208–9
  Cartesian, 272–73, 342
  Christian existentialism, 503–4, 513
  conceptualism, 209
  Demokritos, 42, 47, 159, 272, 590
  Eleatic, 41–42, 54, 56, 79
  Enlightenment, 344–49, 360, 376, 388, 389, 397, 411, 414, 415, 466
  Epictetus, 121, 122
  Epicurean, 120–21, 130, 155
  existentialism, 503–13, 590, 593
  Golden Mean, 56, 57
  Greek, 7, 27, 35–39, 41, 42, 49, 51, 53, 54–56, 57–67, 70, 79, 87, 89, 102, 104, 105, 120, 121, 122, 130, 135, 155, 159
  Herakleitos, 36, 41, 159
  Ionian, 35–39, 41, 56
  liberalism, 429–30
  Lucretius, 121, 126 (overview), 130–32

Marcus Aurelius, 116 (box), 117, 121, 122, 126 (overview), 136–37, 147, 149, 150, 382

Neoplatonism, 122, 186, 187, 208, 242, 293, 301

nominalism, 208

Philosopher-kings, 55

Philosophes, 348, 381, 384

Plato, 27, 42, 51, 54–56, 57–67, 70, 79, 87, 99, 102, 104, 105, 120, 121, 122, 155, 159, 187, 191, 192, 208, 270, 293, 429, 503

Protagoras, 47

Pythagorean, 36–39, 56

reality, concept of, 6, 7, 54, 56, 122, 187, 205, 208–9

Roman, 119–22

Romanticism, 213, 217

St. Augustine, 55, 122, 126 (overview), 186, 188, 194, 207, 208, 212, 259, 275, 276

St. Thomas, 209, 211–12, 213, 214, 215, 216

Scholasticism, 208–9, 213

Sokrates, 6, 42, 51, 52, 53n, 54, 55, 56, 57–67, **58,** 99, 120, 121, 208, 382, 429

Sophists, 47, 51, 58

Stoicism, 120–22

Thales, 35, 36

Zeno the Stoic, 121

Phrygian mode, 100, 100n, 105

Piano Concerto (Khachaturian), 572

Picasso, Pablo, Spanish artist (1881–1973), 12, 15, 481, 482, 524–26, 527, 557

Pickens, Alton, American painter (b. 1917), 531, 532

Pico della Mirandola, Giovanni, humanist writer (1463–1494), 270

Pieta (Michelangelo), 300–301, **301**

Pilgrimage to Cythera, A (Watteau), 377, **377**

Pindar, Greek poet-musician (518?–ca. 439 B.C.), 102

Pippin, Horace, American painter (1888–1946), 548

Piranesi, Giambattista, Italian artist (1720–1778), 174–75

Pirelli Tower (Ponti, Nervi, Danosso), Milan, 550, **550**

Pisa

Cathedral with baptistery, **240**

Cathedral and campanile, **240**

Pisistratus, Athenian reformer (605–527 B.C.), 33

Pitt, William, English statesman (1708–1778), 349

Pizarro, Francisco, Spanish conquistador (1471–1541), 274

Plague, The (Camus), 513, 591

Planck, Max, German physicist (1858–1947), 488

Plato, Greek philosopher (427–347 B.C.), 27, 42, 51, 54–56, 57–67, 70, 79, 87, 99, 102, 104, 105, 120, 121, 122, 155, 159, 187, 191, 192, 208, 270, 293, 429, 503

Platonic Academy, Florence, 270, 293, 301

Plautus, Latin dramatist (254?–184 B.C.), 126 (overview)

Play of Daniel, 255

Play of the Three Kings, The, 254–55

Play of the Virtues (Hildegard), 255

Plays

Miracle, 197

Morality, 197–204 (text), 210, 213

musical, 570

Mystery, 197, 213, 255

Pliny the Elder, Roman naturalist and historian (ca. 23–79), 94, 117–18, 126 (overview)

Pliny the Younger, Roman orator and statesman (62?–ca. 123), 125, 126 (overview)

Plotinus, Hellenistic philosopher, founder of Neoplatonism (fl. 205–270), 270

Plow that Broke the Plains, The (Thomson), 570

Plutarch, Greek biographer (ca. 46–ca. 120), 103, 113 (quotation), 126 (overview), 140

Poe, Edgar Allen, American author (1809–1849), 434

Poème Electronique (Varèse), 568

Poetry

Greek, 102–3, 105–6

medieval, 256–58

realism, 436, 441

Renaissance, 326, 330

Roman, 126 (overview), 130–35

Romantic, 415, 419, 420, 422, 423, 424, 433, 434, 435

seventeenth century, 349–59

troubadour, 256–59

twentieth century, 592–93

Victorian, 430, 431, 432

Politics (Aristotle), 56

Pollock, Jackson, American painter (1912–1956), 535

Polo, Marco, Venetian traveler (1254–1324), 274

Polykleitos of Argos, Greek sculptor, (fl. 430 B.C.), 84, 94

Pompadour, Jeanne Antoinette Poisson, Marquise (Madame) de, Mistress of Louis XV (1721–1764), 377, 381

Pompeii, 118, 141, 146, 151, 381

Pompey the Great, Roman general and triumvir (106–48 B.C.), 114, 115

Pompidou National Center for Art and Culture (Piano and Rogers), Paris, 554, **554**

Ponce de León, Michael, American artist (b. 1922), 548

Pont du Gard, France, Roman aqueduct, 143–44, **144**

Ponti, Gio, Italian architect (1891–1971), 550

Pop art, 535–39, 543, 548, 566

Pope, Alexander, English poet (1688–1744), 345 (quotation), 352–55, 360

Popes, 117, 148, 171, 177, 188, 189, 190, 210, 212, 235, 249, 251, 255, 275, 276, 277, 299, 302

Porgy and Bess (Gershwin), 570

Portable Roman Reader, The (Davenport), 114n (quotation)

"Portent, The" (Melville), 436 (text)

Portrait Head from Delos, 97, **97**

Portrait of a Lady (van der Weyden), 297, **297**

Portrait of an Officer (Hals), 374, **374**

Portrait of Henri Mihaux (Dubuffet), 542, **542**

Poseidon, 29, 30 (box), 86, 90, 97, 119, 171

Poseidon (Greek), 83, **83**

Poseidon, Temple of, Sounion, 91, **91**

Post and lintel system, 84–85, **85,** 143, 146, 147

Pottery, Greek, 139

Archaic, 78–79

black-figure, 78–79

Classical, 82, 91–92

Geometric, 76

manufacture of, 76, 91

Minoan, 7

red-figure, 82, 91, **102, 103, 104**

white-ground, 91–92

Poulenc, Francis, French composer (1899–1963), 571

Poussin, Nicolas, French painter (1594–1665), 372–73, 377, 478, 481

Poussinists, 372, 447, 467

Praise of Folly (Erasmus), 327

Praxiteles of Athens, Greek sculptor (fl. 340 B.C.), 92–93, 146

Preludes, Les (Liszt), 454–55 (music)

Prelude to the Afternoon of a Faun (Debussy), 460, 461 (music)

Presentation in the Temple, The (Memling), 297–98, **298**

Prigioniero, Il (Dallapiccola), 570

Prince, The (Machiavelli), 327, 328–30 (text)

Principia (Mathematical Principles of Natural Philosophy) (Newton), 344

Procesión del Rocio, La (Turina), 572

Progressive jazz, 583–84

Prokofiev, Sergei, Russian composer (1891–1953), 388, 561–62, 583

Prolog to *The Canterbury Tales* (Chaucer), 210–11, 219–26 (text)

"Prometheus" (Byron), 419–20 (text)

Prometheus Unbound (Shelley), 420

Prophet (Donatello), 287, **287**

Prophet, The, Abbey Church of St. Pierre, Moissac, 239, **239**

Proposal for a Giant Balloon in the Form of a Typewriter Eraser—Structural Model (Oldenburg), 538, **539**

Propylaia, Athens, 86

Protagoras, Greek Sophist philosopher (ca. 481–411 B.C.), 47

Protestant, 276, 277, 280, 311, 342, 351, 360, 374

Psalms (Bible), 24, 137, 150, 161 (text)

Psalter of St. Swithin, 239, colorplate 16

Psychopathology of Everyday Life, The (Freud), 490

Ptolemy (Claudius Ptolemaeus), Graeco-Egyptian mathematician and astronomer (fl. 2d c. A.D.), 244, 271–72

Puccini, Giacomo, Italian opera composer (1858–1924), 458–59
Pugin, Augustus Welby, Gothic revivalist architect (1812–1852), 468
Punic Wars, 113–14, 127, 140 (overview)
Purgatory (Dante), 213, 214
Pygmalion, 77
Pygmalion (Daumier), 470, **471**
Pythagoras of Samos, Ionian philosopher (ca. 582–ca. 507 B.C.), 36–39, **37,** 41, 42, 54, 56, 79, 99, 211, 244
Pythagoreans of Krotona, 36, 39, 112, 261, 308
Pythagorean theorem, 37
Pythian Games (Delphi), 102
Pythokritos of Rhodes, Greek sculptor (fl. 200–190 B.C.), 95

Q

Quadrille at the Moulin Rouge (Toulouse-Lautrec), 481, **481**
Quadrivium, 210, 300
Quakers, 277
Quantum theory, 488–90, 569
Quartet no. 2 (Janáček), 571
Queen's House (Jones), 380, **380**
Queen's Megaron, Knossos (Minoan), 74, **74**
Quintilian, Marcus Fabius, Roman rhetorician and critic (ca. 35–ca. 100), 126 (overview), 151

R

Rachmaninoff, Sergei, Russian composer (1873–1943), 16
Racine, Jean Baptiste, French dramatic poet (1639–1699), 394
Radio Tubes (Davis), 526, **527**
Raft of the Medusa (Henze), 572
Raft of the Medusa, The (Gericault), 466, **466**
Ragtime, 573, 579–80, 582, 585, 587
Rape of the Daughters of Leucippus (Rubens), 372, colorplate 34
Raphael (Raffaello Sanzio), Italian artist (1483–1520), 8, 14, 317, 370, 372, 525
Rauschenberg, Robert, American artist (b. 1925), 536
Ravel, Maurice, French composer (1875–1937), 459, 583
Ravenna, Italy, 117, 176–78, 186, 190, 235, 236, 280, 287, 299, 302, 303–4, 305, 307
Realism, 208–9
    in art, 468–72, 532–33, 546–47
    in literature, 430–33, 436–43, 458–59
Rebec, **217,** 254, **254**
Recorder, 254, **321**
Red Badge of Courage, The (Crane), 443
"Reeve's Tale, The," *The Canterbury Tales* (Chaucer), 226–29 (text)
Reformation, 188, 274–77, 281, 298, 299, 310, 341, 342, 351, 387
Regent Square, 21 (music)
Reign of Terror, 466
Relativity, Theory of, 486, 488–90

Religion. *See also* Philosophy
    Christianity, 7, 55, 56, 57, 117, 120, 121, 122, 124, 125, 126 (overview), 149, 151, 152, 155–81 (unit 3), 186, 187, 188, 191, 193, 194, 232, 233, 234, 235, 237, 238, 261, 275, 305, 573, 576
    Cult of Cybele, 119, 120, 155
    Cult of Isis, 119, 120, 155
    Cult of the Virgin, 205, 207, 213, 217, 244
    Egyptian, 71–72, 119
    Greek, 28–31, 71, 86–91, 120. *See also* Gods
    Islam, 191, 231, 232, 249, 466
    Judaism, 7, 156–62, 347
    Minoan, 27
    Mithraism, 120, 155
    Norse, 191
    Pythagorean, 39
    Roman, 119–22
Reliquary (Rhenish), 239, colorplate 15
Rembrandt van Rijn, Dutch painter (1606–1669), 297, 365, 366, 375, 376, 464, 470, 536
Renaissance, 7, 91, 94, 97, 112, 119, 178, 180, 206, 215, 243, 267–337 (unit 5), 341, 365, 370, 371, 372, 374, 376, 380, 387, 388, 390, 396, 459, 464, 473, 475, 521, 525, 531, 542, 543, 586
Renaissance, Carolingian, 189–90, 270
Renault, Mary, English author (b. 1905), 27
Renoir, Pierre Auguste, French painter (1841–1919), 377, 443, 459, 473, 476, 477
Republic (Plato), 55–56, 105, 121, 127
Requiem (Ligeti), 572
Retablo (de Falla), 572
Return of the Hunters (Bruegel), 13, colorplate 2
Revelation (Bible), 162; **6:1–8; 21:1–4,** 166–67 (text)
Revelation and Fall (Davies), 571
Revolution
    American, 343, 360, 376, 426
    French, 245, 348, 349, 376, 379, 382, 405, 406, 415, 416, 426
Revolutionary Étude (Chopin), 449
Reynolds, Sir Joshua, English portrait painter (1723–1792), 303 (quotation)
Rhadamanthys, Queen of Crete, 48 (box)
Rhapsody in Blue (Gershwin), 570
Rhodes, Cecil, English imperialist (1853–1902), 428
"Rhodora, The" (Emerson), 424–35 (text)
Richard the Lion-Heart, King of England, (1157–1199), 238, 258
Richelieu, Cardinal, Chief minister of Louis XIII (1585–1642), 343
Riegger, Wallingford, American composer (1885–1961), 570
Rigaud, Hyacinthe, French painter (1659–1743), 15
Rigoletto (Verdi), 458

Riley, Bridget, English artist (b. 1931), 540, 542
Rimbaud, Arthur, French poet (1854–1891), 572
Ring of the Nibelung, The (Wagner), 193
Ring shout, 579, 586
Rite of Spring, The (Stravinsky), 557–58, 561
Rivera, Diego, Mexican artist (1886–1957), 533, 549
Roads, Roman, 118, **118,** 143, 150
Roar of the Greasepaint; The Smell of the Crowd, The (Newley), 570
Robespierre, Maximilian Marie Isidore, Leader in French Revolution (1758–1794), 405
Rochberg, George, American composer (b. 1918), 570
Rockefeller, John D., American industrialist (1839–1937), 428, 429
Rococo style, 459
    in architecture, 378–79
    in art, 376–78, 379–80
    in music, 395
Rodeo (Copland), 570
Rodeo Queen (Jimenez), 548
Rodgers, Richard, American composer (1902–1979), 570
Rodin, August, French sculptor (1840–1917), 477–78, 526, 528
Roi David, Le (Honegger), 571
Roland, Knight of Charlemagne (d. 778), 189, 193, 194, 206, 256
Roman coin, **117**
Roman Empire in A.D. 180, 116 (map)
Romanesque, **231** (overview), 239, 244, 247, 249, 263, 295, 296, 467
    architecture, 181, 237, 238, 239, 240, 241, 242, 260
    art, 238, 240–41
    music, 251–60
    relief, 238, 240, 243
    sculpture, 238, 239
Romans, 6, 57, 70, 91, 96, 97, 103, 156, 160, 170–76, 177, 179, 188, 194, 233, 235, 237, 239, 249, 280, 285, 287, 290, 291, 327, 373, 382
Romanticism, 119, 372, 373, 400, 411–25, 433–36
Romantic movement, 347, 348, 411, 415, 448, 463, 466
Rome
    achievements of, 117–19, 127
    ancient, 54, 57, 97, 111–52 (unit 2), 185–88, 190, 235, 280, 368, 369, 370, 371, 380
    Empire, 6, 113, 114–15, 116 (map), 117–18, 119, 124, 126 (overview), 140, 142, 145, 148, 159, 160, 173, 185–86, 188, 191, 234, 408, 463
    fall of, 117, 140 (overview), 185–86, 270
    founding of, 111–12, 125–27, 140 (overview)
    games and contests, 122–25
    modern, 269, 275, 277, 297, 302, 304, 305, 316, 319, 343
    religion and philosophy, 119–22

Republic, 113, 115–16, 117, 124, 126 (overview), 140 (overview), 141, 142, 381, 384
sack of, 169 (overview), 186, 187, 305
Romulus, 111, 112
Roncevaux, battle of, 193
Rondanini Pieta (Michelangelo), 306, **306**
Roof Gossips (Sloan), 532, **532**
Rorem, Ned, American composer (b. 1923), 4 (quotation)
Roscellinus (Roscelin), Jean, French philosopher (1050–1122), 208, 209
Rose windows, 242, 244, 247 colorplate 18 (Chartres Cathedral)
Rossini, Gioacchino, Italian composer (1792–1868), 448
Rossner, Judith, American writer (b. 1935), 591
Rothko, Mark, Russian-American painter (1903–1970), 535, 540
Rouault, Georges, French painter (1871–1958), 522
Rouen Cathedral, West Façade Sunlight (Monet), 475–76, colorplate 45
Roughing It (Twain), 438
Rousseau, Henri, French painter (1844–1910), 481, 526
Rousseau, Jean Jacques, French philosopher (1712–1778), 348, 411–14, 416, 467, 469, 532, 548
Royal Portal, Chartres Cathedral, 142, **243,** 243–44
Rubenists, 372, 447, 467
Rubens, Peter Paul, Flemish statesman and painter (1577–1640), 312, 371–72, 380, 476
Rubicon, 115
Rucellai Madonna (Duccio), 249, **249**
Rude, François, French sculptor (1784–1855), 467
Rue, Pierre de la, Franco-Flemish composer (1460–1518), 317
Ruggles, Carl, American composer (1876–1971), 570
Ruisdael, Jacob van, Dutch landscape painter (1628–1682), 376
Runner at the Starting Point, Two Wrestlers, Javelin Thrower (Greek), 123, **123**
Russell, Bertrand, English philosopher, mathematician, and writer (1872–1970), 117, 425
Russell, Terry, J. T. and a Levi Jacket (Duecker), 546, colorplate 59

S

Saarinen, Eero, Finnish-American architect (1910–1961), 552
Safdie, Moshe, Israeli architect (b. 1945), 553
Sails (Debussy), 460, 461 (music)
St. Anne, 21 (music)
Sant' Apollinare Nuovo, Ravenna, 177, **177**
Sainte Chapelle, Paris, **245,** 245–46, **246**
St. Clement, Rome, 174, **174**
St. Denis, Abbey Church of, **241,** 241–42, 249

St. Étienne (Abbaye Aux Hommes), Caen, France, 237, **237**
St. Irene, Constantinople, 178
St. John Lateran, Rome, 174
Ste.-Madeleine, Vézelay, France, **238,** 238–39, **239,** 249
Saint Mark, *Gospel Book of Archbishop Ebbo of Reims,* 236, **236**
St. Mark's Cathedral, Venice, 180, **180,** 181, 316, 319, **319, 320,** 320 (floor plan)
St. Martin du Canigou, France, 237, **237**
St. Martin-in-the-Fields (Gibbs), 380, **381**
St. Paul's Cathedral (Wren), 380, **381**
St. Paul's Outside the Walls, Rome, 174–75, **175**
St. Peter's, Old, Rome, 291, 302, 369
St. Peter's Basilica, Rome, 148, 174, 301, 302, 306–7, **307, 368,** 368–69, 371
St. Pierre, Abbey Church of, 239
Salamis, Battle of, 35, 78, 82, 91
Salinas, Porfirio, American painter (b. 1912), 548
Salle, David, American artist (b. 1952), 549
Sallust (Caius Sallustius Crispus), Roman historian (86–ca. 34 B.C.), 118 (quotation), 126 (overview)
Salzburg Cathedral (Solari), 366, **366**
S. Carlo alle Quattro Fontane (Borromini), 369, **369**
"Sanctuary" (Wylie), 194 (text)
San Moise (Tremignon and Meyring), Venice, 370, **370**
Santa Maria della Salute (Longhena), Venice, 370, **370**
Santa Maria Maggiore, Rome, 176
Santa Maria Novella, Florence (Alberti), 286, 290–91, **291,** 308, 366
Santa Pudenziana, Rome, 175–76, **176**
Santa Sabina, Rome, 171, **171**
San Vitale, Ravenna, 178, **178,** 190, 235 colorplate 10
Sappho of Lesbos, Greek poet-musician (fl. 6th c. B.C.), 102–3, **103,** 103 (text), 133, 258
Sarcophagi, 170, 172–73
Sarcophagus of Junius Bassus, The (Roman), 172–73, **173**
Sartre, Jean Paul, French novelist and philosopher (1905–1980), 503, 504–10, 511
Saunders, Raymond, American artist (b. 1934), 549
Savonarola, Girolamo, Italian religious reformer (1452–1498), 301
Sayers, Dorothy L., English writer and translator (1893–1957), 193
Scarlatti, Domenico, Italian composer (1687–1757), 395
Scenes de la Vie en Bohème (Murger), 458
Schat, Peter, Dutch composer (b. 1935), 572
Schillebeeckx, Edward, Dutch Roman Catholic theologian (b. 1914), 513
Schiller, Friedrich von, German dramatist, poet, and historian (1759–1805), 415

Schilling, Friedrich William Joseph von, German philosopher (1775–1854), 415
Schliemann, Heinrich, German archeologist (1822–1890), 75
Schnabel, Julian, American artist (b. 1951), 549
Schoenberg, Arnold, Austrian composer (1874–1951), 559, 566, 567, 571, 583
Scholasticism, 208–9, 213
Scholder, Fritz, American painter (b. 1937), 543
Schonzeit, Ben, American painter (b. 1942), 546, 547
Schopenhauer, Arthur, German philosopher (1788–1860), 415
Schubert, Franz, Viennese composer (1797–1828), 16, 448–49, 463
Schuller, Gunther, American composer (b. 1925), 570
Schuman, William, American composer (b. 1910), 570
Schumann, Robert, German composer (1810–1856), 20 (quotation), 448
Schwitters, Kurt, German artist (1887–1948), 530
Science fiction, 590, 594–95
Scipio Africanus the Elder, Roman general (236–183 B.C.), 127
Scipio Africanus the Younger, Roman general (ca. 185–129 B.C.), 127
"Scipio's Dream," *On the Republic* (Cicero), 127–30 (text)
Scott, Sir Walter, Scottish novelist and poet (1771–1832), 410, 467
Scream, The (Munch), 482, **482**
Sculpture
architectural, 88–90, 237, 239, 242, 243–44, 249
Baroque, 368, 369, 370
canon of, 84
Cycladic, 73
early Christian, 171–73
Egyptian, 70–71, 78, 84, 94, 171
Etruscan, 139–40
Gothic, 243, 244
Greek, 76–84, 88–89, 92–97, 119, 142, 146, 170, 171
Greek Archaic, 77–82, 170, 171
Greek Classical, 82–84, 88–89, 92–94
Greek Geometric, 76–77
Hellenistic, 94–97
Impressionism, 477–78
Islamic, 233
Minoan, 74–75
Mycenaean, 75
Neoclassical, 384
relief, 238, 247, 467
Renaissance, 287, 289–90, 291, 292, 300–301, 306
Rococo, 378, 379
Roman, 141–43, 147–49, 150, 171
Romanesque, 238, 239
Romantic, 467
twentieth century, 528, 531, 538, 539, 540, 541, 544, 545, 546
"Second Coming, The" (Yeats), 494 (text)

Second Coming of Christ, 166, 243
"Second Inaugural Address" (Lincoln), 409 (text)
Second Isaiah, Hebrew Prophet (6th c. B.C.), 157n; 40:1–9; 53:3–6, 158, 159
Second Shepherd's Play, The, 197
Second Treatise on Civil Government (Locke), 345
Secretariat building of the United Nations (Harrison and Le Corbusier), 550, **550**
Seikolos Song (Greek), 106 (music)
Seize the Day (Bellow), 590, 591
Self-Portrait (Gauguin), 479, colorplate 48
Self-Portrait (Leyster), 374, **375**
Senate, Roman, 113, 114, 115, 149
Seneca, Marcus Annaeus, Roman rhetorician (fl. 1st c. B.C.), 114 (quotation), 119 (quotation), 121, 125, 126 (overview), 151
Sentaro (DeLap), 544, **545**
Sept repons des tenebras (Poulenc), 571
Sequences, in music, 253, 254
Sequenzas (Berio), 572
Sermon on the Mount (Jesus), 162–64 (text)
"Service of Song, A" (Dickinson), 441 (text)
Sessions, Roger, American composer (b. 1896), 570
Seurat, Georges, French painter (1859–1891), 480–81, 482
Seven Studies on Themes of Paul Klee (Schuller), 570
Shakespeare, William, English playwright (1564–1616), 8, 9, 115 (quotation), 160, 197, 280, 337, 349, 358, 422, 430, 452, 453, 467, 492, 590
Shelley, Mary Wollstonecraft Godwin, English writer (1797–1851), 422, 448
Shelley, Percy Bysshe, English poet (1792–1822), 415, 420–22, 467, 570
Shepard, Sam, American playwright (b. 1943), 593
Sheridan, Mrs. Richard Brinsley. See Mrs. Richard Brinsley Sheridan
"Shiloh" (Melville), 437 (text)
"Shine Perishing Republic" (Jeffers), 495 (text), 592
Shivering Woman (Barlach), 522, **523**
Shostakovitch, Dmitri, Russian composer (1906–1975), 564, 569–70
Sic et Non (Abelard), 209
Sichtbar (Schwitters), 530, **530**
Sicily, 26, 32, 50, 79, 127, 181
Side Frames (di Suvero), 544, **545**
Siena Cathedral (Pisano), Italy, 247, **247**
Simon, Father Richard, Biblical scholar (1638–1712), 347–48
Simonides of Keos, Greek poet-musician (556–468 B.C.), 33
Sinfonietta (Janáček), 571
Siqueiros, David Alfaro, Mexican artist (1896–1974), 533, 549
Sir Thomas More (Holbein the Younger), **331**
Sistine Chapel, 301, 470
Sitwell, Edith, Dame, English poet, critic, and novelist (1887–1964), 571

Sixtus IV, Pope (1414–1484), 275, 299
Sleeping Beauty (Tchaikovsky), 456
Sleep of Reason Produces Monsters, The (Goya), 466
Sloan, John, American artist (1871–1951), 532
Sluter, Claus, Dutch-Burgundian sculptor (d. 1406), 316
Small Crucifixion, The (Grünewald), 311, colorplate 32
Smith, Adam, Scottish economist (1723–1790), 345–46
Smith, David, American sculptor (1906–1965), 544, 546
Snake Goddess (Minoan), **74**, 74–75
Social Contract (Rousseau), 411
Social Darwinism, 428–29
Society of Jesus (Jesuits), 365, 366
Sokrates, Greek philosopher (469–399 B.C.), 6, 42, 51, 52, 53n, 54, 55, 56, 57–67 (text), **58**, 99, 120, 121, 192, 208, 382, 429
"Soldier's Embrace, A" (Gordimer), 515–20 (text), 596
Solo for Electronic Instrument with Reverberation (Stockhausen), 569
Solomon, King of Palestine, 156, 179
Solomon, Temple of, 146, 156
Solon, Athenian lawgiver (640–558 B.C.), 33, 34, 102, 105, 113
Solzhenitsyn, Aleksandr, Russian-American writer (b. 1918), 596
Sonata da Chiesa in E minor (Corelli), 391–92 (music)
Sonata form, 397–98, 400, 563
Sondheim, Stephen, American composer and lyricist (b. 1930), 570
"Song" (Donne), 349 (text)
Song of Roland, 193–94. *See also* Chanson de Roland
Song of the Ass, 255 (music)
Song-sermon, 579
Songs of Innocence (Blake), 415
Sonnets (Michelangelo)
  V, 302 (text)
  XXX, 330–31 (text)
  XXXII, 331 (text)
  LXI, 331 (text)
Sonnets (Petrarch)
  III, 326 (text)
  XLVII, 326 (text)
  LXIX, 326 (text)
  CCXCII, 326 (text)
  CCCXIII, 326 (text)
Sophists, Greek, 47, 51, 57
Sophokles, Greek dramatist (ca. 496–406 B.C.), 29, 31, **48**, 48–49, 84, 92, 100, 105, 119, 270, 591
Sorbonne, College de, Paris, 210
"Sorrowful Woman, A" (Godwin), 609–11 (text)
Sorrows of Young Werther, The (Goethe), 415, 424
Soul jazz, 584–85
Sound of Music, The (Rodgers and Hammerstein), 570
Sounds and Words (Babbitt), 568
South Pacific (Rodgers and Hammerstein), 570

Sower, The (Millet), 469, **470**
Spanish Armada, 280, 309
Spanish Inquisition, 277, 311
Sparta, 26, 50, 51, 53, 80, 91, 92, 102, 103, 105, 122
Spartans, 34–35, 91
Spencer, Herbert, English philosopher (1820–1903), 428–29
Sphinx and Great Pyramid, 70, **70**
Spinoza, Baruch de, Dutch-Jewish philosopher (1632–1677), 347, 348
Spirit of the Laws, The (Montesquieu), 345, 348
Spiritual Exercises (Ignatius of Loyola), 369
Spirituals, 573, 578, 579, 580, 586
Spy Who Came in from the Cold, The (Le Carré), 590, 591
Stabat Mater (Poulenc), 571
Stained glass, 242, 244, 245, 246, 247
Stalin, Joseph, Soviet dictator (1879–1953), 373, 486
Starry Night, The (van Gogh), 13, 14, 479, colorplate 4
Star Spangled Banner, The, 259
Statuette of Youth, 76, **77**
Statuettes, Greek, 76
Steele, Wilbur Daniel, American writer (1886–1970), 11 (quotation)
Stein, Gertrude, American poet (1874–1946), 9 (quotation), 482
Steinbeck, John, American novelist (1902–1968), 595
Stele of Hegesco, 92, **92**
Stereobate, 85, **87**
Sterne, Laurence, English writer (1713–1768), 590
Stieglitz, Alfred, American photographer (1864–1946), 526, 530
Still Life (Picasso), 525, colorplate 51
Stockhausen, Karl Heinz, German composer (b. 1928), 568, 569, 572
Stoicism, 120–22, 125, 126, 127, 135, 149, 159, 382
Stone in the Tree, The (Tanguy), 532, **532**
Storm, The (Nóvak), 571
Stranger, The (Camus), 511
Strategie (Xenakis), 572
Strauss, Johann, Jr., Austrian composer (1825–1899), 388, 572
Strauss, Richard, Austrian composer (1864–1949), 17, 460
Stravinsky, Igor, Russian-American composer (1882–1971), 16, 254, 388, 557, 567, 568, 583
Street cry, 577
String Quartet in F major, op. 3, no. 5 (Haydn), 398 (music)
Stuart, Gilbert, American painter (1755–1828), **384**, 384–85
Sturm und Drang, 414
Stylobate, 85, **87**
Subjection of Women (Mill), 430
Suchon, Eugen, Czech composer (b. 1908), 571
Sueno de Eros, El (Esplá), 572
Suetonius (Caius Suetonius Tranquillus), Roman biographer (ca. 69-ca. 140), 126 (overview)

Suger, Abbot, of St. Denis (12th c.), 241, 242
Suleymaniye Camii Mosque (Sinan), Istanbul, 232, **232**, 249
Sullivan, Louis, American architect (1856–1924), 550
Summum bonum (Aristotle), 57
Sunday Afternoon on the Island of La Grande Jatte (Seurat), 480–81, colorplate 49
Sun-Treader (Ruggles), 570
Supper at Emmaus (Caravaggio), **367,** 367–68
Surrealism, in art, 530–32, 543–44
Suvero, Mark di, American artist (b. 1933), 544, 545
Swan Lake (Tchaikovsky), 456
Sweeney Todd (Sondheim), 570
Swift, Jonathan, Anglo-Irish author (1667–1745), 355–58
Swing style jazz, 581, 582, 583, 584, 585, 586, 587
Sybaris, Italy, 26, 112
Sydney Opera House (Utzon), 553, **554**
"Sympathy" (Dickinson), 442 (text)
Symphonic poem. *See* Tone poem
Symphonie Fantastique (Berlioz), 452, 453 (music)
Symphony for Small Orchestra (Webern), 567, 567 (music)
Symphony No. 2 (Rochberg), 570
Symphony No. 3 (Harris), 570
Symphony No. 3 (Riegger), 570
Symphony No. 3 (Sessions), 570
Symphony No. 3 in E-flat major, op. 55 (Beethoven), 400
Symphony No. 4 in A major, op. 90 (Mendelssohn), 452 (music)
Symphony No. 5 (Shostakovich), 569
Symphony No. 5 in B-flat major, op. 100 (Prokofiev), 561–62 (music)
Symphony No. 5 in C minor, op. 67 (Beethoven), 8, 400, 401 (music)
Symphony No. 5 in E minor, op. 64 (Tchaikovsky), 456–57 (music)
Symphony No. 6 (W. Schuman), 570
Symphony No. 7 (Leningrad) (Shostakovitch), 569
Symphony No. 9 (Beethoven), 400
Symphony No. 40 in G minor (Mozart), 399 (music)
Symphony on G (Harrison), 570
Symphony orchestra, 451, 451 (table)
Symposium (Plato), 55
Synchrony (Cowell), 570
Syncopation, 575–76
Syracuse, Sicily, 26, 50, 112, 170

T

Tabula Rasa, 347
Tacitus, Publius Cornelius, Roman historian (ca. 55-ca. 117), 114 (quotation), 115, 126 (overview)
Talleyrand, Charles Maurice de, French statesman (1754–1838), 406
Talmud, 29
Tamayo, Rufino, Mexican painter (b. 1899), 548

Tanguy, Yves, French-American painter (1900–1955), 528, 532
Tanner, Henry O., American painter (1859–1937), 548
Tarquin the Proud, Etruscan king (fl. 509 B.C.), 113, 139 (overview)
Tchaikovsky, Peter Ilyich, Russian composer (1840–1893), 16, 372, 451, 452, 456–57
Tempietto (Bramante), 302, **303,** 380
Temple of
    Amon (Egyptian), 6, 72, **72,** 89, 175, 244
    Amon-Mut-Khonsu (Egyptian), 72, **72,** 89
    Athena (Parthenon), 5, 6, 47, 80, 86, 87, **87,** 88
    Athena Nike (Greek), 86, **90,** 90–91
    Hera I, Paestum (Greek), 79–80, **80,** 86
    Hera II, Paestum (Greek), 86, **86**
    Olympian Zeus (Greek), 96, **96**
    Poseidon, Sounion (Greek), 91, **91**
    Queen Hatshepsut (Egyptian), 72, **72**
"Tenebrae" (Levertov), 515 (text)
Tennyson, Alfred, Lord, English poet (1809–1892), 408, 430–31
Terence, Latin dramatist (190?–159 B.C.), 126 (overview)
Terpander of Lesbos, Greek musician (ca. 675 B.C.), 101–2
Tertullian, Roman Christian theologian (ca. 160-ca. 230), 126 (overview), 351
Tetractys of the decad, 38
Texas Sweet Funk (Jimenez), 548
Thackeray, William Makepeace, English novelist (1811–1863), 438
Thales, Ionian philosopher (ca. 636–546 B.C.), 35, 36
Theatre, Greek, 42, 146
Thebes, Greece, 48, 48 (box), 53, 102
Themistokles, Greek general and statesman (ca. 524-ca. 460 B.C.), 34, 35
Theodora, empress, wife of Justinian I (d. 548), 278, colorplate 12
Theodoric I, Ostrogothic emperor (454?–526), 169 (overview), 177, 192, 236
Theodosius I, the Great, Roman emperor (346?–395), 116 (box), 117, 124
Theogony (Hesiod), 29
Thera (Santorini), Aegean island, 27, 28
Thermopylai, Battle of, 34–35
Thespis, Greek dramatist (fl. 534 B.C.), 42
Thinker, The (Rodin), 478, **478**
Third Piano Sonata (Boulez), 568
Thirty Years' War, 280, 341, 371
Thomas, Dylan, Welsh poet (1914–1953), 592, 596 (text)
Thomas à Becket, Saint, Archbishop of Canterbury (1118–1170), 210
Thomson, Virgil, American composer (b. 1896), 570
Thoreau, Henry David, American author and naturalist (1817–1862), 434, 435, 436, 566
Three-Cornered Hat, The (de Falla), 572
Three Goddesses, Parthenon, **89**

Threepenny Opera (Brecht and Weill), 395, 570
Three Places in New England (Ives), 566 (text)
Throne room, Knossos (Minoan), 74, **74**
Thucydides, Athenian historian (471–399 B.C.), 51, 270
Thyrsis? Sleepest Thou? (Bennet), 322 (music)
Tiberius (Claudius Nero Caesar), Roman emperor (42 B.C.–A.D. 37), 116 (box), 120
Tibia. *See* Aulos
Tiffany, Louis Comfort, American designer of stained glass (1848–1933), 533
"Tiger, The" (Blake), 416 (text)
Till Eulenspiegel's Merry Pranks (Strauss), 455–56 (music)
Time Charts (listed chronologically)
    Greek Civilization, 107–8
    Middle Ages, 264
    Renaissance, 283
    Early Modern World, 1600–1789, 362–63
    Middle Modern World, 1789–1914, 444–46
    Twentieth century, 614–15
Time Cycle, Four Songs for Soprano and Orchestra (Foss), 570
Tintoretto (Jacopo Robusti), Venetian painter (1518–1594), 307–8, **308,** 370, 372
Tippett, Michael, English composer (b. 1905), 571
Tiresias, Greek seer, 49, 100
Titian (Tiziano Vecelli), Venetian painter (ca. 1490–1576), 294, 304, 307, 308, 370, 464
Titus (Flavius Sabinus Vespasianus), Roman emperor (ca. 40–81), 110 (box), 146, 147
"To a Skylark" (Shelley), 420–21 (text)
"To His Coy Mistress" (Marvell), 350 (text)
Tom the Taylor (Purcell), 323 (text)
Tone poem, 455
Tone row, 559, 560
Tools (Schonzeit), 546, **547**
Torah, 156, 160, 162
Toreutics (metal craftsmanship), 75
Tosca (Puccini), 458
Toulouse-Lautrec, Henri, French artist (1864–1901), 481, 526
Tragedy, The (Picasso), 524, **524**
Trajan (Marcus Ulpius Trajanus), Roman emperor (52–117), 116 (box), 145, 147, 148, 149, 150
Trajan, Column of, 147, **147,** 148, **148**
Transicion (Kagel), 572
Transmigration of souls, 39
Trash (Andrews), 549
Treatise of Human Nature Being an Attempt to Introduce the Experimental Method of Reasoning into Moral Subjects, A (Hume), 347
Treaty of Versailles, 485, 486
Tribute Money (Masaccio), 287–88, **288,** 525

Triforium, 174, 178, 244, 246
Triglyphs, 85, 86, 302
Trinity, 26, 171, 175, 177, 186
Trio sonata, 388, 391
Tristan und Isolde (Wagner), 458
Tristram Shandy (Sterne), 590
Tristus est anima mea (Lassus), 318 (music)
Trivium, 210, 300
Trois poèmes d'Henri Michaux (Lutoslawski), 572
Trojans, 97, 126, 127, 309
Trojan War, 28, 31, 43, 50, 75, 79
Trojan Women, The (Euripides), 50
Tropes, in music, 253, 254
Trotsky, Leon, Russian revolutionary (1877–1940), 486
Troubadour Song (Beatritz), 258 (text)
Troubadour Song (William IX), 250–57 (text)
Troubadour-trouvère, 195n, 206, 256–59
Troy, 25n, 43, 44, 50, 75, 97, 112, 126, 309, 602
True West (Shepard), 593
Tuchman, Barbara, American historian (b. 1912), 410
Turina, Joaquin, Spanish composer (1882–1949), 572
Turks, 91, 169 (overview), 179, 232, 407
Twain, Mark. *See* Clemens, Samuel Langhorne
TWA Terminal (Saarinen), 552, **552**, 553, **553**
Twelve Tables of Law, Roman, 113
Twelve-tone system. *See* Atonality
Two Treatises of Government (Locke), 345
Tyler, Anne, American novelist (b. 1941), 591
Tympanum, 238, 244, 247
Tyrants, Greek, 32–33

U

Uccello, Paolo, Florentine painter (1397–1475), 289
"Ulysses" (Tennyson), 431 (text)
"Unhorsing of Bernardino della Carda, The," *Battle of San Romano* (Uccello), 289, **289**
Unitarian church, 277
United Nations, 502
Universities, 209, 210, 211, 255
    Bologna, 209, 269
    Cambridge, 209
    Muslim, 231–32
    Oxford, 209
    Paris, 208, 209, 210
    rise of, 209
    Salerno, 209
"Unmoved Mover" (Aquinas), 56, 211–12
"Unmoved Mover" (Aristotle), 56–57
Updike, John, American writer (b. 1932), 595
Urban II, Pope (ca. 1042–1099), 238
"Use of Force, The" (Williams), 592
Utilitarianism, 429
"Utilitarian View of the Monitor's Fight, A" (Melville), 437 (text), 438

Utopia, 274, 331
Utopia (More), 274, 331–36 (text)
Utzon, Joern, Danish architect (b. 1918), 553, 554

V

Valhalla, 191
van der Weyden, Flemish painter (1400–1464), 297, 315
van Dyck, Anthony, Flemish painter (1599–1641), 372
van Eyck, Jan, Flemish painter (1390–1441), 288, 294, 295–96, 304, 311, 315, 376
van Gogh, Vincent, Dutch painter (1853–1890), 13, 14–15, 478–79, 482, 522, 526
Varèse, Edgard, French composer (1883–1965), 566, 568
Variations for Orchestra (Webern), 567
Vasari, Giorgio, Italian architect, writer, and painter (1511–1574), 270, 293, 295, 299, 304, 305
Velasquez, Diego, Spanish painter (1599–1660), 366, 370–71, **371**, 464, 542, 543
Velasquez Painting Gongora (Gongora), 543, **543**
Venice, 176, 180–81, 274, 304, 308, 319, 321
"Veni sponsa Christi" (Palestrina), 319 (music)
Ventre, Legislatif, Le (Daumier), 470, **470**
Venus, 30 (box), 119, 142, 293, 377
Venus Consoling Love (Boucher), 377, colorplate 39
Venus with a Mirror (Titian), 307, colorplate 29
Verdi, Giuseppe, Italian opera composer (1813–1901), 372, 448, 458
Verlaine, Paul, French poet (1844–1896), 459
Vermeer, Jan, Dutch painter (1632–1675), 375–76
Verne, Jules, English novelist (1828–1905), 595
Veronese, Paolo, Venetian painter (1528–1588), 308–9
Verrocchio, Andrea di Cione, Florentine sculptor (1435–1488), 291, 299, 301, 544
Versailles, Palace of (Le Vau; Hardouin Mansart), 343, 373, **373**, 374, **374**, 381, 387
Versuch uber Schweine (Henze), 572
Vespasian (Titus Flavius Vespasianus), Roman emperor (9–79), 116 (box), 119 (quotation), 146
Vesuvius, Mount, 141, 151
Victimae paschali laudes, 392
Victor Emmanuel II, King of Italy (1820–1878), 408
Victoria, Queen of Great Britain and Ireland (1819–1901), 407, 408, 409
Victorian Gothic mansion, California, 468, **469**
Victorian period, 430, 467, 468
Victory Boogie Woogie (Mondrian), 528

Victory Untying Her Sandal, Temple of Athena Nike, 92, **92**
Vietnam War, 502, 515, 535, 536, 590
Vietnam War Memorial, Washington, D.C., 546
Vikings, 190, 192, 236, 237, 274
Village Bride, The (Greuze), 381, **382**
Villa Rotunda (Palladio), 308, **308**
Villa Savoye (Le Corbusier), 534, **534**
Vindication of the Rights of Women (Wollstonecraft), 422
Vin herbé, Le (Martin), 572
Violin Concerto (Berg), 559–61 (music)
Violin Concerto (Khachaturian), 572
Virgil (Publius Vergilius Maro), Latin poet (70–19 B.C.), 111, 125, 126 (overview), 127, 142, 214, 270, 325
Virginia, University of (Jefferson), 143
Virginia State Capitol (Jefferson), 143, 385, **385**
Virgin Mary, 207, 208, 213, 244
    in art, 181, 248, 249, 293, 296, 300, 311
Virgin with the Monkey, The (Dürer), 310, **310**
Vision after the Sermon (Jacob Wrestling with the Angel) (Gauguin), 479, **480**
Vision and Prayer (Babbitt), 568
Vitruvius Pollio, Marcus, Roman architect (1st c. B.C.), 146, 290
Vivaldi, Antonio, Italian composer (1678–1741), 392
Voltaire (François Marie de Arouet), French political philosopher and writer (1694–1778), 348, 352, 360, 377, 384
Voltaire (Houdon), 384, **384**
Vonnegut, Kurt, American novelist (b. 1922), 602–6
Voodoo (Vodun), 579
Vox clamantis (Eben), 571

W

Wagner, Richard, German composer (1813–1883), 193, 259, 448, 452, 453, 457, 458, 459, 460, 559
Waiting for Godot (Beckett), 593
Waiting Indian No. 4 (Scholder), 543
Walden (Thoreau), 415
Waldo, Peter, French religious reformer (d. 1217), 275
Walking Man, The (Rodin), **477**, 477–78
"Wall, The" (Sartre), 505–11 (text)
Wallace, Alfred Russel, English naturalist (1823–1913), 427
Walpole, Robert, English statesman (1676–1745), 349
Walton, William, English composer (1902–1982), 571
Wanted Poster (White), 549
Warhol, Andy, American artist (b. 1925), 538
War Requiem (Britten), 570
Washerwoman, The (Daumier), 470, **471**
Washington, George, American general and president (1732–1799), 384
Wasps, The (Aristophanes), 51
Wasteland, The (Eliot), 590, 592

Waterloo, 405, 406

Watermill With the Great Red Roof, The (Hobbema), 13, colorplate 3

Watt, James, Scottish scientist and inventor (1736–1819), 407

Watteau, Jean Antoine, French painter (1684–1721), 374–77, 395

"Way to Jerusalem, The" sacred dance, 261

Weber, Carl Maria von, German composer (1786–1826), 463

Webern, Anton, Austrian composer (1883–1945), 566, 567, 568

Weill, Kurt, German-American composer (1900–1950), 570

Wellesz, Egon, Austrian composer (1885–1974), 571

Wells, H(erbert) G(eorge), English writer (1866–1946), 595

West Side Story (Bernstein and Sondheim), 570, 593

Westwood Children, The (Johnson), 548, **548**

Wheatfields (Ruisdael), 376, colorplate 36

Wheel-lyre (organistrum), 254, **254**

"When All My Five and Country Senses See" (Thomas), 592, 596 (text)

"When a Man Has No Freedom to Fight for at Home" (Byron), 419 (text)

"When Lilacs Last in the Dooryard Bloom'd" (Whitman), 436

Where Do We Come From? What Are We? Where Are We Going? (Gauguin), 12–13, 480, colorplate 1

Whistler, James McNeil, American painter (1834–1903), 476–77

Whistler's Mother (Whistler), 477, **477**

White, Charles, American artist (b. 1918), 549

Whitman, Walt, American poet (1819–1892), 435, 436, 566

Wiclif, John (or Wycliffe), English religious reformer (1320–1384), 275

Wife of Bath, 258, 591

Wilde, Oscar, English author (1854–1900), 8 (quotation)

William of Champeaux, Scholastic philosopher (ca. 1070–1121), 208, 209

William the Conqueror, duke of Normandy (1027?–1087), 237, 241

William I, Emperor of Germany (1797–1888), 407

William II, Emperor of Germany (1859–1941), 407

William III of Orange, King of England (1650–1702), 343

William IX, duke of Aquitaine, troubadour (1071–1126), 256–57

Williams, William Carlos, American physician and author (1883–1963), 591–92

Will to Power, The (Nietzsche), 503

Wilson, Woodrow, American president (1856–1924), 485

Windows (Druckman), 570

Witches Hammer, The (1498), 298

"With Rue My Heart is Laden" (Housman), 10 (text)

Wivenhoe Park, Essex (Constable), 467, colorplate 41

Wollstonecraft Godwin, Mary, English feminist and writer (1759–1797), 422

Woman Holding a Balance (Vermeer), 376, **376**

Woman 1 (de Kooning), 535, colorplate 56

Woodruff, Hale, American painter (b. 1900), 548, 549

Wordsworth, William, English poet (1770–1850), 13, 416–18, 429, 463, 467

Works and Days (Hesiod), 31–32

Workshop of the Bauhaus (Gropius), Dessau, Germany, 534, **534**

Work song, 577, 585

World Exploration 1271–1295; 1486–1611 (map), 275

"World Is Too Much With Us, The" (Wordsworth), 418 (text)

World of Will and Idea, The (Schopenhauer), 415

World War I, 405, 407, 410, 411, 485, 490, 492, 522, 523, 530, 559, 592, 595

World War II, 229, 407, 411, 485, 486, 495, 576, 582, 589, 590, 595

Wren, Sir Christopher, English architect (1632–1723), 380

Wright, Frank Lloyd, American architect (1867–1959), 534, 535, 550

Wright, Richard, American writer (1908–1960), 495–99

Wuorinen, Charles, American composer (b. 1938), 571

Wylie, Elinor, American poet (1885–1928), 194

X

X (Bladen), 546, **546**

Xenakis, Iannis, Greek composer (b. 1922), 572

Xenophon, Greek historian and general (434?–355? B.C.), 51

Xerxes, Persian king (519–465 B.C.), 82

X–P (Khi-rho) page, *Lindisfarne Gospels* (Hiberno-Saxon), 234, colorplate 13

Y

Yahweh, Hebrew god, 156, 157

Yeats, William Butler, Irish poet (1865–1939), 494

"Yet Do I Marvel" (Cullen), 495 (text)

Young Girl Reading, A (Fragonard), 378, **378**

"Young Girls Dancing Around the Altar," **104**

Z

Zen Buddhism, 569

Zeno the Stoic, Greek philosopher (335?–263? B.C.), 121

Zeus, 29, 30 (box), 43 (box), **88**, 100, 119, 121, 123, 171

Zodiac, 238, 260, 294

Zola, Émile, French novelist (1840–1902), 407, 438, 458, 476

Zurbarán, Francisco de, Spanish painter (1598–1664), 370

Zwingli, Ulrich, Swiss leader of Reformation (1484–1531), 276